GHOST DIVISION

The 11th "Gespenster" Panzer Division
and the German Armored Force in World War II

A. Harding Ganz

STACKPOLE
BOOKS

Published by
STACKPOLE BOOKS
5067 Ritter Road
Mechanicsburg, PA 17055
www.stackpolebooks.com

Printed in the United States of America

10 9 8 7 6 5 4 3 2 1

First edition

Library of Congress Cataloging-in-Publication Data

Ganz, Albert Harding, 1938- author.
Ghost division : the 11th "Gespenster" Panzer Division and the German Armored Force / A. Harding Ganz. — First edition.
pages cm
Includes bibliographical references and index.
ISBN 978-0-8117-1659-8
1. Germany. Heer. Panzerdivision, 11—History. 2. World War, 1939–1945—Regimental histories—Germany. 3. World War, 1939–1945—Tank warfare. 4. World War, 1939–1945—Campaigns—Eastern Front. 5. World War, 1939–1945—Campaigns—Western Front. I. Title. II. Title: 11th "Gespenster" Panzer Division and the German Armored Force.
D757.5611th G36 2015
940.54'1343—dc23
2015031335

CONTENTS

LIST OF ILLUSTRATIONS

List of Maps

Preface

The 11. Panzer-Division was activated by an Oberkommando des Heeres (OKH, Army High Command) order of 17 July 1940. Organized around the 11. Schützenbrigade (mot) (motorized 11. Rifle Brigade), the unit was combined with Panzer-Regiment 15 by an OKH order of 6 September 1940. It adopted the symbol of a sword-wielding specter on a half-track, and identification as the "Gespenster" ("Ghost") Division. Nine more panzer divisions were formed in the months that followed, doubling the number of panzer divisions in the German Wehrmacht to twenty.

This buildup reflected the decisive role the German Panzerwaffe (armored force) had played in the Polish campaign in 1939 and the campaigns in the West in 1940—the offensives that introduced the phrase *Blitzkrieg*, or lightning war. The Gespenster-Division would fight in Yugoslavia in 1941, in Russia in 1941–44, and in the West in 1944–45. Its operations would exemplify the role the Panzerwaffe played in World War II and influence future developments in armored warfare. At the same time, the unit would uphold the traditional principles of honor and chivalry in warfare, and earn the respect of its opponents.

As a young boy growing up in New York City during World War II, and then as a student of history, I developed an interest in armored warfare. I was captivated by Desmond Young's *Rommel* (1950) and von Mellenthin's *Panzer Battles* (1956). After college, I gained experience in armor operations while serving as a tank platoon leader (M60s) with the US 4th Armored Division (1964–66). I was stationed at Crailsheim, Germany, a posting that gave me the opportunity to visit many of the World War II battlefields of the European Theater alongside fellow Armor officers Lts. Jim Jackson and Art Walz, and I gained additional knowledge through correspondence with my Officer Candidate School and Armor School classmate Robert Wells.

My postdoctoral studies of the 4th Armored in World War II revealed that the division was constantly engaged with the German 11. Panzer-Division from September to December 1944. I made contact with Karl Heinz Loschke of Braunschweig, secretary of the 11. Panzer Veterans Association, an introduction that resulted in communications with many Gespensters and invitations to the unit's annual May reunions at Kötzting, Bavaria, the site of the division's negotiated surrender to Patton's Third Army in May 1945.

Among the many "Elften" noted in this book, instrumental for providing details were Klaus Bardt, Walter Rahn, Ansgar Pawelke, Gerhard Winkler, Karl Thieme (who had my *Armor* article on the 11. Panzer translated into German and who nicknamed me "Professor Panzerganz"!), Friedrich Karl von Eggeling, Ernst August von Fersen, Walter Schaefer-Kehnert, and Kurt Nentwig. American veterans were also of assistance, especially Jimmie Leach and Sam Schenker of the US 4th Armored Division and William Molla of the 26th "Yankee" Division. One caveat is that many personal accounts and experiences cannot be corroborated, but reflect what was known at the time or was remembered.

Academics who have given great support are Allan R. Millett of the Ohio State University, Michael J. Lyons of North Dakota State University, the Scholarly Activity Committee of the Ohio State University Newark Campus, OSUN Associate Deans Howard Federspiel and Paul Panek, and Tauni Graham and John Crissinger of the OSUN Library. Others who have given assistance are Jeff Danby and Guy Franz Arend, as well as my wife, Diane, and Erik and Victoria, who have helped in so many ways. I must also acknowledge the congenial working with Stackpole editors Dave Reisch and Brittany Stoner. There is much more to the history of the 11. Gespenster-Division, and I would greatly appreciate corrections and additions.

A. Harding Ganz
Associate Professor Emeritus, History
Ohio State University
Newark, Ohio 43055

A Note on German Terminology and Unit Nomenclature

I have endeavored to incorporate German terms and abbreviations as actually used in World War II. For example, "Landser" is the generic term for the German soldier, while "Wagen" or "Panzer" was the Panzerkampfwagen (tank). One characteristic of German pronunciation is that the "v" is pronounced as "f," and the "w" as "v;" thus the VW is the "Fau Vay," the Lkw (Lastwagen, truck) is the "Ell kah vay," and "Vagen" is a panzer. The artillery forward observer (FO) is the "Fau Bay" (VB, Vorgeschobener Beobachter), and the half-track SPW (Schützenpanzerwagen) was the "Es Pay Vay." Other common terms included the "Acht-komma-acht," the 8,8cm gun ("eighty-eight"), and "Das Zweibein," the "bi-pod," for the MG 42. German gun measurements were in centimeters with commas, not millimeters and decimal points as in American practice. (German sources also use commas with times, as in 05,15 hours.)

In German usage, Arabic numerals were employed for platoons, companies, regiments, brigades, divisions, and armies. Roman numerals were used for battalions *within* a regiment, and for corps, but Arabic was used for separate battalions (and Abteilungen). The numeral followed the unit name in the case of regiments and panzer groups, but preceded it in most other cases. Thus 1./6./II. Abt./Pz.Rgt.15/11.Pz.Div. in XXXXVI. (not XLVI) A.K. in Pz.Gp. 4 (but redesignated 4.Pz.Armee) was the 1st Platoon, 6th Company, 2nd Battalion of Panzer Regiment 15 of the 11th Panzer Division in the Forty-First Army Corps, Panzer Group 4 (but redesignated as 4th Panzer Army). Pz.Jäg.Abt. 61 was Panzerjägerabteilung (Tank Destroyer Battalion) 61. *Abteilung* here meant battalion, but the terms were *not* interchangeable. In orders and records, units may be hyphenated or not (e.g., 11.Panzer-Division/11.Panzerdivision, 11.Pz.-Div./11.Pz.Div).

In American practice, letters were used for companies, artillery batteries, and combat commands; Roman numerals were employed for corps; and Arabic numerals were used in most other cases. Numbered armies were spelled out. Thus 2/B/37 Tk/CCA/4th AD in XII Corps, Third Army, 12th Army Group, was 2nd Platoon, B Company, 37th Tank Battalion, Combat Command A, 4th Armored Division in the Twelfth Corps, Third Army, Twelfth Army Group. To differentiate German from American (and other national) units, the proper designations will be used. German ranks and unit terminology—and their abbreviations—will also be used, for reasons including familiarization and as an aid in research in original language or records sources. Examples here might include LXXXX. A.K. (not XC.) and XXXXVII. Pz.K. (not XLVII.), Pz.G.R. for Panzergrenadier-Regiment (not PGR), and I.D. for Infanterie-Division, but Pz.Div. (not P.D.) for Panzer-Division.

GLOSSARY

Abteilung	detachment; also, battalion
Angriff	attack
Arko/Artilleriekommandeur	artillery commander
Auffrischung	replenishment, rehabilitation, refitting, rebuilding
Aufklärung	reconnaissance
Ausf./Ausführung	model (e.g., of a panzer)
Ausbildung	instruction, training
Besatzung	crew
Befehlswagen/-panzer	command vehicle/-tank
Bordfunk	intercom (communications)
Brückenkopf	bridgehead
DNF, Dinafü/Division Nachschubführer	division supply leader
Erdloch	foxhole
Ersatz	replacement
Feuerbefehl	fire command
Einsatzbereit	combat-ready
Fla[k]/Fliegerabwehr[kanone]	air defense [gun]
Flivo/Fliegerverbindungsoffizier	air liaison officer
Gef.Std./Gefechtsstand	(forward) command post
Gefechtsstärke	fighting strength
gef./gefallen	killed in action
Geschütz	gun; artillery piece; assault gun
Granatwerfer	mortar
Halbkettenfahrzeug	half-track
Hiwi/Hilfsfreiwillige	auxiliary volunteer
HKL/Hauptkampflinie	MLR/main line of resistance
HVP/Hauptverbandplatz	main (medical) clearing station
Igel	"Hedgehog" (all-around defensive position)
I-Gruppe/-Staffel (Instandssetzungs-)	maintenance group/staff
Kampfbereit	battle-ready
Kesselschlacht	cauldron battle
Kettenfahrzeuge	tracked vehicles
Kettenkrad/Kettenkraftrad	(half-)tracked motorcycle
Kgf/Kriegsgefangene	prisoners of war
Kfz/Kraftfahrzeug	motor vehicle
Kommandant	(panzer) commander
Kdr/Kommandeur	(unit) commander
Krad/Kraftrad	motorcycle
KTB/Kriegstagebuch	war diary
Lagebericht/-besprechung	situation report/-meeting, conference
Lkw/Lastkraftwagen	truck
MPi/Maschinenpistole	submachine gun
Mot/motorisiert	motorized
Nachr./Nachrichten	signals
Nachschub	supply (materiel)
Nebelwerfer/Raketen NbW	("smoke mortar")/rocket launcher
Ordonnanzoffizier	orderly officer
Pak/Panzerabwehrkanone	antitank gun
Pz.Kpfw./Panzerkampfwagen	armored fighting vehicle; tank (also Panzer, Wagen)
Panzergranate	armor-piercing shell
Panzerjäger	tank-destroyer
Panzerspähwagen	armored scout vehicle (armored car or light half-track)
Pi/Pionier	engineer
Pkw/Personenkraftwagen	personnel motor vehicle
Räderfahrzeuge	wheeled vehicles
Richtschütze	gunner
Rohr	barrel; artillery tube
Rollbahn	roadway designated for motor transport, excluding horse-drawn or foot units
Sani/Sanitäter	medic; aid man
Schützengraben	(rifle) trench
Sfl./Selbstfahrlafette	self-propelled mount; motor carriage
SPW/Schützenpanzerwagen	armored personnel vehicle; half-track
Sprenggranate	high-explosive shell
Stellung	position
Stoss (Gegen-/Vor-)	thrust (counter-/advance-)
Tagesbefehl	order of the day
Tarnung	camouflage
Treffer (Voll-)	hit (direct)
Tr.Ü.Pl./Truppenübungsplatz	troop training area
Turmluke	turret hatch
Überläufer	deserter
Verpflegungsstärke	ration strength
Vers./Versorgung	supply (provisions)
verw./verwundet	wounded in action
V.B./Vorgeschobener Beobachter	(artillery) forward observer
Wurfgerät	multiple rocket launcher frame
Ziel erkannt!	Target identified!
Zugführer	platoon leader
Zugmaschine, Schlepper	prime mover

CHAPTER ONE

Antecedents

BY THE TIME THE GUNS FELL SILENT ON THE WESTERN FRONT ON 11 November 1918, it had become obvious that the tank was now a major factor in the equations of warfare. The British had been the first to introduce the tank. Lieutenant Colonel of Engineers Ernest Dunlop Swinton is credited with outfitting an armored car with caterpillar tracks to create a machine that could cross trenches and flatten barbed-wire entanglements, all while protected against the deadly machine guns that dominated the no-man's-land between opposing trench lines. Supported by Winston Churchill, First Lord of the Admiralty, against official resistance, production of the machines was organized by the Landships Committee in 1915, and testing was undertaken by a special unit of the Machine Gun Corps under Swinton. The term "tank" was possibly adopted by Colonel Swinton after he heard workmen in the plant where the chassis and hull were being produced refer to it as a "water carrier for Mesopotamia" and as "that tank thing." British Mark I tanks were first employed at Flers during the Battle of the Somme on 15 September 1916, albeit without great success; design improvements continued for later Marks, and they became operational under The Tank Corps (as redesignated 27 July 1917).[1]

In France, Colonel d'Artillerie Baptiste Estienne was inspired after seeing some American-made Holt Manufacturing Company caterpillar tractors behind the front lines. He also encountered opposition to developing an armored machine, but the French high command ultimately acquiesced in the development of such a vehicle. The firms of Schneider and St. Chamond began to produce tanks in 1916, and these machines were first used at Berry-au-Bac on 16 April 1917 during the disastrous Chemin des Dames offensive. Other allied nations soon followed suit: the Italians obtained a Schneider and some French-made Renault light tanks in 1918, inspirations that stimulated Italian tank design and production, while the infant American Tank Corps used French Renaults and British Mark Vs on the Western Front.

The first demonstrated success of tanks came during the Battle of Cambrai on 20 November 1917, when in a surprise attack without extensive artillery preparation 381 Mark IV tanks of the British Tank Corps broke through the German lines to a depth of 8 kilometers (5 miles) before most were knocked out or suffered mechanical failure. The success had equally caught the British commanders by surprise, as they had made no provision for enabling the infantry to keep pace with the tanks.

The introduction of British tanks on the Somme belatedly prompted the German Kriegsministerium (War Ministry) to consider armored fighting vehicles, and in 1917 engineer Josef Vollmer and motor transport officer Hauptmann (Captain) Wegner produced designs for a prototype. The result was the A7V Sturmpanzerwagen (armored assault vehicle), its numerical designation coming from the War Department's Division 7 (Traffic). It was tested on 14 May 1917 and subsequently put into production by the Daimler automotive company. At 32 tons and a length of 7.3 meters (24 feet, 6 inches), its size was comparable to the British Mark IV's 28 tons and 26-foot, 5-inch overall length. It had two 100-horsepower Daimler four-cylinder engines driving each track, engines that produced a maximum speed of 8 km/h (5 mph) compared to the Mark IV's 105 hp and top speed of 6 km/h (3.7 mph). It mounted a 5,7cm gun in the bow with limited traverse and bristled with six machine guns and armor up to 30mm (1.18 inches) thick. The British Mark IV mounted a 6-pounder (5,7cm) Hotchkiss gun in each side sponson, along with four Lewis machine guns in the "Male" version (mounting cannon), and six machine guns in the "Female" version (mounting machine guns only). Its armor thickness was only 12mm (.5 inches). However, the A7V had a crew of eighteen packed inside, while the Mark IV carried eight; an armored citadel overhung the A7V's tracks to protect the crewmen, but limited the vehicle's trench-crossing and climbing capability. The Mark IV, on the other hand, had exposed overhead tracks protruding beyond the hull.

Only twenty A7Vs were produced, as the Germans instead used captured British models in the March 1918 offensives.[2] Thirteen A7Vs did lead a German attack on 24 April 1918 that captured Villers-Bretonneux near Amiens, a battle that included history's first tank-versus-tank engagement. An A7V damaged and drove off two Mark IV Females with its 5,7cm gun, but in turn was engaged by a Male and overturned on a steep bank. Two more A7Vs arrived and were also engaged. One was hit and abandoned, and the other retreated.[3] The engagement demonstrated that tanks could now expect to fight enemy tanks; following the fight the British modified a number of Females with one 6-pounder gun sponson, referring to them as "Hermaphrodites."

As the role of tanks was expanding beyond trench-crossing and breakthrough to pursuit and exploitation, lighter 14-ton British Medium Mark A Whippets, capable of reaching 13 km/h (8 mph), and 7-ton French Renault FTs with top speeds of 9.6 km/h (6 mph) were produced. Hundreds of Allied tanks took part in the counteroffensives of 1918, and the British breakthrough at Amiens—with 604 tanks—caused German Gen. Erich Ludendorff to refer to 8 August as the "Black Day" of the German Army. As World War I ended with the Armistice of 11 November 1918, it was clear that tanks would play a crucial if not decisive role in future conflicts.

The fighting in Europe demonstrated to perceptive observers that heavy tanks in support of infantry could break through enemy defensive systems, and fast, light tanks could be used for exploitation. Villers-Bretonneux proved that tanks could expect to engage enemy tanks, and Cambrai showed the need for the three combat arms—armor, infantry, and artillery—to coordinate with one another.

Certain individuals of vision began to formulate armored warfare doctrine in the postwar period, although novel concepts were often subordinated to institutional interests and tank production was susceptible to budgetary constraints. As early as November 1916, Capt. Geoffrey le Q. Martel of the British Tank Corps staff wrote a paper envisioning clashes between future tank armies. Col. J. F. C. Fuller of the Tank Corps proposed reorganizing each infantry battalion to include a tank company in a 1919 memorandum, and in his 1920 book *Tanks in the Great War 1914–1918*, he elaborated on the principle of mechanization of the combat arms.

Another British tank advocate was infantry Capt. Basil H. Liddell Hart. Disabled by gas on the Somme during World War I, Liddell Hart subsequently became a prolific military commentator. After rewriting the tactics portion of the army's Infantry Training Manual in 1920, Liddell Hart became military correspondent for first the *Daily Telegraph* and then the *Times*, and he issued a stream of works in 1925, 1927, 1932, and 1933 (he would continue writing until after his death in 1970).[4] He advanced the "expanding torrent" concept of deep penetration by mechanized units, proposing in 1922 a "New Model Division" composed of composite brigades with tank battalions, infantry battalions in armored carriers, and mechanized artillery; the War Office ultimately authorized such an Experimental Mechanised Force for testing on Salisbury Plain in 1927, but it was disbanded the next year. By the 1930s, Liddell Hart had concluded that antitank defenses qualified the capabilities of armor, though his continued advocacy of the "indirect approach" as Britain's military strategy found favor among armor tacticians.

For his part, Fuller apparently became convinced that the focus should be on all-tank brigades to which infantry or other elements might be attached. This trend, of "fleets of tanks" like warships, was reflected in the first armored force manual, *Mechanised and Armoured Formations*, issued in 1929.[5] Accordingly, British tank design in the 1930s began to diverge between heavily armored infantry tanks and more mobile medium cruiser tanks. The 26-ton Matilda and the slightly smaller Valentine had up to 76mm (3 inches) of armor and a speed of 24 km/h (15 mph), while the cruiser tank A13 had only 14mm (.5 inches) of armor but a speed of 48 km/h (30 mph). All three models would go to war mounting only a 2-pounder (39mm) gun, inferior to the 7,5cm guns of the French, Germans, and Russians.

In 1938 the Mobile Division was formed; it was redesignated the Armoured Division the next year. It counted some 321 light and cruiser tanks in two armored brigades. There was also a Support Group consisting of a motorized rifle battalion and a small motorized artillery regiment. The formation would prove to be unbalanced, with a ratio of six tank battalions to only one of infantry. It would be Britain's sole armored division when World War II broke out in 1939. The heavy Matilda IIs were in the separate 1st Army Tank Brigade.

In France tank development had been initiated under Col. Baptiste Estienne, who was authorized to work with the Schneider and Renault companies in 1916. After his promotion to Général, he had commanded the French tank units (Artillerie d'Assaut) during World War I and subsequently urged mechanization of the infantry and artillery, and with tanks, organized as a separate mechanized arm. Instead, the tanks were subordinated to the Infantry Department, and in 1929 the French began the *defensive* border fortification system named after Defense Minister André Maginot (who as a sergeant was wounded in the terrible battle of Verdun in 1916). *La Ligne Maginot* reflected not only a renewed faith in fortifications—a result of the struggles around Forts Vaux and Douaumont during World War I—but also the "paralyzing pessimism" caused by the casualties that crippled France.[6]

In the 1930s France produced a number of very capable tanks, perhaps the best being the Somua S35, which mounted a 47mm gun and coaxial machine gun in an electric-power traverse turret, weighed 20 tons, and had a speed of 46 km/h (29 mph) and a 230-kilometer (143-mile) radius of action. The formidable Char B1 had a 37mm gun in its turret plus a short 75mm howitzer mounted in the front hull. But the 30-ton tank's speed was only 29 km/h (18 mph) and the 75mm howitzer had no traverse; it was instead aimed by moving the tank itself. The improved B1bis had a 47mm gun in the turret, increased armor (60mm compared to 40mm), and a more powerful engine, but was heavier and the fuel endurance was reduced from 200 kilometers (125 miles) to 140 kilometers (87 miles), or about three hours. Although the French tanks were perhaps superior to those of other nations of the time, they had a major drawback: all had only a small, one-man turret, which meant the tank commander also had to be his own loader and gunner.

More significantly, French tactical doctrine did not keep pace with the evolving capabilities of the tanks being produced. The cavalry vied with the infantry for armored fighting vehicles more powerful than its armored cars, and in 1934 formed the Division Légère Mécanique (DLM), the first of three light mechanized divisions by 1940. It achieved a certain tactical balance, being composed of a reconnaissance brigade of armored cars and motorcycles, a tank brigade of Somua S35s and Hotchkiss H35s, a rifle brigade in Laffly armored wheeled carriers, a towed artillery regiment, and engineer and service units. The DLM's strike force potential, however, was constrained by its traditional light cavalry role of reconnaissance, security, and delaying missions, and in the later 1940 campaign, the three DLMs simply screened the Anglo-French advance north into Belgium.

The French main battle tanks were organized into battalions to accompany the infantry, both in pace and in tactical operations. Their mission was defined in the 1930 *Instruction on the Employment of Tanks*, which declared that "the tank is an infantry-supporting weapon." The Germans, meanwhile, were beginning to evolve a doctrine of mobile warfare, and their *Truppenführung* manual stated that "in the zone of action of tanks, the action of other arms is to be based on that of tanks."[7] The doctrinal contrast with the French is obvious.

In vain did more far-sighted French officers argue for mechanization. Lt. Col. Charles de Gaulle, a member of the secretariat of the Council of National Defense, advocated this stance in his *Vers l'armée de métier (Toward a Professional Army)*, published in Paris by Berger-Levrault in 1934. It was translated and published in German the following year as *Frankreichs Stossarmee (France's Shock Army)*, and translations in other languages followed (though not in English until 1941, as *The Army of the Future*).[8] But the book was written in a style that was flamboyant, patriotic, and unspecific, and the professionalism issue served only to antagonize his conservative superiors as well as politicians and retard his career. During the Great War, Capitaine de Gaulle, wounded and captured at Douaumont village at Verdun 3 March 1916, had never *himself* seen tanks in action, as he was a prisoner of war in Germany for the next two years. More effective changes—if less dramatic than those proposed by de Gaulle—were incrementally implemented by Générals Pierre Héring and Gaston Billotte, and Général Maxime Weygand, who initiated the first DLM in 1934.[9]

If the participation of tanks in the Spanish Civil War of 1936–39 and the increasingly aggressive foreign policy of Adolf Hitler's Germany gave pause, it was the dramatic *Blitzkrieg* (Lightning War) of panzer divisions overrunning Poland in September 1939 that finally galvanized the French high command into the realization that actual armored division-level formations were needed.

Four battalions of heavy Char Bs were divided into two half or demi-brigades, each with a battalion of motorized infantry, in September 1939. Subsequently these and the newly formed battalions were reorganized on 16 January 1940 into two armored divisions: 1ère and 2ème Division Cuirassée de Reserve (DCR). Each DCR had a strength of 6,510 personnel, and sixty-two Char B and eighty-four Hotchkiss H39 tanks in two tank brigades. The divisions had been hastily improvised and were poorly balanced, each with four battalions of tanks, two of towed artillery, and only one battalion of infantry in Lorraine tracked armored carriers. The 3ème DCR was formed in March 1940 and the 4ème, under Colonel de Gaulle, only assembled five days *after* the German Blitzkrieg struck on 10 May 1940 with ten panzer divisions.[10] The DCRs—belatedly formed, ill-equipped, poorly organized, and having had no time to practice training maneuvers much less develop tactical concepts—were overwhelmed and destroyed one by one.

Because of their production and employment of tanks in World War I, the French and British experience and examples had significant influence on developments in other countries. Italy has the distinction of being the first nation to use motor vehicles in battle, when armored cars and Fiat trucks carrying troops were employed in the Italian-Turkish campaign in Tripolitania (western Libya) in 1912. Lancia armored car units were formed when Italy entered World War I against Austria, but the mountainous Tyrolean and rugged Isonzo terrain discouraged mobile warfare.

Thus the first postwar Italian-produced tanks were based on French and English models. The Carro Armato Modello 21 produced by Fiat was a two-man tank with twin machine guns based on the Renault FT, and the Carro Veloce (fast tank) 3/33 and later CV 3/35 (both redesignated L3) were small, two-man tracked vehicles with machine guns produced by Ansaldo, modeled after the British Carden Lloyd Mark VI machine-gun carrier. The L3s proved useful working with infantry in Ethiopia and in Spain, but were outclassed in the latter conflict by the Republican forces equipped with the Russian T-26 tank mounting a 45mm gun. This prompted production of the M 11, though its 37mm gun (47mm in the M 11/39) was mounted in the hull with limited traverse, the turret having only twin machine guns.

More advanced was the organization of Italian tanks into battalions and brigades, and then into three armored divisions (Divisione Corazzata) formed through 1939: Ariete, Centauro, and Littorio, all of which would fight in North Africa. It was even proposed that the armored divisions be paired with motorized infantry divisions (Trieste and Trento were formed) in armored corps. In practice, however, the Italian tanks were too lightly armed and armored to carry out a strike role, and exploitation was the mission of the Division Celere, which by 1939 was still mounted on horses and bicycles.[11]

British and French tanks were utilized by other nations in the 1920s as well, before they ventured into their own designs in the 1930s. Models included the little Vickers Carden Lloyd Mark VI machine-gun carrier, the Vickers Medium C, and the ubiquitous Renault FT 1917, over 4,000 of which had been produced.[12] An expansionist Japan produced tankettes and light tanks mounting a 37mm gun, and mediums mounting a short 57mm gun, the mainstay by 1939 being the Type 97 Chiha (later improved with a high-velocity quick-firing (QF) 47mm, as the Shinhoto Chiha). Three Japanese tank regiments were formed in 1933 and a tank brigade including a motorized infantry and a motorized artillery regiment followed in 1934; all were successfully employed against the poorly equipped Nationalist Chinese forces. But in the 1938 and 1939 border engagements with the Soviet Union, Japanese tanks and tactics, supporting the infantry, proved inferior.

In eastern Europe the reborn Poland was supported and influenced by France, especially in the Russo-Polish War of 1920–21. By 1939 the Polish Army included a battalion of French Renault R35s with a 37mm gun and two 7TP battalions of their own design. The latter mounted a high-velocity Bofors 37mm gun, evolved from the Vickers-Armstrong 6-ton light tank. Machine gun–carrying TK and TKS tankettes and armored cars supported the infantry and cavalry reconnaissance units. With some 190 gun-carrying tanks, the Poles had more tanks than either Britain or the United States. But Germany had far more and, with the Polish leadership compelled to disperse its ground forces to defend the country's entire border, they would be overwhelmed in September 1939.

The new Czechoslovak Army had also been organized under French guidance, though by 1936 the excellent Skoda Works was producing its own medium tank, the LT 35, mounting a 37mm gun. When Nazi Germany occupied Bohemia in March 1939, the Germans took some 218 of these into service as the Panzer 35(t), the "t" meaning tschechisch or Czech. The Germans also took over the prototype of the newer, lighter TNHP, or LT 38, mounting a high-velocity 37mm Skoda gun. Recognizing this tank as superior to the German Panzers I and II, and possibly the III, Germany put it into production as the Panzer 38(t). These would be used by several German panzer divisions, and after 1942 the now obsolete chassis was still being utilized for self-propelled artillery and antitank and tank destroyer armored vehicles.[13]

While many nations were evolving tanks and armored organization and concepts in the interwar period from 1919 to 1939, the United States had retreated into trans-Atlantic isolationism and military budgets had suffered accordingly. Interbranch rivalry also retarded the development of an American armored force. While a Tank Corps was established 26 January 1918 during World War I, its units first saw action only on 12 September when the 304th Tank Brigade, under Lt. Col. George S. Patton Jr., attacked the St. Mihiel salient. The four *total* American tank battalions were equipped with French Renault and British Mark V tanks, with no American-built versions reaching the theater. Under the National Defense Act of 1920 the Tank Corps was abolished, and tanks were subordinated to the Infantry branch.

There were some who urged mechanization, especially Col. Daniel Van Voorhis and later Col. Adna Chaffee, but experimental mechanized forces in 1928 and in 1930 were quickly dissolved. A number of tank designs reached prototype stage, but most did not go into production. A light cavalry tank did emerge in 1935, designated the M1 "Combat Car" (as "tanks" belonged to the Infantry), and this was followed by the M2 series. These had only machine guns, in one or in twin turrets. By 1939 the medium M2 tank had been developed, but its 37mm gun was wholly inadequate by then. When war broke out in 1939, the Germans, Italians, and French all had armored division formations, while the US Army had just one mechanized cavalry brigade (the 7th). American Chief of Cavalry Maj. Gen. John Herr would not be misled "to assume that the untried machine can displace the proved and tried horse." It was only after Poland, Scandinavia, the Low Countries, and France all fell before the German Blitzkrieg, and Britain was threatened with invasion, that the US War Department finally established an Armored Force on 10 July 1940 ("for purposes of service test"); two armored divisions, the 1st and 2nd, were authorized five days later.[14]

The one unique American contribution to armored development was the design of an erratic and abrasive inventor, J. Walter Christie. His 1928 prototype tank had four large bogie wheels supporting each track, the wheels being independently sprung, providing a good cross-country ride. The 8-ton vehicle had a 338 bhp Liberty 12-cylinder V-type engine producing a very high power-to-weight ratio of 25:1. Christie's original was also convertible, with a removable track that allowed 68 km/h (42 mph) on its tracks and an incredible 112 km/h (70 mph) on its wheels. A number of Christie–type tanks were procured, but by 1936 the Ordnance Department determined to stay with the sturdy volute (vertical) spring suspension that became characteristic of American tanks. The British did adopt the Christie suspension (though not the convertibility feature) for their cruiser tanks, but the most notable adoption was by the new Soviet Union.

After the upheavals of revolutions and civil war, an exhausted and traumatized Russia finally emerged in late 1922 as the Union of Soviet Socialist Republics. This first Communist country, ostracized by the democratic West, cemented a relationship with the defeated Germany's Weimar Republic with the Rapallo Agreement of 1922. Diplomatic recognition and trade agreements led to military cooperation, and the German Republic, denied viable weaponry by the 1919 Treaty of Versailles, was able to establish bases and training facilities in Russia. Initially, Russia's tanks were British and French, mostly captured from the White Russians during the Red-White Civil War of 1918–19. But as Russian industry recovered and as Communist Party General Secretary Josef Stalin consolidated his power, the dictator was determined on rapid (if brutal) industrialization, with the first Five-Year Plan of coordinated production introduced at the 15th Party Congress in 1927.

The driving force behind Soviet tank development may have been Red Army Chief of Staff Marshal Mikhail Tukhachevsky; he was supported by Stalin, at least until the paranoid ruler liquidated his high command (and several million other Russians) in the Great Purges from 1936 to 1938. Among the first Soviet-built tanks were the MS-I/T-18, a copy of the Renault FT, and the T-26 after 1928, copied from the British Vickers 6-ton light tank. The Russians constructed higher turrets to accommodate larger guns and their recoil at all elevations above the small turret ring. They included a 45mm gun in the T-26's B and C models and a 76mm howitzer in the D model of 1934. Some also had the characteristically Russian radio tube aerial around the turret top; this served as an additional handhold for troops riding on the tank, but it also identified a commander's tank to a foe. In any case, few Russian tanks would have radios.

Of significance were the BT series (Bystry Tank, fast tank) with four large bogie wheels on each side, developed from two revolutionary Christie tanks acquired in 1931. Models were upgunned from 37mm to 45mm, and the BT-5A and 7A mounted a 76.2mm howitzer. Russian tanks would continue to feature gun calibers larger than those of other nations, though penetration was more from the kinetic energy of a heavy projectile than from high velocity. Diesel engines also became characteristic while gasoline fueled the tanks of other nations. The T-26 and the BT were dispatched to aid Communist (Republican) forces in the Spanish Civil War, and were the mainstay of the armored force in 1939. Other Russian tanks ranged from the little machine-gun carriers (the T-37 and T-38 reconnaissance tankettes, which also had an amphibious capability) to the three-turreted T-28 with a 76.2mm howitzer and four machine guns to the gigantic 45-ton T-35 with a crew of ten and five turrets—one with a 76.2mm gun, two with 45mm guns, and two with machine guns.

The great number of Russian tanks were increasingly obsolete by 1939 but, unrevealed to the outside world, two new models were already in production and would catch the Germans by surprise in 1941. The first was the KV heavy tank (named for Klim Voroshilov, Soviet Defense Commissar). It mounted a 76.2mm gun and had armor 76mm (3 inches) thick, making its weight 43 tons. The second was the T-34 medium tank, considered by some the best tank of World War II. Evolved from the BT, it had the Christie suspension and a high power-to-weight ratio. It weighed 26 tons and mounted a 76.2mm gun with a muzzle velocity of 612 meters per second (2,007 feet per second). Its armor was only 45mm (1.8 inches) thick in the A model, but more significantly its turret and hull armor were sloped, up to 60 degrees on the bow, increasing relative thickness and ricochet effect. Its tracks were 478mm (19 inches) wide, giving it excellent maneuverability in the extremes of Russia's terrain and weather. One limitation was the four-man crew, which forced the tank commander to be his own gunner. (This would be corrected with the T-34/85 of 1944, when a larger turret provided space for a fifth crew member and a powerful 85mm gun.)[15]

By 1941 the Germans estimated the Russians had over 24,000 tanks, a figure that was actually too low. If the Russians had the largest tank force in the world, and the most heavily gunned, their armored warfare organization and doctrine were less impressive. Each infantry division had a battalion of light tanks, and there were a large number of tank brigades of 100 tanks, each with three battalions of light or medium tanks. There were also seven division-sized mechanized corps by 1939, each with two or three mechanized brigades, a motorized infantry brigade, and a motorized field artillery regiment. There seems, however, to have been little concept of coordination between the tanks and the infantry, who often rode the tanks into the attack.

Future Red Army marshals—notably Generals Pavlov, Konev, Malinovsky, and Rokossovsky—served in Spain, where the Russian T-26 and BT tanks outgunned the Italian L 3s and German Panzer Is armed only with machine guns. Nonetheless none of the tank units achieved dramatic successes, leading many observers to comment on the efficacy of defensive antitank guns, and reconfirm that tanks worked best when supporting the infantry. If there were any more original ideas, they were apparently stifled by the pervasive terror of the Great Purges and the NKVD secret police. In the Far East, however, in a border engagement along the river Khalkhin in August 1939, Gen. Georgi Zhukov fixed the Japanese forces with a frontal assault and then launched his 6th Tank Brigade to encircle them. But such originality was not generally encouraged in Stalin's Soviet Union, and no revolutionary concepts of armored warfare would be coming to fruition.

The nation that would dramatically revolutionize warfare by restoring offensive mobility with its panzer divisions—thus influencing armored forces tactically, operationally, and strategically into the twenty-first century—was Germany. To some extent, Germany's novel armored warfare concepts resulted from her parlous situation after 1919, when the country was virtually disarmed by the Armistice of 11 November 1918 and the Treaty of Versailles of 28 June 1919, as the Weimar Republic began to emerge. The treaty's denial in Articles 171, 181, and 198 of tanks, combat aircraft, and submarines, in addition to heavy artillery and modern battleships, served to emphasize the perceived importance of these weapons. With the Reichswehr (Reich Defense Forces) limited by the treaty to 100,000 personnel, only rapid mobility could concentrate Germany's forces at a threatened part of her extensive frontier—(Germany bordered ten countries)—and offset any numerical superiority an opponent might have.

While universal arms reduction had been implied by Versailles, the France of ardent nationalist President Raymond Poincaré and Premier Georges Clemenceau had no intention of doing so. The French-equipped army of the new, belligerently expansionist Poland invaded the exhausted Soviet Union in 1920, an implied threat also against Germany to the west.

German Gen. Hans von Seeckt, who served as chief of staff of Generaloberst (Colonel General) August von Mackensen's 11. Armee during the Gorlice–Tarnow breakthrough in 1915 and served in Serbia, Rumania, and Turkey, became Chef der Heeresleitung (Chief of the Army Command) in the new, truncated Reichswehr 17 March 1920.[16] Von Seeckt was primarily concerned with keeping the armed forces isolated from politics (both radical and democratic), preserving the Gross Generalstab (Great General Staff) tradition through the Truppenamt (Office of Troops), and linking the new units with historical regimental lineage to develop a renewed esprit de corps.

The Versailles Treaty mandated long-term service: twelve years for enlisted personnel and twenty-five years for officers. This was meant to prevent the rapid training and passing into the reserves of men, the practice by which Generalmajor Gerhard von Scharnhorst's reformers had evaded Napoleon's limit of 42,000 troops for the Prussian Army after the emperor's Jena–Auerstädt victory of 1806; and which also generated the large national Prussian Army of trained reserves that rose against Napoleon in the 1813 War of Liberation. Von Seeckt, responsible for national defense, compromised these restrictions by mandating highly selective recruiting and training an officer and non-commissioned officer (NCO) cadre to prepare for future military expansion: "Not an army of soldiers, but an army of leaders (Führerheer)." Yet prejudiced against a mass "democratic" army of conscripts, he also saw the small Reichsheer as an elite army, and of necessity mobile, and as early as 1921 held exercises in the Harz Mountains employing truck-borne motorized infantry.

Also of significance was von Seeckt's initiation of contacts with the Soviet Union, a *rapprochement* between Germany and Russia prompted by the belligerence of French-supported Poland. Soviet leader Lenin needed to industrialize, and he postponed his Marxist Communist goals with the New Economic Policy (NEP); by March 1921 negotiations were opened for the transfer of prohibited German industries to Russia. Von Seeckt saw the opportunity to produce and test new weaponry and develop new tactical concepts, and convinced the new chancellor, Dr. Josef Wirth, and Foreign Secretary Ago Freiherr von Maltzahn of the advantages to Germany. He personally received Karl Radek, the Soviet Comintern (Communist International) agent who had supported the German Communist Spartacist uprising in 1918–19 and had helped organize the Communist revolt in the Ruhr in 1920. Establishing "Special Branch R" in the Reichswehr Ministry and collaborating with the Society for the Furthering of Industrial Enterprises (GEFU), von Seeckt played a major role in the resulting Rapallo Agreement of 16 April 1922, at the time of the international Genoa Conference. By 1923 a tank training center was opened in Kazan on the Volga, an air training base operated at Lipetsk, and a chemical warfare facility opened at Saratov. German officers and pilots were working with their Russian counterparts developing concepts of armored warfare, aerial bombing, and parachute troops, all laying the basis for the Blitzkrieg.[17]

When Gustav Stresemann became chancellor in 1923, and subsequently as foreign secretary until his death in 1929, he followed a two-pronged foreign policy: 1) *détente* with France and accommodation with the Western powers through the "fulfillment" of the terms of Versailles, and 2) pursuing policies and contacts abroad to strengthen Germany's national defense. The first tactic resulted in American Dawes Plan credits and the Locarno Pact of 1925, which guaranteed the European borders (*western* but not the *eastern*) and provided for Germany's entry into the League of Nations, generating the "Spirit of Locarno" of international goodwill that resulted in Stresemann's sharing the 1926 Nobel Peace Prize with French Foreign Minister Aristide Briand.

Stresemann's second tactic helped Germany circumvent the terms of Versailles. The Inter-Allied Control Commission (IACC) was established in 1919 to monitor German compliance with Versailles; the IAMCC (IMKK to the Germans), the branch charged with monitoring the treaty's military provisions, continually found its on-site inspection teams thwarted, evaded, and compromised. German firm Krupp gained control of the Bofors ordnance works in Sweden, Fokker displaced to the Netherlands, and Japanese firm Kawasaki built eight U-boats. In Germany cryptanalysts in the Abwehr (Defense) Section were disguised as newspaper translators and provided advanced warning of IACC inspections, while the Heinkel He 70 "mail carrier" was the forerunner of the He 111 bomber of 1934, and advertising skywriter squadrons and glider clubs trained future pilots like Adolf Galland, later general of the Luftwaffe's Fighter Command. Krupp's "Koch and Kienzle Development Firm" designed tanks ("agricultural tractors"), and Rheinmetall's railroad car department constructed artillery.[18]

Of greatest significance was Germany's covert relationship with Russia. Krupp technicians supervised artillery shell manufacturing at the Putilov arms works in Leningrad, Junkers established an aircraft plant at Fili near Moscow, and there was a rifle works at Tula. German officers traveled as tourists and businessmen, and even as "Communist Party delegates." The air training center at Lipetsk was disguised as an "Agricultural Pest Control Unit" and those killed in accidents might be returned to Germany in cases labeled "engine parts," all to evade the IACC. Despite IACC reports of German evasion and occasional probes, Western political leaders in particular were unwilling to jeopardize the spirit of *détente* by following up on intelligence that had awkward political implications, dismissing these complaints as "petty detail" and "technical controversies."[19] Stresemann was finally able to secure the withdrawal of the IAMCC in January 1927, despite the group's final report concluding that "Germany had never disarmed, had never had the intention of disarming, and for seven years had done everything in her power to deceive and 'counter-control' the Commission appointed to control her disarmament."[20]

The euphoric "Spirit of Locarno" culminated in 1928 with the Kellogg-Briand Pact to "outlaw war," signed by sixty-three nations. Yet at the Geneva Disarmament Conference, which began in 1930, the France of Aristide Briand repulsed any attempts to reduce her armed forces and maintained the largest standing army in Europe. When Adolf Hitler became chancellor of Germany in 1933 resulting from the world Depression, he withdrew the country from the League of Nations and intended to rearm Germany to right what he saw as the *Diktat* of Versailles. The rise of the Nazi regime ended the collaboration with the Communist Soviet Union, which was now embroiled in the violence of Stalin's "Second Revolution," thus ending the NEP, and the brutal collectivization of agriculture. Nonetheless, Stresemann and von Seeckt had served well their nation's national security interests, if not the idealistic concept of "world peace," and the atmosphere and circumstances were conducive to the revolutionary concepts of armored warfare that would evolve as Blitzkrieg.

CHAPTER TWO

Origins of the Panzerwaffe

DEFEATED IN WORLD WAR I DUE IN NO SMALL MEASURE TO THE Allied tank forces, and denied tanks by the Treaty of Versailles' Article 171, the new Reichsheer was very conscious of the importance of these revolutionary weapons. The question of what kind of tanks, what unit organization, and what operational concepts would be appropriate to create a German Panzerwaffe (Armored Force), however, would divide the German military as these issues divided the militaries of other nations—and in Germany's case in 1919 they were a moot point anyway.

While the Daimler A7V was the only German tank model actually put into production and committed to combat in World War I, a variety of additional types of tanks were being constructed or had reached prototype stage when the war ended. These included the A7V-U, which had overhead tracks similar to the British Marks, and the super-heavy Grosskampfwagen (or "K-Wagen") weighing 165 tons, having a twenty-two-man crew, and mounting four 7,7cm guns in side sponsons along with six machine guns. The K-Wagen was so large it could only be transported in twenty 5-ton sections. Two prototypes were built, both powered by Daimler-Benz engines. Conversely, the Krupp–built LK II, which looked like the British Whippet, weighed 10 tons and mounted either a 5,7cm gun or two machine guns in a fixed turret, and the prototype LK I had a revolving turret. While some of these models were destroyed under the treaty terms and the remaining wartime A7Vs were given to Poland, the LK II design and two prototypes were sold to Sweden. Ten light tanks were assembled from component parts there under the supervision of Josef Vollmer, the German engineer who had designed the LK II and the A7V, and were organized into the first Swedish tank unit in 1920. The LK II was produced by the Landsverk Company of Landskrona in southern Sweden as the M 21 (improved later as the M 21/29).[1]

With the Rapallo Agreement and the establishment of the tank center at Kazan in the Soviet Union by 1926, the Reichsheer produced and tested "agricultural tractors," among them the 10-ton Leichter Traktor with a 3,7cm gun in a revolving turret and Rheinmetall's Grosstraktor of 20 tons mounting a 7,5cm or 10,5cm gun in a revolving turret and two machine-gun turrets. In 1933 Rheinmetall also produced the multi-turreted Neubaufahrzeug, or New Model Vehicle (NbFz); this prompted the Russian T-28, which became the standard Russian medium tank by 1939. Prototype A had a short 7,5cm gun and a 3,7cm coaxially in the turret, while the B version mounted 10,5cm and a 3,7cm guns. Both had machine-gun turrets, one fore and one aft. However, these formidable-appearing tanks had only thin 14.5mm (.5-inch) armor, thus weighing only 23 tons. The Germans subsequently produced a total of just six of the NbFz, though when they were offloaded at the Oslo docks during the 1940 Scandinavian campaign they created quite a sensation.[2]

Later German panzer commanders who trained at Kazan (code-named "Kama") included Wilhelm Ritter von Thoma, subsequently commander of the panzer component of the Legion Condor sent to Spain and finally the Deutsches Afrika Korps (DAK) in North Africa. The Rapallo relationship ended after Hitler and his NSDAP came to power in January 1933, and by autumn of that year the German bases in Russia were closed. Nonetheless Marshal Mikhail Tukachevsky, head of the Red Army, helped facilitate the return of some of the prototypes to Germany, including six of the large and three of the light "tractors." The cooperation had been mutually beneficial for both the German and Russian armed forces, though ultimately they would clash as opponents.[3]

In Germany, thanks to the favorable atmosphere created by von Seeckt's policies, progress toward mechanization was carried out by the Inspektion der Kraftfahrtruppen (Inspectorate of Motorized Transport Troops) under Oberst (later General der Infanterie) Erich von Tschischwitz. He requested a general staff officer from the Truppenamt, which assigned Hauptmann Heinz Guderian—the man who would become "Vater der Panzerwaffe" (Father of the Armored Force)—effective 1 April 1922. Born 17 June 1888 at Kulm (Polish Chelmno) on the Vistula, Guderian trained with the 10. Hannöversch Jäger Bataillon (Hannoverian Light Infantry Battalion) and was commissioned an officer in 1908. During World War I he served on the Western Front as a staff and signals officer, including at the battles of Verdun and the Aisne, where he learned the importance of communications.

After the war, it was determined that Guderian should acquire some practical experience with transport troops, so in 1922 he was attached for three months to the 7. Bayerische Kraftfahr Bataillon (Bavarian Motorized Transport Battalion) in Munich. This unit was commanded by Maj. Oswald Lutz, with whom Guderian was to work closely in the years to come.[4] While serving in various positions with the Motorized Troops Department, Guderian quickly became aware of the operational possibilities of mobile warfare, especially when Oberstleutnant Walther von Brauchitsch, later commander in chief of the army, organized maneuvers during the winter of 1923–24 to test possible coordination between mobile ground forces and tactical airpower. While Reichsheer maneuvers had to be conducted with canvas and wood mock-ups over wheeled vehicles to simulate "tanks" (at least for the world news media), Guderian was familiar with the tank warfare developments at Kazan and in 1929 witnessed the German-influenced Swedish developments. Guderian was "particularly delighted" to be sent to Sweden for four weeks in 1929, where he actually drove an LK II and witnessed tank maneuvers of the Strijdsvagn Battalion of the Gota Guards.[5] He was also developing the concept of tactical armored formations being *balanced* formations of tanks and mobile infantry and artillery, the concept of the combined arms team:

> In this year, 1929, I became convinced that tanks working on their own or in conjunction with infantry could never achieve decisive importance. My historical studies, the exercises carried out in England and our own experiences with mock-ups had persuaded me that tanks would never be able to produce their full effect until the other weapons on whose support they must inevitably rely were brought up to their standard of speed and of cross-country performance. In such a formation of all arms, the tanks must play the primary role, the other weapons being subordinated to the requirements of the armor. It would be wrong to include tanks in infantry divisions: what was needed were armored divisions which would include all the supporting arms needed to allow the tanks to fight with full effect.[6]

Major Guderian's conclusions were also the result of his reading the flood of writing on tanks and mechanization of the 1920s, and he acknowledged the work of the English thinkers such as Fuller, Martel, and Liddell Hart. (While some writers also credit the work of Charles de Gaulle as being an influence, de Gaulle's major book was published in 1934, at a time when Guderian had already formulated his concepts and the first three panzer divisions were already being organized.)[7]

Yet even in the German military there was resistance to mechanization. Tschischwitz's successor at the Transport Troops Inspectorate, Oberst Oldwig von Natzmer, told Guderian motorized units were only "supposed to carry flour!" and after the 1929 maneuvers the new inspector, Gen. Otto von Stülpnagel, said that whole panzer divisions were a "Utopian dream."[8] But the chief of staff of the Inspectorate was Guderian's friend, now Oberst Lutz, who secured Guderian command of the 3. Preussisch Kraftfahr Bataillon (Prussian Motorized Battalion) in 1930. Guderian reorganized the unit as a panzer reconnaissance battalion with armored cars, motorcycles, (dummy) tanks, and (wooden) antitank guns. In the following year Lutz, promoted to general, was named chief of the Inspectorate, and he made now Oberstleutnant Guderian his chief of staff. As in other countries, resistance to mechanization came from the infantry and cavalry branches. The Inspector of Cavalry, General von Hirschberg, was committed to developing heavy horse cavalry, although he was willing to pass reconnaissance operations to the motorized troops; but General von Knochenhauer, who succeeded him, sought to regain control of any such units.

Nonetheless, because of the Versailles constraints, the advocates of mechanization in the Reichswehr had support in various departments. In addition, denied tanks, these men could contemplate the types of tanks required to implement the evolving doctrine and organization, rather than fabricating operational and organizational concepts around inventories of (increasingly obsolete) tanks. To equip the battalions of the eventual panzer divisions, a light tank with a 3,7cm gun and a medium tank with a 7,5cm gun were envisioned. Guderian says that he and Lutz felt that the lighter tank should mount a 5cm gun with an armor-piercing shell given the trend toward heavier guns and thicker armor abroad, but the Heereswaffenamt (Army Ordnance Office) insisted on the 3,7cm because it was already in production as an antitank weapon.

The tank types would be similar, however: they had their weight limited to 24 tons (as German field engineer bridging weight limits were a factor), a speed of 40 km/h (25 mph), and a five-man Besatzung (crew) consisting of a Kommandant (commander), Richtschütze (gunner), and Ladeschütze (loader) in the turret, and Fahrer (driver) and Funker (radio operator and bow gunner) in the front hull. Crew intercommunications would be by larynx microphones, and all tanks would have radios. Thus while other national armies too often concentrated on firepower and armor—leading to tanks with poor communications systems and a tank commander acting also as gunner—the German concept would emphasize tactical coordination of tank platoons and tank companies, with individual tank commanders receiving orders and controlling the firing and maneuvering of their tanks. Though German tanks would be outgunned by heavier enemy tanks in 1940 and 1941, their tactical flexibility would enable panzer units to prevail.

In the interim, a small training tank could be more quickly produced, and in 1933 the Heereswaffenamt put out orders to Krupp, MAN, Henschel, Daimler-Benz, and Rheinmetall-Borsig to submit designs under the designation of Landwirtschaftlicher Schlepper (LaS) or "agricultural tractor." In December 1933 the Krupp chassis and the Daimler-Benz turret and superstructure were selected for development, and production began in 1934. The small, two-man, 5.3-ton tankette had two 7,92mm machine guns mounted in its turret. The LaS model A used a girder to steady the outboard ends of the suspension wheel axles. The B model had a more powerful engine (100 bhp to 57 bhp) and an additional bogie wheel on each side.

When an experimental vehicle was accepted for service, it was given a specific Ordnance inventory number as a Sonderkraftfahrzeug (special-purpose motor vehicle), abbreviated as Sd.Kfz. After Hitler's Germany announced rearmament, this "agricultural tractor" was redesignated as the Panzerkampfwagen I (armored fighting vehicle) or Pz.Kpfw. I (Sd.Kfz. 101). While it served well its initial purpose as a trainer, it was also available to equip the first panzer divisions. "Nobody in 1932," Guderian later said, "could have guessed that one day we should have to go into action with this little training tank."[9] Panzer or Wagen became the term for a tank, though "panzer" in its broader sense came to mean armored forces as a concept.

On 30 January 1933 Adolf Hitler was named Kanzler (chancellor) of a nationalist coalition government. Whatever his ultimate racial and geopolitical policies, there is no question that mechanization of the German armed forces received dramatic stimulation through the personal interest and encouragement of the leader of the government. Guderian first sensed this when the chancellor himself opened the Berlin Automobile Exhibition at the beginning of February. In early 1934 Hitler inspected new equipment at Kummersdorf, sponsored by the Heeresamt, and Guderian was able to demonstrate the components of a panzer force: a motorcycle platoon, an antitank platoon, Panzer Is, and armored reconnaissance cars. The speed and precision movements of these units prompted Hitler to exclaim: "That's what I need! That's what I want to have!"[10]

Meanwhile the insistent demands of Hitler's brown-uniformed Sturmabteilungen (SA), or Storm Troop Detachments, for the "Second (Socialist) Revolution" and the replacement of the Reichswehr with a "people's army" culminated in the bloody purging of Ernst Röhm and the SA leaders on the night of 29–30 June 1934. While the suppression of the turbulent storm troopers was generally greeted with relief, many German officers were uneasy when Hitler assumed the office of the president with the death of Feldmarschall Paul von Hindenburg on 2 August and they had to swear an oath of allegiance to the Führer himself.

By 1935 German rearmament was underway. Conscription was introduced and the Reichswehr was renamed the Wehrmacht (armed forces) by the Law for the Creation of the Armed Forces of 16 March 1935. On 27 September 1935 the cover name Inspektion der Kraftfahrtruppen was redesignated Kommando der Panzertruppe (Armored Troop Command), and on 15 October the first three panzer divisions were established: the 1. headquartered at Weimar, the 2. at Würzburg, and the 3. at Berlin.[11] These first panzer divisions were originally organized with a panzer brigade of two regiments of two battalions with four companies each, totaling sixteen panzer companies with 561 Panzer Is. The infantry component was a motorized Schützenbrigade (rifle brigade) of a truck-borne rifle regiment of two battalions, and a motorcycle battalion, totaling nine rifle companies. The motorized artillery regiment had twenty-four truck-towed 10,5cm howitzers in two battalions of four-gun batteries. There was an antitank battalion of towed 3,7cm guns, an engineer battalion, a reconnaissance battalion of armored cars and motorcycles, a signals battalion, and medical, maintenance, and supply units. As artillery carried out fire missions from fixed positions, however, its full potential was retarded, subordinated to the overriding focus on mobility. (Self-propelled field artillery would not come into service until 1942.[12])

This organization resulted in a ratio of sixteen panzer companies to nine infantry companies, and peacetime maneuvers demonstrated a need for more infantry. Thus the next three panzer divisions—4., 5., and 10., created in 1938 and 1939—had a rifle brigade with a pair of two-battalion regiments, while the rifle regiment in the first three divisions was increased from two to three battalions each.[13] The Cavalry branch also created armored forces in 1938, with four Leichte (Light) divisions (1., 2., 3., and 4.) very similar to the panzer divisions but with only one tank battalion. Subsequently they passed to the Kommando der Panzertruppe, and after the 1939 Polish campaign were reorganized as panzer divisions 6., 7., 8., and 9. In the 1939 organization the panzer divisions had a panzer brigade of two regiments with two battalions each. The battalions had seventy-eight panzers in a medium/mixed company (nineteen Pz. IIIs and IVs) and two light companies (twenty-four Pz. Is and IIs), and the ratio was now a more balanced one of twelve panzer to twelve infantry companies. With command panzers, the 1939 panzer division had 328 panzers, 3,183 troops in the rifle brigade, 24 artillery pieces, and with other elements had a total strength of 11,792 personnel.[14]

Meanwhile the Panzer II (Sd.Kfz. 121), designed in 1935, entered production in 1937. The first prototypes weighed 7.5 tons and mounted a 2cm cannon and a machine gun in the turret. Though soon outclassed, the Panzer II was the primary panzer of the panzer divisions into 1940. It was characterized by having four or five large road wheels and four return rollers on each side (the drive sprocket being in front), and the chassis would later be utilized for self-propelled artillery, tank destroyer, and reconnaissance vehicles. The three-man crew consisted of a driver, the commander (who also traversed the little turret and loaded and fired the 2cm gun and MG), and a radio operator.

Other types of armored vehicles were developed to complement the panzers in the panzer division, including Panzerspähwagen (armored scout cars) in the Aufklärungsabteilung (reconnaissance battalion). Abteilung meant "detachment," but also meant Bataillon, the two terms <u>not</u> being interchangeable. Thus a panzer battalion was an Abteilung (Abt.), while an infantry battalion was a Bataillon (Btl.).

Like other nations, Germany had wheeled armored cars evolved from World War I. By 1939 the two basic types were the four-wheeled Sd.Kfz. 221 series and the eight-wheeled Sd.Kfz. 231 series. The four-wheeled scout car weighed some 4.8 tons, had a speed of 53 km/h (30 mph), and mounted a 2cm gun in an open turret. The thin armor was well-angled ballistically, the average being 55 degrees. The eight-wheeled armored car, the "Acht-Rad," also mounted a 2cm gun but was larger, weighing 11 tons, with a top speed of 85 km/h (53 mph). Both Panzerspähwagen had full-wheel drive, self-sealing bulletproof tires, and unlike those of other nations, could be driven backward equally well as it could be driven forward, the rearward-facing radio operator serving as rear driver. Variants had the large-frame radio antenna apparatus; later versions of the Acht-Rad mounted a short or a long 7,5cm gun on the hull, while the Puma (Sd.Kfz. 234/2) mounted a high-velocity 5cm gun in an enlarged turret.[15]

In keeping with the panzer division concept of a balanced combined arms team, the infantry and artillery would be motorized to keep pace with the tanks, and capable of cross-country mobility. This was the genesis of the Halbkettenfahrzeuge (half-track vehicles) of the German Army that played a significant role in World War II. Only the United States developed similar vehicles as armored personnel carriers. In addition, field artillery was initially to be towed by half-tracks. The Halbkette principle was to have front wheels for steering and for road movement, while the weight of the chassis was carried on tracks for cross-country movement. Research conducted during World War I had resulted in Daimler's "Marienwagen" and Benz's "Kraftprotze," though the war ended before these went into production.[16]

In 1932 the Ordnance Office awarded at least six contracts for half-track vehicles of different sizes for specific purposes: a 1-ton series by Demag, a 3-ton series by Hansa-Lloyd-Goliath, a 5-ton series by Büssing-NAG, an 8-ton series by Krauss-Maffei, a 12-ton series by Daimler-Benz, and an 18-ton series by FAMO. Maybach supplied most of the six- or twelve-cylinder engines for these half-tracks. Turning of the steering wheel by the driver turned the front wheels, while turning more sharply braked one of the tracks. High road speed required lubricated track links and rubber track pads, though later wartime shortages of rubber resulted in steel tracks and greater track wear.

The 1-ton series vehicles were designated "leichter Zugkraftwagen 1t" (light traction vehicle 1 ton) and allocated Ordnance inventory number Sd.Kfz. 10. It was intended to tow the 3,7cm antitank gun, a light infantry howitzer, or an ammunition trailer. Later mounting the 2cm Flak 38 gun, the Sd.Kfz. 10/4 was the primary self-propelled flak gun. In 1939 it was modified to carry armor while shortening the chassis and eliminating one road wheel on each side. As the "leichter Schützenpanzerwagen" or light armored personnel carrier (Sd.Kfz. 250), at least ten versions later emerged, including command, communications, reconnaissance, mortar, antitank (3,7cm Pak—Panzerabwehrkanone), and fire support (short 7,5cm) vehicles. As combat vehicles these half-tracks weighed some 6 tons and had a road speed of 74 km/h (46 mph), though the 8–14mm (.3–.5-inch) armor only gave protection from small-arms fire, and the open compartment was susceptible to artillery fire.

The 3-ton series (Sd.Kfz. 11) was intended to tow the 10,5cm howitzer or an ammunition trailer. The Schützenpanzerwagen model (Sd.Kfz. 251) was produced in the largest numbers during World War II, with roughly 15,000 being produced in some twenty-three versions including engineer, mortar, medical, flamethrower, antitank, and flak versions. The SPW was the mainstay of the mechanized rifle units (redesignated panzergrenadier units in 1942) of the panzer division. As such it weighed 8.5 tons, mounted one or more machine guns, had a road speed of 52 km/h (32 mph), and carried a ten-man infantry squad who could quickly dismount through rear hull doors or over the sides. Its armor, however, was a thin 8–14mm, and it was open-topped because its function was as a troop carrier, not a fighting vehicle (although in combat, such as in France in 1940, it would often be used as such). The 251 series were technically sophisticated according to collector Guy Franz Arend of Belgium, but were rather underpowered. The American M3 half-track was mechanically more reliable, but the German version's steel tracks gave it better cross-country mobility than did the American vehicle's rubber tracks.[17]

The 5-ton series Zugmaschine (Sd.Kfz. 6) towed engineer bridging equipment trailers or artillery, and later versions were self-propelled mounts for flak or Nebelwerfer (10-barrelled rocket launchers). This was also true of the 8-ton series (Sd.Kfz. 7), the prime mover for the 15cm howitzer or the versatile 8,8cm flak gun, also found to be effective in the antitank role. (In 1944 some were employed to tow the launching platform for the V-2 ballistic rocket and as fire guidance units.) Daimler-Benz produced the first heavy 12-ton half-track in 1931 in collaboration with the Russian government, and later versions of this Sd.Kfz. 8 towed the heavy 21cm mortar, the 24cm long-range gun, or the 10,5cm flak gun, at corps or army level.

The heaviest half-track was the 18-ton Sd.Kfz. 9 series, which provided the standard tank retriever for the army. A spade lowered from the rear gave ground purchase for winching power, and it could tow an eight-wheeled low-bed trailer that could carry the 24-ton Panzer IV. (By 1943, however, the heavier Tiger and Panther tanks required a Panther chassis modified as a Bergepanzer, or tank recovery vehicle.) The lightest tracked vehicle produced was the "Kettenkrad," Kettenkraftrad or tracked motorcycle of 1940, type HK 101 (Sd.Kfz. 2). This 1.7-ton tracked vehicle with motorcycle steering could go 80 km/h (50 mph) and proved especially useful for negotiating rugged terrain and forest trails to resupply forward troops with ammunition and rations and evacuate wounded.

Most troops and supplies of the panzer divisions, however, were transported in Lastkraftwagen (Lkw, trucks). Contracts had been let to at least eleven different manufacturers, including Ford-Werke, Borgward, Mercedes-Benz, Büssing-NAG, Magirus, and MAN. An attempt at standardization was made with the 6x6 Uniform Diesel, but it proved too heavy and too expensive. The Lastkraftwagen were produced with a cargo weight capacity between 1.6 and 6.5 tons. The most numerous Lkw was the 3.6-ton Adam Opel Blitz Typ 3,6-36S, with a six-cylinder 3.6-liter gasoline engine. It proved reliable, and Daimler-Benz also produced the model under license. Some 95,000 of the standard Blitz-S were built, albeit only with two-wheel drive. In 1940 the Opel Blitz Typ 6700A appeared, and 25,000 would be built. This had 4x4 all-wheel drive, with two driving axles. Staff and officers generally rode in a Personenkraftwagen (Pkw, personnel vehicle), such as the medium Horch Kfz.15 (Kraftfahrzeug, motor vehicle) and the light Volkswagen Kfz.1.[18]

Given the deep mud conditions in Russia during that campaign, wheeled Opel, Ford, and Magirus Lkws were also converted as half-tracks by Daimler-Benz. While wheeled vehicles bogged down in the Russian mud, fatally slowing the 1941 German campaign, the production and improvisation of half-tracks gave the Wehrmacht significant capability in subsequent campaigns.

Ordnance in the panzer division included Pak (Panzerabwehrkanone, antitank guns), Flak (Fliegerabwehrkanone, antiaircraft guns), and Artillerie (artillery). The standard antitank gun was the 3,7cm Pak 36. Its maximum range was some 4,000 meters (4,400 yards) though its muzzle velocity at 762 meters per second (2,500 fps) gave it an armor-piercing capability of only 36mm (1.4 inches) at 500 meters (545 yards) against armor inclined 30 degrees to the vertical with a Panzergranate (armor-piercing round).[19] The Pak 36 was adequate against the slab-sided, thinly armor-plated tanks of the early war period, but after 1939 it was recognized that heavier tanks made better antitank guns necessary. The heavy French Char B1bis had 60mm (2.4-inch) frontal armor, and the British Matilda Mark II and Valentine had up to 76mm (3 inches). The 5cm Pak 38 gave a penetration at 500 meters of 61mm (2.4 inches), and the 7,5cm Pak 40 would penetrate 104mm (4 inches) at 500 meters or 89mm (3.5 inches) at 1,000 meters. In comparison, the standard US antitank gun used later in the war, the 57mm M1, penetrated 68mm (2.7 inches) at 1,000 yards. The Russians initially depended on the 14.5mm (.58-caliber) PTRD antitank rifle, but by 1943 had upgunned to a 57mm antitank gun. The Paks were on a two-wheeled carriage and towed, but were also mounted on Panzerjäger (tank destroyer) chassis. Most deadly against enemy tanks would be the 8,8cm (3.5-inch) Flak gun in a ground-firing role, famous as the "Acht-komma-acht" or "Acht-acht" ("eighty-eight" or 88mm to the Allies).

In addition to machine guns, air defense was provided by flak units (under the Luftwaffe). The 2cm automatic gun might be mounted as Zwillingsflak (twin guns), Drillingsflak (triple guns), or Vierlingsflak (quadruple guns). Next larger was the 3,7cm, the 5cm Flak 41, and then the 8,8cm flak gun. As an antitank gun, the 8,8cm Flak 36 was mounted in the later Tiger I panzer; it had a muzzle velocity of 792 m/s (2,600 fps), and when produced as the Pak 43 and mounted in the Königstiger (King Tiger), its muzzle velocity was 1,000 m/s (3,280 fps)—a speed that could penetrate any tank used during the war. The Russians and Americans used machine guns and automatic cannon as antiaircraft guns, though they do not seem to have used the heavier-caliber AA guns in an anti-armor role to the extent the Germans used the ubiquitous Acht-komma-acht. Larger German flak guns were the 10,5cm Flak 38 and the 12,8cm Flak 40.

The standard German divisional field artillery howitzer in the light artillery battalions of the artillery regiment was the 10,5cm leichte Feld Haubitze (light field howitzer) 18. The le.F.H. 18 had a maximum range of 12,250 meters (13,400 yards). In comparison the American 105mm howitzer M2 ranged 11,150 meters (12,200 yards). In 1941 the gun was fitted with a muzzle brake to control recoil. This permitted a longer-range charge to be fired, increasing the range by 1,600 meters (1,899 yards).

The standard German medium battalion howitzer was the 15cm schwere Feld Haubitze (heavy field howitzer) 18. The 15cm s.F.H. 18 had a range of 13,300 meters (14,630 yards). The later s.F.H. 18/40 had a muzzle brake and higher velocity, increasing the range to 15,000 meters (16,500 yards). The US medium 155mm howitzer M1 ranged a comparable 16,400 yards. The Russian 122mm howitzer M1938 ranged 11,800 meters (12,800 yards), and the 152mm gun-howitzer M1937 ranged 17,620 meters (18,000 yards). Of the longer-ranged Kanone (guns) with higher velocities, the 10cm K 18 had a range of 18,900 meters (20,850 yards) and the 15cm K 18 ranged 24,600 meters (27,000 yards). By comparison the Russian 122mm cannon M1931/37 had a range of 20,800 meters (22,600 yards), while the American 155mm ("Long Tom") used in corps artillery ranged 23,600 meters (26,000 yards).

In Russia the Germans would encounter the "Katyusha" ("Little Kate") multiple rocket launcher M13, organized in separate rocket regiments. Though inaccurate, a salvo of sixteen rockets from each launcher flared through the air with a terrifying scream, earning the launcher the nickname "Stalins Orgel" ("Stalin's Organ") from the German Landsers. The Russians used the Katyushas as short-range (9,000 meters or 9,800 yards) field artillery, firing massed salvos to saturate a target area, the flaring smoke trails arcing across the sky. Western armies, with their more precise fire-control computing and better communications, could fire accurate concentrations of regular artillery and carry out fire missions within minutes, even if they could not match the massive bombardments of the Russians.

Nonetheless the Germans had also developed multiple rocket launchers, including the Nebelwerfer, or chemical smoke mortar (to be feared in turn by American GIs as the "Screaming Meemie"). The Nebelwerfer was originally the larger 10cm version of the 5cm and 8cm infantry Granatwerfer (mortar) smoothbore, muzzle-loaded, projectile-firing ordnance. But the Nebelwerfer, first designed by Dr. Walter Dornberger ("father" of the later V-2 ballistic missile), were rocket-firing by 1931, evading the restrictions on artillery of the Treaty of Versailles because rockets were not covered.

The rockets were later organized in separate battalions and even regiments. Werfers ranged from the six-tubed 15cm NbW 41 firing its meter-long rockets in sequence, to larger 21cm, 28cm, and 32cm Werfers. A regiment of heavy Nebelwerfer could saturate a target area with 6 tons of explosive in five seconds, and repeat the barrage every minute. The rockets were also fired from frames mounted on the sides of half-tracks, and in 1944 they were mounted on the small 2-ton Opel Maultier (Mule). The Americans later utilized rocket launchers, including a sixty-tubed structure atop the M4 Sherman tank, and in landing craft supporting amphibious operations.

In 1939 the German Schützenkompanie (rifle company) had some 157 personnel in three rifle platoons. Each Zug in turn numbered forty-nine in three squads, and each Gruppe numbered thirteen. The standard Gewehr (rifle) was the reliable Mauser Karabiner 98k (kurz, or short carbine). It was a bolt-action 7,92mm rifle with a five-round magazine capacity. Other nations also had bolt-action rifles, such as the British Lee-Enfield and the Russian Mosin-Nagant. The Americans, however, were equipped with the semiautomatic M1 Garand firing an eight-round clip. But unlike American and British squad tactics, which emphasized marksmanship and support by a bipod-mounted automatic rifle, the German concept was volume of fire based on the squad light machine gun.

The American Browning Automatic Rifle (BAR), the British Bren Gun, and the Russian Degtyarev automatic rifles fired from a removable box or drum magazine. The Mauser Werke air-cooled Maschinengewehr 34 was also bipod-mounted, but was a belt-fed machine gun, yet light enough to be carried by one man. It had a rate of fire of over 850 rounds per minute. (It would be succeeded by the even better MG 42 with a rate of fire of over 1,200 rpm, with a quick barrel-change feature given the excessive heat generated.) On a more stable tripod mount both functioned as a schwere (medium) machine gun in weapons companies like those of other infantries.[20]

German officers and vehicle crewmen, in addition to being issued the 9mm Walther Pistole 38, were authorized the submachine gun Maschinenpistole 38, later the MPi 40. Commonly misnamed the "Schmeisser," the 9mm Ermawerke MPi fired at 500 rpm from a thirty-two-round box magazine, and was nicknamed the "Kugelspritzer" ("bullet-squirter"). Panzer crews and motorized infantry (later Panzergrenadiers) appreciated the metal folding stock of the MPi in the confines of a panzer or a Halbkette. The infantry also used antipersonnel and antitank Handgranate (hand grenades). Little changed from World War I was the Stielhandgranate 39 stick grenade ("potato masher" to the Western Allies), lobbed some 30 meters (33 yards) to explode within four to five seconds. Variants included a fragmentation sleeve, smoke, and illumination versions, as well as the lighter Eihandgranate 39 (egg-shaped grenades). Grenades could also be launched from the Karabiner 98k with a muzzle attachment and a propelling cartridge, extending the range to some 240 meters (265 yards).

Standard infantry-support weapons included mortars, flamethrowers, and mines. The muzzle-loaded 5cm leichte Granatwerfer (light mortar), comparable to the US 60mm mortar, had a range of 518 meters (570 yards). The 8cm schwere Granatwerfer, similar to the US 81mm mortar, had a range of 2,400 meters (2,625 yards). Encountering the large Russian 120mm mortar on the Eastern Front, the Germans copied it as the 12cm Granatwerfer 42, which had a range of 6,000 meters (6,700 yards).

Against fortifications the Pioniere (combat engineers) used hollow-charge explosives and flamethrowers. The Hohlladung (hollow- or shaped-charge) explosive was point-initiating and base-detonating, the blast focused by a cone forward at a standoff distance, "shaping" a jet stream to penetrate armor or concrete, and was used in a variety of munitions. The Flammenwerfer 35 was succeeded by the Flammenwerfer 41. This had two cylinders, one with compressed nitrogen for projection, the other with fuel, ignited by triggering hydrogen. Duration of the fire was ten seconds, in short bursts.

There were a variety of antipersonnel and antitank mines. The Schü-Mine (Schützen, or defense mine) was a bounding type. The 4-kilogram (9-pound) S-Mine 35 was triggered either by 7 kilograms (15 pounds) of foot pressure or by trip wire pull igniter, and a canister was propelled one meter (one yard) above the ground, spewing 360 steel balls or scrap steel with a killing radius of 10 meters (12 yards). The small half-kilogram (one-pound) Schü-Mine 42 was a handy booby trap that would cripple a soldier. Varieties of these AP mines were encased in wood or glass to foil metallic mine detectors, and usually had explosive anti-lifting devices; the only sure way to clear minefields was to probe for them with a bayonet on hands and knees.

There were some forty types of antitank mines. Typical was the 10-kilogram (21 lb) Teller (plate) Panzermine 35 triggered by 180 kilograms (400 pounds) of pressure on the pressure plate. This would disable a tank by breaking the track and often damaging a road wheel. The Soviets would be the most prolific at laying minefields, utilizing their TMB-2 and TM-41 antitank mines. Minefields were most effective with a pattern of AP and AT mines underground, and covered by defensive fire.

Tactically, German infantry procedures were closely related to their artillery operations, though these varied greatly depending on the mission, enemy forces and capabilities, available troops, and terrain and weather. Ideally there were four levels to a linear defense in depth manned by infantry units (though this formation was seldom employed until later in the war when German forces were increasingly on the defensive). The HKL (Hauptkampflinie) was the main line of resistance (US MLR), meant to repulse an enemy attack. The Gefechtsvorposten (combat outposts) were 1,800–4,500 meters (2,000–5,000 yards) ahead of the HKL, within range of the main line's light artillery (10,5cm le.F.H. 18) batteries; these were more thinly manned than the HKL and intended to absorb the enemy attack. In front of the combat outposts was the Vorgeschobene Stellung (advanced position), some 4,500–6,000 meters (5,000–7,000 yards) beyond the HKL and covered by the longer-range medium artillery (15cm s.F.H. 18); it was manned by light forces tasked with delaying the enemy attack and perhaps forcing premature deployment. A Reserve position was to be several thousand meters behind the HKL, beyond range of enemy artillery, forcing a delay in their displacing batteries forward, and served as a position to which forces could fall back from the HKL and from which counterattacks could be mounted.

Defensive frontage width for an infantry unit was about double the attack frontage. A Kompanie (company) defended 400–1,000 meters (440–1,100 yards), a Bataillon defended 800–2,000 meters (880–2,200 yards), a Regiment defended 2,000–3,000 meters (2,200–3,300 yards), and a Division defended 6,000–10,000 meters (6,600–11,000 yards) or about 6–10 kilometers (4–6 miles). Defensive positions entailed entrenchments, wire entanglements, cleared fields of fire, and primary direction of fire and final protective lines for machine guns. Since World War I, minefields, laid with both AP and AT mines, had strengthened a defensive position. Mortars, AT guns, and artillery would also be sited. More permanent fortifications like the Westwall along the German border had steel-and-concrete bunkers (British "pillboxes"), gun positions, and antitank obstacles built by Organisation Todt (OT) construction units. Preferably field positions were disposed in depth for an elastic defense utilizing counterattack forces to restore a penetrated position, not a strictly linear defense.[21]

Attack tactics had evolved since World War I, moving from the British "wave" tactics slaughtered by the machine guns on the Somme in 1916 to a new model of infiltration and surprise artillery tactics. This approach was developed by artillery Oberst Georg Bruchmüller and Gen. Oskar von Hutier in the Riga attack in 1917 and employed in the Westfront offensives of 1918. The new Panzerwaffe would play a significant role in this tactical evolution, though there were divergent concepts as to what this role would be. Some thought it should decisively strengthen an infantry breakthrough of an opponent's main defenses. Others believed the primary role should be flanking, flank-and-frontal envelopment, and encirclement maneuvers and attacks. Political and international events in the 1930s began to be factors that determined what the role of the Panzerwaffe would be.

CHAPTER THREE

The First Operations

IN JULY 1936 GEN. FRANCISCO FRANCO CHALLENGED THE Popular Front coalition government in Spain, beginning the three-year Spanish Civil War. Stalin's Soviet Union sent forces to support the Republic, and Hitler's Germany and Benito Mussolini's Italy supported Franco's nationalist and fascist movement. Other Western powers sympathized with the Republicans but did not become involved, except for some volunteers, leaving Communist influence dominant.

While Mussolini contributed a large contingent of air and ground forces, Hitler and his high command refused Franco's request for three German divisions. Hermann Göring, World War I fighter ace and founder of Nazi Germany's Luftwaffe, however, saw the struggle as one to stop the spread of Communism, gain a potential ally, and test new airpower concepts and technology. Luftwaffe units, including four fighter-bomber and four fighter squadrons, were committed, and the Heinkel He 111 twin-engine bomber, the Junkers Ju 87 Stuka dive-bomber, and the Messerschmitt Bf 109 fighter plane all first saw combat here. Future German Luftwaffe leaders and aces also first saw combat in Spain, including Adolf Galland, later head of Fighter Command. He sailed from Hamburg with other pilots in civilian clothes masquerading as a Kraft durch Freude (Strength through Joy, KdF) tourist group, and flew uniformed as a Spanish captain.[1]

This "Legion Condor" was augmented by some panzer training units and totaled some 12,000 personnel. Oberstleutnant Wilhelm Ritter von Thoma had administrative control of the three Lehrkompanien (training companies) of Panzer Is and IIs, Panzerabteilung 88, from volunteers from Panzer-Regiment 6 of 3. Panzer-Division.[2] Von Thoma did not expect, nor did he deduce, significant lessons for armored warfare tactics or doctrine in this internecine conflict. The need for larger-caliber guns and stronger armor was confirmed, however, as the Italian and German tankettes, mostly mounting only machine guns, were outclassed by the Russian BTs and T-26s with their 76mm cannon.

By 1938 Hitler was ready to undertake a more aggressive foreign policy, initially to right the "Diktat" of Versailles, on behalf of the pro-German population in truncated Austria and German minorities (Volksdeutsch) in the Sudetenland of Czechoslovakia and in the "Corridor" to Danzig in Poland separating East Prussia from the Reich. The resistance from conservative elements in the German high command, opposed to both his aggressive foreign policy and to the revolutionary mechanization of the army, came to a head in January 1938. The outcome on 4 February of that year was the restructuring of the Wehrmacht unified under Hitler himself, with the Oberkommando der Wehrmacht (OKW, High Command of the Armed Forces) assumed by General der Artillerie Wilhelm Keitel. There were three branches: OKH (Heer, Army), under Generaloberst Walter von Brauchitsch; OKL (Luftwaffe, Air Force), under Generalfeldmarschall Hermann Göring; and OKM (Marine, Navy), under Adm. Erich Raeder.[3]

On 12 March 1938 came the *Anschluss* (union with Germany) of Austria, dubbed the "Blumenkrieg" ("War of Flowers") by journalists as pro-German citizens greeted the German military columns with bouquets, the vehicles themselves bedecked with flags and greenery. For the Panzerwaffe the event served as a practical test: the 2. Panzer-Division undertook a 676-kilometer (420-mile) road march from Würzburg to Vienna. While observers critical of Hitler's *Anschluss* ridiculed the apparent logistical and maintenance difficulties, this served to underestimate the potential of armored forces by future enemies.[4] In Germany, the rapid movement of the 2. Pz.Div. in forty-eight hours over icy roads confirmed the operational possibilities of such forces, and resulted in the formation of the 4. and 5. Panzer-Divisionen by November. The fact that now-Generalleutnant Guderian accompanied Hitler as the Austrian-born Führer made a triumphal entry into Linz also boded well for support from the highest authority.

In October 1938, following the Munich Agreement over the Sudeten issue, Guderian's XVI. Armee-Korps with the 1. Pz.Div. and the 13. and 20. Infanterie-Divisionen (motorisiert) rolled across the Czech border to liberate the German-populated Sudetenland. By now it was commonplace for mechanized units equipped with Panzer Is and IIs to be featured at parades and at the annual Nazi *Parteitagen* (Party Days) of the Nürnberg rallies—and as part of the implementation of an increasingly forward foreign policy. Hitler's successes ever since the reoccupation of the Rhineland in 1936 generated rising enthusiasm and impatience among German Volksdeutsch minorities under foreign rule. The disintegration of Czechoslovakia with the independence of Slovakia and the occupation of Bohemia and Moravia in the spring of 1939 was followed by tense negotiations with Poland over Danzig (Polish Gdansk) and the "Korridor," and the subsequent German-Soviet Pact of August 1939, which sealed the fate of Poland.

Meanwhile, production had finally begun on the two panzer models intended to be the mainstay of the Panzerwaffe, the Panzers III and IV, as the Panzers I and II had always been intended to be only stopgap training tanks. In 1935 the Waffenamt put out bids for a medium tank in the 15-ton class, originally camouflaged as a Zugführerwagen (ZW, Troop Commander's Vehicle). Daimler-Benz received the contract and prototypes were developed and tested, with the Ausführung E (Model E) going into limited production in December 1938 as the Pz.Kpfw. III (Sd.Kfz. 141). These saw service in the Polish campaign of 1939.

The original frontal armor of the Panzer III was 30mm (1 1/8 inches) thick and the tank's weight was 15 tons, while later models had frontal armor 50mm (2 inches) thick and weighed some 22 tons. The Maybach 12-cylinder engine developed 300 bhp with a road speed of 39 km/h (24 mph) and a road operating range of 175 km (100 miles). There were two MG 34s mounted, one in the front hull and one coaxially mounted to the right of the main gun.

While the Panzer branch wanted a 5cm tank gun for the Panzer III, Ordnance insisted on the 3,7cm gun already in production as an infantry antitank gun. However, the turret ring was designed large enough so the panzer could be upgunned later. After the French campaign in 1940, Hitler himself ordered the 5cm Kw.K. L/60 (Kampfwagen Kanone)—with a barrel length of 60 calibers, or a length sixty times longer than the gun's bore diameter—installed in all Panzer IIIs. But Ordnance substituted the shorter Kw.K. L/42, which had a lower muzzle velocity of 685 meters per second (2,247 feet per second) compared to the L/60's 823 m/s (2,700 fps), and lower penetrating capability, in the Model G, and the L/60 gun was not mounted until the Model J in 1941. Writing of the critical tank battles in the Western Desert during this time, Generalmajor Friedrich W. von Mellenthin, a staff officer in most of the panzer campaigns during the war, said he felt that "this disobedience went far to lose us the war."[5]

Like the Panzer III, the larger Panzer IV's design was camouflaged as a Bataillonsführerwagen (BW,

Battalion Commander's Vehicle). Krupp's prototype for the 24-ton-class medium was accepted in 1936 as the Pz.Kpfw. IV (Sd.Kfz. 161). Its configuration was visually very similar to the Panzer III for silhouette recognition by the infantry, though it had eight road wheels and four return rollers on each side, rather than the six road wheels and three return rollers of the Pz. III. The drive sprocket was at the front and the idler wheel at the rear on both. It was intended as a close-support tank, with its short, low-velocity 385 m/s (1,263 fps) 7,5cm Kw.K. L/24 firing primarily Sprenggranate (HE, high-explosive) rounds against infantry and "soft" (i.e., unarmored) targets like vehicles and artillery. Subsequent models had increased armor (5cm/2 inches frontal armor in Ausführung E of 1940) with larger engines to power the increased weight.

The French campaign would demonstrate the need for an armor-defeating capability, though it wasn't until March 1942 that the Model F2 mounted a long, high-velocity 7,5cm Kw.K. L/43 gun with muzzle brake (or blast deflector). This had a muzzle velocity of 740 m/s (2,428 fps) and could penetrate 89mm (3.5 inches) of 30-degree sloped armor at 1,000 meters (3,028 feet), adequate to penetrate the excellent 60-degree-sloped frontal armor of the Russian T-34. The Model G of late 1942 had a more powerful 7,5cm Kw.K. L/48 gun and a muzzle velocity of 751 m/s (2,461 fps).[6] Though later outclassed, the basic design of the Panzer IV enabled it to be up-armored and improved, and it remained in production until the end of the war. Like the Panzer III, its reliable chassis was also later utilized for tank destroyers and self-propelled artillery.

By the summer of 1939, a modern German Wehrmacht had emerged with powerful ground forces and a formidable air force. The Luftwaffe was equipped primarily as a tactical air force with a significant close air support capability for the ground forces. The spearheads of any offensive campaign would feature the six panzer divisions and four light divisions, supported by the motorized divisions. The six panzer divisions (numbered 1.–5. and 10.) varied in size and organization, generally having a panzer brigade of some 328 panzers in two regiments of two battalions each, and a motorized rifle brigade of two regiments and a motorcycle battalion, as well as an organic artillery regiment with twenty-four 10,5cm towed howitzers in two battalions, and reconnaissance, engineer, antitank, and signals battalions, and medical, maintenance, and supply companies. Strength was 11,000–12,000 personnel. The four light divisions had two motorized rifle regiments but only one panzer battalion. Numbered 1.–4., they were converted to panzer divisions after the Polish campaign, and were renumbered 6.–9.[7]

The Panzer Force perhaps lacked the number of medium battle tanks of powers like France and Russia; there were only 98 Panzer IIIs and 211 Panzer IVs as opposed to 1,445 Panzer Is and 1,233 Panzer IIs.[8] But more importantly, the Panzerwaffe had evolved a doctrine of the balanced, combined-arms panzer division, and coordinated tactics featuring radio communications, that gave it tremendous operational mobility and flexibility. In addition there were junior officers trained at the Panzertruppenschule (armored troops school) at Wünsdorf south of Berlin, imbued with the spirit of aggressive leadership from the front, ready to take the initiative during the fast pace of panzer operations. This doctrine complemented well the more traditional German concept of Auftragstaktik (mission-oriented tactics), which encouraged operational flexibility as opportunity offered, rather than strict adherence to detailed orders.

At the operational campaign level, however, there were still differences as to how the panzer and motorized divisions were to be employed—whether they were to be massed as panzer corps for deep penetration, or used to lead the advance of the infantry divisions whose equipment was horse-drawn. In Fall WEISS (Case WHITE), Germany's operational plan for the defeat of Poland, the Oberkommando des Heeres planned a large encircling strategy. In the north Heeresgruppe Nord (Army Group North) under Generaloberst Fedor von Bock had two armies: 4. Armee would slice across the Corridor and link up with 3. Armee in East Prussia, with both then driving south on Warsaw. They would meet 10. Armee, with 8. Armee on its left flank, of Heeresgruppe Süd (Army Group South) under Generaloberst Gerd von Rundstedt as they swung north. Von Rundstedt's 14. Armee on the right flank would drive into Galicia. Von Bock favored a deeper envelopment beyond the Weichsel (Vistula) to the Bug, but this was not accepted at the time.

Although the OKH plan was one of penetration, maneuver, and encirclement, the two army groups differed in their concepts about the mobile forces. The sixty divisions arrayed against Poland included all six panzer and four light divisions and four motorized infantry divisions. While one panzer and two motorized divisions in Heeresgruppe Nord were concentrated in XIX. Armee-Korps under aggressive General der Panzertruppen Guderian, those in H.Gr. Süd were under four different corps with infantry divisions, as well as in reserve.

As the Wehrmacht deployed against Poland in August 1939, individuals and elements of the future 11. Panzer-Division participated, and would gain valuable combat experience. Oberst Günther Angern had command of 3. Schützenbrigade in the 3. Panzer-Division in Guderian's XIX. A.K. in H.Gr. Nord. Born in Kolberg in eastern Prussia 5 March 1893, Angern served in the infantry in World War I. He would later command the 11. Schützenbrigade (mot) (motorized Rifle Brigade) in both the Danish and French campaigns; that unit in turn would become the infantry component of the 11. Pz. Div., and in 1941 Angern would command the division itself.[9] The first division commander actually would be Oberst Ludwig Crüwell, a staff officer in the West at the time.

In Heeresgruppe Süd Panzer-Regiment 15 under Oberstleutnant Johannes Streich was in the 5. Panzer-Division in 14. Armee. Later the panzer component of the 11.Pz. Div., Pz. Rgt. 15 traced its lineage from the Leibkürassier-Regiments "Grosser Kurfürst" (Schlesisches) Nr.1 (Guard Cuirassier Regiment "Great Elector" (Silesian) Nr.1) and 1. Eskadron Hüterin der 7. (Preussische) Reiter Regiment (1. Watch Squadron of the 7. (Prussian) Cavalry Regiment).[10] Originated in Breslau, Silesia, 16 July 1646 as a heavy dragoon cavalry company, it was named 7 July 1674 and expanded and redesignated as a cuirassier regiment in 1717. Battle honors included Fehrbellin and Hochstädt, and the Marne and Pinsk in World War I. In 1916 it was reorganized as an infantry storm regiment and participated in the 1918 offensives on the Western Front.

The legacy continued as the 1. Schwadron of the 7. (Preussisch) Reiter Regiment in 1920 in Breslau, but with Hitler's expansion of the armed forces in 1935, the 1. Kompanie evolved as the 5. Kompanie of Panzer-Regiment 2 in the garrison city of Eisenach in Thuringia on 15 October 1935 under Hauptmann Manfred Graf Strachwitz. The 5. Kompanie became the nucleus for Panzer-Regiment 15, organized 12 October 1937 in Sagan auf der Bober in northern Silesia southeast of Berlin (subsequently Polish Zagan on the Bobr after 1945). Sagan would later be considered the home of the 11. Panzer-Division. Oberstlt. Streich, who had served in Poland, Serbia, Rumania, and France in World War I, became commander of the regiment until 9 February 1941, leading it as part of the 5. Panzer-Division in Poland and in France.[11]

The new panzer regiment had two battalions: I. Abteilung under Major Sieckenius, and II. Abteilung under Major von Drabich-Waechter. Each battalion had three numbered companies, two light (Panzer Is and IIs) and one mixed (Panzer IIIs and IVs). The units undertook training in gunnery and in unit maneuvers at Neuhammer and Wildflecken. The regiment paraded its panzers at the Nürnberg party rally in September 1938, and then rolled into Czechoslovakia in October during the Sudeten crisis, and did so again in March 1939 as Slovakia became independent and Germany occupied Bohemia and Moravia. In November 1938 the 5. Panzer-Division was organized, commanded by Generalleutnant Heinrich von Vietinghoff. Streich's Panzer-Regiment 15 was brigaded with Pz.Rgt. 31 in the 8. Panzerbrigade.

As tensions with Poland increased during the summer of 1939, the regiment was in a state of increased readiness. At the time of the Polish campaign the regiment numbered 141 panzers: 57 Panzer Is, 74 Pz. IIs, 3 Pz. IIIs, and 7 Pz. IVs.[12] On the night of 20 August, Pz. Rgt. 15 received marching orders for 06,00 the next morning. Leutnant Siegfried Schönstedt, a Panzer II Zugführer (platoon leader) in I. Abteilung, recounted how his unit road-marched through the quiet early streets of Sagan to load their "steel steeds" on railway cars. At 09,12 Uhr the train pulled out of the railyard heading south, reaching Leobschütz in Upper Silesia by midnight, and the regiment then road-marched through the darkness to Jägerndorf and its assembly area. At 04,45 on 1 September 1939 the unit crossed the border as the Wehrmacht invaded Poland.[13] Vietinghoff's 5. Pz. Div. was in VIII. A.K. commanded by General der Infanterie Ernst Busch with two infantry divisions, in Generaloberst Wilhelm List's 14. Armee in Heeresgruppe Süd.

On that 1 September the Wehrmacht struck Poland with an all-out assault. The Luftwaffe annihilated the Polish air force and mechanized forces rolled across the border. Journalists would coin a new word—*Blitzkrieg*, or Lightning War. Hitler may have been surprised when England and France declared war on Germany two days later, especially considering the Nazi-Soviet pact that was to deter them had been concluded just ten days earlier, but the assault continued unabated. The 4. Armee of Heeresgruppe Nord under Generaloberst von Bock cut across the Corridor, shattering the Pomorze Army with 3. Armee, and then they drove south up the Vistula toward Warsaw. At the same time 8. and 10. Armee of H.Gr.Süd uder Generaloberst von Rundstedt drove up from Silesia. Most of the Poznań and Lodz Armies were encircled, and on 6 September the Polish government fled to Lublin ahead of 14. Armee and then on to Rumania. Civilian refugees, retreating Poles, and advancing Germans all headed east, creating massive dust clouds that made it difficult for the strafing aircraft of Luftflotte (Air Fleets) 1. and 2. to differentiate friend from foe.

Almost the entire panzer force, some 1,500 panzers, was committed, though most were Panzer I tankettes (two MGs) and Pz. IIs (2cm guns); only a few were Pz. IIIs (short 3,7cm) and Pz. IVs (short 7,5cm).[14] The thirty active Polish divisions, being infantry, and the eleven horse cavalry brigades were no match for the mechanized forces that attacked them, neither by weaponry nor doctrine. The Polish forces included some 190 Polish 7TP, French R35, and English Vickers tanks, 470 reconnaissance tankettes, and 90 obsolescent armored cars, mostly attached to the infantry divisions and cavalry brigades. Guderian may have been exaggerating when he said, "The Polish *Pomorska* Cavalry Brigade, in ignorance of the nature of our tanks, had charged them [3. Panzer-Division] with swords and lances and had suffered tremendous losses." Though he was reflecting the contrast in combat doctrine, the image quickly spread: "the ignorant Polish cavalry rode in the attack against heavy German panzers," A. E. Johann wrote in *Zwischen Westwall und Maginotlinie* (1939).[15]

Given its weaponry and tactics, the Polish military was little more "obsolete" than were other military forces; it was the mechanized German Wehrmacht that now set the standard against which other militaries would be measured. Yet Polish strategy was to disperse their forces to defend *all* their territory; and when Polish hopes that England and France, having declared war on Germany 3 September, might distract some German forces, and hopes that autumn rains might slow the invasion, proved in vain, the panzer spearheads essentially defeated the Polish ground forces in two weeks.

Five of the six panzer divisions and three of the four light divisions—though only two of the four motorized infantry divisions—were among the forty-four divisions committed in the initial assault. In the 10. Armee drive of H.Gr. Süd, 1. and 4. Panzer-Divisionen soon outran the two regular (i.e., nonmotorized) infantry divisions in their XVI. A.K. Farther south in 14. Armee, 5. Panzer-Division with Streich's Pz. Rgt. 15 was tied to the pace of the two infantry divisions, 8. and 28., in Busch's VIII. A.K. After a few days the 5. Pz. Div. was shifted to the right flank of the 14. Armee, driving through Galicia, skirting the foothills of the Carpathian Mountains. The rapid defeat of the Polish forces, however, minimized the defects of these corps organizations.

Crakow was captured on 6 September and the 14. Armee advance continued toward Lemberg (Lwów). Reluctant to get committed east of the Vistula, on 11 September OKH nonetheless agreed to a second, deeper envelopment to the Bug, as Bock had recommended. But Guderian's XIX. A.K., including Angern's 3. Schützenbrigade in 3. Pz. Div., joined by 10. Pz. Div., swept *east* of the Bug, fighting into the citadel of the fortress city of Brest (Brzesc) by 17 September, and making radio contact with 10. Armee from the south at Włodawa on the Bug.

On that same 17 September however, by the secret terms of the Nazi-Soviet Pact, the Red Army advanced into eastern Poland, and Poland once again disappeared from the map of Europe. With the Bug as the demarcation line, Guderian's and the other German forces had to withdraw westward. Defiant Warsaw was bombed into submission by 27 September. Many of the retreating Polish forces fell into Russian hands, and the officer corps disappeared. (In 1943 the Germans uncovered the remains of some 4,300 Polish officers executed by the Soviets in the Katyn Forest near Smolensk. The Western Allies accepted the Soviet accusation at the time of German responsibility until postwar political shifts and finally Russian admission revealed otherwise.)

Unfortunately wartime atrocities occasionally occurred, and on 10 September Panzer-Regiment 15's band was returning by bus through Stobnica when it was shot up by Polish troops and seventeen members captured were shot and burned, save only Feldwebel Rösner, who escaped and later returned to the German lines in civilian clothes.[16] The most publicized incident was the Polish massacre of German-language civilians in Bromberg (Bydgoszcz) on 3 September; according to Polish sources the population had risen against retreating Polish soldiers.[17] (These incidents would pale, however, before the brutal occupation policies of Heinrich Himmler's SS police forces.)

The Polish campaign vindicated the panzer force concept pressed by Heinz Guderian, and he vividly demonstrated the leadership style expected of a panzer leader—bold initiative and aggressive leadership from the front. Guderian emphasized that commanders needed to lead from the front, in armored vehicles, and be well equipped with radios. His command vehicle was an SPW half-track that offered cross-country mobility, with radios for communication with higher headquarters and his subordinate units, which he visited during the day. It was armored against small-arms fire, although Guderian's adjutant was mortally wounded by a Polish sniper.[18] Guderian's aphorisms would become panzer doctrine—"Plan carefully, execute violently"—as he urged his units across the Brahe (Brda) and then the Narev River lines, and he was with the lead infantry regiment attacking the citadel at Brest-Litovsk. Aggressive leadership was reflected in his "Boot them, don't spatter them," and driving the operation to its conclusion in his "ticket to the end of the line."[19]

While the Polenfeldzug had been dramatically successful, post-campaign analysis identified several aspects that needed to be addressed. These included the need for greater precision between the Luftwaffe and the ground forces, as friendly units were sometimes mistakenly attacked. There were also stoppage problems with the infantry squad's Model 34 machine gun (that resulted in the excellent MG 42 later). The 8,8cm flak gun proved especially effective against bunkers and prepared fortifications and could be expected to have a significant direct-fire role in addition to its antiaircraft role.

Among the panzer forces, it was concluded that the light divisions had little staying power, and thus they were converted into regular panzer divisions. The motorized infantry divisions were found to be unwieldy, especially for motor traffic control, and one of the three infantry regiments was deleted from each division. As expected, the Panzer Is and IIs were too light and too poorly armed for any role other than reconnaissance, and too vulnerable to any Polish gunfire. Increased production of the Pz. IIIs and IVs was needed, including better frontal armor and longer, more powerful high-velocity guns. Guderian said as much to Hitler during the Führer's surprise visit to his corps near Plevno on 5 September.[20] Panzer losses in street-fighting did indicate that armor needed infantry accompaniment in urban fighting, or such conflict was to be avoided.

On 30 November 1939 the companies of Panzer-Regiment 15 rail-loaded at Sorau. The trains rolled through the night back across Germany to offload on 1 December down the ramps at Soest, southwest of Paderborn in Westphalia. From there the regiment road-marched 20 kilometers to their assigned quarters around Nordbögge and Unna, east of Dortmund. Training was undertaken in the cold, snowy winter days, but the quarters were comfortable, the local Wirtshäusern were hospitable, and "great quantities of alcoholic beverages were consumed."[21]

In December 1939 new motorized formations were organized, based on the success and lessons of the Polish campaign. The 11. Schützenbrigade (mot) was organized 1 December 1939 with Schützenregiment 110 and S.R. 111, later the infantry component of the 11. Panzer-Division. The brigade staff formed at Meinigen, and the regiments at Hamburg and Magdeburg. The brigade's first commander was Oberst Günther Angern, who had commanded 3. Schützenbrigade of 3. Pz. Div. in Poland. Unit training ensued at the training area Altengrabow east of Magdeburg in March 1940 followed by brigade-level exercises in the Lüneburger Heide south of Hamburg.[22]

While England and France had not responded to Hitler's offer of a negotiated settlement in his Reichstag speech of 6 October, the inactive Westfront was characterized by Western journalists as the "Sitzkrieg" ("Sitting War") and as the "Phony War." For the Christmas holidays in 1939 married personnel in particular received fourteen days leave to be with their families. As Hitler's hope for a *rapprochement* with the Western powers failed to materialize and British forces began to be transported to France, he ordered preparations for Fall GELB (Case YELLOW), an offensive against France.

But then on 16 February 1940 the British destroyer HMS *Cossack* attacked the German Trosschiff (supply ship) *Altmark* in the territorial waters of neutral Norway in order to rescue British prisoners on board. The *Altmark* was returning from the South Atlantic where it had supplied the commerce raider Panzerschiff (pocket battleship) *Admiral Graf Spee*. The Norwegian coastal waterway was a vital route for German ships carrying iron ore down from the Swedish Kiruna mines. Two-thirds of Germany's iron ore for steel came from Sweden. During the winter months when the Gulf of Bothnia and the port of

The West, 1940

Legend: Allied, German Armies

Luleå were blocked by ice, the iron ore was railroaded across the mountains and transported through the Norwegian port of Narvik.

Grossadmiral Erich Raeder had earlier proposed the possible occupation of Norway, but Gen. Franz Halder, Chef des Generalstabes des Heeres (Chief of the Army General Staff), determined it would be impossible to defend such a long coastline, especially in view of British sea power, and it was hoped Norwegian neutrality would be respected by the British and the French.[23] However, the Western Allies had already developed plans to land an expeditionary force at Narvik, ostensibly to assist the Finns in the Russo-Finnish "Winter War" initiated by Stalin the previous November, but more obviously to deny the crucial iron ore resources to Germany. The Finns did not request Allied aid, nor would Norway or Sweden allow passage rights for fear of a violent German military reaction. Nor did England and France want to fight Russia as well as Germany. But the *Altmark* incident convinced Hitler the British would no longer respect Norwegian neutrality, and two days later he ordered the implementation of Fall WESERÜBUNG (Case WESER EXERCISE) for the occupation of Norway and the seizure of Denmark as a "bridge" across the Skagerrak.[24]

Angern's 11. Schützenbrigade (mot) was alerted for movement north for Operation WESERÜBUNG SÜD, the occupation of Denmark, as part of the Scandinavian campaign. Controlled by XXXI. Armeekorps, the rifle brigade and the 170. Infanterie-Division were reinforced by Panzer Is and IIs, and two motorized machine-gun battalions. They were to drive up the Jutland Peninsula by the end of W Tag (day of attack) to Aalborg, which was to be occupied by a parachute platoon and an airborne battalion on W-plus two hours. Naval forces were to land at Esbjerg and Tyborön on the North Sea coast. The 198. Infanterie-Division, reinforced, was to occupy Sjaelland, with landings at Gedser, Nyborg, Korsör, and Copenhagen itself. The 11. Schützenbrigade bivouacked at Schleswig and Rendsburg on 8 April, and rolled across the Danish border at 05,15 Uhr the next morning, 9 April, as the operation began. Special units had infiltrated before W Hour to seize key bridges, and the panzers discouraged resistance by the weak Danish border forces.

German forces in fast warships and transports also made landings at seven Norwegian ports from Oslo to Narvik despite the Royal Navy's superiority, while air units landed at Stavanger and the Oslo airfield. In most cases there was no resistance as the Norwegian forces were taken by surprise. German forces overran Denmark on 9 April, the government surrendering at 07,20 that morning—two hours and five minutes after the border was crossed—under threat of Luftwaffe bombing. The Danish military was ordered by the government to cease hostilities by 08,00. The panzers and motorcyclists of 11. Schützenbrigade accompanied by Infanterie Rgt. 401 of the 170. Inf. Div. in trucks raced up the western side of the Jutland Peninsula to Aalborg in the north of the peninsula, where airborne forces had landed on the airfield a few hours earlier. Elements of the 198. I.D. were transported by ship to occupy Sjaelland and Copenhagen itself.

The rest of the campaign was completed according to OKW planning. On 10 April Skagen at the extreme tip of the Jutland Peninsula was occupied by the 11. Schützenbrigade and the mission was accomplished. The brigade staff and Schützenregiment 110 secured the area of Aalborg and S.R. 111 that of Tisted.

In Norway, the elements of six German divisions and paratroopers who had landed on 9 April were Gruppe XXI under corps commander General der Infanterie Nikolaus von Falkenhorst. They were covered by the fighters and bombers of X Flieger Korps (air division) and the warships of the Kriegsmarine. Some ships were lost, including three cruisers, but the ground forces consolidated their positions and moved inland. The German landings preempted the Anglo-French expedition intended as a response to German aggression for the Allied mining of neutral Norwegian waters (announced the day before, 8 April)—the original rationale of assisting Finland being obviated by the Finnish capitulation to the Soviet Union on 12 March.

Panzers were also landed, as Panzer-Abteilung z.b.V. 40 (zur besonderen Verwendung, for special purposes). It had been formed by Oberstleutnant Ernst Volckheim, a prolific armored theorist, in early March. Three light companies had been selected from three panzer regiments, with 3. Kompanie under Hauptmann Niedrieck being 5. Kp. of Streich's Pz. Rgt. 15. Two companies had driven north through Jutland to be shipped across the Skagerrak by 24 April, 3. Kompanie being shipped directly and landing 17 April. But the steamship *Urundi* ran aground, and *Atlantis H* was sunk with five panzers aboard.[25]

Attached to 163. Inf.-Div., Niedrieck had five Panzer Is, six Pz. IIs, and a small Panzer Befehlswagen (command tank). The panzers led the infantry columns as they advanced up the icy, snow-covered roads of the Gudbrandsdal valley from Oslo toward Trondheim. Three of the multiturreted NbFz panzers were offloaded in Oslo as well; they appeared formidable, but were only thinly armored prototypes. They were attached to the 196. I.D. advancing up the parallel Østerdal valley to the east.

The Norwegian Army had no tanks or antitank guns, and could only slow the German advance with roadblocks. The German advance toward Trondheim did encounter the British 148th and 15th Brigades after their landing at Åndalsnes, though those units' Boys antitank rifles did not prove effective. A Panzer II in the lead firing Sprenggranate (high-explosive shells) usually overcame any opposition. Even one or two panzers could demoralize an opponent who had no defense against them. (A need for greater gun elevation to engage targets up steep mountainsides was recommended, however.) Contact with the German force landed at Trondheim was made 30 April.

Much more extensive fighting took place at Narvik where the British battleship HMS *Warspite* smashed ten German destroyers in the narrow fjord, and British troops landed to seize the port. But with the expectation that battle would shortly ensue along the Western Front in France, the Allies evacuated Åndalsnes and Namsos by 3 May, as Norwegian units surrendered. At Narvik Anglo-French forces fought longer, but with disaster unfolding on the Western Front they were evacuated by 8 June, even as Schlachtkreuzer (battle cruisers) *Scharnhorst* and *Gneisenau* sank six ships including aircraft carrier HMS *Glorious*. The Norwegian high command surrendered the next day, King Haakon VII having fled to Britain. Some of the panzers were later transferred to the Finnish Front after the German invasion of Russia, and subsequently incorporated into the 25. Panzer-Division formed in occupied Norway.

Jutland had been turned over to the 160. Inf.-Div. for occupation duty, and on 24 April Angern's 11. Schützenbrigade returned to Germany in the area of Hannover. Losses were negligible, and for them the Danish campaign served as a useful experience in a quasi-war environment of traffic control, unit coordination, maintenance, and supply.

The Scandinavian campaign was a dramatic example of rapid but careful and detailed planning by OKW, and mutual support among all three branches of the German military—the army, navy, and the Luftwaffe—especially in the face of British sea power. The iron ore shipments were assured, German U-boats and surface raiders could more easily debouch into the North Atlantic, and warships and aircraft based in Norway would later savage the Allied Lend-Lease convoys around the North Cape to Murmansk. Hitler could justly gloat that the operation was "not only bold, but one of the sauciest undertakings in the history of modern warfare," and American historian Earl Ziemke concluded that, "well planned and skillfully executed, it showed the Wehrmacht at its best."[26]

CHAPTER FOUR

The French Campaign

IN THE SPRING OF 1940 THE TEN GERMAN PANZER DIVISIONS, including 5. Panzer-Division (commanded by Generalleutnant Max von Hartlieb since the previous October), were deployed westward in preparation for Fall GELB. By 3 March Streich's Panzer-Regiment 15 was stationed around Witterschlick-Duisdorf bei Bonn, west of the Rhine River. The troops were granted passes to Bonn and the large city of Köln, and home leaves as well. But there was also training in the Hardt heights at Truppenübungsplatz Wahn.

As the Scandinavian campaign concluded, there was general expectation that the "Sitzkrieg" in the West was about to end. At 15,00 Uhr on 9 May a motorcycle messenger brought the alert signal to Pz.-Rgt. 15: "Receive ammunition, turn in training equipment and other materials." There had been alerts before, but this time the Landsers knew it was the real thing. In a flurry of activity leaves were canceled, vehicles were loaded, and by evening orders had been distributed for the regiment to march the next morning.[1]

On A Tag (day of attack), 10 May 1940, the long-awaited German Blitzkrieg exploded into the Low Countries, heralding the offensive in the West. The Luftwaffe swarmed over targets and cities, paratroopers dropped from Ju 52 trimotor transport planes, artillery concentrations smashed into border defenses, and panzer divisions rolled into action. The assault in the north seemed to be a repeat of the famous Schlieffen Plan of 1914, by which the German forces swung north *around* the wooded hill country of the Ardennes and French border fortresses through Belgium to come down on Paris. But this time the Allies thought they were prepared, and the British Expeditionary Force (BEF) and the French 1ère Armee mécanique confidently crossed the Belgian border to advance north to the Dyle River line to meet the German offensive head-on.

It was all a ruse: only three of Germany's ten panzer divisions were with Generaloberst Fedor von Bock's Heeresgruppe B invading Belgium and the Netherlands. The real Schwerpunkt (point of main effort) of the German offensive was with the other seven panzer divisions of Generaloberst Gerd von Rundstedt's

Heeresgruppe A, which were beginning to thread their way *through* the wooded hills and valleys of the Ardennes in the *center* to split the Allied forces by driving to the sea, thus cutting off and trapping the mechanized forces lured north into Flanders. H.Gr. C defended the Saar and upper Rhine borders. This strategic concept was the unique plan of General der Infanterie Erich von Manstein, chief of staff of Rundstedt's H.Gr. A.

The original OKH plans for Fall GELB were indeed merely a repeat of the old Schlieffen Plan.[2] Manstein remembered, "Significantly enough, my first reaction to the plan laid down in these two Operation Orders was emotional rather than intellectual." He believed that the Allies were well prepared to thwart such an attack, and so he proposed a plan whereby H.Gr. B's attack drew the Allied mechanized forces north into Belgium, to be encircled in a Kessel (cauldron) by panzer forces passing *through* the Ardennes and swinging up behind them, resulting in the collapse of the Allied armies.[3] Manstein got the support of von Rundstedt and Guderian, and most importantly Hitler (who was also questioning the OKH plan) when he met with him on 17 February 1940. In the meantime, on 10 January the Chef des Stabes of 7. Luftlandedivision (Air Landing Division) accidently crash-landed near Mechelen, Belgium, in fog, and part of the Fall GELB plans were presumed to have been given to the Allies. This further contributed to the adoption of Manstein's revised plan instead of the unoriginal OKH plan. (Actually, the Allies were suspicious the GELB plans recovered at Mechelen were a "plant.")

It is now generally acknowledged that the Allies had more gun tanks than did the Wehrmacht—2,689 to 2,439—and some models were of better quality than the panzers, such as the French Somua S35, the heavy French Char B1bis, and British Matilda.[4] Nor was Allied strategy completely defensive, the so-called "Maginot Line mentality." In May 1940 the French had six armored or mechanized divisions: three armored divisions cuirassée de reserve (DCRs), three mechanized divisions légères mécanisées (DLMs), and seven motorized divisions, and the British were deploying three armored brigades to form their Armoured Division.

While about half the French tank battalions were attached to infantry formations, these were generally equipped with older models (six had old 1918 Renaults). But there were twenty-four battalions with the DCRs and DLMs, and the French 1ère Armée mécanique under Général Georges M. J. Blanchard, as well as the motorized BEF under General Lord Gort, were poised to advance into Belgium under Allied Plan D to the Dyle River Line. The three DCRs were still forming in the Châlons-sur-Marne training area as a GHQ Reserve however. Their organization was tank-heavy with 146 tanks in two brigades but only one motorized infantry battalion each, and the French high command in particular had no concept of massing the armor for decisive mobile warfare.

As the Allied mechanized forces were lured north into Belgium, the real mass of German armor was moving through the rugged Ardennes against minimal resistance as Panzergruppe Kleist under General der Kavallerie Ewald von Kleist. It contained three panzer divisions in Guderian's XIX. Armeekorps (mot) on the left and two in the XXXXI. A.K.(mot) in the center. Two more panzer divisions were in XV. A.K.(mot) on Kleist's right flank. As in Poland and Scandinavia, components of the future 11. Panzer-Division participated in the campaign: Oberst Johannes Streich's Panzer-Regiment 15 in 5. Pz.Div. and, later, Oberst Günther Angern's 11. Schützenbrigade (mot). 5. Pz.Div. under Generalleutnant von Hartlieb was part of XV. A.K. (mot) under General der Infanterie Hermann Hoth on the northern flank. Each battalion of Pz.Rgt. 15 had one medium and two light panzer companies, totaling fifty-one Panzer Is, sixty-one Pz.IIs, twenty-four Pz.IIIs, sixteen Pz.IVs, and fifteen command panzers, a total of 167 panzers for the regiment.[5]

On its left was 7. Panz.-Div. under General Major Erwin Rommel. Rommel was an aggressive commander who had earned Germany's highest award in World War I, the *Pour le Mérite*, as a Hauptmann in the Alpenkorps mountain division that helped collapse the Italians at Karfreit (Caporetto) in 1917. His later lectures were published as *Infanterie Greift An* (Infantry Attacks) in 1937; this helped bring him to Hitler's attention, and he commanded an escort battalion from the Grossdeutschland Infanterie-Regiment assigned to Hitler's headquarters before being transferred to the Panzerwaffe in 1940 and receiving command of the 7. Pz.Div.

The panzer drive through the Ardennes was headed toward the Meuse River, which wound its way from France north through Belgium as the geologic western boundary of the rugged Ardennes, and then out to the North Sea through Holland as the Maas. Isolated French aerial reconnaissance indeed indicated all the roads through the Ardennes to be thronged with vehicle traffic, even running with headlights full-on at night. The French commander-in-chief, Gen. Maurice Gamelin, was surprised at reports that even tanks were moving through the "impassable" Ardennes. But he believed an orthodox advance would require the deployment of infantry and artillery before crossing the Meuse River barrier could be attempted. Additional forces were ordered to move north to strengthen Gen. André-Georges Corap's 9ème Armée stretching north as right flank protection for the Anglo-French mechanized advance to the Dyle.

But the key to Blitzkrieg was *un*orthodoxy. The panzers raced through the woods scattering the Chasseurs Ardennais, crossed the river gorges, and rolled through little villages as startled townspeople gawked from their windows. The panzer units ensured their engineers were well forward and maintenance equipment and personnel and fuel trucks kept pace, and the crews had rations for three days. Roads were dedicated for the panzer units, the infantry having to use byways.

Late on Whitsunday (Pentecost), 12 May, Rommel's motorcyclists reached the Meuse. The Dinant bridge had been demolished, as had a railway bridge upriver at Anseremme, and a third at Yvoir was damaged. Using their initiative, the motorcycle troops found an old stone weir at Houx, some 6 kilometers north of Dinant and, though having no heavy weapons or support, nonetheless aggressively worked their way across and established a bridgehead that night. Meanwhile Hartlieb's 5. Pz.Div. had been delayed by demolitions on the Salm and by elements of the Belgian 2ème Division de Cavalerie. But a vanguard under Oberst Paul Hermann Werner, commander of Pz.Rgt. 31, clashed with the French 4ème Division Légère de Cavalerie at Hotton on the Ourthe before reaching Yvoir on that 12th, at which time French sappers blew the bridge as the first German armored car rolled on to it. Streich's Pz.Rgt. 15 had been following in the division columns, moving through Losheim on the 11th and St.Vith on the 12th, and then crossing the Ourthe at Hotton on the 13th.[6]

At dawn on 13 May infantry of Rommel's Schützenregiment 6 tried to cross the Meuse at Bouvignes a kilometer north of Dinant but their inflatable rubber rafts were holed by heavy fire from elements of the French 18ème Division. When Rommel arrived he ordered some houses set on fire to create a smoke screen at the crossing site, and then he deployed some Panzer IVs to give direct-fire support with their 7,5cm cannon. Rommel personally crossed in a boat to energize the assault, and then had the engineers use pontoon rafts to begin ferrying panzers across that night.

Because the Panzer IIIs and IVs of Pz.Rgt. 15 were too heavy for the improvised Meuse bridge at Houx, they were diverted south by XV Corps commander Hoth to cross with the 7. Pz.Div., where they were arbitrarily commandeered by Rommel whose 7. Panzer primarily had 3,7cm-gunned Czech Skoda 38(t)s. In addition, Rommel commandeered the bridging train from 5. Pz.Div. despite protests from Hartlieb, and by Tuesday 14 May the panzer columns were pouring across the Meuse headed west. Rommel again personally took the lead, leaving his Acht-rad armored command car for a Panzer III, though at Onhaye the Wagen was hit twice, and Rommel was cut by shattered periscope glass.[7] It was Hartlieb's misfortune to pace such an aggressive and recognized figure; Rommel even had to be restrained to allow the Allies to become more deeply committed west of the Meuse River as the attack unfolded. On the left 6. Pz.Div. troops of Gen.Lt. Georg-Hans Reinhardt's XXXXI. A.K.(mot) crossed the Meuse at Montherme on the 13th by lashing wood planks to the girders of the downed bridge there, and 8. Pz.Div. approached Nouzonville.

The third major crossing of the Meuse was by Guderian's XIX. A.K.(mot) at Sedan, at the southern edge of the Ardennes. On 13 May, supported by heavy direct fire from panzers and 8,8cm flak guns—and strafing and bombing relays of Stuka Ju 87 dive-bombers that unnerved the defending French reservists of the 55ème Division d'Infanterie—elements of 1., 2., and 10. Panzer-Divisionen crossed the river, and put in a 16-ton pontoon bridge at Glaire that night. The role of close air support as "flying artillery" striking targets was decisive in maintaining the pace of the advance while the field artillery was still back in the columns. Guderian himself crossed in an assault boat, only to be cheerfully greeted on the far bank by Oberstleutnant Hermann Balck of Schützenregiment 1 of 1. Pz.Div. telling him, "Joyriding in canoes on the Meuse is forbidden!"—phrasing Guderian had used during the planning of the operation much earlier. (Balck was a later commander of the 11. Panzer.) The Sedan crossing had been meticulously war-gamed out at Koblenz, and Oberst Walther Nehring, Guderian's chief of staff, had issued the necessary orders based on this, only changing the times and dates.[8] By the 14th Guderian's panzers had broken into the open and began driving toward the Channel coast.

As the French forces began to collapse, the panzer columns rounded up many fugitives, had them throw their weapons down to be crushed under the tracks of the panzers, and motioned them to the rear as Kriegsgefangene (prisoners of war). French command, control, and communications broke down as headquarters and command posts displaced to new locations, hampered by refugees in flight and often under Luftwaffe attack. With growing awareness of the coming debacle French leaders began to panic. On the morning of 15 May a despairing Prime Minister Paul Reynaud telephoned English Prime Minister Winston Churchill: "We are beaten, we have lost the battle."[9] At that point the direction of the German offensive remained unclear: Were they driving east behind the Maginot Line? South to Paris? Or west to the English Channel and the sea?

The Grand-Quartier Général (GQG) released the three DCRs in an effort to stop the German drive, but there was no concept of massing the armor for a counterattack. (The three DLMs—the 1ère with 7ème Armée and the 2ème and 3ème with the mechanized 1ère Armée—had already been committed in the drive north.) The 1ère DCR was ordered up to Charleroi on the Sambre in Belgium, with the tracked vehicles moving by rail and the wheeled vehicles by road. The tracked vehicles required twenty-eight trains to be moved, an operation interrupted when Luftwaffe bombing cut the rail lines. The 2ème was to move to Hirson and the 3ème was to move to Sedan. But on 15 May the three French armored divisions encountered the hard-driving German spearheads.

Général Bruneau had not assembled all his 1ère DCR battalions at Charleroi before he was ordered first to Mettet, then to a position east of Philippeville to block the German forces crossing the Meuse in the Dinant sector. The heavy Char B1s had to be refueled after eight hours, and the even heavier B1bis models after five and a half hours. The 37ème Bataillon along the Flavion–Ermeton road had barely finished refueling and the 28ème was waiting immobile near Morville on the 15th when they were struck by Rommel's 7. Panzer-Division and the covering Stukas. Rommel thrust on to Philippeville as Oberst Werner's Pz.Rgt. 31 of 5. Pz.Div. followed and sent his Panzer IIIs and IVs into the attack. Only two B1s of the immobile 28ème were able to get away, the 37ème was ambushed by 5. Pz.Div. antitank guns, a Hotchkiss battalion was shot up, and the remaining B1s ran out of fuel. But the big B1s were not easy to knock out in the violent clashes of armor. Streich's Pz.Rgt. 15, having crossed the Meuse on the 15th, continued the attack on the 16th through Barbencon and Beaumont and crossed the Belgian border into France south of Maubeuge, engaging French units along the way.

It was intense tank battle: In his Feuerbefehl (fire command) to the Richtschütze (gunner), the Kommandant (commander) through his Bordsprech (intercom) gave deflection by clock direction and the estimated range in meters: *"Achtung! Zehn Uhr, feindlicher Panzer! Entfernung dreihundert! Schuss!"* ("Alert! Ten o'clock, enemy tank! Range three hundred! Fire!") The Ladeschütze (loader) slammed a Panzergranate (armor-piercing round) into the breech while the Fahrer (driver) to the left of the Funker (radio operator) brought the Wagen to a smooth stop. Then: *"Volltreffer . . . Abgepralt!"* ("Direct hit . . . ricochet!") And then a second round: *"Schuss! . . . Ziel!"* ("Fire! . . . Target!")[10]

In the center of the gap being torn open in the French lines, the 2ème DCR was unloading its tanks at railheads around Hirson on 15 May when it was struck by 6. Pz.Div. followed by 8. Pz.Div. The French units were scattered. In the south the 3ème DCR moved toward Sedan, slowed by the need to refuel, and on the 15th the XXI Corps commander, Général J. A. L. R. Flavigny, decided it would be better to disperse the tank units in defensive positions. Guderian's motorized corps had now crossed the Meuse and he dropped off 10. Pz.Div. as flank protection while he forged ahead with the 1. and 2. Panzer-Divisionen and simply swept past the French armor. When Kleist and his superiors, concerned about French counterattacks, ordered a halt, Guderian angrily threatened resignation to get his way and keep going.

On the 17th Colonel de Gaulle, with an ad hoc formation functioning as a fourth DCR but with only ninety-three tanks in the equivalent of three battalions, attacked Guderian's flank from Laon toward Montcornet on the Serre. This was easily fended off by 10. Pz.Div. With reinforcements de Gaulle tried again on the 19th, but the Germans had mined the bridges and deployed antitank guns, and the Stukas ended the foray. The seven panzer divisions that had debouched from the Ardennes and crossed the Meuse were racing each other across northern France between the Somme and the Belgian border toward the Kanal. Rommel's 7. Pz.Div. crossed the Sambre, with Hartlieb's 5. Pz.Div. echeloned on its right flank, overrunning and scattering diverse French units.

At Jamagne north of Philippeville Lt. Kaphengst of Pz.Rgt. 15 rounded up some 300 French as Gefangene from the houses there on the 15th, and Moroccan colonial troops were rounded up near Beaumont on the 16th. But there were also sharp clashes and losses. On the 17th the regiment crossed the French border at Hedruch (Hestrud) where Unteroffizier Frost's panzer Nr. 12 of 4. Kompanie was lost to a mine, and a tank battle ensued past Berlaimont on the Sambre southwest of Maubeuge and into the Forêt de Mormal. Regimental adjutant Oberleutnant von Portatius was killed when his Panzer III was knocked out by a French 2,5cm antitank gun, and Oberst Streich's Panzer III was hit on the turret mantlet before his driver swung the panzer around.[11]

Involved in the fighting in the Forêt de Mormal on 17 May was another component of the future 11. Panzer-Division, Oberst Günther Angern's 11. Schützenbrigade (mot) with Rifle Regiments 110 and 111, fresh from the Danish campaign. At Hannover the brigade had been alerted for the French Feldzug. On 11–12 May the brigade had road-marched to Dillenburg northeast of Koblenz, then via Selters and across the Rhine at Neuweid, through the Eifel via Bad Neuenahr and the Ardennes via St. Vith to Dinant. There it was assigned to the VIII. A.K. of 4. Armee commanded by Günther von Kluge. On 18 May the brigade was attached to Hoth's XV. A.K.(mot) of 4. Armee as the 5. and 7. Pz.Divs cleared the Forêt de Mormal.[12]

The pace of XV Korps advance continued to be set by Rommel. He himself was in the lead with the advance units, sometimes in a command Panzer III, sometimes overhead in a Fieseler Storch light observation plane, to immediately sense opportunities and often give verbal orders to commanders. "Wireless alone—due to the necessity for encoding—would have taken far too long," he later wrote, "first to get the situation reports back to Division and then for Division to issue its orders." Rommel also acknowledged the shock action of armor: "I have found again and again that in encounter actions, the day goes to the side that is the first to plaster its opponent with fire." His lead panzers slashed through surprised French units, firing on the move and continuing through the night. "Much of our ammunition was tracer and the regiment drove on through the new defense line spraying an immense rain of fire far into the country on either side."[13]

The drive continued on the 18th through Lonquignol (Locquignol) where Oberleutnant Anton Graf Magnis-Eckersdorf, commander of 4. Kompanie/ Pz.Rgt. 15 was killed, his men giving him a hasty burial in the woods with a wooden cross, surmounted by his Panzermütze. But the engagements around Jolimetz left French Char B1s, Renault R35s, and armored cars smashed and burning. The heavy French tanks were invulnerable to the undergunned Panzer IIs and even IIIs, but the drum fire pounding against their armor was enough to panic French crews into abandoning their vehicles. Orders sent the regiment from Le Quesnoy southwest through St. Python and St. Aubert, past military cemeteries of World War I, across the Escaut Canal at Cambrai, and on toward Arras. But about 20,00 hours on 21 May there was sudden fighting at Mercatel with the "Tommys," English tanks and troops, which continued through the night.

In an attempt to stem the German drive, Gen. Lord Gort, commander of the BEF, ordered Maj. Gen. H. E. Franklyn of 5 Division to organize an attack south from Arras. "Frankforce" was hastily gathered, comprising two territorial battalions of Durham Light Infantry, six regiments of artillery, and a tank brigade of sixty-eight infantry tanks that included sixteen of the heavily armored Matilda Mark IIs. Under the tactical command of tank expert Maj. Gen. Geoffrey le Q. Martel of 50 Division, the force advanced south in two columns on the afternoon of 21 May. The heavy Matilda IIs, impervious to the German 3,7cm AT guns, overran the infantry and artillery of Rommel's 7. Pz.Div., and broke the motorized SS Totenkopf (Death's Head) Division. But French Somua S35 tanks of the neighboring 3ème DLM mistakenly engaged the British, and Rommel personally brought his powerful, high-velocity 8,8cm flak guns into play to penetrate the Matildas. During the night 5. and 8. Panzer-Divisionen converged on the flanks.[14]

As Hoth's XV. A.K.(mot) blunted this only major threat to the German advance, Guderian's XIX. Motorized Corps swept on. Thus it was the Austrian 2. (Wiener) Pz.Div. that reached Abbeville on the Somme estuary on 20 May, only ten days after Fall

GELB began; it then continued north up the Channel coast, cutting off some forty Allied divisions in Belgium and overrunning their supply depots. The Allies' only recourse without fuel or ammunition was to ration what they had, abandon tanks, planes, artillery, and other equipment, and head for the coast to evacuate from the fishing port of Dunkirk (French Dunkerque, German Dünkirchen).

Hoth's panzers got a chance to pull badly needed maintenance on the 25th and 26th, and the first mailbags from home caught up with the exhausted crews. On the 27th the direction of advance was changed to the north to compress the Dunkirk pocket. The drive was astride the old World War I trench lines of Vimy Ridge, Lens, and Loos, and the column crossed the La Bassée Canal by pontoon bridge. Once again Rommel commandeered Panzer Regiments 15 and 31 from the exasperated Hartlieb, with official authorization from Hoth to do so. Rommel's own 7. Panzer had been converted from 2. Leichte Division and had one panzer regiment instead of two. Half of his 289 panzers were Czech Skoda Panzer 38(t)s, with Rommel noting that "I was extremely impressed by the large numbers of spick-and-span tanks which the 5th Panzer Brigade [*sic*] possessed, far larger than the tank strength of my division." Though junior in time-in-grade, Rommel's favored relationship with the Führerhauptquartier (Hitler's headquarters) was demonstrated when his aide, Oberleutnant Karl Hanke, an ardent Nazi and later Gauleiter (NSDAP regional leader) in Silesia, presented him with the Ritterkreuz (Knight's Cross) for bravery, on Hitler's orders, at a commanders' meeting.[15] The drive continued through Fournes and Lommes between Armentières and Lille, a blur of clashes, wrecked Allied equipment, surrendering soldiers, and gratefully discovered English cigarettes and chocolate.

While Johannes Streich and Panzer-Regiment 15 loyally carried out the missions assigned by the impetuous Rommel while under his command, there was increasing resentment against Rommel's arrogance that other officers would feel as well. On 14 May when Rommel had commandeered 5. Panzer's bridging elements and Panzer IIIs and IVs to cross the Meuse, despite Hartlieb's protests, he was then critical of 5. Pz.Div. for not keeping pace. "Rommel seized this opportunity to filch my own heavy tanks," wrote Streich later, "for use in his division's advance as well. When my general, Hartlieb, protested, he was told that General Hoth had sanctioned it; I myself don't believe for a minute that Rommel asked his permission. Our infantry took very heavy casualties as a consequence." Rommel's 4. Armee commander, Gen. Günther von Kluge, subsequently pointed out to Rommel that many of his claims in his reports for his 7. Pz.Div. were excessive or falsified. Streich later went to Libya as a general, the first commander of 5. Leichte Division as Rommel's DAK was forming. This able fighting commander sometimes defied Rommel, who finally relieved him in May 1941. "You were far too concerned with the well-being of your troops," he said according to Streich, who stiffly replied, "I can imagine no greater words of praise for a division commander."[16]

The panzer drive was getting into the canal-seamed low country of Flanders and the old Ypres salient, not good tank country, and perhaps was one reason for the "Halt" order of 24 May, stopping the panzers as they were poised to overrun the Allies' Dunkirk perimeter. The order was given by Generaloberst von Rundstedt and apparently confirmed by Hitler, who visited the general's headquarters at Charleville near Sedan that morning. Other factors influencing the decision were concerns about the need to pull maintenance on the panzers, which had been driven for two weeks with little break, the need to conserve the armor for defeating the rest of the French Army, and Generalfeldmarschall Hermann Göring's assurances that his Luftwaffe alone would annihilate the trapped Allied forces. The "Halt" order became more controversial later after the British were able to evacuate a third of a million men in Operation DYNAMO by 4 June.[17]

Panzer-Regiment 15 was pulled back to Wavrin on 28 May and then road-marched, in stages, via Beaurains south of Arras–St.Pol–Hesdin to Marenla 20 kilometers from the coast by 1 June. In the shade of the fruit trees of the Hubron Farm, tents were put up, and religious services were held on Sunday, 2 June. After the battle of Arras and the panzers being stopped short of the Dunkirk pocket, other forces of H.Gr. A and B continued to close in. Angern's 11. Schützenbrigade reached Boulogne on 29 May and then advanced toward Cap Griz Nez and the Pas de Calais, fighting withdrawing British forces at Cassel, Kappel, and Rexpoede.

It was apparently during this time that the nickname of the future 11. Panzer-Division evolved, as the "Gespenster-division" ("Ghost Division"). The tradition was that a captured British officer referred to the rapidly moving 11. Rifle Brigade as a "phantom brigade," and the nickname was adopted when the 11. Pz.Div. was later formed. The image portrayed on publications and even painted on panzers and vehicles was of a sword-wielding specter riding a charging half-track. Works often refer to Rommel's 7. Pz.Div. as the "Phantom" or "Ghost" Division.[18] But while the 11. Schützenbrigade (mot) was indeed in Hoth's XV. A.K.(mot) with 7. Pz.Div., it was the 11. Panzer, not the 7. Panzer, that was to be so acknowledged in the Wehrmacht.

As the French attempted to form the so-called "Weygand Line" (Gen. Maxime Weygand having succeeded Général Gamelin on 20 May) along the Somme and the Aisne, the German forces regrouped for Fall ROT (Operation RED), the defeat of the rest of the Allied forces in France. The armor was reorganized into five motorized corps, with two panzer divisions and one motorized division each: Hoth's XV. A.K.(mot) with 5. and 7. Pz.Div., 2. Inf.Div.(mot), and the 11. S.B., remained under Kluge's 4. Armee. Kleist retained XIV. and XVI. A.K.(mot), while Guderian was given command of a panzer group of XXXIX. and XXXXI. A.K.(mot), his former XIX. Corps being dissolved.[19]

At 5. Pz.Div. Hartlieb had been relieved by Hoth, perhaps unfairly, and succeeded by Generalleutnant Joachim Lemelsen from 29. I.D.(mot) on 29 May. (Hartlieb later had rear-area commands in occupied Russia.) The units now moved up to their attack positions, Oberst Streich's Pz.Rgt. 15 making a night road march via Hesdin to Cramont. At 10,00 hours on 5 June the panzers moved to their line of departure, and at 15,30 crossed a floating bridge across the Somme into a bridgehead established by the rifle units at Pont Remy, 8 kilometers upriver from Abbeville, and attacked. Three Panzer IIIs of 1. Kompanie were hit, but the attack gained momentum through the collapsing French 5ème Division Coloniale and 54ème Division d'Infanterie, and by midnight had crossed the Allery–Airaines road.

The next day the panzers attacked south down a secondary road axis through Aumont to the heights of Hornoy where Oblt. Heilmann, commander of 6. Kompanie, was mortally wounded by artillery fire. From Meigneux the advance swung southwest to Romescamps, 4. Kompanie in the lead. There the regiment took up an "Igel" (hedgehog) all-around defense position with Acht-komma-acht flak guns, and the begrimed, exhausted crews got a brief rest. On the 7th the axis of advance led through Formerie approaching Forges-les-Eaux by midnight, Rommel's 7. Pz.Div. paralleling the 5. Pz.Div. on the east through Feuquieres, driving toward Rouen on the Seine west of Paris.

Farther east Panzergruppe Kleist thrust across the Somme between Amiens and Peronne, but upon meeting stiff French resistance it was shifted to the left near Laon to exploit the crossing of the Aisne by Guderian's panzer group. From there Kleist drove across the Marne, bypassing Paris (declared an open city) as Guderian swung southeast to surround the French forces in la Ligne Maginot along the German border from behind.

Any pause in the relentless advance and clashes was welcomed by the Landsers. At Forges on 8 June the panzer troopers of 5. Pz.Div. discovered a small fountain and happily splashed themselves with water using pails found nearby, but the gathering quickly dispersed when two French Morane-Saulnier 406 fighter planes swept over the area. Generally, however, the Luftwaffe had rapidly forward-based to French airfields, and the Messerschmitt Bf 109s were superior to the French Moranes and the RAF Hawker Hurricanes they encountered.

The Forges railroad junction was strongly defended, and English forces laid mines and hastily improvised roadblocks. But by noon Panzer-Regiment 15 was on the move again down the Bouchy road toward Rouen, encountering scattered British and French troops who were taken prisoner. Nightfall found the panzers in the outskirts of the city, and while Pz.Rgt. 15 laagered at Isneauville, skirmishes continued as French and British troops and Germans encountered each other that night in confusion. Flames and clouds of smoke boiled up over Rouen as the British demolished the large oil tanks there.

On that same 8 June, Rommel's 7. Pz.Div. crossed the Andelle at Normanville and hoped to seize the bridges across the Seine upriver at Elbeuf. There he worked his way by foot through the traffic jams in the narrow streets that night to urge the motorcyclists of his Kradschützenabteilung 7 forward, but about 03,00 the French blew the Seine bridges.

New orders on the 9th from Generalleutnant Fedor von Bock's H.Gr. B turned Hoth's XV. Corps to drive to the Channel along the north bank of the Seine to prevent Allied forces evacuating from the port city of Le Havre. Rommel rode with his Panzer-Regiment 25 and reached the sea at Dalles, sharing with his men the satisfaction of walking down the shingle beach to the water's edge. Then the panzers drove up along the coast to Fecamp and St. Valéry en Caux against increasing resistance from the Allied troops now trapped, and 2.Inf.Div.(mot) under Generalmajor Paul Bader came up on their flank.

On the evening of the 11th Rommel sent a delegation of German-speaking prisoners into St. Valéry to demand a surrender, but this was refused. With German artillery and tank fire and converging street fighting, the trapped units began to surrender by the next day. These included the demoralized remnants of four divisions of French Général M. Ihler's IX Corps and English Maj. Gen. Victor Fortune and his 51 Highland Division.

During the 9th after capturing Rouen, Lemelson's 5. Pz.Div. advanced north farther inland through Cleres and toward the road junction of Totes. When 5. Kompanie, leading the regiment through the hilly, forested terrain, got tangled up overtaking a retreating truck column of some thirty vehicles, 4. Kompanie under Leutnant Horst von Buttlar took the lead and by nightfall the panzers were rounding up British prisoners in Totes. That night the Landsers were trying to get some sleep when suddenly the crack of the high-velocity 8,8cm flak guns sent them scrambling for their weapons. The outposts had heard the squeal and clanking of tank tracks and alerted nearby panzer and gun crews as five French tanks blundered into the German positions. They were all knocked out, but artillery fire the next day caused casualties, including Lt. von Buttlar, wounded by shell fragments.

At 19,30 hours the regiment moved out again toward the Channel coast amid intermittent clashes, including some with cavalry units. As the panzer forces pushed deeper into the pocket of Allied forces trapped against the Channel and hoping to be evacuated, they found it expedient to establish Igel laager positions as British and French forces deliberately or inadvertently encountered German units that night. "Soft" vehicles accompanying the attack units—fuel and ammunition Lkws (Lastkraftwagen, trucks)—were protected by a ring of panzers and antitank guns.

On 11 June in St. Pierre Benouville the panzer troops liberated vast amounts of English stores, from tennis balls and golf clubs to cigarettes. As the march columns jumped off again at 15,30 hours with the Channel coast only 30 kilometers away, the day turned out to be the "most exciting and eventful day" for Panzer-Regiment 15 since the French Feldzug began.[20] The men were eager to catch sight of the sea, and they closed in on the seaside community of Veules les Roses south of Dieppe, about 8 kilometers up from St. Valéry where 7. Pz.Div. was attacking. Steep cliffs overlooked the beach where small craft were trying to evacuate Allied soldiers, while artillery and antitank guns attempted to hold outer positions and the perimeter.

The panzers moved to engage in "hull defilade" firing positions, the tank hulls behind the cover of hillocks with only their turrets and guns exposed. Hauptmann Reinhardt's 5. Kp. engaged three French tanks, and Lt. Zügner's panzer and an enemy gun fired at each other simultaneously, hitting each other. His crew bailed out, and Zügner later climbed aboard a Panzer I after convincing the crew he was neither English nor French. The track of his Wagen was wrecked, but later repaired. Given the accuracy of the enemy fire, as ranges and checkpoints had presumably been preregistered it was decided to attack at 20,30 hours when the darkening eastern horizon would make the moving panzers more difficult to engage.

Division commander Lemelson gave Oberst Streich verbal attack orders, but when the regiment jumped off it was alone, the orders apparently not getting to Oberst Werner's Pz.Rgt. 31 in time. Streich led the I. Abteilung guiding to the left side of the coast road, with II. Abteilung on the right side, attacking from the east. A tank attack at night could be more dramatic, and more demoralizing for the defenders, than an attack by day, with tracer streams arcing across the ground, muzzle flashes and explosions sudden and blinding, and the roaring of tank engines and squealing of tracks somehow magnified in the darkness. Tank gunners lost their night vision peering through their telescopic gun sights, but the panzers did not stop for accurate firing and instead lurched cross-country lashing out with cannon Sprenggranate and machine-gun fire toward the enemy positions. Conversely, enemy antitank gunners would try to track the moving silhouettes obscured by the gloom to engage them.

When II. Abt. encountered mines they crossed over to the left side of the coast road as well, and the regiment deployed over the fields in the open. Orienting the axis of attack at night proved difficult. At one point Streich came alongside the Befehlspanzer (command tank) of Maj. Dr. Ludwig Schmahl of I.

Abteilung, who opened his hatch and called out, "General direction of march a hands-breadth to the right of the moon." After a refueling pause, the regiment continued closing in on the shrinking pocket. A British radio message was intercepted: "We are surrounded. Tanks are coming—this is the end."[21] II. Abt. under Hauptmann Theodor-Friedrich Carl Graf von Schimmelmann from 2. Kp. who had succeeded Maj. von Drabich-Waechter, attacked the eastern face of Veules les Roses with 4. and 5. Kompanien. 6. Kp. went with Streich and I. Abt. swinging around to the southwest.

As dawn of the 12th began to break the Panzer IVs of 3. Kp. even opened fire on ships evacuating the seaside harbor below the steep cliffs, and the remaining defenders surrendered. The regiment claimed some 26,000 prisoners, though many more had simply been waved to the rear during the night. Nonetheless the count included French division commander Général Durant, two brigade commanders, Algerians, four French cavalry regiments, and innumerable British troops. For its accomplishment Pz.Rgt. 15 was noted in a Wehrmacht dispatch, and Oberst Streich earned the Ritterkreuz des Eisernen Kreuzes (Knight's Cross of the Iron Cross), the first in the regiment. At 21,00 hours that evening the regiment road-marched back through St. Pierre-Le Vieux and Cruchet to "igel" at Grenville by 01,00 on the 13th. The panzer troops were justifiably proud of their accomplishments. Thus when a brochure was published later, *Die Taten der 7. Panzer-Division* (Deeds of the 7. Panzer Division), as was a propaganda film, *Sieg im Westen* (Victory in the West), that recorded many actions actually carried out by Pz.Rgt. 15 and 5. Pz.Div. and referred to the 7. as the "Gespenster" Division, there was further resentment against General Rommel, who "always allowed war correspondents to swarm around," commented Feldwebel Gustav Schrodek.[22]

On 13 June the final campaign to defeat the remaining French forces began with the crossing of the Seine, Hoth's XV. Korps' objectives being back south to Brest and the Brittany ports some 700 kilometers to the west. Since the bridges at Rouen were not yet usable, Pz.Rgt. 15 crossed on a pontoon bridge at Courcelles some 50 kilometers to the southeast on the 16th and rolled via Evreux, Alençon, and Mayenne. At Rennes on the 19th Gén. Robert Altmayer, commander of the disintegrated 19ème Armée, surrendered to the 5. Pz.Div.[23] Landerneau just northeast of Brest was reached by the 20th. There once again the troops enjoyed captured provisions and went swimming in the Atlantic amid a backdrop of demolished and burning war materiel in the big port city of Brest. Rumors swirled of an armistice and a victory parade through Paris. Meanwhile, British Lt. Gen. Sir Alan Brooke had landed at Cherbourg on 13 June to take command of "Norman Force"—elements of 52 Lowland and 1 Armoured Divisions—but concluded the very next day the task was hopeless and ordered the evacuation of the British troops just landed. Rommel's 7. Pz.Div., crossing the Seine on the 17th, was detached to race into the Cotentin Peninsula and capture Cherbourg by the 19th.[24]

On the southern flank of Hoth's XV. A.K. drive into Brittany was Oberst Günther Angern's 11. Schützenbrigade. After the fighting around the Dunkirk pocket the unit pulled maintenance and replenished north of the Somme, then advanced down along the Channel coast clashing with British units before reaching Dieppe to mop up for three days (12–15 June). On the 16th the motorized brigade was on the move again, crossing the Seine at Vernon west of Paris and rolling through Evreux and Alençon, and Rennes by the 17th. On the 18th they continued through Loudeac, Fontivy, and Châteaulin, to Crozon on the Cap de la Chévre Peninsula on the south side of the bay across from Brest on the 20th.[25]

On 22 June French delegates signed the German armistice terms at Compiègne, in the same railway car where the armistice ending World War I had been signed in 1918. (The car was then taken to Berlin, but apparently subsequently destroyed in an Allied air raid.) The armistice terms, to take effect on the 25th, were more lenient than the French expected. While the Germans would occupy northern France and the Atlantic coast until the conclusion of the war with England, the central and southern area would be independent under the new government forming at Vichy under elderly Marshal Henri Philippe Petain, respected by Hitler for his heroic defense at Verdun in 1916.

While Kleist's panzers rolled across the Loire and down to the Spanish border, the motorized 11. Schütz-Brig. with other units of XV. Corps moved back through Quimper and along the Bay of Biscay coast through the ports of Lorient, Vannes, and St. Nazaire at the mouth of the Loire, disarming any French troops encountered. Whether it was due to the rapid collapse of the French forces, contempt for the politicians of the Fourth Republic, or deep divisions in French society, many French accepted the German victory with equanimity, and treated the young, jubilant troopers with a certain not unfriendly respect.

While many studies understandably focus on analyzing the reasons for the French *defeat*, the overriding factors for the German *victory* were the Blitzkrieg concept of Heinz Guderian, and the strategic vision of Erich von Manstein—and the intuitive comprehension of their originality by Adolf Hitler. Had the original OKH plan been adhered to, there is no reason to believe that the Allied armies would not have performed better than in 1914.

CHAPTER FIVE

Formation of the 11. Panzer-Division

WITH THE END OF THE 1940 FRENCH CAMPAIGN MANY UNITS stayed for temporary occupation duty, while others returned to Germany. The troopers of Panzer-Regiment 15 envisioned themselves as participating in a victory parade through Paris on the way home, and Hauptmann Abraham even suggested to Oberst Streich that the regimental colors might be flown in from the garrison base in Silesia for the grand occasion. This rumor was not fulfilled, but the regiment was going home. The tracked vehicles were loaded on railway cars to be transported from France on 2 July. The wheeled vehicles of the entire 5. Panzer-Division were put under the command of Oberst Streich and departed that day from Brest as well, the road-march column being some 40 kilometers (25 miles) in length.

As there were not enough motorcyclists to direct the vehicle column march serials through the twists and turns typical of many smaller villages, signs with the name "Streich" and an arrow were painted and then located at intersections, those designated to do so being called the "Pinselkolonne"—the "paintbrush unit." Having a sense of humor, the regimental commander himself even mounted a traffic director's box and moved his vehicles by, then lapped the column again. While later serving as a Generalleutnant and Inspecteur der "Schnellen Truppen" (Inspector of the "Fast Troops") and having a training command in Paris, on trips back to Germany Streich sometimes passed through towns whose houses still had signboards bearing his name.

In Reims some, including Streich himself, "secured" bottles of French champagne to take home. Crossing the border at Wasserbillig, Luxembourg, with non-duty-free items could pose a problem, but "Papa Streich" solved this by having the regimental band strike up marching music while the troops staged a small "victory parade" past the customs officials. From Trier the regiment returned to Sagan by road and rail where on Monday 15 July there was a church service followed by panzers parading down Kepplerstrasse, and the "France-fighters" were celebrated by the populace well into the night.[1]

The 11. Schützenbrigade (mot) also returned home from Brittany after relaxing at Carnac on Quiberon Bay near Vannes 24 June–3 July. For his able leadership Oberst Günther Angern was awarded the Ritterkreuz on 5 August 1940. On 8 August the combat veterans participated in a victory parade in Erfurt, capital of Thuringia. Victory in the West in 1940 meant an enthusiastic reception for the returning Landsers, followed by furloughs to homes and garrison duties akin to those of peacetime. But it soon became clear there would be no settlement with Great Britain. The high command reluctantly began to plan for the amphibious invasion of England from occupied France, Unternehmen SEELÖWE (Operation SEA LION); it was canceled, however, in September after the Luftwaffe failed to defeat the Royal Air Force in the aerial Battle of Britain.

Sobering was the expansion westward of Stalin's Soviet Union, with the occupation of the three Baltic states as well as eastern Poland, the defeat of Finland, and the occupation of Bessarabia and northern Bukovina in June 1940 (regaining lands Russia had lost in 1918) threatening the Rumanian oil fields of Ploesti upon which Germany depended. In North Africa Mussolini's Italian forces attacked British Egypt on 13 September from Libya and invaded neutral Greece in the Balkans on 28 October from Albania, though both drives soon stalled. Although Hitler's deep-rooted decision to invade the Soviet Union remained top secret, it was nonetheless obvious that world war would continue, and perhaps escalate.

Ten new panzer divisions were ordered to be organized, the first being the 11. Panzer-Division. This doubled the number of panzer divisions to twenty, but halved the number of panzers in each, from some 328 to 160. Combat had demonstrated the need to increase the infantry-to-tank ratio, from a ratio of sixteen panzer companies to nine infantry in the 1935 organization to a 12:12 ratio in the 1939 organization to six panzer companies to fifteen infantry in the 1940 realignment. In addition, the numerous Panzer Is were clearly obsolete and most were withdrawn from the divisions, retained only for training. All of this increased the mechanization of the Wehrmacht. Not only were the four light divisions converted to panzer divisions and strengthened from a panzer battalion to a regiment, but also five of the ten new divisions were converted from regular infantry divisions. Two came from motorized divisions and three, like the 11. Pz.Div., were formed from various components. Ultimately there were some forty-six numbered or named panzer divisions.[2]

On 1 August 1940 Generalmajor Ludwig Crüwell was named commander of the yet-to-be organized new 11. Panzer-Division. Crüwell, born 20 March 1892 in Dortmund, was a Fahnenjunker (Officer Cadet) in Dragoner Regiment 9 in Metz in 1911, commissioned a Leutnant der Kavallerie in 1912, and served through World War I. He held several positions in the 1930s, including command of Pz.Rgt. 6 of 3. Pz.Div. in 1937–38, and was on the staff of 16. Armee in the French campaign. Crüwell was thus the first commander of the 11. Pz.Div., serving as such through the Yugoslav campaign and into the Russian campaign (1 August 1940–22 August 1941). He later commanded Rommel's DAK in North Africa until his Fieseler Storch was shot down and he was captured 29 May 1942 during the Gazala battle.[3]

The 11. Panzer-Division itself was expanded from the 11. Schützenbrigade (mot) and its staff at Erfurt in Thuringia, Wehrkreis (Military District) IX by an OKH order of 17 July 1940. On 6 September by order of OKH Panzer-Regiment 15 was reassigned from 5. Pz.-Div. to the organizing 11. Pz.-Div. (Pz.-Rgt. 31 stayed with the 5. Pz.-Div.).[4] The incorporation of Pz.Rgt. 15 at Sagan in Niederschlesien (northern or Lower Silesia) in Wehrkreis VIII, for recruiting purposes, identified the 11. Panzer as Silesian, though the new division also adopted the rifle brigade's nickname as the "Gespenster-Division," or the "Ghost Division."

German units were organized by the Kriegsstärkenachweisungen (K.St.N.) tables of organization and equipment (T/O&E in the US Army): Grund Gliederung was the basic-type establishment; Soll Gliederung was the authorized establishment; and Ise (Erste) Gliederung was the initial/actual establishment. Later reports in the Kriegstagebuch (war diary, KTB) by the division Ia (1. Generalstabsoffizier, chief of staff/operations) would differentiate Gefechts-und Verpflegungsstärke (fighting and ration strength), the latter including Beamte, officials such as Zahlmeister (paymaster), personnel on leave or hospitalized and, especially later in Russia, Hiwis or Hilfswillige (civilian volunteers). The 11. Pz.Div. reflected how some other new divisions were formed. Schützenregiment (mot) 111 exchanged its I. Bataillon for I.Btl./S.R. 103 of the new 14.Pz.Div.; Pz. Abwehrabteilung (Antitank Battalion) 61 came from the 231. Inf.Div., redesignated as Panzerjäger-Abteilung (Tank Destroyer Battalion) 61; Krad-schützen-Btl. (Motorcycle Battalion) 61 and Pz. Aufklärungs-Abt. (Reconnaissance Battalion) 231 also came from 231. I.D.; Pz. Nachrichten-Abt. (Signals Battalion) 341 came from 311. I.D.; Pz. Pionier-Btl. (Engineer Battalion.) 209 from 209. I.D.; and Artillerie-Rgt. (Artillery Regiment) 119 (initially designated 231) came from several units: the Stab came from Art.Rgt. 746 (mot), the I. Abt. from I./Art.Rgt. 4 of the 4. I.D., the II. Abt. from III./Art.Rgt. 677, and the III. Abt. from I./Art.Rgt. 643, separate Heeres-truppen (army troops). Other company-sized units forming were numbered 61.[5]

The Stab (Staff) was organized by specific functions. A Chef des Stabes (chief of staff) was usually found at levels higher than division. At division level operations were carried out by the Ia, Der erste Generalstabsoffizier (the First General Staff Officer), Maj. Werner Wolff. The Ib (Nachschub, Supply) was Hauptmann Friedrich von Heuduck, Ic (Nachrichten, Intelligence) for a long time was Leutnant Siegfried Vietor, IIa (Personal/personnel, officers) and adjutant was Maj. Bernhard von Bernuth, and IIb (personnel, enlisted) was Lt. Klaus Knorr. Other positions were III Rechtsoffz. (Judge Advocate), IVa Verwaltung (Administration), IVb Sanitäts (Medical), IVc Veterinär, (Veterinarian, not in panzer divisions), IVd Geistlicher or Seelsorger (Chaplain), and V Kraft-fahrwesen Offz. (Motor Transport Officer). VI would be added later: Nationalsozialistischer Führungsoffizier (NSFO or NaSoFü), National Socialist Leadership Officer for Nazi troop guidance, after the establishment of the NS-Führungsstab in OKW 22 February 1943.

The operational groupings were the Führungsabteilung (tactical or operations group) at the Gefechtsstand (Division Forward Command Post), consisting of the Ia, Ic, liaison officers, and artillery Ia. The rückwärtiger Stab (Division Rear Echelon) was the Nachschub Gruppe (Supply or Quartermaster) under the Ib, with IVa, IVb, (IVc), and V; and the Adjutantur (personnel group) of the adjutant IIa, and IIb, IVd, and the Division Stabs Kompanie (Headquarters Company).

The Tross (Division Trains) were controlled by the DNF or Dinafü (Division Nachschubführer, Division Supply Leader), Oberstleutnant Camillo Neureiter, and included medical, supply, replacement, administration, ordnance, military police, bakery, and postal units, each numbered 61. In the supply columns, Leichte Kolonne I (Light Column I) vehicles carried ammunition, and Leichte Kolonne II vehicles carried gasoline fuel.[6]

Oberst Günther Angern's 11. Schütz.-Brig. still had Schützen-Regiment 110, commanded by Oberst Helwig Luz, and S.R. 111, commanded by Oberst Theodor Bohlmann-Combrinck. Each regiment had two rifle battalions transported in Lkws. Oberst Johannes Streich's Panzer-Regiment 15 had two battalions of two light and one medium company each. The light companies had Panzer IIs mounting the 2cm gun, and even still some Pz.Is with MGs. The medium companies had Pz. IIIs (3,7cm) and IVs (7,5cm). Artl.-Rgt. 119 was under the command of Oberstleutnant Heinz Matena. It had three battalions of light 10,5cm and medium 15cm howitzers, towed by half-tracks.

Ostpreussische Leichte Flakabteilung 71 (Light Antiaircraft Battalion 71) was soon attached to the division for tactical support in January 1941, and remained until May 1942. L./71 was a Luftwaffe unit from East Prussia, their flying eagle insignia and blue-gray uniforms different than the army's eagle and Feldgrau (field gray-green). The commander was Maj. Werner Jacobson. The firepower of the half-track-mounted 3,7cm and 2cm automatic cannon, the latter in single, twin (Zwillingsflak), or quadruple (Vierlingsflak) mounts, against both air and ground targets, would be much appreciated for the year and a half L./71 would work with the 11. Panzer. Other battalions were Kradschützenbataillon 61, Pz. Aufklärungsabteilung 231, Pz. Jäger Abt. 61, Pz. Pionier Btl. 209, and Pz. Nachrichten Abt. 341.[7]

By 1 October 1940 the division elements relocated to the Sagan Kaserne (Barracks) where Pz.Rgt. 15 was housed in a massive, permanent four-story stone building. Other units had more temporary structures, and the division formed at the nearby Neuhammer Truppenübungsplatz (Training Area) where it carried out maneuvers and firing exercises.

Before the war, the service requirement for military-age males was six months in the Reichsarbeitsdienst (RAD, National Labor Service) doing construction projects, then two years in the military. After the war broke out the time obligation was extended. Grundausbildung was basic training, initially sixteen weeks, reduced to eight weeks later during the war. Individual training was followed by Gruppe (squad) and Zug (platoon) unit training.

Soldbuch
zugleich Personalausweis
Nr.
für
den ... (Dienstgrad)
ab ... (Datum) ... (neuer Dienstgrad)
ab ...
ab ...
... (Vor- und Zuname)
Beschriftung und Nummer der Erkennungsmarke
Blutgruppe
Gasmaskengröße 3
Wehrnummer
1

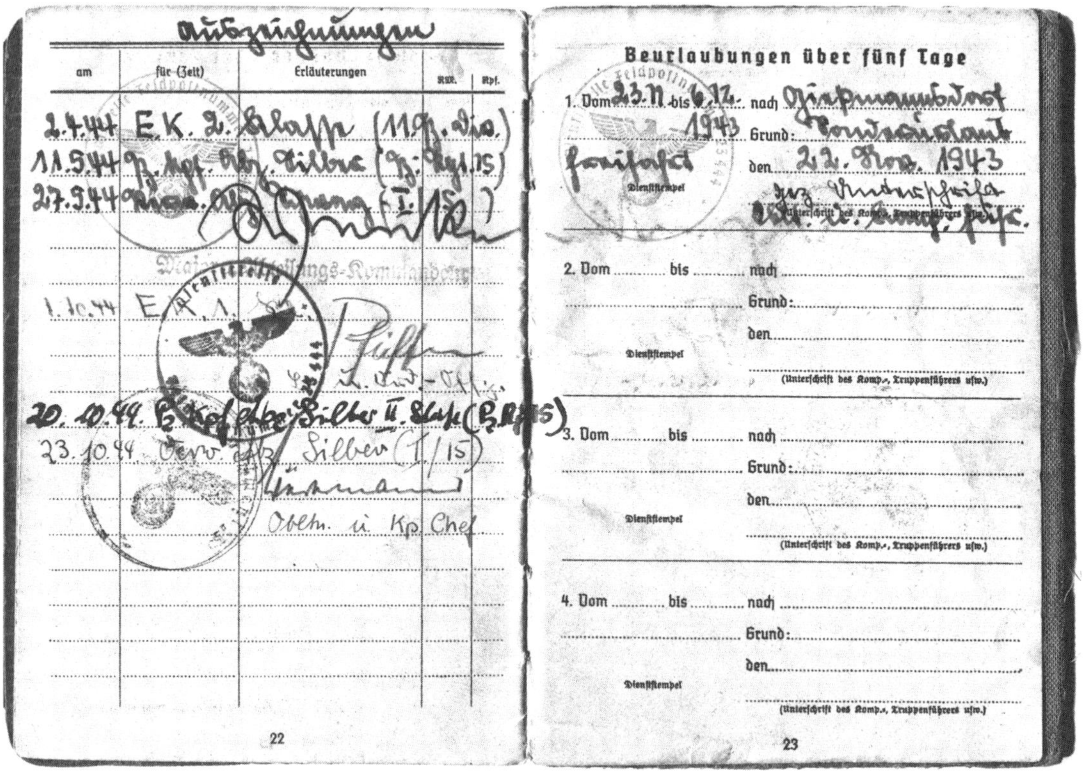

am	für (Zeit)	Erläuterungen	RM.	Rpf.

22

Beurlaubungen über fünf Tage
1. Vom ... bis ... nach ...
Grund: ...
den ...
Dienststempel
(Unterschrift des Komp.-, Truppenführers usw.)
2. Vom ... bis ... nach ...
Grund: ...
den ...
Dienststempel
(Unterschrift des Komp.-, Truppenführers usw.)
3. Vom ... bis ... nach ...
Grund: ...
den ...
Dienststempel
(Unterschrift des Komp.-, Truppenführers usw.)
4. Vom ... bis ... nach ...
Grund: ...
den ...
Dienststempel
(Unterschrift des Komp.-, Truppenführers usw.)
23

Soldbuch (identification book) of Oberleutnant von Eggeling, Pz.Rgt.15, including awards (Iron Cross 2. and 1. Class, Tank Assault Badges in Silver, and Wound Badges in Black and Silver). F. K. VON EGGELING

Upon joining a unit the recruit received his Soldbuch and Erkennungsmarke. The Soldbuch, 105 x 145mm with a soft cover, was no longer a "pay book," but one's personal identification and service record booklet, with photo, personal data, Wehrnummer (original military registration number), promotions, decorations, hospitalizations, and furloughs. These were usually written in by the unit adjutant. It also had the blood type, unit, and serial number as on the two-part metal Erkennungsmarke identification disc worn around the neck (nicknamed "Hundemarke," or "dog tags"), the lower part to be snapped off by graves registration if killed in action.

During a typical day of training in the Kaserne, a Feldwebel (sergeant) rousted the men. Dressing and pulling on their "Knobelbechern" ("dice boxes" or their Marschstiefel jackboots), they fell out for inspection and daily training routines: *"Stillgestanden! Gewehr über! Gewehr umhängen! Abteilung—Marsch! Abteilung—Halt! Gewehr ab! Hinlegen! Auf!"* And hopefully: *"Rührt Euch."* ("Attention! Shoulder arms! Sling arms! Unit—March! Unit—Halt! Order arms! Lie down! Up!" And: "At ease.") The "goose-step" Paradeschritt was not taught recruits.[8]

As in other armies, the "Frosch" ("frogs"—Landsers and Gefreiters) might fear the company first sergeant, "Der Spiess" (from the "pikes" carried by sergeants in the army of Friedrich II der Grosse). Kurt Nentwig found himself in the supply column of Leutnant Urban, in his "Raupensammlung" ("worm collection"). He had been transferred to Pz.Rgt. 15 as a "Bonbongefreiter" ("candy corporal"); after several months a recruit was promoted and got a star on the left arm ("but no increase in pay"), sarcastically referred to as a Bonbon.[9] Physical exercise included sports: swimming, Fussball (soccer), and skiing.

Advanced enlisted men might be selected as officer candidates to be promoted as lieutenants. One process was by attending a military academy (before the war there were four Kriegsschule, at Potsdam, Dresden, Hannover, and München). Halfway through the Lehrgang (course of instruction), the Fahnenjunker (or Offizieranwärter, officer candidate) became a Fähnrich (cadet), and then an Oberfähnrich, before being promoted a Leutnant. There were also special service branch schools, and the program was expanded during the war.[10]

Driver training was done by instructors from the Nationalsozialistisches Kraftfahrkorps (NSKK, National Socialist Motor Transport Corps). The Panzersoldat black uniform had a short field jacket, long trousers, and a soft, round beret, with rose trim and the Totenkopf (death's head) insignia of the hussars. The black wool-rayon material did not show vehicle grease and oil, the jacket was double-breasted against frontal cold wind endured while riding in an open hatch, and there were no cuffs or buttons exposed that might snag in the vehicle interior. The trousers had ankle tapes and fit into laced shoes. The beret covered a vehicle helmet, over which earphones were put. A throat microphone was used for intercommunication by the crew. A switch at the chest changed to company or battalion radio frequency. Later, the regular Feldgrau uniform and Feldmütze (field cap) with turn-down button flaps were worn, though often the panzer jacket was kept.[11] Sometimes the Panzersoldaten referred to the infantry Landsers as "Stoppelhopser"—"stubble-hoppers," as traditionally fall maneuvers were performed in the fields after harvest. With pride, especially with a Bier, Schnaps, and/or Steinhäger at a local Gasthaus when on Kurzurlaub (pass), they could sing the *Panzerlied*, the "Song of the Tanks":

> Ob's stürmt oder schneit, ob die Sonne uns lacht,
> der Tag glühend heiss oder eiskalt die Nacht;
> bestaubt sind die Gesichter, doch froh ist unser Sinn,
> es braust unser Panzer im Sturmwind dahin
>
> (Through storm winds or snow, or the sun's laughing ray,
> the cold of the night, or the heat of the day;
> begrimed are our faces, yet joyful spirits rise,
> our tank roars along in a strong storm of wind)[12]

The five-man Besatzung (crew) of the Panzer IIIs and IVs learned their responsibilities: in the turret the Kommandant had all-around vision in the cupola and controlled the panzer, the Richtschütze sat to the left of the main gun breech and fired the main gun and coaxial machine gun, and the Ladeschütze was to the right, to load the weapons and clear stoppages; in the front hull was the Fahrer, and the Funker who also operated the bow machine gun on the right side.

Through the Bordsprech (intercom) the Kommandant gave deflection to the Richtschütze in his

Feuerbefehl by the clock method, 12 Uhr being directly ahead. On the Panzer III the Richtschütze traversed the turret by manually turning a handwheel with his right hand (which also had the trigger), and elevating or depressing the gun by a handwheel with his left hand. He fired the turret-mounted coax machine gun by working a pedal with his right foot. Panzersoldat Gefreiter Nentwig noted that the Fahrer could accidently hit the pedal behind him and, if the gunner had not put it on Sicher (safe), a burst of deadly machine-gun fire could result.[13] The Panzer IV also had manual elevation, but an electrical traverse, with manual capability used for precise gunlaying. Maneuvers included basic formations for the five-panzer Zug: Reihe (column, for road marches), Doppelreihe (doubled column for approach advance), Linie (line, firepower ahead), and Keil (wedge, spread to flanks). Kompanie formations included the Breitkeil (two platoons abreast in wedge formation, other platoons behind in wedge or Doppelreihe formation).[14]

That the members of a unit all came from a specific Wehrkreis strengthened the bonds of comradeship insofar as they shared a familiarity with locations and communities, and in some cases even families. This also encouraged the mutual sense of duty, as neighbors and school classmates would learn of the conduct of their acquaintances. Many officers of the panzer regiment were of the Schlesische Adel (Silesian nobility) like Lt. Friedrich Karl von Eggeling; to them command came naturally. The common soldiers might be from their estates or adjacent villages. They could easily discuss livestock, horses, tractors, crops, and weather at home. Although there could be a certain paternalistic attitude on the part of noble officers, this was indeed appropriate, to have an obligation to provide for the welfare of their men as much as possible. In the field all ate the same rations, but a good officer ensured his men would be served first. Panzer crews in particular (a Leutnant having his own panzer), who had to depend upon each other in combat, were likely to share rations.

The nobility had deep family traditions that provided a certain cohesiveness, though also a certain antagonism between them and the Nazi regime whose origins and original support were largely working class and lower middle class. This was reflected in numerous ways. In October 1941 sixteen-year-old Friedel von Eggeling was in school when a delegation of SS recruiting officers came into the classroom and determined that tall, blond-haired, blue-eyed Friedrich, among others, seemed well-qualified as Aryan for the SS, the elite Nazi Schutz Staffel under Reichsführer Himmler. To avoid this, his father motored to Sagan as quickly as he could, and within a week had him enlisted as an Offizieranwärter in Pz.Rgt. 15 (which as 1. Kürassierregiment, Leibkürassiers des Königs, The King's Own Cuirassier Regiment, had been the regiment of their ancestors). Von Eggeling, now seventeen, joined the regiment 1 April 1942, and served under a commander, Theodor-Friedrich Carl Graf von Schimmelmann, who was the son of his father's regimental commander; Lt. Freiherr von Wallenberg-Pachaly of 2. Kompanie was a cousin; the regimental Messeoffizier (mess officer) Freiherr von Tschirschky was another cousin, and Freiherr von Loebenstein was an uncle. Von Eggeling did feel that after the 20 July 1944 attempt on Hitler's life by army officers, and the Führer's subsequent determination to "eliminate those blueblooded rascals," personnel were assigned to the regiment from more diverse backgrounds who did not share the regimental mystique.[15]

At least three members of the division attended the same private boarding school, Die Ritterakademie zu Brandenburg a. Havel southwest of Berlin: Wend von Wietersheim (to 1915), later 11. Pz.Div. commander; Ernst August Freiherr von Fersen (to 1938), later Oberleutnant; and Klaus Jürgen Bardt (to 1943, seventeen years old), Fahnenjunker with Pz.Rgt. 15. Students reflected distinguished family names, including von Arnim, von Bülow, von Jagow, von Manteuffel, von Richthofen, and others. Klaus Bardt felt the ideals of respect, dignity, and civility, even chivalry, inculcated in the shared social and educational background, carried over into their military roles: "Certain behavior just was not acceptable." He also noted that most had a rural background in horsemanship since boyhood: "Fast thinking, risk taking and action became part of their attitude," and as hunters they "learned to utilize terrain, wind, and light to be successful. They were excellent marksmen and had keen eyesight and a gift for observing their surroundings. All this helped them to develop into useful members or leaders of tank-crews or units."[16]

Because Panzer-Regiment 15 was recruited in Wehrkreis VIII, Silesia, the Silesian dialect was another bond of comradeship. It did mean that common soldiers could less easily mock their officers (as soldiers are wont to do) in dialect. While understanding the dialect, however, an officer could lose respect by speaking it. Gefreiter (and later Leutnant) Kurt Nentwig's mother had admonished him, *"Junge, tu ock nie a su pauern!"* ("Boy, don't speak like a peasant!") Nonetheless, later non-Silesian officers were sometimes considered "town people," and sometimes their men had trouble understanding "the strange German dialect."[17] Yet even most of these became ardent members of the division. Walter Rahn, born in Giessen, Oberhessen (Upper Hesse), in 1920, was in a youth group at ten years of age, the deutsche Pfadfinderbund (DPB, German Pathfinder Federation). But when the Nazis came to power in 1933, youth groups were dissolved, and Rahn was amalgamated into the deutsches Jungvolk (DJ) of the Hitler Jugend (HJ). After obligatory service in the RAD, he joined the army, underwent artillery officer training at Jüterbog in 1941, and then was assigned to Pz.Rgt. 15 at Sagan. Because his brother had been killed in action, as a "Last Son" he was not to be sent to the front, and he served as a training officer until 1943. Manpower shortages after that saw Leutnant Rahn serving in many positions in the regiment, and after the war he played a major role in organizing contacts with his former comrades.[18]

Those who had Jewish connections felt and resented the discriminatory Nazi policies. Friedrich K. von Eggeling's mother was three-eighths Jewish, but also a quarter direct descendant of the Austrian Habsburg Emperor Franz I, which made her "interesting" to the Nazi regime. She had to report every month to the SS station in their town (where she would be insulted: "Oh, here you are, you Jewish pig"). His father, active in a nationalist political party, had been imprisoned, and had to have SS permission to attend to the family estates in Silesia. Later regimental commander Meinrad von Lauchert had married into the quarter-Jewish Pulvermann family of Hamburg (famous for the Pulvermann Grab in horse-jumping), and even "privileged" upper-class individuals were the object of discrimination.[19]

Nazi policy toward German Juden had been complicated by the problem of definition, as in formulating the discriminatory Nürnberg Laws of 1935, so thoroughly assimilated into German society was the Jewish population. The result was that many who were technically Mischlinge (mixed race) were either simply accepted, or received official exemptions from anti-Jewish legislation, and even served in the Wehrmacht. Quarter-Jew Juergen Krackow enlisted in Pz.Rgt. 15 at Sagan, was promoted to Panzerleutnant, and was awarded EK 2. (Eiserne Kreuz 2. Klasse), EK 1., the Wound Badge in Gold, and the Panzer Assault Badge in Silver while serving later with the 5. and 23. Pz.Div. on the Ostfront. In his 1991 book *Die Genehmigung* (The Exemption) is his official exemption document dated 28 Januar 1943, Führerhauptquartier (gez. Adolf Hitler). Kriegsmarine Adm. Bernhard Rogge was quarter-Jewish, and Luftwaffe Feldmarschall Erhard Milch was half-Jewish. Some 150,000 full Jews and Mischlinge, like panzer leader Fritz Bayerlein and later Kanzler Helmut Schmidt, served in the Wehrmacht.[20]

Some of these men were proud to serve as Germans, though with some bitterness, while others hoped their service would save their families from persecution. Like most Germans, they were generally unaware of the ultimate destruction wrought by the top-secret "Endlösung der Judenfrage" (Final Solution of the Jewish Question), the Holocaust (Shoah). Tragically, many fought and died in combat even as family members suffered and died in the concentration and later death camps in occupied Poland. Eastern Jews in the occupied territories received no exemptions.

In October 1940 the Ib (Nachschub), Hauptmann von Heuduck, recorded for the Kriegstagebuch that OKH was going to equip the division for employment in subtropical zones, which certainly stimulated speculation, especially as the Italians had attacked the British in North Africa.[21] Unit training at Neuhammer was all too short as the division was alerted for a long E-Transport (Eisenbahn, railroad) movement, and those on leave were recalled two days after Christmas. Some of the panzer companies received new Panzer IIIs with a short 5cm gun, replacing those with the short 3,7cm, and new Panzer IVs with a better short 7,5cm gun. As rumors about the division's destination abounded, movement orders were issued on 18 January of the new year to rail-load the division for departure on the 20th.

Trains loaded by company. For tracked vehicles a steam "Lok" backed a line of flatcars down one of the Neuhammer sidings to an end ramp. Then the waiting column of panzers moved forward and up the ramp, clanking ahead and crossing from car to car, the drivers ground-guided by sergeants stepping backward to the car ahead, motioning the drivers to stay centered. Then chock blocks were wedged under the tracks and cable tie-downs affixed to secure the panzers and half-tracks. Wheeled vehicles were side-loaded from platforms the same height as the flatcars, the men jockeying them into position. The crews with their Kleidersacke (duffle bags) of extra clothing and personal equipment climbed aboard the passenger cars at the head end of the train and settled into the various compartments. Despite the winter cold, many troops pushed down the coach windows so they could lean out to watch the activity. Unless a vehicle slipped off a flatcar, a company could load in less than two hours.

Then the trains departed with the shriek of the steam engines' high-pitched whistles, and began rolling through the winter countryside. Rounding a curve one could see the engine pounding ahead, or the long line of flatcars and armored vehicles following. Soon the trains were heading not east or west, but south, and it was announced the division was headed toward Rumania as "Lehrtruppen," instructional troops. The route south went through Breslau, across rugged Slovakia, through Budapest, across the Transylvanian Alps, and over the rolling farmlands of Wallachia. The unit detrained eight days later at Medgidia near Constanta in the Dobrudja on the Black Sea. Three officers of the attached Flak battalion I./71 became famous for playing the card game "Skat" in their compartment for seven days without interruption. The train trip through the Balkans was a new experience for most, though marred when there was a head-on collision on single track near Nagy-Karole on the Hungarian rail lines of the troop train with 2. Panzer Kompanie. Six troopers were killed in the accident.[22]

The 11. Panzer-Division was billeted in various locations among Constanta–Medgidia–Cernavoda, some even in thatched-roof structures where the flavor of an eastern culture was felt. Many also visited the large harbor of Constanta with its impressive casino along the seawall, and scrambled down on the rocks to taste the brackish water of the Black Sea. On a sunny 9 February Panzer-Regiment 15 held a formation in Medgidia, and as the regimental band struck up martial airs Oberst Streich received the Knights Cross of the Iron Cross from General Crüwell, awarded 31 January for the action at Veules les Roses. Then "Papa Streich" reviewed his regiment for the last time, as the next morning he left by train for Berlin, promoted to take command of the 5. Leichte Division soon to be sent to Tripoli as a part of Rommel's Deutsches Afrika Korps (reorganized as 21. Pz.Div. on 1 August 1941). Three weeks later Oberstleutnant Gustav-Adolf Riebel arrived as new regimental commander. "Peter" Riebel had been born 13 March 1896 in Burglehn-Muskau. He served in Ulan Regiment 4. in World War I and was promoted to Leutnant in 1916. He remained in the Reichsheer, and later became adjutant to Heinz Guderian, Kommandeur der Schnelle Truppen, absorbing Guderian's doctrines of panzer warfare. Obst.Lt. Riebel was adjutant in Kleist's XXII. A.K.(mot) through the Polish campaign, and then was adjutant to Guderian again in XIX. A.K.(mot) through the French campaign.[23]

The deployment of the 11. Pz.Div. to Rumania as "Lehrtruppen" was part of a complex realignment of Balkan diplomacy. On 21 July 1940, even as OKW was preparing Unternehmen SEELÖWE against England, Hitler raised the issue of attacking Russia with Generalfeldmarschall Walter von Brauchitsch, and OKH initiated planning. Hitler's motives included suspicions about Stalin's expansionist threat, Churchill's anticipation of Russia's involvement in the war, Hitler's own geopolitical and racial objectives of expanding into the Eurasian "heartland" for Lebensraum (living space) against the inferior Slavic "Untermenschen," and his conviction that the Soviet Union could rapidly be defeated.

For a successful campaign against Russia it was vital that the Balkan countries on the southern flank be stable and friendly, especially to ensure the production and transportation of oil from Rumania. This seemed to be accomplished by shrewd diplomatic moves. To resolve Hungarian and Bulgarian irredentist claims against Rumania from World War I, Hitler pressured the cession of the southern Dobrudja to Bulgaria on 21 August, and the cession of one-third of Transylvania to Hungary on 30 August; he then guaranteed the territorial integrity of the rest of Rumania against the Soviet Union, which had already occupied Bessarabia and northern Bukovina the previous June. This brought Rumanian dictator Gen. Ion Antonescu, who had seized power with the Fascist Iron Guard on 6 September, to request German military assistance. The first German mission, to protect the oil fields and to train the Rumanian military, arrived in Rumania on 7 October 1940. German diplomatic moves in the Balkans, on top of the series of military victories in the West, swayed many Balkan leaders toward closer relationships with Germany.

But then Mussolini, perhaps jealous of Hitler's successes, threw the Balkans and the whole eastern Mediterranean into turmoil with his invasions of

British Egypt and Greece. Retribution was swift. The Greeks stalled the Italians in the mountains and drove them back into Albania, the British Royal Navy's old Fairey Swordfish torpedo bombers from aircraft carrier HMS *Illustrious* sank three battleships in their naval base of Taranto on 11 November, and Gen. Richard O'Connor's Western Desert Force routed Marshal Rodolfo Graziani's 10. Army in December and drove across Cyrenaica.

Even more disturbing from Hitler's perspective was the British occupation of Crete and Limnos in the Aegean on 31 October, the deployment of RAF elements into southern Greece on 4 November, and Britain's preparations to send ground forces from North Africa, ostensibly to aid the Greeks (who didn't need assistance and were chary of Hitler's reaction). The British deployment could adversely influence Balkan diplomatic alignments and bring the Ploesti oil fields within RAF bomber range. On 4 November Hitler ordered the OKH to plan the invasion of Greece, and persuaded Hungary and Rumania to sign the Tripartite Pact (of Axis powers) on 20 and 23 November, respectively. Bulgaria and Yugoslavia were more reluctant but finally also signed, on 1 and 25 March 1941, respectively.[24]

On 13 December 1940 OKW issued Weisung (Directive) Nr. 20 for the invasion of Greece, Unternehmen MARITA, and on 18 December Weisung Nr. 21 for the invasion of Russia, Unternehmen BARBAROSSA. In the preliminary planning for BARBAROSSA it was determined the Schwerpunkt (point of main effort) would be with two army groups north of the Pripet marshes. Nonetheless Heeresgruppe Süd would drive into the Ukraine for a double envelopment; a Kesselschlacht west of the Dnepr would be spearheaded by Panzergruppe 1 and 6. Armee in the north and by 12. Armee from Rumania in the south, with 17. Armee screening the Hungarian border area between them.

Generalfeldmarschall Wilhelm List and 12. Armee was given responsibility for MARITA and by late December his headquarters moved to Rumania, followed by other forces, including 5. and 11. Panzer-Divisionen. On 18 March 1941 it was decided that 12. Armee would occupy Greece, and for BARBAROSSA H.Gr. Süd would lead off with its northern thrust by Pz.Gruppe 1 only, a new 11. Armee being created to defend Rumania. Events were moving rapidly. Luftwaffe units were deployed to Italian air bases in the south, and Generalleutnant Erwin Rommel had arrived in Tripoli on 12 February 1941 and soon counterattacked the British, who had been weakened by having dispatched forces to Greece, even before all elements of his DAK disembarked. General O'Connor was captured 7 April and his WDF forces routed.

Joining the Tripartite Pact on 1 March, Bulgaria allowed the German forces that would attack Greece entrance from Rumania. Upon receipt of Stichwort (code word) "Hammel!" the 11. Pz.Div. rolled out of its Rumanian billets the next day, and by 07,00 hours the division was crossing the Bulgarian border at Silistra on the Danube. The 300-kilometer road march turned inland, through Razgrad and up the Kotel and Vrica Passes of the rugged Balkan Mountains, to assigned billeting between Sliven, Stara Zagora, and Jambol of old eastern Rumelia by the next day. The motorcycles, vehicles, and panzers, with the "Gespenster" image proudly stenciled on, churned up the unpaved roads in clear weather.

Bulgaria was to be home for a month, with units billeted in numerous communities, or bivouacking in fields under camouflaged tents; II. Abt./Art.Rgt. 119 put up a huge tent later nicknamed the "Jannusch Circus" after the commander. Crüwell and the division staff were in Sliven. Cities like Jambol featured Turkish baths, Mocca, and other oriental delights. For the Landsers it was again a novel experience, with street and town names in the Eastern Orthodox Cyrillic alphabet, and the custom of shaking the head to say "Da" (Yes) and nodding to say "Ne" (No). The Zigeuner (Gypsy) areas added romantic color, sometimes with their dancing bears (though many Gypsies would later be exterminated under Nazi policy). Bulgaria had been a German ally in the last war, and the reception was friendly, even if the thatched and tiled peasant huts were primitive by western European standards. Packs of dogs hunting through the villages at night had to be treated with respect. There were maneuvers and training, but the atmosphere was relaxed, and one could catch a "Nickerchen," a short nap, in the warming spring sun.

But formations, reviews, and inspections were also held, as General Crüwell played host to a number of visitors. Important among these were General der Infanterie Gustav von Wietersheim of XIV. Armeekorps (mot) with operational control of the 11. Pz.Div., Generaloberst Ewald von Kleist of Pz.Gruppe 1, and Generalfeldmarschall Wilhelm List commanding 12. Armee. Others included the German

Ambassador Freiherr von Richthofen, and especially Bulgarian Tsar Boris III of the German Saxe–Coburg–Gotha line, who arrived at Jambol by train on 17 March. Field maneuvers were being demonstrated for him when suddenly King Boris clambered aboard one of the 4. Kompanie panzers and greeted the crew with the Bavarian-dialect *"Grüss Gott!"* ("God's greetings"), and was given an orientation of the panzer's controls. To the dismay of his security, he then donned a rubberized motorcyclist coat and was allowed to drive a Panzer III, one of Oberst Riebel's command tanks, number 02.[25]

Other Army and Luftwaffe units concentrated in Rumania and Bulgaria for the invasion of Greece, the target date being on or about 1 April, even as more British forces arrived there. To some extent the obvious German buildup in the Balkans provided cover for the secret major buildup of the Wehrmacht in occupied Poland for the invasion of Russia. To complete a pro-German solidarity in the Balkans Hitler had pressured Yugoslavia as well, and on 25 March Prince Regent Paul's government signed the Tripartite Pact. OKH in particular had urged the use of the Belgrade–Niš–Salonika rail line for MARITA, but Hitler had not pressed to allow the transit of German forces.

The very next night there was a military *coup d'etat* in Belgrade and a new government was formed by (former) air force general Dušan Simonič, with seventeen-year-old King Peter II as titular ruler. On the 29th the Yugoslav armed forces were mobilized. General Sir John Dill, the British chief of staff, flew to Belgrade on 1 April, and on 3 April the new regime sought an agreement with the Soviet Union; British, Greek, and Yugoslav military representatives also met to discuss measures in common against the German threat. Hitler's careful Balkan diplomacy was in jeopardy, and the vital oil barge traffic up the Donau through the narrow Eiserne Tor (Iron Gate) and up past Belgrade was at risk.

Hitler was furious. As soon as he learned of the *coup* on 27 March, Hitler convened a meeting of the high command at 13,00 hours. They then issued Weisung Nr. 25, the Blitzkrieg against Yugoslavia, as Unternehmen 25. Within twenty-four hours OKH developed a combined plan of campaign against Yugoslavia and Greece. At a special conference of the field commanders in Vienna on the 29th, it was determined that the Luftwaffe would annihilate the Yugoslav air force and paralyze the military command structure by bombing Belgrade on 6 April; the 12. Armee led by Pz.Gruppe 1 would attack on the 8th, and the rapidly organized 2. Armee under Generaloberst Maximilian von Weichs would strike from the north on the 10th. List's 12. Armee in Bulgaria now had to reorganize for a dual mission: Kleist's Pz.Gr. 1 would attack Yugoslavia, not Greece, from the south, while the rest of 12. Armee carried out MARITA. The mountainous terrain in both cases posed formidable challenges.

The main assault against Yugoslavia would come from von Weichs's 2. Armee from Austria and Hungary in the northwest, Pz.Gr. 1 in the south, and a third force, XXXXI. A.K.(mot), from Timisoara in Rumania to the northeast; all were to converge on the capital city of Belgrade. Only the Wehrmacht could develop such an audacious campaign to overrun the large nation of Yugoslavia and defeat the significant British forces in Greece, and then redeploy for the invasion of Russia, all in only a few weeks' time. Primitive road networks, inadequate rail lines, limited river bridges, and easily blocked mountain defiles, not to mention poor weather conditions and enemy resistance, all posed challenges that only the most skillful and experienced staff work could plan for and overcome. In addition, even a rapidly concluded campaign meant a postponement of BARBAROSSA. While the OKH operations order of 3 February 1941 anticipated a target date of 15 May, Hitler estimated now a postponement of four to six weeks.

On 28 March the 11. Panzer-Division received its alert order, ready to move on six hours' notice, and on 31 March received code word "Sofia." On 2 April the 11. Panzer rolled out of its billeting areas to follow a route along the Maritza River valley through Plovdiv to assembly areas northeast of Sofia between Breznik and Kalotina, close to the Serbian Yugoslav border. The local villagers were delighted, sensing the Germans were going to attack their ancient enemy the Serbs.

CHAPTER SIX

The Serbian Campaign

AS THE 11. PANZER-DIVISION UNDER GENERALMAJOR LUDWIG Crüwell was poised for its first campaign as a division, it had some 12,220 officers and men and 116 panzers. Oberstleutnant Gustav-Adolf Riebel's Panzer-Regiment 15 had two battalions, each with two light companies (Panzer IIs and IIIs) and one medium company (Pz. IIIs and IVs), a company having twenty-two panzers each (four platoons of five panzers each and two staff panzers). Oberst Günther Angern's 11. Schützenbrigade had two rifle regiments: S.R. 110 under Oberst Helwig Luz and S.R. 111 under Oberst Theodor Bohlmann-Combrinck, each with two battalions of three companies and heavy weapons, transported in trucks, and Kradschützen-Btl. 61 under Obstlt. von Stockhausen with three motorcycle companies and heavy weapons.

Obstlt. Heinz Matena's Art.Rgt. 119 had two light Abteilungen (10,5cm howitzers) and one medium Abt. (15cm howitzers and 10cm guns), the ordnance towed by half-tracks. Pz. Aufklärungs-Abteilung 231 under Hauptmann Horst von Usedom had reconnaissance, armored car, and motorcycle companies. Panz. Jäger-Abt. 61 under Maj. Edgar Schulz had towed 3,7cm Pak 36 and 5cm Pak 38 antitank guns in three companies. Pz. Pionier-Btl. 209 under Maj. Bernhard Scholaster had three engineer companies and bridging columns B and K. Pz. Nachrichten-Abt. 341 under Maj. Franz Bluhm had radio and telephone signals companies. Nachschub Dienste 61 (supply services) under Obstlt. Camillo Neureiter as the Dinafü (DNF) included supply, fuel, and transport companies; there were also administrative services, medical and ambulance companies, field military police, and field post. Attachments included 1. Batterie./608. Flak-Abteilung and Maj. Werner Jacobson's Leichte Flakabteilung 71 with 2cm and 3,7cm flak guns, towed and mounted.

As detailed by the Gefechts- und Verpflegungsstärke chart of 1 April 1941, while the ration strength of the 11. Pz.Div. was 15,800 personnel, the fighting strength was 12,220: 357 officers, 40 officials, 1,896 non-commissioned officers, and 9,927 enlisted men. Weaponry was listed separately (but no vehicles were listed). There were 116 panzers: 53 Pz. IIs (2cm Kw.K—Kampfwagen Kanone, tank guns), 46

Pz. IIIs (22 with 3,7cm, 24 with short 5cm), and 17 Pz. IVs (with short 7,5cm guns). The ground troops had 78 mortars (18 5cm leichte Granatwerfer 36, 30 8cm schwere Gr.W. 34), and 24 towed infantry guns (20 7,5cm leichte Infanterie Geschütz 18, and 4 15cm s.I.G.).

The artillery had thirty-six towed pieces (twenty-four 10,5cm le.F.H. 18, eight 15cm s.F.H. 18, and four long 10cm K 18 guns). Antitank weapons were thirty-eight antitank rifles (thirty-five 7.9mm Panzerbüchse 39 and three captured English Mark I Boys cal.55/13.9mm), and fifty-one towed antitank guns (nine 5cm Pak 38, forty-two 3,7cm Pak 36). There were forty-five antiaircraft guns on half-tracks or two-wheeled trailers (twenty-eight 2cm Flak 30, eight quad-mounted 2cm flak, Vierlingsflak, and nine 3,7cm Flak 36).[1]

A detailed Gliederung (divisional organization) from the schematic (which did not include numerical strengths of personnel) displayed unit types and weaponry. 11. Pz.Div. staff headquarters had two light machine guns (le.M.G. 34), the 61. Motorcycle Platoon, and the 61. Cartographic Section. Pz.-Rgt. 15 headquarters had a signals platoon and a light panzer platoon, and a regimental maintenance company. The I. and II. Abteilungen each had a staff company, two light panzer companies and a medium company (numbered 1.–3. Kp. in I. Abt and 4.–6. Kp./II. Abt.), a maintenance company, and a supply company.

The 11. Schützenbrigade had two rifle regiments and the motorcycle battalion. S.R. 110 and 111 each had a headquarters company with a signals, a Pionier (3 le.M.G.), and a motorcycle platoon. Each then had two rifle battalions transported by truck, each having five companies: three with eighteen le.M.G., two s.M.G., and three 5cm light mortars, a heavy machine-gun company with eight s.M.G. and six 8cm heavy mortars, and a heavy weapons company with two 7,5cm light infantry guns, three towed 3,7cm Pak 36 antitank guns and one le.M.G., and an engineer platoon with three le.M.G. The companies were numbered 1.–5. Kp. in each I. Btl., 6.–11.Kp./II. Btl., and 12. Kp. was the regimental headquarters company with signals, Pionier, and motorcycle platoons. There was also a regimental infantry gun company with four 7,5cm le.I.G.and two 15cm s.I.G. Kradschützen-Bataillon 61 had five companies numbered 1.–5.: three motorcycle companies with eighteen le.M.G., two s.M.G., and three 5cm mortars, an s.M.G. company with eight s.M.G. and six 8cm s.Gr.W., and a reconnaissance company with two 7,5cm le.I.G., three 3,7cm Pak 36 and one le.M.G. and a Pionier platoon with three le.M.G.

Art.Rgt. 119 headquarters had two le.M.G. with a support and a weather section and a signals platoon, and controlled three towed artillery battalions: I. and II. Abteilungen each had a survey section and a signals platoon, and three firing batteries with four 10,5cm le.F.H. and two le.M.G. each, while III. Abt. had a survey section and a signals platoon, and one battery with four 10cm K 18 guns and two le.M.G., and two batteries with four 15cm s.F.H. and two le.M.G. each, totaling thirty-six artillery tubes. The batteries were numbered 1.–3. Battr. in I. Abt., 4.–6. in II. Abt., and 7.–9./ III. Abt.

Pz. Aufklärungs-Abt. 231 headquarters had a signals platoon and two le.M.G., a light supply column, and three companies numbered 1.–3.: an armored car company with 2cm guns on ten Sd.Kfz. 231 Achtrad armored cars and twenty-six le.M.G., a motorcycle company with eighteen le.M.G., two s.M.G., and three 5cm le.Gr.W., and a reconnaissance company with two 7,5cm le.I.G., one le.M.G., and three 3,7cm Pak 36, and an engineer platoon with three le.M.G. Pz.Jäger-Abt. 61 had a signals platoon and one tank destroyer company with three 5cm Pak 38, nine 3,7cm Pak 36, and six le.M.G. while companies 2 and 3 had twelve 3,7cm Pak 36 and six le.M.G. each. Attached was 1. Battr./ 608 Flak-Btl., self-propelled, with ten 2cm flak guns including two Vierlingsflak, and four le.M.G. Pz.Pionier-Btl. 209 had three numbered companies, each with nine le.M.G., a light supply column, bridging columns Brüko B and K, and Construction Troop 49. Pz. Nachrichten-Abt. 341 had a telephone company with two le.M.G., a radio company with thirteen le.M.G., and a light supply column.

The Nachschub Dienste 61 had light supply columns 1.–7., maintenance companies 1.–3., transportation company 61, fuel columns 8.–10., and supply columns 11.–13., with a 60-ton capacity in Nr. 13. The Verwaltungsdienste (Administrative Services) had Bakery Company 61, Butcher Company 61, and Rations Office 61. In addition there was the Sanitäts Dienst with 1. and 2. Medical Companies, and Ambulance Companies 1.–3.; Ordungs Dienst as Field Military Police Troop 61; and Field Post Office 61.[2]

Early on 6 April 1941 the German Blitzkrieg opened the Balkan campaign against Yugoslavia and Greece in all its fury. Stukas and medium bombers of VIII. Fliegerkorps under General der Flieger Wolfram

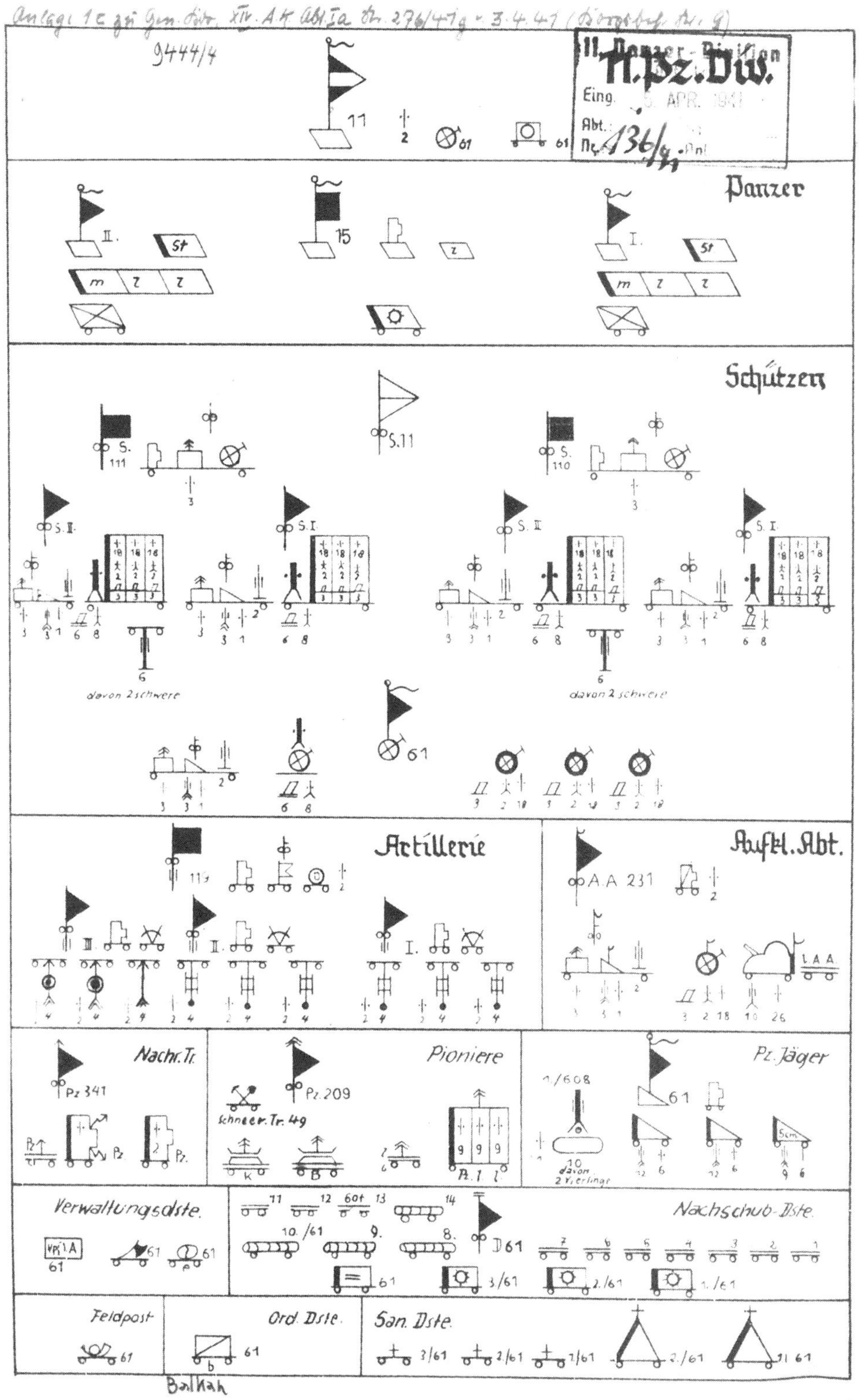

11.Pz.Div. Kriegsgliederung (Order of Battle) for 5 April 1941, prior to the Serbian Campaign, listing two battalions in Pz.Rgt.15, regiments 110 and 111 in Rifle Brigade 11, three battalions in Art.Rgt.119, and other units. NARA T-315/ROLL 585/FRAME 000668

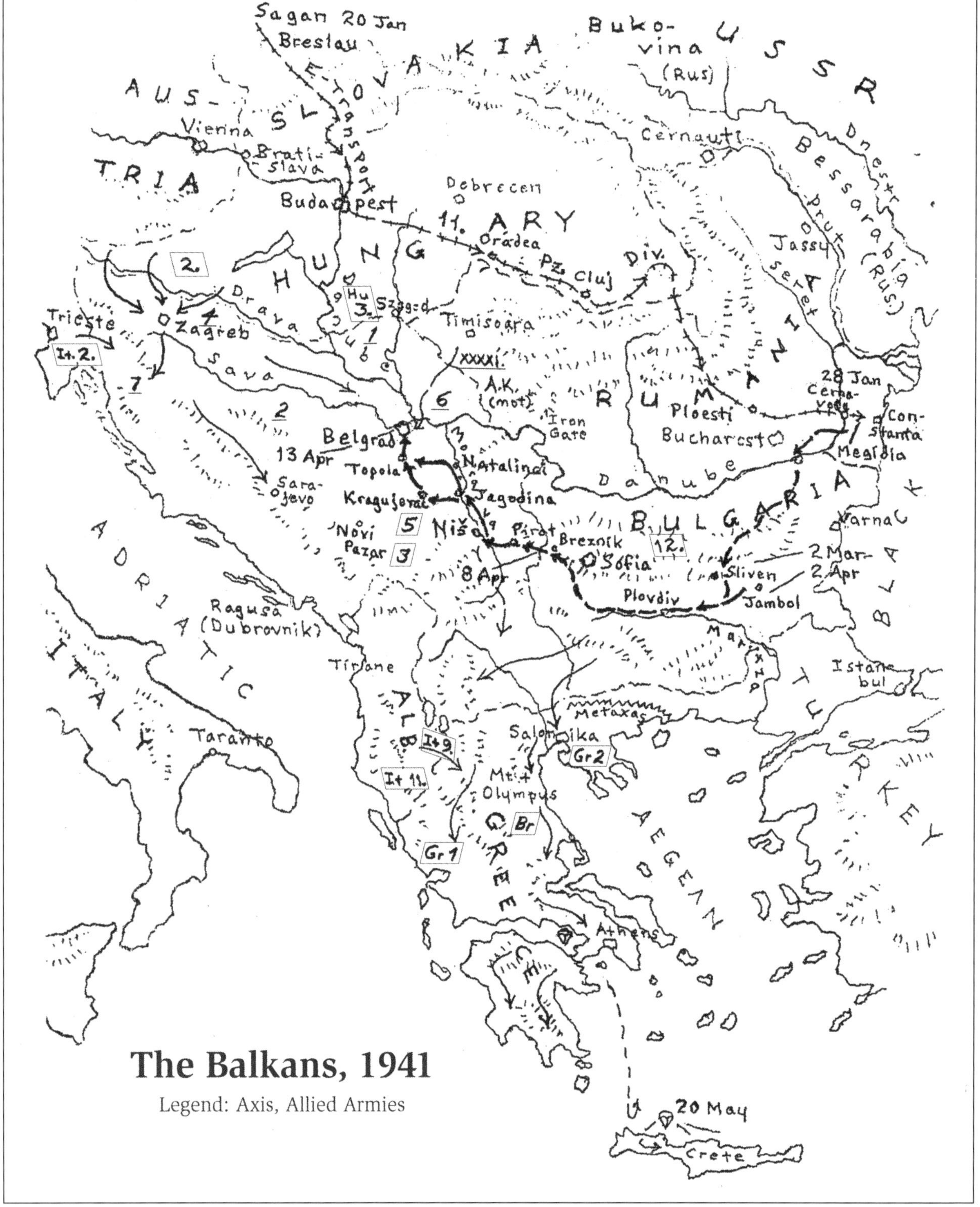

The Balkans, 1941

Legend: Axis, Allied Armies

von Richthofen of 4. Luftflotte from bases in Austria and Rumania swept over Belgrade at rooftop level, targeting government buildings and military installations. As planned, the airstrikes virtually annihilated the Yugoslav air force and air defenses, and crippled Yugoslav command and communications. 2. Armee in the north, still hurriedly deploying, attacked across the border and drove toward Zagreb, and by the 10th Croatian elements in the Serb-commanded Yugoslav army mutinied or deserted, and the northern armies began to disintegrate.

In the south List's Armeeoberkommando (A.O.K.) 12 attacked Greece from Bulgaria through the Metaxas Line fortifications toward Salonika, and its XXXX. Armeekorps spearheaded by 9. Pz.Div. drove across southern Yugoslavia to separate Greek and Yugoslav forces, entering Skoplje on the 7th (even as the Yugoslavs mounted an offensive against the Italians in Albania!). XIV. A.K. under Gen. der Inf. Gustav von Wietersheim of Kleist's Panzergruppe 1 attacked into southern Yugoslavia on 8 April against the Yugoslav 5th Army, one of the few armies fully mobilized.

The 11. Panzer-Division led the way, followed by the 5. Pz.-Div., 294. Infanterie-Division, and 4. Gebirgs (Mountain) Division on the flanks, with the mission of driving to Niš and north down the Morava River valley to Belgrade. Code names had been assigned: Tannhäuser (Pz.Gr. 1), Heckenrose (XIV. A.K.), Erika (11. Pz.Div.), Blaumeise (294. I.D.), and Schulrat (4. Geb.); 11. Pz.Div. code names included Lorelei (Pz.Rgt. 15), Primus (S.R. 110), Knoblauch (S.R. 111), and Waldemar (Art.Rgt. 111).[3]

At 05,00 Uhr on the 8th the lead elements of Crüwell's "Gespenster-Division" crossed the Yugoslav border in a chilling mixture of sleet, rain, and snow. As was becoming standard panzer practice, the division was organized as Kampfgruppen (battle groups) under regimental headquarters, but task-oriented with a mix of panzer, motorized infantry, and combat engineer units. Kampfgruppe Riebel was in the lead, in this case with both battalions of Pz.-Rgt. 15, commanded by Oberstlt. Riebel. Kgr. Riebel's composition demonstrated the battle group mix concept: the two panzer battalions of Pz.Rgt. 15, the reconnaissance battalion Pz.A.A. 231, a company of infantry (2. Kp./ S.R. 110), engineer (3./ Pz. Pi.-Btl. 209) and antitank (1./ Pz. Jäg.-Abt. 61) companies, a bridging column, one artillery battalion (I./ A.R. 119), a flak battery (1./ lei.Flak-Abt. 71), and communications and medical elements.[4] The other battlegroups were Gruppe Luz (Schützenregiment 110) and Gruppe Bohlmann (S.R. 111).

The axis of advance was astride the Sofia–Niš highway through Caribrod and Pirot. At the first enemy contact seven batteries of Oberst Matena's A.R. 119 fired concentrations from map coordinates on barracks and target points in Caribrod. While II. Abteilung/Pz.Rgt. 15 removed mines and its panzers ground their way through primitive roadblocks, the I. Abteilung roared through to Caribrod itself. Some in the following wheeled vehicles fell casualty to Yugoslav machine-gun and infantry fire from the hillsides until these could be cleared by Gruppe Bohlmann.[5] The strategy was to penetrate the Yugoslav linear defenses, thin as they were with a few blockhouses or bunkers, wire, and antitank obstacles at key points, and exploit rapidly along the major axes of advance, bypassing pockets to be mopped up later, to break organized resistance. As in Poland and in France, the speed of the German advance meant that enemy orders from their headquarters to their units were often irrelevant by the time they were received. The Yugoslav 5th Army tried to withdraw behind the upper Morava, but the German drive toward Niš disorganized and isolated the elements.

Two kilometers west of Caribrod Obstlt. Schmahl's I. Abteilung/15 encountered a destroyed bridge over the Yerma River. The engineers began to replace it amid artillery fire, while the panzers turned aside, broke through a line of bunkers, and took up firing position on the high ground before Ruzino-Polje. At noon the bridge was completed for the wheeled vehicles, though 6. Kompanie led by Oblt. Körtge of Major Graf von Schimmelmann's II. Abt./15 found a ford as well for the panzers and halftracks, and Schimmelmann took the lead driving toward Pirot. The Yerma incident exemplified the dynamism of panzer warfare: Instead of the division being checked by a blown bridge, the combat engineers, right behind the vanguard, swung into action to build a new bridge; one panzer battalion simultaneously sought to bypass the obstacle while giving covering fire; and the other battalion located a ford—and the advance continued apace.

The panzers rolled through Pirot and seized a bridge over the Nisava that had been prepared for demolition, while Yugoslav soldiers, in their greatcoats and French/Italian-type helmets, fled over the hills or surrendered and were waved to the rear. At

18,00 hours, still dealing with hostile rifle and machine-gun fire, II./15 took up an Igel position of all-around "hedgehog" defense to await fuel resupply 5 kilometers beyond Pirot. The motorcyclists of Obstlt. von Stockhausen's Kradschützenbataillon 61 with their sidecar-mounted machine guns, and the armored cars and light half-tracks of Hptm. von Usedom's Aufklärungs-Abt. 231, pressed farther along the Rollbahn (major roadway) toward Niš in increasing rain. The first day of action netted three guns, six antitank guns, four heavy machine guns, some 200 Kriegsgefangene, and other enemy losses there was no time to count.[6]

The second day, the 9th, saw continuing sleet and scattered resistance as the 11. Pz.Div. panzers drove through Niš. Protected by its mountainous location in the country's south, Niš was the traditional Serb wartime capital owing to Belgrade's exposed position on the Danube. But in this campaign the German drive was coming up *from* the south. Former comrades in the 5. Pz.Div., now under the command of Gen.Maj. Gustav Fehn, were following the 11. Panzer, but became stalled along the poor roads near Pirot. The 5. Panzer was ordered to turn southward and cut off Yugoslav forces around Leskovac and then, as the drive of the Elfte (Eleventh) was so successful, it was reassigned to the XXXX. A.K.(mot) for the Greek campaign.[7] It was also learned that to the south, in the campaign against Greece, 2. Pz.Div. had entered the Aegean port of Salonika and 9. Pz.Div. had reached the Albanian border, separating the Yugoslavs from the Greeks and British.

As the primitive country roads were quickly chewed to a muddy morass by the tracked vehicles, the wheeled vehicles with their resupply of fuel and munitions had difficulty catching up to the spearheads. On occasion half-tracks had to use tow cables to pull a string of trucks along. At one point some Pz. IIs from a light platoon towed oxcarts to the Niš airport to bring back captured drums of gasoline. Beyond Niš the advance picked up speed in the broadening Morava valley, Kgr. Riebel in the lead astride the Rollbahn, with Gruppe Bohlmann on the left and Gp. Luz on the right. Panzer crews moving cross-country did not have the same lurching, jarring, bone-bruising ride as when they had crossed the mountains and gorges in the border area. Infantry could now also climb aboard the panzers and brace their feet and hang on better as well.

Beyond Paracin the highway paralleled the railroad. On the campaign's third day, the 10th, a steam train was halted and the Yugoslav reserve officers and enlisted personnel going south toward the "front" found they were now Gefangene. They did continue south, but this time on foot and without weapons, long columns forming on the edges of the road while panzer crews passing heading north gazed at them in curiosity and snapped photos as mementos.

The panzers raced on, through Cuprija and Jagodina, smashing through Yugoslav forces whose poor radio communications did not allow them time to alert units behind them of the pace of the armored column. Maj. Werner Jacobson's attached L./71, which had rapidly deployed its flak guns at river crossings, refueling points, and night defense positions, even got a chance to open fire on some Yugoslav bombers that appeared. 1. Batterie supported Kgr. Riebel (Pz.Rgt. 15), 2. Battr. supported Gp. Luz (S.R. 110), 3. Battr. supported Gp. Bohlmann (S.R. 111), and the headquarters units covered the division command group and trains.

Nearing Milosevo II./15 took the lead of Kampfgruppe Riebel, with Hauptmann Zügner's 5. Kompanie in the van. There were seventeen panzers: Zügner's Befehlspanzer III, Lt. Rother's 1. Zug with Pz. IIIs numbered 11–15, Rother's marked 11 for 1st Platoon, first panzer (pronounced 1-1); Lt. Graf Magnis's 2. Zug numbered 21–23; Lt. Becker's 3. Zug numbered 31–33; and the Pz. IIs of Feldwebel Plasa's 4. Leichte Zug numbered 41–45. Number 4–5 ("Vier-Fünf") was commanded by Uffz. Kurt Nentwig. Reconnaissance gave radio warning of an approaching troop train, and orders were to engage it if warning shots didn't stop the engineer. Gustav Schrodek, a Richtschütze in Lt. Anton Magnis's platoon leader's Pz. III, Wagen 2-1 ("Zwei-Eins"), remembered of the incident, "What a meal for us, at that time still very hungry for battle." The gunners traversed their turrets to bring cannon and machine guns to bear.[8] But the train continued on at full speed, whereupon the panzer column opened fire. "The effect was simply fearful, especially as the range was scarcely more than 100 meters," Schrodek said. This brought the troop train to a stop, though the panzer column continued on and following units rounded up the survivors as prisoners of war.

With the column now 170 kilometers into enemy territory, the Elften (Eleveners) found resistance stiffening nearing Lapovo. From Jagodina Gruppe Luz had already swung onto a parallel advance into the high ground heading toward Kragujevac. This was S.R. 110, followed by other elements of 11. S.B. as Kampfgruppe Angern. The panzers of 5. Kp. of II./15 drove into Lapovo, guns firing at scattering Yugoslav soldiers—*"Feuer frei!"* ("Fire at will!")—and bypassing the train station, which was then attacked by the infantry. A Henschel Hs 126 two-seater observation plane flew overhead. All the panzers and vehicles displayed the red, white, and black Hakenkreuz (swastika) cloth panels to allow for recognition by their own aircraft, especially important when the spearheads might be deep behind enemy forces. The observation plane now dropped a smoke flare, this one violet to warn of enemy tanks.

No enemy armor had yet been encountered, and Yugoslav armor was poor and obsolete: some armored cars, some British tracked Vickers Bren gun carriers, and some Czech Skoda 4-ton tanks—though the latter had a barbette-mounted 4,7cm cannon, a caliber larger than the 2cm or 3,7cm guns of the Panzer IIs and IIIs.[9] The panzers were deployed astride the main road, churning through gardens and behind houses, easy victims for any antitank weapons at close range—especially when the tanks were without infantry, who were still clearing the train station. The loaders slammed Panzergranate rounds into the gun breeches, and gunners glued their eyes to their gun optics with their right hands on the traversing wheel with trigger. "Nervous? *Ja*, that we were. Why should one lie about it?" Schrodek remembered. At one point his panzer rounded a bend on the main road, the company commander's panzer right behind it, and Lt. Magnis suddenly shouted "Tank!" through the intercom system. The driver slewed to a stop and Schrodek fired. But simultaneously he saw the crew bailing out of the tank ahead as smoke erupted from a mine it had detonated. It was Wagen 1-4, of Hauptfeldwebel Kurt Linde, the "Spiess," the company first sergeant, which had been forging ahead nearby. Schrodek's round hit the right side of Linde's tank, and it could easily have been a tragic case of "friendly fire." Reflecting on this later could bring on a cold sweat.

The observation plane flew over again, the Beobachter (observer) waggling its wings as a warning of danger farther on. *"Vorsicht!"* ("Caution!") radioed the Flivo to "Erika" (11. Pz.Div.). The Fliegerverbindungsoffizieren (air liaison officers) were with the ground units. Leutnant Magnis peered over the rim of the turret cupola with his binoculars, but his gunner urged him to duck down. His response was lost in the crack of gunfire, and Schrodek sensed the lieutenant's body suddenly jerk. Schrodek turned from his gunner's seat to see the cigarette in Magnis's mouth suddenly turn red, and then blood bespattered him. The other crew members at first thought Schrodek to be critically wounded, as the driver rapidly reversed 2-1 behind a detonating smoke shell, the panzer commander still slumped in the cupola. Unit after-action reports might simply say "light resistance," but combat can be an intensely personal experience.

Sighting the II. Abt. commander, tall Maj. Graf von Schimmelmann, in a commanders' conference, Schrodek ran over to report, but the blood on his uniform told the story. The battalion medical officer returned with Schrodek to 2-1 and pulled the stricken platoon leader out of the cupola and laid him on a canvas tarpaulin. But the bullet wound over the left ear was fatal. Lt. Anton Graf Magnis-Ullersdorf—the well-liked "Toni" Magnis—was gefallen, killed in action.[10]

II./15 had a brief pause while the infantry fought ahead and the engineers cleared the minefield under artillery fire. The Landsers were exhausted and caught catnaps when they could, but they recognized that speed, and keeping the enemy off-balance, meant minimal casualties. I. Abt. bypassed the action, driving toward Markovac. To the west the riflemen of Kampfgruppen Luz and Angern captured Kragujevac, allowing them to converge on Topola with Kgr. Riebel on the 11th, still amid cold, rainy weather.[11] Resistance increased from Yugoslav forces (primarily Serbs) compressed toward Belgrade, now threatened from three directions. In the northwest 14. Pz.Div. of XXXXVI. A.K.(mot) of 2. Armee entered Zagreb in Croatia on 10 April, and 8. Pz.Div., followed by motorized 16. Inf.Div., drove southeast between the Drava and the Sava toward Belgrade. From the northeast motorized 2. Waffen-SS Division Reich and motorized infantry regiment Grossdeutschland of XXXXI. A.K.(mot) thrust toward the Danube, while 11. Pz.Div. led motorized XIV. A.K. north. Croat, Slovene, and Bosnian elements in the Serb-commanded Yugoslav Army mutinied or deserted as the northern forces continued disintegrating.

Near Natalinci on the 12th 4. Kompanie/II. Abt. approached a river crossing shown on the map. But the bridge was of wood and the company commander, not willing to attempt it, sent a panzer to ford the 4–6-meter-wide stream. It drove across and climbed the steep, muddy slope on the far side, even as Yugoslav artillery, which had zeroed in the bridge, smashed it with a concentration. At the same time the company commander's Pz. III. bogged down in the mud. He dismounted and boarded a panzer that had already crossed. It was a platoon leader's Wagen but the radio only had a single transmitting/receiving frequency. Oberfunkmeister (company communications chief) Karl Süss stayed with the stranded headquarters panzer and communicated the radio traffic to the other platoons, and the advance continued without pause. The incident demonstrated once again that radio communication is crucial in armored warfare, ensuring rapid responses to changing situations.[12]

At Natalinci the platoon leader of the Leichte Zug of 4. Kp. destroyed a Yugoslav artillery forward observer in a church tower with the 2cm cannon of his Pz. II. 1. and 4. Züge working with the infantry cleared the town house-by-house. (Tankmen prefer not to fight in constricted urban areas, but if operating in conjunction with mechanized infantry with whom they have trained, the intense sounds of supporting fire of cannon and machine guns—in addition to the churning, squealing tracks of the tank—are magnified by the confining walls and seem to come from all directions, which can panic irresolute defenders.) A Yugoslav commander was captured, and he proceeded to surrender an artillery and an engineer battalion, a signals detachment, and infantry of battalion strength. On the high ground west of the town II./15 battalion commander Graf Schimmelmann praised 4. Kompanie as the "Lions of Natalinci."

North of Topola, a city noted for its tombs of Serb kings in the royal church, an abandoned Skoda tank was passed—the first and last enemy tank actually seen by the 11. Panzer "Gespensters" during this Serbien-Feldzug. The Division Gefechtsstand (Div. Gef.Std., Division Forward Command Post) was advanced to Kragujevac, then to Topola.

Easter Sunday was 13 April, and for the first time during the campaign, the sun came out. The race for Belgrade was on. The armored vehicles roared through Ralja as Yugoslav resistance was collapsing, the end obviously at hand. Angern reported to Division, "8,10 Uhr, Citadel Belgrad occupied, no resistance."[13] At 13,00 hours that day the 11. Panzer "Gespensters" entered Belgrade, the sidewalks thronged with curious crowds, and raised the German flag on the Kalemegdan, the high fortress overlooking the confluence of the Sava and Danube Rivers. At 14,30 Crüwell's division staged an impromptu parade before the Skuptchina (Parliament) building, the panzer crews perched in their hatches, passing in review before Generaloberst von Kleist of Panzergruppe 1, who had complimented Crüwell by radio for his division being the first to enter the Yugoslav capital.

That claim was disputed, however, by the 8. Panzer-Division under Gen. Maj. Walter Neumann-Silkow, entering from the west, and 2. SS Division (mot) Reich under SS Gruppenführer Paul Hausser, from the east. Late on the previous afternoon Hauptsturmführer Fritz Klingenberg of Reich, finding all the Danube bridges down, took a patrol across the river in captured pneumatic rafts. Entering the city unopposed, his patrol raised the Nazi flag atop the German legation building at 17,00 on the 12th. Two hours later Klingenberg, accompanied by a representative of the German Foreign Ministry interned by the Yugoslavs, received the surrender of the city from the mayor. From the west 2. Armee, which had had no reports from its advancing 8. Pz.Div., received Pz.Gr. 1's flash on the 13th noting that the 11. Pz.Div. had been "rolling into the capital since 06,32." At 11,52 2. Armee then received a radio message from the 8. Panzer that it had entered "during the night."[14] No matter, there was honor enough for all.

While some 11. Pz.Div. units were involved in mopping up operations at Smederevo and toward Ragore, most pulled maintenance and cleaned weapons and equipment, ending the six-day drive. On the 14th the Elfte, Pz.Gruppe 1 now under 2. Armee, received the mission of attacking west toward Dubrovnik (Ragusa in Italian) on the Dalmatian coast. The division retraced some of its routes south, though Pz.Rgt. 15 stayed in Belgrade as the panzers were still undergoing maintenance. Only one composite company was formed, under Hauptmann Heinrich Pricken, then dissolved again. An advance force of the 11. Panzer was organized under Maj. von Götz of II. Btl./ 110, led by the armored cars of Pz. A.A. 231, which reached Novi Pazar, the former Serb capital that had been captured by the Turks in 1456. There it was learned a cease-fire had been agreed to on the 17th, and the units returned to Belgrade.[15]

Meanwhile in western Yugoslavia 14. Panzer-Division had driven south toward Sarajevo in

Bosnia-Herzegovina. They were greeted as liberators by the Croatians and Slovenes, ethnic units who then began fighting the Serbs. "Yugoslavia," like "Czecho-Slovakia," was an artificial creation of 1919, the culmination of the Serb ambition of creating "Greater Serbia." Many Croatians and Slovenes, as well as Bosnians and others, would be German allies during World War II. (And when Yugoslavia was re-created after 1945, it disintegrated again into those defiant national entities in the 1990s.) By 15 April 8. and 14. Panzer-Divisionen converged on Sarajevo, and Yugoslav representatives surrendered unconditionally to Generaloberst von Weichs of 2. Armee effective 18 April 1941.

Yugoslavia had been overrun in eleven days. Though resistance had been sporadic, the Wehrmacht had concluded an incredibly successful campaign, given the rugged terrain and conditions of snow, freezing sleet, flooded rivers, and mud. Yet the army high command had needed to quickly improvise a plan of campaign, redeploy a variety of units, and demonstrate that panzer forces could operate decisively under adverse conditions. Guderian's aphorism, "Plan carefully, execute violently," was again vindicated. The emphasis had been on speed, not only to prevent any further organized enemy resistance, but also to release the mobile units for the coming Russian campaign. In bypassing resistance that scattered into the mountains, it was recognized that future pacification would be a challenge. Serb "Četnići" (Chetniks) were planned partisan organizations formed of local militia units to meet such a contingency; and indeed, guerrilla warfare would plague German and Italian occupation forces in the years ahead.[16]

From a military perspective, the Yugoslav campaign had been a complete success. German losses had been unexpectedly light: 558 casualties, including 151 killed, 392 wounded, and 15 missing. Of these the 11. Panzer listed 9 officers and 54 men killed and 16 officers and 157 men wounded. Of the panzer operations, US Department of the Army historian George Blau concluded, "The German tanks and trucks proved capable of negotiating virtually every type of terrain," and "It was here that German motorized equipment surpassed all expectations by covering great distances with lightning speed over primitive, winding roads and through narrow, treacherous mountain passes." In his Tagesbefehl (Order of the Day) of 25 May, division commander Crüwell summarized the accomplishments of his recently organized "Gespenster" division, and noted the praise of Generaloberst von Kleist for the capture of Belgrade, "That you did with your division alone!" Awards bestowed included the Ritterkreuz on Major Graf von Schimmelmann, II./15, and also on Crüwell, both dated 14 May 1941.[17]

On 25 April, after another week of maintenance, relaxing, and viewing the sights of Belgrade including the bomb-damaged royal palace, the Elften were underway to Vienna. Sunshine and warm, noted the Ia, Maj. Werner Wolff, in the KTB. The wheeled vehicle convoys road-marched up the valley of the Danube via Budapest, while the tracked vehicles rail-loaded at Ruma, just northwest of Belgrade, to travel by Eisenbahn-Transport (E-Transport).[18]

To the south the fighting continued as the Blitzkrieg, spearheaded by 2. and 9. Panzer-Divisionen, and then supplemented by 5. Pz.Div., overran Greece and forced the British to evacuate by 1 May. MARITA had been completed in twenty-four days, releasing the mobile units for the Russian campaign. Of the six panzer divisions committed to the Balkans (16. Pz.Div. was stationed on the Bulgarian-Turkish border to encourage neutrality there), the three in Greece were hard-pressed to be redeployed in time. In addition to battle damage, tracks and transmissions of the panzers, and tires and engines of the wheeled vehicles, had all been badly worn in their dramatic mastering of the primitive roads and by their going cross-country over rugged terrain.

On 20 May 1941 Luftwaffe paratroopers, who had seized the Corinthian isthmus, led the invasion and conquest of British-occupied Crete. Though the airborne forces suffered heavy casualties, the British were again routed, and Luftwaffe units now based there sank nine British warships, removed the threat to the Rumanian oil fields, and with Rommel's DAK in North Africa, jeopardized the whole British position in the Near East and the Suez Canal lifeline.

For the Landsers of the Gespenster-Division, flush with their recent victory in Yugoslavia and following a year and a half of Wehrmacht successes, Wien in springtime seemed a delightful culmination, with Austrian Mädels in their colorful Dirndls adding an atmosphere of Gemütlichkeit. The division was in the vicinity for some five weeks, and many became familiar with St. Stephansplatz, the Ring Strasse and the Strassenbahnen, the amusement activities of the Prater Park, and other entertainment sites that too often were "Tabu," or off-limits.

Panzer-Regiment 15 and some staff were quartered in the massive Arsenal, also the location of the Heeresgeschichtliches Museum, the Museum of Military History, with artifacts and paintings related to Prinz Eugen and major figures of the former Austro-Hungarian Empire. There also Panzer IIIs were equipped with stowage boxes behind the turrets, nicknamed "Tropenkiste," or tropical boxes, leading to speculation again that the division might be headed for the Western Desert. Trains and other elements were quartered in the St. Pölten area of Lower Austria west of Vienna. Some troops were given leave, and some of the married personnel were allowed to make arrangements to have wives and family come and stay.

The rather relaxed month in the Vienna area for the 11. Panzer-Division provides further insight into the question of whether the Balkan campaign delayed BARBAROSSA. The Greek operation had been taken into account when planning the deployments for the Russian campaign. It was the coup in Yugoslavia on 27 March that caused Hitler to order the invasion of that country that same evening and a postponement of BARBAROSSA, ultimately set for 22 June. But only a few of the units in the Balkans were scheduled for the attack, and in fact, the unexpectedly rapid defeat of Yugoslavia made available road and railroad transportation routes that actually facilitated the redeployment of units there to central European destinations. In the event, it was excessive rainfall in May that meant a postponement, and the Polish-Russian river valleys were still flooded into June.[19] Mussolini's ill-advised Greek adventure, the consequent British intervention, and the Yugoslav coup all certainly upset Hitler's diplomacy in the Balkans. But whether the volatile Balkans would have remained quiescent on the southern flank of an invasion of Russia, especially given British strategic potential, remains questionable.

On 9 June elements of the 11. Panzer-Division rail-loaded for departure from the Vienna area, bound for training areas in German-occupied southern Poland. There was reluctance in leaving delightful Österreich, with schoolchildren bedecking the vehicles with flower bouquets; yet there was also a nervous anticipation about challenging the unknown ahead, even if they remained confident in the ongoing victories of the Wehrmacht. The trains began rolling, beginning with staff elements on the 10th and Trains by the 12th, across Slovakia and the Carpathian Mountains of Galicia, via Cracow (Polish Kraków) to Nisko on the San. From there the units road-marched to areas around Stalova Vola. Schützenregiment 110 was billeted at Debica (where a fire destroyed the wooden barracks and many vehicles of 6. Kompanie), S.R. 111 was at Pretkov, other 11. Schützenbrigade elements were at Mielec, and Panzer-Regiment 15 was at Stalova Vola. While ostensibly training for an invasion of England, the latest rumors were that the Soviets (with whom Germany had signed a ten-year Non-Aggression Pact in August 1939) would allow transit through the Ukraine and the Caucasus to attack British India, or go through Rumania and Turkey to Syria and Palestine, while Rommel advanced on the vital Suez Canal from Libya.[20]

The Landsers sweated in the humidity, loading extra ordnance and fuel drums on their vehicles, evidence that the Elfte was in for a long movement. A Panzer III might stow 360 liters of extra fuel in cans racked on the back deck behind the turret. Others had ten jerry cans strapped to the turret and towed a trailer with an additional three drums.[21] On the muggy evening of 21 June 1941, with headlights covered and under radio silence, the units began moving up around the Polish village of Lasczov, only 40 kilometers short of the Soviet occupation border. In fact the forests and villages for over 1,000 kilometers were teeming with German panzers, guns, vehicles, and troops moving up to that eastern border, masked by the raucous croaking of the frogs of the River Bug.

CHAPTER SEVEN

Operation BARBAROSSA

AT 03,15 HOURS ON 22 JUNE 1941 THOUSANDS OF GERMAN guns rippled and flashed along the Soviet occupation border in Poland, the thundering cannonading and concussion sweeping in waves back over the waiting troops seconds later. Special units had earlier crossed the River Bug in order to eliminate Russian border guards and seize bridges. Wave after wave of level bombers, dive-bombers, and fighter planes droned overhead, bombing Soviet airfields and targeting identified command centers, and then strafing troops, barracks, and vehicles as targets of opportunity. The Luftwaffe offensive had been preceded by thirty Heinkel He 111 and Junkers Ju 88A twin-engine bombers, which had flown at high altitude to avoid detection and had been overhead to target ten key air bases at 03,15. Once again the Luftwaffe annihilated the enemy air force in the western theater, in the opening hours of another Blitzkrieg. "The world will hold its breath," Hitler said.

Russian airfields, installations, motor parks, and other key points had been precisely identified by secret, high-altitude photo reconnaissance missions carried out by Geschwader Rowehl. This special wing had been formed under Oberst Theodor Rowehl in October 1940, and was composed of modified Heinkel 111s, Dornier 215B2s, Junkers 88Bs and 86Ps, with pressurized cabins for altitudes over 10,000 meters (39,000 feet). One crash-landed in Russia, but its significance was not realized by the Soviets. Now some of the planes were used to drop "Brandenburg" Intelligence Regiment commandos by parachute to seize key points and conduct sabotage activities, and to work with Ukrainian nationalists.[1]

Despite a variety of warnings and indications, Josef Stalin and the Soviet high command were taken by surprise and Russian army units received no notice as Unternehmen BARBAROSSA erupted upon them in the lightening dawn of that Sunday—the summer solstice, the longest day of the year. Seven German armies (with 2.German Armee in OKH reserve), four panzer groups, and three air fleets—3,050,000 troops, 600,000 vehicles including 3,350 armored fighting vehicles, 7,184 guns, and 625,000 horses in 145 divisions, 19 of them panzer and 14 motorized, and 3,760 attack aircraft—all were in motion, and two Rumanian armies were mobilized.

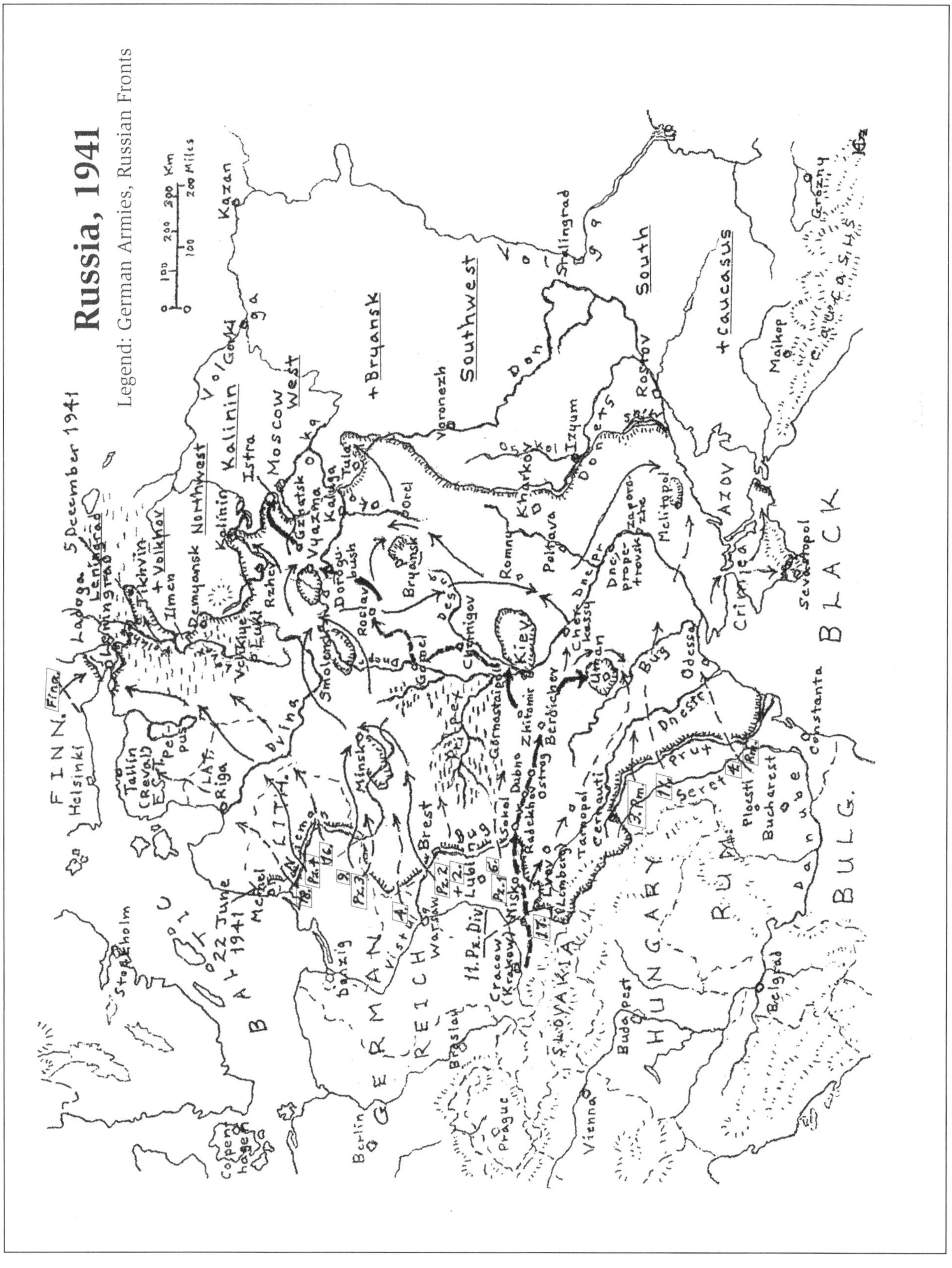

Russia, 1941

Legend: German Armies, Russian Fronts

The Soviets were estimated to have more forces than the Germans massed in the European theater: ten armies with 4,500,000 troops in 170 infantry and cavalry divisions and 41 motorized and tank brigades, with over 10,000 tanks (actually 24,000 tanks), and 6,000 aircraft.[2] But Hitler and the Germans knew that Germany had defeated Russia in World War I, that German forces had crippled the primitive Russian mass armies so badly that Russia had collapsed into revolution. Under the Stalinist Communist dictatorship the Red Army appeared no better, its leadership purged in the Great Terror of the 1930s, its manpower conscripted under brutal conditions, and its equipment vast in numbers but largely obsolete. All of this was demonstrated by the poor showing of Russian units in the Spanish Civil War and in the Russo-Finnish "Winter War" only ended a year earlier. Moreover, the German forces would be advancing into the Baltic states, eastern Poland, and the Ukraine, areas forcibly seized by the Soviet Union, and where hatred of Communism and of Russians suggested that in many areas the Germans would largely be greeted as liberators. Nor was revolution against the Stalinist regime beyond imagining.

It was with some surprise, as there were still rumors of operations against the English, but with equanimity, that the Landsers of the 11. Panzer-Division learned they were attacking the Soviet Union. Politics were beyond them, but the successes of the German recovery under Hitler and then the victories of the Wehrmacht generated a faith in the regime and a readiness, as veterans, to carry out the new missions assigned. Generalmajor Ludwig Crüwell had distributed a divisional Tagesbefehl (Order of the Day) that was read to the troops assembled by their unit commanders that morning:

> Soldiers of the 11. Panzer-Division!
> The Führer calls us to battle against Bolshevism, the core enemy
> of our National Socialist Reich.
> The struggle will be difficult, privation and hardship will be very
> great everywhere.
> The Gespenster Division will fall on the enemy as it did in Serbia,
> wherever we meet him—attack and destroy him.
> I know that I myself, as in the Southeast, can rely on each of you
> absolutely, from the most senior officer to the youngest trooper.
> Our password remains attack, our objective the Dnepr. We want
> to be the first there again, as at Belgrad.
> Heil dem Führer![3]

That fateful morning of the 22nd the men gathered around radios to hear news of the invasion, and at 15,00 hours that afternoon the units crossed the Bug at Sokal to exploit the bridgeheads of the infantry. *"Klar zum Gefecht!"* ("Clear for action!") The division organization and commanders were little changed from the Yugoslav campaign, but there was an increase of the medium Panzer IIIs mounting a 5cm Kw.K.

General Crüwell's 11. Pz.-Div. had some 13,559 personnel fighting strength and 143 panzers. Numbers varied from day to day depending on personnel present for duty or under medical care, and whether vehicles were einsatzbereit (ready for action) or undergoing Instandsetzung (maintenance).[4] His Ia (Operations) was Oberstleutnant Werner Wolff. There were fifty-two Panzer IIs (2cm), twenty-four Pz. IIIs (3,7cm) and forty-seven Pz. IIIs (5cm), and twenty Pz. IVs (7,5cm). Panzer-Regiment 15 under Oberstleutnant Gustav-Adolf Riebel had two battalions, each of two light (Pz. IIs and IIIs) companies and one medium (Pz. IIIs and IVs) company. Each company was still authorized twenty-two panzers in four platoons of five panzers each and two staff panzers, and companies were numbered 1.–3.Kp. in I. Abteilung and 4.–6. in II. Abt.

11. Schützenbrigade (mot) under Oberst Günther Angern had two motorized rifle regiments, S.R. 110 under Oberst Helwig Luz and S.R. 111 under Oberst Theodor Bohlmann-Combrinck. Each regiment had two battalions, and each battalion had three rifle companies, a machine-gun company, and a support platoon (two 7,5cm le.I.G.), an antitank platoon (three 3,7cm Pak 36), and an engineer platoon. Each regiment also had an infantry gun company (two towed 15cm s.I.G. and four 7,5cm le.I.G.). The rifle companies were truck-borne. Artillerie-Regiment 119 commanded by Oberst Heinz Matena had two light Abteilungen with three batteries of four towed 10,5cm le.F.H. each, and a medium Abteilung with three batteries of four towed 15cm s.F.H. each. The 8-ton half-track Sd.Kfz. 7s towed the guns cross-country into firing positions. Attached was Beobachtungsbatterie

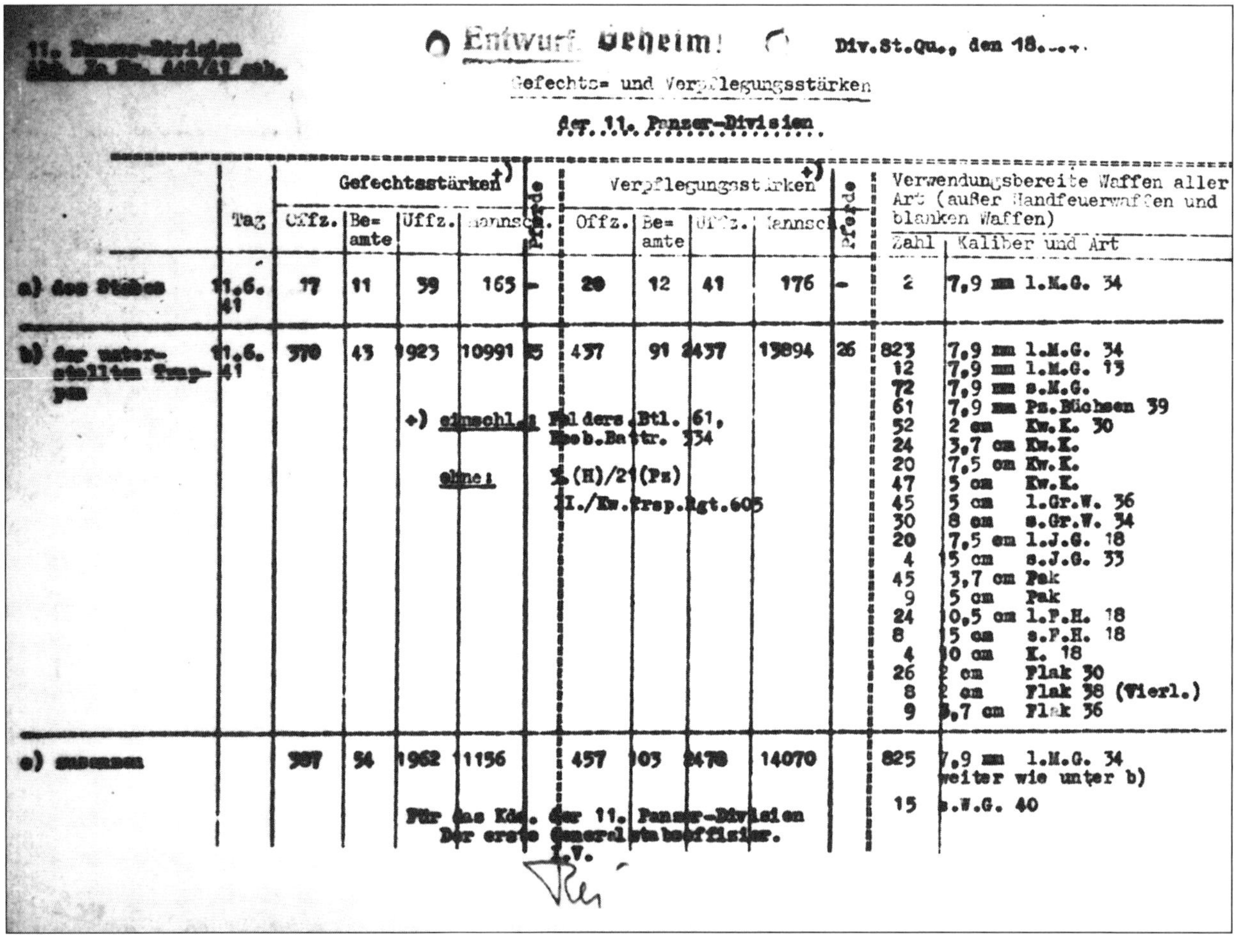

Entwurf Geheim! Div.St.Qu., den 18.

Gefechts= und Verpflegungsstärken

der 11. Panzer-Division

	Tag	Gefechtsstärken +) Offz.	Be= amte	Uffz.	Mannsch.	Pferde	Verpflegungsstärken +) Offz.	Be= amte	Uffz.	Mannsch.	Pferde	Verwendungsbereite Waffen aller Art (außer Handfeuerwaffen und blanken Waffen) Zahl	Kaliber und Art
a) des Stabes	11.6.41	17	11	39	165	–	20	12	41	176	–	2	7,9 mm l.M.G. 34
b) der unterstellten Truppen	11.6.41	370	43	1923	10991	5	437	91	2437	13894	26	823	7,9 mm l.M.G. 34
												12	7,9 mm l.M.G. 13
												72	7,9 mm s.M.G.
												61	7,9 mm Pz.Büchsen 39
												52	2 cm Kw.K. 30
												24	3,7 cm Kw.K.
												20	7,5 cm Kw.K.
												47	5 cm Kw.K.
												45	5 cm l.Gr.W. 36
												30	8 cm s.Gr.W. 34
												20	7,5 cm l.J.G. 18
												4	15 cm s.J.G. 33
												45	3,7 cm Pak
												9	5 cm Pak
												24	10,5 cm l.F.H. 18
												8	15 cm s.F.H. 18
												4	10 cm K. 18
												26	2 cm Flak 30
												8	2 cm Flak 38 (Vierl.)
												9	3,7 cm Flak 36
c) zusammen		387	54	1962	11156		457	103	2478	14070		825	7,9 mm l.M.G. 34 weiter wie unter b)
												15	s.W.G. 40

+) einschl. Kradschtz.Btl. 61, Beob.Battr. 334

ohne: 5.(H)/21(Pz) II./Kw.Trsp.Rgt.605

Für das Kdo. der 11. Panzer-Division
Der erste Generalstabsoffizier.
I.V.

Gefechts- und Verpflegungsstärken (fighting and ration strengths), 18 June 1941, before the invasion of Russia. The 2cm Kw.K.30 was mounted in the Panzer II; Panzerspähwagen (scout cars) had the Kw.K. 36 and 38. NARA T-315/ROLL 2320/ 000176

(Observation Battery) 334 for range plotting and counterbattery missions.

Kradschützen-Bataillon 61 under Obstlt. von Stockhausen had three motorcycle companies, a heavy machine-gun company, and a reconnaissance company. Auto-Union or BMWs were standard, often with sidecars (Beiwagenkrad). Pz. Aufklärungs-Abteilung 231 under Hptm. Horst von Usedom had an armored car company with the four-wheeled Sd.Kfz. 221 or the eight-wheeled Sd.Kfz. 231, with 2cm guns. The motorcycle company had three 5cm mortars, and the heavy reconnaissance company included three 3,7cm antitank guns and two 7,5cm le.I.G. Panzerjäger-Abteilung 61 under Maj. Edgar Schulz had one antitank company with three 5cm Pak 38 and nine 3,7cm Pak 36, and an attached battery, 1. Battr./608, of ten 2cm heavy machine guns. There were no 8,8cm guns organic to the division.

Pz. Pionier-Bataillon 209 under Maj. Bernhard Scholaster had two bridge companies and three engineer companies, using the Hanomag 3-ton half-track. Pz. Nachrichten-Abteilung 89 under Maj. Franz Bluhm had a telephone company, a radio company, and repair and maintenance detachments. The Dinafü (DNF) was Obstlt. Camillo Neureiter, and Nachschub Truppe (Supply Troop) 61 included supply, maintenance, and fuel companies. Other companies included medical, ambulance, bakery, and administration, and Feldgendarmerie and Feld Post units, all numbered 61. Maj. Werner Jacobson's le. Flak-Abt. 71 remained attached to the division. Also attached was a battalion (III./Nebelwerfer Rgt.) of fifteen heavy rocket launchers (schwere Wurfgerät 40); these used 28cm or 32cm rockets fired from wooden crates on towed, two-wheeled tired carriages. With the crew sheltering from the backblast flame, the rockets flared through the sky some 2,000 meters, and resulted in a smashing concentration.

In addition to the white, sword-wielding specter on a half-track stenciled on the sides or rear of the panzers and vehicles of the 11. Gespenster Panzer-Division, there was a large white "K" painted on the rear of vehicles and turrets for Generaloberst Ewald von Kleist, commanding Panzergruppe 1. Pz.Gr. 1 was the principal strike force of Heeresgruppe Süd as it drove into the Ukraine. The Schwerpunkt (point of main effort) of Unternehmen BARBAROSSA was with the three army-sized panzer groups of Heeresgruppe Nord and H.Gr. Mitte north of the Pripet forest and swamp area, especially with Pz.Gr. 2 and 3 under Generals Heinz Guderian and Hermann Hoth. They would advance on the Minsk–Smolensk–Moscow axis while Pz.Gr. 4 under Generaloberst Erich Hoepner attacked through the Baltic states toward Leningrad.

Hitler's objective was *not* the capture of the Soviet capital of Moscow, but rather the destruction of the Red Army via huge Kesselschlachten (encirclement battles). As stated in Weisung Nr. 21 of 18 December 1940, "the bulk of the Russian army stationed in western Russia is to be destroyed in a series of daring operations spearheaded by armored thrusts" that would overrun Belorussia (White Russia), the Baltic area, and Leningrad. "Only then will the offensive operations leading to the seizure of Moscow, the important communications and armaments production center, be continued."[5]

There has always been an argument historically as to whether a campaign's primary strategic objective should be the capture of the enemy's capital, or the destruction of the enemy's armed forces. Military strategists generally consider the latter the more important, though perhaps the same could be accomplished by threatening the capital, the opponent concentrating to defend it. Guderian, who understood what motivated combat soldiers, would later argue vehemently for a continued drive on Moscow rather than the annihilation of the Kievan pocket. In France in 1940 he knew his panzer troops would aggressively drive toward a recognizable objective: "In our case this was—the Channel! That was a clear inspiration to every one of our soldiers, and he could follow it even though he might receive no orders for long periods of time once the attack was launched." Paris was not the objective in 1940; though Moscow in 1941 perhaps had a greater strategic significance.[6]

Initially in Weisung Nr. 21, Feldmarschall Gerd von Rundstedt's Heeresgruppe Süd would also attempt a double envelopment: "Strong forces concentrated on both wings are to achieve the complete annihilation of the Russian troops in the Ukraine west of the Dnepr." In the OKH Operation Order of 3 February 1941, Pz.Gr. 1 and 6. Armee were to act as the northern arm of the pincer, attacking toward Kiev. The southern arm was to be 12. Armee driving across the Prut toward Kirovograd. 17. Armee would screen the Hungarian frontier. With the British deployments to Greece, however, and the decision to invade and occupy Greece, 12. Armee was committed to Unternehmen MARITA, and on 18 March its role in BARBAROSSA was abandoned.

Then, with the Yugoslav *coup*, and the 12. Armee's expanded role in the Balkans campaign, the 11. Armee headquarters under Generaloberst Eugen Ritter von Schobert was assigned to Moldavia along the Prut with now a defensive mission, reinforcing the two Rumanian armies formed there. 17. Armee under Gen. d. Inf. Karl Heinrich von Stülpnagel was to engage the Russian forces in the Przemysl salient west of Lvov (Lemberg).[7] This change also reflected the importance of securing the Rumanian oil fields from a Soviet attack, and an awareness of the sizeable Red Army forces concentrated in the Ukraine having the capability, if not the intent, of invading Rumania, or of thrusting into German-occupied Poland. Thus the primary drive of Heeresgruppe Süd was in the northern Ukraine alone, spearheaded by Kleist's Pz.Gr. 1 followed by 6. Armee under Feldmarschall Walter von Reichenau.

It now seems that Gen. Georgi Zhukov, appointed Red Army chief of staff in February 1941, urged a preemptive attack against the German buildup in occupied Poland, as revealed in a document cosigned by Defense Commissar Semyon Timoshenko and dated 15 May 1941. Zhukov had defeated Japanese forces at the Khalkhin Gol (River) on the disputed Mongolian-Manchurian border in August 1939 and had recently commanded all the Red Army forces in the Kiev Special Military District, massed in the western Ukraine and Russian-occupied Poland. But Stalin would have been aware that the Red Army was in no condition to engage the victorious Wehrmacht, at least at this time, and no planning seems to have ensued. Many German 11. Panzer veterans, however, believed that the massive Russian forces they encountered portended an aggressive intent.[8]

Were the massed forces intended as a deterrent? A deterrent is easily perceived as a threat.

The Red Army forces massed in the western Ukraine and the occupied Polish territories were under Col. Gen. Mikhail Kirponos, the new commander of the Kiev Special Military District. This command was redesignated as the wartime South-Western Front by 22 June, and Kirponos and his staff were moving their headquarters from Kiev to Tarnopol when the Germans attacked. To oppose the some forty-one German divisions—including four motorized divisions and five panzer divisions, of which the 11. Pz.Div. was one, with 728 panzers in H.Gr. Süd—Kirponos had some sixty-one divisions including sixteen tank divisions with 4,536 tanks in four armies, while 9th Army was positioned in Bessarabia behind the Prut.

But the Russian divisions numbered barely 8,000 personnel each, the motorized units generally lacked vehicles, and the tanks were a mismatched collection of light T-26s, obsolete two-turreted BT-2s, three-turreted T-28 mediums, five-turreted T-35 heavies, and T-38 reconnaissance tanks. (Newer KV-1s and T-34s would, however, prove a surprise to the Germans.)[9] Soviet Russia did have border defenses, bunkers, and artillery positions in the "fortified regions" protecting vital avenues of approach along the western border, called the "Stalin Line." But with the occupation of Bessarabia and eastern Poland, a new system of fortified regions was planned, and much of the weaponry and equipment from the older positions had been moved forward some 300 kilometers.

Many of the new positions were still under construction, and units, weapons, and telephone communications were in transition. They comprised isolated strongpoints, while the older positions no longer represented an integrated defense. Even more crippling for the Russian commanders was the paralysis engendered by the Stalinist terror, with the very real threat of execution. When Kirponos ordered second-echelon forces to have more fuel and ammunition ready, his orders were countermanded through the NKVD (Soviet state police) border guards headquarters. In addition, his staff had to use the civilian telephone exchanges for communication because the use of the radio was forbidden.[10]

For the 11. Panzer-Division the invasion began to unfold as in the Operations Orders drawn up for B Day and Y Hour. At 16,45 hours on the 21st the code words "Heldensage, Wotan, Neckar 15" ("Heroic saga, Odin, Neckar 15") were received from the Ia (chief of staff) of Pz.Gr. 1, meaning the campaign was to begin on 22 June at 03,15 hours. The 11. Pz.Div. would spearhead the attack of XXXXVIII. A.K. (mot) commanded by Generalleutnant Werner Kempf, after the infantry divisions—57. on the right, 75. on the left—crossed the Bug and broke through the Russian positions. Farther to the right the 287. I.D. of XXXXIV. A.K. attacked, while to the left 14. Pz.Div. of III. A.K.(mot) attacked on the highway axis Luck (Lutsk)–Rovno–Kiev.

For the Elfte the axis was Sokal–Radekhov–across the Styr–Dubno–Ostrog–Berdichev–Dnepr. The 11. would pass through the infantry lines beyond the Bug and Sokal, with Aufkl.-Abt. 231 and Kradschtz.-Btl. 61 under Pz.Rgt.15. The order of march was organized to deploy into battle formation. Riebel's panzer regiment moved in three battle groups: Kampfgruppe A under Graf Schimmelmann led off with a panzer platoon on the point, followed by a rifle platoon in half-tracks, an 8,8cm flak battery, the command group of II./15, the rest of 6. Panzer Kompanie, the regimental command group, a light flak platoon (with half-track-mounted Vierlingsflak, quad 2cm guns), the rest of II./15, another 8,8cm battery, another light flak platoon, 2. Kp./S.R. 110 (minus one platoon), an engineer platoon, and a battery of towed artillery. Kgr. B, under Maj. Dr. Ludwig Schmahl was I.Abt./Pz.Rgt. 15 with engineers, artillery, and a bridging column. Kgr. C was the Tross (combat trains), protected by light panzer, reconnaissance, and flak platoons.

Axes of advance were marked on 1:100,000- and 1:300,000-scale maps; Hakenkreuz (swastika) aircraft recognition panels were to be displayed beyond the Bug, and all German aircraft would be painted bright yellow on the sky-blue wing undersides one-third in from the wing tips, with a half-meter-wide band around the dark green fuselage behind the insignia for rapid identification from the ground.[11]

The Sokal bridge over the Bug had been captured intact, and the 11. Panzer columns rolled onto the high ground beyond and through the scattered bunkers, deploying over the fields on the bright sunny day, with A.A. 231 reconnaissance elements now ahead, the K.61 Kradschützen in support. Division commander General Crüwell was up front in his command track, an Sd.Kfz. 251/6 with the distinctive tubular radio antennae. Even the truck-mounted infantry could deploy over the dry fields in their 2.5-ton Opel Blitz vehicles. The versatile Opel Lkw had dual rear tires for additional traction, though the low-slung chassis and lack of four-wheel drive later proved very disadvantageous in Russian mud.

Resistance was sporadic, and stunned Russian prisoners were rounded up by the Germans—*"Ruki verkh! Hände hoch!"* ("Hands up!")—and waved to the rear. The experience of Unteroffizier Alfred Höckendorf in a way exemplified this first day of the campaign. A motorcycle messenger of 4. Kp./15, the rear wheel of his Krad was hit by a shell while crossing a field of wheat. Because there were Russian soldiers in the area Feldwebel Bergander stayed with him with his Panzer III. But then Bergander had to continue on. Alone, with friendly infantry a kilometer back, Uffz. Höckendorf took potshots at the brown-clad Ivanen as they materialized out of the tall wheat—who then surrendered to him. By the time friendly troops arrived he had gathered forty Gefangene. Another ten were dead. Leo Prause, another Melder, was less fortunate, and died of a stomach shot. The motorcyclists of K. 61 spread ahead aggressively but were equally vulnerable. Uffz. Werner Strietzel would be one of those wounded.[12] As night fell, 11. Pz.Div. units took up Igel all-around defensive positions west of Stoyanov, 25 kilometers deep in enemy territory. Trains caught up to top off the Fahrzeuge with fuel and resupply ammunition.

Just to the north Gen.Maj. Friedrich Kühn's 14. Panzer-Division of Gen. der Kav. Eberhard von Mackensen's motorized III. A.K. paralleled the 11. Pz.-Div. drive through the collapsing Russian defenses, and shattered an abortive Russian tank attack near Vladimir-Volynskiy. Kleist's panzer spearheads were slicing into the Russian 5th Army of Maj. Gen. Mikhail Potapov, headquartered in Rovno. Already the 124th and 87th Rifle Divisions had been wrecked by the 11. and 14. Pz.Div. drives, their remnants isolated and surrounded.

Col. Petr Pavlov's 41st Tank Division, under orders to move north to concentrate at Kovel, was a powerful force on paper but reflected the defects of the Red Army. The 41st had some 15 twin-turreted BT-2 Christie-type light tanks, 312 T-26s, and 31 new KV-2 heavy tanks, bizarre machines with tall turrets mounting a 15,2cm howitzer. But the KV-2s had just been received, no crews were trained in their use, and no ammunition had been supplied; the BT-2s were obsolete and only mounted machine guns, and as the division artillery had no prime movers, the BTs were used to tow the guns; and the T-26s had a 4,5cm gun but no spare parts, and as only company commanders had radios, the circular pipe antenna around the T-26's turret top immediately identified command tanks to the enemy. When the 87th Division appealed for tank support, Colonel Pavlov detached a battalion of T-26s to help hold Vladimir-Volynskiy. But thirty of the fifty tanks were shot up by the panzers and anti-tank guns of Kühn's 14. Panzer and, with the Russians lacking recovery capability, these were all lost.[13]

On the 23rd the Gespensters moved out at 03,30 hours, Riebel's Panz.-Rgt. 15 in the lead. Following an air observation report of a mass of Russian tanks approaching the village of Radekhov on the southern flank, the regiment deployed facing south at 05,30, I. Abt. on the left and II. on the right, while 8,8cm guns came up in the center and division artillery moved into firing position to receive the Russian tanks. Suddenly a bomber formation flew over from the southwest, red stars clearly visible; but they continued on, either having expended their bomb loads or having another target.

Some Russian tanks appeared but were quickly knocked out, but not before a round hit the cupola of a 1. Kompanie Panzer III and Feldwebel Hans Albrecht was mortally wounded. Advancing south beyond Radekhov, the regiment then stopped short of gently rising ground with a clear 2,000-meter field of fire. Leutnant von Renesse was ordered to take his 2. Zug of 5. Kompanie to reconnoiter ahead. Of his five Panzer IIIs, three had the short 5cm gun; the other two had the 3,7cm gun—one of which was malfunctioning—but with its machine guns and radio, the fifth panzer was still an asset. Renesse continued in wedge formation, the optimum formation for reconnoitering, with firepower to the front, and the wing panzers protecting the flanks from surprise. Halting 100 meters from a road, Renesse had just reported no contact when tank engines were suddenly heard from a copse. First one tank, then a second, a third, and a fourth rolled into view, 50 meters apart. *"Pass auf!"* ("Watch out!")

Though the tank forms were unfamiliar, the red star on the green turret was visible, and Uffz. Gustav Schrodek, Richtschütze of Renesse's Kampfwagen 2-1, slammed a 5cm round into the first tank—with no effect. "For God's sake," he thought, "were the Russian tanks opposite so superior, they could only be penetrated by their own tank guns?" As the platoon blazed away at the Russian tanks, also without effect, the Russian tanks, apparently buttoned up and unsure where the fire was coming from, turned around and drove off. A shaken Renesse reported by radio: "Found ourselves in a fight with four enemy tanks. Type unknown, not recorded on recognition tables. In spite of many hits, our shots had no effect. Have the impression that the shells simply ricochet off. The enemy tanks disengaged without fighting and drove back. Should we push on? Over."[14] Renesse was ordered to return as soon as possible.

This was among the first recorded German contacts with the T-34 tank, a tank more powerful, capable, and better armored than any German panzer, including the Pz. IV. The A model 26-ton tank was powered by a 500 hp V-12 diesel engine and had 478mm (19-inch) tracks on a Christie suspension, providing good cross-country mobility. It had a 7,62cm gun and coaxial and bow machine guns, along with a sloped turret and hull armor, the bow armor angled 60 degrees to increase the relative armor thickness from 45mm (1.8 inches) to 75mm (3 inches). The B model had 482mm (19.3-inch) tracks (550mm/22 inches on the C model by 1942) and its glacis armor was increased to 60mm (2.4 inches). (The early Panzer IV tracks were 400mm/15.75 inches wide, and its glacis armor was 30mm/1.2 inches) The tank turret was traversed by manual or by electric power, able to turn 360 degrees in 14 seconds. The main gun was fired by a foot pedal trigger, though it had a low muzzle velocity of 612 m/s (2,007 fps). The crew members had a padded cloth helmet with earphones and a throat microphone for crew intercom. The driver had two compressed-air bottles that would help start the engine in cold weather. The T-34s were initially produced at Kharkov and Stalingrad.

The T-34's major disadvantage was that it had only a four-man crew, with the tank commander also acting as gunner, when both functions required full concentration. There was no turret basket, the seats being attached to the traversing turret. Tactically, the lack of radios (except for the company commander's tank) was not adequately compensated for by flag and hand-and-arm signals. Russian tank formations maneuvered without much coordination and could be defeated by German tactical expertise. But the thick armor of the rugged T-34 quickly became legendary among the panzer troops.

At one point at Radekhov a lone T-34 drove toward the II.Abteiling/15 and became a target for the whole battalion. Gefreiter Kurt Nentwig in his Panzer II was one of those who engaged the Russian tank, which was hit thirty to fifty times before it stopped. Hauptmann Zügner commanded his 5. Kompanie over the radio: *"Stopfen, stopfen! Der ist doch schon tot!"* ("Stop firing! He is already dead!") The battered T-34 sat silently for the next hour or so while the battalion awaited the next Russian move. Then the T-34's motor suddenly coughed to life and the big tank rumbled back to its own lines—a dramatic display of the ineffectiveness of the 2cm, 3,7cm, and short 5cm panzer guns against it. The infantry were even more vulnerable to the Russian tank threat, their primary Pak being only the 3,7cm Pak 36 soon derisively called the "Panzeranklopfgerät" (tank door knocker).[15]

As Pz.Rgt. 15 braced for the expected Russian tank attack, an artillery concentration hit in the area, though with little effect. Renesse's and Schrodek's Kampfwagen 2-1 had its left idler wheel and some track links damaged and the rations locker/box was holed, but all were quickly repaired. At the same time the division Fieseler Storch reconnaissance plane flew over and threw out a message near the regimental commander's panzer. Glancing at its warning, Riebel gave the order, *"Klar zum Gefecht!"* Within a quarter hour masses of Russian tanks began appearing over the high ground to the south. They began firing, but their rounds were short, throwing up fountains of dirt while the German Panzersoldaten held their fire until they were within a close 400-meter range. As the first wave of Russian tanks were lost to view in a shallow dip in the ground, the gunners re-estimated their ranges to the rise where the tanks would reemerge and present their thinner, more vulnerable belly armor.

Then the panzer commanders shouted their fire commands, and streaks from the green tracer elements in the armor-piercing rounds created a lacework of fire that smashed the Russian tanks. Some blazed up with exploding ammunition, turrets and chunks of armor and track parts clanging through the air; some crew members bailing out only to be cut down by machine-gun fire, while others were a ball of fire screaming in agony as they died. Some of the new T-34s and KV-1 heavy tanks, both mounting the 7,62cm gun, were among those engaged; they were impervious to the 3,7cm antitank guns, but were penetrated by the Acht-komma-acht flak guns the Germans deployed.

German panzer gunners also quickly learned to aim for the tracks of the T-34s and KVs, or the turret ring, where the gun mantlet proved a shell trap. But the flurry of Russian tank shells was likewise deadly to the panzers. Panzer commanders usually rode crouching in their open hatch for better all-around visibility, though this left them vulnerable. Gefreiter Hans Ruland was the Funker in the Panzer IV of his platoon leader, Lt. Prinz-Holstein, 1. Zug of 3. Kp. I./15. The attack had rolled across a cornfield, some panzers loaded with Sprenggranate against antitank teams, when the T-34s were encountered. *"Jungs"* ("Boys"), came over the radio, "shoot what's in the barrel!" (The tactic was faster than having the Ladeschütze unload the round and throw in a Panzergranate.)

Just then a Russian round ricocheted off the commander's cupola and Lt. Prinz-Holstein was killed. The other four crew members bailed out and ran back a kilometer to the Rollbahn. The other four panzer commanders of 1. Zug were also killed, as was Lt. Neur of 2. Zug. Regimental Stabs Arzt Dr. Weinberger and his medical personnel back on the Rollbahn tended to the wounded even as shells screamed overhead.[16] By 16,00 hours on the 23rd the battle of Radekhov was over, the retreating Russians leaving forty-six tanks wrecked and smoking in the open fields, some with their turrets blown off. Only one Pz. III was a complete loss, in Maj. Graf Schimmelmann's II./15, the others being retrieved and repaired.[17]

Meanwhile Oberst Helwig Luz's Schützenregiment 110, reinforced with 2. Kompanie/15 panzers, reached Berestechko and that evening established a bridgehead over the Styr River, 11 kilometers east of Radekhov. The rest of the Gespenster-Division was rolling east as well, deep past myriad Russian forces, the 197. Infanterie-Division protecting the flank. Generaloberst Franz Halder, Chef des Generalstabes of OKH, noted in his diary for 23 June, "The greatest advance has been made by 11. Panzer Division, after battling it out with enemy tanks."

The Russian tank attack at Radekhov had been mounted by the 10th Tank Division under Maj. Gen. Sergei Ogurtsov. It was part of the XV Mechanized Corps under Maj. Gen. Ignatiy Karpezo around Brody, ordered to counterattack the German penetration beyond Sokal by Kirponos late on the 22nd. But 60 percent of the privates in the 37th Tank Division had not completed basic training and its rifle regiment had no transport and thus set out on foot; the 212th Motorized Rifle Division also did not have its organic vehicles, most of the artillery howitzers had no sights, and the communications and engineer battalions were not fully organized or equipped and were immobilized.

Some of the 37th Tank, within 32 kilometers of Radekhov by 14,00 on the 23rd, might have supported the attack of the 10th Tank. But Karpezo ordered Col. Fedor Anikushkin to divert against a reported (but nonexistent) German force at Adama. Thus the 10th, which had started out with some 326 tanks but lost many along the way to air attack and breakdowns, attacked alone, lost 46 at Radekhov, and was ultimately forced to retreat out of the way.

At this time, each Soviet tank division theoretically had 210 T-34s and 63 KVs—but in reality none did, and such an organization would have been unwieldly anyway. In August the mechanized corps were disbanded and their tank divisions reorganized as tank brigades with ninety-three tanks: a company of seven heavy KVs, two companies of eleven T-34s each, and six companies of sixty-four light tanks (T-26, BT-7, or Lend-Lease types). In September, amid losses and low production, the tank brigade was reduced to sixty-seven tanks.[18]

Kirponos, at what was now the South-Western Front, grappled with the collapse of his armies before the German onslaught, as did the other Front commanders. They had been further unnerved by receiving Directive Number 3 from Moscow, ordering a general counteroffensive to destroy the enemy forces and drive into German Polish territory. Received by 23,00 hours on the 22nd, Kirponos's objective was Lublin, 130 kilometers *west* of the occupation border! Prodded by his political commissar, Nikolai Vashugin, Kirponos had to dispatch orders to his army and corps commanders to carry out the unrealistic directive. The next day Chief of the General Staff Col. Gen. Georgi Zhukov and Member of the Military Council Nikita Khrushchev arrived and lambasted Kirponos for his lackluster efforts to attack the Germans.[19]

With dawn on 24 June 11. Pz.-Div. engineers of Maj. Bernhard Scholaster's Pz. Pionier-Btl. 209 began repairing a bridge over the Styr near Berestechko. Unable to stop the 11. on the ground, elements of the Red Air Force mounted some 523 sorties between 22 and 24 June, dropping some 2,500 bombs.[20] Crüwell's Gespensters took casualties, but the momentum continued. The air strikes of Gen. Wolfram Freiherr von Richthofen's VIII. Fliegerkorps were coordinated by Flivos (air liaison officers) riding with the panzer spearheads and the Beobachter (observers) in a Fieseler Storch overhead.

Feldwebel Schrodek reflected the small unit experience. When air reconnaissance reported Russian armor coming north from Lopatin around 07,00 hours, 5.Kp./15 was detached as flank security. Seeking a good position for his 2-1, Leutnant von Renesse had his driver break through the boards at the back of an old barn to get a clear field of fire. Instead, the structure collapsed on top of the panzer, damaging the suspension and a shock absorber. To continue as platoon leader, von Renesse commandeered another panzer, and his crew drove the damaged Wagen back seeking the maintenance company. On the way, three Russian bombers attacked the road jammed with traffic heading east. *"Vollgas! Bomben!"* Many drivers pulled off to the sides and Landsers jumped into the nearest ditch, while the flak units opened up with their quad 2cm guns. 2-1 jerked to a stop at the edge of some woods and the crew jumped out, with no injuries.[21]

The 11. Panzer spearheads were now across the Styr and driving another 50 kilometers toward Dubno, fighting engagements along the way. On the north flank of Kleist's breakthrough, splitting the Russian 5th and 6th Armies apart, 14. Pz.Div. and 13. Pz.Div. encountered stubborn resistance and took casualties from Russian artillery near Voinitsa while heading for the Styr and Lutsk. In the process the Russian XXII Mechanized Corps was mauled and its commander, Maj. Gen. Semon Kondrusev, was killed. On 25 June the 11. Pz.Div. continued to drive east, and reported to Panzergruppe 1 it had flanked, penetrated, and secured Dubno by 14,00 hours and was continuing on toward Ostrog on the Viliya River, a tributary of the Goryn, and the old Soviet border.

The 11. Pz.Div. was now operating in two major Kampfgruppen. Kpfgr. Riebel had Pz.Rgt. 15 and Aufkl.-Abt. 231; Kgr. Angern was the 11. Rifle Brigade (S.R. 110 and 111), supported by Matena's Art.Rgt. 119. Both battle groups had companies of engineers from Pz.Pi.Btl. 209, antitank guns from Pz.Jg.Abt. 61, and flak guns from le.Flak.Abt.(mot) 71. One historian points out that while division artillery supported Kgr. Angern, Kgr. Riebel's panzers also had an artillery capability, if of shorter and more direct range. The Panzer III's normal ammunition load was thirty-six Panzergranate rounds, and fifty-nine Sprenggranate (high-explosive) shells, and five other rounds.[22] In the evening there was a rumor of Soviet armor advancing from Ostrov behind them; this caused confusion among the trains elements, but nothing came of it.

At 02,00 hours on the 26th the advance was resumed and by 06,30 Mlodovna had been taken, albeit against stubborn Russian infantry and artillery. When crossing fields that were mined, the infantry learned to follow in the tracks of the panzers, which detonated antipersonnel mines; they were careful, however, not to follow the panzers *too* closely, as the tanks drew fire and the infantry were vulnerable to shell splinters and metal fragments. Three panzers were lost in the day's fighting and there were more casualties, with Leutnant Duttenhofer of I./15 being killed at noontime. Russian tanks attacked from the northeast around 14,00 hours but Kampfgruppe Angern slugged ahead to 5 kilometers west of the village of Mizoch and 20 kilometers northwest of Ostrog. Russian planes continued to periodically bomb and strafe the ground units, but also lost heavily to flak fire and Luftwaffe Messerschmitt Bf 109s. Obstlt. von Stockhausen's motorcycle battalion K.61 fought their way into Ostrog.

To the north Kühn's 14. Pz.-Div. reached the Styr on the 25th and the 13. Pz.-Div. under Generalleutnant Friedrich Wilhelm von Rothkirch captured Lutsk on the Rovno–Zhitomir–Kiev highway. But increasing Russian resistance in the form of antitank guns, artillery, and tank attacks, though smashed by the advancing Germans, nonetheless caused mounting losses and time delays. Mackensen's two motorized III. Corps panzer divisions were shifted south and exploited the breach made by the 11. Panzer, followed by the 111. and 299. Inf.-Div. 16. Panzer-Division under Generalleutnant Hans Valentin Hube was released from panzer group reserve, and with the follow-on 75. I.D. streamed by Berestechko on the 11.'s route.

Stand-to on the 27th was at 00,30 hours. Pz.-Rgt.15 engaged Russian forces supported by heavy artillery west of Mizoch, but Angern's rifle brigade reached Ostrog by 05,00 and gained a bridgehead over the Viliya River, backing up the K.61 motorcyclists. The road bridge east of Ostrog had been blown, and the railroad bridge was wired with demolition charges and protected by heavy guns. Nonetheless some panzers swept in and seized the railroad bridge, and a bridgehead was also established there.

Losses were accumulating, and temporary cemeteries of Birkenkreuze (birchwood crosses) were left in the villages. These markers carried the deceased's name on the crosspiece, and maybe the rank and date on the post below, and the helmet on top. These graveyards were not the only signs of the intensifying battle: Maj. Dr. Ludwig Schmahl's I./15 was down to twelve panzers ready for action. Crews were becoming proficient at digging Erdlöcher (foxholes) and camouflaging their vehicles and guns from the incessant Russian artillery fire and air attacks. The flat Ukrainian countryside, broken only by occasional copses of woods and thatch-roofed villages, was a bland horizon that seemed to stretch endlessly into the distance, and the clouds of dust from the moving columns and the smoke boiling out of wrecked equipment and charred bodies and burning rubber could be seen over a wide expanse. There was a brief diversion when a twin-engined Heinkel 111 bomber had crash-landed beside the road to Skivra near Dubno, with the crew unscathed.[23]

Riebel's panzer regiment was in action near Mizoch in an all-around Igel formation during the night of the 26th but was ordered to disengage and support the advanced position at Ostrog. Feldwebel Kahl related how the scout platoon reconnoitered a route for the regiment. The platoon was awakened at 00,15 hours early on the 27th in rain and darkness. Lt. Karge briefed his sergeants on a map, then the platoon moved out on motorcycles and scout cars with no lights, machine guns cleared for action. They crossed a railroad line and went through a village, using a compass to guide along the various muddy tracks to maintain direction. They also stopped at certain points and cut their motors, to listen for any ominous sounds. A few kilometers to the left occasional flashes from artillery and machine gun tracer streams lit the darkness.

In predawn twilight some huts began to materialize when suddenly a rifle shot rang out. Immediately all were off their motorcycles and the MGs set up, as Lt. Karge fired some rounds at the buildings with his MPi—reconnaissance by fire. This triggered a firefight, and when larger-caliber shells began to fall it was obvious this village was held in force. "Mount up and pull back!" shouted Lt. Karge, and the platoon leaped to their vehicles. A scout car and two motorcycles were left behind, but all the men rode back. Karge met the regiment coming up within a kilometer, which then deployed. Major Schmahl led his I./15 from his Befehlspanzer. The Russian force was overrun, eleven guns were taken without loss, and the regiment reached Ostrog.[24]

The Russian numbers—of men, tanks, guns, vehicles—seemed endless. They were destroyed by the hundreds, yet more kept coming. The series of uncoordinated but persistent Russian attacks resulted from Kirponos's attempt to blunt the German drive spearheaded by the 11. Panzer. Russian orders of the 24th had been to concentrate four mechanized corps, each with two tank divisions and a motorized rifle division for a total of eight tank and four motorized divisions. Maj. Gen. Mikhail Potapov's 5th Army was to attack from the north with IX and XIX Mechanized Corps, coordinating with VIII and XV Mechanized Corps attacking from the south. Zhukov also insisted the XXXVI and XXXVII Rifle Corps join the attack. The objective was Dubno, to cut off the German spearhead at Ostrog poised to strike toward Shepetovka, a major supply base and railroad junction. The German panzers might also swing south in a drive to outflank the Lvov-area forces.

Once again it was a powerful Russian force—on paper. But a shortage of vehicles meant the infantry and artillery could not support the tanks, and a lack of maps, intelligence, and communications guaranteed poor coordination. The armored forces were decimated by lack of fuel, no spare parts, and Luftwaffe attacks. (Only later would the Russians become proficient in the employment of mines in the defense, and of infantry riding the tanks in the attack.) Maj. Gen. T. A. Mishanin's 12th Tank Division advanced toward Berestechko with three rivers to cross. But no scouting had been done, the bridges were found destroyed or to be too small, signal flags were inadequate to control changes, and tanks milling around were easy targets for German artillery and antitank guns. The German forces were also now prepared to engage the formidable T-34s and KVs. In one tactic, the panzers might delay back, luring the Russian tanks into an ambush of Pak including the Acht-achts, and attack from the flank.

Most of 12th Tank Division's tanks bogged down in the swampy terrain, many elements simply scattered, and Mishanin himself was later knocked unconscious when shell fire collapsed a brick building over his KV in Brody; on the 29th his tank was hit and flamed up and the badly burned general stumbled off into the darkness. His body was never recovered.[25] Liaison with the VVS, Red Air Force, redeploying from the interior, was also lacking. Gen. E. S. Ptukhin, commander Air Forces South-Western Front, and his chief of staff were recalled to Moscow on the

26th, and subsequently both were shot. Other officers were likewise shot, ensuring no one would use their initiative against orders. Corps Commissar Nikolai Vashugin, having threatened commanders into hopeless attacks, finally shot himself on the 28th.[26]

Anti-Soviet Ukrainians, remembering the brutality of defeat in the Red-White Civil War of the 1920s and the murderous collectivization and purges of the 1930s, rose up to support the Germans. In attempting to pass through Lvov on a forced march east to Brody for the attack, VIII Mechanized Corps Russians were embroiled in street-fighting with Organization of Ukrainian Nationalists (OUN) fighters. The NKVD in turn had been executing political prisoners or anyone considered unreliable, culminating in the "Lvov massacre" as the Soviets evacuated the city 29–30 June, by which time some 12,000 Ukrainians had been killed by NKVD units.[27]

In four days of heavy fighting (26–30 June) against the German penetration beyond Dubno, the mechanized forces of Kirponos's South-West Front were crippled. The seemingly reckless expenditure of troops and equipment had at least slowed the drive of Kleist's Panzergruppe 1. The four panzer divisions, supplemented by 9. Pz.Div. under Gen.Lt. Alfred Ritter von Hubicki, and the infantry, artillery, and Luftwaffe, were well occupied in fending off and destroying the uncoordinated but persistent attacks. Generaloberst Halder at OKH wrote in his War Diary on 26 June: "*AGp. South* is advancing slowly, unfortunately with considerable losses. The enemy on this front has energetic leadership. He is continuously throwing new forces against the tank wedge, attacking frontally, as before, and now also the southern flank, and . . . the northern flank"[28]

The resistance against Kleist's panzer group was in contrast to the disaster north of the Pripet overtaking Col. Gen. Fyodor Kuznetsov's North-Western Front and Col. Gen. Dmitry Pavlov's Western Front, for which Kuznetsov was relieved and Pavlov was shot. 8. Pz.Div. of Hoepner's Panzergruppe 4 crossed the Dvina at Dvinsk (Daugavpils) on 26 June, leading the Heeresgruppe Nord drive through the Baltics toward Leningrad, and Hoth's Pz.Gr. 3 and Guderian's Pz.Gr. 2 pincers of H.Gr. Mitte met on the 27th in Belorussia on the Smolensk–Moscow axis encircling twenty Russian divisions of the 3rd and 10th Armies in the Minsk Kessel, claiming some 290,000 prisoners, 2,500 tanks, and 1,400 guns. With understandable optimism Halder at OKH on 3 July could note in his diary the shattering of the Russian army west of the Dvina and Dnepr, and "It is thus probably no overstatement to say that the Russian campaign has been won in the space of two weeks."[29]

The 16th and 19th Armies were among the new Russian armies and fronts being formed. Coming from Siberia, they were first intended for the Ukraine, but on 26 June were ordered north because of the greater catastrophe looming there. But while Lt. Gen. M. F. Lukin's small 16th Army was entraining at Shepetovka, he diverted his 109th Motorized Rifle Division to contest the 11. Panzer Division's advance to Ostrog. Its 173rd Reconnaissance Battalion arrived just before the 11. Panzer's motorcyclists of K. 61, which quickly deployed and drove the Russians into the northeast part of town.

During the night of 26–27 June Lukin forwarded more of his units as Group or Task Force Lukin. Three infantry battalions crossed the Viliya River by a small bridge, by boats, and by swimming, but meanwhile Kampfgruppe Angern's motorized infantry had arrived, followed by Pz.Rgt. 15. Heavy fighting ensued, especially around an old Catholic monastery, and also north of town along the Goryn. The Russians finally retreated back across the Viliya, but two battalions were trapped. Lukin's forces, now with artillery support, kept mounting counterattacks for the next few days. But the two battalions were finally wiped out, and the heavy losses brought the 381st Regiment's commander to shoot himself.[30]

Crüwell's 11. Panzer-Division at Ostrog was some 100 kilometers ahead of Kempf's XXXXVIII. A.K.(mot) front, and the Russian attacks around Dubno behind them made resupply hazardous. Luftwaffe He 111s airlifted some supplies to the Elften at Ostrog, supply canisters dropping by parachute with rations, medical supplies, ammunition, and even some fuel. A medical Hauptverbandplatz (HVP, main clearing station), was set up by 2.Kp.Sanitätsdienst 61 in a large, two-story building at Novo Malin, some 15 kilometers from Ostrog. Between 26 June and 3 July 478 wounded were treated there. The Red Air Force, in turn, mounted desperate attacks, the Gespensters recording up to eighty sorties in a day. Planes were shot down in droves, by flak and by Me 109s, though at least one bomb hit a well and killed a number of I./15 troopers in a water-carrying detail. "Never in its history," related Gustav Schrodek, "did Panzer Regiment 15 experience so many air attacks as here, in and around Ostrog."[31]

If their panzers seemed to be in a static position, some crews dug their foxholes and drove their panzers over them for protection against bomb and shell splinters. Some vehicles in the open were wrecked. The Russians also dropped propaganda leaflets, urging surrender. One Passierschein (permit) in German and in Russian read:

> GO WITH THIS PERMIT THROUGH THE FRONT [Lines].
> German Soldiers! All, who go over to the side of the Red Army,
> are guaranteed: Life, good treatment and return home after the war's end.

Other leaflets included the "Reichs-Küsskarte"—the "Reich Kiss Card," contending that German officers and Hitler's band were turning Germany into a whorehouse. No 11. Panzer trooper seems to have been enticed to desert.[32] Russians, however, were surrendering by the hundreds.

By 1 July the Russian attempt to retake Dubno and Ostrog finally petered out, leaving a wreckage of guns, tanks, armored cars, and bodies too numerous to bury (even amid the July heat) until the fighting ended. "During the afternoon of 1.7.41., while the 11. P.D. [*sic*] was still defending the Ostrog bridgehead in the tenacious, embittered struggle," panzer gunner Schrodek later wrote, "and a thunderstorm turned all roads into a morass, the four day long raging tank battle to the rear—between Dubno and Werba—came to an end. All enemy attacks, in spite of the material superiority in part of the Russian tank force and the fighting determination of the Russian soldiers despite bloody casualties, broke down." The 11. Panzer history also concludes, "There followed days of the hardest challenge for the whole division, which lay far beyond all other divisions." Over 600 Russian tanks were claimed destroyed, 150 by the Gespensters around Ostrog.[33]

On the next day, 2 July, the 11. Panzer-Division was ordered to resume the offensive toward Kiev. The South-Western Front's mechanized forces had been annihilated in the ten days of these border battles. If by mid-July the South-Western Front had less than 300 tanks operational of the 4,536 on 22 June, then some 4,200 tanks total, without counting armored cars, had been lost.[34]

CHAPTER EIGHT

BARBAROSSA: Exploitation

GERMANY'S ALLIES DECLARED WAR ON THE USSR: ITALY AND Rumania on 22 June 1941, Slovakia on the 23rd, Finland on the 26th, and Hungary on the 27th. Each had their own limited national objectives and their military contribution was unexceptional; incredibly so, for their national survival was at risk should Communist Russia ultimately defeat Germany. In the north on 10 July the Finns attacked in Karelia, but only to regain areas lost in 1940, and they would not besiege Leningrad. In the south the border remained quiescent until the German 11. Armee and Rumanian 3. Army attacked across the Prut on 1 July. Generaloberst Eugen Ritter von Schobert's 11. Armee had no panzer divisions, and the Rumanians were primarily interested in regaining Bessarabia, gaining "Transnistria" (between the Dnestr and the Bug), and taking the big port city of Odessa, which was not occupied until 17 October.[1]

Controlling the Russian armies in the south was the new Southern Front organized 25 June under Gen. Ivan Tyulenev with his headquarters at Vinnitsa. This allowed Kirponos's South-Western Front to concentrate on Kleist's Panzergruppe 1 attack in the northern Ukraine. But even if von Schobert's attack was supplementary to von Rundstedt's main drive, all Russian forces in the western Ukraine might still be encircled. Kirponos, comprehending the threat, had already ordered 6th Army in the Lvov salient to pull back to Kremenets, 12th Army conforming, on 26 June. This was initially overruled by Stavka, Stalin's high command, though finally agreed to. Lvov fell on the 30th.[2]

Kirponos's South-Western Front headquarters evacuated Tarnopol for Proskurov, and then for Zhitomir. Tarnopol on the Seret fell to General der Infanterie Karl Heinrich von Stülpnagel's 17. Armee on 2 July as it broke through the Russian 6th Army and pressed hard against the 26th. Actually, if 17. Armee had been ordered not to push hard, the Russian armies in the Lvov salient would have been even more vulnerable to encirclement, given Stalin's general insistence on standing firm; for coming up from the south across the Prut was von Schobert's 11. Armee, heading for the Dnestr and Vinnitsa. The Russians were falling back to the old Polish-Ukrainian border and the fortifications of the Stalin Line.

With the Russian assaults at Ostrog exhausted, Crüwell's 11. Panzer-Division resumed the offensive early on 2 July. The Viliya bridge at Ostrog was too badly damaged for vehicle crossing, but air reconnaissance reported traffic on the railroad bridge at Brodov over the Goryn 12 kilometers to the north. A Kampfgruppe from Riebel's Pz.-Rgt.15 and a motorcycle unit from the motorized 16.Inf.Div approached under cover of a sunken road. Three large-caliber Russian guns were sighted, but were apparently unmanned. Some panzers provided covering fire while the unit deployed in line formation and charged across the last 500 meters of open field to the bridge, where engineers quickly deactivated explosive charges that had been placed. Two Russian tanks were engaged and hit, one exploding and the other driving off in flames. Another bridge over the Goryn was easier for the wheeled vehicles to cross.

In pursuing a Russian armored car, Leutnant von Renesse's Panzer III 2-1 suddenly hit an antitank ditch, jarring the crew, the vehicle smacking into the dirt wall on the other side with the bow and gun tube. The driver was able to back out without assistance and the gun bore was unplugged (an obstruction in the gun tube when fired could burst the barrel and blast out the breech, catastrophic for the crew in the turret).[3] But Wagen Zwo-Eins was not so fortunate the next day, the 3rd. The panzers rolled ahead, regaining the major road east of Ostrog. Driving into the rising dawn a village came into view. "Villages in enemy territory, and especially such on a route of advance, merited a very special attention," related Richtschütze Schrodek. Wagen 2-2, Oberfeldwebel Kurek, led on the left side of the roadway, Zugführer von Renesse's 2-1 ten meters back and to the right side, the other panzers on the flanks.

Except for some chickens, all seemed quiet as the platoon entered the village. Then suddenly two Russian tanks were identified, well-camouflaged, on both sides of the road, only a few meters ahead. Schrodek took the one to the right: *"Abschuss—Einschlag!"* ("Fire—hit!") Again and again. Wagen 2-2 also opened fire as more targets materialized; 2-2 claimed five, 2-1 another three. The Russian tanks were turned into burning junk now, crews scrambling out of the hatches. The panzer crews were left to wonder why the Russians had not fired earlier. Were the crews asleep?

A kilometer beyond the village of Kupiec a convoy of some twelve trucks was encountered, apparently assuming the panzers were friendly. While the following company lashed the trucks with fire, Lt. von Renesse in 2-1 led his platoon after three trucks that had turned around and were trying to escape. Russian guns from ahead now opened fire, and Fahrer Gefreiter Küpper accelerated and swerved from side to side, across the meadow and grain fields, into a tree line. Suddenly one of the crew shouted *"Bunker!"*, and simultaneously there was a loud clang and a flash, followed by steel splinters sweeping around and painful cries and groans. Wagen 2-1 was smacked to a halt. *"Raus! Raus!"* ("Out! Out!") Schrodek yanked open the gunner's side hatch, but immediately closed it because of MG fire. Through the vision slit he could see bunkers, both small and large, ahead and to the left. But what was to the right? 2-1's loader's hatch was open, and the commander, loader, and radio operator had vanished. But driver Küpper slumped groaning before his feet, bloody from the shell splinters.

Other rounds detonated but didn't hit 2-1. "Were the Russians such bad shots, or did they have another target?" Schrodek wondered. He later learned that the Kampfgruppe commander had driven his own panzer up through the barbed-wire entanglements of the bunker line and picked up the other crew members, but in turn the tank was hit on the front glacis plate and the radio operator/bow gunner was killed. After realizing he was not wounded, Schrodek traversed his tank's turret a little to the left, putting the sloping surface toward the enemy and sheltering the turret-side hatch, knowing the Rotarmisten would realize the panzer was coming to life. Sure enough, another shell hit the curved gun mantlet but ricocheted off, though the track fender was bashed away. The radio was knocked out, and peering out the hatch as the tank battle raged, Schrodek realized escape was almost impossible.

Feldwebel Ohnrich of his 2. Zug drove close, but must have concluded those inside were dead, and drove on. But then Unteroffizier Büttner, the "Kettenhund" (watchdog) of the platoon, came up on the left or off side with 2-5. Schrodek dragged the wounded driver up into the gunner's seat, hoping Büttner could help. 2-5 banged into 2-1's left side, and Schrodek shoved Küpper out of the hatch and across to 2-5's fender. He was about to follow, jumping from panzer to panzer, when 2-5 backed away, leaving him stranded. Schrodek wasn't sure how he got back to the German lines, but he automatically slung on his gas mask as he had been trained to do, wore his 08 Pistole (his "constant companion"), and grabbed a Maschinenpistole. He sprang out and ran to the rear of the panzer and out into a wheatfield, covered by the grain and smoke. He found an Offizierkäppi, probably Renesse's beret.

Schrodek continued crawling low through the wheatfield, in danger of being overrun by the Gleiskette (tracks) of other panzers. He had made it back through the mashed wire entanglements when he suddenly encountered tracks of a tank—but were they of a friend or an enemy? Then the words of deliverance: *"Hinten aufspringen!"* ("Jump up behind!") This was easier said than done, but Schrodek was able to climb up and into the loader's hatch on the panzer's right side. They were then pounded by heavy artillery fire, at least 15cm caliber. After the crew bailed out of this panzer, Schrodek finally got out of the zone of fire on another panzer.

It turned out the artillery was German fire that was falling short of the Russian line of bunkers. Schrodek also learned that Uffz. Büttner had backed away in 2-5 to deal with an Ivan with an antitank grenade. The other crew members were okay, and wounded driver Gefr. Küpper recovered and returned to the unit a year later. Panzer 2-1 was retrieved, and Schrodek accompanied it back for repairs by the Werkstatt-Kompanie at Ostrog. It was soon ready for the renewed drive on Berdichev, heading for Kiev. (When a panzer was knocked out, generally most of the crew survived and the panzer was repairable.)[4] Meanwhile Angern's grenadiers, supported by the firepower of flak, Pak, and artillery, and Pioniere with demolitions, punched through the line of bunkers by 21,00 hours on 3 July and the advance continued. The line of bunkers was, in fact, *not* part of the Stalin Line along the pre–1939 frontier, which was a little farther east.

The panzers passed through the muddy Ukrainian towns of Slavuta, Kamionka, Szepetovka, and Polonne on the 4th, sometimes encountering resistance. Long columns of bedraggled Russian Gefangene, with their dirt-brown overcoats and heads shaved to guard against lice, plodded to the rear, and the line of march was a recurring monotony of destroyed tanks and armored cars, shot-up and overturned supply wagons, and dead horses. Near Slovye there was a field covered with bodies of murdered Ukrainians: by the NKVD? By retreating Russian units? The advancing German panzers and vehicles and motorcycles kicked up clouds of drifting, choking dust when the so-called Rollbahn, the designated "highway," was dry; other times the vehicles had to be towed and pushed when rain made the road a slough, all vehicles caked with splattered mud.

The division was operating in two battle groups: Kpfgr. Bohlmann (111, K.61, Pz.Rgt.15) and Kgr. Luz (110, Pz.Jg.61), with flak and A.R.119 support.[5] Early on 5 July the attack from the bridgehead at Polonne proceeded and, supported by the Luftwaffe, advance elements took a bunker at the railroad bridge of Novo Miropol, the first penetration of the Stalin Line fortifications along the old Polish-Russian border. Some of the bunkers had been disguised against aerial Aufklärung.

The Stalin Line was begun in 1936 along the western Soviet border, built with concrete pillboxes, tank traps, and natural obstacles. But the 1939 partition of Poland saw the frontier advanced westward, and the line was not completed. The strongest sectors were in the north, Pskov on Lake Peipus to Polotsk on the Dvina, and south of the Pripet marshes, from Korosten and fronting Berdichev to the Dnestr. Approaches to some key cities, including Minsk and Odessa, were fortified, but there was no continuous line, and many of the positions were denuded of their weaponry or obsolete by 1941. Nonetheless many of the positions afforded rallying points, and some were bitterly defended.[6]

Frenzied Russian counterattacks, with tremendous losses of troops and equipment, hardly slowed the 11.Pz.Div. as it drove ahead through Novo Miropol on the 6th and through Szulayki and Cudnov and across the Teterev on the 7th, heading for Berdichev. Reinforced Inf.Rgt.60 of Gen.Lt. Sigfrid Henrici's 16.I.D.(mot) protected the flank to the south, while motorized brigade LSSAH (Leibstandarte SS Adolf Hitler) did so to the north. By 14,00 hours on the 7th the advance reached Berdichev, a large city with an airport (also noted for its fortified Carmelite monastery, and as the center of Jewish Hasidism before Cossacks, czarist pogroms, and then communist conquest). K.61 and Kfgr. Bohlmann led, followed by Kfgr. Luz.

Feldw. Erhard Englisch was Fahrer for Lt. Dr. Seydlitz, Zugführer of the 3. Platoon of Panzerkompanie 4./15. Graf Schimmelmann came up to coordinate the attack to seize and cross the 40-meter bridge over the Gnilopiat River, which had been prepared for demolition. As Lt. Ripenhausen rolled toward the bridge, he stuck his head out of the Turmluk (turret cupola hatch) of his Wagen for better orienting—and was immediately shot in the head, costing him his eyesight. His driver, Uffz. Vorländer, turned the tank around and the attack faltered, but Bruno Freiher von Brackel, Kompaniechef of 4. Komp., radioed Seydlitz to take the lead with his 3. Zug. "*Klar*" ("Roger"). Englisch drove their Panzer 3-1 on a zigzag course onto and over the bridge, the feared explosion of the demolition charges not occurring. Twenty meters beyond the bridge a Russian tank took aim, but Richtschütze Paul Sylla was faster, and the Russian tank flamed up. Other 4.Kp. Panzers that had given covering fire now also poured over the bridge and into the city.

But Berdichev was going to be contested. Hauptfeldwebel Knofe led a reconnaissance mission beyond the city, and a small village was quickly taken and some weak antitank guns silenced. But then huge Russian tanks emerged, three turrets each, which the Germans recognized from the tank recognition tables as T-28s mounting a 76.2mm gun and four MGs, two of them in the two fore turrets; some had been used in the Russo-Finnish War and were found to have thin armor (30mm/1.2 inches). The German panzers found good cover, and the formidable T-28s, manned by hastily gathered crews, lumbered clumsily into point-blank range. Seven were soon aflame in a real "Schützenfest" (shooting sport). The Germans' discovery of a vat containing 500 liters (132 gallons) of sweet muscatel wine to fill Kantine and gas mask Kanister (the metal Tragbüchse) added an almost festive note.[7]

Fighting intensified in Berdichev itself. Feldw. Sermond of 5.Kp./15 encountered a KV-1 that emerged from a side street, but the Russian tank then plowed into a building, covering and blinding itself with masonry and dust. Sermond dismounted his Wagen, climbed atop the KV, and dropped a Handgranate in—an action for which he would be awarded the Panzer-Nahkämpfer-Abzeichen (tank close-combat badge). The Russian tank Kaserne and base was taken, as was the airfield, and twelve planes, fuel supplies in chaos, were destroyed on the ground. But the Gespenster-Division was two to three days ahead of the parallel drives of Kleist's Panzergruppe 1, and for the next nine days, 7–15 July, it bore the brunt of frantic Soviet counterattacks. As clumsy and as uncoordinated as they were—incurring incredible Russian losses—the Elften were also taking losses. On the 9th there were tank engagements near Machnowka to the southeast, and Crüwell's Div.Gef.Std. at Holodki to the northwest, threatened by attacks, displaced into Berdichev itself. The platoons of L./71, attached to the battle groups, shot down various Russian planes—obsolete Polikarpov I-15s and I-16s and Tupolev SB-2s, and R-5s—as well as engaged ground targets. The airfield was cleared and some wounded were flown out by tri-motored Ju 52s, affectionately nicknamed "*Tante Ju*" (Auntie Yu).

Toward evening of the 11th the 4. Panzerkompanie with Pioniere on board secured some heights near Bialopol to the east when smoke from a railroad locomotive was seen. The panzers shot up the rails, trapping the train, which had some thirty tanks on flatcars. Three panzers attacked and the train crew, some tank crews, and miscellaneous other personnel fled, leaving the tanks abandoned and in German hands. On the 12th Inf.Rgt.92 of the 60.Inf.Div.(mot) came up to relieve the 11.Pz.Div. to continue the advance. Russian counterattacks continued, though they were smashed by Art.Rgt.119 fire and Stuka dive-bombing attacks. Heavy rain on the 13th also created muddy conditions difficult for tactical maneuvering. On the 14th Kgr. Angern captured Nizgorce to the east but ammunition resupply was difficult and about exhausted, and the battle group fell back. The countryside was seamed with *balkas* (ravines) from which the Rotarmisten attacked, or into which they retreated.

The 11.Pz.Div. attacked eastward again on 15 July, but this time against surprisingly little resistance. Nizgorce was taken, as was Bialopol, 20 kilometers to the east, by noon. A blown bridge caused a delay, but the Pioniere of Pz.Pi.Btl.209 put in a new one and the panzers rolled throughout the night, reaching Rozyn on the morning of the 16th and heading along the Rollbahn toward Skvira. The Russian attacks against the Elfte at Berdichev had lessened because the parallel drives being made by the rest of Kleist's Pz.Gr.1 had caught up. On 10 July, three days after the 11. Panzer fought its way into Berdichev, 16.Pz.Div. crossed the Teterev and drove through Krasnopol to Yanuszpol southwest of Berdichev. The division was commanded by Gen.Lt. Hans Hube, and had encountered stiff fighting before breaking through the Stalin Line at Lyuban on the 9th.

On the northern flank 13.Pz.Div. entered Zhitomir on that same 10th. Its commander was Gen.Maj. Friedrich-Wilhelm von Rothkirch und Panthen. The next day, followed by 25.I.D.(mot) and Gen.Maj. Friedrich Kühn's 14.Pz.Div., it reached the River Irpen, less than 16 kilometers (10 miles) from Kiev. Gen.Lt. Alfred Ritter von Hubicki's Austrian 9.Pz.Div. swung down from Zhitomir behind the Russians attacking at Berdichev, reaching Skvira by the 14th. A gap now 60 kilometers wide and up to 120 kilometers deep had been torn in Kirponos's South-Western Front. Kirponos had attacked that penetration with Potapov's 5th Army from the north, along a line from Korosten to Zhitomir, and with Lt. Gen. Ivan Muzychenko's 6th Army from the south. The forces that attacked the 11.Pz.Div. included the 8th Tank Division of Maj. Gen. Andrei Vlasov's IV Mechanized Corps and then elements of Maj. Gen. Andrei Sokolov's XVI Mechanized Corps and Maj. Gen. Sergei Ogurtsov's 10th Tank Division. (Vlasov would be captured in 1942 by the Germans and belatedly allowed to form an anti-Communist "army" from among Russian prisoners of war.)

Stalin consistently demanded that positions be held, and commanders who faltered were removed, relieved, or executed, for "defeatism," "panic-mongering," "cowardice," or other charges leveled by army commissars, especially the malevolent Lev Mekhlis, and by Lavrenti Beria's feared NKVD. New armies were created and were promptly destroyed, and yet more new armies were created. On 10 July Stalin restructured his Front commands with three higher commands, Glavkom: Northern and North-Western Fronts under North-Western Command or Theater under Marshal Kliment Voroshilov, Western Front under West Command, commanded by Marshal Semyon Timoshenko, and South-Western and Southern Fronts under South-Western Command, led by Marshal Semyon Budenny. With incompetent commanders and inadequate staffs this approach was disbanded in 1942, at which time Stavka began controlling the Fronts directly.[8]

On 11 July Kirponos assembled his commanders, including Nikita Khrushchev, the political member of the Front Soviet, and all recognized the necessity of pouring all available forces into the defense of Kiev, capital of the Ukraine. But Field Marshal Gerd von Rundstedt was not driving to Kiev. As Crüwell's 11. Panzer entered Skvira on the 17th after the city had already been taken by 9.Pz.Div., von Kleist's panzer group was ordered to swing sharply south. The objective was to trap and destroy the remaining Russian armies in the western Ukraine, and sweep down the Dnepr River and gain bridgeheads for a continued eastward advance.

To the north further disasters were visited upon the Red Army. In Feldmarschall Wilhelm Ritter von Leeb's Heeresgruppe Nord the panzer divisions of GenLt. Georg-Hans Reinhardt's XXXXI. A.K.(mot) and LVI. A.K.(mot) under Gen.d.Pz.Tr. Erich von Manstein raced each other through the Baltic states toward Leningrad. Riga fell on 30 June, Pskov on 9 July, and the "Luga Line" was pierced by the 12th, retreating Russians running afoul of their own minefields. The pincers of von Bock's H.Gr. Mitte, having enclosed the Kessel at Minsk on 27 June, opened out again, this time to create the Smolensk cauldron. Hoth's Panzergruppe 3 crossed the Dvina and came down from Vitebsk, and Guderian's Pz.Gr.2 crossed the upper Dnepr near Orsha and Mogilev and the 29.I.D.(mot) took Smolensk itself on 16 July. All Russian lines of communication were cut and the Russian 16th, 19th, and 20th Armies were trapped, and some 100,000 prisoners, 2,000 tanks, and 1,900 guns were taken as the pocket was sealed on the 26th. But the fighting was taking its toll on the German forces as well. 18.Pz.Div. was down to twelve operational panzers, and its commander, Gen.Maj. Walther Nehring, said the heavy casualties must stop "if we do not intend to win ourselves to death."[9]

In the Ukraine Pz.Gr.1 bypassed Kiev, driving south toward Uman, while 11. Armee crossed the Dnestr to trap the South-Western forces in a Kessel. On 18 July Pz.Rgt.15 found the bridge over the Roska at Volodarka intact, but too weak for the weight of the panzers. While the engineers put in a new bridge the van elements, with Aufkl.Abt.231 scouting ahead, thrust on 20 kilometers to Staviscze. That afternoon the panzers resumed their advance. On the 19th the Elfte held at Staviscze as a counterattack force, as the spearheads were now deep in enemy territory. The Gespensters attacked against scattered resistance on the 20th; slowed only by rain and mud, they advanced south through Bazovka and reached Sololovka by 15,00 hours. With clearing weather Russian planes attacked, and they were fended off by the 2cm and 3,7cm flak. Four kilometers south of Nestorovka an east–west rail line was sighted, and a trainload that included T-34s was shot up as the panzer column crossed the rails and continued south. 5. Kompanie/15 was at the rear of the column when someone announced, "Look, panzers of 16. Panzer Division!" Indeed, Hube's 16.Pz.Div. was on a parallel drive on the right flank.

But Hptm. Zügner, Kommandeur of 5.Kp., looked more closely through his Feldstecher (field glasses). He pronounced the tanks as Russian, and using his initiative, determined to attack. The other panzers, overhearing the radio communications, were prepared. The riflemen carried on board the panzers now jumped off, as the company swung to the right and into line formation and attacked. The 5cm guns were able to penetrate the flanks of the T-34s and even the 3,7cm Kw.K. could damage the tracks and road wheels. With some tanks knocked out or crippled the remaining Russian tanks sought cover in some woods.

Meanwhile the lead elements drove south, and attacked to secure Hill 251 (hills were named for their map altitude in meters) 25 kilometers north of Uman. Here there was stiff resistance. Rgts.-Kdr. Oberstlt. Riebel came up in his panzer alongside the Befehlspanzer of I.Abt.-Kdr. Hptm. Pricken. At that moment some panzers were retiring as Russian tanks milled around. "Shoot! Shoot!" shouted Riebel. "*Ja,* but I only have a rubber cannon!" retorted Pricken. Command panzers only had a false barrel as room for radios in the turret was needed. *"Scheissegal—schiessen!"* responded the regimental commander ("Crap, I don't care—shoot!"). At another point Riebel and his adjutant, Oblt. Karl Lestmann, had their command panzers in position with two other Panzer IIIs sealing the eastern flank of the Uman pocket when there was a breakout attempt led by twenty heavy tanks. The Befehlspanzer only had machine guns, but Riebel held his position anyway, though it was two 8,8cm guns that primarily thwarted the breakout. Both the other Panzer III Kommandants were killed, and the image of Riebel, with his cropped white hair and black panzer uniform, standing firmly in his turret cupola under fire became legendary.[10] Overhearing all this on their radios, the regiment rallied and overran the hill.

They would have continued on to Uman, but the wheeled supply vehicles with ammunition and fuel were struggling along the muddy route, further churned up by the panzer treads, so Pz.Rgt.15 and its accompanying grenadiers igelt for the night. Back at the railroad line 5.Kp. was tasked to provide flank protection to the west. There were only seven panzers einsatzbereit now. Two 2.Zug panzers, numbers 21 and 24 with 5cm Kw.K, and company command panzers 01 and 02, were on the south side; three with 3,7cm Kw.K. were on the north side. Two 8,8cm flak were assigned as support. Gunner Schrodek's crew of Lt. von Renesse's 2-1 attached tent shelter quarters to their panzer's fender, hoping to stretch their legs outside that night. But pouring rain forced them inside their panzer after all.

The rain finally ended on the morning of 21 July and the hot sun came out. The Panzersoldaten had acquired a goose from a pond in Sokolovka and attempted to cook it in a pail, but the wood fuel was too damp to light even when doused with gasoline, the "universal expedient." But Hptm. Zügner reported to regiment seeing a dust cloud beyond the trees where the Russian tanks had fled, and the goose was not yet cooked by 19,00 hours when Russian tanks suddenly opened fire. Schrodek frantically tried to detach the tenting from his tank's fender so it wouldn't be ripped to shreds, but there wasn't time, as he had to scramble up and into his gunner's seat. Shelter quarters and goose were abandoned. Some twenty Russian tanks emerged, followed by Rotarmisten in battalion strength, all to the south of the railroad embankment.

The four panzers there opened up, but with little effect against the sloped frontal armor of the T-34s. Zügner ordered Sprenggranate fired to decimate the infantry. At that moment a round jammed in the breech of Wagen 2-1. All attempts to free it failed, and the panzer would have to pull under cover so a crewman could dislodge it by using a rammer run up the barrel from the outside. But Lt. von Renesse determined to stay and use the machine guns. Zügner's company Befehlspanzer 01 was hit, and the crew bailed out. Suddenly 2-1 was hit as well. A cry: *"Der Zwo brennt!"* ("The Two is burning!"). The hatches were opened and Richtschütze Schrodek and the Ladeschütze climbed out opposite sides and ran toward Panzer 2-4. Something exploded in 2-1 and it began to burn. But 2-4 turned and drove away, despite their shouts to get attention. When they caught up, they saw the reason: the panzer commander's cupola was shot away. The gunner, loader, and radio operator were crouched on the front plating. What was left of Feldwebel Ohnrich—his head and upper torso had been shot way—was still in the turret. Schrodek and the loader mounted 2-4 and the Fahrer drove back 200 meters, back across the Uman road, and then they jumped off to shelter by the railroad embankment.

Meanwhile the Russian tanks were slowed crossing a marshy stream. The Acht-komma-achts had arrived and engaged them in direct fire, and the Pz.IIIs from north of the railroad track took them under flank fire even with only their 3,7cm Kw.K. The surviving Ivans retreated. Schrodek could light up a cigarette in relief. But a Sani (medic) saw he was bleeding—a wound caused by a shell splinter near the vertebra column above the waist—and he and the loader were evacuated by motorcycle sidecar back to the HVP established by 2.San.Komp.61 in a manor house at Staviscze. After they were treated they fell into exhausted sleep. During the night of the 22nd Schrodek was awakened by the head medical officer, who asked him to identify some from Pz.Rgt.15 who had died, some badly burned. Among them was his platoon leader, Leutnant von Renesse. When a panzer was hit so the ammunition exploded and caught fire, crewmen trapped inside might be burned beyond recognition, and sometimes could only be identified by particular articles of clothing or by their Erkennungsmarke, metal identification disc ("Hundemarke"). After further treatment at a field hospital Schrodek returned to his unit, where he had been believed gefallen (killed in action).[11]

As Kleist's panzer divisions bore south behind the Russian armies in the Uman area, the Red Army forces thrashed about trying to escape. On German Lagekarte (situation maps) the symbols marched forward: triangular pennants representing divisions, black squares for regiments, panzers with a streamer at the top. The Elfte was still in Gen.Lt. Werner Kempf's XXXXVIII.A.K.(mot), with 16.Pz.Div. and 57.I.D. On 23 July Russian tanks were shot up north of Zibermanovka, with more fighting back at Konela and Sokolovka on the 24th. In the atrocious mud conditions half-track SPWs had to tow wheeled vehicles onward, the infantry riding on the panzers. Aufklärungs Kradschützen elements pressed forward on foot, their motorcycles being brought up in the ubiquitous Russian peasant *panje* wagons, one-horse-drawn carts with wood-spoked wheels. (The term *panje* itself was actually a German soldier term from World War I, slang for Poles and Russians.)

A 20-kilometer gap had opened between Crüwell's 11.Pz.Div. and Hube's 16.Pz.Div. to the right, and the latter attacked through Monastyrische on the 21st. The brigade-sized LSSAH Inf.Div.(mot) under Obergruppenführer Josef "Sepp" Dietrich closed the gap by midday on the 25th. Intense clashes continued. Hauptfeldw. Knofe claimed a Russian plane shot down with his MG, while Stukas supported a battalion of the Hermann Göring Regiment at Konela. Lt. Kienitz of 1.Kp./15 was killed and Oblt. Hahm was wounded and lost an arm. The Russian 7,62cm field gun proved deadly; nicknamed the "Ratsch-Bumm" (crash-boom), its flat trajectory meant the shell would burst before the target heard the sound of its firing.

On 5 August Kleist's Pz.Gr.1 completed the encirclement of the Uman pocket, trapping the Russian 6th and 12th Armies and elements of the 18th. These had been unified under the command of Maj. Gen. P. G. Ponedelin of 12th Army and subordinated to Gen. Ivan Tyulenev's Southern Front. Budenny had ordered the 26th Army to mount a relief attack, but Tyulenev was outraged at Ponedelin's dilatory efforts to escape the trap, and the Kessel was complete. The Russians were caught in a Schachspiel Zugzwang (chess-play move-compulsion) where any move would be destroyed. Some 103,000 personnel were lost and both army commanders were captured. Large numbers of Rotarmisten were taken prisoner, searched, and directed to the rear, swelling the totals.[12]

As the Uman pocket was being destroyed, Kempf's motorized XXXXVIII. Korps was ordered to drive south to Nikolaev on the lower Bug to block Russian forces retreating from Bessarabia before von Schobert's advancing 11. Armee. On 8 August the 11. Panzer-Division was detached into panzer group reserve. That meant no rest, however, as elements of the Elfte fought from the 9th to the 16th in the Cherkassy area near the Dnepr. The Soviet VVS continued to launch forays, with an air attack on the night of 10–11 August. Oblt. Bruno Freiherr von Brackel, commander of 4./15, was killed on the 13th. For his bravery he was awarded the Ritterkreuz dated 23 August. The 11.Pz.Div. was put under the operational control of 6. Armee under Feldmarschall Walter von Reichenau, and on the 17th General Crüwell and Ia Maj. Werner Wolff drove to 6. Armee headquarters and reported "heavy materiel and personnel losses." The division was no longer fully operational and "urgently" needed rest and refitting, and it was given a brief reprieve.[13]

On the 17th the Elfte road-marched back to the Zhitomir-Berdichev area, or rather the tracked vehicles hauled the wheeled vehicles along the muddy route. On the 21st there was a Feldgottesdienst ceremonial service in the field for those who had fallen,

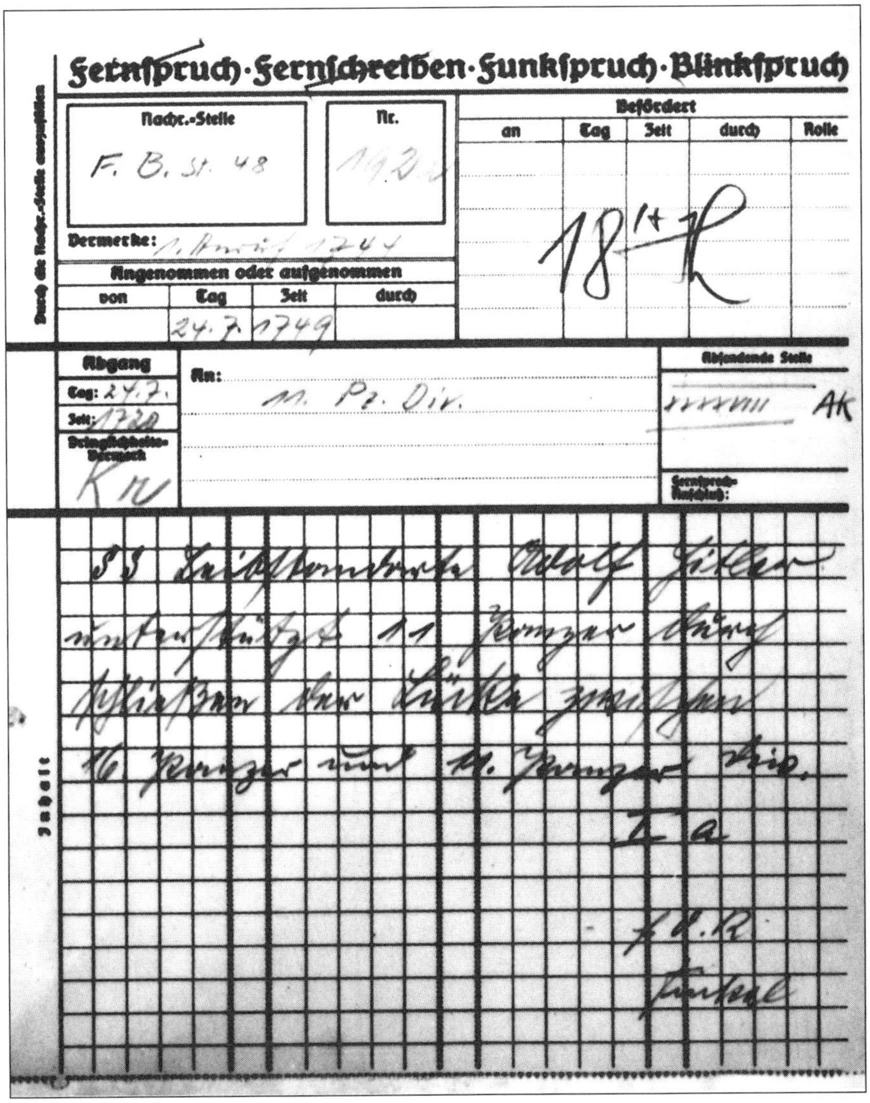
Fernspruch · Fernschreiben · Funkspruch · Blinkspruch

Nachr.-Stelle: F. B. St. 48
Nr.: 192
Befördert: an | Tag | Zeit | durch | Rolle
Vermerke:
Angenommen oder aufgenommen: von | Tag | Zeit | durch
24.7. 1749
Abgang: Tag: 24.7. Zeit: 1720
An: 11. Pz. Div.
Absendende Stelle: XXXXVIII AK

Inhalt:
SS Leibstandarte Adolf Hitler
unterstützt 11 Panzer Div.
Schliessen der Lücke zwischen
16 Panzer und 11. Panzer Div.
Ia

Radio message from XXXXVIII. A.K.(mot), 24 July 1941: SS Leibstandarte Adolf Hitler supports the 11.Pz.Div. to close the gap with 16. Panzer. NARA T-315/ROLL 2321/000487

followed by a pass-in-review parade for a change in command. Gen. Ludwig Crüwell left the 11.Pz.Div. to head Rommel's DAK in North Africa. On the way he was ordered to Hitler's headquarters, where the Führer awarded him Das Eichenlaub zum Ritterkreuz (Oak Leaves to the Knights Cross) for his able leadership of the 11. Panzer, award dated 1 September 1941. Oberst Günther Angern, commander of the 11. Schützenbrigade (mot) since December 1939 and a Ritterkreuzträger from the French campaign, became acting division commander.

There was time to make some awards of the EK 2 (Eisernes Kreuz 2. Klasse/Iron Cross 2nd class), red-white-black ribbons worn at the second buttonhole, earning the recipients appropriate humorous but respectful comments from their Kameraden. General Crüwell also personally made several EK 1 awards, an iron cross pinned at the left breast. Many now qualified for the Sturmabzeichen (assault badge), a bayonet crossing a hand grenade, or in particular, the Panzersturmabzeichen with a panzer, or the Infanteriesturmabzeichen with a bayoneted rifle, all with the eagle and Hakenkreuz. Many also earned the Verwundetenabzeichen (wound badge), a helmet surmounting crossed swords; all these awards were worn on the left breast. German practice was to wear awards on the Feldgrau tunic itself, giving an immediate sense of the wearer's experiences and abilities, as well as recognition if they fell in battle.

The 11.Pz.Div. was on the move again on 22 August, to an assembly area at Malin, with orders to attack toward Gornostaipol, 60 kilometers north of Kiev. It had the only bridge across the Dnepr in the sector north of Kiev capable of carrying all types of vehicles. The Elfte was to exploit through an attack by 111. Infanterie-Division under General der Infanterie Otto Stapf to seize the bridge and establish a bridgehead across the Dnepr. A Kampfgruppe was formed commanded by Oberst Helwig Luz of his Schützenregiment 110 (ohne/minus I.Btl.), Maj. Horst von Usedom's Pz.Aufkl.Abt.231 (ohne one company), Major von Götz's Kradsch.Btl.61, one Pak company, a company of Panzer IIIs, a battery of towed 10,5cm howitzers, and a half-track-mounted engineer company. The 111.Inf.Div. also formed an advanced detachment to seize the bridge: it comprised a bicycle battalion made up of bicycle platoons of the regiments and an assault-gun battery.[14] As Kpfgr. Luz moved to the assembly area south of Malin on the 22nd, it was realized that the dust clouds could not be concealed, so the last 20 kilometers were undertaken under cover of darkness.

At dawn on 23 August after a brief artillery bombardment, the infantry assaulted the Russian positions and reached the planned line of departure for the 11. Panzer. Kgr. Luz advanced, but the unimproved roads were poor, bridges over the numerous rivulets through the marshland had to be reinforced, and the infantry division, unaccustomed to cooperating with panzer forces, occupied the roads with its motorized and horse-drawn vehicles instead of keeping them clear for a rapid panzer movement. Pz.A.A.231 led the way with their Panzerspähwagen, scattering Russian resistance without dismounting their SPWs. Gornostaipol village was cleared and the motorcycle rifle companies, along with the infantry's bicycle riflemen, seized the Dnepr bridge by 17,00 hours.

But the approach to the 1,200-meter-long bridge was over a stone dam and causeway almost 1.5 kilometers long, high above the swamp, and Russian machine-gun fire from the surrounding marshy woodlands, coupled with frantic counterattacks, pinned the Germans down on both east and west sides. In addition stubby green Russian Polikarpov I-16 fighter planes, "Rata" (rat) to the Germans, bombed and strafed the bridge and the approaches. About 1900 that evening acting division commander Oberst Angern, who had come up to the island in the marsh, was wounded and had to be evacuated. For his leadership with the Elfte Angern, already a Ritterkreuzträger, was awarded the Das deutsche Kreuz in Gold (DK) later on 8 March 1942. This was a lesser-known award, conferred upon someone who had already received the EK 1 and EK 2. (After recuperating for a year, Angern assumed command of the 16. Westfalen Pz.Div. but died at Stalingrad.) Angern was succeeded at 11. Schützenbrigade by Oberst Arno von Lenski.

The main body of the 11.Pz.Div. was still struggling forward. The division was now on the edge of the Pripet swamp area, and gnats swarmed everywhere leaving hands and faces swollen. Rocket-firing Soviet fighter planes also made their appearance, forcing careful camouflaging of vehicles and the scattering of personnel when alerted by air-raid warning posts. The three batteries of Major Jacobson's L./71 had numerous engagements with their 3,7cm guns and 2cm Vierlingsflak. Nonetheless a bridgehead had been established, and the reconnaissance elements pressed forward at dawn on the 24th toward Oster on the Desna. Resistance was fierce, however, even after the riflemen and weapons of S.R.110 and then S.R.111 were committed. But, with its primary mission accomplished, the Elfte was to be withdrawn and the forces in the bridgehead came under General Stapf's control.

Russian Ratas, however, supporting a sweep of several river gunboats up the Dnepr from Kiev, succeeded in setting fire to the eastern half of the bridge about 10,00 hours. A rising wind fanned the flames and the engineers were unable to save the bridge. Neither the panzers nor artillery had yet come up, and Oberst Heinz Matena of Art.Rgt.119 found himself on the east bank with only an advanced light (10,5cm) battery and a heavy (15cm) battery, with forty and seventeen shells, respectively, the ammunition resupply still back in Trains. The Russians landed more forces west of Oster and the Desna and were strenuously determined to crush the bridgehead, especially around Karpilovka, Vypolzava, and Lutava. The defenders had Russian prisoners and deserters from five different divisions.

The Ratas also attacked continuously, and with the bridgehead extending 25 kilometers and Major Jacobson's le.Fla.71 still to the west, there were no effective air defenses. The 11.Pz.Div. had been alerted to a new German fighter plane, the Focke-Wulf Fw 190 with its distinctive radial engine, but only a Slovak fighter squadron appeared. "Experience had shown," related Luz, "that the presence of one German fighter plane in the air was sufficient to keep the sky clear of enemy aircraft." The Slovaks were receiving the Messerschmitt Bf 109, but over Gornostaipol they just had Czech-Skoda Aria B354 biplanes.[15]

Nonetheless the Slovak pilots did enable 16-ton ferries to begin ferrying heavy equipment across the Dnepr for the bridgehead, in daytime as well as by night. Nine Panzer IIIs, three assault guns, and several artillery pieces were ferried across by 26 August. Some ammunition, fuel, and rations were dropped by Luftwaffe Ju 52 transports, Kgr. Bohlmann's S.R.111 was committed, and with seventeen medium panzers and more infantry across the Dnepr by the 27th, the bridgehead was secured, although with heavy casualties on both sides. On the 28th a new 10-ton bridge was started below the old bridge site. With this bridgehead the encirclement of Kiev from the north was now feasible. Gen.Lt. Werner Kempf's XXXXVIII. Korps was pulled out for Auffrischung (replenishment and refitting) on 27 August, and Gen.d.Inf. Gustav von Wietersheim's XIV. Korps was pulled out on the 28th. During the night of 28–29 August the 11. Panzer units began to withdraw.

On 24 August the 11. Panzer-Division had received its new division commander, Generalmajor Hans-Karl Freiherr von Esebeck. Born 10 July 1892 in Potsdam, Prussia, von Esebeck served in the cavalry to 1939. A Ritterkreuzträger, he came to the Gespenster-Division from commanding 15. Schützenbrigade and then 15.Pz.Div. in Rommel's DAK, and was wounded 13 May 1941 near Tobruk. After recovering, this panzer commander brought Rommel's audacious style of mobile warfare with him.

With the Dnepr bridge destroyed and the swampy terrain conditions, however, it was finally decided *not* to expand the Gornostaipol bridgehead over the Dnepr. The 11. Panzer-Division was exhausted. On 31 August Major Selmayr, who had replaced Major Wolff as Ia, Erste Generalstabsoffizier, reported that with General Crüwell leaving, Oberst Angern wounded, and a 50 percent officer loss, "The morale of our people [Leute] has suffered a heavy blow;" and the condition of the vehicles was "indescribable." New division commander von Esebeck messaged A.O.K.6 that the division badly needed Auffrischung, and on 2 September Feldmarschall von Reichenau released the 11.Pz.Div. In an Ia report of 10 September, the panzers that were einsatzbereit, compared to those at the beginning of the campaign, were thirty of forty-four Pz.IIs, forty of seventy-six Pz.IIIs, and twelve of twenty-two Pz.IVs, or eighty-two of a total 142. There were fourteen of thirty-one Pz.Spähwagen ready, and motorcycles, half-tracks, trucks, and other vehicles indicated similar loss or were under repair, leaving the division at about 50–65 percent strength.[16]

On 3 September the 11.Pz.-Div. turned over the sector to the 111.Inf.Div. and road-marched back west to Zhitomir for five days' rest spanning 9–14 September. The familiar white divisional symbol, a circle with a vertical line, directed units to their billets. There many Landsers could relax in former Red Army barracks and wash themselves and their vehicles in the Teterev River. They also laundered their clothing, or found Ukrainian women quite happy to do the washing for nominal pay or rations. Movies for the troops were shown in the Zhitomir city theater; films included *Colorful Ukrainian Evenings*, and for the more erudite there was Paul Groener's opera *Friedemann Bach*. Panzer-Propaganda Kompanie 691 made available 1,000 issues of the newspaper *Panzer Voran* for distribution, which included the awarding of the Eichenlaub to the RK to former division commander Gen.Lt. Crüwell.[17] But the "Spiess," the "Top Kicks" or company first sergeants, also ensured their Landsers were kept busy on numerous details.

The Ukrainians in general had greeted the Germans as liberators, a legacy from German occupation and support during World War I, before German withdrawal and Communist conquest and dictatorship. Many Russian soldiers were Überlaufer (deserters) or willingly surrendered to the Germans. Gefreiter Kurt Nentwig was told by several that their fathers or relatives had been captured in World War I and had been well treated in German prisoner of war camps.[18] Unfortunately Nazi occupation policies would alienate much of the Ukrainian population, and many Russians would suffer and die in forced labor and Gefangenenlager (prisoner of war camps) back in Germany.

Local security in Zhitomir was in the hands of the Ukrainian militia, which rounded up former members of the Communist regime. They also rounded up

Jews, and Gustav Schrodek witnessed a truckload of Jews being taken away through the city. Then there was distant machine-gun fire, and he suspected they were shot. "If this really were so," maintained Schrodek at least, who served throughout the war, "it was the first and last time we experienced excesses against the Jews during the campaign in Russia."[19] It is difficult to determine to what extent German *combat* units were aware of, if not complicit in, the operations of the SS security units, especially the notorious SS Einsatzgruppen (Action Groups) in the occupied territories. These SS units also worked with the local indigenous population, and on 19 September the Ukrainian militia emptied the Jewish quarter of Zhitomir and 3,145 Jews were registered and then shot. This was five days after the 11.Pz.Div. had already moved on.

There was a brutality on the Eastern Front in general, which was in contrast to the German-Russian campaigns of twenty years before. Certainly the extremes of the Nazi and the Communist ideologies were new factors. Much of the brutality was generated by the killings during the Red-White Civil War followed by the collectivization and purges of the Stalinist dictatorship, and now massacres of civilians by the NKVD state police followed by executions by the Nazi SS, which inured soldiers and civilians alike to the slaughter.

Top-secret reports were compiled under Obergruppenführer Reinhard Heydrich as chief of the Security Police and SD, for example: 3,000 Ukrainians shot by the NKVD at Lvov (2 July), another 30,000 inhabitants shot by the withdrawing Russians (3 July), and 2,000 Ukrainians murdered by the Soviets at Tarnopol (6 July). The SS carried out their own executions of Communists and Jews, the most infamous being the murder of 33,771 Jews in the steep ravine of Babi Yar outside Kiev after the fighting units had moved on, by Sonderkommando 4 of Brigadeführer Otto Rasch's Einsatzgruppe C.[20] It is difficult to determine to what extent Hitler's notorious "Commissar Order" of 6 June 1941, directing that political commissars simply be shot, was actually carried out before it was retracted 6 May 1942. There seem to be no references to it in the 11. Panzer-Division unit records at least.

Some of the exorbitant Russian battle losses resulted from the practice of simply throwing untrained Muzhiks in successive waves against the German artillery and machine guns. The *Iwanen* came on crying *"Urraa,"* said Lt. Walter Schaefer-Kehnert of Art.Rgt.119. "They are walking on like a herd of sheep. That's incredible and your blood got freezing if you saw an attack by the Russians, the masses coming on and not being impressed by our fire at all." The Russians were often exhausted and afforded little food and no training. Russian Lt. Evgeni Bessonov later remembered, "An overwhelming feeling of indifference set in, an awful apathy; we walked towards the Germans, paying no attention to their fire."[21] The Russians were also put into obsolete or factory-fresh tanks with scarcely any training, the result being hundreds of disabled or burned-out smoking hulks strewn around the battlefields, frequently with their turrets blown off. The crews' charred remains were often inside, or corpses outside.

Any Ivan who deserted or who was simply a straggler from a scattered unit might well be shot by an officer or by a political commissar, or by the field police, or by NKVD squads—as might the officers themselves be shot. There was an aura of death on the Eastern Front, of decomposing, bloated bodies in the summer heat, or mangled corpses frozen in agony in the ice and snow of winter.[22]

CHAPTER NINE

Operation TAIFUN

THE ENCIRCLEMENT OF TIMOSHENKO'S WESTERN FRONT ARMIES at Smolensk by Hoth's Panzergruppe 3 and Guderian's Panzergruppe 2 raised anew the dispute among the German high command about future operations. While the Oberkommando des Heeres and the field commanders urged a drive on Moscow, Hitler had always insisted that the Russian capital was not the primary objective of the campaign, and that to him, "Moscow was simply a place name." In Directive No. 33 of 19 July 1941 Hoth's panzer group, operating with Heeresgruppe Nord, was to thrust *north*eastward to cut the communications between Moscow and Leningrad to isolate the latter while Guderian's Pz.Gr.2 was to drive *south*east to link up with Kleist's Pz.Gr.1 of H.Gr. Süd near Romny, creating a huge encirclement of Budenny's South-West armies around Kiev. Hoepner's Pz.Gr.4 of H.Gr. Nord was driving toward Leningrad. Bock's H.Gr. Mitte would be left with only infantry forces.[1]

In the Supplement to Directive No. 33 issued 23 July, Hitler emphasized that the first objective was the destruction of the enemy forces. In the north Leningrad was to be seized, and in the south an advance made deep through the Ukraine to capture the industrial area of Kharkov and the Donbas (Donets basin), perhaps even advancing to the Caucasus and its supply of oil. Only then might infantry forces capture Moscow. In the earlier Blitzkrieg campaigns, capitals like Warsaw and Paris had also not been the primary objective. In addition, Hitler was aware that Napoleon's capture of Moscow in 1812 had not brought victory, and that forces committed to urban street-fighting would lose their mobility, even if Moscow now was an important communications and industrial center.

Guderian in particular argued strongly for a continued drive on Moscow when Der Führer flew to H.Gr. Mitte headquarters on 4 August and again on the 23d. But once the decision was made, Guderian turned Panzergruppe 2 south on 25 August and with all his energy and ability smashed across the Desna and behind the Russian armies, down toward von Kleist's Pz.Gr.1. Kleist meanwhile had forced crossings of the Dnepr at Kremenchug and Cherkassy below Kiev. In less than three weeks the spearheads were about to meet, creating the largest Kessel of the war. On the other side, Budenny had been relieved on 13 September and flown out, leaving the trapped Russian armies leaderless.

At 18,20 hours on 14 September, German white Very lights flared into the sky, signaling that Walter Model's Berliner 3. "Bär" (Bear) Panzer-Division of Guderian's Pz.Gr.2 and Hans Hube's Westfallen 16.Pz.Div. of Kleist's PzGr.1 had made contact between Lokhvitsa and Lubny south of Romny, some 160 kilometers east of Kiev. Four Russian armies were caught in the huge Kesselschlacht and due to be annihilated: 5th, 21st, 26th, and 37th. In a meeting with Stalin on 29 July Zhukov had urged retreating beyond the Dnepr, abandoning Kiev—for which Stalin had relieved him as chief of the General Staff, replacing him with Marshal Boris Shaposhnikov.

Budenny was replaced as Glavcom over the South-Western and Southern Fronts on 12 September by Marshal Timoshenko who, however, only deferred the question of evacuating Kiev to Stalin. Maj. Gen. V. I. Tupikov, chief of staff to Kirponos, sent a telegram to the general staff: "This is the beginning you know of a catastrophe—a matter of a couple of days." Shaposhnikov simply branded him a "panic-monger," but Kiev indeed fell on 18 September. Kirponos's command group column, trying to escape eastward, was ambushed on the 20th. Kirponos was mortally wounded, and Maj.Gen. Mikhail Potapov of 5th Army was captured. The Germans claimed 665,000 prisoners.[2] It would be the largest encirclement and total of prisoners of the war.

As Leningrad was being isolated in the north, and the Kesselschlacht at Kiev portended the destruction of the major Russian armies in the south, on 6 September Hitler finally issued Directive No. 35 for a converging attack on Moscow. While Kleist's Pz.Gr.1 was to clear the eastern Ukraine and drive toward Kharkov and the Donets, Guderian's Pz.Gp.2 was reoriented to drive northeast toward Moscow. Hoepner's Pz.Gp.4 was shifted laterally from H.Gr. Nord down to the Roslavl area, between Hoth's Pz.Gr.3 and Guderian. This shift of several hundred kilometers across the east–west logistical lines of communication was quite complex, and could only be carried out with staffs as experienced and able as the German Ostheer now was. Guderian, meanwhile, had to turn his axis of advance 180 degrees *back* northeast 650 kilometers.

Unternehmen TAIFUN (Operation TYPHOON) called for a concentration of the three panzer groups attacking toward Moscow under the control of Gen.Feldm. Fedor von Bock's H.Gr. Mitte. The six panzer divisions of Hoepner's Pz.Gr.4—10., 2., and 5.Pz.Div. from OKH reserve, 11. Panzer-Division from H.Gr.Süd, and 19. and 20.Pz.Div. from H.Gr. Nord—were to penetrate the Russian Glavcom West center and break it in half to create two pockets. A northern Kessel around Vyazma would be formed by Hoth's Pz.Gr.3 with three panzer divisions—7.Pz.Div. in the Velizh area and 1. and 6.Pz.Div. transferred from H.Gr. Nord—scything down. A southern Kessel around Bryansk would be formed by Guderian's Pz.Gr.2 with five panzer divisions—3., 4., 9., 17., and 18.—making a wide enveloping sweep from Glukhov toward Orel. Thus fourteen panzer divisions, comprising some 1,350 panzers followed by motorized infantry formations, would segment and annihilate the remaining Soviet armies before Moscow. Deception measures were to conceal the dramatic redeployment of all these forces, with movement by night if possible.[3] In a second phase Pz.Gr.3 would envelop Moscow from the north through Kalinin, Pz.Gr.2 would envelop from the south through Tula, and Hoepner's Pz.Gr.4 would drive directly along the hard-surfaced Smolensk–Moscow Rollbahn to the Russian capital. This was two-lane and cobblestoned, the old post road from Warsaw to Moscow along which Napoleon had advanced.

On 14 September the 11. Panzer-Division under Generalmajor von Esebeck received orders to road-march to the Dnepr where Maj. Bernhard Scholaster's Pz.Pi.Btl.209 organized ferries to float the panzers across to the eastern bank. The Landsers responded to the familiar command: *"Aufgesessen—Motoren anwerfen—Panzer Marsch!"* ("Mount up—start engines—panzers, move out!") Vehicles began crossing pontoon bridges built by the engineers. The route of the main body of the 11. Panzer from the bivouac areas around Zhitomir to Roslavl was 750 kilometers (465 miles), passing through Zhitomir, Korosten, and Gornostaipol; across the now-bridged Dnepr; and on though Oster, Chernigov on the lower Desna, Gomel, Dovsk, Propoisk, Critchev, and Roslavl. Elements were crossing the Dnepr by the 21st and closing their assembly areas west of Roslavl by the 23rd. Quartering parties, five men in a Personenkraftwagen (Pkw, personnel car) each, went ahead to facilitate the arrival of their units in designated areas for refueling and first-echelon (crew) vehicle maintenance after each day's road march. They passed the wreckage of Russian tanks—BTs, T-26Cs, T-34s, even some British A10 Vickers cruiser tanks—and devastated towns, left in the wake of Guderian's earlier drive south that had shattered the Russian 5th Army.

The move was administrative, not tactical, the march serials organized by unit: Marschgruppe C was Pz.Rgt.15, Marschgruppe D was S.R.110, and Marschgruppe B was S.R.111, staff and other units included. Le.Fla.Abt.71 batteries went with the march serials to provide protection from continuing sporadic Soviet air attacks: 1. Batterie went with C, 2.Battr. with D, and 3. with B. Normal vehicle intervals were 25 meters through wooded areas, 50 meters in the open. The Gespenster-Division was still strong, but reflected the hard campaigning. Of some 157 panzers initially committed, including Panzer Is and Befehlspanzer, some 39 were total losses. As of 10 September reported panzer strength was 118, with 20 undergoing maintenance or repair (Instandsetzung), leaving 98 einsatzbereit (ready for action) or 62.4 percent. Of 31 little Pz. Befehlswagen, old Panzer I command panzers, 4 had been lost, 6 were in maintenance, and 21 (67.7 percent) were einsatzbereit.[4]

The Elften had left the Ukraine and were entering Belorussia (White Russia). They were also leaving the flat, featureless steppe country of prairie grasslands and entering the forest and swamp zone north of the Ukraine. This terrain was characterized by birch and alder forests, dense undergrowth, and meadow-like swampland with moors and ponds and sedge islands. Wandering Ivans were rounded up and herded to the rear. Some were Überläufers who came up holding the Propusk/Passierschein leaflets dropped or fired over the Russians encouraging them to desert, and many were adopted by the German units as Hilfswillige (auxiliary volunteers). The "Hiwis" carried out useful tasks for the often shorthanded German units, and would even be carried on personnel reports as a category.[5]

Orders on 28 September found the 11. Panzer moving up to final attack positions around Petrovskoye, 6 kilometers behind the HKL held by infantry. Von Esebeck's division was now in the XXXXVI. A.K.(mot) commanded by General der Panzertruppen Heinrich von Vietinghoff in Hoepner's Pz.Gr.4 under GFM Günther von Kluge's 4. Armee. The axis of advance was along the Roslavl–Moscow Rollbahn. The 11. was to pierce a Russian bridgehead on the upper Desna north of Bryansk, with the 5.Pz.Div. and 252.Inf.Div. on its left. X Tag for Unternehmen TAIFUN was 2 October 1941.

On 30 September Guderian's panzer group, farther south, began its drive toward Bryansk, to take advantage of the still relatively dry weather. On 2 October Bock's other forces began their attack, the Elfte charging into the Desna bridgehead south of the Rollbahn, preceded by a violent assault by Stukas, Nebelwerfer, and artillery bombardment. Once again the Russians were taken by surprise and the Blitzkrieg broke through their positions. Within two days the bridgehead was shattered. The panzers were able to ford the Desna, the water up to their track fenders, the tracks clawing up the eastern bank. One advantage the Germans had was that, except for the Pripet, major Russian rivers flowed north and south from the great divide of the Smolensk–Moscow ridge (known to the Germans as the Orsha Corridor), and the higher western banks overlooked the eastern banks. This provided good height for the artillery Beobachtungsstellen (B-Stellen, forward observation posts) and for covering fire. The rivers themselves, however, could be defensive obstacles for an eastward advance.

While the Pioniere constructed pontoon bridges for the wheeled vehicles, the strike forces forged ahead, though there were casualties from mines and various Russian defensive positions. On the Gespenster spearheads drove, Kampfgruppe von Lenski of 11.S.B. with elements of Pz.Rgt.15 and S.R.110 in the lead, behind the Pz.A.A.231 scout cars and SPWs. They crossed the Desna, the Shuiza, the Snopot, and the Bolva at Utroshino on the 3rd, sweeping north across the Rollbahn at Utrikova to Spass Dyemyensko by the 4th. Close air support was coordinated through the Flivos.

Hitler had distributed a Tagesbefehl on 2 October, reading, "In these three-and-a-half months the conditions have now finally been created for the last powerful blow that should smash [zerschmettern] the opponent still before the onset of winter." Hoepner's Order of the Day commemorated 2 October as the birthday of Generalfeldmarschall von Hindenburg, the man who had won the first great victory over the Russians (Tannenberg); the Panzergruppe's Parole (watchword) was "Hindenburg—Forward—Victory!" and Vietinghoff also urged, "Vorwärts! Vorwärts!" Perhaps the Gespenster Landsers already engaged in combat had no need for such exhortations, and it was noted that neither Hoepner nor Vietinghoff had ended with the traditional, "Heil dem Führer!" The harsh reality of war was generating a certain cynicism among the combat veterans.[6]

On 5 October the spearheads attacked at Vshody on the Ugra—the river where in 1480 Prince Ivan of Moscow gained independence from the Mongol Golden Horde. On that same day the first snow fell. It quickly melted, but was a harbinger of the Russian winter to come. The infantry were wearing their double-breasted, six-button overcoats now, but they were conscious that the wool-rayon material would not be adequate in extreme cold. On the 6th an icy wind and a snowstorm served as further warning; nonetheless the drive continued north across the Volosta at Mirsino and reached Kaidakova by the 8th. On 7 October Vyazma was captured, and 7.Pz.Div. of Hoth's Pz.Gr.3 and 10.Pz.Div. of Hoepner's Pz.Gr.4 met, completing another encirclement. Five Russian armies—the 16th, 19th, 20th, 24th, and 32rd—were caught in the trap.

To the south Guderian's Pz.Gr.2 captured Orel on 3 October; there the 4.Pz.Div. panzers met a streetcar whose passengers cheered them, believing them to be Russian. When 17.Pz.Div. took Bryansk and the bridge over the Desna on the 6th, a convergence with 2. Armee trapped three more Russian armies. *"Rukhi verkh!" "Hände hoch!"* The masterful Doppelschlacht, a double envelopment of the Vyazma-Bryansk pockets netted a further 663,000 Red Army Kriegsgefangene claimed by the Germans, rivaling the Kiev Kesselschlacht of three weeks before; *"Voyna kaput"* (the war is lost), the Bolschevisten Gefangene were saying. Feldmarschall von Bock of H.Gr.Mitte messaged that six Russian armies with 73 rifle and cavalry divisions and 13 tank divisions had been smashed, and 1,277 tanks and 675,098 prisoners taken.[7]

But there were 11. Panzer-Division losses too. On 9 October Major von Götz commanding K.61 fell in a fight in the woods, succeeded by Major von Usedom of A.A.231. On 12 October division commander von Esebeck was hospitalized with pneumonia at Roslavl, and Oberst Arno von Lenski of 11. Schützenbrigade became acting division commander for two weeks (12–27 October). Oberst Helwig Luz temporarily commanded the brigade as well as his own S.R.110. In S.R.111 Hptm. Köpnick took over I.Btl. when Major Kleeburg was wounded on the 11th. Before he was evacuated von Esebeck, recognizing the harsh conditions for the Russian civilian population and the advisability of their support, urged his commanders about procurement, "I deem it unworthy of a German soldier to take food provisions [Lebensmittel] from an inhabitant of an enemy land without payment."[8] Arno von Lenski, acting division commander (in Vertretung), was born 20 July 1893 in Zymochen, eastern Prussia. He had served in cavalry units and staff positions on the Western and then the Eastern Fronts in World War I. Advancing to Oberst by 1938, von Lenski had come to 11.Schtz.-Brig. from 2.S.B./2.Pz.Div. in August.[9]

The division continued operating in three Kampfgruppen under the regimental commanders, task-organized: Kampfgruppe Riebel with his Pz.Rgt.15, K.61, A.A.231, I.Abt./A.R.119, Pz.Jg.Abt.61 (minus 1. and 2. Komp.), 1.Battr. of le.Fla.Abt.71, and 2.Kp./Pz.Pi.Btl.209; Kpfgr. Luz with his S.R.110, III.Abt./A.R.119 and Bb.334 (Beobachtungsbatterie, observation battery), 1.Kp./Pz.Jg.Abt.61, 2.Battr./L./71, Stab 11. Schützenbrigade, and elements of Nachr.Abt.341; and Kgr. Fricke, Oberst Ludwig Fricke acting commander of Oberst Bohlmann-Combrinck's S.R.111 from September to November, with Pz.Pi.Btl.209 (ohne 2.Komp.), A.R.119 (ohne I. and III.Abt. and Bb.334), L./71 (ohne 1. and 2.Battr.), 2.Kp./Pz.Jg. Abt.61, and 1.Zug of San.Kp.61. Oberst Camillo Neureiter as DNF controlled the remaining division support elements in the Tross (trains). Ammunition was delivered to the fighting units by the Lkws of leichte Kolonne I, and fuel by leichte Kolonne II.[10]

While Hoepner's Pz.Gr.4 had been turning north and Guderian's Pz.Gr.2 driving south in mid-September, the Red Army fronts in the center before Moscow had been reorganized. After Timoshenko went to salvage the South-West, Ivan Konev took over the West Front with six armies. Zhukov went to Leningrad and Budenny was given his Reserve Front with two armies, with four armies held in Stavka Western reserve. Andrei Yeremenko held the Bryansk Front with three armies. The three fronts had a total strength of some 800,000 men, 770 tanks, and 364 planes, almost half the entire Red Army strength in men and guns on the Soviet-German front, and one-third of the tanks and planes.[11] (Even at full strength, Russian divisions were numerically equivalent to German brigades; corps roughly equivalent to divisions; armies akin to corps, and fronts similar to large armies. Red Army formations generally did have a higher proportion of combat to support troops, of "teeth to tail.")

On 30 September Guderian's Pz.Gr.2 had broken through the Bryansk Front, and on 2 October twelve

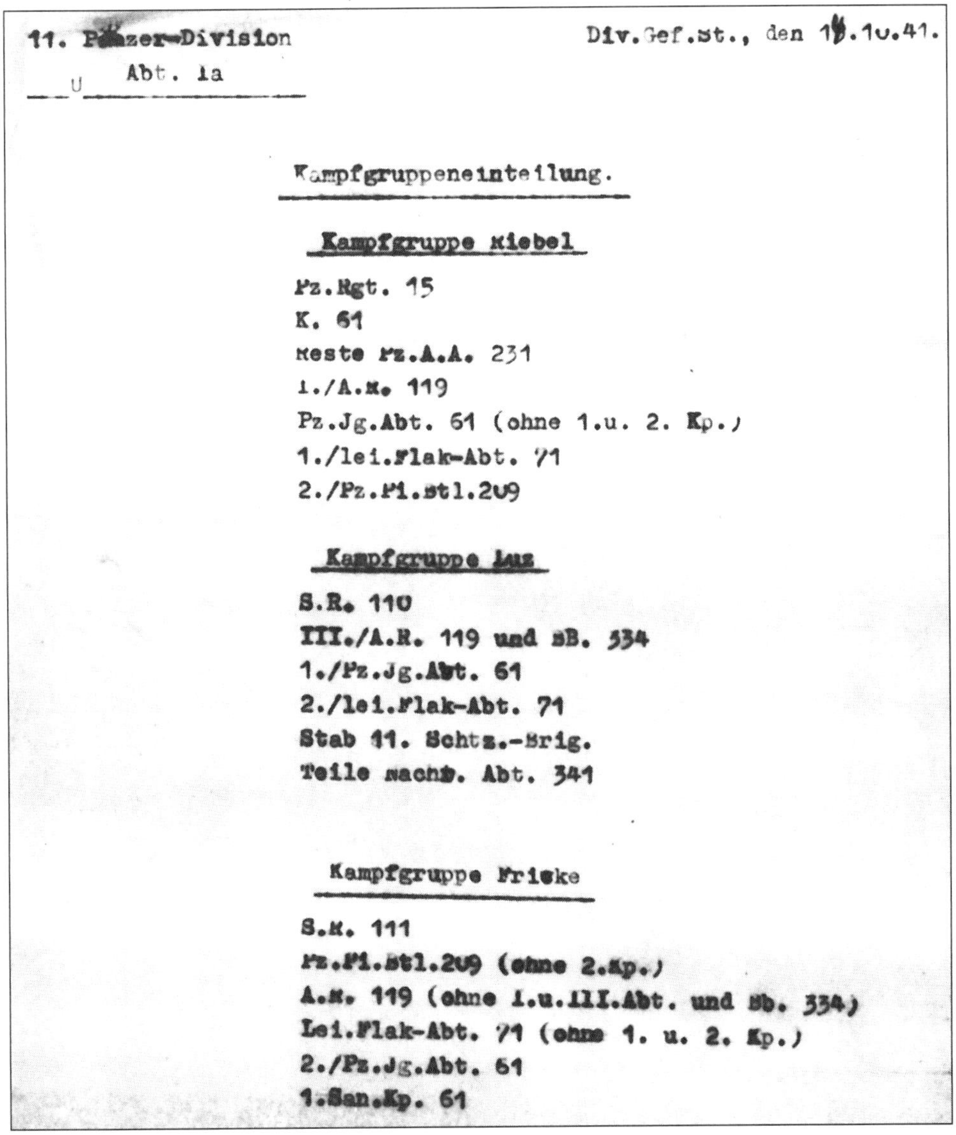

11. Panzer-Division Div.Gef.St., den 14.10.41.
Abt. Ia

Kampfgruppeneinteilung.

Kampfgruppe Riebel

Pz.Rgt. 15
K. 61
Reste Pz.A.A. 231
I./A.R. 119
Pz.Jg.Abt. 61 (ohne 1.u. 2. Kp.)
1./lei.Flak-Abt. 71
2./Pz.Pi.Btl.209

Kampfgruppe Luz

S.R. 110
III./A.R. 119 und sB. 334
1./Pz.Jg.Abt. 61
2./lei.Flak-Abt. 71
Stab 11. Schtz.-Brig.
Teile nachr. Abt. 341

Kampfgruppe Frieke

S.R. 111
Pz.Pi.Btl.209 (ohne 2.Kp.)
A.R. 119 (ohne I.u.III.Abt. und Sb. 334)
Lei.Flak-Abt. 71 (ohne 1. u. 2. Kp.)
2./Pz.Jg.Abt. 61
1.San.Kp. 61

KTB (Kriegstagebuch, War Diary), 14 October 1941—Kampfgruppen list. I. and III. Battalions of Art.Rgt.119 support Kgr. Riebel and Luz. Other units are also distributed. NARA T-315/ROLL 587/000628

German divisions tore a 30-kilometer gap through the West Front north of the Smolensk highway while Pz.Gr.4 ripped into the Reserve armies toward Vyazma. At Stavka Marshal Shaposhnikov refused to believe reports of the new German breakthroughs, Stalin held his commanders responsible for somehow stopping the German offensive, and Lavrenti Beria's NKVD threatened arrests of "panic-mongers" and "provocationists." "But no amount of NKVD intimidation," says historian John Erickson, "could dispose of the brute fact that the Soviet armies at Bryansk had been blasted to pieces."[12] Yeremenko was severely wounded by bomb splinters and flown out, M. F. Lukin of the 19th Army was taken prisoner, Kostantin Rokosssovsky of the 16th Army fought his way out, and M. P. Petrov of the 50th Army died in a Bryansk forest.

On 15 October Foreign Commissar Vyacheslav Molotov warned the British and American ambassadors that the Soviet government was evacuating Moscow for Kuibyshev. Officials were leaving, bridges and factories were prepared for demolition, and looting had broken out. Amid blackout conditions and with air-raid sirens sounding and German bombs exploding, Moscow was a bleak city under siege. The embalmed Lenin, founder of the Soviet Union, was removed from the mausoleum on Red Square to Tyumen, Siberia.

But Stalin indicated a determination to stay and brought Zhukov back on 10 October to command the remnants of West and Reserve Fronts. Muscovite civilians were mobilized to dig antitank ditches, and three lines of fortifications were established to defend the capital. Unlike in 1812, the city would not be allowed to fall to the enemy. On 20 October a state of emergency was declared and provocateurs, spies, deserters, and rumormongers were shot out of hand by the NKVD and security forces.

After the conclusion of the double encirclement battles of Vyazma-Bryansk, the terrible German pincers opened out again, this time to encircle Moscow itself. To the north Pz.Gr.3, now under General Reinhardt since 8 October when Hoth went to command 17. Armee in the Ukraine, drove on Kalinin on the upper Volga to cut the communications between Leningrad and Moscow. To the south Guderian's Pz.Gr.2, redesignated as 2. Panzerarmee on 5 October, drove on Tula. (Kleist's Pz.Gr.1 was redesignated on 25 October, and Pz.Gr.3 and 4 were upgraded 1 January 1942.) Hoepner's Pz.Gr.4, including the Elfte, forged straight ahead on the Smolensk–Moscow Rollbahn toward Mozhaisk. In early October some motorized corps began to be addressed as panzer corps, such as Vietinghoff's XXXXVI. Panz.-Korps, designated as such by the 6th.

But despite the tremendous power of the renewed Blitzkrieg, it was an advance in slow motion—for now the Russian autumn rains brought the *Rasputitsa*, the "season of bad roads." In German this was known as the Schlammperiode, the mud period, and it gripped all movement in its glutinous morass. The seasonal spring and autumn mud periods were not unknown to the Germans, and the launching of Unternehmen BARBAROSSA had originally been timed for the end of the spring Rasputitsa. Many German commanders, including Field Marshals Wilhelm Ritter von Leeb, Gerd von Rundstedt, and Erich von Manstein, had experienced similar conditions on the Russian Front in World War I scarcely twenty years earlier.

Two factors perhaps explain why the Wehrmacht was caught in the autumn mud period and the winter: first, BARBAROSSA had not been launched until the fourth week of June, and the August decision to divert Panzergruppen 3 and 2 to the north and south, respectively, had postponed the final drive on Moscow. Second, both the autumn rains and then the Russian winter came unusually early in 1941 according to records going back to the nineteenth century. While the unpredictability of weather could be assumed, the tight German time schedule allowed no margin for error.

German planning had provided for adequate fuel and ammunition supplies for this expansive campaign, and the Germans were replacing the wide-gauge Russian railroad system of 152.4cm (5 feet) with the standard European (and American) gauge of 143.5cm (4 feet, 8.5 inches). The crews had reached Smolensk 16 August, laying some 23,000 kilometers (14,260 miles) by the end of 1941. But supplies to the forward units depended upon wheeled vehicles, and these failed in the incredibly muddy conditions. Every day 11. Panzer Ia Major Selmayr's reports to Vietinghoff's XXXXVI. Panzer Korps said, "Very great terrain difficulties! Movement only step-by-step!" "Untrafficable." "Every motor movement feared." "Impassable."[13] British military analyst B. H. Liddell Hart concluded: "The Germans lost the chance of victory because they had based their mobility on wheels instead of on tracks. On these mud-roads the wheeled transport was bogged when the tanks could move on. Panzer forces with *tracked* transport might have overrun Russia's vital centres long before the autumn, despite the bad roads."[14] Only the peasant panje wagons could negotiate the mud.

Whether an August drive on Moscow—allowing a Russian retreat east of the Dnepr and leaving the eastern Ukraine and the Donbas unconquered—would have brought victory must remain conjectural. Barring the political collapse of the Stalinist regime, it would seem Hitler and the high command simply overestimated the capabilities of the Wehrmacht, and "we have underestimated the Russian colossus," as Halder at OKH had mused earlier, referring to both its immensity and its resources.[15]

But there was no scorched-earth strategy by Stavka, of deliberate retreat luring the invader ever deeper into Mother Russia, of destroying everything of use to the conqueror. The Red Army was ordered to stand fast, and it died doing so, three million prisoners of war alone attesting to its destruction. With the German invasion the Soviets did begin to evacuate some major armaments plants to the east, as the armor plate mills of Mariupol were shifted to Magnitogorsk, the

Kharkov tank engine plant went to Chelyabinsk in the Urals, and steel mills and heavy machine works were moved as well. Safely beyond German bomber range in the Urals and in western Siberia, the transplanted factories, in concert with the Stalinist industrialization of the 1930s, would enable the Soviet Union to finally prevail against the German onslaught.[16]

Meanwhile the German juggernaut churned ahead. In the south Kleist's Pz.Gr.1 panzers entered Rostov-on-Don on 20 October, the "gateway to the Caucasus," and the industrial center of Kharkov fell on the 24th. In Bock's H.Gr. Mitte drive on Moscow-*"Vorstoss auf Moskau!"* urging the soldiers on—Generalmajor Walter Krüger's 1. Panzer-Division of Reinhardt's Pz.Gr.3 took Kalinin north of Moscow, and in the center Hoepner's Pz.Gr.4 took Mozhaisk on the 19th, the night sky being lit by German bombardment and Russian antiaircraft fire over the capital. On the southern wing Guderian's 2. Panzerarmee struggled toward Tula, 4.Pz.Div. fending off attacks by Col. M. E. Katukov's 4th Tank Brigade. The latter's wide-tracked T-34s could roam where the narrow-tracked panzers could not. Related one panzer gunner, "The Russian tanks are so agile, at close ranges they will climb a slope or cross a piece of swamp faster than you can traverse the turret. And through the noise and the vibration you keep hearing the clangor of shot against armor. When they hit one of our panzers there is so often a deep long explosion, a roar as the fuel burns, a roar too loud, thank God, to let us hear the cries of the crew."[17] Guderian did not reach the edge of Tula until 31 October, with 3.Pz.Div., though the infantry of his LIII. A.K. flanked to the east, advancing toward the Oka and Kolomna.

There were other indications of stiffening Russian resistance as the Blitzkrieg drove forward. The 3., 7., and 18. Panzer-Divisionen all reported encounters with Russian "Minenhunde" (mine dogs), dogs saddled with explosives and trained to run under panzers, tripping a tilt rod as a detonator. It could not be considered worth the effort of the "Moscow Infantry Company" to train such dogs, but it added to the trials of the wary panzer crews who now scrutinized any dog for a saddle pack.[18] "Katyusha" ("Little Kate") rocket barrages, "Stalins Orgel" (Stalin's organ pipes) to the Germans, were now launched in regimental strength, and the German units struggling slowly through the mud became targets for Russian artillery. The mud roads were "corduroyed" with wooden logs laid down crosswise, making for an adequate if bumpy roadway, but still Kettenfahrzeuge (tracked vehicles) were needed to pull the Räderfahrzeuge (wheeled vehicles) through the quagmire by tow cables.

A significant clash took place on 14 October at Borodino on the high road 100 kilometers (62 miles) from Moscow, the site of Napoleon's Pyrrhic victory over Mikhail Kutusov in 1812. There the SS Reich Infanterie-Division (mot) and elements of 10.Pz.Div. fought their way through minefields and bunkers defended stubbornly by Russian troops both well equipped and clothed in quilted *winter* uniforms and fur caps (Ushanka) and boots. These were two regiments of the 32nd Siberian Rifle Division from Vladivostok, supported by two tank brigades with the formidable T-34s and KVs. The elite Waffen-SS troops prevailed, but the fighting was savage and casualties were heavy. What it also meant was that Stalin, reassured that Japan would not be attacking the Soviet Union, was beginning to redeploy forces from Russian Siberia along the Japanese–Manchurian border.

The long hostility between Russia and Japan over Manchuria had seen the Soviets build up their forces in Siberia, and tensed especially when Japan's Tripartite ally, Germany, invaded the USSR in June 1941. That the Japanese leadership had decided not to attack the Soviet Union from behind, but instead attack the Western powers to gain the Southeast Asia resource area, was information provided by a Communist agent in Tokyo, Dr. Richard Sorge. He was part of a vast network of Communist agents coordinated by the Soviet GRU (Chief Intelligence Directorate). A member of the Nazi Party but a longtime secret Communist, Sorge was a correspondent for the *Frankfurter Zeitung* and press attaché for the German ambassador in Tokyo, Eugen Ott. His contacts included Hotsumi Ozaki, advisor to Prime Minister Prince Fumimaro Konoye. While his earlier information that Germany was going to attack the Soviet Union was ignored by Stalin, the revelation now in early October that Japan would attack south, not north, enabled Stalin to shift forces from Siberia to help save Moscow. (Sorge was arrested by the Japanese 18 October, and he was executed in 1944.)

Two other spy rings transmitted crucial information to the director in Moscow: the "Lucy" network in Switzerland and the "Rote Kapelle" (Red Orchestra) in Germany itself. "Lucy" was the codename of a leftist German publisher in Lucerne, Switzerland, named Rudolf Rössler. His sources were ten World

War I companions, five of whom became generals serving in the OKW, including Gen. Fritz Thiele in the OKW cipher department. His associates were Alexander Rado, a Jewish Hungarian Communist, and Englishman Alexander Foote. They had also warned of the German invasion on 22 June, but had also been ignored. Subsequently their information was invaluable. (Tracing the transmissions to Switzerland, the Germans pressured the neutral Swiss, who finally arrested Foote 20 November 1943 and Rössler 19 May 1944. Rado escaped to the French Maquis, though he was ultimately tried in the Soviet Union—for espionage!—but ended up in Communist Hungary.)

The Gestapo and the Funkabwehr (radio counterintelligence) referred to the Soviet network in Germany as Rote Kapelle for the "music boxes," the Soviet term for radio transmitters. The principal agent was Harro Schulze-Boysen, a Luftwaffe Leutnant in the Air Ministry in Berlin. His contacts enabled his network to provide information of production figures, unit movements, and other vital information before he was arrested by the Gestapo 30 August 1942 and subsequently executed. But these GRU networks accomplished their goals in providing invaluable information at the most crucial time in the very existence of the USSR. There were no similar German counterparts.[19]

During the winter the Russians transferred some fifteen rifle divisions, three cavalry divisions, and eight tank brigades with 1,700 tanks, along with 1,500 aircraft, from the Far East across Russia to the fighting fronts. Of greater significance was that these were well-trained troops, experienced in the border clashes with the Japanese, and they were equipped and outfitted for, and inured to, the extreme cold of Siberia.

After the encirclement of the Vyazma pocket, the 11.Pz.Div. took up a Riegelstellung, a blocking position, generally along the Volosta River, against Russian attempts to break out. S.R.111 infantry were on the right, S.R.110 on the left, from 8 to 12 October. The difficulties of strengthening the encirclement pincers were exemplified by the experience of the Leichte Flakabteilung 71 and the wounding of its commander on 12 October. While the firing batteries were detached to the combat units, the L./71 battalion command post was at Mityuschino. Maj. Werner Jacobson's adjutant, Oblt. Ruddies, Ordonnanzoffizier (Orderly Officer) Lt. Eggert, and two messengers were in a small house on a street corner near the other staff personnel. Ruddies related that he and the Major had driven toward Vyasma during the day to coordinate with another flak unit. Returning in the darkness through a sinister wood they saw some soldiers with a machine gun but not in any front line, which he thought peculiar but, "Since the commander didn't say anything, neither did I."

At 22,00 hours the usual sign-off music, Lale Andersen's haunting "Lili-Marleen," came over the radio and they lay on their field cots half-dressed, with thoughts of home:

> Vor der Kaserne, vor dem grossen Tor,
> stand eine Laterne, und steht sie noch davor
>
> Underneath the lamppost, by the barrack gate,
> Darling I remember, the way you used to wait

But then distant firing came closer, and when Ruddies heard Russian voices, he pulled back the shelter half covering the window. *Russen!* Lt. Eggert, in his socks, grabbed his MPi and emptied a magazine through the window. With the cry of *"Urrah! Urrah!"* Russians were flitting through the village streets while tracers and grenade explosions gave off flashes of light. Major Jacobson went down, shot through the window. A Melder ran across the street to the battalion doctor, but was hit. With the wooden house on fire there was only one option: "*Raus*, as fast as possible." Ruddies and Eggert dragged their wounded Major out through the window—also taking the unit's KTB—and across the street to the battalion staff's Igel, where the Nachrichten Zug's Lt. Hochreuter had already been fatally wounded.

In Lt. Eggert's account the village was Losmino. The Melder was O.Gefr. Schleicher, shot in the leg, and Major Jacobson had been badly hit again as he was hoisted over the window ledge. Oberarzt Dr. Born himself was wounded, shot in the hip. As senior battery commander, Oblt. Gröning of 2.Battr. succeeded to command. Elsewhere the half-track–mounted 2cm Zwillings- and Vierlingsflak automatic cannon, along with machine guns and small arms, shattered many of the hordes of Rotarmisten, many having thrown away their weapons, who came flooding through the woods and across the fields. Some survivors surrendered, others simply disappeared into the countryside again.[20]

With the elimination of the Vyazma pocket the Elfte advanced again along the Rollbahn toward Moscow, but so extreme was the mud that the division was forced to a standstill in the Gzhatsk area on the 23rd. In addition, the 11.Pz.Div. was down 134 panzers and 427 other motor vehicles, and 504 were reported killed so far by the middle of October.[21] Lead units secured a bridgehead north of Borodino over the Rusa, a tributary of the Moskva River flowing into Moscow itself.

On 24 October Generalmajor Walter Scheller, a Hanoverian infantry officer, arrived to command the 11. Panzer-Division. Born 27 January 1892, he came from 8. Schützenbrigade, 8.Pz.Div. Von Esebeck had been ill most of October and was finally hospitalized, and Oberst Arno von Lenski had been acting commander. Von Lenski reverted to commanding 11.Schtz.-Brig. and then was reassigned as commander of the Schule für Schnelltruppen (School for Mobile Troops) at Krampnitz near Berlin by December, when Oberst Helwig Luz officially took over the brigade.

After he recovered, von Esebeck went to the 2.Pz.Div. on 17 February 1942, and when he went to XXXXVI. Panzer Korps, von Lenski, as a Generalmajor, succeeded him. Von Esebeck subsequently had other corps commands but was implicated in the 20 July 1944 conspiracy against Hitler and sent to a concentration camp. After the 2.Pz.Div. von Lenski commanded 24.Pz.Div., which he had to surrender at Stalingrad 2 February 1943; he then became a founder of the Soviet-sponsored Nationalkomitee Freies Deutschland and urged his former Kameraden to support the Soviet cause.[22]

On 31 October Gen.d.Pz.Tr. Heinrich von Vietinghoff ordered the 11.Pz.Div. on to Volokolamsk but even the tracked vehicles were almost immobile. Rain poured down, supplies were short, and mail didn't arrive, and any who sought shelter in evacuated Russian buildings found themselves crawling with lice. On 6 November there was frost, but on the 7th there was a thaw. At this point, with restricted fuel, an attack force was formed to push ahead under Oberstlt. Riebel. The force was composed of his Pz.-Rgt.15, with its I. Abteilung (ohne II.Abt.), one artillery battalion (I./119), and one company each of riflemen (2./S.R.110), of engineers (2./Pz.Pi.Btl.209), one battery of light flak (1./le.Fla.Abt.71), and a Panzerjäger company (from Pz.Jg.Abt.61).

The fighting was bitter. Vietinghoff's XXXXVI. Pz.Korps warned again about Russian Brandflaschen, "Molotowcoktails" (Molotov cocktails); these improvised bombs, made of bottles of gasoline with an igniter or a wick to be lit, would be tossed onto a panzer and then break, spreading flaming gasoline. In a report on 1 November Oberstlt. Riebel said that they were most dangerous when thrown on the rear deck (the engine compartment). Fire extinguishers had no effect; sand was the best retardant (though Riebel didn't elaborate on how this would be used, nor the negative effects it would have on the engine).[23]

On 9 November, because of losses, Pz. Aufklärungsabteilung 231 was dissolved, and its elements incorporated into the motorcycle battalion. Maj. Horst von Usedom of Krad-Schützen Bataillon 61 commanded the amalgamated unit as K.61. Von Usedom had commanded A.A.231 but succeeded Major von Götz at K.61 when Götz had been killed in action near Vyasma on 9 October. The new organization, dated 13 November 1941, listed 1. Kompanie with fourteen light Spähwagen and two Achtrad armored cars; 2., 3., and 4. motorcycle companies, each with three light platoons mounting six le.MG on the Kradbeiwagen (sidecar) and one light mortar, one heavy MG squad with two sMG, and one heavy mortar squad with two 8cm Granatwerfer; and 5.(schw.) Komp. with an I.G. platoon with four guns, a Pak platoon with six guns, and a Pionier platoon.[24]

On the 16th a hard freeze enabled the panzers to begin attacking again over new-fallen snow. XXXXVI. Pz. Korps had 5. and 11. Panzer-Divisionen break through defenses on both sides of the railroad station at Petrovskoye and drive to the Istra River reservoir, which they reached by the 24th. Attempts were made to whiten the panzers with chalk whitewash, and to provide scout patrols with improvised winter outfits. The temperature fell to –18 degrees Celsius (zero Fahrenheit). Though the reservoir was not yet frozen enough for vehicles to cross, K.61 established a bridgehead. The suffering of the ill-clad Landsers was becoming intense, but the magnet of "Moskau" drew them on.

Panzer strength in Pz.Rgt.15 was down to thirty-seven: I.Abt. had two Pz.II, eleven Pz.III, and five Pz.IV, totaling eighteen; II.Abt. had three Pz.II, eleven Pz.III, and five Pz.IV, totaling nineteen. The Panzer II with its little 2cm gun was useless in tank engagements—a "Schmetterlingsbüchse" (butterfly-collecting box) to the crews. They were of use with the reconnaissance battalion, though on firm ground the wheeled armored cars might get too far ahead. But with panzer losses, even the Pz.IIs were needed. Gefreiter Kurt Nentwig in his Wagen 4-5 of 5.Kp.

found himself in an attack with four Panzer IIIs to make it a larger "force." Suddenly he sighted a T-34 in a building. He wanted to alert the others, but only the platoon leader's Panzer II, 4-1, had a transmitter; 4-5 only had a receiver. In addition, his turret was frozen and wouldn't traverse.

Nonetheless Nentwig had his driver pivot 4-5 toward the building and Sprenggranate caught the roof on fire, forcing the Russian tank out to be engaged. In the meantime one Pz.III had been hit. The commander, Feldwebel Oskar Scholle, lost his legs, but the truncated stumps froze and he survived to have amputations and prostheses. The loader died of head wounds, but the other three crew members survived. The T-34 was knocked out and the attack pressed on.[25]

On 25 November the Pioniere put in a 300-meter-long plank bridge across the Istra Reservoir ice to get 5-ton vehicles and weapons across to support the K.61 bridgehead, only to see it smashed by a Russian shell and the ice broken. The Gespensters of II./S.R.110 also were able to get across, but the heavy weapons and artillery were held on the west bank. During the night Pz.Pi.Btl.209 prepared a 12-ton ferry that crunched through the thin ice and got twelve trucks across. Other elements crossed the Istra farther upstream behind 5.Pz.Div. and others worked around the south end of the reservoir.

By the 29th the 11. Panzer, supported by Stuka attacks, converged southward on Alabushevo on the railroad line northwest of Moscow, and the highway to Klin and Kalinin at Matushkino. By the last day of November Kampfgruppe Fricke, Oberst Ludwig Fricke commanding S.R.111, and Kgr. Luz, S.R.110, igelt around Alabushevo and Matushkino. Elements of Gen.Maj. Gustav Fehn's 5. Silesian Pz.Div. and the 35.Inf.Div. on the left flank also fought south toward Moscow. At Kryukovo the Elfte's lead elements were only 25 kilometers (16 miles) from Moscow.[26]

In the first days of December the drive on Moscow continued against fierce Russian resistance, including rocket barrages of the Stalins Orgel and clashes with T-34 tanks. Significantly, some of the Russian troops had white padded cotton-wool Siberian snow outfits. On 2 December the temperature was down to minus-25 degrees (minus-13 F) and by the 5th had dropped to minus-30 (minus-22 F). The ground was so hard that only hand grenades tamped might blast a shallow grave for the gefallen, and automatic weapons refused to function. Yet at night fires from bombing raids on Moscow lit the sky and indicated how close the objective was. On the night of 5–6 December Hauptmann Walter Schaefer-Kehnert, with the division since 1940 and now signals officer with III.Abteilung/A.R.119, had a long-range 10cm cannon brought forward to shell the Kremlin. With its maximum range of 18,900 meters (18.9 kilometers) it could at least reach the suburbs, and Schaefer-Kehnert could believe this was the only German artillery to actually shell the city.[27]

On 5 December the Ia's KTB registered –32 degrees (–26 F) and noted that "Entrenching troops in the stone-hard, frozen ground is simply not possible."[28] At 15,30 hours that day division commander Scheller advised Oberstlt. Riebel of Pz.Rgt.15 that if the situation deteriorated, the front-line units should fall back to a line stretching between Andreyevskoye and Alexandrovka. On the 6th, a second day at –32 degrees, the Ia of XXXXVI. Pz.Korps met with the division Ia's at the command post of the 5.Pz.Div., to announce the decision that the battle for Moscow would *not* be continued, and the corps would fall back behind the Istra River. Construction of the Hauptkampflinie with log bunkers would begin. There were also command changes. After von Lenski left, Oberst Luz took over 11.S.B., Oberst Ludwig Fricke took over 110, and Oberst Bohlmann-Combrinck resumed command of Schützenregiment 111.

In the three weeks between 17 November and 9 December, the 11.Pz.Div. had 1,188 casualties, including 6 officers and 226 men killed in action and 37 missing. Not surprisingly, the largest losses were among the infantry, with the reconnaissance unit having the highest proportion: K.61 (including A.A.231) lost 281, including 1 officer and 67 men killed, and 14 missing; S.R.111 lost 360 including 1 officer and 67 men killed, and 2 missing; S.R.110 lost 319 including 3 officers and 65 men killed, and 4 missing; Pz.Rgt.15 lost 85 including 13 men killed, and 4 missing; Pz.Jg.Abt.61 lost 48 including 1 officer and 10 men killed; Pz.Pi.Btl.209 lost 40 men including 9 killed; Art.Rgt.119 lost 40 men including 6 killed; Pz.Nachr.Abt.341 lost 13 men including 5 killed, and 1 missing; and the Sanitätsdienst 61 reported 2 wounded.[29]

On 7 December the retreat began, with the sarcastic codeword "*Weihnachtsurlaub, 1. Reisetag*" —Christmas vacation, first travel day.[30]

CHAPTER TEN

Russian Winter: 1941–42

THE DAY OF 6 DECEMBER 1941 WAS THE HIGH-WATER MARK OF Operation BARBAROSSA. Heeresgruppe Nord had isolated Leningrad by reaching Lake Ladoga and Tikhvin. In Heeresgruppe Mitte Panzergruppe 3 had reached Kalinin, Pz.Gr. 4 had taken Klin and reached the Moskva–Volga Canal north of Moscow, and 2. Panzerarmee was beyond Tula almost to Kolomna and the Oka. H.Gr. Süd had taken Kharkov and most of the Ukraine, and was besieging Sevastopol in the Crimea. 1. Pz.Armee had given up Rostov on the Don but had stabilized a position along the Mius River in the Donbas.

Nevertheless, the objective of the campaign, the defeat of the Soviet Union, had not been accomplished. In retrospect Russia's resources, weather, terrain, and resilience had all been underestimated, as numerous analysts have discussed. The weather aspects had not been ignored by the German command. Meteorological statistics dating back to the nineteenth century indicated heavy snow and subzero temperatures should not be expected before mid-December. In addition, many German commanders were familiar with weather and terrain conditions from World War I, even if they were unsure how mechanized forces might fare. The winter of 1941–42 was exceptional. Yet the USSR had still been brought to the verge of defeat, and in 1941 few expected it to survive the Blitzkrieg that had overrun the rest of Europe. That massive Russia had collapsed into revolution and surrender in World War I was a precedent to be considered seriously. The German onslaught would be renewed, as the spring of 1942 would prove. But in 1941 the Wehrmacht was indeed stopped by "General Mud and Marshal Winter."

In the meantime, it was gradually being recognized that the Soviet Union still had tremendous resources, and that its war production was able to replace material losses. On 1 December an intelligence summary from the Eastern Intelligence Division of OKH gave a sobering estimate of Soviet forces: 263 rifle divisions, 41.5 cavalry divisions, and 51 tank brigades, of which 200, 35, and 40 of these, respectively, were facing the Wehrmacht. The 136 German divisions were qualitatively still superior, but had suffered losses up to 50 percent. The 11. Panzer-Division alone had lost almost 1,200 men in the preceding three weeks. Hitler's Weisung Nr. 39 of 8 December acknowledged the difficulties and ordered the cessation of offensive operations, and the order was implemented in detailed instructions by OKH that same day.[1]

By the 7th the Russians had begun a series of attacks, though poorly coordinated, all along the German front, and these assaults grew in intensity. On that same 7 December (8 December Tokyo time) the Japanese launched a surprise attack that crippled American naval and airpower at Pearl Harbor and in the Philippines. Hitler seems to have been caught unawares by the Japanese action but dutifully supported his Axis ally by declaring war on the United States on 11 December. Many were now fully conscious that the Reich was embroiled in a world war.

North of Moscow Ivan Konev's Kalinin Front began attacks on Reinhardt's Panzergruppe 3 on the 5th, and Zhukov's West Front joined in against Hoepner's Pz.Gr.4 on the 6th on the Klin sector. South of Moscow Zhukov's left flank armies assaulted Guderian's 2. Panzerarmee, and Zhukov optimistically contemplated the encirclement and destruction of all the panzer forces. But the Germans slowly withdrew—Klin was given up on 15 December, Kalinin the next day—and were able to consolidate their lines. Although the 11. Panzer-Division blunted the Russian attacks on the 7th by committing all reserves, at 17,00 hours the ordered retreat began. Deep snow and fuel shortages forced the abandoning of a number of Fahrzeuge. Instead the ubiquitous Russian panje wagons, the shaggy horses now pulling sleighs, once again kept supplies moving, causing some Gespensters to refer to their division as the "Panjedivision."

While the panzer units suffered in the harsh winter weather, the infantry—the "Fusslatscher" (foot-sloggers) fighting in the open—suffered more so. And having less firepower, they were hard-pressed by the Rotarmisten attacks. On 13 December Oberleutnant Kaphengst with a reduced company of panzers, antitank weapons from S.R.110, and a company of combat engineers, was detached to support the 35.I.D. to the left. On the 15th elements of the Elfte pulled back from the Istra to the so-called Boldenka Line, and then to the Rusa River Line. A humiliation followed on 18 December, when General Vietinghoff at XXXXVI. Pz.Korps ordered the combat-capable units of the 11.Pz.Div. to be subordinated to the command of Gustav Fehn's 5.Pz.Div. as "Kampfverbandes Scheller" (Battle Unit Scheller).[2] Fehn indeed later went on to corps commands including XXXX. Pz.Korps and the DAK, and may have been considered the more able commander. (After leaving the 11.Pz.Div. in May 1942 Scheller commanded the 9.Pz.Div. but was relieved by Feldmarschall Walter Model and returned to infantry commands.) The remaining units of the Gespenster-Division at least retained their proud identity.

What was becoming the harshest Russian winter in 140 years put personnel, vehicles, and equipment to the extreme test. At –30 degrees Celsius (–22 Fahrenheit) lubricants froze up, and recoil-operated automatic weapons cycled sluggishly or refused to cycle at all. The charging handle and bolt had to be worked to get off single shots. All oil and grease had to be wiped off, and ordinary sunflower seed oil was found best to keep weapons from freezing. Oil was added to the MG 34 only when warmed, by firing short bursts ("*Angstschiessen,*" or fear shooting) at night. Handgranate were the most effective infantry weapon.

While Hitler forbade major withdrawals and preparing rear positions ("driveling nonsense" Franz Halder at OKH recorded him saying), his insistence that units roll up in "Igelstellen" ("hedgehog positions") around towns and villages, instead of maintaining an HKL in the open, enabled the Wehrmacht to survive the winter weather that had caused Napoleon's *Grande Armee* to collapse in panicked retreat in 1812.[3] Even the primitive Russian huts provided a source of warmth for the wounded and those manning exposed positions. Psychologically too, knowing there was a chance of rotating back to warmth to thaw out every few hours enabled the Landsers to maintain their discipline. Conversely, the villages were also targets of Russian artillery to destroy them as havens, and the izbas (huts) were usually infested with lice.

Newsprint, even Russian propaganda pamphlets, were stuffed behind the Germans' thin field jackets and overcoats as insulation. Paper was also stuffed in boots, for the hobnails conducted cold temperatures. Panzer troops, at least, had high-laced leather shoes. Captured Russians, it was noted, had oversized boots with room for cloth or paper stuffing. Russian felt boots were highly desirable, said Gefreiter Werner von Koblinski, as panzers had no heater other than the engine, as was the Russian fur Ushanka hat. Pump-pressure benzin stoves inside panzers were Verboten after one tipped over while the crew was asleep and detonated the ammunition.

Ice froze hatches shut, and even when covered with canvas tarpaulins (which froze in position) armored vehicles in the open froze up amid the icy wind. In one account, "The method we used to thaw out the engine was to partly fill empty ration tins with earth and to pour on to these either methylated spirits or petrol which we set fire to and put one under the engine and another under the differential." This was done under the cover of the tarpaulin acting as a wind shield, and also to hide the light from the occasional Russian Rata aircraft.[4] The Russian T-34, on the other hand, had a compressed-air starter that enabled the engine to turn over even in extreme cold.

Tracked vehicles had to be parked on pine boughs or straw, or the Ketten would freeze solid to the ground. Sentries had to start the engines every hour or so and run them for 10–15 minutes. Running the engines and burning fires kept engine oils and fuel lines from freezing, though 9–10 centimeters of frost might still form in the interior of a panzer. Once thawed, water dripped down the hull causing electrical shorts until maintenance could dry out or replace the wiring for starters, fuel pumps, and oil pumps.[5] Just as summer dust and sand demanded constant attention to engine filters, so did deep winter require constant efforts by crews and maintenance personnel. But vehicle steel was blistering cold, and touching the metal with ungloved hands could result in tearing off the skin while trying to unstick them.

The artillery found that breech blocks, recoil systems, and sensitive elevating and traversing gear all had to be protected and heated to work. Propellant charges affected the flight of projectiles, and adjustment of fire was made difficult by the shells burying themselves in the deep snowfields. Dysentery and exposing body parts while answering a call of nature resulted in massive casualties, and frostbite to limbs resulted in amputations. In field hospitals there was the stench of gangrene, and soldiers dreaded the black line drawn on limbs by attendants marking the frozen part for amputation.

Those who survived that winter were awarded the specially struck *Ostmedaille* for the Winter Battle in the East 1941/42, sarcastically referred to as the "*Gefrierfleisch Orden*," the "Order of the Frozen Meat." The center stripes of the dark red ribbon were not the national colors, but the decree stated the red represented blood, the white was for snow, and the black for the fallen. It was later worn at the second buttonhole, usually reserved for the EK 2. ribbon.[6]

The other services also faced winter challenges. Luftwaffe Feldwebel Fritz Waldmann said ground crews could be shocked on awakening to find the entire airfield empty of planes—almost completely buried under several meters of snow. The primary task of sentries, in fact, was to keep the entrances and smokestacks of the makeshift bunkers shoveled out, or the men sleeping might be suffocated by woodfire smoke inhalation. OKH subsequently distributed a handbook, *Taschenbuch für den Winterkrieg* (August 1942), of how to cope with Russia's winters, like building hard-packed snow walls and revetments to provide shelter from the freezing wind and even some protection from small-arms fire and shell fragments.[7]

In the December crisis Hitler's determination to hold firm, realizing that a retreat could degenerate into a rout, resulted in dramatic changes in command. Of all three army groups, Wilhelm Ritter von Leeb of H.Gr. Nord and (earlier) Gerd von Rundstedt of H.Gr. Süd, both of whom advocated retreating to Poland, were removed (replaced by Georg von Küchler and Walter von Reichenau, respectively), Fedor von Bock of H.Gr. Mitte resigned with ill health (replaced by Günther von Kluge), two of the four panzer group commanders, Heinz Guderian and Erich Hoepner, were relieved, and thirty-five corps and divisional commanders were relieved or reassigned.

At OKH GFM Walter von Brauchitsch, Oberbefehlshaber des Heeres (ObdH), resigned 7 December. It was accepted on the 19th, with Hitler assuming direct command with the comment, "Anybody can do that bit of operational planning." Generaloberst Franz Halder thought it his duty to stay on as Chef des Generalstabes des Heeres to ameliorate the most drastic decisions that might be forthcoming from Der Führer. Ever more distrustful of the officers of the General Staff, Hitler would increasingly make operational and even tactical decisions from his *Wolfsschanze* (Wolf's Lair) headquarters in the recesses of the Rastenburg east Prussian forests.[8]

By 20 December the 11. Panzer-Division elements were back west of Gzhatsk northeast of Vyazma, and the division Gefechtsstand was at Chernovo. Replacements could not offset losses, leaving all units understrength. Oberst Heinz Matena of Art.Rgt.119 was seriously ill. He left in February and never returned to the division, but after recovering was posted to a training area. With Christmas Eve on 24 December some units were able to celebrate Weihnacht, some even with a decorated Tannenbaum, a little fir tree, in a Russian izba. Schnaps and a cigar supplemented the meager rations, though emotions turned to home and family, singing the familiar, *Ihr Kinderlein Kommet*, *Es ist ein Ros' Entsprungen*, *O du Frohliche*, and *Stille Nacht, Heilige Nacht.*

During this time combat elements were subordinated to the 5.Pz.Div., and when the last six panzers were handed over on Christmas Day, the proud Elfte had no panzers. Some wits sarcastically referred to themselves as "Panzersoldaten zu Fuss" (Armored Foot Troops). Many Gespensters, still clad in their black panzer uniforms—layered with any other clothing for warmth—now manned front positions as infantry.[9]

The 1941 fighting in Russia had seen many casualties, but also acts of bravery and leadership. Numerous Iron Crosses had been awarded, both the EK 2 and the higher EK 1. Six Ritterkreuz were also awarded in 1941, to be worn at the neck. Three were awarded to unit commanders: Oberst Helwig Luz of S.R.110, Oberst Theodor Bohlmann-Combrinck of S.R.111, and Maj. Horst von Usedom of K.61. Division commander Crüwell had received the Eichenlaub in September. The other three were Oberleutnant Bruno Freiherr von Brackel and Oberfeldwebel Gerhard Hensel of Pz.Rgt.15, and Hauptmann Willi Welsch of S.R.110. Infantry Assault, Panzer Engagement, and Wound badges were also awarded and worn.

Proving very useful were the Hilfsfreiwillige, auxiliary Russian volunteers. Some Hiwis were Überläufer, and some had been captured or had surrendered but were not yet processed as Kriegsgefangene. They began to be listed as a category in the Ia's Verpflegungsstärke (ration strength) reports. Kurt Nentwig recalled three Hiwis working with his 5.Kp. of Pz.Rgt.15 as mechanics or truck drivers. He remembered in particular one "Alexei," an engineer from Tula drafted into the Red Army, convinced he would return to Tula after a German victory even after many Landsers no longer believed such a thing possible (perhaps knowing his fate if he fell into Soviet hands again). When the unit's Küchenwagen (mess truck) developed a crack in the motor in the extreme cold, the I-Staffel and Werkstattkompanie gave up on it. But Alexei worked in the subzero temperatures and bored holes and hammered in short pieces of welding wire and repaired it, winning him the admiration of the men. The vehicle served for almost a year before being destroyed by a Russian bomb near Rostov-on-Don. Nentwig met Alexei again at Sagan after the Elfte was transferred to the West in 1944, this time in a German uniform. At a postwar regimental reunion he understood that Alexei had emigrated to Australia, or at least Nentwig hoped that was the case.[10]

By 1 January 1942 the HKL with the combat elements attached to the 5.Pz.Div. was just east of Gzhatsk astride the Rollbahn, the snow-covered main highway connecting Smolensk, Vyasma, and Moscow. The temperature could still drop to –25 C but was "better" than the record low of –53 C (–63 F) recorded northwest of Moscow on the 26th. While the Gespenster-Division awaited rebuilding (what some called the days of "Nichtstun," or downtime), three Sicherungsgruppe (security groups) were ordered formed by General Richard Ruoff, now commanding 4. Panzerarmee (the redesignated Pz.Gr.4). These units were to provide security at key vehicle and railroad bridges in the sector around Dorogobush on the upper Dnepr. Partisan attacks were becoming more frequent and more sophisticated, and would evolve into "Bandenkrieg," or anti-guerrilla warfare.[11]

The panzer troops were not prepared for this type of conflict, and the first methods tried were improvised. Security outposts might be a log-constructed MG position, and patrols might be reinforced by a small Panzer II, with its 2cm cannon useless in tank warfare, but providing additional firepower for anti-guerrilla operations. Initially the strongpoints were not harassed. On a day of moderating temperatures one group of Gespensters for variety thought to use hand grenades to go fishing in the Dnepr, but the river ice was too thick.[12]

While Russia had a tradition of guerrilla warfare against an invader, as against Napoleon's French forces, there seems to have been no significant prewar policy or preparation for this. In the 1930s the Defense Commissariat did planning for Communist Party cadre as partisan nuclei and for secret bases in an invader's rear, but during the 1937 purges of the military Stalin had the members shot or imprisoned because he believed such preparations were "defeatist." On 3 July 1941, in his first public statement to the Soviet people since the shock of the German invasion twelve days earlier, Stalin called for the evacuation or destruction of anything of value to the enemy, and "In areas occupied by the enemy, partisan units, mounted and on foot, must be formed; sabotage groups must be organized to combat enemy units, to foment partisan warfare everywhere, blow up bridges and roads, damage telephone and telegraph lines, set fires to forests, stores, and transport."[13] But in the confusion of collapsing Red armies and the rapid German advances there was little popular resistance, especially among a population only too glad to see the hated commissars and other apparatchiki of the Communist Party and NKVD leave. What resistance there was came from Red Army units cut off and bypassed, and was often random, as they more often sought to escape.

On 10 July the Partisan Movement was officially organized and placed under Lev Mekhlis, chief of the Main Administration of the Political Propaganda of the Red Army. On the 11th Mekhlis issued orders to political commissars of the army fronts and in the republics endangered by the German advance to form and equip partisan combat battalions. Companies or platoons were to operate only at night and from ambush, attacking troop columns and convoys, camps, transports of fuel and ammunition, headquarters, air bases, and railroad trains stopped by rail demolitions. In addition, smaller diversionary units were to be formed to undertake sabotage, cut telephone lines, and attack individuals and small groups of enemy vehicles. There was no mention regarding taking prisoners of war. "Partisany! Avenge Without Mercy!" urged the recruiting posters.[14]

The motive was threefold: first, to harass the German forces; secondly, to reassert Soviet political influence over the populations under German occupation; and thirdly, to generate German reprisals that would alienate the populations of occupied areas. Regarding irregular warfare, Article One of The Hague Convention for Land Warfare of 1907 stated:

> The laws, rights, and duties of war apply not only to armies, but also to militia and volunteer corps fulfilling the following conditions:
>
> 1. To be commanded by a person responsible for his subordinates.
> 2. To have a fixed distinctive emblem recognizable at a distance.
> 3. To carry arms openly.
> 4. To conduct their operations in accordance with the laws and customs of war.[15]

But adhering to these conditions would negate the advantages of having partisans *indistinguishable* from the local population; nor did the Soviets, like other guerrilla-sponsoring agencies, have any intention of doing so. Although the Soviet Union considered itself bound by The Hague Convention and the first Geneva Convention regarding the rules of war, it had never ratified the Geneva Covenant of 1929 on treatment of prisoners of war.

Germany had signed the relevant agreements, though on 3 July OKH issued a clarifying directive that soldiers in uniform, or in civilian clothes, were to be accorded rights as prisoners of war. But "Civilians in mufti or half uniform found with arms are to be considered guerrillas." On 18 July OKH elaborated that members of partisan units, when not wearing a uniform or recognizable insignia, as well as inhabitants who aided them, were to be considered guerrillas and treated as such (i.e., executed). Some of the German field armies announced a time limit before which Red soldiers in the rear should surrender or be considered guerrillas. In September 1941 Hitler further defined their status by stating that this would only apply to combat troops belonging to units that had previously surrendered. Those on a definite mission behind the German lines would be treated as prisoners of war if captured. Brutal German rear-area occupation policies, reflecting Hitler's personal hatreds, however, soon began to alienate the Russian population, and partisan numbers would grow.[16]

With heavy losses, the 11. Panzer-Division was withdrawn west of Gzhatsk. Units sent individuals to two-week "winter courses" in Gzhatsk conducted by instructors from the Heereshochgebirgsschule (Army High Mountain School). Subjects included weapons maintenance, hygiene, and other preparations for winter. Ski and sled techniques were taught for those who would lead Jagdkommandos (Hunter Commands) against partisans.[17] But the winter was already proving far harsher than expected.

As it had been anticipated that Russia would be defeated in the 1941 campaign, occupation policy was still in its formative stages. The army administered the Operationsgebiet (Operations Zone) adjacent to the front, with sectors behind each army controlled by an appointed Korück (Kommandant Rückwärtiges Armeegebiet, Commandant Army Rear Area). OKH had organized nine security divisions composed of older soldiers outfitted with captured French and Czech weapons. On 1 September 1941 the occupied Russian areas came under two civilian Reich commissariats (Ostland for the Baltic states and Belorussia, and Ukraine), whose military security was responsible to the OKW, not OKH. The SS police units also operated in these zones though they were primarily responsible to the Reichssicherheitshauptamt (RSHA, Reich Security Main Office) under SS Obergruppenführer Reinhard Heydrich.[18]

In the Pz.A.O.K. 4 (Armee Oberkommando) rear area, Scheller's 11. Panzer elements were formed into Sicherungsgruppen to protect and defend the Rollbahn and railroad supply lines from parachute, air-landed, cavalry, and partisan units, which were sometimes supplemented by Red Army units. Gespenster units might "igelt" around the villages as Hitler ordered, but the lines of communication also had to be kept open. With losses and detachments, including to 5.Pz.Div., "the division is being plundered," complained the Ia, Major Selmayr, to XXXXVI. Pz.Korps.[19] Without panzers, even panzer companies were now "zu Fuss."

By 13 January 1942 the 11.Pz.-Div. and other units, including battalions of Inf.Rgt.309 and 338 of the 208.I.D. and of Schützenregiment 13 of 5.Pz.Div., took over protection of the Rollbahn and Eisenbahn between Smolensk and Vyasma, including the Dnepr crossings. Two armored trains also patrolled the rail line. The hit-and-run Russian raids, with the Russian units unable (or unwilling) to take prisoners, contributed to the brutality of Bandenkrieg. Caught in the middle were the civilian populations who often assisted the paramilitary groups, whether willingly or unwilling. In one Strafexpedition (punishment expedition) under Hauptmann Paul von Hauser against Bogdanovchina the suspect population was removed from the village, after which "It went up in flames."[20]

The Russian winter offensive consisted of attacks all along the front lines from the Volkhov near Leningrad and Izyum south of Kharkov, to the Kerch Peninsula on the Crimea. In Heeresgruppe Mitte, 4. and 2. Panzerarmee fell back from the Kaluga and Tula areas to a Vyazma–Orel–Kursk line. Astride the H.Gr. Nord and Mitte boundary Konev's Kalinin Front armies had thrust toward Vitebsk on the Dvina. But the northern shoulder held at Demyansk, and Walter Model's 9. and Richard Ruoff's 4. Pz.Armee held a salient at Rzhev. On 20 January the separated elements of Scheller's 11. Panzer-Division were put under IX. Armee Korps. The ration strength of the Gespenster-Division on the 20th was 4,805 (including 140 officers, 25 Beamte, 874 non-commissioned officers, and 3,766 enlisted men). Weapons included only 147 machine guns and 26 heavier ordnance. Pz.Pi.Btl.209 was with IX. A.K., and two Kampfbataillonen were with 5.Pz.Div.[21]

In addition to Russian attacks and partisan actions, Red Army parachutists were dropped in the Vyazma area and cavalry swept out of the snow and gloom with billowing cloaks and flashing sabers. As thinly stretched as the German forces were, however, the Russian attacks were dissipated all along the front instead of being concentrated, and ultimately did not achieve any significant objective. Gen. Georgi Zhukov of West Front had argued for a concentrated offensive against H.Gr. Mitte in a Stavka conference on 5 January, but had been overruled by Stalin.[22]

Nonetheless it seemed that Russian forces were everywhere. In the Gzhatsk-Vyazma area the cavalry were of Maj. Gen. Pavel Belov's I Guards Cavalry Corps, while Col. S. V. Sokolov's XI Cavalry Corps struck from the north, and the major parachute drops were from Maj. Gen. A. F. Levashov's IV Parachute Corps. But the Luftwaffe bombed the relevant airfields, and some 2,000 parachutists were dropped over several nights and scattered over wide areas. They often tumbled out at low altitude into deep snowfields, and thus had difficulty forming as organized units. On 15 January Hitler did allow consolidation along the Königsberg Line (K-Line) stretching between Rzhev, Gzhatsk, Orel, and Kursk, as proposed by Bock earlier.[23]

In the fighting at Golotshelevo, which occurred amid snowstorms and poor visibility against a cavalry force on 27 January, Sicherungsbataillon Hauser's companies had an average strength of thirty-four, and the unit lost six killed and ten wounded. Similar to reports of other security units Btl. Hauser claimed eighty Russian casualties, and reported three machine guns, four Pak, and three Pz. Büchsen (antitank rifles) captured. But unlike in the other unit reports, here twenty Gefangene were listed as "erschossen."[24] Operations were mounted to make areas "gesäubert" (cleansed), "Feind-frei" (free of enemy).

On 6 February 1942 Scheller signed off on a basic order regarding the civilian population in the rear area of Ruoff's Panz.A.O.K. 4 ; the order included a stipulation that all who were military-capable between sixteen and fifty years of age who had received military training were to be handled as Kriegsgefangene, and taken to Durchgangslager (Dulag, Transit Camp) 155 at Dorogobush on the upper Dnepr and Dulag 164 at Bahnhof Dorogobush. Decrees were to be posted in villages warning that anyone taking hostile action against German soldiers would be shot.[25] These were fairly standard procedures. But rear-area security and anti-partisan actions were not anything that front-line combat soldiers relished. Eighty-five members of 1. Batterie/Art.Rgt.119 (zu Fuss) were part of the garrison of 429 under a Major Sichler at Dorogobush when it was attacked by Russian air-landed, regular, and partisan forces. Major Sichler of Korück 4. Pz. Armee was wounded, and the city had to be evacuated on 15 February. Two officers and twenty-nine men of the garrison had been missing since 9 February, presumably seized by partisans.[26]

Gen. Walter von Unruh, Korück 4. Armee, felt that improvised patrols and raids were inadequate to suppress the partisan activity and that major operations were required. After partisans and regular troops encircled the German garrison at Yelnya on 13 March, and still occupied Dorogobush, Unternehmen MÜNCHEN (Operation MUNICH) was planned, under Korück H.Gr. Mitte. 221.Sicherungsdivision commanded by Generalleutnant Pflugbeil was to control elements of Gen.Maj. Wolfgang Fischer's 10.Pz.Div. and Scheller's 11.Pz.Div. The plan was to drive on Yelnya from Pochinok on the Smolensk–Roslavl rail line to relieve the encircled garrison, then advance north to link up with an attack toward Dorogobush down from the Smolensk–Vyazma rail line and clear the Dorogobush–Smolensk–Yelnya triangle.

MÜNCHEN was put into motion on 19 March, and the Yelnya garrison relieved on the 28th. On the 22nd the Elfte recorded fighting strength as 5,300 personnel, along with one howitzer and six panzers. The use of airpower was significant: an anti-partisan squadron of VIII. Fliegerkorps based at Bobryusk carried out bombing, strafing, and reconnaissance missions. But with partisan counterattacks and continuing fighting into April, MÜNCHEN was not completed.[27]

In May a much larger operation was planned, Unternehmen HANNOVER. Under 4. Armee command two corps with elements of nine divisions would drive westward across the Vyazma–Bryansk railroad line toward Smolensk compressing partisan forces toward a cordon line, a "hammer-and-anvil" concept. Vietinghoff's XXXXVI. Panzerkorps with 5.Pz.Div. and 23. and 197.Inf.Div. would advance from the northeast and XXXXIII. A.K. with 19.Pz.Div. and 34. and 131.I.D. would advance from the southeast. The cordon forces were 11.Pz.Div. on the north side, Polizei Rgt. Mitte on the west side, and 221. Sicherungsdivision and composite 442. Division along the south side.

Because the units were understrength, the German units perhaps numbered 30,000–45,000, while the Germans estimated the Soviet forces at around 20,000. On 24 May HANNOVER began, and the drives continued into June. On 9 June General Belov with at least 2,000 men broke out south through the 221.Sicherungsdivision. Most of the fighters joined partisan forces around Kirov and Bryansk, and Belov was flown out for future commands. German casualties totaled some 2,200, while Soviet casualties were some 10,500, including 5,000 Kriegsgefangene. Other Russian fighters melted away, and HANNOVER was generally considered successful.[28]

At this time the 11.Pz.Div. was under the acting command of Oberst Helwig Luz of 11. Schützenbrigade while Scheller was on extended leave, and pending the arrival of Oberst Hermann Balck as new division commander. It is not clear what Gespenster elements were involved in HANNOVER, as the division was being withdrawn for Auffrischung (refitting). In any case, on 29 May a Vorbefehl (Alert Order) was issued for moving the division to a new sector near Kursk for the coming 1942 summer offensive.[29]

While front-line units were committed in Bandenkrieg, elements of the Wehrmacht were not to be involved with the anti-Jewish policies of the regime (though some evidently were). On 24 April 1942 a Summary of Instructions in the Heeresgruppe Mitte (rear area) distributed at least to divisions, included Point 4: "Any communication with Jews is forbidden. Troops on duty or off are to abstain from participating in actions of the police against Jews."[30] This can be read as an awareness of anti-Jewish policies, though in general these were already known to a certain extent. In any case, the 11.Pz.Div. was refitting for battle.

Chaotic fighting continued into the spring before the Russian offensives were exhausted and the Rasputitsa/Schlammperiode of March saw operations coming to an end. Spring came to Russia with a rush, the river ice breaking up with echoing cracking and a profusion of bright flowers suddenly blanketing the countryside in color. Russian folksongs—"The Red Sarafan," "In Praise of Raspberries"—reflected springtime love anew. But the magic of spring was a nightmare for the mechanized forces. The melting snow and recurrent thaws flooded the waterways and the fields became knee-deep in mud. Roadways were a morass into which vehicles sank up to their fenders, and even the Kettenfahrzeuge barely struggled on. Only by horse-drawn panje carts or by railroad was movement possible.[31]

On 12 April OKH had ordered the Auffrischung of the 11. Panzer-Division. At the time it had a Gefechtsstärke of 5,045, with a Grabenstärke (infantry trench strength) of 2,316, with two artillery pieces and six panzers einsatzbereit. On the 13th the Gespensters took over the sector around Yartsevo northeast of Smolensk and some of the equipment of Fischer's 10.Pz.Div. The 10. had suffered such heavy losses that it was sent back to the Amiens area of occupied France to rebuild in May. Thus the Elfte was to be refitted while simultaneously carrying out combat missions. On the 15th Scheller issued a Tagesbefehl ending with a barely concealed irony:

> The Winter Campaign 1941/42 is at an end. At its conclusion the German soldier stands as victor of the Russian soldier and his space and climate.[32]

Concentrated in the Borisov area, the division received replacement personnel and equipment from Sagan and its recruiting district, Wehrkreis VIII Schlesien. Some of the new Gespensters had very varied backgrounds. In 1940 Heinz Kutscheid, after hearing an address by Luftwaffe Ritterkreuzträger ace Maj. Werner Mölders, volunteered for the Luftwaffe, but then was ordered to Ochamps Kaserne in Wiesbaden for infantry communications training. Declared medically fit for the tropics, Kutscheid was destined for the Afrika Korps. But his ship in the Italian convoy was torpedoed by a British submarine off Benghazi, and the survivors were transported to Tripoli. From there, however, he was returned to the Continent, reassigned to the 11.Pz.Div. in Russia, and served in S.R.111.[33]

Some company members of Pz.Rgt.15 went back to Magdeburg to accompany new panzers forward. These were upgunned Panzer III and Pz.IV models, while the Panzer Is and IIs were withdrawn, fit only for security roles. The Pz.Kpfw. III was upgunned from the short 3,7cm L/45 and short 5cm L/42 to the long, high-velocity 5cm L/60. Hitler had ordered this more accurate and more powerful gun in 1940, but Ordnance had substituted the inferior short, low-velocity 5cm L/42 Kw.K. Hitler was "extremely angry," though exactly how the specifications were changed has never been determined. Thus the Ausführung G had the shorter 5cm L/42. Some earlier models (A–F) were retrofitted as well. The H model had additional 30mm armor plates bolted onto the 30mm frontal hull and turret armor.

The J model (as Sd.Kfz. 141/1) first mounted the 5cm L/60 gun with a muzzle velocity of 823 m/s (2,700 fps). Penetrating 60mm (2.4-inch) armor at 30 degrees, L/60 rounds could even knock out the early models (A and B) of the dreaded T-34. The J model carried fewer main gun rounds (eighty-four instead of ninety-nine) because of the bigger gun, and its weight increased to 22 tons with better 50mm (2-inch) armor, necessitating reinforced suspension and wider tracks. Extra steel track sections carried on the bow plates provided further protection.[34]

Supplementing the Pz. III in the panzer divisions was the Pz.Kpfw. IV. In the F2 model, produced after March 1942, the short 7,5cm Kw.K L/24 of the A–F models, known as the "Stummel" (Stump or Stubby One), was replaced by the long, high-velocity 7,5cm L/43 with its distinctive Mündungsbremse (muzzle brake or blast deflector) to lessen recoil and to reduce target obscuration. With a muzzle velocity of 740 m/s (2,248 fps) this gun could penetrate 89mm (3.5 inches) of 30-degree sloped armor at 1,000 m (3,028 ft), including the frontal armor of the C model T-34. This armament raised the vehicle weight to 23.5 tons and reduced its top speed to 40 km/h (25 mph). Further model changes meant the Panzer IV remained the mainstay of the panzer divisions throughout the war.

But already the heavy Pz.Kpfw.VI Tiger with the 8,8cm gun was about to enter production (August 1942), and the sloped-armor Panzer V Panther prototypes were undergoing trials. In addition, a hollow-(shaped-) charge armor-piercing artillery round had been developed, *Rotkopf* (Red Top). Hitler originally forbade its use to keep it secret, but released it in the December 1941 crisis. Fired from the 8,8cm or even field howitzers, its impact being independent of velocity, it could destroy a T-34.[35]

Panzer units were also reorganized according to new K.St.N. tables produced by OKH. A fourth panzer company was added to each panzer battalion, with each company authorized twenty-two panzers; in many cases these additional tanks were taken from panzer divisions in the northern sectors in order to strengthen those in the southern areas. Speculation was thus rife about where the objectives of a renewed campaign would be. The 11. Panzer-Division was among those selected for expansion.

The commander of Pz.-Rgt.15, Oberstleutnant Gustav-Adolf Riebel, had been promoted to Oberst on 1 October and was awarded das deutsche Kreuz (DK) in Gold, the first in the division, on 24 December 1941. Günther Angern later received the DK on 8 March 1942. (The DK, to be worn on the right breast below the eagle, was awarded for bravery and leadership.) In December 1941 Riebel was posted to Pz.Rgt.24 of the new 24. "Der Springende Reiter" Panzer-Division, converted from the 1. Kavalleriedivision on 28 November 1941, and he joined it at Paris 3 January 1942. (He would be killed by a Russian shell splinter on the back deck of his Panzer III on the Kalmyck Steppe near Stalingrad 23 August 1942.)[36]

Riebel had been succeeded as regimental commander 1 January 1942 by Maj. Theodor-Friedrich Carl Graf von Schimmelmann of II. Abteilung. Schimmelmann had been with the regiment since its founding in Sagan in 1937, and had commanded 2.Kp./I.Abt. in Poland and II.Abt. in France, Yugoslavia, and Russia. A tall, distinguished officer and a noted equestrian, Schimmelmann was unflappable, and had already been awarded the Ritterkreuz for his service in the Yugoslav campaign 14 May 1941. As an Oberst later, he would insist on being addressed as Graf: "Anyone can be a Colonel, you have to be *born* a Count." As someone who delighted in vexing authority, Gefreiter Kurt Nentwig might address him deliberately as "Herr Oberst," but there were certain occupational risks in doing so. But later Nentwig became a promoted Leutnant ("I made up my mind now to become an officer in order to minimize the number of idiots who could give orders to me," in his words). He felt as an Reserveoffizierbewerber (ROB, applicant as a Reserve Officer) that Schimmelmann delayed his transfer to a military academy. But as a leader he felt "Schimmelgraf" was "the fairest, bravest and most careful officer I have met in the German army."[37]

Schimmelmann's Pz.-Rgt.15 was increased with a third panzer battalion, II./35 taken from 4.Pz.Div. in H.Gr. Mitte. It was designated as III.Pz.Abt. under Major von Burstin. The 4.Pz.Div. under Generalmajor Heinrich Eberbach remained in the central sector, and was one of several other panzer divisions whose panzer regiment was reduced to one battalion. The artillery regiment under Oberst Oskar Schmidt, now designated *Panzer*-Art.-Rgt. 119, was also expanded, with Heeresflakartillerie Abteliung 277, equipped with 8,8cm guns, becoming its IV.Abt. Aufkl.Abt.231 had been amalgamated with Kradsch.Btl.61. Motorcycles were too vulnerable to enemy fire and less able to negotiate deep mud and snow than Radfahrzeuge and Kettenfahrzeuge, but K.61 also had Spähwagen, half-tracks and armored cars. The reliable motorcycle BMW R75 and sidecar was still useful for staff and liaison duties however. Hptm. Paul von Hauser succeeded Major Horst von Usedom at K.61.[38]

On 5 May 11. Schützenbrigade was redesignated as 11. Panzergrenadier-Brigade, the term "Panzergrenadier" (armored infantry) denoting a more aggressive role than "Schützen" (rifle) units, Oberst Helwig Luz remaining commander. The two rifle regiments were also redesignated, as Pz.Gren.Rgt. 110 and 111. In the 11.Pz.Div. orders and reports and the KTB, however, the older designations 11.S.B. and S.R.110 and S.R.111 are referred to until August when 11.Pz.Gren.Brig. and Pz.Gren.Rgt. 110 and 111 begin to be used.[39] Given the rates of industrial production, however, only one panzergrenadier battalion in some panzer divisions could be equipped with the Sd.Kfz. 251 armored half-track, the battalion listed as gp (gepanzerte). The other battalions were still transported in Lastwagen, to de-truck behind the attack line of departure to deploy as regular infantry or to ride on the panzers. Motorized divisions were redesignated as panzergrenadier divisions in 1943.

Oberst Luz of 11.S.B. had been acting division commander for a time in May after Scheller left. On 16 May 1942 the Gespenster-Division received a new division commander, Oberst Hermann Balck. The Ia, Erste Generalstabsoffizier Major Selmayr, had been succeeded by Oberstleutnant Franz-Joachim Kinitz in March. While Kinitz was on leave 4–25 May, the Ib, Hptm. Reidel, noted in the KTB on 21 May that Balck was the new commander, as of the 16th. He arrived at the Div.Gef.St. on 24 May.[40] Born 12 December 1893 in Danzig-Langfur, Prussia, Balck came from a distinguished military background. Interestingly, his great-grandfather served on the staff of the English Duke of Wellington in the British King's German Legion (KGL), and his grandfather was an officer in the 93rd Argyll and Sutherland Highlander Regiment. His father, William [*sic*] Balck was a Generalleutnant commanding a German division in World War I, receiving the *Pour le Mérite*.

Entering the Kaiserliche Heer 10 April 1913 as a Fahnenjunker (officer candidate) Hermann Balck served as a Leutnant with Jäger Btl. 10 and 22 and

- 99 -

Tag Uhrzeit Ort und Art der Unterkunft	Darstellung der Ereignisse
21.5.42 Mjassojedowa	1 russ. Leuchtpistole 2 automatische Gewehre 4 deutsche Gewehre 4 russ. Gewehre 1 Sanitätstasche.
	Am Vormittag meldet sich der Kommandeur der Heeres Fla. Abt. 277 beim stellv. Div.- Kdr. und Ia. Im Anschluss daran findet beim Ia eine Besprechung über die kraftfahrzeugmässige Auffrischung der Division,sowie über die Transportanmeldung der Kettenteile statt, an der Hauptmann Guderian (Ib) und Hauptmann.Dr. Lindner (bisheriger stellv. Ib) teilnehmen.
11,oo Uhr	Um 11,oo Uhr trifft der Korück Pz. 3, Generalleutnant Schmidt-Bolsow, auf dem Div. Gef. Stand ein. In einer Besprechung mit dem stellv. Div.-Kdr. und Ia lässt er sich über die Lage des zu übernehmenden Gebietes einweisen.
1o,35 Uhr	Um 1o,35 Uhr Anruf von Oberstleutnant Böhm, Chef des Stabes beim Befh. i. H.G. Mitte, dass Generalmajor Scheller mit Wirkung vom 16.5. zur Führerreserve OKH versetzt ist. Oberst Balck, Leiter der Dienststelle des Generals der Schnellen Truppen beim ObdH., wird mit Wirkung vom 16.5. mit der Führung der 11. Panzer-Division beauftragt.
	Der Nachmittag verläuft ruhig. Feindliches s. M.G.- Feuer liegt auf Südrand Micheilowskoje (6,5 km nordostwärts Dorogobush-Stadt). In den übrigen Abschnitten keine besonderen Ereignisse.

KTB, 21 May 1942—Oberst Hermann Balck assigned to command the 11.Pz.Div. succeeding Gen.Maj. Scheller, effective 16 May. NARA T-315/ROLL 590/000352 saw action on both the Western and the Eastern Fronts in World War I, being awarded the EK 2 and EK 1, and being nominated for the *Pour le Mérite* in October 1918. Obstlt. Balck commanded Schützenregiment 1 of 1.Pz.Div. in the 1940 French Feldzug. At Sedan he crossed his riflemen in collapsible rubber boats over the Meuse after a Stuka airstrike and led his Schützen up the high ground on foot. He thrust south during the night without awaiting panzers and antitank guns, and then destroyed a counterattacking French armored brigade as the heavy weapons began arriving.[41]

In the 1941 Greek campaign as commander of Panzer-Regiment 3 in 2.Pz.Div., Oberst Balck led a Kampfgruppe that routed the 21 New Zealand Battalion by flanking with his infantry at night over the slopes of Mount Olympus; he then forded his panzers across the Pinios River and through the Tempe Gorge, flanking 16 Australian Brigade, while oxen and donkeys were commandeered to bring up fuel drums before a bridge was completed. A captured British intelligence report stated, "The German Panzer Regiment 3 knows no going difficulties and negotiates terrain which was regarded as absolutely safe against armor."[42]

Arriving 24 May 1942, Balck came to the Gespenster-Division after a tour on the staff of the Inspectorate of Mobile Troops at OKH, and would command the 11.Pz.Div. until March 1943, being promoted to Generalmajor (1 August 1942) and Generalleutnant (1 January 1943). He later commanded Panzergrenadierdivision Grossdeutschland, XXXX. and XXXXVIII. Panzerkorps, and (after promotion), as General der Panzertruppen, 4. Panzer Armee, and finally Heeresgruppe G in the West. Among his awards Balck would be one of the very few who received the Knights Cross with Oak Leaves, Swords, and Diamonds.[43]

Beginning 1 June 1942 the 11. Panzer-Division rail-loaded its tracked vehicles and by E-Transport and by road moved southeast through Smolensk, Roslavl, and Orel to Novo Archangelsk east of Kursk. In his diary Oberst Balck related his own difficulties in moving with the division. On 7 June at 04,00 he left Kursk but his vehicle broke down. After being repaired at an army maintenance facility it then broke down again, all while rain poured down. Finally a truck came by and took him in tow through the mud. He arrived at Novo Archangelsk after midnight in another vehicle. The division itself was ill-prepared for action, still lacking 40 percent of its vehicles. And meanwhile, Balck noted, the weather was "Rain, rain—nothing but rain. The land of the black earth was turned into a bottomless morass."[44] But the massing of forces by 22 June suggested a renewal of the power that had invaded Russia the year before, heightened by the news of the fall of Tobruk in Libya to Erwin Rommel's Panzerarmee Afrika on the 21st, for which Rommel was promoted by Hitler as Feldmarschall that same day.

The primary objective of Hitler's 1942 campaign were the oil fields of the Caucasus Mountains in the far southeast, to secure this vital resource for the German war machine and deny it to the Russians. The details of Fall BLAU (Operation BLUE) were promulgated in Weisung Nr. 41 of 5 April 1942. (BLAU was originally code-named Fall SIEGFRIED but renamed by Hitler, apparently as heroic names were now considered a bad omen.) Generaloberst Georg von Küchler's Heeresgruppe Nord was to seize Leningrad with the Finns, Feldmarschall Günther von Kluge's H.Gr. Mitte was to stand on the defensive, and in the south Generaloberst Erich von Manstein's 11. Armee was to capture Sevastopol and secure the Crimea. Deception measures, known as Operation KREML, were to persuade Stalin and the Stavka that the main German drive was to cross the upper Don and thrust *north*east toward Moscow. But the primary drive would actually be to the *south*east, under H.G. Süd, commanded by Fedor von Bock, recovered from his illness of December.

Operation BLAU would unfold in four stages: First, two enveloping forces—Hoth's 4. Panzerarmee and 2. Armee under Generaloberst Maximilian Freiherr von Weichs, east of Kursk—would pinch out the Russian forces fronting Voronezh on the upper Don. (The 11. Panzer-Division was assigned to XIII. Armeekorps in 4. Pz.Armee.) Then a second envelopment would result from 6. Armee under Gen.Obst. Friedrich Paulus driving northeast from the Kharkov sector. Thirdly, 4. Pz.Armee would swing down along the Don, followed by 6. Armee, and meet an attack by Kleist's 1. Pz.Armee, which would capture Rostov and the lower Don.

After this was accomplished, H.Gr. Süd would be divided into H.Gr. B under Bock to drive to Stalingrad on the Volga, and H.Gr. A under Feldmarschall Wilhelm List would continue south to the Caucasus oil fields as the fourth phase, implied though not explicit in Weisung Nr. 41. Stalingrad was to be neutralized and its industrial production wrecked, but the city itself was *not* to be captured. Like Leningrad and Moscow, Hitler was aware of the dangers of becoming embroiled in street-to-street and building-to-building urban warfare for Stalingrad—but its capture was to become a fatal obsession later.

The Caucasus oil fields, on the other hand, had always been an important if distant objective. An Oil Detachment Caucasus, tasked with repairing the captured oil fields and organized in the spring of 1941, had been expanded into a brigade. In October 1941 the Operations Division of OKH had begun detailed planning of a six-phase operation that included an advance across Transcaucasia toward the Turkish and Iranian borders and the capture of the border passes into Iraq, opening up the possibility of seizing Middle East oil resources. On 7 November, however, the Führer told Feldmarschall von Brauchitsch he did not intend to go beyond the Russian border. On 19 November he told General Halder that the Caucasus would be the first objective for 1942.[45]

A preliminary to Operation BLAU was the elimination of the Losovaya pocket, a Soviet salient protruding west of Izyum on the middle Donets. At the beginning of May Bock began concentrating Paulus's 6. Armee in the Belgorod-Kharkov sector on the northern shoulder, and Kleist's 1. Pz.Armee around Pavlograd on the south, in anticipation of a pincers movement. Petre Dumitrescu's 3. Rumanian Army fronted the salient on the western side. This operation, FRIDERICUS, was to begin on 17 May—but on the 12th the Russians struck first.

Marshal Timoshenko's Southwest Front intended a pincers movement in the same area, from Volchansk on the right and Izyum on the left, to capture the major communications center of Kharkov. Masses of tanks spearheaded the Russian drives, but the attacks actually, and fatally, complemented the German operation. The Volchansk attack encountered the concentrated power of Paulus's 6. Armee and was stopped in a vicious melee. The Izyum attack broke the Rumanians, and the Russian armies, preceded by cavalry, swept victoriously beyond Krasnograd toward Poltava and even Dnepropetrovsk on the Dnepr, while Gen. A. M. Gorodnyanski's 6th Army swung up behind Kharkov.

But as the Russian forces plunged deep through the collapsing Rumanians—80, 90, 100 kilometers—their flanks became more vulnerable. Hitler sensed the opportunity, and on the 17th Bock initiated Operation FRIDERICUS, made easier by the Russian attack. Paulus's forces assaulted from the north, and Kleist's panzers sliced into the flank from the south. Timoshenko urged withdrawal from what was now a trap, as did political commissar Nikita Khrushchev and Chief of Staff Ivan Bagramyan, but Stalin was obdurate, insisting that the offensive continue forward to capture Kharkov. On the 23rd Paulus's panzers met Kleist's at Balakleya, and Timoshenko's forces were annihilated. Gorodnyanski shot himself and Lt. Gen. Podlas of 57th Army was killed, and while Moscow admitted only 5,000 dead, 70,000 missing, and 300 tanks destroyed, the Germans claimed another huge Kesselschlacht victory, recording 240,000 prisoners and some 1,200 tanks destroyed.[46]

Farther south on the Crimea, the hated and incompetent Lev Mekhlis lost twenty-one divisions in three armies as Manstein overwhelmed his positions on the Kerch Peninsula. He also lost his position as Defense Commissar. Manstein could now concentrate on the siege of Sevastopol, and the Crimea was becoming a base for German Luftwaffe and naval units to dominate the Black Sea and secure the flank of the German drive to the Caucasus. With Russian reserves expended in the Kharkov disaster, the Russian forces in the south were in disarray as the German 1942 offensive was about to begin.

On the morning of 19 June Maj. Joachim Reichel, operations officer of 23.Pz.Div., crash-landed in his Fieseler Storch just inside Russian lines. Contrary to Hitler's orders about security, he had in his briefcase the operations orders for Gen.d.Pz.Tr. Georg Stumme's XXXX. Pz.Korps and the first stage of Operation BLAU. A German patrol discovered the wrecked plane but not the major's body or the briefcase, and it was realized Operation BLAU was probably revealed to the Russians. Nonetheless all the preparations had been made, and Hitler ordered the Operation (renamed BRAUNSCHWEIG on the 30th) to proceed.

The Reichel documents had indeed been recovered by the Russians; they were so detailed, in fact, that some believed they might be a plant. When the documents were laid before Stalin by Lt.Gen. Filipp Golikov of Bryansk Front on the 26th, the dictator swept them aside, said he didn't believe a word of BLAU, lashed out at the incompetence of the intelligence staff, and ordered the Bryansk Front to attack Orel. On the German side Stumme and his chief of staff were relieved of their positions (though Stumme later went to Panzerarmee Afrika), and Gen.d.Pz.Tr. Geyr Freiherr von Schweppenburg took over XXXX. Pz.Korps.

As eleven panzer divisions moved up to their assembly areas, the massed power on the open steppe-country grasslands was reminiscent of the beginning of BARBAROSSA the year before. Once again the Blitzkrieg was to be launched; would the outcome this year be different? Balck's 11. Panzer-Division was now at strength, with Gefechtsstärke (fighting strength) of 13,297 and Verpflegungsstärke (ration strength) of 17,463. Balck later tried to clarify for his unit commanders who was to be included in the strength figures. The Gefechtsstärke was *not* to include medical or radio personnel, vehicle drivers (but include panzer Fahrer), certain officials, Hiwis, or supply and maintenance personnel; the Verpflegungsstärke *was* to include these, including the Hiwis and even Russian Kriegsgefangene (used as labor units), though not personnel on Urlaub (leave).[47] (Grabenstärke, trench strength, of only infantry-type elements, was another category sometimes reported.)

On Balck's staff the Ia was Obstlt. Kinitz and his IIa, the adjutant, was Major von Webski. Gen. Heinz Guderian's older son, Hptm. Heinz-Günther Guderian, was Ib before he went to 116.Pz.Div. as its Ia. At Pz.Rgt.15, fighting strength of 1,734, Oberst Graf Schimmelmann, with Oberstleutnant Max Roth as acting commander, had three Abteilungen, each with two light and one medium company. The companies were still authorized twenty-two panzers of four platoons of five each, and two headquarters panzers. With its third panzer battalion Pz.Rgt.15 actually had 156 panzers total: 5 Panzer IIs, 124 Pz.IIIs (110 of which had the new long 5cm L/60 gun), 13 Pz.IVs (12 with the longer 7,5cm L/43 gun), and 4 command panzers.[48]

The 11. Rifle Brigade, now officially redesignated 11. Panzergrenadierbrigade, was under Oberst Luz, though the two regiments were still referred to as rifle regiments: S.R.110, 2,254 fighting strength, was under Oberst Albert Henze who had succeeded Oberst Ludwig Fricke in April; and S.R.111, 2,190 fighting strength, was under Oberst Alexander von Bosse who had succeeded Oberst Bohlmann-Combrinck in May. Bohlmann was named to command the Schnelle Truppen in Wehrkreis IV (Sachsen) effective 1 May, and Fricke went into the OKH Führer Reserve officers' pool.[49] Henze's S.R.110 had two battalions, each with two Panzergrenadier companies and a heavy weapons company. But now one of the companies, and the Pionier and Panzerjäger Züge, were equipped with the Sd.Kfz. 251 SPW half-tracks. Von Bosse's S.R.111 also had two battalions with three infantry companies and a heavy weapons company, but they were still all truck-borne.

At Pz.Art.Rgt.119, strength of 2,038, Oberst Oskar Schmidt had succeeded the ill Oberst Matena at the beginning of March. The artillery was organized into two light Abteilungen, each with three batteries of four 10,5cm le.F.H., and a medium Abteilung with two batteries of four 15cm s.F.H. and a battery of four long 10cm K 18 guns, though the actual number of tubes was lower. Heeresflakart.-Abt. 277 with eight 8,8cm flak guns in an antitank role was the IV. Abteilung. The ordnance actually totaled eighteen light 10,5cm howitzers, six medium 15cm howitzers, four 10cm K 18 guns, and the eight Acht-komma-acht Flak 18/36 guns.

Kradschützenbataillon 61 was under Hptm. Paul von Hauser. K.61 still listed two motorcycle companies with machine guns, but, having incorporated A.A.231, more potent were the Pz. Spähwagen Sd.Kfz. 231 Achtrad armored cars with the 2cm Kw.K. 36 and 38 guns, and also Typ 233 mounting a short 7,5cm L/24 Sturm Kanone (Stu.K., assault gun), and 8cm Granatwerfer and 5cm Pak 38 antitank guns. K.61 had a strength of 1,008. There was also the Kradschützen-Lehrbataillon (K.L.B., Motorcycle Training or Instruction Battalion), training in the field with 1,086 fighting strength.

At Pz.Pionier-Batl.209, strength 715, Maj. Bernhard Scholaster had been succeeded by Maj. Heinrich Bullerdieck. One company was now in Halbkette, the other still in Lastwagen. Pz.Jäger-Abt.61, with only 77 personnel, was now under Maj. Friedrich Guttmacher who succeeded Maj. Edgar Schulz in May. The battalion had two companies with towed 5cm Pak 38 guns, and an attached Flak Kompanie, 1./608, strength 71, with 2cm guns. For the initial attack I.Abt. from Flak Rgt. 38 with its Acht-komma-acht guns joined the division. At Pz. Nachrichten-Abt. 341, strength 362, the radio and telephone signals companies were commanded by Hptm. Theodor Poretschkin who had succeeded Maj. Franz Bluhm in January.

The medical, supply, and other elements of the division Tross were now coordinated by Hauptmann, promoted to Major, Günther von Zamory as DNF, having succeeded Oberst Camillo Neureiter in April. The Luftwaffe Ostpreussische Leichte Flakabteilung 71, which had provided valuable antiaircraft defense to the division since January 1941 in the Yugoslav and Russian campaigns, was detached in May for reassignment to the 18. Flakdivision of Luftwaffenkommando Ost. Hptm./Maj. Sperling had succeeded Maj. Werner Jacobson, wounded back in October 1941. The 1. Battr. under Hptm. Hugo Novak had already been detached for the air defense of Vyasma railroad stations. When General Scheller spoke of "unsere" L/71. in a farewell Tagesbefehl, it emphasized the deep respect that had evolved.[50] With a nucleus of combat veterans and under able and experienced commanders, and led by aggressive Oberst Hermann Balck, the 11. Gespenster Panzer-Division was well prepared for the new 1942 campaign.

As the Russians also girded for the coming summer campaign, they had absorbed some of the lessons from the 1941 campaign. One organizational change was to dissolve the unwieldy tank and motorized divisions of 1941, and reorganize them into brigades, grouped as tank, mechanized, or rifle corps. Though not yet a balanced combined-arms formation, the Germans considered the evolving Russian corps as approximating a German division in size (thus hereafter, Arabic numbers will be used for Russian corps, not Roman numerals).

CHAPTER ELEVEN

Operations BLAU and WIRBELWIND

AT 02,15 HOURS ON 28 JUNE 1942—G TAG FOR OPERATION BLAU—a massive artillery barrage ripped apart the predawn quiet as the eastern horizon was beginning to lighten through the overcast. Stukas and bombers of the VIII. Fliegerkorps of Generaloberst Wolfram Freiherr von Richthofen smashed the Russian positions along the Voronezh sector. *"Aufgesessen! Motoren anwerfen! Panzer Marsch!"* ("Mount up! Start engines! Panzers Move out!") Two armies of Feldmarschall Fedor von Bock's large Heeresgruppe B, as Armeegruppe Weichs—2. Armee commanded by Generaloberst Maximilian Freiherr von Weichs and 4. Panzer under Generaloberst Hermann Hoth—slashed into Lt. Gen. Filipp Golikov's Bryansk Front positions driving toward Voronezh on the upper Don, with 2. Hungarian Army under Gustáv von Jány on the right flank.

Armeegruppe Weichs attacked with three panzer divisions and three motorized infantry divisions, with infantry divisions following up. The Schwerpunkt was with XXXXVIII. Panzerkorps under Generalleutnant Werner Kempf of Hoth's 4. Pz.Armee, led by 24.Pz.Div. with 16.Inf.Div.(mot) on its right and motorized division Grossdeutschland on its left. Hoth's XXIV. Pz.Korps under Gen.Lt. Willibald Freiherr von Langermann attacked on the left with 9.Pz.Div. and 3.I.D.(mot). The 11. Panzer-Division spearheaded the attack of XIII. Armee-Korps commanded by General der Infanterie Erich Straube with two infantry divisions on the north flank of 4. Pz.Armee. Two days later Paulus's 6. Armee started its drive north from Kharkov across the Oskol to entrap the Russian forces fronting Voronezh.

Balck's 11.Pz.-Div. jumped off from its attack positions on the 28th with 82.Inf.Div. on the right and 385.I.D. on the left. Engineers had improved the roads and strengthened the bridges to move up the heavy equipment. 6. Kompanie of Maj. Gerhard Florin's II.Btl. of Schützenregiment 111 (the new term Panzergrenadier not yet familiar) forded the Tim River.[1] Engineers in pneumatic rubber boats established a footbridge for the riflemen to cross over with their heavy weapons, and then began reinforcing the muddy ford with steel planking to accommodate the panzers and the 8,8cm flak guns needed to protect the bridgehead from both Russian air attack and

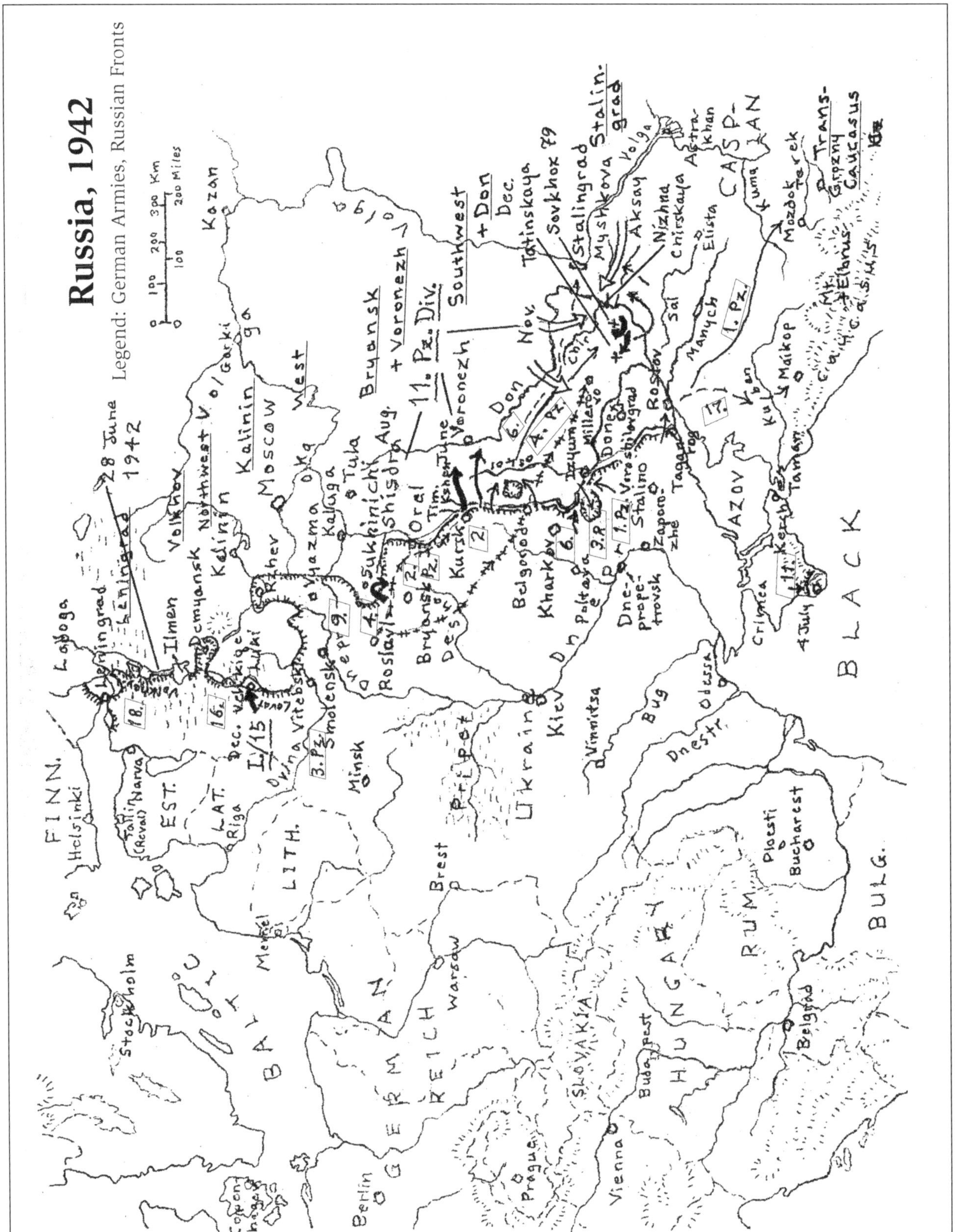

Russia, 1942

Legend: German Armies, Russian Fronts

armored counterattack. The image of engineers in the river with steel helmets and field jackets, but stripped from the waist down, generated much levity.

The first panzer crossed the "underwater" bridge, marked only by hand railings, at 08,00 hours. Others crossed despite some inaccurate Russian artillery fire, but Balck was returning to his Kübelwagen when his adjutant, Major von Webski, was struck by a shell splinter and killed while next to him. The Pioniere began construction of a heavy-duty B-Gerät bridge across the Tim.[2] The panzers and half-tracks began fanning out over the fields of sunflowers and wheat; the prairie grassland steppes were treeless, broken only by occasional balkas (ravines). Russian tanks were engaged and knocked out, the new 5cm Pak proving its worth, as well as the upgunned Panzer IIIs and IVs. Russian resistance was uncoordinated, and prisoners were simply waved to the rear.

By midday the two Gratshevka villages were taken, and Russian trains elements were overrun and eight more tanks destroyed, two by the Panzer-Nahkämpfertrupps (tank close-combat section) of the Pioniere. In addition to T-34s and KV-1s, there were English tanks, the Cruiser A10 Mark II and also the heavy infantry tank Mark II Matilda, both mounting the inferior 2-pounder (3,9cm) gun (the Germans referring to "Mark IIs" without differentiating). Other Elften took Mikailovka and crossed the rail line north of the village, and the first day's objectives had been reached.

Oberstlt. Max Roth, acting commander of Pz.-Rgt.15, received orders to continue the advance to the Kshen River with his panzers, passing through the S.R.111 bridgehead. Roth had his Pz.Rgt.15, along with a battalion of infantry (I./110), a company of engineers (3./209), an artillery battery (6./119), a 2cm flak battery (10./110), and a battery of 8,8cm guns (2./Flak 38).[3] On the left Inf.Rgt.539 of the 385.I.D. under Oberstlt. Erler had also crossed the Tim. Generaloberst Hoth, Pz.A.O.K.4, came up to the division command post at 13,00, finding the attack progressing well. Sudden rainstorms that night challenged the supply services, and once again the ubiquitous horse-drawn panje wagons were utilized to bring up fuel and ammunition. Riflemen forded the Kshen, and on the 29th the bridgehead was enlarged. Panzers and tracked vehicles pulled the supply Opel Lkws across the ford even as the 3.Kp./Pz.Pi.Btl.209 erected an improvised vehicle bridge.

In Hoth's main drive Gen.Maj. Bruno Ritter von Hauenschild's 24.Pz.Div. of XXXXVIII. Pz.Korps had swept across the Tim and then the Kshen, tearing a gap between the Russian 13th and 40th Armies and dispersing the rear-area headquarters of the 40th Army. They plunged 16 kilometers farther on that first day. "Der Springende Reiter" (the Leaping Horseman) was reflecting its spirited origins as the only cavalry division (1.Kav.Div.) converted to a panzer division; former Gespenster Oberst Riebel was commanding its Pz.Rgt.24. XXIV. Panzerkorps was reaching the Kshen as well.

On 30 June Hoth came up again and briefed Balck on the ongoing operation, and praised S.R.111 for the river crossings. He had departed when at 09,40 six Russian planes flew over and dropped bombs on the Div.Gef.Std, damaging a command vehicle and causing casualties of one killed and eleven wounded. The muddy roads further delayed the advance, but the Luftwaffe delivered ammunition and fuel and the panzers thrust on. Two battalions of the 82.I.D. gave more infantry support.

At this time the operational panzer strength of the Elfte was 126: 6 Panzer IIs, 111 Panzer IIIs, and 9 Pz.IVs. Because the Panzer IIIs were the greatest number, it was gratifying that the new long L/60 5cm guns were able to penetrate the formidable T-34s. The Kradschützen-Lehrbataillon (K.L.B.) complemented the 11.Pz.Div. strength with its five companies: armored car, motorcycle, rifle (in half-tracks and trucks), heavy weapons, and Volkswagen companies, with two le.I.G.and three 5cm mittlere Pak. The Feld Ersatzbataillon (Field Replacement Battalion, F.E.B.), with 1,344 personnel, was operational with the division as well, a rather unusual practice. Its function was to process and train replacements for the organic units, but it might be used for security or helping process prisoners. On 1 July it had six le.MG and one 3,7cm antitank gun.[4]

From prisoners Division Ic (Intelligence) reported the Russian opposition as Rifle Regiments 47 and 676 of the 15th Rifle Division and Mortar Regiment 106 of 13th Army along the Tim sector, and 15th Motorized Rifle Brigade and at least sixteen heavy tanks in the Kshen sector.[5] More Gefangene were taken as the advance progressed. But the Gespensters had casualties too. Maj. Gerhard Florin, a Ritterkreuzträger who had led the II./S.R.111 attack across the Tim, was severely wounded on 1 July and evacuated. War correspondent Rudolf Eiche of Panzer Propaganda-Kompanie 694 was with the Gespenster-Division and wrote a piece for the *Brüsseler Zeitung* and the *Berliner Lokalanzeiger* about the assault titled "Bravo Florin!"[6]

The panzer drive continued toward Voronezh, units taking up Igel positions at night. They were harassed by Russian planes and struggling to get fuel and munitions forward, but the panzers were moving too quickly for Russian artillery to register. On 2 July beyond Volovo and Vitrovka-West the panzers crossed the Olym at Nabereshnoye, and the infantry established a bridgehead at Olkovatka. At midday the 11.Pz.Div. was reassigned from XIII. A.K. to XXIV. Panzerkorps under General von Langermann, joining the 9.Pz.Div. commanded by Generalmajor Johannes Baessler, and 3.Inf.Div.(mot) and 377.I.D. On the 3rd the Elfte reached Beresovka, 15 kilometers beyond Nabereshnoye. Russian counterattacks against the 377. Infanterie-Division caused a Kampfgruppe to be diverted to assist them.

By 4 July, after seven days of fighting, the Elfte claimed 160 Russian tanks destroyed, 70 percent being heavy KV-1s and T-34s, and including British "Mark IIs" (actually A10s and Matildas). But on that 4th Major von Burstin of the added III.Abt./Pz.Rgt.15 was killed along with his crew; they were buried by a nearby windmill. It was one of the fifteen panzers lost of the 156 since 28 June as reported by Oberstlt. Roth: one Panzer II, eleven Pz.III l (lang, being the long L/60 gunned-panzers), two Pz.IV lang (being the long L/43 model), and one Befehlspanzerkampfwagen. He reported eighty-six einsatzbereit: ten Pz.II, eleven Pz.III k (kurz, short barrel) and fifty-three Pz.III lang, nine Pz.IV l, and three Bef.Wg, with presumably fifty-five under repair. By the 9th 196 Russian tanks and 6 planes were reported destroyed by the unit for the 12 days since the beginning of the Voronezh offensive. By type the tanks destroyed were 137 T-34s, 25 T-60s, 13 KV-1s, 10 English Mark IIs, and 11 undetermined.[7]

On 9 July the 340. Infanterie-Division established a defensive flank position and the 11.Pz.Dv., after twelve days of attacking, went into reserve to pull maintenance and get some rest. The I.Abt./Flak Rgt.38 with its 8,8cm guns was detached, but 119 still had six 8,8s of IV.Abteilung. Nonetheless, when Russian tanks broke through the infantry on the 11th, Pz.Rgt.15 was called upon to deal with them. As the infantry were not well equipped to fight tanks, it was the panzer forces that not only spearheaded the attack, but also mounted a mobile defense. Psychologically, the panzergrenadiers had an advantage over the regular infantry, as they had trained with their own panzer units, knew them, and could count on their ready support.

On the 11th orders were received detaching Baessler's 9.Pz.Div. and Balck's 11.Pz.Div. from XXIV. Pz.Korps for a new mission to the north. On the 14th the 11. Panzer assembled around Kastornoye to road-march up to south of Orel, with the unit now assigned to VII. A.K. of 2. Panzerarmee under Generaloberst Rudolf Schmidt, in H.Gr. Mitte under von Kluge. The status of the Elfte as reported to VII. A.K. on 12 July showed the division up to strength. Its fighting strength, not counting the division or 11.Pz.Gren.Brig. staffs, was 10,832 personnel. Higher headquarters in particular tracked the status of combat-ready panzers, and at this time Pz.Rgt.15 reported 105 panzers: 14 Pz.IIs, 82 Pz.IIIs (including 73 lang), and 9 Pz.IVs (all lang).[8]

Meanwhile Hitler had flown to Poltava on 3 July and urged Bock not to get his armor bogged down in Voronezh, directing him to reorient the drive southeast as the Russians were in retreat. General der Panzertruppen Geyr von Schweppenburg's XXXX. Pz.Korps of Paulus's 6. Armee, which had been driving up from Kharkov, was now ordered to attack due east. Hoth's 24.Pz.Div. and the motorized GD took Voronezh on the 6th, with the city having already been evacuated. As BLAU entered its third phase and the drive continued to the southeast, the 11. Panzer-Division remained with von Kluge's H.G. Mitte. July found the Elfte undergoing changing assignments: it went from VII. A.K. to Weichs's A.O.K. 2 on 14 July (now under Gen.d.Inf. Hans von Salmuth), then to Schmidt's Pz.A.O.K. 2 on 24 July, then to LVII. A.K.(mot) as it was redesignated a panzer corps, and finally to LIII. A.K. on 30 July.

Hoth's 4. Panzerarmee drove southeast along the Don River followed by Paulus's 6. Armee for the third stage envelopment with 1. Pz.Armee. The southern armies, 17. Armee under Gen. d. Inf. Richard Ruoff and Kleist's 1. Pz.Armee, attacked across the Donets, while Manstein's 11. Armee captured Sevastopol in the Crimea on 4 July. He had cleared the Kerch Peninsula and was prepared to cross the Taman Strait to secure Novorossiysk and Tuapse and the eastern shore of the Black Sea on the flank of a drive to the Caucasus.

On 7 July these southern armies were redesignated as Heeresgruppe A under Feldmarschall Wilhelm List. On the 9th the northern armies of H.Gr. Süd were redesignated as H.Gr. B under Fedor von Bock. But Hitler had become impatient with Bock who, remembering the problems caused in 1941 when masses of Russian forces were bypassed by the Blitzkrieg, had committed 4. Pz.Armee at Voronezh too long for the Führer's liking. On 13 July Hitler retired the Feldmarschall, and he was never to hold a command again. He was succeeded at H.Gr. B by Generaloberst Maximilian von Weichs from 2. Armee (now under von Salmuth).

As 4.Panzerarmee drove south into the Don bend, Kleist's 1. Pz.Armee slugged its way into Rostov-on-Don, the "Gateway to the Caucasus," by 23 July, completing another envelopment—though the Russians had generally retreated.[9] 4. Pz.Armee had thus played a decisive role in the Kesselschacht, even if in the original planning for BLAU it was supposed to spearhead a 6. Armee drive to Stalingrad on the Volga. In fact, after the war, Kleist told B. H. Liddell Hart, "The 4th Panzer Army was advancing on that line, on my left. It could have taken Stalingrad without a fight, at the end of July, but was diverted south to help me in crossing the Don. I did not need its aid, and it merely congested the roads I was using. When it turned north again, a fortnight later, the Russians had gathered just sufficient forces at Stalingrad to check it."[10]

Whether Stalingrad could have been easily taken is debatable, though in any case the original plan had been to invest it, not capture it. Paulus's 6. Armee, predominantly infantry, advanced alone toward the Don bend and Stalingrad. XIV. Panzerkorps had been attached with three fast divisions, but these were immobilized for at least ten days in July by lack of fuel. List's H.Gr. A had priority for the advance to the oil fields and the Caucasus. On 23 July Hitler issued Weisung Nr. 45, which shifted the primary objective to be the *capture* of Stalingrad, though the Caucasus was to be reached too. XXIV. Pz.Korps was transferred from Hoth's 4. Pz.Armee to Paulus. Paulus could now undertake a two-pronged encirclement drive into the Don bend where the 62nd Russian Army had fortified a bridgehead west of the bend fronting Kalach. Elements of the 1st and 4th Tank Armies were committed as well. When the pincers met at Kalach by 8 August after fierce fighting, most of 62nd Army was trapped and destroyed. The Germans claimed over 600 tanks destroyed and over 50,000 prisoners taken.[11] After clearing the Kalach Kessel, 6. Armee was poised to continue the advance across the isthmus, 55 kilometers (35 miles) between the Don bend and Stalingrad on the Volga.

In Weisung Nr. 45 Hitler had been jubilant, saying that in little more than three weeks the Blitzkrieg had achieved its initial objectives, and annihilated Timoshenko's armies. On 15 July Hitler had said to OKH Chief of Staff Halder, "The Russian is finished," to which the latter replied, "I must say, it is beginning to look uncommonly like it." Halder, in his diary for that day, noted the enveloping movement by 1. and 4. Pz.Armee and stated that the enemy was "being ground up" by the armor and infantry.[12] On 16 July Hitler moved into a newly constructed forward headquarters of camouflaged blockhouses in a pine forest near Vinnitsa, deep in the Ukraine. The code name for this compound was "Werwolf." (The next year, the corpses of 10,000 Ukrainians, executed by the NKVD in 1938, were discovered nearby.)[13]

If Stalin had indeed refused to accept the authenticity of the Reichel BLAU documents, and then saw the drive on Voronezh as a portent of the German offensive being *north*east, behind Moscow, rapid decisions were now made in the Kremlin to readjust to the reality of the German drive *south*east. In fact, the Germans sensed that in many cases the Russians were undertaking deliberate retreats, rather than being surrounded because of Stalin's insistence on standfast orders. A major reason for this was that on 26 June Col. Gen. Aleksandr Vasilevsky had replaced the ailing Marshal Shaposhnikov as chief of the General Staff, and persuaded Stalin and the Stavka to be more flexible.

But with the threat to Stalingrad and the rail links south of the city, and with the Russian forces disintegrating, on 28 July Stalin issued Stavka Order No. 227 titled, *"Ni Shagu Nazad!"* ("Not a step back!"). Any commander or political officer who retreated would be removed and assigned to a punishment battalion (human fodder used to clear minefields, dig entrenchments, and absorb artillery fire). Panicmongers, cowards, and defeatists would be shot (or tried in military or NKVD tribunals first).[14] The next day German panzer units cut the last rail link from central Russia to the Caucasus region. Contact with Russian forces in the south would have to be by the Volga or by the Caspian Sea.

As the German armies surged across the lower Don, the final defeat of Soviet Russia in that summer of 1942 seemed almost inevitable. Hitler was ebullient. In North Africa Rommel's Panzerarmee Afrika was driving into British Egypt toward the Suez Canal, and in the Far East the Japanese had expanded throughout the Pacific and Southeast Asia. In the Atlantic German U-boats savaged the convoy shipping lanes between the United States and Britain, and air and naval units based in Norway destroyed Allied Lend-Lease Convoy PQ 17, sinking twenty-three of its thirty-six merchantmen.

Manstein, after securing Sevastopol and the Crimea, was transferred north to capture Leningrad, taking five of eleven divisions and the heavy artillery of 11. Armee to do so. It was felt by Hitler and OKW that the remaining forces of H.Gr. A and B were adequate to capture the Caucasus oil fields *and* secure the Volga at Stalingrad. More sober analysis at OKH, however, reflected replacement and panzer shortages as well as fuel limitations that were already immobilizing entire divisions for days at a time, and the Caucasus oil fields were at vast distances from Rostov—over 300 kilometers (200 miles) to Maikop, and over 600 kilometers (400 miles) to Grozny.

As in Weisung Nr. 45, List's H.Gr. A, 1. Panzer and 17. Armee, with 4. Panzer temporarily attached, drove southeast toward the Caucasus Mountains oil fields in Unternehmen EDELWEISS. Weichs's H.Gr. B continued the advance on Stalingrad. A danger implicit in the original planning now became fact: the Schwerpunkt of the campaign was not only to be divided, but the objectives divergent—south to the Caucasus oil fields, and east to Stalingrad. It is not clear how or when the *capture* of Stalingrad finally became an obsession for Hitler. Rail communications and Volga River traffic could be cut north or south of the city, and industrial production could at least be curtailed by air and artillery bombardment. But perhaps it was the grim determination to capture "Stalin's City" (renamed from Tsaritsyn in 1925) that gave it a greater significance, and it became a test of wills.

List's mobile forces swept south across the torrid, featureless Kuban steppe where temperatures of 55 degrees Celsius (130 F) blasted both men and vehicles. Maikop was taken on 9 August, though the oil fields would have to be repaired, and Grozny was another 500 kilometers (300 miles) distant. German units did penetrate into the Caucasus Mountains, and on 21 August Gebirgsjäger planted the Hakenkreuz flag on Mount Elbrus, at 5,645 meters (18,510 feet) the highest peak in the mountain range.

Reconnaissance elements of the 11.Pz.Div. may have participated in EDELWEISS. They moved beyond Pyatigorsk and into the foothills of the Caucasus, crossing an engineer bridge over a steep, fast-moving river near Georgiyevsk and passing the burned-out wreckage of a Soviet armored train destroyed near Mozdok on the Terek on the way to Grozny. The Aufklärungstruppen also forayed into the upper elevations toward Ordzhonikidze up the Tsarist Grusinian military highway to Georgia, negotiating mountain gorges and retrieving a bogged-down Lkw at Uspenskaya; the rugged terrain was more a challenge than Russian resistance, and the Fieseler Storch might be the only contact with the far-flung units beyond normal radio communication.[15]

Feeling that List's objectives in the Caucasus were now to be achieved simply by pursuit operations, on 31 July OKH had ordered Hoth's 4. Pz.Armee to swing back north 400 kilometers (250 miles) against Stalingrad, where Paulus's 6. Armee was meeting increasingly stubborn Russian resistance. Hoth's mobile forces drove north through the searing, vacant Kalymk steppe country, welcomed by occasional tribesmen, past Bactrian camels in the shimmering haze, slowed only by fuel and lubricant shortages. Long-range patrols reached the approaches to Astrakhan and the Caspian Sea. While 4. Pz.Armee advanced from the south, Paulus's 6. Armee fought across the Don bend at Kalach by 21 August, and 16.Pz.Div. penetrated the northern suburbs of Stalingrad and reached the Volga on the 23rd. 4. Pz.Armee made contact with 6. Armee on 3 September.

Although there was confidence that Stalingrad would soon fall, more perceptive officers were increasingly uneasy that the long, extended flanks were protected not by German forces, but allied forces that were evaluated as weak, poorly equipped, and generally of low morale. South of the 6. and 4. Panzer-Armee embroiled at Stalingrad was the 4. Rumanian Army, and the northern flank along the middle and upper Don toward Voronezh was held by three allied armies: 3. Rumanian, 8. Italian, and 2. Hungarian, the Italians inserted between the Rumanians and the Hungarians because of their national animosities, especially over Transylvania. There was also increasing evidence of the Russian recovery and building up of forces against those flanks.

If attention was focused on the dramatic campaigns in the south, there were also clashes at other points along the Ostfront. Von Küchler's H.Gr. Nord was fighting for Leningrad and held out at Demyansk, and von Kluge's H.Gr. Mitte held at Rzhev down past Orel. As the panzer forces in the north had been reduced for Operation BLAU, only local attacks and counterattacks could be undertaken. The 11. Panzer-Division, more powerful with three panzer battalions, was in Rudolf Schmidt's 2. Panzerarmee.

On 5 July, to forestall the German offensive still considered to be directed against Moscow, Stavka had Zhukov's West Front launch three armies in a spoiling attack against Schmidt's 2. Pz.Armee around Bolkhov, north of Orel. On the 30th Konev's Kalinin Front and Zhukov assaulted 9. Armee under acting commander General der Panzertruppen Heinrich von Vietinghoff in the Rzhev salient to the north. Hitler in turn ordered H.Gr. Mitte to launch a pincers attack against the Russian salient around Sukhinichi northeast of Bryansk in early August, with 4. Armee under Gen.d.Inf. Gotthard Heinrici and Schmidt's 2. Pz.Armee. Feldmarschall von Kluge objected, arguing that consolidating the Rzhev front was more urgent. At a conference at Hitler's Werwolf headquarters near Vinnitsa on 7 August Kluge said he would not disobey a direct order, but that the responsibility was Hitler's.

The original operation was to be a two-pronged attack named ORKAN (Hurricane), but with Zhukov's attacks on 4. Armee in the Rzhev salient, it was reduced to a single attack from the south with four panzer divisions of 2. Pz.Armee, and renamed WIRBELWIND (Whirlwind).[16] The Sukhinichi salient, held by the Russian 16th Army, was well fortified with bunkers, minefields, and barbed-wire entanglements, including defenses in the balkas that were unobservable. When the Soviets attacked near Rzhev the X Tag (attack day) was postponed twenty-four hours until 11 August. The four panzer divisions (9., 11., 17., and 20.) were to attack, two from each side of Ulyanovo, through 25 kilometers (15 miles) of heavily wooded terrain to converge on the Shisdra (Zhisdra) River, and then sweep north 80 kilometers (50 miles) over open terrain past Sukhinichi to Mosalsk.

11. Panzer-Division under Balck, who had been promoted Gen.Maj. 1 August, was on the eastern flank and was to attack northwest, followed by the Austrian 9. Pz.Div. now commanded by Gen.Lt. Walter Scheller (former Elfte commander). The Gespenster-Division was at strength, and Pz.-Rgt.15 had its three panzer battalions, once again commanded by Oberst Graf von Schimmelmann. But there had been an especially tragic loss on 2 August. At an Unteroffizier training course in Bryansk a sudden Russian bombing raid resulted in twenty killed and thirty-five wounded, not even in battle. As Balck's Elften moved up to their attack positions, Oberst Oskar Schmidt's Pz.Art.Rgt.119 was supplemented for the attack by the long-barreled heavy howitzers of 2.Battr./schwere Artillerie-Regiment 604 (21cm Mörser).

The 11. Panzer would attack with two battle groups abreast, under Oberst Helwig Luz commanding 11. Panzergrenadierbrigade (as it was now termed), and Oberst Karl Körner, Kdr. Pz.Gren.Rgt.111. Kampfgruppe Luz was composed of the brigade staff and regimental troops of Pz.Gren.Rgt.110, including a battalion of panzergrenadiers (II./110), a battalion of panzers (I./15), 1. Kp./Pz.Jäger Abt. 61, K.61, K.L.B., and Pz.Pi.Btl.209 (minus one company). Kgr. Körner had Pz.Gr.Rgt.111 and staff, II./15, 2./Pz.Jg.Abt.61, Heeres Pionier-Btl. 630, Brüko K/79, and a light artillery battalion and the heavy battery. Schmidt's Pz.A.R.119 coordinated its fires through the corps Arko (artillery command). Schimmelmann had the follow-on reserve Kampfgruppe including III./15 and I./110, ready to move forward once a breach had been made.[17]

At 04,00 Uhr on 11 August, after a violent artillery barrage and Stuka attack, the grenadiere, pioniere, and panzers moved forward. The day dawned sunny and dry. By 07,23 Kampfgruppe Luz was in Oserenskiy and by 08,30 II.Abt./Pz.Rgt.15 led Kpfgr. Körner past Markovka, and by 09,20 the Sorokino–Goskova Rollbahn was reached. 56.Inf.Div. on the left made good progress, and at 10,50 Gen.Lt. Scheller of 9.Pz.Div. arrived at the Div.Gef.Std. to coordinate his attack. While the 11.Pz.Div. was in XIII. A.K. for supplies, the attack orders came from XXXXI. Pz.Korps under Gen.Lt. Josef Harpe.[18] Balck committed Kgr. Schimmelmann and at 14,25 III.Abt./15 was crossing the Odronka at Debri. The bridge was a little damaged, and the panzers forded the river nearby. Kgr. Körner crossed at Sorokino.

The Panzerwagen of I./15 with Luz seized a bridge over the Shisdra at Durnevo, and Schimmelmann's Pz.Rgt.15 crossed the Wytebet at 15,30 to capture Retshnitsa. I./110 panzergrenadiers secured the village. The K.L.B. reported reaching the Shisdra at

Dretovo and igelt that night at Slobodka. But the fighting was brutal. "Every gorge must be taken by riflemen in heavy fighting," was the Ia Kriegstagebuch entry for that day, "every height, with a deep, organized defense system must be stormed, numerous bunkers must be reduced. The difficulty of the struggle is made plain by the high level of casualties." The Pioniere, who were charged with clearing minefields, repairing or building bridges, and preparing fording sites, all while under enemy fire, suffered "considerable casualties."[19] This was infantry fighting, with the panzers giving support after the engineers cleared the mines. For the grenadiers it meant demolitions and flamethrowers and trench fighting, with sharpened entrenching tools to cleave an Ivan's body, Handgranate, and bursts from their MPi.

Columns of Russian tanks were reported, sighted, or heard by the squealing of their tracks that night, as fierce Rotarmisten counterattacks became manifest on the 12th. Though the major German offensive was in the south, driving into Stalingrad and the Caucasus, the 2. Pz.Armee attack on the Sukhinichi sector threatened a thrust toward Kaluga and Moscow, and thus was encountering the full strength of the Red Army. The K.L.B. was unable to hold its Slobodka Brückenkopf over the Shisdra, as it lacked antitank weapons against the Red tanks. But Schimmelmann seized Hill 243.9 by 09,15 and Luz attacked into Bely Verk. The Ivans were driven back from Debri with two tanks knocked out by 8,8cm flak as Pak, but KV-1s, T-34s, and English Mark IIs were all along the Shisdra.

On 13 August, as II.Btl./I.R.119 of the 25.Inf. Div.(mot) was ordered not to cross the Wytebet by VIII. A.K., Balck met with the Ia of the 56.I.D. about artillery support to assist its advance. 18.Pz.Div. under acting commander Oberst Albert Praun was committed and took Hill 227.5 and Kolmkshchi. At 14,40 hours the 11.Pz.Div. received orders to change the direction of its drive from the west to the north and establish bridgeheads over the Shisdra at Dretovo. Körner's Pz.G.R.111 was in its assembly area when tragically Luftwaffe Stuka bombs fell short and caused eighty-five casualties, including some thirty who died, "by our own fliers." In anger and frustration the wounded were attended to, and the attack was postponed.[20]

The 11.Pz.Div. continued to slug forward, alternating the three battle groups: Luz, Schimmelmann, and Körner. Kampfgruppe Luz led first, with K.61, I.Abt./Pz.Rgt.15, Pz.Pi.Btl.209, and II.Btl./Pz.Gren. Rgt.110. The intensity of the fighting around Bely Verk was reflected in the Tagesmeldung of Luz to Division, 14 August: "The enemy tenaciously defending, each meter must be struggled for through the gorge-filled terrain." Three trench systems, with trenches 1.8m (6 feet) deep, eighteen fieldworks, and twelve bunkers were assaulted and taken. Intricate positioning of Pak and heavy weapons among the hollows made flanking difficult in the tangled woods. Luz reported 120 Russians killed and eighty men and two officers taken prisoner; nine Russian tanks were knocked out, six by I./15, and three by the 8,8cm of IV.(Flak)/A.R.119. One Pak, one antitank rifle, and four machine guns were also destroyed. The battle group's own losses were twenty-six men and two officers—both battalion commanders were killed—with five officers and eighty men wounded.

On the 15th Graf Schimmelmann reported losses to Pz.Rgt.15 of fourteen Pz.III lang and one Pz.IV lang, but the regiment was still at strength with eighty-nine panzers: ten Pz.II, ten Pz.III k, fifty-eight Pz.III l, eight Pz.IV l, and three Bef.Wg. In a Fernschreiben (teleprinter) to Harpe's XXXXI. Pz.Korps that day the 11.Pz.Div. listed its "Kampfstärke" (battle strength), including eighty-nine panzers, artillery including three 8,8cm guns, and the four rifle battalions having about 575 men each. On the 19th the division reported a Grabenstärke (infantry trench strength) of 4,544.[21] Photographs of Schimmelmann investigating the "Panzergrab" (tank graveyard) of Bely Verk with the burned-out hulks of KV-1s, T-34s, T-60s, and English Mark IIs, show a pensive visage. In the battle from 11 August to the 17th the division reported to XXXXI. Pz.K. 2,095 Russians killed, 1,692 prisoners taken, and 123 tanks, 69 guns, 13 mortars, 67 MGs, and numerous firearms destroyed or captured.[22]

The Gespensters struggled ahead against heavy resistance and counterattacks. At OKH Halder mused in his diary that "Operation WHIRLWIND has made gains, but is approaching its objective only slowly in very difficult, fortified terrain and against very strong opposition." Luz told Balck the difficulty was not the Russian infantry, but the superior tank forces. On the 16th he messaged Balck that the panzers couldn't negotiate the marshy terrain and that even a KV-1 would get stuck, adding, "The troops are tired and urgently need rest." Balck responded "that carrying out of the attacks was of decisive importance for the continuation of the advance. A troop leader under these circumstances must be hard, and in regard to the particular situation demand the utmost from the *Truppe*. It must be made clear to the troops that clearing the Shisdra crossings is the last difficult task, and that the terrain north of the Shisdra is more open with fewer ravines." But the advance would not get that far. K.61 was repulsed three times in its attack, and the K.L.B. reported a new type of KV-1 with 120 mm (4.8 inches) of armor, with an all-officer crew (probably the KV-1B with additional armor welded on).[23]

The next day Gen. Rudolf Schmundt, Hitler's adjutant, lectured Balck and hurriedly assembled commanders including Gen.Maj. Kurowski, Chef des Stabes Pz.A.O.K. 2. "*Meine Herren*, the Führer wants to express to you through me his displeasure that the battle is stalemated!" Schmundt told the officers. After a quick visit to the front, after which he said, "*Danke*, I've seen enough," Schmundt left again.[24] Despite the reshuffling of units in Kampfgruppen Luz, Körner, and Schimmelmann, and tactical thrusts, WIRBELWIND made no progress. In retrospect, it is difficult to justify panzer forces, whose forte was maneuver, being committed to a struggle of attrition in a marshy, forested, and heavily fortified area.

On 22 August the exhausted panzergrenadiers of I./110 were relieved by II.Btl./Pz.Gren.Rgt.59 of Gen.Maj. Walter Düveert's 20.Pz.Div., and II./15 turned over a sector of the forming H.K.L. to 56.Inf. Div. The K.L.B. lost its third battalion commander in the fighting. The Russian VVS was active with night bombers ("Nähmaschinen"—sewing machines, from their engine noises) as well as day attacks. At OKH Halder noted on 22 August, "Operation WHIRLWIND is being diluted from a full-stage offensive to a containing action."[25]

On 25 August the 11. Panzer-Division was withdrawn for badly needed Auffrischung (refitting). It was apparent that Unternehmen BLAU was not bringing Russia to defeat, and the division was ordered to prepare a "Winterstellung" (winter position) behind the H.K.L. Two construction battalions were assigned to help build this around Orel. Panzers and vehicles would be emplaced in "Fahrzeugboxen" (vehicle boxes), sheltered places in sunken roads or hollowed out from slopes, some even with folding doors. These provided protection against cold and shellfire, and they would also be camouflaged from aerial observation. Left behind were gefallene Kameraden, to be interred later, in little divisional cemeteries with strange names, far from home—Retschnitsa, Goyana, Dolgoya.

Nonetheless Gespenster units would still be called on as "Feuerwehr" (fire brigades) for the H.K.L. On 29 August Russian air attacks and artillery Trommelfeuer (drum fire) pounded the front lines and tanks broke through. Sperrfeuer (barrier fire) from the German artillery separated the Russian infantry from their tanks, and an Eingreifgruppe (counterattack group) from the Elfte went in. The troops claimed ninety-one tanks destroyed, and "heaps" of dead Russians were seen. Kolosovo and Kuchina also saw attacks repulsed.

Demoralization was apparent among the Russians. Ivans could be seen driven forward at pistol-point, and Russian tanks fired at deserters. On the 24th there were a group of Überläufer who beat their Commissar to death and deserted. On the 30th a senior Commissar himself deserted (declaring, "It's all over"), and the next day his appeal by loudspeaker brought forty-eight more Überläufer over to the German lines. A tank even drove across, its barrel raised and white cloth on the turret.[26]

September 1942 found Balck's Elfte acting as Feuerwehr and even holding a sector of the main line of resistance of Harpe's XXXXI. Pz.Korps along the Shisdra. Kampfgruppen Luz (11.Pz.Gren.Brig. Stab with K.61, the K.L.B., and II./110) and Körner (Pz.Gr .Rgt.111 Stab with I./110 and I. and II./111) were in almost constant combat. The fighting strength of the infantry had been much reduced: 110 reported 469 officers and men for the whole regiment, 111 reported 494, K.61 had 203, and the K.L.B. had 242.[27]

On 3 September the Russians mounted a fierce attack that broke through between the division's left flank and Scheller's 9.Pz.Div. Schimmelmann's Panzer-Regiment 15 was at strength with ninety-nine panzers, and in the intense tank actions they claimed twenty-eight Russian tanks: Maj. Heinrich Pricken's I. Abteilung knocked out three KV-1s and five English Mark IIs; II.Abt. under Hptm. Karl Lestmann who had replaced wounded Major Leinberger, knocked out ten KV-1s, four T-34s, and one T-60 flame-throwing tank; and III.Abt., now under Oblt. Edel Zachariae-Lingenthal from 2. Kompanie, claimed two T-34s and three T-60s. The regiment lost two Panzer IV lang to mechanical problems and eight Pz.III l to Russian gunfire. The Panzer III lang with the high-velocity 5cm L/60 gun, able to knock out the heavy T-34s and KV-1s, was the mainstay of the panzer divisions.

Nonetheless, with Russian pressure, a new H.K.L. had to be established south of Volosovo. Maj. Friedrich Guttmacher's Panz.Jg.Abt.61 positioned its 5cm Pak 38s with Oberst Albert Henze's 110, and the attached army engineer battalion He.Pi.Btl.(mot) 630 laid 2,000 antitank T-Minen and 1,000 antipersonnel S-Minen, strung barbed wire, and worked on other defenses. The Teller Panzermine would wreck the track of a tank or destroy a vehicle; it was activated by some 180 kilograms (400 pounds) of pressure on the pressure plate. The Schü-Mine detonated about a meter above the ground and caused casualties over a radius of 100 meters.[28] The bunkers built by the engineers for machine-gun positions generally were for four Landsers, and they also constructed bunkers for the 5cm Pak.

Heavy-weapons sections were positioned among the line companies, Luz commanding on the left with K.61 (strength 234), II.Btl./110 (with 397), and the K.L.B. (248); Körner commanded on the right with I./111 (153), I./110 (208), and 87 troopers from Pz.Gr.Rgt.111 support units. II./111 (150) and Pz.Rgt.15 (with 72 panzers and also 12 Sturmgeschütze) were in reserve, the units rotating. (The infantry were severely understrength, as a panzergrenadier battalion was authorized some 800 personnel.) Oberst Oskar Schmidt positioned his Pz.A.R. 119 batteries for artillery support, with fire missions called in by the Vorgeschobener Beobachter. He had six le.F.H. batteries with twenty 10,5cm howitzers, two s.F.H. batteries with six 15cm howitzers, one Kanone Batterie with four 10cm guns, and one s.Flak Battr. with four 8,8cm guns (the other battery was nonoperational because it had no guns).[29]

An interesting experiment was carried out by Oberwachtmeister (Oberfeldwebel, First Sergeant) Hennecke of Pz. Propaganda Kp.694 with II./110. He brought his loudspeaker vehicles up to the front lines and made appeals in the Tatar and Kirghiz languages to the Kazakhstanis in the Russian units opposite. "The success was surprising," reported the battalion commander. Eighty deserters came across into the II.Btl. lines, and 100 into the neighboring sector. The Russians retaliated with heavy artillery and MG fire and his apparatus was damaged. But it was repaired and put on a knocked-out tank, and the Überläufer continued coming across anyway.[30]

The Russian deserters were a crucial source of information for the Ic section (division intelligence), especially when it was provided willingly through Vernehmung (interrogation). Orders of battle, unit strengths, equipment, and morale could all be deduced. Thus the divisions and regiments facing XXXXI. Pz.K. could be identified as being from the 16th and 61st Armies, the 1st Guards Cavalry Corps, and the 10th Tank Corps, and their regiments as well. Name, age, family, residence, occupation, and unit details were all gathered.

The interrogation of deserter Semon Petrovich Chernyavski through translator Volksdeutscher Petkau revealed such information: Chernyavski was twenty-seven years old, married, had one child, was a Ukrainian from Stalino, and had been a coal miner; he was a first sergeant in the supply company of the 1166th Rifle Regiment of the 346th Rifle Division, 61st Army; Chernyavski deserted because of aversion to the Soviet regime, and because his family was behind the German lines.

A Sergeant Korbunov deserted 17 August at Polyana through Henze's 110 sector. He was a member of the 4th Rifle Brigade, activated at Moscow in January–February 1942; after action on the Smolensk front the brigade was transferred to Orel, and on 12 August it went by truck to the woods near Polyana where defensive positions and bunkers were built. The brigade had three battalions totaling about 4,000 troops, and had suffered 30 percent casualties. They had 82mm and 120mm mortars and 45mm and 76mm antitank guns. Complete gas equipment was at hand. In Korbunov's company there were many Sträflinge (convicts) and older people. War-weariness—and supervision and pressure by commissars—was very great, and the troops had seen the German propaganda leaflets that promised German success in the war.[31]

On 9 September the Russians sent two armies against Model's 9. Armee in the Rzhev salient. Model argued his army was on the verge of collapse, and Hitler reluctantly released the Grossdeutschland motorized division for counterattacks. The GD exhausted itself over the next few days, but the salient held. General Zhukov had gone south to the Stalingrad area on 26 August, though Ivan Konev, now at West Front, continued the attacks along the Sukhinichi sector lines.

For the Gespensters the period of the "Voronezh" offensive was over. On 13 September Maj. Heinrich Pricken's I.Abteilung was separated from Panzer-Regiment 15 for independent assignment, leaving the regiment with two battalions, and II./15 was detached to support the 56.I.D. On the 13th the 11.Pz.Div. left

2. Panzerarmee and went into army group reserve. In his message of 14 September Generaloberst Rudolf Schmidt could praise the division as the "pace-maker in the advance to the Shisdra," but it was obvious that Operation WIRBELWIND to destroy the Sukhinichi salient had failed.[32]

Attention was increasingly riveted on the brutal struggle for Stalingrad, the "Rattenkrieg" (rats' war) to the Landsers, characterized by heroic determination of German and Russian soldiers alike. Intelligence summaries from Oberstleutnant Reinhard Gehlen's Fremde Heere Ost (Foreign Armies, East) of Abwehr (military intelligence) continued to be optimistic, maintaining that the Red Army was exhausted and had no reserves. Commanders at the front had a very different opinion.

In frustration Hitler, having already abused numerous army leaders, relieved List of command of H.Gr. A on 9 September and took over himself (assigning Kleist on 22 November). He replaced the evermore critical Halder as chief of staff at OKH with Generalleutnant Kurt Zeitzler—who promptly also urged ending the battle—on 24 September; he sent Generalleutnant Walter Warlimont, deputy chief to Gen. Alfred Jodl at OKW, on extended leave; and he further subordinated Feldmarschall Wilhelm Keitel as chief of staff at OKW. At 6. Armee Paulus in turn relieved Generals Gustav von Wietersheim of XIV. Pz.Korps and Viktor von Schwedler of IV. A.K. (Infanterie) over the battle.

In Stalingrad casualties on both sides mounted in the fighting in the industrial ruins of the Dzerzhinski Traktor, the Barrikady, and the Krasny Oktyabr factories. By November the Germans occupied nine-tenths of the city, but Col. Gen. V. I. Chuikov's 62nd Army defenders—dug into the steep riverbanks sheltered from German artillery, and receiving reinforcements crossing the Volga from the east bank despite Stuka attacks—continued to hold out, suffering incredible losses. German forces were also being consumed in the struggle, including mobile forces: three panzer divisions (14., 16., 24.) and three motorized divisions (3., 29., 60.) whose equipment, personnel, and capabilities were wasted in the building-to-building and hand-to-hand combat. This was in addition to fourteen infantry divisions.

As 6. Armee and elements of 4. Pz.Armee were committed and expended in this holocaust, the long flanks were left increasingly vulnerable as the temperatures began to drop and the blowing snow of the coming winter sifted over the devastated ruins. The Rumanians, whose 3. and 4. Army frontages were extended as Paulus pulled in his German divisions, objected to their expected roles but were ignored. (Nor apparently were extensive fieldworks and antitank ditches undertaken.) There were few antitank guns of adequate caliber and in general no mobile forces for counterattack, and the Germans had not provided them. The German mobile forces were being ground down in Stalingrad. Hitler, who had opposed this misuse of mobile forces at Kiev and Voronezh, incomprehensibly and fatally demanded they be used for the capture of this city.[33]

The 11. Panzerdivision, having begun construction of defensive positions for the winter around Orel, was ordered to march back to Bryansk for Auffrischung, to pull maintenance and incorporate replacements and equipment. Then came orders to rail-load, a process begun on 26 September, in order to move south to Millerovo north of Voroshilovgrad (later Lugansk) on the Donets in the operational area of H.Gr. B. But then the orders were canceled, and the E-Transports were stopped at Voronezh and diverted back to an area around Kastornoye east of Kursk. On 27 September the K.L.B., Kradschützen Lehr Bataillon, was reassigned to the Schule für Schnelle Truppen at Krampnitz near Berlin.[34]

Assembled by 4 October, the Gespensters again began construction of winter quarters. Construction of bunkers and shelters for vehicles was much more difficult than at Orel, where wood for lumber was plentiful. Russian houses were in some cases commandeered and the population displaced, though many smaller peasant izbas, even if having the pech (oven) for warmth and built in the protective balkas, were primitive and crawling with lice. (There were reasons why Red Army soldiers had their hair cut off upon induction.) Nonetheless the Landsers generally felt the population was friendly, and harvest festivals when the Russians dressed in colorful folk clothing provided a time to relax. "And so passed October '42," says the division history, "in tranquility—no fire brigade actions—only the work of winter accommodations; to be sure, there were inspections within units and organizations to bring men, weapons, and equipment into working order. *Ja*—and then came the Schlammperiode—and that then was really tranquil!"[35]

Along with rebuilding the division, training was renewed, with an Unteroffizier Lehrgang (course of instruction) at Orel, and engineer training for all, to begin 10 November. The Schlammperiode again saw the usefulness of the small horse-drawn panje wagons. There was frost on the night of 22–23 October, and snow flurries by the end of the month were a harbinger of winter. Felt boots, white camouflage parkas, and wider Ostkette (eastern tracks) for the Panzerwagen meant better preparation for the 1942–43 winter than for the previous winter.

On 1 November 1942 the 11.Pz.Div. was displaced again, this time back to Roslavl west of the Desna in H.Gr. Mitte reserve, but also to mount anti-partisan operations in the vast forest areas north of Bryansk. The Elften could hope that units inheriting their winter positions appreciated their labors, but this crack division was not in major combat for most of October and much of November as it absorbed and trained replacements for the battles to come. In November sobering news came from North Africa, where Anglo-American forces landed from Casablanca to Algiers on 8 November, even as Rommel's Panzerarmee Afrika retreated from El Alamein in British Egypt.

While the 11. Panzer-Division was in 4. Armee reserve under Korück A.O.K. 4 around Roslavl, the 11. Panzergrenadier-Brigade headquarters was deactivated 16 November as being superfluous, its last commander being Oberst Hans Ulrich Back since September. Back went to the Schnelle Truppen Schule, and later commanded a rebuilt 16.Pz.Div. The staff and materials were reassigned or distributed among the divisional units. Oberleutnant Karl Thieme, for example, was reassigned to Pz.Gr.Rgt.110 for employment as a company commander.[36]

Various units were employed in the Bandenbekämpfung or Partisanenkrieg, combating the partisans. Gen.d.Inf. Gotthard Heinrici's 4. Armee issued instructions that the Unternehmungen (operations) were not to be portrayed as Strafexpedition (punishment actions) against the population, but as Befriedung (pacification). One deterrent to partisan activities was the rounding up of males of military age, sixteen to sixty years, who might be drafted or recruited by partisan bands, and transporting them to the Dulag (transit camp) in Roslavl. Another was the billeting of units in the local villages. The platoons of Pz.Gr.Rgt.110 were quartered in some ten villages, their strengths ranging from 76 to 253, while Pz.Rgt.15 was also quartered in ten villages, with strengths of 91 to 230, related to village size.[37]

In some cases the operations against bands that were trapped or aggressive resulted in deadly encounters; in other cases the partisans slipped away, leaving empty bunkers, depots, and cooking ovens. Early on 15 November a four-day operation was mounted in a forested area south of the rail line into Roslavl. It was a hammer-and-anvil tactic with Guttmacher's Pz.Jg. Abt.61 blocking to the east, Hauser's K.61 to the south, and Henze's 110 driving in from the railroad. In support was Schmidt's Pz.A.R.119 and Bullerdieck's 209 engineers. Five panzers of 3.Kp./15 under Oberlt. Maiwald moved in too, and reconnaissance aircraft flew low overhead. Horse patrols were used to go through the forests and underbrush, though at one point Fahnenjunker Friedrich Karl von Eggeling of Pz.Rgt.15 had a patrol that was shot up in an ambush. His horse was shot and he plunged into an icy stream and hid in the reeds. But Lt. Werner von Rupprecht had heard the gunfire and came to the rescue with his light Spähwagen half-track, getting von Eggeling back to the German lines and into warm clothing.[38]

In his Ia report to 4. Armee on 21 November Major Kinitz noted the loss of two killed and five wounded, and an SPW, an Lkw, and a motorcycle damaged on mines. Enemy losses were 20–30 dead, and 550 men (between 16 and 65 years of military age) and 40 women were transported to the Roslavl Dulag. The weapons taken included a biplane, a carbine, and a machine pistol, while some 100 bunkers and fighting positions were destroyed by the engineers. Some suspect buildings were also destroyed. But, as so often, "The bands themselves were no longer in the vicinity"—a common theme in the reports.

The resources confiscated included some livestock and vegetable and grain products. The primary purpose of seizing these goods was to deny their use by the partisan bands. Undoubtedly this caused some hardship among the civilian population, but there was resentment that in many ways they had probably supported the partisans, and now would be dependent upon the Germans for necessities; and if the German cooks and troops could also benefit from the booty, well that was hard to dismiss. The various reports included recommendations emphasizing moving into position under cover of darkness to achieve surprise, and in Oberst Schmidt's *Erfahrungen* (experiences) he urged that "The numbers of translators can never be large enough," for interrogations and announcements and explanations.[39]

In the third week of November 1942 rumors began to spread about Russian attacks around Stalingrad, and on 25 November there was a Wehrmacht radio report that there was a major Russian breakthrough into the great bend of the Don, behind 6. Armee. Once again the 11. Panzer-Division, alerted on the 21st, began rail-loading their Kettenfahrzeuge with crews in passenger cars on the 25th. Trains bore them 700 kilometers (400 miles) south from Roslavl via Belgorod to Millerovo, the major rail center serving Rostov, completing the movement by 7 December. On 1 December at Morosovskaye on the bleak, snow-swept Kalmyk steppe, fleeing Rumanians headed for Rostov, as if seeking refuge from a major disaster, and intending to travel home. There were also Italian rear-area elements at Millerovo who nervously shot at anything moving. It was only by their bad aim that the Gespensters didn't suffer casualties. "Against the enemy we'll hold our own," said Balck, "but may God save us from our allies!"[40] Initially assigned to 3. Rumanian Army, by 6 December Balck's 11.Pz.Div. had been reassigned, to Hoth's 4. Panzerarmee again, in XXXXVIII. Pz.K. It deployed up behind the Chir River, a tributary of the Don joining it at Nizhne Chirskaya, east of the Donbas and fronting Rostov.

On 19 November the Red Army had struck—not against the German 6. Armee *in* Stalingrad, but against the extended flanks, against the poorly equipped 3. Rumanian Army in the north and 4. Rumanian Army in the south. As late as 6 November Gehlen's Fremde Heere Ost intelligence appreciation indicated that any major Soviet offensive would probably be mounted against 2.Pz.Armee of H.Gr. Mitte, not farther south. But the Soviet offensive around Stalingrad was, in fact, Operation URANUS, masterminded by Marshal Vasilevsky and General Zhukov.

The Russians had been able to mass formidable forces, and Konstantin Rokossovsky's Don Front and Nikolai Vatutin's Southwest Front spearheaded by Col. Gen. P. L. Romanenko's 5th Tank Army smashed through Petre Dumitrescu's 3. Rumanian Army in the north across the Don, and Andrei Yeremenko's armies of Stalingrad Front collapsed Constantin Constantinescu's 4. Rumanian Army in the south. In their defense, the Rumanians had only inferior 4,7cm anti-tank guns, incapable of stopping the formidable T-34s. Within five days, by the 23rd, the Russian spearheads had penetrated deep around Paulus's 6.Armee. The vital Don bridge at Kalach was taken by *coup de main* that morning, and the spearheads met that afternoon, encircling 21 divisions, some 330,000 men, in the Stalingrad Kessel.

The Germans might have sensed a new sophistication to the Red Army operations. On 9 October under Stavka Order No. 307, the principle of "unitary command," the political commissars lost their operational role. While the Zampolits were still deputy commanders for political affairs, Stalin was now beginning to entrust the conduct of military operations to the rising new commanders who had actually fought in the bitter campaigns. In addition, on 16 October Stalin issued Order No. 325 to analyze the cause of previous failures and acknowledging the new roles for tank and mechanized units. Massing of tank forces in tank armies was beginning, to carry out armor missions as the German panzer corps and panzer armies had done, though these were ad hoc formations, not coherent combined-arms formations.[41] Nonetheless the ingrained habit of unquestioning obedience, reinforced by the pervasive fear of punishment, still limited the initiative of field- and company-grade officers and NCOs, the type of individual initiative that explains much of the German success. But the weight of vast Russian resources of manpower and industrial production was beginning to be felt, along with emerging operational skills.

CHAPTER TWELVE

Battles of the River Chir

THE SOVIET OFFENSIVE ENCIRCLING PAULUS'S 6. ARMEE IN Stalingrad had caught the Germans by surprise, but it was some time before the revived power of the Red Army was realized. Throughout the summer and autumn of 1942 the Wehrmacht had encircled and destroyed the Russian armies and had reached the Volga and the Caucasus Mountains. Allied Lend-Lease materiel had been suspended after Arctic convoy PQ 17 to Murmansk had been slaughtered off the North Cape of occupied Norway in July, and it seemed as if the Soviet Union was on the verge of collapse. German decisions about Stalingrad can only be understood through this perspective.

A first attempt to counterattack the Russian drives was mounted by XXXXVIII. Panzerkorps under Generalleutnant Ferdinand Heim behind the former 3. Rumanian Army sector of the Don. Heim's corps included General Radu's 1. Rumanian Armored Division, some units of Generalmajor Johannes Baessler's 14. Pz.Div., and Oberst Eberhard Rodt's 22.Pz.Div. But the 1. Rumanian was equipped with some 108 obsolete Czech Panzer 38(t) with 3,7cm guns; the 14.Pz.Div. was exhausted from the Stalingrad urban warfare; and the 22.Pz.Div., minus its Pz.Gren.Rgt.140 sent to reinforce 2. Armee in the Voronezh area, was in process of reequipping its Pz.Rgt.204 with Panzer IIIs and IVs from its 38(t)s.

In addition, while the 22. Panzer had been in reserve behind the 8. Italian Army, its panzers were immobilized for lack of fuel and dug in for the winter among bundles of straw. When the regiment tried to move out, most of its 104 panzers wouldn't start, or quickly dropped out. Mice from the straw had chewed the rubber insulation of the electrical wiring, causing sparking short circuits and even electrical fires.[1]

On 19 November the 22.Pz.Div. attacked the 5th Tank Army, but its twenty available panzers and Panzerjägers barely survived the Soviet onslaught. Corps commander Ferdinand Heim was ordered arrested by an enraged Hitler on 26 November and was court-martialed and imprisoned, though he was later released. His chief of staff was also relieved, replaced by Oberst Friedrich von Mellenthin, staff officer with Panzerarmee Afrika until that September. On 30 November

General der Panzertruppen Hans Cramer took over XXXXVIII. Pz.K. temporarily until Gen.d.Pz.Tr. Otto von Knobelsdorff took over (Knobelsdorff was officially assigned on 10 December, but he arrived on the 4th). On 4 December the corps Hauptquartier was relocated from Petrovka to Nizhne Chirskaya, at the confluence of the Chir and the Don, east of Rostov.

The German command structure had been reorganized, and Feldmarschall Erich von Manstein, planner of the French campaign and conqueror of Sevastopol, left his 11. Armee in the north and arrived by train from Vitebsk to take over the newly created Heeresgruppe Don on 27 November. The new army group was given overall control of Paulus's 6.Armee, Hoth's 4. Pz.Armee, remnants of the 3. and 4. Rumanian Armies, and army-sized Armee-Abteilung (Army Detachment) Hollidt. The latter unit was made responsible for the sector along the Chir River, a tributary west of the Don. A.A.Hollidt was organized with the staff of XVII. A.K. under General der Infanterie Karl-Adolf Hollidt, and included XXXXVIII. Pz.K. That in turn was to command Generalmajor Balck's 11. Panzer-Division closing into its Versammlingsraum (assembly area) on 6 and 7 December, Generalmajor Walter Lucht's 336. Sächsisch (Saxon) Infanterie-Division defending along the Chir, and 7. Luftwaffenfelddivision arriving by the 9th. (These Luftwaffe divisions were Hermann Göring's attempt to ensure a role with the ground forces, but for which they were poorly trained and, said Mellenthin, "They were commanded by air force men who knew nothing about land fighting."[2])

Manstein's mission was to relieve the surrounded 6. Armee, and he assumed Paulus would also attempt a breakout. At 23,45 hours on 23 November Paulus sent a message to Hitler at OKW urging that he have freedom of action. But at 08,38 on the 24th Hitler responded that his position on the Volga must be held, and the pocket would be supplied by air. While the Demyansk pocket had indeed been supplied by the Luftwaffe during the winter of 1941–42, the 6. Armee was a much larger force. The flight distances from the Tatsinskaya and Morozovsk airfields were some 200 kilometers (125 miles), a three-hour flight, while the airfields in the pocket at Pitomnik and Gumrak were under air (and soon artillery) attack. But Hitler was persuaded that the Luftwaffe could supply 6. Armee by Reichsmarschall Göring, although perhaps with more qualifications than is generally acknowledged.

The decisive conversation at the Berghof at Berchtesgaden was conducted, not by Göring, but by his chief of staff, Generaloberst Hans Jeschonnek, whose conditions included close airfields and passable flying weather. Paulus estimated 700 tons a day would be needed; Göring told his staff 500 tons, but the staff replied 350 tons would be the maximum possible. Russian ground advances and winter weather made such resupply very questionable. Manstein reported to the Führer's headquarters that Generaloberst von Richthofen, now commanding Luftflotte IV and the man who would have to carry out the resupply mission with the trimotor Ju 52s (1-ton capacity) and converted twin-engine Heinkel 111s (half-ton capacity), said only 200 tons a day average could be counted on.[3]

Regardless, Manstein felt his relief attack, Unternehmen WINTERGEWITTER (Winter Storm) should be met by a 6. Armee thrust, Operation DONNERSCHLAG (Thunderclap), and Manstein sent his chief of staff, General Friedrich Schulz, and later his chief of operations, Oberst Theodor Busse, into the pocket to urge the joint operations. Manstein's plan was for Hoth's 4. Pz.Armee to attack from the southwest with Generalleutnant Friedrich Kirchner's LVII. Pz.K: 23.Pz.Div., 6.Pz.Div., which had arrived from France having been rebuilt after the 1941–42 winter, and to be joined by 17.Pz.Div. from the Orel sector. A converging attack was to be mounted from across the Don at Nizhne Chirskaya by XXXXVIII. Panzerkorps, spearheaded by 11. Panzer-Division.

Meanwhile the Red Army had struck elsewhere along the Ostfront. To the north, Operation MARS was mounted on 25 November against 9. Armee in the Rzhev salient of Kluge's H.Gr. Mitte by Gen. Maksim Purkayev's Kalinin Front and Col. Gen. Ivan Konev's West Front. Zhukov had direct control of this operation, and there is evidence that MARS was intended to be even more important than URANUS, and that it would expand to destroy H.Gr. Mitte and end the threat to Moscow. But 9. Armee was commanded by tough and resourceful Generaloberst Walter Model, and the Russians were not attacking poorly equipped German allied forces, but veteran German units. By the middle of December MARS had been blunted by panzer counterattacks, with devastating Russian casualties of some 300,000.[4]

Even as Operation RING was to wear down and destroy 6. Armee in Stalingrad, Stavka was also planning Operation SATURN, to break through Italo

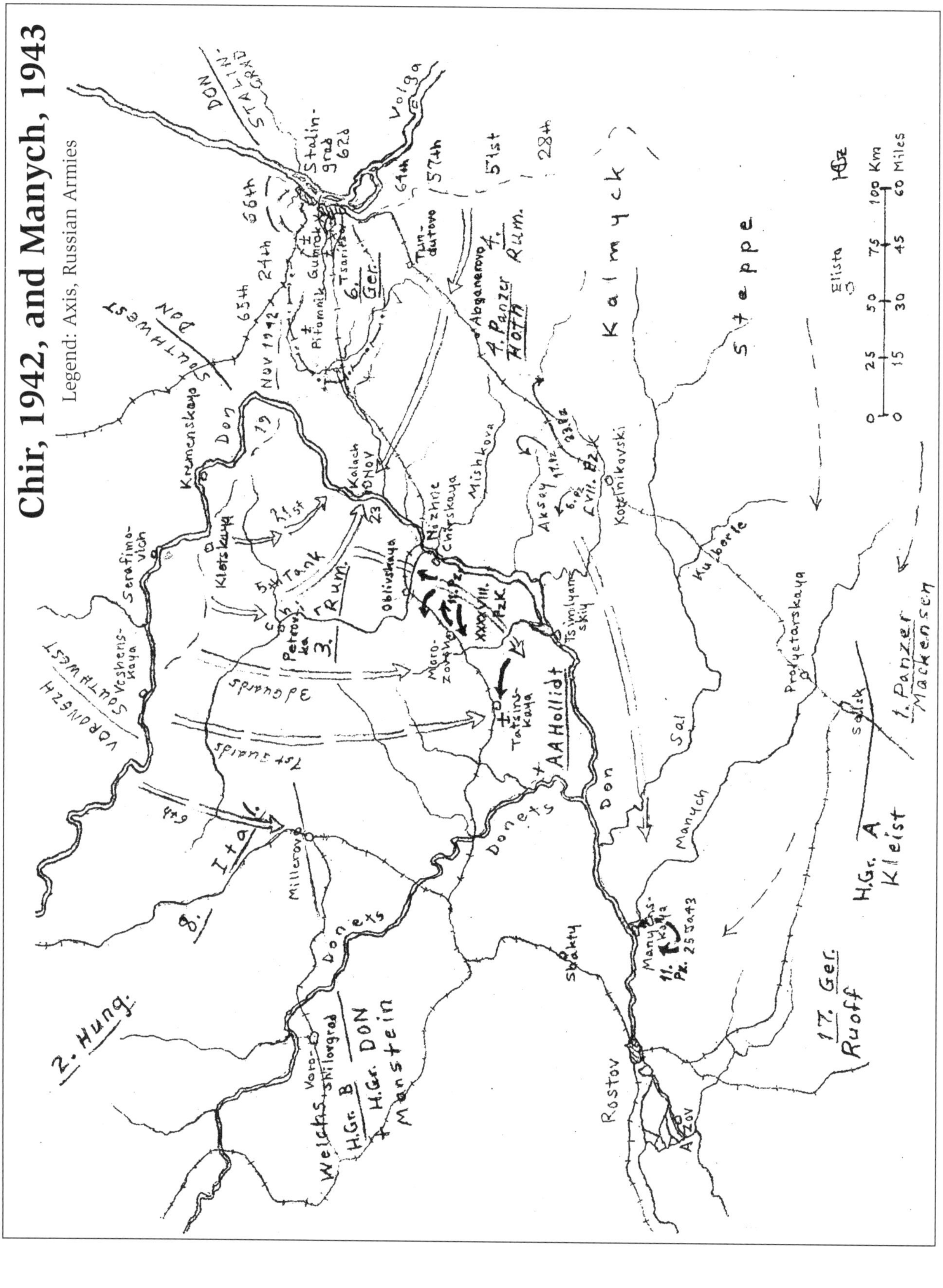

Chir, 1942, and Manych, 1943

Legend: Axis, Russian Armies

Gariboldi's 8. Italian Army on the middle Don and drive south to the Sea of Azov to trap the 1. Panzer and 17. Armee of H.Gr. A to the south. Hitler had finally passed the command of H.G. A on to Kleist on 22 November, with General Richard Ruoff at 17. Armee and Generaloberst Eberhard von Mackensen succeeding to Pz.A.O.K. 1. But first Russian steps were taken to widen the breach isolating 6. Armee in the Stalingrad Kessel from the rest of H.Gr. Don's forces, and mount spoiling attacks to disrupt Manstein's relief plans.

After the 3. Rumanian Army was shattered along the Don, German forces fell back to rally behind the Chir under XXXXVIII. Pz.K. The 40 kilometers (25-mile) river line was primarily held by Lucht's 336.I.D. between Nizhne Chirskaya northwest to Surovikino, all three regiments (658., 686., and 687. Grenadier Rgt.) on line. Alarmeinheiten (units on alert for action) were on the left flank, and Gruppe Adam, comprising various elements under Oberst Wilhem Adam, was holding a small bridgehead across the Chir at Nizhne Chirskaya on the right. The Alarmeinheiten were actually just miscellaneous rallied units, including 6. Armee rear-area personnel. The 7. Luftwaffenfelddivision would arrive by the 9th.

On 6 December General Balck arrived at Nizhne Chirskaya to reconnoiter the sector where his 11.Pz.Div. was to cross the Don to join Hoth's 4. Pz.Armee relief attack. "It was absolutely vital," Manstein said, "that we should continue to hold this stretch of river, as our bridgehead in the angle between the Chir and the Don, including the Don bridge at Nizhne Chirskaya, was of fundamental importance for the relief of Sixth Army. Apart from that, an enemy breakthrough over the Chir would have cleared the way to the Morosovsky and Tatsinskaya airfields, which were only 25 (40 kilometers) and 50 (80 kilometers) miles away, as well as to the Donetz crossings and Rostov."[5]

At this time Gen.Maj. Balck's 11.Pz.-Div. staff included Maj. Franz-Joachim Kinitz, his Ia as Erste Generalstabsoffizier, Major Kaldrack as IIa (adjutant), and Lt. Klaus Knorr as Gehilfe (Assistant) Ia. In the coming operations Balck had basically four maneuver elements: Kampfgruppen of Pz.Rgt.15 under the command of the very able Oberst Graf Schimmelman, Pz.Gren.Rgt.110 led by the imperturbable Oberst Albert Henze, Pz.G.R.111 under Oberst Alexander von Bosse (a Balt later to command a Cossack division), and Kradschützen-Bataillon 61 led by Hauptmann Paul Freiherr von Hauser, its astute Austrian commander. K.61 was basically the reconnaissance battalion, and motorcycles had generally been replaced with SPW half-tracks and Achtrad armored cars.[6]

Companies were assigned to these from Pz.Pionier-Btl.209 now under Hptm. Erhard Grevendorf, and Paks from Guttmacher's Pz.Jäger-Abt.61. Pz.Art.Rgt.119 under Oberst Oskar Schmidt gave artillery support, and Heeres Flak Art.Abt.277 with its Acht-komma-achts was its IV. Abteilung. Other division units included Pz.Nachrichten-Abt.341 (Signals) under Hptm. Theodor Poretschkin; division services, including Sanitäts-Tr.Abt.61 and Nachschub-Abt.61 under Dinafü Maj. Günther von Zamory; and units of the Dinatru (Divisionsnachschubtruppen, division supply troops) moving as the Tross (trains). Ia Kinitz reported the division fighting strength as 4,293, and the ration strength as 9,900. Pz.-Rgt.15, now just two battalions again (II. and III., Major Pricken's I.Abt./15 being separated 13 September), had 103 panzers: twenty-eight Panzer IIs, sixty-four Pz.IIIs, and eleven Pz.IVs. Pz.Art.Rgt.119 had thirty-two Rohre (tubes): twenty-three 10,5cm le.F.H., five 15cm s.F.H., and four 10cm Kan. There were eight 8,8cm flak guns, and there were forty-six antitank guns: twenty 3,7cm le.Pak and twenty-six 5cm m.Pak.[7]

On 7 December Russian forces crossed the upper Chir and broke through the left flank of the 336.Inf.Div. and drove south. XXXXVIII. Pz.Korps Ia Oberstlt. von Mellenthin alerted the 11. Panzer-Division that 51 Russian tanks had broken through and directed them to attack with Pz.-Rgt.15; *"Eile geboten!"* ("Make haste!") he added.[8] This was the Russian 1st Tank Corps under Maj. Gen. V. V. Butkov of Col. Gen. P. L. Romanenko's 5th Tank Army. Romanenko's army had six rifle divisions, two cavalry divisions, Butkov's 1st Tank Corps, one separate tank brigade, and eight artillery regiments reinforced by four additional rifle divisions from the 21st and 65th Armies. Its strength was about 70,000 men, 182 tanks, and 1,213 guns and mortars. On 6 December the 5th Tank Army was reinforced further, with 5th Mechanized Corps adding another 193 tanks, totaling 375 tanks.[9]

As the Russian armor reached the site of Sovkhoz 79 (State Farm 79; the Kolkhoz was a Soviet collective farm), some 25 kilometers (15 miles) deep, they encountered elements of Pz.Rgt.15. With orders to repulse the Soviet breakthrough, Balck set up his Gefechtsstand co-located with Lucht's 336.I.D. headquarters at Verkhne Solonovski southeast of

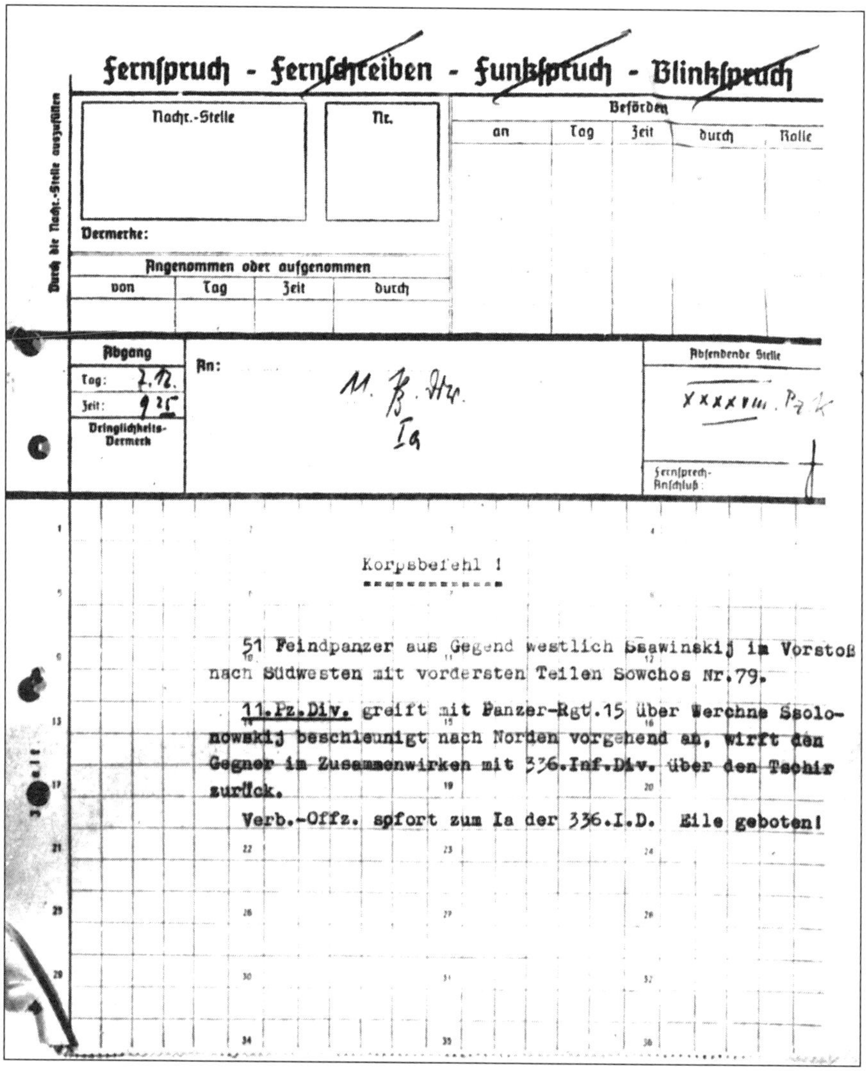

Fernspruch - ~~Fernschreiben~~ - ~~Funkspruch~~ - ~~Blinkspruch~~

Nachr.-Stelle | Nr. | Befördert: an | Tag | Zeit | durch | Rolle

Vermerke:

Angenommen oder aufgenommen: von | Tag | Zeit | durch

Abgang: Tag: 7.12. Zeit: 9 25

Dringlichkeits-Vermerk

An: 11. Pz. Div. Ia

Absendende Stelle: XXXXVIII. Pz.K.

Fernsprech-Anschluß:

Korpsbefehl !

51 Feindpanzer aus Gegend westlich Ssawinskij im Vorstoß nach Südwesten mit vordersten Teilen Sowchos Nr. 79.

11.Pz.Div. greift mit Panzer-Rgt.15 über Werchne Ssolo-nowskij beschleunigt nach Norden vorgehend an, wirft den Gegner im Zusammenwirken mit 336.Inf.Div. über den Tschir zurück.

Verb.-Offz. sofort zum Ia der 336.I.D. Eile geboten!

Telephone message from XXXXVIII. Pz.K.: "51 enemy tanks . . . State Farm 79 . . . Make haste!!"

NARA T-315/ROLL 595/000030

Sovkhoz 79. While this risked making a lucrative target for Soviet airstrikes, it enabled the staffs and the two division commanders to have personal contact and greatly facilitated joint planning and decision making. Lucht wanted Balck to attack immediately with a frontal assault, but Balck insisted it would be better not just to push the Russians back from the farm building complex, but to use his mobility to flank and destroy the Russian force. This plan was confirmed by a corps order at 17,25 hours.

As the 11. Panzer units arrived, Balck positioned the Pz.Pi.Batl.209 combat engineers and Pz.Jg.Abt.61 with 8,8cm flak guns south of the state farm, directed Henze's Pz.G.R.110 to deliver a holding attack from the southwest, and ordered the decisive thrust to be mounted by Oberst Graf Schimmelmann's Pz.Rgt.15 Kampfgruppe supported by von Bosse's Pz.G.R.111 flanking around to the west and attacking into the rear of Butkov's 1st Tank Corps. The infantry's Artillerie-Regiment 336 to the northeast was tied in with the batteries of Pz.A.R.119, Feuerbereit, to fire concentrations.

During the night of 7–8 December Balck's strike force moved over the high ground to the west, over terrain that was snow-covered and unmapped, to attack at 04,30 Uhr before that winter dawn, in freezing rain with the temperature hovering at zero degrees Celsius (32 F).[10] Sighting through the gloom a long

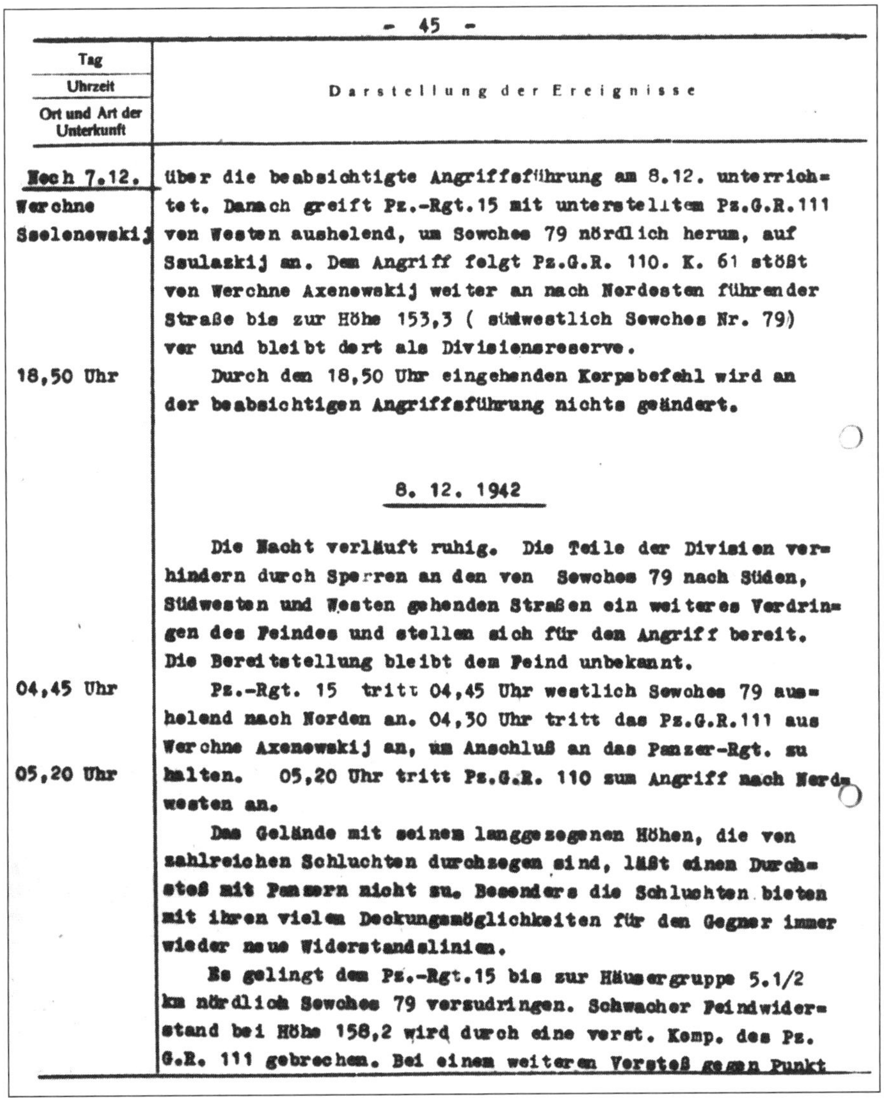

- 45 -

Tag / Uhrzeit / Ort und Art der Unterkunft	Darstellung der Ereignisse
Nach 7.12. Werchne Ssolenewskij	über die beabsichtigte Angriffsführung am 8.12. unterrichtet. Danach greift Pz.-Rgt.15 mit unterstelltem Pz.G.R.111 von Westen ausholend, um Sowchos 79 nördlich herum, auf Ssulaskij an. Dem Angriff folgt Pz.G.R. 110. K. 61 stößt von Werchne Axenowskij weiter an nach Nordosten führender Straße bis zur Höhe 153,3 (südwestlich Sowchos Nr. 79) vor und bleibt dort als Divisionsreserve.
18,50 Uhr	Durch den 18,50 Uhr eingehenden Korpsbefehl wird an der beabsichtigen Angriffsführung nichts geändert.
	8. 12. 1942
	Die Nacht verläuft ruhig. Die Teile der Division verhindern durch Sperren an den von Sowchos 79 nach Süden, Südwesten und Westen gehenden Straßen ein weiteres Vordringen des Feindes und stellen sich für den Angriff bereit. Die Bereitstellung bleibt dem Feind unbekannt.
04,45 Uhr	Pz.-Rgt. 15 tritt 04,45 Uhr westlich Sowchos 79 ausholend nach Norden an. 04,30 Uhr tritt das Pz.G.R.111 aus Werchne Axenowskij an, um Anschluß an das Panzer-Rgt. zu halten.
05,20 Uhr	05,20 Uhr tritt Pz.G.R. 110 zum Angriff nach Nordwesten an.
	Das Gelände mit seinen langgezogenen Höhen, die von zahlreichen Schluchten durchzogen sind, läßt einen Durchstoß mit Panzern nicht zu. Besonders die Schluchten bieten mit ihren vielen Deckungsmöglichkeiten für den Gegner immer wieder neue Widerstandslinien.
	Es gelingt dem Pz.-Rgt.15 bis zur Häusergruppe 5.1/2 km nördlich Sowchos 79 vorzudringen. Schwacher Feindwiderstand bei Höhe 158,2 wird durch eine verst. Komp. des Pz. G.R. 111 gebrochen. Bei einem weiteren Vorstoß gegen Punkt

KTB, 8 December 1942—Balck maneuvers Pz.Rgt.15, Pz.G.R.110 and 111, and K.61 around Sovkhoz 79. NARA T-315/ROLL 594/000548

column of truck-mounted infantry heading south to support the Russian armor assembled at Sovkhoz 79, the panzers swept down behind the vehicles. They laced the trucks with Sprenggranate and machine-gun fire, conserving their main gun anti-armor rounds. The Rotarmisten drivers careened their trucks askew and the Ivans tumbled out, many to fall in the bloody snow. Schimmelgraf's panzers continued south to Sovkhoz 79 behind the Russian armor, which was already moving out to attack what they believed was the weak left flank of the 336.I.D.

Instead the KVs and T-34s encountered the high-velocity fire of the deadly Acht-achts, and then the panzers struck from behind, the 5cm Kw.K. of the Pz.IIIs as well as the 7,5cm Kw.K. of the Pz.IVs penetrating the thinner rear armor of the heavy Russian tanks with Panzergranate. The German rounds—*Volltreffer!* (Direct Hit!)—smashed into the engine compartments, detonating the onboard ammunition and exploding the diesel fuel into flames. The surging tank battle claimed fifty-three Red tanks, wrecking the two brigades of Butkov's 1st Tank Corps.

This was the first of a series of actions over the next two weeks that demonstrated armor in a mobile counterattack role, the panzers destroying Russian tank thrusts that had penetrated the infantry-held HKL along the Chir. These actions enhanced the already impressive reputations of Hermann Balck and the tireless officers and men of the 11. Gespenster Panzer-Division. It is instructive to analyze the command methods of Balck in particular, who would go on to army and army group commands.[11]

In the mold of panzer commanders like Guderian and Rommel, Balck led from the front with the units that were his Schwerpunkt, quickly analyzing terrain and enemy resistance and making decisions transmitted by radio in the clear. This bypassed time-consuming encryption, and imparted the commander's vigorous presence to his units—the panzer concept of *Sattelbefehle*, Orders from the Saddle (the later American Frag[mentary] Orders). Even if the enemy intercepted the radio transmission it was too late to respond, as the maneuver was already being carried out. Von Mellenthin at XXXXVIII. Pz.K., later Balck's chief of staff at 4. Pz.Armee and then at H.Gr. G, repeated Guderian's maxim: *"Klotzen, nicht kleckern"* ("Boot 'em, don't spatter 'em"). "Mobile tactics of this kind saved dangerous situations on numerous occasions and inflicted huge losses on the enemy."[12]

Balck often drove up to the front in his Kübelwagen or led in his armored command vehicle, an Sd.Kfz. 250 Halbkette, accompanied by Major Kinitz, his Ia. Mellenthin reflected this was the same as Rommel's style: "This was contrary to the accepted general staff principle, that the chief of staff is the deputy of the commander in chief during the latter's absence. But Rommel liked to have his principal adviser always at his elbow, and if he became a casualty, well—he could always be replaced." Heinz Gaedke, as a Major Ia in 25.I.D.(mot) and later chief of staff to Balck commanding 6. Armee in 1944 (and a Bundeswehr corps commander) said, "My division commander and I would sit together in a half-track vehicle with the map on our laps, [and] exchange opinions . . . then we'd scribble down our instructions, give them to the driver next to us, and he'd pass the orders along to a couple of radio operators in the back of our vehicle." Balck did not give written orders: "Orders were exclusively verbal. The divisional commander made his decision for the next day during the evening, and he gave the necessary orders verbally to his regimental commanders on the battlefield; then he returned to his main headquarters and discussed his intentions with the chief of staff of the 48th Panzer Corps."[13] This was Auftragstaktik (mission tactics): lower commanders were encouraged to make their own decisions, knowing the commander's intent.

The Gefechtsstand was the commander's forward command post. The rear-echelon headquarters were where the reports were collated: intelligence by the Ic, fuel and munitions requisitions by Ib (Supply), and casualties, replacements, and other personnel aspects by IIa (for officers) and IIb (for enlisted personnel). Operational reports were marked on the message pads whether they transmitted by telephone, teletype, radio, or signal lamp—lining out those not applicable—with sender, recipient, and time noted. These formed the basis for the Kriegstagebuch, or daily War Diary entries, and the reports back to corps and army headquarters, kept as Anlagen (Annexes). Balck worked well with corps Chief of Staff Oberst von Mellenthin: "A very happy relationship between Mellenthin and myself began in these days and held for the entire war."[14]

Von Knobelsdorff, Kommandeur XXXXVIII. Pz.K., came forward in the evening to meet with Balck and his staff, be briefed on situations and conditions, and give his orders. In panzer units, superior commanders did not call their unit commanders *back* to headquarters, away from their units; superior commanders went *forward* to the front-line units. Most significantly, Balck was one of those unique leaders who had "Fingerspitzengefühl" (fingertip feel), that instinctive sixth sense to be at the Schwerpunkt, to sense terrain and appropriate tactics and opportunity, and act decisively.

As the 11. Panzergrenadiere mopped up the state farm area on the 9th, they made a gruesome discovery: over one hundred corpses of German soldiers of the 336.I.D. rear-area supply elements who had been captured, killed, and mutilated by Butkov's 1st Soviet Tank Corps. Some were mashed flat by the tank treads, some were dismembered with spades, others had their genitals smashed and penises cut off, or were impaled with metal pieces. Still others were dragged from the field hospital and mangled, or doused with water to freeze to death. Gefreiter Günther Dörr of Pz.G.R.110, firing his MG 34 from the hip, had fought into Sovkhoz 79 alongside Zugführer Lt. Steffen firing his MPi and others with fixed bayonets; they discovered the massacre. "What we then saw exceeded in cruelty anything we had previously experienced on the Ostfront," Dörr said.[15]

On the 14th an angry Balck distributed a Tagesbefehl to his division about the soldiers "butchered like animals." A Soviet Gefangener, Under-Sergeant Ivan Yakovevitch Korilko, 1st Company, Tank Battalion

346 of Tank Brigade 157, said that at an assembly shortly before the 19 November offensive against the 3. Rumanian Army, they were told that Rumanians were allowed to be taken prisoner, but not Germans. Rumanians were never allowed to be shot before the eyes of the Germans, but it was okay for Germans to be shot before Rumanian eyes. Kameraden! Balck urged his men, there would be much hard fighting, but the horrible sight at Sovkhoz 79 showed clearly what fate awaited them if they were not victorious in this struggle. But there was no call for revenge to be exacted by the Gespensters; their discipline was to be maintained.[16]

The 7. Luftwaffe Feld Division had arrived to help hold the Chir HKL, going into position on the left of Lucht's 336.I.D. It had the newest equipment like the MG 42 replacing the MG 34 and six Sturmgeschütze per battalion, but its men were ignorant of infantry operations and the reality of the Ostfront. The infantry had a front of some 65 kilometers (40 miles), and the role of the 11. Panzer-Division as a mobile counterattack force was crucial. The Russians were able to penetrate those defenses in several places, and the bridgeheads established were quickly fortified with mines and Pak, and with rapid force buildup posed significant threats. On the morning of 10 December the Ivans attacked through the HKL but encountered the Elfte around Ostrovskoi. A lighter episode occurred in the fighting when a 5cm Pak dueled with a KV-1. The Russian tank reversed—and then vanished into a steep balka and toppled down the slope, to the cheers of the German gun crew.

Nevertheless Knobelsdorff felt it more important to protect the German bridgehead at Nizhne Chirskaya as a jumping-off position for the Operation WINTERGEWITTER attack, and that evening of the 10th he ordered Balck's 11.Pz.Div. south to repulse Russian penetrations of the perimeter. That night the Elften road-marched south to attack the next day. The German artillery bombardment began, enhanced by the 336.I.D. artillery and some heavy mortars; Balck was leery about the frozen creeks and balkas where the Chir flowed into the Don, places where the panzers might bog down.

Panzerregiment 15 was ready to attack when Balck received a message from Lucht: "Enemy broken through at Lissinski and at Nizhna Kalinovski, the one breakthrough 22 km [15 miles] as the crow flies from the other."[17] Balck and Knobelsdorff quickly conferred, and decided to call off the counterattack at Nizhne Chirskaya and send the 11.Pz.Div. north to deal with these crises. The artillery barrage might at least cause the Russians, who were expecting an attack, to go over to the defensive. Once more the Gespensters made a night road march, and at dawn on 12 December Pz.Rgt.15 led the attack that destroyed the Russian penetration at Lissinski. Mellenthin emphasized how important it was to attack these bridgeheads before the 7,62cm "Ratsch-Bumms" could be dug into position, mines laid, and the buildup forces could be organized. At least Lucht's Saxons did not retreat, but held their positions, crouching in their Erdlöcher and allowing the tanks to run over them before rising to engage the Russian infantry.

That afternoon the 11.Pz.Div. drove the 22 kilometers to attack the penetration at Nizhna Kalinovski, deploying straight from the approach march. "Our engines have been warm, and our gun barrels, too, ever since we arrived on the Chir," wrote one lieutenant.[18] But the Russians had crossed nearly sixty T-34s across the Chir and two companies advanced eastward toward the gunfire reverberating from the Lissinski battle. By the time the 11.Pz.Div. broke this force, the other Red tanks were in hull-down position and the attack stalled. On the morning of the 13th a more coordinated attack was mounted but the Gespensters were exhausted after a week of constant movement and combat, used as a Feuerwehr. Mechanical breakdowns were increasing, and attacking silhouetted against a wintry sun led to losses. A Russian attack on the right flank temporarily encircled a panzergrenadier battalion under Major Wrede and dislocated Balck's attack. By nightfall the Elfte had lost half its November strength, and could only take up position to contain the Kalinovski bridgehead, turning it over to the 7. Lw.Felddivision.

Based on a Tagesmeldung to XXXXVIII. Pz.K., a Wehrmachtsbericht reported, "A Silesian panzer division under the personal leadership of its division commander threw the enemy back across the Don bend, rubbed out three tank brigades in heavy fighting, and in two days destroyed 39 tanks. The enemy lost much materiel and had heavy losses in men." But an 11.Pz.Div. Tagesmeldung to XXXXVIII. Pz.K. on the 15th also reported the Panzerlage as only twenty-seven operational panzers: eighteen Pz.III lang, three Pz.III kurz, five Pz.IV l, and one Pz.IV k, and on the 16th I/110 had only 271 panzergrenadiers. At the end of the month Pz.Jäger-Abt.61 was dissolved (until May 1943), 1. Kompanie going to Pz.G.R.110 and

2.Kp. going to 111. Weather conditions were reflected in Mellenthin at corps reporting to the Elfte the availability of three Schneepflügen (S-pflüge, snowplows) of Schneeräumtruppe 14.[19]

The 11.Pz.Div. pulled back into reserve, to retrieve and restore broken-down or damaged panzers and vehicles. During the constant movement the troops had only been able to get brief catnaps while slumped in their vehicles. If a column stopped, drivers fell asleep. It took company Offiziere and Unteroffiziere, themselves exhausted, to pound on the vehicles and get them moving again. When commanders and men are exhausted, the necessary coordination among units falters, clear thinking and decision making becomes muddled, mistakes are made, and the mission might well fail. The Gespensters had pushed to their limits. But "Night march saves blood," Balck later wrote. "Each day was like the next. Russian penetration at Point X, counterattack, everything cleared up by evening. Then, another report 20 kilometers eastwards of a deep penetration into some hasty defensive position. About face. Panzers, infantry, and artillery march through the winter night with burning headlights. In position by dawn at the Russians' most sensitive point. Take them by surprise. Crush them. Then repeat the process the next day some 10 or 20 kilometers farther west or east."[20]

Meanwhile, on 12 December Hoth had launched his 4. Panzerarmee in WINTERGEWITTER to relieve 6. Armee in Stalingrad. LVII. Panzerkorps under Gen.Lt. Friedrich Kirchner led the way, with 6. and 23. Panzer divisions and two Luftwaffe field divisions and elements of 4. Rumanian Army on the flanks, and some 800 vehicles to carry 3,000 tons of supplies into the Kessel and to evacuate wounded. Manstein had urged also having 17.Pz.Div. and 16.I.D. (mot), but these were not yet released to him. The Soviets should have been aware of the relief operation, but Maj. Gen. K. G. Trufanov's 51st Army was caught by surprise. In addition, three tank brigades had been forwarded to attack the Nizhne Chirskaya bridgehead, and his army had been weakened by previous fighting. Hoth's panzers, which included the first use in the south of the heavy Panzer VI Tigers with their 100 mm (4 inches) of frontal armor and powerful 8,8cm gun, rolled 20 kilometers (12 miles) a day over the open, frozen ground. The spearheads crossed the Aksay River and reached the Myshkova, 50 kilometers (30 miles) from the 6. Armee perimeter, by the 19th.

But XXXXVIII. Pz.K. was embroiled along the Chir and unable to mount its thrust, leaving only Hoth's attack from the south. At 6. Armee Paulus, either feeling bound by Hitler's orders not to leave the Volga, or persuaded by his chief of staff, Generalmajor Arthur Schmidt, that his forces should hold out until relieved, procrastinated. Hitler may also have been reluctant to admit the drastic change in fortune, and perhaps also believed the SS Panzerkorps (three panzergrenadier divisions) would counterattack (though it was only just arriving from the West at Kharkov, 560 kilometers [350 miles] distant). On the 18th Manstein flew his intelligence chief, Maj. Hans Eismann, into Gumrak to press Paulus. But Paulus had made no plans to break out in DONNERSCHLAG and had no intention of doing so, and Eismann flew out the next day. Whether Paulus could have facilitated the relief operation and still hold the position on the Volga remains contentious.

Stavka Chief of Staff Aleksandr Vasilevsky was at 51st Army headquarters (with Commissar Khrushchev) on 12 December when Hoth attacked. Unable to contact Stalin in Moscow, he contacted Gen. Konstantin Rokossovsky of Don Front to transfer Gen. Andrei Yeremenko's Stalingrad Front to stop Hoth's advance. Stalin was angry at Vasilevsky's initiative, but finally agreed. Yeremenko had already ordered the 4th Mechanized Corps and 13th Tank Corps into action, but had to be prepared also for a 6. Armee attack, not knowing it would not be mounted.

More significantly, Zhukov and Vasilevsky knew the way to thwart Manstein's attack was not to defend against it, but to attack the German front elsewhere. This plan became Operation SATURN: Vatutin's Southwest and F. I. Golikov's Voronezh Fronts were to collapse the 8. Italian Army, stretched along the upper Don and linked with the weak 2. Hungarian Army, and then drive to the Sea of Azov to cut off 1. Panzerarmee and 17. Armee of H.Gr. A. This was modified as LITTLE SATURN, with an objective of driving into the rear of H.Gr. Don short of the Donets rather than across the Donets to Rostov. On 16 December the 1st and 3rd Guards Armies and the adjacent 6th Army assaulted Gariboldi's 8. Italian Army and collapsed it. The Don was no longer a barrier; the river had frozen enough for the Russian tanks to cross over the ice. There was no mobile counterattack force, as 17.Pz. Div. had finally been transferred to Hoth's drive, too late to facilitate a breakthrough to 6. Armee.

The German line along the Chir seemed to have been stabilized prior to LITTLE SATURN, thanks to Lucht's 336.I.D. holding firm and Balck's 11.Pz.Div. mounting its mobile counterattacks. The Russians did hold the Kalinovski bridgehead; they were contained by Luftwaffe Alarmeinheiten, but the river had frozen enough to support tanks. On 15 December the 11. Panzer moved from the Nizhna Kalinovski sector down to Nizhne Chirskaya, closing into assembly areas on the 16th. Knobelsdorff at XXXXVIII. Pz.Korps planned for Balck to attack across the Don on the 17th as the northern arm of WINTERGEWITTER, as Hoth's 4. Pz.Armee had advanced to the Aksay.

But then came the LITTLE SATURN assault on 8. Italian Army farther west. At the same time Romanenko's 5th Tank Army renewed its assaults on Lucht's 336.I.D. holding the Chir River line. There seemed to be little tactical skill in these attacks—simply masses of armored forces thrusting through at one point or another. Four infantry divisions had eliminated the tenuous German bridgehead across the Don at Nizhne Chirskaya, two more crossings on either side of Lissinski were made the evening of the 17th, and on the morning of the 18th an armored brigade and a motorized corps thrust against the 7. Luftwaffe Felddivision on the left farther up the Chir at Oblivskaya. There was no alternative but to postpone the XXXXVIII. Pz.K. role in WINTERGEWITTER and for the 11.Pz.Div. to again deal with the Russian breakthroughs.

On 17 December Balck drove the Russian forces around Lissinski back to the river; he was going to complete their destruction on the 18th when Knobelsdorff learned that a motorized corps had broken out of the bridgehead at Nizhna Kalinovski and the Luftwaffe Alarmeinheiten dissolved. Of the Luftwaffe field divisions Balck said, "After a few days they were gone—finished—in spite of good mechanical equipment. Their training left everything to be desired, and they had no experienced leaders. They were a creation of Hermann Göring's, a creation which had no sound military foundation—the rank and file paid with their lives for this absurdity."[21]

Balck would have preferred to finish off the Lissinski threats, but the breach farther west created a crisis. Such was their relationship that Mellenthin could order Balck, "No, Herr General, this time this is more delicate, the 11.Pz.Div. must go there immediately, every second is costly." *"Na schön,"* Balck replied, *"Machen wir."* ("Well fine, we'll do it.")[22] Once again the Gespensters were moving at night, this time to attack the Russian motorized corps advancing from Kalinovski west of Sovkhoz 79 at dawn on the 19th. When Pz.Rgt.15 attacked at Lissinski on the 17th, it had forty-seven panzers available, including twenty-seven Pz.III lang; of a total of eighty-three panzers, twenty-one others needed limited repairs and fifteen required extensive repairs. For the attack on Kalinovski Schimmelgraf had only twenty-nine einsatzbereit. On the night march north some ten panzers had slid off the icy roadway and had to be retrieved.[23]

Nonetheless Balck formulated his plan: Pz.Gren.Rgt.110 was to take up a frontal blocking position, Pz.Rgt.15 was to attack the Russians' eastern flank, and Pz.G.R.111 was to follow in the right rear, on call. By 05,00 hours on 19 December Balck's 11.Pz.Div. elements were in position. At first light the lead elements of Pz.Rgt.15 saw numerous tanks of the Russian motorized corps deployed and moving south. This was the 5th Mechanized Corps under Maj. Gen. M. V. Volkov with some 193 tanks. As the regiment's approach route had been concealed, its now twenty-five panzers remaining swung in behind the Russian formation—allowing them to knock out forty-two Russian tanks before the Ivans realized the "second wave" following them were German!

The dominating height of Hill 148.8 was captured. From there another formation of tanks was seen, and Hauptmann Karl Lestmann attacked them from behind as well, destroying another twenty-three tanks, totaling sixty-five Soviet tanks claimed. That evening the Russian 3rd Mechanized Brigade attacked the left flank of the 11.Pz.Div. and overran I.Btl. of Pz.Gren.Rgt.110, but Pz.Rgt.15 soon restored the situation.

On 20 December Balck resumed his advance, but then a Russian counterattack on the right flank broke into the rear of Pz.G.R.111. In the swirling tank battles another 10 Rotarmisten tanks were claimed. But it was close combat. Fahnenjunker (Officer Candidate) squad leader Heinz Kutscheid was wounded and his company commander and platoon leader, Lts. Keller and Crewannek, were killed with antitank explosives in their hands.[24] There was a full moon that night over the frosty snow, and both Henze's 110 and von Bosse's 111 reported penetrations by Russian tanks and infantry. Balck sent Hauser's Kradschützen-Batl. 61 to counterattack the Russians at the boundary between the two Panzergrenadier regiments, and dawn revealed hundreds of fallen Russians in the area. On 22 December the front lines were quiet, the Russian motorized corps apparently exhausted by its assaults.

But farther west the collapse of 8. Italian Army saw the Russian 1st Guards Army under Col. Gen. Fyodor Kuznetsov pouring through the gap between the 2. Hungarian Army and Armee Abteilung Hollidt, driving south toward Rostov. Maj. Gen.Vasily M. Badanov's 24th Tank Corps plunged 240 kilometers (150 miles) by 23 December. Now not only was the survival of 6. Armee at Stalingrad threatened, but if the Russians drove on to Rostov, the fate of Kleist's Heeresgruppe A in the Caucasus was at risk. On that same 23rd Hoth, now also being engaged by Col. Gen. Rodion Malinovsky's 2nd Guards Army, received orders to pull back and consolidate along the Aksay. Manstein was only too well aware that the distance from Kazanskaya on the Italian Don front to Rostov was only 300 kilometers (185 miles); 4.Pz.Armee was 400 kilometers (250 miles) away, and the left wing of H.Gr. A was 600 kilometers (375 miles) farther distant. In addition, the lines of communication crossing the vital rail bridges of the Dnepr back at Dnepropetrovsk and Zaporozhe were within 420 kilometers (260 miles) of the Russian forces swarming across the Don.

Knobelsdorff's XXXXVIII. Pz.Korps was ordered to retreat from the Chir sector back to Tatsinskaya, 145 kilometers (90 miles) to the west. Tatsinskaya's airfield was the primary airfield for flying supplies into the 6. Armee Kessel. In commenting on the Russian methods and their horrendous losses in the battles of the Chir, Balck observed, "The fighting on the Chir river was made easier by the methods adopted by the command of the Russian Fifth Tank Army [Romanenko]. They sent their various corps into battle without co-ordinating the timing of their attacks, and without the co-operation of the numerous infantry divisions. Thus the 11th Panzer-Division was enabled to smash one corps after the other, until the hitting power of the Fifth Tank Army had been weakened to such an extent that it was possible for the division to withdraw and start the game all over again with another Russian Tank Army."

Of the Russian operations Mellenthin commented, "Russian tactics are a queer mixture; in spite of their brilliance at infiltration and their exceptional mastery of field fortifications, yet the rigidity of Russian attacks was almost proverbial. . . . The foolish repetition of attacks on the same spot, the rigidity of Russian artillery fire, and the selection of the terrain for the attack, betrayed a total lack of imagination and mental mobility." But the resources of Soviet Russia enabled the Stavka to create new armies and rebuild old ones, and hurl them, with scant training and little tactical finesse, continually into the fray. "That is why fighting with Russians resembles the classic contest between Hercules and the [many-headed] Hydra," Mellenthin said.[25]

Tactics notwithstanding, the Russian attacks along the Chir, even if blocked, effectively disrupted the intended operations of Knobelsdorff's XXXXVIII. Panzerkorps in the relief of 6. Armee at Stalingrad.

CHAPTER THIRTEEN

Back to the Donets

THE RUSSIAN ATTACKS ON THE CHIR RIVER LINE AND THE collapse of 8. Italian Army spelled doom for Paulus's 6. Armee in the Stalingrad Kessel. Knobelsdorff's XXXXVIII. Panzerkorps could not support Hoth's 4. Panzerarmee advance to relieve 6. Armee, and Hoth had to release 6.Pz.Div. on 23 December to try and stop the Russian flood. Therefore Hoth only had thirty-five panzers, grouped under 17.Pz.Div., to resume the attack from the Aksay on 24 December 1942, 70 kilometers (45 miles) from the 6. Armee perimeter. Nonetheless, a foray south by 6. Armee might still have opened a corridor and facilitated a retreat from the Volga. There were no illusions now about the looming fate of 6. Armee. Desperation might have prompted a breakout attempt. But Paulus had a career as a staff officer, not a combat commander, and he seems to have been simply incapable of making drastic decisions; additionally, he might have been dominated by his chief of staff, Gen.Maj. Arthur Schmidt.

For Hitler, it is hard to see where a strategic withdrawal from the ruins along the Volga could be worse than the destruction of a German army and the loss of Stalingrad anyway. But Hitler, unwilling to admit defeat, was adamant, and Paulus was not the commander to defy him. By Weihnacht it was clear that Hoth's offensive was thwarted, and on 26 December LVII. Pz.K. retreated south from the Aksay.

Having retreated from the Chir to Morozovskaya, XXXXVIII. Pz.Korps established its headquarters near Tatsinskaya, just east of the Donets. But the 1st Guards Army under Fyodor Kuznetsov was thrusting south, and by Weihnachtsabend its spearheads were 130 kilometers (80 miles) from Rostov, through which Mackensen's 1. Pz.Armee would have to retreat. Richard Ruoff's 17. Armee was pulling back to the Taman Peninsula by the Sea of Azov, Hitler intending to keep a "balcony" by which a renewed offensive to the Caucasus could be mounted.

The Russian forces of Badanov's 24th Tank Corps had overrun the airfield west of Tatsinskaya, for which the corps was rewarded with the title 2nd *Guards* Tank Corps. When the airfield was recaptured, Oberlt. Franz Thelen, adjutant of Pz.Gren.Rgt.111, later reported that many of the German Ju 52 crews, supply, and other personnel captured by the Russians had again been slain and mutilated, with eyes gouged out and ears and noses cut off, as at Sovkhoz 79.[1] Taking control of Gen.Lt. Erhard Raus's 6.Pz.Div. and Balck's 11.Pz.Div., Knobelsdorff ordered the 6. Panzer to attack north of Tatinskaya to cut off the retreat of Badanov's Tank Corps, while 11. Panzer attacked the force itself.

Manstein continued to pull his H.Gr. Don units back to the Donets. XXXXVIII. Pz.K. gained 7.Pz. Div. under Gen.Lt. Frhr. Hans von Funck, and the 306. Infanterie-Division arrived from France. On 23 December the Elfte was temporarily reassigned from XXXXVIII. Pz.K. to Dumitrescu's 3. Rumanian Army in Armee Abteiling Hollidt. For the Tatsinskaya attack Balck could at least coordinate with the remnants of 3. Rumanian Army, as its chief of staff was German Oberst Walther Wenck, a strong-nerved officer and the former Ia of 1.Pz.Div. "Thank God," thought Balck. (Wenck would command 12. Armee in 1945.)

On the 24th, though with only twenty panzers einsatzbereit, Balck's Gespensters drove into Skassyrskaya on the Bystraya north of Tatsinskaya. On 25 December—Christmas—the Rotarmisten were driven out of Tatsinskaya, but Balck's 11. Panzer lacked the strength to destroy the 24th Tank Corps now trapped in a Kessel around Hill 175. But then Balck received units of 6.Pz.Div. to aid in crushing the Russian position: Pz.Gren.Rgt.4 under energetic Oberst Martin Unrein, Aufkl.Abteilung 6, and Sturmgeschütz Abt. 228.

On the 26th Hptm. Paul von Hauser's K.61 SPWs and Karl Lestmann's panzers took Krykov on the Bystraya to the north behind the Russian corps, but the Sturmgeschütz Abteiling didn't arrive. With only eight panzers now at his disposal, Balck could only ball his fists in helpless rage. On the 27th a concentric attack was launched, with Pz.Gren.Rgt. 111 coming from the east, Pz.G.R.110 from the northeast, and Pz.Rgt.15 and the attached Pz.G.R.4 from the north.[2] There was considerable resistance but the Russians were ground down and twelve tanks were destroyed. The Russian tank corps radioed frantic messages for help, most in the clear, receiving the message: "See it through, five infantry divisions are coming." Stranded, and down to fifty tanks, Badanov's crews mixed captured (and volatile) aviation fuel with aviation lubricants to try and keep them operational.[3]

At one point a Russian plane landed amid the German forces. Both flyers were shot down, and as the papers on board were not of significance, Balck speculated that maybe their mission was to fly the commander (Badanov) out. In any case, the plane landed where his headquarters had been two days prior.

It did not appear that Russian reinforcements were coming in time, and with a clear, moonlit night on the 28th Balck ordered a night attack. At 05,00 his orderly officer reported the Russians attempting a breakout to the northwest through the spread-out Pz.Gren.Rgt.4. But Unrein's Panzergrenadiere, now supported by the Sturmgeschützen, were sealing off the escape option of Badanov's Corps.

When Raus's 6.Pz.Div. had arrived from France it had been hastily committed for the relief of Stalingrad. The infantry had not yet been issued white camouflage snow suits and the vehicles were not yet whitewashed. Against the snow-covered terrain they simply made "good aiming points," thought Oberleutnant Horst Scheibert, the commander of 6. Kompanie/Pz.Rgt.11. Uffz. Wolfgarten of 1.Kp./Pz.G.R.4 fought into Tatsinskaya through the deep snow and the icy wind, the mortar and artillery barrages punctuated by the rattle of MGs and the bark of tank cannon. He favored fighting in towns rather than attacking over the open ground: "Here there was at least more cover and one could—with hand grenades through the window and pause for the detonation—work well from house to house." There was also the horror at finding murdered and mutilated bodies of German soldiers from the Russian occupation three days earlier. Tatsinskaya was a village of blackened ruins and flaming buildings, and it contained the wreckage of some forty planes on its airfield.[4]

As the Germans closed in on the burning ruins and the numerous strewn dead and scattered Buckelhelm (Russian helmets), twelve Russian tanks and thirty trucks sought to escape but were hunted down and also destroyed. It was the end of Badanov's 24th Tank Corps, an end accomplished by a tired division finishing with eight operational panzers. (Badanov managed to escape, and would command 4th Tank Army after July 1943.) The Gespenster division staff received the nickname "Hannibal" for the veritable Cannae that had been orchestrated. Some Elften had even been able to briefly acknowledge Weihnacht during the action, and at 5. Panzer Kompanie/15 its promoted commander, Lt. Wilhelm Gross, had played the role of Weihnachtsmann (Father Christmas) and distributed Schnaps and Schokolade, "joy to the Landser's heart."[5]

No sooner had Tatsinskaya been cleared than a new enemy approached from the north, the Russian 266th Infantry Division. But Henze with Pz.Gren. Rgt.110 and some panzers threw them out of Skassyrskaya and back across the Bystraya. 6.Pz.Div. also blunted a drive, by 25th Tank Corps, in a night action on 31 December–1 January and threw them back across the Bystraya as well.

Yet Yeremenko's Stalingrad Front armies continued their relentless drive down both banks of the Don toward Rostov. To the south, Hoth's 4. Panzerarmee had to allow LVII. Pz.Korps to withdraw back past Kotelnikovski to the Sal River, exposing A.A.Hollidt's right flank. Along the north bank 5th Shock Army under Maj. Gen. Markian M. Popov also stormed down from the Chir. On 29 December Hollidt had to shift Balck's Gespensters 112 kilometers (70 miles) downriver to Zmlyanskiy to block the drive. But the 11.Pz.Div. was a division in name only. Both panzergrenadier regiments scarcely formed a Kampfbataillon, the Pz.Jäger Abt. 61 was dissolved, and there were only a handful of panzers.

Elements of the division road-marched back toward Shakhty north of Rostov, any drivable vehicle generally towing two or three disabled vehicles. In a letter written from a hospital after he was wounded, Lt. Gross said, "Nobody knew any more where we really were. During the movement I tried to sleep in the gunner's seat." Moving again on the 31st, "We are dog-tired, only brief sleep in 24 hours." At the same time there was continuous fighting and shell and rocket fire. In the Tatsinskaya fighting, "There were no prisoners," Gross said. "The Russians didn't take any, and therefore neither did we. Is this still war or a great mass slaughter?"[6] Some Schnaps and comradeship kept them going.

The Ia reports to XXXXVIII. Pz.Korps revealed the Gespenster-Division status: by 28 December there were only five panzers (two Pz.III k, two Pz.III lg, and one Pz.IV lg). As last reported on the 26th, there were 856 panzergrenadiers in the two regiments, scarcely comprising a battalion: Pz.Gr.Rgt.110 had 170 in I. Bataillon and 233 in II. Btl., and Pz.G.R.111 had 226 and 227 in I. and II. Btl., respectively; K.61 had 342. There were twenty-six 5cm Pak, and five 8,8cm flak guns. A.R.119 still had twenty-six tubes: eighteen 10,5cm, four 15cm, and four 10cm Kanone.

On 30 December Balck protested: "After these heavy and pronounced ever-changing battles the division's vehicle capability is completely broken down. On these grounds I have to reorganize the division as one infantry regiment, one motorcycle battalion, dissolve the panzerjäger battalion, hope however that if I now receive the [announced] new panzers, I can have a very strong panzer regiment, so that in some measure then I am operationally serviceable. The artillery is still fairly intact." The repairs by the Werkstattkompanien were constantly interrupted by the frequent moves—"marching every night, fighting every day"—and the division *had* to be aufgefrischt (here, rebuilt), with the new year.[7] Balck's protest at least prompted the arrival of new panzers the next day, giving the division thirty-eight Wagens einsatzbereit: eleven Pz.IIs, twenty-three Pz.IIIs, and four Pz.IVs. The division's fighting strength was 3,890. That night Sturmbootkdo. 912 (assault boat command) was able to emplace defensive mines along the Zymla sector.[8]

The Wehrmacht's second Sylvesternacht (New Year's Eve) in Russia found the embattled 11. Panzer-Division satisfied with their victories between the Don and the Donets. But there were many losses too. Some were grateful for a Heimatschuss (homeward wound, the British "Blighty" or the American "million-dollar wound"), though many were wounded multiple times and returned to duty. Others found a Russian grave, their burials presided over by division Pfarrer (Pastor) Paul Herb. In combat, regimental bands had to serve as graves registration personnel. The Germans made a point of trying to recover their Gefallen (the Ivans generally did not).

For three weeks in January of the new year, the 11.Pz.-Div., as a reserve for Korpsgruppe Mieth behind the Donets, theoretically underwent Auffrischung—refitting, rehabilitation, replenishment, gaining new equipment, absorbing replacements, and becoming Kampfbereit again. But its units were also called upon as Feuerwehr to blunt Soviet penetrations and maintain the HKL. Almost every day the Russians attacked the infantry front. White signal flares soared into the wintry sky, the call for help by the infantry of Lucht's 336.I.D. Then a small Kampfgruppe as a reaction force on alert would sally forth to stabilize the situation.

On one of these forays Lt. Gross was hit in the foot by a round from a Russian antitank rifle. "I suddenly had the feeling someone had struck me on the foot with an iron crowbar," Gross said. "I sprang from the Wagen and hopped around with the pain. There was nothing to see, but I soon perceived that the felt boot was damp, and I realized the 'distribution of

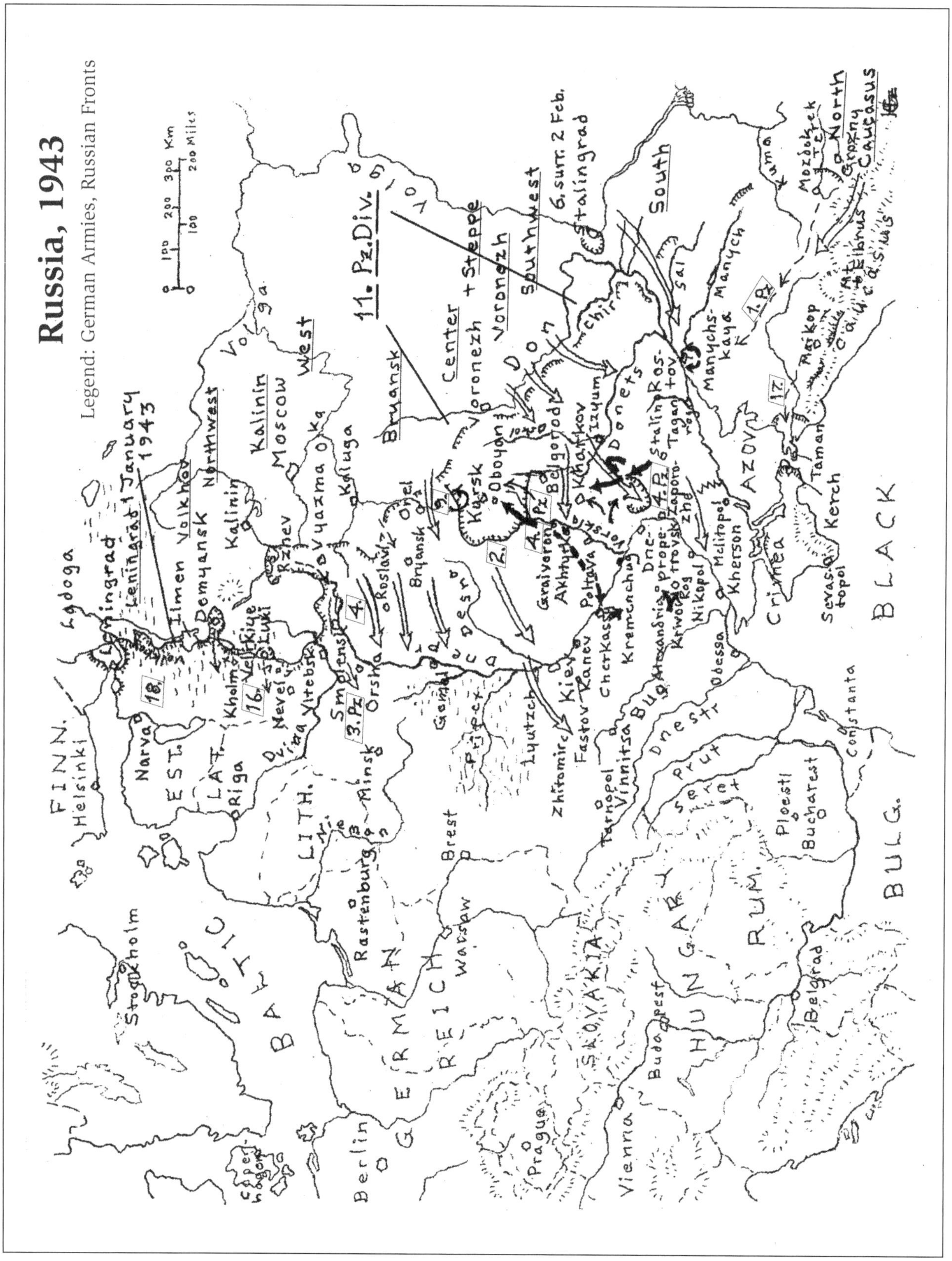

Russia, 1943

Legend: German Armies, Russian Fronts

presents.'" In "this idiotic situation" he was soon disabled. His crew piled him onto his panzer and they drove back.

At the Verbandplatz (VP, field aid station) he received "best greetings for the homeland. *Ja*—and from there I led a peculiar war. Namely the war of the Lazarett [hospital]." When the Ivans were approaching he was evacuated by ambulance. "This march was a chapter in itself," Gross noted. The roads were in the "usual condition" and many vehicles sank in the mud, and his Sanitätsauto overturned. Finally he saw a Lastwagen with the familiar Gespenster symbol of his own division, and he hitched a ride. His wounded foot was attended to, and put in a plaster cast—under which the lice were stirring. "That would heal again," Gross said. "That, my Kameraden, is a genuine Heimatschuss."[9]

Auffrischung was a much-needed rest for many of the Gespensters, with *ruhe* (tranquility) the term used by some. But being in reserve, "ruhe" could be relative. On 3 January the Russians attacked in regimental strength with two KV-1 tanks, leaving 400 counted dead behind; on the 4th the Russians were repulsed "with high losses"; on the 5th three T-70s and one Pak were destroyed; on the 6th 600 dead were counted, and on the 8th two tanks and eleven 7,62cm Ratsch-Bumm Paks were destroyed, and there were 150 Russian dead and 46 prisoners.[10]

Amid the fighting there was time to make awards, and Balck himself received the Eichenlaub to his Ritterkreuz as of 20 December 1942 for his leadership of the division. There were three other RKs for 1942, in S.R.111, Pz.Art.Rgt.119, and Pz.Jäger Abt.61. In addition to Generalmajor Günther Angern, recipients of the Das deutsche Kreuz (DK) in Gold in 1942 included Oberstleutnant Georg Sparre commanding II.Btl./110, Hptm. Heinrich Pricken of 1./15, and Oblt. Klaus Piontek of Pz.Rgt.15.[11] Antitank battalion Pz.Jg.Abt.61 had been deactivated as had reconnaissance A.A.231 earlier, and each panzergrenadier regiment was consolidated as a battalion, which at least made the division more maneuverable. Of the period 1–21 January 1943 Balck could write, "Im Osten nichts Neues" ("All quiet on the Eastern Front")—at least relatively so, for the Gespenster-Division.[12]

During this "calm" period, new vehicles were becoming available to deal with the extreme snow and mud conditions of Russia. One was the "Ost-Mulis" (slang, "East mules"), trucks modified with track suspensions replacing the rear wheels. These were improvised, and might be a 2-ton Ford-Werke Lastkraftwagen with British Carden-Loyd track bogies, or a 3-ton Adam Opel Lkw. As most Lastwagen did not have front-wheel drive (like the American 6x6 2.5-ton truck being sent to Russia), their trafficability was still limited. Another development was the full-tracked Raupenschlepper Ost (RSO, caterpillar tractor), which could carry two tons of supplies or ammunition or be used for towing. The Kettenkrad (motorcycle tractor) with tracks and a front steering wheel remained handy for bringing up replacements or supplies and evacuating wounded.[13]

The wider "Ost-Kette" (east tracks) for the panzers gave better "floatation," felt Lt. Eberhard Schöne, though bridge widths had to be considered in any movement. On the other hand, said Panzersoldat Kurt Nentwig, the proximity of the track to the hull only allowed grousers on the outside. As "Winterkette" these tended to break off when crossing frozen, rutted vehicle tracks, sometimes breaking the track center guides as well. The crews rebolted the center guides to be no more than three blocks apart, though Nentwig's Panzer III once went into action missing eight track guides in a row, putting it at great risk of throwing its track. Friedrich von Eggeling's Panzer IV's Ostkette also broke, and Pz.Rgt.15 simply didn't use them any more after 1943. Crews who had not had time before to whitewash their Fahrzeuge in winter white now did so. The lime-based whitewash was sprayed or painted on by hand, though wet snow or frost sometimes scaled some off, leaving blotchy patches.[14]

While the Gespenster-Division refitted, Andrei Yeremenko's armies of Stalingrad Front, redesignated South Front on 1 January 1943, pressed Hoth's 4. Panzerarmee, south of Rostov, back from the Aksay, back from Kotelnikovski, and then from its positions along the Sal to the River Manych. The spearhead 3rd Guards Tank Corps under Pavel Rotmistrov of Rodion Malinovsky's 2nd Guards Army crossed the Manych where it flowed into the Don from the east at Manychskaya, only 30 kilometers (20 miles) from Rostov and the line of communication of the retreating 1. Pz.Armee. On 22 January Manstein detached the 11.Pz.Div. from XXXXVIII. Pz.K. and ordered it south across the Don to strengthen a counterattack by 4. Pz.Armee.

Balck's 11. Panzer had consolidated its units; it had a Gefechtsstärke of 3,820. Schimmelmann's Pz.Rgt.15 had thirty-three panzers (one Pz.II, five

Pz.III kurz, and twenty-two Pz.III lang, three Pz.IV lang, and two Befehlswagen) in two Abteilungen, each with one medium and two light companies; the panzergrenadiers were under the command of Henze's Pz.G.R.110 of two battalions, each with one rifle and one heavy weapons company, and regimental elements with a heavy infantry gun company and a flak company. Hauser's K.61 battalion had four companies: armored car, SPW half-track, motorcycle, and weapons, and Hptm. Erhard Grevendorf's Pz.Pi. Btl.209 had three engineer companies and a flamethrower troop. Oskar Schmidt's Pz.Art.Rgt.119 was at strength with twenty-six tubes (seventeen 10,5cm le.F.H., five 15cm s.F.H., and four 10cm Kan.) in two Abteilungen, one with two light and one medium howitzer battery, the other with two light and the cannon battery and a Werfer battery. There were also two 8,8cm flak guns.[15]

The 11. Panzer was joined by Gen.Maj. Gerhard Graf von Schwerin-Krosigk's 16. Infanteriedivision (motorisiert), which had retreated all the way from Elista near the Caspian Sea. Technically the "Windhund" (Greyhound) Division was now a Panzergrenadier division, but it was known by the older term under which it had gained fame. (In 1944 it would be reorganized as 116.Pz.Div. in the West.) The 16.I.D.(mot) attacked 2nd Guards Mechanized Corps of Malinovsky's 2nd Guards Tank Army from behind at Sporny on the Manych on the 15th and penetrated Rotmistrov's flank at Samodurovka. In addition, a company of Tiger panzers had been attached from Schwere Panzerabteilung 503.

On 23 January Balck's Elften made a frontal attack against Colonel Yegorov's T-34s at the Lenin Kolkhoz at Bataysk just south of the Don and Rostov. Schwerin's Pz.Abt.116 and Inf.Rgt.156 (mot) attacked from the southeast, and the Ivans were rolled back into the village of Manychskaya. Here the Gespensters were thwarted by a snow-covered antitank ditch and Russian antitank fire. Balck drove up to the outskirts in his Kübel, but was almost shot by a Russian with a PPSh submachine gun.

On the 24th they attacked again, with the goal of capturing the big bridge at Manychskaya that had enabled the Russians to secure their bridgehead for a continuing advance on Rostov from the east, but were thwarted again. Already the Rotarmisten were digging their tanks in between the buildings to serve as bunkers. To lure the Russian tanks from their defilade emplacements in the southern part of the village, Balck determined on a feint to threaten an attack from the east against the northern part with the bridge.

On the next day Schmidt's A.R.119 batteries fired a tremendous concentration as Stukas peeled down on the *northern* part, and armored cars and half-tracks maneuvered into attack position covered by a smokescreen. Then the VBs suddenly shifted the fires to the *southern* part, leaving one battery to support the feint with smoke shell, and Schimmelgraf's panzers charged in, buttoned up against their own artillery shelling, Balck watching the attack from a hill. The Russians had taken the bait, and their tanks left their hull-down emplacements and moved against the feint in the north, believing the Germans would not attack where they had failed before. The panzers maneuvered through the streets and struck the Russian tanks from behind. Hauser's Kradschützen Batl.61 Spähwagen headed in to seize the bridge intact and cut off the now fleeing Russian infantry. At the cost of one German killed and fourteen wounded, the Gespensters claimed some twenty tanks knocked out and 500–600 Russian casualties and eliminated the Russian bridgehead. Once again, Balck's careful planning and violent execution had gained a major tactical victory, ending this immediate threat to Rostov.[16]

On 28 January the 11.Pz.Div. was assigned to Friedrich Kirchner's LVII. Panzerkorps, the nucleus of Hoth's 4. Pz.Armee, which was holding a bridgehead around Rostov south of the Don. Behind them Eberhard von Mackensen's 1. Pz.Armee from the Caucasus was funneling back through Rostov. On the evening of the 28th Balck distributed his orders for a four-column attack against the advancing Russians in the morning. He sat in the house of a teacher, and could briefly contemplate the balalaika on the wall. They were in the land of the Don Cossacks. Everything was clean and cultivated, and the population was unsettled about the return of the Communists. A picture featured the Bogatyr, the hero of the old legends.

On 29 January the four columns moved out to the east: Hauser's K.61 on the right, then Pz.Gren. Rgt.110, Pz.G.R.111, and Pz.Rgt.15 on the left. Balck was watching the panzers moving through the snowy mist when Schimmelmann drove up in a Pkw and reported, "Yesterday Lestmann received the Ritterkreuz, and now they're all drunk. We two must lead the point ourselves." And so they spurred on their "herd of elephants."[17] At the village of Kamenyi they surprised and destroyed an antitank brigade, capturing thirty-two guns. To the north SS Gruppenführer Felix

Steiner's veteran 5. SS Panzergrenadierdivision Wiking advanced on the flank toward Mechitinskaya. The attack continued, and by the evening of the 30th the Russian 248th Rifle Division and two other rifle brigades were shattered, and the Elfte had taken Sernograd. The Russian division's staff officers cut off their rank insignia, but then began to commit suicide anyway.

The captured equipment tallied seventeen Pak 4,7cm, eighty-one Pak 7,62cm, three howitzers 10,5cm, four guns 12cm, two infantry guns, ninety-two antitank rifles, twenty-four mortars, one thousand prisoners—and twenty-two camels; the latter a reminder they were in "Asia." (The camels had been used to draw Russian artillery.) The Gespensters found the two-humped Bactrian camels useful for pulling a panje wagon, and even for "camel patrols"; they also found, as others had, that camels could be stubborn and unpredictable.[18] Among the prisoners were old women and children accompanying the soldiers, a practice that the Landsers always found perplexing.

On the 31st there was a sudden thaw. Some 30cm (one inch) of meltwater covered the frozen ground, ensuring footwear would be soaking wet while vehicles slithered on the ice underneath. Then came an equally sudden freeze that night at –15 degrees (10 F). Balck also learned that he had been promoted to Generalleutnant as of 1 January 1943. The Russian advance on Rostov from the south was thwarted for the time being, and the 11.Pz.Div. pulled back to Kagalnitzkaya. But a new crisis to the north found the 11. Panzer ordered up to the Donets again, crossing to the north bank of the Don by 2 February.

Farther north the German front was further ripped open on 15 January 1943 when Col. Gen. Filipp Golikov's Voronezh Front attacked and collapsed von Jány's 2. Hungarian Army along the upper Don south of Voronezh. On the 24th Bryansk Front assaulted the German 2. Armee commanded by General der Infanterie Hans von Salmuth, and within days two of its three corps were encircled. Then Nikolai Vatutin's Southwest Front, spearheaded by Mobile Group Popov under Gen. Markian Popov burst through the ad hoc formations north of Rostov and headed southwest toward the Dnepr crossings at Dnepropetrovsk and Zaporozhe, the latter the main supply depot for Manstein's Heeresgruppe Don. Of Maximilian von Weichs's four armies in his H.Gr.B, the three allied armies had all disintegrated, and 2. Armee was in danger of being encircled. On 13 February what was left of H.Gr.B was amalgamated with H.Gr. Don as H.Gr. Süd under Manstein. (As Generalfeldmarschall, Weichs was later named commander Südost, Balkans, H.Gr. F.)

To the east Paulus's isolated 6. Armee was undergoing its final tribulation in the ruins of Stalingrad. The starving Germans, huddled in their frozen trenches and bunkers, were bundled in blankets and rags and ceaselessly bombarded by Russian artillery and Katyusha rockets. Ominous, demoralizing loudspeaker messages wafted on the wind: "Every seven seconds a German soldier falls in Russia—Stalingrad—mass grave." This was followed by the ticking off of seven seconds, and then the dolorous repetition: *"Jeden sieben Sekunde ein deutscher Soldat in Russland gefallen ist—Stalingrad—Massgrab."*

With the Kessel split in two, Paulus—made Feldmarschall at the last minute by Hitler, who expected him to thus commit soldierly suicide and not surrender—and Chef des Stabes Schmidt surrendered in their headquarters at the Univermag department store on Red Square on 31 January 1943 to Marshals Nikolai Voronov and Konstantin Rokossovsky of Don Front. On 2 February General Karl Strecker of XI. A.K. in the northern pocket around the tractor factory surrendered as well, signaling the end of 6. Armee and the battle of Stalingrad.

Statistics of strengths and losses on both sides vary greatly, depending on date parameters, extent of operational commitment, auxiliaries, and other factors. In the struggle for Stalingrad the Red Army had perhaps suffered over one million casualties, including 485,000 dead. Of some 230,000 Wehrmacht soldiers in the Kessel, including Rumanians and Russian Hiwis in German service, the majority died. The Soviets announced some 91,000 marched into final captivity, but most died of disease, starvation, and shootings while they were being marched, transported, or incarcerated in Soviet camps. Small numbers of prisoners were released after the war, and in 1955 there were 9,626, including some 2,000 Stalingrad survivors, finally returned to Germany. (In the balance of brutality it is well to remark that of 4.5 million Russians in German captivity, only 1.8 million survived the war.)

The destruction of 6. Armee at Stalingrad was acknowledged around the world as a turning point in the colossal struggle. In Germany, instead of disguising the extent of the disaster, Minister of Propaganda

Dr. Paul Josef Goebbels arranged three days of mourning, solemn music played on all radio stations, and entertainment and sport banned. This funereal heroic fatalism, combined with Goebbels's mass rally in the Berlin Sportpalast on 18 February urging defiant solidarity and commitment to total war, could only sober the most ardent Nazi about the reality of the struggle. Publicizing the Allied demand for "unconditional surrender" announced at the Casablanca Conference in January 1943 by US president Franklin Roosevelt and British prime minister Winston Churchill added to the grim tone of the aftermath of this catastrophic defeat.

The sacrificial stand of 6. Armee had at least preoccupied Russian forces and facilitated the retreat of the German armies from the Caucasus back across the Don at Rostov, the capture of which might have resulted in an even greater catastrophe. By early February the German forces from the Caucasus had generally withdrawn back across the Don. Mackensen's 1. Pz.Armee had withdrawn through Rostov followed by Hoth's 4. Pz.Armee, while the light units of General Sigfrid Henrici's XXXX. Pz.Korps crossed the ice of the frozen Sea of Azov to Taganrog. Generaloberst Richard Ruoff's 17. Armee pulled back beyond the Kuban and fortified the "Gothic Line" fronting the Taman Peninsula across the Kerch Strait from the Crimea, maintaining Hitler's bridgehead for a future drive east.

It was farther north, where the Red armies were driving down behind the Donets and toward the Dnepr to trap Manstein's H.Gr. Süd, that there was a continuing crisis. Golikov's Voronezh Front armies were across the Oskol and the upper Donets, Vatutin's Southwest Front was across the middle Donets past Voroshilovgrad, Yeremenko's South Front closed on Rostov, and Rokossovsky's Don Front, currently mopping up at Stalingrad, was coming up. Ivan Petrov's new North Caucasus Front pressed 17. Armee, along with Ivan Tyulenev's Trans-Caucasus Front. After the collapse of the flank allied armies, only improvised forces were attempting to stem the Russian onslaught in the 300-kilometer (200-mile) gap between Belgorod and Voroshilovgrad. These troops were organized in "detachments," though they were under able commanders: Armee Abteilung Lanz under General der Gebirgstruppen Hubert Lanz, whose 1. Gebirgsdivision had raised the Hakenkreuz flag on Mt. Elbrus; Armee Abteilung Fretter Pico under General der Artillerie Maximilian Fretter-Pico of XXX. A.K.; and Armee Abteilung Hollidt under Gen.d.Inf. Karl-Adolf Hollidt of XVII. A.K.

But Manstein was now regrouping Mackensen's 1. Pz.Armee and Hoth's 4. Pz.Armee for a counterstroke once he could consolidate a firm position in the south. This position would follow the line of the Mius River up from Taganrog; it was a strong position that had been held the previous winter, although it required giving up Rostov and the lower Donets and the eastern Don Basin. Hitler was opposed to giving up any of the industrial Donbas region, and on 5 February he summoned Manstein to fly *back* by four-engined Condor Fw 200 to report at the Wolfsschanze, Hitler's headquarters at Rastenburg, east Prussia, on the 6th. But Manstein argued forcefully for stabilizing a line along the Mius, behind which he could concentrate his forces to drive north and cut off the Russian spearheads. As Mellenthin believed, perhaps the surrender of Paulus six days earlier—Manstein quoted Hitler as [correctly] admitting, "*I alone* bear the responsibility for Stalingrad!"—put the Führer in a more receptive frame of mind, and he reluctantly agreed to Manstein's plan.[19] Rostov was evacuated on 14 February and entered by Russian forces of South Front now under Rodion Malinovsky.

Encouraged by the disintegration of the German allied armies along the Don, and knowing of Hitler's stand-fast orders in general, the retreat of the German forces from Rostov and the lower Donets apparently led Stalin and the Stavka to believe that the Germans were in precipitous flight, and the subsequent Russian operations were more in the nature of pursuit to cut off and annihilate the entire southern German wing. In Operation GALLOP, Vatutin's Southwest Front, now including General Kharitonov's 6th Army from Voronezh Front, was to exploit the gap torn in the German front with the collapse of the 2. Hungarian and 8. Italian Armies, cross the middle Donets, and drive south behind H.Gr. Süd to Mariupol on the Sea of Azov, liberating the Donbas. The 6th Army was to advance across the eastern Ukraine to seize crossings of the Dnepr at Dnepropetrovsk and Zaporozhe. Lt. Gen. Markian Popov in particular led a Mobile Group of four tank corps with 212 tanks that would be the spearhead south once Fyodor Kuznetsov's 1st Guards Army crossed the Donets.

In Operation STAR, Golikov's Voronezh Front with five armies, including Pavel Rybalko's 3rd Tank Army, would attack west against improvised Armee Abteilung Lanz and von Salmuth's 2. Armee of

Kluge's H.Gr. Mitte to seize Kharkov and Kursk. GALLOP was initiated on 29 January and STAR on 2 February.[20] Distressed at the seemingly unstoppable Red Army tidal wave, Hitler was determined that Kharkov, the fourth-largest city in the Soviet Union, be held. On 11 February a categorical order was given to General Hubert Lanz that his Abteilung *must* defend Kharkov, though it was already being isolated by Russian armies passing on either side: Lt. Gen. Pavel Rybalko's 3rd Tank to the south, and Lt. Gen. M. I. Kazakov's 69th and Lt. Gen. K. S. Moskalenko's 40th to the north.

Lanz had been given the newly raised Waffen-SS Panzerkorps, and Hitler was convinced these fresh and fiercely loyal elite troops of his drittes deutsches Reich would prevail or fight to the bitter end in Kharkov. The corps was under the command of SS-Obergruppenführer Paul Hausser, and two of its three panzergrenadier divisions—1. Leibstandarte Adolf Hitler and 2. Das Reich—had just arrived from France, with 3.Totenkopf (Death's Head) to follow. "Papa" Hausser, the "Vater" of the Waffen-SS, had been badly wounded by shrapnel 14 October 1941 and lost his right eye. Wearing a distinctive black eye patch, he had recovered to organize the SS Pz.Korps in May 1942.

The urban warfare in the rubble and ruins of Stalingrad, however, had already demonstrated that committing mobile forces to city street-fighting was a poor utilization of resources, and sure to result in tremendous casualties with no strategic advantage. Manstein knew this, of course, but Lanz was subordinated to the leaderless H.Gr. B (Hitler), not Manstein's H.Gr. Süd (until the H.Gr. B headquarters was dissolved). Nonetheless, Manstein strongly opposed the commitment of Hausser's Panzerkorps in Kharkov, arguing that the corps would be better employed poised to strike at the flank of the Russian drive from the north. But Lanz was in no position to defy a Führer order. By 14 February Russian forces of three armies had penetrated the outskirts of Kharkov and the main supply route from Poltava was under Soviet artillery fire. Hausser requested Lanz to authorize a breakout, but Lanz, though he sympathized, could only respond that it was Hitler's order to hold the city.

"This order was impracticable," felt Hausser, who acted on his own initiative, defying both Lanz and Hitler. On 15 February he ordered his SS Panzerkorps to evacuate Kharkov ("quite rightly," thought Manstein). Generalleutnant Walter Hörnlein also pulled his Panzergrenadierdivison Grossdeutschland to the northwest back through the blazing streets of Kharkov when he realized Hausser's troops were leaving.[21] Hitler was furious, but Hausser was no martinet. A staff officer in the regular army in World War I, he retired as a Generalleutnant from the Reichswehr in 1932. He was selected by Reichsführer-SS Heinrich Himmler to form what became the Waffen-SS (Armed SS) as a military force. Hausser did so, determined that its units would be an elite, but regular, combat force, distinct from the police and the security elements of the rest of the SS. In combat operations, indeed, W-SS units were subordinate to army commands. Unwilling to discipline his combat SS even given Hausser's disobedience, Hitler relieved Hubert Lanz instead.

Hausser's unauthorized withdrawal from Kharkov had an unexpected benefit for Manstein's planned counterstroke. That Hitler's elite SS units had retreated, despite Hitler's presumed orders to fight on, further encouraged the conviction of Stalin and the Stavka that the Germans were in rout, and the Russian spearheads now recklessly plunged onward toward the Dnepr and behind H.Gr. Süd. Farther north Rokossovsky, freed from Stalingrad, was given command of a new Center Front with which to assault H.Gr. Mitte. But Manstein knew that if the shoulders of the penetration held, then the deeper the Russians were committed, the more decisive would be a counterattack to cut them off.

On 17 February Hitler, accompanied by Jodl and Zeitzler, flew in his Condor to meet with Manstein at his army group headquarters at Zaporozhe, and demanded the immediate recapture of Kharkov. By the next day Manstein had been able to convince Hitler of his planned counterstroke and postpone a decision about recapturing Kharkov, especially as the third W-SS panzergrenadier division, Theodor Eicke's 3. Totenkopf, had not come up yet after detraining from the West at Kiev. On the 19th, even as Russian tanks were reported scarcely 70 kilometers (40 miles) from Zaporozhe, Hitler flew back out after agreeing to Manstein's plans.

In the south Armee Abteilung Hollidt was able to hold the Mius River line, and A.A. Fretter-Pico held the shoulder as Mackensen's 1. Pz.Armee regrouped. Hoth's 4. Pz.Armee redeployed to its left (west) as the southern attack force—chess master Manstein's "Rochieren" ("castling") move. To the north Armee Abteilung Lanz, now commanded by General der

Panzertruppen Werner Kempf, held the northern shoulder around Poltava adjoining von Salmuth's 2. Armee, which was now under von Kluge's H.Gr. Mitte. Hausser's SS Pz.Korps was poised as the northern attack force. 15.Inf.Div. from the west arrived at Dnepropetrovsk to block a Russian thrust to Sinelnikovo on the rail line east. Time was of the essence now for a counteroffensive, as the spring thaw, the Schlammperiode, would soon paralyze ground operations.

In addition, intercepted wireless messages indicated that the advancing Russian forces were exhausted, and outrunning their logistics support. Nonetheless the forward Russian commanders were ordered to drive on. Popov's Mobile Group drove past Slavyansk on the Torets near the Donets around the left flank of 1. Pz.Armee and down toward Krasnoarmeiskoye by 12 February, cutting the vital railway from Dnepropetrovsk to Stalino and the heart of the Donets basin. There it was slowed by Felix Steiner's 5. SS Wiking Pz.Gren.Div. But that division was exhausted by the earlier fighting, and two of its three regiments—Nordland and Westland—were composed of Scandinavian and Dutch volunteers, and there was a shortage of officers fluent in their languages beyond basic commands. The division artillery, however, was able to put down formidable fires, and the Wikinger were stubborn soldiers.

The winter of 1942–43 was coming to an end. For the Wehrmacht it had been a series of disasters following the Stalingrad debacle punctuated by stubborn fighting. But in the south, von Manstein was beginning to turn the fluid situation to his advantage, and Balck's 11. Panzer-Division would play an important role in the operations ahead.

Meanwhile, much farther north, the I. Abteilung of Panzer-Regiment 15 under Major Heinrich Pricken, which had been detached from the 11.Pz.-Div., was used as a Feuerwehr reinforcement for a number of sectors of H.Gr. Mitte in the autumn of 1942. On 13 September the battalion had left Bolkhov north of Orel and road-marched to Spasdemenskoye. Then on 5 October the Kettenfahrzeuge were rail-loaded on E-Transport, arriving at Smolensk on the 9th. On the 14th the battalion road-marched again, 140 kilometers via Rudnya and Demidov to Yelissekhenski where I./15 was located for the next two months. In December 1942 it became embroiled in the fighting at Velikiye Luki on the Lovat south of Lake Ilmen.

In November 1942, as components of Zhukov's Operation MARS and working in conjunction with URANUS at Stalingrad, Russian forces assaulted all along the German front. At Leningrad, Kirill Meretskov's Volkhov Front finally slugged through Georg Lindemann's 18. Armee forces by 18 January 1943 to open a route south of Lake Ladoga and end the extended siege of that tortured city. Involved in the fighting were the stubborn volunteers of the Spanish "División Azul" (250. "Blaue" Inf.Div.), Franco's contribution to fighting Communism.

Hitler had originally intended that Leningrad be surrounded and starved into submission. But the Russians managed a trickle of supplies across Lake Ladoga, even constructing a railroad across the meter-thick ice in the frozen winter months, and kept the war industries producing. In addition, German and Finnish forces tied down in siege operations might have been better employed in severing the Murman railroad through Karelia, which had been bringing increased Allied Lend-Lease war materiel down from the Arctic Ocean port of Murmansk.

At Demyansk on the Valdai hills northwest of Moscow, Gen.d.Inf. Ernst Busch's 16. Armee maintained a salient for a future drive on the Russian capital. Cut off during the winter of 1941–42, the Kessel had been successfully resupplied by air until reconnected to the front. Now in November 1942 it was assaulted again, this time by Timoshenko's Northwest Front armies. With German reserves concentrated for the Stalingrad fighting, Hitler finally authorized the evacuation of the Demyansk salient on 31 January 1943, and by the end of February some twelve divisions had slowly contracted the salient back to the Lovat, shortening the front and allowing the formation of a reserve.

West of Moscow on the upper Volga, the larger Rzhev salient held by Walter Model's 9. Armee had also fended off Russian assaults by Konev's Kalinin and Zhukov's West Front armies the previous winter, and was once again under massive attacks from the Kalinin and West Fronts now under Vasiliy Sokolovsky and Konev, respectively. The final surrender of Paulus's 6. Armee at Stalingrad on 2 February 1943 prompted Hitler to reluctantly agree to the evacuation of the Rzhev Frontbogen on the 6th, as it was also vulnerable to encirclement and reserves were lacking. For the Führer it was a bitter decision because it was an admission that the momentous invasion of Soviet Russia had failed, that there would be no future advance on Moscow. By 22 March that salient with some twenty-two divisions, a quarter of a million troops, had been successfully contracted back toward Smolensk. Unternehmen BÜFFELBEWEGUNG (Buffalo Maneuver) shortened the front by some 300 kilometers (200 miles), from 500 kilometers (330 miles) to 200 kilometers (125 miles), releasing badly needed forces.

Between the large Demyansk and Rzhev salients was the much smaller salient at Velikiye Luki on the Lovat. There 7,500 troops of Inf.Rgt.277 of the 83.Inf.Div. and other elements under Oberstleutnant Eduard Freiherr von Sass held the town and its citadel astride important communications routes running down from Leningrad. Ever since it had been captured in August 1941 the salient had seen constant Russian attempts to recapture it, sometimes only being resupplied by armored trains. On 24 November 1942 there was a renewed Russian offensive that surrounded the German forces both in the town and in two other pockets farther south. This attack was mounted by Col. Gen. K. N. Galitsky's 3rd Shock Army of General Maksim Purkayev's Kalinin Front as part of Operation MARS, with over 100,000 troops.[22]

As German forces of H.Gr. Mitte were stretched thin with the Rzhev fighting, Kluge requested authorization for the three isolated pockets to break out to the west, reforming a defensive position while still covering the important north–south Nasva–Novosokolniki–Nevel railroad line supplying H.Gr. Nord. But this would require pulling back some 16–25 kilometers (10–15 miles), and Hitler, preoccupied with Stalingrad, forbade it. The two southern pockets, held by elements of Gen. Theodor Scherer's 83.I.D. and Gen.Lt. Hans Kreising's 3. Gebirgsjägerdivision, were able to fight their way out, but Velikiye Luki was to be held. Supplies and rations grew short despite varied attempts to resupply by air—by parachute, supply "bombs," transport glider, and even by Stuka dive-bombers that could more accurately pinpoint supplies dropped into the perimeter. Pounded by Russian artillery and airstrikes, reduced to eating horsemeat in the smoldering ruins, Sass's garrison tried to hold out.

The first relief attempt was made by Gen.Lt. Erich Brandenberger's 8.Pz.Div. down from Kholm, attacking on 28 November. But it collided with Russian armor and, though having a few Panzer IVs, Pz.Rgt.10 was equipped with twenty-seven obsolete Czech Panzer 38(t)s and captured Russian tanks, and thus made no headway. Gen.d.Inf. Erich Jaschke's 20.I.D.(mot) and Gen.Lt. Werner Göritz's 291.I.D. were also committed, hard pressed to block the Russian avalanche toward Novosokolniki. Gen.d.Inf. Kurt von der Chevallerie at LIX. A.K. covering Vitebsk requested the 11. Panzer's I.Abt./Pz.Rgt.15 from north of Smolensk, on 7 and again on 8 December, but the requests were disapproved by OKH, which was anticipating a Soviet assault in that sector. The 197. Sturmgeschütz Abt. was also requested from Gotthard Heinrici's 4. Armee but it could not be spared, and the Luftwaffe was unwilling to release the 7. Fliegerdivision (redesignated in April 1943 as the 1. Fallschirmjägerdivision), nor even a paratroop battalion.

Finally Maj. Heinrich Pricken's I./15 was released, on 14 December. From Yelissekhenski near Smolensk the Gespenster Abteilung road-marched to Rudnya, rail-loaded there, and was transported via Vitebsk and Nevel to Opukhliki to unload by that evening. The battalion was at strength, with thirty Pz.IIIs and four Pz.IVs. It then continued via Spaskoye to Lameshino by the 18th.[23] On 15 December a provisional corps was formed under Gen. der Inf. Otto Wöhler, Chef des Stabes of H.Gr. Mitte, for a renewed attempt to reach Velikiye Luki. Wöhler's corps apparently included 20.I.D.(mot), 291.I.D., and elements of 83.I.D., 3.Gebirgs.Div., 1. and 3. Jäger Btls, 343. Sicherheits Btl., and 743. Pionierbattalion. Though not listed, the thirty-four panzers of I./15 would be crucial.[24]

On 19 December 1942 Wöhler's attack began. Blanketed in deep snow, with penetrating cold and snow squalls, the terrain was a featureless wasteland. As the Gespenster panzers of I.Abt./Pz.Rgt.15 encountered the first Russian positions, the unit's commander, Maj. Heinrich Pricken, with the battalion since he was an Oberleutnant in 1938, was killed. Lt. Albrecht of 1. Kompanie, whose panzer was close by, shot at the Russian riflemen with his MPi but was also killed, shot through the head. Oblt. Walter succeeded to command as the battalion churned on, then igelt with darkness.

On the 20th the drive continued, the Jägers taking heavy casualties from Russian artillery and mortar fire, but capturing two towns. On the 21st the 20.I.D.(mot), supported by the Gespenster panzers captured the hills west of Alekseikovo and then the town itself, while the 291.I.D. cleared the forest east of Butitlno. Estonians dragooned into the Red Army deserted to the Germans *en masse*, the I. Abteilung claiming at least a battalion.[25] Panzers were lost to

Russian fire and the treacherous terrain conditions; and on the 22nd the panzers encountered a well-organized Russian Pakfront. With more losses, and the panzers needing to be refueled, the drive stalled. They had thrust 25 kilometers (15 miles), halfway to besieged Velikiye Luki.

As Wöhler reported his forces depleted and exhausted, Chevallerie ordered them to stand down for two days to be refitted and regrouped. The supply and repair elements of I./15 tried to stay close to the fighting units, managing to at least dig a one-meter-deep shelter trough in the frozen ground and cover it with canvas as some protection against the wind and biting cold. A couple of small ovens helped keep hands and equipment (almost) thawed out. Von Sass in the besieged ruins of Velikiye Luki pleaded for supplies and a relief expedition, receiving exhortations to hold out from Scherer—who had held out in Kholm for 104 days—Chevallerie, Kluge, and even Hitler, and Sass was awarded the Knight's Cross—but no relief. Christmas 1942 passed, and on 26 December the Russians segmented the perimeter, isolating the Kreml (citadel) on the Lovat under Hauptmann Erich Danedde from the eastern part of the town under von Sass.

As the Austrian 331.I.D. under General Franz Beyer and the 205.I.D. under Gen.Lt. Paul Seyffardt were now provided, Chevallerie and Wöhler planned a new relief attack, Unternehmen TOTILA, for 4 January 1943. With these and other units Wöhler got to within 4 kilometers (2.5 miles) of Velikiye Luki, and scouts could even make out the spires of the citadel. On the 9th there was a renewed thrust under the command of Maj. Günther Tribukait of 5. Jäger Batl. I./15 was down to five panzers, led by Lt. Kloske. The orders were to charge forward without pause; crews of any knocked-out vehicles were to abandon them and ride on others. Tribukait's force finally got to the citadel at 15,06 hours, to the hoarse cheers of Danebbe and his remaining 427 men.

Nineteen-year-old Gefreiter Werner Bürkner, a Funker on Pz.III Nr. 31, was one whose panzer was knocked out. Hit on the left side, the engine conked out. Fahrer Robert Fürst tried to start it again, but then, "'*Raus*, it's burning!" The crew scrambled out, Bürkner taking the radio knobs with him so the Russians couldn't use the radio. They wanted to follow the column but came under Russian fire. Fortunately Wagen Nr. 35 returned and they scrambled aboard. Farther on, however, the column was stalled. Bürkner and Fürst, exposed, jumped into an SPW that gave some protection, and the other three crew members piled into the one ahead. (These rescuers were Halbketten with Tyrolers from Jäger-Btl. 5.)

Then Bürkner and Fürst's half-track was hit, and they sought refuge in an abandoned bunker. The rest of the column continued on. They hoped to remain unseen until nightfall, though they could hear scattered shooting. But to their horror they saw a wisp of cigarette smoke coming from a shell hole, from "*ein kompletter Idiot.*" The Russians saw it as well. Soon Rotarmisten closed in, saying in broken German, *"Komm Bruder, komm her, nix schiessen Kamerad."* Several Germans were rounded up in a line; when a Russian officer appeared, he pulled his pistol out and in a sudden blood-frenzy (Blutrausch) shot one after the other. As he reached Bürkner at the end of the line, his pistol went *click*—empty! He thrust his hand into Bürkner's coat and pulled out his Luger Pistole 08, but just as suddenly recovered his composure. *"Du jung, Du mein Gefangener!"* Seven shot Germans lay in the bloody snow, in front of the Russian soldiers who looked on impassively.

As a stunned Bürkner and others were taken into captivity and interrogated, at one point he saw a Russian female soldier with a handful of German Soldbücher (identification booklets). He recognized Fürst's, with blood on it, and knew his comrade, Robert, had been shot. Later a Russian saw Bürkner's black panzer uniform under his heavy coat and almost shot him as SS. He also had to act as an intermediate interpreter when the Russian interrogator couldn't understand the Tyrolean dialect of Jäger Christian Meyer. Bürkner survived Russian captivity, though he would not be repatriated until 1948.[26]

At the citadel fifteen armored vehicles, SPWs, assault guns, and panzers—Lt. Kloske had only three left—entered the ramparts. But furious Russian artillery fire smashed into the old fortress. When it was determined to move the vehicles out of the citadel, one was hit and blocked the exit. Over the next few days all fifteen gepanzerte Fahrzeuge were destroyed and the crews joined the defenders as infantry. The plan now was to coordinate a breakout during the night of 14–15 January. But the parachute battalion, finally released from 7. Fliegerdivision, got lost in the featureless snow-covered terrain, and Russian artillery pounded the citadel in what was now a trap.

On the 15th the last radio message from von Sass in the eastern pocket was received, a sign that it had been overrun. Gen. Wöhler now authorized Jäger Major Tribukait at the citadel to fight his way back to the west, but the wounded had to be left behind to fall into Russian hands. About 150 Germans managed to escape that night, including Lt. Kloske, as well as several individuals from the eastern pocket. But the Velikiye Luki garrisons had fallen. (On 29 January 1946 the Soviets executed von Sass and ten others, one selected from each rank, of the Velikiye Luki prisoners. Only eleven survived Russian captivity to return to Germany, between 1953 and 1958.) The fighting around Velikiye Luki cost the Germans some 17,000 casualties. But the lines defending the railroad held, and the Germans estimated the Russians lost over 30,000 killed alone. Entire divisions were shattered as the Ivans attacked under horrendous winter conditions against the German forces and "perished in staggering numbers."[27]

For the exhausted surviving Gespensters of the I.Abt./Pz.Rgt.15, rumor spread that the unit was to return to Germany. With February 1943 rumor became fact, as I./15, now under Rittmeister (Cavalry Captain) Karl von Sivers, was indeed ordered back to Germany. Von Sivers was born 8 February 1912 in Allenstein, eastern Prussia. Joining Reiter-Rgt. 2 in Osterode, East Prussia, he was promoted Oberlt. 1 October 1937. The spirited young cavalryman was awarded the EK 2 on 20 September 1939 and the EK 1 on 15 October, and promoted to Rittmeister 1 August 1940. When his 1. Kavalleriedivision was reorganized 28 November 1941 as the 24. Der Springende Reiter (The Leaping Horseman) Panzer-Division, Sivers commanded 6. Schwadron (Company, but the 24. retained the cavalry tradition) in II.Abt./Pz.Rgt.24, and then II.Btl./Pz.Gren.Rgt. 21 in the drive on Stalingrad. On 21 September 1942 he was reassigned to OKH Führerreserve for training as a panzer battalion commander, and appointed to I.Abt./Pz.Rgt.15 on 28 December (even as his old division was trapped and would be destroyed at Stalingrad).[28]

On 3 February the Abteiling marched on foot to Opochluki where they entrained on freight cars, fifty men each. The discomfort of the cold, barren freight cars was offset by the relief of leaving the bleak, winter battleground of Velikiye Luki. The kilometers rattled slowly past: Polodz on the 4th, Dünaburg (Dvinsk) on the 5th, Krotinnen, Memel, Königsberg, Schneidemühl/Küstrin, and Frankfurt am Oder by the 10th, and then down through Cottbus, Zwickau, Plauen, and Hof, to Truppenübungsplatz Grafenwöhr in Bavaria east of Nürnberg by 19,00 hours that day. The clean, stone barracks with cots and mattresses seemed like paradise after the nightmare of Velikiye Luki, and those allowed on Heimaturlaub were fortunate indeed.[29]

CHAPTER FOURTEEN

Kharkov Counterattack

WITH THE NORTHERN AND CENTRAL BATTLE LINES BEGINNING to stabilize by February 1943, the focus of the Ostfront turned to the still-fluid south. As the Russian spearheads plunged onward toward the Dnepr, Manstein began to deploy his forces for a complex series of maneuvers of mobile warfare that would effectively destroy the Russian advance and regain the line of the Donets from Belgorod down to the Mius position. According to the plan, Hoth's Pz.A.O.K.4 was to shift from the Mius sector to Dnepropetrovsk and assume control of Hausser's SS Panzerkorps from Armee Abteilung Kempf and Knobelsdorff's XXXXVIII. Pz.-Korps from A.A. Hollidt. Then Hausser would attack southeast with 2.SS Das Reich and 3.SS Totenkopf with 1.SS Leibstandarte Adolf Hitler holding the flank, while Knobelsdorff attacked north with 6. and 17.Pz.Div. to converge on Losovaya to cut off and annihilate Kharitonov's 6th Army.

Mackensen's 1. Pz.Armee would hold the southern flank with Generalleutnant Hermann Breith's III. Pz.K. with 3. and 19. Pz.Div. while Gen.Lt. Sigfrid Henrici's XXXX. Pz.K. destroyed the Popov Mobile Group with 7. and 11. Pz.Div. and 5.SS Pz.Gren.Div. Wiking. Henrici would advance north to Barvenkovo east of Losovaya, and then the two forces would converge as they drove north to Kharkov.

After recrossing the Don at Rostov and taking position near Taganrog, on 3 February the 11. Panzer-Division was ordered north to the gap in the Donets Bend that had opened with the disintegration of 2. Hungarian Army. They were assigned to Henrici's XXXX. Pz.K. Oberst Schimmelmann's Panzer-Regiment 15 detrained its first sixteen panzers by midday on the 6th in Konstantinovka north of Stalino (later Donetsk), joining division elements that had road-marched through the ice and snow. But the constant movement allowed little time for pulling maintenance on the vehicles. Both tracked and wheeled vehicles "were falling out like flies," said division commander Balck.[1]

Nonetheless the Elfte began a drive north that same day through 24 kilometers (15 miles) of a series of industrial settlements from Konstantinovka to the factory city of Kramatorskaya south of Slavyansk. But when the SPW-Btl. (I.) of Oberst

Albert Henze's Pz.Gren.Rgt.110 debouched from Konstantinovka it encountered heavy antitank fire at Drushkovka and had to fall back, minus ten of the half-tracks and its antitank guns. The 11. Panzer was running head-on into the Russian 3rd Tank Corps under Lt. Gen. M. D. Sinenko, which had joined the 4th Guards Tank Corps under Maj. Gen. P. P. Poluboyarov of Popov's Mobile Group. But reinforced with a Pak Kompanie of 333.Inf.Div., Stukas, and Schimmelmann's Pz.-Rgt.15, the Gespensters slugged ahead up the road through the villages of Novosselovka, Drushkova, Surovo, Krassnotorka, and Ivanovka on the outskirts of Kramatorskaya by the 9th. The temperature hovered around freezing.

The pattern of fighting saw Schmidt's Pz.Art. Rgt.119 batteries' fire missions adjusted by the VBs, and Stukas when the weather allowed, pounding the next village positions. Henze's panzergrenadiers would be following or riding on Schimmelgraf's panzers—*"Einsteigen!"* ("On board!")—charging forward. In many ways these frontal assaults were contrary to panzer principles, especially as the Russians were adept at fortifying the village positions. Manstein was a little disgruntled at Mackensen's insistence that deep snows in the Krivoi Torets valley on the left made flanking maneuvers impossible.[2] But the wider tracks of the T-34 gave it a floatation capability over the snow-covered terrain that restricted the panzers, even with their Ostkette. It was the coordination of the 11.Pz.Div. units, and the skill of the crews and rifle squads, that enabled them to prevail. The roadway and villages from Konstantinovka to the north were littered with the wreckage of Russian tanks and vehicles, the Gespensters claiming at least forty-eight tanks destroyed since the 6th. On the 8th Oberst Alexander von Bosse's Pz.G.R.111 had been ordered back to Makeyevka to be reconstituted.

On the left flank was Gruppe Schmidt, Grenadierregiment 679 of the 333.Inf.Div., as well as two Turkish battalions, I./Turk Btl.94 and I./Turk Btl.371, recruited from the Caucasus. In addition, fire support came from Eisenbahn Panzerzug (Railroad Armored Train) 10 B under Hptm. Richter. On the 9th the locomotive boiler was holed by two 7,5cm rounds and the train had to go back to Konstantinovka Bahnhof for repairs, but soon returned. But the Elften, according to KTB entries, felt "Attachment of Eisb.Pz.Zug 10 B was not effective." The Luftwaffe, on the other hand, was complimented for its continuous air support and Stuka dive-bomber attacks coordinated through the Flivo. The KTB noted "Excellent teamwork with Flieger-Division Donez," and "Very good cooperation the Luftwaffe ground elements. They marked targets with precise smoke, explosive, or flare shells."[3]

On the 10th 7.Pz.-Div., which held at Slavyansk, reported that one of its assault groups attacking to the south had entered Kramatorskaya, but that turned out to be wrong; it was only at Ssozgorod instead. 11 February proved to be "a surprisingly quiet day" for the Eleveners. The reason, determined German radio intercept intelligence, was that the battered 3rd Tank Corps had misread Popov's ordered map coordinates and had been attacking south*east*—into the 11. Panzer drive—rather than south*west*, toward the Dnepr. (Actually, Stavka pressed Vatutin to drive on to the Dnepr, and Vatutin pressed Popov to have 4th Guards Tank Corps leave the defense of Kramatorskaya to 3rd Tank Corps and thrust on to Krasnoarmeiskoye.)

With the Ivans in confusion, III.Abt./Pz.Rgt.15 flanked into Kramatorskaya on the 12th and by the 13th could claim to have cut Popov's supply route through Slavyansk on the Torets from the Donets. But the 333.I.D. fell back through Losovaya with the Russian pressure. More Russian tanks materialized: Maj. Gen. V. G. Burkov's 10th Tank Corps arrived, followed by the 18th Tank Corps, and the fighting in Kramatorskaya devolved into bitter street-fighting.[4]

Balck says he had always pleaded to leave congested Kramatorskaya alone, instead advocating a swing south of the city into the flank and rear of Popov's advance. However, Henrici at XXXX. Pz.K. felt the snowfields in the Krivoi Torets valley were too deep, and that the Russians at least considered the snow an absolutely effective flank protection. As XXXX. Pz.K. staff headquarters were south of Kramatorskaya, Balck took a proposal directly to Mackensen of 1. Pz.Armee when he saw him, asking that the 11.Pz.-Div. be redeployed to attack south behind Popov's 4th Guards Tank Corps, which was continuing on toward the Dnepr. Mackensen agreed, and on 18 February Balck pulled the Elfte out of the city. The Russians reported this as a success. Mackensen also had 7.Pz.Div. leave Slavyansk to 3.Pz.Div. and road-march south to intercept Popov. Mackensen had Breith's III. Pz.K. take over the Slavyansk sector, freeing Henrici's XXXX. Panzerkorps for the renewed drive, with three panzer divisions: Gen.Lt. Hans Freiherr von Funck's Thuringian 7.Pz.Div., made famous under Rommel in the French Feldzug,

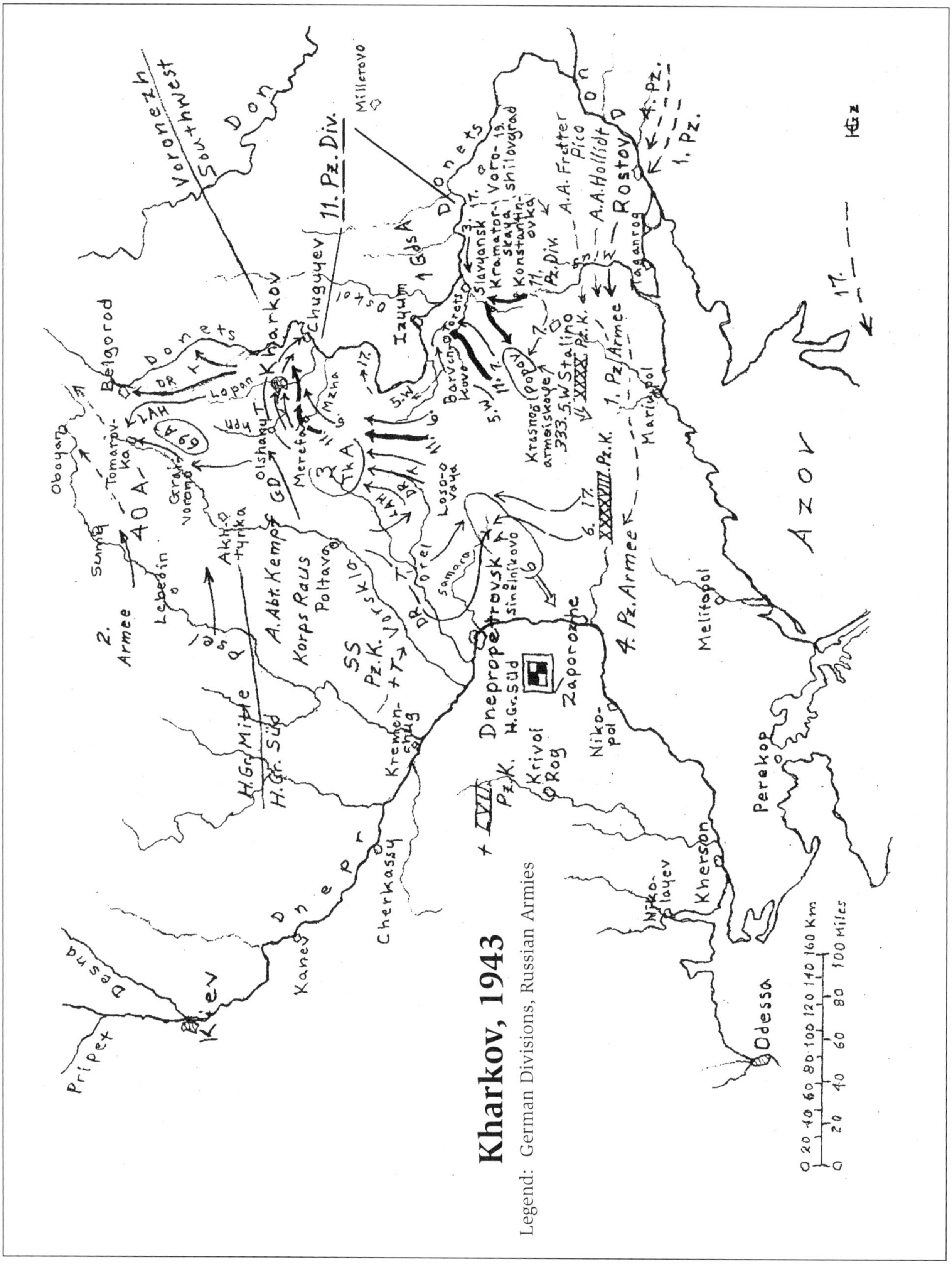

Kharkov, 1943

Legend: German Divisions, Russian Armies

Balck's Silesian 11. Gespenster Panzer-Division, and Gruppenführer Felix Steiner's 5.SS Wiking. 11.Pz.Div. would attack from the north, 7. and 5.SS from the south.

On the morning of 19 February the 11. Panzer advance began; vehicles with snowplows led the way, followed by motorcycles and panzers. The two snowplows belonged to Schneeräumtrupp 63 (Snow-Clearing Troop 63) from XXXX. Pz.K. The Schneepflüge were mounted on MAN and Büssing trucks with all-wheel drive. The division staff was right behind the snowplows as they cleared a pathway across the frozen Krivoi Torets to the Russian Rollbahn south. The fighting strength of the division was some 3,174, with now some thirty-five panzers (two Pz.IIs, twenty-seven Pz.III lang, and six Pz.IVs) einsatzbereit. There were twenty-seven other panzers in short-term repair and forty-one in long-term repair, over fourteen days.

Pz.Art.Rgt.119 had thirty-two tubes: thirteen 10,5cm le.F.H. towed and self-propelled, four 15cm s.F.H., and four 10cm Kan. There were five 8,8cm flak guns in IV.(Flak)/Pz.-A.R.119. There were also eighteen Pak (nine 3,7cm, eight 5cm, and one 7,5cm), with the units. With von Bosse re-forming Pz.G.R.111, Henze's two 110 panzergrenadier battalions were the infantry strength. Kampfgruppe Schimmelmann had Pz.Rgt.15, I./110, K.61, and 3.Battr./119; Grevendorf's 209 engineers and the Acht-achts were in support; the artillery fires were supplemented by the rocket launchers of II./Werfer Rgt. 52; and Henze's Kampfgruppe with the 110 regimental units and II./110 were the division reserve.[5]

The Gespensters drove south, overrunning Russian maintenance and repair elements. Attacking the village of Novo Troizkoye, Balck was in his Kübel near the panzer of Graf Schimmelmann. Their relationship was exemplified by an exchange they had there: Balck had his IIa (adjutant) Maj. Günther Kaldrack tell Schimmelmann to ride with him. But Kaldrack returned saying, "The Herr Graf says there's still violent fighting in the town, would you not prefer to go in his panzer?" "*Ach was*, one can't see anything from inside a panzer. Schimmelmannn should come to me." Kaldrack appeared again: "The Herr Graf announced if the Herr General wasn't polite and wouldn't join him in the panzer, he wouldn't lead with him." There was no alternative, and laughing, Balck climbed on Schimmelmann's panzer.[6]

On 20 February the 11. Panzer swept down on the main elements of Popov's Mobile Group from the north, while Steiner's 5.SS-Wiking and von Funck's 7.Pz.-Div. assaulted from the south. Cut off and trapped, the Popov group was essentially destroyed, mopped up by the 333.Inf.Div. Mackensen's 1. Pz.Armee then turned for a drive north, 17.Pz.Div. of XXXXVIII. Pz.K. on the left paralleling 5.SS Wiking. The 11.Pz.-Div. drove north toward Barvenkovo on the Torets, flanking to the right across the river and coming down on the town from the north by the 28th, while 7.Pz.Div. also thrust across the river. Hptm. Karl Lestmann, commanding II./15, was mortally wounded in his turret when it was hit by a Russian shell.

Over open ground and when the terrain permitted, the attack formation was the Panzerstosskeil (panzer assault wedge) with the heavier panzers leading in a V formation followed by the lighter panzers, with panzergrenadiers and Pioniers in their SPWs, or riding on the panzers if the ground was poor going for the half-tracks. Despite the deep snow and winter conditions, Balck had ably maneuvered his Kampfgruppe—or more accurately his commanders did, as Balck allowed them latitude: Schimmelmann of 15, Henze of 110, von Bossse of 111, Krad.61 under Hptm. Ladewig when Hptm. Paul von Hauser left for reassignment on the 6th, and Grevendorf's Pz.Pi.Btl.209, supported by Schmidt's 119 artillery. They performed a series of nimble actions, pinning the Ivans in front, flanking from one flank or the other, erupting into the Russian rear, and fully demonstrating the effectiveness of panzer warfare correctly led. (Paul von Hauser later went to the Panzerlehrdivision.)

In the twenty-one day battle the Germans claimed the Popov Mobile Group lost 251 tanks, 125 antitank guns, 73 artillery pieces, 217 machine guns, 425 trucks, and some 3,000 dead. Hitler followed the battle closely, and on the 28th messaged, "This dashing attack will fundamentally change the situation on the southern flank of the Ostfront." In a teleprinter message on 2 March Mackensen praised the 11. Panzer-Division and its commander as "the soul of the attack of the Armee."[7]

The fighting continued. Signals Uffz. Schönfelder of 1.Kompanie, Nachrichtenabteilung 89, recorded the radio communications of Hauptmann Klaus Piontek, the new commander of II.Abt./15 as Pz.-Rgt.15 was in action east of Barvenkovo. It was an example of controlled fires. The sergeant was at Schimmelmann's

Befehlspanzer: "Piontek to Schimmelmann—Piontek to Schimmelmann—on the road toward Schimmelmann, ten T-34s approaching!—Understood?" The Funker confirmed: "Understood—Ready!" Then: "Piontek to Pohl—Piontek to Pohl—Pohl, those coming on the left, those belong to me—understood?" "*Verstanden—Fertig!*" Then all the panzers opened fire in unison, destroying the Russian tanks in seconds. Schimmelmann did have to remind Hptm. Piontek that his regimental command panzer only had a wooden barrel. Klaus Piontek was killed in his cupola in a later clash with a KV-1. His body was treated with a ceremonial lying in state in a Russian Orthodox church. Both Lestmann and Piontek had been with the regiment since 1938 as lieutenants.[8]

On another occasion Schimmelmann displayed his *sangfroid* when a Russian tank column stopped outside the regimental command post in a house in Butovo, and the crews dismounted. Schimmelmann calmly ordered: "Get me through to Division," and spoke to the Division Ia, Maj. Franz-Joachim Kinitz: "*Ja*, Kinitz, what to do? Some Muzhiks are hanging around in front of my door. Fortunately they haven't seen us yet since my Wagen is in the courtyard behind. What'll happen? I can't hang a sign on the door saying 'Temporarily closed' or something." But the situation resolved itself when the Russian tank crews remounted and drove off, and the Gefechtsstand resumed its work.

At one point Oblt. Maiwald on Schimmelgraf's staff came up to him with two Russian girls in uniform. "*Ja*, Maiwald, what'll we do with the ladies? Well, we'll ask the Ia!" Over the transmitter to Major Kinitz: "Kinitz, I have two young women in uniform. What'll we do with them?" "Are they at least pretty?" "I'm afraid they are covered with lice." One of the Russian girls immediately said in faultless German, "Oh please, we don't have lice." It was finally decided they could be helpful in organizing regimental quarters in Barvenkovo (with nothing inappropriate hinted).[9]

"Der Graf" had already received the Ritterkreuz, and (as of 3 February) was awarded the Deutsches Kreuz in Gold. The adjutant was told to get a couple of Wagens together and have the crews fall in for a brief ceremony in the field, interrupted by a Stalinsorgel rocket barrage. Schimmelmann met Balck with his coat open, no cap, a cigarette still in his hand, and his faint sardonic smile. They greeted each other and with a few words Balck pinned the award on Schimmelmann's right breast. "Herr General, that thing certainly spoils the dress uniform!" Balck recommended Schimmelmann for a division command, but his successor didn't appreciate Schimmelmann's wit and nonchalance, and it was not forthcoming. It was this mix of mutual affection and respect, and knowing each other's abilities, that allowed the confidence and discretion of Auftragstaktik and Sattelbefehle, and enabled Balck and the 11. Gespensters to work together so effectively in combat.[10]

On 13 March 1943 Balck left the 11.Pz.Div. after ten months, having led it to a number of tactical successes. For the earlier two months fighting on the Chir and the Manych, 7 December 1942 to 31 January 1943, Balck listed Russian losses compared to 11. Panzer-Division losses:

	Enemy losses	Own losses
Tanks:	225	16
Armored reconnaissance vehicles:	12	4
Artillery pieces:	35	—
Antitank guns:	347	12

But 11.Pz.Div. losses were high among other vehicles, due as much to terrain, high mileage, and weather as to enemy action: 745 vehicles, of which 450 were under repair, and 280 motorcycles of which 100 were under repair. Russian casualties included some 30,700 dead—a number attributed, Balck felt, very much to Russian organization and tactics of masses of men, poorly supported, thrown against the Germans in dense formations, to be mown down by panzer, MG, and artillery fire.

11.Pz.Div. losses were:

Died: 215 including 15 officers
Wounded: 1,019 including 47 officers
Missing: 155 including 3 officers

On the day Balck left the division, the Gespensters claimed their 1,000th Russian tank destroyed. (Again, the term "claimed" is used advisedly, as many tanks that were hit were repairable, and whoever controlled the battlefield could retrieve their own armored fighting vehicles.)[11]

Balck was reassigned to the Führerreserve at OKH, and then became acting commander of the big Panzergrenadierdivision Grossdeutschland at Poltava before being assigned to Italy. Like the W-SS divisions, the GD had so much equipment it was equal to *two* panzer divisions. Compared to the 11.Pz.Div. Balck felt it was not combat-efficient, but rather ponderous and difficult to lead. Upon departing the Gespenster-Division Balck met with Hitler, and received 1,500 Reichsmarks for his accomplishments with the 11. Panzer. He was to use it for a vacation with his wife in Slovakia, but there wasn't much time for that. Instead, in November of 1944 when the 11.Pz.Dv. was in his command as part of Heeresgruppe G in the West, the now General der Panzertruppe visited his old division and treated those Gespensters who had served with him in Russia to a gracious and festive evening.[12]

While Mackensen's 1. Panzerarmee had stabilized the southern shoulder of the Russian breakthrough and maneuvered to destroy the Popov Mobile Group drive, Manstein had redeployed Hoth's 4. Pz.Armee around to its left. There it was poised to attack Kharitonov's 6th Army and elements of Lt. Gen. Mikhail Katukov's 1st Guards Army of Vatutin's Southwest Front nearing the Dnepr. Hausser's SS Panzerkorps was at Poltava behind Armee-Abteilung Kempf firming up the northern shoulder of the Russian breakthrough, a gap more than 400 kilometers (250 miles) wide, longer than the Western Front in World War I. By this time 3.SS Panzergrenadierdivision Totenkopf under SS OGruf. Theodor Eicke had come up.

Manstein assigned three corps to Hoth to cut off and destroy the Russian 6th Army: Hausser's SS Panzerkorps from A.A.Kempf was to attack from the northwest, and Knobelsdorff's XXXXVIII. Pz.K. was to attack from the southeast while Gen.d.Pz.Tr. Friedrich Kirchner's LVII. Pz.K. assembled in the Dnepr bend. Local Russian commanders began to warn of the German force buildup, but Stavka and Stalin still urged the drive on. "Without a doubt," estimated Vatutin on 17 February, "the enemy is hurrying to withdraw his forces from the Donbas across the Dnepr" to thwart the Russian advance.[13]

On 19 February, even as the 11.Pz.Div. was driving south to converge with 5.SS-W and 7. Panzer against the Popov Mobile Group, Hoth's attack began. Although Hausser's SS Panzerkorps was separated to the north, Manstein knew it was better for *one* commander—in this case Hoth—to coordinate the pincers attack. Brigadeführer Matthias Kleinheisterkamp's 2.SS Das Reich led Hausser's panzer corps in the drive south towards Pavlograd, supported by Stukas of Feldmarschall Wolfram von Richthofen's IV. Luftflotte; from the south Knobelsdorff's XXXXVIII. Pz.Korps panzer divisions, Oberst Walter von Hünersdorff's 6. and Generalmajor Fridolin von Senger und Etterlin's 17., swept north to shatter the 6th Army spearheads of the 25th Tank Corps under Maj. Gen. P. P. Pavlov, which had reached Slavgorod near the Dnepr on the 22nd. But Pavlov was 100 kilometers (60 miles) beyond the Russian supply trains and running short of fuel, munitions, and rations. The next day, the 23rd, saw Das Reich and 6.Pz.Div. converge on Pavlograd in his rear. The Russians abandoned their tanks, vehicles, and equipment, and isolated groups and soldiers wandered back over the winter landscape. Then, as Obergruppenführer Josef "Sepp" Dietrich's 1. Leibstandarte Adolf Hitler mounted a fixing attack, 2.SS-DR and Eicke's 3.SS-Totenkopf wheeled and began driving north again. They paralleled 6. and 17.Pz.Div. through Losovaya to Taranovka. Henrici's 5.SS-W, 7., along with 11.Pz.Div., joined from the right to sweep north. By the 24th, despite insistent orders to continue the advance, Vatutin finally realized the catastrophe that was overtaking Popov and Kharitonov and suspended all offensive operations. But it was too late. Both Mackensen's and Hoth's panzer divisions were driving north, across the Torets, and Generalmajor Franz Westhoven's Berlin 3. Bär Pz.Div. cut the Izyum–Slavyansk Rollbahn, thrusting to regain the line of the Donets.

By the end of February 1943, 1. and 4. Panzer-Armee had smashed the armies of Vatutin's Southwest Front, which had been sweeping forward to the Dnepr to cut off the entire German southern front only a couple of weeks before. Six tank corps, ten rifle divisions, and several other brigades had been mauled. The Germans claimed 615 tanks, 400 guns, and 600 antitank guns destroyed. Some 23,000 Russians had died, out of perhaps 100,000 casualties. Only 9,000 prisoners were taken, but this was explained by the fact that the panzer forces could not seal off the Kessels as well as infantry and the intense cold encouraged the Germans to seek shelter and made them less watchful, and many Ivans were able to escape across the still-frozen Donets River.[14]

Manstein's panzer divisions reprovisioned in anticipation of a renewed drive north to retake Kharkov. The German victory was a tremendous one and demonstrated how mobile maneuvering, even in winter conditions, could defeat much larger Russian forces. Few militaries could match the agile flanking and reversing maneuvers of the counterattacks of Manstein and his experienced panzer commanders that sliced up the opposing forces and destroyed them.

Russian penetrations had been made at Kursk, Belgorod, and Kharkov, but Manstein's victories over Vatutin's Southwest Front forces exposed these to destruction as well. Lt. Gen. Pavel Rybalko's 3rd Tank Army was redeployed from Golikov's Voronezh Front south as reinforcement, and was committed south of Kharkov on 3 March. To continue the next phase of his counteroffensive north, Manstein massed six panzer divisions in two panzer corps under Hoth's 4. Pz.Armee, while Mackensen's 1. Pz.Armee guarded the right flank along the Donets up past Izyum. The 11. Panzer-Division was reassigned from XXXX. Pz.Korps to XXXXVIII. Pz.K. in 4. Pz.Armee. Hausser's SS Pz.K. with 1.LSSAH, 2.SS-DR, and 3.SS-T was on the left, and Knobelsdorff's XXXXVIII. Pz.K. with 11., 6., and 17.Pz.Div. was on the right. A.A.Kempf held the western sector of the Russian bulge with three infantry divisions and Gen.Lt. Walter Hörnlein's Pz.Gren.Div. GD in a provisional corps under Generalleutnant Erhard Raus, ready to advance as the SS came up.

Technically termed panzergrenadier divisions until redesignated as panzer divisions in October 1943, the three Waffen-SS divisions, as well as GD, actually had more armored fighting vehicles than regular panzer divisions. In addition, each also had a company of the heavy Tiger panzers. The Tiger design had been developed as a heavy panzer following combat experience against the British Matilda II and the French Char B1bis during the 1940 French campaign. Unfortunately Hitler had ordered the first Tigers into action before they could be produced and employed en masse for maximum physical and psychological impact. In August 1942 four Tigers of 1. Kompanie of Schwere Panzerabteilung (Heavy Panzer Battalion) 502 were committed near Leningrad. In January 1943 the Russians captured a Tiger, which enabled them to analyze its strengths (8,8cm gun, 100 mm/4-inch frontal armor, wide tracks) and weaknesses (weight of 56 tons with the attendant limitations of bridges and terrain floatation, and vulnerable flanks, rear, and tracks). One company of the 501. attached to the 10.Pz.Div. saw action at Kasserine Pass in Tunisia in February 1943, and there one Tiger was captured by the Americans. The 503. had been deployed to southern Russia in December 1942.

Manstein would have preferred to drive *across* the Donets and sweep *behind* the Russian forces: "One felt a strong temptation to chase the enemy across the still frozen river and take him in the rear in and west of Kharkov." But with the expected coming thaw, "the ice was liable to break up at any time and no pontoon bridges would have held against the drift-ice." Manstein had his operational goal: "Thus an attempt had to be made to roll up the enemy from the flank and to force him away from Kharkov in the process. . . . At all costs the Army Group wished to avoid Kharkov's becoming a second Stalingrad in which our assault forces might become irretrievably committed."[15]

On the left Hausser's SS Pz.K. advanced north from Pavlograd through heavy snowdrifts against Rybalko's 3rd Tank Army. Hausser wheeled Totenkopf in encircling the Russians in a Kessel west of Bereka by 4 March, and Stukas and the SS destroyed Rybalko's units. (SS-T was now led by Brigadeführer Max Simon after Eicke's Fieseler Storch was shot down 26 February and he was killed).

Knobelsdorff's XXXXVIII. Panzerkorps on the right pushed across the railway line from Losovaya to Kharkov 40 kilometers (25 miles) distant, contested by Maj. Gen. Shafarenko's 25th Guards Rifle Division near Taranovka, Zmiyev, and Merefa. There was a sudden thaw, but 11.Pz.Div. managed to flank around through Merefa and across the Mzha from the west. Von Bosse's Pz.Gren.Rgt.111, reestablished in the rear area, rejoined the division by 5 March, with the Stab, Stabskompanie, and II. Bataillon designated as Pz.G.R.111 without I.Btl. I./111 remained as II./110. The original II./110 under Major Lindner was reconstituted in the rear. Pz.Art.Rgt.119 was organized in two le.F.H. and one s.F.H. Abteilungen (with one Kanone batterie).

For the attack on 6 March, the Elfte attacked with two battle groups: Kampfgruppe Schimmelmann with Pz.Rgt.15 and I.Btl./Pz.G.R.110 and I.Abt./A.R.119, the mobile armored group; and Kgr. Henze with Pz.G.R.110 (ohne I.Btl.), and Hptm. Ladewig's K.61 supported by Pz.A.R.119 (ohne I.Abt.)—Oberst Julius Werner having succeeded Oskar Schmidt—and IV.(Flak)119. Hptm. Grevendorf's Pz.Pi.Btl.209 was in division reserve as was 12.Kp.(Flak)/Pz.A.R.119. Von Bosse's Pz.G.R.111 was assembling in Oktyabrskiy ready for use.[16]

On 9 March Hausser received orders from Hoth at 4. Pz.Armee to swing around Kharkov to the west and north. Manstein was suspicious, noting that "It was inevitable, however, that the name of Kharkov should act as a magic stimulus on the fighting troops and less senior command staffs. The SS Panzer

Corps, wishing to lay the recaptured city at 'its Führer's feet as a symbol of victory, was eager to take the shortest route there, so that the Army Group had to intervene vigorously on more than one occasion to ensure that the corps did not become tied down there while enemy elements still fighting to the west of the city were able to make good their escape."[17] With Totenkopf on the left flank, Leibstandarte and Das Reich drove north to the west of Kharkov.

On the 10th Erhard Raus's provisional corps joined in from Poltava in a frontal attack from the west to fix the Russian forces of Lt. Gen. M. I. Kazakov's 69th Army being pressed by the SS. With Grossdeutschland leading on the right, Raus's forces captured Bogodukhov and made contact with SS-T at Olshany, 24 kilometers (15 miles) to the northeast, and 16 kilometers (10 miles) northwest of Kharkov, separating the 69th and Rybalko's 3rd Tank Army. While the SS turned inward to flank Kharkov, Raus turned north to Akhtyrka and the upper Vorskla in order to close the gap to VII. A.K. of Salmuth's 2. Armee. Lt. Gen. K. S. Moskalenko's 40th Army fell back to a position between the Vorskla and the Psel. Manstein had urged that Kluge's H.Gr. Mitte forces attack south to trap the remaining Russians, but there was antagonism between Manstein and Kluge, and the latter was unwilling or unable to coordinate.

GD drove up to Graivoron, then along the Vorskla toward Borisovka on the 13th, and then to Tomarovka east of Belgorod by the 15th. The 167.I.D. covered the Vorskla flank and cleaned out pockets of cut-off 40th and 69th Army elements. Raus claimed that two Tigers of the GD's Tiger Company alone destroyed a large pack of T-34s. Normally the T-34s would remain beyond effective panzer gun range, at 1,200 meters (1,350 yards), waiting for a German advance. But at Tomarovka two Tigers in concealed positions knocked out sixteen T-34s in the open at long range with their powerful 8,8cm Kw.K. 43 gun, and when the others turned around and fled, the Tigers pursued and picked off another eighteen. "It was observed that the 88mm armor-piercing shells had such a terrific impact that they ripped off the turrets of many T-34s and hurled them several yards," Raus noted. While thirty-four T-34s destroyed was probably an exaggeration, Raus's account does suggest the tremendous morale boast the Tiger gave to the German forces.[18]

While Totenkopf flanked around north of Kharkov, LAH and Das Reich did indeed fight their way into the city itself, and Russian commander Maj. Gen. E. E. Belov shifted forces to meet them. Hausser had disobeyed Manstein. But Hoth's orders of the 9th did allow, "Opportunities to seize the city by a coup are to be utilized," and on the 10th, "SS Panzer Corps will take Kharkov." On the 11th Leibstandarte fought its way in from the northwest to the Dzerzhinsky or Red Square, and on the 12th Das Reich penetrated from the west to the main railroad station.

But now Hoth, perhaps pressured by Manstein, insisted that Das Reich flank around to the north like Totenkopf. Hausser did detach Kampfgruppe Harmel to do so, though he believed that driving through the city on hard-surfaced roads and collapsing Russian resistance was preferable to negotiating the increasingly muddy byways around to the north. By 15 March the last resistance in Kharkov was eliminated even as Kgr. Harmel worked around and down to Rogan. SS-T advanced to Chuguyev on the Donets, cutting the communications of Rybalko's 3rd Tank Army, and behind the forces at Zimiyev holding up Knobelsdorff's XXXXVIII. Pz.K. south of Kharkov. Hausser reported SS losses of 365 officers and 11,154 men in the fighting around this "third" battle of Kharkov.[19] The Waffen-SS were elite soldiers, and the fighting was brutal. The Russians had learned that it was useless to interrogate SS prisoners and simply shot them; the W-SS acted likewise. By now, amid German manpower shortages, even the Waffen-SS had to accept draftees. But it can be argued that the veteran cadre generally indoctrinated them with the Nazi political and racial ideological ethos.[20]

South of Kharkov a new commander of the 11. Panzer-Division was familiarizing himself with the division in the midst of operations, as the Gespensters drove from Merefa on the Mzha to the Udy just south of the city, followed by the 106.Inf.Div. Taking over on 13 March, Generalleutnant Dietrich von Choltitz succeeded Balck in command of the 11.Pz.Div., a post he would hold for only a couple of months, from 13 March to 17 May 1943. Like his division he was also a Silesian, born 9 November 1894 at Wiesegräflich, Kreis Neustadt, but for most of his career he was an infantry officer. In World War I he fought on the Western Front, and in 1939 commanded III.Btl./Infanterie-Regiment 16, then the regiment itself, and in 1942 the 250.I.D. He came to the Elfte from being acting commander of XVII. A.K.[21]

With the capture of Kharkov by Hausser's SS Pz.K. on 15 March and the advance east to Volchansk and Chuguyev, 1. LSSAH drove northeast up the valley of the Lopan toward Belgorod to meet Grossdeutschland advancing east from Tomarovka. They threatened to trap Kazakov's 69th Army, which had already been split from Moskalenkos's 40th. South of Kharkov the 11.Pz.Div. advanced along the Udy River while the 6.Pz.Div. was advancing from the Mzha to the Udy against the Soviet 62nd Guards Rifle Division to link up with Totenkopf to surround and destroy Rybalko's battered 3rd Tank Army.

With a bridge laid across the Udy by Brüko 57 of 6.Pz.Div., the Elfte attack on14 March was led by Kgr. Henze with his Pz.G.R.110 (ohne I.Btl.) with the 8,8cm guns of IV. (Flak)/119, II.Btl./Pz.G.R.111, and one Kp. of panzers from Pz.Rgt.15. Pz.Pi.Btl.209 and K.61 held the south sector of the bridgehead and the 2cm flak guns of 12.Komp./119 protected the site. Kgr. Schimmelmann's gepanzerte Gruppe of Pz. Rgt.15, I./110, along with I./119, was ready to exploit, with eleven self-propelled Panzerjägers of 1.Kp.(Sfl.) representing Maj. Friedrich Guttmacher's Pz.Jäger Abt. 61 attached by the 17th. The fighting strength of the division was 3,539 (ration strength 10,962), with seventy-one panzers (twelve IIs, forty-six IIIs, and thirteen IVs), twenty-eight artillery pieces (twenty 10,5cm le.F.H., five 15cm s.F.H., and three 10cm Kan.), twenty-one Pak (3,7cm, 5cm, and 7,5cm), and six 8,8cm flak, and two 28cm s.Wurfgerät (rocket launchers).[22]

On the evening of 14–15 March Rybalko had received permission from Voronezh Front commander Golikov to withdraw to the northern Donets, but it was already too late. Totenkopf tightened its grip on the Rogan highway to Chuguyev on the Donets, and on the 16th the 6.Pz.Div. linked up with Das Reich, thus surrounding many 3rd Tank elements, while a Kampfgruppe met the 11. Panzer at Bezlyudovka, segmenting the Kessel. 3rd Tank Army disintegrated, the surviving elements escaping across the Donets. Golikov appealed to the Stavka for assistance, and it began to transfer divisions from Vatutin's Southwest Front to restore the front east of Kharkov.

The SS Panzerkorps was now ordered to drive north toward Belgorod, while XXXXVIII. Pz.K. drove east, the 11. and 6.Pz.Div. slugging the 1st Guards Cavalry Corps back across the Donets by 26 March. At 04,00 hours on 18 March Hausser's SS Pz.K. began its sweep north, LAH, Das Reich, and Totenkopf abreast from west to east, between the Kharkov–Belgorod rail line and the northern Donets, trapping Kazakov's 69th Army in the "Udy Kessel," with Korps Raus and GD to the north. By 19,00 that same day LAH and Das Reich entered Belgorod, while Totenkopf secured the line of the Donets.

The Leibstandarte then swung westward establishing blocking positions west of the rail line, and by the 19th met up with Grossdeutschland near Tomarovka, completing the encirclement. Some of the Rotarmisten of the 40th and 69th Armies managed to escape, but all their heavy equipment and ordnance was abandoned. On the 19th the 11.Pz.Div. closed along the Donets; Kmpfgr. Henze took Molodovo, and Kgr. Schimmelmann took Verkniy Saltov. On the 23rd Oberstlt. von Bosse, who had been controlling reserve units, again took command of I. and II.Btl. of Pz.G.R.111.

Stavka rushed new armies in to re-form the front: Lt. Gen. I. M. Chistyakov's 21st Army east of Kharkov, Lt. Gen. M. S. Shumilov's 64th Army east of Belgorod, and Lt. Gen. Mikhail Katukov's 1st Tank Army north of that city. The wrecked 3rd Tank Army was rebuilt as the 57th Army.[23] Manstein might well have continued a drive north to Kursk, but Kluge was not going to play a role, and after 23 March the seasonal Schlammperiode, the Russian Rasputitsa, and the resulting morass of mud brought operations to an end. In addition, the panzer divisions had been in action continuously for weeks on end, and the vehicles and panzers in particular needed maintenance and replacements. On 29 March the 11.Pz.Div. was ordered to turn over its sector to the 39.Inf.Div.

The winter campaign resulted in the Ostfront lines being basically what they had been before the 1942 Operation BLAU. The loss of 6. Armee and four Axis armies was to some extent offset by the destruction of some four Soviet armies and Mobile Group Popov. The Russian victory at Stalingrad might have had even greater strategic impact had a more carefully conceived drive south across the Donets to Rostov to trap Heeresgruppe A been implemented. The drive to the Dnepr to cut off H.Gr. Süd as well was bold, but overly optimistic to the point of recklessness—and ended in the annihilation of those Russian armies. The veteran Wehrmacht was not to be treated so cavalierly.

While both opponents had suffered massive casualties, the Russian losses could be better absorbed because of Russia's vast resources. Nonetheless Manstein's brilliant and carefully planned operations that defeated the Russian drive, recaptured Kharkov and Belgorod, and regained the line of the Donets, did much to restore the confidence of the Wehrmacht, soldiers and commanders alike. Panic was not a German characteristic, as it was of their allies and of their Russian foe, and defeats by overwhelming forces had been received stubbornly and stoically.

Manstein's counteroffensive had reflected once again the tremendous flexible aggressiveness of the German panzer divisions. Paul Hausser's SS Panzerkorps, operating as a larger entity for the first time, in particular came of age in its skillful wheeling maneuvers and switching of directions and objectives that resulted in the recapture of Kharkov and Belgorod. The 11. Gespenster-Division added to its reputation as one of the best panzer divisions of the Wehrmacht. If von Choltitz was new to the panzer division and had yet to demonstrate he was a worthy successor to Hermann Balck, nonetheless the division itself, with confidence in the veteran expertise of the unit commanders—Schimmelmann, Henze, von Bosse, von Hauser, Schmidt—swung automatically into action confidently and smoothly. Losses in battalion and company commanders had to be borne, but experienced junior officers arose to succeed them. After Auffrischung, the Gespensters would be prepared to carry out the new missions given them.

CHAPTER FIFTEEN

Interlude: Spring 1943

AFTER THE SUCCESSFUL RECAPTURE OF KHARKOV AND THE onset of the Schlammperiode in March 1943, the panzer units including the 11. Panzer-Division were withdrawn for refitting. The 11. Panzer, along with the 3.Pz.Div. and Grossdeutschland, were under von Knobelsdorff's XXXXVIII. Panzerkorps. A Kampfgruppe under Oberst Graf Schimmelmann composed of Panzer-Regiment 15, I.Bataillon/Panzergrenadier-Regiment 110—the tracked Schützenpanzerwagen (SPW) battalion with Sd.Kfz.251 half-tracks—and the Spähwagen (armored scout cars) of K.61 stayed as a mobile counterattack force for the infantry units on the HKL during 1–9 April. The rest of the division pulled back to bivouac areas east of Poltava.

Leave was granted for many after months of intense fighting, and the Kharkov main railway station received a new sign: "CHARKOV—HBF" (Hauptbahnhof). It became an eagerly anticipated boarding point for leave trains. Treasured were the Entlausungsschein (E-Schein, delousing certificate) and Wehrmachtfahrschein (Wehrmacht railway ticket) authorizing travel to a home Bahnhof. The city under German occupation was cleared of rubble, and those who got at least a pass might gaze at St. Michael's Church with its Orthodox tile work and "Zwiebeltürmen" ("onion domes"), as well as the "green tank," a British World War I Mark IV tank with its overhead tracks, on permanent display in "Der Rote Platz" (Dzerzhinsky Square). There could also be time for some levity, as when Bäckerei-Kompanie 61 had a ceremony with a massive cake commemorating supplying the two millionth loaf of bread to the division.[1]

The Auffrischung areas were in attractive spring settings with undulating hills and fruit orchards and vegetable gardens. The Ukrainian population was friendly, and partisan activity was not a concern. Sports competitions—swimming at Golovtchino, 100-meter sprints, sack races, tugs-of-war—generated relaxation and camaraderie, especially as a means to integrate replacements into the veteran units of the renowned Gespenster-Division. Companies might put on mock theater productions and musical events in the evenings after duties and training; one was advertised as beginning at 18,00 Uhr and ending "When everyone is tipsy" (besoffen).[2]

But replenishment and re-equipping the division was top priority given casualties, losses, and worn equipment. When Oblt. Kurt Rühmkorf of 5. Kompanie was named to command the Pz.-Rgt.15 Werkstattkompanie (maintenance) by Oberst Schimmelmann on 10 April, he asked Gustav Schrodek to come with him as acting Hauptfeldwebel, the "Spiess" ("Top Kick"). As a young "Beschnuppern" ("first-grader"), Schrodek was unsure how the veteran mechanics would respond to him, but two years on panzers had given him plenty of experience. He was also a good "scrounger," and worked a deal with local German agricultural officials in which he traded used engine oil sitting in barrels (which they used in their tractors) in exchange for cows, potatoes, flour, molasses, and, not least, vodka. All of this enhanced the unit's cooking and baking. Hitler's birthday, 20 April 1943, was at least a feast day, as was Osterfest (Easter). Repairs to damaged tracked and wheeled vehicles kept the maintenance company busy, and that unit was temporarily expanded to 340 men. In addition, new armored vehicles from the homeland had to be passed by the W.Kp. Some piston rings were found defective, which could be catastrophic for crews in battle, and made Schrodek suspicious of deliberate sabotage.

This was also a time when the Dinafü (DNF), Hptm. Günther Zamory—clad in a distinctive camouflage jacket he had acquired somehow—had to handle mass amounts of requisitions, receipts, and inventories. Staff surgeons Drs. Urban and Jeschonnek and dentist Dr. Rothe and their assistants of Sanitätsdienste 61 treated long-delayed medical problems at the Hauptverbandplatz in Ochotsaya.

In weaponry, the reliable Mauser Kar.98k bolt-action 7.92mm infantry rifle with a five-round magazine remained standard. After 1942 receiver markings dou and dot appeared, codes for Waffen Werke Brünn (Brno) in occupied Czechoslovakia, in addition to byf (Mauser Oberndorf) and many other factory codes. Later models had a hooded sight, stamped stock barrel band, and cupped butt plate. Prompted by the Russian semiautomatic (self-loading) Tokarev SVT-40, and the more successful American M1 Garand, the Walther ordnance works produced a semiautomatic, gas-operated rifle, the Gewehr 41 and then the Gewehr 43, with ten-round magazines. These proved overly sensitive under combat conditions, though some Elften used them as sniper rifles. The 9mm Walther P 38 was the standard sidearm with the older, more complex Luger Pistole 08 (the null acht) as substitute standard, with some parts now made by Fabrique Nationale (FN, proof stamp 140) in occupied Belgium. The 9mm pistol round was also used in the popular blowback recoil-operated submachine gun, the Erma Werke MP 38/40, the handy MPi.

Meanwhile, a truly revolutionary firearm was being developed by Hugo Schmeisser at the C.G.Haenel Waffenfabrik in Suhl (in competition with Carl Walther) to fire a shortened 7.92mm round, Kurzpatrone. Designated the Maschinenkarabiner 42, models were issued to selected units on the Ostfront in 1942–1943. The Haenel design was selected, but produced as the MP 43 and then the MP 44, termed Maschine*pistole*, ostensibly as Hitler was opposed to its designation as a carbine, insisting on a longer range for a rifle cartridge. When Hitler did authorize it, it was officially redesignated the StG 44 (Sturmgewehr), the world's first true "assault rifle." Gas-operated, it had a pistol grip and a thirty-round "banana" magazine. It had a push-through selector button for *semi*automatic rifle fire effective to 800 meters (875 yards) and for *full* automatic fire in the final assault phase of the attack; it could fire 800 rounds per minute. Few regular infantry units would be issued the self-loading weapons, however. The 11.Pz.Div., for example, listed 192 authorized 1 June 1943 and 240 on 1 July, but had none at the time, though the StG 44 would be used later.[3]

Infantry and panzergrenadier squad tactics were still based on the firepower of the recoil-operated, belt-fed, bipod-mounted MG 34, which was also mounted on a tripod as a heavy machine gun and on SPW Halbkette and many other vehicles. Now it was being superseded by the MG 42, also designed and produced by the Mauser-Werke. The MG 42 was mounted similarly, but was cheaper and simpler to manufacture. In particular, the bolt drove a feed arm in the top cover that operated pawls that fed the ammunition belt links smoothly and reliably, and the rate of fire was increased to 1,200 rpm with a deadly ripping sound. A saddle-type dual drum with seventy-five rounds could also be fitted. Critics have said this wasted ammunition; but it equalized Russian mass assaults, short bursts could be fired, and German doctrine was based on firepower of the squad machine gun, the riflemen often carrying additional belts of ammo draped around their shoulders. Equally unique was the barrel quick-change feature. Hitting the barrel latch on the right side open with the heel of the hand allowed the hot barrel to slide out of the square air-cooled barrel casing and a new barrel to be pushed in and locked, in less than five seconds! The MG 42, nicknamed "Das Zweibein" (the bipod) would serve the Wehrmacht well during the war, and its features would be widely replicated.[4]

Given the threat posed by the Soviet T-34 and KV-1 tanks, with frontal armor of 75mm (3 inches) and 90mm (3.5 inches), respectively, antitank capabilities had to be improved. The 3,7cm Panzerabwehrkanone, Pak 36, had generally been replaced by the 5cm Pak 38; with a dense tungsten-cored, armor-piercing composite rigid shot (APCR) Panzergranate 40, it could penetrate 86mm (3.4-inch) armor angled 30 degrees to the vertical at 500 meters (545 yards), but was less effective at longer ranges. In addition, there was a shortage of tungsten, needed for machine tools. The standard Pak became the Rheinmettal-Borsig 7,5cm Pak 40. Its APCR round with a velocity of 990 meters per second (3,250 fps) could penetrate 96mm (3.8 inches) of armor angled 30 degrees at 1,000 meters. The effective Russian 76.2mm AT gun was also used, as the Pak 36(r). Most deadly remained the 8,8cm gun, the "Acht-komma-acht." Krupp produced it as the Pak 43; it was transported on a pair of two-wheeled trailers, and lowered as a cruciform ground mount, with armor shield. Its APCR round with a velocity of 1,130 m/s (3,710 fps) could penetrate 192mm (7.68 inches) of armor angled 30 degrees at 1,000 meters and even 136mm (5.4 inches) at 2,000 meters.[5]

By 1943 captured American 2.36-inch (60mm) rocket launchers, "bazookas," prompted the development for the infantry of the 8,8cm Raketenpanzerbüchse, a shoulder-fired rocket launcher propelling a hollow-charge rocket 150 meters (164 yards). It could penetrate 100mm (4 inches) of armor, but only at a very close range. The RPzB. 43 required a two-man team, a firer and a loader. The later RPzB. 54 had a protective shield, as the rocket flared out from the tube. It was nicknamed "Ofenrohr" (stovepipe) from the flame and smoke blast to the rear, as well as "Panzerschreck" (tank terror). A one-shot Panzerfaust (armored fist) was developed subsequently.

Antitank guns emplaced and organized as Pak fronts were formidable, as were the short-range weapons; but these were primarily defensive weapons. For the offensive, panzers were the spearhead, but they also had to engage enemy tanks. The Panzer II was only useful in a reconnaissance role or for giving the engineers support, and even the Pz.III could not compete with the newer Russian T-34s, the C model having 75mm (3 inches) of frontal armor. The Pz.III's 5cm L/60 calibers long Kw.K. 39 could only penetrate 61mm (2.4 inches) of armor angled 30 degrees at 500 meters (545 yards). This could knock out the Russian light T-70s and Lend-Lease tanks like the American M3 General Lee with its 65mm (2.5-inch) armor, as well as the light M3 and M5 Stuarts and the 65mm (2.5-inch) armor of the British Valentine. But it could not penetrate the 76mm (3-inch) armor of the Matilda or the American M4 Sherman (some GMC diesel-engine M4A2s of which were reaching Russia). The Lend-Lease tanks were not as rugged or as powerful as the Russian tanks, but they were arriving in increasing numbers. (The Russians portrayed their *own* tanks in photographs; but *German* photos of knocked-out enemy tanks, as well as unit reports, reflect foreign tanks' extensive use by the Russians.)[6]

The Pz.Kpfw. IV had become the main battle tank of the panzer divisions. The F2 and G models mounted the 7,5cm Kw.K.40 L/43 gun, and they had increased track width (40cm/15.75 inches) and thicker armor (80 mm/3.2 inches). Additional armor skirts or aprons, Panzerschürzen, were spot-welded or hung by hooks on rails along the tracks and around the turrets of both the Pz.III and Pz.IV as protection against Soviet AT rounds, and they also proved effective against the later hollow- or shaped-charge projectiles by changing the standoff distance. Extra track sections bolted on the hull front also added protection, but negated the ricochet potential. This all increased the weight and reduced power, as the 300-horsepower Maybach HL 108 engine was the same. The late G and H models had a longer, more powerful 7,5cm L/48 gun, velocity 750 m/s (2,461 fps), able to penetrate 100mm (4-inch) armor. (Data varies, depending on tank model, type of armor, and type of anti-armor round.)

Innovative camouflage patterns also appeared, many in the dull green, ochre, and russet colors from World War I, replacing the traditional panzer gray. Camouflage broke up the vehicle shape in various light and shadow conditions. In February 1943 OKH had outlined a new paint system. The manufacturer issued the armored vehicle with an earthy, dark yellow ochre base, and the field units then applied the reddish brown russet and dark green color paste, which were issued in packages. Using air compressors, the Werkstattkompanien brushed on or sprayed on these paints in a variety of patterns, from blotches to stripes. Water or gasoline was used to thin the paint paste, and gasoline used to clear it off. But the water-mixed paint often washed off in rain, said Lt. Eberhard Schöne, and gasoline was always in short supply. (On 19 August 1944 OKH issued a directive that camouflage painting would be done at the factory with additional spotting in the three colors. On 31 October 1944 OKH ordered that the reddish primer coat be the base with ochre and green added, and on 31 November dark green became the base color with russet and ochre patches added. By 1945 many panzers were left in their dark green—not gray—base color.)[7]

The proven heavy panzer was the Henschel-designed Tiger (Pz.Kpfw. VI, Sd.Kfz. 181) with its frontal armor of 110mm (4 inches) and powerful 8,8cm Kw.K.36 L/56 gun, which had a muzzle velocity of 792 m/s (2,600 fps) penetrating 110mm (4 inches) at 500 meters and at much longer ranges. Oberst Friedrich von Mellenthin, Chef des Stabes of Knobelsdorff's XXXXVIII. Pz.K., said, "I personally set out to make myself proficient in handling the Tiger tank; I learned to drive this massive vehicle and fire its 88-mm gun. With this powerful gun and very strong armor the Tiger was the most successful and effective tank in the world until the end of the war; it had already shown what it could do in the counterattack on Kharkov. The Russian Stalin tank of 1944 was a very formidable opponent, but I do not consider it the equal of the Tiger."[8] The heavy 56-ton Tigers were not organic to panzer divisions, being grouped in separate heavy panzer battalions, but often attached as companies.

While Henschel had earlier developed a prototype for a medium main battle panzer heavier than the Pz.IV, this had been given impetus by the shock of encountering the Russian T-34. Guderian in particular urged the Waffenamt to develop such a panzer when a commission visited his Panzergruppe 2 in November 1941, though some officers said to simply copy the T-34. A MAN prototype was the one adopted, and production began in November 1942. Design changes resulted in the now-named Panther (Pz.Kpfw. V, Sd.Kfz.171) weighing 43 tons with wide 66cm (26-inch) tracks and interleaved large-diameter road wheels (like the half-tracks and the Tigers) on a double torsion-bar suspension giving a smooth cross-country mobility. It had a 650 bhp Maybach HL 230 engine that gave a road speed of 46 km/h (29 mph). The Panther had angled hull and turret armor, the front hull being 80mm (3.2 inches) at 35 degrees, and a long high-velocity 7,5cm Kw.K.42 L/70 gun with muzzle brake giving a velocity of 935 m/s (3,068 fps) and penetrating 141mm (5.5 inches) of armor angled 30 degrees at 500 meters, a higher velocity and penetration than even the Tiger's 8,8cm Kw.K.36 L/56.[9]

Under pressure from Hitler to rapidly produce the new panzer, the increased weight in particular put heavy strain on the transmission, gearbox, and suspension. In addition, the first model (Ausführung D) had no bow machine gun, which had become a standard feature in panzers—only a port for one. Other problems included hydrostatic lock of the engine, which could only be started by an external rear hand crank, and the front drives sometimes broke when neutral-steered, a problem never solved.[10]

It was obvious that additional testing was needed before the Panther was committed to battle, but Hitler was insistent that the new panzer be ready by the end of the Schlammperiode when mobile operations would resume. The detached I. Abteilung of Pz.Rgt.15 returned from the Velikiye Luki battle to Truppenübungsplatz Grafenwöhr, was one of two battalions slated to be equipped with the new Panther, on 6 February 1943. The other was II.Abt. of Pz.Rgt.33, 9.Pz.Div., on 9 January 1943.[11]

To increase the number of armored fighting vehicles, Hitler demanded production of Sturmgeschütze (assault guns). Already, captured or obsolete chassis had been equipped with a potent gun, though behind a gun shield or in a fixed casemate with limited traverse, rather than in a turret. These were cheaper and faster to produce than panzers, and those with a lower silhouette were of advantage in the open expanses of Russia. Generically, these were more broadly Selbstfahrlafetten, self-propelled motor carriages (Sfl.) and were of three basic types: Sturmpanzer (armored assault), Panzerjäger or Jagdpanzer (tank destroyer), and self-propelled artillery. Initially intended to increase the mobility and firepower of infantry divisions, many were increasingly also equipping the panzer units, and type variations seemed endless.

The little Pz.I chassis early mounted a 4,7cm Pak as a Panzerjäger, or a 15cm s.I.G. (heavy infantry gun). The French Hotchkiss, Renault, or Lorraine chassis might mount a 10,5cm le.F.H. (light field howitzer) or a 15cm s.F.H. (heavy [medium] field howitzer) as self-propelled artillery, or a 7,5cm Pak as the Marder (Marten) I. The excellent Czech 38 chassis mounted the German 7,5cm Pak or captured Russian 7,62cm Pak as the Marder 38 or III, but also the 15cm s.I.G. or a 2cm flak gun. The 7,5cm Pak 40 had a muzzle velocity of 792 m/s (2,600 fps) penetrating 89mm (3.5 inches) of armor sloped 30 degrees, and the 7,62cm Pak 36(r) with a velocity of 740.6 m/s (2,430 fps) penetrated 83mm (3.2 inches) of sloped 30-degree armor, with both guns capable of knocking out the Russian T-34 and the early KV-1. The KV-1A and KV-1B had extra armor bolted or welded on. (By 1944 a 7,5cm Pak was mounted in a redesigned 38(t) chassis as the Hetzer [Baiter] for infantry tank destroyer battalions.)

The reliable Pz.II chassis mounted the 7,5 or 7,62 Pak as the Panzerjäger Marder II, or a 15cm s.I.G. for infantry support; and the Wespe (Wasp) with the 10,5cm le.F.H. 18/2 L/28 with a range of 12,000 meters (13,000 yards) became the standard self-propelled light artillery piece for panzer division artillery.

The Pz.III chassis had already been utilized as an infantry Sturmgeschütz assault gun mounting a short, low-velocity 7,5cm 37 Sturmkanone (Stu.K., assault cannon), and after 1942 a 10,5cm Stu.H. 42 L/28 assault howitzer. To increase its versatility with an antitank role, a longer, high-velocity 7,5cm Stu.K. was mounted, an L/43 in 1942, and then an L/48. Over 9,000 Stu.G. III were produced during the war, and equipped Panzerjäger battalions and even panzer battalions in the panzer divisions.

Although models of the Pz.IV were in production to the end of the war as a panzer, the chassis was also used as an assault gun, a tank destroyer, and self-propelled artillery. The Brummbär (Grizzly Bear) was a Sturmpanzer mounting a short 15cm Stu.H. L/12, and the Hummel (Bumblebee) with a 15cm s.F.H. 18/1 L/30 complemented the 10,5cm Wespe howitzer panzer division artillery battalions in heavy (medium) batteries. Tank destroyer versions included the Hornisse (Hornet), renamed the Nashorn (Rhinoceros) by 1944; it mounted the 8,8cm Pak 43/1 L/71 gun. (By 1944 they were joined by the Jagdpanzer IV with the 7,5cm Pak 39 L/48 gun, and a few with the longer L/70 gun.) Initially organized in separate tank destroyer detachments, many of these self-propelled guns were issued to the panzer divisions, and show up in 11.Pz.Div. reports and returns.

Panzerspähwagen (armored reconnaissance vehicles) might be armored cars or, in 1943, the light half-track Sd.Kfz.250 in the Pz.Aufklärungs-Abteilungen of the panzer divisions. The eight-wheeled Sd.Kfz.234 might mount the 7,5cm Pak or the short 7,5cm Stu.K. L/24, or the 2cm Kw.K. 36 in a turret (and by 1944 the longer 7,5cm L/48, or the 5cm Kw.K. L/60 in a turret as the Puma). The regular infantry Sd.Kfz.251 SPW half-tracks, as well as the Sd.Kfz.250 Schützenpanzerwagen, also mounted heavier ordnance, from 3,7cm Pak to 7,5cm Kw.K. and Stu.K., giving additional firepower to the reconnaissance and panzergrenadier battalions.

A unique tank destroyer arrived on the Ostfront in the spring of 1943, the Ferdinand (redesignated in 1944 as the Elefant). Named for its designer, Dr. Ferdinand Porsche, it was the prototype for the heavy Tiger panzer contract that was ultimately awarded to Henschel instead. Nonetheless more than ninety chassis had been produced and fitted with the most powerful antitank gun yet, the very long 8,8cm Pak 43/2 L/71. With a muzzle velocity of 1,000 m/s (3,280 fps) it could penetrate any armor in World War II: 192mm (7.68 inches) of 30-degree armor at 1,000 meters (1,090 yards) and 139mm (5.56 inches) at 2,000 meters (2,180 yards), the same gun as in the later Nashorn and Königstiger. It was rear-mounted in a very tall box casemate, the vehicle height reaching 3.2 meters (10.5 feet). It was later maligned for not having an integral machine gun for close-in defense; but neither had the Stu.G. III, the Marder series, or the Hornisse. It was a tank *destroyer*, *not* an assault gun. If properly employed in a supporting or overwatch role it could effectively destroy any Russian tank from beyond their gun range. Both Tigers and Ferdinands would be attached to the 11.Pz.Div. later.

More potent tank gun ammunition was also being developed. The standard rounds were the Panzerbrechendegranate (armor-piercing shot, AP) and the Sprenggranate (high-explosive shell, HE). By 1941 the Germans had developed a round with a hard tungsten carbide core in a soft, light metal jacket, the smaller diameter of the sub-caliber bore giving higher velocity and greater penetration. The Allies also developed this round as armor-piercing composite rigid (APCR) or high-velocity armor-piercing (HVAP), and then armor-piercing composite ballistic capped (APCBC). To penetrate armor these rounds depended on high-velocity kinetic energy impacting on a small area.

But a new chemical energy round independent of velocity was developed by 1942, the Panzersprenggranate (high-explosive anti-tank, HEAT), on the

Hohlladungseffekt (hollow- or shaped-charge principle). When the soft nose of this explosive round impacted armor the fuse instantaneously detonated the explosive in a conical container, which shaped a long, thin jet piercing the armor at some 9,000 m/s (30,000 fps). The Panzer IV and Sturmgeschütze were the first panzers to use this round. The artillery hollow-charge round, Rotkopf, had already been employed in December 1941, and hollow-charge explosives had been used for demolitions by engineers. The Soviets began using the advanced munitions, including the hollow-charge rounds, in the B and C models of the T-34.

The German external Panzerschürzen spaced armor on the panzers counteracted this principle by changing the standoff distance. Thus the round would detonate on this outer armor and the shaped jet would dissipate before hitting the hull or turret proper. The thin metal skirt sections, 8mm (5/16 inch) on the turret, 5mm (3/16 inch) on the sides, could be handled by one man and did not obstruct maintenance and repair work to the suspension system, according to Gefreiter (later Lt.) Kurt Nentwig, but they were hung on welded metal bands and frequently tore off. Oberleutnant von Fersen also did not feel the skirts too effective, and said crews generally did not bother to have them replaced. This was truer on the Ostfront than in the West, as the Soviets did not develop infantry hollow-charge antitank munitions like the American bazooka or the British PIAT.[12]

When an anti-armor projectile did penetrate the armor or even smashed against it, it created "spalling"—red-hot shards of metal that killed crew members and destroyed interior wiring, instruments, and controls. But unless the onboard fuel or ammunition also exploded, the vehicle generally could be repaired. Therefore, controlling the battlefield was important: it allowed an army to recover one's own knocked-out armored vehicles, and deny the enemy theirs.[13]

The increased development of German armor was due to three individuals in particular: Albert Speer, who had succeeded Fritz Todt as Reich Minister for Armaments and Munitions when the latter died in a plane crash 8 February 1942, and who greatly increased arms production; Generaloberst Heinz Guderian, "Father of the Panzerwaffe," relieved by Hitler on 26 December 1941 but recalled 28 February 1943 as Generalinspekteur der Panzertruppen (Inspector General of the Armored Troops), to coordinate the development and organization of all Wehrmacht armored forces, including those of the Waffen-SS and the Luftwaffe; and Adolf Hitler, who had recognized the importance of mechanized forces ever since his ascension to power in 1933, and, despite controversial strategic and operational decisions, sought to strengthen them.

Impatient with the bureaucratic complexities as in the laggardly development of the Panther, Hitler urged the development of the assault guns, tank destroyers, and self-propelled artillery on existing chassis. These had been under the Artillery branch, indicated by the smaller units being referred to as batteries, not companies, and the armored fighting vehicles as Geschütze (guns). But Guderian had negotiated to control these as well, and this was agreed to by Hitler in the "Assignment of Duties" drafted 28 February 1943, only for Guderian to subsequently find his control over assault guns limited to *heavy* assault guns (larger than the 7,5cm on the Pz.IV chassis). The majority of assault guns remained under the Artillery.

Gradually the production of the Panzerwaffe began to improve. Panzer production increased from 5,966 in 1943 to 9,161 in 1944, and Sturmgeschütze and Jagdpanzer production increased from 3,406 in 1943 to 8,682 in 1944, totaling 9,372 armored fighting vehicles produced in 1943 and 17,843 in 1944. But during the same periods the Russians were producing some 30,000 annually, plus receiving Allied Lend-Lease tanks.[14]

As spring 1943 wore on, the 11.Pz.-Div. underwent changes with new K.St.N. tables of organization and equipment, and changes in the division's Kriegsgliederung (Order of Battle). Like most panzer divisions, the 11.Pz.Div. had no Panthers or Tigers organic under the K.St.N. But the Elfte might have received a company of the huge Ferdinand Panzerjägers to augment its striking power. A battalion of forty-five Ferdinands was originally assigned to 4. Panzerarmee and Hoth was going to provide one company to each of the three panzer divisions in XXXXVIII. Pz.Korps (as the three Waffen-SS divisions and Grossdeutschland would have a Tiger company each), but on 15 June both battalions of Ferdinands were assigned to 9. Armee in the north.[15] Nor was the 11.Pz.Div. allocated Tigers. Gefreiter Kurt Nentwig recalled the order that each company of Pz.-Rgt.15 had to detach two crews to man new units: "Each master-sergeant was glad about this singular opportunity to get rid of the worst types of all ranks. Months later we saw these *'Blindgänger'* ('misfires' or 'duds') grinning in brand new Tigers."[16]

Detailed listings of the division by unit of personnel and weapons as of 1 June 1943 was reported by the Ia, now Oberstleutnant Kinitz.[17] The division numbered a fighting strength of 6,274 including 205 officers, and a total ration strength of 15,382. That included 183 Russian Hiwis in the units, like 14 with Pz.Gren.Rgt.111, 26 with Pz.Art.Rgt.119, and 42 under the commander of Division Nachschubtruppen, Supply Troops (Dinatru) 61, division trains.

Oberst Graf Schimmelmann's Pz.Rgt.15 had just two Abteilungen, II. under Hptm. Edel Zachariae-Lingenthal and III. (former II./Pz.Rgt.35/4.Pz.Div.) under Hptm. von Bülow, as I./15 remained detached under Maj. Karl von Sivers at Tr.Ü.Platz Grafenwöhr to be reequipped as a Panther battalion. Pz.Rgt.15 numbered 565 men (1,526 ration strength) and the two panzer battalions had two light and one medium company each. The companies were still authorized twenty-two panzers in four platoons of five each and two staff/headquarters panzers. Of the authorized 136 panzers, the Elfte listed 116 gun panzers: 8 Pz.II (2cm), 48 Pz.III (5cm), 53 Pz.IV (7,5cm lang), and 1 Pz.IV with the short 7,5cm L/24 ("Stummel"), assigned to Pz.G.R.110, and 6 Flammpanzer. This was the Pz.III, Ausf. L, Sd.Kfz.141/3, modified with a flamethrower in place of the gun. It had seventy to eighty "shots" of 2–3 seconds duration, firing its flaming stream 50 to 60 meters (55 to 65 yards). 835 liters (225 gallons) of fuel were held in tanks inside the panzer (which would make any crew uncomfortable).[18]

The 11.Pz.Gren.Brig. headquarters had been dissolved as superfluous 16 November 1942, and Pz.Gren.Rgts 110 and 111 were placed directly under division control, 1,245 men (2,187 ration strength) in 110 and 1,265 (2,066) in 111. Oberst Albert Henze still commanded Pz.G.R.110, its I.Btl.(gepanzerte) being equipped with Sd.Kfz.251 half-track SPWs in at least two of its three rifle companies, and a heavy weapons company with mortars and towed infantry guns. Pz.G.R.110 was only a little larger by 1 July, with 2,605 ration strength personnel of 44 Offiziere, 409 Unteroffiziere, 2,130 Mannschaften, and 22 Russian Hiwis.[19] The II.Btl. was similarly organized, though transported in trucks. One source indicates on 15 June the towed infantry gun company was converted as a self-propelled company with six 15cm s.I.G. utilizing the Czech 38 or Pz.II chassis.[20]

At Pz.Gren.Rgt.111 Oberst Alexander von Bosse was succeeded on 15 May by Oberst Dr. Hans Boelsen. Von Bosse was transferred to a cavalry unit, Reiterverband von Pommwitz.[21] The regiment's two battalions were also truck-mounted. The 3.6-ton Opel-Blitz was the standard medium Lastkraftwagen (Lkw, cargo vehicle), also carrying personnel. Some considered it "der Zuverlässige" ("the reliable"), better than the Ford or Daimler-Benz. Some versions had double rear wheels, but most did not have front- or all-wheel drive, a serious liability in mud and snow. The Horch Kfz.15 or 16 (Kraftfahrzeug, motor vehicle) remained the standard Pkw for commanders, staff, or other personnel. The 2.45-ton vehicle with its convertible canvas top did have four-wheel drive. Earlier Kfz.15s also had reserve wheels mounted on the sides, which helped the vehicle ride over rough terrain. The leichter Pkw was the Volkswagen Typ 82 (Kfz.1) designed by Porsche, 725 kilograms (three-quarter ton). It was popular as the little "Kübelwagen" ("bucket car"), but had only rear-wheel drive. The VW Schwimmwagen Typ 66 (Kfz.1/20), weighing 910 kilograms (1 ton), was the very successful amphibious version and did have all-wheel drive.[22]

Pz.Art.Rgt.119, Oberst Oskar Schmidt having been succeeded by Oberst Julius Werner in February, listed a fighting strength of 896 (1,685 ration strength). Of its three battalions, I. and II. Abteilungen had twenty-three 10,5cm le.F.H. in three four-gun firing batteries each, and III.Abt. had two batteries with nine 15cm s.F.H. and a 10cm Kanone battery with three tubes. All were towed, though by July some 10,5cm Wespen and 15cm Hummeln began to appear.[23] Beobachtungs (Observation) Batterie 334 had been reorganized as Beob.Battr.(Pz.)119. Hptm. Hans Bergmann succeeded Hptm. Schlesiger in June. IV.Abt./119 became separate again on 27 April as Heeres-Flakart.Abt.277, Maj. Peter Baack succeeding Major Manger. It numbered eight 8,8cm flak guns towed by medium half-tracks (Sd.Kfz.7), and twenty-one 2cm flak guns in three batteries.

For the reconnaissance role, Kradsch.Btl.61 (which had absorbed A.A.231 back on 9 November 1941) was redesignated as Panzer Aufklärungs-Abteilung 11 on 23 April, under Maj. Horst Lindner.[24] His Befehlswagen was an open-topped Sd.Kfz. 250/3 light half-track with its tube radio antenna, and he commanded an armored car company with four- and eight-wheeled Panzerspähwagen mounting 2cm guns, along with a half-track company, a truck company carrying mortars or towing infantry guns, and two motorcycle platoons and an engineer platoon.

Pz.Pionier Batl.209 was commanded by Hptm. Hans Schnur who succeeded Hptm. Erhard Grevendorf in March, and then by Hptm. Heinz Bödicker. There were two engineer companies mounted in Lkw, with mortars and light machine guns, and a Brüko K (bridging column). Twenty Flammenwerfer were provided for use against Russian bunkers and field fortifications and trenches. The signals battalion, Pz.Nachrichten-Abt.341, was redesignated Pz.Nachr. Abt. 89 on 1 June, under the command of Maj. Arnold Steuer. Its radio and telephone companies moved in wheeled vehicles, as did the light supply column.

The tank destroyer battalion, Pz.Jäger-Abteilung 61, had been inactivated 30 December 1942, though components had subsequently been identified as such. It was listed again in April 1943, though initially only as a training battalion. Its personnel were apparently joined with the attached assault gun battalion, Sturmgeschütz-Abteilung 911. Pz.Jg.Abt.61 was finally reactivated 24 May 1943, Maj. Arnold Kessler succeeding Maj. Friedrich Guttmacher, who left for reassignment by the OKH Führer Reserve on 22 April. By 1 June, with four officers and 132 men it was small, with ten self-propelled s.Pak 7,5cm in two companies.[25] Hauptmann Günther Zamory as the Dinafü coordinated the medical, maintenance, transport, supply, and other division services, all designated as 61.

Attached to the 11.Pz.-Div. on 1 April were the twenty-two assault guns of leichte Sturmgeschütz-Abteilung 911, activated in March in Brandenburg. The unit's coat of arms had St. George slaying the dragon, and its personnel came from Oberschlesien, commanded by Oberstleutnant Georg Wilhelm. The detachment (all Sturmgeschütz Abteilungen being redesignated brigades in summer 1944 to emphasize their independent status) had three batteries, each with seven Stu.G. III with the short 7,5cm Sturmkanone, the "Stummel" ("stump"), Stu.K.37 L/24 or L/33, or longer Stu.K.40 L/43, and three Stu.G. III with a 10,5cm Sturmhaubitze (assault howitzer) Stu.H.42 L/28. Although like other assault gun units the 911 remained army troops, not divisional troops, the 911 was attached to the 11.Pz.Div. for over a year, from 1 April 1943 until 6 May 1944 when the 11. Panzer was transferred to the West; the 911 stayed in Russia.

The battalion's original 1. Batterie under Hauptmann Hoppe had been redesignated Stu.Geschtz.Battr. 247 and sent from Italy to Sardinia. (Two Geschütze and a Pkw were lost to a British submarine during the voyage.) Ever since arriving near Kharkov in the spring, Stu.Geschtz.Abt. 911 had been training to support the infantry, with Pz.Gren.Rgt.110 and 111. Wilhelm's Stu.Gesch.Abt. 911's initial association with the 11.Pz.Div. was marred by a terrible training accident on 14 April. In an engineer Lehrgang (training course) in Resunenkovo for personnel of Pz.Rgt.15 and Stu.G.A. 911, a wood-encased Teller mine exploded. Twenty-five were killed, including thirteen Sturmartilleristen from the assault gun battalion, and fourteen were wounded. Even combat training could be dangerous.[26]

On 15 May 1943 the Gespensters received a new division commander, Generalmajor Johann Mickl, taking command on the 17th. Generalleutnant Dietrich von Choltitz, commander since March, went on sick leave. Choltitz then became assistant commander of XXXXVIII. Panzerkorps under Gen.Lt. Otto von Knobelsdorff for the next three months, and then was assigned to other commands in the West. Gen.Maj. Johann Mickl, an Ostmärker (Austrian), was born 18 April 1893 at Zeltnig, Austria-Hungary. Like von Choltitz, his background was infantry, coming from Pz.Gren.Rgt.25/12.Pz.Div. Also like von Choltitz, he was inheriting the command of a veteran panzer division with experienced unit commanders. Mickl would command the Elften for the next three months, until 10 August, but doesn't seem to have earned their respect.

Unteroffizier Kurt Nentwig related how General Mickl once climbed up behind the turret of his Panzer III for a local attack, but only gave proposals, not orders, that Nentwig transmitted over the radio—labeling him "more a spectator than a leader." An anecdote that circulated through the panzer regiment was that at another time there was a commanders' conference along the Rollbahn where there were pits along the edge, when Russian Rata fighter planes appeared. Mickl said, "Gentlemen, I guess we better jump into the holes!" Graf Schimmelmann put his hand to his brow, turned his head around, and said, "I can see here only *Arschlöcher*!"[27]

Apocryphal or not, such anecdotes reflected the feelings of some veteran Landsers about their

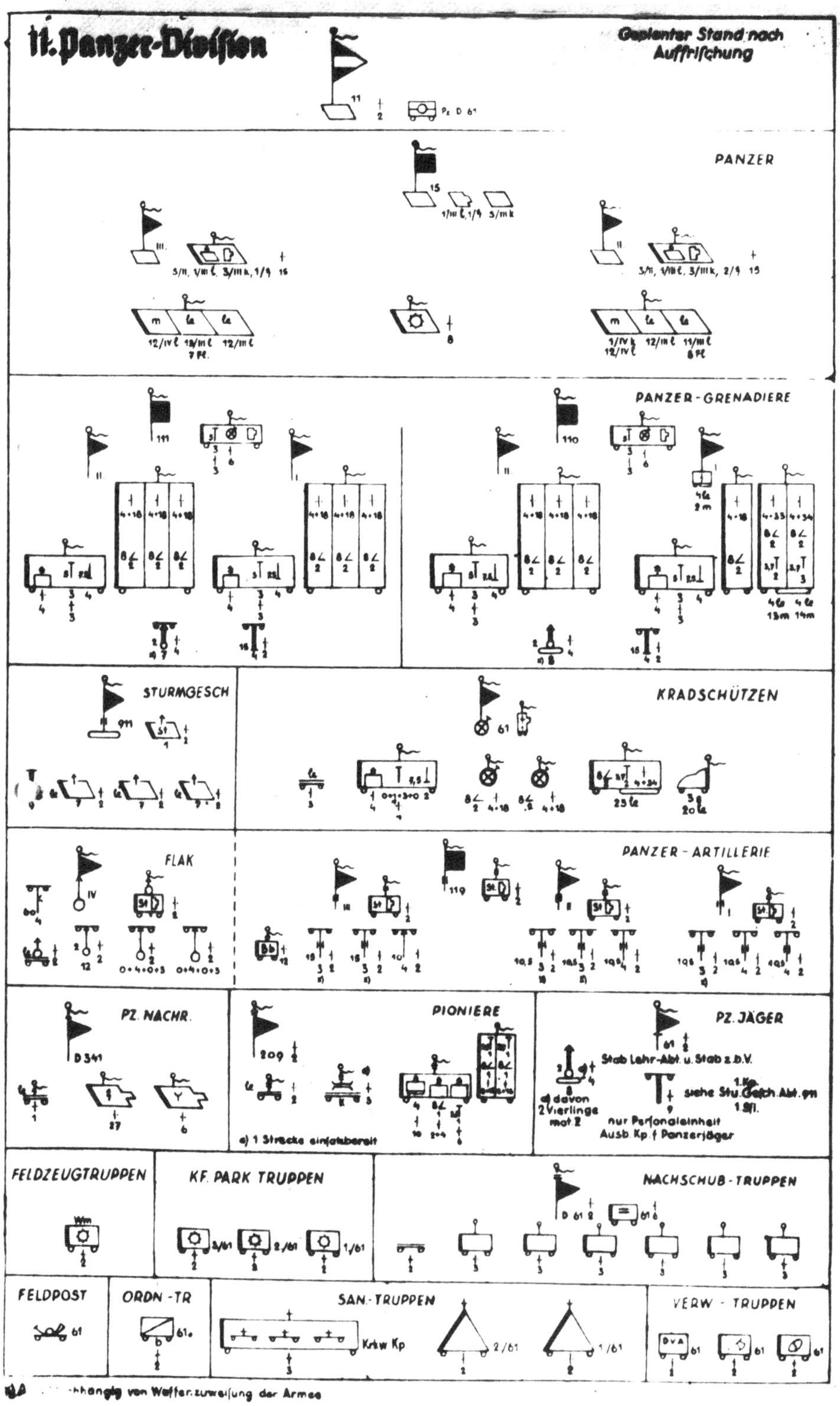

Planned Order of Battle, 10 April 1943 (after refitting). Pz.Rgt.15 has II. and III. Abteilungen, I.Abt. being detached. Pz.Jäger Abt.61 had been deactivated, its personnel assigned to Assault Gun Battalion 911.

NARA T-315/ROLL 599/ 000619

commanders. On the other hand, as commander of Schützenregiment 155 of 90. Leichte Division in North Africa, Mickl had been captured by New Zealanders near Sidi Rezegh in November 1941 but daringly escaped. And in Russia, commanding Pz.Gren.Rgt.25 of the 12.Pz.Div., Oberst Mickl was awarded the Eichenlaub to the Ritterkreuz (awarded 6 March 1943).[28]

Meanwhile the Red Army was maturing by the spring of 1943 based on the experience of war. The rifle corps was becoming standardized at three rifle divisions and support units. Each rifle division was authorized 9,380 men in three rifle regiments, each regiment having an artillery battery of four 76mm guns and an antitank battery of twelve 45mm guns. The divisional artillery regiment numbered twelve 122mm guns and twenty 76mm guns, and the antitank battalion had twelve 45mm antitank guns. Most divisions were very understrength, however, although Guards divisions had higher strengths.

The tank corps strength was increased from 7,800 to 10,977 men and from168 tanks to 209, most to be T-34s. The corps generally had three tank brigades with two or three battalions of sixty-five tanks each, a motorized rifle brigade, a mortar regiment, an antiaircraft regiment, a self-propelled artillery (76mm) regiment, an antitank (45mm) regiment, and a heavier antitank (85mm) battalion. In the sector south of Kursk across from the 11.Pz.Div. area, the Russian 6th Tank Corps under Maj. Gen. A. L. Getman had the 22nd, 112th, and 200th Tank Brigades with 179 tanks, along with the 6th Motorized Rifle Brigade, 270th Mortar Regiment, 1461st SP (Self-Propelled) Artillery Regiment, and 538th and 1008th Antitank Regiments.

The mechanized corps was increased to 15,018 men and from 102 to 204 tanks in three motorized rifle brigades, one or two tank brigades, and supporting regiments as above. A reinforced rifle corps approximated a German infantry division, which had 12,352 personnel in three two-battalion regiments and an artillery regiment. A panzer division had 13,726 personnel and 103 panzers in a panzer regiment, two panzergrenadier regiments, and a panzer artillery regiment; a panzergrenadier division had 13,876 personnel and 48 panzers organized in a panzer battalion, two three-battalion panzergrenadier regiments, and a panzer artillery regiment. Von Manstein considered a Russian tank corps to correspond to a panzer division, and a Russian mechanized corps to correspond to a panzergrenadier division. In both cases there were additional antitank and assault gun units.[29]

Soviet practice was still to support smaller organizations with Army and Front artillery and antitank, engineer, and other units rather than have these organic as combined arms as in the panzer division. Five tank armies were created by 1943 (with a sixth in 1944), to have two tank corps, one mechanized corps, and supporting regiments (46,000–48,000 personnel, 800 tanks), these approximating an average panzer corps (which had no set organization) of three to five divisions.

As the weeks went by that spring of 1943, there was a tense expectation that the front would soon erupt in violent battle. In the North Atlantic there was intense action in the U-boat-convoy war, and in the skies over Germany the Luftwaffe was heavily engaged against the Anglo-American bombing campaign. In North Africa, even though Rommel had held the British at the Mareth Line and panzer forces had shocked the Americans at Kasserine Pass, there was the final surrender in Tunisia on 13 May 1943 of some 170,000 Axis troops, including some 125,000 Germans, actually more than had surrendered at Stalingrad. All of southern Europe, the "soft underbelly" in Prime Minister Winston Churchill's phrase, was exposed to Allied invasion.

CHAPTER SIXTEEN

Preparations for Operation ZITADELLE

IN THE GERMAN HIGH COMMAND THERE WAS A FUNDAMENTAL debate about strategy in the spring of 1943. Anglo-American commitments in North Africa had convinced Hitler the Allierten would not attempt a cross-Channel invasion in 1943, and so divisions in France had been redeployed to Russia for Manstein's counterstroke to Kharkov in March. As the two previous campaigns had failed to conquer Soviet Russia, and the evacuation of the Rzhev salient was a tacit admission there would be no further drive toward Moscow, the consensus was that limited offensives might wear down Stalin to a negotiated stalemate.

Manstein argued for a mobile defense strategy in which he would allow the Russians to attack and then hit them hard *"aus der Nachhand"* ("on the backhand"), rather than a *"Schlag aus der Vorhand"* ("strike a blow on the forehand").[1] In particular, Manstein conceived the Russians attacking again across the Donets driving toward the Dnepr, whereupon Heeresgruppe Süd would fall back from the Mius Line and again annihilate the spearheads. But this would abandon the industrial resources of the Donbas with no certainty the Russians would oblige Manstein's "plan," and Hitler forbade it.

Manstein then proposed the alternate concept, a "forehand" stroke, in particular a pincers attack from north and south to destroy Russian forces in the salient projecting westward from Kursk. It would need to be launched as soon as the ground dried in May, while the Soviets were still rebuilding from the earlier battles and before they consolidated defensive positions.

While OKW (Oberkommando der Wehrmacht), headed by Gen.Feldm. Wilhelm Keitel, dealt with the other theaters of war, Oberkommando des Heeres focused exclusively on the Eastern Front. OKH had also been attracted to the concept of an offensive against the Kursk salient, and on 13 March 1943 Generaloberst Kurt Zeitzler, Chef des OKH, issued Operations Order Nr. 5 outlining a two-pronged attack to destroy the Russian forces in the Kursker Frontbogen. To better secure the Donets industrial area another pincer operation was briefly considered, to drive the Russians back from the Donets southeast of Kharkov; it would include HABICHT

(Hawk) from Chuguyev in the north, and PANTHER from Izyum in the south. But it was determined these would detract from the Kursk operation and thus were canceled.

The Kursk operation was given the code name Unternehmen ZITADELLE (Citadel), and Operations Order Nr. 6 on 15 April detailed the offensive to be launched on six days' notice at any time after 28 April. Generaloberst Hermann Hoth's 4. Panzerarmee of Manstein's H.Gr. Süd was to attack north from the Belgorod-Kharkov area, and Generaloberst Walter Model's 9. Armee of GFM Günther von Kluge's H.Gr. Mitte was to attack south from the Orel sector, the salient base being about 200 kilometers (125 miles) across.

But then vacillation ensued, as Hitler felt it necessary to have more of the heavy armor weaponry produced—the Ferdinands, Tigers, the new Panthers, and assault guns—to ensure the breakthrough of the Russian defenses. As April turned into May, Manstein for one realized the Soviets were using the time to build up formidable defenses in the salient as they too could deduce the possibility of a two-pronged German attack. In a conference at Munich on 3–4 May Model produced intelligence based on aerial photography that the Russians were preparing deep and very strong defenses in the salient and were withdrawing the mobile forces, and insisted that ZITADELLE should be abandoned. Manstein also argued that while an attack in April might have succeeded, it now was doubtful. Generaloberst Heinz Guderian, as Inspector-General of the Armored Troops, supported by Minister of Munitions Albert Speer, said the new armor, especially the Panthers, were not ready for battle, and ZITADELLE would not succeed, that it was "pointless."

Kluge, who had clashed with Guderian in the 1941 campaign and even challenged him to a duel after the conference, apparently still favored the assault as did Zeitzler and the OKH staff and Feldmarschall Keitel. Generaloberst Alfred Jodl, Chef des Wehrmachtführungsstabes im OKW (Chief of Operations), however, was opposed to committing the strategic reserve considering the uncertainties in the Mediterranean. Hoth presumably shared Manstein's misgivings. Perplexed by the divided counsel, Hitler only postponed a decision. On 10 May at the chancellery in Berlin, Guderian pointedly asked Hitler, "Why do you want to attack in the East at all this year?" Keitel, reflecting Hitler's concern about the perception of German power by other nations, said, "We must attack for political reasons." Guderian repeated his question, whereupon Hitler replied, "You're quite right. Whenever I think of this attack my stomach turns over." This reply led Guderian to implore Hitler to "Leave it alone!"[2]

As May turned into June with neither side moving, but with the evident German buildup for an offensive against the Kursk Frontbogen, a certain fatalistic foreboding came to dominate the thoughts of German commanders. Officers could scrutinize the seemingly vacant landscape through the artillery observation scissor-type binoculars, the dual stereoscopic optics providing some range estimation. The grassy plains and cornfields had numerous valleys, woodlots, brooks, and small rivers, and were dotted with thatch-roofed villages from which the Soviets had evacuated the population to a depth of 25 kilometers (15 miles). Yet they could also sense the teeming activity at night, the Rotarmisten emplacing thousands of antipersonnel and antitank mines and barbed-wire entanglements, all invisible in the waving grasses, the digging of trenches and hull-down positions for tanks, the construction of machine-gun nests and interlocked antitank gun positions, and the fortifying of the abandoned villages into strongpoints.

"For two months the shadow of *Citadel* hung over the Eastern Front and affected all our thoughts and planning," observed Oberst von Mellenthin, Chef des Stabes of XXXXVIII. Panzerkorps. "It was disquieting to reflect that after all our training, our profound study of the art of war, and the bitter experiences of the past year, the German General Staff should be dabbling with a dangerous gamble in which we were to stake our last reserves. As the weeks slipped by it became abundantly clear that this was an operation in which we had little to gain and probably a great deal to lose." He continued: "Instead of seeking to create conditions in which maneuver would be possible—by strategic withdrawals or surprise attacks in quiet sectors—the German Supreme Command could think of nothing better than to fling our magnificent panzer divisions against Kursk, which had now become the strongest fortress in the world." Hitler kept postponing X Tag (day of attack), ostensibly awaiting the new armor, but in fact he distrusted the whole concept of *Citadel*—"on this occasion his intuition did not play him false."[3]

Ironically, Stalin had impatiently wanted to attack the "Hitlerite Fascists" as Manstein had hoped, but was dissuaded by Zhukov and Stavka Chief of Staff

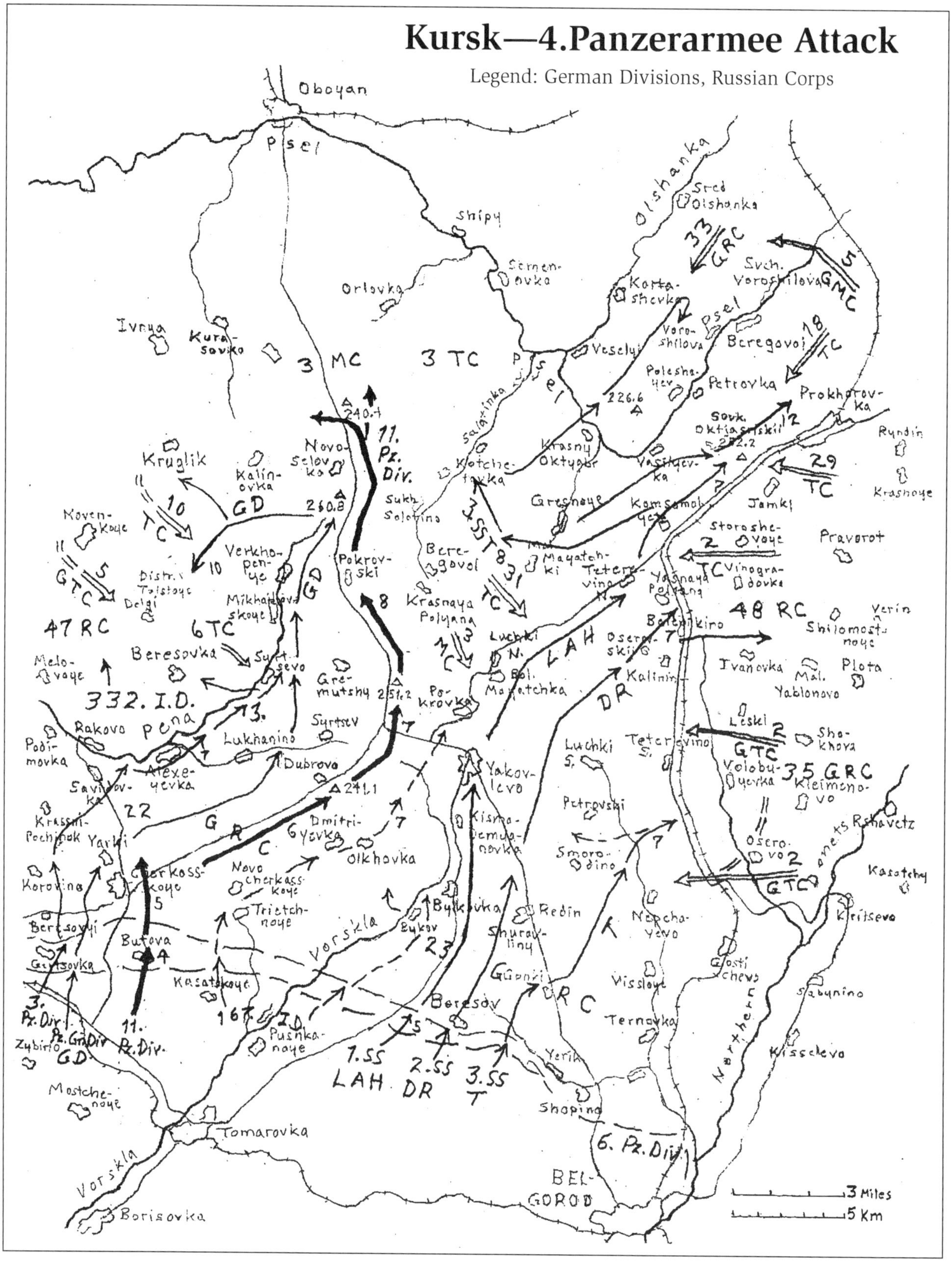

Kursk—4.Panzerarmee Attack

Legend: German Divisions, Russian Corps

Aleksandr Vasilevsky. After the premature attack at Izyum the previous spring, the failure of MARS, and Manstein's counterattack to Kharkov, there was a sobering realism in Stavka. But there was also a new sophistication to Red Army operations, with more able rising commanders rapidly gaining experience. The Kursk salient would be strongly defended to bog down the anticipated German concentric offensive, while building up forces to mount a counteroffensive at the shoulders, Orel and Belgorod. Thus it was the Red Army that would strike "on the backhand." Rokossovsky's Center Front would absorb the attack by Model's 9. Armee from the north, and Vatutin's Voronezh Front faced Hoth's 4. Pz.Armee assault from the south. Popov's Bryansk Front and Sokolovsky's Western Front would mount a counterattack in the north, and Konev's Steppe Front was created as a reserve, to then mount a counterattack in the south.

The Soviet defense system would not be a rigid system, nor a mobile defense, but rather an elastic defense in great depth. A rifle corps had a depth of some 20 kilometers (12 miles) with an outpost line with machine gun and antitank gun positions. The first main line of resistance of a division might have two rifle battalions of a regiment with interlocked strongpoints of antitank guns enmeshed in minefields and barbed wire, linked by communications trenches, about 2 kilometers (1.5 miles) in depth; a third battalion of the regiment would be about 2 kilometers behind that; and the other regiments similarly echeloned or in a third line 5 kilometers farther back. Another rifle division of the corps would be abreast or in a second main line some 15 kilometers (9 miles) from the front.

A third main line of prepared field fortifications was 15 kilometers farther back again, into which the front units—having been exhausted in stemming the assault—would retreat, joined by forces coming forward. Tank forces could move up into prepared hull-down positions or mount counterattacks. There were up to eight major lines in the defensive belt. The lines were separated enough that German divisional artillery, ranging 12,000 meters (13,000 yards), would have to displace forward to bombard the next series of positions.

On one sector of the south (where the 11.Pz.Div. and Pz.Abt.52 [Panther] would attack) west of Belgorod was Maj. Gen. A. I. Baksov's 67th Guards Rifle Division of Maj. Gen. N. B. Ibiansky's 22nd Guards Rifle Corps of Lt. Gen. I. M. Chistiakov's 6th Guards Army in Vatutin's Voronezh Front. Baksov deployed his 67th Guards Division astride the road from Borisovka and Tomarovka northward through Butovo and Cherkasskoye on to Oboyan on the Psel and the (only) paved highway to Kursk from the south. On Baksov's left flank Col. I. M. Nekrasov's 52nd Guards Rifle Division (of 23rd Guards Rifle Corps) was astride the Vorskla River and the road from Tomarovka to Prokhorovka, and on his right was Col. I. P. Sivakov's 71st Guards Rifle Division in front of the Pena. Ten kilometers (6 miles) to the rear was the 90th Guards Rifle Division backed up by Lt. Gen. M. E. Katukov's 1st Tank Army. Baksov's sector was 14 kilometers (9 miles) wide along a generally treeless ridge with mine-infested ravines and copses of trees. His three Guards Rifle Regiments were on line but echeloned in depth: 196th, 199th, and 201st, from right to left. Across from its front, the 11.Pz.Div. identified the 1st Battalions of the 199th and of the 196th in Butovo, the 3rd Battalion of the 199th in a gorge 3 kilometers east of Butovo, and the 2nd and 3rd Battalions of the 196th in Cherkasskoye. A Minenhundebataillon was in a ravine 1 kilometer east of Cherkasskoye. From Überläufer it was determined there were three companies of fifty Minenhunde each, and sixteen Panzerbüchse. Tank and antitank positions were also noted.[4]

The ridgeline screened from German view Baksov's mortars, the 138th Guards Artillery Regiment batteries, and positions of the 73rd Guards Separate Antitank Battalion; they were also camouflaged against German aerial reconnaissance. The 67th Division numbered 8,000 personnel, smaller than a German division, but strongly reinforced with batteries of two attached antitank regiments, two additional artillery regiments, and the assault guns of the 1440th Self-propelled Artillery Regiment, with tanks and assault guns to the rear. The assault guns were the SU-76, a 76.2mm gun on a T-70 light tank chassis. Baksov formed four antitank strongpoints, each with eight to ten antitank guns, protected with machine-gun positions. Twenty-one kilometers (13 miles) of barbed wire were strung, and over 30,000 antipersonnel and antitank mines were emplaced.

The Soviet antitank mine TM-41 weighed 5.5 kilograms (12 pounds). Its explosive charge of 3.6 kilograms (8 pounds) of Amatol or TNT, set off by a pressure of 161 kilograms (350 pounds), was enough to blow off a tank track or demolish a vehicle.

Clearing was done by probing a field with a bayonet or rod to find the mine, as electronic metal mine-detectors were useless in the shrapnel-strewn ground. Disarming involved clearing away the earth, feeling carefully for anti-lifting explosive devices, and then gently unscrewing the pressure cap and pulling out the fuse and attached detonator. Any hasty or careless move could result in explosive death.

The Red Army *Frontovik*, generally disdaining a helmet for his *pilotka* (side cap), with his overcoat rolled over his left shoulder and a simple sack serving as a knapsack, burrowed into the ground. Should he want next of kin notified if he became a casualty, he had to enroll in the Communist Party. Nikolai Litvin, a gun-layer on a 45mm antitank gun, noted the *Frontoviki* were now trained to crouch in their trenches and allow the panzers to overrun them, then attack them from behind with AT mines and satchel charges, while the *Avtomatchiki*, PPSh submachine gun squads, engaged the accompanying grenadiers at close range.[5]

The Russians practiced their deployments with sand table and map exercises, checked bridges and alternate fording sites, calculated artillery concentration targets, and perfected their defenses—and awaited the German offensive. The German buildup was monitored by traditional means of intelligence gathering including aerial reconnaissance, radio traffic analysis, cryptography, and ground probes. Panzer officers, as with the 11.Pz.Div., were to wear normal army Feldgrau uniforms and not their black panzer uniforms when studying the terrain at the front held by the infantry, but no one felt the Ivans were fooled by this. Some sources attribute detailed Soviet intelligence data also to the network of Soviet agents. By this time Dr. Richard Sorge had been arrested in Japan, and "Coro," Luftwaffe Lt. Harro Schulze-Boysen, had been exposed by Adm. Wilhelm Canaris's Abwehr (counterintelligence), thus breaking the "Rote Kapelle." But intelligence continued to flow to Moscow's "Director" through "Dora" (Alexander Rado), "Lucy" (Rudolf Rössler in Lucerne), and an agent code-named "Werther" (still unknown), among others.[6]

Still convinced that heavy armor would break the Russian defenses, Hitler urged increased armor production for ZITADELLE, especially the Panther tank. He also was intrigued with a wooden model of a "Maus" (Mouse) designed by Ferdinand Porsche and the Krupp Company, which would mount a 15cm gun and a coaxial 7,5cm gun in a huge turret, and weigh over 175 tons. (Two prototypes were actually built in 1944, but were destroyed in April 1945.) While the heavy panzers would be formidable, veteran Panzer-soldaten knew that tracks and suspension always remained vulnerable, especially to AT mines, and the heavy weight posed challenges for transportation and recovery, bridge and road capacities, and cross-terrain floatation. They also knew mechanical or technical malfunctions could disable even the most powerful armored fighting vehicles.

Guderian worried about the Panther, "our problem child." There were problems with the track suspension, the drive, and the optics. On 18 June he flew to meet with Hitler at Berchtesgaden and on the way landed at Truppen Übungs Platz Grafenwöhr to again investigate the troubles of Panzer Abteilungen 51 and 52, units that would employ the Panther. "Apart from the technical weaknesses of the not yet perfected tanks," he wrote, "neither the crews nor the commanders were by then sufficiently experienced in their handling, while some of them even lacked adequate battle experience."[7]

Maj. Karl von Sivers's Pz.Abt. (Panther) 52, as the 11. Panzer's I.Abt./Pz.Rgt.15, did have some experienced personnel, the Major himself a Ritterkreuzträger, but they had to absorb many replacements after the Velikiye Luki battle. The crews also had to deal with the problems of the new panzer at the expense of unit training. In addition to the wear on the suspension and gears, and connecting rod and bearing failures caused by the 45-ton weight and the strain on the transmission from the 700 hp production Maybach engine, there were engine fires. These resulted from gasoline and oil leaks and insufficient engine cooling and ventilation, due to watertight sealing of the engine compartment for river fording as standard bridges could often not be used.

On 4 March 1943 the Gespensters of I.Abt./15 had moved from Tr.Ü.Pl. Grafenwöhr to the Panzerkaserne at Erlangen, just northwest of Nürnberg, where they received some of their wheeled vehicles. On 12 April the battalion entrained for Mailly le Camp in occupied France near Troyes east of Paris, having been redesignated as Panzer-Abteilung (Panther) 52 on 6 February. Rittmeister von Sivers was commander with the rank of major, and the staff included Oberlt. Graf Siersdorff as adjutant and Oberlt. Urban commanding the Stabskompanie. As Ordonnanz Offizier (Orderly Officer) Sivers requested Lt. Walter Rahn, who had been a training officer at Sagan. The four panzer company commanders were Oblt. Walter at 1.Komp., Oblt. Pfundtner at 2., Oblt.von Wallenberg at 3., and Oblt. Gabriel at 4. But French railway tunnels turned out to be too narrow and too low for the large Panthers, so on 8 May the battalion returned to Grafenwöhr. They wondered when they might rejoin the rest of their division, still in southern Russia.[8]

Hitler delayed ZITADELLE to allow time for more Tigers and Panthers to be produced, though many realized the Soviet Union was outproducing the Reich. In the three-month period between April and June 1943, 2,816 panzers and self-propelled guns were produced. Of these 484 were Panthers and 156 were Tigers, adding to the 84 of the latter already built. But during the same three months the Red Army received over 6,000 tanks and assault guns. These were mostly of existing types: the T-34, KV-1, and T-70 light tank. Like the Germans the Russians were also beginning to produce assault guns on existing chassis, as *Samokhodnaya Ustanovka* (self-propelled carriage). The SU-76 was the 76.2mm gun on the T-70 chassis, and the SU-122 would be a 122mm gun on a T-34 chassis. To counter the German Tiger the SU-152 was developed; it was a casemated 152mm howitzer cannon on a KV chassis, low-velocity but powerful, and forty-eight were produced by June. It was later nicknamed by the Russian soldiers "Zveroboi"—animal hunter, to hunt the Tigers and Panthers.[9]

At a top-secret conference at the Wolfsschanze at Rastenburg on 1 July with the relevant top commanders, Hitler fixed the date for ZITADELLE as 5 July—four days away. While most attacking units were in their assembly areas prepared to move up to their designated attack positions, the two Panther battalions, 51 and 52, had to be rapidly transferred from Grafenwöhr. A special factory at Berlin-Falkensee and maintenance shops at Grafenwöhr and Erlangen had worked feverishly to get 200 Panthers ready, though on 16 June Guderian had reported to Hitler that 65 of them had problems.

The two Panther Abteilungen were assigned to von Knobelsdorff's XXXXVIII. Panzerkorps in Hoth's 4. Pz.Armee in the south. On 29 June it was decided they would follow the panzer regiment of Grossdeutschland in the attack. Pz.Abt.51 arrived at Borisovka that day. But the Gespensters of Pz.Abt.52 only began rail-loading their 100 Panthers on 28 June, the gun barrels secured in the travel locks on the front hulls. After a rapid movement through Schlesien-Krakau (Silesian Krakow) on 30 June and Smerinka on 1 July, they arrived at Kiev by 2 July. Because of railroad bridge weight restrictions, only six Panthers could be handled at a time, necessitating nineteen trains. On 3 July they began arriving at Odnoborovka east of Poltava, still 35 kilometers from Novo Borisovka, the last reaching the disembark station on the evening of the next day, 4 July—the *same* day as 4. Panzerarmee was beginning ZITADELLE! Movement was further delayed when a Panther broke through a bridge in Borisovka and then overturned and caught fire, destroying both panzer and bridge.

Maj. Karl von Sivers was commander of Pz.Abt.52 but ill at Grafenwöhr. Oberstleutnant Köhnen may have acted as commander, but Hauptmann Baumunk led the battalion at Kursk. Sivers returned as commander 22 July.[10] With Pz.Abt.51, the battalion was in "Panzer Regiment v.L." This reflected the name of the commander assigned on 5 June, Maj. Meinrad von Lauchert, who had attempted to train the units at Grafenwöhr. Von Lauchert was an experienced panzer leader, coming from I.Abt./Pz.Rgt.35 of the 4.Pz.Div. (as II./35 became III.Abt./Pz.Rgt.15), and then from Grafenwöhr. A rather cold and distant figure, he was a noted equestrian, and had been with a cavalry regiment stationed at Bamberg in Bavaria. An excellent commander, he had already received the Ritterkreuz (8 September 1941). Lauchert later commanded Pz.Rgt.15 (1 August 1943 to August 1944), and then 2.Pz.Div. after 13 December 1944.[11]

Ostensibly, there were 204 Panthers that arrived for ZITADELLE. Each battalion had ninety-eight, comprising four companies of twenty-two Panthers (four five-panzer platoons and two headquarters panzers) plus three for staff and five in a signals platoon at battalion, and two Bergepanthers (retrievers). There was also a flak platoon with 2cm Vierlingsflak on three Sd.Kfz. 7/1 half-tracks. Eight Panthers were also assigned for the regimental staff.[12] Panzer Abteilungen 51 and 52, as a "regiment" under von Lauchert, were to be under an improvised brigade headquarters, the 10., under Oberst Karl Decker. Most of the brigade staff came from Pz.Rgt.39 of 17.Pz.Div. which was in XXIV. Pz.Korps in H.Gr. Süd reserve. Decker had been awarded the RK (13 June 1941) and came from commanding Pz.Rgt.4/13.Pz.Div. and then Pz.Rgt.3/2. Pz.Div.

But the brigade headquarters, communications equipment, and vehicles did not leave Berlin until 3 July. Decker and his adjutant belatedly arrived but had nothing to work with. Nor is it evident what the regiment/brigade had in the way of standard maintenance, signals, and supply assets. Lauchert and Sivers had worked together at Grafenwöhr, not always smoothly, but Sivers was ill and it seems that Lauchert had to command both Panther battalions by himself, borrowing vehicles for his headquarters from Grossdeutschland. At Grafenwöhr Oberstleutnant Werner Mildebrath had attempted to get an extension of the training period, but in vain. (Mildebrath had experience; he had been awarded the RK 12 August 1942 with Pz.Rgt.5, 21.Pz.Div. in North Africa.) The manifest problems with the accelerated production of the Panther, the inadequate training, and the improvised formation as a "regiment" (or "brigade"), did not bode well for the combat debut of the Panzer V.

Almost as an afterthought, von Lauchert's regiment/brigade was assigned to the Panzergrenadierdivision Grossdeutschland, and was to work with Oberstlt. Hyacinth Graf von Strachwitz who already commanded the division's panzer regiment plus a Tiger company. The GD, its vehicles marked with its White Helmet symbol, was considered an elite division, like the Waffen-SS divisions, though the latter's script sleeve band was worn on the left cuff, the GD's on the right. In essence a panzer division, it was already too large and unwieldy (as Balck had felt). By 4 July, with some 200 Panthers, Strachwitz's panzer "regiment" had 293 panzers including 12 Tigers. By contrast, of the other two panzer divisions in XXXXVIII. Pz.K., the 11.Pz.Div. had 72 panzers and 3.Pz.Div. had 68.[13]

Nonetheless, poised to assault the fortified salient of Kursk was the greatest concentration of panzer forces in World War II: nineteen panzer or panzergrenadier divisions plus detachments, comprising some 2,928 panzers and assault guns (though the Red Army had 5,128 around the salient). In the Orel sector to the north, Generaloberst Walter Model's 9. Armee of von Kluge's H.Gr. Mitte included one panzergrenadier and six panzer divisions, and fourteen German and three Hungarian infantry divisions, with 1,014 panzers and assault guns. In the Belgorod sector to the south in von Manstein's H.Gr. Süd, Generaloberst Hermann Hoth's 4. Pz.Armee included four panzergrenadier and two panzer divisions (the Waffen-SS panzergrenadier divisions actually being larger than the panzer divisions) and four infantry divisions, with 1,095 panzers and assault guns.

Armee Abteilung Kempf on Hoth's right flank under General der Panzertruppen Werner Kempf included three panzer divisions and six infantry divisions, with 499 panzers and assault guns. There were two panzer divisions and a panzergrenadier division in Army Group reserve. 2. Armee of Generaloberst Walter Weiss held along the western face of the salient with eight infantry divisions.[14]

In the first days of July the panzer divisions moved up to their attack positions, the 11.Pz.Div. up to areas between Tomarovka and Graivoron along the Vorskla, behind the Hauptkampflinie manned by the 167. Infanterie-Division. Rations were issued for five days. For ZITADELLE von Knobelsdorff's XXXXVIII. Pz.Korps included, from the left (west), Generalleutnant Franz Westhoven's 3.Pz.Div., Pz.Gren.Div. Grossdeutschland under Generalleutnant Walter Hörnlein, and Generalmajor Mickl's 11.Pz.Div., behind the 167.Inf.Div. commanded by Generalleutnant Wolf Trierenberg. The three Waffen-SS panzergrenadier divisions of SS Obergruppenführer Paul Hausser's II.SS Pz.Korps were to the right. (I. SS Pz.K. was to be formed in the West 27 July.)

Hoth felt that if the low ridge to the front could be acquired for artillery observation, 4. Pz.Armee's offensive would be more successful, and Manstein concurred. In the late evening of 3 July, under cover of a sultry night marked by rain showers and flashes of lightning, engineer platoons snaked forward in the grassy fields leading to the Rotarmisten outposts, clearing lanes through the minefields and barbed-wire entanglements. It was difficult and dangerous work—inching forward, salt sweat in the eyes from the heat and from fear, probing until a mine was discovered, freezing in position when a Soviet flare flickered until it drifted down. Then carefully feeling for anti-lifting devices, unscrewing and removing the fuse, setting the mine aside, and then inching forward again. Wire cutters were used to cut through entanglements. Then tape was laid along the lane, with care taken to keep the tape, and the silent activity, down in the grasses. GD's engineers lifted 2,700 mines during five hours, with none detonating nor the Russian outposts being alerted.

Expecting the German offensive, but not sure precisely when, the Soviet forces were on the alert before dawn, but then relaxed as the day of 4 July passed without attack. But Hoth intended to strike the day *before* ZITADELLE actually jumped off on the 5th, to secure the ridgeline. The 11.Pz.Div. attack order for X-1.Tag was to seize Butovo and the high ground, and then Cherkasskoye on X Tag. On the right was Pz.Gren.Rgt.110 (ohne I.Btl.) with 2. Kp./Pi.Btl.209,

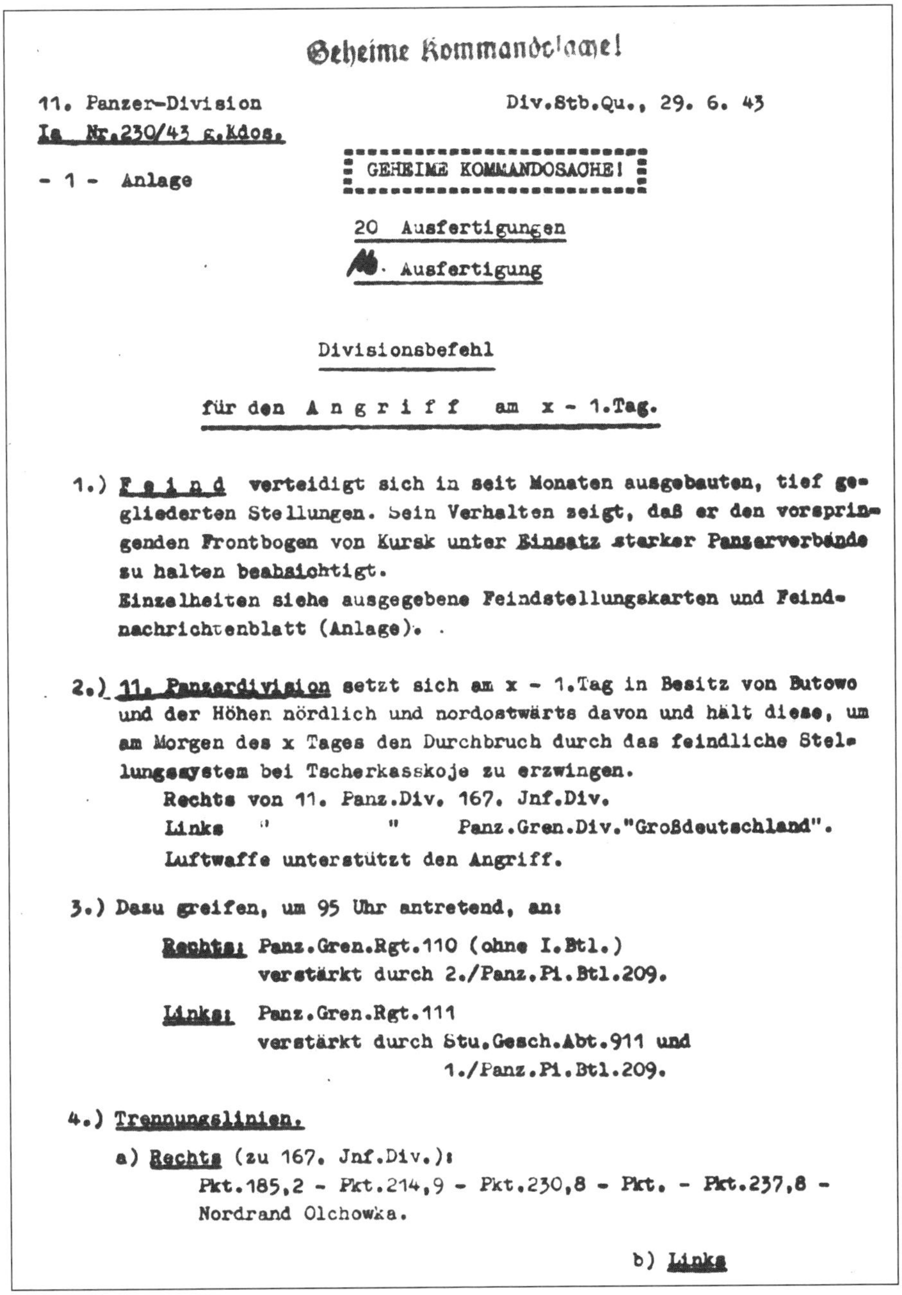

Geheime Kommandosache!

11. Panzer-Division Div.Stb.Qu., 29. 6. 43
Ia Nr.230/43 g.Kdos.

- 1 - Anlage

GEHEIME KOMMANDOSACHE!

20 Ausfertigungen
16. Ausfertigung

Divisionsbefehl

für den A n g r i f f am x - 1.Tag.

1.) F e i n d verteidigt sich in seit Monaten ausgebauten, tief gegliederten Stellungen. Sein Verhalten zeigt, daß er den vorspringenden Frontbogen von Kursk unter Einsatz starker Panzerverbände zu halten beabsichtigt.
Einzelheiten siehe ausgegebene Feindstellungskarten und Feindnachrichtenblatt (Anlage).

2.) 11. Panzerdivision setzt sich am x - 1.Tag in Besitz von Butowo und der Höhen nördlich und nordostwärts davon und hält diese, um am Morgen des x Tages den Durchbruch durch das feindliche Stellungssystem bei Tscherkasskoje zu erzwingen.
Rechts von 11. Panz.Div. 167. Jnf.Div.
Links " " Panz.Gren.Div."Großdeutschland".
Luftwaffe unterstützt den Angriff.

3.) Dazu greifen, um 95 Uhr antretend, an:

Rechts: Panz.Gren.Rgt.110 (ohne I.Btl.)
verstärkt durch 2./Panz.Pi.Btl.209.

Links: Panz.Gren.Rgt.111
verstärkt durch Stu.Gesch.Abt.911 und
1./Panz.Pi.Btl.209.

4.) Trennungslinien.

a) Rechts (zu 167. Jnf.Div.):
Pkt.185,2 - Pkt.214,9 - Pkt.230,8 - Pkt. - Pkt.237,8 -
Nordrand Olchowka.

b) Links

ZITADELLE—Division Attack Order, 29 June 1943: 11.Pz.Div. to occupy Butovo on X-1 Tag, and on X Tag force a breakthrough at Cherkasskoye. NARA T-315/ROLL 599/000974

and on the left was Pz.G.R.111 to be mounted *on* the assault guns of Stu.Gesch.Abt.911, with 1.Kp./Pi. Btl.209. The assault was to be by surprise, with *no* preceding artillery preparation.[15]

Pz.Rgt.15, A.A.11, I.Btl./110, and Pz.Jäg.Abt.61 were to move up the high ground that first night. Then, with better observation by the artillery Vorgeschobener Beobachter, II.Abt./Pz.Art.Rgt.119 would be on call to support 110, and I./119 would support 111, with *observed* fire. H.Flak Abt.277's initial mission, with attached Fla.Btl.(mot) 616, was air defense. The HVP was at Kustovoye, and the Div.Gef.Std. was at Novaya Glinka-Nordwest. The code word for X-1.Tag was "Blücher-Julius."

About 16,00 Uhr that afternoon of the 4th, flights of Stukas suddenly droned overhead and then peeled off and attacked the Russian outpost line and strongpoints. German artillery opened fire and smashed into the Russian positions, and assault forces raced along the cleared lanes even as Soviet machine guns began to open up. Panzergrenadier squads from II./110 of the Elfte reached the high ground to the east of Butovo while 111 attacked from the south, and GD units seized terrain to the left. This isolated the defending Russian battalion, 3rd Battalion/199th Guards Regiment of Baksov's 67th Guards Rifle Division, and ultimately destroyed it. The enemy was "surprised," the Russian artillery fire was "slight," and the infantry defenses were "weak," noted Ia Kinitz in the KTB.

By the evening of the 4th, Hoth had secured the high ground from Gertsova in the west (where 3.Pz.Div. encountered stiff resistance from 71st Guards Rifle Division) to Iakhontov in the east (where Waffen-SS troopers assaulted the 52nd Guards Rifle Division outposts later that night). Defensive positions were rapidly secured and observation posts established, and now the VBs could more accurately plot their concentrations and call in and adjust fire missions. Signals personnel and vehicles also came up to establish wire and radio communications to the batteries displacing forward. The intent was for the Russian main line of resistance to be within the 12,000-meter (13,000-yard) range of the divisional 10,5cm howitzers.[16]

As the main German attack forces moved into their final attack positions during the night of 4–5 July, thunder, lightning, and torrential rain bedeviled them, joined about 02,20 hours early on the 5th by sudden and intense Russian artillery bombardment. Above the din came the drone of Russian bombers also entering the fray. VVS bombers had already been mounting air raids by night, targeting assembly areas and railroad junctions where trains were stalled by partisan attacks on railroad bridges. The Russian bombardment and approaching air raid confirmed suspicions that the Soviets were not caught by surprise.

Indeed, the capture of a German private from the 168.Inf.Div. in the south, and a combat engineer from the 6.Inf.Div. in the north, alerted the Russian command that ZITADELLE would begin by 03,00 hours on 5 July. Marshal Vasilevsky at Voronezh Front authorized Vatutin to begin his preemptive counteroffensive artillery bombardment to disrupt the German plans in the south, and informed Marshal Zhukov at Center Front. Zhukov in turn authorized Rokossovsky to fire his preplanned bombardment in the north, and so informed Stalin in Moscow.

Against Model's 9. Armee positions the bombardment struck located and plotted assembly areas and artillery batteries, as well as probable attack positions, with high explosives and Katyusha rocket barrages. Many German gun crews were caught as they were preparing for opening ZITADELLE with their own bombardment at 03,30 hours, though underground dugouts had long been prepared. But OKH agreed to delay the attack for two hours. Against Hoth's 4.Pz.Armee the bombardment was less effective; perhaps because of the early start to gain the high ground, units had already changed positions from where Russian intelligence and aerial photographs had located them.

The air assault by the Soviet Air Force was also less effective. Though not as sophisticated as the Luftwaffe systems in the West to defend the Reich from Allied strategic bombing, defenses were in place. These included the Freya search-and-acquisition radar scanning about 160 kilometers (100 miles) and the Würzburg tracking radar, a narrow-beam radar with a radius of 60 kilometers (36 miles) that could fix the moving hostile aircraft so the control room could plot the course and vector the fighter interceptors.

Due to take off for the 03,30 assault, 1,800 German bombers and ground-attack airplanes had warmed up their engines, and some flights were airborne from the numerous airfields and airstrips, when Freya signaled the alert. Normally the bombers took off first and assembled into formations, followed by the fighters as escort, as they held less fuel. But now, with minutes to spare, the fighters were scrambled; and the German pilots, better trained and with better planes, including the Messerschmitt Bf 109G and the Focke-Wulf Fw 190F, intercepted and savaged the Russian force. The fighters shot down 132 VVS planes in the first hours, and with the flak joining in, the Germans claimed 432 Russian planes downed on 5 July. In desperation Russian pilots even tried to use ramming tactics against their foe, but the Luftwaffe prevailed, as its bombers began to strike their designated targets.[17]

In the lightening dawn of 5 July, the Landsers on the ground double-checked their weapons and equipment, Panzersoldaten double-checked their gages and optics, and Artilleristen ensured their elevation and traversing dials were correct and their ammunition charges as ordered, and awaited the attack signal.

CHAPTER SEVENTEEN

ZITADELLE: The German Offensive

AT 04,30 UHR ON 5 JULY MODEL'S 9. ARMEE ARTILLERY bombardment in the north commenced in conjunction with the air attacks by the 1. Luftdivision under Luftwaffe Generalleutnant Paul Deichmann of Generaloberst Ritter von Greim's 6. Luftflotte. Aware of the extensive Soviet antitank defenses, Model launched his Angriff at 05,30 hours with his infantry divisions, the only armor committed in the initial assault being the 20. Panzer-Division. The infantry and engineers advanced into a swirling maelstrom of darkness pierced by blinding flashes of explosions from detonating mines, high-explosive artillery barrages, screaming mortars, Stalins Orgel rockets, and strafing and bombing from aircraft, all laced with flat-trajectory 7,62cm "Ratsch-bumms" and machine-gun tracers.

To get through the minefields the 78. Infanterie-Division employed the "Goliaths" of Pz.Kompanien 811 and 813. These were leichte Ladungsträger (light charge carrier), wire-controlled miniature panzers 1.7 meters (66.9 inches) long and carrying a 112.5-kilogram (250-lb) explosive charge to be detonated in the minefields to self-explode mines and obstacles. To clear lanes for the heavy armor there were three companies (312, 313, 314) of the larger-tracked Funklenk (radio-controlled) Ladungsträger Borgward IV, which emplaced a 500-kilogram (1,100-lb) time-delayed explosive that would detonate as the vehicle backed away. Though both could also be effective against tanks, paks, or bunkers, they were quite vulnerable to artillery and gun fire.[1]

Model's 9. Armee also employed eighty-nine of the much-maligned Ferdinand tank destroyers of the schwere Panzerjäger-Abteilungen 653 and 654 in XXXXI. Panzerkorps. These were the hulking Tiger (P), the discontinued Porsche prototypes. Armed with the very deadly 8,8cm Pak 43/2 L/71 high-velocity gun capable of penetrating 139mm (5.56 inches) of 30-degree armor at 2,000 meters (2,180 yards), it was best employed to destroy Russian tanks and antitank positions beyond the range of the Russian guns. Guderian, however, who visited both fronts 10–15 July, was contemptuous of the models, especially as they lacked a machine gun: "Once they had broken into the enemy's infantry zones they literally had to go quail-shooting with cannons." But again, though heavily armored, these were tank destroyers, *not* assault guns. The Hornisse (Hornet) also mounted the 8,8cm Pak 43 L/71 and no MG, and it proved effective. At Kursk some forty-five Hornisse were deployed with schwere Panzerjäger-Abteiling 560 with Armeeabteilung Kempf in the south.[2]

The Ferdinands, however, were awkwardly designed, and suffered from mechanical problems. Almost half of them broke down in the first few days, or were put out of action by mines. But their 200mm (7.9-inch) frontal armor meant few were disabled by Russian fire. The two companies of Tiger panzers with 9. Armee (thirty-one Tigers and fifteen Pz.IIIs of s.Heeres Pz.Abt.505) were almost as powerful with their 8,8cm Kw.K. L/56 guns, and knocked out many Russian positions; a third company joined by 9 July. 9. Armee also employed 66 Sturmpanzer Brummbär (Grizzly Bear) with its stubby 15cm Stu.H. on a Pz.IV chassis in s.Pz.Abt.216 in XXXXI. Pz.K. against bunkers with success. Still, 9. Armee only penetrated the first defensive belt on 5 July up to 8 kilometers (5 miles) deep, west of Ponyri. This advance came at heavy cost, as Rokossovsky threw in counterattack forces.

Hoth's 4. Pz.Armee offensive in the south began after a delay on 5 July, the artillery bombardment in conjunction with the bombing and strafing of Russian positions by 4. Luftflotte of Gen. Otto Desloch. XXXXVIII. Panzerkorps and II. SS Pz.Korps attacked up two routes converging on Oboyan on the Psel and on to Kursk. In addition to its important bridge over the Psel, Oboyan was also the headquarters of Vatutin's Voronezh Front. Unlike Model, Manstein and Hoth chose to spearhead their attack with the armor. Grossdeutschland and the three Waffen-SS divisions each had a heavy panzer company of some fourteen Tigers (and ten Pz.IIIs). The heavily armored Tigers led in the Panzerkeil wedge formation: in a three-platoon company two platoons led, each with four Tigers in their own wedge formation, and their lighter Pz.IIIs, headquarters, and third platoon followed. If there was an anticipated threat given the terrain on either flank, then that flank could be "refused" by the flank panzer dropping back, or by going into a Staffelformation (echelon formation) right or left.

The other panzer units followed, including tank destroyers and assault guns. As the panzers had to stop in order to fire their main gun accurately at enemy tanks or AT gun positions, good control was needed to have a coordinated advance. For divisions without Tigers, heavy assault guns and Panzer IVs had to provide the armored spearhead. The panzergrenadiers and combat engineers followed in their thinner armored half-tracks or rode the panzers, dropping off when they came under fire. With the heavy shellfire and machine-gun fire there were casualties. The battle was rapidly becoming a struggle of attrition, with little opportunity for tactical maneuvering.

XXXXVIII. Panzerkorps, with 464 panzers and 89 assault guns, attacked with the three panzer divisions abreast: Westhoven's 3.Pz.Div. with the Berlin Bär painted on its turrets, Hörnlein's Grossdeutschland with its GD helmet markings, and Mickl's 11.Pz.Div. sporting the white Gespenster image on panzers and vehicles, with Trierenberg's Bayerische 167.Inf.Div. now on the right flank, connecting to Hausser's II.SS Pz.K. The big Grossdeutschland was given the Schwerpunkt, the point of main effort. Oberstlt. Graf Strachwitz had two panzer battalions, and a Tiger company with fourteen Tigers. In addition, Pz.Rgt. von Lauchert with the two Panther battalions, Pz.Abt.51 and 52, were under his control as well. With some 200 Panthers, these battalions were awkward to control, as was the whole division. There were no Panthers with other divisions.

Supported by some 350 panzers and assault guns, GD's infantry advanced from the high ground around Butovo on a front only 3,000 meters (3,300 yards) wide. The Panzerfüsilier-regiment of Oberst Erich Kassnitz led across the open ground, which fronted a ravine and a marsh along the course of the Berezovyi rivulet toward the evacuated hamlets of Alekseevka and Lukhanino. GD's Panzergrenadier-Regiment advanced astride the track from Butovo toward Cherkasskoye. The Fusilier's III.Btl. had gone ahead, but the panzer force failed to keep up. This was the GD's own I.Abt. under Major Pössel, followed by von Lauchert's Panther regiment, with the Gespensters of Pz.Abt.52 under Hptm. Baumunk.

Having eagerly anticipated the powerful new Panthers, the front-line Landsers were dismayed to see flames belching from their exhaust pipes and some even flaring up with carburetor fires. Two were lost, earning the Panther the nickname "Feuerzeug" (matchbox, or lighter). Not only that, there was an undiscovered minefield in the ravine into which the panzers and then the Panthers blundered, even as Baksov's 67th Guards Rifle Division Russians of the 22nd Guards Rifle Corps, who had occupied and fortified the deserted villages, opened fire. In addition, the rainstorm the night before had turned the normally dry ravine into a swamp. Grossdeutschland's artillery commander, Oberstleutnant Albrecht related, "Suddenly tanks appear behind us, more and more of them: they have a very long gun, a completely new type. Oh yes, the new Panther! Once again, however, our enthusiasm is dampened straight away: our tanks which have been able to free themselves from the minefield are now bogged down in a swamp which extends along a small stream." He continued: "It was enough to make one sick. Soldiers and officers alike feared that the entire affair was going to pot. The tanks were stuck fast, some bogged down to the tops of their tracks, and to make matters worse the enemy was firing at them with antitank rifles, antitank guns, and artillery."[3] Continuing alone, the Fusiliers were decimated, as pioneers worked to clear the mines.

On the left 3.Pz.Div. had secured Gertsovka on the 4th and attacked the 71st Guards Rifle Division of the 22nd Guards Rifle Corps on the 5th, reaching Korovino that evening. Lt. von Weltheim of Pz.Rgt.6 pressed on to Krasny Pochinok, and was the first to reach the Pena River. While Grossdeutschland's Fusiliers and panzers were stalled along the Berezovyi stream, there was better progress on the right. There Oberstlt. Karl Lorenz's Grenadierregiment, supported by assault guns, Hptm. Wallroth's 9.s.Pz.Kp. with fourteen Tigers and ten Pz.IIIs, and Major Graf Saurma's II.Abt. of the Panzer-Regiment, made better progress toward Cherkasskoye. Saurma was mortally wounded, but Hörnlein shifted Kassnitz's Fusiliers and von Lauchert's Panthers to reinforce Lorenz's advance. Left behind was Kassnitz, badly wounded.

The Panthers' first day of combat travails continued. By nightfall, as crews and Werkstatt personnel were laboring to make their disabled Panthers einsatzbereit again, perhaps half of the 200 Panthers were out of operation, and perhaps more than thirty-six were irreparable. Fähnrich Friedrich von Eggeling, earlier a Fahnenjunker gunner on a Pz.IV and now a Panther platoon leader, lost his whole platoon in the first three days.[4] By any measure it was a humiliating and damaging loss.

The Panthers' technical problems, their hasty organization and deployment, the lack of time to reconnoiter mission objectives and approaches—or even to test radio communications and zero their weapons—and the impromptu attachment to Hörnlein's Grossdeutschland and then to Graf Strachwitz's Panzer-Regiment, with little coordination with infantry, artillery, and engineers, all combined to ensure the commitment of the new Panthers would be a failure. Nor were the Panther battalions a "brigade." In his report to Generaloberst Kurt Zeitzler at OKH on 17 July, Guderian said, "Because of friction between personnel this Brigade headquarters did not function at the start."[5]

With the chain of command and their roles unclear, it is not surprising that von Strachwitz, von Lauchert, and Decker were at odds on many issues. On 6 July the Panther "regiment" had been officially put under Strachwitz's command, and Decker, with no staff yet, was simply assigned to XXXXVIII. Pz.Korps. Ironically, when Strachwitz was wounded on 10 July, Knobelsdorff assigned Decker to command what was now Grossdeutschland's panzer brigade after Hptm. von Wietersheim had temporarily assumed command.[6] Why was Pz.Abt.52 not returned to its parent 11. Panzer-Division? Meinrad von Lauchert and his Panthersoldaten deserved better.

As the GD infantry approached Cherkasskoye, they could see German panzers and infantry to their right, ahead of them; these were the Gespensters of the 11.Pz.-Div. The evening before, Generaloberst Hoth had turned up at the Div.Gef.Std., emphasizing the importance of the role of the Gespenster-Division in the offensive. On 4 July there were seventy-two Pz.IIIs and IVs einsatzbereit. There were also eight Flammpanzer IIIs, and a battery of six Hummel 15cm self-propelled pieces in Pz.-Art.-Rgt. 119. The spearhead would be the armor of Kampfgruppe Schimmelmann including: II.Abt./Pz.Rgt.15 under Hptm. Edel Lingenthal, who had been with the regiment since Poland in 1939 when he had been Oberleutnant and adjutant of I./15; I./Pz.Gren.Rgt.110(gp) the half-track battalion under Hptm. Karl Thieme, an able and aggressive commander already making a name for himself; I./Pz.Art.Rgt.119 with the six Hummels; a half-track platoon of Pz.Pi.Btl.209; and some twenty-two of the thirty-one assault guns of Oberstlt. Georg Wilhelm's attached Sturmgeschütz-Abteilung 911 Gefechts-Batterien.[7] Like most of the regular panzer divisions the 11. did not have the Tigers or the latest assault guns. But the Panzerschürzen protecting the turrets and flanks of the Panzer IIIs and IVs enhanced their capabilities. Heeres Flak-Abt.277 gave air defense with its motorized 2cm and 3,7cm guns.

The attack began following a heavy artillery and Stuka bombardment. II./110 advanced on the right,

II./111 on the left, and then the gepanzerte Gruppe was committed. The panzergrenadiers took Butovo, though a deep antitank ditch and a large minefield beyond delayed the armored vehicles. Nonetheless the momentum of the attack continued, with the flame-throwing Panzer IIIs burning out bunkers and trenches of Baksov's 67th Guards Division with their fearsome spurts of fire. Eight Russian tanks of the attached 245th Tank Regiment launched a counterattack, but five were knocked out. More tanks and assault guns from the attached 1440th Self-propelled Artillery Regiment challenged the Panzergrenadiers taking Hill 244.5.

The rest of the Elfte was also now in action, taking the smoking ruins of Cherkasskoye, and by nightfall, Schimmelmann's battle group igelt in some woods. Increasingly, the gepanzerte Gruppe was used as the division's spearhead, instead of more balanced Kampfgruppe as earlier. Four hundred Gefangene had been taken, primarily from the 196th Guards Rifle Regiment and the 611th Antitank Regiment in Cherkasskoye. Baksov's division, though reinforced, was shattered, the remnants escaping north to Col. V. G. Chernov's 90th Guards Rifle Division. The advance of the Gespensters now enabled Grossdeutschland to move ahead as well.

But fierce Russian air attacks, mines, and defensive fires had taken their toll, especially among aggressively leading officers. In Pz.Rgt.15 Oberlt. Hubertus Graf Strachwitz, son of GD's Oberst Graf Strachwitz, and Lt. Graf Schaesberg were badly wounded. With losses, 4. and 5. Kompanien were combined under Lt. Eberhard Schöne, and Leutnant Heinze took over 6.Kp. The commander of III.Abt./15, was killed, as was the adjutant, Oblt. Wagner. Hauptmann von Bülow took over the battalion. About 22,30 hours a shell hit an SPW of 3.Kp./110 in the Igel and the vehicle's gasoline flared up. That illuminated the other vehicles in the evening twilight for Russian aircraft, and soon high-explosive bombs set on fire two half-tracks used to tow 5cm Pak guns, and the fire spread to a third.[8]

To the right of XXXXVIII. Pz.K. was II.SS Panzerkorps under Obergruppenführer Paul Hausser, with 494 panzers including the Tiger companies and 95 assault guns, and a Nebelwerfer multiple rocket launcher brigade, in addition to its artillery and other assets. The three divisions struck abreast: 1.Leibstandarte SS Adolf Hitler under Standartenführer Theodor Wisch on the left, 2.SS Das Reich under Gruppenführer Walter Krüger in the center, and 3.SS Totenkopf under Brigadeführer Hermann Priess on the right. With the heavy Tigers in the lead, the SS smashed through Col. I. M. Nekrasov's 52nd Guards Rifle Division of the 23rd Guards Rifle Corps.

The LAH slugged through Bykovka east of the Vorskla almost to Yakovlevo, the DR drove through Berezov, and SS-T seized Gremuchi and flanked Yerik. Hausser had thrust some 20 kilometers (12 miles) through the Russian defenses by the evening of 5 July, but had lost some thirty panzers, including Tigers, to the mines and antitank gun positions. Normally when a panzer was disabled the crew bailed out. But with the heavily armored Tigers, the crews were ordered to remain aboard and give fire support with their powerful 8,8cm cannon.[9]

On 4. Pz.Armee's right flank Armee Abteilung Kempf, including forty-five Tigers of s.Pz.Abt.503 in III. Pz.K., made assault crossings of the Northern Donets River, across from Belgorod. Stymied by Red Army defenses in the northern sector, Gen. Werner Kempf then committed 6.Pz.Div. farther south where 19. and 7.Pz.Div. had established a bridgehead against the defending 7th Guards Army. But the penetration was not deep enough to carry out the division's mission of providing flank protection for the II.SS Pz.Korps advance.

On 6 July in the north Model's 9. Armee forces became embroiled in massive tank engagements west of Ponyri, while air battles dotted the skies with screaming engines barely heard above the din on the ground, and debris flaming down. Russian armor counterattacks mounted by Rokossovsky's Center Front were savaged, especially by the Tigers of the schwere Panzer-Abteilung 505.

In the south Hoth's 4. Pz.Armee resumed the offensive at midmorning of the 6th, after a fierce artillery bombardment, the concussions sweeping back in waves over the waiting German attackers. 3.Pz.Div. reached the Pena, though it found the abrupt and muddy riverbanks difficult to ford. As the course of the Pena was from the northeast before it turned northwest beyond Alekseevka, the XXXXVIII. Pz.K. axis of advance was now northeast, as separate Russian tank regiments of Lt. Gen. I. M. Chistiakov's 6th Guards Army began to mount counterattacks.

GD and the 11. Panzer forged ahead against the stubborn but disintegrating Russian infantry positions, Mickl's Elfte with the mission objective of the bridge across the Psel at Oboyan some 22 kilometers

(14 miles) ahead. But there was no breakthrough, as the GD advanced on Lukhanino and the 11.Pz.Div. on Syrtsev. Noted XXXXVIII. Pz.K. Ia Oberst von Mellenthin, "The entire area had been infested with mines; and the Russian defense along the whole line was supported by tanks operating with all the advantages of high ground." Indeed, now there was increased Russian tank fire in addition to the antitank fire. Grossdeutschland recorded, "Earth bunkers, deep positions with built-in flame-throwers, and especially well dug-in T-34s, excellently camouflaged, made the advance extremely difficult."[10]

Nonetheless Gespenster panzergrenadiers cleared Cherkasskoye and took Hill 246.0 to the east. Maj. Horst Lindner's Pz.Aufkl.Abt.11 Spähwagen flanked Dmitrievka on the Vorskalets, a western tributary of the Vorskla, while Hptm. Hans Schnur's Pi.Btl.209 cleared an antitank ditch. Abreast of Knobelsdorff's corps was Hausser's II.SS Pz.Korps; it made good progress, LAH driving through Yakovlevo toward Pokrovka and DR toward Luchki. But here also there was increased armor combat. Hausser had to employ Totenkopf along his right flank as elements of 167.Inf.Div. were trying to come up and A.A.Kempf was battling along the Northern Donets.

In the Russian flexible defense-in-depth concept, remnants of the forward infantry formations of Chistiakov's 6th Guards Army battered by Hoth's 4. Pz.Armee fell back—the 67th Guards Rifle Division to the 90th Guards Rifle Division in position behind the Pena, the 52nd Guards Rifle Division beyond the northern Vorskla. At the same time Vatutin had already ordered his Voronezh Front tank forces forward to counterattack the German spearheads; this comprised the three tank and mechanized corps of Lieutenant General Katukov's 1st Tank Army and the separate 2nd Guards and 5th Guards Tank Corps. At some 200 tanks each, a Russian tank corps roughly approximated a German panzer division's strength. Over 1,000 tanks—T-34s, T-70s, some KV-1s, and a few Lend-Lease English Churchills and American M3 General Lees—were in motion forward to stop Hoth's 4. Pz.Armee advance.

Overhead swarmed the bombers and fighters of both sides, attacking the dense concentrations of armor and gun positions. Hakenkreuz flag recognition panels were spread on the turret or back deck of the panzers when German planes appeared. The Germans had developed a ground-attack plane, the twin-engined Henschel Hs 129 with an automatic 3cm cannon. It was deadly, but armored and rather underpowered. Twin-engined He 111 and Ju 88 bombers were also used in a ground-attack role, especially dropping cluster bomb canisters (Splitterbomben, fragmentation bombs) which opened to release time- or impact-fused submunition bomblets. The SD-1 dispersed 360 1-kilogram bomblets, and the SD-2 dispersed 180 2-kilogram bomblets. Developed by 1939, they were devastating against Russian open-pit artillery, antiaircraft, and antitank crews.

It was about at this time that Oberleutnant Hans Ulrich Rudel demonstrated his Stuka Ju 87 as a ground-attack "tank-buster." A Staffelkapitän of 1.Staffel/Sturzkampfgeschwader 2 "Immelmann" (1st Squadron/Stuka Wing 2), Rudel came from a test unit on the Crimea with his Stuka armed with two Bordkanone (BK) 3,7cm Flak 18 semiautomatic cannon in detachable pods under the wings. Swooping down on the Russian tanks from behind where the engine compartments were vulnerable, "In the first attack four tanks explode under the hammer blows of my cannons [*sic*]; by the evening the total rises to twelve. We are all seized with a kind of passion for the chase from the glorious feeling of having saved much German bloodshed with every tank destroyed . . . the evil spell is broken, and in this aircraft we possess a weapon which can speedily be employed everywhere and is capable of dealing successfully with the formidable numbers of Soviet tanks." His Stuka became the Ju 87G "Kanonenvogel" (cannon bird), and he was authorized to form a Panzerjäger Staffel. With tungsten-cored 3,7cm rounds, the Stukas were potent tank-killers. The single-engined Stuka was also more maneuverable than the Hs 129.[11]

The Soviet Air Force too employed a ground-support plane, the armored Ilyushin Il-2 Shturmovik ("attack plane") armed with two 23mm automatic cannon and rockets or bombs. By October 1942 the Il-2m3 model was in production; it included a rear-seat gunner, which gave effective defense against German fighters. Built in great numbers, the Shturmovik became a formidable threat to the German panzers. Initially, however, the failure of the Soviet preemptive air strikes early on the 5th gave the Luftwaffe local air superiority over the Kursk battlefield. Concluded one historian, "A week passed before the VVS could reassert a strong air presence in the Belgorod-Kharkov sector."[12]

But Katukov's 1st Tank Army forces were taking up prepared defensive positions. Originally they were to mount counterattacks, with 6th Tank Corps under Maj. Gen. A. L. Getman and 3rd Mechanized Corps under Maj. Gen. S. M. Krivoshein pushing against XXXXVIII. Pz.K., with 31st Tank Corps under Maj. Gen. D. Kh. Chernienko in reserve. At the same time 2nd Guards Tank Corps under Maj. Gen. A. S. Burdeiny and 5th Guards Tank Corps under Maj. Gen. A. G. Kravchenko were to stop Hausser's II.SS Panzerkorps.

It became obvious, however, that Chistyakov's 6th Guards Army was unable to stem Hoth's 4. Pz.Armee attack, and a main line of resistance should be stabilized before mounting counterattacks. In addition, there were heavy tank losses as the tanks moved over the open ground, pulverized by Stuka and bomber airstrikes and, as they neared the battle area, German panzer and antitank gunfire and artillery fire.

Katukov urged that his tank forces simply move up into the prepared hull defilade positions of the second defensive belt, and Voronezh Front commander Vatutin approved this. Zhukov and Stalin were critical of this decision when they learned of it, wanting a more aggressive role for the armor; but they deferred to Vatutin, Marshal Vasilevsky, (chief of staff and Stavka representative with Voronezh Front), and Political Commissar at the Front Lt. Gen. Nikita Khrushchev, who were on-site. Katukov's tanks thus dug in. Lt. Walter Rahn, later Ordonnanz Offizier of Pz.Abt.52 (I.Abt./15) related, "Our Richtschützen had no chance. Of the enemy tanks they saw only the muzzle blasts, and were blinded by the rising sun."[13]

Many of von Lauchert's Panthers had been retrieved from the swamps and minefields and repaired, but still were not integrated into the Grossdeutschland's operations. The long L/70 7,5cm Kw.K.42 was accurate and powerful, engaging out to 3,000 meters, but the Panthers were vulnerable to infantry and antitank gun attack, especially on the flanks. These first models were the Ausführung D with no bow machine gun, though with a port through which an MG 34 could (awkwardly) be mounted. Its machine gun was in the turret, coaxially mounted with the main gun; but the gunner could only fire one or the other. (The later A and G models did have a hull ball-mounted machine gun like other panzers, and an external machine gun could also be mounted at the tank commander's hatch.)

The Gespensters of the 11. Panzer itself ground ahead through the Russian defenses, engaging now Krivoshein's 3rd Mechanized Corps, at 250 tanks the strongest of Katukov's three corps. Again the Germans demonstrated the teamwork borne of experience: calling in airstrikes through the Flivo, and calling in mortar and artillery fire missions through the VBs operating from a Panzer III or SPW, the panzers firing on point targets with their high-velocity guns and giving suppressive area coverage with their machine guns. This enabled the Panzergrenadieren to advance and eliminate antitank and machine-gun positions, and to cover the Pioniere clearing obstacles and passages through the minefields for the panzers.

This was intense tank battle, and panzer crews proved the value of their training. On a Panzer IV the Kommandant constantly scanned the terrain with his binoculars for targets to engage, giving his Feuerbefehl over the Bordfunk with type of ammunition and Zielanweisung (target direction), and estimated range in meters. A good Fahrer was always conscious of the undulations of terrain, sensing the best defilade if a fire command came, braking his 24-ton panzer smoothly so the optics were not left bouncing for the gunner. The Funker intently listened for radio messages through his earphones above the roar of the engine and transmitted as directed, and fired the bow MG 34 at infantry and antitank position threats.

The Richtschütze seated to the left of the cannon breech identified the target through his binocular double-optic sight, switched to main gun or coaxial MG, used his electrical power rocking foot pedal to traverse the turret—toe for right, heel for left—and then manipulated the manual traverse and elevation handwheels to precisely adjust on target with the range markings on the right reticle. The Ladeschütze, braced to the right, opened the breech and thrust in a round, and also fed the ammunition belts into the coaxial MG and cleared any stoppages. The gun was fired by a trigger, or the MG by foot pedal.

Kommandant: *"Panzergranate! Drei Uhr! Entfernung zweihundert! Links von der Hausecke!"* Richtschütze: *"Ziel erkannt!"* Kommandant: *"Schuss!"* Then: *"Volltreffer!"* ("Armor-piercing! Three o'clock! Range two hundred! Left of the house corner!" "Identified!" "Fire!" Then: "Direct hit!")[14] The crew heard the fire command through their headsets over their black Feldmütze, which had replaced the Schutzmütze. Their earphones muffled the ear-splitting *crack!* of the high-velocity gun fire to a dull thud. The panzer rocked back on its suspension, the gun flashed into recoil and rode back into battery, the concussion swept back over the turret top, and the hot shell casing clanged out onto the turret basket platform or into the casing bag, the shells tossed out a hatch when there was a chance. The Ladeschütze threw in a new round, tripping the extractors, with the sliding breech block slamming up into position again.

As an enemy tank might not explode into flame when hit, it was best to immediately fire a second round as the muzzle blast obscuration cleared, as the small penetration hole did not reflect the devastation to the crew inside. Faced with packs of T-34s when they swarmed over the landscape, the panzer had to blast one target and then shift to the next, all while the ventilator blower and the cordite fumes stung the eyes of the crew, and muscles were tensely knotted to exhaustion.

If a panzer threw a track or it was damaged by enemy fire or a mine—*"Besatzung! Ausbooten!"* ("Crew! Bail out!")—the crew would often laboriously repair it by breaking track, removing the damaged sections, winching the track over the return rollers with the front drive sprocket, and bolting on new sections. A panzer could also run on just one track, and even turn if on a hard surface, rapidly accelerating and pivoting on the dead road wheels. If a panzer was disabled, it could be towed by another panzer, crisscrossing the steel tow cables and slipping the ends over the hull tow pintles and hooks.

Sometimes the fighting among the hedges, fences, bushes, and small woods around the wooden houses of the village strongpoints was at close range. Here the Russian Panzerbüchse, antitank rifles, were "much feared," said Uffz. Kurt Nentwig. Well-trained Ivans would aim for the vision slits of the driver. The vision blocks had seven layers of thick glass, but still if hit sent splintered glass into the eyes of the driver, blinding him. They could also penetrate the side armor of the Panzer IV without Schürzen.

In earlier fighting at one village, the characteristic bang of a big 152mm cannon on an SU-152 was heard, and the 5. Kompanie Elften in their Panzer IIIs and IVs felt attacking the position would be suicide. Young Oblt. Graf Strachwitz ordered by radio that if no panzers would move, then each Unteroffizier should dismount their Kampfwagen and lead them by foot. Nentwig said he radioed back, *"Vormachen!"* ("Demonstrate that yourself first!")

By the 6th, with 5.Kp. down to five or six panzers operational of its twenty-two, the company lost another Pz.IV when Nentwig's Wagen was hit on the left side. In a cornfield with no panzergrenadiers, and unable to locate the Russian Pak, Nentwig ordered his Fahrer, *"Zurücksetzen!"* ("Backward!") But his Funker said, "The driver has bailed out!" "Let's bail out too!" Nentwig replied. The crew scrambled out—Nentwig with his Null Acht (Luger Pistole 08), though he forgot his camera—and met behind their panzer, and made their way across the field to a small valley, where the camp kitchen of A.A.11 had located forward. A year later, himself wounded, Nentwig met his runaway driver in the Sagan Kaserne. A splinter from their panzer when hit had destroyed his knee joint. "Panic is an excellent accelerating power!" Despite the resistance, the drive on Dubrova was "getting on forward well" noted Ia Kinitz in the KTB that 6 July.[15]

By the evening of the 6th Kampfgruppe Schimmelmann had penetrated the woods southeast of Dubrova. Pz.Rgt.15 reported it still had seventy-two panzers total: forty-eight Pz.IIIs and twenty-four Pz.IVs, as well as eight Flammpanzer IIIs. By contrast, Grossdeutschland, of its original 293 panzers, had only 33 panzers and 40–50 Panthers still einsatzbereit. A little later a tank with sloped armor and a long gun approached the Gespenster Kampfgruppe Igel "from the enemy's side" in the dusk. A Panzer IV of III. Abteilung on outpost fired and flamed it up at scarcely 100 meters. Tragically it was a Panther; the men had never seen one before. Only one of the five crew members bailed out.[16]

Despite the primary role of the panzers in the struggle, the Panzergrenadiere were also emboldened to deal with the numbers of Russian tanks, even those that were dug in, if they could neutralize the protecting infantry positions. Covered by the ripping sound of the squad "Zweibein" MG 42 and the explosions of the Granatwerfers, the panzergrenadiers crawled forward through the fields of sunflowers and wheat, and through the Maxim machine-gun fire. Then it was close combat in the Russian trenches, Handgranate and MPi against the PPSh *Avtomatchiki*, in areas where the panzers had not pivoted atop the trenches to mash the Russian defenders into the ground.

Although the rocket launcher RPzB. 43 "Ofenrohr" with its hollow-charge warhead was not yet available, the infantry and engineers did have the "exceptionally effective" magnetic hollow-charge grenade. There were several models, the Heft Hohlladung Granate 3 KG penetrating 110mm (4 inches) of steel or 500mm (20 inches) of reinforced concrete. To emplace this on a tank held by its three magnets, or to position it on a Russian bunker, was very close combat, and reflected the intensity of the Kursk fighting.[17]

To the right on the 6th the Waffen-SS divisions surged ahead. Leibstandarte pounded through the 51st Guards Rifle Division to take Yakovlevo and Pokrovka, while Das Reich took Luchki "South" to its right. Russian tanks charged head-on into the LAH Tigers' guns and were wrecked. These were the separate Kravchenko's 5th Guards and Burdeiny's 2nd Guards Tank Corps from Voronezh reserve. They counterattacked over the open according to their original orders; Katukov would seem to have been vindicated in having his 1st Tank Army take up defensive defilade positions instead. Other tank forces from across the Donets were repulsed, largely by the Luftwaffe's ground-attack Hs 129s and Focke-Wulf 190s.

As Hausser punched through the 6th Guards Army defenses, Katukov deployed Chernienko's 31st Tank Corps from reserve to Hausser's left flank. Two motorized infantry regiments were thrown into the gap. "After two hours all that was left of them was their numbers," recorded Maj. Gen. N. K. Popel, the Military Council Commissar with 1st Tank Army. Reconnaissance elements of the LAH raced another 12 kilometers (7 miles) to seize the Luchki "North" and Teterevino villages to the north, though these were up the Prokhorovka road to the north*east*, not the Oboyan axis to the north*west*.[18] Totenkopf fought eastward toward the Lipovyi Donets River attempting to link up with A.A. Kempf forces pressing up the Northern Donets against the 7th Army. On 7 July in the north the bitter struggle for Ponyri continued unabated, and Model's forces had an equally bloody struggle trying to take the Olkhovatka ridge, as Rokossovsky threw in his reserves.

In the south XXXXVIII. Pz.Korps drove north to intersect the Belgorod-Oboyan Rollbahn to Kursk, Grossdeutschland on the left, 11. Panzerdivision on the right. The Gespenster drive was again led by the gepanzerte Gruppe: Pz.Rgt.15, Stu.Gesch.Abt.911, I.Btl./Pz.G.R.110, and the gep. Zug in half-tracks of Pz.Pi.Btl.209. Pz.Jäg.Abt.61 supported II.Btl./Pz.G.R.111. Then A.A.11, II./15, and 111 crossed the Rollbahn and swung north through minefields, swamp areas, and Russian fire. Despite their heavy losses, the Germans controlled the battlefield, and were able to recover and repair their panzers amid the smoldering wrecks of Russian T-34s. Some 300 panzers including Tigers and up to forty Panthers churned ahead. Shattered though their forces were, the Ivans continued to put up stubborn resistance, and minefields took their toll. The Russians sometimes claimed knocking out Tigers, but in many cases these were Panzer IVs—a misidentification explained by the apprehension about the new heavy panzers, and the boxlike appearance of the Pz.IVs with Schürzen around their turrets and on their flanks (3. and 11.Pz.Div. had no Tigers).

Nonetheless the drive picked up momentum, but that afternoon the GD was stopped at Syrtsevo on the Pena by heavy defensive fire and counterattacking Russian tanks. "However, on the right wing we seemed within reach of a big victory," related the Panzerkorps Ia, Oberst Mellenthin. "The grenadier regiment of Grossdeutschland was reported to have reached Werchopenje [Verkhopenye]." This was several kilometers up the Rollbahn, and a Kampfgruppe was improvised to exploit this and advance to Hill 260.08, just short of Novoselovka. But when this force reached Gremuchy, they found the grenadiers consolidating their position: "The grenadiers were under the illusion that they were in Nowosselowka and could not believe they were only in Gremutshy . . . things like that happen in every war and particularly in Russia."[19] Just in the southern sector villages there were at least two Gremuchys, two Luchkis, two Novoselovkas, and two Teterevinos, complicated by inaccuracies on some maps and inventive German transliterations from the Cyrillic alphabet characters.

The new Russian force at Syrtsevo was the 112th Tank Brigade of Major General Getman's 6th Tank Corps, ordered by Katukov to extend eastward across the Pena to support Krivoshein's battered 3rd Mechanized Corps. It included the new Soviet assault gun, the SU-122, a stubby 122mm howitzer on a T-34 chassis. On the 8th GD, stymied at Syrtsevo, flanked through Gremuchy to Verkhopenye. The 11.Pz.Div. advanced astride the Oboyan Rollbahn, 110 on the left side, 111 on the right, and pushed ahead 6 kilometers. They made contact with the LAH north of Pokrovka, those units quickly recognized by the green-splotched Waffen-SS summer Tarnjacke camouflage smocks and helmet covers. Grenadierregiment 339 of 167.Inf.Div. came up behind, occupying Pokrovka. But, noted the KTB, "The attack only slowly goes forward, since the opponent occupies the high ground with strong tank forces and remains dug in." Up to forty Russian tanks were engaged at a time.[20]

Despite the concentration of Russian forces on the left flank west of the Pena, Knobelsdorff on the night of the 8th nonetheless ordered the Elfte and the GD to initially drive straight ahead up the Oboyan road, and take the commanding Hill 260.8. On 9 July the battle groups moved out, Grossdeutschland's on the left of the Rollbahn, 11.Panzer's on the right. Strachwitz and von Lauchert had a mixed force of some ten Tigers, ten Panthers, and nineteen Pz.IVs, and Schimmelmann had twenty-six Panzer IIIs and thirteen IVs as well as five Flammpanzers and six Hummels. They were engaging "Panzerrudel" (tank packs) of twenty to forty T-34s and the new SU-122s of Krivoshein's 3rd Mechanized Corps. But Hptm. Edel Lingenthal's II./Pz.Rgt.15 rolled up the Rotarmisten flank from the east and the Gespensters seized Hill 260.8, and then pushed on to Novoselovka with Hans Rudels's Stukas striking hard ahead. From the hill, the highest point up the Rollbahn, the spires of Oboyan could be made out with field glasses, 20 kilometers (12 miles) ahead. It was now the deepest penetration of ZITADELLE, 20 kilometers, and the Gespensters were halfway to Oboyan and the Psel.[21]

But Grossdeutschland was then to swing west behind the Russian forces on the Pena, as Westhoven's 3.Pz.-Div., which finally crossed the Pena north of Alekseevka by the 10th, advanced on Beresovka. The 11.Pz.-Div. was to block the Rollbahn to the north, and 332.Inf.-Div. of LII. A.K. was to provide flank protection to the west. Maj. Horst Lindner's A.A.11 probed to the northeast, covering Grossdeutschland's movement. With Luftwaffe attacks and the firepower of artillery and Strachwitz's panzers, the GD finally secured Hill 243 north of Verkhopenye and Hill 247 south of Kruglik on the 10th. Strachwitz himself was badly injured when he fell behind the breech of the gun in his panzer just as it fired, the recoiling breech slamming back and crushing his arm and shoulder. After Hptm. von Wietersheim took over, von Knobelsdorff sent Oberst Decker from XXXXVIII. Pz.K. Hauptquartier to assume command of GD's panzer "brigade" (GD's Pz.Rgt. and Decker's "10.Pz.Brig." of Lauchert's "Regiment").[22]

Alone, the Gespensters could not advance farther, and Novoselovka marked the extent of the offensive for XXXXVIII. Pz.-Korps, short of Oboyan on the Psel. On the 10th Oberst Henze's 110 on the left, with Lindner's A.A.11 Spähwagen and Lingenthal's panzers of II./15, did take Hill 232.8, which gave good observation for the artillery, by 15,30 hours. On the right 111 fended off tank attacks. Exhaustion was setting in. Panzer crews catnapped as they could, in or often under their panzer, which provided shelter from artillery shrapnel and the heat of the sun or rain. But if the ground was sodden from the frequent thunderstorms, there was a risk the panzer might sink lower and crush them.

Panzergrenadiere or Pioniere might seek the same, but if the driver was not alerted the vehicle might begin to move. In the open, they dug their Erdlöcher, covering them with a Zeltbahn (shelter quarter) against the elements. Mess crews tried to get Kaffee and even meals up to the front units, but more often the Landsers had only their Eiserne Portion (iron rations): a can of compressed meat, a biscuit, and a tin of Schokakola pieces (dark chocolate with caffeine). To heat rations there was a little Eisbitkocher (fuel tablet stove)—"which we never had," said Lt. von Fersen.[23]

Casualties were heavy. The attached leichte Sturmgeschütz-Abteilung 911 lost its adjutant, Oberlt. Jesse, wounded on the first day (4 July), and battalion Kommandeur Oberstlt. Georg Wilhelm was badly injured when a Geschütz (gun) of 2.Batterie ran over him on the 6th (dying on the 14th). Oblt. Brandt commanding 3.Battr. was wounded on the 7th, Oblt. Wolfgang Müller, Chef of 2.Battr., was killed on the 8th, and Oblt. Schulte-Strathaus, Chef of 1.Battr. and acting Abteilungsführer, on that same day was wounded for his seventh time. Twenty-one were killed and ninety-seven wounded that July at Kursk. Le.Stu.G.Abt.911 was put under Oberst Graf Schimmelmann's Pz.-Rgt.15, but the assault gun batteries worked best with A.A.11's SPWs and Kradschützen and with Pz.Gren.Rgt.111.[24]

In addition, there seems to have been some Gespenster dissatisfaction with General Mickl's command style. The regimental and battalion commanders were used to operating with "loose reins" and using their own initiative. The Div.-Kdr. was often up front and corps orders were received by the Ia at the Div.-Gef.-Std. But Mickl then wanted clarification, which caused delays, and the unit commanders found him intervening in operations that were underway. In a photograph of this time the general is up front, helping his men pushing a motorcycle up a muddy embankment—though his sunglasses and clean uniform suggest the photo was staged.[25]

To the east Leibstandarte and Das Reich drove 5th Guards Tank Corps beyond Teterevino and up the Prokhorovka road on 7 July. But this was divergent, and on the 8th the LAH was turned northwest to link up with 11. Panzer, pounding 31st Tank Corps back from Greznoe and thrusting toward the Psel. The Russians did evade a possible flanking maneuver by Leibstandarte. At the same time, Totenkopf was being relieved of its right flank role by 167.Inf.Div., SS-T coming up on Leibstandarte's left. But Vatutin shifted the 10th Tank Corps and the 5th Guards Tank Corps from the Prokhorovka axis around to the Oboyan sector to block this drive.

Nonetheless Russian tank forces to the east advanced to the attack from along the Lipovyi Donets near Nepkhaevo. This was a brigade of Burdeiny's 2nd Guards Tank Corps, which had already been battered in earlier fighting. Totenkopf's panzer regiment was still in the vicinity and engaged them. More dramatically, Luftwaffe reconnaissance sighted them, and four Staffels from IV. Gruppe of 9. Schlachtgeschwader (Ground-Attack Wing) of Hs 129 "tank buster" aircraft as well as Fw 190s swarmed over them smashing them with bombs, rockets, and cannon fire. Some fifty of sixty tanks were claimed knocked out by air *alone*, and the Russian thrust was repulsed.[26]

On the 9th Totenkopf and the LAH rolled through the remnants of the Russian 3rd Mechanized and 3rd Tank Corps, reaching the Psel River bend, and on the 10th SS-T panzergrenadiers secured a crossing at Krasnyi Oktyabr and took Hill 226.6 east of Kliuchi. But to the right up the Prokhorovka road, Das Reich was confronting new and powerful Russian forces. As this was the direction from which fresh Russian troops would be arriving, late on the 9th Hoth issued new orders for Hausser's II.SS Pz.Korps to change direction from the Oboyan axis now to the northeast toward Prokhorovka. Luftwaffe efforts were to be altered as well. The Schwerpunkt was with Teddy Wisch's 1. Leibstandarte, with Priess's 3.Totenkopf astride the Psel to the left and Krüger's 2.Das Reich on the right flank.

The new Russian forces had been released by Stalin and Stavka on 6 July as the extent and direction of Manstein's assault in the south became clear. The Red Army troops arrayed included 2nd Tank Corps from Southwest Front and the 10th Tank Corps from Konev's Reserve (designated Steppe Front on 10 July), as well as Lt. Gen. P. A. Rotmistrov's 5th Guards Tank Army including 5th Guards Mechanized Corps and 29th and 18th Tank Corps. Some 904 tanks and 58 self-propelled assault guns were entering into the battle. On 9 July Lt. Gen. A. S. Zhadov's 5th Guards Army was released from Steppe Military District with the 32nd Guards and 33rd Guards Rifle Corps, 10th Tank Corps having been released earlier. Other antitank, tank, and artillery brigades and regiments reinforced Vatutin's forces.

In Knobelsdorff's XXXXVIII. Pz.K. sector 3.Pz.Div. was to take over Grossdeutschland's positions so the GD could rejoin the 11.Pz.Div. in the drive north up the Oboyan axis. In Guderian's report to OKH of 17 July, he noted that of von Lauchert's 200 Panthers, only ten were operational on 10 July. Due to enemy action and mechanical failure twenty-five were total losses, one hundred were in need of repair (fifty-six damaged by hits and mines and forty-four by mechanical breakdown), forty were returning from repair, and some twenty-five had not yet been recovered.[27]

With the three Waffen-SS divisions reoriented northeast on the Prokhorovka axis, and with no end of Russian defenses and reinforcements in sight, there was no longer any optimism about a breakthrough to Kursk. It was also obvious that in the north, Model's 9. Armee offensive had stalemated. On that same 10 July, it was learned that British and American forces, fresh from victory in North Africa, had invaded the Italian island of Sicily in the Mediterranean, the stepping-stone to Mussolini's Fascist Italy.

CHAPTER EIGHTEEN

ZITADELLE: The Russian Counteroffensive

GENERAL DER PANZERTRUPPEN OTTO VON KNOBELSDORFF'S XXXXVIII. Panzerkorps regrouped to renew the advance up the road to Oboyan on the Psel on 11 July, and Obergruppenführer Paul Hausser's II.SS Panzerkorps prepared to advance up the Prokhorovka road. The new Russian forces were positioning to block the advance and to mount a counteroffensive against the flanks of Hoth's penetration. The 10th Tank Corps and 5th Guards Tank Corps moved around to the west of the Oboyan sector behind Katukov's depleted 3rd Mechanized and 31st Tank Corps; 5th Guards Army took position along the Psel and 5th Guards Tank Army moved to attack positions around Prokhorovka on the east.

On 10 July, while Priess's 3.Totenkopf established a bridgehead north of the Psel, SS Panzergrenadier-Regiment 2 of the Leibstandarte drove remnants of 2nd Tank Corps from the Komsomolets Sovkhoz (state farm) and Hill 241.6 on the Prokhorovka axis. Vatutin intended Rotmistrov to attack on the 12th, but Hausser struck first, launching his assault the day before. Having reoriented his LAH for the drive to the northeast, at 05,00 hours on 11 July Wisch jumped off with his SS Pz.Gren.Rgt.2,, soon joined by SS Pz.G.R.1. led by Tiger panzers, astride the Prokhorovka road and parallel the railroad embankment. Das Reich's Pz.G.R. Deutschland protected the right flank. The sky was overcast, but the Stukas and artillery smashed into the Russian positions. The panzergrenadiers fought their way up Hill 252.2, captured the Oktyabrskii Sovkhoz, and reached Prokhorokov station. The LAH armor strength was down to ninety panzers, assault guns, and tank destroyers, including four Tigers, and by evening the unit reported sixty-three einsatzbereit.[1]

The decisive day of battle at Prokhorovka would be 12 July, which dawned warm, humid, and cloudy. The stage was being set for what some have considered the greatest tank battle in history, a dramatic clash between Hitler's elite Waffen-SS and Rotmistrov's 5th Guards Tank Army, which in many ways has come to epitomize the epic Battle of Kursk: "Some 1,500 tanks and assault guns were racing, firing, exploding, burning, thundering, and smoking on that minute sea of hills and valleys around Prokhorovka," according to one writer. Yet this may be vastly misleading.[2]

As the day opened Hausser resumed his advance, Totenkopf primarily north of the Psel, and Das Reich south of the railroad embankment intending to link up with III.Pz.K. of Armee Abteilung Kempf advancing up the branches of the Donets. At 06,50 hours on the 12th Leibstandarte advanced in the center south of the Psel and astride the railroad embankment, a width of some 7 kilometers (4 miles). Then a violet smoke signal was seen, and then more and more flares wafted into the air: tank warning! Indeed, packs of Russian tanks emerged from the woodlands, wheatfields, sunflower patches, hedges, hamlets, and balkas and swarmed to meet the German advance head-on, while artillery concentrations and Katyusha rocket barrages pounded the W-SS forces.

But it was *not* two armored forces charging each other. German panzers might fire Sprenggranate shells on the move, but they stopped to fire accurate Panzergranate rounds at point targets. Tank after Russian tank was knocked out, many exploding and the crew bailing out on fire, but still the Rotarmisten tanks came on, firing on the move at random. As the range closed, it became a melee in which the Red tanks might hit the more vulnerable flanks of even the heavy Tigers. The German crews couldn't load, traverse, and fire their guns fast enough to engage all the targets at ranges down to 100 meters, particularly with the field now shrouded in dust and smoke. It was not a uniform Russian charge over a flat field, but rather a series of tank duels fought throughout the undulating landscape. Ivan infantry rode their tanks as long as they could, then dropped off to fight the SS panzergrenadiers.

All German accounts reflect their amazement at the frantic assaults and chaos of vicious, close-quarter fighting. "They were around us, on top of us, and between us," related Untersturmführer Gührs. "We fought man-to-man, jumping out of our foxholes to lob our magnetic hollow-charge grenades at the enemy tanks, leaping on our Schützenpanzerwagens to take on any enemy vehicle or man we spotted. It was hell!" Leibstandarte's Tagesmeldung reported the Russian tanks "drove at high speed," and claimed over forty tanks destroyed "im Nahkampf" (close combat).[3]

As Rotmistrov's tank corps charged over the terrain, all the defects of the T-34/76 tank were made abundantly clear. Having no radios except for the company commander's tank, each lurched forward like a mindless beast. With the four-man crew, the tank commander, doubling as gunner, either tried to command his tank through limited optics (the heavy turret hatch opened *forward*, blocking his hatch-rim view) and was unable to fire the main gun or the coaxial machine gun, or he tried to locate and engage targets through the bouncing gunner's sights while moving, unable to scan the terrain, with the driver simply plowing ahead.

As there was no rotating turret basket floor—the seats attached to struts—the loader had to pull rounds from the floor boxes while stumbling around and over the matting cover and empty shell casings, to follow the breech of the traversing gun mount. An avalanche of unaimed rounds was fired in the general direction of the enemy. The driver sat on a hard bench, having to use a mallet to pound the gearshift, barely able to sense the terrain irregularities through the vision slit as the tank rocked forward. The assistant driver braced himself while spraying bullets ahead from the bow machine gun.

Some tanks now had the 9-R radio transmitter-receiver installed, the antenna on the right front, and a circular commander's cupola with vision blocks for 360-degree vision; but most T-34s just raced forward, vaguely orienting on the company commander's tank (until hit) or in the perceived direction of the enemy. One German unit had equipped itself with captured T-34s: 2.SS Das Reich, with a company of eighteen on 4 July, prominently displaying the German Balkenkreuz insignia. The first thing Das Reich did upon receiving the tanks was to install radios.

Russian infantry who rode the T-34s in the charge hardly had a chance to fire their PPSh submachine guns while clinging on to the turret and hull handrails of the bucking tank. Many tanks dropped out, not from being hit, but simply with mechanical problems. The diesel engines were good, but the transmissions were primitive with poor steel in the friction clutches. The electrical power traverse of the turret had a weak motor heavily overloaded, and with a tank commander/gunner unable to scan for and simultaneously engage targets, a panzer could fire three to four rounds for every one of the T-34's aimed rounds, especially if the panzer could maneuver beyond the field of vision, stop, and fire again. Knocked-out tanks littered the battlefield, many on fire and exploding, especially if a German shell detonated the ammunition or hit the cylindrical extra fuel tanks many T-34s carried on their flanks. But shells kept streaking across the terrain, some bound to hit somewhere, and more and more tanks kept surging ahead.[4]

The blind confusion of the Russian tankers was reflected by SS-Rottenführer Johannes Bräuer as the Russian tanks encountered an antitank ditch too late to stop, some slamming into the far side. "In an instant we were hemmed in by T-34s which were firing wildly in all directions, some even ramming each other. While many tanks were exploding in flames . . . new T-34s kept coming over the ridge, racing down the slope and turning over in the tank ditch behind which we were assembled."[5]

Overhead intense aerial dogfights filled the skies with flashing wings, explosions, and tumbling planes arcing to the ground, streaming smoke trails before impacting. Black, oily clouds of smoke from burning wrecks of tanks billowed skyward. In the afternoon thunderstorms and mutual exhaustion saw the two sides separate. The panzer retrievers and medical teams began to work on the armored and human wreckage.

The Russian tactic of charging for close-quarter fighting had been deliberate. As Rotmistrov had explained to Vatutin and Vasilevsky at the Voronezh Front headquarters at Oboyan on 10 July, the best way to defeat the Tigers and Ferdinands with their thick frontal armor and long-range 8,8cm guns was to close rapidly, and to attack their flanks. "In other words," understood Vatutin, "engage in hand-to-hand fight and board them." The German advance had indeed been thwarted, but the tactic of charging the Fritzes was an expensive experiment, scarcely to be repeated. It was better to ambush the enemy attack at close range from the ravines and hull-down defilade positions, as Katukov had done. Fully half the Russian tank force committed had been wrecked, though it was soon replaced. The LAH alone claimed 192 Soviet tanks destroyed, while the whole SS corps lost 60–70 armored vehicles on the 12th.

One definitive source calculates 572 Russian and German tanks and assault guns (not 1,500) were involved in the Prokhorovka battle on 12 July. This included 172 of the LAH and DR, and some 400 from the three Russian tank corps directly involved: 18th and 29th Tank Corps of Rotmistrov's 5th Guards Tank Army, and the weakened remnants of 2nd Tank Corps. On the actual battlefield—the corridor between the Psel and the railroad embankment—another source concludes that 583 were engaged: LAH with only 63 panzers including 4 Tigers, against 520 of Rotmistrov's 18th and 29th Tank Corps and other elements. The LAH lost 17 panzers including 1 Tiger, while Rotmistrov lost at least 160 tanks that day.[6]

Rotmistrov's 5th Guards Mechanized Corps had to be diverted to where Priess's Totenkopf pierced Lt. Gen. A. S. Zhadov's 5th Guards Army north of the Psel. Burdeiny's 2nd Guards Tank Corps was wrecked attacking Standartenführer Sylvestr "Vestl" Stadler's Der Führer Regiment of Das Reich, even as Generalleutnant Gustav Schmidt's 19.Pz.Div. of III.Pz.K. in Armeeabteilung Kempf advanced from the south.

Even if the Germans would be increasingly (and fatally) outnumbered, at least three famous German "aces" emerged at this time. SS Untersturmführer Michael "Michel" Wittmann commanded 3.Zug of 13.Kompanie (Tiger) of the LSSAH at Prokhorovka, and claimed thirty Russian tanks destroyed at Kursk. (The practice was to paint rings around the gun barrel to indicate enemy tank victims.) Wittmann would go on to become the most well-known "tank ace" of the war, claiming some 138 enemy tanks destroyed before being killed in his Tiger in Normandy, 8 August 1944. The top "Panzerheld" (hero) would be Uffz. Kurt Knispel of s.Pz.Abt. (Tiger) 503 with A.A.Kempf. He was ultimately credited with over 168 tanks destroyed before he was killed in Czechoslovakia 28 April 1945. In the skies over the battle Lt. Erich "Bubi" Hartmann, flying his Bf 109G of 7.Staffel, Jagdgeschwader 52 (7 Squadron, Fighter Wing 52), increased to fifty his number of enemy planes shot down. As a "Fliegerheld" he would become the most famous air ace of the war, with a claim of 352 planes downed—and he would survive.

Dramatic perhaps as was the meeting engagement at Prokhorovka, the more direct drive on Kursk was by Knobelsdorff's XXXXVIII. Pz.Korps up the Oboyan axis of advance. While Hörnlein's Grossdeutschland had swung west to assist Westhoven's 3.Pz.Div. across the Pena on the 10th, the 11. Panzer had covered the movement and, after taking Hill 232.2, remained poised to drive up the Oboyan Rollbahn beyond Novoselovka. That evening a surprise night attack by II./Pz.Gren.Rgt.111 was planned to further expand a defensive position. But when orderly officers went forward they couldn't find the battalion, which had been fired on by the neighboring SS-T troops to the right. The battalion had crossed an iron ore deposit, not uncommon in the area, and the magnetic compass needles had deviated 30 degrees.[7]

At 06,25 hours on 11 July Henze's Pz.Gren. Rgt.110 reported Russian tanks infiltrating the gorge near Malinovka. With the heavy overcast a Stuka strike would be difficult. At 07,45 General Mickl ordered an attack by Schimmelmann's Pz.Rgt.15 and elements of Maj. Arnold Kessler's Pz.Jäg.Abt.61. But the soaked ground and approach inclines of over 11 percent brought objections from Graf Schimmelmann. Instead, other units came up and the panzers extended to defensive positions on the right flank on the northern edge of a woodland to the east. Heavy tank and Pak fire to the left indicated strong Russian forces.

Ahead up the Oboyan road was Hill 244.8, strongly held, and Russian attacks from here overran a company of Boelsen's Pz.Gren.Rgt.111. But a Soviet command group of 10th Tank Corps, including its deputy commander, was intercepted. Documents captured revealed its attack plans against XXXXVIII. Pz.Korps' western flank.[8] An attack against Hill 244.8 failed, but farther to the right a thrust reached toward Orlovka, less than 5 kilometers from the Psel. The Russian tank and vehicle columns moving west were the 5th Guards Tank Corps.

On the night of 11/12 July Grossdeutschland moved back to the Oboyan road sector as it was relieved by 3.Pz.Div. in stages. In turn, the 332. and 255. Infanterie-Divisionen of General d. Inf. Eugen Ott's LII.A.K. extended the left flank northward. But heavy artillery fire that night in the 3.Panzer sector was foreboding: "Their fears—alas—came true," related panzer corps Chef des Stabes Oberst von Mellenthin, "for that very night the 3rd Panzer Division was thrown out of its forward positions." In the morning of the 12th heavy Russian tank attacks drove the 332.I.D. from Beresovka back to the Pena, and drove 3.Pz.Div. off Hill 247 and back to Verkhopenye.[9] Grossdeutschland would have to postpone the Oboyan Angriff.

The Elften were also attacked by Russian tanks on the 12th, the Ivans riding on board clinging to the handrails, until they jumped off to go into action or were shot off by 11. Panzer guns. "The opponent threw himself during the night along the entire front with tanks and infantry up to the HKL," messaged 11.Panzer to corps. "Around 04,30 he attacked the left flank, around 05,00 against the right flank." II.Btl./111 apparently broke, but restored their position in a counterattack with panzers. Nonetheless panzergrenadier companies scarcely had twenty to thirty men and Pz.Rgt.15 was down to thirty-four panzers (twenty-three IIIs, eleven IVs), and so Mickl received permission to fall back for a more stable defense and restore contact with Totenkopf.[10]

It was on the same night of 11–12 July that on the far right of Manstein's offensive that 6.Pz.Div. of A.A.Kempf seized a crossing of the Northern Donets at Rzhavets by *coup de main*, closing the gap toward Hausser's SS Panzerkorps. But on the 12th Vatutin mounted his fierce counterattack at Prokhorovka, and Rotmistrov formed a group from 2nd Guards Tank and 5th Guards Mechanized Corps under his deputy Maj. Gen. K. G. Trufanov that attacked and effectively blocked Kempf's advance.

The attacks on the Oboyan axis were also the result of Vatutin's attacks on the 12th, simultaneous if not necessarily coordinated. The attacks on the western flank were mounted by Maj. Gen. A. G. Kravchenko's 5th Guards Tank Corps against the 332.Inf.Div. and Maj. Gen. V. G. Burkov's 10th Tank Corps against 3.Pz.Div. The Russian units were reinforcements from the Voronezh (5th Corps) and Steppe (10th Corps) Fronts, respectively. The 6th Tank Corps and 22nd Guards Rifle Corps, fought out, were pulled back into reserve. The 11.Panzer was attacked by badly battered but still-determined elements driven forward from 23rd Guards Rifle Corps of Chistyakov's 6th Guards Army, and Krivoshein's 3rd Mechanized Corps and Chernienko's 31st Tank Corps of Katukov's 1st Tank Army, joined by the fresh 32nd Guards Rifle Corps led by Maj. Gen. A. I. Rodimtsev of Zhadov's 5th Guards Army from Konev's Steppe Front.

On the afternoon of 13 July Knobelsdorff appeared at the Gef.Std.of Grossdeutschland and ordered Hörnlein, who was to rejoin the 11.Pz.Div. for the advance to Oboyan, to instead counterattack back to the west again to assist the 3.Pz.Div., "which left no hope for any advance to the north," realized Ia Mellenthin.[11] Of the some three hundred original panzers (350 with assault guns), GD's panzer brigade under Decker now had only forty-seven: twenty Panzer IIIs and IVs, two Tigers, and twenty-five Panthers under von Lauchert.[12]

While 11. Panzer was buffeted by Russian attacks, with Schimmelmann's panzers and the Sturmgeschützen supporting the panzergrenadiers, Grossdeutschland attacked the flank of 10th Tank Corps, enabling Westhoven's 3.Pz.Div. to hold Beresovka. On 14 July the GD attacked again, retaking Hill 243.0 and regaining contact with 3. Panzer north of

Beresovka. This reestablished the left flank of XXXXVIII. Pz.K., but the GD was in no condition to renew the advance to the north alongside the Elfte. Pionier-Lehr-Btl.1 was attached to Boelsen's Pz.G.R.111 to firm up an HKL, and Hptm. Heinz Bödicker's 209 engineers laid minefields. "Waves of attackers against the entire division sector," reported the Ic to XXXXVIII. Pz.K. Ic, "supported by some 50 tanks, led to breakthroughs, which were counterattacked."[13]

To the east Das Reich attacked to link up with 19.Pz.Div. of A.A.Kempf, but the Russians stubbornly resisted. On 13 July Hitler summoned his two army group commanders, von Manstein of Süd and von Kluge of Mitte, back to his Wolfsschanze headquarters at Rastenburg. There Hitler declared that ZITADELLE must be called off immediately, as the Westmächte (Western Powers) had landed in Sicily on the 10th and the Italians were not fighting at all. With the next step a landing in the Balkans or in lower Italy, forces must be taken from the Ostheer. He was also concerned about the Russian buildup along the Donets–Mius front in the south, and the attack on Model's Orel sector the day before, the 12th, which forced Model to divert some of his attack forces to his eastern flank.

Kluge was concerned that the attacks of Colonel Generals Vasiliy Sokolovsky's West and Markian Popov's Bryansk Front—assaults that were spreading against Generaloberst Rudolf Schmidt's 2.Pz.Armee as well—signified a major counteroffensive, and he was in agreement with Hitler. Manstein (who had a sarcastic sign—"What would the Führer say to it?"—behind his desk in his Befehlszug, command train headquarters) disagreed. He felt that Hoth had penetrated the third and last major belt of defenses of the Kursker Bogen, and to halt now meant *"Sieg verschenkte!"* ("Victory would be given away!") 4.Pz.Armee's armor strength totaled 450 armored fighting vehicles: II.SS Pz.K. had four Pz.IIs, eighty Pz.IIIs, sixty-nine Pz.IVs, three Tigers, thirty command panzers, eleven (captured) T-34s, and sixty-four assault guns; XXXXVIII. Pz.K. had forty-two Pz.IIIs, fifty-six Pz.IVs, forty-three Panthers, six Tigers, twelve Flammpanzers, and forty assault guns.

In addition, Manstein had ordered his army group reserve, XXIV. Pz.Korps, comprising ninety-seven panzers in 23.Pz.Div. and 5.SS Wiking Pz.Gren.Div., under Genlt. Walther Nehring, to move up from Kharkov to Belgorod. Nehring had been Rommel's experienced DAK commander until the former was wounded. Behind Mackensen's 1.Pz.Armee along the Donets-Mius front were 17.Pz.Div. and 16.Pz. Gren.Div. The Feldmarschall argued strongly for continuing the offensive.[14]

Hitler would only concede that Manstein might continue to cripple Russian operational reserves, in order to facilitate the withdrawal of the German forces. That same evening Manstein ordered Hausser and Kempf to attack to pinch off the Russian forces in the gap between them but the Russians had withdrawn. GD and 3.Pz.Div. were consolidating the western flank. But Hitler refused the commitment of XXIV. Pz.Korps, and on the 17th OKH ordered II.SS Panzerkorps withdrawn for transportation to Italy. The next day two divisions, including Grossdeutschland, were transferred from Manstein to von Kluge's H.Gr. Mitte. Any disabled equipment that could not be retrieved was to be destroyed.

It is hard to see how Manstein was defining "victory." Certainly there was little point in slugging on toward Kursk. Model's 9.Armee offensive as the northern "pincer" had been aborted, and there was no "Kessel" of Russian forces to be trapped. Further advance simply meant more casualties, at a time when it was realized that Red Army forces were building up on the flanks. Nor would Russian reserves be exhausted. For, as Manstein admitted, they were fighting a Hydra: "that for each head cut off two new ones appeared to grow."[15] Perceptive officers sensed that the Russians were skillfully enmeshing the German panzer forces in the intricate defenses, and preparing their own counteroffensive "backhand."

Now was the time when Manstein, the master of *mobile* warfare, might extricate his panzer units and prepare a mobile defense against the anticipated Russian operations, not churn farther ahead in a struggle of attrition they were bound to lose. ZITADELLE was indeed a "fiasco," the "swan song of the German armored force," as Marshal Konev put it. Kursk was not a demonstration of tactical armored finesse, but rather an exercise of attrition warfare, and the techniques of breeching fortified positions. In addition, the German commanders seemed so focused on Kursk—as at Stalingrad—as to not be fully cognizant of the threatening Soviet buildup looming on the flanks.

Regarding the Russian defense measures, XXXXVIII. Pz.K. Chef des Stabes Oberst von Mellenthin later offered his analysis. The Red Army adopted the German Pakfront concept, in which as many as ten antitank guns were grouped under a single command to concentrate fire, the groups in depth "to draw the attacking armor into a web of enfilade fire." The Rotarmisten fortified these Pakfronts with minefields or antitank ditches. Camouflage and fire discipline at optimum ranges enhanced their effectiveness. For armor to penetrate these defenses, Mellenthin said the Panzerkeil (armored wedge) was replaced with the Panzerglocke (armored bell), which placed super-heavy panzers in the center, medium panzers on the flanks in an arch, and light panzers behind the center ready for pursuit.

Just behind the forward panzers were the commander, artillery and air forward observers, and engineers in half-tracks to clear mines and obstacles. The close cooperation of all arms and continuous radio communication was essential. Mellenthin also commented on the stoicism of the Russian soldiers, making them insensible to losses, and the rigid adherence of commanders to their orders.[16] This was beginning to change, however, as Stalin gained confidence in his rising commanders and their abilities, allowing more initiative than before.

The 11.Panzer-Division was briefly under Hausser's II.SS Pz.Korps (17–18 July) as part of Unternehmen ROLAND, an action to clear the enemy forces from southeast of Oboyan with 2.SS Das Reich. But then the LSSAH and DR went south to Belgorod for railroad transfer West. 3.Totenkopf withdrew from its bridgehead over the Psel to form a new HKL with the Elfte south of the river. On the 18th II.SS Pz.Korps Hauptquartier also went back, and the 11.Pz.Div. and SS-T came under XXXXVIII. Pz.K. SS-T was then ordered to Belgorod as well. The 11.Panzer went on the defense in support of the infantry and ROLAND was canceled.[17]

With Grossdeutschland and the W-SS formations being withdrawn, the area gained by Hoth's 4. Pz.Armee had to be evacuated, and the remaining units began retreating to the original start line of 4 July. The 11.Pz.Div. withdrawal began on the 19th. The eastern march route was back through Bykovka, the western route through Olkovka, to Tomarovka on the Vorskla. How heartbreaking it was to the Eleveners, to move back across that tortured ground and its burned-out hulks of tanks, scattered equipment, and the memory of Kameraden who died there.

On 21 July Russian forces following up vigorously attacked the 3. and 11.Pz.Div. When the GD had moved to H.Gr. Mitte it had left von Lauchert's Panthers behind. Now Pz.Abt.52 (I./15) with forty-one Panthers was assigned to its parent division, the Gespenster-Division, if only for a day. But with that power, Graf Schimmelmann's Pz.Rgt.15 was able to mount counterattacks that stopped the Russian attacks. Le.Sturmgesch.Abt.911, now under Hptm. Voss, had its most successful day on that 21st, claiming fifty-five Russian tanks destroyed. But the Chef der 2.Battr., Oberlt. Liedtke, and his three crew members were wounded when their Geschütz was hit; Maj. Horst Lindner, Kommandeur of Pz.Aufkl.Abt.11, riding with them, was killed. He was succeeded by Hptm. Wilhelm Pirch.[18]

The next day, 22 July, Karl von Sivers, a Major but always known as Rittmeister, returned from his illness to take command of Pz.Abt.52 (Panther). Orders to the remaining 3. and 11.Pz.Div. saw them withdrawing behind the old HKL of 4 July, held by the stretched 332.Inf.Div., the Elfte back to west of Graivoron.

To the north in the Orel sector, the attacks on Model's 9.Armee flank after 12 July expanded along the front held by 2. Panzerarmee, and it became obvious that a major Russian counteroffensive was underway. Matters weren't helped any by the fact that 2.Pz.Armee's commander, Generaloberst Rudolf Schmidt, was arrested by the Gestapo on 10 July for his continued criticism of the Hitler regime in correspondence with his brother. Gen. der Inf. Heinrich Clössner became acting commander, but Model took over controlling 2.Pz.Armee as well as his 9.Armee.[19] Despite its name, 2.Pz.Armee now had only three mobile divisions and some fourteen infantry divisions. (This had been Guderian's famous panzer army in 1941.) In September the headquarters would be reassigned to H.Gr.F in the Balkans for anti-partisan operations.

The Russian counteroffensive was Operation KUTUZOV, its goal to destroy the Orel salient after Model's attacks at Kursk had spent themselves. Sokolovsky's West Front attacked 2.Pz.Armee's left flank, driving south to sever the Bryansk–Orel rail line near Karachev, while Popov's Bryansk Front attacked the nose of the salient. Grossdeutschland moved by rail and by road to the Karachev sector. With an army being roughly equivalent to a German corps, Sokolovsky attacked with two armies and two tank corps, with another army and the new 4th Tank Army in reserve: 313,458 troops and 1,427 tanks and self-propelled guns. 2.Pz.Armee had some 160,000 troops and 325 panzers and assault guns. Popov's Bryansk Front had three armies and a tank and a rifle corps, with the new 3rd Guards Tank Army in reserve, comprising 470,882 troops and 2,309 tanks and self-propelled guns. The Russian reserves seemed inexhaustible. When they recuperated from fighting Model, Rokossovsky's Center Front would join in a converging attack.[20]

As the power of KUTUZOV became apparent by 16 July, little detected by Oberst Reinhard Gehlen's Fremde Heere Ost (FHO, Foreign Armies East) intelligence, Model ordered work begun on HAGEN, a defense line along the Desna fronting Bryansk. Hitler forbade any retreat, but then acquiesced by the 22nd. One of the units caught up in the Orel fighting was the Austrian 9.Pz.Div. under Gen.Maj. Walter Scheller, former commander of the 11.Pz.Div. from October 1941 to May 1942. When he objected to a planned assault near Krasnikov as a suicide attack and offered an alternative, he was relieved by General der Panzertruppen Josef Harpe of XXXXI. Pz.K. and Model on 21 July. An infantryman, he subsequently commanded the 334., and then the 337.Inf.Div. (He would be killed 22 July 1944 defending Brest-Litovsk.)[21]

Model began retreating 2.Panzer and 9.Armee from the Orel sector on 31 July in stubborn phases in Unternehmen HERBSTREISE (Autumn Journey), and by 16 August was fortifying the HAGEN line. The Red Army had not been able to cut off Model; but it had eliminated the Orel salient, though at the cost of half a million casualties.

On 17 July Russian forces assaulted Manstein's Donets Basin salient in the south, Mackensen's 1.Panzerarmee at Izyum and along the middle Donets, and Karl Adolf Hollidt's reestablished 6.Armee along the Mius River line. These attacks were launched by Rodion Malinovsky's Southwest and Fyodor Tolbukhin's South Front armies. Anticipating this offensive, Hitler had held back Nehring's XXIV. Pz.Korps for commitment there. Westhoven's 3.Pz.Div. left XXXXVIII. Pz.K. for the south, and Hausser's II.SS Pz.K., originally intended to go to Italy, now saw only the 1.LSSAH and later the corps headquarters going, while 2.Das Reich and 3.Totenkopf were diverted to the Donbas. The still-formidable SS panzer units slashed into the Russian attacks, preventing any breakthrough, and the Izyum offensive terminated on 27 July, and the Mius offensive likewise by 3 August.

With Grossdeutschland drawn north, and 3.Pz.Div. and the SS divisions diverted to the south, Hoth's 4.Pz.Armee had been stripped of five of its six panzer units. Only the 11.Panzer-Division remained to support the infantry divisions along the dangerously overextended HKL. The Gespensterdivision, southeast of Tomarovka, was regaining its strength. On 22 July the division reported to XXXXVIII. Pz.Korps it had forty-four panzers (four Flammpz., twenty III lg, twelve IV lg, two III kz, two II, two Bef.Wg.) in Schimmelmann's Pz.Rgt.15. Pz.Art.Rgt.119 was increasingly mobile, with five self-propelled Hummeln and twelve Wespen in addition to its seven half-track-towed Kanonen and three Haubitzen. Heavy 7,5cm antitank guns were six s.Pak(Sf) assault guns and three s.Pak(mot Z) towed. There were five towed 8,8cm flak guns in Major Peter Baack's H.Fla.Abt. 277. The assault gun battalion, le. Stu.Gesch.Abt.911, was still attached, with some twenty-two Geschütze.[22]

Like the field artillery towed by Halbkette, the self-propelled batteries went into position, put out their aiming stakes to lay the guns parallel, and leveled the bubbles in their cross-level vial instruments. The Artillerieleitstand (fire direction center) plotted concentrations by map coordinates, and determined the gun-target azimuth correlated with the observer-target azimuth when fire missions were called for. The Vorgeschobener Beobachter would then adjust fires by radio. As tracked vehicles the self-propelled guns could displace and move more quickly and go cross-country better than the ordnance on wheels, even if those were towed by Zugmaschinen.

While the 4. Panzerarmee front was relatively quiescent for the rest of July, the 11.Pz.Div., in separate Kampfgruppen, found itself again the Feuerwehr for the infantry divisions of Eugen Ott's LII. A.K., and often in the front lines. But "Panzerpanik" was beginning to plague the German infantry. On 23 July 332.Inf.Div. signaled "twenty enemy tanks have broken through!" When Schimmelmann's Kampfgruppe arrived they found only two T-34s in the Vorskla valley.[23]

But there were clashes around Bykovka up the Rollbahn, and elsewhere probes by fifty to sixty Russian tanks were reported. On that 23rd Schimmelmann's armored group—Pz.Rgt.15, I./110, and I./119—coordinated with 6.Pz.Div. of III.Pz.K. in Armeeabteilung Kempf to close a gap ripped open on 332.I.D.'s right flank. Generalmajor Walter von Hünersdorff had been mortally wounded by a sharpshooter at Kursk on 14 July, and Oberst Wilhelm Crisolli was acting commander of 6.Pz-Div. Artillery and ground-attack planes supported the intense fighting. Pz.Rgt.15 lost Lt. Meier of III. Abteilung, and Hptm. Lingenthal of II.Abt. was badly wounded and succeeded by Lt. Heinze, Oberfeldwebel Schwidder taking over his 6. Kompanie.

When wry little General Hoth flew to the Div.Gef.Std. on the 24th he was critical of the division's actions he had ordered through LII. A.K.—"the division completely broken into pieces, no clear sectors, unclear conditions of orders. A panzer division should never be positioned in the HKL. This mission falls to the infantry divisions alone. The current actions of the division are out and out not in the spirit of the [4.Panzer] Armee." He criticized General Ott at LII. A.K. as well.[24]

The Gespenster officers felt this criticism was unfair. The infantry from the beginning lacked adequate antitank weapons nor did they have their own panzer units, and the planned Sturmgeschütz units always were needed elsewhere. The infantry felt much alone without the panzers. Indeed, they feared not so much being overrun as being encircled. The proper role of the panzer units in mobile defense was concentrated Gegenangriff, but with the infantry so stretched along the HKL this was not always feasible.[25] Hoth may have felt Mickl was not properly coordinating the various counterattacks, but in any case Hoth may have been reflecting the frustrations of a failed offensive and the recent weakening of his 4. Panzerarmee.

On the 26th the KTB entry claimed the 2,001st Soviet tank destroyed since the beginning of the Russlandfeldzeug, and the milestone was announced in a Wehrmacht Bericht. On the 27th the 11.Pz.Div. was relieved along the HKL by the 332.I.D. and was withdrawn west of Graivoron.[26] At the end of July Meinrad von Lauchert from the disbanded Panther "regiment," as now Oberstleutnant, succeeded the ill Oberst Graf Schimmelmann as commander of Panzer-Regiment 15, taking command on 1 August. "Schimmelgraf" later commanded occupation forces in southern Jutland, Denmark. He had been "our 'Papa,'" said Fähnrich Friedrich von Eggeling, a Zugführer in 3.Kp. Schimmelmann would draw alongside the panzers while standing in his Horch Kfz.15 command car, and then climb on the tanks to hand out Schokolade and cigarettes and words of encouragement. Gefreiter Kurt Nentwig also admired Schimmelmann, the "fairest, bravest and most careful officer" he had met. Of the new commander, however, Lt. Eggeling was later to say, "Lauchert was ambitious to the extreme, very snippy and behaved like a little king. . . . But he was also extremely brave and was always in the front line. Nobody liked him much but everybody was impressed by his bravery and the 'fortune' he had in battle."

There were those who felt he had "Halzschmerz"—award-hunger, a yearning for the higher Ritterkreuz awards hung around the neck. (Lauchert had received the RK 8 September 1941 with I./Pz.Rgt.35/ 4.Pz.Div., and would receive the Eichenlaub as Kommandeur Pz.Rgt.15 on 12 February 1944.) He would be the able commander of Pz.Rgt.15 for the next year.[27] Panzerabteilung 52 (Panther) stayed directly under XXXXVIII. Pz.Korps control. Pz.Abt.51 rejoined Grossdeutschland, receiving ninety-six new Panthers in early August.

CHAPTER NINETEEN

The Kessel of Graivoron

AT 05,00 HOURS ON 3 AUGUST 1943 THE QUIET OF THE GERMAN front lines northwest and east of Belgorod erupted in a violent storm of Russian artillery barrages, sheets of Katyusha rockets, screaming mortars, and direct gunfire from "Ratsch-bumm" 76.2mm guns and those of every other caliber. Fighters, bombers, and Ilyushin ground-attack planes swarmed over the battle area. The night before, simultaneous partisan assaults and demolitions had shut down all the rail lines behind Heeresgruppen Mitte and Süd for the next two days. That afternoon of the 3rd, hundreds of Russian tanks and assault guns, with infantry riding or following, poured into and through the German lines. The German HKL had not been strongly fortified after the recent Operation ZITADELLE, and so sudden was the Russian assault that the *"Achtung Minen"* warning signs had not even been removed to activate the defensive minefields. On the right flank of 4. Panzerarmee 167. Infanterie-Division was disintegrated.

By evening the Russian tank spearheads had plunged 25 kilometers (15 miles), overrunning command posts and maintenance and supply areas, and spreading "tank panic" even among front-line troops. The thrust severed the Tomarovka–Belgorod Rollbahn. A gap 10 kilometers (6 miles) wide was torn between Hoth's 4. Pz.Armee and Armee Abteilung Kempf to its right. With German attention and resources drawn to Operation KUTUZOV against the Orel sector to the north, and the Donets–Mius Line in the south, all evidence is that the Germans were taken completely by surprise in this Belgorod sector. The surprise was further enhanced by twenty-two "underwater" bridges across the Northern Donets and its tributaries; constructed just below the river surfaces, they were now being crossed by streams of tanks.

This was Red Army Operation RUMIANTSEV, planned by Zhukov of Stavka and the two Front commanders involved. Seven armies were committed: three from Konev's Steppe Front attacking Belgorod and A.A.Kempf from the east, and two from Vatutin's Voronezh Front to the northwest against 4. Pz.Armee, with two tank armies then passing through in exploitation. The objective of the tank armies was the rail center of Bogodukhov and then the encirclement of Kharkov, with

Katukov's 1st Tank Army on the western flank and Rotmistrov's 5th Guards Tank Army closer in. The 2nd and 5th Air Armies of the VVS gave wide-ranging close air support to the advancing tanks.

Then two more of Vatutin's armies were to broaden the offensive, and two armies of Malinovsky's Southwest Front were to drive toward Kharkov from the southeast. Belgorod fell on 4 August, and the next day Stalin ordered a massive salute from 125 cannon in Moscow to celebrate the liberation of Orel and Belgorod, and the end of the Kursk battle begun one month before. One definitive source says Stavka concentrated 980,588 troops, 12,627 guns and mortars, and 2,439 tanks and self-propelled guns for the attack. German forces were 210,000 troops and some 250 panzers and assault guns. The Red Army had odds of 5:1 in troops and almost 10:1 in armor. Kampfgruppen of 11.Pz.Div., and 19. and 6.Pz.Div. of A.A.Kempf, could not stem the flood of Russian tanks.[1]

Eugen Ott's LII. A.K. Hauptquartier was dispersed by Russian tanks and Knobelsdorff's XXXXVIII. Panz.-Korps assumed control. Panzergrenadierdivision Grossdeutschland was recalled from H.Gr. Mitte, and Paul Hausser, who had just issued a congratulatory Korpstagesbefehl (Corps Order of the Day) on 2 August to his II.SS Pz.K., had orders for 2.Das Reich and 3.Totenkopf to rail-load for movement back north again.[2] The full weight of the Russian offensive northwest of Belgorod struck the 332.Inf.Div. fronting Tomarovka and Generalleutnant Hans Schäfer was badly wounded.

II.Btl./Panz.Gren.Rgt.111 Gespensters held strongpoints along 8 kilometers (5 miles) of the line but could hardly cover the gap between the 255.Inf.Div. and the 57.I.D. on the left flank. Most of Generalmajor Johann Mickl's 11.Pz.-Div. had been withdrawn to the Saretshye-Lugovka area on the Vorskla with the Div.-Gef.-Std. at Duneika, about 8 kilometers (5 miles) west and northwest of Graivoron, by 31 July.

On 1 August the Elfte had reported by teleprinter to XXXXVIII. Pz.K. that in armored fighting vehicles it had sixty-six panzers, twenty-five assault guns of Stu.-Gesch.Abt.911, and eight Wespen (10,5cm) and three Hummeln (15cm) of Pz.Art.Rgt.119 einsatzbereit. The panzers included six Pz.III kz, twenty-five Pz.III lg, six Flammpz., one Pz.IV kz, twenty-one Pz.IV lg, four Pz.Bef.Wg., and three Beob.Pz.III, along with one Sd.Kfz. 250/5 (Beobachtungswagen). The Sturmgeschützen were nineteeen Stu.Kan. lg (7,5cm StuK. L/48) and six Stu.Haub. (10,5cm StuH. 42 L/28).[3]

In a Tagesmeldung on the 5th XXXXVIII. Pz.K. related, "Since 06,25 hours unbroken attacks along the entire front . . . Heavy and costly battles . . . casualties among commanders makes all more difficult . . . especially strong enemy air activity . . . rolling attacks by bombers . . . III./Gren.Rgt.678 [of 332.I.D.] rubbed out."[4] Russian tank forces swept down from the northwest and on 6 August reached Borisovka on the Rollbahn paralleling the Vorskla along the south bank to Akhtyrka, behind the III.Pz.K. and infantry forces of LII. Korps around Tomarovka.

Oberstlt. von Lauchert, now commanding Pz.-Rgt.15, received orders to counterattack the Russian flank at Ivanovskaya Lisiza, and III.Abt./15 and the half-track battalion, I.Btl./Pz.G.R.110, went into action. But even as they did so, more reports came in of Soviet infantry in Pokrovka, and more tanks in Golovchino farther along the highway toward Graivoron. II.Abteilung/15, now under Oberlt. Dieter von Portatius, was detailed to attack the Ivans at Golovchino. Hptm. von Bülow's III.Abt./15 fought into the southwest part of Ivanovskaya Lisiza but lacked infantry strength to drive on toward Pokrovka. They were to contact the 255.I.D. remnants coming down from the north. II./15 was able to swing northeast against Chotmyshk at 13,40 hours.

While the two Elften panzer battalions and the panzergrenadiers were dealing with the tank thrusts, Russian tanks were reported in Graivoron even farther southwest along the Rollbahn to Akhtyrka. German units were cut off and communications broken, and division had to report to corps that "Stu. Gesch.Abt.911 is completely splintered and through the loss of the commander is at present leaderless." Pz.Rgt.15's Werkstatt Kompanie was ordered to block the highway with any panzers back for maintenance or repair, and establish a defense of the town with Pz.Pi.Btl.209 under Hptm. Heinz Bödicker, soon joined by II/15. Reflecting the confusion, the KTB noted, "The fate of II./Pz.G.R.110 and I./Gren. Rgt.678 [of 332.I.D.] is uncertain."[5]

While Graivoron was held, other sections on the Hauptnachschubweg (main supply route) back to Akhtyrka were periodically cut. On the 7th maintenance personnel of II.Abt./15 were captured in the woods north of Lomnaya, and the supply group of

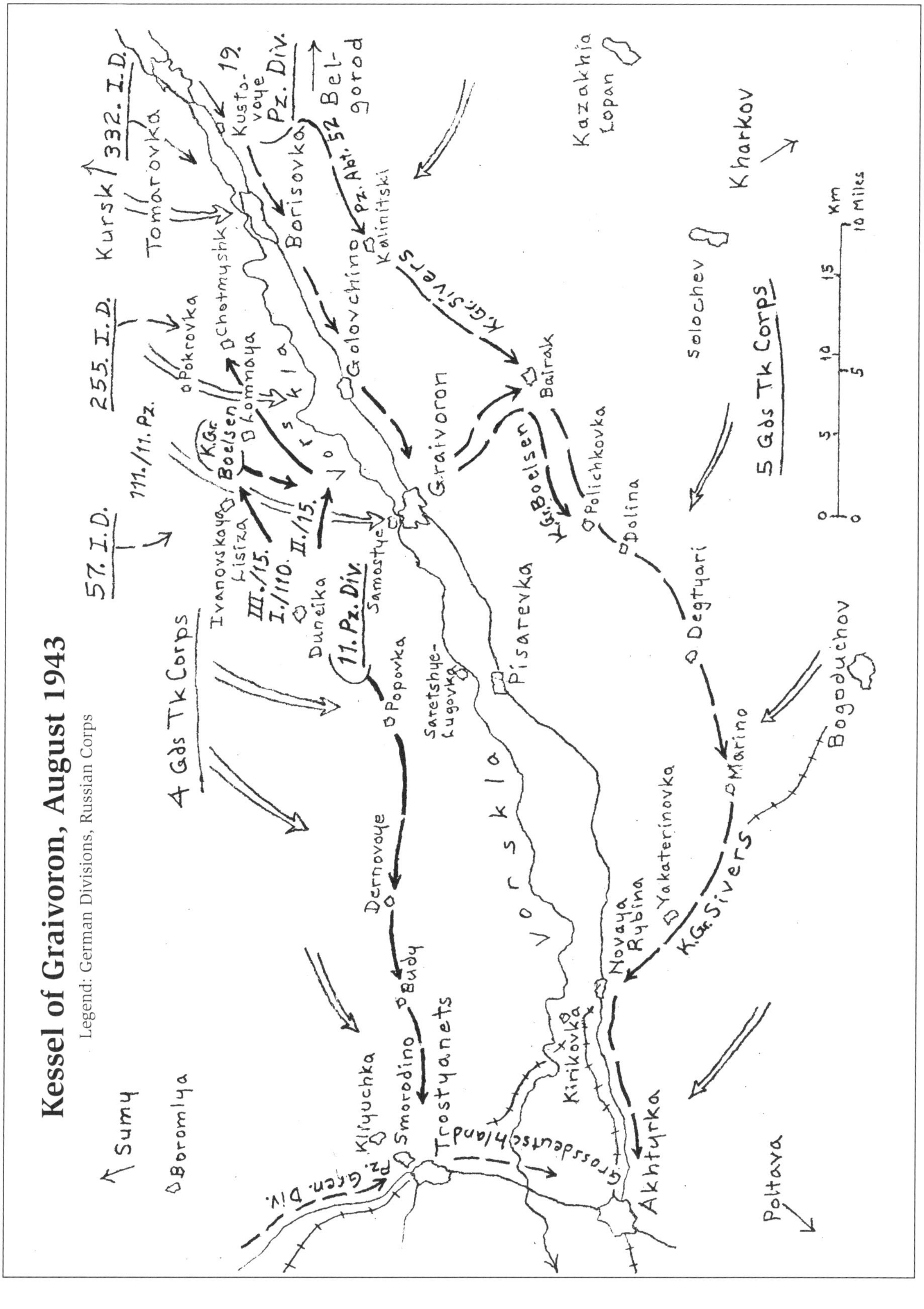

Kessel of Graivoron, August 1943

Legend: German Divisions, Russian Corps

III./15 was almost completely wiped out. Other rear-area personnel of the front-line units streamed to the rear with "tank panic"—understandable, but still unusual for German soldiers. Transport units of 19. Panzer-Division drove back along the Rollbahn to Akhtyrka without incident, but when Generalleutnant Gustav Schmidt and his staff drove back as well that day they were ambushed by T-34s near Borisovka. They scattered into the woods, and Schmidt and his aide died.[6]

By 8 August elements of five German divisions—57., 255., 332. Infanterie-Divisionen and 19.Pz.Div., with Oberst Oskar Sörgel acting commander, and elements of 11.Pz.Div., were cut off and trapped from Graivoron to Borisovka, a Kessel in German accounts. The assault gun batteries of Sturmgeschütz Abt.911 were working with the Elfte units. Oberlt. Günzel took over as commander when Hptm. Voss was killed on 6 August; Hptm. Baythier became commander on the 18th but was badly wounded on the 21st and died two days later, and 3.Battr. fought as infantry after all their guns were lost.

The Russian tank thrusts were by Katukov's 1st Tank Army of Vatutin's Voronezh Front, paralleled on its left by Rotmistrov's 5th Guards Tank Army of Konev's Steppe Front. Maj. Gen. D. Kh. Chernienko's 31st Tank Corps became embroiled at Tomarovka, but A. L. Getman's 6th Tank Corps and S. M. Krivoshein's 3rd Mechanized Corps bore down on Borisovka and points farther west through the porous, undermanned HKL of 57.I.D. and 255.I.D. I.M. Chistyakov's 6th Guards Army infantry rode the T-34s. The Soviet rifle units may not have been able to keep pace with the marauding packs of T-34s, but these were enough to keep the German forces defending and retreating back along the Rollbahn to Akhtyrka in confusion.[7]

While the 11. Panzer engaged in a fighting retreat north of the Graivoron Rollbahn and the Vorskla valley, its sister element fended off the Russian thrusts while retreating parallel to but south of the highway. This was the Panther battalion, Pz.Abt.52, under Major Rittmeister Karl von Sivers again after 22 July. It was still independently directly under von Knobelsdorff's XXXXVIII. Pz.Korps, and was deployed around Tomarovka. A postwar study of Kampfgruppe von Sivers was prepared by Walter Rahn, Leutnant and battalion Ordonnanzoffizier (Orderly Officer), and Klaus Groeger, lieutenant and adjutant to Sivers at the time, for Edel Lingenthal, then a Bundeswehr general in NATO, entitled, "Fighting Withdrawal of 'Combat Group von Sivers' as 'Floating Bubble' in the Vorskla valley . . . August 1943."[8]

After ZITADELLE and the Russian counteroffensives against Orel and the Donets–Mius lines, it was believed the Russian operational reserves had been fully employed, and no offensives were anticipated in the Belgorod–Kharkov sector. But Rittmeister von Sivers, proficient in the Russian language, monitored the enemy radio traffic with a captured radio set and scrutinized the terrain through a sighting telescope mounted on the cupola of his headquarters panzer. He came to a different estimate of the situation: that the Russians were marshalling for a major attack. At first his warnings were dismissed, but later Pz.Abt.52 was ordered to prepare an all-around defensive position at Tomarovka, and if necessary block the highway to the north and west. The battalion had some twenty-seven Panthers einsatzbereit. Nonrepairable panzers were emplaced in fixed positions in a perimeter defense.

In early August, "Repeated attacks launched by a few Russian tanks could be repulsed immediately," said Rahn and Groeger in their postwar study. "But from that moment a suspicious silence reigned in the combat sector in front of Tomarovka. During night-time, the distinct noise of tracked vehicles could be heard in front of the left and right neighboring sectors. After dawn, there could be recognised [*sic*] concentrations of tanks, part of them skillfully concealed by straw bales."[9]

Not liking the Russian buildup, and aware of the thinly held HKL, Sivers took some precautionary measures on his own initiative. He ordered the supply and maintenance companies, installed around Borisovka, to relocate to west of Akhtyrka, about 100 kilometers (60 miles) back. He also ordered that disabled Panthers be towed to the rear area. The I-Staffel did stop their work and prepare for the movement of the damaged Panthers, and the Ordonnanz Offizier, Lt. Rahn, was able to get XXXXVIII. Pz.Korps to make available additional towing vehicles at Graivoron. The commander of the service company, however, was not convinced of the urgency, based on an optimistic situation report from corps, and felt the following afternoon would be time enough.

But that night, 3 August, an ever-increasing noise of battle could be heard from the front. The Soviet offensive had begun. Over half the damaged Panthers were still around in Graivoron, and none of the service company vehicles had yet gone back. Therefore Lt.

Retreat from Graivoron, 1943

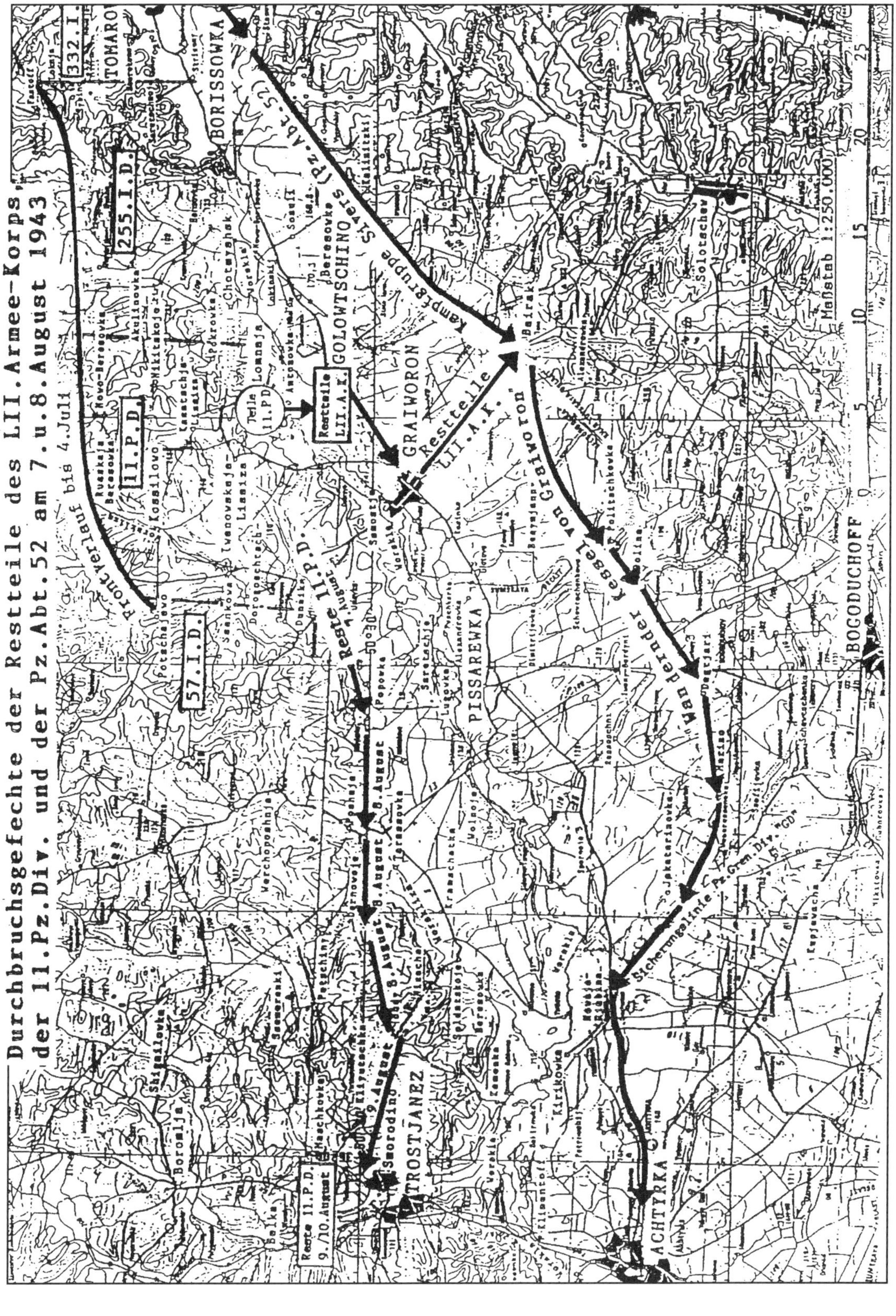

WALTER RAHN

Rahn drove back up to Borisovka to speed the withdrawal, but he had to drive parallel to the Rollbahn because rear elements of the infantry divisions were already beginning to stream back. Some seven T-34s attacked the retreating trains between Tomarovka and Borisovka, and it was obvious the Russians had broken through from the northwest. With tank fighting beginning to flare up, the installations at Graivoron were now threatened, including the remaining deadlined Panthers. With a standing order that no Panthers should fall into enemy hands, Lt. Rahn and Abt. Adju Lt. Groeger made the fateful decision to destroy these Panthers, apparently on their own initiative.

The Pionier Zug of the battalion was ready to carry out this unhappy task. "As there were not sufficient demolition charges at hand," say Rahn and Groeger, "hand grenades and matches setting tanks on fire helped to achieve this destructive effort. Thus ended the 'Panther' drama of Graivoron in an inferno of detonations, flames and smoke, in which a few engineer soldiers sustained minor burns." The authors say forty of eighty damaged Panthers were destroyed, which seems unlikely, though this number was affirmed by Zugführer Lt. Friedrich von Eggeling. 4.Pz.Armee O.Qu.Abt.V (Oberquartiermeister Abt., Higher Quartermaster Detachment), not differentiating between Pz.Abt.51 and 52, reported "Pz.Rgt.39" receiving twenty-one replacement Panthers by 31 July. On that date, of the 212 total, 20 were operational, 108 were needing repair, and 84 were total write-offs; but on 11 August, of the 212 total, 9 were operational, 47 were needing repair, and *156* were total write-offs!—another depressing chapter in the saga of the first ill-fated Panther Ds.[10]

By 6 August it was obvious that the defensive position at Tomarovka was untenable, and Rittmeister von Sivers organized his own Panther battalion, adding stragglers from other units who sought the protection of the Panthers, to form a combat group to stage a fighting withdrawal back to Akhtyrka. As the Russian tank thrusts were primarily coming down from the northwest against the Rollbahn, von Sivers determined on a route farther south. After redistributing available rations and fuel, with the armored vehicles being the top priority, other vehicles were destroyed and the group moved out and cross-country to the southwest at dusk on the 6th. Twenty-two Panthers and a few assault guns led out, followed by SPWs, Lkws, and towing vehicles, with five Panthers as a rear guard. Von Sivers lapped the column in a Kfz.15 command car.

The Kampfgruppe moved as a "Wandernder Kessel" ("floating bubble" or roving pocket). Near Borisovka some twenty T-34s were engaged, of which the German force claimed seventeen knocked out. Kgr. von Sivers igelt for the night at Bairak where various LII. A.K. elements joined them from Graivoron 10 kilometers (6 miles) to the northwest. German forces indeed still held Graivoron, and I-Staffel personnel were able to salvage some needed parts from the smoke-blackened, burned-out Panthers there on the 7th. The Kampfgruppe had also made contact for aerial fuel resupply, and on the 8th a squadron of trimotor Ju 52s, the faithful "Tante Ju," dropped fuel canisters south of Graivoron, the white parachutes facilitating retrieval.

In the afternoon of the 8th the movement resumed. An Me 109 dropped a container, marked by yellow smoke, giving the corps details for a route between Pisarevka on the Rollbahn and Bogodukhov to the south. During the night of 8–9 August Kgr. Sivers continued the withdrawal. Artillery and fighting flashed around the horizon as the men maneuvered their vehicles through the darkness. Flares ahead signaled the security outposts of the Grossdeutschland HKL as the Kampfgruppe struck the Rollbahn again at Novaya Ryabina 15 kilometers (9 miles) from Akhtyrka. The GD Division had begun moving by E-Transport down from Bryansk and H.Gr. Mitte on 5 August, detraining the first elements at Trostyanets and the rest at Akhtyrka, and started building a defensive position to stabilize the retreating forces.[11]

Though Kpfgr. Sivers was down to eleven operational Panthers, mostly because of continuing technical failures, Karl von Sivers had brought his battalion and numerous stragglers, including 2,000 Landsers, as a roving pocket, isolated and only refueled by air, back some 100 kilometers (60 miles) through uncertain and now mostly enemy territory, while claiming some forty Russian tanks knocked out. Lt. Friedrich von Eggeling, Zug Führer in 3.Kp. and later Ordonnanzoffizier of the Panther Abteilung and then adjutant of Pz.Rgt.15, felt "Sivers was a little bit crazy—he slept usually with his pistol under his pillow and it happened more than one time that he shot at the man who tried to wake him. The result was that he was waked with a long stick from far out. But he was a very brave man too and I liked him very much."

And in combat von Sivers was as skillful as he was fearless.[12]

North of the Rollbahn and the Vorskla Mickl's 11. Panzer-Division was fighting its way back westward. On the 7th Krivoshein's 3rd Mechanized Corps drove through a gap to Samostye just north of Graivoron, dividing the division's elements. At Lomnaya to the northeast Oberst Dr. Hans Boelsen, his contact with division having been "torn apart," had I.Btl. of his Pz.Gren.Rgt.111, Pz.Aufklärungs-Abteilung 11 (under Hptm. Wilhelm Pirch, having succeeded Major Horst Lindner killed 21 July), and II./Pz.A.R.119. He was joined by the gepanzerte Gruppe: von Lauchert's II. and III.Abt./Pz.Rgt.15, Karl Thieme's SPW-equipped I.Btl./Pz.G.R.110, and I.Abt./Pz.A.R.119. Boelsen had orders to hold this important position and enable the divisions in the Kessel of Graivoron to withdraw. These Gespensters came under the control of Generalleutnant Poppe whose 255.Inf.Div. elements were retreating.[13]

The rest of the Elfte, including Oberst Albert Henze's Pz.Gren.Rgt.110 and Panz.Art.Rgt.119, were delaying back from Duneika. Oberst Herworth Schmeling had taken over the artillery after Oberst Julius Werner was killed in July. It was an orderly withdrawal, the Feldküchen ensuring Kaffee for the fighting Landsers. Boelsen's Lomnaya Kampfgruppe now acted as rear guard covering the retreat of the infantry divisions. With Russian tank forces cutting the Vorskla valley Rollbahn route back to Akhtyrka, Kgr. Boelsen left Graivoron for Bairak and basically followed Sivers's route west, clashing with Russian tanks up from the Bogodukhov area at Dolina, Degtyari, and Marino, finally contacting Grossdeutschland outposts at Yekaterinovka on the night of the 9th.

The remainder of the division left Duneika and retreated north of the Vorskla through Popovka, Dernovoye, and Budy to reach Trostyanets north of Akhtyrka. But they had to fight for it, supported by the Tiger Abteilung of GD. The Ia KTB noted, "In the course of the day, [was] the extraordinarily difficult work in ascertaining the individual scattered parts of the division. The armored group arrived in Trostyanets. Pz.G.R.111 assembled in Klimentov and must be completely newly equipped and given weapons." Twenty panzers assembled at Trostyanets: "The fighting strengths have sunk to a minimum. The physical and especially the morale condition of the men is critical."[14]

Major Eitel-Friedrich Binder, acting Ia of XXXXVIII. Pz.K., took over the responsibilities as Ia 11.Pz.Div. for Oberstlt. Kinitz, who had gone on leave on the 6th (returning on the 28th). The Elfte was to take over a sector from Trostyanets north to Boromlya, 110 on the right and 111 on the left. The last operational assault gun knocked out two T-34s. Grossdeutschland, trying to establish a defensive position east of Akhtyrka, was now also assaulted by the main Russian offensive. There were gaps everywhere. The Russians "then simply advanced through these gaps. This forced our troops to improvise even further, meaning the rapid transfer of the defence to that point. There were simply shortages everywhere." The Russian numbers were too great. "All in all 10 August demonstrated that the present, new positions were untenable, because the large number of armoured groups fielded by the enemy, up to thirty-six T-34s were counted in places, were repeatedly able to infiltrate through the gaps."[15]

On 10 August Johann Mickl left the 11.Panz.-Div., being transferred to Yugoslavia where he commanded the Croatian 392.Inf.Div. (until the end of March 1945 when he was killed in action near Karlobey). Mickl was succeeded as Kommandeur of the 11. Panzer-Division by Oberst Wend von Wietersheim on that 10th; von Wietersheim would be the respected and beloved leader of the Gespensters until the end of the war.[16]

Wend von Wietersheim was born 18 April 1900 at Neuland at Löwenberg on the Bober, east of Görlitz in Silesia. He was a graduate of the Lauban Gymnasium and of the Ritterakademie zu Brandenburg on the Havel. He entered the Kadettenkorps Lichterfelde, and on 6 August 1918 became a Fähnrich (officer cadet) in Husaren Regiment von Schill 1, Schlesien Nr.4, and commissioned as Leutnant in 1919. Briefly involved in banking, he reentered the now Reichsheer in 1923, and six years later married Rosi-Dorothee née von Cölln, eighteen years old. From 1934 to 1937 Wietersheim was Kompaniechef of Aufklärungsabteilung Stahnsdorf at Berlin, and then in 1938 as a Major he became the adjutant of the 3.Berlin "Bär" Panzer-Division through the Polish campaign, being awarded the EK 2 on 1 October 1939. He was a distant relative of General der Infanterie Gustav von Wietersheim commanding XIV. Armeekorps, and two nephews, Walter and Axel, served in Pz.-Rgt.15.

- 77 -

Tag / Uhrzeit / Ort und Art der Unterkunft	Darstellung der Ereignisse

Wald südwestl. Trostjanez

Noch 9.8.1943

Die Gefechtsstärken sind auf ein Minimum herabgesunken. Körperlicher und besonders moralischer Zustand der Mannschaften ist bedenklich.
Ein Zusammenspiel der einzelnen Waffengattungen ist nicht möglich.
Panz.Gren.Rgt.110 ist im Zusammenwirken mit dem in Trostjanez eingetroffenen Panz.Rgt.15 zum Angriff auf Ssmorodino angetreten und hat den Ort genommen.

18,30 Lage in Trostjanez unverändert.
In Belka Inf.-Feind in Kp.-Stärke mit 2 Granatwerfer und einer Pak.
Eigene dort eingesetzte Sicherungen (Ersatzmannschaften Panz.Gren.Rgt.110) sind auf die Höhenstellungen südlich des Ortes ausgewichen.

Befehl an Panz.Gren.Rgt.111:
Rgt. erkundet:
a) Vormarschstrasse aus seinem Auffrischungsraum Klimentoff über Ssossonka-Maschtschanka-Stanowa-Belka.
b) Gedeckte Annäherung auf Trostjanez.
Einsatz des Rgt. am 10.8. früh auf beiden Vormarschwegen möglich.

Absicht der Div.:
Unter der Voraussetzung, dass die Lage im Abschnitt der Div. weiterhin ruhig bleibt, Einsatz des Panz.Gren.Rgt.111 am 10.8. über Belka - Aleksino - Maschkowka Südrand.
Dort Verbindungsaufnahme mit 7.Panz.-Div.

19,20 Befehl zur Artl.-Umgruppierung.

19,50 Vororientierung XXXXVIII.Panz.-Korps:
Angriff ist einzustellen. Korps verteidigt sich hinter

KTB, 9 August 1943—"The fighting strengths have sunk to a minimum." Retreat from the Kessel of Graivoron along the Vorskla to Trostyanets. NARA T-315/ROLL 600/001239

Rittmeister Karl von Sivers, I.Abt./Pz.Rgt.15. WALTER RAHN

Generalmajor Wend von Wietersheim, 11.Pz.Div. BUNDESARCHIV PHOTO II 4-5982

In March 1940 Major von Wietersheim became commander of Kradschützen-Btl.1, the motorcycle battalion of the Weimar 1.Pz.Div., and for his leadership in the French campaign was awarded the EK 1. on 20 May 1940. Promoted to Oberstleutnant on 1 April 1941, as the Russian campaign began Wietersheim was named commander of the 1. Panzer's Schützenregiment 113 (mot). As part of 4. Pz.Gruppe, 1.Pz.Div. advanced on Leningrad and then on Moscow, but was decimated in the Rzhev salient fighting. For his bravery Wietersheim received Das deutsche Kreuz in Gold 24 December 1941 and the Ritterkreuz 10 January 1942, and was promoted to Oberst 1 April 1942, still commanding S.R.113.

During the 1942 campaign the 1.Pz.-Div. was with 9.Armee in H.G. Mitte, Wietersheim being awarded the Eichenlaub to the RK 12 January 1943. With losses, the 1.Pz.Div. was withdrawn in January for refitting in France, and then deployed to Greece (prompted by a successful Allied deception operation preceding the actual invasion, that of Sicily). This extensive wartime panzer experience was brought by Oberst von Wietersheim—a Ritterkreuzträger who had also earned Verwundeten- and Panzersturm Abzeichene—to command of the 11. Panzer-Division.[17]

The division von Wietersheim took over on 10 August had been badly battered in the fighting retreat along the Vorskla back to Akhtyrka and Trostyanets, led by an unpopular commander. 255. and 332. Infanterie-Divisionen were so crippled they were withdrawn from combat, and von Lauchert's Pz.Rgt.15 could only report six panzers einsatzbereit. Tasked with a counterattack on 10 August, Oberst Boelsen could only protest that the strength of the units he controlled was "much too weak." A.A.11 had some fifty men, and of his Panz.G.R.111, I.Btl. had eighty men and II.Btl. had 100. On the 11th the remnants of

Oberst Oskar Sörgel's 19.Pz.Div. were subordinated to von Wietersheim's Elfte.[18]

The Russian tank thrusts from the north against the 11.Pz.Dv. retreating from Duneika were probably T-34s of Maj. Gen. P. P. Poluboyarov's 4th Guards Tank Corps of the 27th Army under Lt. Gen. S. G. Trofimenko on the western flank of Katukov's 1st Tank Army. The attacks on Kampfgruppe Boelsen retreating from Bairak south of the Vorskla were probably from Maj. Gen. A. G. Kravchenko's 5th Guards Tank Corps attached to Katukov's 1st Tank Army driving southwest on Bogodukhov. [19]

As Konev's Steppe Front armies drove directly against Kharkov, Vatutin's Voronezh Front armies and Rotmistrov's 5th Guards Tank Army were thrusting down past Poltava to encircle the German forces in that fought-over city. Malinovsky's Southwest Front joined in, attacking from the southeast. Now Manstein had to redeploy forces again to prevent this. SS Pz.Gren.Div. 2. Das Reich and 3. Totenkopf, sent south to bolster the Donets–Mius position, were railroaded back north and, with the depleted 3.Pz.Div., were put under the headquarters of Gen.d.Pz.Tr. Hermann Breith's III.Pz.Korps (as Hausser and II.SS Pz.Korps headquarters, as well as 1.Leibstandarte, had left for Italy). SS 5. Wiking reinforced A.A.Kempf.

On 12 August Manstein's SS forces collided with Katukov's 1st Tank Army in a meeting engagement around Bogodukhov to block the Soviet drive: "The result was a remarkable series of complex, vicious, seesawing, mobile battles first around Bogodukhov and then to the west around the key road junction at Akhtyrka." SS-T surrounded some advanced elements that cost the Ivans 100 tanks. The 6th Guards Army with 5th Guards Mechanized Corps of 5th Tank Army was able to cut the Poltava–Kharkov rail line, then DR and Wiking drove them back.[20]

But Manstein had no intention of Kharkov becoming another Stalingrad—"I would rather lose a city than an army"—and supported General Werner Kempf's request to abandon the ruined city. Hitler, however, characteristically ordered it to be held at all costs. On the 14th Kempf was replaced by Gen.d.Inf. Otto Wöhler, Manstein's former chief of staff, and four days later the Armee Abteilung was redesignated as 8. Armee—but the threat to the German force was unchanged.[21]

On 17 August Hoth's 4. Pz.Armee mounted an attack from Akhtyrka southward that met Totenkopf in a pincers movement by the 20th. Although Hoth's force was not strong enough to complete an encirclement of the 6th Guards and 27th Armies, which were assisted by Lt. Gen. Kulik's 4th Guards Army, the fighting did force the Rotarmisten to retreat. The attack was led by a Kampfgruppe that had been formed under Grossdeutschland's Ia, Oberst Walter von Natzmer, including fifteen Tigers, and initially 10.Pz.Gren.Div. on the right and 7.Pz.Div. on the left.

Of the flank attack that caught the Russians by surprise and led to them abandoning much equipment in panic, von Mellenthin of XXXXVIII. Pz.K. concluded, "During World War II such incidents occurred on many occasions, and we learned that skilful use of a few tanks, or well-executed tank raids, often brought much greater results than very heavy artillery fire or massed bombing attacks. In dealing with Russians the rapier is far preferable to the bludgeon."[22]

On 17 August von Wietersheim outlined defense policies for the Trostyanets-Boromlya sector, including 19.Pz.-Div., subordinated to the Elfte: All members of the Tross (trains) would put in three hours a day to strengthen the position, as well as the work by the engineers and combat troops. Pz.Pi.Btl.209 laid minefields before the HKL. Pz.Art.Rgt.119 under Oberstlt. Herworth Schmeling coordinated and registered artillery concentrations with the infantry: EIDER 1, 2, 3, 4, ROSA 1, 2, 3, DORA 1, 2, 3, and others on the map overlay for immediate response when fire missions were called for. But because of the extent of the defense sectors, said Wietersheim, and the limited forces available, regular defense "was not possible." Instead, Widerstandsnestern (resistance nests) supported by Pz.-Rgt.15, Stu.-Gesch.Abt.911, and Panz.Jäg.Abt. 61 would have to suffice. The civilian population had to be evacuated from the sector, with provisions for four weeks: "The last cow is left for them."[23]

Even though badly depleted, the Elften remained effective. Officers in particular had to be versatile. Lt. Franz Thelen, who was assigned to Boelsen's Pz.G.R.111 earlier in 1943, served as regimental Ordonnanz Offizier, commander of the short-range 15cm gun company, and then regimental adjutant; he also commanded I. or II. Bataillon at times when the commanders became casualties. The units coordinated well because the officers and non-commissioned officers knew each other, knew each others' strengths and weaknesses, and could depend on each other.

In addition, said Thelen, the men, though few in number, felt "armed to the teeth," with Das Zweibein and the MPi being the dependable favorite weapons. The 1,200 rounds-per-minute rate of fire of the MG 42 meant that ammunition resupply was an enduring concern, but this was offset by the tremendous firepower. The panzergrenadiers were transported in Lkws, but the sixteen different types of vehicles used was a challenge for maintenance, especially regarding parts procurement.[24]

But Russian attacks were unrelenting. On 17 August Lt. Gen. R. R. Korzun's 47th Army smashed through the 57.Inf.-Div. at Boromlya, and Lt. Gen. N. E. Chibisov's 38th Army drove the 68.I.D. back to the Psel south of Sumy. An 11.Pz.-Div. Kampfgruppe with 112.I.D. infantry sought to block the advance but the Russian forces were too strong. Partisans were also a threat, and the popular Hauptmann Johannes Knaut, commander of the division staff company, was shot near Oleshnya.

The components of the 11.Panzer-Division, having successfully retreated from the Kessel of Graivoron, had assembled in the area around Gadyach on the Psel, and were now holding the sector around Trostyanets, coming under XXXXVIII. Panzerkorps again. On the 18th 19.Pz.-Div. reverted to 4. Pz.Armee control, though Pz.G.R.73 and an artillery battalion stayed with the Elfte. The Gespensters were badly in need of Auffrischung. On 20 August Wietersheim reported, "Fighting strength has become so weak there is only one soldier every 100–200 meters. It is a wonder that the front has held this long." On the 22d I.Btl./110, the half-track battalion, had forty-three fighting men, and on the 23rd Pz.-Rgt.15 had fifteen panzers (eleven Pz.IV lg, three Pz.III lg, and one Pz.III kz) of which only eight were combat-ready, and four assault guns.[25]

On 20 August Russian forces broke through at Lebedin, northwest of Akhtyrka. A small Kampfgruppe composed of von Lauchert's Pz.Rgt.15 and some Panthers of Sivers's Pz.Abt.52 sealed off the breakthrough. Lebedin was evacuated, however, and Moskalenko's 40th Army thrust down the Psel. Russian attacks north of Akhtyrka forced that town to be abandoned and Trostyanets as well, and Hitler finally acquiesced in the abandonment of Kharkov itself on 22 August. On the 26th Division ordered 1.Battr./Panz.Art.Rgt.119 to be an infantry company ("zu Fuss") on the right flank of Pz.G.R.110, and the same for a battery of H.Flak-Abt.277 and a battery of the assault gun battalion. In each panzergrenadier battalion the three companies were to be reduced to two, while Stu.Gesch.Abt.911 consolidated as two batteries and Pz.Jäg.Abt.61 as one company.[26]

Fighting in the Vorskla sector continued as the Germans fell back, but each HKL was "only thinly occupied." Division casualties suffered in August 1943 were 2,855, out of whom 402 were killed, 1,634 were wounded, 464 were missing, and 355 were ill or "other." The determination of the Gespensters may be reflected by Lt. Martin Dietrich, adjutant of A.A.11, who lost his leg in action but insisted on returning to front-line service with his Gespenster-Division using an artificial limb. (He was later killed in action near Spremberg south of Berlin 18 April 1945.)[27]

Even with such critical manpower shortages, the need to upgrade the training of personnel continued. On 28 August four personnel of Pz.Art.Rgt.119 were to participate in a six-week H.Gr. Süd Funkerschule Lehrgang (radio school course of instruction) at Krivoi Rog beginning 1 September, and four personnel from the line units were to attend a Heeresmotorisierung (army motor school) course about winter equipment back at Wünsdorf, Kreis Teltow, 4–9 October. These troops in turn became instructors upon returning to their units.

Selected Mannschaften (enlisted men) might go to Unteroffizier (non-commissioned officer) Schule as at Metz, and those promoted as Fähnrich (officer cadet) would go through a vigorous six-month program as an Offizieranwärter (officer candidate) to be promoted as an officer (as Leutnant). The Germans felt it important that officers had experience as enlisted men first. There were other training schools, and at the Panzertruppen Schule at Ohrdruf in Thuringia in 1943, Oberfähnrich von Eggeling met instructor Major Jürgen Reichardt who later took command of I.Abt./Pz.Rgt.15, then the regiment itself in March 1945.[28]

But the Russian summer offensive "Dampfwalze" (steamroller) continued unabated. "We hoped," wrote von Manstein, "the opponent to have been struck so hard in the course of Operation 'Zitadelle,' that on this front we could count on a certain pause in battle."[29] But clearly the Germans had underestimated the resurgent power of the Red Army. In the south, Ivan Petrov's North Caucasus Front pressed Gen.Obst. Richard Ruoff's 17. Armee back to the Kerch Strait and the Crimea, Fyodor Tolbukhin's South Front drove through the Mius position in the Donets Bend against Hollidt's reconstituted 6. Armee, and Colonel General Malinovsky's Southwest Front drove across the Donets against Mackensen's 1. Pz.Armee. Konev's Steppe Front and Vatutin's Voronezh Front pushed Wöhler's 8. Armee and Hoth's 4. Pz.Armee back toward Poltava. Rokossovsky's Central Front forced 2. Armee under Gen.d.Inf. Walter Weiss of Kluge's H.Gr. Mitte back to the Desna.

Hitler met with Manstein and his army commanders at the Werwolf headquarters at Vinnitsa on 27 August, where Manstein pressed for reinforcements or the Donets region would be lost. But von Küchler's H.Gr. Nord and von Kluge's H.Gr. Mitte were also stretched thin, and could not release any forces to H.Gr. Süd. On 3 September Manstein and Kluge flew back to meet with Hitler at his Wolfsschanze in east Prussia. They pressed for retreat in several sectors, and also insisted that there be a single Oberbefehlshaber Ost, a military commander in chief for the whole Eastern Front—presumably either of them, despite their mutual animosity.

Hitler reluctantly agreed that H.Gr. Mitte could retreat behind the Desna, 17. Armee could cross back to the Crimea, and 6. Armee could pull back to the so-called SCHILDKRÖTE (Tortoise) Line from the Mius—but he was unwilling to give up the Donbas industrial area. Not unexpectedly, he adamantly refused any diminution of his command power, certainly not one that would greatly increase the authority of one of his aristocratic field marshals. OKH remained in command of the Ostfront exclusively, and that was controlled by Hitler.

That same evening of the 3rd it was learned that British forces had landed on the Italian mainland across from Sicily. On 25 July Benito Mussolini had been forced to resign by his government and the Fascist Il Duce was imprisoned (though rescued in a dramatic mountaintop air-landing raid by SS Hauptsturmführer Otto Skorzeny on 12 September). Marshal Pietro Badoglio became premier while King Victor Emmanuel III assumed command of the Italian armed forces. When Axis resistance on Sicily ceased on 17 August, it became obvious that Italy was about to leave the war, and German forces prepared to occupy the country.

In the East on 6 September Malinovsky's Southwest Front tore a gap in the SCHILDKRÖTE Line and was driving for Dnepropetrovsk on the Dnepr, and Rokossovsky's Central Front broke through Weiss's 2. Armee toward Gomel. Manstein demanded reinforcements, or at least a free hand to retreat to a shortened line. On the 8th Hitler flew out to Manstein's headquarters at Zaporozhe on the Dnepr. He at least promised reinforcements for H.Gr. Süd to secure the major crossings of the Dnepr, beginning to acquiesce in the idea of retreating to a fortified position behind that major river. But no reinforcements were forthcoming, and little work was undertaken to fortify the Dnepr line.

On the next day, the 9th, Allied forces landed at Salerno near Naples in Italy and British airborne forces occupied the naval base of Taranto. German forces reacted quickly in occupying the country and moving to contain the landings. But now the American Fifth Army and British 8 Army had a foothold on the Italian peninsula, ready to advance north.

With the Red Army advancing inexorably toward the Dnepr, Manstein warned OKH that he was ordering his armies to retreat to the river before they were cut off. At a fourth meeting, at the Wolfsschanze on 15 September, Hitler finally agreed to a retreat behind the Dnepr; but this would be done while holding the Desna north of Kiev, and the WOTAN (Odin) Line south from Zaporozhe to Melitopol to maintain a link with 17. Armee on the Crimea, under Gen. d. Pioniere Erwin Jaenecke since 8 September. Manstein's orders for the withdrawal went out on the 18th.

The Dnepr had always been a natural barrier to an advance from the east. The river was up to 3 kilometers (2 miles) wide, and its western (right) bank was generally higher than the east bank, providing observation over the flat Ukrainian steppe country. It also guarded the mineral and agricultural resources of the western Ukraine. The retreat of Manstein's army group would be on a broad front of orderly, staged withdrawals, with Russian breakthrough thrusts counterattacked. There would be no encirclements as the Russians had suffered in the German Kessels of 1941.

In addition, the Russian pursuing advance would be slowed by a deliberate policy of "verbrannte Erde" (scorched earth), the removal or destruction of crops and livestock and the destruction of railroads and bridges in a zone 30 kilometers (19 miles) in front of the Dnepr. This was analogous to Operation ALBERICH, the carefully planned German retreat on the Western Front in 1917 back to the fortified SIEGFRIED Stellung (called the Hindenburg Line by the Allies), though much less thorough. The scorched-earth policy had a long tradition in Russia, from denying Napoleon the resources during his advance in 1812 all the way back to the "Scythian Plan" of those early tribes in Ukraine against Darius's Persians in 512 B.C.

In 1943 there was also a removal of much of the civilian population as well. It was noted that in the Soviet advance after Kursk, all males of military age (16 to 60) in the liberated regions were drafted into the Red Army as "cannon fodder." Those who came into German hands, as Überläufer or as Gefangene, reflected only perfunctory training, lack of equipment, and harsh discipline. Hans Buhr was a Russian-German Mennonite from Chortitza across the lower Dnepr from Zaporozhe who alone of his family survived Soviet persecution and deportation to Siberia. Impressed into the Red Army, he was captured by the Germans and worked in the Organisation Todt (OT) labor organization. Captured in turn by the Russians, he surrendered to the 11. Panzer-Division in the Ukraine in 1943, and as a Hilfswillige served as a translator and in other functions in Hauptmann Walter Schaefer-Kehnert's artillery battalion headquarters ("mein Bursche Hans," my lad Hans) for the next two years. (In 1947 Hans married Maria, another Mennonite refugee, and they finally settled near Calgary, Canada.)[30]

In a preemptive move, the Germans also rounded up those of military age. Many Ukrainians would serve as forced labor, but many, out of necessity or preference, became Hiwis in the Wehrmacht. Many German units had Hiwis, the 11.Pz.Div. reporting 153 Hiwis on 26 August. In many cases, their families moved westward as well, to accompany their menfolk, or to escape the return of the Communist authority. In total, the Germans estimated some 600,000 persons, one-tenth the population, were removed, about 280,000 of whom crossed the Dnepr. The Germans also carried off 268,000 tons of grain and destroyed 941,000 tons, but left over 1,656,000 tons, much in the fields for the fall harvest. The Soviets, of course, defined the German measures as a war crime. Some 200,000 Axis wounded, and hospital staffs, had to be evacuated as well.[31]

Even before Hitler's approval (on 15 September), units including the 11.Pz.-Div. were already carrying out evacuation and the "work of destruction" in their sectors. In evacuating its division rear area between 5 and 20 September, the Elfte recorded removing 5,391 Ukrainian civilians, 833 military-capable (Wehrfähige) males, 3,233 head of cattle, 905 calves, 1,354 horses, 1,521.7 tons of grain, 9 tractors, 40 other pieces of farm machinery, and 11 traction engines. Nonetheless at the personal level there must have been some empathy for the plight of the refugees, for Wietersheim had to issue a warning on 13 September, "False humanity only costs our blood!"[32]

On 2 September von Lauchert's Panzer-Regiment 15 underwent a change. III. Abteilung personnel returned to Sagan for training on Panthers, and von Sivers's Panther Abt.52 was to become I.Abt./Pz.Rgt.15 again. The division had been informed by 28 August, though the Panther battalion at the time was ordered to Dnepropetrovsk for Auffrischung, and then was attached to the 23.Pz.-Div. (not returning to the division until 31 October).[33] For now, the panzer regiment had only one battalion (II./15).

The fighting went on. On 9 September the panzergrenadiers were attacked but restored their position. Von Knobelsdorff's XXXXVIII. Pz.K. closely monitored the crucial armor situation of the divisions through daily reports. On 12 September the Elfte reported "the strongpoint occupation of the HKL daily becomes weaker," and the armor strength was twelve panzers (three Pz.IV lg, seven III. lg, and two Bef.Wg.); eight self-propelled artillery (seven Wespen, one Hummel); five assault guns (four Sturm-Kanone, 7,5cm, and one Sturm-Haubitze, 15cm) of Stu.Gesch.Abt.911; and two schwere Pak (Sf). By now the Panzer IIIs and IVs all mounted long-barreled guns.[34]

On the 13th the Russians broke through 19.Pz.-Div. At 07,00 hours von Lauchert received the order to form a Kampfgruppe, and in conjunction with a Panzergruppe from Grossdeutschland mount a counterattack. But GD's force could not be ready before 11,00 hours, and von Lauchert could only help contain the Russian penetration. On the 14th at 12,00 Pz.-Rgt.15 was ordered to be ready to counterattack in Pz.Gren.Rgt.111's sector, but I./111 was able to repulse a Russian attack on its own. At 14,00 Lauchert attacked and took Novoselovka by 15,00 and the Russians, suffering heavy losses, fell back toward Logodi. At 16,30 the panzers and II./110 drove beyond Novoselovka.

But the Russians had broken through between XXIV. Pz.Korps under Gen.d.Pz.Tr. Walther Nehring and von Knobelsdorff's XXXXVIII. Pz.K., though the Gespensters cleared the Rotarmisten infantry from a hollow west of Logodi around 1900 on the 15th. On the night of the 16th Oberstlt. von Lauchert dispatched six panzers to support the staff and two batteries of II./Art.Rgt.818 in containing a Russian bridgehead as the division prepared to withdraw to a new HKL. The movement was carried out though heavy rain and the mud posed problems getting fuel to the panzers, which had secured the left flank of the 72.Inf.Div.

On 18 September Manstein's order for the retreat to the Dnepr by H.Gr. Süd set the units in motion. Poltava was lost—grimly recalled as the battle site of the destruction of King Charles XII's Swedish Army by Tsar Peter the Great in 1709. Hoth's 4. Pz.Armee was to cross the Dnepr at Kiev, though Nehring's XXIV. Pz.K. crossed at Kanev farther south, first forming a defensive bridgehead, and coming under Wöhler's 8. Armee command. 8. Armee headed for the crossings at Cherkassy and Kremenchug, while Mackensen's 1. Pz.Armee withdrew toward Dnepropetrovsk and Zaporozhe. Hollidt's 6. Armee was to hold the WOTAN Line from Zaporozhe down to Melitopol across the barren Nogai Steppe country and maintain contact with Jaenecke's 17. Armee in the Crimea.

The mud that slowed the German withdrawal, and the first attempts at scorched-earth warfare, should have slowed the Rotarmisten as well. But 3rd Tank Army under Lt. Gen. P. S. Rybalko of Vatutin's Voronezh Front in particular pressed ahead, toward Kiev. Konev's Steppe Front was also driving ahead, but Rotmistrov's 5th Guards Tank Army had only fifty of its original 500 tanks operational, and the Germans were staging a fighting withdrawal with sharp counterattacks.

Well-trained and experienced staff officers like Oberst von Mellenthin of Knobelsdorff's XXXXVIII. Pz.K. were instrumental in conducting such a large-scale withdrawal in an orderly way. In analyzing the challenges later, he related the importance of prior planning: of identifying the important routes and improving the bridges, railroad tracks, and river crossings and defending them with flak units while also preparing them for demolition; of selecting assembly areas and rear command and defense positions; and of traffic control for the rapid displacement of withdrawing units and canalizing the expected refugee population along secondary routes, while also ensuring medical and ration provision locations for them as well as for the combat units. Refueling points were essential.

The pursuing enemy should be delayed by minefields, roadblocks, and demolitions, which were most effective if covered by fire to slow their clearance. The front-line units should fall back under cover of darkness to planned positions, the rearguard units conducting an active defense and having the mobility to then rapidly disengage and fall back through the new HKL. Feldpolizei, guides, and liaison and staff officers at key points would facilitate the orderly routing and movement to avoid traffic jams, which provided targets for enemy artillery or airstrikes. Forward airfields provided crucial air support, but they should also be prepared with bombs for demolition and the cratering of the air strips. In general, Manstein's H.Gr. Süd, including the 11.Pz.Div., carried out this withdrawal in a systematic manner.[35]

XXXXVIII. Pz.K., now in Wöhler's 8. Armee, fell back to the Kremenchug crossing of the Dnepr, held the contracting bridgehead, and crossed to the western side by 27 September. Wietersheim's 11. Panzer also fell back, but toward the Cherkassy crossing farther north up the Dnepr, while making panzer counterattacks at Nikolayevka and Shorshevka. The Gefectsstärke reported on the 19th was 3,425, while the Verpflegungsstärke was 10,247, including 180 Hiwis. At midnight on 20 September the 11.Pz.Div. was relieved by Grossdeutschland. The division now was assigned to III. Panzerkorps under General der Panzertruppen Hermann Breith in 8. Armee, and on the 22nd it moved into the contracting perimeter, crossing the Dnepr to the west on the 23rd using ferries as well as the bridge to establish the HKL on the southwestern bank.[36]

While the PANTHER Line defenses along the Dnepr had been barely begun, and in some cases were only antitank ditches, the 11.Pz.Div. found bunkers built by the Organisation Todt labor units to be "luxurious" even if they were not to be occupied by the Gespensters for long. The Div.Gef.Std. was located in the southern part of Cherkassy. The division then undertook a 180 kilometers (110-mile) road march via the industrial center of Krivoi Rog to Shirokoye for a couple of days "Ruhe," the tracked vehicles going by E-Transport.[37]

CHAPTER TWENTY

Defense of the Dnepr

EVEN WHEN MANSTEIN'S HEERESGRUPPE SÜD SUCCESSFULLY withdrew behind the Dnepr in September 1943, evading attempts at encirclement and the capturing of the six crossing sites—Kiev, Kanev, Cherkassy, Kremenchug, Dnepropetrovsk, and Zaporozhe—the Russian pursuit was relentless. As the Red Army approached the Dnepr, Russian commanders were encouraged to work with local partisan groups to get some troops across the wide river by any means and dig in a bridgehead even before any bridging material was forwarded. Between 19 and 26 September Vatutin's Voronezh Front established some forty bridgeheads, most south of Kiev. Though most were just as quickly crushed, as Mellenthin observed, "Russian bridgeheads, however small and harmless they may appear, are bound to grow into formidable danger-points in a very brief time and soon become insuperable strong-points." There was also the possibility of Russian scouts and parachutists in German uniform.[1]

The German units pulling back through the six Dnepr crossing sites then had to fan out on the western bank to cover some 500 kilometers (300 miles) of river from Kiev to Zaporozhe. Wietersheim's 11. Panzer-Division reported to III. Panzer-Korps it had a fighting strength of 2,875, and a ration strength of 9,927 (including 73 Beamte and 114 Hiwis). It characterized most of its units as "weak," and its now three Pz.Gren. Bataillonen as only 58 percent *beweglich* (mobile). It had only five Panzer IIIs and eight Panzer IVs operational, though there were nineteen assault guns between Stu.Gesch.Abt.911 and attached Sturmgeschütz-Abteilung 261 (ohne 2.Battr.). There were thirty artillery pieces and two 8,8cm guns.[2] On 8–9 October the division rolled south in five march serials to Andrusovka, west of Kremenchug, now under XXXXVII. Pz.Korps commanded by General der Panzertruppen Erhard Raus.[3]

On 22 September partisans assisted elements of Rybalko's 3rd Guards Tank Army in crossing the Dnepr to establish a bridgehead at Bukrin north of the Kanev crossing, upriver from Cherkassy. The four divisions of Nehring's XXIV. Pz.K. had just established a defensive bridgehead on the east side as the Germans began crossing the Dnepr at Kanev to the west bank. With 19.Pz.Div. ordered down from Kiev, Nehring's troops proceeded to attack the Russians at Bukrin, who had now been reinforced with tanks ferried across.

At 05,00 hours on the 24th, by which time all German units had crossed the Dnepr, the bridge was blown, and Nehring could concentrate on dealing with the Russian bridgehead at Bukrin. That evening Russian parachutists were dropped at several related sites, only to be annihilated by the German forces already moving through the area. There were three parachute brigades, 7,000 men, who were to reinforce the Bukrin force, and the linkup would be followed by a larger-scale air-landing operation. The failure of the parachute drop apparently soured Stalin on any future airborne operations. But the bridgehead itself was held.[4]

There were other Russian crossings to deal with. On 27 September XXXXVIII. Pz.K. under von Knobelsdorff had withdrawn from its Kremenchug bridgehead, in time to be ordered to eliminate a Russian crossing near Pereyaslav south of Kiev. 7.Pz.Div. and 20.Pz.Gren.Div. immediately moved north and battered the Rotarmisten back into a bend in the river. To the north of Kiev Vatutin's forces captured Chernigov on the Desna 22 September, and then the village of Lyutezh on the Dnepr itself during the night of the 27–28th. But this was contained, and as this was the swampy area downriver from where the Pripet joined the Dnepr, the German commanders felt it was unlikely to be a bridgehead for mobile forces. However, the local populations were used to make corduroy crossings of the marsh areas, and with ferries more troops and guns were brought into the bridgehead. In addition, Vatutin and Military Council member Khrushchev had Lt. Gen. A. G. Kravchenko seal up the tanks of his 5th Guards Tank Corps and simply charge across the swamps and streams to get to the bridgehead on 4 October. Some tanks—and their crews—were lost, but most got across. By the end of the month Rybalko's whole 3rd Guards Tank Army was concentrated in the Lyutezh bridgehead.[5]

While the German forces had generally fallen back behind the Dnepr in September, to the south they held a bridgehead over the river at Zaporozhe linking to the WOTAN Line. This was to protect the mining of iron ore at Krivoi Rog, and the manganese, copper, and nickel at Zaporozhe and Nikopol. At Zaporozhe also was the massive dam and hydroelectric plant, whose turbines generated over 550,000 kilowatts of electricity that provided power for the whole west Ukrainian industrial region. The Russians had badly damaged the dam when retreating in 1941, but the Germans had since repaired the power plant to capacity.[6] Beyond the Ukraine were the oil fields of Rumania, the Reich's primary source of that vital product. Thus these areas were crucial to the German war effort, and it was for the same reasons the Russians placed top priority on gaining them.

Yet now the Red Army was powerful enough to mount a continuing offensive farther north as well, against Kluge's H.Gr. Mitte. Popov's Bryansk Front captured Bryansk on 17 September from Model's 9. Armee, while Rokossovsky's Center Front drove Weiss's 2. Armee back to the Dnepr. Sokolovsky's West Front advanced against Heinrici's 4. Armee and took Smolensk by the 24th, and Yeremenko's Kalinin Front took Nevel, severing lateral communications with Feldmarschall Georg von Küchler's H.Gr. Nord, whose 16. and 18. Armee positions remained unchanged.

Reinhardt's 3. Pz.Armee, however, was unable to hold the PANTHER Line positions north of the Dvina. With losses and Rudolf Schmidt's arrest in July, 2. Pz.Armee had been dissolved and its headquarters, under Gen.Oberst Dr. Lothar Rendulic was transferred in September to H.Gr. F under Generalfeldmarschall Maximilian von Weichs in the Balkans. There it was to control forces disarming Italian units, anticipate an Allied invasion, and fight partisans.

The primary Russian drive remained in the south against Manstein's H.Gr. Süd in the Ukraine. On 9 October Tolbukhin's South Front charged into Hollidt's 6. Armee positions in the WOTAN Line between Zaporozhe and the Sea of Azov after a tremendous bombardment of artillery and rockets. In fierce fighting the German forces initially held their own, but Melitopol fell on the 23rd and by the end of the month 6. Armee had been split in half. Lt. Gen. Matvei Zakharov's 2nd Guards Army thrust on toward the Dnepr estuary at Kherson, cutting communications to Jaenecke's 17. Armee in the Crimea, now stranded. Hitler demanded a bridgehead be held across the lower Dnepr protecting the Nikopol manganese ore deposits. He may also have been hoping it might serve as a jumping-off place for a counterthrust to cut off the Russian spearheads, but Manstein no longer had forces strong enough to do so.

It seemed that everywhere south of Kiev the line of the Dnepr, never in fact really fortified, was breached by the Russian advance. Konev's Steppe Front had expanding bridgeheads at Cherkassy and Kremenchug barely contained by Wöhler's 8. Armee, and Malinovsky's Southwest Front assaulted the German Zaporozhe bridgehead anew on 10 October against Gen.d.Pz.Tr. Sigfrid Henrici's XXXX. Pz.Korps of Mackensen's 1. Pz.Armee. XXXX. Pz.K. included Jagdpanzer Tiger (P) Ferdinands in Heeres-Panzerjägerabteilung 656; these panzerjägers destroyed numbers of T-34s, but the numbers remained overwhelming.

Henrici prepared the Zaporozhian dam and hydroelectric power plant for demolition, but was unable to secure permission from OKH (i.e., Hitler). Russian artillery was already within range of the dam and power plant. After contacting Mackensen, Henrici took the responsibility upon himself to order the lowering of the water level so as not to flood 6. Armee bridges downriver. Henrici evacuated the bridgehead, and then, just before midnight on 14 October ordered the destruction of the dam and power plant. Rear guard elements of 16.Pz.Gren.Div. crossed to the west bank by boats and vehicle ferries.[7]

Even though the Germans still held Dnepropetrovsk and the Dnepr across from Zaporozhe, in the Kremenchug area Konev's forces pressed beyond Novo Georgievsk to swing down against Mackensen's 1. Pz.Armee to Krivoi Rog and behind 6. Armee. With the strategic advantage of interior lines, German forces could be railroaded from the Western theaters to the Ostfront. In an unusual move OKW, believing it now too late in the campaigning season for an Allied invasion in the West, offered mobile forces to the OKH for commitment in the East: 14. and 24.Pz.Div., then 1., 25., and 1.LSSAH Panzer Divisions and 384.Inf.Div. These, in addition to 11. Panzer and 3.SS Totenkopf from 8. Armee, would give Manstein a powerful force to counterattack in the Ukraine. But on 21 October Konev drove toward Krivoi Rog, a major rail center and the site of large ammunition and supply depots for H.Gr. Süd. The reinforcements offered by OKW could not arrive in time, and Mackensen had to use the 11. Panzer and 3.SS-T divisions to stem the Russian flood.[8]

Once again Wietersheim's Gespenster-Division was called upon to thwart the Russian drives, and fought a series of sharp tactical engagements. September had cost the division almost 2,000 casualties, including 233 killed, 1,095 wounded, 169 missing, 376 ill, and 123 other. On 12 October Panz.Gren. Rgt.111, II.Abt./Pz.Rgt.15, and I.Abt./Pz.A.R.119, under staff officer Maj. Günther Kaldrack, were placed at the disposal of XXXXVIII. Pz.K. On the 15th long-experienced Oberstlt. Franz-Joachim Kinitz left the division, succeeded as Ia, Der erste Generalstabsoffizier, by Major Werner Drews, Ia of XXXXVII. Pz.K. Drews would be the capable chief of staff for the division until the end of the war.[9]

On the 17th the Elfte moved by E-Transport to Alexandria where the Div.Gef.Std. was established, under XXXX. Pz.K., the ill Henrici having been succeeded by General der Gebirgstruppen Ferdinand Schörner. Sometimes elements of other units were put under 11.Pz.Div. command, as when on 22 October Gepanzerte Gruppe von Lauchert was formed with elements of 3.SS-T, including some of its panzer regiment, an SPW company, a Wespe (10,5cm) battery, and a Sturmgeschütz battery. The Gruppe also had six Wespen of 23.Pz.Div. and the Elfte's own Pz.Rgt.15 (II.Abt.), an SPW company of Panz.A.A.11, I./Pz.A.R.119, 1.Battr. of Stu.Gesch.Abt.911, the rest of Pz.A.A.11, and an engineer platoon of Pz.Pi. Btl.209. Lauchert's Pz.Rgt.15 had only its second battalion. Though assigned to the Elfte, I.Abt. (Panther)/Pz.Rgt.15 was noted as undergoing Auffrischung by Pz.A.O.K. 1.[10]

While attached to 23.Pz.Div. under Gen. Lt. Nikolaus von Vormann, Pz.Abt.52 (I./15) engaged a Russian drive to Pyatishatki near Krivoi Rog. Lt. Werner Stoll and Lt. Koske had a Kampfgruppe of ten Panthers, joined by four Panzer IVs of Pz.Rgt.23. Three hospital trains left the station for Krivoi Rog, but the third was intercepted and blocked by T-34s on the track. The next day, 19 October, Hptm. Euler of 23.Pz.Div. with two Panthers on either side of a locomotive returned to the Bahnhof to rescue the third hospital train, but found all the wounded had been murdered by the Russians, with only two survivors.[11]

On 24 October A.A.11, Major Anton Donnhauser having succeeded Hptm. Wilhelm Pirch, was ordered to reconnoiter toward Varvarovka, while a Kgr. of II./Pz.Rgt.15 and I./Pz.Gr.Rgt.111 thrust east in a dogged engagement. (Major Kaldrack took over Pz.G.R.111.) Nonetheless Russian forces entered Krivoi Rog on 25 October—though they were then forced out again—and they captured Dnepropetrovsk that same day. With the division near Krivoi Rog and the maintenance shops 300 kilometers (186 miles) back north at Smela near Cherkassy, on the 26th Wietersheim ordered the I-Dienste forward, sending

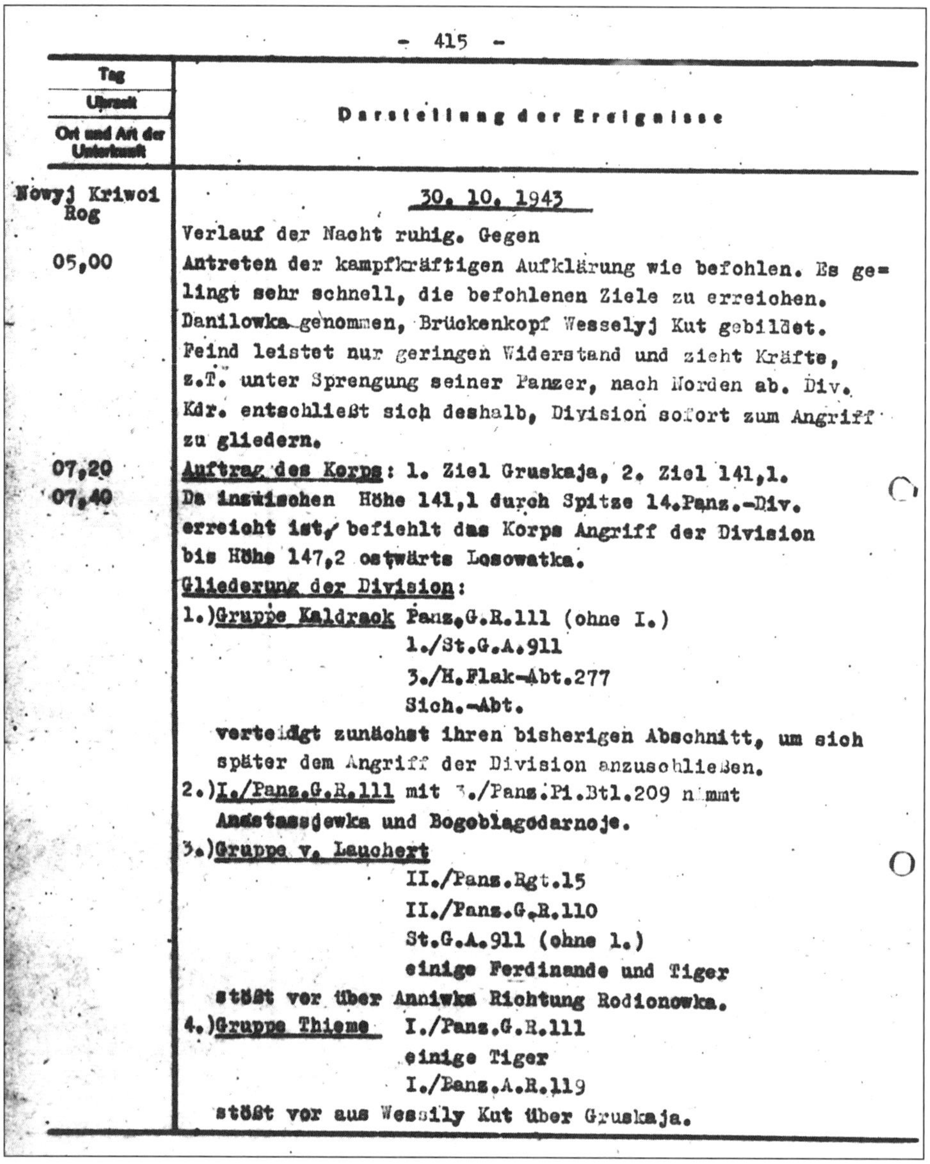

\- 415 -

Tag / Uhrzeit / Ort und Art der Unterkunft	Darstellung der Ereignisse
Nowyj Kriwoi Rog	30. 10. 1943
	Verlauf der Nacht ruhig. Gegen
05,00	Antreten der kampfkräftigen Aufklärung wie befohlen. Es gelingt sehr schnell, die befohlenen Ziele zu erreichen. Danilowka genommen, Brückenkopf Wesselyj Kut gebildet. Feind leistet nur geringen Widerstand und zieht Kräfte, z.T. unter Sprengung seiner Panzer, nach Norden ab. Div. Kdr. entschließt sich deshalb, Division sofort zum Angriff zu gliedern.
07,20	Auftrag des Korps: 1. Ziel Gruskaja, 2. Ziel 141,1.
07,40	Da inzwischen Höhe 141,1 durch Spitze 14.Panz.-Div. erreicht ist, befiehlt das Korps Angriff der Division bis Höhe 147,2 ostwärts Losowatka.
	Gliederung der Division:
	1.) Gruppe Kaldrack Panz.G.R.111 (ohne I.) 1./St.G.A.911 3./H.Flak-Abt.277 Sich.-Abt. verteidigt zunächst ihren bisherigen Abschnitt, um sich später dem Angriff der Division anzuschließen.
	2.) I./Panz.G.R.111 mit 3./Panz.Pi.Btl.209 nimmt Anastassjewka und Bogoblagodarnoje.
	3.) Gruppe v. Lauchert II./Panz.Rgt.15 II./Panz.G.R.110 St.G.A.911 (ohne 1.) einige Ferdinande und Tiger stößt vor über Anniwka Richtung Rodionowka.
	4.) Gruppe Thieme I./Panz.G.R.111 einige Tiger I./Panz.A.R.119 stößt vor aus Wessily Kut über Gruskaja.

KTB, 30 October 1943—Ferdinands and Tigers attached to Gruppen von Lauchert and Thieme, fighting around Krivoi Rog. NARA T-315/ROLL 600/ 001531

vehicles lacking replacement parts or not repairable in ten days back to the Berdichev depots.[12]

On the 27th the Tigers of schwere Panzerabteilung 506 (Tiger) with their high-velocity 8,8cm Kw.K. L/56 guns were attached to Kgr. Henze. The next day six of the ungainly but formidable Ferdinands with their deadly 8,8cm Pak 43/2 L/71 guns of 2./s.Pz. Jg.Rgt. [*sic*] 653 (Ferdinand) were attached to the 11.Panzer-Division as well, along with an armored train, Eisenbahnpanzerzug 26. Like others, Panzerleutnant von Eggeling considered the Tigers and Ferdinands "very, very slow in motion in the muddy black soil of the Ukraine in late October and early winter," nor was there a bridge in the land that could bear the weight of the Ferdinand. But "The gun of course was wonderful!"[13]

On the 29th orders were given for Gruppe Thieme with I./Panz.G.R.111, elements of a Pionier Kompanie, and the six Ferdinands to attack toward Danilovka, while I./Pz.G.R.110, supported by the self-propelled artillery of I./Pz.A.R.119 and a Pionier Gruppe, had three Tigers to attack toward

Kydashevka. Eisb.-Panzerzug 28 probed to the northwest along with reconnaissance by Pz.A.A.11. With the force increased to six Tigers and nine Ferdinands as well as eight Sturmgeschützen and six Panzerjäger, the Gespensters smashed into the Russians. At least forty-three Russian tanks and assault guns were claimed, along with six antitank guns and six artillery pieces among others, with 160 Ivans killed and twenty taken prisoner. By the next day seventeen more tanks had been claimed, and in three days of armored battle a total of 101 enemy tanks and assault guns were destroyed or captured. For the 31st it was planned to build a bridgehead over the Ingules and destroy the Russian forces between the Ingules and Losovatka, and link up with the 23.Pz.Div.[14] On 29 October Mackensen at 1. Panzerarmee was replaced by tough Gen.d.Pz.Tr. Hans Valentin Hube—he had lost an arm at Verdun in 1916—who also sought to block Konev's advance. (Mackensen went to command 14. Armee in Italy.)

The fighting around Krivoi Rog continued. The attached Tigers and Ferdinands as well as the panzers, and the Geschützen of Stu.Gesch.Abt.911 and the Acht-komma-achts of Heeres Flak-Abt.277, were responsible for knocking out scores of T-34s. Many of the Russian crews were poorly trained, and the veteran Panzersoldaten of Lauchert's Pz.Rgt.15 could still outmaneuver them, but the numbers put them at a disadvantage. Nonetheless at one point, said an amazed Lt. von Eggeling, regimental adjutant at the time, von Lauchert had the regiment charge in line formation, like the cavalry charge of "Seydlitz at Rossbach" in 1757.[15]

All along the Ostfront the Russian offensives continued. Their advance was represented by the renaming of the Fronts on 20 October: Tolkukhin's South driving on Kherson became the Fourth Ukrainian, Malinovsky's Southwest capturing Zaporozhe became Third Ukrainian, Konev's Steppe across at Kremenchug became Second Ukrainian, and Vatutin's Voronezh threatening Kiev became First Ukrainian. Farther north Bryansk and Center became the Belorussian (White Russian), and Kalinin and Northwest became First and Second Baltic Fronts respectively. (In 1944 West was divided into Second and Third Belorussian Fronts.)

On 3 November Sivers's Panthers (former Pz.Abt.52), having been working with 23.Pz.Div., were finally reunited with the Elfte as I.Abteilung/Pz.Rgt.15 (Panther). The few panzers of III./15 were absorbed into II.Abt., and the third battalion was dissolved. On 2 November the Ia's KTB had complained, "I.(Panther)/Panz.Rgt.15 is still not arrived from the 23.Panz.Div.," but "Panther" and "I./Panz. Rgt.15" are then mentioned on the 3rd.[16] The Tigers, Ferdinands, and armored train reverted to 8. Armee control.[17]

On 1 November Oberst von Wietersheim learned he had been promoted to Generalmajor. His division, including Stu.Gesch.Abt.911 and now the Panthers, was to be sure to proudly display the old "Gespenst" marking in white on all vehicles. But the fighting continued, the 11.Pz.Div. now in LVII. Pz.Korps commanded by General der Panzertruppen Friedrich Kirchner.

On 3 November Lt. Gen. K. S. Moskalenko's 38th Army followed by Rybalko's 3rd Guards Tank Army of Vatutin's First Ukrainian Front erupted out of the Lyutezh bridgehead across the Dnepr north of Kiev, the tanks brazenly with full headlights on and unnerving sirens wailing. Within three days the Ukrainian capital was in Russian hands, the capture coinciding with the anniversary of the Bolshevik Revolution, 6 November 1917. But the Russian spearheads were driving west around the city and then down to the railroad center of Fastov in the rear of Manstein's H.Gr. Süd as well, again threatening the encirclement of the whole army group.

Manstein flew to Rastenburg to appeal for the release of panzer forces offered by OKW for a counterstroke but Hitler, still more concerned on holding the lower Dnepr and the Crimea—that "aircraft carrier" from which the Rumanian oil fields would be threatened—resisted moving forces up toward Kiev. He finally released two panzer divisions, but they were distant—1.Pz.Div. coming from Greece and 1.LSSAH from northern Italy. At 4. Pz.Armee Hoth had to commit 25.Pz.Div. at Fastov. It had Tiger Abteilung 509 assigned, but the division had been organized in Norway and was coming from France, with little unit training or experience. The wheeled vehicle elements were diverted to Berdichev west of Fastov, but all the armored tracked elements were railroaded on to Kirovograd 200 kilometers (125 miles) to the south, the original destination. It was a tragic error. Gen.Lt. Adolf von Schell attacked with what he had on 7 November but was routed by the Russian tanks. Hitler blamed Hermann Hoth, who was replaced at 4. Pz.Armee by Gen.d.Pz.Truppen Erhard Raus from XXXXVII. Pz.K. on 15 November—with the able and experienced panzer general Hoth never to hold another significant position.[18]

Meanwhile Manstein was assembling six panzer divisions (1., 7., 19., 25., LAH, and DR) under XXXXVIII. Pz.Korps to mount a counterstrike. Dietrich von Choltitz had been acting corps commander while Knobelsdorff was on leave. On the eve of the attack on 15 November, Hermann Balck was appointed corps commander, "to my great joy," said the corps Ia Oberst von Mellenthin, who had worked with Balck when he commanded 11.Pz.Div. during the Chir battles. (Knobelsdorff later commanded XXXX. Pz.K., and then 1. Armee in the West.) Mellenthin felt "Balck has strong claims to be regarded as our finest field commander," and in working smoothly with his Ia, "Between him and myself there was that ideal co-operation, based on unlimited mutual faith," especially as "we both hailed from the cavalry and had the same views on armored warfare."[19]

The plan was to attack from Fastov toward Kiev directly, cutting into the flank of the Russian spearheads. But Raus felt it was better to recapture Zhitomir and block the advance frontally. Nonetheless Balck's panzer Angriff hit the southern flank of the 3rd Tank Army, and turned left to recapture Zhitomir. Balck then thrust east to surround the forces at Brusilov, flanked and overran 60th Army at Radomyshl on 6 December, and maneuvered a pincers attack from Korosten and Malin to trap the Russian forces at Meleni on the Irsha on the 16th. The Russian losses were heavy, and the offensive disrupted, even if recapturing Kiev was beyond the German means. These deftly handled attacks demonstrated what experienced units under a determined and skillful commander could accomplish, even against superior numbers.[20]

But then Vatutin attacked through Walther Nehring's XXIV. Pz.K. at Brusilov, and Balck had to take three panzer divisions south to stabilize that sector. If Kiev was not recaptured, at least Balck had thwarted the encirclement of H.Gr. Süd, and prevented it being separated from H.Gr. Mitte. Amassing six panzer divisions for the Kiev counterstroke had been the exception, however, for Manstein's southern army group's capabilities. The Russians were able to continue to build up formidable forces, and the Germans could only react to the Russian assaults.

Farther south Konev's Second Ukrainian Front with Rotmistrov's 5th Guards Tank Army expanded the bridgehead against the Krivoi Rog area. Wietersheim's 11.Pz.Div., much reduced in strength, was embroiled in the fighting around Alexandria and the Ingulets through much of November, working with 3.SS-Totenkopf commanded by Brigadeführer Hermann Priess, in Wöhler's A.O.K.8. Now, instead of evenly divided Kampfgruppen, the gepanzerte elements were more often combined as a Stossgruppe (shock group) for an attack, the other elements being held in support or for consolidation and defense. For an attack on 16 November to regain contact with the 384.Inf.Div., Stossgruppe Lauchert was formed under Oberstlt. von Lauchert. It comprised Pz.-Rgt.15 (now including von Sivers's Panther battalion), the half-track battalion I./110, the armored parts of A.A.11, the Wespen and Hummeln self-propelled artillery of I.(Sf)/119, and a mine-clearing troop from Pz.Pi. Btl.209. Gruppe Henze was in support with the rest of his Pz.G.R.110, II./119, 1 Kp./209, and the assault guns of Stu.Gesch.Abt.911.

On the left flank of the Stossgruppe was I.Bataillon/111; the II.Btl. moved behind the Stossgruppe to secure against the expected enemy Gegenangriff. Major Heinz Bödicker's Pi.Btl.209 would clear anti-tank mines and then establish a defensive position supported by three tank destroyers of Major Arnold Kessler's Pz.Jg.Abt.61. Pz.A.A.11 provided flank security, and fire support was by the rest of Pz.Art.Rgt.119 and Heer.Flak-Abt.277. Major Arnold Steuer's Nachr.Abt.89 coordinated radio communications. The medical services of the H.V.Pl. were at Novo-Shevtshenkovo, and the Div.Gef.Std. was at Alexeyevka.[21] One consolidation was the Division Security Detachment being reorganized as the Division Begleit Kompanie (Escort Company). The Div.Begl.Kp. was to have two panzergrenadier platoons and a Panzerjäger Zug (Sf) commanded by Hptm. Freiherr von Ledebur.[22]

On 19 November the Gespensters were to be shifted from the Krivoi Rog area to Cherkassy by rail and by road, leaving Assault Gun Battalion 911. The movement was delayed until the 21st, and not all elements went. The E-Transport was for the gepanzerte Fahrzeuge of Pz.Rgt.15, I.Btl./110, and I.Abt./119, under the command of von Lauchert. The road march by the rest of the division was under Major Anton Donnhauser as commander of Pz.Gren.Rgt.111. The armor of the division was seventeen Panthers (one a command panzer), two Panzer IVs, one Panzer III, four light SPWs and fourteen medium SPWs, three Hummeln and seven Wespen, and four Panzerjäger.

Working in the field with SS-T must have been cordial, as reflected in the message, "Thanks, and returning greetings with the wish, 'Auf Wiedersehen'" (Until we meet again), from Priess, Kdr. 3.SS-Pz.Div. Totenkopf.[23]

But the Russians fought their way into Alexandria during the night of 23 November, and Elfte elements had to drive them out again. A gepanzerte Gruppe under von Sivers went on into Beresovka and struggled for Alexandrovka. But the Russian pressure was too great, and on the 26th any vehicles not immediately needed were ordered back across the Ingulets. At this time Gruppe Henze with II./110 and II./119 was detached to the 16. Windhund Panzergrenadierdivision under Gerhard Graf von Schwerin-Krosigk. The armored strength of the Elfte was fifteen Panthers, seven Panzer IVs, one Pz.III, two Befehlswagen, four Wespen and seven Hummeln. The fighting strength was 3,217, the ration strength being 10,030, with attachments and detachments. The mobility of the division was reported as 60 percent. A half-company of Tigers of schwere Panzer Abteilung 503 was attached to the division, as was a company of engineers from 6.Pz.Div. (1./Panz.Pi.Btl.57) and the armored Kampfgruppe of 14.Pz.Div.[24]

The infantry by now had a potent new weapon to fight the Russian tanks. This was the light (5 kilograms/11 lb) one-man, one-shot Faustpatrone 2 or Panzerfaust (armored fist) 30, produced after October 1943. It was a tube, held under the arm, that launched a hollow charge grenade that penetrated 200 mm (8 inches) at a 30-degree angle at 30 meters (33 yards). It could be fired from a standing, kneeling, or prone position, but obviously required steady nerves to engage an enemy tank at such a short range. Later models extended the range, and the Panzerfaust proved a deadly close-combat antitank weapon. New panzers in turn were receiving some additional protection against hollow charge magnetic antitank grenades or mines, with a rippled surface of factory-applied Zimmerit paste that prevented adhesion. Ironically, the Allies never did develop a hollow-charge magnetic mine like the very effective German Heft Hohlladung Granate, and the application of Zimmerit was discontinued a year later, in September 1944.[25]

Increasingly on the defensive, it was important for the Germans to retrieve damaged panzers from the battlefield, sometimes under fire. Heavy half-track Zugmaschine were used as panzer retrievers, and often panzers recovered other panzers with their tow cables. But the Panther was too heavy, so the Bergepanther had been developed as a heavy panzer retriever. It had a turretless Panther chassis with a winch that allowed it to tow disabled Panthers to a sheltered area for repair.

At 11. Panzer-Division there were command changes. At Pz.Aufkl.Abt.11 Hauptmann Wilhelm Pirch had succeeded Major Horst Lindner when Lindner was killed in ZITADELLE. Pirch was awarded the DK and then the Ritterkreuz 13 September 1943; when he went on leave, A.A.11 was commanded by Major Donnhauser who had taken over Pz.G.R.111 earlier in October. He in turn was succeeded at 111 by Oberstlt. Guido von Wartenberg. Major Joachim Menzel succeeded Major Helmut Klugmann at H.Flak.Abt.277 in November.

At the end of November the Elften were pulled out of the line back to Kirovograd for a few days rest. This respite proved all too brief, as the Russian attacks were unrelenting. On 3 December I.Abt. (Panther)/Pz.Rgt.31 of 5.Pz.Div. under Gen.Maj. Karl Decker was attached to the 11.Pz.Div. for counterattacks, and on the 5th elements of 14.Pz.Div. supported the 376.Inf.Div.[26] On 15 December an assault against Novgorodka was mounted, the grenadiers of I./Pz.Gr.Rgt.111 riding on the panzers. But in the still-dark hour of 05,00, the assault encountered Russian antitank guns organized in depth 2.5 kilometers north of Novgorodka. Half the panzers were knocked out, and the attack failed.

For 18 December the 11.Pz.-Div. was joined by some paratroop elements of the 2. Fallschirmjägerdivision. Though the Fallschirmjäger no longer received airborne jump training, these divisions were not Göring's Luftwaffenfelddivisionen; but rather tough, well-trained, and motivated infantry. The 2.Fallsch.Div. had been in the Rome area after the Salerno landings, and in November it was transferred to Russia. On 6 December it was in a counterattack with 2.SS Das Reich around Radomyshl, but then redeployed from Zhitomir south to block the Russian advance on Kirovograd.

The Fallschirmjäger were well outfitted with quilted snow-camouflage suits, including covers over their distinctive paratrooper helmets with the Luftwaffe eagle. The division was under Generalleutnant Gustav Wilke, acting commander for Gen.Lt. Hermann-Bernhard Ramcke, wounded in Italy. Sturmgeschützabteilung 911, briefly attached to 320.I.D. in October, was now attached to the paratroopers. The operations saw the assault guns and the Gespensters and 2.Fs.Jg.Div. working together. On the 18th six panzers with Fallschirmjäger on the decks cleared the gorge at Sinkova. The weather was generally below freezing now, with light snow. The Elfte reported its fighting strength (including Stu.Gesch.Abt.911 and I./Pz.Rgt.31 of 5.Pz.Div.) as 3,133, and reported 2.Fs.Jg.Div. as 4,201.[27]

On the 20th the Russians counterattacked in battalion strength, but Major von Sivers's Panthers of I./15 with I.Btl./Fs.Jg.Rgt.6 occupied a ridge south of Novgorodka and the Ivans were repulsed. Contact was made with 17.Pz.Div. under Gen.Maj. Karl-Friedrich von der Meden. Then an attack broke into the HKL, but I./110 sealed it off while a group of panzergrenadiers and eight Panthers under Lt. Eisern assisted the Fallschirmjägers. Fs.Jg.Rgt.7 took the high ground southwest of Rybchina. This was the nature of the fighting: bitterly contested struggles for high ground around the Ukrainian villages of Kutsovka, Plavni, and Nikolayevka, on toward Rudenovka. The Russians well coordinated their attacks, with tanks and infantry supported by antitank guns and artillery.

On 21 December the 11.Pz.Div. claimed only two T-34s and two assault guns, but nineteen Paks and six pieces of artillery. On that day nine Panthers of I.Abt./Pz.Rgt.31 assisted the Fallschirmjägers in reaching the eastern exit of Novgorodka. (Sivers's I./15 had only two Panthers left.) 2.Fs.Jg.Div. finally cleared all of Novgorodka on 23 December. III. Pz.Korps, with Gen.Lt. Friedrich Schulz acting commander, ordered the Fallschirmjägers to relieve the 11.Pz.Div. The Elfte then marched back north of Kirovograd into reserve, rejoined by Stu.Gesch. Abt.911. Thus Heiligeabend (Christmas Eve) 1943 found the exhausted Gespensters enjoying a relative peace, and another honorable mention in a Wehrmachtsbericht, though a number of units including Oberstlt. Schmeling's artillery had to help maintain the HKL. The weather was gloomy, with light frost followed by rain and snow showers.[28]

This fifth Christmas of the war, the third in Russia for the Elften—Vyazma 1941, Tatsinskaya or Velikiye Luki 1942, and now around Kirovograd 1943—found those able to celebrate doing so, some with a small Tannenbaum, candles, and Schnaps. General Wietersheim addressed "My dear men of the proud Gespenster Division" in a message, remembering "our fallen comrades," and urging, "If we can keep on fighting as before—but <u>only</u> then—will there once again be a safe Christmas, where you can justly speak of your deeds in this winter in the peaceful circles of your family." Lt. Martin Dietrich, adjutant of A.A.11, wrote a circular, "To all officers of the battalion, who find themselves wounded in a hospital or at home," listing those wounded or killed and summarizing the actions from Belgorod to Alexandria, maintaining the close comradeship of the combat veterans including those far away. Such holidays had ever more poignant significance amid the defeats and retreats and loss of Kameraden. At the panzer replacement depot back at Sagan in Silesia, the ceremony of swearing the oath of allegiance by new recruits was held that Christmas. One of the recruits was Horst Knaut, second son of Hauptmann Johann Knaut, the former commander of the division headquarters company who had been killed in August.[29]

All were conscious of the now overwhelming power of the Red Army. By the end of 1943 the Germans had 2,468,500 troops on the Eastern Front (and 706,000 Axis troops), the Russians had 6,394,500 men; the Germans had 2,304 panzers and assault guns, the Russians had 5,800; the Germans had 8,037 guns and mortars, the Russians had 101,400; the Germans had 3,000 aircraft, and the Russians had 13,400.[30] In addition, Allied Lend-Lease materiel strengthened the Red Army, credit given especially to the American 2.5-ton 6x6-wheeled trucks, which had front-wheel drive. These trucks enabled the Russians to motorize more rifle brigades to keep pace with the tank brigades in the tank and mechanized corps of the tank armies, and also enabled the Russians to concentrate on tank production.

Still, the tremendous wastage the Russians suffered with their constant assaults regardless of casualties convinced many Germans this manpower loss could not continue indefinitely. Said von Mellenthin at XXXXVIII. Pz.Korps, "Once again we got the impression that the spearheads of the Red Army were no longer followed by heavy infantry masses. The numerous prisoners were mostly lads of sixteen and some young boys of thirteen were found amongst them. This slaughter of children sickened even hardened veterans of the Eastern Front—our men spoke of another 'Massacre of the Innocents.'"[31] Despite the Russian materiel superiority, the Panzersoldaten maintained confidence in their own panzers and tactics against the Russian tanks. Panther Zugführer Lt. von Eggeling in 3.Kp./Pz.15 observed that the T-34s still generally did not have radios; "only the leader of the unit had connection to his superior unit and was easily spotted because only this tank had an antenna [on the right front]. So, even when the fight was 1:10 you got the Russian commander-tank first and you had all the others in the sack." It would seem that the high number of Russian tank losses claimed was essentially correct.[32] An experienced crew could engage in less than ten seconds: *"Panzergranate laden! Feuer frei! Schuss—Treffer!"* Traverse the Turm to the next target. "Load armor-piercing! Fire at will! Shoot—hit!" An experienced crew worked smoothly and efficiently.

But the aggressive Russian drives were unrelenting. On the Christian Christmas Vatutin's First Ukrainian Front stormed ahead toward Zhitomir led by the 1st Tank and 3rd Guards Tank Armies, and Konev's Second Ukrainian Front turned away from Krivoi Rog and drove north toward Kirovograd. The Elfte reported a fighting strength, including Stu. Gesch.911, of 3,000, with 638 panzergrenadiers in Pz.Gren.Rgt.110 and 492 in Pz.G.R.111. Pz.Rgt.15 had twelve Panzer Vs, six IVs. one III lang, and three command panzers einsatzbereit. There were nine Sturmgeschützen. An 11. Panzer counterattack was launched on the 27th alongside 3. and 6. Panzer-Divisionen, the Panthers delayed three hours by the "swampy ground." By the 31st, reports noted "The attack goes forward well. . . . Mission for the 1st of January 1944: the division is to hold and defend the line won on 31 December and conform to the [HKL]. The construction of the position is to be strengthened."[33]

Silvesterabend (New Year's Eve) could be acknowledged by some, and Oberfeldwebel Kurt Philipp, director of the Musikkorps of Pz.G.R.111, conducted a Winterhilfskonzert (charity-drive concert) with an orchestra of accordions, strings, and brass (saxophones, trumpets, and slide trombones) on 4 January 1944; but it was held in the City Theater back at Uman.[34] In the field there was barely time to recognize awards for bravery in 1943. Balck had received the Schwerter to the Eichenlaub on his Ritterkreuz as of 4 March 1943, and there were seventeen RKs earned by Gespensters: four in Pz.Rgt.15 including Hptm. Karl Lestmann for his command of II.Abt. and his successor Hptm. Edel-Heinrich Zachariae-Lingenthal, and two Oberfeldwebel platoon leaders; three in Pz.Gren.Rgt.110, including Hptm. Karl Thieme commanding I.Btl.(gp), and five in Pz.G.R.111 including commanders Oberst Dr. Hans Boelsen, Oberstlt. Guido von Wartenberg (who had succeeded Major Donnhauser), and Anton Donnhauser, Hauptmann when he commanded II.Bataillon.

Lt. Dieter Mund received the RK for commanding 1.Kp./Pz.Jäg.Abt.61, as did Hptm. Paul Freiherr von Hauser for commanding Kradschützen Btl.61; Hptm. Wilhelm Pirch was recognized for his leadership of Pz.A.A.11 as was Uffz. Heinz Rothardt of 2.Kp. and engineer Oberleutnant Hans-Georg Borck of 3.Kp./ Pz.Pi.Btl.209. Donnhauser and Thieme were also among those awarded Das deutsche Kreuz in Gold, along with Oberst Albert Henze and Oberstlts Graf von Schimmelmann, Alexander von Bosse, and Herwart Schmeling.

On 5 January 1944 Konev's Second Ukrainian Front launched a massive assault against the Kirovograd sector fronting the Ingul River with artillery, rocket barrages, and ground-attack aircraft, breaking through north and south of the city. The German HKL was only thinly held by Gen.Lt. Nikolaus von Vormann's XXXXVII. Pz.Korps of Wöhler's 8. Armee, with LII. Korps on its right. 10.Pz.Gren.Div. to the northeast had 3,700 troops to cover 18 kilometers (11 miles), and both corps were penetrated by the spearheads. 11. and 14. Panzer-Divisionen also held sectors, with their panzer elements held back for counterattacks. 3.Pz.Div. was released to 8. Armee by H.Gr. Süd, and in the south the Russians were stopped short of the Ingul River. But to the north Wietersheim's Elfte was unable to stop the Russians threatening to swing down behind Kirovograd from the north and casualties were heavy. There were few panzers left that were einsatzbereit, and the panzergrenadier companies, now scarcely fourteen men each, were consolidated simply as an infantry force.[35]

Konev's Front numbered some 550,000 men, and the spearheads were masses of tanks of Rotmistrov's 5th Guards Tank Army. From prisoners of war and documents the Germans estimated 620 Russian tanks; the Germans had 56 panzers and 109 assault guns. They claimed 153 Russian tanks destroyed the first day with flank attacks and Pak traps, but German losses were heavy.[36] On the 6th Konev's drive to encircle the Kirovograd defenders continued, crossing the Ingul at Severinka in the north and cutting the Kirovograd–Novomirgorod Rollbahn, and reaching the southern suburbs of the city in the south that evening.

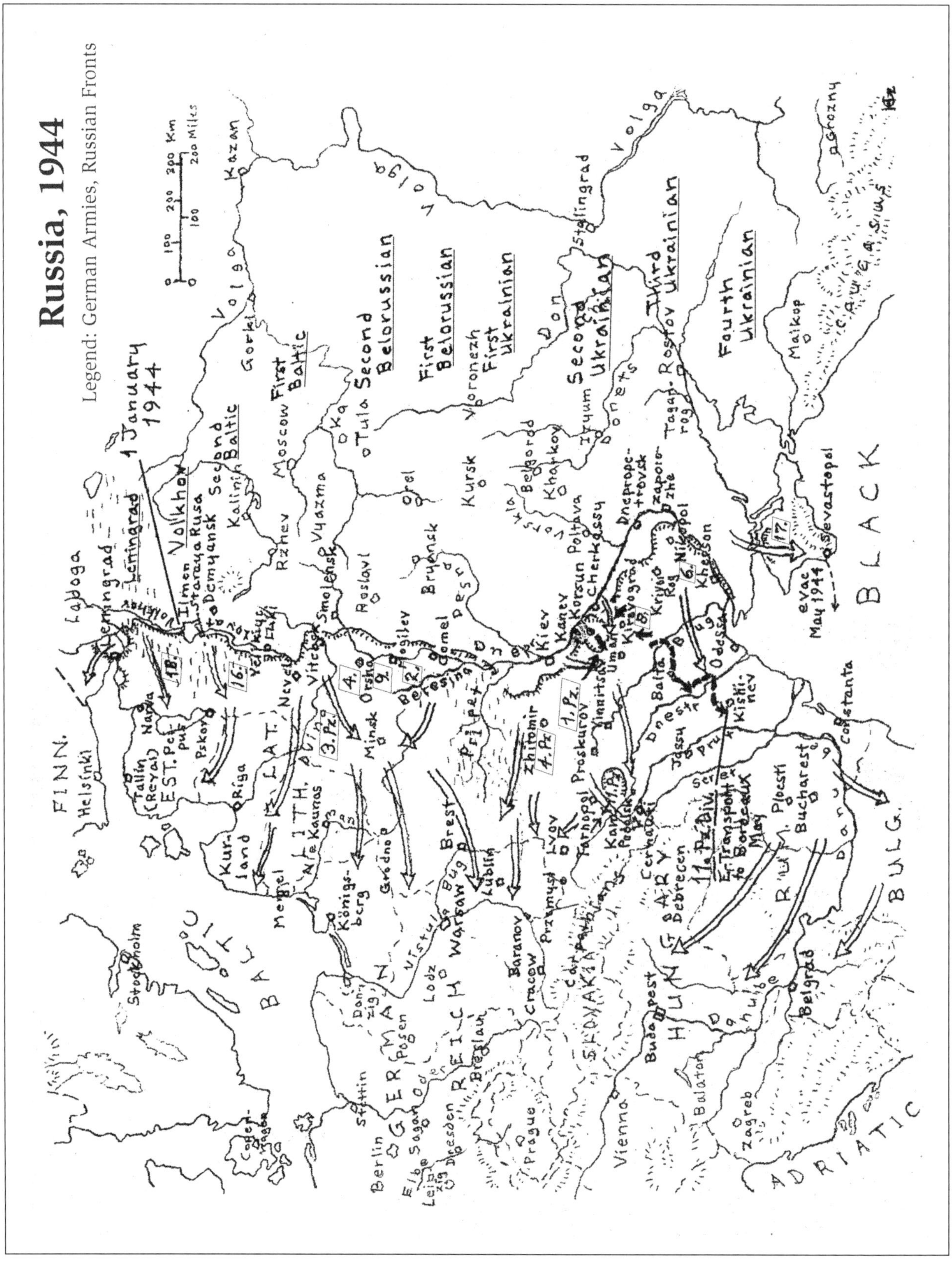

Russia, 1944

Legend: German Armies, Russian Fronts

The 3.Pz.Div. moving up was temporarily commanded by Oberst Rudolf Lang, as Gen.Maj. Fritz Bayerlein had returned to Germany to command a new panzer division. (This would be composed of training instruction units, designated in April the 130. Panzer-Lehr-Division.) But the 3.Berlin Bär panzers were also unable to stem the northern drive, and the three divisions on the HKL east of the Ingul between the enveloping drives—10.Pz.Gren.Div., 14.Pz.Div., and 376.Inf.Div.—delayed back through Adzhamka and formed a perimeter fronting Kirovograd, but still east of the river. To the south the 2.Fs.Jg.Div. fell back from Novgorodka to form a new HKL behind the Ingul, as Hörnlein's Grossdeutschland Pz.Gren.Div. was also released by Manstein to counterattack the southern drive.

During the night of 6–7 January Russian units penetrated Kirovograd in stiff house-to-house fighting, and some withdrawing German forces were isolated at Lelekovka on the north side of the city. The others delayed back to the western bank of the Ingul intact. German delaying tactics and counterattacks slowed the Russian drives, though the Ivans skillfully deployed antitank units echeloned in depth to protect the flanks of these drives. During the night of the 8th a Russian tank foray even overran von Vormann's XXXXVII. Pz.Korps headquarters at Malyye Viski up the Novomirgorod Rollbahn.

From the south Grossdeutschland and the Fallschirmjägers cut off and annihilated the Russian forces that had crossed the Ingul in three days of heavy fighting around Karlovka. 3.Pz.Div. effectively destroyed the Russian foray up the Rollbahn, and on the night of the 9th the isolated force at Lelekovka broke out to link up with a relieving force from Gruznoye. Wietersheim's 11.Pz.Div. was to supplement a 3.Pz.Div. counterattack down to Oboznovka, but was itself hard-pressed to hold the northern shoulder of the penetrations. Vormann's new HKL was formed west of Kirovograd and the Ingul on the line from Vladimirovka to west of Gruznoye-Karlovka as the city itself was abandoned by the 9th, avoiding entrapment. Two infantry divisions, 320. and 106., filled out the HKL north of the 11.Pz.Div. sector to the XI. Armeekorps HKL. The 282.I.D. was brought up as reserve.

Nonetheless Konev displaced his artillery regiments forward, delayed by the muddy conditions, and renewed the massive offensive on 11 January, ultimately breaking through between Vladimirovka and Gruznoye. These penetrations were sealed off, but on the 15th the Russian offensive penetrated the HKL anew, following heavy artillery bombardment and air attacks. There was almost continuous fighting along the whole front. On 12 January Kampfgruppe von Sivers was surrounded at Slatopov for four days, losing six panzers, but knocking out twenty-one Russian tanks.

Finally, with no operational panzers any more, some 220 Gespenster Panzermänner donned white camouflage outfits as infantry. On the 15th they mounted an attack on a small wooded area, but met heavy resistance. Two Sturmgeschützen came up in support on the 16th, but a Russian counterattack forced the Elften back. The commander, Lt. Heinz Grczeska, was killed in the early morning hours. (He had at least been able to see his newborn baby daughter on his last home leave.) Feldwebel Gustav Schrodek was wounded around midnight, and only twenty-seven of the two hundred-some Panzersoldaten returned from their "infantry interlude."[37]

On that 16 January Konev again broke through, but 3.SS Panzer-Division Totenkopf mounted a spoiling attack meeting the Russians head-on. Kirovograd and the line of the Ingul had been lost, but a new Hauptkampflinie was consolidated a few kilometers back to the west. Most of the defending divisions were now barely small battle groups, but the Russians had taken tremendous casualties as well. The Germans estimated that many Russian regiments were reduced to 300–400 men, and by the 17th the Russian tank strength as down to some 120 tanks.[38] Using their mobility, the smaller German forces had delayed, parried, and counterattacked the massive Russian assaults and prevented a breakthrough and encirclement in the twelve days of bitter fighting.

CHAPTER TWENTY-ONE

Cherkassy–Korsun Kessel

OF THE SIX DNEPR RIVER CROSSINGS OVER WHICH MANSTEIN'S Heeresgruppe Süd had crossed in 1943 ahead of the Soviet armies, only around Kanev along the middle Dnepr—the site where three Russian parachute brigades had been wiped out in September—did German forces still have a presence on the river itself as a salient by January 1944. Elsewhere they had been driven back to the west. As Konev's Second Ukrainian Front around Kirovograd to the south and Vatutin's First Ukrainian Front west of Kiev to the north pressed westward, the flanks of the German Kanev salient became ever more vulnerable. Manstein and his commanders all agreed the salient should be evacuated, but Hitler was adamant about retaining it, still hoping to mount a counteroffensive, either north to regain Kiev or south to Kirovograd.

On 24 January there were Russian probes against the Vorposten along the southeast base of the salient where 389. Infanterie-Division of XI. Armeekorps linked to 3. Panzer-Division of Generalleutnant Nikolaus von Vormann's XXXXVII. Panzerkorps along the Kirovograd sector. The clanking of tank treads and the deployment of the Stalinsorgel, indicating a coming assault, had been monitored by German intelligence over the previous days, and the Germans were on the alert. Heavy pressure forced the 389.Inf.Div. back, and the Rotarmisten were busily clearing minefields and wire obstacles that night. General der Artillerie Wilhelm Stemmermann, Kommandeur of XI. A.K. in the eastern part of the salient, ordered his 57.I.D. south to reinforce the 389., and pressed Gen. der Inf. Otto Wöhler of 8. Armee to make available 14.Pz.Div. from XXXXVII. Pz.K. These orders went out, and Wietersheim's 11.Pz.Div., north of Kirovograd, was alerted for movement as well.[1]

At 06,00 hours on 25 January, Konev's artillery and Katyusha rocket regiments exploded in a violent barrage along the eastern base of the salient and against 3.Pz.Div. of Vormann's XXXXVII. Pz.K., and the Russian assault began. Vormann ordered Oberst Lang's 3. Pz.Div. to counterattack. But 3. Panzer was itself under heavy attack by artillery and ground-attack planes, as was indeed Vormann's corps front in general. By afternoon on the 25th the 14.Pz.Div. under Generalmajor Martin Unrein completed its movement from Vormann's right flank around to the threatened left, to blunt the Russian drive. Kampfgruppen of Pz.Gren.Rgt.103 and 108 were to take position at Rossoschovatka and at Kapitanovka to the north, respectively. Pz.Rgt.36 would be prepared to mount an attack, though it only had eleven panzers and assault guns.

To the north a Kampfgruppe of 5.SS Pz.Div. Wiking fought to aid the 389.I.D. and close the gap that had opened between the two corps. What was unclear yet was the Russian axis of advance—was it westward to penetrate behind the salient, or to turn south in a larger operation toward the southern Bug River? Feldmarschall von Manstein might have deduced the Russian objective, but on the 26th he was called from his headquarters at Vinnitsa to a meeting of army and army group commanders of the Ostfront with Hitler on the 27th at Königsberg.[2] On that 26th packs of Soviet T-34s broke through the 14.Pz.Div. near Kapitanovka. Wöhler, before he left for the meeting, put 11. Panzer-Division directly under 8. Armee control to attack from Pisarevka toward Kapitanovka.

But at 11,30 hours reports were received from Generaloberst Hans Valentin Hube's 1. Panzerarmee on the *western* side of the salient that Vatutin's First Ukrainian Front had opened a massive assault against 88.Inf.Div. of XXXXII. A.K. and 34. and 198.Inf.Div. of VII. A.K. It was becoming clear that Vatutin's and Konev's thrusts threatened to drive behind and encircle the German forces in the Kanev salient.

Meanwhile Wietersheim's Elfte had come up and mounted its counterattack. The panzergrenadiers advanced to Kamenovatka, 12 kilometers (7 miles) south of Kapitanovka, and Pz.-Rgt.15 swung through Zlatapol. Major Karl von Sivers had taken over Pz.Rgt.15 for von Lauchert on 24 January when the latter went on Tapferkeitsurlaub (valor leave) following his being awarded the Eichenlaub to the RK; Major Weicke took over Sivers's I. (Panther) Abteilung. By evening the Gespensters had cleared Pisarevka and Tishkovka as they drove toward Kapitanovka, though strong Russian forces held that village as masses of Russian troops, trucks, and guns headed west.[3]

The isolation and destruction of the Kanev salient, which included the town of Korsun, was indeed the Russian objective in their Korsun-Schevchenkovsky Operation (after the full name of the town). Konev's Second Ukrainian Front assaulted the XI. Korps positions with 4th Guards Army under Maj.Gen. Aleksandr Ryshov, and the XXXXVII. Pz.Korps positions with 53rd Army under Lt. Gen. Ivan Galanin. But Konev was impatient to commit Pavel Rotmistrov's 5th Guards Tank Army—on the 25th he replaced Ryshov with General Smirnov—and late on the 25th ordered Maj. Gen. I. G. Lazarov's 20th and Maj. Gen. I. F. Kirichenko's 29th Tank Corps into the attack through Kapitanovka and westward. Rotmistrov had some 22,300 troops and 197 tanks and assault guns.

On the western side of the salient Vatutin committed the 6th Tank Army, newly formed on 20 January under Lt. Gen. Andrei Kravchenko, on the 26th. Initially this attack was thwarted, and Hube's 1. Pz.Armee's headquarters continued concentrating on ongoing fighting farther to the west. But on the 27th Kravchenko's drive swung back southeastward and picked up momentum, and when German intelligence finally confirmed the identity of the new tank army, it was clear that a Russian pincers operation to encircle the Kanev salient was underway.

On the eastern side as Rotmistrov drove west, spearheaded by Lazarov's 20th Tank Corps, Unrein's 14.Pz.Div. was split, with Kampfgruppe Major Heinz von Brese's Pz.Gren.Rgt.108 isolated north of Kapitanovka. Von Vormann now intended a drive north into the flank of Rotmistrov's advance with three panzer divisions, though this had to be coordinated through three headquarters: Lang's 3.Pz.Div. was under XXXXVII. Pz.K. on the right, Unrein's 14. Panzer was under Stemmermann's XI. A.K. in the center, and Wietersheim's 11. Gespenster-Division was directly under 8. Armee on the left.

Nonetheless the attack jumped off at 05,30 Uhr on 27 January. It was led by 11. Panzer-Division, with twelve Panthers, three Pz.IVs, and fifteen Stu.Gesch.IIIs from three assault gun battalions. But the panzergrenadiers had to fight for Pisarevka again, and Sivers's Kampfgruppe, with Thieme's I./110 in half-tracks and II.Abt./Pz.Art.Rgt.119, had to fight for Tishkovka as new waves of T-34s surged westward. Hptm. Walter Schaefer-Kehnert commanded the artillery battalion. He had already been awarded the DK in Gold 5 December 1943 ("Party badge for the nearsighted" he joked because of its large Hakenkreuz in the center). In one of his letters home he related the confused fighting for Tishkovka as the Ivans reoccupied the center of the town, and two of his battery commanders, up with the Beobachtungsposten, were

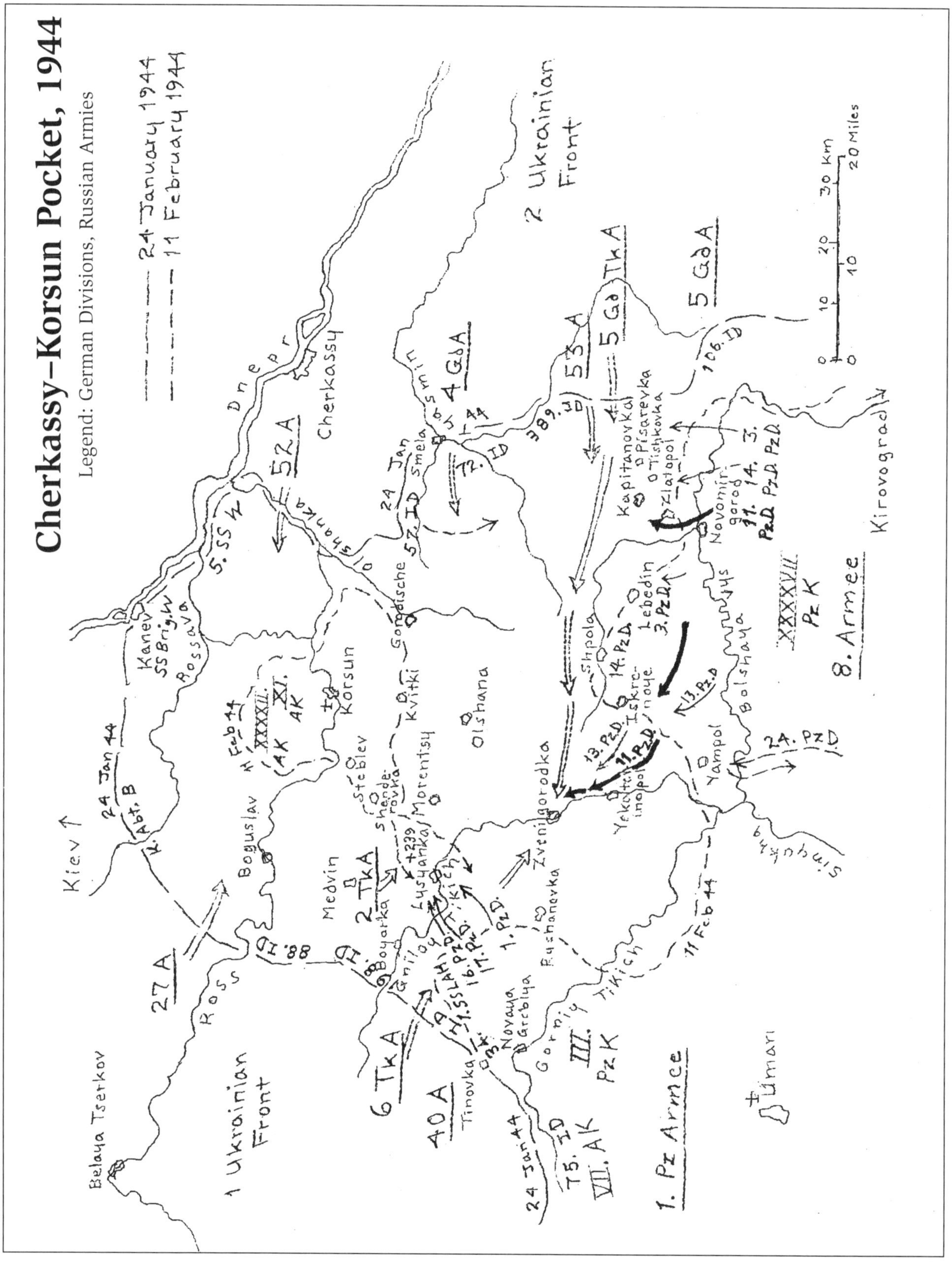

Cherkassy–Korsun Pocket, 1944
Legend: German Divisions, Russian Armies

cut off: "The situation had gotten completely out of control. Our panzers outside of the town had formed a hedgehog for self-defense. . . . On the map, red (for Soviet [tactical symbols]) and blue (for German), were all mixed together. That night, my two battery commanders were able to sneak back through the enemy-occupied town. They were quite a sight to see, and we embraced each other [in joy], when we met up."[4]

To the left the Gespensters reached Kapitanovka and briefly made contact with 14. Panzer's Kampfgruppe von Brese, cutting behind 20th Tank Corps and threatening the destruction of Rotmistrov's spearhead. But 3.Pz.Div. was hard-pressed to hold its own, and the 14.Pz.Div. history related, "More and more armored vehicles festooned with masses of infantry pushed forward in endless columns, closely followed by galloping cavalry formations, [and] flowed around the remaining islands of resistance and continued onward."[5]

Von Vormann recorded:

> Without regard to losses—in the truest sense of the term, the Red masses flooded to the west during the afternoon past the panzers of 3., 11., and 14. Panzer Divisions, who were firing with every barrel, as well as past our heavy artillery fire. An amazing, shatteringly dramatic picture! No other true comparison could fit [this amazing scene]: the dam had broken, and the massive unending flood plunged over the flat landscape, where [our] panzers, surrounded by our few remaining infantry, stood out like cliffs in a firestorm. Our amazement rose further still, when in the late afternoon through the middle of our Sperrfeuer (barrier fire), tightly-packed cavalry formations [of the enemy] galloped towards the west. It was an unforgettable, incredibly shattering scene.[6]

These were the mechanized and three tank brigades of Rotmistrov's third tank corps, the 18th, and the three cavalry divisions of 5th Guards Cossack Cavalry Corps under Maj. Gen. A. G. Selivanov. Their casualties were horrendous, but they swept on regardless.

At 18,00 hours on the 27th the three panzer divisions were put under von Vormann's XXXXVII. Pz.K. control for better coordination, but the 11.Pz.Div. was forced from Tinovka and contact with Kgr. von Brese was lost. 14.Pz.Div. had only six panzers and assault guns left. The Elfte's Pz.Aufkl.Abt.11 now under Maj.Werner von Rupprecht and Pz.Pi.Btl.209 under Maj. Heinz Bödicker were cut off in Tishkovka. The next day the panzer counterattack was ordered to continue, though von Wietersheim and Unrein had scarcely three hundred combat troops each, while Lang's 3. Panzer was stopped by antitank guns.

But Wietersheim had been reinforced with the sixty-one Panthers of I.Abt./Pz.Rgt.26 under Major Glaesgen, temporarily attached from Pz.Gren.Div. Grossdeutschland. The Panthers, accompanied by the assault guns of Stu.Gesch.Abt.911 attacked toward Pisarevka, but had a frontal engagement with a Soviet tank attack from Ossitnyashka. In addition, Konev's spearhead was followed by infantry and antitank units to broaden and defend the penetration. The attack encountered a crossfire from tanks and antitank guns in Pisarevka and Tishkovka. By 11,00 hours the Panthers had knocked out twelve T-34s but lost fifteen of their own, and Major Glaesgen was fatally wounded while in his turret.[7]

By late afternoon on 28 January Lt. Col. Ivan Proshin's 155th Tank Brigade of the 5th Guards Tank Army met Gen. M. I. Savelyev's 233rd Tank Brigade of 6th Tank Army from the north at Zvenigorodka, completing the encirclement of the German forces in the Kanev salient. OKH would term this the Kessel von Tscherkassy—presumably as Cherkassy was on the Dnepr, though no longer held by the Germans. More correctly it was the Korsun Kessel, as that was the site of the crucial airfield and German supply depots.

Konev was convinced that Wöhler's entire 8. Armee was trapped, over ten divisions and 100,000 Germans, as Paulus's 6. Armee had been trapped at Stalingrad. In reality the Kessel had less than that, perhaps 65,000 troops in six understrength divisions and a brigade, the defense complicated by the fact that they were in two corps, each subordinate to a different army: 88.Inf.Div. and division-sized K.Abt.B (Korps Abteilung B, the remnants of 112., 255., and 332.I.D.) in Generalleutnant Theobald Lieb's XXXXII. Armeekorps of Generaloberst Hube's 1. Pz.Armee in the western part, and 57., 72., and 389.Inf.Div., 5.SS Pz.Div. Wiking, and motorized SS Freiwilligen Sturmbrigade Wallonie (French-speaking Belgian volunteers) in General Stemmermann's XI. A.K. of General Wöhler's 8. Armee in the eastern part. In addition, Kampfgruppe von Brese of 14.Pz.Div. and other units were also in the trap, though 11. Panzer's A.A.11 and Pi.209 had extricated themselves from Tishkovka. Because prisoners were captured from all of these, it has been surmised that the Russians deduced their parent units were also in the Kessel, hence Konev's exaggerated estimate.[8]

Nonetheless, even granted the overwhelming strength of the Russian forces and the losses they could endure, the encirclement had been expertly conducted. Deception measures had disguised the timing and direction of the assaults, and the tank spearheads had plunged ahead disregarding the flanks, knowing follow-on infantry and antitank units would deepen and defend the penetrations. Only the artillery was delayed in displacing forward. The weather and terrain hampered the Russians as it did the Germans. The winter in the Ukraine was not as harsh as it was farther east and north, and while the ground might freeze at night, permitting movement, daytime thaws turned the road network into a bog of mud. The roadless Schlammperiode (Rasputitsa) came early in Ukraine. Sunshine, rain, and snow alternated with freeze and thaw to keep the ground a mire.

Whereas the relevant German chiefs of staff had not felt authorized to make major decisions about operations and command arrangements until their commanders returned from Hitler's conference, the commanders did return on the 28th. When Manstein arrived at Uman he immediately placed Lieb's XXXXII. A.K. under 8. Armee and allowed contraction to the Rossava River, abandoning Kanev despite Hitler's wishes. On 7 February Stemmermann by seniority was named to command all the forces in the Kessel.

Manstein also began planning for the relief and retreat of the Kessel, determined it would not become another Stalingrad. Gen.d.Pz.Tr. Hermann Breith's III. Pz.Korps of 1. Pz.Armee and Vormann's XXXXVII. Pz.K. of 8. Armee were alerted for this. Manstein could even contemplate a two-pronged drive that would not only relieve the pocket, but also encircle and destroy the 5th Guards Tank and 6th Tank Army elements that had thrust behind the Kessel. Vormann's panzer divisions however were in poor shape, and badly in need of reinforcements and Auffrischung. On 29 January GD's Panther battalion with 11.Pz.Div. made another foray, but the Rotarmisten were too strong. Of its original sixty-one Panthers I./26 had only seventeen einsatzbereit, and twenty of those disabled were total losses.[9]

While the Kesselkämpfer (cauldron-fighters) initially had adequate supplies, many of their rear-area trains elements, such as supply and medical, had been separated by the encirclement and were sorely needed. As elsewhere, aerial resupply was quickly coordinated through Luftwaffe General der Flieger Hans Seidemann's VIII. Flieger Korps. The ubiquitous trimotor Ju 52s would fly essential supplies, including ammunition and fuel, into Korsun, navigating by radio beacon in darkness; they would also evacuate the wounded. Russian fighters and antiaircraft guns shot a number down, but Oblt. Erich Hartmann's Jagdgeschwader (Fighter Wing) 52 Messerschmitt Bf 109s escorted the flights.

The flight distance from Uman to Korsun was only 100 kilometers (62 miles) and from 27 January to 3 February the Ju 52s and twin-engined Heinkel He 111s were able to fly in 120–140 tons of supply a day, and evacuate 2,800 wounded via racks that fit twelve litters per plane. As the siege continued, however, the situation at Korsun airfield worsened. It was bombed and damaged from weathering and excessive use. When it was finally within range of Russian artillery, it had to be abandoned 13–14 February. From then on supply canisters had to be dropped by parachute, with ever-diminishing results. Ultimately the Luftwaffe airlift flew or dropped 2,026 tons of supplies and evacuated 4,161 wounded. Thirty-two Ju 52s were lost.[10]

While Manstein had to anticipate a Russian offensive beyond the encirclement—whether toward the Bug or south toward the Black Sea, as the Russian offensive had been expanded during Stalingrad—intelligence soon reported the Russians were preparing defensive positions and digging in their tanks against any German relief attack. Breith's III. Pz.K. was transferred from the Vinnitsa sector and was relatively well equipped, with 16. and 17.Pz.Div. and an ad hoc panzer regiment under Oberstleutnant Dr. Franz Bäke (Kdr. Pz.Rgt.11/6.Pz.Div.), followed by 1.Pz.Div. and 1.SS Pz.Div. LAH. Bäke's regiment had thirty-four Tigers of s.Pz.Abt.503 and forty-six Panthers of I./Pz.Rgt.23 of 23.Pz.Div., as well as an assault gun battalion.

Vormann's panzer divisions were much weaker. 13.Pz.Div. from Magdeburg under Gen.Maj. Hans Mikosch was at strength and transferred from LII. A.K., but Unrein's 14.Pz.Div. from Dresden was without its Pz.G.R.108, trapped in the Kessel. Wietersheim's 11. Panzer was working hard to get its few

Panzerwagens einsatzbereit, the GD's Panther battalion made scarcely a company, and Lang's 3.Pz.Div. was burned out. 24.Pz.Div. of Frankfurt was ordered up from Generaloberst Hollidt's 6. Armee southeast of Kirovograd, but it would require several days of road movement along deteriorating roads.[11]

Manstein planned the relief attack to be implemented on 3 February, but apparently Wöhler felt the need for Vormann's panzer corps to keep attempting to break through to Stemmermann before it was up to strength, over Vormann's objections. There were sharp actions where the weakened forces nonetheless aggressively mounted forays. The 11. Panzer gepanzerte Gruppe was led by Major Karl von Sivers. His unit opened a lane through a Russian hasty minefield, drove rapidly north, and opened fire on Russian tanks and forces in the southern part of Lebedin on 31 January. This attack from the rear threw the Ivans into confusion. Russian officers tried to organize a defense and positioned more Paks, but these were destroyed before they could be brought to bear, some by Sivers in his own Wagen.

Meanwhile Sivers sent another element around to the northwest under cover of a snowstorm, and these panzers attacked Lebedin from that direction as well. After engaging Russian columns moving west, Sivers's Kampfgruppe returned to the German positions. Once again it was demonstrated how a foray from an unexpected direction, with rapid maneuvering, could cause confusion and destruction among much larger Rotarmisten units. Kriegsgefangene were from Antitank Regiment 318 and the 31st Tank Brigade of the 29th Tank Corps, and included the chief of staff of the corps, of 5th Guards Tank Army. The Wehrmachtsbericht of 1 February presumably was referring to this attack, of a Panzervorstoss northwest of Kirovograd, claiming seventeen Soviet tanks knocked out.[12]

On 1 February Wietersheim's 11.Pz.Div. launched Vormann's attack, while 14.Pz.Div. took over its sector on the right, linked by 3.Pz.Div. between them. Mikosch's 13.Pz.Div. was to be on Wietersheim's left, but only contributed a small panzer Kampfgruppe and one hundred panzergrenadiers. The Gespensters seized a bridge over the Shpolka River near Iskrenoye, 10 kilometers west of Shpola, and pressed north. But that afternoon rising waters from thawing snow caved in the bridge after only four panzers had crossed. The remaining panzers and the 13.Pz.Div. panzergrenadiers were unable to cross. The 11.Pz.-Div. Kampfgruppe holding the bridgehead was faced with counterattacks by the 18th and 29th Guards Tank corps for the next three days, the Pioniere unable to erect a new bridge under intense fire. The Gespensters claimed sixty-two Soviet tanks destroyed, but the Kgr. was reduced to one panzer and eighty Panzergrenadieren. Oberst von Zychlinski was commanding Pz.G.R.110 because Oberst Albert Henze had gone to command Panzergrenadierdivision FHH (Feldherrnhalle) on the Narva sector in the north, taking command 2 February.

Unrein's 14.Pz.Div. Saxons tried again to regain contact with Pz.Gren.Rgt.108 north of Shpola on 31 January with a small force of two assault guns and a reconnaissance company escorting a resupply column. But they were stopped and driven back, and von Brese's Kampfgruppe had to withdraw north into the Kessel again, on the right flank of 57.I.D. Forced to abandon his panzers due to lack of fuel, von Brese was down to one hundred panzergrenadiers and one light howitzer battery, and was incorporated into 5.SS Wiking.[13] Vormann's XXXXVII. Pz.K. could only await the 24.Pz.Div. before a relief attack was resumed.

To the west Breith's III. Panzerkorps of Hube's 1. Pz.Armee assembled its forces for its relief attempt. Hube urged Manstein that, instead of a drive north to Medvin, Breith first attack east toward Morentsy to link up with Vormann for a more powerful drive north, but Manstein felt this would postpone the relief of Gruppe Stemmermann, hard-pressed to fend off powerful Russian attacks. Breith's attack began at 06,00 on 4 February spearheaded by Bäke's Tigers of s.Pz.Abt.503 and Panthers, with 17.Pz.Div. under Gen.Lt. Karl-Friedrich von der Meden on the right, and 16.Pz.Div. on the left. The 16.Panzer was commanded by Gen.Maj. Hans-Ulrich Back, former commander of the Elfte's 11.Pz.Gren.Brigade. Supported by artillery fire and Stuka attacks Breith drove almost 30 kilometers into the Soviet defenses that day, reaching the Gniloy Tikich Creek, behind Kravchenko's 6th Tank Army.

But thawing mud delayed the arrival of the 1.Pz.Div. and the LAH, fog grounded the Stukas, and Vatutin committed 130 tanks of 6th Tank Army. In addition, Lt. Gen. Semen Bogdanov's 2nd Tank Army was arriving. For the next few days III. Pz.Korps struggled ahead, against Russian tank attacks and against mud. Tigerpanzern were needed to pull lines of two-wheel drive Opel "Blitz" trucks with their vital gasoline and ammunition through the muck. Even panzergrenadiers had to dismount their Sd.Kfz.251 SPWs to lighten the load the Halbketten had to pull forward. At the same time the Kesselkämpfer were forced to contract their lines farther away from the relief point.

In Vormann's XXXXVII. Panzerkorps the rebuilt 24. Der Springende Reiter Pz.Div. under Gen.Maj. Reichsbaron Maximilian von Edelsheim had just begun to arrive on 4 February from the south after struggling for eight days along 300 kilometers (186 miles) of mud-engulfed roads. Incomprehensibly, the order came that same day for the 24.Pz.Div. to disengage and return south, where Malinovsky's Third Ukrainian and Tolbukhin's Fourth Ukrainian Fronts had broken through Hollidt's 6. Armee Nikopol sector. It was Hitler's decision: the Nikopol nickel deposits and refineries could not be lost. Weakened by the wastage from mud and mechanical breakdowns, it was obvious to all that the 24.Pz.Div. would not be able to effectively intervene in the south in time, and its withdrawal now meant Vormann's XXXXVII. Pz.K. could not mount a major part of the relief operation.[14]

The new plan called for Breith's III. Pz.K. to attack eastward towards Lysyanka on the Gniloy Tikich and Morentsy, and for Stemmermann to break out of the pocket toward them. Vormann would attack north on the axis from Zvenigorodka to Olshana, if only as a diversion. To close the gap between 1. Pz. and 8. Armee an ad hoc Kampfgruppe under Gen.Maj. Werner Haack was formed, its nucleus an ad hoc regiment of troops of the besieged units returned from furlough under Oberstlt. Kurt Baake.

In the Kessel, while Stemmermann was in overall command, Lieb, considered the more aggressive leader, would command the breakout force. The battered 389.Inf.Div., with only two hundred infantry and three batteries of artillery, was disbanded, and they were attached to the 57.I.D. Rifle regiments were down to 150 fighting men, less than 10 percent of authorized strength. On 8 February three Russians in an American jeep under a white flag approached the HKL of Korps Abteilung B, and presented letters for Generals Lieb and Stemmermann. It was a surrender ultimatum signed by Zhukov, Konev, and Vatutin. Major Johannes Sepauschke read the contents by telephone to Lieb, who simply said to return them. Sepauschke did treat the envoys to brandy and sandwiches, partly to demonstrate that the Germans still had adequate rations, and then had them blindfolded and returned to their own lines.

On 10 February General Lieb received a letter dropped by an airplane addressed to him by Gen.d.Art. Walter Seydlitz, his old division commander in 1940. Captured at Stalingrad, Seydlitz was now president of the Bund Deutscher Offiziere (League of German Officers) in the Soviet-sponsored Nationalkomitee Freies Deutschland, urging him to desert Hitler and take his command over to the Russians, just as General Graf Yorck von Wartenberg had deserted Napoleon with his Prussian Corps in 1812. Lieb noted in his diary, "I did not answer." Loudspeakers and radio broadcasts, as well as propaganda leaflets dropped by airplane or fired in artillery shells, also bombarded the besieged, promising generous treatment and sumptuous food. There is no evidence the German Landsers believed these promises even as their own situations deteriorated.[15]

As Stemmermann planned his role in the breakout, he reported his strength to 8. Armee as some 56,000 men including 2,000 wounded as of 11 February. Rations and medical shortages were having their deleterious effects, as ammunition and fuel took first priority among the supplies flown in. On 11 February the renewed relief drive began. Breith attacked eastward along the Gniloy Tikich, Back's 16.Pz.Div. with Bäke's Tigers and Panthers and von der Meden's 17.Pz.Div. attacking in parallel north of the creek, the 1. LSSAH under Brigadeführer Wisch guarding the left flank, and 1.Pz.Div. under Gen.Maj. Richard Koll south of the creek on the right flank. Koll had forty-eight Panthers and eighteen Panzer IVs, the strongest division of the four. Breith's III. Pz.K. totaled 165 panzers and assault guns.

Breith attacked along the Gniloy Tikich to capture Lysyanka, which had two bridges. This proved vital, as the heavy bridging companies were still delayed by mud around Uman. With 24.Pz.Div. withdrawn, von Vormann protested that his XXXXVII. Pz.Korps, with only seventeen panzers and assault guns, was too weak to mount the subsidiary attack, now planned for his unit to attack toward Zvenigorodka to at least tie down some of Rotmistrov's 5th Guards Tank Army. Mikosch's 13.Pz.Div., which had taken over the Iskrenoye bridgehead, evacuated it, and the Schwerpunkt of the corps was shifted westward, with the infantry divisions taking over the panzer sectors.

As Lang's 3.Pz.Div. still had to cover the HKL, and Unrein's weak 14.Pz.Div. was relegated to reserve, Wietersheim's 11. Panzer-Division would have to mount the corps drive. Attacking on the morning of 11 February, in conjunction with Kampfgruppe Haack, the Gespensters seized the town of Yerki, captured a bridge over the Shpolka River intact, and headed toward Yekaterinopol until the fuel gave out. Fuel canisters were dropped by air that night, and 13.Pz.Div. came up on Wietersheim's right flank. The drive continued, up the east bank of the Gniloy Tikich, through Skalevatka and Yurkovka, knocking out eighteen Soviet tanks along the way. They also got Stuka ground-attack support from Hans-Ulrich Rudel's Stuka Geschwader "Immelmann." Rudel even claimed a Shturmovik with his underwing-mounted 3,7cm Pak.

The Elfte reached the heights overlooking Zvenigorodka and Hill 204.8. Vormann's spearheads claimed fifty-eight Russian tanks knocked out by 15 February, but Rotmistrov's 20th and then 18th Tank Corps mounted fierce counterattacks. By then Wietersheim and the attached I./26 Panther battalion had only three panzers operational; some fifty-five others were broken down or mud-bound back along the routes from Kapitanovka. With a shortage of canisters and parachutes the Luftwaffe Ju 52s had to drop barrels of fuel and crates of ammunition at low 10-meter altitudes. A discouraged Vormann later wrote:

> This was the last success of 8. Armee in this battle. Its strength was finally spent. In the mud and frost, drizzling rain and snow storms, the troops had performed superhuman feats during the past few days despite insufficient rations—now it had come to an end. Only with panzers, that is, with machines, was it possible to carry out any kind of offensive action in this muddy ground. More was demanded of them than [the panzers] were capable of doing, and they simply broke down without warning, as opposed to men and horses, who gradually reached the limits of their endurance before collapsing.[16]

Meanwhile Breith attacked on the 11th and Bäke's panzers with Back's 16.Pz.-Div. seized a bridge over the Gniloy Tikich near Frankovka, though another bridge across to Bushanka was destroyed as the Germans approached. Koll's 1.Pz.Div. kept pace on the south bank and as a frost hardened the ground surface the Panthers of his advanced Kampfgruppe fought into the parts of Lysyanka south of the creek by 03,00 hours on the 12th. The bridges were demolished by the Russians as 1.Pz.Div. arrived and the creek was unfordable there. But then a patrol found a fording site for the Panthers the next day, panzergrenadiers waded through the ice-cold water, and by 23,00 hours of the 13th Lysyanka was in German hands.

The 1. Panzer's Brückenkolonne-K was still stuck in the mud near Uman, but then a previously unknown bridge with a 40-ton capacity was discovered and captured on the 14th. That evening the forward elements received containers of fuel and ammunition by Seidemann's Ju 52s, flying at rooftop level to drop them, guided by the headlights of vehicles lining the roadway of Lysyanka. There was a shortage of jerry cans, so the panzer crews had to pour gasoline from 200-liter (50-gallon) drums into buckets to refuel the panzers.

On the next day Bäke's Tigers and Panthers led Koll's 1.Pz.Div. to take the village of Oktyabr, consolidated on the 16th, and mounted a foray that briefly ascended the commanding height of Hill 239 beyond Lysyanka. But Bogdanov's 2nd Tank Army had been committed, and Kravchenko's 6th Tank and Rotmistrov's 5th Guards Tank Armies mounted fierce attacks to block the relief attempts. Vormann was under intense pressure from Wöhler to fight ahead. He knew without 24.Pz.Div. his XXXXVII. Pz.K. was too weak to do so; but Wöhler, and Vormann's subordinates, felt the urgency to help save Stemmermann's forces in the Kessel.

Vormann could at least try to close the gap between 1. Pz.Armee and 8. Armee, and attached Wietersheim's five operational panzers to Gruppe Haack to do so. On the 16th Mikosch's 13.Pz.Div.'s and 11.Pz. Div.'s battle groups struggled ahead, and the Gespensters reached Hill 208,9 at Zvenigorodka. Wöhler met with Vormann and the two division commanders at the 11.Pz.Div. Gefechtsstand at Yerki to urge them on. Wietersheim was weak from being abed with Vohlynin Fever, a viral infection like influenza, and his Ia, Oberstlt. Werner Drews, was still sick with the fever. The enervating exhaustion and the strain of constant crises made tempers brittle.[17]

Gruppe Haacke was meanwhile pushing west to link up with Breith's III. Pz.K. Hptm. Schaefer-Kehnert's II./Pz.Art.Rgt.119 gave artillery support to

Baake's infantry in attacking Hill 204,8. Schaefer-Kehnert was forward in a Panther acting as V.B. himself, even using his own panzer's gun to fire on two Russian antitank guns, and then the Panther's machine guns against the Ivans fleeing their trenches atop the hill. But XXXXVII. Pz.Korps could make no progress in facilitating the relief effort.

Thus Gruppe Stemmermann would attempt to break out of the Kessel and meet Breith's III. Panzerkorps at Lysyanka on the Gniloy Tikich the night of 16–17 February, 10 kilometers (6 miles) away. As the perimeter contracted, the lead forces gathered in Shenderovka (Shanderovka). Russian artillery and Stalinsorgel barrages covered most of the Kessel, and the Kesselkämpfer called Shenderovka "Höllentor" (Hell's Gate) with its burning buildings, smashed vehicles and equipment, corpses, and newly wounded and killed. Unit commanders attempted to keep discipline, though there were stragglers, many of them victims of "Kesselpsychose," the panicky feeling of being trapped.

Lieb was to direct the breakout, and orders had been distributed to the divisions on the 15th to move in five waves along three parallel divisional axes. Some 50,000 troops were involved. But these included some 2,000 men too badly wounded to be moved. Lieb consulted Stemmermann and it was decided to leave them, with medical personnel and one doctor from each division, behind. "This is a bitter decision," Lieb noted in his diary for the 16th, "but to take them along would mean their certain death."[18] But perhaps he knew that few would survive Soviet captivity.

At 23,00 hours on 16 February, ordered by Manstein though without Hitler's concurrence, the assault wave moved out. Silently, covered by snow squalls, they hoped to bypass or break through Russian positions in their white camouflaged suits like wraiths in the night, with bayonets and sharpened entrenching spades only. Leaving vehicles behind, the columns moved in single file, following the path trodden through the snowfields. Most of these elements reached the 1.Pz.Div. lines, but a patrol of the center column saw the outlines of T-34s on Hill 239 and experienced the chilling realization that the hill was not in German hands. A company-sized Kampfgruppe of the arriving 1.LSSAH supported by Bäke's Tigers had tried again to take it the previous evening but the Russians were too strong.

At dawn of the 17th came the Russians, now fully alert to the breakout, who opened furious fire and mounted fierce attacks. Tragedy now struck as panic began to overtake the waves of escaping German troops. The breakout had been predicated on the understanding that 1.Pz.Div. held the commanding Hill 239, and radio communication with Stemmermann to inform him otherwise had failed. A terrible misunderstanding had arisen, perhaps due to the lack of unity of command: the Kessel under Stemmermann was of Wöhler's 8. Armee, but the relieving force under Breith's III.Pz.K. was of Hube's 1.Pz.Armee.

Deflected by the Russian tanks and guns on Hill 239, many of the following forces diverged to the south, away from the Lysyanka bridges to the north, and now sought to cross the Gniloy Tikich. The creek, swollen by melting snow, was in flood stage up to 3 meters (10 feet) deep, and 15 meters (50 feet) wide, and the air temperature was –5 degrees Celsius (22 F). In panicked desperation many now plunged into the icy creek only to be swept away and drowned. Lieb himself was carried along on his horse; the mount was lost but he made it across and began to try and rally those reaching the western bank in their frozen clothing. "I remember very well," recalled Lt. von Eggeling of Pz.Rgt.15 many years later, "the sight of thousands and thousands of soldiers, wounded, without their weapons, mostly on foot—a shattered army like Napoleon's army at the Beresina."[19]

Russian tanks lashed the columns with gunfire. Brigadeführer Herbert Otto Gille of Wiking knew he could not leave his SS wounded to the Russians, and brought them along. But two groups of Wiking wounded, 130 in one group and 140 in the other, in panje wagons well marked with Red Cross flags, were attacked by T-34s that massacred them with machine-gun fire and then ran back and forth mashing wagons, horses, and men into bloody pulp under their treads.[20]

In the Kessel artillerymen and Pak-gunners fired off their last rounds and then disabled their guns, as these and most vehicles could not be brought out for lack of fuel. Some Soviet tanks were knocked out by Panzerfausts, but in general it was columns, then groups, of Landsers that moved across the snow-covered terrain and through the balkas with only their small arms. Said Hauptsturmführer Leon Degrelle, commanding the Belgian volunteers of

SS-Freiwilligen Sturmbrigade Wallonie, "The bottom of each ravine was a frightful crush of wrecked vehicles and dozens of dead soldiers sprawled across the red snow. The enemy's guns hammered these passages savagely. We kept falling over wounded and bloody men. We had to take shelter alongside the dead. Carts tipped over. Horses flailed their hooves in the air until the machine-gun bullets spilled their hot intestines into the soiled snow."[21]

But there were not enough Russian infantry following their tanks to seal off the escaping troops, and German soldiers in groups or alone kept filtering through the Russian forces. In addition, some of Bäke's Tigers and Panthers surmounted the Hill 239 ridgeline, and emergency footbridges were emplaced over the Gniloy Tikich downstream. Most of the rearguard units were able to fight their way back to the creek or the 1.Pz.Div. perimeter during the night of 17–18 February, though Stemmermann himself was killed by an antitank round hitting the Kübelwagen in which he was riding.

By 19 February the last escapees from the Kessel seemed to have come into the German lines, and Hube ordered Koll's 1.Pz.Div. and Wisch's LAH, which had fended off numerous Russian assaults, to abandon the Lysyanka bridgehead over the fateful creek. Many wounded were airlifted directly from Lysyanka back to Uman, and the survivors in general were reorganized at Uman. Their three-week ordeal was over. In eliminating the Korsun/Cherkassy Kessel, the Soviets claimed to have completely annihilated the pocket with 55,000 of the Fritzes killed and 18,000 captured, totaling 73,000—more than were actually in the pocket. Hence it was embarrassing to the Russians when photographs were published for the world of three of the commanders being honored at Hitler's Wolfsschanze in Rastenburg on the 18th: Hstuf. Degrelle of the Wallonie received the Ritterkreuz, Gen.Lt. Lieb of XXXXII. A.K. received the Eichenlaub to the RK, and Bgf. Gille of 5.SS Wiking received the Eichenlaub mit Schwerten to his Ritterkreuz. The OKW communiqués simply said the heroic defenders had fought their way out to the relieving forces.

In a more careful analysis, of the 56,000 troops in the Kessel reported by Stemmermann on 11 February, 2,188 wounded were airlifted out, and some 35,000 reached the German lines. Thus German casualties during the week before and including the breakout were some 18,800 killed, and wounded and captured, many of the latter subsequently dying in Soviet captivity. For the siege itself, 28 January to 19 February, of some 60,000 encircled (including Russian Hiwis), 4,161 wounded had been flown out and 36,262 had broken out, totaling 40,423, with casualties of 19,577. One study estimates that the Russians suffered 80,188 casualties during the siege including 24,286 killed or missing.[22]

By allowing the contraction of the Kessel and ordering the breakout, Manstein had avoided another Stalingrad disaster—but in both cases these were in defiance of Hitler's orders. The breakout and relief had been well planned and might have been more successful had the crucial Hill 239 been secured. The belated realization among the retreating Germans that it was not led to demoralization and vast confusion that led directly to the tragedy along the Gniloy Tikich. If some 18,000 had been lost in the last days and in the breakout, some 36,000 had been saved to fight again. But the six and a half divisions had lost all their heavy weapons, vehicles, and equipment, and the units would have to be rebuilt. The Russian achievement was significant as it was.

Beyond Hitler's refusal to abandon the Kanev salient, the absence of a unified command resulted in poor coordination and miscommunication. But there is little criticism regarding the bravery and the abilities of the soldiers involved. They performed as well as they could while simply being vastly outnumbered and outgunned by superior Russian forces. Though it was Breith's III.Pz.K. units that actually relieved Gruppe Stemmermann, the pressure mounted by Vormann's XXXXVII. Panzerkorps helped embroil Rotmistrov's 5th Guards Tank Army and the follow-on infantry armies on that flank. Gen.Lt. Nikolaus von Vormann himself, though criticized by Wöhler and relieved through him, was later promoted to Gen.d.Pz.Tr. and succeeded Gen.d.Inf. Hans Jordan at 9. Armee during the crisis of H.Gr. Mitte in June with a massive new Russian offensive there.

All eight panzer divisions involved in the relief had to be significantly built up again. Wietersheim's 11. Gespenster-Division was withdrawn from along the Gniloy Tikich for Auffrischung and relieved by 2.Fs.Jg.Div., though it was scarcely a battle group. Wend von Wietersheim himself was sick and exhausted, but had given his utmost. This was reflected in an announcement from the Führerhauptquartier on

31 March, that on 26 March Gen.Maj. von Wietersheim was awarded das Eichenlaub mit Schwerten, the 58th recipient in the Wehrmacht of this award since the beginning of the war. The announcement, which noted that the schlesische 11. Panzer-Division had already been named three times in Wehrmachtberichte in 1943, recognized his "outstanding bold and nimble fighting touch" and his "indefatigable energy." When down to four panzers, he "continued the attack with these last four." In not even four weeks the division "destroyed 173 Soviet assault guns as well as 352 antitank guns and artillery."[23] And numerous Russian tanks too, the report might have said, furthering the reputation of the Gespenster-Division.

CHAPTER TWENTY-TWO

From Russia to Southern France

BY THE END OF FEBRUARY 1944 GENERAL VON WIETERSHEIM'S 11. Panzer-Division was withdrawn for refitting around Talnoye, west of Lebedin, northeast of Uman. It was hoped by the exhausted Landsers and their commanders that March would bring the Schlammperiode and bog down the Russians, who in any case would have to bring forward supplies following their winter offensive west of the Dnepr. There would be muddy conditions in the black soil of the Ukraine but, said platoon leader Lt. von Eggeling, "it was always not more than 2–4 days until the always blowing wind dried the mud so far that we could drive in a higher gear than the first."[1] And so could the Russians.

By the spring of 1944 Allied Lend-Lease war materiel was pouring ashore at the Arctic port of Murmansk. The Russians used "every available foot of dock space to unload the freighters as fast as possible," said US Navy Ensign George M. Harding Jr., whose own light cruiser, CL 5 *Milwaukee*, was being transferred to the Russians.[2] The Russian tank and mechanized corps were benefitting significantly from the increased mobility made possible with Lend-Lease vehicles, especially the American 2.5-ton truck, used for cargo, troop transport, and many other functions.

General Motors Corporation had standardized the gasoline-engine GMC Type 353 6x6 with three driving axles for off-road mobility. Known to American GIs as the "Jimmy" or "deuce-and-a-half," over 500,000 6x6s were produced. The version shipped to the Soviet Union was the Studebaker US6, also produced by Reo. Over 100,000 6x6s were shipped. The great advantages over comparable Russian and German trucks were standardization (including the interchangeability of parts), reliability, and the 6x6 three driving axles. The Russian-built 4x2 ZIS-5 and Russian Ford-designed GAZ-AA (made at the Gorky Automobile Factory) had only rear-wheel drive.

The most effective small vehicle was the sturdy American quarter-ton Willys MB "jeep" produced by Willys-Overland Motors Corporation and by Ford Motor Company, with 4x4 all-wheel drive. It proved better than the unreliable Russian GAZ-64/67 or the German Volkswagen, neither of which had front-wheel drive.

The jeeps were fondly remembered by Nikolai Litvin, assigned as a driver for Russian regimental and division headquarters, who referred to them as "My powerful and mobile all-terrain Willys."[3] But no Allied tank matched the Russian T-34.

Most German vehicles were diesel- or gasoline-engined, and most had rear-wheel drive only, or two driving axles with dual rear tires, such as those found on the 3-ton Adam Opel Blitz. "Studebakers" captured from the Russians were highly prized by the Germans. The standard German light Personenkraftwagen was the Volkswagen. The VW Typ 62/82 Pkw Kübelwagen equipped many types of units. It did not have front-wheel drive, although the Typ 128 Schwimmwagen (amphibious version) did. Again, captured American Willys 4x4 jeeps were highly prized by the Germans, as they were by the Russians.[4]

All six Russian tank armies were in the south, and early March 1944 brought a series of consecutive offensives spearheaded by the tank armies. On 4 March, an assault by First Ukrainian Front—directed by Marshal Zhukov himself after Vatutin was mortally wounded on 29 February by Ukrainian nationalist partisans (dying 15 April)—was made against Raus's 4. Panzerarmee south of the Pripet and Hube's 1. Pz.Armee; on 5 March Konev's Second Ukrainian Front attacked Wöhler's 8. Armee fronting Uman; on 6 March Malinovsky's Third Ukrainian Front thrust against Hollidt's 6. Armee in the south; and Tolbukhin's Fourth Ukrainian Front was poised to strike Jaenecke's 17. Armee stranded in the Crimea. Some 2,406,100 Russian troops were committed.

Zhukov opened the massive offensives with the 3rd Guards Tank and 4th Tank Armies driving southwest. Their objective was to tear Manstein's H.Gr. Süd apart and reach Cernauti on the Prut (formerly in Rumanian Moldavia), a move that could drive the German forces back against the Carpathian Mountains and the Black Sea coast. XXXXVIII. Panzerkorps, commanded by Generalleutnant Hermann Balck since November, slowed the drive around Proskurov on the Ukrainian Bug east of Ternopol on the Seret by the 7th. But he only had the LAH and 7. Panzer-Divisionen; the 7. did not have a single operational panzer, and only ten were expected back from maintenance repair.[5]

Katukov's 1st Tank Army added its weight to the offensive, and advanced even at night with headlights on and sirens blaring to further demoralize the German defenders. Proskurov fell on 23 March and the Russians crossed the Dnestr without a pause on the 24th. Some German reserves had been moved up from 8. Armee to help block Zhukov's offensive on 4 March, when Konev opened his assault against 8. Armee the next day, 500,000 strong. Konev had the other three tank armies: 6th Tank under Lt. Gen. A. G. Kravchenko, 2nd Tank under Lt. Gen. S. I. Bogdanov, and 5th Guards Tank Army under Lt. Gen. Pavel Rotmistrov.

8. Armee began to disintegrate as Uman fell on 9 March and the Russians crossed the Ukrainian Bug two days later. Vinnitsa, previously Manstein's headquarters, also fell, Hitler having just ordered in a Führerbefehl on 8 March that these major cities were "fortified places" and must be defended to the end. By 17 March Rotmistrov was crossing the Dnestr.

Wietersheim's 11. Panzer-Division, like other units, was scarcely a battle group, though the attached Sturmgeschütz-Abteilung 911 did receive twelve new assault guns. The division fell back from Talnoye through Uman, then south to cross the Bug at Pervomaysk to Krivoe Osero and to Balta. Sharp counterattacks were mounted when possible, as when Leutnant Kleine with his Panthers of 2.Komp./I.Abt./Pz.-Rgt.15 attacked a patch of woods 7 kilometers north of Slobodka on the 25th and claimed a tank and two antitank guns; but these actions were insignificant amid the general collapse. Oberstlt. Meinrad von Lauchert had returned from his extended leave at the beginning of March; Major Karl von Sivers had been detached from Talnoye earlier to Proskurov, near where he was killed in action on 10 April.[6]

Meanwhile the Russian offensives continued in succession, Malinovsky's Third Ukrainian assault on March 6 reaching Novy Bug the next day, driving 6. Armee from the Ingulets, the Ingul, and then the lower Bug by the 21st. A disgusted Hitler had Hollidt removed from his command of 6. Armee. General der Artillerie Maximilian de Angelis succeeded him on 7 April. On 26 March Kleist and Wöhler agreed to put 8. Armee under H.Gr. A command as it was falling back from the Bug to the southwest.

To the north Zhukov's tank armies drove between Raus's 4.Pz.Armee and Hube's 1. Pz.Armee, crossing the upper Dnestr by 24 March. Konev's 6th Tank Army split Wöhler's 8. Armee from 1. Pz.Armee, crossing the Dnestr near Mogilev Podolskiy. Hube's 1. Pz.Armee was in danger of being encircled east of the Dnestr. Manstein wanted Hube to withdraw to the west, but Hitler forbade it and demanded that

Manstein meet with him. On 25 March the Feldmarschall flew to Berchtesgaden in the Bavarian Alps and then drove to the Berghof in the Obersalzberg complex.[7]

In an acrimonious exchange Hitler accused Manstein of dribbling away his forces, and Manstein blamed Hitler for the disastrous situation and said he *must* order 1. Pz.Armee to break out. In a second meeting that night Hitler reversed himself: he cordially greeted the Feldmarschall, approved a breakout, and said he was dispatching Hausser's II.SS Panzerkorps with 9.Hohenstaufen and 10.Frundsberg SS Panzer Divisions from the West to assist. Although greatly relieved, Manstein then had to deal with Hube, who was preparing his army to break out, but to the *south*, across the Dnestr. Hube was concerned that attacking to the west meant encountering two tank armies and having to cross four tributaries of the Dnestr.

Manstein, however, realized that that meant 1.Pz.Armee would be pressed back into the Carpathian Mountains or south into Rumania, whereas it was more important to rejoin with 4. Pz.Armee in Polish Galicia in the *west*. His order went out on 26 March even as 4th Tank Army took Kamenets-Podolsky behind Hube and forces from the two Russian Fronts met near Khotin south of the Dnestr. Some twenty-two German divisions were in the Kessel, which now began to move west as a Wandernder Kessel (roving pocket). Hube skillfully delayed his pocket back and simultaneously attacked across the Zbruch and the Little Seret. Ammunition and fuel were flown in by 4. Luftflotte and wounded flown out, though there were losses in the intense fighting.

In the Russian 4th Tank Army drive south to Kaments-Podolsk was Lt. Evgeni Bessonov of the 49th Mechanized Brigade. Moved up by Studebaker trucks, he and his platoon were "tank riders," a squad of seven to eight riding each of the three T-34s in a tank platoon. They carried handy PPSh submachine guns while riding on the back deck behind the turret, ready to jump down into action. If their tank was damaged or threw a track, they often assisted the crew with repairs. But as the Fritzes broke out to the west across the Little Seret Bessonov's battalion had 90 percent casualties in the heavy fighting.[8]

It is not clear what 11. Panzer-Division units were involved, but some were with Hube's 1. Pz.Armee north of the upper Dnestr, and others were cut off. Gefreiter Lothar Trenkler of II.Abt./Pz.Rgt.15 was with an element that sought to cross the Dnestr near Kamenets-Podolsky. But there was no bridge at the river gorges, and they had to abandon their vehicles, dividing up the supplies (Trenkler acquired 100 Senator-Zigaretten, "the best German cigarette," in an airtight package). Locating a boat, men could be ferried across, but some were separated. Trenkler and a comrade headed west across Bessarabia with Russian forces advancing all around, with no map or compass, using only the sun for direction.

Getting across the Prut they headed for Darabani and then south to Dorohoi, and across the Seret to Falticeni in the foothills of the Carpathians. The local populations were friendly, the houses and people much cleaner than in Russia, and the people were very fearful of the approaching Russians. This was Bukovina, part of the old Austro-Hungarian Empire, and every house proudly displayed plates with images of Kaiser Franz Josef and Kaiser Wilhelm II. By Easter Sunday (9 April) Trenkler and his comrade reached Vatra Dornei, and the German commandant got them on a train filled with Ukrainian refugees to Debrecen, Hungary. From there a train got them to Przemysl in Galicia where they were deloused, and then on to Sagan, after five weeks of travel.[9]

On 2 April Zhukov, angry at having miscalculated the direction of the breakout, radioed a surrender ultimatum and stated that all captured German officers would be shot—a brutal threat even for that bloody conflict.[10] Under 4. Pz.Armee the Waffen-SS divisions attacked across the Zlota Lipa and then down. On 6 April 10. SS Pz.Div. Frundsberg met 6.Pz.Div. at Buchach on the Strypa, making the linkup. Not only was Hube's 1. Pz.Armee's roving pocket now coalescing with 4. Pz.Armee to reform a solid front, but they had cut behind the Russian tank armies south of the Dnestr. Had there been more German forces Manstein could have isolated and destroyed those spearheads as he had destroyed the Popov spearhead the year before. In any case, the operations of the roving pocket and the relief drive were expertly conducted. But Manstein would not witness the culmination.

On 30 March Hitler's personal Fw 200 Condor had picked up both Kleist and Manstein and flown them to Berchtesgaden to meet with Hitler. Der Führer had courteously received them and presented them both with Swords to their Knights Crosses—and then dismissed the two distinguished field marshals from their commands, never to be employed again. Kleist had pressed Hitler to abandon the Crimea and save 17. Armee, and Manstein had been too outspoken (and able). Hitler said the time for operations was over, that what was needed were commanders who would stand firm. Walter Model was promoted as Generalfeldmarschall to succeed von Manstein, and Ferdinand Schörner was promoted to Generaloberst to succeed von Kleist. On 5 April H.Gr. Süd was renamed H.Gr. Nordukraine and H.Gr. A was renamed Südukraine.

On 8 April Tolbukhin's Fourth Ukrainian Front opened its offensive against 17. Armee in the Crimea and drove down on Sevastopol. Hitler replaced General Jaenecke with corps commander General der Infanterie Karl Allmendinger, but finally agreed to proceed with the evacuation of the German and Rumanian defenders by sea. Heavy casualties in a month of fighting had reduced the defenders from some 150,000 to 60,000. Some 40,000 were evacuated over four nights, but when the end came by 12 May the remaining 20,000 were left to fall into Russian captivity.[11]

Manstein's decision that Hube's 1. Pz.Armee should break out to the west to 4. Pz.Armee did help stabilize the German front reforming in Poland. Generaloberst Hube himself was killed in a plane crash on 21 April near Berchtesgaden just after receiving the Schwerter zum RK from Hitler. He was succeeded at 1. Pz.Armee by Gen.d.Pz.Tr. Erhard Raus, Gen.Obst. Josef Harpe taking command of 4. Pz.Armee. It did however mean the German forces to the south falling back to Rumania were ever weaker, at a time when Regent Adm. Miklos Horthy in Hungary and Marshal Ion Antonescu in Rumania were reassessing their alliance with Hitler's Germany given the Soviet advance.

Hitler even considered occupying Hungary in Unternehmen MARGARETHE, but the necessary German forces were needed to stop the Russians, and the Hungarian army was needed to defend the Carpathian mountain passes. Hitler felt Antonescu of Rumania had no choice but to stay loyal, though the marshal was unrealistically urging the return of territories given Hungary in 1940. Rumanian military units, meanwhile, were proving very unreliable.

Lt. von Eggeling was detached with some Panthers to support a Rumanian division "to give to these poor folks the illusion of infinite strength," and perhaps to encourage their loyalty. But, von Eggeling noted, "My weeks with the Rumanian division was a nightmare all the time. The officers were drunk and had the best food class 1, the sergeants had class 2, and the common soldiers nothing more than 'mammaliga,' which is a mush of maize. They had even no leather boots but rags over their feet. You can imagine how the fighting spirit was." German officers and men of course ate the same rations. The Russians knew the Rumanians were weak and attacked them "nearly every day," but the Panthers maintained their HKL. Von Eggeling received the "King Michael the Brave" decoration from the king himself, who like von Eggeling was young and spoke fluent German, being of the Saxe-Coburg-Gotha family.[12]

The Red Army was even more formidable now with the appearance of two new tank models: the T-34/85 and the heavy IS-2. The tank losses at Kursk had given support to those who argued for upgrading the T-34 rather than just continuing the mass production of the T-34/76. The poor tactical handling of units because of the four-man crew (in which the tank commander was also the gunner), the lack of radios, and the ineffectiveness of the 76.2mm gun against the new German armor, mandated improvement.

While the strengths were maintained—wide tracks, angled armor, and diesel engine—the most notable changes were the enlarged turret for now a five-man crew (with tank commander and gunner having separate functions), and the adaptation of the 85mm gun with a muzzle velocity of 792 m/s (2,599 fps). The turret had electrical traverse, and more radios were now available, and located in the turret, not the hull. The hull was unchanged, having 76mm (3-inch) frontal armor. One disadvantage was that the rear bustle of the larger turret and the protruding gun mount were raised well above the turret base ring to clear the engine compartment during all-round traverse, creating a shot trap for enemy shells.

As powerful as the 85mm gun was, it did not match the velocity and penetration of the Tiger's 8,8cm Kw.K.36 L/56 with the armor-piercing composite ballistic cap (APCBC) round, 810 m/s (2,657 fps), or the Panther's 7,5cm Kw.K.42 L/70, 935 m/s (3,068 fps). Nor did it equal the 8,8cm Kw.K.43 L/71 of the new German heavy panzer, the Königstiger (King Tiger), Tiger B or II: 1,018 m/s (3,340 fps), penetrating 183mm (7.2 inches) of armor. This heavy German panzer weighed 69 tons, with 150mm (6 inches) of frontal armor, which was angled like the Panther's as well.

The new Russian heavy tank was the IS-2 (Iosif Stalin, named for the Soviet ruler). First, the Russians upgraded the KV-1 with an 85mm gun. Then, utilizing the KV chassis but modifying the hull and superstructure, the IS-1 was produced, the A model mounting the 85mm gun and the IS-2B mounting a 100mm gun. Only a few were produced before mounting a 122mm L/43 gun in the IS-2, the largest gun carried by any tank, though its muzzle velocity was only 781 m/s (2,562 fps), and it was slower to load as the heavy ammunition, weighing 39 kilograms (86.5 pounds), was in two parts, projectile and powder casing. The sheer weight of the shot, 75 kilograms (55 pounds) was expected to simply smash an enemy tank. The IS-2 had thick frontal armor of 160mm (6.4 inches). The crew numbered four: tank commander, gunner, loader, and driver—eliminating the bow gunner position. The IS-2 began to be operational in April 1944.[13]

Pressed by Malinovsky's Third Ukrainian Front, and with Konev's tank armies driving beyond the Dnestr, Wöhler's 8. Armee still had to hold at Balta between the Bug and the Dnestr. At any point it was expected that Konev would turn south between or beyond the rivers. 8. Armee had 3.SS Totenkopf, but with four and a half reduced panzer divisions and four battle groups, Wöhler was pressed to retreat back across the Dnestr. It is difficult to determine the strength of the 11.Pz.-Div. by now, or its (improvised) organization. On 27 March in fighting at Kolbasnaya Major Weicke, as well as Lt. Kleine and Lt. von Eggeling of I.(Panther) Abt./15, were wounded.

On the 27th Hitler consented to let the 8. and 6. Armee withdraw to the lower Dnestr, though he insisted that Odessa be held. On the 28th 8. Armee, including Wietersheim's Elften, retreated from the Balta position. The 11. Panzer was going to cross the Dnestr by the bridge at Rybnytsa, but that was taken by the Russians. With four Panthers, and five Sturmgeschütze of Stu.Gesch.Abt.911, delaying actions were fought as the Gespensters retreated 100 kilometers (60 miles) south to Dubossary to finally cross the Dnestr on 6 April. The 11.Pz.Div. came under the command of Korps-Abteilung F, Generalleutnant Louis Tronnier, in 6. Armee, now commanded by Gen.d.Art. Maximilian Fretter-Pico, and took up a defensive position. Ritterkreuzträger Major Joachim Menzel of H.Fla.Abt.277 distinguished himself again by the effect of his 2cm flak guns against the Russian infantry.[14]

The Russian offensives were winding down by the middle of April 1944. Malinovsky's Third Ukrainian Front armies isolated and destroyed the 6. Armee forces at Odessa and gained a bridgehead across the Dnestr south of Tiraspol, but Schörner's H.Gr. Südukraine front began to stabilize along the lower Dnestr and the foothills of the Carpathians. The Red Army offensives had resulted in their own tremendous losses. Of the 2,406,100 Russian troops committed, almost half became casualties: 1,109,528, including 270,198 killed or missing.[15] Many of these were Ukrainians dragooned into the Red Army with scarcely any weapons and equipment, and sacrificed as "cannon fodder."

For the Gespensters now established around Kishinev for a month for rebuilding, this was a "relatively calm time. . . . In the beautiful region we enjoyed this calm; there were sauna steam baths everywhere which were used by all since the enemy situation allowed a continuing relief." Rumors also began to circulate that, the division needing to be completely rebuilt, it would do so—in sunny southern France![16] Indeed, the rumors were true. In early May advance parties were dispatched to the area around Bordeaux on the Garonne near the Bay of Biscay. But not all Gespensters went west. Karl Heinz Loschke of Pz.Art.Rgt.119, for example, was promoted to command a Hummel Abteilung and stayed with the Ostheer. On 6 May Sturmgeschützabteilung 911, with the Elfte since 1 April 1943, was also detached to the Ostheer.

Lt. Karl Zindler of Pz.-Rgt.15 with some 200 men from Sagan established a regimental headquarters site in St. Aigulin bei Liborne, east of the city of Bordeaux. Back at Kishinev on the Ostfront, a last review was held. The division numbered perhaps scarcely 1,000 men present. Lt. von Eggeling was near General von Wietersheim (who was his uncle and godfather) when a captain came up with two men, saluted, and reported: "Second Battalion Grenadierregiment Nr.110 with one officer, one sergeant, and one grenadier ready for entraining."[17]

Leaving the Kettenfahrzeuge behind, on 7 May the Gespensters began boarding their trains. Some were in passenger cars, some in boxcars, some were on flatcars with their vehicles. In the warm spring weather out came accordions and harmonicas, adding to a festive spirit. Photographs show the elation: "Joyful about it, to be able to turn their backs on Russia forever." A.A.11 loaded their motorcycles and armored cars at Stanislau (Stanislavl) farther north in a like mood. One could stretch out and even ride atop the cars in the breeze. Elements of Pz.G.R.111, however, remained in Bessarabia until June, recalled Lt. Horst Loch, adjutant of the II.Btl.[18]

The route of the Gespenster E-Transports was Debreczen–Budapest–Wien, then across Deutschland from Passau to Stuttgart, and then down through Frankreich: Nancy–Paris–Tours and down to Bordeaux by the end of the month, to be greeted by their division commander. Along the way at railroad water plugs the men could wash off soot that had blown back from the steam engine smoke, amid much hilarity. Leaves also were arranged to see families some hadn't seen for some time. Elements still in the east were under Oberst Friedrich Erdmann von Hake of Pz.Rgt.4 of 13.Pz.Div. as acting division commander (7–18 May). Von Hake then took command of 13.Pz.Div. in Rumania.

Bivouac areas were located around Bordeaux, Pz.Rgt.15 being some 60 kilometers (40 miles) north of the city. Other units were located in an arc 50 to 100 kilometers distant, northeast to southeast, Angoulême–Perigeux–Bergerac–Marmande. These were generally Feldlager, tent encampments. For the Ostfrontkämpfer the sudden transition from the horrors of the Russian front now to the beautiful spring in southern France resulted in much incredulous exuberance. Officers indeed were hard-pressed to ensure the discipline of their men, and that foods and goods of the French were paid for. Lt. "Friedel" von Eggeling later felt there was a tacit understanding with the local French partisans, and said he was free to go hunting partridges with a shotgun in the countryside.[19]

The 11. Panzer-Division was to be rebuilt according to the Panzer-Division 44 K.St.N. organization tables. With many qualifications, the division would have 13,726 officers and men, 2,685 motor vehicles (including 103 panzers), and 42 artillery pieces (including 18 self-propelled mounts). Of the personnel, there were 402 officers, 69 Beamte (officials), 2,876 Unteroffiziere (non-commissioned officers), and 10,379 Mannschaften (enlisted personnel). The Beamte were civil service officials without military rank, such as paymasters, construction supervisors, and inspectors. Division headquarters and headquarters company had 360 officers and men.

The panzer regiment had 1,661 personnel in two battalions, a Panther and a Panzer IV battalion, with 103 panzers: forty-two in three companies of three four-panzer platoons and six battalion headquarters panzers in each battalion, and three Panthers and four Pz.IVs in the regimental headquarters company. This meant companies had fourteen panzers including two company headquarters panzers. However, a reconstructed list of officers in Pz.Rgt.15 compiled by Walter Rahn indicates *four* companies in I.(Panther) Abteilung (Nr.1.-4.) and four companies in II.(Pz.IV) Abt. (Nr.5.-8.). In other tables there might be three companies with seventeen panzers each or four companies with twenty-two panzers each, though these numbers were unlikely ever to be achieved in practice.[20]

The allocation of tactical call signs painted on the panzer turrets was as before, stenciled on by the Werkstatt Kp. The headquarters panzers for the commander, the adjutant, and the signals officer were R01, R02, and R03 at regiment, I01, I02, and I03 for the I.(Panther) Abteilung, and II01, II02, and II03 for the II.Abt. (Pz.IV), the headquarters panzers being numbered in sequence II04, etc. In the companies, 101 was the commander and 102 the command sergeant major, with the panzers numbered with three digits for company, platoon, and Panzerwagen. Thus 221 ("Zwei-zwei-eins") was the first Wagen (platoon leader's) of second platoon in second company, 324 was fourth Wagen, second platoon, third company.[21] But in combat, a commander might use any panzer that was operational, though it might not have the requisite radios.

All panzers had shortwave transceiver radio sets on the company frequency. This was the Ultrakurzwelle (ultra short wave) Fu.5 radio. The range of the UKW set was 4–6 kilometers (3–5 miles), depending on topography. The platoon leader's panzer also had an auxiliary receiver to monitor the battalion command net, and the company commander could monitor the regiment. The panzergrenadiers, however, had different radio frequencies, and their commanders usually had to coordinate an operation with the panzer commanders in person.

The panzergrenadiers were organized in two regiments of 2,294 and 2,258 personnel, of two battalions each. Still, only one Bataillon was gepanzerte in Halbkette, with 867 personnel (companies numbered 1.–4.). It had three companies of 183 men each in three rifle platoons, a weapons platoon with four s.M.G., two 8cm mortars, and two 7,5cm howitzers (self-propelled on half-tracks), and a flak platoon with six 2cm flak guns self-propelled. The rifle Zug (platoon) had one officer and twenty-nine men in a platoon headquarters and three Gruppe (squads) in four Sd.Kfz.251 half-track Schützenpanzerwagen. The basic squad was ten panzergrenadiers, including the SPW driver. The emphasis on automatic weapons firepower in lieu of manpower was reflected in the squad having 2 le.M.G. in addition to the vehicle-mounted le.M.G.

The other battalion (companies 5.–8.) and the two battalions of the other regiment used trucks. The company comprised 197 personnel in three platoons and a weapons platoon. The rifle squads had twelve men with two le.M.G. each. The battalions also had a heavy-weapons company with six 2cm flak guns and four 12cm mortars, while the gepanzerte Bataillon also had six 7,5cm guns on half-tracks or Sturmgeschütze. Regimental units included a heavy howitzer company (Nr.9. Kp.), six 15cm self-propelled guns (on a Czech 38(t) chassis or the Brummbär on a Pz.IV chassis), and an engineer company (Nr.10). The headquarters and staff company was 11.Kp.

The panzer artillery regiment of 1,649 personnel had forty-two pieces in three battalions: a mixed Abteilung with three self-propelled batteries of six tubes each, two with six 10,5cm howitzers (le.F.H. Wespe) and one with six 15cm howitzers (s.F.H. Hummel); a light battalion that was half-track-towed, with three batteries of four 10,5cm le.F.H. each; and a schwere (medium) battalion, also half-track-towed, with three batteries of four 15cm s.F.H. each (or 10cm Kanone). Each Abteilung also had a flak battery with three 2cm guns. The former IV.Abt. of the panzer artillery regiment was still "attached," as a Heeres Flakartillerie Abteilung. There were 764 personnel with eight 8,8cm flak guns and six 2cm guns in two batteries, and a light battery with twelve 2cm flak guns, perhaps as the turreted Vierlingsflak Wirbelwind (quad Whirlwind), or nine 3,7cm flak guns on a Pz.IV chassis nicknamed "Möbelwagen" ("furniture van," from the platforms raised), or even as the turreted Ostwind.

The Aufklärungs-Abteilung (Reconnaissance Battalion) of 942 men had thirteen 7,5cm guns, thirty-five 2cm guns, six flamethrowers, ten 8cm mortars, and four s.M.G. These were mounted in Panzerspähwagen, half-tracks or armored cars, mixed in five companies: battalion headquarters, armored car, armored reconnaissance, light armored reconnaissance, and heavy weapons. In A.A.11 practice, the Spähkompanie (1.Kp.) had four- or eight-wheeled armored cars, 2.-4.Kp. had rifle platoons in SPW (Sd.Kfz.250 half-tracks), and 5.Kp. (schwere Kompanie) had heavy machine guns, 3,7cm and 7,5cm Pakwagens, and Granatwerfers as well as a Pionier Zug. There was also a Stabskompanie and a Versorgungs (supply) company.

Lt. Werner Strietzel, commander of 2.Kompanie/A.A.11 until he was wounded in November, felt the ability of the Acht-rad to drive backwards as fast as forwards, the loader or radio operator being the "reverse driver," was of "enormous importance." Strietzel, who had been in reconnaissance since June 1941 when he was in K.61, noted motorcycles had long been discarded as too vulnerable to enemy fire, and with replacement shortfalls of the armored vehicles, increasingly the reconnaissance mission had to depend on VW Kübelwagen (though the VW Schwimmwagen was handy). The recon battalion came up to strength, but many of the personnel had been transferred from the Luftwaffe and had no training or combat experience.[22]

The Panzerjäger-Abteilung (Tank Destroyer Battalion) had 513 personnel with fourteen 7,5cm guns in Jagdpanzer IVs or other Pak vehicles in each of two assault gun companies and three in headquarters, and twelve 7,5cm guns in a third company towed or motorized. The battalion was generally not used tactically as a unit, its companies being attached to battalion Kampfgruppen. The Panzer Pionier-Bataillon (Armored Engineer Battalion) of 885 men had a half-track company and two truck-mounted companies with a mix of 2cm Pak, flamethrowers, 8cm mortars, and s.M.G. The bridging column had Typ K or J bridges. The Panzer Nachrichten-Abteilung (Armored Signals Battalion) with 515 personnel had an Fe (Fernsprech/Fernschreiber, telephone/teleprinter) company, an Fu (Funk, radio) company, and a light signals column. The battalions generally also had headquarters companies and support companies.

The division Nachschub-Dienst (Supply Services) had 1,885 personnel in Versorgung (rations and other provisions), Nachschub (materiel supplies), Verwaltung (administration), Sanitäts (medical), Werkstatt (maintenance), Feldgendarmerie (field police), and Feldpost (postal) components. As earlier, the Nachschubdienst was coordinated by the

Divisionsnachschubführer (Division Supply Leader), the Dinafü or DNF, who reported to the Ib on the division staff.

But when the 11.Pz.-Div. elements assembled around Bordeaux in May, they had no panzers nor other armored vehicles, there were no 8,8cm flak guns, all elements were vastly under strength, and they had to make do with wood-gas trucks. Personnel did begin to return from leaves and from hospital convalescence. (The Wehrmacht strongly believed in returning personnel to their own units, for unit morale and cohesiveness.)

The 11. Panzer-Division was rebuilt in southern France by absorbing the components of the 273. Reserve Panzer-Division. Ordered 19 March, the rebuilding continued to 15 June. The 273. was formed 1 November 1943 from the staff of the Kommandeur der Panzertruppen in Wehrkreis XIII (northern Bayern), headquartered at Würzburg to control motorized and panzer training units and to train the mobile troops from Wehrkreise including XIII and VII (southern Bayern). It was not derived from a replacement division staff as were all other reserve divisions. The 273.Res.Pz.Div. was sent to France and assigned to 1. Armee in a zone between Bordeaux and the Spanish border, carrying out training while also providing some security.

The commander was Generalleutnant Hellmut von der Chevallerie. He had earlier commanded units on the Ostfront until wounded for the seventh time. After his headquarters was amalgamated with Wietersheim's, he went to command Maneuver Area Bergen in Norway. Wietersheim's Ia remained Oberstlt. Werner Drews. Pz.Rgt.15 under Oberst Meinrad von Lauchert absorbed Res.Pz.Abt.35 (Bamberg) and 25 (Erlangen) into its I. and II. Abteilungen, respectively, under Majors Weicke and Berger.

Panzergrenadierregiment 110 under Oberst Heinrich-Georg Hax, who had succeeded Oberstlt. Göttmann on 4 May, was rebuilt from Res.Panz. Gren.Rgt.92: Res.Pz.Gren.Btl.12 (Schweinfurt) and Res.Gren.Btl.(mot) 20 (Regensburg). Pz.Gren.Rgt. 111 under Oberst Wilde absorbed Res.Gren.Rgt. (mot) 73: Res.Pz.Gren.Btl.40 (Augsburg) and Res. Gren.Btl.(mot) 41 (Erlangen). Pz.Artillerieregiment 119 under Oberstlt. Erich Hammon re-created its III.Abt. from Res.Art.Abt.167 (Landsberg am Lech). Pz.Aufklärungsabteilung 11 under Major Karl Bode was reestablished from Res.Pz.Aufkl.Abt.7 (München). Pz.Jäger-Abt. 61 under Major Arnold Kessler absorbed Res.Pz.Jg.Abt.10; and Pz.Pionier-Btl. 209 commanded by Major Heinz Bödicker was re-created from Res.Pz.Pi.Btl.7.[23]

Pz.Nachrichten-Abt.89 under Major Arnold Steuer, and Heeres Flak-Abt. 277 under Major Joachim Menzel, received new personnel as well, bringing the fifteen battalions and supporting units up to strength. There was some consideration given to forming a third battalion of Pz.G.R.110 from the Feldersatzbataillon (Field Replacement Battalion), a rifle company for Pz.Aufkl.Abt.11, a heavy mortar battery for Pz.Art.Rgt.119, and a strengthening of the division headquarters Begleitkompanie (Escort Company).[24]

It would seem, however, that no longer were new personnel predominantly from Wehrkreis VIII Schlesien. Inevitably there was some tension between the battle-tested Ostkämpfer and the influx of so many new drafts. While some were returning wounded combat veterans—many Landsers had already been awarded the Wound Badge in Silver for two to four wounds—perhaps 30 percent were "Neulinge" (novices). In addition, the majority of the Gespensters came from Silesia and eastern Germany and were apprehensive about their families and homes in the path of the advancing Red Army, while many of the new inductees were from Bavaria and western Germany, where Allied bombing and the looming Allied invasion was of primary concern. On the other hand most of the unit commanders and many junior Offiziere and Unteroffiziere had risen within the division and gave it cohesion.

There was an urgency to the reorganization and training of the division in southern France through May. The long-anticipated Anglo-American invasion of Festung Europa (Fortress Europe) of occupied France was expected any day. Also, in expectation of the Allied liberation there was increased activity (and increased participation) on the part of the French underground resistance. Minor acts of sabotage and assassinations began to be carried out, though clashes with regular, well-armed combat troops like the 11.Pz.Div. were avoided.

The British Special Operations Executive (SOE) and then also the American Office of Strategic Services (OSS) parachuted weapons and agents into occupied France to coordinate the partisans as the Forces françaises de l' Intérieur (FFI) under French Lt. Gen. Pierre Koenig in London, appointed by Free French leader Gen. Charles De Gaulle.[25] But instead of seeking confrontations, the Allied high command urged the FFI to bide their time until *after* the invasion had begun, instead concentrating on intelligence about German troop strengths and movements. Three-man "Jedburgh" teams acted as liaisons among the groups. Nonetheless there were many local Maquis (from a Corsican word for the "bush"), some of communist sympathies rather than De Gaullist, who acted independently, especially the Francs-Tireurs et Partisans (FTP). German Alarmeinheiten (units on alert) were formed to respond quickly to any partisan action. Without panzers, Pz.Rgt.15 underwent retraining as infantry. Indeed, on 25 May elements rushed from Moulin-Neuf to reported American airborne landings around Ste. Astier, but it was a false alarm.

On 6 June 1944 came the Allied landings along the French coast in Normandy, Operation OVERLORD. Preceded by airborne landings and naval and air bombardment, amphibious forces came ashore and by nightfall four of the five landing beaches were secure. German counterattacks were unsuccessful and the Allies had established a firm beachhead. The brunt of the Normandy invasion was borne by 7. Armee of Feldmarschall Erwin Rommel's Heeresgruppe B under OB West (Oberbefehlshaber, High Command in the West) Feldm. Gerd von Rundstedt. In southern France south of the Loire, where the invasion was less expected, were the divisions of Armeegruppe G (redesignated H.Gr. G on 11 September) under Generaloberst Johannes Blaskowitz in 1. and 19. Armee. With the Normandy landings many of the units were ordered north, including all four 1944-type infantry divisions, and two of the four mobile divisions, 17.SS Pz.Gren.Div. from the Loire valley, and 2.SS Pz.Div. Das Reich. DR traveled all the way from Toulouse in the far south up through Maquis-infested areas, and then was subject to Allied air attacks when approaching the front.[26]

The remaining divisions were generally static or coast defense. The two mobile divisions were the Austrian 9.Pz.Div. positioned north of Marseille as a counterattack force for the Mediterranean coast sector under 19. Armee, and the 11.Pz.Div. as a counterattack force for the Biscayan-Atlantic coast under 1. Armee; though without panzers and lacking other heavy weapons Wietersheim's Elfte was really not einsatzbereit.

Wietersheim did send a number of officers north to observe how battle conditions differed from the Ostfront. The reports were analyzed and discussed in commanders' conferences to derive tactical responses: Allied air power played a decisive role, already demonstrated in North Africa, Sicily, and Italy. Movement by day was almost completely prevented. Camouflage and cover were essential. Allied artillery had plentiful ammunition, and their effectiveness was enhanced by artillery observation planes, unhindered by the Luftwaffe. Enemy ground advances, however, were methodical and cautious, halting at any resistance and taking no risks, and as a rule ending at nightfall.

In planning vehicle road marches, the time factor should be doubled. With standard vehicle road march procedures a panzer battalion moving by day at 20 km/h and 50-meter vehicle intervals had a time length of about thirty minutes and a road space of some 8,000 meters. But because of the enemy air threat vehicles would have to "spring" from cover to cover in Einzelgruppen—single groups of three to five vehicles. If attacked by "Jabos," enemy Jagdbombers or fighter bombers, all troops would put up fire, especially from 2cm flak guns. Telephonic wire communications would be destroyed; radio communication would have to be relied upon.

Other techniques employed on the Ostfront were still valid, if modified: clear, concise "Sattelbefehle" or frag(mentary) orders were imperative to maintain the pace of panzer warfare. This exemplified the original concept of Auftragstaktik—mission tactics, the basis of German panzer warfare doctrine. The Kampfgruppe concept of mixed battle groups of panzers and panzergrenadiers was still relevant; but mass maneuvers as on the steppes of southern Russia were not practical, given the more varied topography and enemy air power. Instead, training and exercises for smaller, mixed company-sized Panzerkampftrupp elements, including an artillery VB for rapidly transmitted fire missions, would be best.

This required company-grade leaders to take the initiative, and act independently and decisively. Reconnaissance in any situation by every unit was not only necessary for security, but to seize opportunities in an opponent's weak moment—this also required initiative, taking action without orders. Even moving as Einzelgruppen meant alert air lookouts, and if attacked by aircraft, the rapid dismounting from vehicles and firing by all troops with all available weapons. Fire-control exercises emphasized the coordination of artillery and heavy infantry ordnance on concentration points, and rapid displacement to avoid counterbattery fire. Engineer training was emphasized for all units, for mines and obstacles would be necessary to delay an enemy advance.

As in Russia, the practice was to rotate a third of the fighting companies (panzer, panzergrenadier, and reconnaissance) back to the Feldersatzbataillon. While getting a rest, they would constitute a reserve, and provide an experienced cadre in case of extensive casualties in the company, given the tremendous firepower of the opponent. In the coming campaigns in the West, there would be heavy casualties, especially among the unit commanders. In the next eight months the two panzer battalions would have eight different commanders: there would be at least six in the two battalions of Pz.Gren.Rgt.110, and the veterans of Pz.G.R.111 cannot recall all the battalion commanders. Even Hauptmann Franz Thelen, regimental adjutant of 111, could list and date the last five regimental commanders, but "The battalion commanders changed too frequently, one after another" (though the battalion adjutants could name some).[27] The casualties reflect leadership up front; yet it is notable how unit cohesion was maintained and the division remained combat-capable as a result of this rotation policy.

Throughout June and into July the bitter struggle continued in Normandy as the Germans sought to contain the Allied buildup. The summer of 1944 saw the Axis powers being defeated around the globe. The American "island-hopping" advance in the Pacific brought the Mariana Islands within bombing range of the Japanese home islands, and in Italy American forces pierced the Gustav Line and broke out of the Anzio beachhead, entering Rome on 4 June. It was with great anxiety that the Silesian Gespensters learned of the massive offensive of the Red Army against Heeresgruppe Mitte beginning 22 June, Russian Operation BAGRATION. Some twenty-five German divisions simply disappeared in the maelstrom, and the Soviets cleared Bessarabia and were driving into Poland toward the Vistula and Warsaw.

On 1 July von Wietersheim was promoted to Generalleutnant. On 11 July Pz.Rgt.15 removed to La Roche Chalain where they finally began receiving their panzers, and on the 17th moved to Saint Aulage.[28] Von Lauchert's Pz.Rgt.15 was receiving newer models of the Sd.Kfz.171 Panther and the Sd.Kfz.161 Pz.Kpfw. IV. The problems plaguing the first Ausführung D Panthers were being worked out, and an improved model, Ausf. A, went into production in August 1943. It had a bow machine gun, ball-mounted for a wider field of fire, a cast cupola (instead of the forged drum cupola) that afforded better vision for the commander, and transmission, gearbox, and cooling pipe improvements. Frontal armor was increased to 110mm (4.25 inches). The factory-applied Zimmerit antimagnetic paste was discontinued in September 1944 because hollow-charge magnetic antitank ordnance was not used by the Allies.

In February 1944 the Ausf. G entered service. It had more sloped and thicker armor, and increased main armament stowage (from seventy-nine to eighty-two rounds). In addition there was no vision port for the driver; the port had lessened the integrity of the glacis plate and thus it was removed, vision now being provided by the periscopes around the hatches on the hull top. As before, interior heating in cold weather was appreciated; a fan reversed to draw warm air from the left radiator assembly. In the Ausf. G there were ductwork pipes, two to the Fahrer and Funker positions, and two to warm the batteries. The engine exhausts always attracted accompanying cold panzergrenadiers.

The reliable Sd.Kfz.161 Panzer IV was also upgraded, the Ausführung H going into service in March 1943 as the Sd.Kfz.161/2, superseding the F2 and G (Sd.Kfz.161/1) models. It mounted the long 7,5cm L/48 gun, but had increased armor (80mm/ 3.2 inches), which increased the weight (to 25 tons) and reduced the speed (to 38 km/h/ 21 mph). A new cupola had a mount for a 7.92mm flak machine gun, and side vision ports for the driver and radio operator were omitted. The Ausf. J of March 1944 replaced the Panzerschürzen with wire mesh panels; these were lighter and cheaper, yet still effective at detonating hollow charge rounds.[29]

While the Panther's turret traverse was hydraulic, the Panzer IV's traverse was by electric motor powered by a small DKW two-stroke gasoline engine (though the J model was manual only). Asked to compare the two power-traversing systems Jürgen Reichardt, Major later commanding Pz.-Rgt.15, consulted two of his sergeants, Oberfeldwebel Oswald Filla and Feldw. Martin Lange. They felt the advantage of the Panther's oil hydraulic system was that the pumps worked at any time, and if there was an electrical failure it remained Kampfbereit. The motor worked by centrifugal force (later with a crank) and could be started. The disadvantage was that the engine had to be running all the time, as the driveshaft drove the pumps, and traversing speed depended on engine

KARL HEINZ LOSCHKE

KARL THIEME]

Two Ritterkreuz bearers, with Oak Leaves and Swords: Gen.Lt. Wend von Wietersheim and Oberstlt. Karl Thieme.

rpm: 45 seconds to completely traverse 360 degrees at 1,000 rpm, but 15 seconds at 3,000 rpm. But the tactical principle of "fire and movement" meant the panzer had to be ready to move anyway, so "The disadvantage was therefore really an advantage." Lt. Karl Zindler, Zugführer in I./15, also felt the motor running for hydraulic traverse was not a problem.

In turn, the advantage of the Panzer IV's electrical system was that the turret could be traversed with the motor off (sometimes a running engine masked sounds of enemy movement). The disadvantage was that the engine would have to be started to run the generator to keep the batteries charged. Kurt Nentwig found the two-stroke motor on the Panzer IV noisy, and only used it if the panzer were on a slant. Traverse was by foot pedals. The gun could also be traversed and elevated or depressed manually by handwheels, and final precise laying on target was manual.[30]

Perhaps most importantly, the crews had confidence in their panzers. For those who had experienced the Russian T-34/85 and the Iosef Stalin-2, and the assault guns SU-85, SU-122, and SU-152 on the Ostfront, they had little to fear from the American M4 Sherman tank with its short 75mm gun, nor did the Americans have assault guns, except for open-topped tank destroyers. Conversely, American tankers were much intimidated by the heavier German panzers and assault guns with a high-velocity 7,5cm or 7,62cm gun, and the Tiger's 8,8cm gun. And in Normandy they were encountering the King Tiger.

Units continued to be drawn from Blaskowitz's Armeegruppe G, including 1. Armee headquarters and 9.Pz.Div., both sent north to the Normandy front. This left LXIV. Armeekorps with two understrength divisions along the Biscayan coast, and 19. Armee under General der Infanterie Friedrich Wiese with seven infantry divisions of varying quality in three corps headquarters along the Mediterranean coast. Wietersheim's 11. Panzer-Division, in Armeegruppe G reserve, was now the only mobile force in southern France. At the same time, the Maquis were emboldened by the reduced German Wehrmacht presence throughout southern France. The Elften had to mount Terroristeneinsatz (antiterrorist actions) around Castillon sur Dordogne (Le Fleix), and on 21 June there was a fight near St. Foy (Bergerac) in which the SPWs of A.A.11 gave support. There were Gespenster losses in these actions.

On 20 July there was an attempt on the part of some German Army officers to assassinate Hitler in his Wolfsschanze headquarters at Rastenburg east Prussia, but it failed. It was coincident with the collapse of H.Gr. Mitte in the east, and the threatening Allied buildup in Normandy. One reaction to the assassination attempt was to expand the role of the Nationalsozialistische Führungsoffiziere (NSFOs, National Socialist Guidance Officers), sometimes called Nasofüs, to the division level. They had been established by Hitler in late 1943 to imbue officers and men with the National Socialist "spirit." At one point later, Lt. Walter Rahn was told he was the regimental NSFO because no other officer had volunteered, and he had been in the DJ (Deutsches Jungfolk). Veterans took "Troop Information" lectures with some cynicism.

On 25 July, preceded by a massive American carpet-bombing by heavy four-engined bombers, American forces broke through the German HKL near St. Lô on the Normandy front in Operation COBRA. By 31 July the US 4th Armored Division had broken out of Normandy at Avranches into Brittany, and on 1 August the US Third Army became operational under Lt. Gen. George S. Patton Jr., already being recognized by the Germans as an aggressive armor leader from his operations in Tunisia and in Sicily.

On 27 July the 11.Pz.Div. began to displace from the Bordeaux area to the Toulouse-Carcassone-Albi area closer toward Marseille and the Mediterranean coast, as there was a threat of an Allied landing there. Division headquarters was at St. Ferriol by Revel. With not yet a full complement of vehicles—Hptm. Franz Thelen was dispatched to Paris to requisition what he could—many of the personnel had to be shuttled in stages. Yet in the fine summer weather the men could relax, and even the division commander in a bathing suit could try out a Volkswagen Schwimmwagen in a river.

Wietersheim's division was on a three-hour march readiness alert against an Allied landing in southern France. Wietersheim was tasked with responding to three possible landings: a) Simultaneous landings on both sides of Narbonne and the mouth of the Gironde on the Atlantic coast to cut the connection with Fascist Spain; b) a landing in the Rhône delta for a drive up the Rhônetal (Rhône valley) to Lyon to cut off the German forces in southwest France; and c) a landing on the French-Italian Riviera coast, for a drive either into the Rhône valley or into northern Italy. Officers undertook map exercises and route reconnaissance to identify secondary routes and river fording sites, assuming the major bridges and communication routes would be bombed by the Allies. Driving now through Maquis-infested areas had its own risks.

In case of an Allied landing, von Wietersheim felt a beachhead could be defeated by a single panzer division only through an attack by the concentrated division soon after the landing, at the weakest moment of the opponent. But the distances to the Mediterranean coast in Case b was 300 kilometers (186 miles) and in Case c 400–500 kilometers (250–300 miles). Under normal conditions for a panzer unit this meant a march of two to three days to be completely ready for action. With the same conditions as on the Normandy invasion front, even if one didn't want to take losses through the air power of the opponent into account, one must *double* the time required to four to six days! In case of action east of the Rhône a further delay would be caused by the destruction of the Rhône bridges (as was later the case).[31]

On 1 August the Ia reported the division ration strength as 15,059, actually larger than the 13,726 authorized by the KStN: 516 Offz., 3,312 Uffz., 10,480 Mannsch., and 751 Hiwis. During July twenty men and one officer died, whether by illness, accident, or in fighting the French Resistance. There were 139 panzers einsatzbereit: six command Panzer IIIs (with false gun barrels), seventy-four Pz.IVs, and fifty-nine Panthers. There were twenty-five under repair, available in under three weeks. There were eight Sturmgeschützen, 134 SPWs and Pz.Spähwagen, fifteen Marder Panzerjäger, and sixteen Pak, twenty tracked Lkw and nineteen Zugmaschine. There were forty-six artillery pieces (of all types), although no 8,8cm flak guns yet.[32]

But then Wietersheim was ordered to dispatch a detachment of fifty Panzer IVs to Normandie. This meant II.Abteilung/Pz.-Rgt.15 under Major Berger. (Oberst Stenkhoff had succeeded von Lauchert as regimental commander 1 August.) The battalion loaded on two trains on 10 and 11 August, with the panzer commander and driver. A Pkw, a field kitchen, and an Lkw were included. Major Berger commanded one train, Oblt. Edwin Graf Sierstorpff of 8.Kompanie the other. Obergefreiter Lothar Trenkler was one of the Gespensters, after rejoining the division at Bordeaux, having reached Sagan after his trek from Rumania. Ten panzers were nonetheless held back ("inoperable") as a nucleus for refitting the battalion.

A one-day rail journey brought the battalion to Orleans on the middle Loire, but the Eisenbahn bridge there had been bombed out. From Orleans the panzers crossed by ferry and continued by road march, moving by night and using the scattered woods for concealment by day. The route was via Chartres to Dreux where during the night of 15–16 August the panzers were turned over to the 12.SS Panzer-Division Hitler Jugend.[33] They were skirting areas of intense battles to the west. Von Rundstedt had been relieved, and with Patton's divisions pouring down through Avranches, new OB West commander Generalfeldmarschall Günther von Kluge—declaring the situation a *"Riesensauerei"* (one hell of a mess)—urged withdrawal to the Seine.[34]

Instead, Hitler ordered a counterattack, Unternehmen LÜTTICH (Liége). On 7 August four panzer divisions of 5. Panzerarmee under Gen.d.Pz.Tr. Heinrich Eberbach struck west toward Mortain and the coast at Avranches to cut off Patton's drive. But the Americans, alerted by intelligence, including the code-breaking cover-named ULTRA, thwarted the attack and savaged it with air power. Meanwhile Patton, while sending his two lead armored divisions *west* to capture the Breton ports (futile, for the Germans would defend and destroy such fortress ports), turned his other divisions eastward.[35] Three divisions were converging on Le Mans by 8 August and then began swinging north for an encirclement of 5. Panzer and 7. Armee in the Falaise-Argentan Kessel. The II.Abt./15 Gespensters got to Paris, procured and repaired some Wehrmacht and civilian vehicles, and then went southeast via Sens-Troyes (some had been at Mailly-le-Camp the previous year) and Chatillon-Dijon toward Besançon to rejoin the division.

During this time Allied air attacks intensified on 11 and 12 August along the Mediterranean coast sectors between Marseille and the Italian border, but also against the Rhône bridges. On the 12th Luftwaffe air reconnaissance reported the first two escorted convoys of 70–100 ships off the island of Corsica, and it was obvious the Allied invasion of southern France was about to commence. At midday on 13 August Wietersheim's 11. Panzer-Division received a warning order directing them to move east of the Rhône.

CHAPTER TWENTY-THREE

Rhônetal

GENERAL VON WIETERSHEIM WAS AT THE ARMEEGRUPPE G headquarters at Rouffiac by Toulouse on 13 August when he received the alert that the Allied landings were expected east of the Rhône. He was ordered to concentrate in the area of Nimes-Arles south of Avignon in the Rhône delta, and send a gepanzerte Kampfgruppe east of the river. At dark on the 13th elements of the division began to move, following the route of Carcassonne–Beziers–Montpellier–Nimes. Oberstlt. Stenkhoff oversaw the rail-loading of some fifty panzers of Pz.-Rgt.15, mostly Panthers of I.Abt./15, the first train departing Toulouse at 21,00 hours.

The Eisenbahnzug route was Revel–Carcassonne–Trebez–Narbonne–Beziers–Montpelier–Avignon. The first section went into concealment in a forest 4 kilometers from Avignon, where the bridges had been knocked out by Allied bombing. That many of the defending flak guns had been removed to Normandy further meant their vulnerability. Subsequent transports encountered destroyed overhead telephone and telegraph wires and railroad track after a few stations, and had to unload and continue by road march. The other division Räderfahrzeuge, already moving by road, traveled in march groups mixed to be combat ready, as the maquisards were already becoming more active. When moving by day the vehicles moved as Einzelgruppen from cover to cover, already determined upon, though of necessity this was slower than an administrative road march.

Early on the 14th, Division Ia Oberstlt. Werner Drews drove to Gen.d.Inf. Friedrich Wiese's 19. Armee Gefechtsstand at Avignon-Villeneuve to coordinate arrangements to get the division across the Rhône. Other staff officers with unit advance parties went to Nimes. The Div.Gef.Std. located to Remoulins, 25 kilometers west of Avignon. That Menzel's H.Fla Abt.277 still lacked its Acht-achts was "disadvantageous" noted von Wietersheim.

In the early-morning hours of 15 August, as now expected, the Allied invasion of southern France began between Toulon and Cannes, preceded by intense naval and air bombardment. Fifteen kilometers inland paratroopers came down in the night sky around Le Muy near the Argens River, followed by gliders landing, and landing craft headed ashore behind minesweepers and rocket ships. This was the beginning of Allied Operation ANVIL (renamed DRAGOON on 1 August).

The area was thinly held by two divisions of Generalleutnant Ferdinand Neuling's LXII. Armeekorps: 242.Inf.Div. under Gen.Maj. Johannes Baessler and, farther east, the 148.I.D. under Gen.Maj. Otto Fretter-Pico. The personnel of both divisions were ethnic Germans and overage men, and each included an Ost Bataillon of Russians and others who had volunteered or were drafted from eastern countries or prisoner-of-war camps; some of these men had been Hilfswillige on the Ostfront. Both division commanders had been wounded in division commands during the Russian campaign, and OKH had almost retired Neuling after his health broke down in Russia in 1942. Some elements could give stiff resistance, but in general the divisions reflected the parlous manpower situation of the Wehrmacht by 1944.[1]

The paratroopers were British and Americans of the division-sized 1st Airborne Task Force. Nighttime ground fog prevented the pathfinder teams from accurately marking the drop zones, though as in Normandy, the scattering of the paratroopers created additional confusion among the German defenders. Along the coast the brunt of the amphibious assault came against the 765.Inf.Rgt. of Baessler's 242.I.D. The American 3rd Infantry Division came ashore on the St. Tropez peninsula and scattered the 765.Inf. Rgt.'s 4.Bataillon (807. Azerbaijani), and the US 45th Division overwhelmed 1.Btl. The US 36th Division farther east near Cannes met stiffer resistance from 2.Btl. and the naval coast defenses. Nonetheless total Allied casualties in the 15 August invasion were only 95 killed and 385 wounded (compared to some 8,700 to 11,000 casualties on 6 June of the larger Normandy invasion), lighter than expected; and the vast majority of the 2,300 prisoners taken were overage Germans or members of the Ost units.[2]

The landings were made by Maj. Gen. Lucian Truscott's VI Corps of Maj. Gen. Alexander Patch's US Seventh Army. The three American divisions were recent veterans of the Italian campaign; the 3rd and 45th had also been in Sicily, and the 3rd had been in North Africa as well. The American forces rapidly advanced inland, and by the next day the first of seven Free French divisions was also ashore and driving hard.

With the 148.Inf.Div. falling back toward the Alps (it and 157. Reserve Gebirgsdivision around Grenoble would come under OB Südwest in Italy), 242.I.D. shattered, and Neuling's LXII. A.K. generally out of communication, Wiese intended to block a further Allied advance west toward the vital port cities and the Rhône valley with LXXXV. A.K. of Gen.Lt. Baptist Kniess and his two divisions, 244. and 338.I.D.s. At the same time elements of the three divisions west of the Rhône under Gen.Lt. Erich Petersen's IV. Luftwaffe Feldkorps, 189., 198., and 716.I.D.s, were to cross the river, as was the11.Pz.Div. The impediment, of course, was the barrier of the Rhône, with the bridges bombed out. Ferries at Aramon and Tarascon were utilized, mostly at night, as there was little flak defense. Light vehicles up to 5 tons could negotiate a damaged bridge at Montfaucon.

Major Weicke and Lt. Rudolf Graf Hoyos of 2.Kp./I./15 were out on a railway bridge north of Avignon being used as a vehicle crossing to see if it could handle panzers, when seven American P-47 fighter-bombers appeared. The German officers were able to scramble back behind a stone wall, though the bombs wrecked the bridge along with the men and vehicles that were on it. Wietersheim praised acting regimental Ordonnanz Offizier Lt. Karl "Kalle" Zindler of Pz.Rgt.15, who made a suspension bridge at Roquemaure passable for vehicles on his own initiative. He would in turn expect such initiative of each of his officers: "In difficult situations there is *always* a way out, never an impossibility."

Division Ord.-Offz. Lt. Ernst-August Freiherr von Fersen transported staff across the river in a Schwimm-VW. Von Fersen had been an infantry lieutenant with Inf.Rgt.51/18.Inf.Div.(mot) in Russia, when he was wounded in his right upper thigh. No longer capable of the rigors of the infantry, after recuperating he was transferred to the Panzer-Ersatzbataillon of Pz.Rgt.15 in Sagan for retraining, and joined the division at Bordeaux in June as Wietersheim's Begleitoffizier.[3] The Ordonnanzoffizier (Orderly Officer) ensured quarters and vehicles, the Adjutant ensured the functioning of the headquarters, and the Begleitoffizier (Escort Officer) was the general's bodyguard.

By midday on 15 August only one battalion of Pz.Gren.Rgt.110 and a Pz.Pionier Kompanie were across the Rhône. Elements of the division were stretched to Pont St. Esprit 50 kilometers (30 miles) north of Avignon. Pz.Aufklärungsabteilung 11 and Pz.G.R.111 were still 40 kilometers (25 miles) northwest of Montpellier, delayed by a tunnel

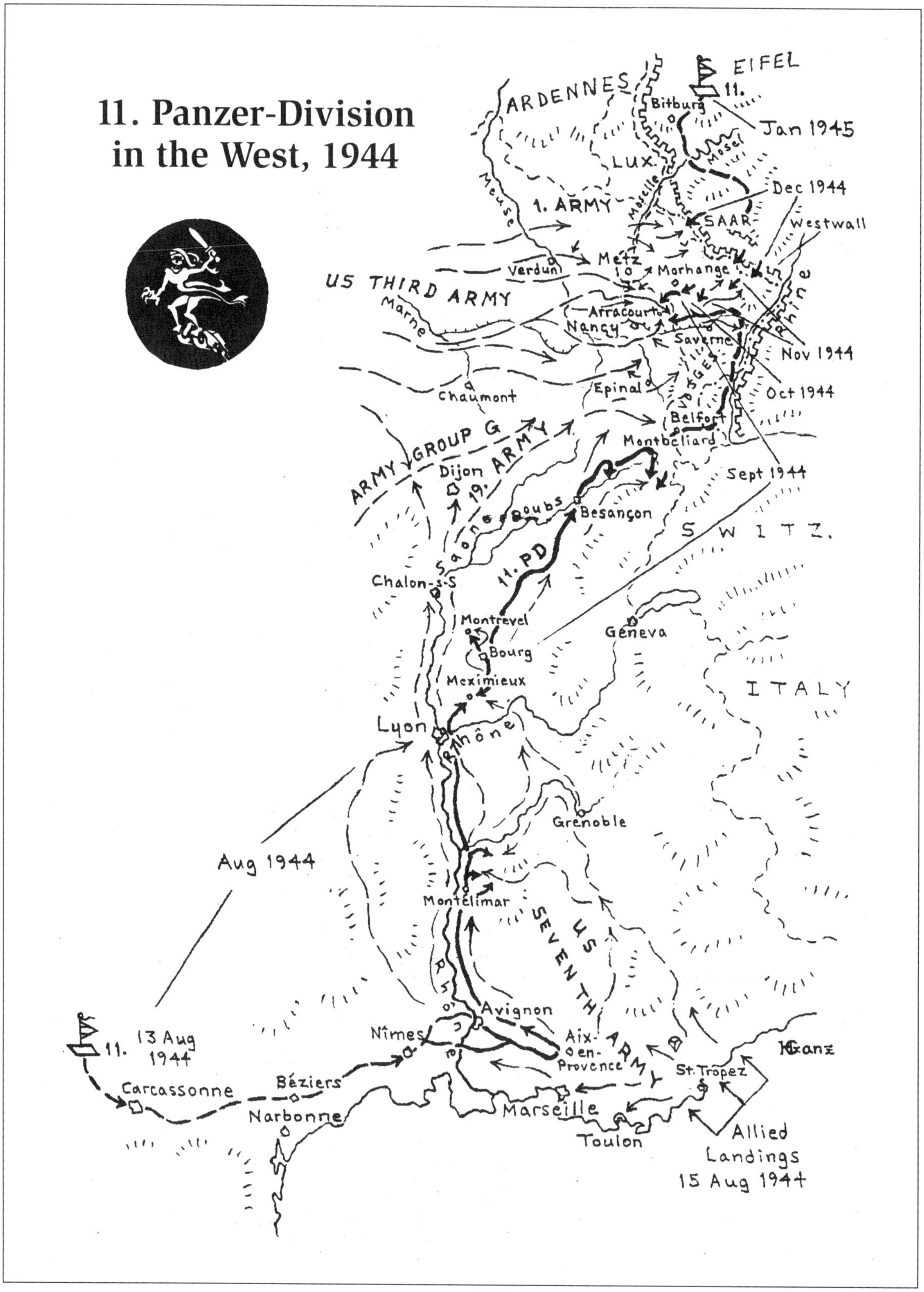

11. Panzer-Division in the West, 1944

demolition by the Maquis. Under cover of night and into the next day bridges at Ardèche north of Pont St. Esprit and at Roquemaure south of Orange enabled vehicles up to 8 tons to cross. The Gespensters began to move into assembly areas between Arles and Aix-en-Provence.[4] The 45-ton Panthers and other heavy gepanzerte Kettenfahrzeuge were more of a challenge, though the engineers modified a coal barge as a ferry with a 60-ton capability at Avignon. The Panthers could only be ferried over one at a time.

On 16 August, the day after the Allied landings, Hitler authorized OKW to order a retreat from southern France, though the major ports must be defended. The disaster overtaking 5. Panzer and 7. Armee in the Falaise-Argentan Kessel in the west was just one challenge facing Germany: the Allies were advancing in Italy; the Polish Underground uprising was underway in Warsaw as the Red Army reached the Vistula; Finland, Rumania, and Bulgaria were deserting the German alliance; and Allied bombing was beginning to cripple the German war machine by concentrating on oil production. ("The Germans viewed the attacks as catastrophic" an American study later concluded, "Consumption of oil exceeded production from May 1944 on.") All this made even Hitler realize the necessity of abandoning all of southern France.[5]

As the elements of the Elfte struggled across the Rhône, the Div.-Gef.-Std. was established at St. Remy north of the Chaine des Alpilles on the east bank on 17 August. To cover the assembly of the division east of the Rhône a security line was formed Etang de Berre–east of Aix-en-Provence-Peyrolles on the Durance. On the 18th at Avignon a 19. Armee commanders' conference outlined the planned retreat north up the Rhônetal. Initially, Petersen's IV. Luftwaffe Korps would move up the west bank, and Kniess's LXXXV. A.K. would move up the east bank. Seven delaying positions were identified. As the sole mobile (and only first-rate) unit in all of Armeegruppe G, Wietersheim's 11. Panzer-Division had the unenviable task of protecting the left flank of 19. Armee and covering the retreat to slow the Allied advance, while somehow avoiding being cut off by Patton's rampaging Third Army in the north. Two days before, on the 16th, Patton's 4th Armored Division had been relieved of impatiently containing Lorient and, leaving the 6th AD before Brest, had captured Orleans on the middle Loire, heading east.

By 18 August only six Panthers had crossed the Rhône, along with Pz.Jäger-Abt.61 and I.Abt./Pz. Art.Rgt.119. Twelve trains with forty Panthers were still west of Carcassonne because of railroad track damage. In late afternoon about 18,00 Uhr the 8-ton bridge at Roquemaure was bombed out, stopping some of the wheeled vehicles from crossing the river. Elements stranded on the railroads were ordered to offload and road-march.[6] Most of the division would not be east of the Rhône until the 22nd, seven days after the landings, a movement that should only have taken two days. Wietersheim felt that better attention to the Rhône-crossing issue—better air defense, alternate crossing sites—would have enabled the 11.Pz.Div. to contest the Allied buildup much sooner.[7] This was all true, though perhaps the necessary resources were simply not available.

As French forces under Général Jean de Lattre de Tassigny, now as II French Corps, advanced on Toulon and Marseille, American forces to their north drove westward toward Avignon on the Rhône. Other American forces rolled up the Durance River to the east, captured Gen.Lt. Ferdinand Neuling and some of his LXII. A.K. staff on the 18th, went through Sisteron on the 19th, and were then reported on the routes heading north to Grenoble and west along the Drôme River, which flowed into the Rhône north of Montelimar.

Desperate to slow down the Allied advance, Wiese ordered Wietersheim to mount a counterattack with what he had. With his division still crossing the Rhône, Wietersheim nonetheless improvised a Kampfgruppe under Oberst Heinrich-George Hax, commanding Pz.Gr.Rgt.110, composed of eight Panthers and some panzergrenadiers. They launched a probing attack toward Aix-en-Provence north of Marseille on 21 August. Panzerleutnant Friedrich von Eggeling of 3.Kp./I./15 had orders to report any tanks and engage them. It was the day after "Friedel's" twentieth birthday, and his crew had some red wine, grapes, and peaches. Sighting and reporting some Americans, he then was ordered to return, which he did so after firing off some high-velocity rounds as a *Salut*.

The probe had the desired effect. As the 30th Infantry Regiment of the US 3rd Infantry Division commanded by Maj. Gen. John O'Daniel advanced to take Aix that day, rumors and reports were rampant: that twelve Panzer IVs were spotted west of Aix, that twenty more panzers, possibly the huge 60-ton Tigers, were seen north of Aix just across the Durance River, that twelve Panthers were reported moving northwest of Aix along National Route 7. Another patrol counted four heavy and five light tanks outside of Aix. The 3rd Infantry Division G-2 (intelligence) did qualify these reports as "(unconfirmed)," and noted, "Many enemy tanks reported as Mk VI [Tiger] may have been Mk V's [Panther]." That the panzers did not seriously contest Aix, but withdrew again, only added to the uncertainty.[8]

This was perhaps the first confrontation between the Gespensters and the "Amis." Indeed, some of Hax's 110 Kampfgruppe was engaged in Aix on the 21st. These included 3.Kompanie under Oberlt. Schlütter of the regiment's I.Btl.(gepanzerte) under Hauptmann Heinz Wolff. Fifteen Landsers were captured by the 3rd Infantry; based on their interrogations, it was estimated at that time 3.Kp. had eighty to ninety-five men. There were ten to twelve half-tracks, each carrying eight to twelve men with three light MGs (two on the vehicle). These represented the three rifle platoons (if excluding the weapons and flak platoons, 4. schwere Zug and 5. le.Fla.Zug.). The two 7,5cm short assault guns on half-tracks noted were of 4.s.Zug (7,5cm Stu.K.37 L/24 on an Sd.Kfz.251/9 or le.SPW Sd.Kfz.250/8), and the platoon would have included two 8cm mortars and four tripod-mounted machine guns on four more half-tracks. The flak platoon with six 2cm flak guns would have been mounted on three half-tracks and two with towing vehicles including a Zwillingsflak.

There was also a PW from a motorized battalion, 6.Kp. of the regiment's II.Btl. [110] under Hauptmann Johannes Schneider. He said the battalion lost a number of vehicles to Allied air attacks during the road movement to west of Aix. Weapons and supplies were transported in requisitioned French wood-gas buses, and ten to twelve men on bicycles were towed by each vehicle. The company had around eighty fighting men in three platoons totaling ten to twelve le.MGs, and one 5cm or 8cm mortar [of 4.schwere Zug].

The American intelligence officer (1st Lt. Henry Huquenin) concluded, "Judging by the 16 PWs captured to date of 110 PGR, the regiment is hardly a crack outfit anymore. The new and untried replacements by far outnumbered the survivors of the old 11 Panzer Division that fought in Russia and are physically unimpressive."[9] This evaluation would prove to be premature.

With elements of the 11.Pz.-Div. also reported moving west of the Rhône, Hax's foray gave pause to Patch at Seventh Army and Truscott at VI Corps. The 36th Division under Maj. Gen. John Dahlquist was headed north and Truscott was going to send the 45th Division, under Maj. Gen. William Eagles, north as well, but now instead ordered the 3rd and 45th Divisions to halt along a north–south line above Marseille in case a counterattack materialized. The 11. Panzer-Division was considered a formidable opponent early on.

As Patch also wanted to ensure that Toulon and Marseille were being secured, the American advance stopped; this allowed Kniess to continue the withdrawal of his LXXXV. Korps forces without interference. Wiese was able to get most of his 19. Armee forces north of the Durance River by 24 August, and Avignon was left to the French and Americans unopposed.[10]

Left behind were elements of Baessler's 242.Inf.-Div. to defend the "fortress" of Toulon, and elements of the 244.I.D. under Gen.Maj. Hans Schaeffer at Marseille, along with some naval and Luftwaffe personnel. The ports had not been heavily fortified, but the French forces under de Lattre did suffer casualties in the street fighting before both port cities were formally surrendered on 28 August. Hitler had demanded that the ports themselves be held; the failure to hold out longer meant early logistical support for the Allied advance north, as Hitler had recognized. Toulon was opened for shipping on 5 September, and Marseille on 15 September, only four weeks after the invasion.

Far to the north three days before, Paris was occupied with little fighting. Its surrender was negotiated by the military Befehlshaber (Commandant) Gen.d.Inf. Dietrich von Choltitz, who had been ordered to make the city a "field of ruins" but who would not do so. Like Rome, the Germans declared Paris an "open city" to spare it the destruction of fighting. Choltitz had commanded the 11.Pz.Div. in 1943 and then LXXXIV. A.K. in Normandy.

By 22 August the Gespenster-Division was assembled east of the Rhône and crossing the Durance to the north. By doctrine and by preference, the 11.Pz.Div. was to be employed as a unified strike force. But except for some Sturmgeschütz III assault guns and Marder tank destroyers with the better infantry divisions, the only armor in southern France was with the 11.Panzer. Thus of necessity, smaller Kampfgruppen would have to carry out diverse and separate missions.

At most, these Kampfgruppen might have a battalion of panzergrenadiers and a company of panzers, though more likely were the mixed company-sized Panzerkampftruppen with only a platoon or section of panzers, as already conceived. Oberst Stenkhoff's Pz.-Rgt.15 would not be employed as such, but its companies were parceled out. Again it was realized that it was crucial that the battalion and company officers be able to act responsibly and with initiative. This tactical reality did have the advantage that the panzer division seemed to be ubiquitous to their enemy, for it was never known whether a few panzers might represent a much larger force.

South of the Durance Oblt. Franz Graf Hoyos of 6.Kompanie had some fifteen Panzer IVs, which represented the strength of II.Abt./Pz.Rgt.15. This force gave caution to O'Daniel's 3rd Infantry Division advance. North of the river some of Major Karl Bode's Aufkl.Abt.11 scouted the American advance, backed up by Lt. Hedtke with five Panthers. Suddenly an estimated twenty-five to thirty enemy armored cars—the six-wheeled M8 mounting only a 37mm gun—were reported. Hedtke let them approach to within 300–400 meters and then opened fire, destroying five of them. He then withdrew behind Lequi. During the night of 25–26 August three Panthers were in a delaying position with Teller antitank mines in front when American M4 Sherman tanks advanced. One tank detonated a mine, illuminating the scene, and after a fierce engagement four Shermans were claimed *captured* and driven back to the German positions.[11]

Other elements of Wietersheim's division had already been ordered north with the American advance toward Grenoble and northwest toward Montélimar and the Rhône valley, threatening to intercept the retreating 19. Armee. It was the ongoing mission of the Elfte to cover the left flank and rear of the German retreat up the Rhônetal from the three advancing American infantry divisions.

Under the 1943 T/O&E 7 (Table of Organization and Equipment), the American infantry division was almost as mobile as the German panzer or panzergrenadier division. (Some of the infantry might be shuttled by quartermaster (QM) truck companies however.) A US division had 14,218 personnel authorized, 16,196 with normal attachments. It had three infantry regiments of three battalions each, an artillery regiment with three 105mm battalions and a 155mm battalion, and a medical and a combat engineer battalion. Normal attachments were a tank battalion (sixty-eight light M5 and medium M4 tanks), a tank destroyer battalion (usually thirty-six M10 tank destroyers), and an antiaircraft battalion.

While the M10 TD mounted a 3-inch (76mm) gun, it had an open-topped turret and thin (2.3-inch/57mm) armor; it had manual traverse and elevation, and did not have a rotating turret basket, nor a bow or coaxial machine gun. It was a stand-off tank destroyer, not a tank. The main battle American tank was the 30-ton M4 Sherman. It was mechanically very reliable, but its short 75mm gun and relatively thin (3-inch/ 76mm) frontal armor was outclassed by the German medium and heavy panzers. The M4 did have an effective hydraulic power turret traverse, and a gyrostabilizer for firing on the move, though the latter was hard to keep in adjustment and crews usually disconnected them. The 15-ton M5 light tank with its 37mm gun and thin (2.5-inch/ 64mm) armor could be used for reconnaissance, but not tank engagements.

Tactically, the US infantry division often operated with three regimental combat teams, each usually with a company attached from the tank, tank destroyer, antiaircraft, engineer, and medical battalions, supported by a 105mm howitzer battalion, with the 155mm howitzer battalion in general support. The regiments in turn usually operated in battalion task forces with attached platoons, mixed according to the mission.

With the port cities secured for the vital importation of oil and other supplies, Patch could focus on the advance northward. De Lattre's expanding French force, with American tanks and equipment, would advance west of the Rhône, Truscott's VI Corps on the east. By 21 August American forces were advancing up N 85, the "Route Napoleon" (from his return from Elba in 1815), toward Grenoble, and also toward the Rhône valley north and south of Montélimar, threatening the 19. Armee retreat along the N 7 highway.

These latter probes were by elements of an American brigade-sized task force under Brig. Gen. Frederick Butler, the VI Corps deputy commander. It had approached from Crest on the Drôme, a tributary of the Rhône north of Montélimar, down to Puy St. Martin. TF Butler was composed of the light tanks and armored cars of the battalion-sized 117th Cavalry Reconnaissance Squadron, Mechanized, including some thirty medium tanks of two tank companies, a company of twelve tank destroyers, a self-propelled armored field artillery battalion with twelve M7 (105mm) pieces, a motorized infantry battalion, and engineer, ordnance, and medical units of the 36th Infantry Division.[12] The rest of Dahlquist's division, the "Texas" Division, followed, while its 143rd Infantry Regiment entered Grenoble to the northeast on the 22nd.

Eagle's 45th "Thunderbird" Infantry Division advanced as well, while O'Daniel's 3rd, the "Rock of the Marne," pressed up N 7 itself. Because of conflicting orders, however, Butler was uncertain whether his mission was north via Grenoble or west toward the Rhône valley, and his units were spread from Aspres and Gap to Crest. Elements did go through the Condillac Pass of the hills above Montélimar that constricted the N 7 highway and the railroad along the east (left) bank of the Rhône. They even took the retreating German motor columns under tank and artillery fire and briefly established a roadblock across the highway near La Coucourde on the 21st.

But now Wietersheim's Gespensters were moving up from the Durance to fend off the American forces on the flank. Major Karl Bode's A.A.11 and elements of Luftwaffe Infanterie Ausbildung (training) Regiment 71 attacked up route D 6 along the Roubion River to Sauzet on the 22nd, and also across the Roubion farther east, to Puy St. Martin and Marsanne behind Task Force Butler, threatening to cut the Amis off. American medium tanks and GIs fought back into Puy that night.

The Aufklärungs-Abteilung with its armored cars and light half-track Sd.Kfz.250s was intended for scouting, not battle. But some of the eight-wheeled Spähwagen Sd.Kfz.234s mounted a 5cm gun in a turret (the Puma) or a 7,5cm gun, Pakwagens, adding formidable firepower. Lt. Werner Strietzel of 2.Kompanie said the companies were sometimes attached to different battle groups, though sometimes the battalion operated as a tactical unit.[13] The versatility of the reconnaissance battalion made it a major maneuver force—though battle losses that reduce the ability of such units to carry out their primary missions has generated an ongoing controversy about the role and weaponry of such units. During this retreat Bode's feints, hit-and-run attacks, and delaying tactics often parried or deterred the American moves.

By 23 August Ami forces were driving in to cut off and segment the 19. Armee retreat. This was Dahlquist's 36th Infantry Division supporting TF Butler: the 143rd Infantry Regiment from Grenoble west to Valence in the north, the 141st Infantry in the center to Montélimar, and the 142nd to Nyons farther south. Eagles's 45th Infantry Division took over the drive north, the 179th Infantry to Grenoble followed by the 180th Infantry, with the 157th in reserve. On that 23rd Bode's Kampfgruppe fought into Sauzet and also crossed the Roubion again, but was thwarted by heavy artillery fire. Passing to the north was the gepanzerte Gruppe under Major Karl Thieme, with his I.Btl./Pz.Gren.Rgt.110, the 15cm Hummeln of I.Abt./Pz.Art.Rgt.119, and ten panzers.

Thieme struck from Sauzet to contest the high ground dominating the N 7 route north of Montélimar. The 198.Inf.Div. under Oberst Alfred Kuhnert was to take over the right flank protection up to Nyons, releasing more of Wietersheim's division. The Div. Gefechtsstand moved to Montélimar. On the 24th Kgr. Thieme counterattacked an advance by the 141st Infantry, even surrounding one battalion, which finally fought its way clear and fell back from Sauzet. The heat was a stifling 40 degrees Celsius (104 F). The 36th Division went over to the defense.

On the evening of the 24th an American liaison officer fled from his jeep when fired on by a small German roadblock, leaving behind a detailed copy of Dahlquist's operational plans for the 25th. With a clearer picture of the 36th Infantry Division deployments, Wiese decided to form a provisional corps under von Wietersheim's command, Korpsgruppe "von Wietersheim": his 11.Pz.Div., the 198.I.D., the Luftwaffe Ausbildung-Rgt.63, Luftwaffe Flak-Rgt.18 with guns from 2cm to 8,8cm, and the 540.Reichsbahn Artillerie Bataillon with five heavy railroad guns 27cm (11 inches) to 38cm (15 inches) in caliber. The availability of this last element was dependent upon the rail lines being kept in repair. Wiese expected Wietersheim to drive back the 36th Infantry Division. In the south Kniess's LXXXV. A.K. was now north of the Durance.

With the extended areas of responsibility, von Wietersheim reverted to the mixed battle group concept previously used. He organized four Gespenster Kampfgruppen under Bode's A.A.11, Thieme's gepanzerte Gruppe, Oberst Hax of Pz.Gren.Rgt.110, and Oberstlt. Wilde of Pz.Gr.Rgt.111. The commander of Pz.Rgt.15 was not included, as the panzer companies were widely distributed; but it may also be that Wietersheim felt Oberstlt. Stenkhoff was new to the division and had yet to prove himself. Stenkhoff was given the responsibility for the administration and supply of the regiment. Bode and Thieme had been with the division in Russia, and Hax had had his

Montelimar, 21–31 August 1944

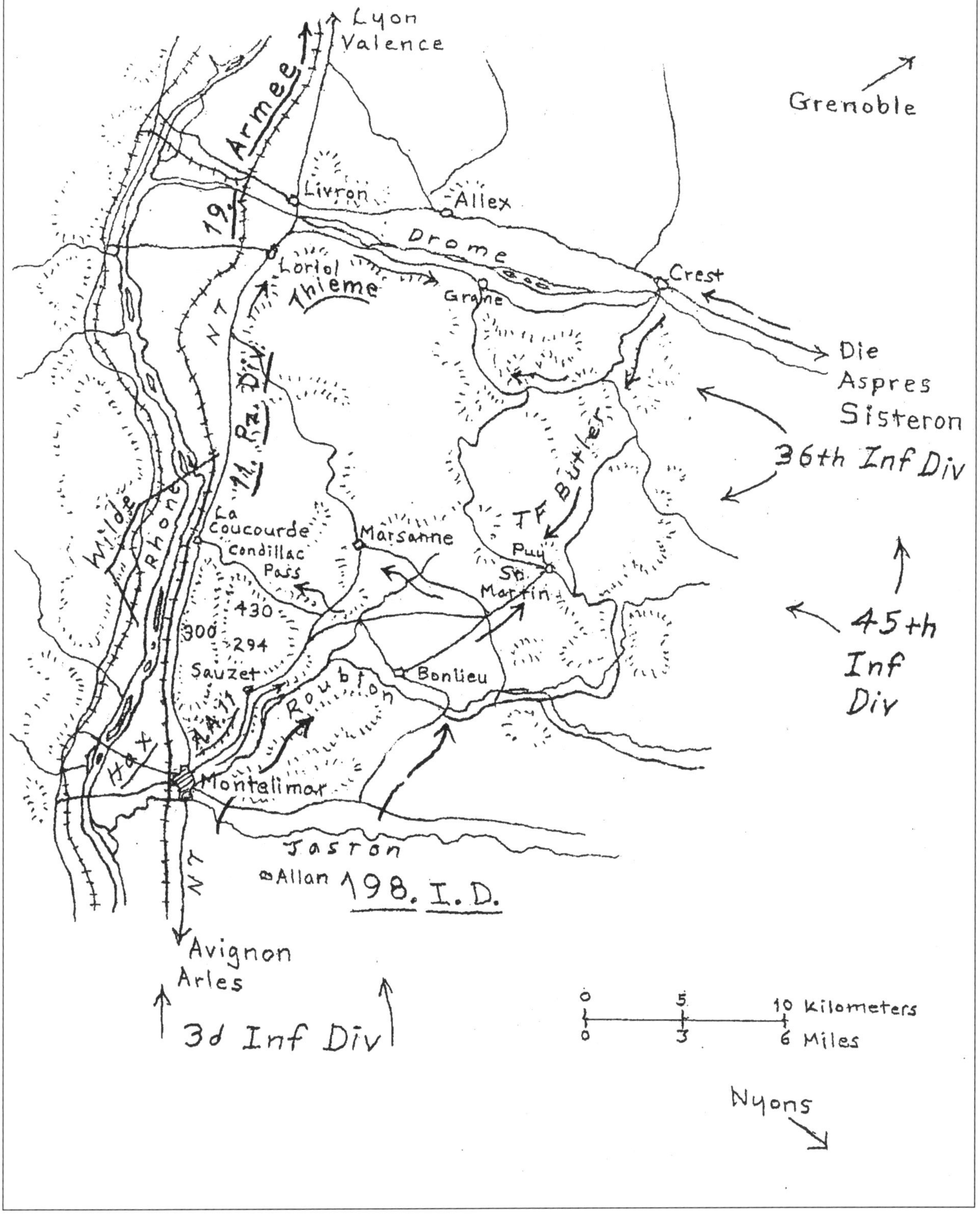

command since May and Wilde since February. Stenkhoff had only joined in August.[14]

Wietersheim also formed two Kampfgruppen built around the 198.Division's 305. and 326. Grenadier Regiments. The artillery was coordinated by a 19. Armee Arko. The 305. was to attack the high ground northeast of Montélimar and close the Condillac Pass, and the 326. would attack across the Roubion near Bonlieu. Kgr. Hax with two panzergrenadier battalions (II. of his own 110 and II./111), two battalions of Luftwaffe Ausbildung-Rgt. 63 (I. and III.), 3.Kp./ Panz.Jg.Abt.61, and panzers and artillery (II./119), was to reinforce the 305. attack. Kgr. Thieme farther north up N 7 with the gp.Gruppe (I./110) and the Gespenster Ersatzbataillon (replacement battalion) 119, would strike eastward from Loriol along the south bank of the Drôme to Grane, 8 kilometers short of Crest.

Kfgr. Wilde, with I.Btl. of his own Pz.Gren. Rgt.111, an artillery battalion (III./119), and a few panzers, would relieve Kgr. Thieme elements outposting N 7 around La Coucourde on the Rhône and be a reserve. Oberstlt. Erich Hammon's Pz.Art.Rgt. 119 battalions were attached to the Kampfgruppen. Bode's A.A.11 would foray into the Puy St. Martin area again behind the American forces. If this complex plan worked out, the 326.Kgr. from the south and Kgr. Thieme from the north might encircle TF Butler and the 36th Infantry Division in a Kessel and destroy them.[15]

There was one factor the panzers were finding they did *not* have to contend with: the Jagdbombers of American tactical air power. In northern France XIX Tactical Air Command was giving devastating support to Patton's hard-driving armored columns. But in southern France the P-47 fighter-bomber and A-20 light bomber squadrons of XII TAC under Brig. Gen. Gordon Saville had been based on Corsica, and the American advance pushed beyond the range even of new airfields being established ashore. In addition, the B-25 and B-26 medium bombers of Mediterranean Allied Tactical Air Force (MATAF) from Sardinia and Corsica were diverted to Italy after 21 August.

Because XII TAC could not give effective close air support when called for by FACs (forward air controllers) with the ground combat units, after 20 August support was limited to attacking ahead of map bomb-lines marking the forward troop units—and these were always changing with battle. While bombing and strafing the German columns retreating up the Rhône valley was destructive, attacking the maneuvering panzer units proved impractical.[16]

Wietersheim's attack began on 25 August. Karl Thieme's Kampfgruppe attacked from Loriol at 11,30 hours along the Drôme against 117th Cavalry Squadron outposts, reaching Grane by 14,00, while other elements from Livron on the north bank seized Allex. Dahlquist, alarmed, sent TF Butler (now scarcely a weak battalion combat team) north from Puy St. Martin toward Crest, and Butler sent a tank platoon toward Grane. But the German force was too strong, and various American units hurriedly set up roadblocks on both sides of the Drôme west of Crest.

Elsewhere the German attacks were less successful, and Major Weicke, commander of I.Abt./ Pz.Rgt.15 was killed in the small village of Saulce-sur-Rhône. At the time he had four Panthers of the battalion staff along with cars, trucks, and motorcycles moving along the highway at night. Fired upon from windows in the village, Weicke had the four panzers form an all-around defense in the marketplace under some chestnut trees. Adju Lt. von Eggeling was running to one of the Panthers to use its radio to call for assistance when a grenade exploded and shards struck him in the face and back. Weicke was also crossing the marketplace when he was shot through the chest. Blood-soaked von Eggeling was able to organize assault groups that finally drove the Maquis away.[17] Weicke was succeeded as Panther battalion commander by Hptm. Freiherr von Rabenau from 1.Kp., who was then killed in action three days later.

From the south the 326. Grenadiers attacked north across the Roubion at Bonlieu through a company of engineers but were driven back by artillery fire. Simultaneously the Amis attacked west from the Condillac Pass to block the N 7 highway at La Coucourde. These were two rifle companies of 1st Battalion, 141st Infantry, four tanks, and seven tank destroyers. Wietersheim himself gathered some Panthers, panzergrenadiers, and self-propelled artillery from Hax and Wilde in the Montélimar and Sauzet area and that night led a furious charge against the American force. The panzergrenadiers never dismounted their SPWs, but fought from their moving vehicles. The American tanks were illuminated by flares fired by a panzer officer. ("Substitute for lacking night-firing equipment," drily commented von Wietersheim.) He had told his leaders, "I wish to see the commanders in the thick of the fray and expect initiative"—and here set a personal example.[18]

Three American tanks and six tank destroyers were knocked out in this sudden Panzervorstoss, and by 01,00 hours on the 26th the rest were forced back into the pass, and the route was open again. Wietersheim also had forces secure the high ground, and Dahlquist's attempt to cut the retreat route of 19. Armee had failed again. On 16 August bombers had seriously damaged the Loriol–Livron railway bridge over the Drôme and that night FFI leader Henri Faure's maquisards set plastic explosives by the massive stone arches of the N 7 highway bridge that blasted a huge gap. Nonetheless the Germans laid planks on the railway bridge, and German engineers improved a ford across the Drôme west of Loriol, keeping the vehicular traffic moving through the Drôme crossing bottleneck.[19] But the traffic jams of vehicles had made lucrative targets for American bombers, and when Task Force Butler had approached on 21 August, his artillery caused much destruction.

It is difficult to judge the effectiveness of the partisans. Obergefreiter Albrecht Englert, a radio operator at 19. Armee headquarters, noted they targeted service, staff, and straggler elements rather than combat units. Most damage during the retreat was the result of Allied bombing and artillery, though there was a pervasive threat throughout an increasingly hostile countryside. The partisans did cut telephone line communications, though radio of course was not affected. Lt. Eggeling said panzer commanders were at risk from snipers if they didn't have accompanying infantry or were exposed in the turret hatch negotiating narrow town streets.[20] Sometimes the FFI worked alongside Allied troops, though in general they did not participate in actual tactical operations, as did partisans on the Russian Front.

With his primary mission being to protect the eastern flank of the 19. Armee withdrawal, Wietersheim's units were widely scattered. It was a significant change in scale from the Ostfront where whole panzer corps were engaged with entire Russian tank armies, and battles were fought involving hundreds of tanks over the open, endless steppe of southern Russia. Now scarcely a platoon of panzers supported understrength infantry or panzergrenadier companies in hilly and often wooded terrain against American battalions or regimental combat teams.

Late on 25 August Wietersheim ordered Pz.Gren. Rgt.110 elements under Hax and Thieme to move north of the Drôme to counter the American forces building up near Crest. He also requested of Wiese that he not try to control all the other forces in his provisional corps, and Wiese redirected these to Kniess's LXXXV. Korps control around Montélimar. The 198. Infanterie-Division was now under Generalmajor Otto Richter. Oberst Alfred Kuhnert had left to attend the divisional commander's Lehrgang (later commanding 26.Pz.Div.).

On the 26th Kniess had Richter's Gren.Rgt.308 as rear guard delay O'Daniel's 3rd Division, advancing north from Avignon, while Gren.Rgt.305 fought the 36th Division's 141st Regiment in the hills north of Montélimar and the 326. clashed with the 142nd Infantry around Bonlieu on the Roubion. There were American forces now around Montélimar as Truscott ordered the 157th Regimental Combat Team and 191st Tank Battalion of Eagles's 45th Division attached to Dahlquist's 36th Division. Moving via Nyons to Marsanne, these were committed to again attempt to cut the German retreat.

On the 26th Kgr. Wilde of Pz.G.R.111 on N 7 fended off an attack from the Condillac Pass and drove the Amis back into the pass. These were elements of TF Butler and 3rd Battalion, 143rd Infantry reinforced with tanks and tank destroyers. North of the Drôme Bode's A.A.11 broke through American roadblocks west of Crest, but the 143rd Infantry was reinforced by the 157th Regimental Combat Team and blocking positions were restored near Grane and Allex. But these were defensive positions and Dahlquist had again failed to reach the N 7 retreat route. Truscott was on the verge of relieving his division commander, though he acknowledged the difficulties of ammunition and fuel resupply and QM truck transportation for the infantry.[21]

By the 27th most of the 11.Pz.-Div., including Oberstlt. Erich Hammon's Pz.Art.Rgt.119, was north of the Drôme, though some of Kmpfgr. Hax and of Wilde were retained to support the 198.Inf.Div. and the 338.I.D. under Gen.Lt. Richard de Courbière, which had crossed the Rhône from the west bank. These were again able to block American attempts to reach N 7, though American artillery ranged on the Rollbahn and littered it with destroyed guns, burned-out vehicles, and dead horses and soldiers. Ia Oberstlt. Werner Drews telephoned 19. Armee that the highway was hopelessly jammed up. Zugmaschine, prime movers, were used to tow vehicles across the Drôme fords, but heavy rain led to flooding. It took twelve hours to get the Elfte units across.[22]

At Allan 8 kilometers southeast of Montélimar, a small American force entered the little village that day on the heels of LXXXV. Korps headquarters units pulling out. Obergefreiter Englert's six-wheeled radio van, equipped with aerials to connect 19. Armee with higher headquarters including OB West and OKW, was among the elements departing. The night before, 19. Armee Chef des Stabes Generalleutnant Walter Botsch had told Englert, "Quicker, quicker, we must go out of Allan and La Coucourde tonight, the 11. Panzer-Division cannot keep the route open, and I cannot operate without my radio-men."[23]

The German rear guard had been reinforced by seven Marder Panzerjägers, the Marder III mounting a 7,62cm Pak 36(r) gun on a Czech 38(t) chassis, and two Sturmgeschütze from Major Arnold Kessler's Pz.Jg.Abt.61. The entering Americans were a 3rd Infantry Division company team of an infantry company reinforced by a tank and a tank destroyer platoon, which knocked out a Marder. But in the tree line overlooking the village was a section of Panthers of 3.Kp./I.Abt./Pz.Rgt.15 under Oberleutnant Erich Stichler. When the leading M4 Sherman debouched from the houses it was immediately knocked out by a high-velocity round and the platoon leader was killed. A German counterattack fought into the village supported by the Panther and a Marder. A number of Amis were surrounded and surrendered. A second Panther was also spotted by the GIs, who stubbornly fought for the village.[24]

It was common practice for a section of Panthers, well-camouflaged, to reveal only one panzer, while a second or third was ready to fire from a different angle. By day's end the German forces had withdrawn to the north and the village was left to additional arriving 3rd Division forces. The American company team lost nine killed and thirteen captured of 130 personnel, with one M4 destroyed and a second disabled. German losses are uncertain beyond the Marder destroyed and a number of Landsers captured. Stichler was badly wounded later northeast of Montélimar, "shot through the breast and left shoulder with an infantry bullet," said von Eggeling, "very likely from a partisan."[25]

On 28 August Truscott again tried, but failed, to cut off the German retreat. The 141st Infantry of the 36th Division advancing on Montélimar from the east was repelled by the 308.Grenadiers of 198.Infanterie-Division. Task Force Butler, now built around 3rd Battalion/157th Infantry of the 45th Division and advancing south of the Drôme, was repulsed at Loriol. The task force lost three medium tanks and two tank destroyers within a few minutes to the Krauts, or Jerries. The fighting at Loriol was against elements of Gren.Rgt.757. of the 338.I.D. and Kampfgruppe Wilde of Pz.G.R.111. Oberleutnant Ernst-August Freiherr von Fersen—"Gustel" to his friends—actually Begleitoffizier (Escort Officer) to division commander von Wietersheim at the time, received the EK 1.Klasse for leading some fifty men in the fighting. He had commandeered machine guns and light flak guns from the road columns and freed the Drôme ford.

Oberlt. Hering, 3.Kompanie commander, had brought some Panthers up from La Coucourde, but had to negotiate not only American artillery fire but also the retreating German traffic. In clearing the way through Loriol he was approached by a large Mercedes with an admiral and his entourage: "Let me drive through immediately, I am the commanding general of the Mediterranean naval forces." "The Herr General may command the Mittelmeer-Seestreitkräfte," retorted Hering, "here I command and please, immediately leave the street free for my panzers." The admiral's Mercedes went to the side and the Panthers thundered through.[26]

At the same time Hptm. Freiherr von Nordeck zur Rabenau, acting Panther battalion commander, who had come into Loriol in his motorcycle sidecar, was killed by American artillery fire. He might have been succeeded by Oblt. Stichler, but Stichler was wounded sometime later. Oblt. von Fersen found himself commanding 2.Kp. and Oblt. von Eggeling switched from adjutant to 3.Kp. "You may imagine how one feels," said the latter, "when day after day another of your best friends is killed."[27] Yet somehow the Gespensters kept functioning.

North of the Drôme the 157th Regiment of the 45th Division attacked toward Livron, but was driven back by the panzers and infantry of Oberst Hax's Pz.G.R.110. General von Wietersheim was everywhere, directing, organizing, leading. According to Oblt. von Fersen the general had a Marke Packard sports car, dark blue splashed with gray. It was a

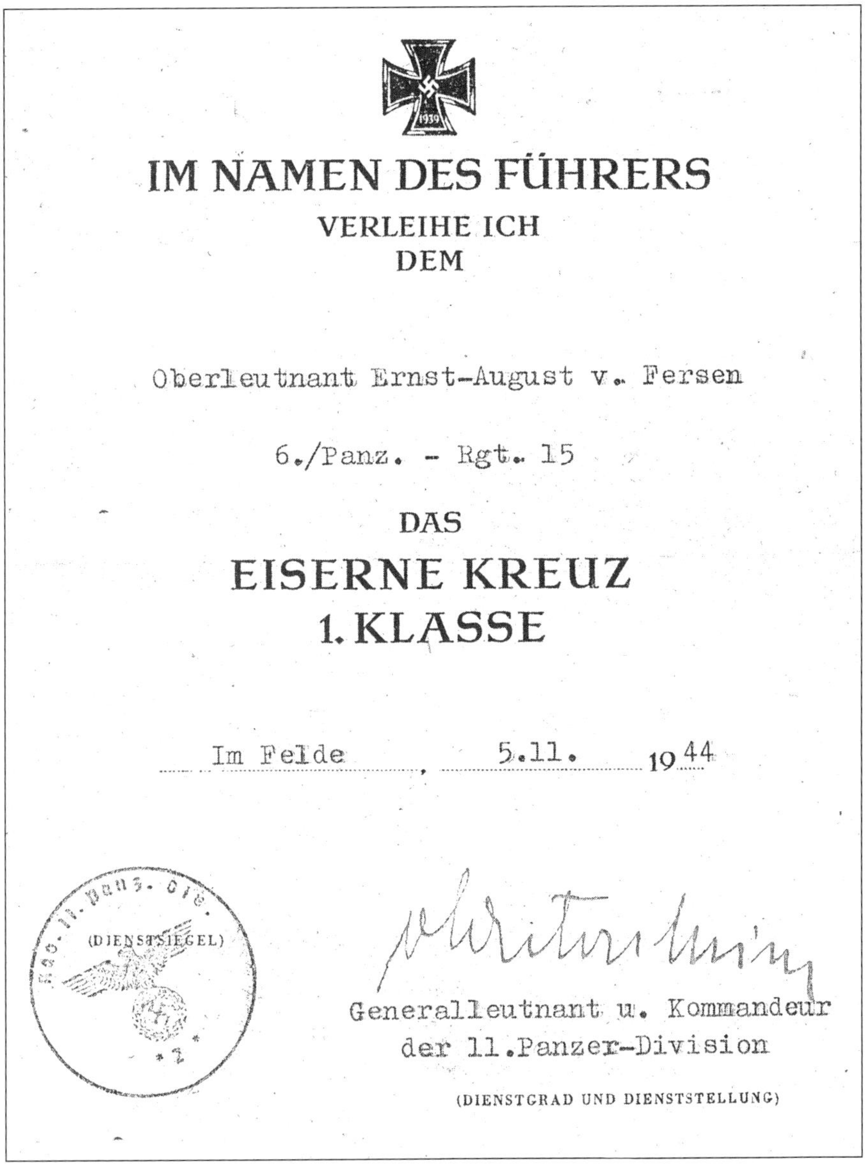

IM NAMEN DES FÜHRERS
VERLEIHE ICH
DEM

Oberleutnant Ernst-August v. Fersen

6./Panz. - Rgt. 15

DAS
EISERNE KREUZ
1. KLASSE

Im Felde, 5.11. 1944

(DIENSTSIEGEL)

Generalleutnant u. Kommandeur
der 11.Panzer-Division

(DIENSTGRAD UND DIENSTSTELLUNG)

Iron Cross 1. Class awarded to Oblt. von Fersen for his actions at Loriol while fighting to free the Drôme ford. ERNST-AUGUST VON FERSEN two-seater with a rumble seat, in which the driver or von Fersen sat with an MPi at the ready: "Mostly, the General drove himself. The escort vehicle with eight men did not come along. So we tore around alone, without regard to the danger." He never saw von Wietersheim in an armored vehicle.[28]

"The General was a 'gentleman' in the best sense," von Fersen observed. Once when headquarters was established in the château of a former French general, von Wietersheim kissed the hand of the lady and said they would only occupy the living room. In the library von Fersen was gratified to find the works, auf deutsch, of von Clausewitz and von Moltke. When his time as escort officer was to end, the Ia, Oberstlt. Werner Drews, told him, "I've seen the face of the general, and now I've seen your face; we will be separating a 'marriage.'"

After some brandy tipples von Fersen said to von Wietersheim, "I'd as willingly be a loader in a panzer as Begleitoffizier." The general, however, said, "That's also no post for you," and said he was needed as a leader in the panzer regiment. Von Fersen later commanded 6.Kp. in II.Abt. (Panzer IVs), then 4.Kp. (Panther), and finally the Panzerjäger Kompanie in the regiment. His radio call-sign was "Der Roller" (The Scooter). Oblt. Tafel was the new Begleitoffizier.

During the night of 28–29 August Kampfgruppe Wilde alone was still south of the Drôme, securing the Loriol crossings along with Gren.Rgt.757 of 338.Inf.Div. against Task Force Butler. The 198.I.D. left Montélimar with Gr.Rgt.305 retreating up route N 7 and the 308. and 326. Grenadieren retreating along the valleys on the east flank. There they collided with the 36th Division's 141st and 143rd Regiments advancing westward anew.

By daylight on the 29th the 141st Infantry converged with the 3rd Infantry Division, which had finally entered Montélimar. There they captured several thousand Germans, including Generalmajor Otto Richter of the 198.Inf.Div. Oberst Otto Schiel became acting commander on 3 September. North of the Drôme the 142nd Infantry entered Livron and TF Butler secured Loriol, though neither could reach the Rhône where Germans continued to cross the Drôme at a few fords. Prisoners and destroyed vehicles abounded, although 1,600 men of the 198.I.D. and 1,100 men of the 338.I.D. managed to escape. Wietersheim's 11.Pz.Div. was needed to the north toward Lyon, and the Div. Gefechtsstand had opened at Valence on the 27th. While the weaker infantry divisions and miscellaneous 19. Armee elements suffered heavy losses and some disintegrated, Wietersheim kept his Kampfgruppen intact and mounted aggressive counterattacks that consistently thwarted the American attempts to cut off the German retreat.

While only losing 750 casualties in the Montélimar battle, these were from the line companies and officers. As the Elfte reached Vienne south of Lyon, it had some 12,500 ration strength troops (of its authorized 13,726). The August fighting had cost the division 1,228 casualties, listed as 255 killed, 487 wounded, 247 missing, 56 ill, and 183 other losses.[29]

Oberst Stenkhoff's Pz.Rgt.15 had thirty Panthers and Panzer IVs (of its authorized 103), Oberst Erich Hammon's Pz.Art.Rgt.119 had thirty-nine tubes (of its forty-two), and the division had 75 percent of its 2,582 other vehicles. Despite the efforts of the Panzer Werkstatt Kompanie under Oblt. Kania and Lt. Habicht during the retreat, some twenty-two immobilized Panthers had had to be destroyed. This was effected by putting an explosive charge into the gun breech, pouring gasoline around, activating the charge detonator, and tossing in a Handgranate with a resulting fire and explosion. Like having to vacate a battleground, a retreat often meant additional losses.

Major Joachim Menzel had finally been able to "procure" four 8,8cm guns for his H.Flak-Art.Abt.277 from a depot near Lyon after overcoming the objections of the paymaster that they were intended for a different unit.[30] As elsewhere, the Acht-komma-achts were formidable guns against ground targets as well as against aircraft, but Menzel was also tasked to be prepared to engage transport planes of an airborne landing. When at strength, Menzel's flak battalion would have six Acht-achts in 1. and 2. Batterien, each battery also having a platoon of four 2cm or 3,7cm flak guns; 3. and 4. Batterien had two platoons with 2cm or 3,7cm guns self-propelled, and one platoon with 2cm Vierlingsflak. What the strength was at any time is uncertain.[31]

And so the retreat up the valley of the Rhône continued, the columns of military personnel swollen by French who had served the Vichy regime or collaborated with the Germans in other ways and now feared retribution by their compatriots, many of whom were eager to demonstrate their newfound loyalty to the advancing Allies. There were also Wehrmacht- and Luftwaffehelferinnen (female auxiliaries) in their gray jackets and skirts who were signals and clerical personnel, and DRK Schwester (German Red Cross

Sisters), apprehensive about being left behind. The Gespensters felt a natural responsibility, especially for the latter females, as the division provided flank and rearguard protection, covered by the Spähwagen of Aufklärungsabteilung 11.[32]

North of Valence the Isère River could be a blocking position, but on 28 August American forces from the Grenoble area took Romans-sur-Isère threatening the pass at Tain; in a sharp action the Elften of I.Btl./Pz.G.R.110 retook the important river crossing. Farther east, however, the Amis crossed the Isère at Moirons, passed through Bourgoin, and crossed the upper Rhône, which flows in from Geneva and turns south at Lyon. By 31 August they even entered Point d'Ain on the Ain River northeast of Lyon and cut the N 84 highway to Geneva at Meximieux.

These were the six-wheeled M8 Greyhound armored cars and jeeps of the battalion-sized 117th Cavalry Reconnaissance Squadron, Mechanized, under Lt. Col. Charles Hodge, the vanguard of Eagles's 45th Infantry Division. It was followed by the French 3ème Division d'Infanterie Algérienne and O'Daniel's 3rd Division, which had swung east after Montélimar and up the north bank of the Isère, while Dahlquist's 36th Infantry Division pressed up the N 7 route along the Rhône itself. A new threat was emerging to be dealt with.

CHAPTER TWENTY-FOUR

From Lyon to the Burgundian Gate

AS WIESE'S 19. ARMEE RETREATED UP THE RHÔNE VALLEY toward Lyon, Kniess's LXXXV. Armeekorps was joined by Petersen's IV. Luftwaffe Korps. Along with elements including the 189. and 716. Infanterie-Divisionen, they crossed the Rhône to the east bank at Vienne, 80 kilometers (50 miles) north of the Drôme. Feldmarschall Walter Model as OB West ordered Generaloberst Johannes Blaskowitz at Armeegruppe G to extend what would be its right wing northeast of Dijon to link up with Heeresgruppe B forces and reunite a western front. It would also enable LXIV. A.K. from the Atlantic coast to join as well.

Forming a defensive line from Dijon through Besançon to neutral Switzerland would secure the approaches to the Burgundische Pforte (Burgundian Gateway, or Belfort Gap) to the upper Rhein (Rhine) valley. In addition, from a salient at Dijon west of the Vogesen (Vosges Mountains) Hitler optimistically wanted to mount a counterattack into the southern flank of Patton's hard-driving US Third Army. Der Führer was now being contemptuously—though privately—referred to as "Gröfaz" (Grösster Feldherr aller Zeiten, the Greatest Field Marshal of all time).[1] Thus the primary route of 19. Armee retreat was to continue straight north toward Dijon up the valley of the Saône, which flowed into the Rhône at Lyon.

But with American forces already across the upper Rhône and the Ain north*east* of Lyon at the end of August, the threat of encirclement and a drive behind the German front to the Burgundian Gate meant Wietersheim's 11. Panzer-Division would have to continue to guard that exposed flank. Generalmajor Richard von Schwerin had a Gruppe with elements of his 189.Inf.Div. and Luftwaffe Ausbildungsregiment 71. defending southeast of Lyon to the Rhône, with Wietersheim concentrated to the northeast.

While the units of the Elfte moved northeast toward Bourg-en-Bresse on the N 83 Rollbahn to Besançon and Belfort, Wietersheim detached a Kampfgruppe of Oberstlt. Wilde's Panzergrenadier-Regiment 111 east along N 84 toward Meximieux. Hauptmann Werner Wehrstädt's I.Bataillon/111 with some panzers plowed through a roadblock at La Valbonne about 8 kilometers (5 miles) southwest of Meximieux on the night of 31 August. "As the Jerries closed in on us," said Fred Rennert of Company F, 179th Infantry Regiment of the 45th Infantry Division, "we decided to make a run for it. There was a castle on top of the hill. After crawling, climbing, running and jumping about half the men made it."[2]

Col. Harold Meyer's 179th Regiment had crossed the Rhône and the Ain, its 3rd Battalion guarding the main supply route (MSR) crossings, the 1st Battalion taking position at Meximieux, and the 2nd Battalion moving to Chalamont on the Bourg road. Its F Company had established three roadblocks west of Meximieux. Now on 1 September the Germans struck at Meximieux, and at the river crossings from the south and also from the east; at the latter they attacked the Chazey bridge, held by maquisards, and blew it. They also struck at Pont d'Ain. As they drove against Meximieux, one Panther was knocked out by 155mm artillery fire, and three others held back, supporting the panzergrenadiers with fire.

The Americans in Meximieux were two companies of Lt. Col. Michael Davison's 1st Battalion and two M10 tank destroyers. They were commanded by Col. Preston Murphy, regimental executive officer, who established the unit's command post (CP) in a stone-walled convent. That afternoon six Panthers with panzergrenadiers on board charged into the town. The GIs mounted a last-ditch defense, with clerks, cooks, drivers, and local French Maquis fighting back determinedly with grenades and small arms from windows and cellars. "We are surrounded by a very aggressive enemy," wrote Col. Meyer to his wife in V-mails later, "The dead were all over town."

Of the six Panthers, five were finally knocked out in the center of town according to Colonel Davison, three by the TDs (one careening into the lobby of the Hôtel Lion d'Or), a fourth by a bazooka rocket launcher, and a fifth by an 81mm mortar round that hit on top of the turret and exploded the ammunition. The sixth Panther withdrew—demonstrating once again that tanks are vulnerable in congested urban fighting unless well supported by infantry. In emphasizing the heroism of his 1st Battalion GIs later, Davison could also say, the 11th Panzer "was certainly an outstanding division and performed with distinction."[3]

From a Naples hospital after being wounded later, Colonel Meyer vividly recalled "The great masses of litter, rubble and destruction, the dead bodies of American, German, French and civilians being retrieved, the broken trees, branches, walls and buildings, the great hulks of smoking vehicles of war" that was the aftermath in Meximieux. The 45th "Thunderbirds" had held the town.[4]

But at the château at Perouges just to the west, the American garrison surrendered that night. Two M10 tank destroyers had been abandoned earlier in the day, one out of fuel, the other with a jammed turret. The Gespensters siphoned gasoline from the latter to the former and, said Leutnant Jürgen von Pflug, adjutant of I.Btl./Pz.G.R.111, used its 7,62cm (3-inch) gun to force the surrender of all the Amis and FFI inside by the F Company commander. "He was a Dumkopf," one disgusted GI, Bob Slingerland, snorted later. Slingerland in turn praised the German attackers; he spent the rest of the war as a PW in Stalag IIIC on the Oder.[5] The 179th Regiment lost 185 men "missing and probably captured" at Meximieux.[6]

About five days later Fred Rennert and some thirty Americans and FFI were about halfway to Dôle on the Doubs west of Besançon as prisoners. At one point they were lined up, and a German officer ordered three of the French executed. Shaken, German-born Rennert asked in German for medics to attend the American wounded, and "He [the German officer] smiled at me and finally consented." The officer would not have been of the 11.Pz.-Div. by this point, though captured partisans were likely to be shot. It is unknown how many Germans, captured by the partisans, were not turned over to the Americans as PWs. American historian Arthur Funk says, "I have a sense that well-trained and disciplined regular army units (which would include the 11.Pz. but exclude SS, reserves, Slavs, occupation troops) were essentially correct in their relations with the French."[7]

During the night of 1–2 September 1944 the last Germans evacuated Lyon, and the 11.Pz.-Div. fell back as well, having effectively covered the eastern flank of 19. Armee. With their flak guns, Major Joachim Menzel's Heeres Flak-Abt.277 had played a role in keeping the retreat routes open through the city, the third largest in France. He was named Kampfkommandant under Gen.Maj. von Schwerin.

With liberation imminent, restless Lyonnaise had risen up in revolt on 24 August. But these were mostly Communist FTP partisans and workers at the barricades, intent on seizing political power before the de Gaullist FFI arrived with American forces. It was premature. With thousands of German troops streaming back through the city, Wiese could handily suppress this uprising. Menzel himself met with some

French delegations and warned them of the destruction that could be wrought with his guns or by Stukas.

The FFI commanders, in agreement with the Americans, postponed their intended attack until 3 September, by which time the Germans had blown most of the Rhône and Saône bridges and departed. Thus the city was spared the destruction of heavy fighting, though an orgy of retribution was carried out against collaborators and the Vichy Milice, which had worked with the Gestapo under Hauptsturmführer Klaus Barbie. Many accused, in the words of American Major Alfred Cox of the OSS, were "torn limb from limb" in the "mad hysteria" over the next few days before the FFI gained control.[8]

The 11.Panzer was stretched again to thwart the Allied advance. A Kampfgruppe composed of Pz.Gren.Rgt.110, II.Abt./Pz.Art.Rgt.119, 2.Kp./Pz. Pionier-Batl.209, 3.Kp./Pz.Jäger-Abt.61, and four Panzer IVs was shifted north toward Louhans, while a Gruppe with Pz.Gren.Rgt.111, Pz.Aufkl.Abt.11, Feld-Ersatz-Bataillon 209, III.Abt./Pz.Art.Rgt.119, 3.Kp./Pz.Pi.Btl.209, and eight Panthers remained around Bourg-en-Bresse.[9] The division Gefechtsstand was established east of the highway intersections at Bourg-en-Bresse north of Meximieux.

On 2 September heavier American forces advanced on Bourg but were held in stiff fighting in which Oberlt. Hering was killed. These were the 157th and 180th Regiments of the 45th Division, passing through the embattled 179th Infantry. Coming up on their left were the 142nd and 143rd Regiments of the 36th Division, having left Lyon to be occupied by French forces. VI Corps G-2 (intelligence) estimated the 11.Pz.Div. had some fifty panzers. Actually, Pz.-Rgt.15 had only twelve Panthers and four Panzer IVs einsatzbereit. Eight Panthers and two Panzer IVs of the 9.SS Panzer-Division at Dijon were ordered diverted to the 11.Pz.Div., the Hohenstaufen itself being in the Netherlands.[10]

To the north, light Ami forces fought into Marboz and even westward to the town of Montrevel on N 75 north of Bourg that evening, but were thrown back out. General Truscott believed that Wiese's 19. Armee would later be turning eastward toward Besançon and Belfort, and got Patch's Seventh Army approval for a VI Corps drive northeast up N 83 to preempt Wiese's movement. (Actually, 19. Armee was ordered to retreat due north to Dijon, while 11.Pz.Div. covered to the northeast.) For flank protection Truscott ordered Lt. Col. Charles Hodge's 117th Cavalry Recon Squadron to capture Montrevel. Conscious that the Germans had a strong presence in the area, and that his cavalry troops were widely scattered, Hodge objected to the mission but was overruled.

At daylight on the 3rd, company-sized B Troop (ten M8 armored cars and eighteen jeeps with machine guns or mortars and 124 men), to be followed by A Troop and five M5 light tanks of Troop F, attacked Montrevel again. They rounded up some sixty to seventy German prisoners—not combat troops, but administrative and supply personnel who had sheltered in the town from the heavy rain.

As soon as Wietersheim learned of the American probe, he dispatched Major Karl Bode's Aufkl.-Abt.11 up from Bourg, reinforced by six Panthers, a self-propelled artillery battery, and a company of Pioniere with mines.[11] Bode sent some of his elements around to the east, cutting the road to Marboz, while others drove up directly astride the highway. The Americans were surrounded and driven back into the center of town, defending a stone-walled city building (which they called "the schoolhouse"). One of the Panthers was put out of action, but the 37mm guns of the M8 armored cars and the M5 light tanks were no match for the 7,5cm high-velocity guns of the Panthers, and three of the five M5s were destroyed. Against infantry and light vehicles the Maschinengewehr was effective. *"Vollgas! Turm MG, Funker MG—Feuer frei!"* And the Pantherkampfwagen bolted forward, spitting fire.

One of the Panthers drove up to within 50 meters of the city building. The Amis sent a hail of bullets at the vision slits of the panzer and at the panzergrenadiers closing in. But then the Panther fired, its round punching right through the stone wall and exploding in the hall inside, followed up by more point-blank Sprengranate rounds. American reinforcements were coming up, but they were thwarted; the trapped American leaders, faced with destruction, surrendered. Maj. Karl Bode met with Captains John Wood and Tom Piddington of B and A Troops. It was fully in character that Bode explained to them that they had been fighting the veteran 11.Panzerdivision, and complimented them on their tough resistance.

In addition, Lt. Col. Charles Hodge later recorded in his personal memoirs: "It is noteworthy to note here that the Commanding General of the 11th Panzer Division [Wietersheim] sent me a message through the doctor whom we had left in Montrevel. The CG said, 'We just don't believe that there is a small armored force here. We believe it is a big operation, and when we found out it is only a squadron, we were utterly amazed, and would you please convey my congratulations to your commanding officer, who is putting up the strongest fight that we have had in the war.'"[12]

The American official history listed the losses of the two troops as twenty jeeps, fifteen armored cars, and two light tanks destroyed, and three damaged. A total of 126 men were surrendered, including thirty-one wounded, while five were killed. The Gespensters left twelve of the most seriously wounded GIs behind, with the doctor. The Elfte lost a Panther, two Spähwagen, and four other vehicles, though personnel losses are not known. The fighting had been fierce, and cavalry troopers were awarded two Distinguished Service Crosses and a Medal of Honor.

Unlike the compliments of the German commanders, VI Corps commander Lucian Truscott later wrote that the Cavalry "go to sleep and are surrounded and captured." This was unfair; their orders had been ill-conceived and they had fought courageously to hold an untenable position.[13] Truscott might have been reflecting the frustration at finding his flanking moves constantly thwarted. The American official history concluded of Wietersheim's fierce counterattacks, "His primary mission, protecting the retreating army's flank, had thus been accomplished," as 19. Armee had moved well north up the Saône valley toward Dijon. Wietersheim felt he had given the infantry units some "breathing space." In American captivity later, von Wietersheim said, "it would have been possible for the Americans to capture the entire Army Group (1st and 19th Armies) if the American forces had not attacked so timidly and cautiously." For the Americans who experienced battle with the 11. Panzer-Division, it was no "champagne campaign" as some GIs had begun to call it.[14]

Tasked with reuniting the Armeegruppe G forces with H.Gr. B to the north and forming the Dijon salient for Hitler's intended counterattack, but also wanting to facilitate the LXIV. A.K. retreat from the Atlantic Bay of Biscay coast, Blaskowitz hoped to establish a defense line of Petersen's IV. Luftwaffe Feldkorps in the south and LXIV. A.K. under Gen.Lt. Karl Sachs from the west, while LXVI. A.K. to the north was assigned to the army group on 27 August by OB West.

Acknowledging the axis of advance of Truscott's three divisions to be northeast astride N 83 through Besançon toward the Burgundian Gate (Belfort Gap) and the upper Rhine valley, Blaskowitz intended a delaying position south of the Doubs River, which flowed southwest into the Saône below Dijon. Kniess's LXXXV. A.K. with 198. and 338. Divisionen was to stretch eastward from the Saône through Dôle on the Doubs to Mouchard on N 83. The 11. Panzer was to cover from Mouchard to the Swiss border.

But the advance of Patch's US Seventh Army and de Lattre's French Armeé B was relentless. To the west the 1ère Division Blindée (1st Armored Division) of Maj. Gén. Aime de Monsabert's II Corps attacked up the right bank of the Saône capturing Givry and Chalôns-sur-Saône on 5 September and Beaume by the 8th. In the center O'Daniel's 3rd Division advanced up N 83 toward Mouchard and Besançon, with Dahlquist's 36th Infantry Division on the left and Eagles's 45th Division following. On the right skirting the Swiss border was the rapidly moving 3ème Division d'Infanterie Algerienne leading Lt. Gen. Emile Bethouart's I Corps.

The German defense line never really formed as the Allies were already thrusting through it. At Besançon the Germans garrisoned the formidable citadel and its fortified outworks dating from French engineer the Marquis de Vauban of the seventeenth century. Truscott was considering bypassing it, as the French Algerians with American tanks and equipment crossed the Doubs at Baume-les-Dames farther east on 5 September.

Wietersheim had disengaged his units enough to move them north from Bourg to cross the Doubs at Dôle where, despite Allied bombing, a crucial bridge remained intact. But wrecked vehicles were everywhere, and movement by night was now required. Establishing the Div.Gef.Std. in Besançon North, the Gespensters were spread along the Doubs. With such an extended area of responsibility, the "HKL" was only a security/outpost line with forces to mount counterattacks. When the commanding general learned of an enemy crossing at Baume-les-Dames he formed a Kampfgruppe around Major Arnold Kessler's Pak Spähwagen and Halbketten of his Pz.Jäger-Abt.61 and committed nine Panthers, which fiercely counterattacked. Hptm. Otto Grumbt of II./111 was awarded the RK for his bravery. "An outstanding commander," felt his adjutant, Lt. Horst Loch. It was the French Algerians who were "severely mauled" and thrown back.[15]

That led Truscott to decide it was too risky to bypass the German strongpoints. At Besançon the US

3rd Division with tanks and tank destroyers assaulted the thick-walled outlying works on both banks of the Doubs, and bombarded the citadel. On 7 September the infantry crossed the moat and scaled the walls, and on the 8th the garrison, mostly of the 159.I.D., surrendered.[16] Wiese had Kniess's LXXXV. A.K. headquarters relocate east during the night of 5–6 September to coordinate the defenses of the Burgundian Gateway. Korps Dehner—a provisional headquarters with 159.I.D. and other elements under administration commander General Ernst Dehner—and Petersen's IV. Luftwaffe Korps covered the approaches to the Vosges Mountains.

The 11.Pz.Div. was withdrawn from the Besançon-Baume region and shifted well east, from the L'Isle-s.-le.Doubs fronting Montbeliard just south of Belfort to near the Swiss border. During this time unit organizations often deviated from the Panzer-Division 44 K.St.N. Bode's Aufklärungsabteilung 11 had a fourth reconnaissance company, and Nr.5.Kp. was the heavy company with 7,5cm Paks on half-tracks, though 1.Kp. at least had only Pkws, no armored cars. Bödicker's Pz.Pi.Btl.209 had a fourth company recently organized from older and wounded personnel.

5.Kp./110, truck-mounted, had eighty men in two panzergrenadier platoons not three, with four le.MGs in each. The schwere Zug had two s.MGs not four, and only one of two 8cm Granatwerfer. Pz.G.R.110's 8.Kp., weapons, had 120 men with six 2cm flak and six 8cm Gr.W. 10.Kompanie/110 was the engineer company with two platoons, a Flammenwerfer platoon with four half-tracks, and an 8cm Gr.W. platoon. Regimental headquarters company (Nr.11) had rocket launchers. Kessler's Pz.Jäger-Abt.61 had three Pak companies and a Versorgungskompanie, Nr.3 Kp. having eighty men and nine 7,5cm guns, towed or assault guns.

While the low silhouette of the turretless assault guns had proved their worth on the open steppe terrain of southern Russia, in the West panzer soldiers were finding some disadvantages to them. For example, Gen.Lt. Heinrich Freiherr von Lüttwitz, commander of 2.Pz.Div., noted that in Normandy in particular the Sturmgeschütze were unable to fire over hedgerows and stone walls. They were best utilized in concealment well-camouflaged at the sides of roads, positioned to engage an enemy's flank.[17]

Around 17,00 hours on 8 September Jochen Menzel was holding a position with his H.Flak-Abt.277 when he heard the rumble of tank engines and the squeal of tracks coming up the Pont de Roide-Audincourt road south of Montbeliard, as a Piper Cub L-4 observation plane flew overhead. The enemy tank column stopped while the tank commanders scanned the sides of the hill pass ahead with their binoculars, then started forward. The M4s were of the 3ème French Algerians again. The Pak 43 8,8cm guns of Menzel's flak battalion were well camouflaged with branches, and the officers did not use their binoculars lest the light glint off the lenses. The Acht-achts had a velocity of 1,000 m/s (3,280 fps) and a flat, accurate trajectory; the best range for them to engage the short-barreled M4 Sherman, said Menzel, was between 800 and 1,200 meters. The 8,8s also operated most efficiently in pairs.

In this case the French tanks were coming within 200 meters. The 2cm Zwillingsflak were ready if infantry appeared. Hauptmann Giesebrecht had two guns tracking the leading tanks, while Menzel himself was with the second pair on the other side of the pass, sited to knock out the tanks at the rear, trapping the column. He felt the same expectant tension as when he hunted in peacetime. Accompanying him during this time was Swiss journalist Marcel Sutter of the *Baseler Zeitung*. The battery vehicles and prime movers were 500 meters back in the woods.

At Menzel's command *"Feuer!"* the deadly guns blasted their targeted tanks simultaneously. They were using Panzergranate rounds capable of penetrating the heavy Russian Iosef Stalins. Within seconds the column was a blazing shambles, while the 2cm flak guns downed the L-4. Six tanks and the airplane were claimed. The French were halted until Bethouart's I Corps could bring more forces up.[18]

As the German front began to coalesce, 1. Armee returned to Armeegruppe G from H.Gr. B on 8 September. It was commanded by Gen. der Panzertruppen Otto von Knobelsdorff who had succeeded Gen.d.Inf. Kurt von der Chevallerie two days earlier. (Chevallerie's younger brother Hellmut had commanded the 273. Res. Panzer-Division absorbed by the 11.Pz.Div. in May.) On the 11th Blaskowitz's Armeegruppe G was raised to the status of *Heeres*gruppe G.

LXIV. Korps was allowed to abandon Dijon and fall back to the Langres plateau before the Vosges, north of which LXVI. A.K. under Gen.d.Art. Walther Lucht stretched to Chaumont and on to Nancy behind the Mosel (Moselle). From now on, the rivers were flowing north. On 11 September US Seventh Army reconnaissance elements made contact with Patton's Third Army at Sombernon east of Dijon, and tank destroyers of 1ère Division Motorisée d'Infanterie met a patrol of the 6th Armored Division at Saulieu, marking the union of the Allied armies in the West.

Most of the Wehrmacht personnel from southwestern France had already passed into the Dijon salient, except for units left behind to garrison the Biscayen ports and deny the Allies supplies through them. But the rear columns of LXIV. Korps under Gen.Maj. Botho Elster, former commandant of Biarritz, had become stranded. They were mostly rear echelon administrative and service personnel from all branches of the Wehrmacht. Elster negotiated to surrender 19,614 personnel through the US 83rd Infantry Division on 10 September. Nonetheless, the extraction of some 68,000 of 88,000 personnel from southwestern France, many on foot, had been successfully engineered by Gen. Karl Sachs of LXIV. A.K. Bombarded by demands from Blaskowitz to hasten the retreat, Sachs had been relieved of his command 3 September anyway, succeeded by (ill) Gen.Lt. Otto Lasch.

Despite heavy losses, Blaskowitz's army group had effectively pulled back to reform a German Westfront. On 26 August Model at OB West had stated in a conference that "not much of the Nineteenth Army would get back," but it was important that the 11.Pz.Div. fight its way out. The Gespenster-Division had done that and more, enabling 19. Armee to fall back relatively intact.[19]

Indeed, the threat of an encirclement had been very real, *if* General Patton had swung his Third Army forces down in a pincers move to meet Truscott's VI Corps. But Patton was focused on driving *east* to the Rhine, though Gen. Dwight Eisenhower, the Supreme Allied Commander (SAC) at Supreme Headquarters Allied Expeditionary Force (SHAEF), caustically observed, "there is no point getting there until we are in a position to do something about it."[20] Nor were there any plans for an encirclement, leaving Truscott's flanking attempts to be frustrated by the evanescent Wietersheim and his 11. Gespenster-Division.

Already there was dissension in the Allied high command about the conduct of operations. Eisenhower, thinking in infantry terms, sought a steady "broad front" advance to the German frontier, acquiesced to by loyal Lt. Gen. Omar Bradley, commanding the 12th Army Group (First, Third, and, after 5 September, Ninth US Armies). To the north British Field Marshal Sir Bernard Montgomery, commanding 21 Army Group (2 British and 1 Canadian Armies) argued for a more decisive thrust on a "narrow front."

American armor commanders, thinking in terms of mobile warfare, conceived of maneuver and flanking encirclements. Maj. Gen. John Wood of the US 4th Armored Division indeed sensed an opportunity for an encirclement with the defeat of the German Mortain counterattack. He was exasperated that armor leader Patton insisted on sending his lead 4th and 6th Armored Divisions *west*ward to capture the Brittany ports according to the original planning, knowing they would be defended or destroyed as Cherbourg had been. The one encirclement that resulted by default, the Falaise-Argentan pocket, was not as decisive as it might have been with a deeper envelopment.[21]

While great encirclement battles had been fought by the Germans and the Russians on the Ostfront, and Rommel had frequently used flanking maneuvers in the Western Desert, these were not the American way of war, despite a small encirclement at Mons. Patton briefly suggested a swing up to Beauvais, but this was back north*west* of Paris, and nothing came of it. There was an analogy with the 1941 invasion of Russia. Just as the Pripet forested swamp area divided that front north and south, so the Ardennes-Eifel forested hill country divided the approaches to Germany. The Allied Schwerpunkt was in the *northern* region toward the Ruhr industrial area and Berlin; though by force of personality Patton, *south* of the Ardennes-Eifel, made his "subsidiary" Third Army drive of equal significance. While a drive on the Saar industrial area, if not to the Rhine, was a legitimate objective, more controlled flanking attacks to north and south to destroy the German forces, including Armeegruppe G, *west* of the German frontier Westwall, might have been more productive than just a "broad front" advance.

But, of Eisenhower and the infantry commanders, noted Bruce Clarke, combat commander of the 4th Armored, "A deep envelopment by armor was not in their experience or concept." The "infantry mindset" was well reflected by General Eisenhower who had earlier admonished his armor commander, General Patton, as a corps commander, for being too aggressive; that "in actual battle, a commander can best direct his outfit from a command post where he can be in touch with all of his staff and subordinates"—completely opposite to the panzer and armor concept of leadership up front.[22]

In addition, American corps organization generally paired one armored division with one or two infantry divisions. While the infantry divisions were more mobile than the German infantry divisions (still dependent on horse-drawn ordnance and equipment), only one regiment was fully transportable with organic trucking. More importantly, most commanders did not share the mobile warfare doctrine of those from the Armor branch. American strategy in 1944, beyond the logistical limitations, does not compare well with Manstein's strategy in 1940, where seven of the ten German panzer divisions were concentrated as the Schwerpunkt to decisively flank, trap, and destroy the Allied forces in Belgium in conjunction with the other three, in some two weeks. Nor were there counterparts to the panzer corps, much less the panzer armies that had engineered the Kesselschlachten of the Blitzkrieg, or the Russian tank armies by 1943.

While American armored divisions were manifesting tremendous mobility, they were intended for pursuit operations, *not* breakthrough and battle engagements. American armor was characterized by the M4 Sherman medium tank, at a time when heavier and more powerful German and Russian tanks were being built to spearhead as well as exploit the attack. The armored division field manual emphasized that its "*primary role is in offensive operations against hostile rear areas*." The infantry was to make the breakthrough, and the armored division was "to exploit it." The tank *gunnery* manual itself even stated: "The ultimate objective of the armored division is vital rear installations. These are attacked less with cannon than with the crushing power of the tank and with its machine guns. . . . While this manual concerns itself with the gunnery of tank cannon, commanders must constantly emphasize the great importance of the tank machine guns."[23]

Like the German panzer division 1944, the standard "light" US armored division had fifteen battalions, and was fairly well balanced. It aggregated 12,774 personnel including the routinely attached tank destroyer and self-propelled antiaircraft gun battalions, and its 2,500 vehicles included 269 tanks, 36 tank destroyers (M18 Hellcats), and 54 self-propelled M7s mounting 105mm howitzers. Organic to the division were three tank battalions, three armored infantry battalions, three armored artillery battalions, a battalion-sized cavalry reconnaissance squadron (mechanized), and armored engineer, armored ordnance maintenance, and armored medical battalions, trains, and attachments.

For operations there were two combat command headquarters, CCA and CCB, and a smaller Reserve Command, to control a mix of the tank, armored infantry, and armored artillery battalions, with companies of engineers, tank destroyers, and the other units. In principle this was similar to the German Kampfgruppe of "combined arms teams," and companies were cross-reinforced in battalion-sized task forces, and platoons were exchanged to form mixed company teams.

All the armored infantry were mounted in M3 half-tracks, whereas the Germans could only equip one of the four panzergrenadier battalions with the Sd.Kfz.251-series Halbketten, the others being transported by trucks. The armored artillery was all self-propelled, but the M7 105mm howitzers only had a range of 11,000 meters (12,000 yards), whereas the panzer division included 15cm pieces with a longer range of 15,000 meters. But the Americans recognized this with combat, and a 155mm battalion was routinely attached to or in support from corps. In France, the panzer artillery regiment had only one Abteilung self-propelled, with two 10,5cm Wespe batteries and a 15cm Hummel battery, the light (10,5cm) and medium (15cm) battalions being half-track towed.

The weakness of the American armored division was the three tank battalions, each having three medium tank companies based on the M4 (a company having seventeen M4s with the short 75mm gun and one with a 105mm howitzer, the latter usually grouped with the two from the other companies as a gun section in support), and a light tank company of M5s with a 37mm gun. These did not compare well with the two Abteilungen, Panther and Panzer IV, of the panzer division with their high-velocity 7,5cm guns. More potent was the tank destroyer battalion with the M18 Hellcats with their 76mm gun and hydraulic traverse, but they had open-top turrets and thin armor like the M10, as opposed to the Jagdpanzers of the German Panzerjäger-Abteilung. In addition, the German Flak-Abteilung had the formidable 8,8cm flak gun to employ against enemy armor.[24]

Heeresgruppe G losses in the south were heavy enough as it was. In the four weeks from 15 August through 14 September, there were at least 143,250 German casualties, over half the original strength (excluding the Atlantic coast garrisons). Of these,

131,250 were prisoners of war, thus 12,000 were killed and wounded. Of 1,592 guns and howitzers, 1,038 pieces were in fixed positions and could not be moved. Of the 544 mobile pieces 379 were lost, 165 extricated. The US VI Corps had some 9,900 casualties, the French slightly more, thus totaling some 20,000.[25] But perhaps the majority of the German losses were noncombat troops. Many of the units would be rebuilt to face the Allies again.

Wietersheim's 11.Pz.-Div. had only 6,500 men (of its authorized 13,726), only 2,500 being of fighting strength; it retained 12 panzers (of 103), and 2 self-propelled guns by 14 September. On the 11th it had had 30 panzers einsatzbereit.[26] The Gespensters could take pride when 19. Armee informed them an English-language report called them "an elite division," and the American soldiers' magazine *Yank* later said of fighting the 11., "It was not so easy!" The German *Die Wacht* claimed two or three enemy divisions were so badly damaged they had to be withdrawn for refitting—"Every soldier knows what that means."[27]

Blaskowitz continued to withdraw 19. Armee toward the Vosges and the Burgundian Gate, though he also now had 1. Armee, which was trying to fall back to the Moselle. By 15 September de Lattre de Tassigny had unilaterally declared his forces to be 1ère Armée Française, the First French Army; with Patch's Seventh Army they now composed the 6th Army Group under Lt. Gen. Jacob Devers. Coming under Eisenhower's control, they found their role subordinate to the major drives farther north. Patch was to advance to and across the rugged Vosges Mountains, while de Lattre was to advance through the Belfort Gap to Mulhouse and the Rhine valley.

In northern France the German forces were in disarray as the Allies surged onward. On 3 September the British Guards Armoured Division drove into Brussels, and the next day the British 11 Armoured captured the huge port of Antwerp with its facilities intact (though the maritime approaches through the Scheldt estuary had yet to be cleared). The American First Army under Lt. Gen. Courtney Hodges took Liège on 7 September and Luxembourg City on the 10th. Patton's Third Army had swept across the lines of the Seine, the Marne, and the Meuse, and was approaching Nancy in Alsace-Lorraine and the forts of Metz on the Moselle.

But already by the end of August the baleful tyranny of logistics was beginning to restrict the Allied advance, what British military analyst B. H. Liddell Hart called the "law of overstretch"—that the momentum of mechanized warfare was heavily dependent on petrol, oil, and lubricants (POL), and these were rapidly diminishing in the forward areas. An armored division used over 1,000 gallons of fuel per mile, and the tanks were racing 50 miles (80 kilometers) a day. When Maj. Gen. Hugh Gaffey, Third Army chief of staff, had the armored units hold up, Patton overruled him: "I told Gaffey to run till his engines stop and then go on, on foot."[28] Now was the time to tailor operations to the logistical realities.

Hitler had realized these logistical limitations for the Allies, and they were a major reason for his demand that ports be defended and destroyed. At the same time he acquiesced in his defeated armies retreating from France and Belgium back to the Westwall defenses on the German border, shortening their supply lines and lengthening those of the Allies. The Allied planning estimated 45,000 tons of supplies needed to be landed daily by D+90 (6 September, ninety days from the day of the Normandy invasion). While port facilities were established for landing over the invasion beaches, the next problem was getting the supplies forward to the advancing spearheads.

Ironically, the Allied pre-invasion interdiction bombing, which had effectively isolated the Normandy invasion area, now meant bridges, highways, and railroad lines and yards all had to be repaired to sustain the advance. But the damage was extensive, and fuel pipelines from the beaches had leaks and shutdowns. Airlifting bulk supplies by C-47 transport planes would preclude airborne operations, and the improvised "Red Ball Express" of round-trip trucking between St. Lô and the Chartres area could only deliver 7,000 tons daily.[29] The fuel shortages were exacerbated by the "broad front" strategy, whereby seven armies, including two from southern France, were fanning out from the North Sea to the Swiss border.

In the late summer of 1944, however, the German panzer forces were badly depleted, and the Allied mechanized armor was lancing into Belgium and eastern France. In the East the Red Army had reached the Vistula deep in Poland and was sweeping through the Balkans and up the Danube valley toward Belgrade, and there was a euphoric sense among the Allies that Germany was on the verge of total collapse.

CHAPTER TWENTY-FIVE

The German Recovery

BY MID-SEPTEMBER 1944 THE WESTERN ALLIES FOUND German resistance stiffening. Despite the debacle of the Falaise-Argentan Kessel, many unit commanders and staffs managed to escape and begin rebuilding their units. An innate sense of discipline and organization began to reassert itself. New units also began to appear in the OKW orders of battle. In mid-August Hitler had ordered the formation of twenty-five new infantry divisions, to be termed Volksgrenadier, appealing to the nationalist instincts of the German folk. In addition to eighteen divisions raised in July, now also so designated, there were thus 43 V.G.D.s. Some were to go to the Ostfront, the majority to the Westfront. Most were numbered in the 500 series, though some older divisions were rebuilt as Volksgrenadier divisions. The V.G.D.s were to have a reduced number of personnel, reflecting German manpower shortages, but increased numbers of automatic weapons.

The regular infantry division Typ 1944 had 12,352 personnel authorized by the K.St.N. tables. It had three infantry regiments of two battalions each and an artillery regiment with three 10,5cm battalions and a 15cm battalion, and a Pak, an engineer, a signals, and a Füsilier Bataillon, the latter mostly on Fahrräder (bicycles) for reconnaissance. By contrast, the Volksgrenadierdivision, while still having three regiments of two battalions each, had only 10,072 personnel. Its artillery regiment had two 10,5cm battalions, a 15cm battalion, and a 7,5cm Pak battalion in addition to a Panzerjäger battalion with Sturmgeschütze. It also had an engineer, a signals, and a Füsilier (bicycle) battalion.

In small arms, the V.G.D. had fewer Mauser 98k rifles than the Division 44, 6,054 to 9,069, but 2,064 Maschinenpistole to 1,503. In addition, 216 R.Pz.B., rocket launchers, were authorized, as opposed to 108. Down in the line companies, there were two submachine gun platoons and a rifle platoon, not three rifle platoons. Squads were nine men, the rifle squad including a Zweibein, MG 42.[1]

In July 1944 Hitler also ordered the formation of ten new panzer brigades numbered 101 through 110, the idea being they would be smaller and more flexible than divisions, if not to increase numbers on orders of battle charts. Guderian strenuously objected, believing that new panzer production (Panther Ausf. G's) would go to these brigades rather than to reequip existing, experienced panzer divisions.

The brigade was to number 1,902 personnel (including 75 Hiwis). It was to have a Panzerabteilung and a Panzergrenadierbataillon, a Stabs and a Panzerpionierkompanie, and a Werkstatt Zug. The panzer Abteilung would have thirty-three Panthers in three companies and three command Panthers, a fourth company with eleven Panzerjäger IVs, and a Versorgungskompanie. The Pz.Gren.Btl. was half-track-mounted, with four Panzergrenadier companies, two 12cm Granatwerfer Battr., an s.I.G. Kompanie, and a Flak Battr.[2]

The most glaring weaknesses of the brigades were their lack of artillery or reconnaissance units, their limited signals, medical, and support elements, and limited recovery and bridging capabilities—all of which had made the combined arms concept of the panzer divisions so effective. An attempt was made to have experienced commanders and cadre. Oberst Dr. Franz Bäke, to command Panzerbrigade 106 FHH (Feldherrnhalle), had already been awarded the Eichenlaub mit Schwertern zum Ritterkreuz des Eisernen Kreuzes with 6.Pz.Div., and had three tank close-combat destruction awards on his right sleeve. He was noted for leading his regiment of Tigers and Panthers during the Cherkassy-Korsun Kessel fighting in 1943. Hptm. Erich Oberwöhrmann, to command the Panzerabteilung, was also a Ritterkreuzträger. But most of the personnel were recruits with no experience and little training, and those who did have experience gained it on the Ostfront. Allied air power and precision artillery meant different conditions in the West altogether.

Three more Panzerbrigaden were also raised, numbered 111–113, but they were larger, with a Panther *and* a Panzer IV battalion, totaling ninety-eight panzers at full strength, and a *two*-battalion Panzergrenadier-Regiment, though still lacking organic artillery and other elements. They also included elements of divisions being refitted: I.Abt.(Panther)/Pz.Rgt.16 of the 116. "Windhund" ("Greyhound") Pz.Div. going to Pz.Brig.111, I.Abt.(Panther)/Pz.Rgt.29 of 12.Pz.Div. going to Pz.Brig.112, and I.Abt.(Panther)/Pz.Rgt.130 of the Panzer-Lehr-Division equipping Pz.Brig.113.[3]

As the defeated German forces retreated toward the German border, it was hoped they could man the defenses of the Westwall (called the "Siegfried Line" by the Allies; while the Siegfried Stellung of World War I had been called the "Hindenburg Line"). Begun in 1936 after the remilitarization of Germany's Rhineland by the Todt construction organization and intensified during the 1938 Sudetenland crisis, the Westwall was a system of fortifications along the western German border from Kleve near the Netherlands to Basel in Switzerland. There were double belts around the industrial areas of Aachen and the Saar, with an additional line back across the Hunsrück Mountains to the Haardt Mountains.

While the French Maginot Line fortifications along the Franco-German border consisted of self-contained underground forts, the Westwall featured reinforced concrete bunkers ("pillboxes" to the Allies) with machine guns and antitank guns sited for mutual support. Fronting the bunker line and covered by them were antitank obstacles zigzagging across the countryside. These were generally pyramid-shaped reinforced concrete blocks set in a foundation, upon which a tank might be caught. They were arranged in five rows rising from 1 meter in front to 2 meters (6 feet) in the back. They were nicknamed *"Panzerhöcker"* or *"Drachenzähne"* ("tank humps" or "dragon's teeth").[4]

After the conquest of France in 1940 the Westwall was neglected, and with the construction of the Atlantikwall by 1944 much electrical and telephone wiring had been removed. Now, however, the Westwall might provide a significant defense of the homeland, but much rehabilitation needed to be done: apertures enlarged to accommodate the weaponry of 1944, communications restored, minefields laid, and barbed wire strung. Thus while work was undertaken to restore the defensibility of the position, it became imperative to slow the Allied advance *before* reaching the Westwall, if possible.

The Westfront was beginning to recover. Elderly sixty-eight-year-old Generalfeldmarschall Gerd von Rundstedt was reinstated as Oberbefehlshaber West on 5 September by Hitler, having been relieved on 3 July during the Normandy bloodbath ("Make peace, you fools," he had responded to GFM Wilhelm Keitel at OKW. "What else can you do?").[5] He brought the aura of distinguished command experience, though major decisions would still be made by OKW (Hitler). This allowed GFM Walter Model, who had held the responsibilities of OB West in addition to his command of Heeresgruppe B, to concentrate on his armies north of the Loire.

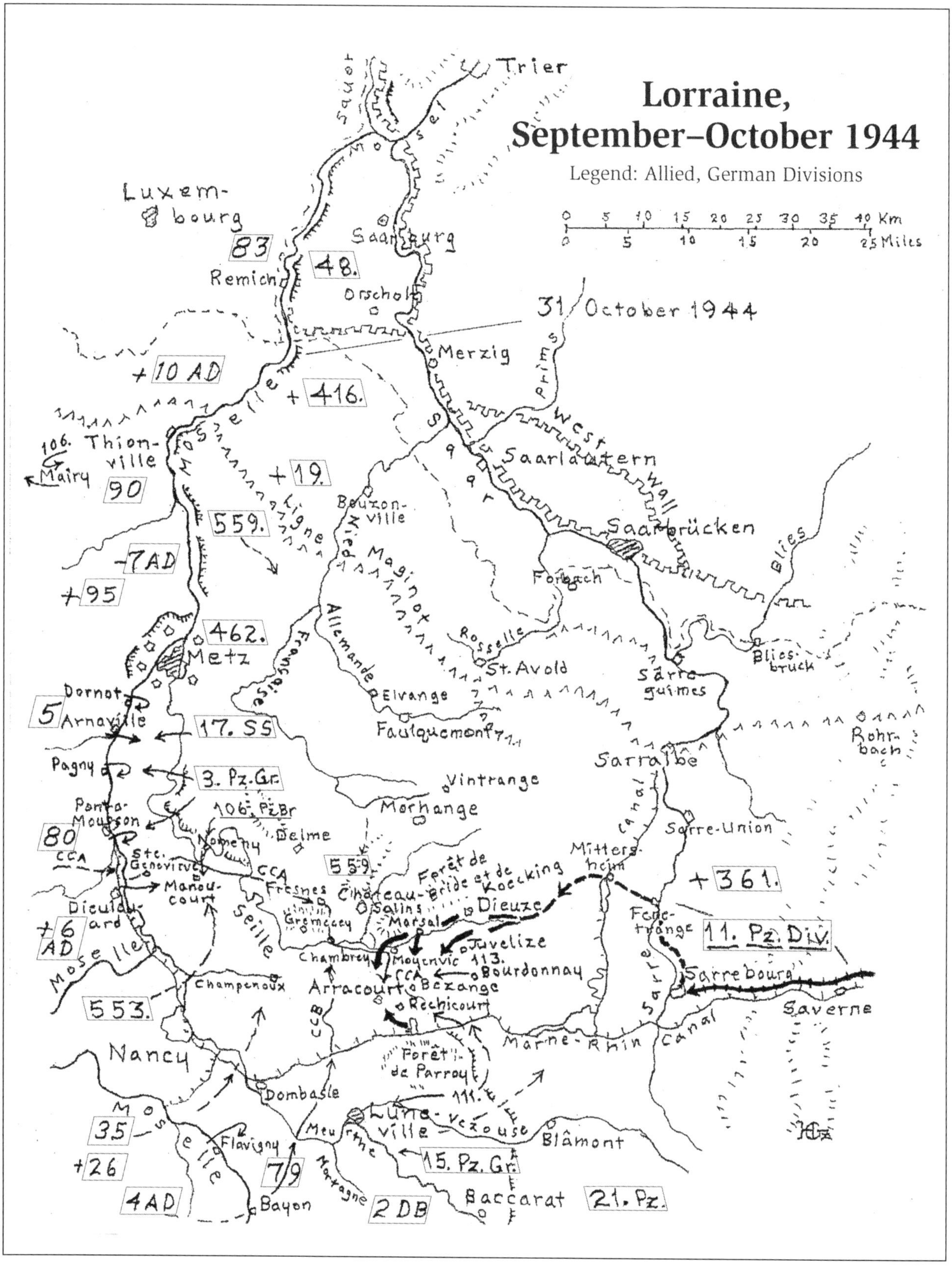

Lorraine, September–October 1944

Legend: Allied, German Divisions

In the north 15. Armee under General der Infanterie Gustav von Zangen ferried his forces across the Scheldt. (They still controlled the maritime approaches to the big port of Antwerp, even after the British had taken the port itself on 4 September.) In the Netherlands Generaloberst Kurt Student with his newly created 1. Fallschirm-Armee gathered the forces he could along the Albert and Meuse-Escaut Canals, the West Stellung, to slow the advance of the British 2 Army to the Dutch border. General der Panzertruppen Erich Brandenberger, newly appointed 3 September as commander of 7. Armee, controlled the retreating German forces from Maastricht on the Maas (French-Belgian Meuse) River south into the rugged Ardennes-Eifel. He had little to slow the American drive north of Aachen but numerous roadblocks reinforced by mines and an occasional Pak, along with stubborn Grenadiers.

In the path of an American advance through the major city of Aachen to the Ruhr, Brandenberger had the remnants of several divisions, while 116.Pz.Div. (with only three panzers) was to defend the city itself. On 13 September, however, the Americans bypassed the city to the south and penetrated the Westwall defenses before they were stopped by fuel shortages and various German units. In the dank gloom of the Hürtgenwald, the Schnee Eifel, and the deep Ardennes the Allies' probes of the Westwall were also repulsed. Meanwhile, 5. Panzerarmee headquarters was reorganizing in Belgium.

The American penetrations were gambles. Following the exhilarating breakout from Normandy, they were eager in pursuing the defeated foe. The forces were suffering from logistical "overstretch," and they lacked the engineer demolitions, flamethrowers, and other weaponry that proved to be needed to attack the Westwall fortifications, even if those defenses were hastily manned and underequipped. South of Luxembourg the German border since 1919, and thus the Westwall, turned sharply east, fronting the Saar industrial basin to the Rhine, and then ran south to Basel in Switzerland.

But Patton's Third Army was now approaching Elsass-Lothringen (Alsace-Lorraine to the French), territories that had been German from 1871 until 1919, and indeed Germanic since well before expansionist French King Louis XIV. Just as Aachen had been the capital of Emperor Karl der Grosse (Carolus Magnus, or Charlemagne in French), so Metz was the capital after 843 A.D. of his grandson, the Emperor Lothair.[6] The Third Army, which had swept across the river lines as well as the tortured battlefields of World War I (as the Blitzkrieg had done in 1940), now suddenly found German resistance stiffening along the line of the Moselle (the German Mosel up past Trier) well ahead of the German frontier.

This was the sector of Knobelsdorff's 1. Armee, now in Armeegruppe G, and new units were arriving: 3. and 15. Panzergrenadierdivisionen from Italy (though not yet their organic panzer battalions), and 553. and 559. Volksgrenadierdivisionen and Pz.Brig. 106 detraining and moving up, with 19.Inf.Div. and 36.V.G.D. scheduled to reinforce. At the same time retreating elements of the 48.I.D. were taking up position while 17.SS Panzergrenadierdivision Götz von Berlichingen was being rebuilt, absorbing the remnants of 49. and 51.SS Panzergrenadierbrigaden; the latter two units had fought the US 4th Armored Division at Troyes 25 August, as SS Panzergrenadier-Regimente 37 and 38, respectively.[7]

On a bright, clear 5 September, the Amis came out of the tree line at Pagny-sur-Moselle and at Pont-à-Mousson south of Metz to launch rubber assault boats to cross the river. The Americans were of the 80th Infantry Division of XII Corps of Patton's Third Army. The 3.Pz.Gren.Div. defenders were well prepared on the east bank high ground and lashed them with mortar, artillery, and machine-gun fire, and at Pont-à-Mousson the grenadiers attacked the battalion that had crossed with bayonets, grenades and Maschinenpistole, and wiped out the position. "*Hände hoch!*" ("Hands up!")

Farther south Luftwaffe Feldregiment 92 caused heavy casualties among the Americans who crossed at Marbache, as did Fallschirmjäger Ersatz Regiment 3 where the Moselle loops west around Nancy past Toul. The 553. V.G.D. reinforced sharp counterattacks. Closer to the defended forts around the city of Metz, 17.SS-Pz.Gren.Div. was positioned on the eastern bank of the Moselle. When American infantry crossed the river at Dornot on 8 September they were quickly pinned down by a fierce Gegenangriff of II.Btl./ SS Pz.Gren.Rgt.37.

On the 10th a bridgehead was finally established at Arnaville. It was covered by a smoke screen, with strong support from artillery, tank destroyers, and P-47 fighter-bombers. This was the 5th Infantry Division of the US XX Corps. But the GIs at Dornot were fiercely attacked by assault guns and grenadiers of Pz.Gr.Rgt. 8/ 3.Pz.Gren.Div. and SS of II.Btl./ 51.SS

Pz.Gren.Brig. (SS Pz.G.R.38) of 17.SS Pz.Gren.Div., and the survivors abandoned the little bridgehead on the night of the 10th. The forts around Metz itself were being manned by the ad hoc Division Nummer 462 of stragglers and others; but it also included officer candidates of the Fahnenjunkerschule and non-commissioned officer candidates of the Unterführerschule who, if not trained as units, nonetheless were selected and dedicated fighters.

As American forces advanced on Metz and Thionville to the north, they encountered fierce resistance from the 462. in the steel-and-concrete forts surrounded by minefields, wire entanglements, and enfilading fields of fire. The American troops were the 7th Armored and 90th Infantry Divisions, cross-reinforced, of the XX corps. Knobelsdorff even launched a counterattack with Oberst Franz Bäke's Pz.Brig.106 FHH on 8 September that penetrated through the widely spread American forces and overran the 90th Division Command Post near Mairy north of Briey. Despite this early success, the attack was a mistake. It was intended as a spoiling attack to cover the retreat behind the Moselle, but it brought out the defects of the panzer brigade organization. Without organic reconnaissance, antitank, or artillery elements, the panzers fell prey to the 90th Division units that closed around them. Of Pz.Brig.106 FHH's some thirty-nine operational panzers and assault guns, thirty were lost, along with sixty half-tracks and almost a hundred other vehicles.[8] Nonetheless the attack did give the 90th Division pause; the 559. V.G.D. abandoned Thionville on the 12th but stabilized the Hauptkampflinie on the east side of the Moselle, discouraging American plans to cross the river barrier.

If the defense line of the Moselle was being consolidated, the situation south of Nancy held by the 553. V.G.D. remained in flux. Yet even here German resistance was becoming evident. Pz.Gren.Rgt.104 of 15.Pz.Gren.Div. on the 553.'s left could only stretch outposts south along the upper Moselle. But when an American infantry battalion crossed a bridge at Flavigny on 10 September, the German artillery smashed the bridge and the panzergrenadiers with panzers overran the position, the surviving GIs swimming or wading back to the west bank.

With its other regiment (Pz.G.R.115) farther north, 15.Pz.Gren.Div. still could only have Vorposten for alerting of enemy crossings and perhaps fighting delaying actions until a counterattack could be mounted. The next day the Amis were crossing at Crévéchamps and Neuviller-sur-Moselle, and also farther south upriver at Bainville-aux-Miroirs and Bayon, where tanks forded the associated canal and other small waterways. After failed counterattacks, the Pz.G.R.104 elements fell back behind the Meurthe, the next barrier.

American and French forces were also pressing into the Neufchâteau area where only 16.Inf.Div. and various other units reflected where 19. and 1. Armee had rejoined the Westfront. It was from this area that Hitler on 3 September ordered a counterattack into the southern flank of Patton's hard-driving Third Army. The Germans would mount a formidable force: 3., 15., and 17.SS Panzergrenadier Divisions, three new panzer brigades (111., 112., and 113.), Panzerlehr, 11. Panzer, and 21. Panzer-Divisionen, and Panzerbrigade 106 as well as 107 and 108. The 5. Panzerarmee headquarters was brought down to Strasbourg (Strassburg), where newly appointed commander General der Panzertruppen Hasso von Manteuffel, coming from command of Panzergrenadierdivision Grossdeutschland on the Ostfront, arrived on 11 September. LVIII. Panzerkorps under Gen.d.Pz.Tr. Walter Krüger was to control the operation.

But in the meantime the three panzergrenadier divisions were already committed from Nancy up past Metz, Panzerlehr and 21.Pz.Div. needed to be rebuilt, 11.Panzer had stopped the Allied advance from the south at Audincourt and was covering the Burgundian Gate west of Belfort, and the panzer brigades had yet to come up except for Pz.Brig.106, which had been decimated north of Metz. At OB West Model and then von Rundstedt said they needed many more forces, and Blaskowitz at Armeegruppe G (redesignated Heeresgruppe G on 11 September) sought postponements.

As the 16.Inf.Div. was being driven from the Neufchâteau area, Blaskowitz felt pressured to order an attack on 12 September, the order being passed down to Manteuffel who passed it down to Generalleutnant Heinrich Freiherr von Lüttwitz who gave it to the new Pz.Brig.112. Lüttwitz had just been promoted on the 5th from 2.Pz.Div. to command XXXXVII. Pz.Korps. Pz.Brig.112 had its Panther and Panzer IV battalions at strength, some ninety-six panzers. It advanced that same day from Epinal toward Vittel, backed up by 21.Pz.Div. But there was no reconnaissance and no artillery support. The 21.Pz.-Div. contingent was only a Kampfgruppe under Oberstlt. Hans von Luck, composed of about 240 grenadiers and a few assault guns from Pz.Gren.Rgt.192, and with no panzers. The Panther battalion of 112. igelt that night at Dompaire and the Pz.IV battalion on the south flank at Darney.

On the 13th the Panther Abteilung at Dompaire in a valley was assaulted by Free French armor from two sides and devastated by American P-47 Thunderbolts. When the Pz.IV Abteilung moved up it was engaged as well, as was Kgr. Luck. The inexperienced Pz.Brig.112 lost sixty of its ninety-six panzers in its first battle. Forewarned, French Général Jacques Leclerc had positioned the combat commands of his 2ème Division Blindée to annihilate the Panthers trapped at Dompaire before the other German forces could intervene. "The plan worked," von Luck said later. "Perhaps, remembering 1940, we underestimated the French." This was the "Debacle at Epinal."[9] The battle again demonstrated the inherent weaknesses of Hitler's panzer brigade concept.

To the left of Leclerc's armored division the US 79th Infantry Division, both in XV Corps and having just joined Third Army, had crossed the upper Moselle at Charmes on the 12th. North of Nancy the US 80th Division, which had lost its bridgehead over the Moselle at Pont-à-Mousson on 5 September, crossed again at Dieulouard 7 kilometers (4 miles) to the south on the 12th. The river had only been lightly outposted, but on the 13th a battalion of Pz.Gren.Rgt.29 of 3.Pz.Div. counterattacked, seizing the dominant St. Genevieve ridge, and driving the Amis back to the bridges their engineers were installing.

Even while this fighting was continuing, an American armored column erupted out of the Dieulouard bridgehead, ascended the hills, and rapidly drove east. It was a tactical road march, with a time-length of three hours, the column firing at any enemy along the highway; the Americans crashed through roadblocks and drove past Nomeny, through Letricourt, across the Seille River at Aulnois and on through Lemoncourt to laager at Fresnes-en-Saulnois 5 kilometers from Château-Salins (Salzburgen) by that evening, 30 kilometers (18 miles) deep behind the German forces. This was Combat Command A under Col. Bruce Clarke of Wood's 4th Armored Division; the unit claimed 354 prisoners of war, along with twelve panzers, eighty-five other vehicles, and five large-caliber guns taken or destroyed, with little loss to themselves. The next day CCA continued its penetration swinging south, crossing the Seille again at Chambrey, cutting the N 74 Rollbahn from Nancy, through Moyenvic to Arracourt and Valhey just north of the Marne-Rhin Canal.

From the south more American armor drove north from the upper Moselle, crossing the Meurthe and reaching the Marne-Rhin Canal west of Lunéville on the 14th. This was CCB of the 4th Armored under Brig. Gen. Holmes Dager, and its advance meant the double envelopment of the Nancy salient, tearing a gaping hole in the Moselle defense line. German forces surrounded included the 553.V.G.D., elements of Pz.G.R.104 of 15.Pz.Gren.Div., and their rear echelons and headquarters.

The US 4th Armored Division, which had spearheaded Patton's drive across France, had been activated 15 April 1941 at Pine Camp in upstate New York. Converted as a "light" armored division in 1943 like other armored divisions (except the 2nd and 3rd ADs), it had been restlessly training for three years in the continental United States and then in England before coming ashore over the UTAH landing beach in Normandy after D-plus-36. The aggressive style of armor leadership in the 4th Armored was set by division commander Maj. Gen. John Wood during the breakout when his division drove south to Coutances. There he personally captured a German soldier, found a way through the minefields, and scribbled a message sent *back* to his CCB commander: "General Dager—Send the infantry through after me."[10]

The 35th Infantry Division crossed the Meurthe on the left of CCB advancing on Nancy, which was evacuated eastward by the 553.V.G.D. on the 14th. But the 4th Armored encirclement of the Nancy Kessel was, as often with armor encirclements, not solid. Blaskowitz was gathering forces behind CCA along its MSR from Dieulouard to cut off the armor penetration, and also to crush the 80th Division bridgehead.

On 14 September Pz.Gren.Rgt.29 of 3.Pz.Gren. Div. mounted attacks against the Brückenkopf as did Volksgrenadierregiment 1119. of 553.V.G.D. from the south. They were joined on the 15th by SS Pz.G.R.37 (the former 49.SS Pz.Gren.Brig.) of 17.SS Pz.Gren.Div. and Pz.Aufkl.Abt.115/ 15.Pz.Gren.Div. Bäke's Pz.Brig.106 FHH came down from Metz; it was much reduced after the Mairy debacle and now had only five panzers einsatzbereit. But Pz.Jäger Abt.3 of 3.Pz.Gren.Div. was attached, and Bäke blocked the Dieulouard-Château-Salins highway near Nomeny, and regained contact with 553.V.G.D. at Manoucourt.[11]

Just before dark on the 15th American tanks leading a convoy west from Fresnes along the highway appeared, and they were ambushed by the panzers and Pak guns of Pz.Brig.106. This was a tank company escorting an infantry battalion of the 80th Division attached to CCA/4th AD, now ordered to return to the bridgehead. Through the night they fought their way back to Dieulouard and, though Pz.G.R. 115/15.Pz.Gren.Div. also arrived from the north to assault the bridgehead, the 80th Division secured its perimeter.

The Rollbahn to Fresnes and Château-Salins, however, was back under German control, while the 553.V.G.D. stubbornly resisted the 35th Division in the hills and woods northeast of Nancy. The 4th Armored's Reserve Command under Col. Wendell Blanchard and the mechanized 42nd Cavalry Squadron occupied Lunéville on the 16th. But when CCB advanced north behind CCA, which outposted the hills east of Arracourt, Dager reported "some of the fiercest enemy resistance to date," from Volks. Gren.Rgt.1120.[12] From Mazerulles CCB moved north across the Seille at Chambrey to Fresnes by the 18th.

At Heeresgruppe G Blaskowitz, under heavy pressure from OKW and Hitler to mount a counteroffensive to stop Patton's advance, had to inform von Rundstedt at OB West on 14 September that an offensive *west* of the Moselle was impossible; he instead proposed a smaller counterattack *east* of the Moselle to secure Lunéville, at the confluence of the Vezouse and Meurthe Rivers, and attack north to Château-Salins. Rundstedt simply forwarded this to OKW. Hitler, impatient that *some* action be taken, approved, and directed that it be mounted by 18 September. But the forces Hitler had initially identified for the Gegenangriff were lacking. The three panzergrenadier divisions were thoroughly committed, the 106. and 112. Panzer Brigades had been wrecked, 21.Pz.Div. had no panzers, and Panzerlehr was engaged in the Eifel. The other four panzer brigades were in the process of arriving at railheads.

The only armored force reasonably intact was Wietersheim's 11. Gespenster Panzer-Division, and Wiese was desperate to keep that unit covering the Burgundian Gate at Belfort and blocking Allied entrance to the Rhine valley. After thwarting the advance of the 3ème Algerienne on 8 September, the division held a sector from l'Isle-sur-le-Doubs to Pont de Roide and the Swiss border, where the Doubs twists out of Schweiz and north to where it flows west and southwest past Audincourt and Montbeliard. From 10 to 15 September the Div. Gefechtsstand was at Montbeliard. Pz.Aufkl.Abt.11 linked on the right to Gruppe Degener, a collection of various units, and 159.Inf.Div., now under Kniess's LXXXV. A.K. with headquarters at Belfort.

The French were relatively quiescent and the Gespensters took the opportunity for some Auffrischung. Some 1,000 Luftwaffe personnel had been "taken in" after apparently having been forgotten in some training garrisons in France, and had to be assimilated and trained. The Pz. Werkstatt Kompanie of Pz.-Rgt.15 worked diligently to get the panzers combat-ready. The Panthers required major maintenance after 800 kilometers, but some of the original ones now had over 1,500 kilometers on their odometers. The WK was at Delle scarcely 500 meters from the Swiss border, and the border guards could watch them at work. By 11 September perhaps over thirty Panthers and Panzer IVs were once again einsatzbereit.[13]

One reason for the apparent lull, though they did not know it, was that French Général de Lattre had Bethouart's I Corps hold up while de Monsabert's II Corps was redeployed from Dijon and the western flank of the US Seventh Army around to the right flank so a united 1ère Armée Française could mount a coordinated drive through the Belfort Gap to Mulhouse and the Rhine valley. In addition, Seventh Army's VI Corps divisions were now oriented to attack northeast into the forbidding and high Vosges Mountains, and they had to prepare for the forested terrain that gave advantage to the German infantry divisions. The 11.Pz.-Div. was relieved after 15 September in order to proceed north to participate in the armored counteroffensive in Lorraine. 19. Armee would have to fend for itself.

On 17 September came the electrifying news of the Allied airborne invasion of the Netherlands. An airborne carpet of transport planes towing gliders, followed by parachutes blossoming forth, covered a corridor 80 kilometers (50 miles) long, from Eindhoven to Arnhem across the Neder Rijn, the Lower Rhine. Thousands of British and American paratroopers "hit the silk" on that sunny Sunday afternoon. Except for some flak, occasional skirmishes on the ground, and a brief foray by some Luftwaffe Focke-Wulf 190 fighter planes near Wesel, there was no organized resistance. Surprise had been achieved.

After briefly admiring the spectacle as a paratrooper himself, Generaloberst Kurt Student began coordinating the units of his 1. Fallschirm-Armee to deal with the invasion. Even more immediate was the response of Generalfeldmarschall Walter Model, whose headquarters in the Hartenstein Hotel in Oosterbeek in the western outskirts of Arnheim (Arnhem) was within 3 kilometers of a British drop zone. He immediately drove to the headquarters of II.SS Panzerkorps under SS Obergruppenführer Willi Bittrich to order the nearby 9.SS Pz.Div. Hohenstaufen into action at Arnhem. Model also coordinated the movements of other forces including 10.SS Pz.Div. Frundsberg, and rerouted Pz.Brig. 107, which was being sent to Aachen. It was the Allies' misfortune that the two relevant senior German commanders were present, and that the two Waffen-SS panzer divisions, though badly understrength, were refitting in the Arnhem area. In addition, a copy of the Allied operations order was recovered from an American glider that was shot down, and within two hours, said General Student, it was on his desk.

At 14,35 hours that afternoon, following an intense rolling artillery barrage, British tanks charged out of a bridgehead over the Meuse-Escaut Canal while Hawker Typhoons strafed ahead with 20mm cannon and rockets. This was the beginning of Allied Operation MARKET-GARDEN, an attempt to drop three airborne divisions of the First Allied Airborne Army to seize the water crossings from Eindhoven through Nijmegen to Arnhem on the Neder Rijn (MARKET), with an armored ground assault by British 30 Corps (GARDEN). This would set up an Allied drive to capture the Ruhr industrial complex from the north. There was Allied hope the war would be won before winter.

Supreme Allied Commander General Eisenhower had been vacillating about his "broad front" versus the "narrow front" strategy, alternately promising British Field Marshal Montgomery that he favored the primary effort and resources supporting a drive *north* of the Ardennes to the Ruhr, but also acknowledging Bradley's support of Patton driving *south* of the Ardennes through the Saar and across the Rhine. The result was that Lt. Gen. Courtney Hodges's US First Army was stretched from Aachen to Luxembourg, not concentrated enough at any point to be decisive.

First Army might still have advanced on the right flank of Montgomery's 2 British Army and an airborne operation for a drive east toward the Ruhr. But the RAF and USAAF felt the flak defenses around the Ruhr were too strong for air operations. In addition, the first V-2 rockets began to strike London, and they were launched from along the Dutch coast. Since 13 June V-1 gyro-guided, jet-propelled flying bombs ("Buzz Bombs") had begun to target the Normandy beaches and England, and now also the port of Antwerp. Their visible trails up through the skies gave promise of new "Wunderwaffen." These were Hitler's Vergeltungswaffen, weapons of retaliation for the terror bombing of German cities.

While the V-1s were subsonic and vulnerable to antiaircraft guns and fighter interceptors, the V-2 rocket was a ballistic missile that was supersonic, coming down upon its target without warning, and its warhead could destroy a city block of buildings. There was no defense against the V-2. Earlier, Prime Minister Winston Churchill had urged the bombing of the V-1 launching sites, but Operation CROSSBOW had failed. The English people, who had endured the nighttime "Blitz" of 1941, were becoming demoralized by the helplessness when faced with this new assault from the skies. The V-weapon destruction would only be ended by ground forces overrunning the launch sites themselves. For a number of reasons then, MARKET-GARDEN was oriented north, not east. But there would be no significant flank protection, and in fact the Guards Armoured Division had to lead 30 Corps up a single highway on a one-tank front.

German preset demolitions destroyed some of the eight bridges that needed to be crossed before the airborne troops could capture them, fog and rain delayed the subsequent landing of artillery and heavy weapons, and German attacks with panzers and assault guns periodically cut the route of advance. After nine days 43 Division finally reached the Neder Rijn at Arnhem, but it was too late. The exhausted survivors of 1 British Airborne Division withdrew across the river by boat or by swimming during the night of 25–26 September, the rest being captured. While a significant salient had been projected into the German lines, the ultimate objective of MARKET-GARDEN had failed. Nor was the Netherlands liberated, and the V weapons continued to rain down on England. It proved to be, as Lt. Gen. Frederick Browning of 1 British Airborne Corps had cautioned Montgomery, simply "a bridge too far."[14]

Consternation had gripped the German high command when the first reports of the paratroop landings had been received on 17 September, including Hitler at his Rastenburg Wolfsschanze. But it soon became evident that Student and Model could deal with the Allied operation with their own Heeresgruppe B resources. At Heeresgruppe G Blaskowitz was still obligated to carry out the attack in Lorraine on the 18th, and these orders remained unchanged.

CHAPTER TWENTY-SIX

Counterattack in Lorraine

IN LORRAINE, GENERAL VON MANTEUFFEL OF 5. PANZERARMEE was in a quandary as how to carry out the attack ordered for 18 September to restore the breech made by Patton's 4th Armored Division in its envelopment of Nancy, its combat commands positioned from Luneville through Arracourt to Fresnes-en-Saulnois. As developed, General Krüger's LVIII. Pz.Korps with Panzerbrigade 113 and elements of 15.Pz.Gren.Div. would attack from north of the Rhein–Marne Kanal (Canal la Marne au Rhin); XXXXVII. Pz.Korps under General von Lüttwitz with 111. and 112. Panzerbrigaden and 21.Pz.Div. would secure the highway junction of Luneville and then drive north over the canal to join Krüger.

Pz.Brig.113 under Oberst Freiherr von Seckendorff was detraining at Saarburg (Sarrebourg) with its Panther Abteilung (I./130.Pz.Lehr Div.) and Panzer IV Abt. 2113, and its two-battalion Pz.Gren.Rgt.2113, I.Btl. in Halbketten, II.Btl. in Lastwagen. Generalleutnant Eberhard Rodt's 15.Pz.Gren.Div., however, was spread from Dieulouard to Luneville. The battered Pz.Brig.112 and a panzer battalion of Oberst Heinrich Bronsart von Schellendorf's Pz.Brig.111 were still engaged with 2ème Division Blindée in the Châtel area on the upper Moselle after the Dompaire battle.

Schellendorf's brigade moved into Rambervillers south of Luneville. It had most of its Panther and Panzer IV battalions but was down eleven Panthers from air attack and mechanical failures. Others were still near Châtel, and the brigade had not yet received its Panzerjäger company. Gen.Lt. Edgar Feuchtinger's 21.Pz.Div. had only Pz.Gren.Rgt.192, but had finally received twenty-four panzers, though was also committed. Manteuffel was ordered to attack on the 18th without waiting for 11. Panzer-Division or the other disparate units. It would mean an attack piecemeal, but Blaskowitz, already suspect with Hitler, was not in a position to challenge the order.

On 18 September Krüger had Pz.Brig.113 move from Sarrebourg to Blamont. They crossed the Marne-Rhin Canal to the north side at Lagarde and Moussey that

Arracourt—4th Armored vs. 11. Panzer, September 1944

(showing American and German unit symbology)

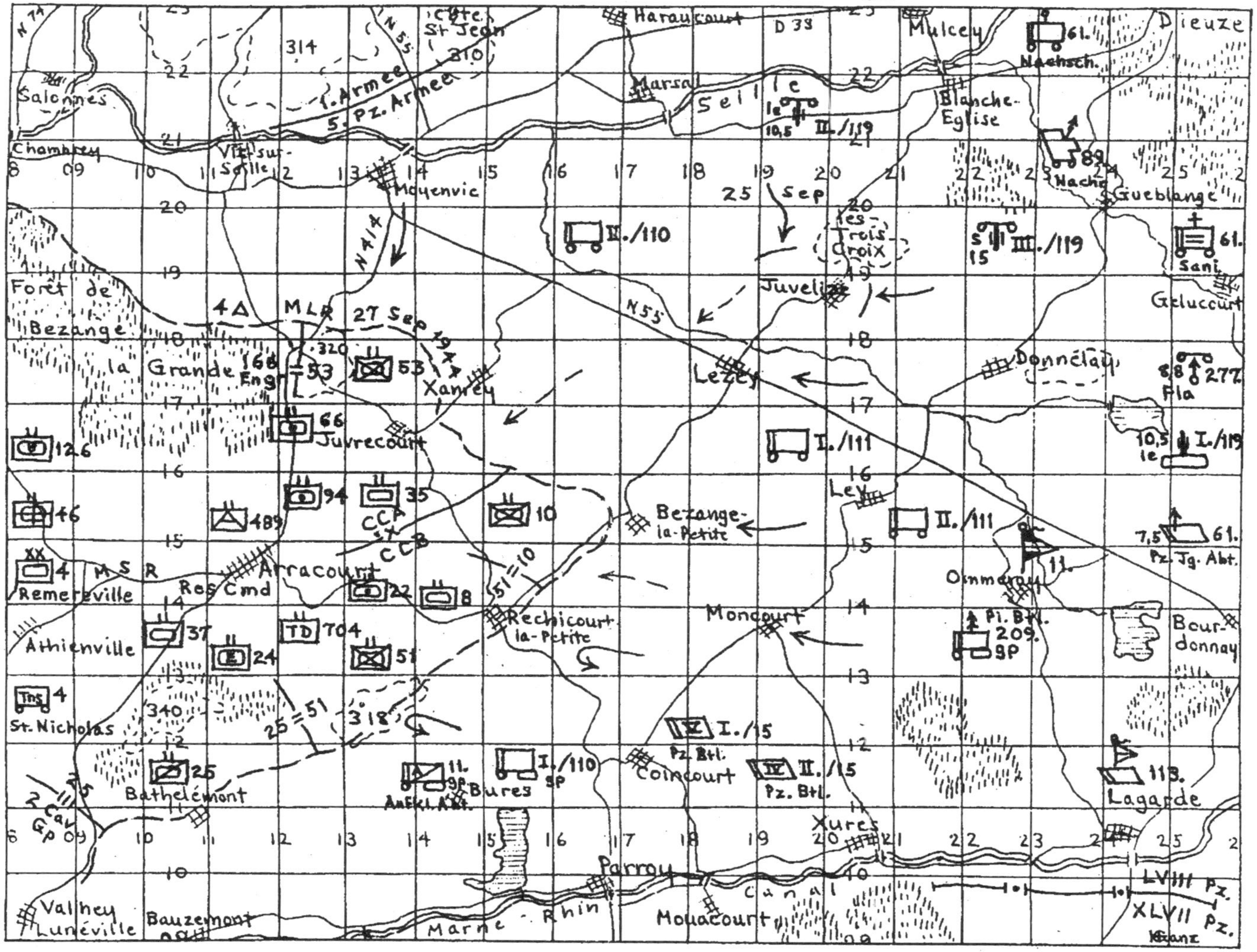

night in order to attack on the 19th. Lüttwitz did have Schellendorf's Pz.Brig.111 advance on Luneville about 07,00 hours on the 18th led by seventeen panzers, but they encountered American mechanized cavalry elements. This was the battalion-sized 42nd Cavalry Reconnaissance Squadron, Mechanized, of the 2nd Cavalry Group, Mechanized, outposting Luneville. Six "assault guns" from that unit's E Troop were rushed forward, but these were M8s with a short 75mm pack howitzer on an M5 light tank chassis, and three were quickly destroyed by the Panthers.

Schellendorf drove on into Luneville, now joined by elements of Pz.G.R.104 of 15.Pz.-Gren.Div. and 100 grenadiers of Pz.G.R.192 of 21.Pz.-Div. There they encountered some tanks and tank destroyers of the US 4th Armored Division. This was the small Reserve Command under Col. Wendell Blanchard, including only a tank, an armored infantry, and a tank destroyer company, though with a self-propelled artillery battalion in direct support. While other ADs utilized Reserve Command as a third combat command (CCR), the 4th generally employed it as originally intended. In the close fighting the American cavalry squadron commander was killed, the cavalry group commander badly wounded and evacuated, and the TD battalion commander was killed the next day.[1]

But now Schellendorf found American reinforcements arriving, and tank destroyers with a high-velocity 76mm gun began to take a toll, as did increased American artillery fire. (While US infantry divisions had tank destroyer battalions attached with M10 or M36 TDs with 3-inch and 90mm guns, the armored divisions had TD battalions attached with the more agile M18 Hellcat with a high-velocity 76.2mm gun.) That evening Manteuffel ordered the Pz.Brig.111 to disengage and move to Parroy north of the canal for a concerted drive with Pz.Brig.113.

The reinforcements were a 4th Armored task force from Combat Command A at Arracourt including a second armored field artillery battalion, and fire support from two more field artillery battalions. Combat Command B of the 6th Armored Division also began to arrive. The 6th AD had been left in Brittany ever since early August, and only now was its CCB catching up to Third Army.[2]

Luneville could not be held amid the American buildup, and other French and American forces were approaching from the southwest as the German forces there fell back from the Mortagne to the Meurthe. The Allied troops were the US 79th Infantry Division and the French armor of XV Corps, resisted by Kampfgruppe Luck with II.Btl. of Luck's own Pz.G.R.125, only 140 grenadiers. Manteuffel now intended to attack toward Champenoux east of Nancy with Pz.Brig.113. It would be joined by Pz.Brig.111 under Krüger's LVIII. Pz.K., to assist the 553.V.G.D. being pressed by the 35th Infantry Division. Driving all the way up to Pont-à-Mousson and restoring the line of the Moselle seemed remote.

Early on 19 September Seckendorff's Panzerbrigade 113 advanced west from Bourdonnay with forty-two Panthers and Pz.Gren.Rgt.2113 in the lead, to attack the American force around Arracourt between the Marne-Rhin Canal and the Seille River to the north. There was heavy morning ground fog, typical this time of year, and with only Volkswagens in the Aufklärungskompanie there was no effective reconnaissance as to what lay ahead. In addition, Pz.Brig.111 had not yet crossed the canal, nor was there organic artillery support as the brigade attacked alone.

As the Panthers deployed over the rolling terrain of fields, woodlots, and small stone villages, American M4 tanks were suddenly encountered in the murk—*Feindpanzer!*—scarcely 75 meters away. The Americans were on alert and three Panthers were claimed quickly destroyed in a frantic exchange of tank fire. The Panthers had hydraulic traverse, but with barely trained, inexperienced crews there was scarcely time to identify and engage in the thick fog, and the long-range accuracy of the deadly 7,5cm L/70 gun was negated. West of Bezange-la-Petite they encountered M18 tank destroyers in hull-down defilade. Green and red tracers lanced through the gloom and three of the four TDs were destroyed, but seven Panthers were lost.

The American force was CCA of the 4th Armored under Col. Bruce Clarke: 37th Tank Battalion, 53rd Armored Infantry Battalion, 166th Combat Engineer Battalion, and three artillery battalions and attached companies, soon rejoined by the task force sent to Luneville. The initial clash was with Lt. Col. Creighton Abrams's 37th Tank Battalion. At 09,45 hours that morning Division was alerted: "From CCA (voice)/ Having tank battle in our vic/ Abe ko'd 2 tks—TDs 1/ about 20 en tks came thru Ley—believe we have enough to take care of them." This began eleven days of armored battles around Arracourt.[3]

Even with the short-barreled 75mm guns of their M4 Shermans, the highly trained and experienced tankers of the 4th Armored maneuvered to hull defilade behind a ridge, racing to another position, wheeling south through Réchicourt, catching the Panthers in flank, and mopping up the panzergrenadiers west of Moncourt. *"Sani!"* (Medic!) came the cry of the Verwundete (wounded). CCA claimed forty-three Panthers and Panzer IVs knocked out to eight lost of their own armor. Pz.Brig.113 had been wrecked.

By the next day Oberst von Schellendorf's Pz.Brig.111 was north of the canal but Manteuffel did not press Krüger to attack, despite pressure from Blaskowitz; Manteuffel argued that piecemeal attacks were fruitless. The veteran 11.Pz.-Div. would add significant weight to a renewed attack, but the Gespensters, having been ordered north from the Burgundische Pforte, were just now rail-loading ten panzers of Pz.-Rgt.15 at Montbeliard. Because of the omnipresent American airpower, the trains went by night, remaining in tunnels during the day. There the men remained uncomfortable because of the smoke from the idling steam engines, which couldn't drop their fires.

The Eisenbahntransport with the Kettenfahrzeuge had better cover in the Rhine valley because of the low-lying autumn mist. They moved on the route through Colmar and Strassburg (Strasbourg), then on to Zabern (Saverne) and detraining at Saarburg (Sarrebourg). The Räderfahrzeuge generally marched by road, also covered by morning fog, and could move by day. The remaining panzers would follow on the 22nd, organized by Oblt. Rahn, Ordonnanz Offizier of I.Abt. A Zug with 2.Kp./Pz.Rgt.15 near Colmar, however, left its tunnel near twilight, but light enough so the P-47 Jabos sighted it and attacked with rockets and their eight .50-caliber machine guns. Nonetheless the Reichsbahn rerouted trains, repaired damage from air attacks, and, said the division history, "The achievements of the railroads here in the West, as earlier in the East, was astonishing!"[4]

With the exception of a battle group that remained in the Belfort area, the Elfte moved to Lorraine. The Kampfgruppe was under Oberstleutnant Erich Hammon, commander of Pz.Art.Rgt.119. It consisted of a Nachrichtenzug (signals platoon), ten Panzer IVs of 6.Kp./Pz.Rgt.15 under Oberlt. Franz Graf Hoyos, a rifle company, an engineer company, and an artillery detachment with self-propelled pieces and flak guns that had operated directly under division control. Hammon's battle group did not return to the division until November. There was some feeling that Hammon was an ardent Nazi and was not too well-liked, one reason he was detached with rather a small command. On the other hand this was an independent command, and the appearance of just a few panzers and panzergrenadiers in the Belfort area had an impact on the enemy, out of all proportion to their actual numbers.

As the 11. Panzer assembled near Sarrebourg 20–27 September (most combat units by the 24th), Pz.Rgt.15 had twenty Panthers and ten Panzer IVs, both panzergrenadier regiments, the armored reconnaissance battalion, and the armored engineer battalion, at about 70 percent of K.St.N. strength. Panz.Art.Rgt.119 had three light (10,5cm) batteries but reduced to four tubes each, and three medium (15cm) batteries of four Röhre each. Pz.Jäger Abt.61 remained in the Saverne area training, and awaiting their new Jagdpanzer IV tank destroyers mounting the 7,5cm Pak 39 L/48 on a Pz.IV chassis, with Panzerschürzen protecting the Laufwerk (tracks and suspension). Because of the Feldersatzbataillon (Field Replacement Battalion) there was a reserve of some 2,000 men, not yet fully trained. About half were the Luftwaffe personnel incorporated earlier—young flight volunteers released by Göring due to lack of planes and fuel.[5]

Meanwhile south of the Marne-Rhin Canal Lüttwitz's XXXXVII. Pz.K. with elements of 21.Pz.Div. and Pz.Brig.112, pressed by the US XV Corps, delayed back from the Mortagne to the Meurthe and abandoned Luneville. Pz.Gr.Rgt.104 of 15.Pz.Gren. Div. formed a blocking position north of the canal. Thus Krüger only had Pz.Brig.111 and the remnants of Pz.Brig.113 to engage the 4th Armored's CCA around Arracourt. On 20 September two American armored columns advanced again, northeast, one crossing the Seille at Moyenvic driving toward Hampont, the other thrusting to Dusz (Dieuze), Patton still intending to drive to the Saar and beyond. But Dager's CCB was bogged down fighting through Château-Salins, which was defended by several units including 954. Sicherheitsbataillon (Security Battalion). This battalion may only have had three companies of eighty men each, and a German study characterized the garrison as "weak" and "mostly encircled," but they kept an entire combat command at bay.[6]

Pressured hard by Blaskowitz, Manteuffel ordered Krüger at LVIII. Pz.Korps to attack *now* with Oberst von Schellendorf's Pz.Brig.111, another piecemeal commitment. A Kampfgruppe with eight panzers thrust up toward Arracourt from the canal, attacking a field artillery battalion just about to limber up and join the CCA advance. But the Amis depressed their 155mm howitzers to fire at the panzers point-blank, and tanks and tank destroyers arrived to send the battle group back.[7]

Another Kampfgruppe advanced to the high ground west of Ommeray with Pz. IVs from Pz.Abt.2111 and some 8,8cm guns. They encountered an American tank company cresting Mannecourt Hill, and in a fierce gun battle five or six M4s were knocked out, as were the same number of panzers. More American tanks arrived, and the engagement continued until each side had lost eleven or twelve tanks. The Americans were from the three tank companies of the 37th Tank Battalion under Lieutenant Colonel Abrams, recalled from the advance to Dieuze. At nightfall Abrams took Moncourt and then took up night defensive positions back at Lezey. Another force advanced down toward Bures but was driven back by the panzers there.

Manteuffel wanted to withdraw and await the 11.Pz.-Div. arrival, but Blaskowitz insisted on the attack orders he had received. Rundstedt at OB West now ordered Knobelsdorff at 1. Armee to attack southeast from Delme to meet a 5. Pz.-Armee attack northeast in a pincers operation to encircle the 4th Armored Division. But Hitler also took the opportunity of the stalled attack to relieve Blaskowitz at Heeresgruppe G, and the next day, the 21st, appointed Gen.d.Pz.Tr. Hermann Balck to that position, with Oberst Friedrich von Mellenthin as the Ia. Balck, of course, had commanded the 11.Pz.Div. with distinction, and had worked well with von Mellenthin as Ia of XXXXVIII. Pz.Korps in Russia.

In addition, if Balck was aggressive and rather abrasive, Mellenthin was a close friend of Gen.Lt. Siegfried Westphal, Chef des Stabes to OB West, from the Afrikafeldzug, and Knobelsdorff had been his commander at XXXXVIII. Pz.K. Such close professional relationships did much to facilitate operational coordination. On the other hand, Hitler ordered Balck to renew the offensive deep into Patton's Third Army flank, as Blaskowitz had failed to do, though Mellenthin commented, "The absurdity of this criticism soon became clear to us."[8]

Patton's XII Corps, spearheaded by the 4th Armored, had to be stopped, and Balck ordered Knobelsdorff and Manteuffel to renew the pincers operation against the 4th AD. On that 21st the Amis paused to concentrate against Château-Salins, while Schellendorf's Pz.Brig.111 redeployed to attack the Arracourt area from the northeast instead of from the southeast. White marking tape was laid by patrols that night up to the American lines. On 22 September, under cover of the normal autumn morning fog, the Panthers of Major Gerhard Tebbe's I.Abt. (of Pz.Rgt.16, 116. Pz.Div.) and panzergrenadiers came in north of Juvelize, the Panzervorstoss overrunning the American outpost lines and destroying seven light M5 tanks.

But M18 tank destroyers in hull defilade knocked out three panzers, American M4 mediums arrived supported by artillery fire, and as the sun burned off the ground fog P-47 Thunderbolt fighter-bombers, the dreaded "Jabos," flew in strafing and bombing. By day's end Panzerbrigade 111 was reduced to seven panzers and eighty men, and Kommandeur Oberst Heinrich Bronsart von Schellendorf himself was among the slain. Major Tebbe, Stabsoffizier Oblt. Walter Schubert, and I.Abt. Adjutant Oblt. Horst Gittermann later felt that their commander, depressed at a rebuke by Manteuffel that morning, dismounted his command SPW and deliberately walked into American automatic weapons fire to seek a battlefield death.[9]

The 11. Panzer's Pz.Gren.Rgt.111, temporarily under Major Karl Thieme after Oberst Wilde was wounded, was arriving to continue the attack, but fortunately Manteuffel called it off. Oberst Freiherr von Seckendorff of Pz.Brig.113 was killed by a Jagdbomber the next day. The 4th Armored's outpost line had been held by its 25th Cavalry Recon Squadron, Mechanized, supported by C/704th TD Battalion. Lt. Col. Abrams had counterattacked with his 37th Tank and 10th Armored Infantry Battalions. Clarke's CCA had lost twenty-one tanks, but both panzer brigades had been wrecked and their commanders killed. In addition, the deficient recovery and maintenance capabilities of these brigades, and the loss of the battlefield, meant disabled panzers could not be retrieved and repaired.

South of the Marne-Rhin Canal Lüttwitz's XXXXVII. Pz.K. was very much on the defensive. Pz.Gr.Rgt.104 of Rodt's 15.Pz.Gren.Div. was delaying back from Luneville into the Forêt de Parroy, and Feuchtinger's 21.Pz.Div., barely regiment-sized, and the remnants of Pz.Brig.112 (seven panzers) crossed behind the Vezouse by 24 September. They were pressed by the US 79th Infantry Division and the armor of the French 2 ème Division Blindée of Third Army's XV Corps.

Patton's third corps, the XX on the left of XII Corps, was stalled along the line of the Moselle and the forts at Metz. Von Rundstedt was thus able to move 559. Volksgrenadierdivision from north of Metz and assemble it at Mörchingen (Morhange) for Knobelsdorff's 1. Armee attack with Pz.Brig.106 FHH near Château-Salins, which was still in German hands. Though with heavy losses, Oberst Erich Löhr was extracting his 553.V.G.D. from the Nancy Kessel, pressed by the US 35th Infantry Division and CCB of the 6th Armored Division, while Wood's 4th AD drew in, anticipating renewed German attacks.

On 24 September Oberst Franz Bäke's Pz.Brig.106 Feldherrnhalle and the 559.V.G.D. under Generalmajor Kurt Freiherr von Mühlen assaulted the 4th Armored's CCB between Fresnes-en-Saulnois and Château-Salins. The Angriff was coordinated by XIII.SS-Korps under SS Gruppenführer und General der Waffen-SS Hermann Priess, formed 7 September. When the skies cleared the Jabos swarmed in, and with the punishing American artillery fire, the Germans had to fall back into the city of Château-Salins and the shelter of the Forêt d'Amelécourt (Forêt de Château-Salins on US maps). Clarke's CCA retrieved and repaired its damaged tanks and consolidated its position around Arracourt on that 24th and braced for the next attack.

That night Wietersheim's 11. Panzer-Division moved up to its attack positions, less Kgr.Hammon at Belfort. Oberst Stenkhoff's Pz.-Rgt.15 had perhaps only sixteen Panzerwagen einsatzbereit of its twenty Panthers in I.Abt.(Panther) under Major Jürgen Reichardt and ten Panzer IVs in II.Abt. under Hptm. Rodenhauser. Pz.Gren.Rgt.110 under Oberst Heinrich-Georg Hax had the gepanzerte I. Bataillon Schützenpanzerwagen of Major Karl Thieme and II.Btl. under Hptm. Johannes Schneider. Pz.G.R.111 was now under Oberstlt. Werner von Rupprecht, with Hptm. Werner Wehrstädt commanding I.Btl. and Hptm. Otto Grumbt commanding II.Btl.

Hammon's Pz.Art.Rgt.119 theoretically had three battalions, I.Abt. under Hptm. Günther Rahm, II.Abt. under Hptm. Hoffmann, and III.Abt. under Hptm. Walter Schaefer-Kehnert. The battalions had mixed light 10,5cm and schwere (medium) 15cm batteries, and self-propelled Wespen (10,5cm) and Hummeln (15cm). But some of these had been detached with Kgr. Hammon, and perhaps only two battalions moved into Feuerstellungen that night.

Maj. Jochen Menzel's Heeresflakabteilung 277 with its 8,8cm guns was moving up, as were the other division elements including Maj. Heinz Bödicker's Pz.Pi.Btl.209, Maj. Arnold Steuer's Pz.Nachrichtenabteilung 89, and the Tross (trains) elements. The Div.Gefechtsstand was at Alteville south of the reservoir Etang de Lindre, south of Dieuz. Maj. Karl Bode's Pz.Aufkl.Abt.11 was not ready yet, and Maj. Arnold Kessler's Pz.Jg.Abt.61 was getting its Jagdpanzer IVs. The death of Schellendorf essentially put the remnants of Pz.Brig.111 under 11.Pz.Div. operational control.[10]

Wooded areas for concealment from the Jabos were sparse, but the open rolling farmland, 12 kilometers (7 miles) between the Seille and the Canal, was ideal armor country. The landscape was dotted with little villages of stone stuccoed buildings, often connected, with the inevitable manure pile out front. Tactically, Wietersheim preferred an attack from Bourdonnay just north of the canal against the CCA salient. But Manteuffel was under orders to regain contact with 1. Armee, and thus the 11. Panzer movement routes from Sarrebourg had been more northerly, along the Fénétrange-Mittersheim axis to Dieuze for an attack along the valley of the Seille.

The Pz.Brig.111 elements were gradually incorporated into the division, ultimately thirty Panthers, while other vehicles were distributed according to unit requirements. These were generally much newer vehicles than their own. Of the personnel, many returned to the Reich for reassignment. Pz.G.R.111 covered the division's assembly, from the remnants of Pz.Brig.111 near Blanche-Eglise down to Pz.Brig.113 around Ommeray.

On 24 September Wietersheim received the Angriffsbefehl to attack the next day, though units were still moving up. The operational panzers of Pz.Rgt.15 assembled in the forest area south of Dieuze, with a smaller group in the woods a kilometer northeast of Marimont. The panzer companies and platoons, however, would work with the panzergrenadiers in company-sized teams.

One artillery battalion of 119. was positioned in the wooded ridge of the Forêt de Bride et de Koecking north of the Seille for converging fire on the Juvelize area. The panzer brigades had not had their own artillery. The other battalion was near Gelucourt

Panther (Model A) like Oblt. Walter Rahn's. WALTER RAHN

Oblt. von Fersen and crew on his well-camouflaged Panzer IV: gunner Uffz. Franke, loader Gefr. Triller, driver Gefr. Bob, and radio operator/bow gunner Gefr. Meiler. ERNST-AUGUST VON FERSEN

with H.Flak Abt.277 employing its Acht-komma-acht guns in a direct-fire role, concealed from air observation in patches of woods. At nightfall Pz.G.R.110, with a combat battalion organized from the Feldersatzbataillon, took up its attack position near Blanche-Eglise and a small woods just south of it with a Pionierkompanie from 209.

At 09,00 Uhr on 25 September the Angriff began, in heavy rain that had delayed deployment but also kept off the Jabos. Artillery fire and the high-velocity 8,8cm as Pak guns slashed the American salient. The Americans responded in kind. The open ground was crisscrossed by a lacework of red and green-white tracers, long streaks from armor-piercing rounds, and dashed lines of machine gun bullets, the tracers every fifth round in the belt.

One Kampfgruppe under Hptm. Schneider from Mulcey crossed the Seille at Marsal and came down on the American outposts, while Hax's Schwerpunkt under Karl Thieme drove directly at Juvelize. Another force drove along the Seille, taking Moyenvic and reaching Vic-sur-Seille and making the contact with 559.V.G.D. of 1. Armee that closed the gap in the front.

The 4th Armored Division's CCA held a salient whose eastern apex was at Juvelize. The Kampfgruppen now attacked both sides of the Frontbogen, Pz.Gr.Rgt.110 elements from the north and east taking Hill 264, against the 53rd Armored Infantry Battalion and 37th Tank Battalion, while Pz.G.R.111 struck the 10th AIB and captured Moncourt. A Troop/ 25th Cavalry Recon Squadron had manned the outpost line. But Clarke's Fourthers fought stubbornly and mounted counterattacks, with strong artillery support from the organic 66th and 94th Armored Field Artillery Battalions (SP), and the attached 696th AFA Battalion M7s and 191st FA Battalion with its 155mm howitzers; a ceaseless Trommelfeuer beat down on the attackers. Companies from the 24th Armored Engineer Battalion and the routinely attached 704th TD Battalion and 489th Anti Aircraft Artillery (Automatic Weapons) Battalion (SP) supplemented CCA. 35th Tank Battalion was in reserve.

That night the 119. artillery batteries displaced forward to support a further advance. Patrols found the Amis had retreated. General Wood abandoned the Juvelize salient and brought Dager's CCB—8th Tk Bn, 51st AIB, and 22nd AFA—down from the Fresnes-Château-Salins sector to replace the 320th Infantry Regiment on CCA's south flank, the infantry moving north to rejoin its 35th Infantry Division in the Forêt de Gremecey.

The 4th Armored Trains with the shops of the 126th Armored Ordnance Maintenance Battalion and aid stations of the 46th Armored Medical Battalion moved back from the Arracourt area, and Wood's Forward Echelon Command Post moved 7 kilometers back from Athienville to Remereville on that 26th. The 37th Tank also went into reserve, to make good its earlier losses. The armored doughs dug foxholes and MG positions on the high ground as the 4th Armored, its fifteen battalions now consolidated, readied for the continuation of the Arracourt battles.

Now they were facing the experienced veterans of the 11. Panzer-Division who, even if leavened with new recruits, had enough dependable commanders to coordinate the attacks. This "certainly put us on notice," said Capt. Jimmie Leach, commanding B Company of Abrams's 37th Tank Battalion, "that some real pros were joining the opposition." The apprehension that many GI tankers had about engaging the Panther was not encouraged by a XII Corps G-3 Operations Notes of 10 September, with diagrams, distributed to units advising flank engagements, and warning that at 1,000 yards the 75mm rounds might penetrate "only when hitting the lower half of the mantlett [*sic*], when they are deflected down, penetrating thin hull top-plate," but that the "Hull is invulnerable to all calibers."[11]

Pz.G.R.110 took over the sector Moyenvic-Juvelize-Donnelay supported by some panzers and an engineer company. They dug their Erdlöcher and Schützengräben and emplaced their MG 42s and Granatwerfer. They were able to utilize some concrete fortifications from World War I that provided protection from Ami artillery and air attack. Most of Pz.Rgt.15 and Pz.G.R.111 were shifted down to the left to the Ommeray-Bourdonnay axis for an attack against the south flank of the 4th Armored. The much-reduced Pz.Brig.113 was in the forested high ground southwest of Ommeray.

Wietersheim's Gefechtsstand was at a farm along the road Gelucourt-Maizieres les Vic 2.5 kilometers southeast of Gelucourt. He did argue that the mission of closing the gap between 1. Armee and 5. Pz.Armee had been accomplished and it would be best to go over to the defensive.[12] But Manteuffel was under orders to continue the attack. Krüger massed twenty-five panzers for an attack on the 27th, from the remnants of the two panzer brigades, from 15.Pz.

Gren.Div., and from Pz.Rgt.15. In addition, Major Karl Bode's Pz.Aufkl.Abt.11 had arrived from 19. Armee and was also committed.

Wietersheim objected that American artillery and air power made such massing mistaken, that his smaller mixed company-sized Panzerkampftruppen combat groups would be more effective. But Manteuffel and Balck were from the Ostfront where massed armor could be decisive, the Luftwaffe had promised fifty planes as cover, and they were adamant. The armored units moved along a narrow road between the Etang de Parroy lake and the canal during the night.

At 08,00 Uhr on 27 September a diversionary force drove from Coincourt and Moncourt against the 10th AIB holding the sector from Hill 265 behind Bezange-la-Petite at the point of the new MLR back southwest to Rechicourt, CCB now holding the southern parts of the 4th AD salient. This was Nahkampf, close combat—the *pow! pow! bling!* of the M1 Garand clip and chatter of the Thompson submachine gun, the *crack!* of the Gewehr 98k and *brrrp!* of the MPi 40. American 1st Lt. James Fields, though shot through the face, nonetheless rallied his platoon on Hill 265, actions for which he later received the Congressional Medal of Honor.

On the right flank Pz.Gren.Rgt.110 fought into Xanrey toward Juvrecourt, which was held by CCA's 53rd armored infantry. At 10,00 the larger panzer force advanced against the camelback Hills 293 and 318 toward Arracourt itself against the 51st AIB, which had relieved the 320th Infantry Regiment. But there was no Luftwaffe, and six battalions of American field artillery smashed into the force, stopping it around Fourasse Farm west of Bures. That night Wietersheim transferred Pz.G.R.110 around from the north to the south flank.

Simultaneously, north of the Seille Knobelsdorff had Priess's XIII.SS Korps attack in conjunction with 5. Pz.Armee on the 27th. II.Btl./ Inf.Rgt.1127 of Generalmajor von Mühlen's 559. Volksgrenadierdivision, spearheaded by Oberst Bäke's Pz.Brig.106, struck along the Chambrey-Pettoncourt road, achieving surprise.[13] They fought their way into Pettoncourt where the MSR of Maj. Gen. Paul Baade's 35th "Santa Fe" Infantry Division crossed the Seille, with the objective of Moncel on the Nancy-Dieuze Rollbahn.

The attack struck the right flank of Baade's 137th Infantry Regiment, but reinforcements from the 320th Infantry in reserve repelled the thrust. Mühlen's 559., reinforced by Volksgrenadierregiment 59 of the 19.V.G.D., also attacked across the gap from the Forêt d'Amelécourt by Château-Salins and drove the 35th Division back into the Forêt de Gremecey. Baade committed his routinely attached 737th Tank Battalion and 654th TD Battalion, though the narrow trails through the dense woods limited their effectiveness. On the 28th the Germans fought through Pettoncourt again. Ami artillery and air attacks blunted a further advance, though fierce hand-to-hand combat ensued in the forest itself.

On that 28 September Wietersheim's panzers and panzergrenadiers fought onto the dominating Hill 318 on his southern flank but the 51st AIB was stubborn, and a bitter battle surged back and forth over the crest. The fighting continued through the night and into the next day, and Hptm. Johannes Schneider's II.Btl./Pz.G.R.110 took Hill 293 and even penetrated the Bois du Bénamont south of Arracourt. But a tank platoon of M4s from 8th Tank Battalion got to the top of Hill 318, and as the morning fog burned off, the P-47 Jabos of Brig. Gen. O. P. Weyland's XIX TAC joined with accurate artillery fire to break the German force.

Strafed by the fighter-bombers, pounded by the ear-shattering artillery explosions, and lashed by direct tank and infantry fire, eighteen panzers and several half-tracks were smashed and the German grenadiers streamed back in retreat. They were rallied finally east of Parroy by General von Wietersheim himself. As Oberst von Mellenthin, Balck's chief of staff, had observed, "it was clear that American air power put our panzers at a hopeless disadvantage, and that the normal principles of armored warfare did not apply in this theater," something von Wietersheim had tried to argue, in vain. After the war, General von Wietersheim said to William Molla, at the time a captain, assistant S-3, 101st Infantry Regiment, 26th Infantry Division, "Proper employment of a panzer division in mass tank attack was no longer possible because of American air and artillery, especially because of your spotter planes. You could mass tanks and we couldn't."[14]

Elsewhere along the American perimeter, more localized but intense attacks and counterattacks continued. Oberstlt. Rupprecht's Pz.Gren.111 battalions stretched from Vic-sur-Seille through Bezange-la-Petite to Rechicourt. Lt. von Eggeling's 3.Kp./15 with five or six Panthers fought on Hill 265, "Dreifinger-Wäldchen" (three-fingered woodlot). His friend and former neighbor Hptm. Graf von Pfeil und

Klein Ellguth and two panzergrenadiers would creep through the oak brush of the hill to find a position where a Panther might fire on an exposed Ami tank. Then von Eggeling, on foot, would lead one of the Panthers into a firing position covered by the noise and machine-gun fire of the other Panthers. He claimed "quite a few Shermans," but lost three Panthers to the US artillery, and finally Hill 265 had to be abandoned.

Von Eggeling also lost a Richtschütze to a shell fragment while urinating outside the panzer, something strictly forbidden in action; shell casings were the "chamber pots." Hauptmann Pfeil then learned his parents had been imprisoned by the Gestapo and, because he knew his association with some of the 20 July conspirators would implicate him, he walked openly toward the US lines and was shot dead. "You see," said von Eggeling, "that besides the terror of the war we sometimes had to suffer the terror of the Nazi-regime."[15]

On 29 September Balck visited von Rundstedt's headquarters at Bad Kreuznach and told the OB West he still intended to restore the defense line of the Moselle, but demanded significant reinforcements. Although the Allied airborne operation had failed to cross the lower Rhine, the British 2 Army was pressing 15. Armee in the Netherlands and the US First Army was engaged in the struggle for Aachen, and Rundstedt had few reserves to give Heeresgruppe G. Balck had to go over to the defensive, the Elfte's HKL stabilized from Moyenvic on the Seille down through Bezange-la-Petite and the small forest west of Moncourt to the Etang de Parroy on the Marne-Rhin Canal.

North of the Seille Priess's XIII.SS-Korps lost Pz.Brig.106 FHH and the assault guns of Pz. Abt.103 of 3.Pz.Gren.Div., transferred down to Belfort by E-Transport. But Priess did receive reinforcements: Füsilier Btl.115 of 15.Pz.Gren.Div. and Volksgrenadierregiment 73 of Oberst Karl Britzelmayr's 19.V.G.D., sent down from Thionville where Patton's XX Corps remained stymied by the forts around Metz. With these forces strengthening Mühlen's 559.V.G.D., on 30 September Priess assaulted the 35th Division in the Forêt de Gremecey, first against the 134th Infantry Regiment on the left, and then spreading against the 137th on the right as well. General Baade was hard-pressed, and his battalions in the woods were pushed back.

XII Corps commander Maj. Gen. Manton Eddy had no confidence in his infantry commanders. Baade of the 35th was "quiet and almost timid," he confided to his diary, and Maj. Gen. Horace McBride of the 80th was "convinced his division is whipped."[16] In a commanders' conference Eddy finally ordered General Baade's 35th Infantry Division to abandon the Forêt de Gremecey and retreat behind the Seille, alerting the 4th Armored to withdraw as well. Baade must have wondered why the 6th Armored Division's Combat Command B couldn't be employed to restore the situation, as Maj. Gen. Robert Grow's 6th AD was in XII Corps reserve.

As soon as he learned of Eddy's retreat order, Patton countermanded it, and indeed ordered Grow's 6th Armored combat commands up to counterattack and salvage the 35th Infantry Division position. CCB was left as a link to the 80th Division pressing against Löhr's 553.V.G.D., but the other two combat commands were to mount a pincers attack around the German forces in the Forêt de Gremecey. Rather than become entangled in the forest itself, the armor was to swing over the open terrain where tanks operated best, and good observation meant effective artillery support.

On 1 October, though rain prevented air support, CCA bridged Osson Creek and swept through Jallaucourt to the Lemoncourt-Fresnes ridge behind Priess's forces, while CCR to the south drove through Pettoncourt along the Seille to Chambrey.[17] With the threat of encirclement, and under Balck's orders to assume the defensive, Priess's forces abandoned the forest and retreated back to the Forêt d'Amelécourt and Château-Salins to establish the HKL. If Balck had not been able to restore the line of the Moselle, the German attacks had effectively blocked Patton's Third Army, and stabilized the front in Lorraine for the next month.

TWENTY-SEVEN

Linear Defense in Lorraine

BY OCTOBER 1944 STALEMATE PREDOMINATED IN THE WEST, for over a month. If Hitler's demands for a major counteroffensive in Lorraine had been unrealistic and had been frustrated, nonetheless his insistence on defending and/or destroying the coastal ports while his armies rallied along—or in Lorraine, in advance of—the German frontier resulted in the Allied armies coming to a halt due to lack of supplies, especially POL.

On 23 September, with the realization that the airborne operation would end short of the lower Rhine, Eisenhower had ordered his armies to go over to the defensive until a logistical buildup allowed a renewed advance, with only limited operations permitted. In the north Montgomery was to focus on opening the huge port of Antwerp. It was 1 Canadian Army that had to fight across the flooded polder land of the South Beveland peninsula and Walcheren Island to clear the 90-kilometer (56-mile) maritime approaches against Gen.d.Inf. Gustav von Zangen's 15. Armee. Antwerp had been captured with its facilities intact on 4 September, but it was not until 28 November that the first ship negotiated the West Scheldt estuary.

While Student's 1. Fallschirmarmee resisted 2 British Army's push toward the Maas (Meuse), Gen.d.Pz.Tr. Erich Brandenberger's 7. Armee blocked access to the Köln Plain. The US First Army, joined by Ninth Army in October, struggled through the double belt of Westwall fortifications around Aachen. On 23 October Manteuffel's 5. Panzerarmee headquarters from Lorraine took over the Aachen sector. In Lorraine the Third Army had to go onto the defensive as well, much to Patton's exasperation. The 7th Armored Division was transferred north to Montgomery on 8 October, and on 29 September XV Corps had been transferred to Devers's 6th Army Group, as those armies could be supplied through Marseille.

Von Knobelsdorff, with his 1. Armee stretched from Luxembourg to the Seille River, and then south to Baccarat and the Vosges after 5. Pz.Armee went north, was fortunate that Patton chose to concentrate on reducing the forts of Metz west of the Moselle with his three XX Corps divisions. Why the armor commander did not bypass the formidable fortifications has remained a source of debate. Artillery, armor, air strikes and even napalm had little effect and they cost the infantry heavy casualties.

Metz was defended by Division Nummer 462, an ad hoc formation commanded by Generalleutnant Walter Krause, but included able men from the Fahnenjunkerschule and Unterführerschule, as well as a Waffen-SS Nachrichtenschule (Signals School). On its left was 17.SS-Panzergrenadierdivision Götz von Berlichingen under SS Standartenführer Thomas Müller. Fort Driant did not fall until 6 December and Fort Jeanne d'Arc not until 13 December.

In Patton's XII Corps sector the 80th Infantry Division, working with the 6th Armored Division, the "Super Sixth," pushed its way to the Seille River, contested by elements of 3.Pz.Gren.Div. under Generalmajor Hans Hecker and 553.Volksgrenadierdivision under Oberst Erich Löhr, which had withdrawn from the Nancy Kessel. Gen.Maj. Kurt Freiherr von Mühlen's 559.V.G.D. was entrenched in the Forêt d'Amelécourt and Château-Salins across from Baade's 35th Infantry Division, and Wietersheim's 11.Panzer-Division was positioned from the Seille to the Marne-Rhin Canal opposite Wood's 4th Armored Division around Arracourt. The Elfte's Hauptkampflinie was a concave line 18 kilometers (11 miles) long: Moyenvic–Bezange la Petite–Moncourt–Etang de Parroy. An engineer company outposted Bures. The Division Gefechtsstand was at the farm 2.5 kilometers southwest of Gelucourt. Aggressive patrols and raids sometimes flared into small engagements.

The battalion formed from the Ersatzbataillon was now designated as III.Btl./ Pz.Gren.Rgt.110 under Major Julius Dalhaus, or the Einsatz Bataillon (Action Battalion).[1] With Pz.Gren.Rgt.110 on the right and Pz.G.R.111 on the left, Pz.Aufkl.Abt.11 and one battalion from each regiment was held back as a counterattack reserve. Pz.Pi.Btl.209 was also in the line, on the far left. By 3 October Pz.Brig.111 was absorbed into the 11.Pz.Div. raising the strength to sixty panzers, and Pz.Brig.113 was incorporated into Rodt's 15.Pz.Gren.Div. resisting the 79th Infantry Division in the Forêt de Parroy south of the canal.

But on that same 3 October Pz.G.R.111 under Oberstlt. Werner von Rupprecht and ten to twelve Panzer IVs were detached to Lüttwitz's XXXXVII. Panzerkorps fronting St. Die on the upper Meurthe in the foothills of the Vosges. Of Feuchtinger's 21.Pz.Div. there, Pz.Gren.Rgt.s 125 and 192 were at 50 percent strength, though Pz.Rgt.22 had only nine panzers operational. It was holding off the French armor of 2ème DB along the Mortagne east of Rambervillers. The 16. Infanterie-Division (redesignated 16.V.G.D. 9 October) under Generalleutnant Ernst Häckel, however, was being hard-pressed by the US 45th Infantry Division. Supplied through Marseille, Devers's US Seventh and the French 1ère Armée were able to keep advancing against Wiese's 19. Armee and Lüttwitz's corps.

Two regiments of Maj. Gen. Eagles's 45th Division were converging through the wooded hills of the Forêt de Mortagne along the west bank of the upper Mortagne to take Brouvelieures. Rupprecht's Gespensters moved up from St. Die and on 6 October the panzers and panzergrenadiers caught the Amis by surprise along the forest trails. They had not expected armor in the dark woods. The Pz.Gren.Rgt.111 Kampfgruppe was withdrawn the next night, having stalled the 45th Division's advance nearly a week. The action, just like Kampfgruppe Hammon's presence in the Belfort area, hinted that more of the "Ghost Division," as it was called by the Amis, might be lurking nearby.[2]

For the rest of the division the detachments meant that all three battalions of Hax's Pz.Gren.Rgt.110 had to defend the HKL, along with Bödicker's Pz.Pionier Btl.209, and even the division Begleitkompanie. The only reserve was Pz.A.A.11 and two to three panzers positioned at points behind the battalions, giving psychological as well as physical support. The reconnaissance battalion was now commanded by Major Graf von Pfeil. He had been adjutant to Generaloberst Friedrich Fromm of the Reserve Army, implicated in the 20 July assassination plot against Hitler (and subsequently executed). Lt. Werner Strietzel, commanding 2.Kp., understood that von Pfeil, because of that association, was "punished" by being reassigned to a combat unit.[3]

By doctrine and by organization and equipment armored units were not well suited for position defense, but there was no alternative. Pz.-Rgt.15 reserves were under forest cover, one Eingreifgruppe (counterattack group) 2 kilometers south of Blanche Eglise, a second group 3 kilometers southwest of Ommeray. The HKL could only be held as a series of strongpoints, using the stone farm buildings. The strongpoints covered the gaps by fire, and were linked by patrols at night, giving a semblance of a defense in depth. As practiced in Russia, the front lines were thinned out as Vorposten. In addition, some positions after the fighting were on exposed forward slopes.

Wietersheim wanted to pull these back to more defensible reverse-slope terrain, but orders were to hold all ground won. The positions were strengthened by minefields, but they couldn't be supplied during daytimes.

The artillery batteries were deployed so that all sectors had some artillery support. But they were too weak and short of shells to engage the American artillery in duels, and had to prepare alternate firing positions, well camouflaged. According to the 1944 K.St.N., the panzer artillery regiment had three battalions: Hauptmann Günther Rahm's I. Abteilung (self-propelled) mixed, authorized with two light batteries of six Wespen (10,5cm) each and a schwere (medium) battery of six Hummeln (15cm); Hptm. Hoffmann's II.Abt. (half-track-towed) with three light batteries of four 10,5cm howitzers each, and Hptm. Walter Schaefer-Kehnert's III.Abt. (towed) with three batteries of four 15cm howitzers each.

Because the battalions were understrength and widely dispersed, explained Rolf Wandhoff, Oberlt. and adjutant of Pz.A.R.119, they were mixed for greater flexibility so each battalion included a 15cm battery. While I.Abt. still had the Selbstfahrlafette (Battr. Nr. 1–3), II.Abt. traded Nr.5 Battr. to III.Abt. for Nr.9, thus having Battr. 4, 6, and 9 (15cm). Schaefer-Kehnert's III.Abt. had Nr.5 Battr. with 10,5cm Haubitze (12 kilometers range), Nr.7 with 10cm Kanone (20 kilometers), Nr.8 with 15cm Haubitze (15 kilometers), and Nr.10 with six 12cm Russian mortars (6 kilometers), though ammunition resupply was a problem. As battalion commander he preferred his captured American jeep, "kleine Willy" ("Little Willy") from the Willys Overland builder's plate. It was light, maneuverable, easy to cover with a camouflage net, and it was more powerful than the VW-Kübelwagen, especially with its four-wheel drive.[4]

Menzel's 8,8cm guns were positioned for antiaircraft defense of the artillery positions and panzer assembly areas and maintenance shop areas, yet also for direct fire along avenues of armor approach. The division command post was transferred back to Alteville, 6 kilometers southeast of Dieuze. Communications were by radio, but in a static situation telephone wire was laid. This was more secure, and if well-buried from artillery fire, more reliable.

Although stronger, Wood's 4th Armored Division, like the 11.Pz.Div., was not well suited for defense and had even less experience in this. Of the battles around Arracourt Nat Frankel of C Co/8th Tank battalion, said, "I remember a kind of all-pervasive despair as we fought for that village." Joe Kmetz of A Co/10th Armored Infantry Battalion later wrote that his Able Company "lost half the company on Hill 265 as we were not accustomed to HOLDING . . . Hill 265 was the first holding action for us—a disaster."[5]

On 7 October with heavy fighting in the Forêt de Parroy, Pz.A.A.11, the only reserve, was detached south with some panzers to strengthen 15.Pz.Gren. Div., while 119. artillery fired from north of the canal. In return a Festungs MG Bataillon (fortress machine gun battalion) was attached to the Elfte. These had some forty-eight 2cm flak guns, but the guns were Army, not Luftwaffe, and intended for ground combat. The crews were of older age classes, and the batteries were deployed behind Pz.Pi.Btl.209 until they got combat experience.

For several nights engine sounds and vehicle movement in the American lines portended a possible attack. Hptm. Johannes Schneider had his II.Btl./110 panzergrenadiers near Bezange la Petite on alert. He had 5., 6, and 7. Kp. on line with the heavy machine guns and Granatwerfers of 8.Kp. Lt. Rudolph had his platoon of three Panzer IVs nearby. Schneider had his Bataillonsgefechtsstand in the basement of a farm on the northwest edge of the village.

When two young GIs wandered into Schneider's front lines, carrying mess kits and apparently lost, it was learned that the new US 26th Infantry Division was relieving the 4th Armored Division. This was the Massachusetts National Guard "Yankee" Division, the "YD," commanded by Maj. Gen. Willard Paul. It effected the relief of Wood's 4th AD during 7–12 October, though the 4th's veteran artillery and tank destroyer battalions remained to support them. The 704th TD Battalion in particular had learned indirect-fire techniques with their elevation quadrants and azimuth indicators in addition to antitank direct fire. The M18s tied into the 26th Division artillery fire-direction centers, their 76mm guns having a range of 13,000 meters (14,000 yards), greater than the 105mm howitzers' 11,000 meters (12,500 yards).[6]

On 10 October Pz.Gren.Rgt.111 returned to the division, but two days later the 11. Panzer was mandated to take over the sector including the Luneville–Sarrebourg railroad line and much of 111. was kept south of the canal. There were stiff local actions, especially around the Moncourt woods, Coincourt, and Bezange la Petite. On the 12th there was increased artillery and mortar fire on Hill 265, and in the afternoon Amerikaner infantry attacked and forced 5. Kompanie out of their Schützengraben. During the night Schneider coordinated a counterattack force and at first light, with Lt. Rudolph's three Panzerwagens, regained the hill. One panzer crested the ridge but was knocked out by an AT gun. The crew escaped, and the next night the I-Staffel were able to attach tow cables and retrieve the damaged panzer.[7]

On higher orders, a Grosskampfstellung (main battle position) system was to be followed. As earlier, to reduce the effects of enemy artillery fire, the HKL would only be held by one-third of the defending unit, the other two-thirds positioned back 1,000–2,000 meters in strongpoints, to which the front line troops could withdraw. But this was dependent upon the strength of the unit, and in the case of Hax's Pz.G.R.110, it had a fighting strength of about 600 men and a sector 9–10 kilometers wide; if one-third of the Landsers were in the front line, 200, this meant only 20 men per kilometer! In some cases companies fell to 20 men total. With a couple of panzers behind the HKL, camouflaged in defilade positions but also having alternate positions, engine sounds and sometimes the squealing of tracks, magnified at night, perhaps deterred American patrols or probes.[8]

Still, during quiet times, some got a chance to play the card game Skat, catch up on the mail from the Heimat, and read about their division's exploits in the newspapers. The reports said their 11. Panzer-Division had "stood well the test in attack and in defense" (*Mülhauser Tagblatt*, 5 September 1944), and noted how under their "exceptional commander, Schwertträger Generalleutnant von Wietersheim" the "Gespensterdivision . . . masterly fulfilled their difficult task" in fending off the enemy flanking attempts in the Rhônetal (*Die Wacht*, 7 September 1944).[9]

Some in rest areas or on leave might see films with actresses Marika Rökk or Zarah Leander, or actor Heinz Rühmann (in *Quax the Crash Pilot*), or the antics of "*Münchhausen*." On radio there was the ever-popular "Wunschkonzert" (request concert) on Sunday evenings with music ("Erika"), greetings between Landsers and their families, and even birth announcements for soldiers in the field.[10]

During this static defense, the company mess Lastwagen came up at dusk towing the "Gulaschkanone," the field kitchen trailer with its distinctive stovepipe, to deliver hot meals. The company Kettenkrad (halftrack motorcycle), also brought up hot rations, as well as post, ammunition, and other supplies in a small trailer, and evacuated wounded or sick, churning along small, muddy trails trucks couldn't negotiate, and less subject to American harassing and interdiction (H&I) artillery fire.

The mess teams would distribute rations for the next day and depart before dawn. Hot Wurst and Kaffee were always morale-boosters, offsetting the Kommisbrot hard biscuit that was eaten only after being softened in coffee containers. This was in the Eiserne Portion (iron rations) with a Schokakola energy tin, which also contained a tin of cold meat.[11] Army rations were supplemented by local produce, and Hptm. Schaefer-Kehnert of III.Abt./119 wrote his mother that he found himself the "division agriculturist," rounding up hogs and cattle, and that his command post looked like a stockyard.[12] Officers ate with their men, sharing the discomfort of the front lines, unconsciously manifesting that indefinable blend of quiet authority, competence, and camaraderie of true leadership. The panzers were kept topped off with fuel, though the crews sometimes had to lug 20-liter (5-gallon) fuel cans up to the forward positions.

The crews slept in or under their panzers, with two of the five-man Besatzung on watch in two- or three-hour shifts, one manning the turret machine gun (and radio through his earphones), the other often on the ground. Applying lessons learned in Russia, the accompanying panzergrenadiers often slept in their Schlafsack in a shallow pit, over which the panzer drove, straddling it, giving protection from the pervasive artillery fire and the elements, and warmth in colder weather. It was a good precaution. Maj. Ray Mason, S-3 (operations) of the US 4th Armored's 22nd Armored Field Artillery, for example, said the battalion would fire concentrations 45 meters (50 yards) in from a wood line, creating deadly tree bursts.

Gefreiter Martin Lange of the Panther battalion I-Gruppe (Instandsetzungsgruppe, maintenance group) did most of his work at night. Canvas tarpaulins were strung for concealment, so lights and welding equipment could be used. Maintenance sections were located in patches of woods, hidden from spotter planes and fighter bombers, with all signs of tread marks leading into the area carefully swept away. One time a headquarters vehicle openly drove into a wood line—*Idiot!*—followed by several Ami artillery concentrations.[13]

South of the Marne-Rhin Canal on 29 September Balck had shifted 5. Panzerarmee's responsibility south of Rambervillers under Lüttwitz's XXXXVII.

Pz.Korps, while Krüger's LVIII. Pz.K. now included the Forêt de Parroy, both sectors protecting the approach to the Saverne Gap. As the US 79th Infantry Division slugged ahead through the dense forest against Pz.Gren.Rgts.104 and 115 of 15.Pz.Gren. Div., Krüger committed two battalions of Pz. G.R.2113 of Panzerbrigade 113. The Elfte's Pz.Aufklärungsabteilung 11 had been committed as well, the reconnaissance battalion's Spähwagen and Halbketten driving the 315th Infantry Regiment back from the Fait and Bossupre crossroads on 7 October. The American artillery continued to give the 79th Division advance enough power to press ahead, and on 9 October Krüger requested, and received, permission to finally withdraw from the stubbornly contested Forêt de Parroy.

East of the forest in more open terrain, the 79th Division captured Embermenil on the 13th, though elements of the 11. Panzer (of A.A.11, Pz.Pi.Btl.209, and Pz.G.r.111, with some panzers) contested Leintrey south of the Sarrebourg railroad line and mounted Gegenangriffe from Remoncourt to the north. The US XV Corps then paused, as it had to return some artillery and other supporting battalions to Third Army, and was anticipating reinforcement with the new 44th Infantry Division (arriving after 17 October).

During the nights 15–17 October the 553.V.G.D., now commanded by Generalmajor Hans Bruhn (Oberst Erich Löhr had been court-martialed for his "failure" in the Nancy Kessel) came south and replaced 15.Pz.Gren.Div. Much weakened, it was reinforced with some fortress battalions. At the same time Lüttwitz's XXXXVII. Pz.K. headquarters was transferred to 5. Pz.Armee now in H.Gr. B (17 October), replaced by LXXXIX. A.K. under Genlt. Werner von und zu Gilsa. The sector south of the Vezouze was in Wiese's 19. Armee.[14]

On 22 October American troops supported by tank destroyers attacked the Elfte's lines between Bezange-la-Petite and the woods southwest of Moncourt after a heavy artillery bombardment. The attack was resisted by Pz.Gren.Rgt.110 and the Division Begleitkompanie. The Amis were generally unsuccessful, but gained a foothold in the Moncourt woods. These were three companies of the 104th Regiment of the 26th YD supported by two companies of the 704th TD Battalion. The GIs counted fourteen pillboxes in the woods and along the edge of the town. There were mines, booby traps, and shelters, some 4 meters (12 feet) deep. The Gespensters held the eastern part of the woods but it was a much-exposed section of the HKL, especially as the Forêt de Parroy had been evacuated on the 9th. South of the canal Pz.G.R.111 had received another Festung MG Btl. to stiffen resistance.[15]

During the some four weeks of static defense, despite the occasional clashes and casualties from mortar and artillery fire, a certain rapport apparently developed between the antagonists in the Arracourt sector. After Hauptmann Schneider admonished two young Landsers who had fallen asleep in the Vorposten on the night of 10 October, they deserted the next night to the YD, probably fearing harsh punishment (though Schneider knew he needed all the men he had). From them Capt. Bill Molla, assistant S-3 of the 101st Infantry, learned Schneider's name. Molla developed great respect for the Gespensters and after the war facilitated contacts between the former enemies. (In one example of this mutual respect, after recovering the body of an American first lieutenant in front of Bezange-la-Petite, Schneider's men buried him, marking the position of the grave. He subsequently could be identified as Lt. Joseph Clampett.)

After the 22nd October fighting on Hill 265, Leutnant Schwarze, V.B. of Pz.Art.Rgt.119, contacted Schneider on the field telephone. "Hauptmann, on 265 your soldiers are standing together with American soldiers, are talking and smoking cigarettes!" The battalion commander immediately ordered an increased alert and ran to Hill 265 with his adjutant, Leutnant Hoffmann, and two orderlies. Demanding to know who was responsible, he was told a Sani, hearing loud cries for help, left his trench waving his Red Cross flag and had bandaged about five soldiers with throat and head wounds and had led them back. The Yanks then also recovered some of their wounded.

Another soldier said an American officer asked him to send a "Parlamentär" (officer bearing a white flag of truce). Schneider declined, saying the Americans could request a truce, but at 11,00 hours he would consider himself at war again. Subsequently American artillery pounded the hill, but no attack followed. Schneider then determined to man his main HKL on the reverse slope, and that night had engineers mine the forward trench with antipersonnel mines and Teller antitank mines in the open areas.

Photographs of Lt. Karl "Kalle" Zindler of 2./15 with American Gefangene at this time, however, do not seem to reflect hostility.

On the southern flank near the canal was the 2nd Cavalry Group, Mechanized, nicknamed "Patton's Ghosts." The regiment-sized unit was composed of the battalion-sized 2nd and 42nd Cavalry Reconnaissance Squadrons, Mechanized, commanded by Col. C. Hanson Reed, wounded at Luneville and returned to action. After the war Colonel Reed corresponded many times with General von Wietersheim of 11. Panzer, and as he later wrote Lt. Gen Manton Eddy of XII Corps, "Despite several holes they left in my hide and some bad drillings they gave us, evened up, I reckon, by some we gave them, I always had the deepest respect and admiration for them." He continued: "I wonder if you know, we had a working arrangement, even during combat to trade our wounded prisoners back and forth. Von Wietersheim never kept any of our badly wounded and always let me have them back under a white flag."[16]

Over three nights, 26 to 28 October, the Elften were relieved by 361. Volksgrenadierdivision commanded by Oberst Alfred Philippi. It had the reduced organization of two battalions in each of its three regiments, but it had a battery of Panzerjäger 38(t) Hetzer assault guns (7,5cm Pak 39 L/48) and a battery of 7,5cm Pak 40, and while the 952. and 953.V.G. Regiments manned the HKL, Philippi could have his Rgt.951 in reserve. Artillerieregiment 361 was horse-drawn; curiously, this was not a disadvantage as it moved down from north Holland because it had no prime movers needing the limited gasoline. It also had its Füsilier (bicycle) Kompanie, a 3,7cm flak battery, and engineers. Its personnel were generally untrained, coming from the Kriegsmarine, Luftwaffe, and other sources. Some Gespenster panzergrenadiers and elements of Pz.Art.Rgt.119 remained to support the new division.

On 28 October Krüger's LVIII. Pz.K. was ordered north, whereupon von Gilsa's LXXXIX. Korps was put under von Knobelsdorff's 1. Armee. LXIV. A.K. in turn took over the southern sectors of LXXXIX. A.K., which concentrated against the Arracourt sector between the Seille and the Marne-Rhin Canal. On 20 October two squadrons of American P-47s had breached the Etang de Lindre dam south of Dieuze with 1,000-pound bombs. This meant waters could not be released along the Seille and cut off any American forces crossing to the north bank.

By the end of the month the German HKL was stabilized: 361.V.G.D. under LXXXIX. A.K. was positioned from the Marne-Rhin Canal up to Moyenvic on the Seille opposite the 26th Infantry Division; then Priess's XIII.SS-Armeekorps controlled Mühlen's 559.V.G.D. positioned from that point north including Château-Salins to Malaucourt along Osson Creek opposite the 35th Infantry Division; the weak 48. Infanterie-Division commanded by Generalleutnant Karl Casper, which had replaced the 553.V.G.D., along the middle Seille fronting the high Côte de Delme (Delme Ridge) opposite the 80th Division; and 17.SS-Pz.Gren.Div. now under SS Brigadeführer und Generalmajor der Waffen-SS Werner Ostendorff north along the lower Seille to the LXXXII. A.K. under Gen.d.Inf. Walter Hörnlein, which held the line of the Moselle and Metz against Patton's XX Corps commanded by Maj. Gen. Walton Walker. Eddy's XII Corps' two armored divisions, the 4th and 6th, were in reserve.

Balck and Knobelsdorff hoped to bring up Feuchtinger's 21.Panzer-Division from 19. Armee, but Wiese still needed it against the US Seventh Army. Thus Wietersheim's 11.Pz.-Div. was the only operational reserve for Heeresgruppe G west of St. Avold. When it was relieved by 361.V.G.D. the Elfte moved in stages to assembly areas 20 kilometers (12 miles) east of Metz for Auffrischung, and as a reserve astride the axis Metz–St. Avold–Saarbrücken and the Saar industrial region of the German Rheinpfalz (Rhine-Palatinate). The Division Gefechtsstand opened on 29 October at Eltwingen (Elvange) northwest of Falkenberg (Faulquemont).

After a meeting of company commanders on 2 November Hauptmann Schneider collapsed unconscious from exhaustion. He awoke the next morning to find his concerned division commander sitting by his side. Schneider insisted he not be medically evacuated, as his battalion was now in a rest area. The general agreed, but ordered the adjutant to mention in his daily morning report how many hours Schneider had slept during the night. "Yes, General von Wietersheim was 'like a father' with his soldiers!" Schneider recalled. It was during this time that former division commander Hermann Balck, now Heeresgruppe G commander and newly promoted as General der Panzertruppen, came down to the division at Eltwingen. He reviewed some of the Panzersoldaten of 2./15 and then sponsored a pleasant evening visiting with some 100 of his former Gespenster Kameraden of the fighting in Russia in 1942–43. The morale of any military unit is highly dependent on sensing the concern commanders have for the welfare of their men.[17]

A few Elften received leave, and others received additional training. Maj. Karl Thieme, who had already been awarded the Ritterkreuz on 30 October 1943 as commander I.Btl./Pz.Gren.Rgt.110 and now was awarded the Eichenlaub on 23 October 1944 while he commanded Pz.G.R.111, went back for regimental command Lehrgang, and would return as an Oberstleutnant to command his cherished Panzergrenadier-Regiment 110. "For me a dream come true!" he later said.[18] The 11. Panzer received replacements while in bivouac and the armored strength was brought up to forty Panthers and twenty Panzer IVs in Oberstlt. Stenkhoff's Pz.Rgt.15 (of 103 authorized), and ten Jagdpanzer IV turretless assault guns in Major Kessler's Pz.Jäger Abteilung 61 (of thirty-one authorized).[19] The Elfte's positioning was to anticipate a Third Army XX Corps attack from either Thionville or the Pont-à-Mousson area, though also the Third Army XII Corps sector was a concern. The Delme Ridge and then the Nied River fronting Faulquemont were the major first and second defense lines, and minefields and trenches were being constructed.

Wietersheim met with his unit commanders to discuss tactics against Patton's next offensive, expected in November, toward the Saar industrial basin through the traditional "Lorraine Gateway." They knew that American artillery and airpower, even with the anticipated poorer weather, made large-scale armored operations impractical, and Balck's headquarters now acknowledged this. For the infantry manning the HKL, the principles of elastic defense and defense in depth were invoked, despite OKW's (Hitler's) order to hold every meter of ground. Again, Vorposten 2 or 3 kilometers forward of the HKL would withdraw when an attack appeared imminent. Night-fighting was emphasized and immediate sharp, local counterattacks would be mounted. Funkverbindung, radio communications, would be crucial.

For the panzer units the Panzerkampftrupps, panzer battle teams of mixed companies of a panzer platoon (usually two to three panzers) and two panzergrenadier platoons each, would fight these actions, as Wietersheim had planned in southern France. As the lone panzer division for 1. Armee's front, some 135 kilometers (85 miles) long, even battalion-sized Kampfgruppen would have to be scattered to various threatened locations. "Speed, movement, and surprise," recorded Major Thieme, "should offset the numerical and materiel superiority of the enemy." Aggressive company-grade officers would be vital.[20]

Small sections of even one panzer, a half-track, and an artillery forward observer would by their sudden presence and fire magnify their small numbers, encouraging their own infantry and making the advancing Americans more cautious. These tactics did not conform to the principles of mass and concentration, but they seemed the only practical way to slow a powerful American advance along a very broad front. Other panzer forces were moving north, as the continuing American First Army drive toward Aachen threatened to advance through the Westwall, across the Roer River, and onto the Köln Plain and against the Ruhr industrial heartland.

In other theaters of war the Axis forces were being defeated. In the Pacific the Japanese navy had been crippled in the Philippine Sea and American forces were converging on the Philippines, and the British were advancing in Burma. On the Ostfront the Russian armies cut off H.Gr. Nord in Kurland, were advancing on Budapest from the Balkans, and were building up to assault across the Vistula.

In the west, however, German resistance had become firmer. In Italy Luftwaffe Generalfeldmarschall Albert Kesselring, as Oberbefehlshaber Süd, was stalling the British and Americans along the Gothic Line with Heeresgruppe C. On the Westfront von Zangen's 15. Armee was bitterly resisting the 1 Canadian Army's struggle to clear the flooded approaches to Antwerp, and Student's 1. Fallschirm-Armee was stopping the 2 British Army in the Peel marshes west of the Maas. As Hodges's US First Army divisions worked through the Westwall belt of bunkers around Aachen, they encountered stiff resistance. While American artillery and airpower in particular did much to blunt the counterattacks, these served warning that the German forces had recovered.

Farther south Erich Brandenberger's 7. Armee slowed the push into the dark, forbidding fir forest of the Hürtgenwald. The American objective was the crossroads at Schmidt, and protection of the advance on Aachen. It would not be generally recognized by the Americans until the end of November that the real significance of the Hürtgen Forest was the seven flood-control dams including the Urft and the Schwammenauel Dams. These controlled the Roer River athwart any advance eastward from Aachen into the Köln Plain. If any forces crossed the Roer and the river was then flooded, they might be stranded for some two weeks.

On 18 October Eisenhower met with his senior commanders at Brussels to review strategy. Though Antwerp was not yet opened, the logistical buildup of October would support a renewed offensive in early November. With the failure of the airborne operation at Arnhem Eisenhower reiterated his determination to advance on a broad front. Montgomery's 21 Army Group was to open Antwerp and push to the Maas. The new US Ninth Army headquarters under Lt. Gen. William Simpson was inserted between British 2 and US First Armies (to forestall Hodges's army ever coming under Montgomery's control). The primary effort would now be made by Bradley's 12th Army Group's three armies. Devers's 6th Army Group's push into the Vosges and to the Rhine was still subsidiary.

Bradley set a target date of 5 November for First and Ninth Armies' attack, and 10 November for an assault by Patton's Third. With continuing rain, however, Bradley wanted air force support and postponed the D-day (day of attack) until the 10th. But he agreed that restless Patton could begin sooner, regardless of the weather, no later than the 8th. On 21 October the ruined city of Aachen, capital and resting place of Emperor Karl der Grosse, capitulated, the first major German city to fall to the Allies.[21]

On 22 October the chiefs of staff of von Rundstedt's OB West and Model's Heeresgruppe B, General der Kavallerie Siegfried Westphal and Gen. der Infanterie Hans Krebs, were called to the Wolfschanze in east Prussia to learn of a plan, Die Wacht am Rhein—a defensive connotation as in the patriotic song of the 1840s, "The Watch on the Rhine"—for an Abwehrschlacht im Westen (defensive battle in the West). Sworn to secrecy, they then learned from Hitler himself it was, in fact, to be a major *offensive* by three armies of H.Gr. B mounted in the Ardennes to destroy the British and American armies north of the axis Bastogne–Brussels–Antwerp: Manteuffel's 5. Panzerarmee, Brandenberger's 7. Armee on the southern flank, and the Schwerpunkt to be with the new 6. Panzerarmee activated 14 September under SS-Obergruppenführer und Panzer-Generaloberst der Waffen-SS Josef "Sepp" Dietrich, a longtime favorite of Hitler's.

Hitler had broached the idea to Generaloberst Alfred Jodl, Chef des Wehrmachtführungsstabes im OKW by 16 September, but when the three army commanders met on 27 October, the ambitious plan was modified by von Rundstedt and Model to the destruction of the American forces in Belgium *east* of the Meuse, Unternehmen HERBSTNEBEL (Operation Autumn Fog). Hitler, however, insisted on Antwerp as the objective. Secrecy was paramount and exceedingly successful; few German commanders beyond those immediately involved, much less the Allies, learned of or even suspected the planned assault in the Ardennes. In H.Gr. G Chef des Stabes von Mellenthin said that only he and Balck were informed.[22] But first the armies of OB West had to be braced against the anticipated Allied November offensive.

With revised intelligence about the buildup in the American XII Corps area, and the apparent determination of Patton to concentrate XX Corps against Metz, rather than drive toward the Saar, on the night of 7 November the 11. Panzerdivision displaced down to north of Morhange behind the 48. Infanterie and the 559. and 361. Volksgrenadier-Divisionen. The Div.Gef.Std. relocated to Vintrange. Hitler himself added an additional force to 1. Armee, five artillery battalions of the 401. Volksartillerie-Korps that were detraining at St. Avold.

The Gespenster battle groups were dispatched to preselected assembly areas, from Delme to Dieuze. Terrain features were generally gently rolling farm country with stone villages and forests and hills. More significant were the Delme Ridge behind the Seille, sharply steep on the western side, and two long, narrow plateau spurs angling northeast; the Morhange plateau with the Forêt d'Amelécourt north of Château-Salins and the Petite Seille River; and the Dieuze plateau covered by the Forêt de Bride et de Koecking paralleling on the south side. Miserable in the continuing rain, the Landsers readied their weapons and sheltered in their muddy Schützengraben, and waited for the American assault.

CHAPTER TWENTY-EIGHT

Mobile Defense in Lorraine

AS RAIN POURED DOWN AT DAWN ON 8 NOVEMBER 1944, A thundering American artillery barrage erupted along the 50-kilometer (30-mile) front held by 48.Inf.Div. and 559. and 361.V.G.D.s of Knobelsdorff's 1. Armee in Lorraine. This was the beginning of Patton's Third Army offensive by Eddy's XII Corps. Walker's XX Corps around Metz was not involved. For three and a half hours seventeen battalions of heavy corps artillery bombarded the German lines, joined first by twenty battalions of divisional artillery, and then by the sharp crack of direct fire from 90mm antiaircraft artillery battalions, the 3-inch guns of tank destroyers, and the short 105mm howitzers of regimental cannon companies.

Rain had been coming down incessantly since the beginning of November, which at least grounded American air power; but attacking in the rain also meant the front-line Landsers were caught by surprise. Ready to attack any time after the 5th, General Eddy had urged another postponement because the rain meant no air support and turned the ground into a muddy morass, but Patton was adamant and would wait no longer.

On the front of Philippi's 361. Volksgrenadierdivision south of the Petite Seille to the Marne-Rhin Canal, the Americans attacked toward Dieuze as in September, past Bezange-la-Petite and Moncourt against V.G.Rgt.952. But this was only a feint. The major assaults drove across the Seille at Vic-sur-Seille and Moyenvic and began to ascend the dominating Côte St. Jean (Hill 310). But V.G.R.953 with Pionier Btl.361 held the crest, while flanking fire from Marsal on the left pinned the Amis down amid a murderous crossfire. Pi.Btl.559 from the adjacent division reinforced the defenders that night. V.G.R.951 held reserve positions.

The attack was mounted by Paul's 26th Yankee Infantry Division; the feint was made by its 328th Infantry Regiment, and the failed attack against Hill 310 by the 101st Infantry Regiment. "The Germans could see every blade of grass on the forward slope of Hill 310," said Captain Molla of the 101st. "They threw everything they had at us except the kitchen sink," said Pfc Bob Watson of George Company. "We lost a lot of men to the eighty-eights" (the generic GI term for deadly German

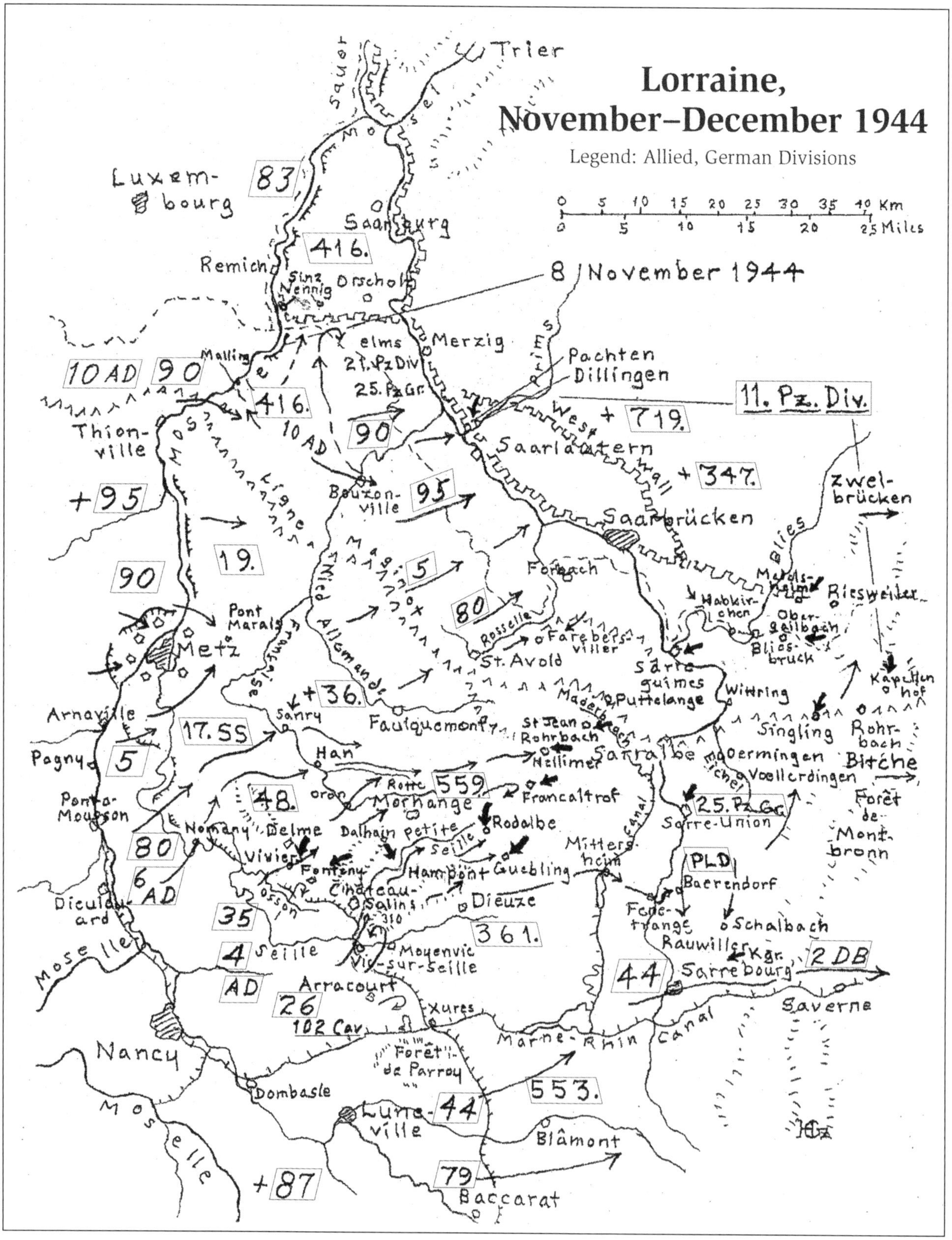
Lorraine,
November–December 1944
Legend: Allied, German Divisions
0 5 10 15 20 25 30 35 40 Km
0 5 10 15 20 25 Miles
8 November 1944
Trier
Luxembourg
Saarburg
Remich
Sinz
Nennig
Orscholz
Merzig
Pachten
Dillingen
11. Pz. Div.
Thionville
Bouzonville
Saarlautern
Saarbrücken
Zweibrücken
Forbach
Metz
Pont Marais
St. Avold
Farebersviller
Sarreguimes
Puttelange
Wittring
Faulquemont
Sanry
Han
Arnaville
Pagny
Pont-a-Mousson
Morhange
Rodalbe
Francaltrof
Hellimer
Sarralbe
Oermingen
Voellerdingen
Bitche
Sarre-Union
Delme
Nomeny
Vivier
Fonteny
Dalhain
Château-Salins
Hampont
Guebling
Dieuze
Mittersheim
Baerendorf
Fenetrange
Schalbach
Rauwiller
Sarrebourg
Saverne
Moyenvic
Vic-sur-Seille
Arracourt
Xures
Marne-Rhin Canal
Nancy
Dombasle
Lunéville
Forêt de Parroy
Blâmont
Baccarat
Forêt de Mont-bronn
Singling
Rohrbach
Kapellenhof
Rieswelier
Ober-Gailbach
Bliesbruck
Habkirchen
Medelsheim
Dieulouard
Moselle
Seille
Saar
Sauer
Mosel
Prims
Blies
Nied Française
Nied Allemande
Rosselle
West Wall
Ligne Maginot
Canal
83
416.
10 AD
90
416.
21. Pz Div
25. Pz Gr.
10 AD
90
+ 719.
+ 347.
+ 95
95
19.
90
5
80
+ 36.
17. SS
5
559
48.
80
6 AD
35
4 AD
361.
26
102 Cav.
44
25. Pz. Gr.
PLD
Kgr.
2 DB
553.
44
79
+ 87

fire).[1] But the 104th Infantry took Morville-les-Vic and crossed the Petite Seille and attacked into Château-Salins the next day from the east. The 2nd Cavalry Group, Mechanized, covered the right flank of the corps to the canal. The attack appeared to be on a northeast axis rather than east as before, toward Morhange, not Dieuze.

West of the Petite Seille the HKL was held by Mühlen's 559.V.G.D.: Volksgrenadierregiment 1127 at Château-Salins through the southern part of the Forêt d'Amelécourt on the Morhange plateau, V.G.R.1125 from Fresnes-en-Saulnois across open terrain to Malaucourt-sur-Seille, and V.G.R.1126 holding reserve positions. It had its Pionierbataillon and Füsilierkompanie but, unlike the 361.V.G.D., it lacked 7,5cm Pak and Pz.Jg.38(t) Hetzer batteries.

The 559.V.G.D. was attacked from the Forêt de Gremecey, and American forces bridged the flooded Osson Creek. Tanks churned through the mud to assist the infantry, but the defenders had been fortifying their positions for the previous month, and minefields, wire entanglements, and covered bunkers made the American advance difficult and costly. The grenadiers had loaded the cartridge belts into their Zweibein MG 42s, slapped the feed cover down, pulled the cocking handle back to open the bolt, and then shoved it forward, and from under their camouflage pressed their triggers and sent streams of tracers at the olive-drab figures moving forward. Baade's 35th Santa Fe Division mounted the attack, the 320th Infantry Regiment passing through the 134th Infantry to assault the forest and Fresnes, and on the left, the 137th Infantry Regiment established a bridgehead across Osson Creek.

The weak 48.Inf.Div. under Gen.Lt. Karl Casper held positions forward of, and on, the Delmer-Rücken (Côte de Delme), and on its right flank was SS Pz.Gren.Rgt.38 of 17.SS Pz.Gren.Div. McBride's 80th "Blue Ridge" Division attacked this sector, its regiments crossing the Seille by fording and by rubber assault boats, engineers putting in footbridges and then treadway bridges so tanks could cross. That night 48.Inf.Div. fell back to the Delme Ridge positions.

Sensing that the region west of the Forêt d'Amelécourt to the Côte de Delme was the most vulnerable, Balck put 11. Panzer-Division under Priess's XIII.SS-A.K. command. Wietersheim's Div.-Gef.-Std. moved to Brehain west of Morhange during the night of 8–9 November, and Wietersheim organized two mixed Kampfgruppen. A "northern" group assembled in the woods northeast of Viviers, and a "southern" group, with elements supporting V.G.R.1126 near Gerbecourt, took position near Fonteny.

On 9 November Patton broadened his offensive with attacks by XX Corps in the Metz sector, against LXXXII. A.K. under Gen.d.Inf. Walter Hörnlein on 1. Armee's right flank. Division Nr.462, now commanded by Generalleutnant Vollrath Lübbe, defended the forts and the city itself. It had been upgraded as 462. Volksgenadierdivision with its own engineers and artillery plus an additional infantry regiment, but its officers and non-commissioned officers in the schools there had graduated and received assignments elsewhere. They had been replaced by overage and poorly trained troops, derisively referred to as "Halbsoldaten."[2] Yet, if not as maneuverable as regular combat troops, they could still man the machine guns and other weapons of the defense.

North of the fortified city the 19.V.G.D. resisted the crossing of the Moselle downriver from Thionville by the US 90th Infantry Division followed by the new 10th Armored Division. 416.I.D., composed of personnel with ailments, held the Moselle north of the 19.V.G.D. South of Metz 17.SS Pz.Gren.Div. of XIII.SS Korps fell back after the 5th Division attacked across the lower Seille. Pz.G.R.35 of 25.Pz.Gren.Div., released from OKW reserve at Baumholder, penetrated almost to the 90th Division bridge at Malling on 12 November before being driven back. The American advances north and south of Metz suggested an intended encirclement.

Farther south on 9 November two American armored columns—one from Malaucourt, the other from Jallaucourt—advanced out of the 35th Division bridgehead across the flooded Osson Creek against Mühlen's V.G.R.1125. Restricted to roadways because of the muddy conditions, the tanks nonetheless charged ahead over roadblocks and gun positions, though losing some tanks to mines. These were two battalion-sized cross-reinforced task forces of the 4th Armored Division's Combat Command B (Task Forces Churchill and Maybach). Wood's 4th Armored was the 11. Panzer's old adversary from the September Arracourt battles. The 4th disdained to have a nickname as the other armored divisions had. The Gespensters acknowledged it as "eine Elitedivision."

They were approaching a German secondary position near Fonteny, when 8,8cm guns of 9. Flakdivision suddenly engaged one of the columns at long range. Wietersheim had also positioned one Kampfgruppe there in the Bois de Serres under Oberstlt. Rupprecht's Pz.Gren.Rgt.111. As the Ami tanks closed, the panzers were in the tree lines festooned with branches as camouflage. There was the soft whine of turret motors as they traversed toward the targets, and then a final adjustment before the command: *Feuer*!

At one point a young Obergefreiter of 5.Kp./ Pz.G.R.111 picked up an "Ofenrohr" (8,8cm Raketen Panzerbüchse 54) from a wounded Kamerad and, though untrained in its use, knocked out four Shermans in ten minutes from the window of a house. This *"Mordskerl"* (devil of a fellow) was rewarded with the EK 2. and 1. Klasse, a tank destruction badge, and a Tapferkeitsurlaub (bravery leave). Task Force Maybach retreated, having lost fifteen tanks, ten half-tracks, and three assault guns (105mm).[3] Panzer commanders talked their drivers back over the intercom. They shed the camouflage branches, keeping their frontal armor toward the enemy, and then shifted to alternate positions.

TF Churchill had rolled on to Hannocourt supported by airstrikes of XIX TAC P-47s, approaching the Nied Française River. But that night a force of panzers and assault guns, along with troops of Pz.G.R.111 and Festungs Btl.43 attacked into Viviers behind the task force. Some of Churchill's tanks returned to reopen the road but were forced off the Rollbahn by Pak and mired down in the boggy fields. Many American tanks had "grouser" or "duckbill" track extensions for better ground pressure and flotation than the M4's 15.1 psi (the Panther's was 12.52 psi), though the mud remained dominant. Infantry of the 35th Division now caught up and fighting continued through the 10th until the Germans withdrew that night. The rain turned to snow and the ground became a muddy slush.

At the same time II.Btl./Pz.Gren.Rgt.110 under Hptm. Johannes Schneider occupied Fonteny, but 35th Division infantry joined the 4th AD task force to renew the battle for the town on the 11th. Losses were heavy: two American battalion commanders died; Lt. Klele's platoon of 8. Kompanie panzergrenadiers was destroyed in the house-to-house fighting; and Schneider was badly wounded by shell fragments and was in hospitals for the rest of the war.[4]

In the valley of the Petite Seille the 361.V.G.D. was forced back as the 26th Infantry Division cleared Château-Salins and Morville-lès-Vic. The Americans were then in position to flank the Côte St. Jean (Hill 310) and V.G.R. 953 retreated back into the Forêt de Bride et de Koecking. The Yankee Division was supported by the attached tank battalion, which had the new M4s with the 76mm gun. These were the colored tankers of the 761st Tank Battalion (Cld). But they were inexperienced, and when their C Company came down a slope in line formation, they stopped upon encountering an antitank ditch—and lost seven tanks to "ripsaw," the German antitank guns.[5]

Instead of masking the forest on the Dieuze plateau, the American infantry began to work their way through it, suffering losses not only from the maze of German defenses but also from ailments caused by the rain, cold, sleet, and snow. "All through this I think we were taking a worse beating than the Jerries," said an officer of the 104th Infantry. "They fought a delaying action, all the way. When things got too tough they could withdraw to their next defense line."[6] The Landsers suffered as well, but they had the defenders' advantages of prepared positions and of falling back on their own supply lines.

On 10 November an American armored column emerged from Morville-lès-Vic and advanced to Hampont in the valley of the Petite Seille. It moved slowly, because of roadblocks, and maneuver was not possible because any tanks or other vehicles that went off the blacktop surface of the highway became mired and had to be winched out of the mud. On the 11th the column continued advancing up the Petite Seille valley. A second column then crossed behind it at Hampont and began ascending a route toward the Bois de Kerperche north of the forest through which the 26th Infantry Division was advancing. These were two battalion-sized, cross-reinforced task forces of Combat Command A now under Lt. Col. Creighton Abrams of Wood's 4th Armored Division.

Oberleutnant Walter Rahn, adjutant of I.Abt. (Panther)/ Pz.Rgt.15 was at the Bataillonsgefechtsstand in the Forêt de Château-Salins when an excited infantry Feldwebel of the 559.V.G.D. burst in reporting that a hundred Ami tanks were advancing up the valley. This was CCA's Task Force Hunter, with a tank battalion, an armored field artillery battalion, two companies of armored infantry, an armored engineer company, a tank destroyer platoon, part of a medical company, and trains. The task force was built around the 37th Tank Battalion, Maj. William Hunter, XO (Executive Officer) commanding. As there could be no off-road maneuvering because of the swampy mud terrain, it was an advance on a one-tank front. As it neared Haboudange, the road was between the river and a railroad embankment on the south side.

Rahn immediately alerted the crews of five Panthers that were nearby awaiting maintenance, and mounted a Kettenkrad to size up the situation for himself. Knowing that the companies and platoons of the regiment were widely dispersed, he realized that these panzers were the only ones immediately available. They were technically dead-lined, and averaged only six rounds of ammunition each. But Rahn found them a reverse slope position near Dalhain from where they could engage the American column at 1,500 meters from hull defilade, the turrets alone being exposed.

The high-velocity rounds of the Panthers streaked across the valley into the left flank of the column. At the same time guns of Flak Btl.111 with a unit of the 361.V.G.D. opened up from the front. But the deadliest fire came from the flank. Four tanks, two half-tracks, and two quarter-ton jeeps were destroyed and at least four officers killed. The American tanks returned the fire, according to tank company commander Capt. Jimmie Leach, even though "they could not see what was firing."

The deadly fire ceased as suddenly as it had begun. Some vehicles continued ahead, and the rest of the column backed up to find an alternate route. At a postwar 11. Panzer reunion Col. (ret.) Jimmie Leach, a captain commanding B Co/37th Tank Battalion at the time, met Walter Rahn. "Why did you stop shooting?" he asked his erstwhile opponent. Walter Rahn simply said, "We were out of ammunition."[7]

On the American left, Eddy's XII Corps was more successful. As the 80th Division had driven the 48.Inf.Div. back to the Delme Ridge position, two combat commands of the 6th Armored Division were committed on 9 November. While aircraft from XIX TAC bombed and strafed the Delme Ridge, enabling the 80th Division to capture it, the 6th AD combat commands, encountering less muddy conditions than farther south, flanked around to the north of the ridge. By the 11th they were across the Nied Française, the next German defense line, at Han-sur-Nied and Sanry-sur-Nied. Priess's XIII.SS Korps had little to resist the American advance, but motored Volksgrenadierregiment 951 of 361.V.G.D. up from the Dieuze area, and committed I.Btl./SS Pz.Gren.Rgt.37 to reinforce SS Pz.Gr.Rgt.38.

Rundstedt at OB West released the 36.V.G.D. under Generalmajor August Wellm to Balck's H.Gr. G, and Balck took Feuchtinger's 21. Panzerdivision from 19. Armee and dispatched it north. Feuchtinger only had some nineteen panzers and three assault guns, and four panzergrenadier battalions with only sixty to seventy riflemen in each. Bäke's small Panzerbrigade 106 FHH went north as well, subordinated to 21.Panzer on the 13th. But 11. Panzer-Division was in action against the 4th Armored advances, so these were all that Balck could make available.[8] The new units mounted counterattacks, but the steady American advance continued beyond the Nied and by 16 November the 6th AD's CCA and the infantry were on the high ground south of Faulquemont.

The US XX Corps had begun its offensive the day after XII Corps and by 19 November contact was made between the 90th Infantry Division from the north and 5th Division from the south, encircling Metz and its garrison. While Walker's XX Corps divisions pressed on toward the German frontier and the Saar River, Generalleutnant Heinrich Kittel, who had succeeded the ill General Lübbe, was badly wounded and captured on 21 November as the Americans fought their way into Metz itself. Outlying forts continued to resist.

In Priess's XIII.SS A.K., on 10 November Wietersheim's Elfte was ordered to delay back to the line Fremery–Haboudange to cover a general retreat to the Nied Stellung. Oberstlt. Werner von Rupprecht's Pz.Gren.Rgt.111 was on the right, and Pz.G.R.110, under acting commander Hptm. Heinz Wolff of I.Btl.(gp) was in the center on the main Rollbahn to Morhange. Major Karl Thieme was the commander-designate, but he was attending the Regimentsführer Lehrgang and would not return until the 17th. He had replaced Oberst Heinrich-Georg Hax who went to 8.Pz.Div. on the Ostfront, which he later commanded.[9]

Near Morhange itself was Pz.Aufkl.Abt.11, commanded by Maj. Graf von Pfeil, who had succeeded Maj. Karl Bode by 15 October. The Div.Gef.Std. was relocated to Harpich north of the town. During fighting on the 11th, an American map was captured that showed the planned axis of advance for the 4th and 6th Armored Divisions leading northeast to Zweibrücken. With this knowledge the 11. Panzer was concentrated east of Morhange. On 11 November the 26th Division infantry pushed beyond the Bois de Kerperche on the Dieuze plateau to Rodalbe.

The American armor column in the Petite Seille valley continued on through Conthil, and reached Rodalbe as well by noon the next day. The task force started north toward Bermering thrusting between the 559. and 361. Volksgrenadierdivisionen, but the road north was thoroughly mined, and the tanks that tried to maneuver off the road became bogged down in the mud and targets for Pak in the Pfaffenhorst Woods. This was Task Force Hunter's 37th Tank Battalion, and the tankers drew back into the Bois de Conthil, 1,000 meters west of Rodalbe.

To restore the break in the front Wietersheim used the Gepanzertefahrzeuge of A.A.11 and elements of Pz.Gr.Rgt.110, with ten Panthers. American artillery broke up the first counterattack but the Elftens attacked again on the 13th with accurate counterbattery fire by Pz.Art.Rgt.119, now commanded by Oberst Daude. The Kampfgruppe elements left at Belfort had rejoined the division, and Oberstlt. Erich Hammon was reassigned. The Panthers rolled down the Bermering road and the panzergrenadiers assaulted the Americans in Rodalbe from all sides that evening. Some 200 GIs were captured, these from the 3rd Battalion/104th Infantry Regiment. "We were in a tight spot," said PFC Dick Courtney of L Company (AT Platoon). "The whole 3rd Battalion was almost wiped out." Hunter's 37th Tank Battalion went into reserve to await new tanks to replace those lost.[10]

Wietersheim then ordered Hauptmann Ferdinand Biedermann, commanding 3. Kompanie/Pz.Rgt.15, to form a Kampfgruppe with seventeen panzers and Hptm. Wolff's I.(gp)/110 in half-tracks, and make a night road march south to mount a spoiling attack near Guebling, where the 26th Infantry Division was debouching from the Forêt de Bride et de Koecking north of Dieuze. The route was back to Bénestroff and down to Bourgaltroff and Guebling, assembling astride Dordal Creek and outposting Kutzeling Farm. American air did not fly at night and American H&I fire at road junctions was predictable, so the column moved freely.

The column was led by a guide on foot or in a VW Kübel with hooded lights. The drivers followed the four marker lights on the panzer ahead, the four lights blurring to two cat-eye images at the correct vehicle interval of 25 meters. (Four images meant too close, one image indicated too far back.) With the constant rain and sleet, dust was not a concern. But when the column occasionally halted, someone had to go back and bang on the fenders to wake drivers who dozed off.

It was important for crewmen to rotate positions, spelling the driver, the others slumped in the seats or curled on the turret basket floor alongside the ammunition in the soft green interior light (American dome lights were red). The pace of fighting and moving was exhausting, and the Besatzungen "just catnapped when we could," said Obergefreiter Martin Lange, driver and mechanic of Pz.Rgt.15, ruefully.[11]

Six Panthers were positioned among the stone buildings of the Kutzeling Farm early on the morning of 14 November when American tanks skirted around the Bois de Kerperche from the north. Panzergranate shells screamed across the open ground and the lead tank was knocked out, blocking the road. The Ami armored infantry scrambled out of their half-tracks, and the fighting continued for the next six hours. This was a 4th Armored task force built around Maj. Arthur West's 10th AIB, part of Task Force Oden of Abrams's CCA. Finally some of the M4s were able to maneuver closer and disable three of the Panthers—*"Ausbooten!"* ("Bail out!")—whereupon the rest pulled back while covered by a smoke screen from their turret-mounted smoke-grenade launchers.

The task force then continued on down toward Guebling, but encountered Biedermann's Panthers where the road angled up and over the Dieuze-Bénestroff railroad and the Dordal Creek. The CCA unit diary recorded, "Weather conditions were extremely bad, it was snowing and raining and soil conditions made all the vehicles road-bound." Nonetheless an artillery observation L-4 plane from the 94th AFA Battalion got up and adjusted fire on to them, forcing the panzer crews to "button up"—*"Luken dicht!"* ("Close hatches!")—and fight half blind, with ground fog reducing visibility to scarcely 25 meters. Instead of being in hull defilade behind the railroad embankment, the Panthers were in the open in front of it. Tanks on both sides were knocked out, including Biedermann's Panther. When the ammunition exploded he was thrown out of his Turmluke with a severe leg wound, and his crew members were killed. The incapacitation of the unit commander may explain why the other Panthers fought in some confusion.[12]

With the Panthers neutralized, Task Force West proceeded toward Guebling. But the lead tank hit a mine approaching the railroad and, when the second and third tanks tried to fan out to the right and left, they were also disabled by mines. The armored doughs dismounted to continue up the slope toward the hamlet while armored engineers cleared the mines and, finding the bridge over the unfordable Dordal Creek blown, put in a treadway bridge under fire. It was well after dark when the tanks and vehicles of the task force moved into Guebling and outposted it. It would have been preferable to occupy the high ground to the north, but it was after 22,00 hours and, said Art West, "I was tired; and I assumed everyone else was." German patrols infiltrated back into the town during the night. One group with a Panzerfaust knocked out the artillery forward observer's tank, killing the FO.[13]

Wietersheim's Div.Gef.Std. was transferred to Torcheveille, and more units concentrated at Bourgaltroff to eliminate the American penetration to Guebling. When the sounds of vehicle movement into Guebling were heard in the early hours of the 15th the Gespensters laid down an accurate and heavy artillery and mortar barrage. Three gasoline trucks that had come up to refuel West's task force were destroyed, and a number of tanks and other vehicles were damaged while the GIs sought shelter in the buildings even as these collapsed around them.

The rest of TF Oden, commanded by Lt. Col. Delk Oden of the 35th Tank Battalion, came up that morning and an attack was mounted to take the high ground. But it was repulsed, laced by heavy indirect and direct fire. That afternoon the Americans were seen to be destroying damaged vehicles and evacuating wounded, and then pulling out of Guebling under cover of a smoke screen, and destroying the treadway bridge over the creek. Oden and West both had recommended retreat from Guebling to Abrams, and General Wood reluctantly concurred. "But we just couldn't break that Goddamn fire, and couldn't get through," said Colonel Oden, and—a compliment for the 11.Pz.Div.—"those Goddamn Germans were the hardest fighting things we had ever tangled with."[14] A document was also captured in which XII Corps commander Maj. Gen. Manton Eddy recognized the 26th Division "for its excellent fighting against the 11.Pz.Div., known as one of the best German units," and he commended the YD by noting "Some of Germany's finest fighting troops are on your front, including the tough and tested 11th Panzer Division."[15]

North of the Petite Seille American forces closed in on Morhange. These were the 35th Infantry Division and Dager's CCB of the 4th Armored. The 559.V.G.D. put up stiff resistance, albeit less effectively because the Elfte was in action against the 4th AD's CCA and the 26th Division and unable to give support. Two 4th Armored task forces now advanced northeast up the valley of the Nied Française; one of them crossed to the north bank at Oron, and the other on the south bank. Karl Casper's 48.Inf.Div. had been shattered, so on 14 November Balck replaced it with the 36.V.G.D. and ordered it to be amalgamated with Mühlen's 559.V.G.D. in the Morhange sector as Kampfgruppe Mühlen. On the morning of the 15th V.G.R.1127 evacuated the battered town of Morhange.

Balck was able to carry out these delaying actions without interference from OKW, and on the night of 17–18 November 1. Armee withdrew to a Faulquemont–Bénestroff–Bourgaltroff line. Both armored divisions in XII Corps (the 4th and the 6th) were exhausted, and on the 16th Eddy had pulled them out of the line. American armor commanders were especially bitter, for the armor, instead of being held for exploitation or maneuver, was being used instead to bludgeon the advance forward. It was a type of fighting for which American armor was neither designed nor equipped, and they felt the whole campaign was an unimaginative and atrocious misuse of that arm. These operations, wrote General Wood of the 4th Armored later, "furnish only a classic example of the way in which armored divisions should never be employed, if avoidable."[16]

Oblt. von Eggeling, Pz.Rgt.15, on leave in November 1944 at his family estate, Schloss Geissmannsdorf, in Silesia. FRIEDRICH KARL VON EGGELING

Lorraine mud: knocked-out Panthers and a Sherman tank of the 4th Armored Division, 25 November 1944. DAVA SC 197268

General von Wietersheim leaving a headquarters with Begleitoffizier (Escort Officer) Oblt. Tafel, who had replaced Oblt. von Fersen. ERNST-AUGUST VON FERSEN

Perhaps there was no good alternative. But Patton, like Eisenhower, was advancing on a "broad front." To the north Patton's other corps, XX under Walker, was preoccupied in surrounding Metz. However, on 18 November the 10th Armored Division crossed the lower Nied at Bouzonville, and the road net was adequate for a thrust *southeast*, between the Sarre and the former French Maginot Line, to St. Avold. OB West was indeed concerned that the armor advance was part of a concentric attack to join the 6th AD near Faulquemont. Instead Patton had Walker pull the 10th Armored *back* and sent *north* across the German frontier toward the Saar–Mosel Dreieck (triangle), the confluence of the Saar and Mosel Rivers. But this was blocked by an extension of the Westwall defenses, the Orscholzriegel (Orscholz barrier), which the Americans called the Orscholz or Siegfried Switch Line. The 416.Inf.Div. held the position, and elements of 21.Pz.Div. and 25.Pz.Gren.Div. mounted counterattacks that denied a breakthrough.[17]

On 18 November Eddy's XII Corps renewed the offensive to the Sarre. On his right the 26th Infantry Division attacked the Dieuze-Bénestroff line held by Philippi's 361. Volksgrenadierdivision, and struggled into Guebling. In the center the 35th Division jumped off from a line of departure (LD) east of Morhange against Kgr. Mühlen (remnants of his 559.V.G.D.and 48.I.D.). On the left the 80th Division remained on the defensive fronting Faulquemont and the 36.V.G.D. The 4th and 6th Armored Divisions were positioned to exploit through them, but would again be used to attack.

Once again Wietersheim's Elfte had to be parceled out in small detachments ready to counterattack, on a Hellimer–Rening–Torcheville–Guinzeling line some 15 kilometers in length. The Div.Gef.Std. was at Hinsingen, south of Sarralbe. On 14 November the 11.Pz.Div. had reported a strength of only 800 men, and indeed, on the 15th there were only twenty-seven panzers and twenty-six assault guns in *all* of 1. Armee.[18] On the 17th and 18th the Gespensters were under LXXXIX. Korps, and then back under XIII.SS Korps. SS Grüppenführer Max Simon had come from Italy to take over XIII.SS A.K. on the 16th, Priess being reassigned to H.Gr. B (slated for I.SS Panzerkorps in the Ardennes offensive). Simon judged the 11.Pz.Div. to be "powerful and trustworthy" relative to his other formations.[19]

There were more losses on the 18th, and Lt. Kurt Nentwig was evacuated after his hand and wrist were smashed by artillery shell splinters before he could close the hatch on his Panzer IV Wagen. The three artillery battalions of Pz.Art.Rgt.119 were more dispersed than ever. To supervise his scattered batteries Hptm. Schaefer-Kehnert, whose III. Abteilung usually supported Pz.Gren.Rgt.111, divided his headquarters into a rear command post administered by his adjutant, and a forward command post from which he himself operated.[20]

On 19 November the XII Corps armor was committed anew. One column moved through Rodalbe after the armored infantry had secured it and, slowed by mines and spots of resistance, advanced through Bermering and Virming toward Francaltroff. This was a 4th Armored task force under Lt. Col. Abrams, who had reverted to command his 37th Tank Battalion after Col. William Withers took over Combat Command A. The second task force (West) followed. Another column emerged from the gutted buildings of Dieuze on the 21st after it was secured from V.G.R.953, and drove east through Loudrefing to cross the Canal des Houillères de la Sarre on the 22nd. It was Dager's CCB of the 4th AD, which continued east to Fénétrange on the Sarre River itself.

On the Kampfgruppe Mühlen HKL northeast of Morhange American tanks and infantry penetrated through Bertring and Gros-Tenquin on 19 November. These were the tanks of Combat Command B under Col. George Read of Grow's 6th AD attacking through Baade's 35th Infantry Division. At first resistance seemed to be light—because Mühlen had dropped his various elements back to his main line of resistance behind antitank ditches, mines, and entrenched machine gun nests. But a small Kampfgruppe of the 11.Pz.-Div. gave caution to the American advance, another force from 17.SS-Pz.Gren.Div. arrived from the Metz sector, and on the 20th Balck committed a part of Oberst Hans-Joachim Deckert's 15.Pz.Gren.Div. from H.Gr. G reserve at Hellimer.

On 22 November tanks broke through the HKL to St. Jean-Rohrbach, and infantry fought into Hilsprich the next day, approaching the Mutterbach (Maderbach), a tributary of the Sarre. It was Read's CCB, and the 35th Division's 1st Battalion, 137th Infantry Regiment. They were resisted by SS Pz.Gren.Rgt.38. Six new Jagdpanzer IVs had arrived for Pz.Jäger Abt.61, and a Gespenster Kampfgruppe led by Oberstleutnant Werner von Rupprecht counterattacked and claimed ten American tanks at St.Jean-Rohrbach. The SS and Eleveners then fought back into Hilsprich that evening surrounding the Amis, though some survivors managed to get back through the Germans. Lt. Jürgen von Pflug, adjutant of I./111, recalled the blue-and-white Santa Fe Trail wheel shoulder patch from 35th Division Kriegsgefangene.[21]

Oberstlt. Rupprecht, commander of Pz.G.R.111, however, was killed. "Avoidable," said Lt. von Pflug, "if he had been sensible about it." He had come up to the Bataillonsgefechtsstand with his Ordonnanzoffizier Lt. Benkert and, despite being warned about the proximity of the Ami riflemen, went boldly forward. "What had to happen happened. A sheaf of automatic weapons fire." Benkert was shot through the head and Rupprecht died shortly thereafter. He was succeeded in the interim by Major von Rintelen, and then by Oberst Johann Adolf Graf von Kielmansegg. The Americans were able to retake Hilsprich on the 24th, and by the end of the month were along the Maderbach. The 11.Pz.Div. command post moved from Hinsingen to Saaralbe, then to Herbitsheim.[22]

After Patton's Third Army led off the American November Offensive on 8 and 9 November, Devers's 6th Army Group attacked on the 13th, and Bradley's D-Day for 12th Army Group's Ninth and First Armies' attack was the 16th. In the north the Ninth Army under Lt. Gen. William Simpson attacked in the Köln Plain between Geilenkirchen and Eschweiler, a land dotted with little industrial stone villages, each turned into a miniature fortress. A heavy air and artillery bombardment preceded the attack. The Americans were driving toward the Roer River, and it was finally realized that they could not cross the river until First Army captured and neutralized the dams controlling the floodwaters up in the Hürtgen Forest.

During the October lull the Germans had assiduously increased their defenses here with antitank ditches and minefields. The sector was defended by General von Zangen's 15. Armee which, together with 1. Fallschirmarmee, was now in Heeresgruppe H. This army group was formed 10 November under General Kurt Student, with General der Fallschirmtruppen Alfred Schlemm taking over 1. Fallschirmarmee on 20 November. Manteuffel's 5. Panzerarmee headquarters had controlled much of this sector but was surreptitiously withdrawn in preparation for the Ardennes offensive.

Brandenberger's 7. Armee of Model's H.Gr. B held the Westwall border positions through the Eifel to Trier. Bradley's Ninth and First Armies battered their way forward. It was a struggle of attrition. Casualties were heavy on both sides, and the Americans did not achieve a breakthrough. In the Netherlands the Canadians and British were slogging through the polder lands to the Maas and broadening the salient to the Neder Rijn of September. In the south, however, where Wiese's 19. Armee was hard-pressed by the French and Americans, a threatened breakthrough loomed.

CHAPTER TWENTY-NINE

Defense of the Saar

EVEN IF THE AMERICAN ARMIES—NINTH, FIRST, AND THIRD—OF Bradley's 12th Army Group would be unable to achieve a breakthrough in their November offensive, sudden ruptures in the German Westfront appeared farther south. General der Infanterie Friedrich Wiese's 19. Armee was stretched thin resisting the two armies of Lt. Gen. Jacob Devers's 6th Army Group. Wiese could slow the Allied advance in the Vosges Mountains, but both his flanks were vulnerable: the Burgundische Pforte (Belfort Gap) on his left by the Swiss border, and the Zabern (Saverne) Gap between the Vosges and the German Haardt Mountains on the right; nor did he have mobile forces such as the 11. Panzerdivision, which had so ably covered his retreat up the Rhônetal.

Devers launched his part of the Allied November offensive in a snowstorm on 13 November. Free French armor, 1ère Division Blindée, dramatically drove through the Belfort Gap on the 16th, and four days later entered Mühlhausen (Mulhouse) and reached the upper Rhine. Simultaneously, 2ème Division Blindée of Seventh Army maneuvered to capture Saverne on the 22nd and reached Strassburg (Strasbourg), capital of Alsace, and the Rhine the next day. The 6th Army Group was poised to cross the Rhine at either location, or to launch a pincers attack to Colmar behind Wiese's divisions in the Vosges.

Of greater concern to Balck at H.Gr. G and von Rundstedt at OB West was the breech opening between 19. and 1. Armee, and an American drive northeast of the Sarre into the Saar industrial area. The 11.Pz.-Div. was committed all along the front against the American XII Corps advance, and other mobile forces were resisting XX Corps. On 21 November von Rundstedt ordered Student's H.Gr. H in the Netherlands to send south the weak 245. and 256. Volksgrenadierdivisionen. He also released four battalions of 401. Volksartilleriekorps, and finally persuaded the OKW that afternoon to release the Panzer-Lehr-Division to counterattack the Franco-American thrust through the Saverne Gap. Pz.Brigade 106 was ordered south from XIII.SS-Armeekorps and passed through Strasbourg on the way to Mulhouse the day before the French tanks arrived.

Panzerlehr (secretly scheduled for the Ardennes offensive) was refitting at Munster, but moved 500 kilometers (300 miles) south to Sarre-Union by the 23rd. Commanded by Gen.Lt. Fritz Bayerlein, the PLD was ordered to attack south that same afternoon with what had arrived: thirty to forty panzers of Oberst Rudolf Gerhardt's Pz.-Lehr-Rgt.130, two of its four panzergrenadier battalions, and about ten assault guns.[1]

Bayerlein attacked south, east of the Sarre in two parallel columns: Pz.Gren.Rgt.901 under Oberst Paul Freiherr von Hauser with twenty to twenty-five Panthers as the eastern column through Eywiller, and Pz.G.R.902 under Major Otto Kuhnow with ten to twelve Panzer IVs as the western column through Postroff to Baerendorf. (Von Hauser had commanded the Elfte's K.61 in 1942–43.) They scattered the light forces of the 106th Cavalry Group, Mechanized, and continuing through the night drove elements of the 44th Infantry Division from Rauwiller and back to Schalbach.

As the PLD drive continued on the 24th, suddenly American tanks attacked into the flank of the western column behind the spearhead, at Baerendorf and Postroff. Dager's CCB of the 4th Armored Division had crossed the Sarre as two task forces. General Wood had objected to his corps commander's plan of advancing north *between* the Canal des Houilleres and the Sarre toward Sarre-Union because the thickly wooded Mosterwald (Bois de Bonnefontaine) had no roads; he instead negotiated to cross into the Seventh Army zone to flank up the open *east* bank of the Sarre. Ironically, the 4th Armored's attack collided with the PLD attack, frustrating Wood's maneuver, just as the 4th AD's move thwarted Bayerlein's attack.[2] Bitter fighting ensued at Baerendorf on the 25th, and artillery fire stopped Pz.G.R.901 at Schalbach.

At the same time, on 24 November Eisenhower and Bradley consulted with Devers and Patch, and the decision was made that Seventh Army's XV Corps axis of advance should now be north, not east, complementing Patton's drive toward the Saar, as von Rundstedt and Balck had anticipated. Realizing Panzerlehr's attack had failed, Rundstedt ordered that Bayerlein go over to the defensive, and the PLD began to withdraw northward to a lateral road linking Wolfskirchen, Eywiller, and Durstel as an HKL. Major Kuhnow, commander of Pz.G.R.902, was captured at Schalbach, succeeded by Oberstlt. Joachim Ritter von Poschinger. 25. Panzergrenadierdivision commanded by Oberst Arnold Burmeister began relieving some Panzerlehr units 25–27 November, though the 25. still had detachments deployed throughout the 1. Armee area.[3]

The 4th Armored Division now began driving north against Bayerlein's division toward Sarre-Union, CCB through Wolfskirchen and Eywiller, and Col Withers's CCA, which Wood had passed behind Dager around to the right, through Gungwiller and Durstel. The 4th AD's lateral move took pressure off 361.V.G.D. and the 11.Pz.Div., and Wietersheim could fall back to an HKL that stretched from Püttlingen (Puttelange), along the Maderbach, in front of Saaralben (Sarralbe), and through Sarre-Union, and linked to Panzerlehr's right flank. Pz.Gren.Rgt.110 under now Oberstleutnant Karl Thieme was on the left east of the Sarre, and Pz.G.R.111 under Oberst von Kielmansegg was on the right west of the Sarre, in contact with 17.SS Pz.Gren.Div., at the end of November.

The Maderbach was in the old French Maginot Line. It was of marginal use to the Germans as the fields of fire were oriented east and the entrances on the reverse slopes were vulnerable from the west; but the concrete forts could provide shelter from artillery and air bombardment, and the antitank obstacles and entanglements posed problems for the attacking Americans.

Farther to the right where 17.SS-Pz.Gren.Div. was defending, the American 6th Armored and 26th Infantry Divisions along the Maderbach "pinched out" the 35th Division, which went into XII Corps reserve for resting and absorbing replacements. General Wellm had gotten permission from Gruppenführer Simon of XIII.SS-A.K. to withdraw his weakened 36.V.G.D. back across the Nied Allemande where the Maginot Line fortifications could provide some measure of defense.

On 25 November the 80th Division of Maj. Gen. McBride, with heavy artillery support and the attached tank and tank destroyer battalions, assaulted the Falkenberg Stellung (Faulquemont Position) and broke through. Wellm was able to delay back the next day and then retreat to a position west of the Sarre, abandoning St. Avold. But when the 80th Division pushed on to the Metz–Saargemünd railroad line through Farebersviller, elements of SS Pz.Gren.Rgt.38 and flak panzers of SS Aufklärungsabteilung 17 counterattacked and held the Amis from the town. The German front remained intact.

Across the upper Sarre, however, the 4th Armored kept driving north toward Sarre-Union. This was now held by 25.Pz.Gren.Div. supported by 11. Pz.-Div. The 1. Armee left flank was defended by LXXXIX. Korps (Gen.Lt. Gustav Höhne having replaced Gen.Lt. Werner von und zu Gilsa on the 22nd) along the Moder River north of the Saverne Gap and Strasbourg: 361.V.G.D., which had absorbed the 553.V.G.D.; 245.V.G.D. from the Netherlands; and 256.V.G.D., across the foothills of the Haardt past Hagenau to Gambsheim on the Rhine.

Wiese's 19. Armee was now separated in the Vosges-Colmar area from the rest of Balck's H.Gr. G. It was subordinated to a new headquarters formed on 10 December, Heeresgruppe Oberrhein (Army Group Upper Rhine) under Heinrich Himmler, the sinister Reichsführer-SS und Chef der deutschen Polizei, as Oberbefehlshaber. The army group reported not to von Rundstedt's OB West, but directly to OKW.

Oberst Arnold Burmeister's 25.Pz.Gren.Div., actually the right wing of LXXXIX. A.K., held Sarre-Union and the hills overlooking it from the north. It had eighteen Panzerwagen, but a Kampfgruppe was also with 21.Pz.-Div. on the 1. Armee right wing in the Merzig sector holding the Saar crossings of the Saarhöhen Stellung (Saar Heights position) west of the Saar against the US XX Corps.

On 1 December the 4th Armored's CCB sought to flank around the right of Sarre-Union while the 101st Infantry Regiment of the 26th Division, which had crossed the Sarre to join the 4th Armored drive, advanced on Sarre-Union itself. But the American armor was stymied by the mud, which restricted the tanks, and panzers from Panzerlehr stiffened the resistance north of Mackwiller and Rimsdorf 3–5 kilometers from Sarre-Union. Two armor battalion commanders and one of the infantry battalion commanders were wounded. Two American infantry companies got into Sarre-Union but met such heavy fire from the hills beyond that they withdrew, and Burmeister reoccupied the town in force.

The next day the infantry attacked into the town again, and the 4th AD cut the Domfessel and Voellerdingen roads to the east. At noon on the 3rd eight panzers and the Begleitkompanie of the 11. Panzer-Division charged down the Oermingen road and into Sarre-Union, overrunning five 57mm AT guns that were ineffective against the heavier panzers anyway. American artillery then came into play and on 4 December more infantry and tanks regained control of the town in house-to-house fighting. The 104th Infantry had reinforced the 101st in the battle, and A Company of the 4th AD's 37th Tank Battalion had joined in. The Gespensters withdrew from Sarre-Union.[4] The 4th Armored then reorganized near Domfessel. The frustrating drive had resulted in Gen. John Wood being relieved by General Patton, succeeded by Patton's Chief of Staff Maj. Gen. Hugh Gaffey. Brig. Gen. Herbert Earnest took over Combat Command A from Withers.

Wietersheim's 11.Pz.Div. still had to hold a sector of the defense line, from south of Puttelange along the Maderbach, and from Sarralbe to Oermingen on the Eichel, generally in the Maginot Line defenses. The ration strength was 3,500, with 800 panzergrenadiers, though there were only 20 panzers and assault guns. The Divisionsgefechtsstand moved from Herbitsheim on the Sarre east across the Eichel to Etting. To the right was 17.SS Pz.Gren.Div. Götz von Berlichingen, commanded now by Standartenführer Hans Lingner who had succeeded Brigadeführer Werner Ostendorff. The division maintained a line from Puttelange to the Rosselle south of Forbach. It had a ration strength of 4,000 including 1,700 infantry, and though its artillery regiment was at strength it had little armor. Its personnel included untrained draftees and unwilling Volksdeutsche (racial Germans) from eastern Europe.[5] The Waffen-SS was far from its elite origins.

Gruppenführer Max Simon's XIII.SS Korps' right flank was held well forward of the Saar and the Westwall by 36. and 347. Volksgrenadierdivisionen to the boundary with Gen.d.Inf. Walter Hörnlein's LXXXII. A.K. Hörnlein's troops continued the 1.Armee line to Orscholz and the Mosel. It was necessary to dispatch some Gespenster panzers to give a modicum of armor support.

On 4 December the three left-wing divisions of Eddy's XII Corps renewed the Third Army advance. The 80th Division took Farebersviller and the 35th Division, committed again, crossed the Maderbach and captured Puttelange from the 17.SS Pz.Gren.Div. Lingner's units fell back behind the Sarre pursued by the 6th AD combat commands, which encountered the new German Stellung the next day. The 35th Division began a five-day battle against the Waffen-SS troops for Saargemünd (Sarreguemines), which was not cleared until 11 December.

The Elfte likewise fell back to delay positions along the Eichel, incorporating the battered 25.Pz. Gren.Div. temporarily, its fighting strength only 600 men, on its left. Wietersheim was permitted, "in case of continuing heavy enemy pressure," to withdraw to the Maginot Line in the Weidesheim–Achen–Bining sector.[6] This barred the northeast axis of advance of the US 4th Armored Division, which was to push toward the road junctions of Rohrbach-les-Bitches and Bitche and ultimately Zweibrücken or Pirmasens. The Div.-Gef.-Std. removed to Obergailbach.

To the north the four divisions of Maj. Gen. Walton Walker's XX Corps continued to slog forward and by 2 December were approaching the Saar River and the Westwall. Hörnlein's LXXXII. A.K. had fallen back across the German border and was ensconced in the Westwall defenses on the east bank of the Saar, but was badly stretched. The 416.Inf.Div. held the Orscholz position and the Saar-Mosel triangle. To its left was 19.V.G.D., reduced to one-third its normal strength with only 630 infantrymen left. Ersatzmänner were of low quality and were untrained, and included a Volkssturm (People's Militia) Bataillon. Hitler had ordered the formation of the Deutsche Volkssturm 8 October 1944, the draft extending to all German males ages sixteen to sixty. Many units would only be identified by an armband on the left sleeve, and were dressed in uniform oddments.

Feuchtinger's 21.Pz.Div. was the counterattack reserve, though on 4 December it had only 200 infantry (barely a company in size); the *total* strength of Kampfgruppe Mühlen (remnants of 559.V.G.D. and 48.I.D) on that date was 360 men. The 719.I.D. was detraining at Saarbrücken after moving south from Holland as an overage garrison unit, and its division artillery was characterized as the "Artillery Museum of Europe." Replacements were pumped into these forces and, as there had been time to improve the Westwall position here, there was a certain defensive capability behind the minefields, entanglements, and antitank obstacles, and in the concrete bunkers. Defending the homeland territory now enhanced a grim determination.

Bad weather limited American air support by XIX TAC, and also restricted the L-4 spotter planes, making Ami artillery fire adjustment more difficult. In addition, the German use of flash-hider salt reduced the muzzle flash, and further limited American artillery flash-ranging techniques and counterbattery fire.

On 3 December Americans of the 95th Infantry Division captured a Saar bridge at Saarlautern (French Saarlouis) and penetrated the heavily fortified east bank suburbs; they also captured two pill boxes of the Westwall there from elements of Kgr. Mühlen. 21.Pz.Div. was spread too thin to make an effective counterattack. Oberstlt. Hans von Luck's Pz.Gren.Rgt.125 was split up, II.Btl. at Saarlautern and I.Btl. sent north to assist a 25.Pz.Gren.Div. Kampfgruppe at Merzig.[7]

Hitler was enraged at the penetration of the Westwall, and ordered an investigation and punitive measures taken. One casualty was Knobelsdorff at 1. Armee, and on 4 December he was succeeded by General der Infanterie Hans Obstfelder. Obstfelder had commanded LXXXVI. A.K. in the West and was nominated by Model as being firm in defense. Oberst Friedrich von Mellenthin, Balck's long-experienced and able chief of staff of H.Gr. G was relieved the next day, for Generalmajor Helmut Städke, a veteran of the Ostfront.[8]

At the same time, OB West was insistent that Panzer-Lehr, 11.Pz.-Div., and 401. and 404. Volksartilleriekorps be transferred to H.Gr. B as ordered by OKW. Across Germany trains had been rolling west, bringing long flatcar loads of Panthers and Tigers and other armored vehicles, while masses of men and materiel moved into assembly areas deep in the forested recesses of the silent and brooding Eifel for Hitler's Ardennes offensive. Balck had to comply, but as of 5 December was able to keep 11.Pz.Div. and 404. Volksartilleriekorps in his H.Gr. G. He dispatched a Gespenster Kampfgruppe to the Saarlautern area that included ten panzers, some Jagdpanzer IVs, and engineers in half-tracks.

The American 90th Division had crossed the Saar just north of Saarlautern and established the Dillingen-Pachten bridgehead. Just before dawn on 7 December four Panzer IVs and two companies of Pioniere launched an attack while other elements infiltrated back to reoccupy bunkers the GIs had cleared earlier. Later in the day six Gespenster panzers supported an attack from the north against the bridgehead. The fighting was at close quarters and the casualties were high on both sides, but the Americans, though they contracted their perimeter, managed to hold. The German attacks lacked a certain coordination because elements of disparate units were committed: panzers from 11.Pz.Div., tank destroyers from Panzerjäger Abt.654, Rgt.59/19.V.G.D., a battalion of Rgt.87/36.V.G.D., two battalions of the arriving Rgt.723/719.I.D., and elements of Pionier-Btl.668. The 8,8cm guns of schwere Pak-Abt.686 also arrived.[9]

On the next day elements of 21.Pz.Div. were involved, and an attack by twelve panzers included the 11. Panzer Kampfgruppe. Such tactics nonetheless made the American advance very costly as Patton's Third Army divisions pushed ahead in frontal attacks along a broad front, and could not achieve a decisive breakthrough.

Meanwhile the rest of Wietersheim's Elfte had withdrawn back across the Eichel west of the Sarre by 4 December. The American 4th Armored Division continued to advance, its two combat commands abreast. Combat Command B fought its way into Voellerdingen after engaging ten panzers, claiming two, and capturing a bridge across the Eichel intact. Just to the south CCA drove into Domfessel, which was lightly held by a Panzerlehr detachment, but lost five tanks to accurate German artillery fire. On the 5th CCB pushed on to Schmittviller and CCA, getting across the Eichel, advanced up the highway to Rahling on the way to Bining and Rohrbach.

Wietersheim pulled back into the Maginot Line defenses, Pz.Gren.Rgt.110 under Oberstlt. Thieme generally on the left, and Oberst Kielmannsegg's Pz.G.R.111 generally on the right. Detachments of Panthers of Major Jürgen Reichardt's I.Abt./Pz.Rgt.15 and Panzer IVs of Hauptmann Rodenhauser's II.Abteilung supported the panzergrenadiers, as did the Jagdpanzers of Maj. Arnold Kessler's Pz.Jäger-Abt.61. The Spähwagen and Halbketten of Maj. Graf von Pfeil's Pz.Aufklärings-Abt.11 covered the withdrawal. The Wespen and Hummeln as well as the towed artillery of Oberst Daude's Pz.Art.Rgt.119 displaced to give fire support to the new HKL, joined by Maj. Jochen Menzel's Acht-komma-achts. Maj. Heinz Bödicker's engineers of Pz.Pi.Btl.209 laid mines to enhance the Maginot Line obstacles. 25.Pz.Gren.Div. elements on the left deployed in the Forêt de Montbronn across the Buttenbach.

The Panzergrenadieren of I.Bataillon/ Pz.G.R.111 were taking up positions in the little hill farm town of Singling when American tanks—*"Feindpanzer!"* an observer warned—appeared on a slight rise about 800 meters to the south in the late afternoon of 5 December. On the previous day the battalion had moved from Hinsingen on the Rode River south of Sarralbe through Sarrable and Voellerdingen to its new HKL position west of Rohrbach. Its commander was Hauptmann Paul Engelmann; he had succeeded the ill Hptm. Wilhelm Gattmann, who in turn had succeeded Hptm. Werner Wehrstädt, killed back in October. 1.Kp./Panz.Jg.Abt.61 with eight Sturmgeschützen and some of II./111 under Ritterkreuzträger Hptm. Otto Grumbt were positioned near Bining.

I./111's three rifle companies and heavy weapons company were understrength, with 150–200 troops. They were supported by a 7,5cm Pak and three 2cm flak, and a two-barreled rocket launcher and five 8cm mortars to the north. There were also two Jagdpanzer IV assault guns and three Panthers in the village, which was on a ridge. Lt. "Kalle" Zindler, now commanding 2. Kompanie I./15, had six Panthers around the stone farm buildings of Welschoff Farm on the next ridgeline 1,100 meters to the north. When the Ami tanks crested the rise at 800 meters in line formation, five M4s were simultaneously knocked out by high-velocity gunfire. Nine others were mired in the mud on the naked high ground and also knocked out. Fourteen M4s were disabled or lost.[10]

On 6 December American tanks appeared again, this time with white phosphorous smoke and high-explosive artillery concentrations smashing into Singling, while another armored column advanced on the Rollbahn toward Bining and Rohrbach. The 4th Armored's CCA was advancing along two axes. When the Gespensters in Singling couldn't be suppressed by fire alone, the Americans mounted a coordinated attack. While one tank company gave supporting fire another tank company with infantry mounted on the tanks attacked into the town.

Lt. Col. Creighton Abrams had tried to advance his 37th Tank Battalion task force along the main highway toward Bining but had received flanking fire from the Forêt de Montbronn on his right. Thus he had received permission to follow a parallel route that passed near Singling, but the heavy fire there determined him to take the village. B/37th Tk Bn and B/51st AIB were given the mission. As the infantry M3 half-tracks bogged down—"The mud was so bad," related the armored infantry battalion after-action report, "that only full-tracked vehicles could maneuver, even on trails"—the armored doughs mounted the tanks.

Thirteen tanks attacked in line formation through the cold gray with guns blazing on the move, and the infantry dropped off when approaching a hedge south of town. Observing this, even as his own Panzer-Lehr-Division was withdrawn, was Generalleutnant Fritz Bayerlein. He recalled later that it was "an outstanding tank attack, such as I have rarely seen, over ideal tank terrain."[11] Capt. Jimmie Leach and 1st Lt.

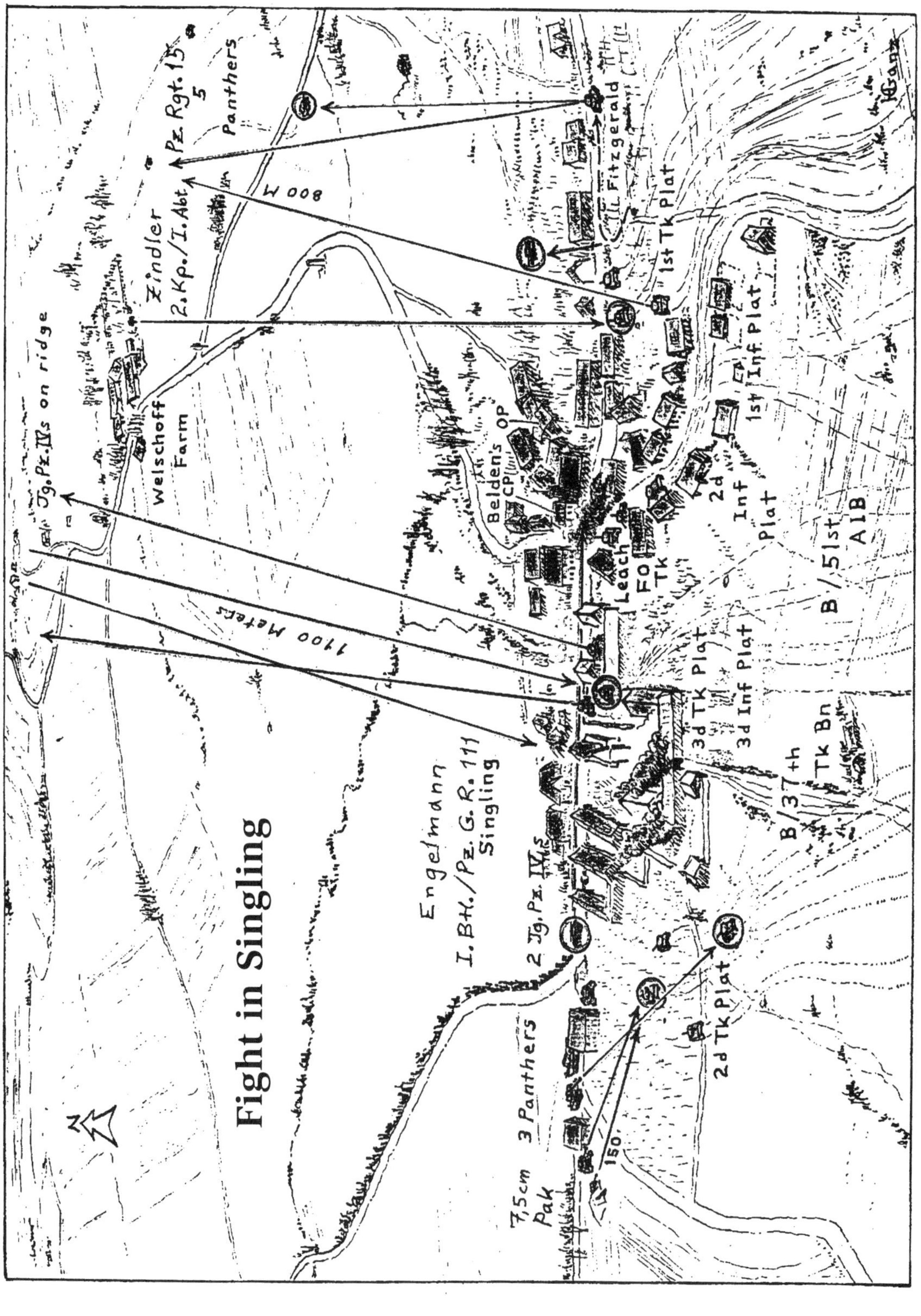
Fight in Singling
Engelmann
I. Btl./Pz. G. R. 111
Singling
2 Jg. Pz. IVs
3 Panthers
7,5cm Pak
150
2d Tk Plat
B/37th Tk Bn
3d Tk Plat
3d Inf Plat
B/51st AIB
Leach
FO
Tk
2d Inf Plat
1st Inf Plat
1st Tk Plat
Fitzgerald
Belden's CP
OP
Welschoff Farm
Jg. Pz. IVs on ridge
1100 Meters
Zindler
2. Kp./I. Abt.
Pz. Rgt. 15
5 Panthers
800 M

Dan Belden were the company commanders. B/37 had fourteen tanks operational of its T/O&E eighteen (one dropped out with a faulty radio), though B/51 had only 57 of its authorized 251 men.

But in the daylong battle the Panthers and Pak in the western part of the town knocked out two tanks, and two more were destroyed by long-range fire from the Welschoff Farm position. One of the German Jagdpanzers was knocked out, however, and, reflecting the low morale of many new replacements, at least fifty-six Germans surrendered. In the farm area several Panthers were poised. New panzer commanders were told, *Nein*, you don't stand tall in your hatch, so proud, so *stolz*—you crouch and grip the rim of the hatch and barely peek out.

Five Panthers under Lt. Karl Zindler emerged and attacked down across the valley, but two were knocked out by an M4 with the new 76mm high-velocity gun. Zindler's Wagen was one of the Panthers knocked out and two of his Besatzung were wounded.[12] The German advantage was in the accurate, long range of their high-velocity guns and in dominating the battle area by fire. Attacking negated this, and the remaining three Panthers pulled back behind smoke. But caught among the buildings with enfilading gunfire from the west and the north, Team B was ordered out by Abrams, and directed to continue down toward Bining. Abrams was to be relieved by CCB, but when its tank-infantry team approached, the tank of one of its platoon leaders was knocked out and that night the 4th AD abandoned Singling.

Meanwhile other American forces took Bining short of Rohrbach, but the next day the advance halted; the tired and weakened 4th Armored Division was relieved in place by the new 12th Armored Division, and passed into reserve. "The famed 'Fourth' was known throughout the whole ETO as the cream of American Armored Divisions," knew the untried 12th Armored "Hellcats" as they moved up against the 11. Panzer with some trepidation. "It was a good thing for them, however, that the Wehrmacht didn't know how much the Hellcats were worried and confused during those first hectic nights on the front."[13]

But the 11. Panzer also abandoned Singling, which was of no significant tactical value, and fell back on the night of 6–7 December to a Wittring–Gros Réderching–Petit Réderching–Lesselberg line, with the Div.Gefechtsstand just west of Riesweiler. This was on German soil for the first time, in the Rheinpfalz or Niederpfalz, the Palatinate.

On 8 December the American XII Corps renewed its offensive. On the right of XIII.SS Korps Wellm's 36.V.G.D. held the line between Forbach and Sarreguemines (Saargemünd) and Lingner's 17.SS Pz.Gren.Div. held on the east along the Sarre to Wittring. The 11.Pz.Div. (and 25.Pz.Gren.Div.) held the left through Rohrbach to the Pfälzer Wald and the Haardt Mountains. The American 80th Division had been pulled out of the line for refitting on the 7th, and the 6th Armored and 2nd Cavalry Group took over its sector as the corps' left flank protection. The 35th Division, already embroiled in the struggle for Sarreguemines, used assault boats to cross the Sarre to advance toward the Blies, and the 26th Division began to fight through the Maginot Line forts around Achen.

A Kampfgruppe of 11.Pz.Div. of thirteen to fifteen panzers with panzergrenadiers of Thieme's Pz.G.R. 110 mounted on them launched a counterattack against the 35th Division from Neunkirch, a suburb of Sarreguemines. But American artillery supporting the river crossings were in range and nine battalions of field artillery smashed the Gegenangriff as it was forming up. Such demonstrations of the deadly American artillery prompted Balck to issue a general directive late on the 8th: "The experiences of the last days have taught that the enemy artillery, employing air or ground observation, easily destroys our own counterattacks before they are actually formed." Counterattacks in the future were to be launched only in twilight or at night or in fog, unless woods or bad weather denied enemy observation.[14]

The 26th Division attack had the support not only of artillery, but also the bombing and strafing by XIX TAC—*"Achtung Jabo!"* was the air warning—which caused heavy Verluste to the Gespensters in le Grand Bois south of Wittring. The Maginot forts gave some trouble, but the Germans had largely withdrawn to the Bois de Blies-Brucken. The Yankee Division took Gros-Réderching on 10 December and the 12th Armored, occupying evacuated Singling on the 9th, also took Rohrbach-lès-Bitche on the 10th. The 26th Division was then withdrawn for refitting, replaced by the newly arrived 87th Division.

In the wet, freezing, demoralizing struggle of attrition, the Americans were suffering almost as many "nonbattle" losses as combat casualties, especially the painfully swollen "trench foot" cases.[15] German veterans of the Ostfront were able to prepare their replacements better. But for the German divisions in the Saar there was no relief. The 17.SS pulled back to the Blies, while the 11. Panzer took position along a ridge west of Obergailbach. On the 11th it received twenty new Panthers to replace losses, but it was critically short of panzergrenadiers.

On 10 December LXXXX. A.K. became operational, taking control of the 11. Panzer and 25. Panzergrenadier Divisions. Under Luftwaffe General der Flieger Erich Petersen, this was the former IV. Luftwaffe Feldkorps headquarters in 19. Armee, redesignated 22 November. Inserted between Simon's XIII.SS A.K. and Höhne's LXXXIX. A.K., its boundaries were between Bitsche (Bitche) and Bliesbruck; but for corps troops it only added a light howitzer battalion and a mixed flak battalion. LXXXIX. A.K. was designated Gruppe Höhne and comprised the remnants of 361., 245., and 256.V.G.D.s. Gen.d.Inf. Gustav Höhne was promised the understrength 21.Pz.Div. The American forces of the Seventh Army struggled into the fortifications around Bitche defended by 25.Pz.Gren.Div., but couldn't take the city itself.

On 12 December the 35th Division crossed the Blies River in plywood boats. The current was swift and the weather alternated between rain, sleet, and snow. As the Amis fought into Habkirchen SS Pz.Gren.Rgt.38 mounted a sharp counterattack and the Amis were reduced to a handful. Some 200 troops of Volksgrenadierregiment 165 of 36.V.G.D. were committed as well. Once again American artillery played a crucial role, and after a three-day battle the Waffen-SS Truppen withdrew.

The 35th also crossed at Bliesbruck, and a regiment of the fresh 87th Division cut off part of the Elfte's Pz.Gren.Rgt.110 and took Obergailbach. Farther south the 87th took Rimling from SS Pz.G.R.37. The Gespensters fell back from Gros-Rédercing but stopped the 12th Armored near Kapellenhof and in the valley of the Schwalbach, their boundary with Burmeister's 25.Pz.Gren.Div. defending the Bitche sector.

Despite orders from above forbidding defensive preparations *in* the Westwall, Wietersheim got Petersen's permission to reconnoiter new positions by the Westwall near Zweibrücken. Divisional Versorgung units and the Feldersatzbataillon were moved into appropriate sectors. But the design of the Westwall was so intricate "it could be compared to a battleship," said von Wietersheim. Even after fourteen days, advance parties scouting in preparation for occupying the positions were not familiar with it all. The bunkers and obstacles were emplaced to canalize enemy movements and provide flanking fire, and interlocking fields of fire needed to be studied. It was a mistake, von Wietersheim said, for the Supreme Command to prohibit systematically preparing to possibly occupy the line as a defeatist "looking to the rear." For units suddenly withdrawn into the unfamiliar defenses, the Westwall was a *Falle*, a trap.[16]

Although the bunker firing apertures were obsolete for the MG 42 and emplacements too small for the larger Pak of 1944, and wire entanglements, minefields, and communications equipment had been removed or were lacking, the bunkers did provide shelter, and a coherent defense behind antitank obstacles could be created. Primary and alternate Feuerstellungen for the artillery could also be prepared. The advantages were that supply lines were shorter, and that panzers and weaponry of all kinds sent back for repair by the Werkstattkompanien could be returned to the units the same day or the next day. The faster resupply of artillery ammunition meant that Pz.A.R.119 could increase its expenditure to 3,000 rounds a day, though it still could not compare with the 6,000–8,000 rounds a day of American artillery.

On 11 December, with the Div.Gef.Std. remaining at a forester's house north of Altheim, the right wing of the division withdrew under pressure to some woods northeast of Obergailbach. Height 362 was the core of the Widerstandslinie. A.A.11 extended the line of resistance east to 25.Pz.Gren.Div. north of Hottviller. When the Americans penetrated to Medelsheim on the 12th, a sudden artillery concentration and an immediate Gegenstoss led by Hptm. Heinz Wolff with only two SPWs of his I./110 routed them "with heavy losses." "Obviously," the enemy division (the 87th Infantry Division) was new and inexperienced. But with superior enemy numbers, the HKL was drawn back to Gersheim and north of Medelsheim.

On 16 December the first units of 257. Volksgrenadierdivision began a relief in place of the 11.Pz.Div. This was completed by the 18th, as Wietersheim's Elfte was ordered north. Patton was preparing a renewed offensive by his Third Army, but reports of German attacks in the Ardennes caused a pause. A 6th Armored attack was canceled on the 17th, the 87th Division was ordered to halt on the 18th, and the 35th Division was ordered to consolidate on the 19th. The German soldiers heard Propaganda Reichsminister Josef Goebbels's voice over the radio: "The Wehrmacht has launched its great offensive. We will destroy the enemy and cut all his lines of communications. Paris is our goal."[17] (Actually, the objective of HERBSTNEBEL was Antwerp to the northeast, not Paris.)

In retrospect, the German forces in Lorraine had effectively stopped Patton's Third Army drive to the Saar and the Rhine, both in September and again in November. In fact, his army had generally been held *short* of the Westwall and the German frontier by December. In no small measure was this due to General Wend von Wietersheim and his 11. Panzer-Division.

Despite an overwhelming preponderance of air, artillery, and materiel resources in the November offensive an American breakthrough had not been achieved. While muddy terrain and bad weather favored the German defenders, Patton's offensive had been an unimaginative frontal assault along a broad expanse, and had degenerated into a costly struggle of attrition—disappointing in an armor commander of his demonstrated capability. Losses on both sides had been high, and the US official history acknowledges that American tank losses "probably were considerably higher than those of the enemy."[18] Balck had been especially insistent that minefields be coordinated at army group level, not merely left to defending units, and that mines be laid in great depth *within* the defender's position, not just in front of the Vorposten where the enemy could clear them. In addition, lots of dummy mines should be laid. "After all," he said, "when a tank moves out and sees signs of mines, he can't know whether they're fake or real."[19]

The American infantry had also suffered. An 11. Panzer Enemy Intelligence Bulletin of 4 December by Lt. Heinz Wassermeyer, Abt.Ic, noted that American prisoners of war under interrogation were demoralized from the mines, machine guns, and German artillery, and that "The prisoners complain about lack of drill of the replacements and about too quick promotions of the lower leaders."[20] (Wassermeyer had succeeded Oberlt. Siegfried Vietor, longtime division Ic, killed on reconnaissance on 19 November at Grosstänchen.) But many German veterans also felt that even the more experienced Ami infantry were "half-hearted," that they preferred to withdraw rather than offer energetic resistance, and in many cases left American tankers without infantry support, leading to high armor losses. Most respected American fighter-bombers, but especially the artillery, fire adjusted by the forward observers, like Lt. Charles "Chuck" Ross of the 26th YD, in the L-4 Piper cubs that flew even in overcast weather.[21]

The well-experienced Generalmajor F. W. von Mellenthin observed, "I think that Patton would have done better if the 4th and 6th Armored Divisions had been grouped together in a single corps, reinforced possibly by the French 2nd Armored Division. These were all very experienced formations and ably commanded; Wood of the 4th Armored Division proved himself an expert in armored tactics, and [General Jacques] Leclerc showed great dash in the advance on Strasbourg." But American doctrine and practice did not favor a concentration for a Schwerpunkt, a point of main effort, which had proved so successful in the panzer Blitzkrieg tactics.

"I think," commented von Mellenthin, "the Americans made a grave mistake in coupling their armored divisions too closely with the infantry; combined as a tank army under one commander, these three armored divisions might well have achieved a decisive breakthrough." Even while the American infantry divisions were mostly motorized, however, the corps commanders were of an infantry background—and mentality.[22]

The autumn fighting in Lorraine had cost the 11.Pz.Div. over 6,000 casualties, including 1,000 killed: 1,668 Verluste including 349 killed in September, 1,947 including 311 killed in October, and 1,748 including 343 gefallen in November, plus the losses in December.[23] Mellenthin noted the "splendid resistance" of the 11. Panzer-Division, and Wietersheim felt justified in the tactics he had employed: a defense in depth in a chessboard deployment offering flanking possibilities with panzers and self-propelled artillery and flak that could rapidly change positions. Retirements and then surprise counterblows kept the opponent off-balance.

The fighting in Lorraine could be described, he felt, "as one continuing crisis." As the most viable panzer force for all of Balck's army group, of necessity the Elfte could not be concentrated as a division. Instead its battle groups had to be dispatched to various danger points. Again, it was vital that the junior commanders, given increased and even independent command and decision-making responsibilities, be able and energetic. The "*Kavallerie-Taktik*," said the general, were mastered by even the smallest Kampfgruppen, and contributed decisively to the defensive successes against an opponent superior in numbers and equipment.[24]

CHAPTER THIRTY

Eifel and Orscholzriegel

WITH THE RELIEF BY 257. VOLKSGRENADIERDIVISION BY 18 December 1944, the 11. Panzer-Division went into reserve, preparatory to its redeployment to the Eifel. This was the wooded, hilly plateau that was the German continuation of the Ardennes, where the German offensive was breaking through the American lines. Panzerregiment 15 began rail-loading its tracked armored vehicles near Kaiserslautern on the 22nd, and then moved by Eisenbahntransport via Zweibrücken and Wemmetsweiler north to the vicinity of Nonweiler. There were delays and reroutings because of Allied bomb damage.

Then the division moved by road march over the icy roads of the rugged Hunsrück Mountains in the dead of winter into the valley of the Mosel by Trier, and then up to cantonments in the Eifel in the area of Bitburg-Kyllburg and Wittlich. The panzers were dug in against air attack even in the forests. The Divisionsgefechtsstand was established at Badem, 15 kilometers (9 miles) northeast of Bitburg. Generalleutnant von Wietersheim had gone ahead and met with von Manteuffel of 5. Panzerarmee. Simultaneously he was informed that the 11.Pz.Div. was in OKW-Reserve, in support of the continuing Ardennes offensive.[1]

On 16 December 1944 Hitler had launched his great offensive in the Ardennes. Some twenty-five German divisions assaulted six American divisions on a 110-kilometer (68-mile) front between Monschau south of Aachen and Echternach northwest of Trier. The Schwerpunkt was with 6. Panzer-Armee under SS Oberstgruppenführer Josef "Sepp" Dietrich, who would drive northeast across the Meuse and take Antwerp, trapping the Allied armies to the north. 5. Panzerarmee under General der Panzertruppen Hasso von Manteuffel advanced parallel on the left, and 7. Armee under Gen.d.Pz.Tr. Erich Brandenberger covered the southern flank. 2.Pz.Div. in 5.Pz.Armee was commanded by former Gespenster Oberst von Lauchert.

Von Rundstedt as OB West had opposed the offensive, offering as an alternative a pincers operation against the Aachen salient. But Hitler rejected this, and the disgruntled Feldmarschall now played only a nominal role. The offensive, finally titled

CHRISTROSE, was under the operational control of Walter Model at H.Gr.B.

Manteuffel had persuaded Hitler to forgo the traditional, planned preparatory bombardment, and instead have a carefully selected Sturmbataillon (assault battalion) from each infantry division infiltrate through the thinly manned American positions simultaneously with artillery concentrations fired on targeted rear areas. Flak unit searchlights were also to create "artificial moonlight" by reflecting their beams off the low cloud cover, providing some dim predawn illumination for the advance, while other beams played across the American outposts, perhaps blinding them, and guiding the assault Truppen.[2]

At 05,30 hours on 16 December, the assault units rapidly penetrated the American positions, while salvoes of V-1 flying bombs flared overhead toward Liége and Antwerp. 6. Pz. Armee plunged through the Losheim Gap spearheaded by Kampfgruppe Peiper, an armored battle group of 1.SS Pz.Div.LAH led by Obersturmbannführer Jochen Peiper, which took Stavelot the next day and headed toward Werbomont.

5. Panzerarmee bridged the Our River, the border with Luxembourg, during the night of the 16th and the next day the panzer divisions were rolling westward toward the road centers of St. Vith and Bastnach (Bastogne) in Belgium, but with strict orders to bypass resistance. Two regiments of the new American 106th Infantry Division were surrounded on the high Schnee Eifel and surrendered by their commanders on the 19th.

Columns of Ami Gefangene were marched to the rear, perhaps unnerved by the massive "King Tigers" with their long 8,8cm guns they had heard about, and the confident if not jubilant German soldiers moving forward on the same roads. The Americans had been taken by surprise, and while there were spots of dogged resistance, there were streams of panic-stricken service and even combat elements, having abandoned vehicles and weapons, jamming the winding Ardennes roads to their rear, pursued by the fear of German tanks.

Adding to the American confusion were German paratroopers dropped behind the lines, and jeeps with English-speaking Germans in American uniforms. These were components of Unternehmen GREIF (Griffin) organized by master commando SS OStubaf. Otto Skorzeny. The Fallschirmspringer were commanded by Oberst Friedrich Freiherr von der Heydte, an experienced paratrooper commander, and in Unternehmen HOHES VENN trimotor Ju 52s dropped them, as well as dummy figures, along the north flank of 6. Pz.Armee.

There were some forty English-speaking Kommandos in GI uniforms in jeeps who worked through the American positions, cutting telephone wires, turning road signs the wrong way, and intercepting dispatch riders, liaison officers, and military police to create traffic confusion. They were to seize the Meuse bridges by coup, the spans to be secured by the captured or disguised American tanks and vehicles of special Panzerbrigade 150 Brandenburger.[3] (Using such uniforms and disguises, of course, denied them the Geneva Convention rights if captured.)

The Allies, however, began to reinforce the line of the Meuse, and Pz.Brig.150 instead attacked toward Malmédy on the 21st but was repulsed. The Fallschirmspringer also did not accomplish much, and von der Heydte was captured on the 23rd. Yet GREIF caused panic, confusion, and numerous erroneous reports and false alarms out of all proportion to the numbers involved. Normal passwords and signs/countersigns were distrusted, and instead officers and others found themselves challenged to answer "Americanism" questions about baseball teams and movie stars. Most of the commandos returned to German lines; some seventeen were caught while wearing American uniforms and shot. In addition, rumors spread like wildfire throughout the American units that American prisoners as well as Belgian civilians had been brutally executed by SS units, and the term "Malmédy Massacre" was voiced. Soon atrocities committed, especially by 1.SS Pz.Div. Leibstandarte, were documented, and retaliations ensued.[4]

Manteuffel's two panzer corps were driving toward the southern road center of Bastogne, though there was an inherent contradiction in the mission: the panzer divisions were to bypass serious resistance, yet the road center was needed to facilitate the advance to the Meuse. Preferably it would be taken in passing, otherwise it would be left to the following infantry. The 116. Windhund and 2.Pz.Div. worked around Bastogne to the north and across the Ourthe River. The day before, von Lauchert's Aufklärungsabteilung 2 of 2.Pz.Div. had captured the doctors, aid men, and medical supplies of a medical company west of Bastogne. The 326th Medical Company wore the "Screaming Eagle" shoulder patch of the 101st Airborne Division, which meant that elite division of paratroopers had arrived to help hold Bastogne.

Approaching Bastogne were Bayerlein's Panzer-Lehr-Division and 26.V.G.D. under Generalmajor Heinz Kokott, having broken through the isolated remnants of the 28th Infantry Division. Encountering American tanks as well as the airborne troops, Bayerlein worked around the city to the south, crossing the West Ourthe at Moircy on the 21st and proceeding westward, while 26.V.G.D. completed surrounding Bastogne. On the south flank 5. Fallschirmjäger-division led the 7. Armee advance, cutting the communications to Bastogne from the south at Martelange on the Sure on the 21st.

The two American airborne divisions had been Eisenhower's only reserve, and they were trucked north, with headlights on, from France. The 82nd Airborne had been directed on to Werbomont while the 101st went into Bastogne, closing on the 19th and joining the remains of CCR/9th Armored Division, and CCB 10th AD, supplemented by tank destroyers and VIII Corps artillery. Gen.d.Pz.Tr. Heinrich Freiherr von Lüttwitz of XXXXVII. Pz.K. essayed to bluff the defenders into surrendering on the 22nd, and was contemptuously refused ("Nuts"). In retrospect this was foolish, as these were highly motivated paratroopers determined to fight (as he well knew), and the incident simply increased their morale.

The skies cleared on 23 December and C-47 cargo planes paradropped much needed supplies into the surrounded forces at Bastogne and the Jagdbombers swarmed over the battlefields. Then the weather closed in again with snow. On Christmas Day, the 25th, the black-uniformed Panzersoldaten of 2.Pz.Div.'s lead Kampfgruppe stood on a rise of ground, thrashing their arms and stamping their feet in the snow to restore circulation in the cold. Below them lay the sparkling waters of the Meuse and the town of Dinant, 100 kilometers (60 miles) from their line of departure nine days before.

Following the unfolding events very closely were Wietersheim and his Gespenster officers at Bitburg, in OKW Reserve. They might be committed at any time, probably with 5. Panzerarmee, and Menzel's 277. Flak guns had already engaged American planes attacking the supply lines. In analyzing the ongoing operations, to the Elfte officers it appeared that in the rugged, wooded Ardennes, rather than a coordinated defensive HKL, roadblocks and strongpoints at river crossings and controlling the roads winding through steep-sided ravines best blocked an opponent's advance. This reality had enabled small, improvised groups of American engineers and service personnel to frustrate the panzer divisions, unlike in 1940.

In the attack, if overwhelming firepower could not be brought to bear, then alternate routes, even forest trails, would have to be located and reconnoitered for flanking moves. Avoiding open fields when the weather was clear for American air power and artillery adjustment observation remained essential. Revealing dirt tracks left by armored vehicle treads across the snow-covered ground somehow had to be avoided.

The sixth Christmas of the war found the Germans on the offensive; they had just shocked their American opponents, shattered their defense, and sent them reeling. In a Weihnachsfest message to his men in the Gespenster newspaper *Nachrichten*, the division commander reviewed "A year full of grave events and the hardest fighting," from Kirovograd and Cherkassy in the East to the Burgundian Gate and Morhange in the West. With their bravery, the enemy had to confess, "*Hier geht es nicht!* Here stands the Elfte!" Thoughts also went to those wounded and those lost, and families in the homeland. And that perhaps, now that they were once again in the attack, the German forces might effect a turning point in the war.[5]

Awards conferred in 1944 included the Eichenlaub mit Schwerten zum Ritterkreuz des Eisernen Kreuzes to von Wietersheim as division commander in Russia, on 26 March 1944. Von Lauchert received the Oak Leaves on 12 February 1944 as Kommandeur Pz.Rgt.15, and Karl Thieme received the Eichenlaub as major, commanding Pz.Gren.Rgt.111 on 23 October.

There were thirteen recipients of the Ritterkreuz: by unit, Pz.Rgt.15 (one), Pz.G.R.110 (three), Pz. G.R.111 (three), Pz.Jg.Abt.61 (two), A.A.11 (one), Pz.Pi.Btl.209 (two) and H.Flak Abt.277 (one). Five RK were awarded in Russia including to Albert Henze as Oberst, 110, on 15 January; Heinz Bödicker as Hptm., Pi.Btl.209, on 9 January; and Karl von Sivers as Major, I./15, on 6 March. Eight RK were awarded in the West including to Maj. Joachim Menzel, 277, 10 September; Maj. Arnold Kessler, Pz.Jäg.Abt.61, 4 October; Hptm. Otto Grumbt, II./111, 28 October; Hptm. Heinz Wolff for commanding 110, 12 December; and Maj. Werner Freiherr von Rupprecht, 111, 12 December. All were officers except Oberfeldwebel Lorenz Harthan, engineer platoon leader in 5.Kp./ Pz.Aufkl.Abt.11, on 12 June 1944.

Sivers and Menzel were also awarded Das deutsche Kreuz in gold, as were Maj. Günther

Kaldrack, Lt. Jürgen von Pflug, and Oblt. Franz Thelen among others. The often hand-to-hand infantry combat in Russia was reflected in awarding the Nahkampfspange (Close Combat Clasp) in gold, worn on the left breast above the pocket, to members of Pz.Gren.Rgt.111 including von Pflug and Thelen, and commander Maj. Anton Donnhauser.[6]

A unique award was the Ritterkreuz des Kriegsverdienstkreuzes (Knights Cross of the War Merit Cross) for noncombat distinction, the only such award in the division. The RK des KVK was conferred 8 December 1944 on Oberfeldwebel Kurt Reuschel of the Pz.-Rgt.15 Werkstattkompanie for his tireless efforts in repairing and maintaining the regiment's panzers. In Russia he had even repaired six factory-new but immobilized T-34s, and captured seven trucks with fuel cans that he turned over to the Versorgungsgruppe.[7]

There were other awards as well. Oberlt. Friedrich Karl von Eggeling of Pz.Rgt.15, who had already received the Iron Cross 2nd Class (2 April 1944) and the Panzersturmabzeichen (Tank Assault Badge) in Silver (11 May 1944) in Russia, in October was awarded the EK 1.Klasse on the 1st, and a second Panzersturmabzeichen in Silver on the 20th. He also was awarded the Wound Badge in Black on 27 May 1944 and in Silver on 23 October, as listed in his Soldbuch by I.Abt. Adju Lt. Dietrich Pfeiffer. (He would be wounded five times, but like many others, was returned to duty.) In late November he was rewarded with a "Tapferkeitsurlaub" to the family estate Schloss Geissmannsdorf bei Löwenberg in Silesia. But of the eight-day leave more than three were spent traveling by train, as most of the stations were bombed, and twice locomotives were destroyed by air strafing.[8]

While at Bitburg the Elfte was undergoing Auffrischung for the panzers, vehicles, and personnel, while also preparing for combat. Feldgendarmerie Trupp 61 military police, their metal gorget and chain prominently displayed over their double-breasted overcoats, kept army traffic moving to supply the offensive, and intercepted stragglers. Fighting continued unabated in the snow-covered Ardennes.

The Americans were solidifying the northern shoulder of the penetration along the Elsenborn ridge and the Ambleve River, and British forces had come down to help hold the line of the Meuse. In the south 7. Armee had taken Diekirch on 20 December and pressed beyond Echternach, but the Americans held Ettelbruck and forces were beginning to drive north from there to Neuf Château to the west. On the 26th, the day after Christmas, CCR of the 4th Armored Division broke through to Bastogne from the southwest, bringing relief to the beleaguered airborne and armored units surrounded there. The 4th Armored was the vanguard of Patton's Third Army, battling up the Martelange axis against 5.Fs.Jg.Div. and 26.V.G.D.

The German salient struggle, with its apex overlooking Dinant, was being referred to by the Americans as the "Battle of the Bulge," from the large protrusion in the American lines. After such an offensive had spent itself, the natural counteroffensive would be to attack from the shoulders to even cut off the spearheads in a Kessel. Pivoting mobile armies around to mount counteroffensives was characteristic of armored warfare—Guderian had swung south behind Kiev in 1941, and Manstein had turned from the Mius and coordinated a pincers drive to Kharkov in 1943. As an armored commander Patton, swinging up from Lorraine, could fully be expected to do the same. He had hinted at such in a somber commanders' meeting with Eisenhower and Bradley at Verdun on 19 December. The deeper the enemy penetration, the more certain his ultimate defeat by counterblow: Manstein's *"aus der Nachhand"* ("on the backhand") stroke.[9]

Hence it was a little surprising that, instead of his armor and infantry *concentrated* to follow the 4th Armored lead up the relatively open Martelange-Bastogne watershed axis, Patton's divisions advanced on a *broad* front through the rugged, forested terrain to the east, athwart which snaked the Sure and Wiltz Rivers. An even deeper counterthrust could be made up the Diekirch–St. Vith highway axis, the former MLR of the US 28th Infantry Division. The 11. Panzer-Division around Bitburg was indeed poised to counter such a drive, and had already sent a Kampfgruppe to strengthen the 7. Armee boundary north of Trier. Had Patton counterattacked up the Diekirch axis, he would have encountered his old foe from Lorraine.

North of the broken American front Field Marshal Montgomery's 21 Army Group had taken command of Bradley's First and Ninth Armies on 20 December, but the British commander apparently felt it necessary to organize his forces better before mounting a major flank attack. Eisenhower, averse to mobile warfare concepts, seemed content merely to compress the "Bulge" back to its line of departure. Hitler, in turn, finally acknowledged that his forces would not be crossing the Meuse, and on 8 January of the new year authorized the withdrawal in stages back to the Westwall, with 6. Pz.Armee to constitute a reserve. Thus when patrols of the US 11th Armored Division of Third Army and of 2nd AD of First Army met just south of Houffalize on 16 January 1945, reuniting the American front, there were no German forces encircled.

The fighting continued, unimaginative and stubborn, unrelieved by any tactical originality by either side. It left the snowy hills of the Ardennes dotted with the derelicts of burned-out tanks, splotched with ugly artillery and bomb craters in the clean snow, and littered with huddled forms of the fallen dusted with a soft blanket of white. While infantry in forested areas suffered from artillery tree bursts, some German grenadier casualties were caused by air bursts in the open. This was the result of the secret American radar proximity fuse initially used in antiaircraft artillery, its first ground use occurring during the crisis in the Ardennes on 21 December.

By January 1945 the 11.Pz.Div. was being built up to its authorized strength of 13,726 men, though some of the replacements had to march in from the Rhine on foot. Panzer-Regiment 15, Oberstlt. Stenkhoff having been succeeded by Oberstlt. Lühl, counted fifty Panthers in Maj. Reichardt's I. Abteilung (Panther) and thirty Panzer IVs in Hptm. Rodenhauser's II.Abt., eighty of the K.St.N.'s total of 103 panzers. Each battalion had four panzer companies (1.–4.Kp. in I.Abt, and 5.–8.Kp. in II.). Pz.Gren.Rgt.110 under Oberstlt. Thieme and Pz.G.R.111 under Oberst Graf von Kielmansegg were also up to strength, with their two battalions of four rifle companies each (1.–4.Kp. in I.., and 5.–8.Kp. in II.), I./110(gp) being the half-track battalion.

There were also twenty-five Jagdpanzers, in Major Kessler's Pz.Jäger-Abt.61 (Pak), but also in Maj. Graf von Pfeil's Pz.A.A.11, and with the panzergrenadiers. Pz.Art.Rgt.119 under Oberst Daude had its three battalions: I.Abt./119 having the self-propelled Wespen (10,5cm) and Hummeln (15cm), (1.–3.Battr.); II.Abt./119 was mixed (4.–6.Battr.), and III.Abt. (7.–10.Battr.) was heavy. Major Menzel's Heeres Flak-Abteilung 277 included the 8,8cm guns. Major Bödicker's Pz.Pion.Btl.209 and Pz.Nachr.Abt.89, as well as the division supply, medical, and service elements were also organized according to the 1944 K.St.N.[10]

At the beginning of January General von Wietersheim reported to the headquarters of Heeresgruppe G near Saarbücken. Blaskowitz had been recalled and replaced Balck on 20 December.[11] It was apparent there would be no Third Army drive up the Diekirch axis nor up a deeper Echternach–Bitburg axis. The Gespenster-Division was now alerted to participate in the winter offensive in Alsace that began 1 January 1945, Unternehmen NORDWIND (Northwind). The Elfte was to be under XXXIX. Panzerkorps, transferred from east Prussia and commanded by Generalleutnant Karl Decker. By 21 December both Hitler and von Rundstedt had realized the Ardennes offensive was losing momentum and, knowing Devers's 6th Army Group had spread itself thin to cover Third Army sectors in Lorraine as Patton redeployed to drive north, contemplated an offensive by H.Gr. G to take advantage of this. NORDWIND would be an offensive south from the Saarbrücken and the Bitche areas to the Saverne Gap that would cut off American and French forces at Strasbourg on the Rhine, blocked by the Colmar Pocket to the south.

Another offensive, tentatively code-named ZAHNARZT (Dentist), might then drive into the rear of Patton's Third Army. Hitler involved himself in these discussions, having moved his headquarters from Berlin to command post "Adlerhorst" (Eagle's Aerie) near Bad Nauheim north of Frankfurt am Main in early December.[12] Twelve divisions were made available for NORDWIND including two panzer and two panzergrenadier divisions. 11.Pz.Div. was to redeploy down from the Eifel.

American intelligence was aware of the German buildup and, realizing how thin 6th Army Group's front was, on 26 December Eisenhower ordered Devers to withdraw to the Vosges Mountains. But this meant abandoning Strasbourg and the parts of Alsace that had been liberated, and not surprisingly the French leaders objected furiously; Eisenhower had to back down.

On 1 January the first of a series of blows of NORDWIND struck, spearheaded by 17.SS Pz.Gren.Div. GvB in the Sarre valley, a few hours before New Year's Day. Nine super-heavy Jagdtiger tank destroyers mounting a 12,8cm cannon lumbered across the terrain. But Devers, and Patch of Seventh Army, had strengthened the sector. Minefields and plotted artillery concentrations stopped the attack short of Singling. East of Bitche, however, in the deep forests,

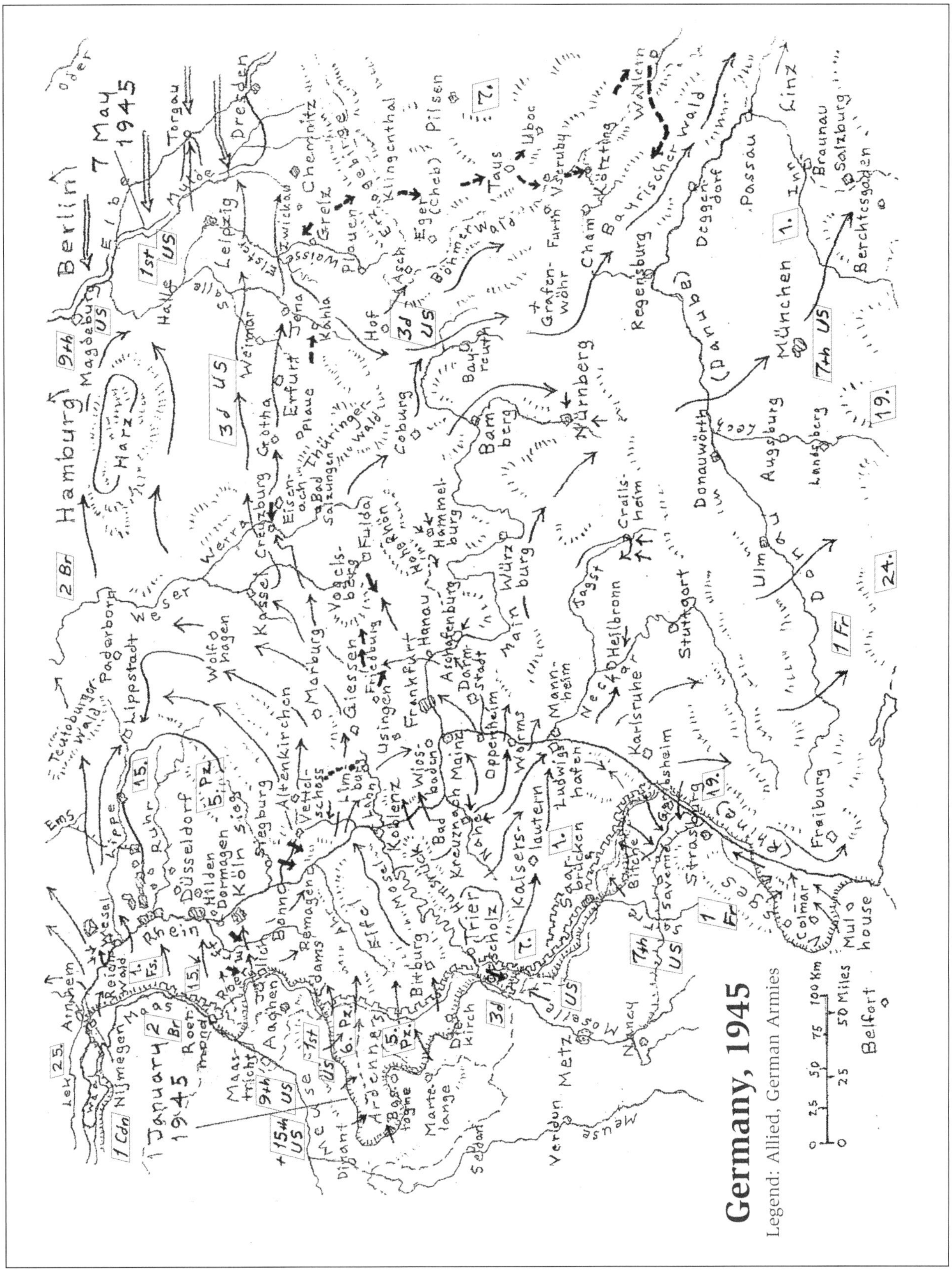

Germany, 1945

Legend: Allied, German Armies

four Volksgrenadier divisions caught the Americans by surprise. Supplemented by 6.SS Gebirgsdivision Nord, newly arrived from the Finnish front, they sent the light tanks and armored cars of the cavalry screening forces reeling back toward the Saverne Gap.

On 5 January Himmler's H.Gr. Oberrhein launched a two-pronged pincer attack on Strasbourg: forces that had been ferried across the Rhine at Gambsheim attacked from the north, and 19. Armee forces spearheaded by Pz.-Brig.106 FHH came from Colmar to the south (SONNENWENDE, Winter Solstice). On the 7th Decker's XXXIX. Pz.K., just arrived, swept south inland from the Rhine with 21.Pz.Div. and 25.Pz. Gren.Div. Wietersheim's Elfte was originally to have been included, but was held back in 1. Armee reserve. (Gen.d.Inf. Hans von Obstfelder had succeeded von Knobelsdorff on 2 December.)

The Americans committed the 14th Armored Division and the Germans committed 7. Fallschirmjäger-division in the desperate struggles in the fields and forests and villages of Alsace. With the cancelation of the ZAHNARZT concept, 10.SS-Pz.Div. Frundsberg was committed to drive south from Lauterbourg along the west bank of the Rhine to the forces at Gambsheim on the 16th. Heard from above was the strange whistle of German Me 262 Düsenjäger (jet fighter planes), which peeled down to strafe the American positions with rockets, bombs, and 3cm cannon fire. Bitter armored and infantry fighting took place at Herrlisheim, resulting by the 18th in the destruction of an American combat command (CCA, 12th Armored Division).

In the center the Americans had retreated to the Moder River line of the Saverne Gap paralleling the Marne-Rhin Canal to the north. In a driving snowstorm the night of 26 January German mountain troops and paratroopers joined with panzergrenadiers and Volksgrenadiers to assault the American positions, but heavy casualties and mutual exhaustion saw the NORDWIND battles finally come to an end by the end of the month. French forces held Strasbourg, and the American Seventh Army had managed to retain the Saverne Gap. But Allied strength had been strained. Even the 101st Airborne Division, battered at Bastogne and relieved into SHAEF reserve, came down to 6th Army Group.

On 12 January the 11. Panzer-Division had left Bitburg for NORDWIND and moved past Trier and the Mosel valley into the high cold of the Hunsrück Mountains. But then for the next five days it was held around Reinsfeld-Kell with the Div.Gef.Std. at Schillingen. As now in Heeresgruppe G reserve, it was to be prepared to move southwest to the Saar–Mosel Dreieck (triangle) south of Trier guarded by the Orscholzriegel (barrier) defenses along the base, or south to Saarlautern (Saarlouis). Blaskowitz assigned the division to LXXXII. Armeekorps under Gen.d.Inf. Walther Hahm, who was responsible for the whole sector, directly under army group control. Elfte participation in NORDWIND was postponed.

On 14 January American forces pushed through the snow and subfreezing cold and attacked Tettingen behind the "dragon's teeth" antitank obstacles on the western sector of the Orscholzriegel. This was the Orscholz Barrier or Siegfried Switch of the Saar-Moselle Triangle to the Americans. It was held by Lt. Reudiger's II.Btl./Gren.Rgt.714 of 416. Infanterie-Division. The Amis then pressed on to Butzdorf, and the next day they also took the village of Nennig on the Mosel. 416.Inf.Div. under Generalleutnant Kurt Pflieger had only two weak regiments to defend the Riegel, and only its Ersatzbataillon as reserve, which counterattacked but could not regain the villages.

These were battalion-sized attacks of the new American 94th Infantry Division, which had relieved the 90th Division seven days before. General Walker of XX Corps told Maj. Gen. Harry Malony of the 94th to probe the position (the same where 10th Armored had been rebuffed in November) to gain experience and perhaps get a foothold, but only in battalion-level strength. But the threat of piercing the Riegel prompted Blaskowitz to commit the 11. Panzer to restore the line; he had been considering an armored raid from the Riegel anyway.

On the 16th Wietersheim was ordered to send a Kampfgruppe to support the 416.I.D., and the next day was to cross the Saar with the whole division to attack on the 18th, down to Perl at the southwest corner of the border on the Mosel. For lack of fuel and with bridge limitations some fifty heavy Panthers (I.Abt./15) were delayed in crossing. The attack would be launched by thirty Panzer IVs (II./15), sixteen assault guns, and the panzergrenadier regiments. The Div.Gef.Std. moved to Beuren.

Wietersheim strongly opposed the plan, as the Riegel terrain was cut up by poor roads, antitank ditches, bunkers, and other obstacles to armored maneuver. In addition, there were no defenses on the western leg of the Dreieck along the Mosel, as the Westwall position had assumed a neutral Luxembourg.

Occupied by the Americans on the left bank, that flank was exposed and vulnerable, and the high ground gave them good artillery observation.[13]

Alerted by American pilots reporting panzers crossing the lower Saar at Saarburg, and through the night of the 17th, spurred by the sound of squealing tracks and engine sounds in the Campholz Woods just to the east, the Americans laid mines and brought up bazookas, pole and satchel charges, and sited antitank guns and tank destroyers and tensely awaited the expected assault.

On the cold dawn of 18 January mortars and artillery barrages smashed into the villages fortified by the Americans, the firing continuing for twenty minutes. "Geysers of dirt flew up from the streets," related the 94th Division history, "as snow, mud and jagged steel fragments ripped through the air." Pz.Gren.Rgt.110 was to attack Butzdorf and Tettingen, and Pz.G.R.111 was to attack Nennig and Wies. Led by the engineers of its 10. Kompanie, Wolff's I.Btl.(gp)/Pz.G.R.110 in their half-track Schützenpanzerwagen deployed and drove down from Sinz along with four Jagdpanzer IVs of Kessler's Pz.Jäger-Abt.61 and several Panzer IVs of 7.Kp./Pz.Rgt.15.

Other forces of II.Btl./Pz.G.R.110 issued forth from Campholz Woods. The right-hand forces drove against Butzdorf, the left-hand forces against Tettingen. The Americans resisted with artillery and mortar fire and tank destroyers, both towed and M36s with their 90mm guns, and also M4 tanks. Mines, and bazookas in the villages, took their toll. But at 11,30 hours ten Panthers of 2.Kp./15 arrived from Sinz and, going into hull defilade, lashed the villages with Panzergranate and Sprenggranate rounds. SPWs brought up the panzergrenadiers closer than usual, who then dismounted and worked into the buildings along with the panzers and 416. Grenadieren in their overcoats. It was Nahkampf, with MPi and Handgranate, and by nightfall the Gespensters captured Butzdorf. Damaged panzers were retrieved.[14]

With heavy fighting continuing at Tettingen-Butzdorf and at Nennig, the Americans mounted an attack on the town of Orscholz itself to the east, high above the Saar, defended by II.Btl./Gren.Rgt.712/416.Inf.Div. The Amis attacked in a snowstorm on the night of 19–20 January but encountered antipersonnel minefields of Schü-mines (S-mines), which blew off a GI's foot, and tangled barbed wire hidden in the snow, and interlocking machine-gun fire from the bunkers. One company had gotten ahead but was then cut off; attempts to reach it failed with heavy casualties from artillery and MG fire, tanks could not cross an antitank ditch, and by the 21st they were forced to surrender. The 10 officers and 230 men were mostly from B Company, 1st Battalion, 301st Infantry, 94th Division.[15]

Pflieger's 416. infantry also attacked the 376th Infantry of the 94th at Nennig on the 18th and 19th, but were thrown back by artillery observers on the Luxembourg side of the Mosel concentrating heavy fire to support the defenders. Then on the 20th panzergrenadiers of Pz.Gren.Rgt.110 aboard five panzers attacked from the north, and that evening four panzers with Pz.G.R.111 led an attack from the east, resulting in tenacious fighting. "A bazooka was a clumsy hunk of iron pipe" whose rounds "simply bounced off the tank," felt GI Bob Kingsbury of Easy Company, 376th Infantry.

With a renewed German assault on the 21st at a dark 21,00 hours under heavy American fire, including from 94th Division mortars across the Mosel, the Gespensters fought their way into the center of Nennig. Panzers blasted holes in the walls of Schloss Berg, and the Americans were forced to abandon the castle and half the town. But the Elften took heavy casualties as American reinforcements arrived.[16]

American tanks and armored infantry entered the battle the next day and fought into Nennig again, but were driven back out. This was Combat Command A of the fresh 8th Armored Division, joined by 2nd Battalion, 376th Infantry. The fighting was as intense as anywhere along the Western Front. Soldiers on both sides fought through snowdrifts, broke through icy trenches, and suffered in the piercing wind. The wounded in the open often froze to death, and at least on a couple of occasions local cease-fires were agreed upon for Sanis and medics to bring them in.

For panzer crews their ice-cold tanks, despite the heating ducts, could be as miserable as frozen mud trenches were for the panzergrenadiers. And the Ami artillery caused "one casualty after another," said Oberfeldwebel Georg Kolodziejczyk of 3.Kp./15, later a recipient of the Ritterkreuz. "The morale of the crews, who only left their Wagens in urgent cases, was further vexed by the ordered radio silence and the prohibition on keeping the engines running, not to be able to warm themselves a little."[17]

The sergeant did have a field telephone line to a commander of one of the 416. infantry regiments they were supporting. When the commander requested assistance to recapture a bunker, Kolodziejczyk said his three Panthers and fifteen or twenty men of the commander's Leute (people) could attack in the morning gray. But first he contacted battalion headquarters, saying in "code," "the doctor has ordered taking a walk and two others should walk as well." Oblt. Walter Rahn, alternatively commanding 1. Kompanie I./15 and the battalion Stabskompanie, replied, "the weather was too bad for a walk, that he might in no case go walking, since he would only catch a cold." *"Verstanden!"* responded the Ofw. But then it was determined to carry out the attack anyway. After retaking the bunker, claiming almost forty Ami Gefangene without loss, he radioed battalion, "The walk did us good, *alles in Ordnumg!*" and the infantry commander greeted him with a bottle of Schnaps.

In the fighting in Nennig on the 22nd Alfred Höckendorf with three panzers joined Ritterkreuzträger Ofw. Willi Frost, Zugführer in 4.Kp./15. "The streets of the place lay full of dead, yet we must go through," Höckendorf said. American artillery pounded the buildings and shell splinters and chunks of masonry rattled against the Panthers. Encountering American tanks Frost moved ahead too far and his Wagen was hit. The crew bailed out and dropped into an antitank ditch, but a shell splinter hit Frost and he died in the Feldlazarett. Höckendorf's panzer suddenly encountered a tank. The two commanders locked eyes, but before Höckendorf's gunner could traverse, the Ami backed around the corner of a building. As Panzergranate rounds streaked across and down streets his Kampfwagen was struck—his Fahrer hit in the head, his Richtschütze had his leg shattered. The Panzerwagen of Uffz. Ries was also hit and exploded into flames, but they were able to carry Ries into the castle, even as it was being blasted by tanks and artillery. In three more days of fighting, by 25 January, the Americans finally recaptured Nennig and Schloss Berg.

On 26 January in a blizzard the 94th Division launched an attack ahead toward Sinz, and again encountered Schü-mines and deadly machine gun crossfire, and then the dreaded panzers. CCA, 8th Armored Division was committed the next day and helped take Sinz, but was withdrawn on the 28th and Sinz was abandoned. Butzdorf was captured, but the 94th went onto the defensive, still amid the pillboxes, minefields, and antitank defenses of the Orscholzriegel—though the Mosel flank had *no* defenses, and might have offered an opening. General Patton was very critical of Malony.[18]

The skies had briefly cleared on 22 January as they had over the Ardennes. Four-engined B-24 Liberators bombed 12cm mortar and artillery positions at Beuren and Kreuzweiler, and on the 23rd P-47 fighter bombers bombed and strafed Sinz and Bannholz Woods where panzers and armored vehicles sheltered. But most of the fighting was in the winter gloom.[19]

The 94th Division began a series of limited-objective attacks again but it was evident that Patton was not mounting a major offensive in the Saar–Mosel Triangle, nor was there an objective of value beyond Trier or the lower Saar to the north and east. Wietersheim was bitter about the losses, and "the division fought on with the feeling that their battle was of no significance for the larger situation." The division commander, exhausted, finally had to report himself ill, though he stayed with his division.[20]

On 5 February the 11.Pz.-Div. began to be replaced by the 256. Volksgrenadierdivision mauled in NORDWIND, commanded by Gen.Maj. Gerhard Franz. The transition was completed by the 10th. Leaving some elements behind to support the 256.V.G.D., the Gespensters began to assemble southeast of Trier with the division command post at Osburg in the foothills of the Hunsrück. Pz.Aufklärungs-Abt.11 had had relatively few Verluste as it had been screening the open right flank along the Mosel, Pz.Art.Rgt.119 was brought up to strength, and sixty Panthers and Panzer IVs equipped Pz.-Rgt.15. Panzer grenadier strengths were low, despite replacements from the Ersatzbataillon, and a supplementary battalion with Pz.Gren. Rgt.110 (no longer identified as III.Btl.) was dissolved.[21]

Some Panthers of 4.Kp./Pz.Rgt.15 under Oblt. Müller-Hagen and II.Btl./111 with some others stayed to support the 256.V.G.D. as the 94th Division continued to struggle through the pillboxes and antitank obstacles and minefields of the Orscholz Barrier, with February bringing ten days of freezing rain.

Companies of M4 Sherman tank and M36 tank destroyer battalion attachments had been joined by M18 Hellcat tank destroyers (76mm). These were of the 704th Tank Destroyer Battalion usually attached to the 4th Armored Division. Just as small detachments of the Gespensters implied the rest of the 11.Pz.Div. might be nearby, so the destroyermen with the 4th Armored shoulder patch gave warning their division, recently in the Ardennes, might be in the vicinity.

There were nine days of bitter fighting for the 94th to gain the Campholz Woods (1–8 February), and in nine more days the Amis had still not secured Sinz and the Bannholz Woods (7–15 February). On 9 February the Panthers of 4.Kp./15 counterattacked in the Bannholz Woods destroying five M18 Hellcats and "are moving down the line with infantry," came the last American distress call, "firing into each foxhole" and taking twenty prisoners.

At Sinz there were so many casualties that on the 10th an American medical officer approached the Panthers on foot waving his helmet emblazoned with the Red Cross and requested treating the wounded. A Gespenster panzer commander came forward and agreed, providing he treat German casualties as well, and later thanked him.[22]

In the aftermath of the Ardennes offensive, with the 11. Panzer-Division withdrawn from the Saar-Moselle Triangle, and feeling that the 94th had finally penetrated the Orscholz Barrier, Patton committed the veteran 10th Armored Division on 20 February. One combat command drove along the open Mosel flank, another worked around with the 94th Division, and by the next day approached the Saar and the *main* part of the Westwall. There was no encirclement.

The Gespenster contingent, II./111 under Oblt. Horst Loch, withdrew across the Saar with the retreating Volksgrenadiers, but would not return to the division until east of the Rhine in early March. Horst Loch had succeeded Hptm. Lüth, gefallen, his body never recovered. Indeed, there were at least five battalion commanders of II./111 in the West through 1945, and four commanders of I./111.[23] Even if the Orscholz struggle had escalated into something more than Patton had intended, it was a threat that had to be met. The Elfte played a crucial role in containing it.

CHAPTER THIRTY-ONE

Defense of the Rhine

THE FATALISTIC SENSE OF DOOM ON THE OSTFRONT WAS realized on 12 January 1945 when the Red Army burst out of its Vistula River bridgeheads and stormed across Poland and into the Reich. At the same time in the West the Allied armies were slowly compressing the "Bulge" in the Ardennes and fending off the NORDWIND attacks. In the north the Third Belorussian Front under Gen. Ivan Chernyakovsky and Second Belorussian Front under Marshal Konstantin Rokossovsky smashed into Heeresgruppe Mitte commanded by Generaloberst Georg-Hans Reinhardt. The Russians drove into east Prussia, further isolating Generaloberst Ferdinand Schörner's H.Gr. Nord in the Kurland Peninsula.

In the center Marshal Zhukov's First Belorussian Front rampaged across western Poland and into eastern Germany and by 3 February reached Frankfurt on the Oder, 70 kilometers (40 miles) from Berlin itself. The First Ukrainian Front under Marshal Ivan Konev swept into Silesia through H.Gr. A under Generaloberst Josef Harpe and by 8 February was north of Breslau (Polish Wrocław), and farther south the Fourth, Second, and Third Ukrainian Fronts drove over Slovakia and Hungary (capturing Budapest 14 February) and into Austria. The Soviet power was overwhelming: 1.5 million troops against 596,000, 3,300 tanks against 700 panzers, 28,000 guns against 8,200, and 10,000 aircraft opposed to 1,300 of the Luftwaffe.

T-34 and IS-2 tanks swarmed across the frozen ground. A wave of fear spread over Germany at the onset of the Red hordes with horrific tales of murder, rape, and destruction that exceeded any embellishment—justified as savage reprisal for Nazi brutality in occupied Russia. On 22 January Hitler ordered Dietrich's 6. Panzerarmee, redesignated 6.SS-Panzerarmee, to the east—but then redirected it *south* instead to relieve Budapest in Hungary. "Of all his many strategic blunders," said Generalmajor von Mellenthin, his own wife and children barely escaping from Breslau, "this was the most incredible."[1]

By the end of January some 3.5 million German civilians were on the move fleeing the Russians, and ultimately there were some 7 million refugees—hundreds of whom were mashed under tank treads when overtaken. For those Gespensters who had homes and family in Schlesien, it was a nightmare they were helpless to affect, especially as the Nazi regime considered any organized evacuation of German civilians as "defeatist," as did Gauleiter Karl Hanke of Breslau.

As Konev's armies drove to the Oder in northern Lower Silesia in January they approached Sagan on the Bober, home base of Panzerregiment 15 and, by extension, of the 11. Panzerdivision. Werner Ellger was in the Ersatz-Abteilung of the panzer regiment, which was mobilized with the panzers at hand, and under Maj. Freiherr von Maerken dispatched southwest to Steinau, northeast of Liegnitz (Polish Legnica). There the battered 4. Panzerarmee under General der Panzertruppen Fritz Gräser was trying to contain a Russian bridgehead established by the 4th Tank Army north of Breslau.

Other elements were collected as infantry companies and given weapons, the training cadre and men from the convalescent company serving as platoon and squad leaders. The recruits were only seventeen to eighteen years old, still half-children, and several cried because they couldn't haul the heavy ammunition boxes on the march from the Dachsberg barracks to the railroad station. Defeated after eight days of fighting in the cold and snow, Ellger and other Fahnenjunker (officer cadets) were then ordered back to Sagan. He later learned that of the 150 men in his company only 26 came back. Major von Maerken's detachment was "rubbed out," and the Major was killed.[2]

One of those who returned from Steinau was Walter Volkmann. Born in Breslau he had just turned eighteen on 14 January. After service with the RAD (Reichsarbeitsdienst, Reich Labor Service) digging antitank ditches in Lithuania, he was in panzer training in Sagan. Later a driver of a Sturmgeschütz in Panzerabteilung Stansdorf II fighting near Cottbus southeast of Berlin, the unit was surrounded on 28 April at Radeland and taken prisoner by the Russians. All the girls were raped; they could hear their screams, and "We couldn't help them." Volkmann survived Russian slave labor at Maikop in the Caucasus, finally being released in April 1948.[3]

Other contingents went south to Oppeln where 17. Armee under Generalleutnant Friedrich Schulz, himself a Silesian, was opposing Konev's bridgehead of 5th Guards Army at Ohlau, south of Breslau. Konev was planning to encircle the fortress city, and by 16 February Breslau was surrounded (though not surrendering until 6 May).

On 27 January the Allied prisoners of war held at Stalag Luft III at Sagan were marched west as the Soviets approached. These were American and British air force personnel, "Kriegies" as they called themselves (from Kriegsgefangene, prisoners of war). After the Russians overran Silesia and occupied Sagan (Polish Zagan), the stone Kaserne on the Dachsberg was used as a prison camp for German soldiers, including Walter Volkmann.[4]

There were other masses moving west, even French and Polish slave laborers, who yet feared "liberation" by the fierce Soviet Red armies, a fear in many cases justified. The contrast between Russian Communist and Western culture had been evident from when the Red armies first entered Poland in 1944. "Immediately upon crossing the Polish border," said Frontovik Nikolai Litvin, "I noticed a change in the landscape. Farms were neatly arranged, and the soil was carefully tilled. You could sense the spirit of individualism." The contrast became stronger as the Rotarmisten entered Germany; the country was "different" and "clean" noted Lt. Evgeni Bessonov.[5]

In the West the Allied counteroffensive in the Ardennes evolved into a revived offensive eastward into the Eifel by February 1945. Buildups behind the Allied positions portended a series of assaults all along a broad front. Oberbefehlshaber West, Generalfeldmarschall Gerd von Rundstedt, had to ration his forces judiciously. In the north where Generaloberst Kurt Student was relieved and replaced at H.Gr. H by Generaloberst Johannes Blaskowitz (from H.Gr. G) on 29 January, General der Infanterie Günther Blumentritt's forces as 25. Armee defended the Netherlands, and 1. Fallschirmarmee under General der Fallschirmtruppen Alfred Schlemm held the Westwall through the Reichswald and along the Maas south to Roermond.

GFM Walter Model at H.Gr. B switched the headquarters of Gen.d.Pz.Tr. Hasso von Manteuffel and Gen.d.Inf. Gustav von Zangen, so Manteuffel's 5. Pz.Armee would defend the open country from the Roer east across the Rhineland to Cologne, the Rhine, and the Ruhr industrial complex of cities. The forces in the rugged Eifel would then be von Zangen's 15. Armee along with Gen.d.Pz.Tr. Erich Brandenberger's 7. Armee.

South of the Mosel the Saarland was still defended by 1. Armee, under Gen.d.Inf. Hans von Obstfelder since 4 December, now the single army in H.Gr. G. Blaskowitz had been replaced 29 January by Oberstgruppenführer und Generaloberst der Waffen-SS Paul Hausser, recovered from his wounding the previous 20 August commanding 7. Armee, though still wearing the right eyepatch from his 1941 wounding.

19. Armee and the Colmar forces had been under Heinrich Himmler as Heeresgruppe Oberrhein. As the longtime commander of 19. Armee, Gen.d.Inf. Friedrich Wiese, was perhaps unenthusiastic about reporting to the Reichsführer-SS, Wiese had been replaced on 15 December by Generalleutnant Siegfried Rasp. On 23 January, however, Hitler had Hausser succeed Himmler who he appointed to command H.Gr. Weichsel (Vistula) to stiffen the collapsing Ostfront. On the 29th Hitler dissolved H.Gr. Oberrhein, Hausser went to H.Gr. G, and 19. Armee reverted to H.Gr. G control. The employment of the 11. Panzer-Division was debated, especially after Hitler personally ordered the division pulled out of the Saar–Mosel Dreieck.

By February 1945 the 1 Canadian and 2 British Armies were poised to drive across the lower Maas toward the Ruhr. The US Ninth Army was ready to attack across the Roer, but the First Army had to seize the dams in the Hürtgen Forest controlling the river flooding before the Allies could safely cross. In the Eifel the aggressive Patton and most of his Third Army were ready to advance; they might drive *north* for an encirclement in the Cologne Plain, or drive *astride* the Mosel axis downriver to the Rhine at Koblenz or to Mainz and Frankfurt, or attack *south* across the Mosel *behind* the Saarland defenses and, possibly in concert with Seventh Army, encircle 7. and 1. Armee in the Saar Palatinate.

The Elfte was in OKW Reserve, but operationally had been controlled by Heeresgruppe G in January. As the Westwall lines of the Saarland had scarcely been penetrated, the primary concern of H.Gr. G was an Allied advance drive north *in* the Rhine valley to Weissenburg (Wissembourg), 30 kilometers (20 miles) west of Karlsruhe, toward Ludwigshafen and Mainz.

In January General von Wietersheim had proposed that his division be redeployed to fight for Silesia in the Ost, but the situation in the West was critical as well, and the Elfte was needed there. Division Ia Oberstlt. Werner Drews was dispatched to Kaiserslautern to prepare for advance parties to go to Wissembourg for a possible counterattack. Some Gespenster units entrained for movement at Zerf and Hermeskeil in the Osburger Hochwald of the Hunsrück Mountains southeast of Trier. Lack of fuel and bombed-out rail sections meant many detours and movement on foot or by Lastwagen shuttles.

But then on 21 February the division commander received a telephone message from GFM Model that he was to report *immediately* at the Gefechtsstand of the LVIII. Pz.Korps west of Köln. There Model met with Wieterseim and told him the division, along with 9.Pz.-Div., would be a reserve for the expected great American attack across the Roer toward the Rhine and the Ruhr. When he said the division must immediately assemble in the Düsseldorf–München–Gladbach/Grevenbroich area, Wietersheim protested that the division was already moving to Kaiserslautern and there was not enough fuel for such a long movement back up north. Model did not react but simply said, "In any case the division must be at Düsseldorf in three days."[6]

In the south on 2 February the French had taken Colmar, and the Americans took Neuf Brisach on the 6th, making the Rhine axis vulnerable. But in the north on 8 February the 1 Canadian Army under Lt. Gen. Henry Crerar attacked Schlemm's 1.Fallschirmarmee in the Reichswald between the Maas and the Rhine, beginning the major Allied offensive toward the Ruhr. By the 10th, the planned D-day for Lt. Gen. William Simpson's US Ninth Army crossing of the Roer, Hodges's First Army had captured the concrete Urft and earthen Schwammenauel Dams. But the Germans had destroyed the machinery and the discharge valves, and engineers calculated the Roer downriver would remain flooded for the next two weeks.

Nonetheless, the 11. Panzer units heading toward Kaiserslautern now had to be turned around and redirected north. Generalmajor Horst Freiherr Treusch von Buttlar-Brandenfels, arriving from the OKW staff, was put in charge of coordinating the complicated reverse movement. He may have been intended as acting division commander, but von Wietersheim stayed with his division, and so von Buttlar might be described as assistant division commander. Born 2 September 1900 in Kassel, von Buttlar had served as a staff officer, most recently on the Wehrmachtführungsstabes im OKW (WFSt.) of Generaloberst Alfred Jodl.[7]

On the 22nd the Div. Gefechtsstand opened at Gubberath west of Grevenbroich, and von Wietersheim met with the commanders of LXXXI. A.K., Gen.d.Inf. Friedrich Köchling, and XII.SS Korps, Gen.Lt. Eduard Crasemann, to coordinate the Elfte's role in the defense. Von Zangen's 15. Armee staff was in the process of exchanging positions with von Manteuffel's 5. Pz.-Armee Stab (an inopportune time to exchange commands felt Gen.Maj. von Mellenthin, now Chef des Stabes of 5. Pz.Armee), as the Roer floodwaters were beginning to recede and an American crossing was imminent. Reconnaissance Aufkl. Abt.11 and some panzers and artillery as they arrived moved up to positions around Titz to Königshoven astride the Düsseldorf–Aachen Rollbahn, supporting the 59. Infanterie and 363. Volksgrenadier Divisionen north of Jülich.

Maj. Jürgen Reichardt, now commanding Panzer-Regiment 15, and his staff detrained at Viersen north of München-Gladbach and set up quarters in Garzweiler. Each train had two or three cars with 2cm Vierlingsflak guns as air defense, and with the threat of Allied paratroop landings, sometimes the bow MG 34s of the panzers were dismounted and taken into quarters to be handy. They could not know that Generals Bradley, Patton, and other American commanders did not favor airborne operations, which required too much advanced planning and were too inflexible (drop zones, landing zones, weapons and equipment apportionment, and coordination with the USAAF); armored units could undertake a change of mission while on the move at 30 miles an hour.

On the left the Austrian 9.Pz.Div. under Gen.Maj. Harald Freiherr Gustav von Elverfeldt assembled along the Erft River covering the Düren-Köln axis. It had only twenty-nine panzers and sixteen assault guns, about the same operational strength as the 11.Pz.Div. The Erft was seen as the second Hauptkampflinie after the Roer HKL. In this more northern sector of the Westfront, the Royal Air Force was in evidence along with the USAAF, and Hptm. Heinz Wolff of I.Btl.(gp)/Pz.Gren.Rgt.110 was killed by a British fighter plane. He was succeeded by Hptm. Adalbert Höfer of II.Btl., having recovered from a wound in January. II.Btl. went to Oblt. Heinrich Stolze.[8]

On 23 February under a massed artillery bombardment, American troops of Ninth Army began the assault crossing of the Roer while the river was still high, to gain surprise, in Operation GRENADE. Under smoke screens from smoke generators and pots and chemical mortar phosphorous shells, the troops launched assault boats while engineers began to construct cable ferries and foot and treadway vehicle bridges. American intelligence estimated American superiority at 5:1 odds.

Model released the 9. and 11.Panzer-Divisionen to von Zangen's 15. Armee, still responsible for the sector, which in turn attached them to Köchling's LXXXI. A.K., though the Gespenster units were still arriving. The Americans captured Jülich the first day. The Germans had prepared minefields, antitank obstacles, and fields of fire, and the stone houses in the villages comprised strongpoints across the flat Köln Plain. But the defending forces were simply too weak to hold for long, and the panzer forces had to be committed piecemeal.

9.Pz.Div. lost its I.Btl./Pz.Gren.Rgt.10, only 200 men, and its commander, captured, along the uncompleted Aachen–Köln Autobahn (a four-lane, limited access, divided superhighway) in the Hambachwald. On the 27th American tanks, including a new model with a long barrel and muzzle brake, penetrated the defenses at Elsdorf. This was a T26 medium tank with a 90mm L/50 gun, a 41-ton vehicle with torsion bar suspension. Known as the "General Pershing," it was in a class with the T-34/85 and the Panther (redesignated M26 as adopted for production).

The drive was by the big 3rd "Spearhead" Armored Division, which reached the Erft fronting Köln. While the fourteen other US armored divisions were reorganized by the 15 September 1943 T/O&E as "light" armored divisions, the 3rd (and 2nd) retained the older ("heavy") organization of *two* tank regiments and an armored infantry regiment as well as the armored artillery and other battalions. There were 14,620 personnel and 390 tanks plus attachments, compared to 12,774 personnel and 269 tanks (including routine attachments) in the "light" ADs by the 12 February 1944 T/O&E. In addition, an infantry regiment was usually attached for balancing out the regimental combat commands.[9]

A Kampfgruppe from Gen.Maj. Walter Denkert's 3. Panzergrenadierdivision came north from the Eifel, but the American drive was too powerful and the German forces too weak to stop it. The wrecked 59.Inf.Div. was put under the 11.Pz.Div. On the 26th

Reichardt, as Kommandeur of Pz.-Rgt.15, received a Funkbefehl for his senior officer to take command of a Volksgrenadier regiment to defend Kirchherten. But considering the dispersed units—one of them reported "30 men including leader. Weapons: 8 Panzerfäuste, no rifles"—Reichardt considered it unworkable.

At the same time his own Panther was destroyed by an artillery shell. He and his crew were able to get out, and at night headed east cross-country, guiding by tracers being fired. Kirchherten was lost, and when Reichardt returned he was blamed and arrested for a court-martial. Thanks to the energetic intervention of his division commander, General von Wietersheim, he was released after two days.[10]

At OB West von Rundstedt sensed that Simpson's Ninth Army was swinging north for an encirclement with 1 Canadian Army. He finally got Hitler's agreement to retreat from a now-exposed salient at Roermond, the confluence of the Roer and the Maas, faced by the British 2 Army. Thus by the time British troops with Crerar's Canadians met the Americans at Geldern on 3 March, Schlemm's forces had withdrawn.

Behind the Roer River defenses 11.Pz.-Div. elements fought what were now delaying actions at Hottorf, Garzweiler, and Grevenbroich. But American armor had been committed in the form of the 8th, the 5th, and the big 2nd Armored Divisions, and with the fast-moving infantry divisions, Ninth Army was entering the exploitation phase across the Köln Plain to the Rhine. München-Gladbach was taken on 1 March with little resistance and the main drive was to Neuss and Düsseldorf.

Manteuffel, taking command of 15. Armee's former sector, ordered a pincers attack from the north by Panzer-Lehr, which had been fighting the Canadian drive, and 11.Pz.Div. from the south. But this clearly was no longer practical. XII.SS Korps fell back to the north, separated from LXXXI. A.K., including the Elfte, and they withdrew back to the Erft. There was talk about concentrating the 11. Panzer and the PLD under its commander, Gen.Lt. Fritz Bayerlein, as Korps Bayerlein, but that was clearly impractical as well.

On 28 February the Gespensters began withdrawing across the Erft, the north flank of LXXXI. A.K., with the battered 59.I.D. and 363.V.G.D. The division command post was removed from Ökoven southeast of Grevenbroich to Ückerath. But there were no prepared positions, and the Elften fell back toward Zons north of Dormagen on the west bank of the Rhine halfway between Düsseldorf and Köln. The Pz.Rgt.15 I-Staffel situated at Dormagen.

On 2 March General von Buttlar, with rolling elements of the division, crossed the Rhine by boats, barges, and ferries to Benrath near Hilden "to at least occupy something as receiving point on the other bank of the Rhine with the [coming] catastrophe," said General von Wietersheim. Somehow the Gespensters retained their cohesion and morale. When four of the men of Pz.Art.Rgt.119 begged to see their families as the division was near Köln, Adjutant Oberleutnant Rolf Wandhoff understood their concern and released them, not expecting them to return. Yet three did return, saying that at the end "we want to be with the old crowd." Both Wandhoff and Schaefer-Kehnert felt that officers, noncoms, and men working together and sharing the same hardships and dangers, was a major factor in the Gespenster morale, of "being welded together."[11]

On the west bank it was a case of mobile defense, with short, radioed Sattelbefehlen to Panzerkampftrupps—single panzers or panzerjägers, SPWs or Spähwagens, some Pioniere and Artillerie V.B.s, and by chance a platoon of Panzergrenadiere. The SPW battalion of 110 was still relatively intact, and on the left flank A.A.11 tried to keep contact with 9.Pz.Div. north of Köln. Late on the night of 3–4 March the Elfte received orders to cross the Rhine.[12]

But there was still heavy fighting along what was now merely a bridgehead on the west bank. The nature of the fighting near Zons was reflected by Feldwebel Friedrich Rüther of 4. Kompanie/Pz.Rgt.15, in a Kampfgruppe led by Lt. Rudolf Graf Hoyos, at Stürzelberg. At 15,45 Uhr on 5 March an order was received for the two best panzers to go in the direction of St. Peter, and report to a rifle battalion commander, Oblt. Mathes. The Bataillonsgefechtsstand was two kilometers back, but the road was exposed to heavy tank and artillery fire.

Rüther, Kommandant of his Panther, had an experienced crew: Richtschütze Uffz. Fritz Burger wore the Panzerkampfabzeichen in Silber, Ladeschütze Ogefr. Heinz Hirschner was dependable even if no Auszeichnung yet, Fahrer Ogefr. Peter Abele, Träger of the EK 2. and Pz.-Kampfabzeichens 2. Stufe (level), and likewise Funker Ogefr. Paul Kowasch. Abele shifted into seventh gear and at a speed of 40 km/h (25 mph)—*Vollgas!*—raced the distance without incident. But

American infantry were already into the houses and factories of the industrial community of Nievenheim.

Without further orders, Rüther positioned his Wagen between houses to cover the Derikum road. Soon two Shermans appeared and, knowing as a Panzermann to engage the most dangerous threat of the opponent, Rüther had Burger engage the first tank, then make a slight turn of the traversing wheel and engage the second, both exploding into flames after four Panzerbrechende Granate rounds. Two other tanks dipped behind a railroad line, but not fast enough, and were hit and flamed up. *Volltreffer!* Rüther then had Abele back up and drive north through the industrial area to engage the American infantry with Sprenggranate.

But suddenly there was an electrical failure on the main gun, so Rüther engaged with bow and turret machine guns. He sighted another tank in a straw rick at 500 meters, and this time the main gun worked again. One hundred meters to the right was a sixth tank that began traversing, but Burger was faster, and Rüther claimed this as well. Yet there were losses: when Wagen 212 was hit by an artillery shell Rüther helped save the crew who bailed out, though Kommandant Lt. Graf Hoyos was wounded.[13]

Despite a panzer's number stenciled on the turret, a commander would use whatever was available. Near Köln company commander Oblt. von Fersen, call sign "Der Roller" ("The Scooter"), had the regimental command Panther ROII in support of the 111. Panzergrenadieren. But it was knocked out with a hit to the track and to the turret gun mantlet. Nonetheless Oberst von Kielmansegg had him and his Funker stay for two hours utilizing the medium-wave radio set tuned to the regimental frequency.[14]

In armored actions, once again the importance of radio communication was demonstrated. Unteroffizier Klaus Bardt was a gunner on Panther number 233, covered with branches, good Tarnung, and positioned at the edge of some woods in a dense overcast—albeit with an inoperative radio. The crew became aware that three panzers on the right were moving back with their turrets at the six o'clock position (facing the enemy). "Did we get a radio order but could not hear it? Unpleasant uncertainty!" The Kommandant then felt it best to pull back as well. Maintenance at Dormagen repaired the radio the next day.

Bardt was one of the recent replacements. Born at Hubertushof in the Warthegau, he was six years old when Hitler came into power, and thirteen when the war broke out. Assigned to Luftwaffe air defense near Spandau in 1944, he had some experience with the 8,8cm flak gun before undergoing panzer training at Sagan for Pz.Rgt.15. In another incident, Lt. Erich von Witzleben's 4.Kp. Panther was knocked out and he and his crew jumped into a cellar. "Surprise: occupied by GIs!" and the Germans were taken prisoner. But when some GIs went for coffee they escaped again. (Witzleben was later killed near Remagen.)[15] Most of the Gespensters crossed the Rhine the night of 4 March, the rearguard elements the night of the 5th. General von Wietersheim and certain staff members crossed in the last assault boat of Pz.Pionier-Btl. 209.

Hitler had demanded that Köln itself be defended, the ruined city badly gutted by two years of RAF bombing. The flak guns of air defense were deadly against the advancing American tanks, as were Panzerfausts in the rubble. Nonetheless tanks entered the city on 5 March followed by infantry. These were tanks of the US 3rd Armored Division. They were resisted by Volksgrenadier, Volkssturm, and other elements, including those of 9.Pz.Div. whose commander, Gen.Maj. von Elverfeldt, was killed. By noon on the 7th Köln was cleared. The retreating Germans demolished the Hohenzollern Rhine Bridge and the last defenders crossed to the east bank between there and Worringen to the north.

As the American forces approached the Rhine they were eager to seize a bridge intact across the fabled river. But in this they were apparently discouraged by Field Marshal Sir Bernard Montgomery. The British leader was planning a massive set-piece offensive to cross the Rhine north of the Ruhr industrial area, and he did not want to be preempted by the Americans. He was supported by Supreme Allied Commander General Eisenhower, perhaps for inter-allied diplomatic reasons.

But the German high command was more concerned with the operations of the American Third Army, recognizing General Patton as the most able and aggressive of the Allied commanders in the West. Positioned in the Ardennes resulting from the Battle of the Bulge, Patton had pushed into the Eifel through the German defenses, his VIII Corps taking Prüm by 12 February, his XII Corps fighting into Bitburg by the 27th. South of the Mosel his XX Corps crossed the Saar on the 22nd, and captured Trier on 2 March.

Patton's offensive was renewed on 5 March from the Prüm and the Kyle River lines. Most dramatically an armored column erupted through and then behind the German positions, and, following a single road through the Hohe Eifel it drove relentlessly eastward, overrunning gun positions and twisting through little towns, the tanks towing half-tracks through the mud of churned-up trails and smashing into approaching German columns or overtaking retreating columns. (General der Kavallerie Edwin Graf von Rothkirch, commander of LIII. A.K., found his command car in a cluster of tanks and was taken prisoner.) The American tanks buttoned up when hit by artillery, and kept firing on the move. They scattered rear-echelon elements, and directed surprised Germans to the American rear as prisoners of war.

By nightfall of the 7th the tankers debouched into the Rhine valley across from Neuweid, just north of Koblenz near Andernach. In two and a half days they had sliced 100 kilometers (65 miles) from the Kyle to the Rhine through the rugged Hohe Eifel. This was Combat Command B of the vaunted 4th Armored Division under Maj. Gen. Hugh Gaffey, led by Brig. Gen. Holmes Dager with Lt. Col. Creighton Abrams's 37th Tank Battalion in the fore, followed by CCA. Patton had ordered the armor to attack boldly on the roads, disregarding the wooded heights, which were left to artillery and fighter-bombers until the infantry came up.[16]

In the process the 4th Armored had cleaved through 7. Armee, commanded by Gen.d.Inf. Hans Felber who had succeeded the ousted Brandenberger on 20 February. (Brandenberger later commanded 19. Armee after 25 March.) On 2 March 7. Armee had been transferred from Model's H.Gr. B to Hausser's H.Gr. G to defend against Patton. At the same time to the north, US First Army forces led by 9th Armored Division crossed the Erft near Euskirchen on 2 March and pressed toward the Rhine south of Köln and the valley of the Ahr, which flowed in at Sinzig.

Learning of Rothkirch's capture, Model subordinated the separated LIII. A.K. under 15. Armee to the north and ordered Generalmajor Walter Botsch, preparing defenses at Bonn and Remagen along the Rhine, to take over its command. As von Zangen's 15. Armee was itself threatened with encirclement from the north, Model ordered the 11. Panzer-Division, recovering near Hilden, to go south, recross the Rhine at Bonn, and attack southwest toward Rheinbach and the Ahr to blunt the American drives.

General von Wietersheim had been called to a Lagebesprechung (situation meeting) at Bad Godesberg just south of Bonn (both towns being on the left or west bank of the Rhine) to discuss such an operation on 7 March. American forces were already approaching Bonn, and von Wietersheim noted the shortage of fuel to move his division from Hilden, and the difficulties of recrossing the river. Upon his return to the division command post that night, he received the report that the Amis had seized the railroad bridge crossing the middle Rhine at Remagen, planked for vehicle transit, by surprise that day.

On the 8th Model ordered von Wietersheim to immediately go to the bridge site, organize whatever troop elements were there, and with his division remove (beseitigen) the Brückenkopf at that location and destroy the bridge. Wietersheim ordered his Elften to prepare to move south, well aware that lack of Betriebsstoff (POL) meant his units could only move piecemeal. He was also skeptical about the value of the Remagen crossing for the Americans, as the river there went through the picturesque but steep gorge formed by the Siebengebirge of the forested Westerwald, blocking approaches to the Ruhr from the south (the Rhine itself had no defenses), and there were better locations at which to cross, especially considering the disintegrating morale and power of the Wehrmacht.[17]

On that 7 March Combat Command B of the US 9th Armored, which was driving for the valley of the Ahr, discovered that the Ludendorff railroad bridge at Remagen was still intact. It hastily threw forces across to hold it. The American commanders—Hodges, Bradley, and Eisenhower—were enthusiastic about the accomplishment, but then Eisenhower began to have second thoughts, for the same reasons that Wietersheim had speculated. Eisenhower was also reluctant to deviate from the broad front concept of closing all along the Rhine and *then* launching Montgomery's offensive north of the Ruhr. This was all true, but Patton's 4th Armored had just demonstrated how even the rugged Eifel could be negotiated with resolute leadership.

In the meantime the American foothold had to be eliminated. To coordinate a counterattack Model designated Generalleutnant Fritz Bayerlein. But his own Panzer-Lehr-Division could only count fifteen panzers and 300 men, and 9.Pz.Div. now under Oberst Helmuth Zollenkopf could only contribute fifteen panzers and 600 men. Pz.Brigade 106 Feldherrnhalle under Oberstlt. Heinrich Drewes, which had been fighting in Köln with the 9.Pz.-Div. and then in Bonn, was now only company-sized with five panzers. The 11. Panzer-Division with its twenty-five panzers, eighteen artillery pieces, and 4,000 men, would be a significant addition—if they could get enough Benzin (gasoline) to move down from Hilden.

Hitler used the occasion of the loss of the Remagen bridge to finally remove stalwart old Feldmarschall Gerd von Rundstedt at OB West on 8 March, and summon Luftwaffe General and Generalfeldmarschall Albert Kesselring up from Italy. As commander of OB Süd he had been effectively delaying the Allied advance there. Noted for his optimism and smile, he greeted his staff on the 10th with the witty remark, "Well, gentlemen, I am the new V.3."[18]

On 9 March First Army's 9th Armored Division met Patton's 11th AD near the Rhine, but many of von Zangen's remnants of 15. Armee were able to get across the river by boats and ferries. At Remagen the arriving panzer forces from the north sought to establish a defense line Ockenfels–Ohlenberg–north bank of the Erpel. On the 9th Model drove down from Essen to Bayerlein's headquarters at Oberpleis across the Rhine from Bad Godesberg, and then they both went to Kalenborn in the hills across from Remagen where von Wietersheim had established the Div.Gef.Std. in the basement of the schoolhouse.

Model approved an attack for the 10th with a Kampfgruppe from Panzer-Lehr and some 11.Panzer elements, but when PLD Kampfgruppe Hudel was delayed in moving down, the idea was dropped. Some Elfte units arrived, having found fuel around Düsseldorf, some even using the four-lane divided Reichsautobahn Köln–Frankfurt highway. The 9th Infantry Division G-2 (Intelligence) tracked them to the Hertscheid exit and toward Rheinbreitbach. Gespenster Ia Drews believed the move on the Autobahn was so brazen that any American air reconnaissance assumed they were American units. The Elften took up position around Bruchhausen.

Oblt. Kurt Störmer, assistant operations officer, recalled the staff's 90-kilometer (50-mile) all-night move from Düsseldorf-Hilden: "It was a ghastly move, full of reminders of how desperate was our situation. When we reached Kalenborn on the morning of the 8th [*sic*; 9th] it was incredibly difficult to get a picture of what had happened from the mish-mash of units then in contact with the enemy. Field Marshal Model paid a visit and bellowed his orders to 'stop the Americans at all costs,' but we needed ideas or guns and ammunition, not empty promises or haranguing. That man was a midget, full of poison."[19]

The Americans were building up their bridgehead, their engineers putting in more bridges and three pontoon ferries. When they attacked Bad Honnef where Pioniere had constructed obstacles, however, the Elfte's A.A.11 mounted a Gegenstoss that drove them back on the 11th. The Amis were expanding the bridgehead toward the Sieg River across from Bonn in the north, and to Andernach in the south, and east toward the Autobahn, with six divisions; but they remained undecided as to whether it might be the basis for an offensive north against the Ruhr, or south toward Frankfurt, or not utilized at all.

More German units were arriving as well, two Volksartillerie Korps with 15cm and 21cm howitzers, and the 340. Volksgrenadierdivision. Von Zangen's 15. Armee Hauptquartier coordinated the defense, though Bayerlein wanted to attack with what he had before the Brückenkopf consolidated. In this he was overruled by Model and Kesselring who felt more concentrated force was needed—and this was always the dilemma, the question of which force could build up faster. Meanwhile the Germans tried to destroy the bridges with Luftwaffe attacks, artillery shelling, and even V-2 rockets from the Netherlands, and seven underwater swimmers. Little damage was done and, although the Ludendorff Brücke itself collapsed on 17 March, the American bridgehead was secured.

Model could rally elements from seven more divisions, but these were scarcely even battalion-sized Kampfgruppen. Three corps headquarters controlled these forces, the panzer forces in the north under Bayerlein, given LIII. Armeekorps, the LXXIV. A.K. Feldgrauen under General der Infanterie Karl Püchler in the center, and LXVII. A.K. under Gen.d.Inf. Otto Hitzfeld in the south. Oberst Horst Niemack from the Grossdeutschland Füsilier-Regiment in the east took command of Panzerlehr. Pz.Brig.106 FHH and Oberst Zollenkopf's weak 9.Pz.Div. were around Bad Honnef, and in the rugged hills to the east of Rheinbreitbach was the Elfte's A.A.11.

The 11.Pz.Div. was coming into the Kalenborn-Vettelschoss area, the Div.Gef.Std. moving back to Günderscheid by the Autobahn on the 11th—to be greeted by an artillery barrage that caused considerable casualties among the staff. In the south Rheinpioniere units put up obstacles supported by the PLD Kampfgruppe around Dattenberg south of Linz.

Generalmajor von Buttlar was named to command a "Panzer-Brigade" including the Panzerlehr Kgr. and some elements of the 11. Panzer in the center. The Americans kept pressing to expand the bridgehead, along the Rhine valley at Bad Honnef in the north and toward Bad Hönning in the south, and into the high hills overlooking the valley, the 11.Pz.Div. fighting at Notscheid and Vettelschoss. On the 14th the Div.Gef.Std. removed east of the Autobahn to Bettenau, and on the 15th to the Kloster (Cloister) Ehrenstein east of Neustadt. Gespenster Panzerkampftrupps had to be formed ad hoc from officers and panzers that were available. These included some Jagdpanthers, and Uffz. Klaus Bardt was assigned as gunner on one as he had become familiar with the 8,8cm flak at Spandau.

Long-experienced Oberleutnant Walter Rahn, commanding 1.Kp./15 since November, was stationed at a military hospital back at Hilden when he was ordered to take command of I. Abteilung (Panther)/ Pz.Rgt.15. He found the Abteilungsgefechtsstand at the schoolhouse in Vettelschoss on 14 March and got a Lagebericht (situation report) briefing. The battalion was subordinated to Oberstlt. Karl Thieme's Pz.G.R.110. At about 23,30 hours Lt. Herbert Henkel of 1. Kompanie reported with five repaired panzers for attack orders for the next day. Afterwards, Henkel and Rahn woke the battalion surgeon, Dr. Knoflach, to congratulate him on his 30th birthday, the 15th. All three had gotten married shortly before, and their new roles as husbands connected them. As a Geburtstag gift all they could offer was a cigarette rolled with the last tobacco crumbs until they could celebrate with a drink.

But at dawn on the 15th Rahn awoke to a heavy artillery Trommelfeuer of Vettelschoss and of the entire section of the front line. The telephone line to regiment was severed. After a quick orientation briefing by radio, Rahn ran up to learn that Lt. Henkel had lost four of five Panthers to artillery shells; then Henkel's Funker signaled, "Commander killed by artillery hit," as well. Thieme ordered Rahn to block a flank attack, and he radioed Lt. Erich von Witzleben of 4.Kp. to prepare with six einsatzbereit Panthers he could gather.

Rahn then rode over in a motorcycle sidecar. But coming under fire, he and the driver stopped in a hollow and he continued alone on foot. Suddenly ten to fifteen olive-drab figures appeared, rifles leveled. Rahn had no choice but to raise his arms, carefully away from his pistol holster. The GIs then took his pistol, wristwatch, medals, and Soldbuch, but returned the photographs of his new wife.

Walter Rahn would always be indignant about his treatment after that. When interrogated, he said he stubbornly cited the Geneva Convention, and was placed on the fender of a combat vehicle exposed to fire. Then he was taken by jeep to a wooden barrack between Kretzhaus and Linz where a German-speaking officer ripped off his shirt and his "Hundemarke" (metal Erkennungsmarke identity disc), took him outside, and put a pistol to the back of his neck, telling him "You aren't registered anywhere and your body will be buried here in the park." This wasn't how the Gespensters treated their Gefangene. "I would have expected this kind of treatment from the Soviets, but not from the Americans," Rahn said.

Taken to a PW collecting point at a schoolyard in Linz, a third interrogator was friendlier and said Rahn might have been considered SS because of the black panzer uniform and death's head insignia, a claim he did not believe. In further discussion about the unbroken fighting spirit of the 11. Panzer-Division, Rahn said he attributed this to General von Wietersheim and the officers always looking after the welfare of their soldiers, and also to the front-line soldiers feeling bound by their soldier's oath.

Rahn subsequently was incarcerated at a PW camp at Attichy near Compiègne, France. He learned Lt. von Witzleben had been killed on the 15th and Dr. Knoflach was mortally wounded and Henkel gefallen, and with his own capture, it was a sad "Ides of March." Erich von Witzleben was related to Generalfeldmarschall Erwin von Witzleben; involved in the 20 July assassination conspiracy, the field marshal was arrested by the Gestapo, tried, and executed.[20]

On 16 March the Americans reached the Reichsautobahn at Brüngsberg. 340.V.G.D. commanded by Generalleutnant Theodor Tolsdorff was inserted between the 9. and 11.Pz.Div. but could not change the situation. On the 19th the American 1st Infantry Division fought into Eudenbach beyond the Autobahn and overran the Sauerwiese airfield. As with other captured airfields, there were camouflaged revetments, and planes abandoned or destroyed, often for lack of fuel. Here there were two Stukas, two Fw 190s, a twin-engined Ju 88, and a Fieseler 56 and 156 Storch.[21]

On the 20th the 340.V.G.D. began to relieve the Elfte, which was to move north to the Sieg River.

That night the first elements began to move, followed by the rest the next night. One third of Artillerie-Rgt.119 and the few elements in Panzer-Brigade Buttlar were to stay behind and support the 340.

One complication was an order to destroy the Autobahn bridge across the Wied. It was more useful for the Remagen defenders shifting forces at that point than of possible use by the Americans, but with a so-called Führerbefehl, after the division crossed, one of the pillars was destroyed. By 23 March the 11.Pz.Div. was assembled south of the Sieg east of Siegburg to refit, and also to block an American northern advance from Remagen.[22] It remained to be seen whether the Americans would mount a major breakout from Remagen—and what role Patton's Third Army would play.

CHAPTER THIRTY-TWO

From Germany to Czechoslovakia

ON 13 MARCH 1945 GENERAL PATTON'S THIRD ARMY BEGAN TO move—but *not* across the Rhine or through the Remagen bridgehead. South of Trier his XX Corps attacked from its Saar bridgehead into the forested Hunsrück against a regiment of 6.SS Gebirgsdivision Nord of LXXXII. Armeekorps. The next day his XII Corps attacked *southeast*, across the Mosel against LXXXIX. A.K. The river itself, with its spectacular terraced vineyards and multitudinous loops, was impossible to defend except on the high plateaus. But LXXXIX. A.K. scarcely had enough forces to do so anyway.

On the 15th two armored spearheads thrust from the XII Corps bridgehead and swept south parallel to the Rhine, reaching the Nahe River near Bad Kreuznach and Gensingen, scarcely twenty-four hours from the Mosel. Gen.d.Inf. Hans Felber, commander of 7. Armee since 20 February, with his staff barely evaded the armored columns—tanks, armored cars, half-tracks, self-propelled artillery—while fighter-bombers strafed retreating Germans trying to infiltrate through the fast-rolling Americans in the bright spring sunshine. These spearheads were Combat Commands B and A of the 4th Armored Division, followed by motorized regimental combat teams of the 5th and 90th Infantry Divisions, fighter-bombers of XIX Tactical Air Command swooping overhead.[1]

The German high command had not been sure where Patton would strike next. In the north Montgomery's 21 Army Group was building up, but not moving. Nor were the Americans apparently going to exploit from their Remagen bridgehead. On that same 15 March Patch's US Seventh Army began a set-piece attack on a broad front from Saarbrücken east to the Rhine against 1. Armee under Gen.d.Inf. Hermann Förtsch (in command since 28 February), but the Westwall fortifications were defended as stubbornly as ever.

Was Patton going to force a crossing above the Rhine gorge between Bingen and Mainz? Was he going to drive toward Frankfurt and then Kassel or Fulda? Or was he going to swing down along the Nahe to meet his XX Corps advance and encircle 7. Armee? Instead his 4th Armored crossed the Nahe driving south*east* and reached

Worms on the Rhine by 20 March. Patton now had three more armored divisions in action and swept across the Saar-Palatinate, the 12th AD taking Ludwigshafen, behind 1. Armee, with the apparent intention of not only encircling 7. Armee, but 1. Armee as well, in a huge Kesselschlacht.

With Patton rampaging behind them, the Westwall defenders collapsed, and the remnants of Hausser's two armies fled eastward to escape across the upper Rhine. On 24 March Patton's 12th AD met 14th AD from Seventh Army at Germersheim on the Rhine south of Speyer, completing the huge encirclement.

No more graphic contrast between the mobile maneuvers of Patton's Third Army, and the set-piece frontal attack along a very wide front by Seventh Army against defended fortifications, can be found than in this eleven-day campaign. Seventh Army slugged forward into the defenses, until 1. Armee disintegrated with Patton *behind* them, and suffered over twice his casualties.[2] And this is why the Germans respected General Patton as the most able American commander.

Patton was already jumping the Rhine downriver at Oppenheim, on 22 March. Indeed, it seems his primary motive was to cross the Rhine before Montgomery's carefully prepared assault crossing planned for the night of the 23rd. But Patton was not being reckless: he sensed the German forces were in disarray and not prepared for a surprise crossing, and his 5th Infantry Division was well versed in river crossings. Assault boats, landing craft, and bridging equipment were rapidly brought up, and under a moonlit sky they crossed the storied river against scattered resistance. On the 23rd with tactical air support the Amis pressed rapidly inland, while tanks began to cross for the exploitation.

The defenders were the remnants of Felber's 7. Armee, which Kesselring at OB West had allowed to retreat across the Rhine. The sector stretched 80 kilometers (50 miles) from Wiesbaden, opposite Mainz, to Mannheim. He had only one corps, XIII. A.K., commanded by Generalleutnant Ralph Graf von Oriola, with four weak divisions—two of them with only 400 men each. At Oppenheim there were students, cadres, convalescent companies, and security elements under Wehrkreis XII, the local military district. This headquarters was summarily upgraded as XII. A.K., but it had no organized units.

Officer candidates from a training school in Wiesbaden with a few panzers and assault guns were sent into a counterattack shortly after midnight on the 23rd, but were soon dispersed by artillery or surrendered to the infantry. There was nothing to stop Patton from sweeping on to Darmstadt or to Frankfurt on the Main River, or both.[3]

Wietersheim's 11. Panzer-Division had scarcely assembled east of Siegburg south of Köln when on 24 March OB West ordered it south to Frankfurt. The next day General von Wietersheim drove ahead to Frankfurt, made telephone contact with 7. Armee, and was ordered to assemble the division north of Hanau just east of Frankfurt. The staff was already putting the division into motion, the route being Altenkirchen–Limburg–Camberg–Esch and then up to Merzhausen to Usingen north of Frankfurt. The movement had to be made in increments and as fuel was available. Any moves were at night, as American airpower was all-pervasive by day. Even cloud cover did not prevent the little low-flying L-4 Piper Cubs from delivering observed artillery fire.

Panzerbrigade Buttlar was held back at Remagen, and Pz.Gren.Rgt.111 under Oberst Graf von Kielmansegg was held to defend the Sieg by Model. Putting Hptm. Rodenhauser, as senior commander, in charge of Pz.-Rgt.15 elements, Reichardt stayed back with ten Panthers. The Gespensters did find that stragglers from other units gravitated to the Elfte as it still reflected organization and cohesion.[4]

But the situation was changing rapidly and dramatically. On 25 March American armor came charging out of the Oppenheim bridgehead and swept south of Darmstadt, and seized crossings of the Main at Aschaffenburg and at Hanau east of Frankfurt. These were Combat Commands B and A of the 4th Armored Division. An armored column even drove 60 kilometers (35 miles) due east to Hammelburg, ostensibly to liberate the American prisoners in the Kriegsgefangenenlager (Stalag XIII C) there, but was destroyed.[5]

There were other crossings of the Rhine as well. Patton's forces crossed in the cliff-edged gorge of the Rhine above Koblenz, at Boppard on 25 March under the frown of medieval Schloss Marksburg at Braubach, and at St. Goar the next day, raising the American flag on the fabled high rock of the siren Loreley. On the 28th another crossing was made at Mainz, though by that time most German defenders had withdrawn.

South of Oppenheim on the 26th the Seventh Army attacked across the river north and south of

Worms. The assault included the use of DD amphibious tanks (Duplex Drive M4s floated by canvas skirts) as had been used at Normandy. American First Army forces also began to break out of the Remagen bridgehead on the 24th but started thrusting east to link up with Third Army, not north across the Sieg toward the Ruhr. Gen. Hans Felber received the blame for not stopping the Americans and late on the 26th was succeeded at 7. Armee by Gen.d.Inf. Hans von Obstfelder from 19. Armee, succeeded there by Erich Brandenberger.

Much farther north Montgomery's 21st Army Group launched its heralded offensive across the Rhine north of the Ruhr on the night of 23–24 March against 1. Fallschirmarmee. Following a massive artillery and air bombardment and behind a smoke screen, the British 2 Army north of Wesel and the US Ninth Army south of the city assaulted across the river in fast storm boats, assault boats, and amphibious tanks followed by landing craft and then the ferry and bridging engineers. On the 24th two airborne divisions dropped north of Wesel and linked up with the ground forces by nightfall.

At Heeresgruppe H Generaloberst Johannes Blaskowitz (having replaced Kurt Student) ordered his mobile units to counterattack. 15.Pz.Gren.Div. did attack the British at Rees but had to fall back. He also ordered General von Lüttwitz of XXXXVII. Pz.K. to have the 116.Pz.-Div. attack the Americans south of the Lippe, but an Allied advance north of the Lippe to Haltern on the 29th forced the Windhund Division to withdraw. Blaskowitz and Gen.d.Inf. Günther Blumentritt, now at 1. Fallschirmarmee, urged a retreat to the rugged Teutoburgerwald and then behind the Weser; but Hitler, and Kesselring at OB West, forbade that. Crossing the north–south Dortmund–Ems Canal, the Allied drive picked up momentum; not south against the Ruhr, but east toward Lippstadt and Paderborn, threatening as the northern arm to encircle the forces defending the Ruhr.

As Wietersheim's 11. Panzerdivision units worked their way south from the Sieg on 25–26 March, Panzer Aufklärungsabteiling 11 reached Bad Vibel just northeast of Frankfurt to cover the movement to Usingen for employment east of Bad Nauheim and Friedburg. Einsatzbereit panzers covered the movement of disabled panzers towing each other, panzers with broken suspensions, turrets binding, and gun defects, the crews working with the I-Staffel to salvage what fighting power they could.[6]

But as the units moved south on the 26th they were assailed all along the route from Altenkirchen to Limburg on the Lahn by American armored forces breaking out from the Remagen bridgehead toward the east, even as Patton's Third Army flooded across the Rhine. The panzers and panzergrenadiers put up desperate resistance and mounted counterattacks from the line of march. On the 27th more American armor swung down from Limburg to Camberg and Idstein northwest of Frankfurt while other forces drove east toward Marburg and Giessen. At Altenkirchen H..Flak-Abt.277 had to destroy some of the 8,8cm flak guns lacking transport and fuel, and divisional service personnel were captured on the route to Limburg.

Hauptmann Walter Schaefer-Kehnert's III.Abt./119 had stayed behind at Remagen positioned in a basalt quarry, and was overrun. With two others in his "kleine Willy" jeep he tried to rejoin his division, but American tanks and troops were everywhere. At one point Schaefer-Kehnert and the other two were hiding in a potting shed when he saw a GI approaching, rifle at the ready. "A rabbit crossed his path and he ran after it. I am convinced that rabbit saved our lives." On 8 May he finally surrendered at an American command post, but escaped from a train taking PWs to France to get back to his family farm in Magdeburg—only to find it taken by the Russians.[7]

6.SS Gebirgsdivision Nord commanded by Gruppenführer Karl-Heinrich Brenner, moving from Wiesbaden to oppose the Oppenheim attack, was ordered by Kesselring up to hold the Lahn at Limburg. With no gasoline the 6,000 mountain troops marched on foot, arriving just south of Limburg late on the 26th to find American tanks already there. Brenner set up a defensive position astride the Autobahn facing north.

The Gespensters had been assaulted by three armored divisions breaking out of the Remagen bridgehead: the 3rd Armored around Altenkirchen after Bayerlein's rump Panzer-Lehr under Oberst Horst Niemack was driven north across the Sieg, the 7th AD at Freilingen and Wallmerod after brushing aside Oberst Helmuth Zollenkopf's 9.Panzer remnants and crossing the Frankfurt Autobahn, and the 9th AD on the southern flank at Limburg on the Lahn.

For most American GIs this was the first experience with the impressive Autobahn system. While amused by the exit ramp "Ausfahrt" signs, many vehicles and tanks negotiated the reversing circles (what the Americans would call a "cloverleaf") the wrong way, "five olive-drab mechanical mice in a concrete maze," observed Col. William Triplet of Combat Command A, 7th Armored Division. As his CCA struck the 11. Panzer on the 26th, "I could see no method, pattern, or reason in the German troop dispositions." That was because the armor had breached the Remagen defenders and was encountering the Gespenster road-march elements moving diagonally across their path.[8]

The German front was shattered—"Corps HQ," said General der Infanterie Gustav Höhne of LXXXIX. A.K., "was no longer in a position to exercise effective command."[9] While 9th Armored turned south on the Autobahn to Idstein on the 27th, making contact with Third Army north of Wiesbaden, the other two armored divisions crossed the Dill eastward on the same day. The 3rd AD took Marburg and the 7th AD took Giessen on the 28th with crossings over the upper Lahn. Thousands of Wehrmacht soldiers, sensing the war was lost and almost over, were surrendering to the Americans en masse, while villagers were quick to hang white sheets and even Daunendecke (eiderdown quilts) from their windows in surrender as the American tank columns roared through.

As Patton's Third Army now drove north from Frankfurt and the Main, the segmented parts of the Elfte worked their way east. At Florstadt east of Friedburg on the 28th Pz.Aufkl.Abt.11 clashed with a powerful armored force. This was Combat Command A of the 4th Armored Division—"an old acquaintance from the battles in Lothringen!" commented Anton Donnhauser and Werner Drews in the division history—the division now commanded by Maj. Gen. William Hoge, whose CCB 9th AD had seized the Remagen bridge.[10]

Elements of Pz.Rgt.15 and Pz.Gren.Rgt.110 that had reached Butzbach west of the Autobahn were isolated, but able to infiltrate through the armor. This was complicated further by two more armored divisions now driving north toward Alsfeld, the 9th and the 6th Armored. As the armored columns sought to bypass towns and resistance to exploit deep into the German rear areas paralleling and on the Autobahn, disparate Gespenster units were able to move cross-country on secondary roads. The remnants of Brenner's 6.SS Nord worked their way back east until being trapped by 2 April; many were then shot because of a rumor (untrue) that in capturing an American field hospital at Altenstadt they had murdered the staff and raped the nurses.[11]

The 11.Panzer Hauptquartier Stab escaped capture near Blafeld, 12 kilometers (7 miles) east of Bad Nauheim, by sheltering in a patch of woods while the tanks and half-tracks went by. A message was broadcast on the division's radio frequencies: "Division assemble at the Vogelsberg." This was a high forested area west of Fulda, a highly visible rallying point. Along the byways through Schoten, Nidda, and Ortenberg the units made their way.

"What one scarcely dared to hope—happened: the troop units of the division by all possible ways began to arrive during the course of 28 and 29 March," says the division history. It was the "single joy" of these days wrote von Wietersheim. It was a tribute to the charisma and ability of leaders like von Wietersheim and Karl Thieme, and the company-grade officers commanding battalions, that while thousands of Wehrmacht Soldaten were heading west to surrender to the Americans, Gespensters were heading east to rejoin their division.[12] But movement was painful: in addition to avoiding the Jabos, moving at night, the elements were clashing with probes of Col. Hank Reed's 2nd Cavalry Group, another old foe.

The division received orders from XII. A.K., the former Wehrkreis XII (Wiesbaden), now commanded by Generaloberst Herbert Osterkamp. It was to block the Fulda Gap, the passage between the Vogelsberg on the north side and the Hohe Rhön on the south, along with Panzerbrigade Munzel on its left. Oberst Oskar Munzel had the remnants of his 2.Pz.Div. amalgamated with an ad hoc formation, Panzerbrigade Thüringen, a training formation with a panzer and an assault gun battalion and a panzergrenadier regiment, all undertstrength. But the American offensive had torn a wide gap between Model's H.Gr. B and Hausser's H.Gr. G, and Kesselring at OB West was hard-pressed to find forces to close it.

On 28 March the three armored divisions of Hodges's First Army attack began to swing north, for the evident encirclement of the Ruhr with the Tommys and Amis of 21 Army Group. The 3rd Armored drove toward Paderborn but met stiff resistance on 30 March and its commander (Maj. Gen. Maurice Rose) was killed. A task force turned back west and on 1 April met a 2nd Armored force at Lippstadt, encircling the Ruhr. Trapped in the large Kessel was most of Model's H.Gr. B, including 5. Panzerarmee, most of 15. Armee, and two corps of 1. Fallschirmarmee. The Elfte's Pz.Gren.Rgt.111 left at the Sieg was entrapped as well.

Patton's Third Army in turn, spearheaded by the 4th Armored Division, turned northeast toward Eisenach in eastern Germany. The 4th skirted around north of the Vogelsberg, drove through Lauterbach and Grossenüder on the 29th, shot up a trainload of panzers but also clashed with panzers at Bad Hersfeld on the 30th, and by the 31st approached the Werra River fronting Eisenach. On the left the 6th AD advanced toward Kassel by the 31st.

Against the 11. Panzer and Pz.Brig. Munzel in the Fulda Gap position came the 11th Armored Division, led by Brig. Gen. Holmes Dager, previously commander of the 4th AD's CCB, and there were other former "acquaintances" as well. The 11th "Thunderbolt" AD was followed by Maj. Gen. Willard Paul's 26th "Yankee" Division, and to the north the 90th Texas-Oklahoma Infantry Division was led by Brig. Gen. Herbert Earnest from the 4th AD's CCA. Covering the southern flank was Colonel Reed's two 2nd Cavalry Group reconnaissance squadrons, which liberated Allied prisoners of war at Bad Orb on 2 April.

In a Lazarett in Bad Salzschlirf northwest of Fulda that fell into American hands was Obergefreiter Lothar Trenkler of II./15, wounded on 21 March at Remagen, who watched the Amerikaner columns go by. "In three hours I saw more tanks and equipment than I had seen German in three years of war. Then I knew that the stick it through slogans and promises of 'Wunderwaffen' were simply empty phrases."[13]

With the 4th Armored astride the Autobahn approaching the Werra short of Eisenach, the Fulda position was outflanked. General von Obstfelder of 7. Armee hoped to form a defensive line against the Third Army behind the Werra, a tributary of the Weser. Replacing General Kniess at LXXXV. A.K. with General der Panzertruppen Smilo Freiherr von Lüttwitz (cousin of Heinrich von Lüttwitz whose XXXXVII. Pz.Korps was entrapped in the Ruhrkessel), Obstfelder charged the corps with defending the Werra sector from Creuzburg, 10 kilometers (6 miles) northwest of Eisenach, to Vacha, 20 kilometers (12 miles) west of Bad Salzungen.

Osterkamp's XII. A.K. delayed back from Fulda, and farther south was LXXXII. A.K. under Gen.d.Inf. Walther Hahm; it also felt pressure from the American Seventh Army, which had crossed the Rhine and was advancing on Würzburg and Nürnberg in Bavaria. On 1 April—Oster Sonntag—the 11. Panzer was ordered back to Bad Salzungen and then to Eisenach. Crossing the Hohe Rhön on icy roads that night, the Elften moved through Fladungen and across the Werra to support defenders from the Panzertruppenschule Eisenach under Oberst Wissmann at Spichra.

On 1 April the 4th Armored Division had reached the Werra near Horschel to find the bridge blown; when they tried for the bridge at Spichra 3 kilometers to the north, they encountered heavy fire, and four tanks were knocked out by Paks. The next attempt was at Creuzburg to the north, but the bridge there was blown and gunfire started fires that burned the town down that night. On the 2nd the Gespensters arrived. The Amis attacked across the river in rubber boats, the fighting continuing into the night as they tried to establish a bridgehead.

Armored engineers began to install a floating treadway to get tanks across, but at 07,00 hours on the 3rd three German planes swooped low out of the morning sun and ripped up four pontoons with fragmentation bombs. With limited ammunition, Pz.Art.Rgt.119 at least gave some support. "The Werra was a tough little river," observed the 4th AD's division history.[14] Luftwaffe sorties from nearby airfields strafed and bombed the Brückenkopf, but the 4th's antiaircraft battalion put up defensive fire and the tankers finally crossed the Werra on 4 April.

In any case the Werra position was outflanked. To the north the 6th AD crossed the Werra and reached Mühlhausen on 4 April, and to the south the 11th Armored had captured Zella-Mehlis (site of the Walther-Waffenfabrik, maker of the P.38 pistol sidearm) on the western side of the Thüringer Wald on 2 April. The 4th AD resumed its advance astride the Autobahn after bypassing Eisenach to the north and entering Gotha, while CCA turned south to Ohrdruf, the location of an underground OKW communications center. It, however, had never been used, and GFM Kesselring and the OB West Hauptquartier had departed the town shortly before. But the Amis did run into an ambush where two batteries of 8,8cm guns knocked out seven tanks and four half-tracks.[15]

To their horror, the 4th Armored also discovered the first of the Nazi concentration camps liberated, with skeleton-like, emaciated survivors and murdered inmates and charred bodies. For Germans who perhaps had little knowledge of the extent of the regime's brutality (not to mention the six actual death camps in occupied Poland), the revelation of these camps by Allied liberation was mortifying. "I vividly recall seeing, for the first time," said young Uffz. Klaus Bardt of Panzerregiment 15, "columns of concentration camp prisoners on a road in the Ohrdruf area. For us it was a shattering experience and the first glimpse into the darkest chapter of that time."[16] Then the 4th AD was stopped at Gotha for a week to allow supplies and the infantry divisions to catch up.

After a roundabout journey Maj. Jürgen Reichardt had rejoined the Elfte in Eisenach (noting the Kaserne where he had been a Leutnant with Pz.Rgt.2), and General von Buttlar with some elements arrived from Fulda by the Oberhof Pass over the Thüringerwald. The Gespensters had been relieved by Gruppe Siry, a remnant of 347. Infanterie-division at Eisenach under Generalleutnant Maximilian Siry. On the 7th it launched a Gegenangriff at Friedrichroda west of Ohrdruf but was basically destroyed. On the night of 8–9 April the 11. Panzer pulled back from west of the Oberhof-Ohrdruf road.

On the 10th near Plaue south of Arnstadt a new Panzergrenadier-Regiment 111 was reconstituted under Oberst Zerbel, replacing the one entrapped in the Ruhrkessel. The personnel came from returning members of the regiment, the Feldersatzbataillon, the flak battalion (which had lost all its guns), and from a battalion (zu Fuss) of Pz.Art.Rgt.119. The artillery regiment itself, with few guns and no ammunition, was later reorganized as an infantry force. Near Sonderhausen some new Panzer IVs, Panthers, and Sturmgeschütze were acquired. Benzin was short, and one Leutnant filled his panzer at a commercial Tankstelle at pistol-point.[17]

The 4th Armored renewed the drive east on the 11th astride the Autobahn past Erfurt and Weimar—its CCB uncovering the terrible reality of the Buchenwald Konzentrationslager. The Elfte held a sector around Kranichfeld, east of Marlishausen-Stadtilm, but as the armor drove on in the north and the infantry advanced in the south, other ad hoc forces gave way and retreated across the Saale River south of Rudolstadt. To the north the 4th Armored passed Jena to cross the Saale on the 12th and, paralleling on its left, 6th AD crossed at Camburg on the 13th. To the south the 11th AD passed down the west side of the Thüringerwald. The 11.Pz.Div. pulled back across the Saale at Kahla the night of 12–13 April and then to the north–south Autobahn to Bayreuth.

On 13 April the news was broadcast that Franklin Delano Roosevelt, four-term president of the United States, had died. Hitler, naming armies with few forces (11. and 12.) in despair as his Reich crumbled, took sudden hope that history was repeating itself; that just as the sudden death of Russian Tsarina Elisabeth in 1762 and the accession of his admirer, Peter III, had saved Friedrich II der Grosse in the Seven Years War, so now the death of one of the three major Allied leaders might reverse the course of this war. But Vice President Harry Truman succeeded to the presidency and the Allied armies forged relentlessly onward.

The 4th AD crossed the Zwickauer Mulde less than 12 kilometers (7 miles) from Chemnitz, and the 6th AD crossed the next day at Rochlitz. There the armor paused, the Mulde apparently being a demarcation line agreed upon with the Red Army advancing from the east. But the infantry divisions continued to close up, and on the 14th Wietersheim's division, fighting delaying actions, was ordered to defend the line of the Weisse Elster with a Brückenkopf at Greiz southwest of Zwickau. At Auma the division had been joined by an infantry replacement regiment from Chemnitz—350 men, barely equipped. The Elfte was still a magnet for other personnel whose units had dissolved and whose homes were under Allied control or gutted by Allied bombing; perhaps they did this for rations and medical provision, but also sensing the cohesiveness retained by the Gespensters.

The 11. Panzer took up position along the river, Pz.Gren.Rgt.110 on the north flank toward Werdau, Pz.G.R.111 on the south forward of Reichenbach, with the available panzers as Eingreifgruppen (counterattack detachments) giving support. A.A.11 covered the southern flank. The position was defined as an HKL, but in reality was only a series of Widerstandsnestern (pockets of resistance).[18]

It was also on 15 April that General von Wietersheim received orders from OKW to turn over his command to General von Buttlar, and for him to proceed to Berlin to take command of XXXXI. Panzerkorps. But it was patently obvious that routes to Berlin were being cut by the Russian and Western armies closing on the Elbe. Von Wietersheim knew XXXXI. Pz.K. existed largely on paper, nor was he ready to leave his Gespensterdivision. Reporting ill with a stomach ailment, he stayed near the Divisionsgefechtsstand in his Wohnwagen (living quarters van) and in communication with Ia Oberstleutnant Werner Drews even though General von Buttlar was now officially in command.[19]

On the 16th the Greiz position was attacked by American units reorienting to move south. The Vorposten west of the Weisse Elster were driven in, and attacks on the flanks threatened encirclement. The Kampfgruppe that was the former 347.Inf.Div., now under Generalleutnant Wolf Trierenberg, was stretched from Hof up to Plauen in Vogtland, and on the right were miscellaneous units around Zwickau. But the Elften knew their flanks were vulnerable; Oberstlt. Thieme's Pz.Gren.Rgt.110 blocked a northern thrust from Werdau, and A.A.11. supported Zerbel's reconstituted Pz.G.R.111 south of Reichenbach.

Nonetheless it was now obvious that Patton's Third Army, instead of driving east or northeast toward Berlin, was held at the Mulde and beginning a major drive southeast. That night the 11.Pz.-Div. withdrew from the Greiz position back across the Dresden Autobahn through Lengenfeld, and to the border of the Sudetenland in the foothills of the Erzgebirge for a new sector, Eibenstock-Klingenthal. They could move more rapidly with headlights on, easily mistaken for one of the American columns that now also used their headlights.

The 11. Panzer may now have had thirty Panthers in Reichardt's Pz.-Rgt.15, though many were not einsatzbereit, and acquired some twenty Panzerjägers from a plant in Plauen. The infantry troop strength was reportedly at 80 percent, and Pz.Art.Rgt.119 under Hptm. Hoffmann still had two battalions, each possibly with three batteries of three tubes again. Lack of fuel and ammunition were severe limitations, and Czech vehicles were commandeered for transport. A 7. Armee return on 21 April showed the 11.Pz.Div. having twelve panzers (ten Pz.IVs and two Panthers) and ten assault guns operational, yet that was more than the rest of 7. Armee. American intelligence based on ULTRA code-breaking rated the 11. Panzer as "by far the prime unit in 7 Army."[20]

As spring 1945 came to war-torn Europe, German defeat was all but assured. In the north the Ruhrkessel was slowly crushed by the Allied armies, and on 21 April Feldmarschall Model of H.Gr. B (and his aide) walked into a forest north of Düsseldorf and, contemptuous of Feldmarschall Paulus for having surrendered at Stalingrad, shot himself. His men buried him. The Gespensters of the original Pz.Gren. Rgt.111 would be surrendered in the Kessel.

Patton's Third Army drove south, the 11th Armored capturing Coburg on 11 April and Bayreuth on the 14th. The 90th Infantry Division, after clashing along the Weisse Elster, took Hof on 18 April and crossed the Czech border at Prex, heading toward Asch and Eger (Czech Cheb), paralleling the 11. Panzer moving southeast. While 6th Armored stayed along the Mulde line, the 4th AD was relieved by two infantry divisions 16–18 April, then backtracked to the north–south Autobahn and raced south past Bayreuth heading for the Danube.

In the south Seventh Army also began to swing southeast while the French entered Freiburg and the Schwarzwald. There was only isolated resistance, with a roadblock or Panzerfausts carried by elderly Volkssturm or Hitler Jugend boys. At Crailsheim on the Jagst, however, the US 10th Armored got overextended, and was forced to withdraw after a fierce six-day battle (6–11 April) with SS trainees and Gebirgstruppen, while 17.SS Pz.Gren.Div. defended the Neckar at Heilbronn. Some SS retained their fanaticism. A Scharführer riding on Oberleutnant von Fersen's Panzer IV shot himself rather than risk being wounded or captured. "To us this was incomprehensible," he said.[21]

The 11.Pz.Div. still maintained defense lines against an American advance across the mountains into Böhmen (Bohemia), with 347.Inf.Div. on its left and now Division Nr.404, a Landesschützen (Local Defense) unit on its right. Motorized Regiment Gruse, composed of training and replacement personnel from Wehrkreis IV Sachsen (Saxony) joined with the division. On 23 April the Elfte received orders from Heeresgruppe G, since 2 April under Gen.d.Inf. Friedrich Schulz from the Ostfront (Hausser having been relieved for proposing consolidation of units), to move with Smilo Frhr. von Lüttwitz's LXXXV. A.K. down to Passau on the Donau (Danube) at the Austrian border. It was to join SS units and defend the so-called "Führerrefugium" at Berchtesgaden (the Alpine or National Redoubt to the Americans).

Lack of fuel made this impractical, especially in the case of the heavier armored vehicles. But the Elfte was prepared to mount a Gegenangriff around Eger. On the 25th only twenty-four of the sixty-nine remaining panzers and assault guns were einsatzbereit, and the II.Abteilung of Reichardt's Pz.Rgt.15 had to be converted into infantry. Thus the regiment was composed of a staff company and supply and maintenance companies, and two battalions: I. Abteilung under Hptm. Rodenhauser was the panzer battalion, with 1. Kompanie (Panzer) under Hptm. Haen, and 2.Kp. (Sturmgeschütze III, 7,5cm L/48) under Oblt. von Fersen (Pz.Jg.Abt.61 having been dissolved some time before); and II.Abt. under Hptm. Mielenhausen was now "Panzergrenadier," with six companies numbered 3.–8.Kp. Uffz. Klaus Bardt had a Gruppe (squad) of eight: two with the MPi 38, three with the K 98, and three with the semi-automatic K 43. The artillery called themselves "Panzergrenadierregiment 119."[22]

On 25 April the Elfte received orders from 7. Armee under General von Obstfelder to move to the area of Taus (Domazlice) to thwart any American advance toward Pilsen (Plzen). With what Benzin was available, General von Buttlar formed a Kampfgruppe from Pz.Gren.Rgt.110, a panzer company, and an artillery detachment, and moved as ordered. The rest of the division moved in stages, closing Taus in the Böhmerwald, 45 kilometers (27 miles) southwest of Pilsen, three days later. It had fuel for only a 20–30-kilometer move.

With new orders to move to Wallern (Volary), 40 kilometers (25 miles) northeast of Passau, von Buttlar took his Kampfgruppe ahead, closing on 2 May. Pz.G.R.111 elements had replaced those of 110. They were to block an American drive on Linz, Österreich. The rest of the Elfte remained in the Taus area lacking fuel, the two parts now 70 kilometers (40 miles) apart. There was no wire communication and transmissions by radio were intermittent in the mountainous terrain. On 29 and 30 April there were clashes with the division's strongpoints north of Waldmünchen and Furth im Wald, and at the Schwarzkopfes (Schwarkoppe/Cerkov) in the rugged Böhmerwald.

Fighting ability could still be recognized, and there were four awards of the Ritterkreuz made for 1945, including Oberstlt. Erich Hammon of 119, and Hptm. Rudolf Kaeppel, commander of the division Begleitkompanie. Oberstlt. Karl Thieme of 110 was awarded the Schwerter as of 9 May as Nummer 156 (of 159 total), but this was unconfirmed as the paperwork, supported by Model, got tangled up at OB West which, admittedly, had other issues to contend with. The award was approved by Grossadmiral Karl Dönitz of the Kriegsmarine, named by Hitler to succeed him as Führer after he committed suicide on 30 April. Ia Oberstlt. Werner Drews was awarded Das deutsche Kreuz, as his predecessor, Obstlt. Kinitz, had received the DK in 1943.

The awards now might ring hollow to some, but as long as the Gespenster-Division was still an intact fighting force, discipline and standard procedures would be maintained. The reputation and mystique of a military formation would last beyond its final dissolution.

CHAPTER THIRTY-THREE

The Gespenster-Division Dismounts

ON 2 MAY 1945 THE DIVISION COMMAND POST AT UBOC (Uborsko) east of Taus received an order from the army group under Generalfeldmarschall Ferdinand Schörner to send a force eastward to Brünn (Brno) with the rest of the division to follow. This of course meant a last-ditch attempt to slow the Russian armies driving up the Donau—Marshal Malinovsky's Second Ukrainian Front—and the inevitable destruction and captivity of the 11. Panzer-Division.[1]

That evening General von Wietersheim called a conference of the available unit commanders at the Div.Gef.Std. at Uboc to discuss the situation. The discussions must have been emotional, as some felt it necessary to obey the order as soldiers; others argued that the war was over and that Hitler's death, announced by radio on 1 May, released them from the personal oath they had taken to Der Führer upon entering the Wehrmacht. Maj. Jürgen Reichardt commanding Pz.-Rgt.15 attended, as did Oberstlt. Karl Thieme of Pz.Gren.Rgt.110. Ritterkreuzträger Thieme was apparently one who argued that an accommodation with the Americans be sought. Von Wietersheim wanted his commanders to come to a consensus for an intact division surrender; the conference adjourned, to convene again on the 3rd, and Thieme said it required "time and persuasion" before the majority came around. Additionally, the later US Third Army IPW (Interrogation of Prisoners of War) report says, "He [von Wietersheim] called a meeting of his ranking officers and informed them of his intention. When all present agreed with these plans, he again took charge of the division."[2]

It was agreed that surrender conditions would include: no dissolution of units in captivity; exclusive German command authority until discharge; retention of all rank insignia and awards; and the officers to retain sidearms, their own jurisdiction over legal issues, their own ration and supply distribution, and the quickest discharge as prisoners of war.[3] It is possible that von Buttlar came up from Wallern and argued against surrender, then returned to his Kampfgruppe. The relationship between him and von Wietersheim was "cool and distant" said Leutnant Klaus

Groeger of Pz.Rgt.15, and in any case the loyalty of the Gespensters was to their former beloved division commander.[4]

Early on 4 May the 11.Pz.-Div. emissaries, Maj. Karl Heinz Voigtmann, Ib (division quartermaster) and Oblt. Klaus Knorr, adjutant, set out in three Kübelwagens with white flags with translators and a letter from von Wietersheim to contact the American lines near Neumark (Vseruby). It was the outposts of Col. Raymond E. Bell's 359th Infantry Regiment, 90th Infantry Division (Texas-Oklahoma, "Tough 'Ombres") that they approached.[5] The Germans first contacted the 3rd Battalion positions but were rebuffed. Lt. Johnny Cochran, commander of M Company (Heavy Weapons), related: "A soldier under a white flag of truce approached us. He was brought to me and I heard his demands. He insisted on being taken to the chief of staff of the 90th Division. No German soldier was going to tell me what to do, so I had him returned to our perimeter. He was told to return to whence he came." Unfortunately, Cochran had not been aware of Wietersheim's letter.[6]

At 07,15 hours the emissaries tried at the 2nd Battalion outpost of Tech 5 Walter Huskey of G Company, and this time Major Voigtmann, in his black panzer uniform, indicated that he had a letter with him and expressed a desire to speak to the divisional commander. At 07,55 battalion called regiment informing Colonel Bell that the 11th Panzer Division was prepared to surrender.[7] At the battalion command post (CP) Capt. Frank A. Turner had Voigtmann and Knorr blindfolded, and they were driven in jeeps back down to the division CP in Cham, where they delivered Wietersheim's letter (typed, in German) to the 90th's CG (Commanding General), Brig. Gen. Herbert L. Earnest:

> Division C.P. 3 May 1945
> 11th Panzer Division
> Commander
>
> The development of the military and political situation makes it desirable to me to avoid further losses on both sides. I have therefore ordered the Major, the bearer of this note, to negotiate with you the cessation of hostilities.
>
> von Wietersheim (signed)
> Lt Gen and Division Commander

General Earnest, who had fought the 11.Pz.Div. as commander of CCA of the 4th AD, contacted General Patton about bringing the German division back across the Czech border. It was still capable of formidable resistance. "Almost to the last day of the war it retained its integrity as a unit and fought throughout as a unit," said the XII Corps history. The Germans recall that Earnest returned and responded: "General Patton is of the opinion, that the 11th Panzer Division was the fairest and bravest German division against which he had fought in this war," and would approve arrangements for its return and disarming.[8]

The 11. Panzer would retain unit integrity and cross over the mountains from Czechoslovakia on two routes, via Eschlkam and via Rittsteig, to open assembly areas around the hilltop town of Kötzting, some 24 kilometers (15 miles) to the southwest. Division allocated the 359th Regiment 15 trucks and 10,000 gallons (36,000 liters) of gasoline to facilitate the move. Tentage and water points would be established, but the 11. would supervise its own Truppen for all administration and quartering. Col. Bell sent Regimental Sgt. Maj. E. W. Beckman to visit the German headquarters to arrange to have the kitchen trains come in first to feed the Landsers with their own rations. General Wietersheim agreed, but smiled when Beckman said prisoners liked American K rations. Upon leaving, Beckman found his jeep had gone elsewhere. A kind German Major volunteered a German Kübelwagen to drive him back, but the sergeant major had to stand uncomfortably all the way so the GIs would see he was American.[9]

General Earnest went forward to meet with General von Wietersheim at Vseruby. By now rumor had spread like wildfire that the famed 11th Panzer "Ghost" Division was coming in, and GIs were milling around with curiosity as Wietersheim and some staff officers drove into the town in a Mercedes command car with its top down. The two CGs met in a badly wrecked farmhouse on the outskirts of Vseruby at 16,00 hours that afternoon, with Capt. Herbert Oemichen as interpreter. The 359th news sheet recorded that General Earnest spoke "with a free and easy manner," and Wietersheim "was a handsome man of well over six feet and built proportionately. Dressed in a long coat minus insignia he kept it buttoned throughout." The weather was cold (with snow at the higher elevations), and Earnest also wore his overcoat. In a US Army Signal Corps photograph, von Wietersheim is seated, explaining map details to

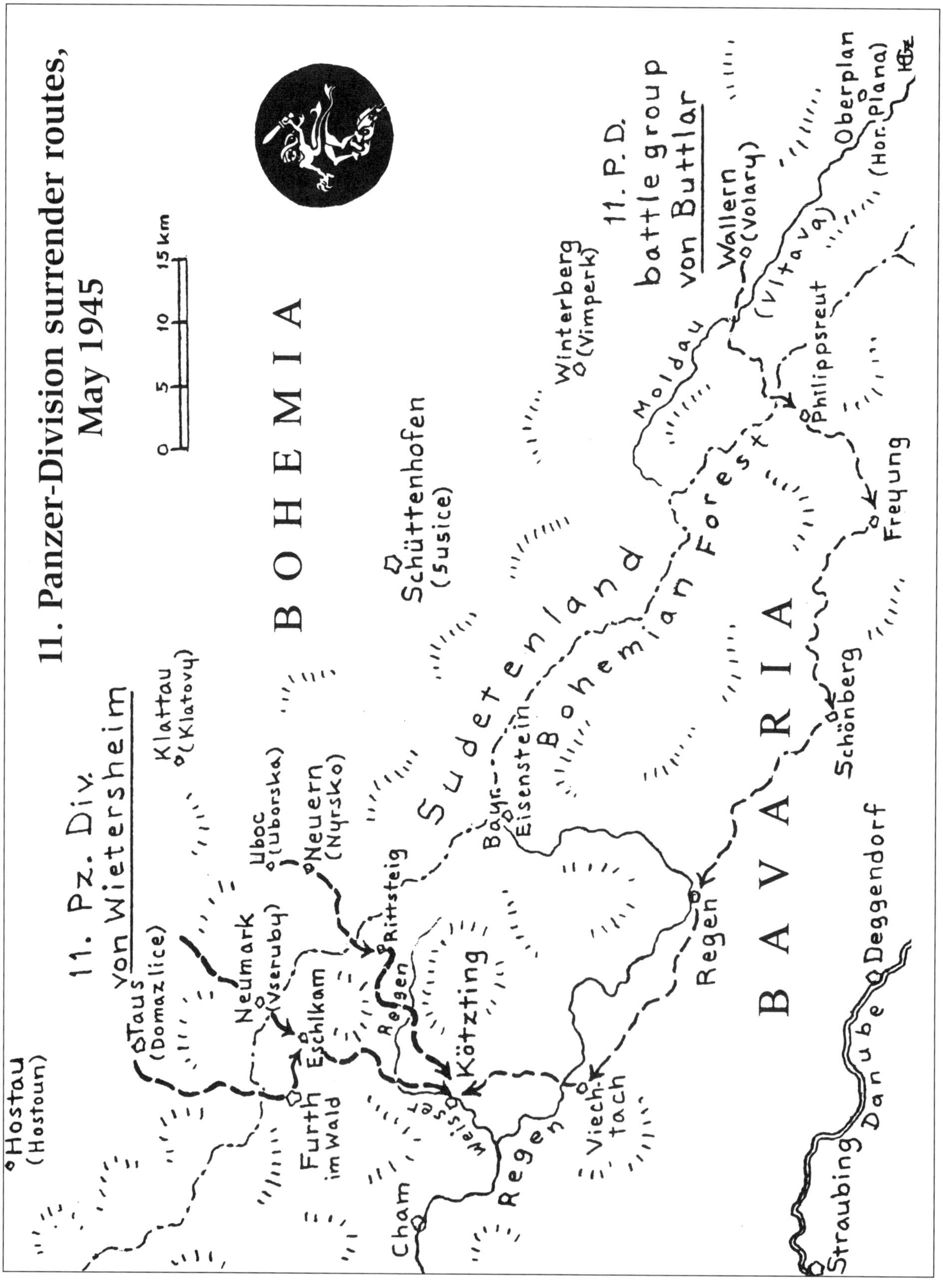

11. Panzer-Division surrender routes, May 1945

Earnest. The Third Army press release said of the German officers, "This was to be a surrender with honor, and they held their heads high." The American officers included Brig. Gen. Ernest Bixby of 90th Div Arty (as colonel, he was commander of 4th AD Artillery) and Colonel Bell.[10]

General Earnest agreed that Wietersheim could use the 90th's radio communications to round up stray elements, and when he learned the 11. was short of gasoline and said some would have to walk, Wietersheim replied with a sad, tired smile, "No, they're used to hauling each other's vehicles." And when it was suggested that units coming in at night might use lights "if they are not afraid of the Luftwaffe," the German officers just laughed.[11]

An observation plane reported the German columns forming, and by 23,10 hours the G-3 journal noted, "It is very dark out, but everything going well." The first 11. Panzer columns began arriving at Kötzting that night. Collecting points were established for small arms, but officers retained their sidearms and later it was decided that each company would be issued five rifles for discipline. Thieme's Pz.Gren. Rgt.110 and Reichardt's Pz.Rgt.15 came from the Neuern (Nyrsko) and Uboc area, crossing at Rittsteig and down the steep switchbacks, while units from the Taus area crossed via Furth and joined the columns from Vseruby at Eschlkam. The 2nd Battalion, 359th was responsible for the units coming via Eschlkam and the 3rd Battalion for those coming down from Rittsteig.[12]

The 3rd's commander, Lt. Col. O. C. Talbott, surrounded his area with tanks and machine guns, though "all these precautions happily proved unnecessary." He worked with a German lieutenant colonel and "The whole affair went very smoothly." Some confusion resulted from the US 2nd Infantry Division advancing through the area, and Talbott had to threaten to arrest an artillery commander who tried to seize a German officer's pistol. The Gespensters were proud though generally relieved that the fighting was over, but two panzers drove into the area with gun barrels elevated as though on parade, with the Panzerkommandanten at stiff attention. Panzerleutnant

Generalleutnant Wend von Wietersheim negotiating the surrender of the Gespenster-Division with Brig. Gen. Herbert Earnest of the 90th Infantry Division at Vseruby, Czechoslovakia, 4 May 1945. DAVA SC 437549

Freiherr von Fersen remembers that when a Capt. [Henry] Morgenthau ordered his element into a field, the regimental adjutant, Lt. Baron (*sic*) von Brockdorff, said they only followed orders from General von Wietersheim. Lt. Traverse Hall of L Company admired the 11th as "without doubt the best disciplined, well-trained outfit of those we captured," with the tanks "all cleaned up and polished."[13]

The Elfte units continued to roll in during the night. To Lt. Klaus Groeger the night was very cold and stormy as his Pz.Rgt.15 vehicles negotiated the steep, twisting road down to Rittsteig. The GIs were friendly and correct, but his own men kept their weapons available against Czech partisans who, anticipating liberation, were beginning to act against stragglers and civilians. BAR (Browning Automatic Rifle) man Allan Tribett's F Co. of the 2nd Battalion was spaced out along the convoy road, the GIs in pairs. A cold, drizzling rain was falling and some of them built small fires, shared by some of the Germans at vehicle halts. They also shared cognac and Schnaps, and "This led to a certain amount of confusion before that night was over," he recalled. More motor vehicles, horse-drawn vehicles, and troops continued to move into the Kötzting assembly areas throughout the next day. A final count list included 9,050 personnel, 137 half-tracks and armored vehicles, and 1,120 trucks, cars, and jeeps. But there were only twenty assault guns and self-propelled howitzers, and only six Panzer IVs and one Panther left.[14]

By 6 May the other regiments of the 90th were advancing across into Czechoslovakia with the 4th Armored to pass through, driving toward Prague. Wietersheim's surrender included von Buttlar's Kampfgruppe at Wallern (Volary) to the southeast, and when he learned of this, von Buttlar canvassed his officers as to whether they should continue east toward Brünn (Brno) or accept internment, most urging the latter. Buttlar was kept abreast of the wider war situation by an LXXXV. A.K. communications unit attached to the 11.Pz.Div. during the Rhôntal Feldzug ("bad luck" said Obergefreiter Franz Oexler) that was still with Buttlar's headquarters.[15] At this time Paul's 26th Yankee Division was driving along the Danube River supporting Dager's 11th AD, and on 4 May assisted in capturing Linz, Austria. By 6 May the YD was advancing up into Czechoslovakia to the Moldau (Vltava) River line southeast of Wallern.

All the bridges were blown and the approaches marshy from rain. Nonetheless, that evening B Company of 1st Battalion, 101st Infantry Regiment reported that two officers from Pz.Gren.Rgt.111 came in to discuss possible surrender, ostensibly after a broadcast from an attached Psychological Broadcasting Unit. Other contacts were made and a railroad bridge was suggested as the only place for a crossing.[16] The Elfte officers returned to Buttlar's Hauptquartier accompanied by 1st Lt. George Largay of the regiment's I&R (Intelligence and Reconnaissance) Platoon. The German envoys said they had received orders at 17,00 hours not to fire unless fired upon, and Col. Walter T. Scott, commander of the 101st Infantry, issued a cease-fire order at 20,00 to allow for negotiations.

Early on 7 May, at 01,30 hours, Lt. Largay radioed from the German HQ through the 1st Battalion that about 5,000 German troops would surrender at 07,00 that morning.[17] Colonel Scott and his XO (Executive Officer), Lt. Col. Dan Murphy, went forward to meet with Generalleutnant von Buttlar. As Buttlar was the official commander of the 11.Pz.Div., the YD would believe (or at least claim) that it had accepted the surrender of their erstwhile foe, the 11th Panzer Division—a claim also made by the 90th Division. An IPW report said that von Buttlar had opposed the surrender by von Wietersheim, and was considered a "ruthless disciplinarian."[18] Other elements surrendered too, including headquarters of LXXXV. Korps, ultimately totaling some 25,000. The unconditional surrender of the German high command took effect on 9 May, and the European war was over.

Several days now passed in sorting out the PWs. General von Buttlar insisted that his 11. Panzer Kampfgruppe be reunited with the rest of the division at Kötzting as provided for in Wietersheim's surrender, and estimated that 135,000 liters of fuel (36,000 gallons) would be needed for the move. Maj. Gen. Paul of the 26th YD acquiesced, and finally on 15 May with MP escort, Buttlar's Elfte units were trucked back to the northwest on the route Philippsreut–Freyung–Schönberg–Regen–Viechtach to Kötzting.[19]

As the 90th Division had continued into Czechoslovakia, the assembling of the 11. Panzer units at Kötzting was passed to Col. Hank Reed's 2nd Cavalry Group. They were a longtime opponent of the German division, yet their respect for Wietersheim's division had increased along with its enhanced fighting reputation. Conversely, it was the advancing Red Army that was treated with suspicion. On 8 May the

11.Pz.Div. vehicles at Kötzting, Bavaria, including a VW Schwimmwagen and assault gun (7,5cm gun). KÖTZTING TREFFEN

Above: US Col. Hank Reed, 2nd Cavalry Group, prevents the Russians from acquiring the 11. Gespenster-Division.
SCHRODEK, *BILD*, 516

Hauptmann Dr. Rudolf Lessing and the Lipizzaner mares "liberated" at Hostau, Sudetenland, by the 2nd Cavalry Group.
KÖTZTING TREFFEN

2nd Cavalry had outposted a forward line in Czechoslovakia, and its "special mission was to prevent the crossing of this line by any Russian troops." On the 11th contact was made with the 4th Russian Tank Corps at Nepomuk moving toward Pilsen (Plzen) and also just north of Klattau (Klatovy). The 2nd Cav's Report of Operations stated, "The attitude of the Russian Forces was extremely uncooperative and upon the occasion at Klattau almost threatening." Reed met with the Soviet commanding general, who was most interested in gaining control of the 11.Pz.Div., but Reed put him off, and finally the Russians "withdrew beyond our established line."[20]

The units of the 11.Pz.Div. were allocated encampment sites, unguarded, around the hill town of Kötzting. Feldwebel Gustav Schrodek, dreading the worst, was so amazed at the "really unexpected generous conditions" that he neglected to shake the hand of the American officer who extended it, though he made up for it later.[21] Ogfr. Franz Oexler was a citizen of the town, waving to his mother in their house as he returned. His knowledge of the town facilitated the arranging of the units. The 2nd Cavalry sector was to the left of Gehringstrasse, the Elften to the right. Under German and American tents Pz.Gren.Rgt.111 was to the east, Pz.G.R.110 was near the Bahnhof on the west, wheeled and tracked vehicles were down by the Weisser Regen River, and the division staff was at the Hotel Amberger Hof.

It was in a hillside meadow behind the Amberger Hof that the men assembled in a formation to hear a farewell speech from von Wietersheim about the division's experiences and tribulations during the years of war. Oblt. von Fersen remembers he urged his Panzersoldaten to continue to live their lives with the principles of discipline and honor that had guided the Gespensters through the war. Then they took his salute as they passed in review before their commanding general for the last time. As Colonel Reed wrote General Eddy, "I never put any of the 11th Panzer Division behind barbed wire, and the general and his staff became very close friends of my staff and myself. . . . They fought with us so hard and were so outstandingly proper in their military procedure over prisoners, wounded, etc, that I could never see my way clear to locking any of them up."[22]

But there was tragedy as well. Thousands of German children had been evacuated from the cities to the country villages to escape the Allied bombing, many to the Sudetenland. These were now forlorn and starving, and many became victims of the vengeful Czechs and Red Army soldiers. The Elften shared their rations as they could, as did the GIs now along the border. "I still see before me today," recalled American Capt. Ferdinand Sperl, an intelligence officer attached to the 2nd Cav, "two boys tearing raw flesh from the cadavers [of dead horses] and trying to eat it."

One who experienced all this was young Christel Bobeth, whose Maria-Wächtler-Schule Gymnasium (grammar school) in Essen had been evacuated to Bohemia in October 1943 because of the Allied bombing of the Ruhr. Now in 1945 on 21 April the girls had packed essentials, and with their teachers, left their children's refugee camp for the German border, some 200 people on foot. A doctor accompanied them in an automobile with some supplies and some weaker children. But with hostile Czechs, German stragglers, displaced persons, and the menace of the advancing Russians, "we saw great misery." Finally they made contact with 11. Panzer elements and the welcoming "Gulaschkanone," and knew they had reached safety.[23]

Colonel Reed arranged for trucks with their friendly white star to pick up wandering children, knowing Czechoslovakia would be in the Soviet occupation zone. The American GIs were conscious of the horrific brutality of the Nazi Konzentrationslager with the liberation of Buchenwald, Flossenbürg, and Dachau in April (the horrors of the Holocaust in the six actual death camps in Poland, overrun by the Red Army, had yet to be comprehended); yet they could still be compassionate to a defeated foe and to the wider human tragedy. These GIs were not humanistically naïve. They were hardened combat veterans: the 26th Division had been in combat since October 1944, the 2nd Cavalry Group since August 1944, and the 90th Division since Normandy in June.

US Captain Sperl, Swiss-born and fluent in German, found himself military "mayor" of Kötzting. Headquarters was established in a bank on the Marktplatz and a process initiated to discharge the German troops. The discharge center was organized into five sections: physical exam, screening, personal data, fingerprinting, and filing. The screening was handled by IPW teams. Names were checked against an alphabetical listing of possible war criminals issued by ETOUSA (European Theater of Operations US Army), though some listings like "Schmidt" were too common to be practical. In any case German unit officers vouched for their men, to prevent SS and

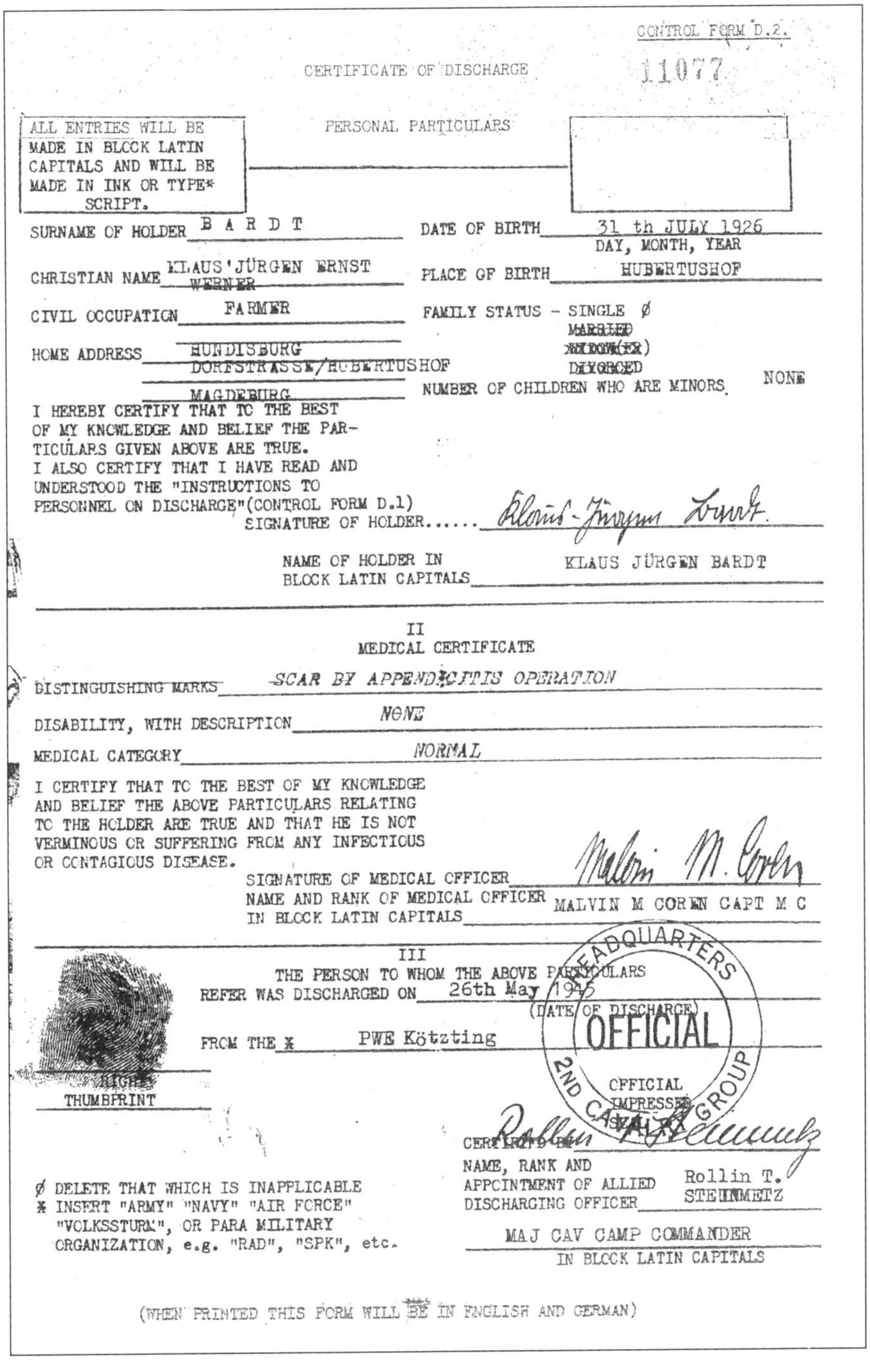

CONTROL FORM D.2.

CERTIFICATE OF DISCHARGE

11077

ALL ENTRIES WILL BE MADE IN BLOCK LATIN CAPITALS AND WILL BE MADE IN INK OR TYPE* SCRIPT.

PERSONAL PARTICULARS

SURNAME OF HOLDER B A R D T

DATE OF BIRTH 31 th JULY 1926
DAY, MONTH, YEAR

CHRISTIAN NAME KLAUS'JÜRGEN ERNST WERNER

PLACE OF BIRTH HUBERTUSHOF

CIVIL OCCUPATION FARMER

FAMILY STATUS - SINGLE Ø
MARRIED
WIDOW(ER)
DIVORCED

HOME ADDRESS HUNDISBURG
DORFSTRASSE/HUBERTUSHOF
MAGDEBURG

NUMBER OF CHILDREN WHO ARE MINORS NONE

I HEREBY CERTIFY THAT TO THE BEST OF MY KNOWLEDGE AND BELIEF THE PARTICULARS GIVEN ABOVE ARE TRUE.
I ALSO CERTIFY THAT I HAVE READ AND UNDERSTOOD THE "INSTRUCTIONS TO PERSONNEL ON DISCHARGE"(CONTROL FORM D.1)

SIGNATURE OF HOLDER...... Klaus-Jürgen Bardt

NAME OF HOLDER IN BLOCK LATIN CAPITALS KLAUS JÜRGEN BARDT

II
MEDICAL CERTIFICATE

DISTINGUISHING MARKS SCAR BY APPENDICITIS OPERATION

DISABILITY, WITH DESCRIPTION NONE

MEDICAL CATEGORY NORMAL

I CERTIFY THAT TO THE BEST OF MY KNOWLEDGE AND BELIEF THE ABOVE PARTICULARS RELATING TO THE HOLDER ARE TRUE AND THAT HE IS NOT VERMINOUS OR SUFFERING FROM ANY INFECTIOUS OR CONTAGIOUS DISEASE.

SIGNATURE OF MEDICAL OFFICER Malvin M. Coren

NAME AND RANK OF MEDICAL OFFICER IN BLOCK LATIN CAPITALS MALVIN M COREN CAPT M C

III
THE PERSON TO WHOM THE ABOVE PARTICULARS REFER WAS DISCHARGED ON 26th May 1945
(DATE OF DISCHARGE)

FROM THE * PWE Kötzting

RIGHT THUMBPRINT

HEADQUARTERS OFFICIAL 2ND CAVALRY GROUP

OFFICIAL IMPRESSED SEAL

CERTIFIED BY Rollin T. Steinmetz

NAME, RANK AND APPOINTMENT OF ALLIED DISCHARGING OFFICER Rollin T. STEINMETZ
MAJ CAV CAMP COMMANDER
IN BLOCK LATIN CAPITALS

Ø DELETE THAT WHICH IS INAPPLICABLE
* INSERT "ARMY" "NAVY" "AIR FORCE" "VOLKSSTURM", OR PARA MILITARY ORGANIZATION, e.g. "RAD", "SPK", etc.

(WHEN PRINTED THIS FORM WILL BE IN ENGLISH AND GERMAN)

Discharge of Klaus Bardt, Pz.Rgt.15, by 2nd Cavalry Group at Kötzting. KLAUS BARDT other elements from passing themselves off as Wehrmacht. The discharge paper was signed by a 2nd Cavalry medical officer and a staff officer (Klaus Jürgen Bardt's was signed by Capt. Malvin Coren and Maj. Rollin Steinmetz). Sperl is still amazed that they processed some 17,000 in twenty-four days.[24]

"According to the terms of surrender," Colonel Reed later wrote Brigadier General Molla, "they had free run of the same valley that we occupied in the Bayerische Wald and none of them were behind barbed wire, no restrictions except that they did not leave until we discharged them. I can assure you that they were the first German soldiers discharged, and by the time the stringent order came out, that all German P.O.W.s would be confined behind barbed wire, I reported that there was no barbed wire in the Bayerische Wald and three weeks later, when the first shipment of wire arrived, there were no 11th Panzer left in the valley—all discharged. . . . They left in honor."[25]

Most of those discharged were trucked to the railroad station at Schwandorf to wend their way home or to seek out relatives. Many whose homes were now under Russian occupation had no desire to leave. Two Service Battalions were formed of 300 men each. One battalion was sent to Coburg to haul food for DPs (displaced persons) there, while the other remained under 2nd Cavalry control under a former panzer captain. "Their discipline and work has been excellent," concluded the 2nd Cav. The German Service Battalion remained in the Disarmed Enemy Force category until 26 January 1946 when they were deactivated and discharged under a 20 January 1946 order from TUSA (Third US Army). Some left, while others were hired on as civilian employees by the now 2nd Constabulary Regiment in Occupation.[26]

The respect and friendship between Colonel Reed and General von Wietersheim ensured an evolving German-American postwar relationship, though as a general, von Wietersheim would be held by the Americans until 1948. "I could wish no greater military return myself than the admiration he had from his soldiers at the end of a losing war," wrote Reed to General Eddy. "It takes a great man to maintain the respect of his troops while losing."[27] It was a relationship that would result in joint reunions between the 2nd Cavalry Regiment Association and the 11. Panzer veterans for the next half century, with members of each attending the alternate reunions of the other, both in the United States and at Kötzting, Bavaria.

Related to the surrender of the 11. Panzer-Division was the saving of a herd of the famous white Lipizzaner horses from the Soviets. In April Captain Sperl of IPW Team No. 10, attached to XII Corps headquarters and working with the 2nd Cavalry, had received a report of a Luftwaffe intelligence group quartered in a hunting castle on the Dianaberg in the Sudetenland. Disguised as a meteorological unit, the group had maps and documents of road nets and bridges in the Soviet Union. On 24 April Sperl went behind the German lines with a captured officer and arranged for their removal, for which he received the Silver Star. The documents were flown to London amid the increasing tension between the West and the Soviets that presaged the coming Cold War.[28]

In one of the officer's wallets Sperl saw a photo of white horses, and learned that the Lipizzaner mares of the Spanish Riding School in Vienna had been evacuated from Piber to the German Army Remount Depot stables at Hostau (Houstoun) in the Sudetenland. He reported this to Colonel Reed, as they were both horse enthusiasts. Reed had also received a report of some 200 British and American PWs working at Hostau. The stud farm manager, Oberstleutnant Hubert Rudofsky, had been refused permission from Berlin to move the herd. But the staff veterinarian, tall Hauptmann Dr. Rudolf Lessing, was allowed to contact the Americans. He rode by horseback through the forest, evading hostile groups of SS, partisans, and others, to the outposts of the 2nd Cavalry Group, who took him to headquarters.

There were apparently over 350 Lipizzan mares and foals, as well as some 200 Russian thoroughbreds brought in by a retreating anti-Soviet Cossack unit. Colonel Reed got quick approval from Patton to save the Lipizzaners, the general being an expert horseman who had won fifth place in the pentathlon at the 1912 Stockholm Olympics. Capt. Tom Stewart of the 42nd Recon Squadron was dispatched to return with Dr. Lessing on horseback to secure the release of the PWs and the horses. Arrangements were made for a "battle" whereupon the Germans would surrender, and on the 29th Stewart with Troop A of the 42nd "captured" Hostau.[29]

The Lipizzaner stallions had been evacuated to the stables of Schloss Arco at St. Martin in Upper Austria. There General Patton and Under Secretary of War Robert Patterson were treated to a dressage (trained movement) riding exhibition on 7 May. Oberst Alois Podhajsky, a bronze medalist in the

1936 Olympic horse competition and director of the Spanish Riding School, urged American protection of the institution and Patton readily agreed.[30] Staff veterinarian Dr. Wolfgang Kroll located sites around Furth im Wald, Bayern, for the Hostau Lipizzaners, and on 15 May the "horse drive" began, foals in trucks, and some 2nd Cavalry GIs now actually riding horses! They were moved in groups of thirty to forty at thirty-minute intervals over the border, and Lt. Bill Quinlan had to face down some Communist Czech partisans blocking the route. Patton justified the rescue of the horses from the Soviet zone by referring to them as Allied "prisoners of war."[31]

Cementing the emerging German-American friendship was the celebrating of the local Catholic festival of Pfingsten (Whitsuntide or Pentecost) that May. After Capt. Sperl had established his headquarters in Kötzting, he had been approached by Bürgermeister Hans Kroher and Pfarrer (Pastor) Josef Dietl sounding him out about celebrating the traditional Pfingsten. The festival had been treated with suspicion by the Nazi regime, and ETOUSA had forbidden large gatherings. But Sperl said the festival should be held and helped organize it. Franz Oexler indeed was to play a leading role, and Sperl gave him Discharge Paper No. 1; at the festival on 20 and 21 May Oexler rode one of the newly liberated Lipizzaners. Congeniality between the former enemies was further demonstrated on 14 October 1946 when Colonel Reed's 2nd Constabulary Regiment staged a military parade in downtown München for American dignitaries including General Eisenhower. Many of the troopers, however, and over half the band, were 11. Panzer veterans, in American uniform. "General Eisenhower never knew that," said Colonel Reed.[32]

CHAPTER THIRTY-FOUR

Epilogue

AT THE WAR'S END, ALLIED SOLDIERS RETURNED TO HOMES AND families and victory parades. Wehrmacht Landsers, however, returned to a land of bombed-out cities, displaced refugees, homes under Soviet and Allied occupation, and possible war crimes trials. Those who were still with the division and discharged through Patton's US 2nd Cavalry Group at Kötzting, Bavaria, were perhaps more fortunate than those captured or surrendered earlier. Lt. Friedrich von Eggeling, wounded for the fifth time near Greiz, was evacuated to a Lazarett in Bohemia. There he fell into the hands of the Russians, but was released in August. Many others were prisoners of the Russians earlier. Some, like Werner Bürkner, survived Soviet captivity; many did not. Bürkner was finally released in 1948. Others were released in Communist East Germany, but apparently could not emigrate to the West. It was only after the reunification of Germany in 1991 that some could attend the Kötzting reunions, and there were some emotional meetings with Kameraden not seen for so many years.

Walter Rahn, captured at Remagen, almost fell into Soviet hands. Like others who had become American prisoners of war, Rahn had been trucked to a collection point in Linz, Austria, then via Belgium to a camp in France, and finally to Camp Attichy, north of Paris. In interrogation at Attichy Rahn acknowledged he had been in the Deutsches Jungvolk of the HJ (but didn't mention his brief time as NSFO). Because he had sent a Red Cross card to his wife Ursula who was staying in Dessau north of Leipzig he found himself, "to my horror," being listed for release to the Soviet occupation zone of eastern Germany. But he had a Kamerad in the camp office who "corrected" his file for release in Giessen north of Frankfurt in the US Zone.

The Americans did not maintain tight control, and factions in the camps emerged, some strongly anti-Fascist, others still National Socialist. On 20 April 1945 some intended to commemorate Hitler's birthday in some way, but Rahn says he refused to participate despite pressure from an angry Hauptmann. In any case, the Americans were on alert for anything unusual on that day. Lt. Kurt Nentwig was later also transferred to Attichy. Conditions were tolerable there, though rations were minimal. Some of the German prisoners worked in the camp kitchen, and Rahn met a Gefreiter of Pz.Pi.Btl.209 working as a cook. One time in Russia the Panzermänner had shared their rations with the attached engineers, so now "it was a pleasure for him to return the act of kindness" and pass on some extras, so "that by the time I was released, I had almost regained my normal weight."

On 12 January 1946 Rahn was released and reunited with his wife and mother, who were living with a cousin in Büdingen in Upper Hesse, the dwelling in Giessen having been destroyed by bombing. He later learned that the senior officer in his tent at Attichy, Generalmajor (actually Oberst) Lemm, had been released to join his wife living in Magdeburg; but when the train rolled over the demarcation line between the American and Soviet zones, the train doors were bolted shut and the prisoners transported to the Soviet Union, the survivors not returning for another ten years.[1]

Those held prisoner by the Americans expected better treatment, but in some cases were betrayed. On 10 March 1945 an apparently vindictive General Eisenhower (*before* any concentration camps in Germany were liberated, revealing their horrendous conditions) ordered deprivation of rations, shelter, and medical care in the PW camps and denied neutral ICRC (International Committee Red Cross) inspections. Subsequently PWs were redesignated as DEF (Disarmed Enemy Forces), evading the treatment requirements of the Geneva Prisoner of War Convention of 1929.

The harshest of these American camps were along the Rhine, and those like Bretzenheim under French control in the later French occupation zone. Period US Signal Corps photographs show masses of German prisoners in open-air wire enclosures with no shelter or facilities evident. The Germans dug shelter holes but died of starvation or disease in the mud and feces, the dead stripped and piled in layers to be destroyed by quicklime as at Rheinberg, north of Düsseldorf. These were the deadly "Hungerwiesen" ("hunger meadows") to the German survivors.[2]

German junior officers were not separated from enlisted prisoners as was usual. Oberleutnant Rolf Wandhoff, adjutant of Pz.Art.Rgt.119, captured near Remagen, suffered in a camp between Remagen and Kripp. "Schrecklich" (dreadful) is all he would ever say. While many died, he survived and was moved to other camps. Finally (as P.W. Nr. 3403548) at a camp at Foucartville, one of some 1,600 camps in France, he got some writing materials to keep a diary for his wife (Sunday 16 September 1945: "I don't know where you are. I don't know whether you're still alive").[3] Lt. Kurt Nentwig also starved at a camp near Bad Kreuznach before being transferred to Camp Attichy in France.

Some of those discharged or finally released, seeing no future in their devastated homeland or whose homes were under Soviet occupation, emigrated abroad and had subsequent careers. Dietrich Pfeiffer of Panzer-Regiment 15 went to Venezuela, and Ernst-August Freiherr von Fersen, having lost Baltic properties, went to Argentina with Margrit and their son Axel in 1951, and celebrated his 94th birthday in 2015. Heinz Kutscheid of Pz.Gren.Rgt.111 attended Heidelberg University in the American Zone of Occupation, joined the Metropolitan Life Insurance Company in Berlin and Frankfurt, and then moved to El Paso, Texas, with Hannelore and taught German language at a community college there. Klaus Bardt moved to Canada in 1949 and was a textile chemist with CEBA and then Crompton & Knowles Company. He and Jutta moved to New Jersey and retired to Charlotte, North Carolina.

Of those who remained in Germany, Walter Rahn of Hamburg became a Generalapotheker (Apothecary General) in the later Bundeswehr. Karl Thieme worked with US Army transportation at Bremerhaven during the Occupation, where his fluency in English proved an asset. Kurt Nentwig served with the Industrial Police organized by the US Army in Bamberg and is living near Frankfurt a/M. Rolf Wandhoff, released in February 1946, studied law, and was District President of Lüneburg. Gerhard Winkler and Irmgard live in Wedel, on the Elbe, Holstein. Mechanic Martin Lange and Ruth lived in Munster, and he was on the staff of the Panzermuseum there.

Walter Schaefer-Kehnert became a professor of agricultural economics at the University of Göttingen and later served with Robert McNamara at the World Bank, and he and Theresa had a home in the diplomatic area of Remagen-Oberwinter overlooking the Rhine valley. Friedrich Karl von Eggeling lost his Silesian estates to Communist Poland, but earned a degree in forestry at Freiburg University, became a forestry official, taught at München and Edinburgh, Scotland, and is involved in the timber export business. Living in Schwaig, Nürnberg, he celebrated his 91st birthday 20 August 2015. Karl Heinz Loschke, longtime Sprecher (secretary) of the 11. Panzer's veterans association, was an architect in Braunschweig. Ansgar Pawelke, Sprecher of Pz.Rgt. 15 veterans, became a lawyer in Bonn. Many others mentioned in this work also had subsequent careers and raised families, though by the twenty-first century an increasing number had passed away.

Like many higher-ranking officers Generalleutnant Wend von Wietersheim was held in American captivity, in his case until 1948 at Allendorf and Neustadt, where he was encouraged to write the historical manuscripts of the 11.Pz.Div. in the West. After being released he was in managerial positions with the DEMAG heavy equipment company. A number of Gespensters later served in the Bundeswehr (Federal Armed Forces), created in 1955 in response to Communist aggression in the Korean War: Anton Donnhauser, Horst Loch, Jürgen von Pflug, and Werner von Koblinski among others. Several Gespensters became generals: Heinz-Günther Guderian, Heinz Guderian's son, on the division staff in 1943; Heinrich-Georg Hax, Oberst commanding Pz.Gren. Rgt.110 in 1944; Johann Adolf Graf von Kielmansegg, Oberst commanding Pz.G.R.111 in 1944; Werner Drews, division Ia; and Edel-Heinrich Zachariae-Lingenthal, commanding II.Abt./Pz.Rgt.15 in 1943 until wounded, who had been with the regiment even in the Polnische Feldzug of 1939.

American military units were stationed in West Germany as occupation troops, including the 2nd Armored Cavalry Regiment, and then as the Cold War with the Soviet Union deepened, they evolved as forces allied with the new Bundeswehr in the NATO alliance. Undoubtedly the changing political situation hastened a reconciliation between former enemies. With the 2nd Cavalry and the 11. Panzer veterans, however, the circumstances had already developed a close relationship, and the discharge papers with an American stamp and signatures are among the proudest mementos of many of these German veterans today.

Colonel Reed visited General von Wietersheim and his wife Rosi-Dorothee, and joint reunions emerged. For the 11. Panzer veterans in particular, May 1945 was less the end of a long and bitter war than the beginning of a new epoch. The Gespenster Treffen (reunions) with the 2nd Cavalry and other American veterans would be held in Kötzting in May every few years with the motto: "Aus Feinden werden Freunde" ("Enemies become friends"). When the 26th Yankee Division was officially deactivated in 1993, Sprecher Karl Heinz Loschke sent a cablegram in English:

> We, like you, revere the memory of all the brave men lost in battles we fought against each other. We remember the common effort to find together after the war in comradeship and friendship to go from enemy to friend which we will preserve in the future.

Annual 11. Panzer greetings to the 2nd Cavalry veterans, as published in the latter's regimental newsletter, "Thoroughbred," reflected the mutual feeling: "In the past 50 years of our personal friendship, we have served as examples and proof of the camaraderie and compatibility of nations and populations." The 2nd Cavalry felt likewise, association chairman Louis Holz of Wayne-Strafford, Pennsylvania, saying: "Very few people outside of our group know of the unique friendship. . . . But we know, because we have lived it."[4]

The fiftieth anniversary of the surrender, 11–14 May 1995, was to be the twentieth and last major Treffen. Though their numbers had dwindled, some 950 11. Panzer veterans and 30 2nd Cavalry veterans from the United States and their wives attended. Jimmie Leach of the 4th Armored and his wife, Marion, were there from Beaufort, South Carolina, as were some other Americans. In blue blazers the American veterans marched with the Gespensters to lay a wreath at the Gedenkstein (memorial stone) at the Bahnhofsplatz to the 18,000 11. Panzer Truppen killed in action during the war and sing the haunting "Ich hatt' einen Kameraden" ("I Had a Comrade"). A special feature was an exhibition of Lipizzanzers, further symbolizing German-American cooperation at the war's end. 11. Panzer veterans in turn have attended American ceremonies and laid a wreath at Patton's grave in the Third Army cemetery at Hamm in Luxembourg.[5]

Yet many have been reluctant to end the reunions, and some still convene in May at Kötzting. In June 2004 I was invited to give a presentation at the reunion of the Traditions-Verband Panzer-Regiment 15 Grosser Kurfürst at Wolfhagen near Kassel. The Bundeswehr's Panzerbataillon 64 was based at Pommern Kaserne, its insignia a springing wolf on a horseshoe, and the Leopard panzers of Hauptmann Schneider's 3. Kompanie displayed the "Ghost" image of the former Gespenster-Division on their turrets.

Above: "Enemies become friends." Walter Rahn, Pz.Rgt.15, meeting Jimmie Leach, 37th Tank Battalion, with the author looking on, at Kötzting in 1995. They had fought in Lorraine in 1944. AUTHOR'S PHOTO

Author and Karl Heinz Loschke, Pz.Art.Rgt.119, secretary of the 11. Panzer Veterans Association, at his home in Braunschweig, 1989. AUTHOR'S PHOTO

The Gespenster legacy lived on with the Leopards of Pz.Batl.64 at Pommern Kaserne, Wolfhagen, near Kassel. Pictured are the author and Gerhard Winkler, Pz.Rgt.15, June 2000. AUTHOR'S PHOTO

Pz.Rgt.15 Treffen (Reunion) at Wolfhagen near Kassel, June 2004. The group includes Hans-Werner Bürkner on the left, Walter Rahn third from left, and Gerhard Otto in the center; the author, Karin Rahn, and author's wife, Diane, are in the back. AUTHOR'S PHOTO

The battalion's predecessor, Pz.Batl.54, was organized at Grafenwöhr in 1956, and based at Wolfhagen in 1960. In 1966 arrangements were made for future reunions of Pz.Rgt.15 to be held at Wolfhagen, and the following year veterans assembled for a Treffen that featured Generalleutnant a.D. (ausser Dienst, retired) Johannes Streich, first commander of the regiment in 1937. In 1981 Pz.Batl.54 was redesignated Pz.Batl.64, with Pz.Rgt.15 reunions continuing. But with the drawdown following the demise of the Soviet Union and the reunification of East and West Germany in 1991, the battalion was deactivated in 2008. Walter Rahn and Ansgar Pawelke arranged the heritage transfer of the Pz.Rgt.15 Traditionsraum to Bad Salzungen near Eisenach and Pz.Batl.393 in the Werratal Kaserne, near where the 11.Pz.Div. had fought in 1945.[6]

Whatever the political and ideological differences that take nations to war, the soldiers of both sides experience the heroism and horror of combat in common. The circumstances of the surrender of the 11. Panzer-Division may be exceptional, though perhaps not unique, among combatants of a similar cultural background and shared values. One senses that the leadership and example set by 11. Panzer commanders, especially the division commander himself, strongly influenced the tone of combat. General Wend von Wietersheim on occasion personally led his troops into attack, rallied them in retreat, was solicitous of their welfare, and treated his opponents with honor and respect. The 11. Panzer's fierce but fair conduct on the field of battle won the regard of their American adversaries, which ultimately became the foundation for the negotiated surrender with honor and the congenial relationships that continued over half a century.

In the broader context of armored warfare, the 11. Panzer-Division well exemplified the organizational and tactical concepts of the Panzerwaffe as articulated and practiced by Heinz Guderian. As the panzer division principle was to combine all the elements of the combat arms supporting each other, so the Kampfgruppen were organized under regimental or battalion headquarters, even down to the mixed company-sized Panzerkampftrupp of a section or platoon of panzers, a platoon of panzergrenadiers, a squad of engineers, and an artillery V.B. to call in supporting fires. The division commander then maneuvered these Kampfgruppen, as Balck deftly so did along the Chir, and von Wietersheim did at Montelimar.

Crucial in the division's successes were able and aggressive leaders like Ludwig Crüwell, Hermann Balck, and Wend von Wietersheim, and unit commanders like Graf Schimmelmann, Albert Henze, and Karl Thieme. At the same time, despite losses, there were well-experienced junior officers capable of commanding battalions when needed, and coordinating together. Able leadership in turn generated a loyalty among the enlisted personnel who felt they were competently led.

The Gespensters also had confidence in their weapons and equipment and their tactical use, from the Panther down to the Panzerfaust and the excellent "Zweibein" MG 42. The Germans had conceived of the role of the panzer divisions not only as infantry support or for exploitation, but as the spearhead in the attack, and capable of defeating enemy armored forces in battle. Even if outnumbered, the panzer units could defeat a foe by skillful tactical maneuvering, and bringing their weaponry and other divisional assets to bear, like the deadly "Acht-komma-achts."

The concepts of the Panzerwaffe, including tactical close air support, the combined arms team, and the Schwerpunkt (point of main effort), and later defense in depth and mobile counterattack, were adapted by other militaries. In the case of the US Army, Patton was one of the first to recognize and practice these concepts, "achieving a masterful example of blitzkrieg at its best," said his biographer Martin Blumenson.[7] The pace of armored warfare was exhibited by his armor commanders as well, especially John Wood of the 4th Armored. "I had spent two days with him shortly before the [Normandy] invasion," said B. H. Liddell Hart, "and he had impressed me as being more conscious of the possibilities of a deep exploitation and the importance of speed than anyone else."[8]

The 1943 reorganization of the US armored division into three combat command headquarters (redesignated brigade headquarters after 1962) to control any combination of divisional units according to mission, endorsed the battle group concept.[9] It was ironic that the tricolor armored division shoulder sleeve insignia—red for artillery, blue for infantry, and yellow for cavalry/armor—symbolized the combined-arms principle before the doctrine was formulated.

Maneuvers emphasized these concepts, as at the Desert Training Center in the Mojave Desert, California, established by Patton in April 1942, and the National Training Center at Fort Irwin, California; they were debated at the Combined Arms Center of the Training and Doctrine Command (TRADOC) at Fort Leavenworth, Kansas, not to mention the Armor School at Fort Knox, Kentucky, and NATO training areas in Germany, including Grafenwöhr. The Coalition mechanized forces that swept across the Iraqi desert in Operation Desert Storm in 1991 with M1A1 Abrams tanks and A-10A Thunderbolt IIs reflected the spirit. "We were playing Rommel," said an Armor friend.

Times change, but the concepts of combined arms teamwork, skillful leadership, and effective weaponry and equipment remain valid. The operations of the 11. Panzerdivision provide examples of these concepts in action.

APPENDIX A

Table of Comparative Ranks

Heer	Waffen-SS	US Army
Generalfeldmarschall	(Reichsführer-SS)	General of the Army
Gen.Feldm./GFM		
Generaloberst	Oberstgruppenführer	General
Gen.Obst.	Obstgruf.	Gen
General der Inf., Pz.Tr., etc.	Obergruppenführer	Lieutenant General
Gen. d. Inf., Pz.Tr.	OGruf.	Lt Gen
Generalleutnant	Gruppenführer	Major General
Gen.Lt.	Gruf.	Maj Gen
Generalmajor	Brigadeführer	Brigadier General
Gen.Maj.	Bgf. /Brig.Fhr.	Br, Brig Gen
	Oberführer	
	Obf. /Oberf.	
Oberst	Standartenführer	Colonel
Oberst	Staf.	Col
Oberstleutnant	Obersturmbannführer	Lieutenant Colonel
Obst.Lt./Oberstlt.	OStubaf.	Lt Col
Major	Sturmbannführer	Major
Maj.	Stubaf.	Maj
Hauptmann	Hauptsturmführer	Captain
Hptm.	Hstuf.	Capt
Oberleutnant	Obersturmführer	First Lieutenant
Ob.Lt./Oblt.	Ostuf.	1st Lt
Leutnant	Untersturmführer	Second Lieutenant
Lt.	Ustuf.	2nd Lt
Hauptfeldwebel		
Hfw.		
Stabsfeldwebel	Sturmscharführer	Master Sergeant
Stabsfeldw.	Stuscha.	M/Sgt
Oberfeldwebel	Hauptscharführer	First Sergeant
Ofw.	Hscha.	1st Sgt
Feldwebel	Oberscharführer	Technical Sergeant
Feldw./Fw.	Oscha.	Tech, T/Sgt
Fähnrich	Standartenjunker	(Cadet)
Fähnr.	St.J.	
Fahnenjunker		(Officer Candidate)
Fhj.		

Heer	Waffen-SS	US Army
Unterfeldwebel	Scharführer	Staff Sergeant
Unt.Feldw.	Scharf.	S/Sgt
Unteroffizier	Unterscharführer	Sergeant
Uffz.	Uscha.	Sgt
Stabsgefreiter		
Stabsgefr.		
Obergefreiter	Rottenführer	(British: Lance Corporal)
Ob.Gefr./Ogefr./Ogfr.	Rttf.	
Gefreiter	Sturmmann	Corporal
Gefr.	Strm.	Corp, Cpl
Oberschütze	Oberschütze	Private First Class
Oschtz.	Oschtz.	Pfc
Schütze, Grenadier	Schütze, SS Mann	Private
Schtz., Gren.	Schtz.	Pvt

Unteroffizier (Uffz.) was a rank, and also the term used for noncommissioned officers (NCO); Mannschaften (Mannsch.) was the term for enlisted men (EM).

APPENDIX B

11. Panzer-Division Units and Commanders, 1940–45

11. Panzer-Division—activated 1 August 1940

Divisionskommandeure[1]	
Generalmajor Crüwell, Ludwig	1 August 1940–22 August 1941
Oberst Angern, Günther	22–24 August 1941[2]
Generalmajor Esebeck, Hans-Karl Frhr. von	24 August–12/20 October 1941
Oberst Lenski, Arno von	12–27 October 1941
Generalmajor Scheller, Walter	20/27 October 1941–16 May 1942
Oberst/Gen.Maj./Gen.Lt. Balck, Hermann	16/24 May 1942–4/13 March 1943
Generalleutnant Choltitz, Dietrich von	13 March–15/17 May 1943
Generalmajor Mickl, Johannes	15/17 May–10 August 1943
Oberst/Gen.Maj./Gen.Lt. Wietersheim, Wend von	10 August 1943–15 April 1945
Oberst Hake, Friedrich Erdmann von	7–18 May 1944
Generalmajor Treusch von Buttlar-Brandenfels, Horst	15 April–5 May 1945

1. Generalstabsoffiziere (Ia)	
Major Wolff, Werner	August 1940–August 1941
Major Selmayr	August 1941–March 1942
Major/Oberstlt. Kinitz, Franz-Joachim	6 March 1942–15 October 1943
Major Binder, Eitel-Friedrich	6–28 August 1943
Major/Oberstlt. Drews, Werner	15 October 1943–5 May 1945

11. Schützenbrigade—activated 8 December 1939; redesignated 5 May 1942 as:

11. Panzergrenadierbrigade—dissolved 16 November 1942	
Oberst Angern, Günther	December 1939–August 1941
Oberst Lenski, Arno von	August–December 1941
Oberst Luz, Helwig	December 1941–September 1942
Oberst Hillebrand, von	May 1942
Oberst Körner, Karl	June 1942
Oberst Back, Hans Ulrich	September–November 1942

Schützen-/Panzergrenadier-Regiment 110	
Oberst Luz, Helwig	December 1939–November 1941
Oberst Fricke, Ludwig	November 1941–April 1942
Oberst Henze, Albert	April 1942–January 1944
Oberstlt. Rauch, Josef	November 1942–January 1943
Oberstlt. Sparre, Georg	December 1942
Major Oertzen, von	August 1943
Oberst Zychlinski, von	January–March 1944
Oberstlt. Göttmann	April–May 1944
Oberst Hax, Heinrich-Georg	May–9 November 1944
Hptm. Wolff, Heinz	9–17 November 1944
Oberstlt Thieme, Karl	10/17 November 1944–5 May 1945

Schützen-/Panzergrenadier-Regiment 111 (reconstituted 10 April 1945)[3]	
Oberst Bohlmann-Combrinck, Theodor	December 1939–May 1942
Oberst Fricke, Ludwig	September–November 1941
Oberst Bosse, Alexander von	May 1942–15 May 1943
Oberst Hillebrand, von	May 1942
Oberst Körner, Karl	August 1942
Oberst Boelsen, Dr. Hans	15 May–October 1943
Major Donnhauser, Anton	October–December 1943
Oberstlt. Wartenberg, Guido von	December 1943–January 1944 k
Major Kaldrack, Günther	January–February 1944
Oberstlt. Wilde	February–August 1944 w
Major Thieme, Karl	August–September 1944
Oberstlt. Rupprecht, Werner von	September–23 November 1944 k
Oberst Kielmansegg, Johann Adolf Graf von	November 1944–April 1945
Oberst Zerbel (111. reconstituted)	10 April–5 May 1945

Panzer-Regiment 15—designated 12 October 1937; from 5.Pz.Div. 6 September 1940

Oberst Streich, Johannes	15 October 1937–15 February 1941
Oberstlt./Oberst Riebel, Gustav-Adolf	23 February–31 December 1941
Oberst Schimmelmann, Theodor-Friedrich Carl Graf von	1 January 1942–1 August 1943
Oberstlt. Roth, Max	May–August 1942
Oberstlt./Oberst Lauchert, Meinrad von	1 August 1943–1 August 1944
Major Sivers, Karl von	24 January–10 April 1944 k
Oberstlt. Stenkhoff, Karl-Gustav	2 August–December 1944
Oberstlt. Lühl	January–February 1945
Major Reichardt, Jürgen	February–5 May 1945

(Pz.) Artillerie-Regiment 119—redesignated from Art.Rgt.231, 10 October 1940

Oberst Matena, Heinz	August 1940–February 1942
Oberst Schmidt, Oskar	March 1942–February 1943
Oberst Werner, Julius	February–July 1943 k
Oberstlt. Schmeling, Herwart	August–December 1943
Oberstlt. Palm	August 1943
Oberstlt. Hammon, Erich	July–November 1944
Oberst Daude	November 44–26 February 1945 k
Oberstlt. (not known)	February–20 March 1945 m
Hptm. Hoffmann	March–5 May 1945

Heeres Flakartillerie Abteilung 277 (as IV.Abt./A.R.119, 22 May 1942–27 April 1943)

Major Manger	
Major Baack, Peter	July–September 1943
Major Klugmann, Helmut	September–November 1943
Major Menzel, Joachim	November 1943–15 January 1945

Kradschützenbataillon 61—redesignated A.A.11, 23 April 1943

Oberstlt. Stockhausen, von	April–July 1941
Major Götz, von	August–9 October 1941 k
Major Usedom, Horst von	October 1941–May 1942
Hptm. Hauser, Paul von	May 1942–6 February 1943
Hptm. Ladewig	March 1943

Pz. Aufklärungsabteilung 231—amalgamated under K.61, 9 November 1941

Hptm./Major Usedom, Horst von	April–9 November 1941
Hptm./Rittmeister Herff, von	April 1941

Pz. Aufklärungsabteilung 11—as redesignated from K.61, 23 April 1943

Major Lindner, Horst	April–21 July 1943 k
Hptm. Pirch, Wilhelm	21 July–September 1943
Major Donnhauser, Anton	October–December 1943
Major Rupprecht, Werner von	January–June 1944
Major Bode, Karl	June–September 1944
Major Thieme, Karl	1–15 October 1944
Major Pfeil, Graf von	15 October–December 1944
Hptm. Riedinger, Fritz	January–February 1945

Panzerjägerabteilung 61 (inactivated 30 December 1942–24 May 1943)

Major Schultz, Edgar	July 1941–May 1942
Major Guttmacher, Friedrich	May 1942–April 1943
Major Kessler, Arnold	May 1943–April 1945

Pz. Pionierbataillon 209

Major Scholaster, Bernhard	September 1939–February 1942
Major Bullerdieck, Heinrich	February–November 1942
Hptm. Grevendorf, Erhard	December 1942–March 1943
Hptm. Schnur, Hans	March 1943
Hptm./Major Bödicker, Heinz	July 1943–9 March 1945
Oblt. Snoek, August	October 1944

Pz. Nachrichtenabteilung 341—redesignated 89, 1 June 1943

Major Bluhm, Franz	November 1939–January 1942
Major Bernuth, Bernhard von	September 1941
Hptm. Poretschkin, Theodor	January 1942–May 1943
Major Steuer, Arnold	May 1943–October 1944

Division Nachschub Führer 61 (DNF, DiNaFü)

Oberstlt./Oberst Neureiter, Camillo	August 1940–April 1942
Hptm./Maj. Zamory, Günther von	April 1942 –

Div.Nachsch.Tr., San.Tr.Abt., Verwaltungs Tr.Abt., Feldpost, Ord.-Dste, Feld Gend. Tr.61; Feldersatz Btl.

1. Dates given when known. In some cases, there is the date of appointment/date actually at headquarters. Some commanders were acting (i.V., in Vertretung). Listings compiled from BA–MA (Bundesarchiv–Militärarchv), Freiburg i.Br., Herr Meyer, 1989; Karl Heinz Loschke list, 1990; Walter Rahn list, 1992; references in the KTBs; and from sources noted in the text.
2. k = killed, w = wounded, m = missing in action.
3. Pz.Gren.Rgt.111 was reconstituted 10 April 1945 when the original regiment was lost in the Ruhr Kessel.

APPENDIX C

11. Panzer-Division Units and Commanders in the West, 1944–45

Div.Kdr.

Gen.Lt. Wietersheim, Wend von	10 August 1943–15 April 1945
Gen.Maj. Buttlar-Brandenfels, Freiherr von	15 April–5 May 1945

Ia

Oberstlt. Drews, Werner	15 October 1943–5 May 1945

Pz.Rgt. 15

Oberst Lauchert, Meinrad von	1 August 1943–1 August 1944
Oberstlt. Stenkhoff, Karl-Gustav	2 August–December 1944
Oberstlt. Lühl	January–February 1945
Major Reichardt, Jürgen	February–5 May 1945

I. Abt. (Panther) (1.-4.Kp.)

Maj. Weicke	5 January–25 August 1944 k
Hptm. von Rabenau	–29 August 1944 k
Maj. Reichardt, Jürgen	August 1944–February 1945
Oblt. Rahn, Walter	March–15 March 1945 m
Hptm. Rodenhauser	15 March–5 May 1945

II. Abt. (PzKpfw IV) (5.-8.Kp.)

Maj. Berger	–15 August 1944
Hptm. Rodenhauser	August 1944–14 March 1945
Hptm. Mielenhausen	March–5 May 1945

Pz.Gren.Rgt. 110

Oberstlt. Göttmann	April–May 1944
Oberst Hax, Heinrich-Georg	4 May–9 November 1944
Hptm. Wolff, Heinz	9–17 November 1944
Oberstlt. Thieme, Karl	10/17 November 1944–5 May 1945

I. Btl.(gp) (1.-4.Kp.)

Maj. Thieme, Karl	May–November 1944
Hptm. Wolff, Heinz	November 1944–22 February 1945 k
Hptm. Höfer, Adalbert	March–May 1945

II. Btl. (5.-8.Kp.)

Hptm. Schneider, Johannes	September–11 November 1944 w
Hptm. Höfer, Adalbert	11 November 1944–January 1945 w
Oblt. Stolze, Heinrich	January–May 1945

(9.–10.Kp.)

III. Btl.

Maj. Dalhaus, Julius	October–November 1944

Pz.Gren.Rgt. 111

Oberstlt. Wilde	February–August 1944 w
Maj. Thieme, Karl	August–September 1944
Oberstlt. Rupprecht, Werner von	September–23 November 1944 k
Oberst Kielmansegg, Johann Adolf Graf von	November 1944–April 1945
Oberst. Zerbel (Pz.G.R.111 reconstituted)	10 April–5 May 1945

I. Btl. (1.-4.Kp.)

Hptm. Wehrstädt, Werner	May–October 1944 k
Hptm. Gattmann, Wilhelm	October–November 1944 ill
Hptm. Engelmann, Paul	November–December 1944
Hptm. Lüttge, Fritz	January–25 February 1945 m

II. Btl. (5.-8.Kp.)

Hptm/Maj. Grumbt, Otto	July–September 1944 w
Hptm. Reuter, Fritz	October–November 1944
Hptm. Lüth	November 1944–January 1945
Oblt. Loch, Horst	January–February 1945
Hptm. Kunze	20–26 February 1945 m

(9.-10.Kp)

Pz.Art.Rgt.119

Oberstlt. Hammon, Erich	July–November 1944
Oberst Daude	November 1944–26 February 1945 k
Oberstlt. (not known)	February–20 March 1945 m
Hptm. Hoffmann	March–5 May 1945

I.Abt. (Sf) (1.-3.Battr.)

Hptm. Rahm, Günther	

II. Abt. (gemischt) (4.-6.Battr.)

Hptm. Hoffmann	

III. Abt. (schw) (7.-10.Battr)

Hptm. Schaefer-Kehnert, Walter	30 March 1945 m

H. Flak Abt. 277

Maj. Menzel, Joachim	November 1943–15 January 1945

Pz.A.A. 11 (Aufkl. Abt.)

Maj. Bode, Karl	June–September 1944
Maj.Thieme, Karl	1–15 October 1944
Maj. Pfeil, Graf von	15 October–December 1944
Hptm. Riedinger, Fritz	January–February 1945

Pz.Jäger Abt. 61 (Pak)

Maj. Kessler, Arnold	May 1943–April 1945

Pz.Pion.Btl. 209

Maj. Bödicker, Heinz	Jul 1943–9 March 1945
Oblt. Snoek, August	–6 October 1944

Pz.Nachr.Abt. 89

Maj. Steuer, Arnold	May 1943–October 1944

DiNaFü

Maj. Zamory, Günther von	April 1942–

Div.Nachsch.Tr., San.Tr.Abt., Verw.Tr.Abt., Feldpost, Ord-Dste, Feld Gend.Tr.61; Feldersatz Btl.

11. Panzer-Division: Die Ritterkreuzträger[1]

Name:	Date awarded:	Rank:	Unit:
Schwerter (Swords)			
Balck, Hermann (Nr. 25.)	4 Mar 1943	Gen.Lt.	Kdr. 11.Pz.Div.
Thieme, Karl (Nr. 156.)	9 May 1945	Oberstlt.	Kdr. Pz.Gren.Rgt.110[2]
Wietersheim, Wend von (Nr. 58.)	26 Mar 1944	Gen.Maj.	Kdr. 11.Pz.Div.
Eichenlaub (Oak Leaves)			
Balck, Hermann (Nr. 155.)	20 Dec 1942	Gen.Maj.	Kdr. 11.Pz.Div.
Crüwell, Ludwig (Nr. 34.)	1 Sept 1941	Gen.Lt.	Kdr. 11.Pz.Div.
Lauchert, Meinrad von (Nr. 396.)	12 Feb 1944	Oberst	Kdr. Pz.Rgt.15
Thieme, Karl (Nr. 627.)	23 Oct 1944	Maj.	Führer Pz.Gren.Rgt.111
Ritterkreuz (Knight's Cross)			
Hq., Stab:			
(Angern, Günther—prior to 11.Pz.Div.	5 Aug 1940	Oberst	Kdr. 11.Schtz.Brig.)
(Streich, Johannes—prior to 11.Pz.Div.	31 Jan 1941	Oberst	Kdr. Pz.Rgt.15)
Crüwell, Ludwig	14 May 1941	Gen.Maj.	Kdr. 11.Pz.Div.
Kaeppel, Rudolf	1 Feb 1945	Hptm.	Chef Div.Begleit Kp.
Panzer Rgt. 15			
Brackel, Bruno Freiherr von	23 Aug 1941	Oblt.	Führer 3.Kp./Pz.Rgt.15
Brockdorf, Cay-Lorenz Baron von	14 Apr 1945	Oblt.	Adju. Pz.Rgt.15
Frost, Willi	24 Sept 1943	Ofw.	Zugfhr. i.d. 4.Kp./Pz.Rgt.15
Hensel, Gerhard	26 Dec 1941	Ofw.	Zugfhr. i.d. 2.Kp./Pz.Rgt.15
Ketterer, Karl	24 Mar 1943	Ofw.	Zugfhr. i.d. 7.Kp./Pz.Rgt.15
Kolodziejczyk, Georg	5 Mar 1945	Ofw.	Zugfhr. i.d. 3.Kp./Pz.Rgt.15
Lestmann, Karl	25 Jan 1943	Hptm.	Kdr. II.Abt./Pz.Rgt.15
Schimmelmann, Theodor Graf von	14 May 1941	Maj.	Kdr. II.Abt./Pz.Rgt.15
Sivers, Karl von	6 Mar 1944	Maj.	Kdr. I.Abt./Pz.Rgt.15
Zachariae-Lingenthal, Edel-Heinrich	18 Sep 1943	Hptm.	Kdr. II.Abt./Pz.Rgt.15
(Brehme, Gerhard	23 Aug 1943	Ofw.	Zugfhr. i.d. 1./Pz.Abt.52 [I./15])

Name:	Date awarded:	Rank:	Unit:
Schützen-/Panzergrenadier-Rgt. 110			
Bartsch, Günter	12 Nov 1943	Uffz.	Gruppenfhr. i.d. 2.Kp./Pz.G.R.110
Grabowski, Josef	18 Jan 1944	Lt.	Fhr. 4.Kp./Pz.G.R.110
Henze, Albert	15 Jan 1944	Oberst	Kdr. Pz.Gren.Rgt.110
Jokisch, Fritz	28 July 1943	Feldw.	Zugfhr. i.d. 3.Kp./Pz.G.R.110
Luz, Helwig	15 Nov 1941	Oberst	Kdr. Schützen Rgt. 110
Thieme, Karl	30 Oct 1943	Hptm.	Kdr. I.Btl./Pz.Gren.Rgt.110
Welsch, Willi	29 Sep 1941	Hptm.	Chef 2.Kp./Schtz.Rgt.110
Wolff, Heinz	12 Dec 1944	Hptm.	Fhr . I.Btl./Pz.G.R.110
Schützen-/Panzergrenadier-Rgt. 111			
Boelsen, Dr. Hans	17 Sep 1943	Oberst	Kdr. Pz.Gren.Rgt.111
Bohlmann-Combrinck, Theodor	8 Aug 1941	Oberst	Kdr. Schtz.Rgt.111
Danowski, Franz	18 Oct 1944	Oblt.	Fhr, 10.(Pi.)Kp./Pz.G.R.111
Donnhauser, Anton	18 Jul 1943	Hptm.	Kdr. II.Btl./Pz.G.R.111
Florin, Gerhard	2 Feb 1942	Hptm.	Kdr. II.Btl./Schtz.Rgt.111
Grumbt, Otto	28 Oct 1944	Hptm.	Kdr. II.Btl./Pz.G.R.111
Kleinschmidt, Ernst	30 Sep 1943	Lt.	Btl. Adju. im Pz.G.R.111
Muenzer, Eberhard	23 Aug 1943	Hptm.	Rgt. Adju. Pz.Gren.Rgt.111
Rupprecht, Werner Frhr. Von	12 Dec 1944	Maj.	Fhr. Pz.Gren.Rgt.111
Wartenberg, Guido von	6 Oct 1943	Maj.	Fhr. Pz.Gren.Rgt.111
Pz. Artillerie Rgt. 119			
Hammon, Erich	1 Feb 1945	Oberstlt.	Kdr. Pz.Art.Rgt.119
Thoma, Helmut	3 May 1942	Oblt.	Chef 9.Battr./Pz.Art.Rgt.119
Panzerjäger Abt. 61			
Assmann, Alois	18 Sep 1942	Ob.Gefr.	Richtschütze i.d. 1./Pz.Jäg.Abt.61
Kessler, Arnold	4 Oct 1944	Maj.	Kdr. Pz.Jäg.Abt.61
Mund, Dieter	19 Sep 1943	Lt.	Fhr. 1./Pz.Jäg.Abt.61
Tilgner, Herbert	18 Dec 1944	Oblt.	Chef 2./Pz.Jäger Abt.61
Kradschützen-Bataillon 61			
Hauser, Paul Freiherr von	25 Jan 1943	Hptm.	Kdr. Kradschtz.Btl.61
Usedom, Horst von	31 Dec 1941	Maj.	Kdr. Kradschtz.Btl.61
Pz. Aufklärungs-Abteilung 11			
Harthan, Lorenz	12 Jun 1944	Ofw.	Pi.Zugführer i.d. 5./Pz.A.A.11
Pirch, Wilhelm	13 Sep 1943	Hptm.	Fhr. Pz.Aufkl.Abt.11
Rothardt, Heinz	30 Sep 1943	Uffz.	Zugfhr. i.d. 2.Kp./Pz.A.A.11

Name:	Date awarded:	Rank:	Unit:
Pz. Pionier-Bataillon 209			
Bödicker, Heinz	9 Jan 1944	Hptm.	Fhr. Pz.Pi.Btl.209
Borck, Hans-Georg	23 Dec 1943	Oblt.	Chef 3.Kp./Pz.Pi.Btl.209
Snoek, August	5 Nov 1944	Oblt.	Fhr. Pz.Pi.Btl.209
Heeres Flakartillerie Abt. 277			
Menzel, Joachim	10 Sep 1944	Maj.	Kdr. H.Flakart.Abt.277

1. Names organized by unit alphabetically. Data from Seemen, *Die Ritterkreuzträger* (1976), updated by Fellgiebel, *Die Träger des Ritterkreuzes* (1986). "Führer" (Fhr.) means "leader" of a unit.

2. The Schwerter for Karl Thieme was unconfirmed, but apparently approved by Grossadmiral Karl Dönitz as Führer, as Schwerter Nr. 156. The Swords and Oakleaves awards were officially listed and numbered, with totals during the war of some 159 and 883 respectively.

Notes

CHAPTER 1: ANTECEDENTS

1. Lt. Col. Robert J. Icks, *Tanks and Armored Vehicles* (New York: Duell, Sloan and Pearce, 1945), 93. Brig. Gen. Sir James Edmonds, *Military Operations: France, Belgium 1917* (London: HM Stationery Office, 1948), 2:148n.
2. A7V from Allgemeines Kriegsdepartement 7, Abteilung Verkehrswesen. No A7Vs survive, though there is a full-sized replica ("Wotan") at the Panzermuseum in Munster near Paderborn. Details of World War I tanks, which sometimes vary, are in many sources; see, for example, Christopher F. Foss, *The Encyclopedia of Tanks and Armored Fighting Vehicles* (San Diego, CA: Thunder Bay, 2002). These details are from the booklets *Germany* (1973), 10, and *Development of the British Tank, Part One 1915–1918* (n.d.), 8–9, RAC (Royal Armoured Corps) Centre Tank Museum, Bovington, Dorset.
3. This first tank clash is described in many sources, including Barrie Pitt, *1918: The Last Act* (New York: Ballantine, 1963), 149–151; accounts differ, however, as in Arch Whitehouse, *Tank* (Garden City, NY: Doubleday, 1960), 105–106. The British official history, utilizing conflicting German sources, says two A7Vs were hit and abandoned, the crew of the third surrendering after suffering (metallic) splash from the 58th Machine-Gun Battalion. Brig. Gen. Sir James Edmonds, *Military Operations: France and Belgium, 1918 (March–April)* (London: MacMillan & Co., 1937), 392, 407. There is only a brief reference in the German official history *Reichsarchiv, Der Weltkrieg 1914–1918*, Bd. XIV (Berlin: E. S. Mittler und Sohn, 1919/1944/1956), 309–310; similarly in Gen. Walther Nehring, *Die Geschichte der deutschen Panzerwaffe 1916 bis 1945* (Berlin: Propyläen Verlag, 1969), 36. General Nehring commanded Rommel's Deutsches Afrika Korps (DAK), later the XXIV Panzerkorps, and finally 1. Panzerarmee on the Eastern Front.
4. A list of B. H. Liddell Hart's publications are in his posthumous *History of the Second World War* (New York: G. P. Putnam's Sons, 1971/Perigee, 1982), 767–768, and in other works.
5. The evolution of armored forces is primarily from Richard M. Ogorkiewicz, *Armor* (New York: Praeger, 1960), a classic if somewhat dated work.
6. Alistair Horne, *The Price of Glory: Verdun 1916* (New York: Penguin, 1978), 341.
7. Data in RAC, *France* (1970); quotations in Ogorkiewicz, *Armor*, 178–179.
8. Nehring, *Panzerwaffe*, bibliography, 44. The German edition of de Gaulle's work was published by Voggenreiter Verlag, Potsdam, 1935.
9. Julian Jackson, *The Fall of France* (New York: Oxford University Press, 2004), 22–23.
10. Organization of the DLMs and DCRs is detailed in Guy Chapman, *Why France Fell* (New York: Holt, Rinehart and Winston, 1968), in Appendix A, 342–344.
11. Icks, *Tanks*, 189–200; Ogorkiewicz, *Armor*, 237–245.
12. RAC booklets by nation; Ogorkiewicz, *Armor*, and Icks, *Tanks*, chapters by nation.
13. In the 1941 invasion of Russia the Panzer 35(t) equipped the 6. Panzer-Division, though it was withdrawn by 1942. The Panzer 38(t) served well with the 2. and 3. Leichte (Light) Divisions in Poland, and in France after those units were upgraded as the 7. and 8. Panzer-Divisionen in 1940. The 12., 19., and 20. Panzer-Divisionen also employed the Pz. 38(t) in 1941. See the discussion in Drs. Stephen and Russell Hart, *German Tanks of World War II* (London: Brown, 1999), 33–43.
14. Mary Lee Stubbs and Stanley Russell Connor, *Armor-Cavalry* Part I (Washington, DC: Office of the Chief of Military History, 1969), 54, 58.
15. Data from tables in RAC booklet *USSR* (1970), here for the T-34/76A with L/30 gun, 37, 40. The B and C models had 60mm (2.4-inch) and 75mm (3-inch) armor, respectively, and the 76.2mm L/41 gun had a muzzle velocity of 680 mps (2,231 fps).
16. Walter Goerlitz, *The German General Staff*, trans. Brian Battershaw (New York: Praeger, 1952), 222ff.
17. Ibid., 228ff; Sondergruppe R in Nehring, *Panzerwaffe*, 43.
18. Barton Whaley, *Covert German Rearmament 1919–1939* (Frederick, MD: University Publications of America, 1984), 9–30. Other sources include Hans W. Gatzke, *Stresemann and the Rearmament of Germany* (1954) and Seymour Melman, ed., *Inspection for Disarmament* (1958). Stresemann's private papers were uncovered in 1953 as part of the Foreign Ministry documents captured in 1945.

19. Quotations of Foreign Minister Briand and of historian Arnold J. Toynbee, who had been a British delegate at the 1919 peace conference, in Whaley, *Covert German Rearmament*, 33.
20. John Wheeler-Bennett, *The Nemesis of Power: The German Army in Politics, 1918–1945* (London: MacMillan, 1953), 185–186.

CHAPTER 2: ORIGINS OF THE PANZERWAFFE

1. RAC *Germany* (1973), 6ff; Ogorkiewicz, *Armor*, 207, 273.
2. Data from Nehring, *Panzerwaffe*, 116, and Ogorkiewicz, *Armor*, 209.
3. Nehring, *Panzerwaffe*, 43–44, 115. Stationsleiter (base directors) were Director Mahlbrand (1927–29), Maj. Ritter von Radlmaier (1929–31), and Major Harpe 1931–33).
4. Heinz Guderian, *Panzer Leader*, trans. Constantine Fitzgibbon (New York: Ballantine, 1957), 6ff.
5. Ibid., 12.
6. Ibid., 13; in his analysis of German conceptualizing, Samuel W. Mitcham Jr., *The Panzer Legions* (Mechanicsburg, PA: Stackpole, 2007), 4, warns that Guderian's memoirs are rather "self-serving." Guderian's influence on combined arms developments is denigrated in Russell A. Hart, *Guderian: Panzer Pioneer or Myth Maker?* (Washington, DC: Potomac Books, 2006), 25–27; Hart writes that Guderian was an "arrogant, ambitious egotist" who "exaggerated" his own role (115) and "hampered the German war machine at every stage" (118).
7. Guderian, *Panzer Leader*, 10; Ogorkiewicz, *Armor*, 21; Nehring. *Panzerwaffe*, 85; Jackson, *Fall of France*, 23, also disputes de Gaulle's influence. Whitehouse, *Tank*, 129, says the Germans "obviously" took notice, and de Gaulle's book "became the war bible of the Hitler regime." Kenneth Macksey in *Tank Warfare* (New York: Stein and Day, 1972), 86n, says it is instructive to note that in the bibliography of Guderian's *Achtung Panzer!* of 1937, de Gaulle is included but not Liddell Hart. In the 1992 introduction to his *Guderian* (London: Greenhill, 1992), xii, xiv, 41, Macksey argues that Fuller was Guderian's primary influence, not Liddell Hart; he adds that Liddell Hart is not mentioned by Guderian in his original *Erinnerungen eines Soldaten*, but was added in the English versions of *Panzer Leader* (in Ballantine, 10), which he facilitated and for which he wrote the foreword. Guderian cannot have been unaware of Liddell Hart's voluminous writings however.
8. Guderian, *Panzer Leader*, 11, 13; also Nehring, *Panzerwaffe*, 50, 59.
9. Guderian, *Panzer Leader*, 18. The British and American terminology would refer to the panzer types as Marks (Mark III for Panzer III, etc.) in World War II.
10. Ibid., 19.
11. Gesetz für den Aufbau der Wehrmacht. Goerlitz, *German General Staff*, 291; Nehring, *Panzerwaffe*, 90. Also note Hubertus Senf, *Die Entwicklung der Panzerwaffe im deutschen Heer zwischen den beiden Weltkriegen* (Frankfurt: E. S. Mittler & Sohn, 1969).
12. For the negligence to develop self-propelled artillery see David T. Zabecki, *Steel Wind* (Westport, CT: Praeger, 1994), 104. Oberst Georg Bruchmüller had developed the concept of massed artillery fire without registration or adjustment for surprise, employed at Riga in 1917 and in the "Ludendorff Offensives" in 1918. In the postwar period only the Red Army expanded on his principles. While assault guns and tank destroyers were developed after 1939, self-propelled artillery was not operational until 1942 (e.g., German Wespe, 10,5cm on a Panzer II chassis; the US M7 Priest, 105mm on an M4 chassis; and the British Bishop, a 25-pounder on a Valentine chassis). The Soviet Samokhodnaya Ustanovka (self-propelled carriages, SUs) diverged as assault guns or tank destroyers, but had a certain indirect fire capability.
13. Organization from Ogorkiewicz, *Armor*, 73–74; also from his "The Structure and Functions of Armored Divisions Part II," *Armor* 67, no. 2 (March–April 1958): 38–42; Wolf Keilig, *Das deutsche Heer* (Bad Nauheim: Podzun Verlag, 1956), Bd. II.
14. Harts, *German Tanks*, 158. Data for 1. Pz. Div., others differed slightly.
15. Dr. Frido von Senger und Etterlin, *Taschenbuch der Panzer 1943-1957* (Munich: J. F. Lehmanns, 1957), 75–81.
16. The German half-tracks are covered in Walter J. Spielberger und Uwe Feist, *Halbkettenfahrzeuge* (Fallbrook, CA: Aero, 1968); and Drs. Matthew Hughes and Chris Mann, *Fighting Techniques of a Panzergrenadier1941–1945* (Osceola, WI: MBI, 2000), chapter 6. Other works include Senger and Etterlin, *Taschenbuch*, and Duncan Crow and Robert J. Icks, *Encyclopedia of Armoured Cars and Half-Tracks* (Secaucus, NJ: Chartwell, 1976), 75ff.
17. SPW, "Es Pay Vay," to the German soldier. Guy Franz Arend began collecting armored vehicles at the end of World War II and had examples of all Sd.Kfz. 251 models, as well as other German and Allied vehicles in his Bastogne Historical Center (BHC) and then in his Arlon Victory Museum. By 2003 the excellent Victory Museum collection had been relocated to Auburn, Indiana, USA. Guy and Lisle now spend their time in Switzerland.

18. Lkws from Reinhard Franks, *Trucks of the Wehrmacht*, trans. Dr. Edward Force (Atglen, PA: Schiffer, 1994). S-Typ was Standardtyp (rear-drive), and A-Typ was Allradgetrieben (all-wheel drive).
19. Ordnance data from (US) War Department Technical Manual TM-E 30-451, *Handbook on German Military Forces 15 March 1945* (Washington: US Government Printing Office, 1945; reprint, Baton Rouge: Louisiana State University Press, 1990). (Hereafter cited as TM-E 30-451.) In his introduction to the reprinted edition American historian Stephen E. Ambrose says, "This volume is unique and valuable beyond measure"; also Ian V. Hogg, *Encyclopedia of Infantry Weapons of World II* (Greenwich, CT: Bison, 1977). Data varies with different models, ammunition types, and other factors.
20. *Die Schützenkompanie*, adapted by Oberstleutnant Ludwig Queckbörner (Berlin: E. S. Mittler & Sohn, 1939), 114ff.
21. TM-E 30-451, 228–231, as modified for late war.

CHAPTER 3: THE FIRST OPERATIONS

1. Adolf Galland, *The First and the Last*, trans. Mervyn Savill (New York: Henry Holt, 1954), vii–viii.
2. Goerlitz, *German General Staff*, 307; Nehring, *Panzerwaffe*, 95; Mitcham, *Panzer Legions*, 53.
3. Goerlitz, *German General Staff*, 317ff.
4. Anschluss is "union" in Cassell's 1939 and Webster's 1942 dictionaries; Ogorkiewicz, *Armor*, 211–212; Guderian, *Panzer Leader*, 30ff; Macksey, *Guderian*, 71ff.
5. Muzzle velocities especially in Ogorkiewicz, *Armor*, 313; Maj. Gen. F. W. von Mellenthin, *Panzer Battles*, trans. H. Betzler, ed. L. C. F. Turner (Norman: University of Oklahoma Press, 1956), 155n; also Guderian, *Panzer Leader*, 114.
6. Data from Harts, *German Tanks*, 76; chart of German tank gun armor penetration in Ogorkiewicz, *Armor*, 314, and in RAC, *Germany*, 36.
7. Variations in divisional organizations are in Harts, *German Tanks*, 158, 167.
8. Ibid., 14, 19.
9. Guderian, *Panzer Leader*, 51; Angern from Keilig, *Das deutsche Heer*, Bd. II, 14.
10. The history of Pz. Rgt. 15 is by Gustav W. Schrodek, *Ihr Glaube galt dem Vaterland* (Their Trust Was in the Fatherland) (Munich: Schild-Verlag, 1976), copy courtesy of Gerhard Winkler of Pz. Rgt. 15. Schrodek was a Feldwebel (sergeant) with Pz. Rgt. 15 who had joined the regiment as a new recruit 15 November 1938.
11. Streich, born in Holstein, later commanded 5. Leichte Division (redesignated 21. Pz. Div.) in Rommel's DAK. He retired as Generalleutnant. An early history of the regiment through 1938 was also given the author by Walter Volkmann in Wolfhagen, June 2000.
12. Panzer inventory from George F. Nafziger, *The German Order of Battle: Panzers and Artillery in World War II* (London: Greenhill Books and Mechanicsburg, PA: Stackpole, 1999), 56. Thomas L. Jentz, ed., *Panzertruppen* (Atglen, PA: Schiffer, 1996), 91, shows seventy-two Pz. Is, eighty-one Pz. IIs, three Pz. IIIs, eight Pz. IVs, and eleven Panzer Befehlswagen as of 1 September 1939.
13. Schönstedt's account of the Polish Feldzug in Schrodek, *Ihr Glaube*, 41–63.
14. Provisional Panzer Division Kempf in East Prussia constituted a seventh panzer division. The German Order of Battle is charted in several sources, including Oberst i.G. Horst Scheibert und Genmaj. a.D. Carl Wagener, *Die deutsche Panzertruppe 1939–1945* (Bad Nauheim: Podzun-Verlag, 1966), 10, and Maj. Robert M. Kennedy, *The German Campaign in Poland* (Washington, DC: Department of the Army Pamphlet No. 20-255, 1956), 74. A political treatment is Nicholas Bethell, *The War Hitler Won: the Fall of Poland* (New York: Holt, Rinehart and Winston, 1972). World War II campaign maps are in Thomas E. Griess, ed., *Campaign Atlas to The Second World War* (Wayne, NJ: Avery, 1989), produced for the US Military Academy at West Point, New York.
15. Ogorkiewicz, *Armor*, 269. Guderian, *Panzer Leader*, 53, repeated in other sources including von Mellenthin, *Panzer Battles*, 3; A. E. Johann, *Zwischen Westwall und Maginotlinie* (Berlin: Im Deutschen Verlag, 1939), 47. Historian Steven Zaloga, however, in "Polish Cavalry Against Panzers," *Armor* 93, no.1 (January–February 1984), 29, clarifies that in a skirmish on 1 September 1939 near the village of Krojanty, two squadrons of the 18th Lancers (*sans* lances) were attacked by two German armored cars and withdrew into nearby woods. Italian journalists visiting the scene the next day were told troopers had been killed while charging tanks, and German propaganda embellished the story. Richard Ogorkiewicz also referred to the account as a "fable" in a letter responding to other points, published in *Armor* 93, no. 2 (March–April 1984), 3.
16. Schönstedt's account in Schrodek, *Ihr Glaube*, 63. Some 22,000 Polish officers and intelligentsia were executed in 1940 by the Soviet NKVD, an act admitted by Soviet leader Mikhail Gorbachev in 1990.
17. Bethell, *The War Hitler Won*, 84. Noted in Mellenthin, *Panzer Battles*, 7, and Kennedy, *Poland*, 92.
18. Guderian, *Panzer Leader*, 61. Guderian's half-track was presumably an Sd.Kfz. 251/6 Kommandowagen, based on the Schützenpanzerwagen.
19. "Klotzen, nicht kleckern" in Guderian, *Panzer Leader*, 83, and "Fahrkarte bis zur Endstation" in Scheibert and Wagener, *Panzertruppen*, 18.

20. Kennedy, *Poland*, 131–135, based on *Armee Korps Erfahrungsberichte*; Guderian, *Panzer Leader*, 54–55.
21. Schrodek, *Ihr Glaube*, 65.
22. Formation and actions of the 11. Schützenbrigade (mot) and Schützen-Regimenter 110 and 111 in Oberstleutnant a.D. Anton J. Donnhauser und Generalmajor Werner Drews, *Der Weg der 11. Panzer-Division* (Bad Wörishofen: Holzmann-Druck-Service, 1982), 9–11, and sketch map; copy courtesy of Karl Heinz Loschke, Sprecher der ehemalige 11. Panzer-Division (secretary of the former 11. Pz. Div.). Donnhauser commanded A.A. 11 and Pz.G.R. 111, and Drews was Ia (chief of operations) 1943–45; and Georg Tessin, *Verbände und Truppen der deutschen Wehrmacht und Waffen SS im Zweiten Weltkrieg 1939–1945*, 14 vols. (Frankfurt a/M: E. S. Mittler & Sohn, 1966–72), Band 3 (volumes are by unit numbers, Bd. 3 having 11s).
23. Earl F. Ziemke, *The German Northern Theater of Operations 1940–1945* (Washington, DC: Department of the Army Pamphlet No. 20-271, 1959), 4ff.
24. Ibid., 16–17.
25. Pz.-Abt. z.b.V. 40 operations from Jentz, *Panzertruppen*, 110–115.
26. Ziemke, *Northern Theater*, 109.

CHAPTER 4: THE FRENCH CAMPAIGN

1. Schrodek, *Ihr Glaube*, 66–67. "Landser" was slang for the common soldier.
2. There are many works (in English) on the campaign in the West. Works that give operational details include Guy Chapman, *Why France Fell* and Len Deighton, *Blitzkrieg* (New York: Alfred A. Knopf, 1980). A series of campaign maps with at least panzer corps [*sic*] are in Griess, *Campaign Atlas*. Orders of battle showing panzer divisions are in Mellenthin, *Panzer Battles*, map "French Campaign 1940," and in Scheibert and Wagener, *Panzertruppe*, 34.
3. Generalfeldmarschall Erich von Manstein, *Verlorene Siege* (Bonn: Athenäum-Verlag, 1955), 96; but using the translated Field Marshal Erich von Manstein, trans. Anthony G. Powell, *Lost Victories* (Novato, CA: Presidio, 1982), 98. Manstein credits British analyst B. H. Liddell Hart for first clarifying Manstein's role in his *The Other Side of the Hill* interviews in 1948, published in the United States as *The German Generals Talk* (New York: William Morrow, 1948), note 113.
4. For example, Michael J. Lyons, *World War II: A Short History*, 4th ed. (Upper Saddle River, NJ: Pearson Prentice Hall, 2004), 86ff. Tank numbers in Brig. Gen. Vincent J. Esposito USA (Ret.), *A Concise History of World War II* (New York: Praeger, 1964), 57. Mellenthin, *Panzer Battles*, 12, gives 4,000 Franco-British tanks to 2,800 German.
5. Jentz, *Panzertruppen*, 120, also Nafziger, *Panzers and Artillery*, 58. Motorized corps were not officially designated Panzerkorps until October 1941.
6. Schrodek, *Ihr Glaube*, 65–70.
7. Rommel in France in Mellenthin, *Panzer Battles*, 18, 20, Deighton, *Blitzkrieg*, 54ff, and Chapman, *Why France Fell*, 109ff, among others. The pace of Rommel's operations is reflected in Hans von Luck, *Panzer Commander* (New York: Praeger, 1989). Von Luck succeeded to command of Rommel's Aufklärungsabteilung 37 (Reconnaissance Battalion) on 28 May, and later served with Rommel in the Western Desert.
8. Guderian, *Panzer Leader*, 80; Deighton, *Blitzkrieg*, 219; Mellenthin, *Panzer Battles*, 13–16. An in-depth treatment of the Sedan operation is Robert A. Doughty, colonel and professor at the USMA at West Point, *The Breaking Point: Sedan and the Fall of France, 1940* (Hamden, CT: Archon, 1990), especially chapter 5. Doughty emphasizes that infantry and artillery were as important as panzers and close air support in the German operations.
9. Quoted in Deighton, *Blitzkrieg*, 233.
10. Feuerbefehl from Pz.Rgt. 15 veterans to author. A semifictional, censored account of the 5. Pz.Div. in the French Campaign is Hans Christern, *Die "Roten Teufel" und Ihr Kommandeur* (Munich: Zentralverlag der NSDAP, Franz Eher Nachf., 1941), copy from Stephen Finney. It features Oberst Paul Hermann Werner, Kdr. Pz.Rgt. 31. Werner died of a heart attack at the end of the campaign, 30 June 1940 (149). Major Christern (here as "Christoph") was Kdr. II. Abt./31; as Oberst he commanded 4. Pz.Div. in 1944 and 7. Pz.Div. in 1945.
11. Pz.Rgt.15 operations are from Schrodek, *Ihr Glaube*, including photos and captions.
12. Donnhauser und Drews, *Der Weg*, 11.
13. B. H. Liddell Hart, ed., *The Rommel Papers* (London: Collins, 1953), 13, 7, 20. Translations slightly different in selections excerpted in John Pimlott, ed., *Rommel and his Art of War* (London: Greenhill, 1994), 41, 38, 44. The paucity of written orders by armor commanders is sometimes a challenge for historians later.
14. The Arras battle is in several sources, including Chapman, *Why France Fell*, 184–187; Deighton, *Blitzkrieg*, 250–254; and George H. Stein, *The Waffen SS* (Ithaca, NY: Cornell University Press, 1966), 67–69. The Waffen-SS (Armed or Combat SS) evolved as an elite fighting force from Reichsführer-SS Heinrich Himmler's Schutz Staffeln (Nazi guard echelons), though under army operational control.
15. Rommel quoted in Liddell Hart, *Rommel Papers*, 38 (actually, 8. Pz.Brig.; 5. Pz.Brig. was with 4. Pz.Div.); Schrodek, *Ihr Glaube*, 77.

16. "Friction" and resentment of Rommel's "arbitrariness" is reflected by Schrodek, *Ihr Glaube*, 70–71; David Irving, *The Trail of the Fox* (New York: E. P. Dutton, 1977), 56, 104. Irving later interviewed the eighty-five-year old Streich in Hamburg, receiving an unpublished typescript "Erinnerungen an Afrika" ("Memoirs of Africa") subsequently deposited in the Sammlung Irving in the IFZ, Institut für Zeitgeschichte (Institute of Contemporary History) in Munich. Irving, 73, 496.
17. In his analysis of the "Halt" order, Liddell Hart, *Second World War*, 80–84, concludes the initiative was Hitler's.
18. 7. Pz.Div. "retrospectively christened 'The Phantom Division'" in Liddell Hart, *German Generals Talk*, 47, and as "Ghost Division" in Desmond Young, *Rommel, the Desert Fox* (New York: Harper & Row, 1950; Berkley, 1971), 49, among others. At the time Nazi publications publicized Rommel's 7. Panzer as the "Gespenster" Division, and later works by Horst Scheibert, Franz Kurowski, Hans von Luck, David Irving, and others do also. Rather defensively, the 1982 11. Pz.Div. history by Donnhauser und Drews, *Der Weg der 11. Panzer-Division*, 13, 18, and 246, differentiates the 11. Schützenbrigade as the "Phantombrigade," noting the British refer to "The Phantom Brigade" and Rommel's 7. Pz.Div. as the "Ghost Division." But the 11. Pz.Div. named itself the "Gespenster-Division"—"And the Gespenst was, is, and remains plainly our image!" They refer to a 1940 OKW-published *Erinnerungsbuch* (Recollections Book) titled "Mit der Gespensterbrigade am Feind," a copy held by former Leutnant Fritz Schleicher, crediting this "Spitzenbrigade [point brigade] which in lightning-quick action and unexpected thrusts in a few days through Belgium and northern France reached the western-most point of the French Atlantic coast," as receiving their name from the English.

    Hasso von Manteuffel, commanding units in the 7.Pz.-Div. and then the division itself in 1943, published a history of the division, *Die 7. Panzer-Division im Zweiten Weltkrieg* (Traditionsverband ehem. 7. Panzer-Division-Kameradenhilfe e.V., n.d. [1965]). The tradition was that a French general, captured at St. Valéry, referred to the 7. as "Die Gespenster-Division," 109. But despite von Manteuffel's subtitle, *Einsatz und Kampf der"Gespenster-Division" 1939–1945*, there is then no ghost symbol nor further reference (e.g., Tagesbefehle 28.11.1941, 237, or 8.10.1943, 362–365). Instead, the divisional field symbol Y (similar to the 11. Panzer's circle with vertical line) was displayed on reunion banners (photo).

    In former Feldwebel G. W. Schrodek's *Die 11. Panzerdivision "Gespensterdivision" Bilddokumente 1940–1945* (Friedberg: Podzun-Pallas-Verlag GmbH, 1984), 10, he says a British officer gave the name "Ghost-brigade" to Kampfgruppe Angern, identifying the battle group as comprising "the heavy fighting vehicles of Pz.Rgt. 15 and the 11. Schützen-Brigade," part of the 5. Pz.Div. praised by Rommel on 15 May 1940 for bridging the Meuse. This is repeated in the outline history by Schrodek in the annual Treffen (reunion) programs of the 11. Panzer (in May in Kötzting, Bayern). In his 1976 Pz.Rgt. 15 history, *Ihr Glaube galt dem Vaterland*, Schrodek noted for 7 June 1940 it was a captured British officer who remarked on the lightning-quick "ghostly" emergence of the independent Schützenbrigade ANGER [*sic*]. The postwar 3. Kompanie of Panzerbataillon 64 of the Bundeswehr stationed at Pommern Kaserne, Wolfhagen, through 2008, proudly displayed the 11. Pz.Div. "Gespenster" on the turrets of their Leopard panzers. *Bilddokumente* was given to this author by Karl Heinz Loschke.
19. Chapman, *Why France Fell*, 346–347.
20. Schrodek, *Ihr Glaube*, 15, 85; also photos, and account and battle deployment map by Leutnant Zügner, 5. Kompanie, 89.
21. Ibid., 87. Many unit commanders are from a list compiled by Walter Rahn, Pz.Rgt.15, reconstructing the officers of Pz.Rgt. 15, by May 1992.
22. Knights Cross awards in Gerhard von Seemen, *Die Ritterkreuzträger 1939–1945* (Friedberg: Podzun-Pallas-Verlag, 1976) and Walther-Peer Fellgiebel, *Die Träger des Ritterkreuzes des Eisernen Kreuzes* (Friedberg: Podzun-Pallas-Verlag, 1986). Fellgiebel updated and corrected von Seemen, keeping the same format. Schrodek, *Ihr Glaube*, 15, 90. It can, however, be argued that a well-earned reputation, enhanced by publicity, contributes to the morale of the home front as well as the armed forces.
23. Chapman, *Why France Fell*, 318.
24. *Rommel Papers*, 68–84.
25. Route map in Donnhauser und Drews, *Der Weg*, 12.

CHAPTER 5: FORMATION OF THE 11. PANZER-DIVISION

1. Schrodek, *Ihr Glaube*, 92–93.
2. Ogorkiewicz, *Armor*. Some have simply attributed the doubling of panzer divisions to Hitler's fascination with numbers. There were sound organizational reasons as noted. Panzer division histories are summarized in Mitcham, *Panzer Legions*, and in Rolf Stoves, *Die gepanzerten und motorisierten deutschen Grossverbände 1935–1945* (Friedberg: Podzun-Pallas-Verlag, 1986). The some forty-six ultimate Panzerdivisionen include the Hermann Göring and seven Waffen-SS divisions, but exclude the reserve, replacement, training, or incomplete divisions.

3. Crüwell in LTC John R. Angolia, *On the Field of Honor*, vol. 2 (Stilwell, KS: John R. Angolia, 1980), 45–46; also Keilig, *deutsche Heer*, Band. II.
4. OKH orders 17 July 1940 and 6 September 1940 reproduced in Donnhauser und Drews, *Der Weg*, 198, 199.
5. The formation of the 11. Pz.Div. is covered by Stoves, *Grossverbände*, 82–83; Mitcham, *Panzer Legions*, 104; and Tessin, *Verbände*. Volumes in the latter are by unit number, here especially Bands 3 (6–14), 4 (15–30), and 6 (71–130).

   The captured 11. Panzer Division unit records, 1940–43, were microfilmed (22 rolls) and are held by the US National Archives and Records Administration (NARA), Washington, DC, in Microcopy T-315 (divisions). The 1944–45 records (in the West) are lacking. The formation of the 11. Pz.Div. is in 11. Pz.Div. Ia (Operations) KTB (Kriegstagebuch, War Diary) 1 August–1 October 1940, T-315/Roll 584/Frames 000007–000017. Hereafter cited as KTB Ia (11. Pz.Div. unless otherwise stated) T-315/Roll number/ Frame number. Documents in the KTBs and Anlagen (annexes) are often signed off by the Ia, F.d.R. (Für der Richtigkeit/for accuracy).
6. In supply, Nachschub was materiel, Versorgung was provisions (including rations and medical supplies). The corresponding US Army staff positions, prefixed S at battalion and regimental level, G at division and above, were: G-1 (IIa), G-2 (Ic), G-3 (Ia), and G-4 (Ib). 11. Pz.Div. officers from lists provided to the author, compiled by Karl Heinz Loschke, Pz.Art.Rgt. 119 and Sprecher (secretary) of the 11. Pz.Div. veterans association, and also by the Bundesarchiv-Militärarchiv, Freiburg i. Br. (BA-MA) Herr Meyer, 1989. Staff functions in TM-E 30-451, 82–84; Mitcham, *Panzer Legions*, appendix 5, 286–287.
7. Units from Donnhauser und Drews, *Der Weg*, 16–17, and commanders from lists noted above. The I./71 history is from Dr. Hugo Novak, Batteriechef 1./71 as Hptm., *Geschichte der ostpreussischen Leichten Flakabteilung 71*, 4 vols. (Siegen, 1980–83), copies via Louis Holz, 2nd Cavalry Association, 1994.
8. TM-E 30-451, 12-13; Soldbuch of F. K. von Eggeling, given to the author, January 2013; Manual of Arms in *Die Schützenkompanie*, 100–114. Landser slang terms from Kurt Nentwig, Klaus Bardt, and other panzer veterans. In comparison, the American soldier's service record, War Department, Adjutant General's Office (WD AGO) Form 53-55 (DD 214 after 1 January 1950) was kept at headquarters until discharge. German officers were "promoted," not "commissioned" as in the US Army.
9. Kurt Nentwig was transferred to Pz.Rgt. 15 on 1 Jan. 1941. Nentwig, letter to author, 1 July 2012.
10. Siegfried Knappe with Ted Brusaw, *Soldat* (New York: Dell, 1992), 116, 113; TM-E 30-451, 74–75.
11. TM-E 30-451, 457.
12. Lyrics by Kurt Wiehle. First verse, author's translation to rhyme. The *Panzerlied* could also be heard at postwar Treffen (reunions), and at Grafenwöhr training area clubs.
13. Kurt Nentwig, letter to author, 1 July 2012.
14. Training Directive 1 March 1939 in Jentz, *Panzertruppen 1933–1942*, 79–81.
15. Friedrich K. von Eggeling, letters to author, 18 July 1997 and 9 June 2012.
16. Klaus Bardt, letter to author, 1 August 1996; also copy of Walter von Meers, ed., *Zöglinge der Ritterakademie zu Brandenburg a.H.* (Cologne: Gerhard Heinrigs, Werdedruck und Verlag, n.d. [1970]).
17. Kurt Nentwig, letter to author, 1 July 2012.
18. Walter Rahn, letter to author, 21 Oktober 2008.
19. Friedrich K. von Eggeling, letters (in English) to author, 6 March and 31 May 2012.
20. For Mischlinge definitions, Raul Hilberg, *The Destruction of the European Jews* (New York, London: Holmes & Meier, 1985), 27–38; Juergen Krackow, *Die Genehmigung* (Mainz-München: v. Hase & Koehler, 1991), 195, copy sent to author by Herr Krackow. For Jews in the Wehrmacht, see Bryan Mark Rigg, *Hitler's Jewish Soldiers* (Lawrence: University Press of Kansas, 2002), especially 65; and Rigg's *Lives of Hitler's Jewish Soldiers* (Lawrence: University Press of Kansas, 2009). The coordinated Final Solution was initiated by Obergruppenführer Reinhard Heydrich as Der Chef der Sicherheitspolizei und des SD in the Wannsee Conference of 20 January 1942.
21. Ausrüstung für Verwendung in subtropischen Zonen, KTB Ib, 30.9.1940. NARA Microcopy T-315/Roll 584/Frame 000014.
22. Schrodek, *Bilddokumente*, 23, and *Ihr Glaube*, 96; railloading from Martin Lange, Ogfr. Pz.Rgt. 15 Werkstatt Kp., discussions with author (1992) when on the staff of the Panzermuseum, Munster, similar to postwar procedures.
23. Schrodek, *Ihr Glaube*, 97; KTB Ia, 8.2.41, T-315/584/000055; Jason D. Mark, *Death of the Leaping Horseman* [24. Pz.Div.] (Sydney: Jason D. Mark, 2003), 427–428.
24. Detailed discussion of German diplomacy and military planning and operations are well presented by Martin L. Van Crefeld, *Hitler's Strategy 1940–1941: The Balkan Clue* (Cambridge: Cambridge University Press, 1973), and in the Department of the Army historical studies by George E. Blau, *The German Campaign in the Balkans* (Department of the Army Pamphlet No. 20-260, November 1953) and *The German Campaign in Russia* (DA No. 20-261a, March 1955). These are hereafter cited as Blau, *Balkans*, and as Blau, *Russia*.
25. Schrodek, *Ihr Glaube*, 99; photographs in Schrodek, *Bild*, 56–65.

CHAPTER 6: THE SERBIAN CAMPAIGN

1. KTB Ia Gefechts- und Verpflegungsstärke of Offz., Bea., Uffz., und Mann., with Verwendungsbereite Waffen aller Art (ausser Handfeuerwaffen und blanken Waffen), as of 1 April 1941, NARA/T-315/584/000164. (Panzers are deduced from weapon types, such as Kw.K.) These reports were generated as of the 1st, 11th, and 21st of every month. Jentz, *Panzertruppen*, 154, shows 45 Pz. IIs, 25 Pz. IIIs (3,7cm), 26 Pz. IIIs (5cm) 16 Pz. IVs, and 14 Pz.Befehlswagen, totaling 126 panzers for Pz.Rgt. 15 as of 6 April 1941, and Nafziger, *Panzers and Artillery* , 82, shows the same for 5 April 1941.
2. Schematic diagram, Anlage to XIV. A.K. Ia 3.4.41 for 11. Pz.Div., T-315/585/000668. Symbols are in *German Military Symbols* (Washington, DC: Military Intelligence Service, January 1943), and W. J. K. Davies, *German Army Handbook 1939–1945* (New York: Arco, 1974); Nafziger, *Panzers and Artillery*, 82–83, is helpful, though inexplicably misidentifies three 11. Pz.Div. units (Pz.Rgt. 15 as 33rd, 341 Signals as 85th, and 209 Engineers as 86th).
3. KTB Ia Anlage Leitungsskizze, 7.4.41, T-315/585/000758.
4. KTB Ia Anlage Divisions Befehl Nr. 1, 7.4.41, T-315/585/000766.
5. Schrodek, *Ihr Glaube*, 102; the map in Donnhauser und Drews, *Der Weg*, 19, implies Gruppe Bohlmann was in the lead.
6. Schrodek, *Ihr Glaube*, 104.
7. Blau, *Balkans*, 50; also Scheibert und Wagener, *Panzertruppe*, 67.
8. Schrodek, *Ihr Glaube*, 106; platoons and crew names listed, 101. Later, panzers would have three numbers painted on their turrets, representing company, platoon, panzer (e.g., 521).
9. Note the photographs in Schrodek, *Bild*, 78; Lage (situation) maps from beyond Niš, KTB Ia Anlagen, 9, 10.4.41, T-315/585/000977.
10. Beobachter and Flivo reports, 10.4.41 in KTB Ia Anlagen, T-315/585/001118.
11. Routes in Donnhauser und Drews, *Der Weg*, 19.
12. Note Obstlt. von Mellenthin's role, *Panzer Battles*, 29, encouraging Croat separatism. He was Ic (Intelligence) at 2. Armee at the time. Karl Süss's account in Schrodek, *Ihr Glaube*, 111.
13. Angern in KTB Ia Anlage 13.4.41, T-315/586/000086.
14. Blau, *Balkans*, 54; Klingenberg also in Stein, *Waffen-SS*, 116, and Paul Hausser, *Waffen-SS im Einsatz* (Göttingen: Plesse Verlag K. W. Schütz, 1953), 41. Standartenführer Klingenberg was later killed in action on 22 March 1945 leading 17. SS Panzergrenadierdivision Götz von Berlichingen.
15. Pricken's "Kompanie" is from Schrodek, *Ihr Glaube*, 113; Bericht of the Vorausabteilung by Götz, 15-19.4.41, is in KTB Ia Anlage, T-315/586/000391-5. Motorized SS Division Reich was retitled *Das* Reich in May 1942.
16. Blau, *Balkans*, 35.
17. 11. Pz.Div. losses KTB Ia 28.4.41, T-315/584/000159; Blau, *Balkans*, 64. Schrodek, *Ihr Glaube*, 115, 113; Donnhauser und Drews, *Der Weg*, 21.
18. Schrodek, *Bild*, 102; KTB Ia 20.4.41/584/000149, 000153. In his earlier *Ihr Glaube* (1976), 115, Schrodek says the tracks rail-loaded at Agram (Zagreb), which is incorrect. The briefer Donnhauser und Drews, *Der Weg*, 21, gives no location.
19. Blau, *Balkans*, 150, also Liddell Hart, *Second World War*, 134. Martin Van Crefeld, *Balkan Clue*, 174–175, analyzes the OKH buildup stages and specific units and says that OKH deployment schedules resulted in a June date, and the shortage of motor vehicles for the equipping and transporting of infantry and motorized units for the attack were primary governing factors leading to the 22 June date. This perhaps does not do justice to the organizational capabilities of OKH. The British imperial forces landed in Greece included the motorized 6 Australian and 2 New Zealand Divisions and 1st Tank Brigade of 2 British Armoured Division.
20. Photos of billeting areas in Schrodek, *Bild*, 107–115. The Debica fire is captioned 9 June.
21. Photo in Uwe Feist, *The German Panzers* (Fallbrook, CA: Aero, 1966), 26; Paul Carell, *Hitler Moves East 1941–1943*, trans. Ewald Osers (Little, Brown & Co., 1965/Bantam, 1966), 2. Paul Carell is the pseudonym of Paul Karl Schmidt, an Obersturmbannführer in the Allgemeine (General) SS, chief press spokesman in the Foreign Ministry. Schmidt was a *prosecution* witness at the Nuremberg Trials.

CHAPTER 7: OPERATION BARBAROSSA

1. Carell, *Hitler Moves East*, 54–56. Page 55 says one plane came down in Russia with engine failure near Minsk on 20 June 1941, but "the crew were able to set their secret machine on fire before they were captured." Walter J. Boyne, *Clash of Wings* (New York: Simon & Schuster, 1994/Touchstone, 1997), 144, says one plane crashed near Rovno 15 April 1941, but "despite the fact that it was obviously a reconnaissance plane, complete with cameras and exposed film, the Soviets did not protest."
2. German estimates primarily from Blau, *Russia*, 38–42, and other sources, all varying depending on definitions. The Russian 26th Army in the Przemysl salient seems to have been missed, and the 2nd mistaken for the 9th in Bessarabia, as in Blau, *Russia*, 43, and in Brig. Gen. Vincent J. Esposito, *The West Point Atlas of American Wars*, vol. 2 (New York: Praeger, 1959/1964), map 24. There are numerous works on the Russian Campaign in

English including works by Alan Clark, *Barbarossa* (New York: William Morrow & Co., 1965/1985), John Erickson, *The Road to Stalingrad* (Boulder, CO: Westview Press, 1975/1984), and David M. Glantz and Jonathan M. House, *When Titans Clashed* (Lawrence: University Press of Kansas, 1995). Excellent works may yet have errors: Clark, for example, mistakes Manteuffel for Mackensen at III Corps (mot), and Glantz and House say the Panther had an 8,8cm gun (though corrected in their 1999 *The Battle of Kursk*). Translations include Heinz Guderian's *Panzer Leader*. Vivid accounts for the initial campaign include Carell, *Hitler Moves East* from the German perspective, and Victor J. Kamenir, *The Bloody Triangle* (Minneapolis: Zenith/MBI, 2008) for the Russian.

3. Divisions-Tagesbefehl, 22. Juni 1941 in Schrodek, *Bild*, 116, also in *Ihr Glaube*, 121.
4. Data from KTB Ia Anlage Gefechts-und Verpflegungsstärke dated 18.7.1941 as of 21.6.41, T-315/2320/000176, 000177. Ration strength was 17,108. Combat strength, including Felders. Btl. 61 and Beob. Battr. 334 was 13,559: 387 Offz., 54 Beamte, 1,962 Uffz., and 11,156 Mannsch. (plus 15 Pferde, horses). Harts, *German Tanks*, 169, give 175 panzers with the 11. Pz.Div. on 22 June 1941; Nafziger, *Panzers and Artillery*, 83, gives 144; Kamenir, *Bloody Triangle*, 280, gives 135; Jentz, *Panzertruppen*, 191, gives 141.
5. Directive No. 21, Operation BARBAROSSA, 18 December 1940. Given in Blau, *Russia*, 22–23.
6. Guderian, *Panzer Leader*, 75. The roles of Washington, DC, and Richmond, Virginia, in the American Civil War come to mind.
7. Blau, *Russia*, 24–34.
8. Glantz and House, *Titans*, 41. On 327n29 they say Soviet émigré V. Rezun, writing under the pen name of Victor Suvorov, has cited this document in arguing Stalin's aggressive plans. Kamenir, *Bloody Triangle*, 30, clarifies defector Victor Suvorov as the pen name of Vladimir Rezun, former Chief of GRU (Chief Intelligence Directorate), accusatory of Stalin. While not mentioning Zhukov's memorandum, Kamenir also concludes the Soviet Union was in no shape to mount an offensive, at least not in 1941. Walter Schaefer-Kehnert, Pz.Art. Rgt. 119, was one who told the author, in 2004, he believed the Red Army was poised to attack.
9. For convenience, as all sources differ, data is primarily from Kamenir. His is the most detailed study of the opening battles in the Ukraine. Numbers, however, can be confusing. On page 7 the 5 panzer divisions total 728 panzers, while on 281 the total is 586; but this miscalculates the number of Panzer IIIs and does not include command panzers. Kamenir's focus is on the "bloody triangle" between Lutsk, Dubno, and Brody, involving 1,500 Russian tanks (p. ix); but the total for the 5 mechanized corps (11 tank divisions) involved is 3,427 (p. 281), and for all 8 corps is 4,536 (p. 34). If South-Western Front had less than 300 operational by mid-July (p.262), some 4,200 tanks had been lost.
10. Ibid., 30–32, 68. Kamenir says the planned system was named the "Molotov Line," after the new Foreign Commissar.
11. Attack order, including Order of March (Gliederung) in Schrodek, *Ihr Glaube*, 119–121; movement of Kampfgruppe A in KTB Ia, 22.6.41, T-315/2320/000013.
12. Schrodek, *Ihr Glaube*, 123–124; Werner Striezel, letter to author, 28 October 1990.
13. Kamenir, *Bloody Triangle*, 81; Pavlov's 25 July 1941 report about the condition of his 41st Tank Division in Kamenir, 36. In Russian usage the patronymic is given as a middle name (e.g., Mikhail Ivanovich Potapov). Kamenir, and Glantz and House, generally use initials.
14. As quoted by Schrodek, *Ihr Glaube*, 126.
15. Kurt Nentwig, account to author, 25 May 2012. T-34 data from RAC, *USSR* (1970), tables 36–37, 40; also Steven Zaloga, *T-34/76* (London: Osprey, 1994), 36–41. Zaloga says the first T-34 attack on Pz.Rgt. 15 was on 22 June by thirty T-34s of the Lvov Tank Training Regiment, knocking out three Pz. IVs and two Pz. IIIs.
16. Hans Ruland, letter to Walter Rahn, 4 März 1991, copy (via Klaus Bardt) to author. The current US military aptly refers to the all-around visibility as better "situational awareness."
17. Radekhov battle sketch maps in Schrodek's *Ihr Glaube*, 128, and in *Bild*, 132, along with photos of knocked-out Russian tanks. Kamenir, *Bloody Triangle*, 144, feels the German account of losses is more reasonable than Soviet reports.
18. 11th Armored Division as translated in Charles Burdick and Hans-Adolf Jacobsen, ed., *The Halder War Diary, 1939–1942* (Novato, CA: Presidio, 1988, abridged), 415; Kamenir, *Bloody Triangle*, 37–41, 99, 143; more briefly in Glantz and House, *Titans*, 54, and Erickson, *Road to Stalingrad*, 164. Organizations in Zaloga, *T-34/76*, 16, 21.
19. Kamenir, *Bloody Triangle*, 101, 107–108; Glantz and House, *Titans*, 51; Erickson, *Road to Stalingrad*, 132. Apparently ordered by Stalin, Directive No. 3 had been drawn up by Defense Commissar Marshal Semyon Timoshenko—with Zhukov's signature added after he had left by plane for Kiev, he later maintained.
20. Kamenir, *Bloody Triangle*, 152.
21. Schrodek, *Ihr Glaube*, 130.
22. KTB Ia, 26.6.41, T-315/2320/000200. Pz. III ammunition load from R. L. DiNardo, *Germany's Panzer Arm* (Westport, CT: Greenwood, 1997), 106.
23. Schrodek, *Bild*, 143, and other photos and captions.
24. Schrodek, *Ihr Glaube*, 132–133.

25. Erickson, *Road to Stalingrad*, 163–166; unit actions detailed in Kamenir, *Bloody Triangle*, and Mishanin's fate is on 185, 202, and 234.
26. Kamenir, *Bloody Triangle*, 192, 218. Voyenno-Vozdushnye Sily (VVS) translates as Military or War Air Force.
27. Erickson, *Road to Stalingrad*, 166, and Kamenir, *Bloody Triangle*, 155. Two factions of the OUN had evolved since forming in 1929, OUN-B (the Bandera group) and OUN-M (the Mel'nyk group). The Germans had set up training units of émigré Ukrainians in 1940, especially from OUN-B. Erickson, 103n.
28. Burdick and Jacobsen, ed., *Halder War Diary*, 424.
29. Blau, *Russia*, 44. Sources differ on numbers, Glantz and House, *Titans*, 53, saying over 417,000 Soviet soldiers were "destroyed or swallowed up." In any case the encirclements were porous, and many Russians, if not units, escaped. Halder in Burdick and Jacobsen, ed., *Halder War Diary*, 446.
30. Erickson, *Road to Stalingrad*, 166; Lukin's operations are detailed by Kamenir, *Bloody Triangle*, 178, 197–199, and 236.
31. Schrodek, *Ihr Glaube* 134; photos of airdrops and HVP, Schrodek, *Bild*, 147 and 151.
32. Photos in Schrodek, *Bild*, 155, 159–160.
33. Schrodek, *Ihr Glaube*, 134–135; Donnhauser und Drews, *Der Weg*, 25.
34. Kamenir, *Bloody Triangle*, 34, 262.

CHAPTER 8: BARBAROSSA: EXPLOITATION

1. Richard L. DiNardo, *Germany and the Axis Powers* (Lawrence: University Press of Kansas, 2005), 113–119.
2. Kamenir, *Bloody Triangle*, 193; Erickson, *Road to Stalingrad*, 166. Erickson follows the various reorganizations of Stavka, "High Command Headquarters," though it was always under Stalin's dictatorial control.
3. Schrodek, *Ihr Glaube*, 135–136, also *Bild*, 168–170.
4. Schrodek's account in *Ihr Glaube*, 137–140.
5. Photograph in Novak, *le.Fla, 71*, II, 81; also detailed maps; Kgr. in KTB Ia, 5.7.41, T-315/2320/000034.
6. OKH intelligence appreciation after penetration, in Clark, *Barbarossa*, 31.
7. Kampfgruppe organization in KTB Ia, 7.7.41, T-315/2320/000037; Feldw. Englisch's account in Schrodek, *Ihr Glaube*, 145–146. T-28 data from RAC, *USSR*, 37. The T-28M, however, was up-armored to 80mm (3.2 inches).
8. Erickson, *Road to Stalingrad*, 168–172. Clark, *Barbarossa*, refers to former cavalry sergeant Budenny as "jovial mediocrity," 131, and "malevolent fatuity" and "imbecile," 137. He was at least loyal to Stalin, a prime requisite. No German commander was ever executed on Hitler's orders for military reasons, though some later feared this.
9. Glantz and House, *Titans*, 60.
10. Incident in Schrodek, *Ihr Glaube*, 154; Mark, *Death of the Leaping Horseman*, 55, including photos of Riebel. Oberst Riebel would later be killed while serving with the 24.Pz.Div. near Stalingrad 23 August 1942.
11. Episode at the railroad in Schrodek's *Ihr Glaube*, 153–162, and in *Bild*, 205–206, sketch maps in both.
12. Erickson, *Road to Stalingrad*, 203; Glantz and House, *Titans*, 336n10, give 79,220 lost, from Soviet sources.
13. As quoted in David Stahel, *Kiev 1941* (New York: Cambridge University Press, 2012), 96, from KTB Ia 18.8.41, T-315/2320/000107.
14. Annex 2, "The 11th Panzer Division in the Fighting for the DNEPR Bridge near GORNOSTAYPOL, 23 to 29 August 1941" by No. 404 (Helwig Luz in American captivity) at Garmisch, 12 June 1947. Commanders are identified by the first letter of the last name, and Luz's report is "Written from memory." Copy at the USAMHI (US Army Military History Institute), Carlisle, PA; corroborated in KTB Ia Anlagenband 23.8.41, T-315/2321/001996ff. The assault guns were from Sturmgeschützabteilung 191. Franz Kurowski and Gottfried Tornau, *Sturmgeschütze* (Würzburg: Verlagshaus, 2008), 56–59.
15. Luz MS "Gornostaypol," 14; air alerts from A.O.K.6, 29.8.1941 in KTB Ia Anlage, T-315/2321/001296.
16. Berichte as Anlage to Ia KTB, 10.9.1941, T-315/2321/001313-001338. Again, numbers of panzers available 22.6.41 vary. Jentz, *Panzertruppen*, 206, for 5 September 1941 has 153 of 200 panzers operational: 9 Pz.Is, 38 IIs, 75 IIIs, 18 IVs, and 13 Bef.Pz.
17. Anlage to KTB Ia Kino 15.9.41, *Panzer Voran*, 5.9.41, T-315/2321/001414-001419.
18. Kurt Nentwig, letters to author, 2012. Von Mellenthin, *Panzer Battles*, 210–211, also comments on the positive reception of the German soldiers, and how occupation policies undermined this.
19. Schrodek, *Ihr Glaube*, 174. This may be viewed with skepticism.
20. Yitzhak Arad, Schmuel Krakowski, and Schmuel Spector, eds., *The Einsatzgruppen Reports*, trans. Stella Schossberger (New York: Holocaust Library, 1989). Ereignismeldungen UdSSR (Operational Situation Reports USSR) dated 2, 3, 6 July, and 2 October 1941; Zhitomir on 7 October 1941. No Wehrmacht units are identified. Note also studies like Raul Hilberg, *The Destruction of the European Jews*.
21. Interview of Walter Schaefer-Kehnert by Laurence Rees, 2001, for a BBC production *Timewatch: War of the Century*, transcript, 12; copy to author by Heinz Kutscheid; Evgeni Bessonov, *Tank Rider*, trans. Bair Irincheev (Mechanicsburg, PA: Stackpole, 2003), 50.

22. Omer Bartov, *The Eastern Front, 1941–45 German Troops and the Barbarisation of Warfare*, 2nd ed. (New York: Palgrave, 2001) says German brutality was the result of Nazi indoctrination. Russel Stolfi, however, documents German reports of "consistent" and "pervasive" Russian atrocities against captured and wounded Germans from the very first day of the campaign in R. H. S. Stolfi, *Hitler's Panzers East* (Norman: University of Oklahoma Press, 1991), 91–93. Very little work seems to have been done on Communist Soviet policies and practices that contributed to this brutality. Focusing on the *Russian* war effort Glantz and House, *Titans*, 57, after discussing German atrocities, simply note, "All this being said, from the very start, the Red Army responded in kind" with no details. In 1995 Jan Philipp Reemtsma's Hamburg Institute of Social Research sponsored a controversial photograph exhibit titled "Vernichtungskrieg, Verbrechen der Wehrmacht 1941 bis 1944" ("War of Extermination. Crimes of the Wehrmacht 1941 to 1944"). It toured Germany and was to come to the United States in 1999, but meanwhile it was determined that some of the photos were actually of Soviet NKVD victims. "The exhibition and the Institute lost credibility," admitted Reemtsma, and it was closed. Omer Bartov, Atina Grossmann, and Mary Nolan, *Crimes of War* (New York: New Press, 2002), 15.

    Note the critical discussion of the Reemtsma exhibit, and the section "Crimes of the Red Army," in Craig W. H. Luther, *Barbarossa Unleashed* (Atglen, PA: Schiffer, 2013), 454–469. Luther, 458 and n231, notes Soviet atrocities recorded by the OKW's War Crimes Bureau microfilmed by the NARA and returned to the BA/MA Freiburg. In his exhaustive study, Luther also says that "recent scholarship supports the conclusion that the great majority of German soldiers in Russia behaved with honor and dignity" (86).

CHAPTER 9: OPERATION TAIFUN

1. Blau, *Russia*, 50–51. From 1703 to 1918 the Russian capital had been at St.Petersburg/Petrograd, the "head" of Russia; but Moscow was the "heart" of Russia, and its capital once again.
2. Carell, *Hitler Moves East*, 128. Encirclement was completed by the 16th. Glantz and House, *Titans*, 77, say the German figure "came close," stating 452,270 men. By comparison, some 91,000 Germans surrendered at Stalingrad in 1943 of some 200,000 encircled, and 325,000 in the Ruhr pocket were surrendered in 1945.
3. Blau, *Russia*, 76–77.
4. Novak, *L./71*, Teil III, 4; Panzer Lage Ia KTB Anlage 18.9.1941, T-315/586/001041-2. Again, sources vary on numbers, often whether Befehlspanzer with no gun are included.
5. German and Russian propaganda leaflet examples in Schrodek, *Bild*, 229, 243, 244.
6. Novak, *L./71*, Teil III, 9; reproduced in Schrodek, *Bild*, 246; in his *Ihr Glaube*, 179 he says these exhortations were "pathetic." David Stahel, *Operation Typhoon* (Cambridge: Cambridge University Press, 2013), 364n55, 249, estimates the 11.Pz.Div. had 199 panzers at the beginning of Typhoon, speculating it may have received additional panzers for the operation. On 24 October it had ninety operational, with sixty-four lost and forty-five out of service.
7. Bock's message in Ia KTB Anhang 19.10.1941, T-315/587/000896.
8. 11.Pz.Div. command losses, changes, in Ia KTB 9., 12.10.41, T-315/2320/000153/000158; 11.Pz.Div. Kdr. Persönlich an die Herren Kommandeure, Ia KTB Anhang 11.10.41, T-315/587/000432.
9. Sources vary greatly on von Lenski's assignments. Keilig, *deutsche Heer*, Bd.2, 195 lists v.Lenski assigned to 11.S.B. 5 August 1941 though Angern of 11.S.B. became acting division commander after Crüwell left on 22 August until he was wounded on the 24th. Mitcham, *Panzer Legions*, 177 says von Lenski came from commanding Schützen *Regiment* 2. Mark, *Death of the Leaping Horseman*, 158, says von Lenski assumed command of 2.S.B. on 1 June 1941 but was "left behind" for BARBAROSSA.
10. Kampfgruppeneinteilung, Abt Ia, Div.Gef.St., den 14.10.41 in Ia KTB Anhang, T-315/587/000628.
11. Data used from Erickson, *Road to Stalingrad*, 213.
12. Ibid., 217.
13. For example, Ia to XXXXVI. Panz.-Korps from Div.Gef.Std. Pitina, 15.10.41, KTB Anlage, T-315/587/000656.
14. Liddell Hart, *The German Generals Talk*, 139–140.
15. Diary entry 11 August 1941 in Burdick and Jacobsen, *Halder War Diary*, 506.
16. Erickson, *Road to Stalingrad*, 233–234.
17. Quoted in Clark, *Barbarossa*, 164.
18. Carell, *Hitler Moves East*, 134–136; photo of a killed Minenhund in Scheibert und Wagener, *Panzertruppe*, 144.
19. David Kahn, *The Code Breakers* (New York: MacMillan, 1967), 654–661. Kahn also details the Soviet codes and ciphers used.
20. Accounts related in Novak, *L./71*, Teil III, 31–34. "Lili Marleen" was written by German soldier Hans Leip in 1915, set to music by Norbert Schultze in 1938, and recorded by Lale Andersen in 1939. In North Africa Rommel urged it as a sign-off song for Wehrmacht Radio Belgrad broadcasts, and it became popular especially with the British 8 Army as well.

21. Zustandsbericht für Monat Oktober, KTB Ia, 16.10.41, T-315/2320/000204.
22. Keilig, *deutsche Heer*, Bd. 2, 195, says von Lenski became commander of the Schule f. Schnelle Tr. "Herbst" (autumn) 1941, and doesn't include his role as acting division commander; Mitcham, *Panzer Legions*, 177 simply says he commanded the School for Mobile Troops (1941–42); Mark, *Death of the Leaping Horseman*, 158, says he "resumed command" of the brigade until "the gates of Moscow," and then returned to Germany to command the Schule.
23. Bericht KTB Ia Anlage, 1.11.1941, in T-315/587/001298.
24. Kriegsgliederung including named personnel and motorcycle and vehicle numbers, KTB Ia Anlage 13.11.41, in T-315/587/001394.
25. Panzer strength as of 21 November 1941 in Schrodek, *Ihr Glaube*, 189; Kurt Nentwig, letter to author, 25 May 2012.
26. Detailed map in Novak, *L./71*, III, 39.
27. Walter Schaefer-Kehnert, *Kriegstagebuch in Feldpostbriefen, 1940–1945*, 125, privately published from his wartime letters home, copy provided the author; and discussions with Professor Schaefer-Kehnert at his Remagen-Oberwinter home in 2004.
28. KTB Ia Anlage 5.12.41, in T-315/587/001041. Of the mud and winter being decisive, many historians conclude, as does Luther, *Barbarossa Unleashed*, "Yet the factor most responsible for the German failure to capture Moscow was the dramatic change in the weather" (642) and "Frostbite began to cause more casualties than action in battle" (647).
29. Verluste für die Zeit vom 17.11.-9.12. [1941], KTB Ia Anlage, T-315/588/000446.
30. Stichwort "Weihnachtsurlaub, 1.Reisetag," KTB Ia Anlage 7.12.41, T-315/587/001046; in Schrodek, *Ihr Glaube*, 197, and *Bild*, 291.

CHAPTER 10: RUSSIAN WINTER: 1941–42

1. Blau, *Russia*, 83, 92–95. These figures were not far off. Erickson, *Road to Stalingrad*, 269, calculates 219 Russian rifle divisions on the German front 1 December 1941.
2. Schrodek, *Ihr Glaube*, 199; Donnhauser und Drews, *Der Weg*, 52, 54.
3. 16 December entry in Burdick and Jacobsen, *The Halder War Diary*, 590.
4. Werner von Koblinski, letter to author, 21 April 1996; account in James Lucas, *War on the Eastern Front* (Novato, CA: Presidio, 1979), 138.
5. Gary L. Simpson, *Tiger Ace* (Atglen, PA: Schiffer, 1994), 110.
6. Conditions noted by Kurt Nentwig, letter to author, 25 May 2012; *Ostmedaille* in Robin Lumsden, *Third Reich Militaria* (London: Ian Allan, 1987/1990), 41, 45.
7. Experiences related by Fritz Waldmann of Crailsheim, Germany, to the author, 1965; Lucas, *Eastern Front*, 96, 208.
8. Goerlitz, *German General Staff*, 404–406; Clark, *Barbarossa*, 182.
9. Weihnachtsfest deduced from photos and poems in Schrodek, *Bild*, 293–305.
10. Kurt Nentwig, letter to author, 13 June 2012.
11. Donnhauser und Drews, *Der Weg*, 58.
12. Schrodek, *Bild*, 319.
13. Erickson, *Road to Stalingrad*, 27–28; Edgar M. Howell, *The Soviet Partisan Movement*, Department of the Army Pamphlet 20–244 (Washington: Department of the Army, 1956), 45–46.
14. Howell, *Soviet Partisan Movement*, 47–48; poster in Earl F. Ziemke and Magna E. Bauer, *Moscow to Stalingrad* (New York: Military Heritage Press, 1987), 201.
15. Brigadier C. Aubrey and Otto Heilbrunn, *Communist Guerilla Warfare* (London: George Allen & Unwin, 1954), 85. The focus of John A. Armstrong, ed., *Soviet Partisans in World War II* (Madison: University of Wisconsin Press, 1964), is partisan organization, not legal or moral aspects.
16. Howell, *Soviet Partisan Movement*, 57–58; Alexander Dallin, *German Rule in Russia* (New York: St. Martin's Press, 1957).
17. KTB Ia 1-11.12.41, T-315/588/000529-000532.
18. Ziemke and Bauer, *Moscow to Stalingrad*, 208.
19. Ia to XXXXVI. Pz.Korps 31.12.41. in KTB, T-315/588/000792.
20. Quoted in KTB Ia 28.1.42, T-315/588/000913.
21. Donnhauser und Drews, *Der Weg*, 59.
22. Erickson, *Road to Stalingrad*, 297–298.
23. Ibid., 313–315; Ziemke and Bauer, *Moscow to Stalingrad*, 94, 121.
24. KTB Ia Anlagen reports 26-31.1.42, T-315/588/001307-001311.
25. Scheller's Grundlegender Befehl 6.2.1942, in KTB Ia Anlagen T-315/588/001394-001399.
26. Bericht über die Räumung der Stadt Dorogobush am 15.2.42, KTB Ia Anlage 16.2.42, T-315/588/001540-001543.
27. Plan concept in Gerhard L. Weinberg, "The Yelnya-Dorogobuzh [*sic*] area, 1941" in Armstrong, ed., *Soviet Partisans*, though on 423 he states "German operations are of no interest." 11.Pz.Div. strength in KTB Ia 22.3.1942, T-315/588/001081, operations in 001071ff.
28. Weinberg in Ibid., 438–448.
29. KTB Ia 18.5.42; Vorbefehl 29.5.42, in T-315/590/000318, 000378.
30. Auszug aus dem Merkblatt für die in Heeres-Gebiet untergebrachten Truppen, eight-page summary, Anl.1 zu 11.Pz.Div.-Ia-v.24.4.42., initialed by an unidentified

Leutnant. The full quote: "4.) Jeder Verkehr mit Juden ist untersagt. Bei Aktionen der Polizei gegen Juden hat sich die Truppe jeder dienstlichen oder ausserdienstlichen Teilnahme zu enthalten." KTB Ia 24.4.42, T-315/590/000545.

31. Department of the Army Pamphlets No. 20-290, *Terrain Factors in the Russian Campaign* (July 1951) and No. 20-291, *Effects of Climate on Combat in European Russia* (February 1952).
32. KTB Ia 12.4.42, T-315/588/001144, 001146; Tagesbefehl 15.4.42 in KTB Ia, T-315/588/001158-001160, also quoted in Schrodek, *Ihr Glaube*, 217, and Donnhauser und Drews, *Der Weg*, 62.
33. Heinz J. W. Kutscheid, letter to Karl Thieme, 25 July 1995, copied to author.
34. Guderian, *Panzer Leader*, 114; Mellenthin, *Panzer Battles*, 155n. According to the Harts, *German Tanks*, 52, the G model had entered service in *April* 1940. Data from Ogorkiewicz, *Armor*, 314, RAC *Germany*, and Harts, 52–53.
35. Harts, *German Tanks*, 76ff; Ziemke and Bauer, *Moscow to Stalingrad*, 92, 126.
36. Horst Scheibert, *Die Träger des deutschen Kreuzes in Gold: Das Heer* (Friedberg: Podzun-Pallas-Verlag, 1992), alphabetical listing of Angern and Riebel. The DK was between the EK 1 and RK, rather as the Distinguished Service Cross was between the Silver Star and the Medal of Honor in the US Army. Riebel's death in Mark, *Death of the Leaping Horseman*, 54.
37. Kurt Nentwig, letter to author, 25 May 2012.
38. Schrodek, *Bild*, 381, captions list Hptm. von Hauser as commanding A.A.11. But A.A.231 had been amalgamated with K.61 on 9 November 1941 and A.A.11 was not activated until 27 April 1943.
39. Schrodek, *Ihr Glaube*, 218; Tessin, *Verbände*, Band 3, 202–204; 11.Pz.Div. KTB entries May–August 1942, T-315/590-591.
40. KTB Ia 21.5.42 and 24.5.42, T-315/590/000352 and 000364.
41. Balck's background is in his memoirs, *Ordnung im Chaos: Erinnerungen 1893–1948* (Osnabrück: Biblio Verlag, 1981); Mellenthin, *Panzer Battles*, 13–16; Doughty, *Breaking Point*, 140ff. Kinitz was sometimes misspelled Kienitz.
42. Quoted in Mellenthin, *Panzer Battles*, 36.
43. Balck's Diamonds for 4. Pz.Armee 31 August 1944, Number 19 of 27 total during the war, Träger des Eichenlaubs mit Schwertern und Brillanten zum Ritterkreuz des Eisernen Kreuzes listed in Seemen and in Fellgiebel.
44. Quoted in Donnhauser und Drews, *Der Weg*, 63–65. Balck's dates may be off.
45. Blau, *Russia*, 130, 110–113; Ziemke and Bauer, *Moscow to Stalingrad*, 287–289, include the 6. Armee drive in Phase I. Fall BLAU would be the last time "Fall" was used meaning "Operation," replaced by "Unternehmen."
46. Erickson, *Road to Stalingrad*, 344–347; Clark, *Barbarossa*, 200–203; Carell, *Hitler Moves East*, 495–497; Ziemke and Bauer, *Moscow to Stalingrad*, 282. Most sources state 6,000–8,000 Russian tanks lost, though they accept the 240,000 prisoners taken number.
47. The Reichel incident is from Erickson, *Road to Stalingrad*, 354–355, Carell, *Hitler Moves East*, 518–519, and Ziemke and Bauer, *Moscow to Stalingrad*, 330–332. Unit strengths given are fighting strengths. Gefechts- und Verpflegungsstärke as of 1 July 1942. With strikeouts and written changes on the report, the totals here do not exactly match the 13,316 and 16,494 Insgesamt (totals) on the record. Weapons are listed by caliber, not by type or vehicle. Anlage zum KTB Ia 1.7.1942, T-315/593/000727-9. Balck's clarification actually in Anlage zum KTB Ia 17.10.1942, T-315/593/000654.
48. Panzerlage in KTB Ia 28.6.1942 in T-315/591/000260. Jentz has the same in *Panzertruppen*, chart 237 for 25 June 1942.
49. Ic Anlage zum KTB, Tätigkeitsbericht der Abt.IIa vom 21.4.-30.6.42, in T-315/591/000232.
50. Novak, *L/71.*, Teil III, 110, Teil IV, 3.

CHAPTER 11: OPERATIONS BLAU AND WIRBELWIND

1. Divisionsbefehl, Angriff über der Tim, 25.6.1942, KTB Ia Anlage, T-315/591/000157.
2. Balck, *Ordnung im Chaos*, 379; Tim crossing in Schrodek, *Ihr Glaube*, 218, Donnhauser und Drews, *Der Weg*, 65–66, and KTB Ia 28.6.42, T-315/591/000251ff; photos of Pioniere bridges in Schrodek, *Bild*, 333–336.
3. KTB Ia Anlage 28.6.42, in T-315/591/000620. Schrodek, *Ihr Glaube*, 218, lists the same except has 1 Gep.Schtz.Kp. instead of all I./S.R.110, and does not include 3./209.
4. Panzer Lage in KTB Ia 30.6.42, T-315/591/000262, 000264; K.L.B. in 11.Pz.Div. Schematische Kriegsgliederung KTB Ia Anlage 20.7.42, T-315/592/000627 and 1.7.42 Truppenteil 593/000728; F.E.B. in KTB Ia Anlage 1.7.42, 593/000728-9.
5. Tätigkeitsbericht 29.6.1942 in KTB Ic Anlage, T-315/593/000887.
6. Kriegsberichter Rudolf Eiche's article in Anlage zum Tätigkeitsbericht der Abt.Ic zum KTB 2.7.42, in T-315/593/001356.
7. Photos of British tanks (knocked out) in Schrodek, *Bild*, 343, 354; Roth, Ausfälle, Gesamt Panzer 4.7.42 Anlage zum KTB Ia, T-315/591/001220-1; Panzer-Abschusszahlen 28.6.-10.7.42, Anlage zum KTB Ia T-315/592/000182-3. Reported by unit; for example,

K.L.B. claimed four undetermined, and Pz.Pi.Btl.209 claimed one T-34 and one KV-1.

8. Kampfstärke Stand 11.7.42 an VII. A.K., KTB Ia Anlage 12.7.42, T-315/592/000343. The reports all differ, depending on units attached or detached and what is counted (here including the K.L.B. but not the F.E.B. or staffs).
9. Mellenthin, *Panzer Battles*, 159, claimed 240,000 prisoners; Glantz and House, *Titans*, 120, say 54,000; Erickson, 363, Carell, 541, Blau, 153, and Ziemke and Bauer, 356, only say most had escaped.
10. Blau, *Russia*, 152–153; Kleist in Liddell Hart, *German Generals Talk*, 171, quoted in Mellenthin, 159, and in other sources.
11. Ziemke and Bauer, *Moscow to Stalingrad*, 363, 384; operations are detailed in Carell, *Hitler Moves East*, 581ff.
12. Anthony Beevor, *Stalingrad* (New York: Viking, 1998), 79; Burdick and Jacobsen, eds., *Halder War Diary* 640.
13. Beevor, *Stalingrad*, 79.
14. Glantz and House, *Titans*, 121; Erickson, *Road to Stalingrad*, 371.
15. This is based on photos in Schrodek, *Bild*, 394–396, captioned A.A.11, if correct. But A.A.11 wasn't established with the 11.Pz.Div. until 27 April 1943, and A.A.231 had been amalgamated with K.61 9 November 1941. In fact, *Bild* consistently captions the reconnaissance battalion as "A.A.11." There are, however, some scribbled messages from "A.A.11" in September 1942 in KTB Ia Anlage T-315/593/000356-000359.
16. Blau, *Russia*, 159; Ziemke and Bauer, *Moscow to Stalingrad*, 398–405.
17. Donnhauser und Drews, *Der Weg*, 72; Kampfgruppen list in KTB Ia 11.8.1942, T-315/591/000376, 000391. The Sukhinichi struggle is detailed in the KTB, *Der Weg*, 73–77, and in Schrodek, *Ihr Glaube*, 224–227.
18. Arrangement in KTB Ia 14.8.42, T-315/591/000425.
19. KTB Ia 11.8.1942, T-315/591/000367.
20. Schrodek, *Ihr Glaube*, 225; Tagesmeldung an LIII. A.K. 13.8.1942, KTB Ia Anlage, T-315/592/001006.
21. Messages in KTB Ia Anlagen: Tagesmeldung Kgr. Luz an Div. 14.8.42, T-315/592/001097; Schimmelmanns Panzerlage an Div. 15.8.42, T-315/592/001174; Kampfstärkemeldung an XXXXI. Pz.K., 15.8.42, T-315/592/001181; Grabenstärke an XXXXI. Pz.K. 19.8.42, T-315/592/001259.
22. Schrodek, *Bild*, 353; Zwischenmeldung Fernspruch an XXXXI. Pz.K. 18.8.42, KTB Ia Anlage, T-315/592/001241.
23. Halder's diary entry 14 August 1942 in Burdick and Jacobsen, eds., *The Halder War Diary*, 657; KTB Ia 16.8.42, T-315/591/000441, 000446.
24. Quoted in Schrodek, *Ihr Glaube*, 226; Schmundt's visit only mentioned in the KTB; Donnhauser und Drews, *Der Weg*, 76, say the Armeeoberbefehlshaber (Schmidt) was present, but the KTB says it was his Ia. KTB Ia 17.8.42, T-315/591/000448.
25. Burdick and Jacobsen, eds., *The Halder War Diary*, 660.
26. Donnhauser und Drews, *Der Weg*, 77, 76; Schrodek, *Ihr Glaube*, 226; Unit Gefechtsberichte of the August fighting in KTB Ia Anlagen, T-315/593/000147-000205.
27. KTB Ia Anlage 2.9.42, T-315/593/000057, and Gefechtsstärke as of 29.8.42, T-315/593/000016.
28. TM-E 30-451, 486–494.
29. KTB Ia Anlagen 5.–9.9.42, T-315/593/000241, 000295, 000214. The artillery sketch map in 000241 unfortunately does not include scale.
30. Tätigkeits-Bericht of Oberwachtmeister Hennecke 8.9.1942 and Kdr. II./Pz.Gren.Rgt.110 in Anlagen zum Abt. Ic zum KTB, T-315/594/000083, 000145. Hennecke was with the battalion 1–4 September 1942.
31. There are many more details in the records. Vernehmungen in Anlageband zum Tätigkeitsbericht der Abt.Ic zum KTB 4.8.1942 and 17.8.1942, T-315/594/000458/000330.
32. I./15 separated, KTB Ia 13.9.42, T-315/591/000578; Schmidt's 14 September 1942 message reproduced in Schrodek, *Ihr Glaube*, 277, and in *Bild*, 365.
33. Blau, *Russia*, 168; DiNardo, *Axis Powers*, 140 for the plight of the allied forces.
34. KTB Ia 27.9-2.10.1942, T-315/591/000588-000590.
35. Donnhauser und Drews, *Der Weg*, 82; Schrodek, *Ihr Glaube*, 229, only refers to winter preparations in October, and that there was no battle action into November.
36. Auflösung der Stab des 11.Pz.Gren.Brig., 15.11.1942. in KTB Ia Anlage, T-315/594/000725.
37. 4. Armee 12.11.42, KTB Ia Anlage, T-315/594/000724; Bandenbekämpfung 17.11.42, in 000532; Belegungssstärke 12.11.42, in 000701.
38. Friedrich von Eggeling, letter to author, 12 July 2013. Von Eggeling was promoted Leutnant in December 1942.
39. Map in Anlage zum Ia KTB 19.11.42; quotes from Erfahrungen Kgr. Henze 19.11.42, Ia Bericht 21.11.42, and Schmidt's Erfahrungen 19.11.42, in T-315/594/000960-000984, 001026-001028.
40. Schrodek, *Bild*, 374; E-Transport in KTB Ia 21.-25.11.1942, T-315/594/000534-000536.
41. Erickson, *Road to Stalingrad*, 452, 365.

CHAPTER 12: BATTLES OF THE RIVER CHIR

1. Carell, *Hitler Moves East*, 622; Mellenthin, *Panzer Battles*, 170, though this was the 22.Pz.Div., not the 13. 13.Pz.Div. was with H.Gr. A south of Rostov.
2. Mellenthin, *Panzer Battles*, 175n.

3. Carell, *Hitler Moves East*, 636. Beevor, *Stalingrad*, 270, says Goering's assurance was with "breath-taking irresponsibility," and Glantz and House, *Titans*, 134, say it was "impulsively promised."
4. Glantz and House, *Titans*, 136–139.
5. Manstein, *Lost Victories*, 326.
6. Leaders characterized by Balck, *Ordnung*, 442–443.
7. Gefechts- und Verpflegungsstärke 1.12.1942, Anlage zum Ia KTB, T-315/596/000196. These reports were generated as of the 1st, the 11th, and the 21st of a month.
8. Fernspruch (telephone) XXXXVIII. Pz.K. an 11.Pz.Div., Anlage zum Ia KTB 7.12.1942, T-315/595/000030. The Chir River engagements are detailed in the Tagesmeldungen (daily reports) and messages in the 11.Pz.Div. Ia Anlagen., 8.12.42ff, in T-315/594/000548ff.
9. Strengths from David M. Glantz, *From the Don to the Dnepr* (London: Frank Cass, 1991), 15 and n8 on 400–401. The Chir battles against XXXXVIII. Pz.K. are only mentioned briefly, 15; *Titans*, 140, says that the "11th Panzer Division performed herculean feats to parry these attacks."
10. KTB Ia 8.12.42, T-315/594/000582.
11. These actions are well covered by Mellenthin, *Panzer Battles*, 175–184, and by Balck, *Ordnung im Chaos*. They have also been the subject of several analytical studies. David Zabecki portrays Balck's command qualities in "The Greatest German General No One Ever Heard Of," *World War II* (April–May 2008), and US Army Capt. Robert G. Walters studies Balck's *Auftragstaktik* and their relevance to the US Army's Air-Land Battle maneuvers doctrine in an unpublished master's thesis, "Order Out of Chaos" (Monterey, CA: Naval Postgraduate School, 1989). Russel Stolfi's "The Chir River Battles," contributed to a 1984 Art of War Symposium at the US Army War College, Carlisle Barracks, Pennsylvania. Balck and Knobelsdorff have also collaborated with American historians on a number of occasions.
12. Mellenthin, *Panzer Battles*, 251, 183.
13. Ibid., 46, 183–184; Gaedke in Walters, "Order Out of Chaos," 10. One of Rommel's C/S, Gen.Lt. Alfred Gause, in fact was wounded in the Gazala battle, 1 June 1942.
14. Balck, *Ordnung*, 399. Message headings were: Fernspruch-Fernschreiben-Funkspruch-Blinkspruch.
15. Dörr's statement to Walter Rahn (later of Pz.Rgt.15), copy provided to author in 2008.
16. Balck's Tagesbefehl, Abt. Ic KTB 14.12.42 Anlage, T-315/595/000508-000509, reproduced in Schrodek, *Bild*, 377; also in Balck, *Ordnung*, 401, and Donnhauser und Drews, *Der Weg*, 84.
17. Mellenthin, *Panzer Battles*, 178.
18. Clark, *Barbarossa*, 263, identified as being from the 115th Panzergrenadier Regiment, probably meaning 15.Pz.Rgt.; Pz.G.R.115 was in 15.Pz.Div. in Africa.
19. Wehrmachtsbericht 9 Dez. 1942 in Ia KTB Anlage, T-315/595/000212; Panzerlage in Tagesmeldung an XXXXVIII. Pz.K. 15.12.1942 in Ia KTB Anlage, T-315/595/000539; Pz.Jg.Abt.61 aufgelöst 30.12.1942 in Ia KTB, T-315/594/000612; Stärkemeldung 16.12.1942 Ia KTB Anlage, T-315/594/000590; S-pflüge by Mellenthin 19. Dez. 1942 in Ia KTB Anlage, T-315/595/000725.
20. Balck, *Ordnung*, 403.
21. Mellenthin, *Panzer Battles*, 184.
22. Balck, *Ordnung*, 405. "Heikel" as "ticklish" in F. W. von Mellenthin, *German Generals of World War II As I Saw Them* (Norman: University of Oklahoma Press, 1977), 203.
23. Fernspruch an XXXXVIII. Pz.K. 16.12.42 KTB Ia Anlage, T-315/595/000591; Meldung Pz.Rgt.15 an Division, Ia KTB Anlage, T-315/595/000634.
24. Heinz Kutscheid, letter to Karl Thieme, 25 July 1995, copy provided to author.
25. Balck in Mellenthin, *Panzer Battles*, 184, and Mellenthin, 186.

CHAPTER 13: BACK TO THE DONETS

1. Statement of Franz Thelen, copy provided to author via Walter Rahn, 13 January 2008.
2. Balck's sketch map in *Ordnung*, 409.
3. Balck, *Ordnung*, 411; Glantz, *From the Don to the Dnepr*, 69.
4. Scheibert, and Wolfgarten's account, in Oberstlt. Horst Scheibert, *Panzer Zwischen Don und Donez* (Friedberg: Podzun-Pallas-Verlag, 1979). 44, 50–54; Russian operations are described in Glantz, *From the Don to the Dnepr*, 65ff.
5. Leutnant Gross in Schrodek, *Ihr Glaube*, 233.
6. Ziemke and Bauer, *Moscow to Stalingrad*, 492; Donnhauser und Drews, *Der Weg*, 94; Leutnant Gross Feldpostbrief 27 December 1942, rewritten 5 January 1943 in Schrodek, *Ihr Glaube*, 234.
7. Tagesmeldung an XXXXVIII. Pz.K. 28.12.1942 and Stärkemeldung 26.12.1942, Anlage zum Ia KTB, T-315/595/001443, 001204; Balck to "Lieber Cramer" (?) 30.12.1942, KTB Anlage, T-315/595/001557.
8. Gefechtsstärke in Ia Tätigkeitsbericht 31.12.1942, T-315/596/000192; Stab Humbert an 11.Pz.Div. 31.12.1942 in Ia KTB Anlage, T-315/595/001606.
9. Leutnant Gross's experience in Schrodek, *Ihr Glaube*, 235–237.
10. Tagesmeldung an A.A.Hollidt, Anlagen zum Ia KTB, T-315/596/000505-000867.
11. Scheibert, *Die Träger des deutschen Kreuzes in Gold*.
12. Balck, *Ordnung*, 417.

13. Donnhauser und Drews, *Der Weg*, 110. Examples of these vehicles may be found in the Panzermuseum Munster, and in the collection by Guy Franz Arend, originally known as the Victory Museum in Arlon, Belgium and relocated to Auburn, Indiana, USA, after 1991.
14. Eberhard Schöne, e-mail to author, 9 March 2012; Kurt Nentwig, letter to author, 15 March 2012; von Eggeling, letter to author, 6 March 2012.
15. Gefechtsstärke 21.1.1943 Anlage zum Ia KTB; organization 19.1.1943 Ia KTB; T-315/596/001079, 000283.
16. Mellenthin, *Panzer Battles*, 203–205 with sketch maps; for 16.I.D.(mot), Paul Carell, *Scorched Earth*, trans. Ewald Osers (New York: Little, Brown and Co., 1966/Ballantine, 1971), 134–140; Balck, *Ordnung*, 420–423; Ia KTB 21-27.1.1943, also Anlagen. Russian loss figures vary; numbers used here are found in T-315/596/000283-000305, 001097ff.
17. Balck, *Ordnung*, 426.
18. Ibid., 426–427; Schrodek, *Bild*, 384.
19. Carell, *Scorched Earth*, 191; Manstein, *Lost Victories*, 365; Mellenthin, *Panzer Battles*, 206, says Hitler came *forward* to Manstein's headquarters near Zaporozhe.
20. Glantz, *From the Don to the Dnepr*, 82ff and Orders of Battle in Appendices 2 and 3 on 382–391. Glantz also has day-to-day operations maps, German units being shown at the division level.
21. Hausser, *Waffen-SS im Einsatz*, 83–84; Manstein, *Lost Victories*, 422; "richtiger-weise" in *Verlorene Siege*, 453; Helmuth Spaeter, *The History of the Panzerkorps Grossdeutschland*, trans. David Johnston (Winnipeg, Manitoba: J. J. Fedorowicz, 1995), vol. 2, 43. Works on the Waffen-SS include Stein, *Waffen-SS*, and Marc J. Rikmenspoel, *Waffen-SS, The Encyclopedia* (Garden City, NY: Aegis, 2002). Note also *Waffen-SS im Bild* (Göttingen: Plesse Verlag, 1957).
22. Glantz and House, *Titans*, 139. Sources for the I.Abt./Pz.Rgt.15 in the Velikiye Luki struggle include Schrodek, *Ihr Glaube*, 264–266, Schrodek, *Bild*, 369, and Carell, *Scorched Earth*, 316–333; *Operations of Encircled Forces*, Dept. of the Army Pamphlet No. 20-234 (January 1952), 7–14, is detailed though incomplete; and Franz Kurowski, *Deadlock Before Moscow* (West Chester, PA: Schiffer, 1992) is detailed though the panzer forces have errors. A Department of the Army caveat about their pamphlets (iii) is: "The reader is reminded that publications in the German Report Series were written by Germans from the German point of view and are presented without interpretation by American personnel." Written by (unnamed) German officers in American captivity, the project was done in the context of the Korean War after intervention by Communist China, with possible escalation involving Russia.

    A good discussion of this US Army Historical Division project, resulting in some 2,500 manuscripts by some 730 former German general, field, and staff officers, 1946–61, is in Lt. Col. (ret.) Peter G. Tsouras, ed., *Panzers on the Eastern Front* [papers by Gen. Erhard Raus] (Mechanicsburg, PA: Stackpole, 2002), 234–244. Some critics—not American NATO officers facing the Soviet threat—have complained about the German anti-Russian bias.
23. Schrodek, *Ihr Glaube*, 264–266, and Kurowski, *Deadlock*, 246ff, though confusing; also the I./15 Report 365-366.
24. Kurowski, *Deadlock*, 249, not including I./15. Sources vary greatly, most not listing I./15. Carell, *Scorched Earth*, 322, says combat groups of 291. and 331.I.D.s, parts of Pz.Gren.Rgt.76 [of 20.I.D.(mot)], Pz.Rgt.10 [of 8.Pz.Div.], and Sturmgeschütz Abt. 237. DA 20-234, 10, implies elements of 83.I.D., 20.I.D.(mot), a Jäger Batl., two batteries of 10,5cm artillery, and a Nebelwerfer (rocket) brigade.
25. Kurowski, *Deadlock*, 253, says this attack continued through the night and in pouring rain that reduced visibility to 100 meters.
26. Unpublished manuscript of H.-Werner Bürkner, "Die letzten Beissen die Hunde" (1990), copy given to the author by Herr Bürkner at a Pz.Rgt.15 Treffen (reunion) in Wolfhagen, 2003. Bürkner identifies Lt. Kloske as Lt. Koske.
27. Carell, *Scorched Earth*, 332–333; Glantz and House, *Titans*, 347n17.
28. Sivers from Mark, *Death of the Leaping Horseman [24.Pz.Div.]*, 437–438, and Eberhard Schöne, Pz.Rgt.15, e-mail to author, 9 March 2012. Schrodek spells Sivers as Sievers, but the former spelling is on lists.
29. Schrodek, *Ihr Glaube*, 266.

CHAPTER 14: KHARKOV COUNTERATTACK

1. Balck, *Ordnung*, 427; also Donnhauser und Drews, *Der Weg*, 99; Ia KTB 6.2.1943, T-315/597/000012.
2. Manstein, *Lost Victories*, 416–417.
3. KTB Ia entries 9.2.1943, 13.2.1943, and 8.2.1943, T-315/597/000024, 000047, 000023.
4. The panzer drive is in Donnhauser und Drews, *Der Weg*, 101–104 and Schrodek, *Ihr Glaube*, 241–243, especially the map on 240; photos in Schrodek, *Bild*, 399–400; Colonel Glantz, *From the Don to the Dnepr*, has excellent day-to-day sketch maps and unit details. Operations are also in Dana V. Sadarananda, *Beyond Stalingrad* (Mechanicsburg, PA: Stackpole, 1990), 104ff.

5. Gefechtsstärke as reported 11.2.1943, T-315/597/000272; attack Gliederung 19.2.1943 in Ia KTB, 000067.
6. Balck, *Ordnung*, 437; 11.Pz.Div. flanking movements on Balck's sketch map, 432.
7. Popov losses from Carell, *Scorched Earth*, 214; Balck, *Ordnung*, 438; Hitler, forwarded to 11.Pz.Div. by H.Gr. Süd, 28.2.1943, Ia KTB Anlage, T-315/597/000766; Manteuffel, *7. Panzer-Division*, 326–327.
8. Schrodek, *Ihr Glaube*, 245, 252, and *Bild*, 411.
9. Schrodek, *Ihr Glaube*, 246, 245.
10. Ibid., 245–246; Scheibert, *deutschen Kreuzes in Gold*, Schimmelmann listed by name; Balck, *Ordnung*, 442.
11. Balck, *Ordnung*, 441; Balck's 12 March 1943 farewell letter is reproduced in Schrodek, *Bild*, 408.
12. Balck, *Ordnung*, 445, 444.
13. Vatutin quoted in Glantz, *From the Don to the Dnepr*, 120.
14. Figures from Carell, *Scorched Earth*, 214, similar in Manstein, *Lost Victories*, 433; Glantz and House, *Titans*, 349n32, note the German figures, and add that Soviet sources are "silent" on the losses.
15. Manstein, *Lost Victories*, 432, 434–435.
16. Bemerkungen zum Ia KTB, 5.3.1943, T-315/598/000017-000018.
17. Manstein, *Lost Victories*, 435–436.
18. "Frontal Counterattack" in *German Defense Tactics against Russian Break-Throughs*, Department of the Army Pamphlet No. 20-233 (October 1951), 7.
19. Hoth's orders from Carell, *Scorched Earth*, 217; Hausser's argument in his *Waffen-SS im Einsatz*, 94, and losses on 95; 3rd Tank Army in Glantz, *From the Don to the Dnepr*, 202.
20. This was especially true of SS-Totenkopf, coming from Eicke and the brutal Konzentrationslager background (even if before Heydrich's "Endlösung"). Charles W. Sydnor Jr., *Soldiers of Destruction* (Princeton, NJ: Princeton University Press, 1977), 261, 315. But in 1943 Himmler undertook a Europe-wide anti-Communist recruiting campaign that resulted in *non*-Germanic French, Russian, and Asian Waffen-SS units, including the 13.Waffen-Gebirgsdivision SS "Handschar" (scimitar) of Bosnian Muslims whose motivations were more nationalistic.
21. Bemerkungen zum Ia KTB 13.3.1943, T-315/598/000053; Donnhauser und Drews, *Der Weg*, 107, also say Balck left after Merefa, 13 March 1943.
22. KTB Ia 14. and 17.3.1943, T-315/598/000058, 000069; Gefechts- und Verpflegungsstärke 11.3.43 in Ia KTB Anlage, T-315/598/000563. It is not clear if all of Pz.Jäger Abt.61 was reactivated after being deactivated 30 December 1942.
23. KTB Ia 29.3.1943, T-315/598/000102; operations and detailed situation maps in Glantz, *From the Don to the Dnepr*, 199–210.

CHAPTER 15: INTERLUDE: SPRING 1943

1. Photos in Schrodek, *Bild*, 412–414, 359.
2. Ibid., 426–432, 420.
3. The 11.Pz.Div. listed 192 Selbstladegewehre authorized, then 240, but had none. Anlagen 1.6.43 and 1.7.43 zum Ia KTB, T-315/599/000834, 001115. Sources on firearms include Hogg, *Infantry Weapons*, and W. H. B. Smith, *Small Arms of the World* 7th ed. (Harrisburg: Stackpole, 1962). It might be noted that the MP 38/40 was designed under Berthold Giepel of Erma Werke; "Schmeisser" is a misnomer, as in Smith, 443.
4. Comments by Hptm. Franz Thelen, Adju/111, letter to author, 21 August 1990. The postwar Bundeswehr simply produced the MG 42 as the MG 1, in 7.62mm NATO caliber. In designing a new machine gun, the M60, the United States adopted the belt feed pawl mechanism of the MG 42, and the bolt assembly of the German paratroopers' FG 42, but it is considered inferior in many ways; for the quick-change barrel feature, the spare barrels all had a bipod, gas cylinder, and front sight attached!
5. Hogg, *Infantry Weapons*, 130, 134, 136; TM-E 30-451, 339, 340, 342 are similar.
6. See photos in Schrodek, *Bild*, 343, 354. Tank data sources include RAC booklets, TM-E 30-451, and Harts, *German Tanks*.
7. Eberhard Schöne to author; information from Mark Thrasher from Internet sources; Franks, *Trucks of the Wehrmacht*, 196–198.
8. Mellenthin, *Panzer Battles*, 212. For the Tiger in action, note Otto Carius, *Tigers in the Mud*, trans. Robert J. Edwards (Mechanicsburg, PA: Stackpole, 2003), especially the technical issues in the after-action reports. Copy via Mike Kirk. Carius was in schw. Pz.Abt.502 in Russia.
9. Guderian, *Panzer Leader*, 215; Panther development history in many sources including Harts, *German Tanks*, and Thomas L. Jentz, *Germany's Panther Tank* (Atglen, PA: Schiffer, 1995). Data from Harts, RAC booklet *Germany*, and Ogorkiewicz, *Armor*. MAN—Maschinenfabrik Augsburg-Nürnberg, in München.
10. Author's discussions with Martin Lange (Ogfr. Pz.Rgt.15 W.Kp.), on staff at Panzermuseum Munster, 1992.
11. Jentz, *Panther*, 130.
12. Nentwig, letter to author, 11 June 2012; Fersen, e-mail to author, 26 June 2012; PIAT (Projector, Infantry, Anti-tank) was spring-fired. The Soviets did develop the hand-thrown RPG-43 grenade. Hogg, *Infantry Weapons*, 148, 168. Panzerschürzen in Walter J. Spielberger, *Der Panzerkampfwagen IV und Seine Abarten* (Stuttgart: Motorbuch Verlag, 1975), 66.
13. Sources on armor and munitions include Ogorkiewicz, *Armor*, 311–317.

14. Guderian, *Panzer Leader*, 227–231; Clark, *Barbarossa*, 313–316; production figures used by Clark, 313n, from Orgorkiewicz, *Armor*, 217–218; Walter S. Dunn, *Kursk* (Westport, CT: Praeger, 1997), 95, gives 10,747 German tanks produced in 1943 compared to 27,300 Russian.
15. George M. Nipe, *Blood, Steel and Myth* (Stamford, CT: RZM, 2011), 43. Hereafter cited as *Myth*.
16. Kurt Nentwig, letter to author, 25 May 2012.
17. Gefechts- und Verpflegungsstärken der 11. Panzer-Division, 1.6.1943, Anlagen zum Ia KTB, T-315/599/000815-000819; Kriegsgliederung, Geplanter Stand nach Auffrischung (planned order of battle after rehabilitation) an XXXXVIII. Pz.K. 10.4.43, including K.61 and attached le.Sturmgeschütz Abt. 911, which included Pz.Jäger Abt.61.
18. Flammenwerferpanzer III in Senger und Etterlin, *Taschenbuch*, 34, and TM-E 30-451, 536. Photo of flamethrower demonstration in Schrodek, *Bild*, 427.
19. Anlage zum Ia KTB 1.7.43, T-315/601/000015.
20. Nafziger, *Panzers and Artillery*, 85; though he also says the 11.Pz.Div. was "destroyed" at Stalingrad, and misidentifies some units (e.g., Pz.Rgt. 15 as the 25th, Pz.G.R.111 as the 4th, and Pz.A.R.119 as the 76th). One is tempted to use his very detailed organizations, down to platoons, but not without corroboration.
21. Versetzte Offiziere 1.-31.5.1943, Ia KTB, T-315/599/000739.
22. The VW was, of course, pronounced "Fau Vay." Vehicles in the Panzermuseum Munster booklet, 84, 88, 92, 90, and in the Victory Museum booklet, 19, 26, 48, 49.
23. Six Hummeln are reported 2 July 1943 in Wochenmeldung, and twelve Wespen by 22 July 1943, Anlagen zum Ia KTB, T-315/599/001006, 001008, and 600/000481.
24. Unbenennung des Kradschtz.-Btl.61 in Panzer-Aufklärungs Abteilung 11. Bemerkungen zum Ia KTB 23.4.1943, T-315/599/000396.
25. For Pz.Jäger Abt.61, the planned Kriegsgliederung, 10.4.43 an XXXXVIII. Pz.K. shows "nur Personaleinheit," and "1.Kp. siehe Stu.Gesch.Abt.911," Anlage zum Ia KTB, T-315/599/000619; Wiederaufstellung der Pz.Jäger Abt.61, 24.5.43, 599/000787; Versetze Offiziere 22.4.43, 599/000374; Gefechts- und Verpflegungsstärken, 1.6.43, 599/000816, 000817.
26. Geschichte der Sturmgeschützbrigade 911 in Donnhauser und Drews, *Der Weg*, 259ff; also in Kurowski und Tornau, *Sturmgeschütze*, 205–207. Abt. organization from Nipe, *Myth*, 99; and Harts, *German Tanks*, 66. The four-man Geschütz crew were the Geschützführer, Richthtunteroffizier, Ladekanonier und Funker, and the Fahrer. Kurowski und Tornau, *Sturmgeschütze*, 321. Accident in 911. Geschichte in *Der Weg*, 261, and KTB Ia 14.4.1943, T-315/599/000391.
27. Von Choltitz was beurlaubt on the 17th. Veränderungen in der Kriegsrangliste 1.-31.5.1943, KTB Ia T-315/599/000377; Kurt Nentwig, letter to author, 15 March 2012. Rata (rat) was the nickname of the stubby Polikarpov I-16 fighter plane.
28. Mickl coming from Pz.G.R.25/12.Pz.Div. in LTC John R. Angolia, *On the Field of Honor*, vol. 2, 183; from 12. Schützenbrigade in Keilig, *deutsche Heer*, 221; from Inf.Rgt.155 [90.le.Div., DAK] in Mitcham, *Panzer Legions*, 107.
29. Glantz, *From the Don to the Dnepr*, 220–221; David M. Glantz and Jonathan M. House, *The Battle of Kursk* (Lawrence: University Press of Kansas, 1999), 315–316; Manstein, *Verlorene Siege*, 509n; German divisional strengths are 1944 K.St.N. in TM-E 30-451, 93–103, as being realistic comparative strengths.

CHAPTER 16: PREPARATIONS FOR OPERATION ZITADELLE

1. Manstein, *Verlorene Siege*, 483, also *Lost Victories*, 445–446. In *Verlorene Siege*, Manstein has twenty-four pages arguing about ZITADELLE, only seven on the operation itself (perhaps reflecting his despair about it).
2. Guderian, *Panzer Leader*, 245–247. Others, including Clark, *Barbarossa*, 275, 325, and Glantz and House, *Kursk*, 3, accept Guderian's account.
3. Mellenthin, *Panzer Battles*, 216–217.
4. Feindlage in Divisionsbefehl für den Angriff am X-1.Tag, Anlage zum Ia KTB 29.6.1943, T-315/599/000979; Minenhunde in Ic Tätigkeitsbericht 6.7.1943, T-315/600/000695; Soviet defense measures from Dunn, *Kursk*, 100–105; 67th Guards Rifle Division and Orders of Battle from Glantz and House, *Kursk*, 68–73, 307.
5. Nik Cornish, *Images of Kursk* (London: Brassey's, 2002), 11, 76, 196; Nikolai Litvin, *800 Days on the Eastern Front*, trans. and ed. Stuart Britton (Lawrence: University Press of Kansas, 2007), 10–13. Litvin was in the 4th Guards Airborne Division in the northern sector of the salient.
6. Carell, *Scorched Earth*, 103ff; Kahn, *Codebreakers*, 650–661; David Glantz, *Soviet Military Intelligence in War* (London: Frank Cass, 1990), 266, says the Werther intelligence was "contradictory and often unreliable."
7. Guderian, *Panzer Leader*, 247, 250; Panther problems in Harts, *German Tanks*, 97–98; technical reports and modifications in Jentz, *Panther Tank*.
8. Schrodek, *Ihr Glaube*, 266–267; I./15 redesignated as Pz.Abt.52 6 February 1943 in both Jentz, *Panther Tank*, 130, and Nafziger, *Panzers and Artillery*, 359.
9. Harts, *German Tanks*, 97–98; Dunn, *Kursk*, 86–87; Glantz and House, *Kursk*, 19, 36–37; Senger und Etterlin, *Taschenbuch*, 245–252; photos in Icks, *Tanks and Armored Vehicles*, 168.

10. Ernst Klink, *Das Gesetz des Handelns* (Stuttgart: Deutsche Verlags-Anstalt, 1966), 333; Nipe, *Myth*, 46; Schrodek, *Ihr Glaube*, 267; Sivers, Köhnen, and Baumunk in Walter Rahn Liste of May 1992, clarified by Lt. Eberhard Schöne in e-mail to author, 9 March 2012.
11. Lt. Friedrich K. von Eggeling, letter to author, 6 March 2012; Lauchert's commands in Mitcham, *Panzer Legions*, 51.
12. Jentz, *Panther Tank*, 130, based on K.St.N. 1150a, 10 January 1943, and K.St.N. 1177, 10 January 1943; Nafziger, *Panzers and Artillery*, 359, totals 104 Panthers in Pz.Abt.51, but only 76 in "a second organization" that had been authorized 17 Panthers per company.
13. Nipe, *Myth*, 39.
14. Sources vary. Panzer numbers from ibid., 39; total forces are based on Glantz and House, *Kursk*, 283–338. German data excludes 2. Pz.Armee, but includes XXIV. Pz.K. Soviet data restricted to the Central, Voronezh, and Steppe Fronts.
15. Divisionsbefehl für den Angriff am X-1.Tag, Anlage zum Ia KTB 29.6.1943, T-315/599/000974ff.
16. Carell, *Scorched Earth*, 12–13; Glantz and House, *Kursk*, 81, 83; KTB Ia 4.7.1943, T-315/599/00437.
17. Boyne, *Clash of Wings*, 301, 162. Soviet sources "remain vague about this air debacle" says Von Hardesty, *Red Phoenix* (Washington, DC: Smithsonian Institution Press, 1982/1991), 160.

CHAPTER 17: ZITADELLE: THE GERMAN OFFENSIVE

1. See Icks, *Tanks and Armored Vehicles*, 209; also Mark Healy, *Zitadelle* (Brimscombe Port Stroud, Gloucestershire: The History Press, 2008), 181, 223. Later Goliaths were radio-controlled and were nicknamed "Beetle," "Doodlebug," or "Minedog" by the Western Allies at Anzio in 1944.
2. Harts, *German Tanks*, 155; Guderian, *Panzer Leader*, 251. Dunn, *Kursk*, 89, notes the 665th Battalion of Hornets while Glantz and House, *Kursk*, do not. Glantz and House, 284, note 105 Elefants (Fredinands). Dunn also attributes a Panther battalion to 2.Pz.Div. (55), as well as 2nd SS Corps (125), but that is not correct.
3. George Nipe, *Myth*, 93, demonstrates that Strachwitz's panzers got stuck first, that the Panthers followed; Carell, *Scorched Earth*, 43–45; Spaeter, *Grossdeutschland*, 116–118; Mellenthin, *Panzer Battles*, 218n notes the Gren.Rgt. was similar to the Füs.Rgt., though with a higher proportion of heavy weapons.
4. Glantz and House, *Kursk*, 97, say thirty-six "lay as smoking hulks in the deadly ravine"; Dunn, *Kursk*, 113, says forty "were out of action from Soviet fire"; Harts, *German Tanks*, 97–98, say of 250 [*sic*] Panthers, 51.Abt. lost "56 percent," and by the second day "just one-fifth" remained operational (i.e., 50 of 250); Friedrich von Eggeling, letter to author, 31 May 2012. Books on the Grossdeutschland Division by Horst Scheibert (1970) and James Lucas (1978) make no mention of the Panther battalions.
5. Quoted in Jentz, *Panther Tank*, 130.
6. Nipe, *Myth*, is very critical of Strachwitz, 110, 147, 270.
7. Tagesmeldung an XXXXVIII. Panzerkorps 2.7.43, Anlage zum Ia KTB, T-315/599/001008.
8. 11.Pz.Div. operations in Schrodek, *Ihr Glaube*, 268ff, and Donnhauser und Drews, *Der Weg*, 111ff; note the excellent maps in Nipe, *Myth*; Russian units and Orders of Battle in Glantz and House, *Kursk*, 94ff, and 250ff, and using those figures; 11.Pz.Div. officer losses in *Ihr Glaube*, 268, and from Rahn's list. For some other German accounts, see Steven H. Newton, *Kursk: The German View* (Cambridge, MA: DaCapo, 2002), though there are many errors about 11. Pz.Div. units.
9. Figures from Glantz and House, *Kursk*, 287; Silvester Stadler, *Die Offensive gegen Kursk 1943* (Osnabrück: Munin Verlag, 1980), 34, totals 493 SS panzers as of 2 July 1943; Simpson, *Tiger Ace*, 176, 182; a vivid account of the SS Tigers is Will Fey, *Panzer im Brennpunkt der Fronten* (Munich: J. F. Lehmanns Verlag, 1960), 25ff. Fey's SS Tiger Company was with DR, and later became s.Pz.Abt.102 (Tiger), then s.Pz.Abt. 502 (Königstiger). Panzer crew experiences are reflected in his *Armor Battles of the Waffen-SS*, trans. Henri Henschler (Mechanicsburg, PA: Stackpole, 1990).
10. Mellenthin, *Panzer Battles*, 220; GD quoted in Glantz and House, *Kursk*, 107.
11. Boyne, *Clash of Wings*, 162, 163, 142, 154; Carell, *Scorched Earth*, 58; Hans Ulrich Rudel, *Stuka Pilot* (New York: Ballantine, 1963), 85–86. Rudel gives no date for his first attack, but it is unlikely it was 5 July. The Luftwaffe's direct intervention in armored combat "remained minimal," says Richard Muller, *The German Air War in Russia* (Baltimore: Nautical & Aviation Pub. Co. of America, 1992), 123.
12. Hardesty, *Red Phoenix*, 160.
13. Unpublished MS, presentation of Gen. Walter Rahn, *"Einsatz der 'Elften', Zitadelle-Kursker Bogen Juli 1943,"* at 11.Pz.Div. Treffen (reunion) in Kötzting, Bavaria, 23 May 1992.
14. Zugführer Olt. Ernst-August Freiherr von Fersen, e-mail to author, 26 June 2012.
15. Nentwig, letter to author, 15 March 2012; Glantz and House, *Kursk*, 310ff, list several "Self-propelled Artillery Regiment (152mm)," as well as 76mm, 85mm, and 122mm (the SU-85 later); KTB Ia 6.7.1943, T-315/599/000451.
16. Nipe, *Myth*, 189n43, 148; Schrodek, *Ihr Glaube*, 269.

17. Evaluation of British Army weapons authority Ian Hogg in his *Infantry Weapons*, 171.
18. Quote by Carell, *Scorched Earth*, 60; the Luftwaffe attack, however, is dated on the 8th. George Nipe, *Myth*, 226, argues the Prokhorovka axis had always been planned.
19. Mellenthin, *Panzer Battles*, 221–223; Nipe, *Myth*, 214, dates this incident as on the 8th, not the 7th.
20. KTB Ia 8.7.1943, T-315/599/000461.
21. Tagesmeldung an XXXXVIII. Panzerkorps 9.7.1943, Anlage zum Ia KTB, T-315/599/001534.
22. Nipe, *Myth*, 270.
23. Freiherr von Fersen, e-mail to author, 15 July 2012; also Eberhard Schöne, 9 March 2012.
24. Geschichte der Sturmgeschützbrigade 911 in Donnhauser und Drews, *Der Weg*, 262, 282, 283.
25. Donnhauser und Drews, *Der Weg*, 114. Compare Rommel's supporting his Ia, Oberstlt. Siegfried Westphal, who felt compelled to countermand one of his orders in Africa in 1941 in Mellenthin, *Panzer Battles*, 46. For Kursk, Mellenthin relates Grossdeutschland's operations, but says little about Mickl's 11.Pz.Div. Photo with Mickl in Nipe, *Myth*, 244.
26. Carell, *Scorched Earth*, 70, claims "for the first time in military history a large armoured formation was opposed from the air alone." At least "dramatic" in Muller, *German Air War*, 123.
27. Jentz, *Panther*, 132.

CHAPTER 18: ZITADELLE: THE RUSSIAN COUNTEROFFENSIVE

1. Ninety from Glantz and House, *Kursk*, 178, and sixty-three in Nipe, *Myth*, 427. These are the primary accounts of the Prokhorovka fighting utilized.
2. Fifteen hundred tanks and assault guns involved in Carell, *Scorched Earth*, 76; likewise 1,500 tanks in Martin Caidin, *The Tigers Are Burning* (New York: Hawthorne Books, 1974), 218.
3. Gühr's quote in Glantz and House, *Kursk*, 185; LAH Tagesmeldung 12 Juli 1943 in Stadler, *Die Offensive gegen Kursk*, 100–102. Nipe, *Myth*, 318, says LAH did not intend to advance until that afternoon, after SS-T attacked south *across* the Psel near Petrowka, 310.
4. Zaloga, *T-34/76*; RAC, *USSR*; Stadler, *Die Offensive gegen Kursk*, 34, for DR's T-34s.
5. Nipe, *Myth*, 321. George Nipe does not discount the dramatic Russian charge, but demonstrates that only Leibstandarte was on the actual battlefield of "Prokhorovka," and its strength was sixty-three panzers—nor was it advancing at the time, leading Nipe to label the armored collision a "myth."
6. Glantz and House, *Kursk*, 414n5; Nipe, *Myth*, 427, 438, 441. Fifteen hundred tanks and assault guns in Carell, *Scorched Earth*, and in Caidin, *The Tigers Are Burning*. With German records unavailable to Carell at the time, he apparently accepted figures much exaggerated by General Rotmistrov (possibly to justify his own horrendous losses to Stalin). Other writers followed suit. Caidin also incorrectly includes Panthers, with 8,8cm guns (82), and says, "Hausser was removed from his command by an enraged Hitler" (221). There were no Panthers present, nor did they mount the 8,8cm gun, and Hausser was awarded the Eichenlaub to the Ritterkreuz 28 July.
7. Schrodek, *Ihr Glaube*, 270, 271; Donnhauser und Drews, *Der Weg*, 114–115.
8. Beutekarte in Ia KTB 11.7.1943, T-315/599/000482.
9. Nipe, *Myth*, 302–303; Mellenthin, *Panzer Battles*, 226.
10. Nipe, *Myth*, 352–354; Meldung an XXXXVIII. Panzerkorps 12.7.43. Anlage zum Ia KTB, T-315/600/000098.
11. Mellenthin, *Panzer Battles*, 226–227. Mitcham, *Panzer Legions*, 266, says Knobelsdorff was on leave during ZITADELLE, 7 May to 20 August 1943, and his "Deputy," Dietrich von Choltitz, was acting corps commander. But Mellenthin places him at GD headquarters on 13 July, and says Knobelsdorff was on leave in October (248). Unfortunately, very seldom are names given in the KTBs or other unit records.
12. Nipe, *Myth*, 353. Guderian's 17 July Report to OKH said only ten Panthers were operational on 10 July. Jentz, *Panther*, 132.
13. Pi.Lehr-Btl.1 (ohne 1.Kp.) in KTB Ia 14.7.43, T-315/599/000497; Ic Abendmeldung 14.7.43 an Gen.Kdo. XXXXVIII. Pz.Korps Ic, T-315/600/001058.
14. Führer sign in Janusz Piekalkiewicz, *Operation "Citadel,"* trans. Michaela Nierhaus (Novato, CA: Presidio, 1987), 30; Manstein, *Verlorene Siege*, 501–502, though he has 17. and 23.Pz.Div. reversed; panzer numbers in Klink, *Gesetzt*, 266, including panzers under repair.
15. Manstein, *Verlorene Siege*, 509.
16. Mellenthin, *Panzer Battles*, 230–234.
17. ROLAND in Stadler, *Die Offensive gegen Kursk*, 140–145; Nipe, *Myth*, 417–422; also in KTB Ia 17.7.1943, T-315/599/000503.
18. KTB Ia 21.7.43, T-315/599/000527, 000521; Geschichte der Sturmgeschützbrigade 911 in Donnhauser und Drews, *Der Weg*, 262–263.
19. Glantz and House, *Kursk*, 232; Mitcham, *Panzer Legions*,43; Mitcham also has Clössner commanding 2.Pz.Armee 10–15 July 1943 (259).
20. Orders of Battle data from Glantz and House, *Kursk*, Appendices A and B, 283ff.
21. Piekalkiewicz, *Operation "Citadel,"* 251-252; Mitcham, *Panzer Legions*, 98, says Scheller had been wounded.
22. 11.Panzer-Division Ia an XXXXVIII. Panzerkorps 22.7.43, Anlage zum KTB, T-315/600/000481.

23. Donnhauser und Drews, *Der Weg*, 120.
24. Ia KTB 24.7.1943, T-315/599/000552.
25. Donnhauser und Drews, *Der Weg*, 120–121.
26. KTB Ia Bemerkungen 26.7.1943, T-315/599/000562; Donnhauser und Drews, *Der Weg*, 120–122 and Schrodek, *Ihr Glaube*, 272–274 are at variance about this period of operations; Walter Rahn, "Einsatz der Elften."
27. Friedrich K. von Eggeling, letters (in English) to author, 31 May 2012 and 12 January 2013; Kurt Nentwig, letter to author, 25 May 2012.

CHAPTER 19: THE KESSEL OF GRAIVORON

1. Hardesty, *Red Phoenix*, 169; data, and details of RUMIANTSEV in Glantz and House, *Kursk*, 246.
2. Stadler, *Die Offensive gegen Kursk*, 203.
3. KTB Ia 3.8.1943, T-315/600/001166; Fernschreiben 1.8.43 an XXXXVIII. Pz.K., Anlage zum Ia KTB, T-315/601/000003. The 19 Geschützen probably mounted the L/48 gun of Ausf. G, as there were only 120 of the L/43 gun of the Ausf. F produced. Harts, *German Tanks*, 64.
4. XXXXVIII. Pz.K. Tagesmeldung, Anlage zum Ia KTB 5.8.1943, T-315/601/000105ff.
5. Meldung an XXXXVIII. Pz.K. 6.8.43 and KTB Ia 7.8.43, T-315/600/001219, 001224. Graivoron operations are compiled from Donnhauser und Drews, *Der Weg*, 122–126, Schrodek, *Ihr Glaube*, 275–280, and Rahn, "Einstaz der 'Elften,'" as well as the KTB Ia 1.8.-20.9.1943, T-315/600/001166ff. Russian operations are primarily from Glantz and House, *Kursk* 241ff.
6. Schrodek, *Ihr Glaube*, 276, says 52 of the Versorgungsgruppe were captured, more than in the battalion group. Carell, *Scorched Earth*, 347, implies Schmidt and his aide committed suicide. The Russians allowed their men to bury them.
7. Sörgel in Carell, *Scorched Earth*, 349, as Kdr. 19.Pz.Div, also as Soergel in KTB Ia 11.8.1943, T-315/600/001251; Spaeter, *Grossdeutschland*, 155, has Oberst Terwitz; Geschichte der Sturmgeschützbrigade 911 in Donnhauser und Drews, *Der Weg*, 264. Glantz and House, *Kursk*, 248 refer to the "overall weakness of the Soviet forces," but this was not apparent to the Germans facing them, nor in their statistics given on 246.
8. "Fighting Withdrawal of 'Combat Group von Sivers' as 'Floating Bubble' in the Vorskla Valley . . . August 1943" hereafter cited as 'von Sivers' (translated MS, n.d.); map of routes from Rahn, "Einsatz der 'Elften.'"
9. Rahn and Groeger, 'von Sivers,' 3.
10. Rahn and Groeger, 'von Sivers,' 6; Friedrich von Eggeling to author, 20 March 2013; Jentz, *Panther Tank*, 134. Neither Donnhauser und Drews, *Der Weg*, 123–124, nor Schrodek, *Ihr Glaube*, 275, treat the movements of Pz.Abt.52 here.
11. Rahn and Groeger, 'von Sivers,' 10; Spaeter, *Grossdeutschland*, 146–156. Spaeter says that on a road north of Zaphorozhets "stood six Panthers of a newly-arrived panzer unit, apparently the 19th Panzer Division" (156). But 19.Pz.Div. had no Panthers, so unless these were the GD's (former Pz.Abt.51), these must have been of Kgr. Sivers. The next Panther Abteilung went to SS Das Reich in August, then to 23.Pz.Div. Jentz, *Panther Tank*, 137.
12. Letter (in English) from Friedrich von Eggeling to author, 31 May 2012.
13. Pirch in Gefechts-Bericht Oberst Boelsen über Pz.A.A.11, 4.8. bis 9.8.1943 für KTB, 12.8.1943, in T-315/601/000685.
14. Boelsen's Gefechts-Bericht 12.8.43 for 5.-9.8.43, T-315/601/000681; Tigers in Anlage zum Ia KTB 9.8.43, T-315/601/000535; KTB Ia 9.8.43, T-315/600/001237-001241.
15. Spaeter, *Grossdeutschland*, 156. The movements of the 11.Pz.Div. are obscure; this account follows Rahn's route maps in "Einsatz der 'Elften.'"
16. Keilig, *Das deutsche Heer*, 221, though giving Mickl's dates with 11.Pz.Div. as 15 May–12 August 1943; Mitcham, *Panzer Legions*, 106, has May 11–August 8, 1943; Anglia, *On the Field of Honor*, v.2, 183, says Mickl was killed in action 10 April 1945; the 11.Pz.Div. KTB only says Oberst von Wietersheim took over on 10.8.1943, KTB Ia 10.8.1943, T-315/600/001248.
17. Von Wietersheim's early life in particular, is from Walter von Leers, ed., *Zöglinge der Ritterakademie zu Brandenburg a.H.*, which is arranged by graduate number. Copy provided the author by Klaus Bardt, Nr.2270; von Wietersheim was graduate Nr.1886.
18. KTB Ia 11.8.1943, T-315/600/001253, 001251.
19. Glantz and House, *Kursk*, 248–249, say Poluboiarov "pushed back a combat group of the 11th Panzer Division and advanced steadily to the south." The movements of the Russian 4th and 5th GTC are depicted in Glantz, *From the Don to the Dnepr*, especially map 65 on 287.
20. Glantz and House, *Kursk*, 249.
21. Carell, *Scorched Earth*, 349.
22. Spaeter, *Grossdeutschland*, 161–162; Glantz and House, *Kursk*, 251, identify 7. and 19.Pz.Div. as well as GD, though the map, 243, shows 11. and 19.Pz.Div. and GD; in Glantz, *From the Don to the Dnepr*, 337, and map, 338, the force is given as GD, 7.Pz.Div., and 10.Pz.Gren.Div.; Mellenthin, *Panzer Battles*, 239, referring to the attack as 20 August, but presumably meaning the 18th.

23. Divisionsbefehl zur Verteidigung des Vorskla- und Boromlja-Abschnittes, 17.8.1943, Anlage zum Ia KTB, T-315/601/000732-000736. Oberstlt. Palm is noted as Kdr. Pz.Art.Rgt.119 on 16 August in 601/000736.
24. Franz Thelen, letter to author 21 August 1990.
25. 19.Pz.Div. in KTB Ia 18.8.43, Wietersheim 20.8.43, I./110 22.8.43, in T-315/600/001275, 001282, 001291; Panzerlage in Tagesmeldung 23.8.43, Anlage zum Ia KTB, T-315/001182.
26. KTB Ia 26.8.1943, T-315/600/001311-001312. Schrodek, *Ihr Glaube*, 281, says the 11.Pz.Div. undertook a long march on 23 August back behind the Dnepr; but there is no reference to this in Donnhauser und Drews, *Der Weg*, 126, or in the KTB, which refers to fighting at Staro Iwanowka and Oleschnja.
27. KTB Ia 1.9.43, T-315/600/001337; Verluste 1.-31.8.43 in Personelle Lage 1.9.43, Anlage zum Ia KTB, T-315/601/001614; Dietrich in Schrodek, *Bild*, 447.
28. Orders signed 28 August 1943 by Ia Kinitz (who returned to duty on the 28th), Anlage zum Ia KTB, T-315/601/001366, 001368; Friedrich von Eggeling, letters to Jeff Danby 16 May, and to author 17 May, 2013.
29. Manstein, *Verlorene Siege*, 515.
30. Walter Schaefer-Kehnert to author, 11 October 1996, and his privately published booklet, "Die Geschichte von Hans Buhr."
31. Hiwis in the 11.Pz.Div., Ia an XXXXVIII. Pz.K. 26.8.43, Anlage zum KTB, T-315/601/001311; Earl F. Ziemke, *Stalingrad to Berlin* (Washington, DC: OCMH, 1968), 172; Carell, *Scorched Earth*, 380–381. Carell also notes, 383, that a number of German officers, Germany having lost the war, were convicted of this "atrocity" in the Soviet Union, as was Manstein himself—by a *British* military court in 1949. On Manstein's trial see [British] Major General Mungo Melvin, *Manstein* (New York: St. Martin's Press, 2010), chapter 16 "Crime and Punishment," 451–484.
32. Zerstörungsarbeiten KTB Ia 11.9.43 Bemerkungen, T-315/600/001385; Abtransportiert 5.-20. September 1943, Ia Anlage zum KTB, and Div.Gef.Std. (Wietersheim, signed by Ia Kinitz) 13.9.43, Ia Anlage, T-315/601/001491, 001633.
33. KTB Ia 2.9.43 Bemerkungen, T-315/600/001334; Betr. Umgliederung 28.8.43 Anlage zum Ia KTB, T-315/601/001367. Jentz, *Panther Tank*, 134, notes Pz.Abt.52 was redesignated I./15 on 24 August 1943.
34. Tagesmeldung an XXXXVIII. Pz.K. 12.9.1943, Ia Anlage zum KTB, T-315/601/001623.
35. Mellenthin, *Panzer Battles*, 241–245; 11.Pz.Div. Marschdisziplin an III. Pz.K. 23.9.43, Anlage zum Ia KTB, T-315/602/000187.
36. Ia an XXXXVIII. Pz.K. 19.9.43, Anlage zum KTB, T-315/601/001736; KTB Ia 24.9.1943, T-315/600/001440.
37. Donnhauser und Drews, *Der Weg*, 127; KTB Ia 26.9.1943, T-315/600/001444; Schrodek, *Ihr Glaube*, 283.

CHAPTER 20: DEFENSE OF THE DNEPR

1. Mellenthin, *Panzer Battles*, 185; III. Pz.Korps warning 26.9.1943 Anlage zum Ia KTB, T-315/602/000256.
2. Stand and Wochenmeldung an III.Pz.K. 25.9.43 and Tagesmeldung 24.9.43, Anlagen zum Ia KTB, T-315/602/000231, 000229, 000189.
3. Marschgliederung, Ia an Feldgend.-Tr.61, 8.10.43, Anlage zum KTB, T-315/602/000300.
4. The Bukrin bridgehead actions are vividly portrayed in Carell, *Scorched Earth*, 390–411.
5. Carell, *Scorched Earth*, 415–417; Glantz and House, *Titans*, 173.
6. Carell, *Scorched Earth*, 375, 377–378.
7. Account based on Ibid., 432–439. Carell, 434, says Heeres-Panzerabteilung 656 had two *battalions* of Ferdinands. Harts, *German Tanks*, 155, say after Kursk, the few surviving Elefants (Ferdinands renamed) were redeployed to Italy in early 1944. Mitcham, *Panzer Legions*, 198, 265, says Henrici was seriously ill on 30 September, and succeeded on 10 October by Gen.d.Gebirgstruppen Ferdinand Schörner.
8. Ziemke, *Stalingrad to Berlin*, 182–183.
9. Total casualties were 1,996. Meldung an III.Pz.K., 1.10.43 Anlage zum Ia KTB, T-315/602/000305; KTB Ia 12.10.43 Bemerkungen, and 16.10.43, T-315/600/001470, 001477; Drews in Ia KTB 15.10.43 Bemerkungen, T-315/600/001476.
10. Note on Gliederung chart, Stand 1.10.43, under Pz.Rgr.15: "I.(Panther)/Panzer Rgt.15 zur Zeit in Auffrischung bei Pz.A.O.K.1." Anlage zum Ia KTB, T-315/602/000307.
11. Schrodek, *Ihr Glaube*, 283; Report of Lt. Werner Stoll, copy provided to author by Walter Rahn, Pz.Rgt.15, 13 January 2008.
12. XXXX. Pz.Korpsbefehl 24.10.43, KTB Ia, T-315/600/001506; Div. Befehl für Instandsetzungsdienste aus Smela, Anlage zum Ia KTB, T-315/602/000856. Normally, short-term repair was that made within fourteen days, long-term after.
13. KTB Ia 27.-29.10.1943 in T-315/600/001517, 001521, 001527; Donnhauser und Drews, *Der Weg*, 131; letter Friedrich von Eggeling to author, 17 May 2013.
14. KTB Ia 27.-31.10.1943, T-315/600/001517-001531.
15. Von Eggeling to author 27 October 2014, 15 January 2015.
16. I./15 in KTB Ia 2 and 3 November 1943, T-315/600/001538, 001546. Regarding I./15 rejoining the 11.Pz.Div. (3 November 1943), Schrodek, *Ihr Glaube*, 286, gives 31 October; Donnhauser und Drews, *Der Weg*, 132, give no date but the context is end of Octo-

ber; Stoves, *Grossverbände*, 85, says October; Tessin, *Verbände*, Bd. 3, 202, says "Herbst"; Nafziger, *Panzers*, 359, says 24 August; and Rahn's list of company commanders says 21 August (1943).

17. KTB Ia 31.10.1943, T-315/600/001536, 001537.
18. Carell, *Scorched Earth*, 430, indicates 4. Pz.Armee failed to reroute the 25.Pz.Div. armor, while Mellenthin, *Panzer Battles*, 250 says it was H.Gr. Süd's mistake.
19. Mellenthin, *Panzer Battles*, 251–252. Mitcham, *Panzer Legions*, 266, says that Gen.d.Pz.Tr. Heinrich Eberbach took command of XXXXVIII. Pz.K. on 1 October until Knobelsdorff returned in November, but also notes on 107 that Choltitz was deputy corps commander.
20. Actions detailed in Mellenthin, *Panzer Battles*, 253–264. Glantz and House, *Titans*, 174, say Manstein "achieved initial but fleeting success."
21. Fernschreiben and Tagesmeldung an LII. Armeekorps 15.11.1943, Anlagen zum Ia KTB, T-315/603/000069-000079.
22. Umgliederung der Div.Sich.Abt. in Div.Begl.Kp. 7.11.43 Anlage zum Ia KTB, T-315/602/001157.
23. Tagesmeldung an LII. Panzerkorps (*sic*; *LVII*) 18.11.43 and Befehl zur Verladung 19.11.43, Anlagen zum Ia KTB, T-315/603/000096-99, KTB Ia 19.11.43, T-315/600/001580; Meldung an 11.Pz.Div. from Priesz (sic) 19.11.43, Anlage zum Ia KTB, T-315/603/000114.
24. Tagesmeldung an XI. A.K. 26.11.43 and Wochenmeldung an XI. A.K. 27.11.43, Anlagen zum Ia KTB, T-315/603/000238-000244. 16.Pz.Gren.Div was rebuilt in the West as 116.Pz.Div. in 1944.
25. Hogg, *Infantry Weapons*, 152–154; TM-E 30-451, 318.; Zimmerit was named after the Chemische Werke Zimmer AG of Berlin. Hogg, *Infantry Weapons*, 171, Harts, *German Tanks*, 98. The British "Sticky Bomb" issued to Home Guard and partisans had an adhesive, and the Hawkins grenade, notably strapped by American paratroopers to their leg, was a small antitank mine; neither was magnetic or hollow charge.
26. KTB Ia 3. 5.12.1943, T-315/600/001639, 001645.
27. 11.Pz.Div. Fernschreiben an LII.A.K. 19.12.1943, Anlage zum Ia KTB, T-315/603/000595.
28. Schrodek, *Ihr Glaube*, 289–294; Volker Griesser, *The Lions of Carentan* [Fs.Jg.Rgt.5] (Drexel Hill, PA: Casemate, 2011), 48–51, copy via Robert Barrett; KTB Ia 25.12.1943, T-315/600/001722-3.
29. Wietersheim's Christmas message in Div.Gef.Std., 24.12.1943, T-315/603/000659, and in Schrodek, *Bild*, 461; Lt. Dietrich in *Bild*, 455–457; Vereidigung at Sagan, *Bild*, 458.
30. Glantz and House, *Titans*, 184.
31. Mellenthin, *Panzer Battles*, 269 (referring to the "Kinderkorps" volunteers attacking the B.E.F. at Ypres in 1914), and reflected in Donnhauser und Drews, *Der Weg*, 132–133. Mellenthin, 266n, notes that Erich Ludendorff had also commented on the Russian losses by 1916 in World War I, and that revolution came a few months later.
32. Friedrich von Eggeling, letter to author (in English), 27 November 2012.
33. Gefechtsstärke list 26.12.1943, Panzerlage 27.12.1943, Anlagen zum Ia KTB, T-315/603/000667, 000669; KTB Ia 27.12. and 31.12.1943, T-315/600/001728, 001748.
34. Schrodek, *Bild*, 464–465.
35. Schrodek, *Ihr Glaube*, 293; the Kirovograd battle is well detailed in "Defense Against Break-throughs—A Combination of Defense Tactics," in DA Pamphlet No. 20-233, *German Defense Tactics Against Russian Breakthroughs* (October 1951), 72–77, especially in maps 11a, b, c; note also Griesser, *Lions*, 53–54.
36. Glantz and House, *Titans*, 355n10; DA Pamphlet No. 20-233 *German Defense Tactics*, 74, 73; Carell, *Scorched Earth*, 454, says at one point Wietersheim lured a Russian armored brigade into a ravine and Lauchert's Pz.Rgt.15 ambushed them, destroying "three dozen" Soviet tanks.
37. Schrodek, *Bild*, 466–467; Grzeczka is the spelling in Schrodek's earlier *Ihr Glaube*, 294, with some other differences about this episode.
38. DA Pamphlet No.20-233 *German Defense Tactics*, 77.

CHAPTER 21: CHERKASSY–KORSUN KESSEL

1. The available 11. Panzer-Division Kriegstagebücher and Anlagen end in 1943. For the Cherkassy (Korsun) pocket battle operations, Douglas E. Nash, *Hell's Gate* (Southbury, CT: RZM Imports, 2002); Carell, *Scorched Earth*, 465–505; "The Pocket West of Cherkassy," in DA Pamphlet No. 20-234, *Operations of Encircled Forces* (January 1952), 15–42; Niklas Zetterling and Anders Frankson, *The Korsun Pocket* (Drexel Hill, PA: Casemate, 2008).
2. Ziemke, *Stalingrad to Berlin*, 256; Nash, *Hell's Gate*, 64, says Hitler ordered the meeting to emphasize the need for National Socialist philosophy and education.
3. Schrodek, *Ihr Glaube*, 295; von Lauchert's Urlaub clarified by Friedrich von Eggeling, Pz.Rgt.15, letter to author 12 February 2013; operations in Nash, *Hell's Gate*, 65, though Pz.Rgt.15 is misidentified as Pz.Rgt.8 (actually lost in Tunisia). The Sturmgeschütz Abteilung attached is given as 905., but was 911.
4. 11.Pz.-Div. armor strength in Zetterling and Frankson, *Korsun Pocket*, 74 and 304n169. The assault guns were from its attached Stu.Gesch.Abt.911, Stu.G.A.905, and Pz.Rgt.8 (of 20.Pz.Gr.Div.). As quoted by Nash, *Hell's Gate*, 83, from Schaefer-Kehnert, *Kriegstagebuch in Feldpostbriefen*, 246–248.
5. As quoted in Nash, *Hell's Gate*, 83.

6. Translation as in Ibid., 83; similar in Carell, *Scorched Earth*, 466.
7. Donnhauser und Drews, *Der Weg*, 267; Nash, *Hell's Gate*, 80, 88–89.
8. Carell, *Scorched Earth*, 469–470.
9. Nash, *Hell's Gate*, 97.
10. Ibid., 114–119.
11. Carell, *Scorched Earth*, 474 says the 24.Pz.Div. movement was ordered by Hitler; Nash, *Hell's Gate*, 128 says it was ordered by Manstein, and on 1 February Hitler transferred 6. Armee to Kleist's H.Gr.A in the south to prevent Manstein from transferring additional forces without his permission. Division home stations are generally from Mitcham, *Panzer Legions*.
12. As related in Schrodek, *Ihr Glaube*, 295.
13. Nash, *Hell's Gate*, 131.
14. Zetterling und Frankson, *Korsun Pocket*, 169–171. Hitler's orders moving a single panzer division is an excellent example of "micromanagement," of which American presidents from Abraham Lincoln through Lyndon B. Johnson have also been accused.
15. DA Pamphlet No. 20-234, *Encircled Forces*, 23; Nash, *Hell's Gate*, 194 notes that some of these German officers served Communist East Germany later, though Seydlitz was tried for war crimes in 1950 by the Soviets and sentenced to twenty-five years in prison.
16. Vormann quoted in Nash, *Hell's Gate*, 231.
17. Ibid., 275.
18. DA Pamphlet No. 20-234, *Encircled Forces*, 25.
19. Von Eggeling, letter to author, 12 January 2013, referring to Napoleon's retreat from Moscow in 1812.
20. Carell, *Scorched Earth*, 495–496; Nash, *Hell's Gate*, 308.
21. Quoted in Nash, *Hell's Gate*, 314. Degrelle succeeded Obersturmbannführer Lucien Lippert, who was killed 13 February 1944.
22. Casualty figures differ among Carell, *Scorched Earth*, 505, DA Pamphlet No. 20-234 *Encircled Forces*, 32, and most detailed in Nash, *Hell's Gate*, 364–366, 375, and Zeterling and Frankson, *Korsun Pocket*, 277. Glantz and House, *Titans*, 188, 356n give Soviet losses, but, however, accept the Russian estimate of 73,000 German losses as "far more credible" than the German figures.
23. Führerhauptquartier announcement reproduced in Schrodek, *Bild*, 468.

CHAPTER 22: FROM RUSSIA TO SOUTHERN FRANCE

1. Von Eggeling, letter to author, 12 January 2013 (in English).
2. E-mail from G. M. Harding Jr. to author, March 5, 2014. Harding was the son of US Marine Corps combat artist Capt. George M. Harding, great-uncle of the author.
3. Litvin, *800 Days on the Eastern Front*, 44. Litvin was with the 9th Guards Airborne Regiment and then the 354th Rifle Division. Examples of most of these vehicles were in the Victory Museum of Guy Franz Arend, later in Auburn, Indiana.
4. Data and descriptions from Franks, *Trucks of the Wehrmacht*.
5. Ziemke, *Stalingrad to Berlin*, 276; operations also in Glantz and House, *Titans*, 189ff and 356n14, 18.
6. Stu.Gesch.Abt.911 in Donnhauser und Drews, *Der Weg*, 267; Schrodek, *Ihr Glaube*, 297; on 296 Schrodek says Sivers, with crews of disabled panzers and the wheeled vehicles of the 11.Pz.Div., was transferred to "den neuen Einsatzraum von Prosskurow." In Schrodek's *Bilddokumente*, 470, there is a photo of Sivers's grave, the Birkenkreuz inscribed "Ritterkreuzträger Major Karl v. Sivers, Kdr. I. Panther Pz.Rgt.15, 10.4.44," and captioned "Major Karl von Sievers [*sic*] fell near Proskurov while leading an armored battle group." But Proskurov had fallen well before 10 April, and German forces had long since retreated. Friedrich von Eggeling, I./15, 12 January 2013, understands Sivers was with "another unit," and that Lauchert remained in command of the regiment.
7. The Kehlsteinhaus, nicknamed "Eagle's Nest," apparently by a French diplomat, was further accessed by a road and elevator up the Kehlstein Mountain, though seldom used by Hitler. The meeting at the Berghof is, perhaps dramatically, presented in Carell, *Scorched Earth*, 515–523.
8. Bessonov, *Tank Rider*, 76, 88. Lieutenant Bessonov's platoon was in the 1st Rifle Battalion of the 49th Mechanized Brigade, 6th Guards Mechanized Corps of 4th Tank Army.
9. Lothar Trenkler's letters and diary edited and published by his nephew, Thomas Trenkler, *Wiedersehen im Niemansland: Die Geschichte dreier Brüder, 1940–1949* (Wien: Czernin Verlag, 2000), 70–80. Some details given the author by Lothar Trenkler at Wolfhagen, June 2004.
10. Ziemke, *Stalingrad to Berlin*, 282; Carell, *Scorched Earth*, 526–527.These operations are covered in two DA pamphlets: "Encirclement of a Panzer Army near Kamenets-Podolsky" in DA No. 20-234 *Operations of Encircled Forces*, 43–51, and "Flank Attack" in DA No. 20-33 *German Defense Tactics against Russian Break-Throughs*, 9–14. At the end of March the 11.Pz.-Div. is listed as a strength of only two battalions with nine panzers, four Paks, and two artillery batteries in Werner Haupt, *Army Group South*, trans. Josef G. Welsh (Atglen, PA: Schiffer, 1998), 344.
11. There are discrepancies between the accounts of Glantz and House, *Titans*, 357n22, Ziemke, *Stalingrad to Berlin*, 294–295, and Carell, *Scorched Earth*, 552–560.

12. Letters (in English) from von Eggeling to author, 31 May 2012 and 12 February 2013. Eggeling was nineteen years old and King Michael was twenty-two.
13. Data especially from tables in RAC booklets *USSR* and *Germany*; note also Richard Joachimsen, "Der legendäre T-34" in *DMZ (Deutsche Militärzeitschrift)* Nr.43 (Januar-Februar 2005), 8–13. Some authors say the IS-1 was used at Kursk, and that the T-34/85 was used at Cherkassy-Korsun, but these need corroboration. The IS-3 was produced in 1945, but too late to see battle in World War II.
14. Schrodek, *Ihr Glaube*, 297, 298. The 11.Pz.Div. operations are sketched in *Geschichte der Sturmgeschützbrigade 911* in *Der Weg*, 268. Stu.G.A.911 also in Kurowski und Tornau, *Sturmgeschütze*, 250. Hptm. Gottfried Tornau was a later commander of Sturmartillerie-Brigade 911 in the West as redesignated. Mitcham, *Panzer Legions*, 105, says the 11.Pz.Div. absorbed the remnants of Gren.Rgt.416 of 123.Inf.Div. "which had also been smashed on the Eastern Front;" though he also says the 11. was "surrounded" at Cherkassy (Korsun).
15. Using figures accepted by Glantz and House, *Titans*, 356n.
16. Donnhauser und Drews, *Der Weg*, 139. This account also says that half the division traveled with much improvisation to France, while the other half carried out a difficult movement in the Carpathians that cost not only men, but especially much materiel. No dates or details are given.
17. Von Eggeling, letter to author, 31 May 2012, perhaps at least reflecting a general perception. Stoves, *Grossverbände*, 84 says the 11.Pz.Div. numbered some 8,000.
18. Photos and captions in Schrodek, *Bild*, 472–475. The movement to southern France is in Donnhauser und Drews, *Der Weg*, 139–143 and Schrodek, *Ihr Glaube*, 298–301. Pz.G.R.111 in Horst Loch letter to author, 30 October 1994.
19. Von Hake from Mitcham, *Panzer Legions*, 106, 114, 116. The Stu.Gesch.Abt.911 account in Donnhauser und Drews, *Der Weg*, 268 refers to von Hake as the division Ia. Von Eggeling, letter to author, 20 March 2013.
20. Lists of officers of Pz.Rgt.15 compiled by Walter Rahn, with input from other Kameraden. Data for the Panz.Div.44 K.St.N. (Kriegsstärkenachweisung) tables derived form NARA Microcopy T-78/Roll 410 Personelle Stärkeberechnung 15 August 1944 Frame 6878410, Waffen-Soll 410/6378412, Soll an Panz. und gp.Kfz. 410/6378591, and Soll an ungp. Kfz. 410/6378593. The Schematische Kriegsgliederung of 15 August 1944 shows two panzer battalions with *four* companies of twenty-two panzers each, totaling 176 plus headquarters panzers, though "Vorläufige Ausstatung" (interim equipment) lists seventeen panzers each, totaling 136 plus headquarters panzers, instead of 103; though 103 was closer to the actuality. There are other variations as well. Again, Grundgliederung was basic establishment, Soll- was intended, and Ise was actual.

    The data was tabulated by the US War Department in TM-E 30-451 of 15 March 1945; as reproduced by Louisiana State University Press, 1990 (adding page numbers for convenience), it has the panzer division tables on pages 103ff; these are Part II-25ff in the original TM-E. George Nafziger, *Panzers and Artillery*, 27–29, is useful here, though the totals don't add correctly.
21. W. J. K. Davies, *Panzer Regiments* (London: Almark, 1978), 15. At the Panzermuseum Munster, the author remarked that the Panther was marked *II*01; II. Abteilung was usually Panzer IVs.
22. Werner Strietzel, letter to author, 28 October 1990. Except for being wounded five times, and Komp. Führerlehrgang, Strietzel was in all the campaigns of the division.
23. Mitcham, *Panzer Legions*, 219–220; Tessin, *Verbände*, volumes by unit number.
24. Donnhauser und Drews, *Der Weg*, 142. It is unclear to what extent these were carried out. Tessin, *Verbände*, Bd.6, 227 lists a III./110 activated in November 1944.
25. See Arthur L. Funk, *Hidden Ally* (Westport, CT: Greenwood, 1992). Funk does not discuss the legal status of the partisans under the 1907 The Hague Convention however.
26. Operations in southern France are well treated in Jeffrey J. Clarke and Robert Ross Smith, *Riviera to the Rhine* (Washington, DC: Center of Military History, 1993). For an overview of 11.Pz.Div. operations note this author's "The 11th Panzers in the Defense, 1944" in *Armor* 103, no. 2, (March–April 1994), 26–37.
27. Franz Thelen, letter to author, 21 August 1990; points listed and discussed in Donnhauser und Drews, *Der Weg*, 143–145, though reference is to "Feldersatz*regiment*." Policies discussed by General von Wietersheim in a series of manuscripts written while in US prison camps at Allendorf and Neustadt near Marburg in 1947–1948. These were collected and printed as "11. Panzer-Division August 1944–Mai 1945" by Karl Heinz Loschke, Sprecher (Secretary) of the 11.Pz.Div. veterans association in 1996, copy presented to the author. There are MS copies at the USAMHI (US Army Military History Institute) archives at the US Army Heritage and Education Center in Carlisle, PA. Clarke and Smith, *Riviera*, 66n, refer to an unpaginated report dated 4 June 1946 in the John E. Dahlquist Papers there, which may be the first MS in the collection. Hereafter these will be cited by the Wietersheim MS number.
28. Schrodek, *Ihr Glaube*, 301 says maybe the panzers were from "I./Pz.Rgt.27(?)" (*sic*); but Pz.Rgt.27 was in 19.Pz.Div. on the Russian front.

29. Panzer data from Harts, *German Tanks*, Senger und Etterlin, *Taschenbuch*, RAC Bovington booklet *Germany*, as well as Jentz, *Panther Tank*, and Spielberger, *Panzerkampfwagen IV*. Heating in Jentz, 78, 97.
30. Letters to author from Jürgen Reichardt, 17 September 1990, Karl Zindler, 1 October 1990, and Kurt Nentwig, 11 June 2012. The American M4 (and later tanks) also traversed 360 degrees in fifteen seconds. Many American military histories incorrectly say the German panzers did not have power traverse.
31. MS #A-880 (Wietersheim) "Süd-Frankreich (15. August–14. September 1944)," 2–3; also in Donnhauser und Drews, *Der Weg*, 145–146. This approximates Nachträglicher Bericht 11. Panzer-Division Süd-Frankreich 15.8.44-14.9.44 Rapport Gen. von Wietersheim, RH 27-11/135 BA-MA (Bundesarchiv-Militärchiv, Freiburg i. Breisgau).
32. Anlage zum Ia KTB 5.8.44, Zustandsbericht Meldung reproduced in Thierry Chazalon, *Nationale 7: La Route de la Mort* (2008), 20. The Gliederung chart of 5 July 1944 reproduced on page 18 does not show a III.Btl./Pz.Gren.Rgt.110. This booklet, copy via Jeff Danby, includes excerpted journal entries of Gefreiter Hans Werner, Funker for Lt. Karl Zindler as Ordonnanz Offz. of I./15, headquarters Panther numbered I02.
33. Account of Oblt. Sierstorpff in Schrodek, *Ihr Glaube*, 301–302; ten panzers held back in Donnhauser und Drews, *Der Weg*, 142. MS #A-880 (Wietersheim), 1, written without access to records, says at "Ende Juni" some fifty Pz.IVs had to be given up. But the division was still around Bordeaux, and from Schrodek it is clear this was "Anfang August" and the rail route was from Toulouse.
34. Martin Blumenson, *Breakout and Pursuit* (Washington, DC: Dept. of the Army, 1961), 322. Operations also in Chester Wilmot, *The Struggle for Europe* (London: Collins, 1952) and Russell Weigley, *Eisenhower's Lieutenants* (Bloomington: Indiana University Press, 1981).
35. Note the author's "Questionable Objective: The Brittany Ports, 1944," *Journal of Military History* 59, no. 1 (January 1995): 77–95.

CHAPTER 23: RHÔNETAL

1. German operations are well presented in Clarke and Smith, *Riviera*, 68ff. To a large extent they are based on a series of manuscripts by Charles V. P. von Luttichau for the Office of the Chief of Military History (Washington, DC, 1958); copies provided the author by Thomas Crecca, Center of Military History, 2013. American units and organizations are in Shelby L. Stanton, *World War II Order of Battle* (New York: Galahad, 1991).
2. Clarke and Smith, *Riviera*, 122; Normandy casualties from Esposito, *Concise History of World War II*, 88, and Wilmot, *Struggle for Europe*, 293n. Normandy operations are in Gordon A. Harrison, *Cross-Channel Attack* (Washington, DC: Department of the Army, 1951).
3. Wietersheim's letter from Div.Gef.Std. den 19.8.44 in Schrodek, *Ihr Glaube*, 305; e-mail from von Fersen to author, 27 August 2009.
4. Jörg Staiger, *Rückzug durchs Rhônetal* (Neckargemünd: Kurt Vowinckel Verlag, 1965), 43, 47–48; though he misidentifies Pz.A.A.11 as Pz.A.A.61. Movements also in Donnhauser und Drews, *Der Weg*, 146–149.
5. United States Strategic Bombing Survey, Summary Report (European War), September 30, 1945 (Washington, DC: Government Printing Office, 1945), vol.1. The USSBS study was sponsored by the US Army Air Forces, hopefully to demonstrate the efficacy of air power.
6. Staiger, *Rückzug*, 58, also says seven dead-lined Panthers had to be destroyed for lack of transport.
7. MS #A-880 (Wietersheim) "Süd-Frankreich," 5.
8. Von Eggeling, letter to author, 20 March 2013, and also to Jeff Danby, 10 March 2013, letters shared by both; Clarke and Smith, *Riviera*, 142, says ten panzers; 3d ID G-2 Periodic Reports 20, 21, 22 August 1944, quoted in Jeff Danby, *The Day of the Panzer* (Drexel Hill, PA: Casemate, 2008), 94, 100. Copies also shared with the author.
9. 3d ID G-2 Periodic Reports No. 7 and No. 8, 22 and 23 August 1944, copies via Jeff Danby. Names of the PWs were not included. Feldpost numbers were collected, thus 01015 equals I./110, and 30563 equals 6./II./110. Lacking 11.Pz.Div. KTBs for the West, the American G-2 reports provide some insight into actual unit organization and morale.
10. Clarke and Smith, *Riviera*, 142–143. This US Army official history is critical of the American caution that "may have sacrificed an opportunity to cut off major portions of Kniess' corps south of the Durance."
11. These actions are in Schrodek, *Ihr Glaube*, 306–307, though not in *Der Weg* or in Wietersheim's MS; nor are they confirmed by *Riviera* or other American sources, and the M8s would not be so massed.
12. US T/O&E 7 *The Infantry Division*, 15 July 1943; Clarke and Smith, *Riviera*, 80, 132, 144.
13. Werner Strietzel, letter to author, 28 October 1990.
14. Lt. von Eggeling, for one, felt the regimental commander "was a real catastrophe." Letter to author, 17 May 2013.
15. Luttichau, unpublished MS #R-111 chapter 13 "The Battle of Montélimar," 25–27; Clarke and Smith, *Riviera*, 157–158. Because of the wooded hills, Luttichau, 29, felt Wietersheim might better have sent the 198.I.D.

up N 7, with his 11.Pz.Div. attacking through the Roubion valley on Grâne.

16. Clarke and Smith, *Riviera*, 213–216. The battle of Montélimar is well detailed in *Riviera*, 144–170.
17. Account by Friedrich von Eggeling to author 20 March 2013; he emphatically said the village was not Sauzet as in Schrodek, *Ihr Glaube*, 305. Schrodek simply says, "von Partisanen erschossen."
18. MS #A-880 (Wietersheim) "Süd-Frankreich," 10; Luttichau, R-111, 24, 31; Clarke and Smith, *Riviera*, 160.
19. Funk, *Hidden Ally*, 155.
20. Albrecht Englert to author, 23 May 1995; von Eggeling to author, 20 March 2013.
21. Clarke and Smith, *Riviera*, 163; Lt. General L. K. Truscott Jr., *Command Missions* (New York: E. P. Dutton & Co., 1954), 430–431; Joachim Ludewig in his *Rückzug* (Maj. Gen. David Zabecki, ed., Lexington: University Press of Kentucky, 2012), 179, comments that the Americans never blocked the valley road permanently, and the attempt to stop the German withdrawal primarily with artillery fire failed.
22. Staiger, *Rückzug*, 82.
23. Albrecht Englert to author, 28 August 2004 (improving on his apologetic "my english in catastrophe").
24. Letters from von Eggeling (I.Abteilung Ordonnanz Offizier at the time) to author, and to Jeff Danby, 15 January 2013. Danby had published *The Day of the Panzer* (2008), an excellent study of Allan as an American small-unit action, esp. 167ff. The 3rd Division units involved were: L Co/3rd Bn/15th IR; 3rd Plat/B Co/756th Tk Bn; 3rd Plat/B Co/601st TD Bn; and M8s from Cannon Company/15th IR. His grandfather, Lt. Edgar Danby, was the tank platoon leader killed.
25. Letters from von Eggeling to Danby, 15 January and 7 April 2013, shared with the author. Danby, *The Day of the Panzer*, 236, speculates that a Panther knocked out the next day was the Panther at Allan. Von Eggeling says Stichler was wounded the next day (the 28th); Schrodek, *Ihr Glaube*, 309, says it was on 5 September.
26. Episode related by Freiherr von Fersen, e-mail to author, 24 June 2009. This may have been Vize Admiral Ernst Scheurlen, who held that position 17 August–5 September 1944. Samuel W. Mitcham Jr., *Retreat to the Reich* (Westport, CT: Praeger, 2000), 169. Fersen's EK 1.Kl. certificate dated 5 November 1944, recommendation by Major Bertram, A.O.K.19 NSFO, 18.10.1944.
27. Testimonial Bericht about the circumstances of Rabenau's death to Pz.Rgt.15 by Oblt. von Fersen, 22 November 1944; Von Eggeling to Danby, 15 January 2013.
28. Von Fersen, letter to author, 24 June 2009, and e-mail, 27 August 2009.
29. Zustandsbericht Meldung vom 1.9.1944, Verluste 1.-31.8.1944, Anlage zum Ia KTB in BA-MA RH 10-149. There are numerous reports in the BA-MA.
30. Jochen Menzel, *Der Löwe von Lyon* (Berg am See: Kurt Vowinckel, 1988), 25, 33. Copy sent to the author by Herr Menzel. 11.Pz.Div. figures from Clarke and Smith, *Riviera*, 168. The authors do surprisingly say, "the 11th had not really done much during the campaign." Some GIs and their commanders might differ. Twenty-two Panthers destroyed from Schrodek, *Ihr Glaube*, 307.
31. Jochen Menzel to author, July 1990.
32. Menzel, *Der Löwe*, 128, photographs; and Werner Strietzel, A.A.11, letter to author, 28 October 1990.

CHAPTER 24: FROM LYON TO THE BURGUNDIAN GATE

1. Von Eggeling letter to Danby, 10 March 2013, also Oberstlt. Hans von Luck [Pz.G.R.125/21.Pz.Div.], *Panzer Commander*, 191.
2. Fred Rennert, letter to fellow veteran Peter Gaidosh, n.d., copy provided to author by Gaidosh, 23 January 2001.
3. Colonel Meyer's letters and MS about "Mex" courtesy of Col. Harlos Hatter, S-4 (Supply) of 179th RCT at the time, 45th Infantry Division Museum, Oklahoma City, OK to author, 27 April 1994: General Davison's extensive letter is in *Armor* (July–August 1994), 2, responding to the author's article, "The 11th Panzers in the Defense, 1944" in *Armor* (March–April 1994). There is very little about the battle in Donnhauser und Drews, *Der Weg*, 154, Schrodek, *Ihr Glaube*, 309, or Wietersheim's MS, 12, nor in Staiger, *Rückzug*, 103. The battle is described by Funk, *Hidden Ally*, 243–248.
4. Colonel Meyer's MS V-mailed home from Naples 14 October 1944, courtesy of Col. Harlos Hatter, 45th Infantry Division Museum to author, 27 April 1994.
5. Davison's 1994 *Armor* letter; Funk, *Hidden Ally*, 246–247; Jürgen von Pflug to author, 27 September1990 (though he referred to a captured "Sherman-Panzer"); Bob Slingerland letter to von Pflug, 7 May 1991, and correspondence with both with the author in October and November 1990.
6. Clarke and Smith, *Riviera*, 177, though saying the 179th had only three men killed, which cannot be correct. Funk, *Hidden Ally*, 248, has eleven Americans killed and fifty as prisoners, the French thirty-nine killed and twelve as prisoners. German losses according to the 179th Regiment were eighty-five killed and forty-one captured, and twelve panzers, three self-propelled guns, and seven other vehicles destroyed. The 45th Div. lost two TDs, two armored cars, one half-track, and two jeeps.

7. Fred Rennert letter via Peter Gaidosh to author, 23 January 2001; Arthur Funk to author, 16 August 2001.
8. Menzel, *Der Löwe*, 38, 115; Funk, *Hidden Ally*, 238, 248–252. Barbie later escaped to Bolivia but was extradited back to France, was convicted of crimes against humanity, and died in prison in 1991.
9. Staiger, *Rückzug*, 103.
10. Arthur L. Funk, "Mandate for Surrender," *World War II* (March 1990), 27–33, 28; Schrodek, *Ihr Glaube*, 309; ref. 9.SS Pz.Div. in Staiger, *Rückzug*, 106.
11. MS #A-880 (Wietersheim), "Süd-Frankreich," 13; Luttichau, R-112, chapter 14, "Breakout and Withdrawal to the Dijon Salient," 25–26.
12. Funk, "Mandate," 33. Staiger, *Rückzug*, 106, says the 117. Einheit was "completely rubbed out."
13. Clarke and Smith, *Riviera*, 180; Funk, "Mandate," 27, 33. Truscott, 439, quoting from his aide's journal in his *Command Missions*, published in 1954.
14. Clarke and Smith, *Riviera*, 180–181; Wietersheim's MS #A-880, "Süd-Frankreich," 14; (US) Third Army Interrogation Report, 19 October 1945, M/Sgt Ernst Simon, Mobile Mission Dept., AG Translation Branch 8 Dec 45. Additional remarks (after responding to fourteen questions). At USAMHI No. B-805.
15. The 4th Tunisian Tirailleurs Regiment, Clarke and Smith, *Riviera*, 188; 11.Pz.Div. units in MS #A-880 (Wietersheim), 14, Donnhauser und Drews, *Der Weg*, 156, and nine Panthers from Schrodek, *Ihr Glaube*, 309; Grumbt's RK, and "outstanding," in Jürgen von Pflug letters to author, 6 June and 30 October 1994.
16. Weigley, *Eisenhower's Lieutenants*, 235.
17. Organizations deduced by 3rd Infantry Division G-2 Intelligence, based on PW interrogations, whose information might not always be accurate. G-2 Periodic Reports No. 14 (29 August 1944), No. 17 (2 September), No. 21 (6 September), No. 22 (7 September) and No. 23 (8 September). Lüttwitz's report dated 17 July 1944, seventeen copies distributed, translated as Annex "C" in Periodic Report No. 25 (10 September 1944), copies from Jeff Danby.
18. Account by Menzel, *Der Löwe*, 203–208; letter to author, July 1990. Clarke and Smith, *Riviera* , 190, say the 3rd Algerian was "firmly halted" by the 11th Panzer Division.
19. Blumenson, *Breakout and Pursuit*, 655; Luttichau in MS #R-113, chapter 15, "The German Withdrawal from Southwestern France," 35, 36, says "it is doubtful whether another general in Sach's place could have done any better," and calls the accomplishment "impressive." Model in Luttichau MS #R-112, chapter 14, "Breakout and Withdrawal to the Dijon Salient," 5.
20. Eisenhower, letter to Gen. George C. Marshall, Chief of Staff of the US Army, 24 August 1944, in Alfred D. Chandler Jr., ed., *The Papers of Dwight David Eisenhower*, 5 vols., *The War Years* (Baltimore and London: Johns Hopkins University Press, 1970), 4:2092–94.
21. Wood is supported by the author in his "Questionable Objective;" Wood's reasoning is paraphrased in Blumenson, *Breakout and Pursuit*, 359.
22. Gen. Bruce Clarke (ret.) letter to author, 16 June 1977. The "broad front" strategy is treated in many sources, as diverse as Forrest C. Pogue, *The Supreme Command* (Washington, DC: Department of the Army, 1954), and, critically, by Chester Wilmot, *Struggle for Europe*. Eisenhower quoted by Capt. Harry C. Butcher, USNR, *My Three Years with Eisenhower* (New York: Simon and Schuster, 1946), 273, on 7 March 1943 in Tunisia; Butcher was Eisenhower's naval aide.
23. FM 17-100, *The Armored Division*, 15 January 1944, 2, emphasis in original; FM 17-12, *Tank Gunnery*, 22 April 1943, 1, 4.
24. US T/O&E 17 *The Armored Division*, 12 February 1944, with changes. The M4 with 105mm howitzer was termed an "assault gun," but not used as such, rather in fire support.
25. Calculations in Clarke and Smith, *Riviera*, 196–197; German artillery calculations in Luttichau MS R-112, 28.
26. Clarke and Smith, *Riviera*, 198; Schrodek, *Ihr Glaube*, 310. Luttichau, MS R-112, 30, credits 11.Panzer with 14,832 men on 1 September, which appears excessive. On page 32, 11.Pz.Div. casualties for 1–31 August are given as 747: 123 killed, 447 wounded, and 177 missing.
27. Report of 2 September 1944 forwarded 8 September 1944, *Yank* of 17 June 1945, *Die Wacht* of 7 September 1944, in Schrodek, *Ihr Glaube*, 310–311. *Yank* also in Wietersheim's MS #A-880 "Süd-Frankreich," 19.
28. Patton's diary entry, 30 August 1944, in Martin Blumenson, ed., *The Patton Papers*, (Boston: Houghton Mifflin, 1974), vol. 2, 531.
29. American logistical difficulties are treated in Roland G. Ruppenthal, *Logistical Support of the Armies*, 2 vols. (Washington, DC: Department of the Army, 1953–1959), especially I: 491, 550, 574, and 559.

CHAPTER 25: THE GERMAN RECOVERY

1. Figures from numerous charts in TM-E 30-451; relevant K.St.N. tables are in NARS microcopy T-78/Roll 410/frames 6378533-4, though strength is listed as 10,506 (plus 691 Hiwis); the Grundgliederung is in T-78/410/6378531.
2. K.St.N. and Gliederung charts as reproduced in Friedrich Bruns, *Die Panzerbrigade 106 FHH* (Celle: Friedrich Bruns, 1991), copy presented to the author. There are not corresponding charts in the 1945 TM-E 30-451, presumably as most of the brigades were incorporated into existing panzer divisions after October 1944.

3. Jean Paul Pallud, "Panzer Attack in Lorraine," *After the Battle*, No.83 (London: Battle of Britain Prints International., 1994), 30.
4. Charles B. MacDonald, *The Siegfried Line Campaign* (Washington, DC: Office of the Chief of Military History, 1963), 30-35, including diagrams of the bunkers.
5. Wilmot, *Struggle for Europe*, 347.
6. There are still sharp cultural and linguistic differences among this "border" population as the author found on trips in the 1990s between say, Arracourt and Morhange, and Bärendorf and Wolfskirchen east of the Saar (Sarre) River.
7. Rikmenspoel, *Waffen SS, The Encyclopedia*, 38, 46–47. Operations are well detailed in Hugh M. Cole, *The Lorraine Campaign* (Washington, DC: Dept. of the Army, 1950).
8. Cole, *Lorraine Campaign*, 159 and 159n; Wilmot, *Struggle for Europe*, 537n, has thirty-three Panthers and eleven assault guns. Both sources say only nine were left. The KTB of Pz.Brig.106, 9.9.1944 in Bruns, *Pz.Brig.106 FHH*, 66, says twenty-six panzers and eight Panzerspähwagen were destroyed.
9. Hans von Luck, *Panzer Commander*, 171–172. Luck commanded Pz.G.R.125, but took over Pz.G.R.192 as Oberst Rauch went on sick leave. Other details from Cole, *Lorraine Campaign*, 199-201.
10. Hanson Baldwin, *Tiger Jack* (Ft. Collins. CO: Old Army Press, 1979), 30. "Tiger Jack" was a journalist's nickname for General Wood, not known in the 4th Armored. Sources on the 4th AD include Kenneth Koyen, *The Fourth Armored Division* (Munich: Herder-Druck, 1946), and, through December 1944, Don M. Fox, *Patton's Vanguard* (Jefferson, NC: McFarland & Co., 2003). Operations are well-covered in the US Army official histories. Note also US Army Armor School Manuscripts (ARMS), including "The Nancy Bridgehead" (Fort Knox, Kentucky: 1946). The unit records are in NARS Record Group 604.
11. Pz.Brig.106 KTB 15.9.44 in Bruns, *Panzerbrigade 106 FHH*, 82; Erich Spiwoks und Hans Stöber, *Endkampf zwischen Mosel und Inn* (Osnabrück: Munin Verlag, 1976), 146.
12. Cole, *Lorraine Campaign*, 105.
13. Donnhauser und Drews, *Der Weg*, 157; Schrodek, *Ihr Gaube*, 310; Clarke and Smith, *Riviera*, 237, say there were twenty-five panzers operational. It is interesting to contrast American armor operational readiness, because of the mechanical reliability of the vehicles and recovery, especially in controlling the battlefield. For example, with the sixty-seven "runners" of the 756th Tk Bn and thirty-three M10s of the 601st TD Bn on 31 August 1944 attached to 3d Inf Div, one TD in maintenance would be "Fit in 24 Hrs," one TD and one M5 in "48 Hrs," and the twenty back in Ordnance were all "mechanical failure (Non-Battle Loss)" and would be repaired. 3d Inf Div G-3 (Operations) Report No.24, 31 August 1944.
14. Quoted in Cornelius Ryan, *A Bridge Too Far* (NY: Simon & Schuster, 1974), Frontispiece.

CHAPTER 26: COUNTERATTACK IN LORRAINE

1. Maj. J. H. Pitman, Col. C. Hancock ("Hank") Reed, and Lt. Col. Bill Bailey respectively. The 696th Armored Field Artillery Battalion is also in Robert W. McCormick, *Cockney* (Worthington, OH: Cottonwood, 1983).
2. 4th AD AARs (After Action Reports) are in NARA Record Group 604; the 704th TD is covered in Lonnie Gill, ed., *Code Name: Harpoon* (LaPiente, CA: Baron, 1982); and the 6th AD in George F. Hofmann, *The Super Sixth* (Louisville, KY: 6th Armored Division Association, 1975).
3. 4th AD G-3 Journal, 19 September 1944, NARA 604-3.2; the CCA Troop List: 37 Tk Bn (-A), 53 AIB (-B), C/10 AIB, 166 (C) Engr Bn (-B), C/24 Armd Engr Bn, C/704 TD Bn (-2d Plat), 66 AFA Bn, 94 AFA Bn (-C), and 191 FA Bn (155mm), plus the returning TF Hunter companies. The Arracourt tank battles are well detailed in Cole, *Lorraine Campaign*, 209–255, with its excellent maps.
4. Schrodek, *Ihr Glaube*, 312; Donnhauser und Drews, *Der Weg*, 159, which implies the movement began on 15 September, as does the English translation of MS #B-364 (Wietersheim) "Rheinland Teil I," though not the original manuscript.
5. MS #B-364 (Wietersheim) "Rheinland Teil I," 1–2. The German usage of schwere (heavy) for 15cm artillery was termed "medium" by the US Army (155mm howitzers).
6. US Third Army G-2 Periodic Report No.104, 20–21 September 1944 dated 220600 A , report of a PW from 2nd Company/954th Security Battalion captured in the vicinity of Château-Salins; Spiwoks und Stöber, *Endkampf*, 66.
7. 191st FA Bn. Battle details primarily from Cole, *Lorraine Campaign*, 227–229.
8. Mellenthin, *Panzer Battles*, 312.
9. The three officers revisited the battle area in 1992 with Jean Paul Pallud, who authored "Panzer Attack in Lorraine," copy courtesy of Richard Buchanan (704th TD Bn, 1996).
10. Donnhauser und Drews, *Der Weg*, 160–162; MS #B-364 (Wietersheim) "Rheinland Teil I" refers to two artillery *battalions* , while Cole, *Lorraine Campaign*, 237, says two *batteries*. Since "Abteilung" could mean "battalion" or "detachment," it is not clear if Kgr. Hammon included one of the organic battalions, or an ad hoc formation—probably the latter.

11. Koyen, *Beach*, 292; correspondence and conversations with Col. (ret.) Jimmie Leach; XII Corps G-3 Operations Notes No. 4, 10 September 1944.
12. MS #B-364 (Wietersheim), 13–14. The date is probably 26 September not the 27th. Cole, *Lorraine Campaign*, 239–240 may be more accurate here.
13. 559.Volks-Gren.Div.: Gren.Rgts. 1125, 1126, 1127; Art.Rgt.1559; Pak 1559; Pi.Btl.1559; Div. Einheiten 1559 (Füs.Kp., Nachr.Btl. [*sic*], Sich.Kp., Ausb.Kp.). Tessin, *Verbände*, Bd. 6. MS #A-972 (Mühlen). George F. Nafziger, *The German Order of Battle: Infantry in World War II* (London: Greenhill, 2000), 351, notes the Pz.Jäger Kp. was probably expanded into a battalion with 7,5cm Pak 40, le.Pz.Jg.38(t) Hetzer, and 3,7cm flak batteries.
14. Donnhauser und Drews, *Der Weg*, 163; MS #B-364 (Wietersheim), 7; Mellenthin, *Panzer Battles*, 317, after the panzer brigades were wrecked; conversation of Brig. Gen. (ret.) William Molla with Wietersheim and Balck in 1971, in *Yankee Doings* (Boston: Yankee Division Veterans Association) March–April 1987, 15. *Yankee Doings* is the bimonthly newsletter of the 26th Infantry Division (Massachusetts National Guard). Bill Molla had much contact with his former Gespenster enemies, and shared his work with the author.
15. Letters from von Eggeling to author, 28 August 1997 and 20 March 2013.
16. Maj. Gen. Manton Eddy Diary entries of 16 and 22 September 1944, at USAMHI, Carlisle, PA.
17. Hofmann, *Super Sixth*, 141–148.

CHAPTER 27: LINEAR DEFENSE IN LORRAINE

1. MS #364 (Wietersheim), 8. Wietersheim also says twenty half-tracks were captured by the Pi-Kp. of Pz.G.R.111 in a night attack and used until the end of the war, but neither Schrodek, *Ihr Glaube*, 312, nor Donnhauser und Drews, *Der Weg*, 163, mention this, nor do 4th Armored Division sources.
2. Clarke and Smith, *Riviera*, 277–280.
3. Werner Strietzel, letter to author 28 October 1990. Hptm. von Pfeil was also related to this Silesian noble family.
4. Rolf Wandhoff letter to author, 17 July 1990; Schaefer-Kehnert, Anmerkungen to his *Kriegstagebuch in Feldpostbriefen 1940–1945*, 278–279.
5. Nat Frankel and Larry Smith, *Patton's Best* (New York: Hawthorne, 1978), 69; Joseph Kmetz, letter to Paul D'Angelo, editor of the 26th Inf Div newsletter *Yankee Doings* (March–April 1987), 15.
6. Schneider's account in *Yankee Doings* (March–April 1986), 14-16, facilitated by Brig. Gen. (ret.) William Molla; Cole, *Lorraine Campaign*, 290; Gill, *Harpoon*, I-10, II-10. The 11.Pz.Div. activities are primarily from MS #364 (Wietersheim) and Donnhauser und Drews, *Der Weg*, 163–165.
7. Schneider's account in *Yankee Doings* (March–April 1986), 15.
8. MS #364 (Wietersheim), 12; Donnhauser und Drews, *Der Weg*, 165. The fear of German tracked vehicles at night is well reflected in Charles B. MacDonald, *Company Commander* (New York: Ballantine, 1947/1984), 24–36. MacDonald first commanded I Co/23rd Inf Rgt/2nd ID in the Schnee Eifel, and finally determined, 41, that it was simply the sounds of a supply vehicle (Kettenkrad, half-track motorcycle) bringing up rations at night that had unnerved the unit. The tracked American M29 Weasel and the British Universal (Bren gun) carrier served the same supply function.
9. Zeitung pages in Schrodek, *Bild*, 492–493.
10. Klaus Bardt, Pz.Rgt.15, e-mail to author 8 December 2007; entries in Christian Zentner and Friedemann Bedürftig, eds., *The Encyclopedia of the Third Reich*, 2 vols., trans. Amy Hackett (New York: Macmillan, 1991).
11. Pz.Rgt.15 Lts Eberhard Schöne letter to author, 9 March 2012, and von Fersen, e-mail, 15 July 2012. The packaged ration, comparable to the American three-meal K ration, weighed 825 grams (1.82 lbs). The Grosskampfpäckchen (combat ration) of caffeinated chocolate Schokakola or fruit bars was analogous to the American 4-ounce chocolate emergency combat D ration. TM-E 30-451, 299–300.
12. Walter Schaefer-Kehnert, 30 September 1944, in his *Feldpostbriefen*, 271.
13. Author's discussions with Ray Mason, Columbus, Ohio; and with Ogfr Martin Lange, 23 and 30 May 1992, when he was on the staff of Panzermuseum Munster.
14. These operations and changes are in MS #B-364 (Wietersheim), 10–11; Donnhauser und Drews, *Der Weg*, 164–165; and Clarke and Smith, *Riviera*, 268–270.
15. MS #B-364, 13; Donnhauser und Drews, Der Weg, 165; *26th Infantry Division History in World War II* ("Weisermühl" Wels-Klischee: Krammer Linz, 1946), 8.
16. Schneider in *Yankee Doings* (March–April 1986), 15, though in MS #B-364, 13 (not in *Der Weg*, 165), on 20 October II./110 was "given to the left neighbor of the Division"; von Eggeling, letter to author, 10 October 2012; Lt. Zindler photos as in Schrodek, *Bild*, 495 and *Ihr Glaube*, 341; Reed letter to Eddy, n.d., copy to author via General Molla, also in *Yankee Doings* (January–February 1987), 18.
17. Schneider in *Yankee Doings* (March–April 1986), 16, who locates this at Dieuze; for Balck's visit one photo caption in Schrodek, *Bild*, 498, says November, the other October.
18. Thieme, letter to author, 28 October 1993.
19. Donnhauser und Drews, *Der Weg*, 166; MS #B-416 (Wietersheim) "Die Kämpfe der 11. Panzer-Division

zwischen Chateau-Salins und Zweibrücken" (28.10.44-18.12.44 in Lothringen), 1; Cole, *Lorraine Campaign*, 313, gives fifty new Panthers and nineteen Panzer IVs but not more than one or two tank destroyers on 8 November.

20. Thieme, letter to author, 28 October 1993, quoting Wietersheim, MS #B-416, 1.
21. MacDonald, *The Siegfried Line Campaign*, 390–392, 317; also for 12th Army Group October operations.
22. German planning in many sources, here from Hugh M. Cole, *The Ardennes: Battle of the Bulge* (Washington, DC: Office of the Chief of Military History, 1965), 16–28; Mellenthin, *Panzer Battles*, 339.

CHAPTER 28: MOBILE DEFENSE IN LORRAINE

1. Brig. Gen. (ret.) Bill Molla, who walked the German position a year later, in an address to 101st Infantry veterans, 1 April 1989; author's discussion with Bob Watson, 31 October 2014.
2. MS #B-416 (Wietersheim), 2; Cole, *Lorraine Campaign*, 417–418.
3. Of his 4th AD General Wood had said, "They shall be known by their deeds alone." "Elitedivision," and Ofenrohr, in Nachrichtenblatt für die verwundeten Offiziere des I./Pz.Gren.Rgt.111, 15 December 1944, 2, via Kuno Heilmann through Franz Thelen to author 5 August 1990; and in MS #B-416 (Wietersheim), 2, referring to a "Bazooka (Ofenrohr)" though 559.V.G.D. is misidentified as 259.V.G.D.; operations in Cole, *Lorraine Campaign*, 342ff. The M4 with a short 105mm howitzer was intended for fire support, not an anti-armor role.
4. Schneider's account in *Yankee Doings* (March–April 1986), 16. The mortally wounded American commanders were Lt. Col. William Slade of the 253rd AFA Bn and Lt. Col. Alfred Maybach of the 4th AD's 51st AIB, succeeded by Maj. Harry Van Arnam. Cole, *Lorraine Campaign*, 346.
5. Trezzvant W. Anderson, *Come Out Fighting* (Salzburg: Salzburger Druckerei und Verlag, 1945), 32.
6. Cole, *Lorraine Campaign*, 333.
7. Combat interview of Capt. Leach by Capt. Dayton at Riche, France, 24 November 1944, NARA Record Group 604 Box 24092 Folder 273; Leach met Rahn at the 1995 Treffen of the Gespenster-Division, and Leach and the author then drove to the battle site, including the position near Dalhain from which the Panthers fired across the valley. Account by Rahn (1974) sent to William Molla and shared with the author; reproduced by Schrodek in *Ihr Glaube* (1976), 312–313. The TF Hunter troop list was: 37 Tk (-C), 66 AFA, A/53 AIB, C/10 AIB, A/46 Med (-), plats C/24 Engr, plat C/704 TD.
8. Spiwoks und Stöber, *Endkampf.* 75, 82; Bruns, *Panzerbrigade 106 FHH*, 275, 290.
9. Karl Thieme, letter to author, 23 September 1990.
10. Cole, *Lorraine Campaign*, 328–330; MS #B-416 (Wietersheim), 7, says it was Pz.G.R.111 at Rodalbe, and 400 American Gefangene; Pfc. Richard D. Courtney, *Normandy to the Bulge* (Carbondale & Edwardsville: Southern Illinois University Press, 1977), 38.
11. Author's discussions with Ogfr Lange, 23 and 30 May 1992.
12. CCA S-3 Log NARA Record Group 604 (4th AD); Biedermann interview with Bill Molla published in *Yankee Doings* (September–October 1976), 3. Observation about defilade by the author (former tank platoon leader) after visiting the site in 1992.
13. West letter to author, 6 September 1980; and interview 31 March 1976 in the "General Abrams Story" Oral History Project, USAMHI.
14. Oden USAMHI interview, 18 March 1977; Maj. Gen. Delk Oden letter to author, September 1980.
15. MS #B-416 (Wietersheim), 4; *26th Infantry Division History in World War II*, n.p.
16. Wood's Foreword to ARMS, "Armor vs. Mud and Mines" (Fort Knox, 1950).
17. OB West KTB, 16 November 1944, in Cole, *Lorraine Campaign*, 408n.
18. MS #B-416 (Wietersheim), 5; Cole, *Lorraine Campaign*, 450n.
19. In 1947 Simon (MS #C-023, "Bericht ueber den Feldzug 'Rheinland' und 'Sueddeutschland',") said the 11.Pz.Div. was at 50–70 percent strength with 30–40 panzers, but he was writing from memory.
20. Nentwig, letter to author, 28 March 2013; Schaefer-Kehnert, "Kriegstagebuch."
21. Cole, *Lorraine Campaign*, 476–478; MS #B-416 (Wietersheim), 5, refers to "Panzerabwehrgeschütze," though the translator uses "tank destroyers," and Donnhauser und Drews, *Der Weg*, 169, says "Panzerjäger IV." Hofmann, *Super Sixth*, 231, has a photo of a Jagdpanzer IV L/48 knocked out outside St. Jean-Rohrbach.
22. Jürgen von Pflug, letter to author, 23 March 1994.

CHAPTER 29: DEFENSE OF THE SAAR

1. Panzerlehr's attack is in Clarke and Smith, *Riviera*, 377–386, and Cole, *Lorraine Campaign*, 464–471; Helmut Ritgen, *Die Geschichte der Panzer-Lehr-Division im Westen 1944–1945* (Stuttgart: Motorbuch, 1979), 204–214. Major Ritgen was commander of II./130 and (212) was wounded 25 November. There is less detail in Franz Kurowski, *Die Panzer-Lehr-Division* (Bad Nauheim: Podzun-Verlag, 1964).

2. Wood had approached his old friend and classmate, Maj. Gen. Wade Haislip, commanding the neighboring XV Corps, and Patton approved. But clashes with his corps commander, Eddy, resulted in Patton relieving Wood on 3 December. Note the author's "Patton's Relief of General Wood," *Journal of Military History* 53 (July 1989), 257–273.
3. Kurowski, *Panzer-Lehr*, 149. In a report, Oberst Kurt von Einem, Chef d.Gen.St. of XIII.SS-A.K., says Panzerlehr, 25.Pz.Gren.Div., and 11.Pz.Div. were formed as Gruppe "Bayerlein" 25 November–1 December 1944, and then the weak 25.Pz.Gren.Div. was subordinated to the 11.Pz.Div. Spiwoks und Stöber, *Endkampf*, 89–91.
4. Cole, *Lorraine Campaign*, 521–525. The fight for Sarre-Union in Schrodek, *Ihr Glaube*, 314–318, is an account written by Brig. Gen. William Molla of the US 26th Inf. Div. experience. Wietersheim in MS #B-416, 13, repeated in *Der Weg*, 170, has the 11.Pz.Div. *right* boundary from the Sarre at Witring north of the Blies at Bliesbrück, well *east* of the Saar and Saargemünd, on 28 November. But the US XII Corps was still *west* of the Maderbach on 30 November and Saargemünd (Sarreguemines) did not fall until 11 December. These sources also say it was I./110 that charged into Sarre-Union, and on 29 November; but prisoners taken were from the Begleit Kp. on 3 December.
5. Cole, *Lorraine Campaign*, 526–527. This is at variance with a monatliche Zustandsbericht for 6 December 1944 that totals 12,702, of which 3,593 are panzergrenadiers, and 74 panzers. Anlage zum Ia KTB in RH 10/149 in BA-MA Freiburg i. Br.
6. MS #B-416 (Wietersheim), 7; dated 30 November 1944 but more likely early December. Several dates are off by a few days.
7. Cole, *Lorraine Campaign*, 552–553; Luck, *Panzer Commander*, 178.
8. Hugh Cole, *Lorraine Campaign*, 566, speculates that von Mellenthin had criticized Generaloberst Heinz Guderian, chief of staff at OKH, at various times. Mellenthin, *Panzer Battles*, 336, simply says "Hitler and his entourage" were seeking scapegoats for the "blunders of the Supreme Command." Knobelsdorff and Mellenthin both were later given positions again. Guderian had been appointed Chef des Stabes des Heeres on 21 July 1944 after Gen.Oberst Kurt Zeitzler had resigned 1 July.
9. Cole, *Lorraine Campaign*, 567n.
10. This destroyed C Company/37th Tk Bn and included two artillery forward observer tanks. Note the author's "Return to Singling," *Armor* 94, no. 5 (September–October 1985), 32–39. This was based largely on discussions with Jimmie Leach, B/37, and on Gordon A. Harrison, "Singling," in *Small Unit Actions* (Washington, DC: Historical Division, War Department, 1946), 175–212. MS #B-416 (Wietersheim), 8, incorrectly dates the Singling battle as on 4 December.
11. AAR 6 December 1944 in NARA 604 - INF (51)—0.3; Bayerlein in Harrison, "Singling," 177.
12. Panzer commander advice actually in a lecture by a Bundeswehr Oberst, former Hptm. in 116.Pz.Div. in 1944, to Armor Officer Basic (AOB) Class No. 13 at the Armor School, Fort Knox, Kentucky, May 1964; Karl Zindler letter to author, 1 October 1990. Jimmie Leach wrote Zindler on 2 December 1991 that he believed it was Sgt. Bob Fitzgerald's tank that had knocked him out.
13. *A History of the United States Twelfth Armored Division* (Baton Rouge, LA: Army and Navy Publishing Co., 1947), 27.
14. Cole, *Lorraine Campaign*, 537n.
15. In November, Third Army reported 22,773 battle casualties and at least 15,737 *non*battle casualties. Ibid., 593.
16. MS #B-416 (Wietersheim), 8–9.
17. Luck, *Panzer Commander*, 178.
18. Cole, *Lorraine Campaign*, 592.
19. Transcript of interview of Gen. Hermann Balck by Battelle Laboratories, Columbus, Ohio, 1979, for USAF A-10 project, 11–13.
20. Feindnachrichtenblatt Abt.Ic 4 Dezember 1944, copy to author via Brig. Gen. Bill Molla.
21. Von Eggeling, letter to author 18 July 1997, and Kurt Nentwig among others; discussions with Lt. Col. (ret) Charles Ross.
22. Mellenthin, *Panzer Battles*, 334. Walton Walker alone was from Armor. Note the doctrinal clashes in the author's "Patton's Relief of General Wood," above.
23. Zustandsberichte Meldungen 1.10.1944, 1.11.1944, and 1.12.1944 in BA-MA RH 10/149. The high statistics for the October lull must overlap in some way.
24. Mellenthin, *Panzer Battles*, 332; MS #B-416 (Wietersheim), 8, 10.

CHAPTER 30: EIFEL AND ORSCHOLZRIEGEL

1. Schrodek, *Ihr Glaube*, 319; MS #B-417 (Wietersheim), "Rheinland, Teil III (20. 12.44–10.2.45),"1. The dates of the movement are not clear.
2. Liddell Hart, *German Generals Talk*, 280–281. There are many works on the Ardennes offensive, including Cole, *The Ardennes: Battle of the Bulge*. 6. Pz.Armee was referred to as 6.SS Panzerarmee, though not officially retitled until 1945.
3. Greif, wrote Manteuffel to Robert C. Ringer of the 106th ID, 26 January 1970, "was absolutely against martial law, against the usage of war, and against my feelings."

4. On 17 December Kgr. Peiper had collided with an American convoy of Battery B, 285th Field Artillery Observation Battalion near Malmédy. As the vanguard continued on, American prisoners were rounded up, and shot down by a follow-on element. Subsequently there were incidents when German PWs were shot by their American captors, and there was at least one written order (by HQ 328th IR, 26th ID) of 21 December 1944 that "No SS troops or paratroopers will be taken prisoners but will be shot on sight." There are eighty-four names on the Malmédy memorial at the Baugnez crossroads. Autopsies performed after the recovery of the bodies on 13 January 1945 by the 3060th Quartermaster Graves Registration Company proved that at least forty of the Americans had been deliberately shot in the head. On the other hand, the atrocities of the LAH, and American retaliations, seem to have been isolated incidents.

   After the war a trial was held at Dachau in 1946. Seventy-four Waffen-SS men, including Sepp Dietrich, were tried; forty-three were sentenced to death, and thirty-one to prison terms. But after American Defense Counsel Lt. Col. Willis Everett revealed that "confessions" were extracted by torture, the death sentences were commuted and the Germans paroled after thirteen years at Dachau. Peiper is believed to have been killed while living in Traves, France, by French Communists on 14 July 1976. There are numerous works on the Malmédy case. The military context is in Cole, *Ardennes*, 261–264; note the discussion of "Der Malmedy-Prozess" in Hausser, *Waffen-SS im Einsatz*, 244–261.
5. "Nachrichten" reproduced in Schrodek, *Bild*, 504, and also quoted in *Ihr Glaube*, 319.
6. Scheibert, *Die Träger des deutschen Kreuzes in Gold*; Manfred Dörr und Franz Thomas, *Die Träger der Nahkampfspange in Gold* (Osnabrück: Biblio, 1986).
7. Awards from Fellgiebel, *Die Träger*; Reuschel (photo) in Schrodek, *Bild*, 502. Of the RK des KVK, the award had to be approved by Hitler. Lumsden, *Third Reich Militaria*, 23, says only 225 were awarded; only 137 in Ron Manion, *German Military Collectibles* (Dubuque, IA: Antique Trader Books, 1995), 223.
8. Von Eggeling, letter to author, 10 October 2012, and awards from his Soldbuch (identification booklet) graciously given the author. Urlaub was 1–12 December, per 17 July 2013 letter.
9. Patton: "Hell, let's have the guts to let the ---- -- ------- go all the way to Paris. Then we'll really cut 'em off and chew 'em up." As quoted by Gen. Dwight D. Eisenhower, *Crusade in Europe* (Garden City, NY: Doubleday, 1948), 350.
10. MS #B-417 (Wietersheim), 1. There are discrepancies in dates, Lühl succeeding Stenkhoff 20 December 1944 in Rahn's List, 1 January 1945 in Loschke's List, and the two are not listed in the BA-MA listing.
11. Mellenthin, *Panzer Battles*, 336, refers to "various unsavory intrigues ending in Balck's dismissal," but also that Guderian arranged for him to become commander of 6. Armee in Hungary. Guderian also got Generalmajor von Mellenthin reinstated, if not to the general staff, at least attached to 9.Pz.Div. in the Ardennes, 338.
12. Planning and operations are in Clarke and Smith, *Riviera to the Rhine*, 492ff. Note map on 506.
13. MS #B-417 (Wietersheim), 3; Donnhauser und Drews, *Der Weg*, 174–175. Operations in the Saar–Moselle triangle are in Charles B. MacDonald, *The Last Offensive* (Washington, DC: Office of the Chief of Military History, 1973), 116–134.
14. Lt. Laurence G. Byrnes, ed., *History of the 94th Infantry Division in World War II* (94th Infantry Division Association, 1948; reprinted Nashville, TN: The Battery Press, 1982), 84–130, copy courtesy of Bob Kingsbury, 94th ID; updated by Tony Le Tissier, *Patton's Pawns* (Tuscaloosa: University of Alabama Press, 2007), 37–45. 11.Pz.Div. unit details apparently from PW interrogations. 1st Bn/376th IR held the Tettingen-Butzdorf villages, and companies were attached from 774th TD Bn (towed), 607th TD Bn (M36), and 748th Tk Bn. Attachments listed in Byrnes, 516–517; note the 774th was reequipped with M36s after 26 January. Stanton, *Order of Battle*, 334, 336.
15. Le Tissier, *Pawns*, 55; Byrnes, *94th*, 138; MacDonald, *Last Offensive*, 123. 1st and 2nd Bn, 301st IR had been involved, supported by A Co, 748th Tk Bn.
16. 3rd Bn/302nd IR had relieved 3rd Bn/376th IR. Lt. Col. (ret) Robert Kingsbury, scout in E/376 IR, letter to author 8 May 2006, reproduced as "First Scout for General Patton" (Boston, MA: Camp Constitution Press, 2013), 17.
17. Accounts in Schrodek, *Ihr Glaube*, 320–322.
18. On 30 January Patton and Walker visited the 94th Division and were critical of the fact that nonbattle casualties exceeded battle casualties, along with the high number of surrenders, and threatened to relieve General Malony. Le Tissier, *Pawns*, 83–84. The 8th AD was transferred to Ninth Army in Holland.
19. Byrnes, *94th*, 146–147.
20. MS #B-417 (Wietersheim), 7.
21. Byrnes, *94th*, 154 (and Le Tissier, *Pawns*, 67), refer to the III Battalion of the 110th Panzergrenadiers, though Donnhauser u Drews, *Der Weg*, 177, only refer to "das zusätzliche Bataillon beim Regiment 110 . . . aufgelöst werden."
22. Byrnes, *94th*, 217, 225 (and Le Tissier, *Pawns*, 106, 110). Medical officer Lt. Percy Heidelberger later received the Silver Star with oak leaf cluster. Both authors refer to the Panthers' 75mm gun as "88s," and also mention "Tigers." The travail of the 704th TD Bn is in Gill, *Harpoon*, II-13–II-17.

23. Commanders of I./111 determined by Adjutant Lt. Jürgen von Pflug, letter to author, 6 June 1994, and of II./111 by Adju Ob.Lt. Horst Loch, 30 October 1994, and von Pflug. These contacts had been suggested by Hptm. Franz Thelen, regimental adjutant, in a letter to author, 21 August 1990.

CHAPTER 31: DEFENSE OF THE RHINE

1. Mellenthin, *Panzer Battles*, 343n; statistics in Lyons, *World War II, A Short History*, 269. On 25 January the German army groups were redesignated—Nord becoming Kurland, Weichsel added, Mitte becoming Nord, and A becoming Mitte—with command changes as well. Russian Col. Gen. Aleksandr Vasilevsky succeeded Chernyakovsky when the latter was killed 18 February.
2. Werner Ellger's account in Schrodek, *Ihr Glaube*, 322–323; operations in Christopher Duffy, *Red Storm on the Reich* (New York: Atheneum, 1991), 94ff.
3. Discussion with Walter Volkmann about his "Erinnerung" at Wolfhagen Pz.Rgt.15 Treffen, June 2000. Evgeni Bessonov, *Tank Rider*, 184, denied robbing and raping, "at least" not in his company.
4. Stalag III Luft was the site of a mass escape in 1943 of British RAF personnel (not American), though only three of seventy-six escapees were successful. Stalag was a contraction of Stammlager (main camp); Oflag was Offizierlager.
5. Litvin, *800 Days on the Eastern Front*, 82. Bessonov, *Tank Rider*, 181. There are numerous accounts of the Soviet brutality, including in John Toland, *The Last 100 Days* (New York: Random House, 1966) and Cornelius Ryan, *The Last Battle* (New York: Simon & Schuster, 1966).
6. MS #B-742 (Wietersheim) "Die Kämpfe der 11. Panzer-Division zwischen Roer und Rhein (Rheinland Teil IV) 11.02.45–05.03.45" (Neustadt, 20.11.1947), 3–4.
7. Wolf Keilig, *Das deutsche Heer*, Bd. 2, 211 p.342; Wietersheim in MS #B-742, 4, only refers to "der zur Division kommendierte Generalmajor von Buttlar." Some sources, for example Mitcham, *Panzer Legions*, 106, list him as commander in January 1945. Movements in Donnhauser und Drews, *Der Weg*, 178, and by Jürgen Reichardt, Pz.Rgt.15, in Schrodek, *Ihr Glaube*, 324, though he dates the move north as *19* February.
8. Flak defense and airborne threat from Klaus Bardt, 2002. Command changes from Karl Thieme, letter to author, 23 September 1990.
9. Stanton, *Order of Battle*, 18.
10. Reichardt's account in Schrodek, *Ihr Glaube*, 324–325. He identifies Volks-Grenadier-Regiment 1103, but perhaps Gren.Rgt. 1034, 1035, or 1036 in 59.Inf.Div. was meant.
11. Adju Oblt. Rolf Wandhoff, related by Hptm. Walter Schaefer-Kehnert in letter to author, 26 January 1993.
12. MS #B-742 (Wietersheim), 12–13. Donnhauser und Drews in *Der Weg*, 180, say the order to cross was late on 3/4 March; Wietersheim, 16, says the official permission came on 5/6 March, that before then he could be court-martialed for crossing.
13. Rüther's account in Schrodek, *Ihr Glaube*, 325–326. Assuming its veracity, the American tanks may have been from the 786th Tk Bn attached to the 99th ID, or from 3rd AD.
14. Von Fersen e-mail to author 19 March 2015.
15. Klaus Bardt to author, 12 July 1996.
16. CCB/4th AD drive in Koyen, *Beach to Bavaria*, 89–95 and MacDonald, *Last Offensive*, 201–205. On 8 March Dager went to command 11th AD, and Abrams took over CCB.
17. MS #B-590 (Wietersheim) "Rheinland Teil V (6–21 March 1945)," 2–3; Donnhauser und Drews, *Der Weg*, 181.
18. Mellenthin, *Panzer Battles*, 349; documents related to the movements of Pz.Brig.106 FHH are in Bruns, *Die Panzerbrigade 106 FHH*, 590–602; Henry G. Philipps, *Remagen: Springboard to Victory* (Penn Valley, CA: H. G. Philipps, 1995), 37, says schw.Pz.Jäger Abt. 654 with Jagdpanthers was also available. It had last been in NORDWIND from Colmar. Philipps had been a lieutenant with M Co./47th IR/9th ID.
19. Störmer quoted in Philipps, *Remagen*, 38.
20. Walter Rahn's account in his "Ides of March," 15 March 1994, shared with the author and also Henry Philipps, though slightly different in the latter's *Remagen*, 41–43. In subsequent correspondence, "Red" Philipps and the author conclude Rahn was captured by the 52nd AIB of the 9th AD, attached to the 310th RCT (78th ID) which in turn was attached to the 9th ID in the Kretzlar area.
21. US Strategic Air Force in Europe, Office of the Director of Intelligence, Techn.Int.Rep A 316, 1 May 1945, reproduced in Wilbert Fuhr, *Der Einsatz(flug)hafen Eudenbach* (Königswinter: Wilbert Fuhr, 1998), 197, 202.
22. Donnhauser und Drews, *Der Weg*, 186–187; MS #B-590 (Wietersheim), 9.

CHAPTER 32: FROM GERMANY TO CZECHOSLOVAKIA

1. "Magnificent," messaged Bradley to Patton, quoted in Koyen, *Beach to Bavaria*, 97; "spectacular," says the US official history, MacDonald, *Last Offensive*, 248; Patton's "favorite division," says Weigley, *Eisenhower's Lieutenants*, 953. The 4th AD was one of only three US divisions (of eighty-nine) to be awarded the Presidential Unit Citation (the other two being the 101st Airborne and the 3rd Division).

2. Seventh Army had 12,000 casualties, Third Army had 5,220. Third Army estimated 113,000 German losses including 68,000 PWs opposing it. Seventh Army claimed 22,000 PWs. MacDonald, *Last Offensive*, 264.
3. Ibid., 266–286.
4. MS #B-755 (Wietersheim), "Die Kämpfe der 11.Pz.Div. Zwischen Rhein und Tschechischer Grenze vom 21.3.–15.4.1945" I. Teil, 1–4; March order (for Pz.Rgt.15) 25.3.1945 in Schrodek, *Ihr Glaube*, 327; stragglers from Donnhauser und Drews, *Der Weg*, 187.
5. This was small Task Force Baum ordered by Patton, about which 4th AD veterans are still bitter.
6. Schrodek, *Ihr Glaube*, 330. One is reminded of Rudyard Kipling's "Cripple" towing "Paralytic," disabled British destroyers at Jutland (Skaggerakschlacht), 1916.
7. As reported in the (London) *Daily Mail*, March 20, 1995, 31–32, "Trapped behind enemy lines and saved by a rabbit," copy to author from Professor Schaefer-Kehnert.
8. William S. Triplet, *A Colonel in the Armored Divisions*, ed. Robert H. Ferrell (Columbia and London: University of Missouri Press, 2001), 233, 239. Admiring the German national Autobahn network, General Eisenhower, as later president, championed the construction of a US interstate highway system in 1956.
9. Quoted in MacDonald, *Last Offensive*, 349.
10. Donnhauser und Drews, *Der Weg*, 189.
11. MacDonald, *Last Offensive*, 350. This was the 16th Field Hospital. Koyen, *Beach to Bavaria*, 113 says "the doctors and nurses were released" (by the W-SS).
12. Donnhauser und Drews, *Der Weg*, 189–190; MS #B-755 (Wietersheim), 6. It is not easy to judge when a commander should acknowledge that a conflict is lost, and surrender his forces. Should Friedrich II der Grosse, his forces exhausted and abandoned by his English ally, have surrendered to his enemies in 1761? In American history, should Gen. George Washington, beset with betrayal and mutiny in the Continental Army, have given up in early 1781? Should Confederate general Robert E. Lee have surrendered with the fall of Petersburg and Richmond in April 1865?
13. Lothar Trenkler to author, June 2004.
14. Koyen, *Beach to Bavaria*, 112–113.
15. MacDonald, *Last Offensive*, 376–377; not in Koyen, *Beach to Bavaria*, 115.
16. Klaus Bardt to author, 25 September 1996. That the extent of the Nazi criminality was generally not known was also true of Jews and part-Jewish Mischlinge who received exemptions to fight in the Wehrmacht even as relatives died in the Holocaust. Rigg, *Lives of Hitler's Jewish Soldiers*, 130, 276.
17. Reichardt in Schrodek, *Ihr Glaube*, 330; MS #B-755 (Wietersheim), 10–13; Donnhauser und Drews, *Der Weg*, 192–193; reconstitution of Pz.G.R.111 from correspondence of Hptm. Franz Thelen, Adju of Pz.G.R.111, and Lt. Jürgen von Pflug, Adju of I.Btl./111 with Henry G. Philipps, January 1995, and with author.
18. Sketch map of Greiz positions in Schrodek, *Ihr Glaube*, 331, and in his *Bild*, 514.
19. Donnhauser und Drews, *Der Weg*, 193; Schrodek, *Ihr Glaube*, 331; MS #B-755 (Wietersheim), 16.
20. Panzerjägers from Donnhauser und Drews, *Der Weg*, 193, other numbers in MS #B-756 by Ia Werner Drews, "Die Kämpfe der 11. Panzer-Division zwischen Rhein und tschechischer Grenze vom 16. April bis 4. Mai 1945"; written by Drews while in American captivity at Neustadt in 1948, the numbers are suspect; 7. Armee return of 21 April 1945 in MacDonald, *Last Offensive*, 466; Ralph Bennett, *Ultra in the West* (London: Hutchinson & Co., 1979), 233.
21. MacDonald, *Last Offensive*, 416–417, 480; Frhr. von Fersen e-mail to author, 13 April 2012.
22. MS #B-756 (Drews), 6; Frhr. von Fersen e-mail to author 18 Juli 2014, and 1 September 2014; Schrodek, *Ihr Glaube*, 335–337; Klaus Bardt to author 19 April 1996.

CHAPTER 33: THE GESPENSTER-DIVISION DISMOUNTS

1. The negotiated surrender of the 11. Panzer-Division was the subject of the author's "Die 11.PD sitz ab" (The 11th Panzer Division Dismounts—an old cavalry term, suggested by Klaus Bardt), trans. Klaus Bardt and facilitated by Gerhard Winkler (both of Pz.Rgt.15), in *Deutsche Militärzeitschrift (DMZ)* (Bad Soden-Salmünster) Teil I Heft Nr.34 (Juli–August 2003): 87–90; Teil II Nr.35 (Sept.–Okt. 2003): 62–66; also in *Soldat im Volk* (Bonn), 1.Teil in Heft 53. Jahrgang Nr.3 (Mai–Juni 2004): 89–97; 2. Teil Nr.4 (Juli–August 2004): 146–150.
2. Karl Thieme, letter to Gen. William Molla (26th YD), 14 December 1994, copy to author; IPW report quoted in Lt. Col. George Dyer, *XII Corps: Spearhead of Patton's Third Army* (Baton Rouge: Military Press of Louisiana, c. 1947), 426.
3. The German account is by Oblt. Klaus Knorr, "Die letzten Stunden der 11. Panzer-Division," and has been reprinted in the annual programs of the division Treffen (reunions) in May in Kötzting, Bavaria.
4. Schrodek, *Bild*, 524, says Buttlar came up the night of 4/5 May; Klaus Groeger, letter to author, 8 November 1995.
5. The three vehicles were identified as "peeps" (tankers' term for jeeps) in the account in "Carry On," the newssheet of the 359th IR, 90th ID for Saturday 5 May 1945, copy provided by Allan Tribett, a BAR man with F Company, to author 8 January 1996. "Three small armored cars" were referred to in Gene Currivan's

article as published by The *New York Times* and the *Boston Herald* on Sunday 6 May 1945, copies provided by Brig. Gen. Raymond E. Bell Jr., son of Colonel Bell, who has shared his own research on the topic with the author. Bell published his account of the role the 359th IR played in "Giving Up the Ghost," *WW II History* magazine (September 2005). Klaus Knorr was unable to confirm details when the author asked him at the 1995 Treffen, and he passed away the next year.

6. John Colby, *War from the Ground Up* [90th Infantry Division] (Austin, TX: Nortex Press, 1991), 466–467.
7. 359th IR newssheet "Carry On" for Friday 4 May 1945. The surrender episode is compiled from personal accounts and the NARA unit records, the 90th ID indexed as 390-INF, including the 90th G-3 Journal, the 359th Regimental Journal, and the A/A Rpts (After Action Reports).
8. Dyer, *XII Corps*, 426; Knorr, 11.Pz.Div. Treffen programs; Wietersheim's offer is photocopied in Schrodek, *Bild*, 515, and translated in Colby, *War from the Ground Up*, 467, and in other sources.
9. E. W. Beckman to author, 27 December 1995. Surrender arrangements are best detailed in the 359th Regimental Journal of 4 May 1945 and in the A/A Rpt.
10. 359th IR newssheet "Carry On," 4 May 1945; photos reflect the atmosphere of the meeting with GIs milling around the farm area, as in Colby, Schrodek's *Bild*, and the 90th Division and regimental history books, *The 90th* (1946) and *Album 359* (1945). Knorr says the meeting took place in a farmhouse near Eschlkam, but the after-action reports and other contemporary sources identify Vseruby. The photo in *Bild*, 515, is captioned Oberst Reed, but the star on the helmet indicates Brig. Gen. Earnest. In May 1995 this author joined with Generals Ray Bell Jr. and William Molla, and Gespenster veterans Walter Rahn and Gerhard Otto, in driving around the area, identifying routes and sites of the surrender. In 2000 General Bell identified the house itself, in a letter to author of 2 October 2001.
11. 359th IR "Carry On" and the *New York Times* and *Boston Herald* articles, 6 May 1945.
12. 90th ID G-3 journal, 4 May 1945; routes corroborated by Oberstlt. Karl Thieme to author 11 July 1995 as in 90th ID after-action report, and some details from Maj. Jürgen Reichardt to author 17 September 1990; Schrodek, *Ihr Glaube*, 337–338; Donnhauser und Drews, *Der Weg*, 196 gives routes as Furth im Wald and Bayerisch Eisenstein, repeated in several accounts, but the latter was not a major route.
13. Lt. Gen. O. C. Talbott, letter to author, 22 September 1995; Colby, *War from the Ground Up*, 467–469; Traverse Hall, letter to author, 26 December 1995; Frhr. von Fersen, letter to author, 16 August 1997.
14. Klaus Groeger, letter to author, 29 June 1995; Allan Tribett, letter to author, January 8, 1996. A detailed list, broken down by unit, is in the 90th Division's after-action report for 5 May 1945.
15. Details of this unit are from Franz Oexler, letter to author, 4 October 1995; Kgr. Buttlar is in Schrodek, *Bild*, 524–525.
16. 101st regimental journal; 26th ID records are in NARA II RG 407, 326-INF (101)-0. US Army World War II unit records were moved from NA Suitland, Maryland, to NA II College Park, Maryland.
17. 101st regimental journal; also War Diary of Commanding Officer, 101st Infantry, 1–9 May 1945. Details are from General Molla, then Assistant S-3 of the 101st, and by Bill Connors, 26th ID, to author 21 September 1994. Pfc Richard Courtney of L Co., in his *Normandy to the Bulge*, 103–104, relates being approached by a tank column and a general in a Mercedes who offered to surrender the 11th Panzer Division to *him*—but he may be embellishing a bit.
18. IPW Reports 06 2000 May 1945 and 07 1900 May 1945 by Lt. Col. John Cotter, AC of S, G-2 (26th Division).
19. Details in Donnhauser und Drews, *Der Weg*, 195; Schrodek, *Bild*, 524–525; and in unit journal of 3rd Bn/101st Inf. Route confirmed to author by Franz Oexler in a letter 4 October 1995.
20. 2nd Cav Group (M) report of operations, 30 Oct 1945, in Constabulary Reports in NA II RG 94. Note also the revealing photos of Reed and the Soviets in Schrodek, *Bild*, 516.
21. Schrodek, *Ihr Glaube*, 339.
22. Unit sites identified by Oexler, Thieme, and Groeger. Photos of the last review in Schrodek, *Bild*, 518–521. Franz Oexler was instrumental in organizing the post-war German-American reunions at Kötzting until his death in 1996. Reed, letter to Eddy, copy provided to author by General Molla, and quoted in *Yankee Doings* (January–February 1987), 18. The brief reference in the US Army official history, *The Last Offensive*, 467, which says "the remnants of the division marched with their commander, General von Wietersheim, to prisoner-of-war cages," is incorrect. Drs. Martin Blumenson and Hugh Cole, military historians with Third Army earlier, do not have direct knowledge of the 11. Panzer surrender. Letters to author of 28 July and 7 September 2000, respectively.
23. Quoted in *Mittelbayerische Zeitung*, 6/7 May 1995, 8, covering the fiftieth anniversary Treffen in Kötzting, and in author's conversations with Sperl there. The author is indebted to Werner von Koblinski, 11.Pz.Div., who compiled, photocopied, and collated the special reports in the area newspapers related to the reunion, sending them 22 June 1995. Christel Bobeth's experiences, copy to author, August 1995.

24. Process from Ferdinand Sperl, telephone interview, 2 May 1995, and conversations at Kötzting in June 1995; Klaus Bardt, Pz.Rgt.15, copy of discharge paper and letter, 12 June 2000; discharge center organization in S-3 report in 2nd Cav Group (M) report of operations, 30 Oct 1945, in NA II RG 94.
25. Col. C. Hancock Reed, letter to General Molla, January 4, 1974. This attitude and treatment is in marked contrast to that befalling thousands of German PWs held in American barbed-wire enclosures exposed to the elements, even if perhaps the numbers of deaths given in James Bacque's *Other Losses* (Don Mills, Ontario: Stoddard, 1989; Toronto: General Paperbacks, 1991) are exaggerated.
26. 2nd Cav Group (M) Reports of Operations, 30 Oct 1945, 29 Jan 1946, 30 Apr 1946, in NA II RG 94.
27. Reed, letter to Eddy, in *Yankee Doings* (January–February 1987), 18.
28. Sperl to author by telephone, 2 May 1995; Dyer, *XII Corps*, 426.
29. Details are from Sperl; Dr.med.vet. Rudolf Lessing, "Die Lipizzaner in Hostau 1945," in the 11.Pz.Div. Jahrestreffen programs; Dyer, *XII Corps*, 426; Mary E. Lightstone of the US Lipizzan Association, discussions at Kötzting in June 1995 and letter to author, 18 December 2001; specials in the *Kötztinger Zeitung*, 11 Mai 1995, 14, and in the *Mittelbayerische Zeitung*, 6/7 Mai 1995, 8–9.
30. Dyer, 426; Patton's diary entry for 7 May 1945 with Podhajsky's address in Blumenson, ed., *The Patton Papers*, vol. 2. Patton attended another demonstration in August.
31. The episode was the subject of a 1963 Walt Disney movie, *Miracle of the White Stallions* [*sic*; the horses were mares]. Dr. Lessing related the experience to the author's wife, Diane, on a visit back to Hostoun, Czech Republic, 12 May 1995.
32. Accounts by Sperl in May 1995 articles in *Mittelbayerische Zeitung* and *Kötztinger Zeitung*; 2nd Constabulary Report of Operations, 11 Nov 1946, in NA II, RG 94, CNRG-2-0.3.

CHAPTER 34: EPILOGUE

1. "Memories of My Time as a Prisoner of the US Army in France," by Walter Rahn, n.d., copy to author 15 December 1995. William E. "Buddy" Warren translated a number of Walter Rahn's writings into English. After release from Soviet captivity in 1950, Oberst Heinz-Georg Lemm served in the Bundeswehr, retiring as a Generalleutnant.
2. The conditions and details are vividly portrayed in James Bacque's *Other Losses*. His evidence of Eisenhower's callousness has been challenged by American historian Stephen Ambrose and English historian John Keegan among others, though admitting further investigation is needed. Note the caustic comments of British Brig. Gen. Desmond Young (himself a prisoner of war) about Eisenhower's "crusade" convictions in his *Rommel* (1950), chapter 8.III. "Civil War" (138–139). PW camps in the United States were also ordered to reduce rations and services in March 1945 as at Aliceville, Alabama, presumably by the War Department through the OPMG (Office of the Provost Marshal General). Note the exhibits in the Aliceville Camp Museum. Here at least local produce alleviated the harshness, and a number of former German PWs would revisit the camp years later, because of the fairness of the American guards and generosity of the local population.
3. Tagebuch, copy to author from Walter Schaefer-Kehnert, who received it from his friend's widow in 1995.
4. Cablegram from 11.Pz.Div. to Yankee Division Veterans Association 26 August 1993, copies to author from General Molla (26th YD) and from Karl Heinz Loschke (11.Pz.Div.); 2nd Cavalry Association newsletter *Thoroughbred* (March 1996); address by Louis Holz (2nd Cavalry) given, and printed in the 11.Panzer's 50. Jahrestreffen program, for the Kötzting reunion 11–14 May 1995.
5. It might be noted that the US 4th Armored Division had 1,519 KIA (killed in action) in its ten months of combat, July 1944 to May 1945. Koyen, *Beach to Bavaria*, dedication.
6. Schrodek, *Ihr Glaube*, 342, 347–348; annual "Rundschreiben" of ehemalige (circular of the former) Pz.Rgt.15 by Sprecher Ansgar Pawelke.
7. Martin Blumenson, *Patton* (New York: William Morrow and Co., 1985), 239.
8. Liddell Hart, *History of the Second World War*, 557n.
9. As quoted in *The Tank Commander's Guide*, ed. William L. Warnick, Lt. Col. John G. Cook, USA, Ret., and Dr. Robert A. Baker (Harrisburg, PA: Stackpole, 1963), 78–79: "The ROAD [Reorganization Objective Army Division, 1962] concept permits the formation of tailor-made units, utilizing various combinations or 'mixes' of six to fifteen combat battalions . . . as interchangeable building blocks added to the common division base . . . tailored to a particular task."

BIBLIOGRAPHY

Unpublished sources essential to this study were communications with 11. Panzer veterans and the division unit records microfilmed by the US National Archives and Records Administration (NARA) in Microfilm Publication T315 (Records of Army Divisions). The 11. Pz.Div. records date from 1940 to 1943 (22 DVDs) but lack the records for 1944–45. Other unpublished materials are located at the Bundesarchiv-Militärarchiv (BA-MA), Freiburg im Breisgau; the USAMHI (US Army Military History Institute) archives at the US Army Heritage and Education Center (USAHEC), Carlisle, Pennsylvania; and the US Army Center of Military History (CMH), Washington, DC. The published sources are limited only to works actually cited.

Anderson, Trezzvant W. *Come Out Fighting*. Salzburg: Salzburger Druckerei und Verlag, 1945.

Angolia, LTC John R. *On the Field of Honor*. Vol. 2. Stillwell, KS: John R. Angolia, 1980.

Arad, Yitzhak, Schmuel Krakowski, and Schmuel Spector, eds. *The Einsatzgruppen Reports*. Translated by Stella Schossberger. New York: Holocaust Library, 1989.

"Armor vs. Mud and Mines." Ft. Knox, KY: Armor School Manuscript (ARMS), 1950.

Armstrong, John A., ed. *Soviet Partisans in World War II*. Madison: University of Wisconsin Press, 1964.

Aubrey, Brigadier C., and Otto Heilbrunn. *Communist Guerilla Warfare*. London: George Allen & Unwin, 1951.

Bacque, James. *Other Losses*. Don Mills, Ontario: Stoddard, 1989. Reprint, Toronto: General Paperbacks, 1991.

Balck, Hermann. *Ordnung im Chaos. Erinnerungen 1893–1948*. Osnabrück: Biblio Verlag, 1981.

Baldwin, Hanson. *Tiger Jack*. Ft. Collins, CO: Old Army Press, 1979.

Bartov, Omer, Atina Grossmann, and Mary Nolan. *Crimes of War*. New York: New Press, 2002.

Bartov, Omer. *The Eastern Front, 1941–1945*. 2nd ed. New York: Palgrave, 2001.

———. *Hitler's Army*. New York: Oxford University Press, 1991.

Beevor, Antony. *Stalingrad*. New York: Viking, 1998.

Bell, Brig. Gen. Raymond E., Jr. "Giving up the Ghost." *WWII History* (September 2005).

Bennett, Ralph. *Ultra in the West*. London: Hutchinson & Co., 1979.

Bessonov, Evgeni. *Tank Rider*. Translated by Bair Irincheev. Mechanicsburg, PA: Stackpole, 2003.

Bethell, Nicholas. *The War Hitler Won: The Fall of Poland*. New York: Holt, Rinehart and Winston, 1972.

Blau, George E. *The German Campaigns in the Balkans*. Washington, DC: Department of the Army Pamphlet No. 20-260, November 1953.

———. *The German Campaign in Russia*. Washington, DC: Department of the Army Pamphlet No. 20-261, March 1955.

Blumenson, Martin. *Breakout and Pursuit*. Washington, DC: Department of the Army, 1961.

———, ed. *The Patton Papers*. Vol. 2. Boston: Houghton Mifflin, 1974.

———. *Patton*. New York: William Morrow and Co., 1985.

Boyne, Walter J. *Clash of Wings*. New York: Simon & Schuster, 1994. Reprint, New York: Touchstone, 1997.

Bruns, Friedrich. *Die Panzerbrigade 106 FHH*. Celle: Friedrich Bruns, 1991.

Burdick, Charles, and Hans-Adolf Jacobsen, eds. *The Halder War Diary, 1939–1942*. Novato, CA: Presidio, 1988. Abridged.

Butcher, Captain Harry C., USNR. *My Three Years with Eisenhower*. New York: Simon & Schuster, 1946.

Byrnes, Lt. Laurence G., ed. *History of the 94th Infantry Division in World War II*. 94th Infantry Division Association, 1948. Reprint, Nashville, TN: The Battery Press, 1982.

Caidin, Martin. *The Tigers Are Burning*. New York: Hawthorne Books, 1974.

Carell, Paul. *Hitler Moves East 1941–1943*. Translated by Ewald Osers. Boston: Little, Brown & Co., 1965. Reprint, New York: Bantam, 1966.

———. *Scorched Earth*. Translated by Ewald Osers. New York: Ballantine, 1966. Reprint, 1971.

Carius, Otto. *Tigers in the Mud*. Translated by Robert J. Edwards. Mechanicsburg, PA: Stackpole, 2003.

Chandler, Alfred D., Jr., ed. *The Papers of Dwight D. Eisenhower*. 5 vols. *The War Years*. Baltimore and London: John Hopkins University Press, 1970.

Chapman, Guy. *Why France Fell*. New York: Holt, Rinehart and Winston, 1968.

Chazalon, Thierry. *Nationale 7: La Route de la Mort*. Privately printed, 2008.

Christern, Hans. *Die "Roten Teufel" und Ihr Kommandeur*. Munich: Zentral Verlag der NSDAP, Franz Eher Nachf., 1941.

Clark, Alan. *Barbarossa*. New York: William Morrow & Co., 1965. Reprint, 1985.

Clarke, Jeffrey J., and Robert Ross Smith. *Riviera to the Rhine*. Washington, DC: Center of Military History, 1993.

Colby, John. *War from the Ground Up*. Austin, TX: Nortex Press, 1991.

Cole, Hugh M. *The Ardennes: Battle of the Bulge*. Washington, DC: Office of the Chief of Military History, 1965.

———. *The Lorraine Campaign*. Washington, DC: Department of the Army, 1950.

Cornish, Nik. *Images of Kursk*. London: Brassey's, 2002.

Courtney, Pfc Richard D. *Normandy to the Bulge*. Carbondale & Edwardsville: Southern Illinois University Press, 1977.

Crow, Duncan, and Robert J. Ickes. *Encyclopedia of Armoured Cars and Half-tracks*. Secaucus, NJ: Chartwell Books, 1976.

Dallin, Alexander. *German Rule in Russia*. New York: St. Martin's Press, 1957.

Danby, Jeff. *The Day of the Panzer*. Drexel Hill, PA: Casemate, 2008.

Davies, W. J. K. *German Army Handbook 1939–1945*. New York: Arco, 1974.

———. *Panzer Regiments*. London: Almark, 1978.

Deighton, Len. *Blitzkrieg*. New York: Alfred A. Knopf, 1980.

DiNardo, Richard L. *Germany and the Axis Powers*. Lawrence: University Press of Kansas, 2005.

———. *Germany's Panzer Arm*. Westport, CT: Greenwood, 1997.

Dörr, Manfred, and Franz Thomas. *Die Träger der Nahkampfspange in Gold*. Osnabrück: Biblio Verlag, 1986.

Donnhauser, Oberstleutnant a.D. Anton J., and Generalmajor Werner Drews. *Der Weg der 11. Panzer-Division*. Bad Wörishofen: Holzmann-Druck-Service, 1982.

Doughty, Col. Robert A. *The Breaking Point: Sedan and the Fall of France, 1940*. Hamden, CT: Archon, 1990.

Duffy, Christopher. *Red Storm on the Reich*. New York: Atheneum, 1991.

Dunn, Walter S., Jr. *Kursk*. Westport, CT: Praeger, 1997.

Dyer, Lt. Col. George. *XII Corps: Spearhead of Patton's Third Army*. Baton Rouge, LA: Military Press of Louisiana., ca. 1947.

Edmonds, Brig. Gen. Sir James. *France and Belgium 1917*. Vol. 2. London: H. M. Stationary Office, 1948.

———. *Military Operations: France and Belgium, 1918 (March–April)*. London: MacMillan & Co., 1937.

Effects of Climate on Combat in European Russia. Washington, DC: Department of the Army Pamphlet No. 20-291, February 1952.

Eisenhower, Dwight D. *Crusade in Europe*. Garden City, New York: Doubleday & Co., 1948.

Erickson, John. *The Road to Stalingrad*. Boulder, CO: Westview, 1975. Reprint, 1984.

Esposito, Brig. Gen. Vincent J. *A Concise History of World War II*. New York: Praeger, 1964.

———. *The West Point Atlas of American Wars*. Vol. II. New York: Praeger, 1959. Reprint, 1964.

Feist, Uwe. *The German Panzers*. Fallbrook, CA: Arco, 1966.

Fellgiebel, Walther-Peer. *Die Träger des Ritterkreuzes des Eisernen Kreuzes 1939–1945*. Friedberg: Podzun-Pallas Verlag, 1986.

Fey, Will. *Armor Battles of the Waffen-SS*. Translated by Henri Henschler. Mechanicsburg, PA: Stackpole, 1990.

———. *Panzer im Brennpunkt der Fronten*. Munich: J. F. Lehmanns Verlag, 1960.

Field Manual 17-100. *The Armored Division*. Washington, DC: War Department, 15 January 1944.

Field Manual 17-12. *Tank Gunnery*. Washington, DC: War Department, 22 April 1943.

Foss, Christopher F., ed. *The Encyclopedia of Tanks and Armored Fighting Vehicles*. San Diego, CA: Thunder Bay, 2002.

Fox, Don M. *Patton's Vanguard*. Jefferson, NC: McFarland & Co., 2003.

Frankel, Nat, and Larry Smith. *Patton's Best*. New York: Hawthorne, 1978.

Franks, Reinhard. *Trucks of the Wehrmacht*. Translated by Dr. Edward Force. Atglen, PA: Schiffer, 1994.

Fuhr, Wilbert. *Der Einsatz(flug)hafen Eudenbach*. Königswiter: Wilbert Fuhr, 1998.

Funk, Arthur L. *Hidden Ally*. Westport, CT: Greenwood, 1992.

———. "Mandate for Surrender." *World War II* (March 1990): 27–33.

Galland, Adolf. *The First and the Last*. Translated by Mervyn Savill. New York: Henry Holt & Co., 1954.

Ganz, A. Harding. "Die 11. PD sitzt ab." Translated by Klaus Bardt. *Deutsche Militärzeitschrift (DMZ)*. Bad Soden-Salmünster. Teil I Heft Nr. 34 (July/August 2003): 87–90; Teil II Nr. 35 (September/October 2003): 62–66. Also in *Soldat im Volk*. Bonn. 1. Teil in Heft 53. Jahrgang Nr. 3 (May/June 2004): 89–97; 2. Teil Nr. 4 (July/August 2004): 145–150.

———. "The 11th Panzers in the Defense, 1944." *Armor* 103, no. 2 (March/April 1994): 26–37.

———. "Patton's Relief of General Wood." *Journal of Military History* 53, no. 3 (July 1989): 257–273.

———. "Questionable Objective: The Brittany Ports, 1944." *Journal of Military History* 59, no. 1 (January 1995): 77–95.

———. "Return to Singling." *Armor* 94, no. 5 (September/October 1985): 32–39.

German Defense Tactics against Russian Break-Throughs. Washington, DC: Department of the Army Pamphlet No. 20-233, October 1951.

German Military Symbols. Washington, DC: Military Intelligence Service, January 1943.

Gill, Lonnie, ed. *Code Name: Harpoon*. La Puente, CA: Baron, 1982.

Glantz, David M. and Jonathan M. House. *The Battle of Kursk*. Lawrence: University Press of Kansas, 1999.

Glantz, David M. *From the Don to the Dnepr*. London: Frank Cass, 1991.

———. *Soviet Military Intelligence in War*. London: Frank Cass, 1990.

Glantz, David M., and Jonathan M. House. *When Titans Clashed*. Lawrence: University Press of Kansas, 1995.

Goerlitz, Walter. *The German General Staff*. Translated by Brian Battershaw. New York: Praeger, 1952.

Griess, Thomas E., ed. *Campaign Atlas to the Second World War*. Wayne, NJ: Avery, 1989.

Griesser, Volker. *The Lions of Carentan*. Drexel Hill, PA: Casemate, 2011.

Guderian, Heinz. *Panzer Leader*. Translated by Constantine Fitzgibbon. New York: Ballantine, 1957.

Hart, Russell A. *Guderian: Panzer Pioneer or Myth Maker?* Washington, DC: Potomac Books, 2006.

Hart, Drs. Stephen and Russell. *German Tanks of World War II*. London: Brown, 1999.

Hardesty, Von. *Red Phoenix*. Washington, DC: Smithsonian Institution Press, 1982. Reprint, 1991.

Harrison, Gordon A. *Cross Channel Attack*. Washington, DC: Department of the Army, 1951.

———. "Singling." In *Small Unit Actions*. Washington, DC: Historical Division, War Department, 1946: 175–212.

Haupt,, Werner. *Army Group South*. Translated by Joseph G. Welsh. Atglen, PA: Schiffer, 1998.

Hausser, Paul. *Waffen-SS im Einsatz*. Göttingen: Plesse Verlag K. W. Schütz, 1953.

Healy, Mark. *Zitadelle*. Brimscombe Port Stroud, Gloucestershire: History Press, 2008.

Hilberg, Raul. *The Destruction of the European Jews*. New York: Holmes & Meier, 1985.

A History of the United States Twelfth Armored Division. Baton Rouge, LA: Army and Navy Publishing Co., 1947.

Hofmann, George F. *The Super Sixth*. Louisville, KY: 6th Armored Division Association, 1975.

Hogg, Ian V. *Encyclopedia of Infantry Weapons of World War II*. Greenwich, CT: Bison, 1977.

Horne, Alistair. *The Price of Glory: Verdun 1916*. New York: Penguin, 1978.

Howell, Edgar M. *The Soviet Partisan Movement*. DA 20-244. Washington, DC: Department of the Army, 1956.

Hughes, Dr. Matthew, and Dr. Chris Mann. *Fighting Techniques of a Panzergrenadier 1941–1945*. Osceola, WI: MBI, 2000.

Icks, Lt. Col. Robert S. *Tanks and Armored Vehicles*. New York: Duell, Sloan and Pearce, 1945.

Irving, David. *The Trail of the Fox*. New York: E. P. Dutton, 1977.

Jackson, Julian. *The Fall of France*. New York: Oxford University Press, 2004.

Jentz, Thomas L. *Germany's Panther Tank*. Atglen, PA: Schiffer, 1995.

———, ed. *Panzertruppen*. Atglen, PA: Schiffer, 1996.

Johann, A. E. *Zwischen Westwall und Maginotlinie*. Berlin: Im Deutschen Verlag, 1939.

Kahn, David. *The Code Breakers*. New York: MacMillan, 1967.

Kamenir, Victor J. *The Bloody Triangle*. Minneapolis: Zenith, 2008.

Keilig, Wolf. *Das deutsche Heer*. Band II. Bad Nauheim: Podzun Verlag, 1956.

Kennedy, Maj. Robert M. *The German Campaign in Poland*. DA No. 20-255. Washington, DC: Department of the Army, 1956.

Klink, Ernst. *Das Gesetz des Handelns*. Stuttgart: Deutsche Verlags-Anstalt, 1966.

Knappe, Siegfried, with Ted Brusaw. *Soldat*. New York: Dell, 1992.

Knorr, Klaus. "Die letzen Stunden der 11. Panzer-Division." *Jahrestreffen* (annual reunion programs of the former 11. Panzer-Division).

Koyen, Kenneth. *The Fourth Armored Division from the Beach to Bavaria*. Munich: Herder Druck, 1946.

Krackow, Juergen. *Die Genehmigung*. Mainz-Munich: v. Hase & Koehler Verlag, 1991.

Kurowski, Franz. *Deadlock Before Moscow*. West Chester, PA: Schiffer, 1992.

———. *Die Panzer-Lehr-Division*. Bad Nauheim: Podzun-Verlag, 1964.

———, and Gottfried Tornau. *Sturmgeschütze*. Würzburg: Verlagshaus Würzburg GmbH & Co., 2008.

Leers, Walter von, ed. *Zöglinge der Ritterakademie zu Brandenburg a.H.* Cologne: Gerhard Heinrigs, Werdedruck und Verlag, n.d. [1970].

Le Tissier, Tony. *Patton's Pawns*. Tuscaloosa: University of Alabama Press, 2007.

Liddell Hart, B. H. *The German Generals Talk*. New York: William Morrow, 1948.

———. *History of the Second World War*. New York: G. P. Putnam's Sons, 1971. Reprint, New York: Perigee, 1982.

———, ed. *The Rommel Papers*. London: Collins, 1953.

Litvin, Nikolai. *800 Days on the Eastern Front*. Translated and edited by Stuart Britton. Lawrence: University Press of Kansas, 2007.

Lucas, James. *War on the Eastern Front*. Novato, CA: Presidio Press,1979.

Luck, Hans von. *Panzer Commander*. New York: Praeger, 1989.

Ludewig, Joachim. *Rückzug*. Edited by Maj. Gen. David Zabecki. Lexington: University Press of Kentucky, 2012.

Lumsden, Robin. *Third Reich Militaria*. London: Ian Allen, 1987. Reprint, 1990.

Luther, Craig W. H. *Barbarossa Unleashed*. Atglen, PA: Schiffer, 2013.

Luttichau, Charles V. P. von. Unpublished manuscript for Office of the Chief of Military History, Washington, DC: 1958; esp. MS Nos. R-106, R-111, R-112, R-113.

Lyons, Michael J. *World War II: A Short History*. 4th ed. Upper Saddle River, NJ: Pearson Prentice Hall, 2004.

MacDonald, Charles B. *Company Commander*. New York: Ballantine, 1947. Reprint, 1984.

———. *The Last Offensive*. Washington, DC: Office of the Chief of Military History, 1973.

———. *The Siegfried Line Campaign*. Washington, DC: Office of the Chief of Military History, 1963.

Macksey, Kenneth. *Guderian*. London: Greenhill Books, 1992.

———. *Tank Warfare*. New York: Stein and Day, 1972.

Manion, Ron. *German Military Collectibles*. Dubuque, IA: Antique Trader Books, 1995.

Manstein, Field Marshal Erich von. *Lost Victories*. Translated by Anthony G. Powell. Novato, CA: Presidio, 1982.

———, Generalfeldmarschall. *Verlorene Siege*. Bonn: Athenäum-Verlag, 1955.

Manteuffel, Hasso von. *Die 7. Panzer-Division im Zweiten Weltkrieg*. Traditionsverband ehem. 7. Panzer-Division-Kameradenhilfe e.V., n.d. [1965].

Mark, Jason D. *Death of the Leaping Horseman*. Sydney: Jason D. Mark, 2003.

McCormick, Robert W. *Cockney*. Worthington, OH: Cottonwood, 1983.

Mellenthin, Maj. Gen. F. W. von. *German Generals of World War II As I Saw Them*. Norman: University of Oklahoma Press, 1977.

———. *Panzer Battles*. Translated by H. Betzler, edited by L. C. F. Turner. Norman: University of Oklahoma Press, 1956.

Melvin, [British] Maj. Gen. Mungo. *Manstein*. New York: St. Martin's Press, 2010.

Menzel, Jochen. *Der Löwe von Lyon*. Berg am See: Kurt Vowinckel Verlag, 1988.

Mitcham, Samuel W., Jr. *The Panzer Legions*. Mechanicsburg, PA: Stackpole, 2007.

———. *Retreat to the Reich*. Westport, CT: Praeger, 2000.

Muller, Richard. *The German Air War in Russia*. Baltimore: Nautical & Aviation Publishing Co., 1992.

Nafziger, George F. *German Order of Battle: Infantry in World War II*. London: Greenhill Books, and Mechanicsburg, PA: Stackpole, 2000.

———. *German Order of Battle: Panzers and Artillery in World War II*. London: Greenhill Books, and Mechanicsburg, PA: Stackpole, 1999.

"The Nancy Bridgehead." Ft. Knox, KY: Armor School Manuscript (ARMS), 1946.

Nash, Douglas E. *Hell's Gate*. Southbury, CT: RZM Imports, 2002.

Nehring, General Walther. *Die Geschichte der deutschen Panzerwaffe, 1919 bis 1945*. Berlin: Propyläen Verlag, 1969.

Newton, Steven H. *Kursk: The German View*. Cambridge, MA: DaCapo, 2002.

Nipe, George M. *Blood, Steel and Myth*. Stamford, CT: RZM, 2011.

Novak, Dr. Hugo. *Geschichte der ostpreussischen Leichten Flakabteilung 71*. 4 vols. Siegen: n.p., 1980–1983.

Ogorkiewicz, Richard M. *Armor: A History of Mechanized Forces*. New York: Praeger, 1960.

———. "The Structure and Functions of Armored Divisions." Part II. *Armor* 67, no. 2 (March/April 1958): 38–42.

Operations of Encircled Forces. Washington, DC: Department of the Army Pamphlet No. 20-234, January 1952.

Pallud, Jean Paul. "Panzer Attack in Lorraine." *After the Battle*, no. 83. London: Battle of Britain Prints International, 1994: 30–53.

Philipps, Henry G. *Remagen: Springboard to Victory*. Penn Valley, CA: H. G. Philipps, 1995.

Piekalkiewicz, Janusz. *Operation "Citadel"*. Translated by Michaela Nierhaus. Novato, CA: Presidio, 1987.

Pimlott, John, ed. *Rommel and his Art of War*. London: Greenhill, 1994; Mechanicsburg, PA: Stackpole, 2003.

Pitt, Barrie. 1918: *The Last Act*. New York: Ballantine, 1963.

Pogue, Forrest C. *The Supreme Command*. Washington, DC: Department of the Army, 1954.

Reichsarchiv. *Der Weltkrieg 1914–1918*. Bd. 14. Berlin: Ernst Siegfried Mittler und Sohn, 1919/1944/1956.

Rigg, Bryan Mark. *Hitler's Jewish Soldiers*. Lawrence: University Press of Kansas, 2002.

———. *Lives of Hitler's Jewish Soldiers*. Lawrence: University Press of Kansas, 2009.

Rikmenspoel, Marc J. *Waffen-SS Encyclopedia*. Bedford, PA: Aberjona Press, 2004.

Ritgen, Helmut. *Die Geschichte der Panzer-Lehr-Division im Westen 1944–1945*. Stuttgart: Motorbuch Verlag, 1979.

Royal Armoured Corps Centre Tank Museum booklets (by nation). Bovington Camp, Wareham, Dorset.

Rudel, Hans Ulrich. *Stuka Pilot*. New York: Ballantine, 1963.

Ruppenthal, Roland G. *Logistical Support of the Armies*. 2 vols. Washington, DC: Department of the Army, 1953–59.

Ryan, Cornelius. *A Bridge Too Far*. New York: Simon & Schuster, 1974.

———. *The Last Battle*. New York: Simon & Schuster, 1966.

Sadarananda, Dana V. *Beyond Stalingrad*. Mechanicsburg, PA: Stackpole, 1990.

Schaefer-Kehnert, Walter. *Kriegstagebuch in Feldpostbriefen, 1940–1945*. n.p., n.d.

Scheibert, Oberst i. G. Horst and Genmaj. A. D. Carl Wagener. *Die deutsche Panzertruppe 1939–1945*. Bad Nauheim: Podzun-Verlag, 1966.

Scheibert, Horst. *Panzer Zwischen Don und Donez*. Friedberg: Podzun-Pallas-Verlag, 1979.

———. *Die Träger des deutschen Kreuzes in Gold: Das Heer*. Friedberg: Podzun-Pallas-Verlag, 1992.

Die Schützenkompanie. Adapted by Oberstleutnant Ludwig Queckbörner. Berlin: E. S. Mittler & Sohn, 1939.

Schrodek, G. W. *Die 11. Panzerdivision "Gespensterdivision" Bilddokumente 1940–1945*. Friedberg: Podzun-Pallas-Verlag, 1984.

———. *Ihr Glaube galt dem Vaterland*. Munich: Schild-Verlag, 1976.

Seemen, Gerhard von. *Die Ritterkreuzträger, 1939–1945*. Friedberg: Podzun-Pallas-Verlag, 1978.

Senff, Hubertus. *Die Entwicklung der Panzerwaffe im deutschen Heer zwischen den beiden Weltkriegen*. Frankfurt: E. S. Mittler & Sohn, 1969.

Senger und Etterlin, Dr. Frido von. *Taschenbuch der Panzer, 1943–1957*. Munich: J. F. Lehmanns Verlag, 1957.

Simpson, Gary L. *Tiger Ace*. Atglen, PA: Schiffer, 1994.

Smith, W. H. B. *Small Arms of the World*. 7th ed. Harrisburg, PA: Stackpole, 1962.

Spaeter, Helmuth. *The History of the Panzerkorps Grossdeutschland*. Vol. 2. Translated by David Johnston. Winnipeg, Manitoba: J. J. Fedorowicz, 1995.

Spielberger, Walter J. *Der Panzerkampfwagen IV und seine Abarten*. Stuttgart: Motorbuch Verlag, 1975.

Spielberger, Walter J., and Uwe Feist. *Halbkettenfahrzeuge*. Fallbrook, CA: Aero, 1968.

Spiwoks, Erich und Hans Stöber. *Endkampf zwischen Mosel und Inn*. Osnabrück: Munin Verlag, 1976.

Stadler, Silvester. *Die Offensive gegen Kursk 1943*. Osnabrück: Munin Verlag, 1980.

Staiger, Jörg. *Rückzug durchs Rhônetal*. Neckargemünd: Kurt Vowinckel, 1965.

Stahel, David. *Kiev 1941*. New York: Cambridge University Press, 2012.

———. *Operation Typhoon*. Cambridge: Cambridge University Press, 2013.

Stanton, Shelby L. *World War II Order of Battle*. New York: Galahad Books, 1991.

Stein, George H. *The Waffen SS*. Ithaca, NY: Cornell University Press, 1966.

Stolfi, R. H. S. *Hitler's Panzers East*. Norman: University of Oklahoma Press, 1991.

Stoves, Rolf. *Die gepanzerten und motorisierten deutschen Grossverbände 1935–1945*. Friedberg: Podzun-Pallas-Verlag, 1986.

Stubbs, Mary Lee, and Stanley Russell Connor. *Armor-Cavalry*. Part I. Washington, DC: Office of the Chief of Military History, 1969.

Sydnor, Charles W., Jr. *Soldiers of Destruction*. Princeton, NJ: Princeton University Press, 1977.

Terrain Factors in the Russian Campaign. Washington, DC: Department of the Army Pamphlet No. 20-290, July 1951.

Tessin, Georg. *Verbände und Truppen der deutschen Wehrmacht und Waffen SS im Zweiten Weltkrieg 1939–1945*. Bd. 3, 4, 6. Frankfurt: Verlag E. S. Mittler & Sohn, 1966–1972.

Toland, John. *The Last 100 Days*. New York: Random House, 1966.

Trenkler, Thomas, ed. *Wiedersehen im Niemansland: Die Geschichte dreier Brüder, 1940–1949*. Wien: Czernin Verlag, 2000.

Triplet, William S. *A Colonel in the Armored Divisions*. Edited by Robert H. Ferrell. Columbia and London: University of Missouri Press, 2001.

Truscott, Lt. General L. K., Jr. *Command Missions*. New York: E. P. Dutton & Co., 1954.

Tsouras, Lt. Col. (Ret.), ed. *Panzers on the Eastern Front*. [Papers by Gen. Erhard Raus] Mechanicsburg, PA: Stackpole, 2002.

26 Infantry Division History in World War II. "Weisermühl" Wels-Klischee: Krammer Linz, 1946.

United States Strategic Bombing Survey. Vol. 1. Summary Report (European War), September 30, 1945. Washington, DC: Government Printing Office, 1945.

Van Crefeld, Martin L. *Hitler's Strategy 1940–1941: The Balkan Clue*. Cambridge: Cambridge University Press, 1973.

Walters, Robert G., Captain US Army. "Order Out of Chaos." Unpublished master's thesis. Monterey, CA: Naval Postgraduate School, 1989.

Waffen-SS im Bild. Göttingen: Plesse Verlag, 1957.

War Department Technical Manual TM-E 30-451. *Handbook on German Military Forces, 15 March 1945*. Washington, DC: US Government Printing Office, 1945. Reprint, Baton Rouge: Louisiana State University Press, 1990.

Warnick, William L., Lt. Col. John G. Cook (USA, Ret.), and Dr. Robert A. Baker. *The Tank Commander's Guide*. Harrisburg, PA: Stackpole, 1963.

Weigley, Russell. *Eisenhower's Lieutenants*. Bloomington: Indiana University Press, 1981.

Whaley, Barton. *Covert German Rearmament 1919–1939*. Frederick, MD: University Publications of America, 1984.

Wheeler-Bennett, John. *The Nemesis of Power: The German Army in Politics, 1918–1945*. London: MacMillan, 1953.

Whitehouse, Arch. *Tank*. Garden City, New York: Doubleday, 1960.

Wietersheim, Generalleutnant Wend von. *11. Panzer-Division, August 1944–Mai 1945*. Unpublished manuscripts collected by Karl Heinz Loschke, Sprecher der Traditionsverbandes der ehemaligen 11. Panzer-Division, 1996.

Wilmot, Chester. *The Struggle for Europe*. London: Collins, 1952.

Young, Desmond. *Rommel, The Desert Fox*. New York: Harper & Row, 1950; Berkley, 1971.

Zabecki, David T. "The Greatest German General No One Ever Heard Of." *World War II* (April/May 2008).

———. *Steel Wind*. Westport, CT: Praeger, 1994.

Zaloga, Steven. "Polish Cavalry Against Panzers." *Armor* 93, no. 1 (January/February 1984): 26–31.

———. *T-34/76*. London: Osprey, 1994.

Zentner, Christian, and Friedemann Bedürftig, eds. *The Encyclopedia of the Third Reich*. 2 vols. Translated by Amy Hackett. New York: MacMillan, 1991.

Zetterling, Niklas, and Anders Frankson. *The Korsun Pocket*. Drexel Hill, PA: Casemate: 2008.

Ziemke, Earl F. *The German Northern Theater of Operations 1940–1945*. Washington, DC: Department of the Army Pamphlet No. 20-271, 1959.

Ziemke, Earl F., and Magna E. Bauer. *Moscow to Stalingrad*. New York: Military Heritage Press, 1987.

Ziemke, Earl F. *Stalingrad to Berlin*. Washington, DC: Office of the Chief of Military History, 1968.

Index

Page numbers in italics indicates illustrations.